MANAGING FOR THE FUTURE

Organizational Behavior & Processes

Ancona
Kochan
Scully
Van Maanen
Westney

Massachusetts Institute of Technology

THOMSON
SOUTH-WESTERN

Australia · Canada · Mexico · Singapore · Spain · United Kingdom · United States

MANAGING FOR THE FUTURE
Organizational Behavior & Processes, Third Edition

Deborah Ancona
Sloan School of Management
Massachusetts Institute of Technology

John Van Maanen
Sloan School of Management
Massachusetts Institute of Technology

Thomas A. Kochan
Sloan School of Management
Massachusetts Institute of Technology

D. Eleanor Westney
Sloan School of Management
Massachusetts Institute of Technology

Maureen Scully
Graduate School of Management
Simmons College

Dedicated to those who have inspired us to try to be better students and teachers.
Special thanks to: Professor Jack Barbash • Professor Arthur H. Gladstein • Professor Marius B. Jansen • Professor Joanne Martin • Professor Edgar H. Schein

VP/Editorial Director
Jack W. Calhoun

Marketing Manager
Jacquelyn Carrillo

Internal Designer
Bethany Casey

VP/Editor-in-Chief
Michael P. Roche

Production Editor
Emily Gross

Cover Designer
Bethany Casey

Senior Publisher
Melissa S. Acuña

Manufacturing Coordinator
Rhonda Utley

Photographs
©PhotoDisc

Executive Editor
John Szilagyi

Compositor
Trejo Production

Design Project Manager
Bethany Casey

Senior Developmental Editor
Judith O'Neill

Printer
Von Hoffmann Press, Inc.
Frederick, MD

COPYRIGHT ©2005
by South-Western, a division of Thomson Learning.
Thomson Learning™ is a trademark used herein under license.

Printed in the United States of America
1 2 3 4 5 07 06 05 04 03

For more information contact
South-Western College Publishing,
5191 Natorp Boulevard,
Mason, Ohio, 45040
Or you can visit our Internet site at:
http://www.swlearning.com

ALL RIGHTS RESERVED
No part of this work covered by the copyright hereon may be reproduced or used in any form or by any means—graphic, electronic, or mechanical, including photocopying, recording, taping, Web distribution or information storage and retrieval systems—without the written permission of the publisher.

For permission to use material from this text or product, contact us by
Tel: (800) 730-2214
Fax: (800) 730-2215
http://www.thomsonrights.com

Library of Congress Control Number: 2003113908
ISBN 0-324-05575-7

Brief Table of Contents

Overview of the Modules

Analytics

Module 1   The "New" Organization: Taking Action in an Era of Organizational Transformation

Module 2   Three Lenses on Organizational Analysis and Action

Teams

Module 3   Making Teams Work

Module 4   Diverse Cognitive Styles in Teams

Module 5   Team Processes

Module 6   Teams in Organizations

Organizations

Module 7   Workforce Management: Employment Relationships in Changing Organizations

Module 8   Managing Change in Organizations

Module 9   Organizational Actions in Complex Environments

Module 10   Learning Across Borders: Disneyland on the Move

Skills

Module 11   Managing Cultural Diversity

Module 12   Negotiation and Conflict Resolutions

Module 13   Change From Within: Roads to Successful Issue Selling

Module 14   Leadership

Index

Table of Contents

Analytics

Module 1	**The "New" Organization: Taking Action in an Era of Organizational Transformation**	
Overview		6

Core

Class Note	**Changing Organizational Models**	10
	Key Features of the "Old" Model of the Organization 11	
	Key Features of the "New" Model of the Organization 13	
	Taking Action in the New Model 18	
	References 21	
The Press	**A Sampling of Analyses of the New Organization**	22
	The Coming of the New Organization 22	
	The New Managerial Work 22	
	The American Corporation as an Employer 23	
	Designing Effective Organizations 23	
	The Mind of the CEO 23	
	. . . and Some Skeptical Voices 24	
	Beyond the Hype 24	
	Will the Organization of the Future Make the Mistakes of the Past? 24	
	Coda to the New Organization 24	
	The Twenty-first Century Firm 25	
Questionnaire	**Mapping Your Organization**	27

Elective

Class Note	**Reading the Business Press**	30
The Press	**The Search for the Organization of Tomorrow**	31
	Management by Web	39
	Ephemeral 39	
	Digitization 42	
	Cultural Change 42	
	Feedback 43	
	Delivering the Goods 43	
	Connections 44	
	Talent Hunt 45	
	Incubator 45	

Index

Module 2 Three Lenses on Organizational Analysis and Action

Overview — 4

Core

Class Note — **Introduction** — 8
- Our Personal "Schemas" 8
- Building More Complete Models 10
- Three Classic Lenses on Organizations 10
- The Three Lenses in Action 11
- References 11

Class Note — **The Strategic Design Lens** — 13
- Overview 13
- Assignment Summary 13
- Additional Suggested Readings 13
- The Organization as Strategic Design 14
- References 27

Case — **Strategic Design at Dynacorp** — 28
- Dynacorp's Design: The Functional Organization 28
- Internal Investigation: Diagnosing the Organizational Problems 30
- External Investigation: Identifying Alternative Designs 33

Class Note — **The Political Lens** — 33
- Overview 33
- Assignment Summary 33
- Suggested Further Readings 33
- The Organization as a Political System 34
- Power 36
- Using the Political Lens to Take More Effective Action in Organizations 41
- References 45

The Press — **Informal Network: The Company Behind the Chart** — 47
- The Steps of Network Analysis 48
- Whom Do You Trust? 49
- Whom Do You Talk To? 52
- Network Holes and Other Problems 53

Class Note — **The Cultural Lens** — 57
- Overview 57
- Assignment Summary 57
- The Centrality of Symbolism 57
- Toward a Working Definition of Culture 58
- Organizational Culture 59
- Toward a Cultural Diagnosis of Organizations 64
- Postscript: The "New" Organization 66
- Recommended Further Reading 66

The Press	**Organizational Culture**	67
	A Historical Note 67	
	Definition of Organizational Culture 69	
	The Levels of Culture 70	
	Deciphering the "Content" of Culture 71	
	Two Case Examples 72	
	Cultural Dynamics: How Is Culture Created? 75	
	Cultural Dynamics: Preservation Through Socialization 75	
	Cultural Dynamics: Natural Evolution 76	
	Cultural Dynamics: Guided Evolution and Managed Change 77	
	The Role of the Organizational Psychologist 78	
	References 78	
Class Note	**Applying the Three Lenses**	83
	Taking Effective Action Steps 84	
	Assignment Summary 84	
Case	**Dynacorp Revisited: The Front/Back Organization**	85
	The Front/Back Design at Dynacorp 85	
	Your Role 86	
	The Situation 86	
	The Visits and Discussions 87	
	Dynacorp Video Transcript Northeast Region 88	

Index

Teams

Module 3   Making Teams Work

Overview		6

Core

Class Note	**A Team Primer**	10
	Key Terms 10	
	Types of Teams 11	
	Teams versus Individuals 12	
	A Team Effectiveness Model 13	
	References 15	

Handbook

	Overview	3
	I. Who Are We?	3
	• *Description 3*	
	• *Suggestions 4*	
	II. What Do We Want to Accomplish?	5
	• *Description 5*	
	• *Suggestions 5*	

III. How Can We Organize Ourselves to Meet Our Goals? 6
- *Description 6*
- *Suggestions—Work Structure 7*
- *Suggestions—The Facilitator Role 7*
- *Suggestions—The Project Manager Role 8*
- *Suggestions—The Boundary Manager Role 8*
- *Suggestions—Agreeing Upon Norms 9*

IV. How Will We Operate? 10
- *Discussion 10*
- *Suggestions—Planning an Agenda 10*
- *Suggestions—Brainstorming 11*
- *Suggestions—Multivoting 11*
- *Suggestions—Communicating Cross-culturally 12*

V. How Can We Continuously Learn and Improve? 13
- *Suggestions—Giving Feedback 13*
- *Suggestions—Assessing Yourself and the Team 14*

Assessment   Team Assessment Survey   17

Index

Module 4   Diverse Cognitive Styles in Teams

Overview   4

Core

Assessment   Cognitive Style Self-Assessment   6
Scoring Scheme 8
Summary Score 9

Class Note   Mapping Multiple Perspectives   11

The Press   Mapping Managerial Styles   13
Managerial Mapping 13
Personal Work Styles 15
Work Preferences 15
A Basis for Self-Understanding 21

Elective

The Press   Give Me an E. Give Me an S.   28

Index

Module 5 — Team Processes

    Overview   4

Core

    Class Note   Team Process Observation Guide   8
        Membership 8
        Organizational Context 8
        Team Processes 8
        Task and Maintenance Functions 9
        Task Functions 9
        Maintenance Functions 9
        Decision Making 9
        Communication 11
        Influence 12
        Conflict 13
        Atmosphere 13
        Emotional Issues 14
        Taking Action 14
        References 15

    The Press   Virtually There?   16
        Doctors: Not Just Cheaper, Smarter 17
        Developers: Even Better Than the Real Thing? 18
        Consultants: New Behaviors for New Technologies 20
        Bankers: Less Paper Means More Backers 20

        The Trouble with Teams   21

Index

Module 6 — Teams in Organizations

    Overview   4

Core

    Class Note   Outward Bound: Linking Teams to Their Organization   8
        Team Effectiveness 9
        Moving Outward 9
        Analyzing and Managing the External Environment Using the Three Lenses 9
        References 10

    Case   Aston-Blair, Inc.   11
        Company Background 11
        Formation of the Task Force 12
        Initial Meeting of the Task Force 12
        Preparation of the Task Force Report 14
        The August 4 Report of the Task Force 15

Elective

The Press	**The Comparative Advantage of X-Teams**	22
	Five Components That Make X-Teams Successful 22	
	Is the X-Team for Your Company? 29	

Index

Organization

Module 7 — Workforce Management: Employment Relationships in Changing Organizations

Overview		6

Core

Class Note	**Managing a Changing Workforce in Turbulent Times**	12
	The "Old" Versus "New" Employment Relationship 13	
	Flexibility: What Kind, What Is Changing, and for Whom? 17	
	Putting More Options on the Menu for the New Employment Relationship 20	
	Human Assets and Twenty-First Century Organizational Forms 20	
	Attending to Perceived Inconsistencies and Unintended Consequences 21	
	Summary 22	
	References 23	
The Press	**The Changing Social Contract for White-Collar Workers**	25
	The Theoretical Challenge 25	
	A Return to the Past? The Limits of Loyalty 25	
	Moving On: Free Agency and Professionalism 26	
	The Conditions for Professionalism 26	
	Building Competitive Advantage Through People	29
	The Role of the Executive in the "War for Talent" Era 29	
	Implications for HR Professionals 31	
	The Heart of Strategy 35	
	What's Wrong with Management Practices in Silicon Valley? A Lot.	36
	Silicon Valley's Approach to Management 36	
	The Consequences 36	
	In Silicon Valley, Loyalty Means Paying a High Price; Cultural Strengths Help Offset Loss of Paper Wealth	38
	For a New Insider, It Was a Risk Worth Taking 40	

Elective

Case	The Part-Time Partner (A)	44
	Should Meeker, Needham & Ames Make Julie Ross a Partner? 48	
	The Part-Time Partner Redux: So We Solved the Problem, Didn't We? (B)	52
The Press	Integrating Work and Family Life: A Holistic Approach	54
	Executive Summary: Reframing the Debate 54	
	A Call to Action 57	
	Addressing the Crisis in Confidence in Corporations: Root Causes, Victims, and Strategies for Reform	58
	Root Causes 58	
	The Victims 59	
	Remedies 60	
	References 61	

Index

Module 8 Managing Change in Organizations

	Overview	4

Core

Class Note	Organizational Change: An Overview	6
	Why Is Organizational Change So Difficult? 6	
	Organizational Change at Procter & Gamble: Organization 2005 8	
	Stage Models of Change Processes 11	
	Dimensions of Change 15	
	Being a More Effective Change Agent 18	
	References 21	
Case	The Strategy That Wouldn't Travel 22	
	Inside Wichita 23	
	Cookie-Cutter Conundrum 24	

Elective

Readings	The Life Cycle of Typical Change Initiatives	28
	The Leadership of Profound Change	32
	The Myth of the Hero-CEO 32	
	A Different View of Executive Leadership 33	
	What Is Leadership and Who Are the Leaders? 35	
	Culture Change at General Electric	38
	Stage One: Work-Outs and the "RAMMP" Matrix 38	
	The Payoff Matrix 40	
	Stage Two: Best Practices 40	

Stage Three: Process Maps 41
Stage Four: Change Acceleration 41
Stage Five: Strategic Initiatives 42
Stage Six: Making Customers Winners 42
Stage Seven: Six Sigma Quality 42
The Integrated Learning Process 42

Index

Module 9   Organizational Action in Complex Environments

    Overview   4

Core

Class Note   **Organizations and Their Environments: Sets, Stakeholders, and Organizational Fields**   8
The Strategic Design Perspective: The "Organization Set" 8
The Political Perspective: The Stakeholders Model 13
The Cultural Perspective: Institutional Fields 17
Integrating Perspectives: Seeing the Environment Through Three Lenses 22
References 22

Case   **RU-486: The Handling by Roussel-Uclaf of a Double Dilemma**   23
The Company 23
The Product 23
The French Government's Authorization 24
The Debate: Proceed to Market, or Not? 25
The Decision 27
Reactions 28
The Government's Order 28
Reactions 28
RU-486 in the Rest of Europe 29
RU-486 in Asia 30
RU-486 in the United States 30

Index

Module 10   Learning Across Borders: Disneyland on the Move

    Overview   4

Core

Class Note   **Disneyland in the US of A**   8
The Copy: Disneyland Goes to Florida 10
References 13

The Press	The Smile Factory: Work at Disneyland *It's a Small World 14* *The Disney Way 22* *References 23*	13
Class Note	Disney Goes to Tokyo: Crossing the Pacific *The Cultural Marketplace 26* *References 28*	25
The Press	Displacing Disney: Some Notes on the Flow of Culture *The Transformation 28* *Cultural Experience Revisited 32* *References 33*	28
Class Note	Disney Goes to Paris: Crossing the Atlantic *References 39*	35
The Press	Mouse Trap *Mickey's Misfires 40* *Disney Knows Best 40* *Tarnished Image 40* *Corporate Hubris 41* *Ballooning Costs 41* *Good Attendance 42* *High Prices 43*	39
Class Note	Disney Goes to Hong Kong: An Uncertain Journey *A World with Mouse Ears? 49* *References 49*	45
The Press	The Ever-Expanding, Profit-Maximizing, Cultural-Imperialist, Wonderful World of Disney	50

Index

Skills

Module 11 Managing Cultural Diversity

Overview		6

Core

Class Note	Managing Cultural Diversity: From Understanding to Action *The Meaning of Diversity 10* *Background: The U.S. Societal and Policy Context 13* *Organizational Processes 14* *Managing Diversity for High Performance 17* *References and Additional Readings 17*	10

	Bystander Awareness: Skills for Effective Managers	20
	From Valuing Diversity to Taking Action 20	
	Historical and Conceptual Background 21	
	The Bystander in the Workplace 21	
	The Courage of One's Convictions 21	
	Collusion 22	
	Cultural Variation in Intervention Styles 22	
	Ideas for Bystanders 23	
	Structural Solutions 23	
	A Closing Thought 24	
Exercise	**Bystander Scenarios: What Would You Do?**	25
	Scenario 1: Introducing the Invisible Colleague 26	
	Scenario 2: Is It Really About Race? 26	
	Scenario 3: The Awkward Invitation 27	
	Scenario 4: Is It the Nature of the Project? 27	
	Scenario 5: Counting on a Colleague 28	
	Scenario 6: I Was Just Trying to Be Sensitive! 28	
	Scenario 7: You Just Weren't Listening 29	

Elective

The Press	**Making Differences Matter: A New Paradigm for Managing Diversity**	32
	The Discrimination-and-Fairness Paradigm 33	
	The Access-and-Legitimacy Paradigm 35	
	The Emerging Paradigm: Connecting Diversity to Work Perspectives 36	
	Eight Preconditions for Making the Paradigm Shift 37	
	First Interstate Bank: A Paradigm Shift in Progress 38	
	Shift Complete: Third-Paradigm Companies in Action 39	

Index

Module 12 Negotiation and Conflict Resolution

Overview		4

Core

Class Note	**Negotiation and Conflict Resolution: An Introduction**	6
	Purpose of This Module 7	
	Negotiation as a Form of Conflict Management 7	
	Dealmaking: The Building Blocks of Negotiation 8	
	Conclusion 19	
	References 19	

Elective

The Press	**Dealcrafting: The Substance of Three-Dimensional Negotiations**	22
	Basic Dealcrafting Orientation 1: A Relentless Focus of Creating Maximum Value 24	
	Basic Dealcrafting Orientation 2: A Relentless Focus on Differences as the Raw Material for Joint Gains 26	

Differences in Cost/Revenue Structure 26
Differences in Capability 27
Differences in Interest and Priority 27
Implication: Agenda Management 28
Differences in Forecast or Belief About the Future 28
Contingent Agreements Based on Forecast Differences: A 3-D Extension 30
Differences in Attitudes Toward Risk 30
Differences in Attitudes Toward Time 32
Differences in Tax Status 33
Differences in Accounting Treatment and Reporting Sensitivity 33
Crafting Value from a Variety of Differences 34
Conclusion 35
About the Authors 35
References 35

Breakthrough Bargaining 36
Power Moves 36
Process Moves 38
Appreciative Moves 40
About the Authors 42

Index

Module 13 Change From Within: Roads to Successful Issue Selling

Overview 4

Core

Class Note **Issue Selling From Within** 6
The Choice to Sell Issues in Organizations 7
The Challenge of Charged Issues 10
Conclusion 11

Exercise **Issue Selling** 12
Instructions 12
Chris Peters and the "People" Issue 12

Case **Inex** 14
Inex Company 16
Company Structure 16
The Management Committee 19
Jones's Dilemma 19

Elective

The Press **Dinosaurs or Dynamos? Recognizing Middle Management's Strategic Role** 22
Executive Overview 22
The Misunderstood Middle Manager 23
Competitive Advantage and Middle Management Strategic Roles 23
Championing Strategic Alternatives 24

Synthesizing Information 24
Facilitating Adaptability 24
Implementing Deliberate Strategy 25
Linking Strategic Roles to Core Capability 25
Middle Management's Role in the Reengineered Organization 26
Realizing Middle Management's Strategic Value 27
Everyone a Middle Manager? 29
About the Authors 29

Index

Module 14 Leadership

Overview		4

Core

Class Note	Leadership in an Age of Uncertainty	8
	The Framework 9	
	The Four Capabilities 14	
	The Change Signature 14	
	References 16	
Exercise	Your Change Signature	19
	Step 1: Past Self 19	
	Step 2: Developed Self 19	
	Step 3: Underdeveloped Self 20	
	Step 4: Future Self 20	
	Step 5: Integration 20	
Case	Re-engineering MIT: How President Charles Vest Put MIT Back on Track	21
	Carly Fiorina: A Story of Leadership Development	26
	Early Fiorina 27	
	The AT&T and Lucent Years 28	
	HP 29	
	Epilogue 32	

Elective

The Press	What Should I Do With My Life?	36
	MONEY Doesn't Fund Dreams 37	
	SMARTS Can't Answer The Question 38	
	PLACE Defines You 39	
	ATTITUDE Is the Biggest Obstacle 39	
	Excerpts from Geeks & Geezers: How Era, Values, and Defining Moments Shape Leaders	42
	The Power of the Crucible 42	
	Creating Meaning Out of the Crucible Experience 43	
	What Makes a Leader 44	

Crucibles of Leadership 44
The Importance of Individual Factors 46
Adaptive Capacity Is Key 46
The Difference Between Fasting and Starving 48
Adaptive Capacity as Applied Creativity 49
Seeing the World in a New Light 51

Index

Introduction

Managing for the Future consists of 14 instructional modules on organizational behavior and processes that focus on the *new* organization and on how organizations deal with change. The modules, initially, were the product of a cross-functional team that came together to teach the graduate course in organizational behavior at MIT. More recently, those of us from MIT, representing the disciplines of anthropology, social psychology, sociology, and industrial relations, have been joined in our endeavors by others. A number of new Sloan faculty and visitors have taught with us and contributed to our thinking and writing, including Professors Mitch Abolafia, Stuart Albert, Ella Bell, Paul Carlile, Deborah Kolb, and Amy Segal. We have also gone beyond MIT's borders to recruit scholars from other schools to contribute modules. Module 13 on issue selling was contributed by Professors Susan Ashford and Jane Dutton of the University of Michigan. The negotiations module, Module 12, was written by Professor Deborah Kolb from the Progam on Negotiations at Harvard Law School and the Simmons Center for Gender in Organizations.

Our analysis of the new organization, inclining decisively toward the flat, the networked, the flexible, the diverse, and the global, has always concerned itself with balancing the extravagant claims made in its favor with the harsher reality of implementing and sustaining it. Since *Managing for the Future* was first published, we have persisted in our attempts to separate the hype from the reality and to talk more freely about the unintended consequences brought about by this recent era of change in the firm. Taking up three theoretical lenses—strategic design, political, and cultural—we show how they can be used to analyze organizations and direct managerial action. Placing considerably more emphasis on skills in this new edition, we augment our work with a new module on leadership. The actions that managers can take to cope effectively with change remains a persistent concern. And, as our students have been known to complain about excessive reading, we again break modules down into core and elective pieces so that instructors can choose the length and depth of reading assigned for a given class.

The organizational behavior course at MIT continues to be molded around the features of the new organization: a networked, flat, flexible entity made up of a diverse workforce operating in a global environment. Our modules are similarly shaped. We arrange them into four major groupings—Analytics, Teams, Organizations, and Skills—reflecting how we teach the course. We examine changes in the firm using the strategic design, political, and cultural lenses, intensively teaching these lenses. These two frameworks—the lenses plus the new organization—compose the analytic grouping of modules and form the foundational core of the course. We then move on to use the frameworks to analyze and plan managerial action in teams and organizations. When looking at both teams and organizations, we include an analysis of the environment to show how context influences structures and processes. Finally, we bring skills sessions into the mix so that students gain a sense of how to manage in a shifting corporate landscape. We also to stress international issues and cases and organizational links to strategy.

Our aim is not to teach the correct way to manage or the perfect way to design an organization. There is no one best way to manage, build, and lead. Rather, our aim is to provide a general understanding of possible managerial approaches to particular problems and to introduce ways to sort out the various social costs and benefits typically associated with them. Because we exist in a time of considerable tumult and flux, many different managerial approaches, some vastly different and contradictory, circulate among academics, consultants, and chroniclers of the popular press. We include a variety of readings from these quarters so that students can debate what the future will look like, assess what actions are appropriate in various situations, gauge what is hype versus what is reality, and, in the process, become more critical readers of both the business and the academic press and more informed users of consultant services.

Because students learn in different ways, the modules include varied instructional media including cases, experiential exercises, readings, questionnaires, teamwork, discussions, papers, projects, and videotapes. One of our goals is to get students to be more aware of their own beliefs and actions, to compare these and their responses in exercises and in class with the conceptual material, and perhaps to change the way they think and act as managers. Thus, we want students to learn new theories and models, but also to learn more about themselves now and how they need to develop in the future. Students should leave the course with a better sense of their learning styles, the roles that they take on in teams, and how they respond to new managerial challenges, such as downsizing or the taking of new products to market.

Given our varied goals (including learning theory, applying that theory, examining one's own beliefs and behaviors, and becoming more capable organizational participants), these modules and the course they support require that the professor take on different roles. On some days the professor is a lecturer; on others, a case leader. During experiential exercises the professor is a facilitator, whereas during certain team exercises he or she may be required to act as a coach. Thus, the teacher is not always the "expert," just as the goals of the day are not always to memorize a given set of concepts. Although, like us, instructors may sometimes find it difficult to teach in new ways, the Detailed Teaching Notes included in the accompanying Instructor's Module should help make the transitions a lot easier.

The modules mirror the way we teach the organizational behavior course at MIT and are organized as a set that can be used together as a full course, as an addition to an existing course, or individually as one-day seminars or as executive education courses on particular topics. The modules examine current practices in real companies around the world, but also provide concise readings on key up-to-date theoretical contributions. We rely on fewer readings and examples than most texts, because we have found it more effective to teach less material but to teach it in a way that obliges students to retain and apply it. For example, students will not be exposed to all the social-psychological theory of groups, but they will learn skills in creating work teams along with some key concepts and models of teams, and they will have to fit those concepts and models to cases, to their own behavior in teams, and to team diagnoses. In this way learning is not rote memorization. Instead students internalize concepts that hereafter can be tested in new situations. A module can be taught in one three-hour session, in two one-and-a-half-hour sessions, or in three one-hour sessions.

Although we provide cases, experiential exercises, and conceptual material, we believe that students learn best when they must apply what they have learned to a real situation. Thus, we strongly suggest that classes be broken up into small teams that work together throughout the term and that these teams be given the task of analyzing real organizations or teams. Module 3, "Making Teams Work," provides a listing of alternative assignments for bringing real-world experiences into the classroom as well as materials to help teams work productively and learn about their own team process. Again, these assignments help motivate students to learn the material in the course and engage them in the process of making theory useful.

Thus, our specific objectives in this book, and the courses it supports, can be summarized as follows:

1. Introduce students to the "new" organization and to three lenses—strategic design, political, and cultural—from the behavioral sciences that help students to analyze it.
2. Provide opportunities to apply these lenses to real organizational and managerial problems.
3. Participate in ongoing work teams in which students can learn about teamwork.
4. Allow students to examine their own behavior and beliefs about organizations so that they can contrast them with the theories and observations of others.
5. Encourage students to become critical readers of the business press, the trends it discusses, and the services offered by different organizational consultants.
6. Enable students to be informed and engaged participants in organizational transformation.

The Modules in Detail

Analytics

Two frameworks—three lenses plus the concept of the *new* organization—compose the analytic grouping of modules in *Managing for the Future* and form the foundational core of the course. We mold Module 1 around the features of the new organization: a networked, flat, flexible entity made up of a diverse workforce operating in a global environment. Module 2 introduces the three lenses—strategic design, political, and cultural—that we use to analyze teams and organizations and to win support for change.

Module 1   The "New" Organization: Taking Action in an Era of Organizational Transformation

Module 2   Three Lenses on Organizational Analysis and Action

Module 1
The "New" Organization: Taking Action in an Era of Organizational Transformation

In Module 1, we examine some of the features that characterize the ascendent "new" organizational form, one that is networked, flat, flexible, diverse, and global, and set the norms for a course based on experiential learning. We contrast the new organization with its traditional predecessor and discuss the pros and cons of each. For example, the traditional bureaucratic form of organization achieves control and stability whereas the new form facilitates coordination and rapid adaptation. The traditional bureaucratic form stresses distance and buffering from the external environment; the new form is networked, continually and tightly linked to other firms, both competitors and allies. We try to scrutinize the hype that heralded the emergence of the new organizational model and look at the costs associated with new organizational designs. We emphasize that the jury is still out as to what the "new" organization will ultimately look like. New to this module's mix of resources is an article written at the height of the dot-com bubble, which makes useful points about the impact of the Internet on the boundaries and activities of twenty-first century organizations. We discuss some of the forces that push organizations to adopt new forms and some of the forces that inhibit making changes—even changes that sound so promising—including the role that managers have in quashing or upholding change. Finally, we recognize that many organizations are currently in a state of flux, caught between the old and the new and exhibiting features of each. This ongoing situation calls for the analysis of contradictory forces and makes the understanding of organizational change paramount. An organizational mapping exercise asks students to characterize an organization with which they are familiar in terms of how well it fits the model of the "new" organization.

Module 2
Three Lenses on Organizational Analysis and Action

The behavioral sciences provide three powerful lenses with which to observe, analyze, and understand organizations: the **strategic design** lens, the **political** lens, and the **cultural** lens. The strategic design lens views the organization as a goal-directed entity in which an engineering approach can be used to craft an organizational structure and system of rewards, careers, controls, and tasks that fit a given environment. The political lens, in contrast, views the organization and its environment as a set of changing interests and coalitions that are in conflict over scarce resources and over which multiple stakeholders negotiate. The cultural lens views the organization as a set of deeply held assumptions that are acquired early in a firm's history and that are passed on through stories, symbols, myths, and socialization procedures. These deeply held assumptions signal to people how to act and react to events around them and may explain why people may sabotage major change efforts. The three lenses highlight very different aspects of organizational behavior, but only through an understanding of all three can a complete organizational diagnosis and understanding of change take place.

Module 2 is divided into five parts. The first part introduces the three lenses, contrasting them with ways, or schemas, each of us has of looking at the world. The second part introduces the strategic design lens and includes a case for application. The third part introduces the political design lens and uses a role-playing exercise to practice stakeholder analysis. The fourth part provides the conceptual basis for the cultural lens and includes a cultural diagnostic exercise. The fifth part showcases the three lenses in combination, underscoring their essential complementarity, and revisits the earlier case, to explore an integrated plan for managerial action.

Teams

Managing for the Future places a rather large emphasis on teams. Teams are, after all, a key structural element in the "new" organization, and students are expected to improve their team design and management skills over the run of the course. Teams can be used within the course framework to carry out organizational analyses and further train students in using the three lenses. Thus, the next four modules are devoted to teams, but the diversity and negotiations modules can also be adapted to a team orientation.

Module 3	Making Teams Work
Module 4	Diverse Cognitive Styles in Teams
Module 5	Team Processes
Module 6	Teams in Organizations

Module 3
Making Teams Work

Module 3 is somewhat unique in that it does not correspond to a specific class in our course outline but, rather, is a tool we distribute to help students work productively in their ongoing teams. This module could be adopted in any course that uses teams extensively or that assigns a major team project. It serves two major functions: (1) it provides a conceptual introduction to the nature and vocabulary of teams; and (2) it provides a handbook that helps students create effective working teams and keep them on track. In addition, the module includes a Team Assessment Survey that allows teams to do mid-term evaluations of how well they are operating.

Not surprisingly students often have differing notions of what a team is, when a team should be created, and what different types of teams exist. The Class Note in Module 3 serves as a primer on teams, giving students a common language about teams and a model of team effectiveness. This module is also motivated by the fact that teams often suffer from process problems. Most courses provide conceptual aid, but not pragmatic advice about how to go about setting goals, creating a team structure, defining a team process, and learning to deal with problems over time. The self-contained Team Handbook included in this module provides actual steps to follow and barriers to avoid in answering the questions: Who are we? What do we want to accomplish? How can we organize ourselves to meet our goals? How will we operate? and How can we continuously learn and improve?

Module 4
Diverse Cognitive Styles in Teams

Teams underscore the need to work with diverse sets of people in changing sets of configurations. Team successes also require a greater understanding of one's own style, the style of coworkers, and how those styles interact. Module 4 takes students through an assessment of their cognitive styles, and an accompanying experiential exercise helps them see what style means with regard to their interactions with others. The particular diagnostic device that we use is not promoted as the "answer" to understanding all interpersonal interactions but, rather, is given as a starting point for assessing similarities and differences between individuals and how to deal with them.

The diagnostic device used for the self-assessment part of this module is similar to the Myers-Briggs Type Indicator®. It focuses on an individual's information environment and illuminates a person's preferences in how to take in information and how to make decisions. This approach fits the manager's world of highly interpersonal and informational tasks, high levels of problem solving with others, and the need for fast-paced decision making. Students are encouraged to think about the kinds of activities they enjoy, the ways in which they like to get information, how they see others, and how others may see them.

The experiential exercise calls for students to engage in a problem-solving exercise with a specially configured group. Students then report on how they worked together. Later, when students learn about the nature of the group configuration, they are asked to compare and contrast what it is like to work with similar versus different types of individuals. They also discuss how multiple valid solutions to the same problem can be derived and how people's different preferences for solutions can enhance or inhibit organizational change.

Module 5
Team Processes

Module 5 concentrates on internal team dynamics and how to improve team decision making. The focus here is on what can go wrong in teams, how to improve and lead teams, and how to observe ongoing processes, particularly decision making. This module contains conceptual material on how to observe a team and team decision making. (If this module is used in the same course as Module 2, then students can also apply the strategic design, political, and cultural diagnostic lenses to team behavior. The connections between how team processes are viewed through strategic design, political, and cultural lenses have been strengthened in this edition.) We also provide a choice of exercises that push students to apply the conceptual material to actual teams in action. Experiential exercises involving either the viewing of *Twelve Angry Men* or a product development task, in which teams must design and build a product that will compete with products created by the other teams, or both may be implemented.

The conceptual material examines what to observe in teams (e.g., communication, influence, task and maintenance behaviors, decision making, conflict, atmosphere, and emotional issues) and covers problems that teams often encounter, such as poor organization, groupthink, and biased information. A listing of key influence tactics that team members and leaders can use to shape and shift team processes is also included.

Students seem to remember and internalize these concepts most readily when they have to apply them. *Twelve Angry Men* is a wonderful example of the complexity of team decision making, which not only helps to illustrate many team phenomena, but also allows students to try to predict what will happen as the jury ponders how best to manage its processes. The product development task calls on students to engage in a time-limited task that requires multiple skills, creativity, and coordination. Afterward students must evaluate how well their teams allocated roles, made decisions, communicated, and handled conflict.

A new article from *Fast Company* ("Virtually, There?"), designated as an elective reading, has been added. It looks at the ever-growing collection of electronic collaboration tools and suggests new modes in which teams may work together.

Module 6
Teams in Organizations

While Module 5 concentrates on internal team dynamics, Module 6 contemplates the relationships between a team and its external environment, putting the focus on how organizational context influences teams with respect to the impact of team design, rewards, and supervision. How internal dynamics and external boundary management interact is another key dimension of this module. What team members need to do—obtain resources, influence key stakeholders, and obtain feedback—to effectively manage their environment is addressed. Students apply the conceptual material to a case study of a task force run by a recent MBA graduate. This in-depth case provides a longitudinal look at one team leader's struggle to meet his goals. By examining the design of the team, its early processes, the ways in which outsiders are handled, and the nature of the organizational context, students learn a lot about how to manage and how not to manage a team. A new article on X-Teams, an adaptive, flexible team structure, replaces the two older readings, and brings the theoretical component of this module up to date. The issues of how to design an organization to facilitate effective teamwork can also be emphasized in Module 6.

Organizations

When looking at both teams and organizations, we include an analysis of the environment to show how context influences structures and processes. We also to stress international issues and cases and organizational links to strategy.

Module 7		Workforce Management: Employment Relationships in Changing Organizations
Module 8		Managing Change in Organizations
Module 9		Organizational Action in Complex Environments
Module 10		Learning Across Borders: Disneyland on the Move

Module 7
Workforce Management: Employment Relationships in Changing Organizations

Module 7 examines changing employment relationships in organizations that are trying to be flatter and more flexible. It examines the departures from old models of lifelong employment security, the nature of flexible and varied work arrangements (e.g., part-time work, working from home, and the use of temporary workers), the unintentional contradictions that often emerge when firms institute multiple employment arrangements, and the issues of equity and fairness that these new arrangements create. The conceptual material presented identifies two types of flexibility: (1) flexibility for employees, and (2) flexibility for organizations. The former involves flexibility about time, space, the division of labor, careers, skills, and assignments as seen in the introduction of flextime, job sharing, telecommuting, nonlinear careers, and multiskilling. Flexibility for organizations means a greater ability to expand and contract employee numbers. These two forms of flexibility are, however, often hard to reconcile and create numerous managerial dilemmas.

Students analyze a case that centers on the the difficulties of simultaneously evaluating employees with different employment arrangements for promotion. A new part added to the case illustrates the broader significance of the case themes (coherence, legitimacy, multiple constituencies, setting precedents, and recruiting and retaining women).

Students also participate in an experiential exercise where concurrent downsizing, redeployment, and teamwork create particular challenges. It is an exercise that students seldom forget. As a managerial transformation that looks great on paper is actually implemented, the personal and human resource consequences of creating a flatter and more flexible organization are uncovered.

All in all, Module 7 has been the target of a thorough revision. New content relates to the talent war that preceded the dot-com bust and the implications for workforce management that followed in its wake (e.g., worthless stock options and rescinded job offers), and new readings replace older ones, ensuring that the theoretical contributions remain up to date.

Module 8
Managing Change in Organizations

Don't let anyone snow you. Changing organizations is no easy task. As generations of theorists have proclaimed, organizations are characterized by inertia; yet increasingly organizations are looking to their employees to take on the role of "change agents" in their effort to become more flexible, more productive, more responsive to customers, more competitive—in short, more successful. In Module 8, students receive and use information about how to be more effective in organizational change initiatives that they may participate in or lead. The Class Note provides a basic framework for understanding change, again relying on our three lenses, and for taking useful action in change initiatives. It follows the extensive changes made by Procter & Gamble as the corporation moved from a geographic to a product grouping structure.

The accompanying case looks at a change initiative that succeeds in one location but runs into trouble when attempts are made to replicate it elsewhere. The accompanying readings, new to this edition, are all gleaned from *The Dance of Change* by Peter Senge and colleagues.

Module 9
Organizational Action in Complex Environments

Module 9 helps to develop an understanding of how to analyze an organization's environment, especially with regard to other organizations that are important for its survival and success. As organizations become more networked, flexible, and global, interaction with the external environment increases and becomes even more critical to success. Again turning to our three lenses, we present different but complementary perspectives on the environment and examine the intricacies of environmental analysis in a global context.

A new section on integrating the strategic, political, and cultural perspectives has been added as a lead-in to the case material. The RU-486 case, a particularly complex case that was originally developed at INSEAD, has been adapted for inclusion in this module. As the drug's manufacturer tries, at least on the surface, to frame the environment in "neutral" business terms, holding fast to a strategic design perspective, powerful external stakeholders mobilize to influence the company's actions. The institutional environment also constrains the company's actions in ways that may not be immediately evident until application of the cultural lens comes into play.

Module 10
Learning Across Borders: Disneyland on the Move

One of the most difficult aspects of operating in a global context is determining how a particular product or process will fare when transplanted into a rather different and distinctive cultural context. When a company takes its operations abroad, learning and change always figure into the equation. Module 10 takes a look at all of Disney's theme park operations, which will grow to five in 2005 with the anticipated opening of Hong Kong Disneyland, but reserves special attention for Disneyland Paris. Disney was successful beyond all expectations in its first venture abroad, Tokyo Dislneyland, but it was troubled beyond all expectations in its second global venture in France. And the troubles continue to this day even though Disneyland Paris is far and away the number 1 tourist site in Europe, when measured by yearly park visitors.

Module 10 functions as an extended case study of the Walt Disney Company and includes input from scholarly papers, consultant reports, and business press accounts. From this mixture of readings students receive an extensive analysis of Disney in its home environments (Anaheim and Orlando) and are then asked to contrast that experience with Disneyland in France, Japan, and Hong Kong, putting the the focus on what Disney has learned across borders and what it still needs to learn to survive.

Skills

The Skills section of *Managing for the Future* continues to promote the development of management skills by focusing on the range of actions managers can take to cope effectively with change and has been expanded to include a new module on leadership.

Module 11   Managing Cultural Diversity
Module 12   Negotiation and Conflict Resolution
Module 13   Change from Within: Roads to Successful Issue Selling
Module 14   Leadership

Module 11
Managing Cultural Diversity

Module 11 has been substantially reworked to emphasize the role of diversity, not just for labor markets and consumer niches but also for enhancing organizational learning and effectiveness. This module introduces students to the bystander perspective and includes videotaped vignettes that focus on building skills for intervening in workplace situations where respect for diversity is being undermined. Students learn about their responsibilities as bystanders, see the result of action and nonaction in these situations, and come to understand their own biases. A new elective reading on the "third paradigm" for diversity management (identified by Thomas and Ely)—the learning-and-effectiveness paradigm—replaces an older work on affirmative action. Content has also been expanded to include more on the relevance of diversity outside the United States, with additional references cited on women around the globe.

Module 12
Negotiation and Conflict Resolution

Working in a diverse and changing organization with extensive external contact means greater interpersonal interaction and often greater conflict. In this type of environment—in the *new* organization—negotiation skills are of paramount importance. Module 12 provides a complete overview of the key concepts that managers need to engage in negotiations and has been revised to sharpen its emphasis on how to create the conditions for success when negotiating. New readings and references have been added to provide a forum for the latest thinking on a host of issues related to negotiation and conflict. The Mango Systems role play has been retained. This in-class exercise, followed by a structured debriefing (outlined in full in the Detailed Teaching Notes), ensures that negotiation skills are both discussed and applied. In it students have to read the signals given off by various organizational actors and then decide what to do. Module 12 also includes an optional video companion that specifically looks at how people set the stage for negotiations. The video can be used to illustrate how openings shape what subsequently happens in a negotiation and to supplement discussions of gender and style.

Module 13
Change from Within: Roads to Successful Issue Selling

In Module 13, the ability to generate trust for new ideas plays large as do the issues surrounding legitimate versus illegitimate organizational players, timing, and framing. First six essential issue selling processes—bundling, framing, language, involvement, approach, and timing—are explained in detail. Then, from this tactical foundation, students explore the challenge of selling charged, or undiscussable, issues in a variety of corporate environments. Focusing on the best methods to raise both comfortable and charged issues within the firm, Module 13 convincingly shows that today's managers must be prepared to sell ideas both up and down the organization.

The Inex case concentrates on the difficulties of selling a charged issue in an unresponsive organization. Students are asked to map out a tactical strategy for having the issue heard and supported by middle management, and in so doing, discover that an issue is frequently not sold solely on its own merits.

Module 14
Leadership

Module 14 is a new addition to *Managing for the Future*. It develops an integrative framework for studying leadership that blends four leadership capabilities—sensemaking, relating, visioning, and inventing—with the leader's unique "change signature," or the characteristic way that he or she makes things happen. Particular emphasis is placed on the distributive nature of leadership in today's flat, networked, and flexible organizations, where leadership permeates all levels, and on how leaders can act to gain credibility under threat. Two cases explore the contrasting leadership of Carly Fiorina, chairman and CEO of Hewlett-Packard, and MIT president Charles Vest. An exercise centering on students' change signatures complements the conceptual framework. Two elective readings, an article from *Fast Company* and an excerpt from *Geeks and Geezers*, by W. G. Bennis and R. J. Thomas, explore how change signatures develop.

The Modules in Toto

Taken together, the 14 modules in *Managing for the Future* include most topics covered by conventional texts on organizational behavior, from perception, interpersonal communication, and cognitive styles, to group process, team performance, and intergroup relations, to organizational environments, change, and rewards. Admittedly, our approach to teaching the subject is eclectic. We meld case studies, experiential exercises, theory, and video with our individual preferences and rely on the supporting framework of the strategic design, political, and cultural lenses to hold everything together. Although we try to examine and predict the directions that the "new" organization will take in future, we are quick to acknowledge that no one can be sure. Will future organizations be large sets of integrated firms similar to those in Japan, or will we see lots of smaller virtual firms that pull together the manufacturing, service, and distribution of other specialized companies? Will we be able to manage our diversity and link across the globe, or will we fall back to keeping within our own borders? We do not know the answers to these questions, but we do know that it is fun and motivating to think about organizational forms of the future and the skills and capabilities that will be needed when we get there.

In conclusion, these modules represent our sense of what works best in the limited time allocated to teach an introductory course in organizational behavior, and we are committed to updating and adding to them. We also would like to think of these modules as a product of the whole field. That is, we encourage you to let us know of changes that you would like to see, or ideas that you have. If you think that you have a module that would fit into the framework of the course and would add to the breadth or depth of the material covered, please get in touch with us. We hope that our approach and materials work as well for you as they have worked for us.

Support Materials

Instructor's Manual (ISBN 0-324-05576-5). Prepared by the text authors, the Instructor's Manual provides faculty with comprehensive and integrated teaching support. Each Instructor's Module includes an overview of key learning principles, a recap of Student Module content, explanations of preclass assignments (if applicable), a brief teaching plan (including various options for segmenting the class into manageable chunks), and Detailed Teaching Notes, which offer (1) practical advice for directing in-class exercises and discussions, and (2) insights for reaching consistently constructive conclusions. The authors relate their particular experiences in running the course at MIT and allow plenty of room for adapting their methods to individual styles and preferences. Transparencies and handouts are also included.

PowerPoint. A set of PowerPoint slides accompanies every module, providing instructors with a complete set of basic notes for lectures, cases, exercises, and handouts. Available for download at http://ancona.swlearning.com.

Video (ISBN0-324-23254-3). Optional video companions to accompany four modules are available on VHS cassette to instructors who adopt *Managing for the Future.*

- **Module 2** The video companion for Module 2 corresponds to the Dynacorp case. It records the remarks of key informants in Dynacorp's Customer Operations group and provides useful inputs for diagnosing what has been facilitating and hindering the change initiative at the firm.
- **Module 10** A short CNN news segment about EuroDisney (later renamed Disneyland Paris), which was first broadcast on the one-year anniversary of the park's opening, dramatizes Disney's continuing struggle to transplant the Disneyland experience in France.
- **Module 11** Written and produced by the Sloan School of Management and used in MIT's own skills training focus groups and courses, the video companion for Module 11 is an enactment of the eight bystander exercises that appear in the module.
- **Module 12** The video companion for Module 12 complements the Mango Systems role-playing exercise featured in the module. It captures the opening sequences of several pairs of Mango Systems negotiators, which can be used to illustrate how opening exchanges shape what subsequently happens in a negotiation.

Managing for the Future **Web Site.** Online support is provided at http://ancona.swlearning.com.

Acknowledgments

We would like to express our appreciation to colleagues who have taught with us and contributed to our thinking and writing: Mitch Abolafia, Stuart Albert, Ella Bell, Paul Carlile, Deborah Kolb, Amy Segal, Susan Ashford, and Jane Dutton. Our thanks also go to Gordon E. Dehler, Jean A. Grube, Ali Mir, Bruce H. Kemelgor, Gil Preuss, Sandy Kristin Piderit, and Ivan Manev, whose constructive reviews helped to fine-tune our revision plans.

About the Authors

Deborah Ancona

Deborah Ancona is the Seley Distinguished Professor of Management at the Sloan School of Management at MIT. She received bachelor's and master's degrees in psychology from the University of Pennsylvania and a Ph.D. in organizational behavior from Columbia University. Prior to joining MIT, she was on the faculty of the Amos Tuck School at Dartmouth College. Professor Ancona's major research interests include group processes, team performance, boundary management, time and timing in organizations, and "entrainment" and "temporal leadership," which push companies to reorganize in ways that better mesh with the key cycles and rhythms of business. In her current research, she proposes a new organizational structure—the "X-team"—that allows teams to manage complex tasks while facilitating movement across stages of the value chain and adapting to business environment changes. She has published in *Administrative Science Quarterly, Academy of Management Journal, Organization Science,* and *Group and Organization Studies.*

Thomas A. Kochan

Thomas A. Kochan is the George M. Bunker Professor of Management at the Sloan School of Management at MIT. He received his bachelor's, master's, and Ph.D. degrees in industrial relations from the University of Wisconsin. Prior to joining MIT, he was on the faculty of the School of Industrial and Labor Relations at Cornell University. Professor Kochan's research focuses on the rate of diffusion of innovative human resource policies across U.S. industries. Arguing that the U.S. employment relations system is at a historic crossroads equivalent to that of the 1930s, Kochan examines options for a new public policy for employment relations and describes changes that business and labor must make in order to achieve "mutual gains' in employment relationships. His recent books include *After Lean Production: Evolving Employment Practices in the World Auto Industry* (1997), *The Mutual Gains Enterprise* (1994), *Transforming Organizations* (1992), and *The Transformation of American Industrial Relations* (1986). He has also published in *Administrative Science Quarterly,* the *Academy of Management Journal, Industrial and Labor Relations Review, Industrial Relations,* the *Quarterly Journal of Economics,* and other journals. He is a past president of the International Industrial Relations Association.

Maureen A. Scully

Maureen Scully is Faculty Affiliate at the Center for Gender in Organizations, Simmons School of Management. She also serves as Research Associate for the Initiative for Social Innovation through Business (ISIB) at the Aspen Institute. Her research addresses how the ideal of meritocracy can make inequality in organizations appear as a legitimate outcome of a fair advancement contest. She also focuses on employee caucus groups and diversity in work organizations. Before coming to CGO, Maureen was on the faculty at the MIT Sloan School of Management and a Fellow in the Program on Ethics and the Professions at Harvard University. She has designed and taught courses on human resource management and organizational behavior. She has also consulted with joint labor/management teams to find collaborative pathways to participation, teamwork, and respect for workers across classes. She is currently working on a book, *Luck, Pluck, or Merit? How Americans Make Sense of Inequality* (forthcoming). She received her bachelor's degree in social studies from Harvard-Radcliffe and her master's degree in sociology and Ph.D. in organizational behavior from Stanford University.

John Van Maanen

John Van Maanen is the Erwin Schell Professor of Organization Studies at the Sloan School of Management at MIT. He has been a visiting professor at Yale University, University of Surrey (UK), and INSEAD (France). Professor Van Maanen works in the general area of occupational and organizational sociology. Professor Van Maanen studies people ethnographically—by living with them under the same conditions. Among the groups he has studied intensively are Gloucester fishermen, Disneyland employees, U.S. patrol officers, and London detectives and their superiors. Cultural descriptions figure prominently in his writings about occupational conflicts, organizational careers, and work routines. His recent writings examine the social history of ethnographic understandings of work organizations and the various ways particular occupation identities take shape and change in work settings. He is the author of numerous articles and books including *Essays in Interpersonal Relations, Organizational Careers, Tales of the Field,* and most recently, *Representation in Ethnography*. He currently serves on the editorial boards of *Administrative Science Quarterly, Journal of Contemporary Ethnography,* and *Qualitative Sociology,* and he is a member of the American Sociological Association and the Society for Applied Anthropology.

D. Eleanor Westney

D. Eleanor Westney is the Sloan Fellows Professor of International Management at the Sloan School of Management at MIT. She received her undergraduate education at the University of Toronto and her Ph.D. in sociology from Princeton University. Professor Westney's long-term research interest is learning across borders: how organizational patterns developed in one social context are adapted in other societies. She has worked extensively on Japan, and is the author of *Imitation and Innovation: The Transfer of Western Organizational Forms to Meiji Japan* (Harvard University Press, 1987) and a number of articles and book chapters on the Japanese business system. Since joining the Sloan faculty in 1982, she has conducted research on cross-border management issues and is the editor (with Sumantra Ghoshal) of *Organization Theory and the Multinational Corporation* (Macmillan, 1993).

Deborah M. Kolb

Deborah Kolb is Professor of Management at the Simmons School of Management and Faculty Affiliate at the Center for Gender in Organizations. She is also a Senior Fellow at the Program on Negotiation at Harvard Law School, where she codirects the Negotiations in the Workplace program. Her research studies how people can become more effective problem solvers by mastering the dual requirements of empowerment and connection in negotiation. Deborah also participates in international research and consulting projects linking strategic business concerns with gender and diversity. She has published several books and numerous articles, including *The Mediators* (MIT Press, 1983), *Making Talk Work: Profiles of Mediators* (Jossey-Bass, 1994), *The Shadow Negotiation: How Women Can Master the Hidden Agendas That Determine Bargaining Success* (with Judith Williams; Simon and Schuster, 2000), and *Everyday Negotiation: Navigating the Hidden Agendas in Bargaining* (with Judith Williams; Jossey-Bass, 2003). She is a faculty co-editor of the *Negotiation Journal* and on the editorial board of the *Journal of Conflict Resolution*. Deborah received her Ph.D. from Sloan School of Management at the Massachusetts Institute of Technology where her dissertation won the Zannetos Prize for outstanding doctoral scholarship. She has a B.A. from Vassar College and an MBA from the University of Colorado.

Jane E. Dutton

Jane E. Dutton is the William Russell Kelly Professor of Business Administration at the University of Michigan Business School. Her research is focused on how organizational conditions enable human thriving. In particular, she focuses on how the quality of connection between people at work affects individual and organizational flourishing. Her research has explored compassion and organizations, resilience and organizations, as well as energy and organizations. This research stream is part of a growing domain of expertise at the University of Michigan called Positive Organizational Scholarship (http://www.bus.umich.edu/Positive). Her past research has explored processes of organizational adaptation, focusing on how strategic issues are interpreted and managed in organizations, as well as issues of organizational identity and change. She earned her bachelor's degree at Colby College, and her M.A. and Ph.D. at Northwestern.

Susan J. Ashford

Susan J. Ashford is the Michael and Susan Jandernoa Professor of Business Administration, Professor of Organizational Behavior and Human Resource Management, and Director of the Executive MBA Program at the University of Michigan Business School. Her current research interests include leadership and managerial effectiveness, issue selling, self-management, and organizational change. She has studied this work in the context of interpersonal relations, organizational change, and employee socialization, Dr. Ashford teaches in the areas of organizational behavior, leadership, negotiation, and the management of organizational change. Her work has been published in a variety of outlets including: the *Academy of Management Review*, *Academy of Management Journal*, *Journal of Applied Psychology*, *Organizational Behavior and Human Decision Processes*, *Research in Organizational Behavior*, and *Strategic Management Journal*, among other outlets. She received her bachelor's degree at San Jose State University, and her M.S. and Ph.D. at Northwestern University.

MANAGING FOR THE FUTURE

Organizational Behavior & Processes

ANALYTICS

Module 1
The "New" Organization:
Taking Action in an Era of
Organizational Transformation

Module 2
Lenses on Organizational
Analysis and Action

Ancona • Kochan • Scully
Van Maanen • Westney

MANAGING FOR THE FUTURE

Organizational Behavior & Processes

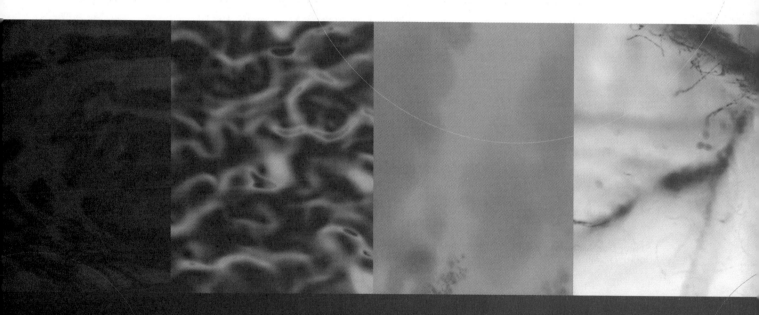

The "New" Organization: Taking Action in an Era of Organizational Transformation

Module 1

MANAGING FOR THE FUTURE
Organizational Behavior & Processes, Third Edition

Deborah Ancona
Sloan School of Management
Massachusetts Institute of Technology

John Van Maanen
Sloan School of Management
Massachusetts Institute of Technology

Thomas A. Kochan
Sloan School of Management
Massachusetts Institute of Technology

D. Eleanor Westney
Sloan School of Management
Massachusetts Institute of Technology

Maureen Scully
Graduate School of Management
Simmons College

Dedicated to those who have inspired us to try to be better students and teachers.
Special thanks to: Professor Jack Barbash • Professor Arthur H. Gladstein • Professor Marius B. Jansen • Professor Joanne Martin • Professor Edgar H. Schein

---

VP/Editorial Director
Jack W. Calhoun

Marketing Manager
Jacquelyn Carrillo

Internal Designer
Bethany Casey

VP/Editor-in-Chief
Michael P. Roche

Production Editor
Emily Gross

Cover Designer
Bethany Casey

Senior Publisher
Melissa S. Acuña

Manufacturing Coordinator
Rhonda Utley

Photographs
©PhotoDisc

Executive Editor
John Szilagyi

Compositor
Trejo Production

Design Project Manager
Bethany Casey

Senior Developmental Editor
Judith O'Neill

Printer
Von Hoffmann Press, Inc.
Frederick, MD

COPYRIGHT ©2005
by South-Western, a division of Thomson Learning.
Thomson Learning™ is a trademark used herein under license.

Printed in the United States of America
1 2 3 4 5 07 06 05 04 03

For more information contact
South-Western College Publishing,
5191 Natorp Boulevard,
Mason, Ohio, 45040
Or you can visit our Internet site at:
http://www.swlearning.com

ALL RIGHTS RESERVED
No part of this work covered by the copyright hereon may be reproduced or used in any form or by any means—graphic, electronic, or mechanical, including photocopying, recording, taping, Web distribution or information storage and retrieval systems—without the written permission of the publisher.

For permission to use material from this text or product, contact us by
Tel: (800) 730-2214
Fax: (800) 730-2215
http://www.thomsonrights.com

Library of Congress Control Number: 2003113908
ISBN 0-324-05575-7

Contents

The "New" Organization: Taking Action in an Era of Organizational Transformation

	Overview	6

Core

	Class Note	**Changing Organizational Models**	10
		Key Features of the "Old" Model of the Organization 11	
		Key Features of the "New" Model of the Organization 13	
		Taking Action in the New Model 18	
		References 21	
	The Press	**A Sampling of Analyses of the New Organization**	22
		The Coming of the New Organization 22	
		The New Managerial Work 22	
		The American Corporation as an Employer 23	
		Designing Effective Organizations 23	
		The Mind of the CEO 23	
		. . . and Some Skeptical Voices	24
		Beyond the Hype 24	
		Will the Organization of the Future Make the Mistakes of the Past? 24	
		Coda to the New Organization 24	
		The Twenty-first Century Firm 25	
	Questionnaire	**Mapping Your Organization**	27

Elective

	Class Note	**Reading the Business Press**	30
	The Press	**The Search for the Organization of Tomorrow**	31
		Management by Web	39
		Ephemeral 39	
		Digitization 42	
		Cultural Change 42	
		Feedback 43	
		Delivering the Goods 43	
		Connections 44	
		Talent Hunt 45	
		Incubator 45	

Index

Overview

Companies, nonprofit institutions, and public-sector organizations today all seem to be demanding that the people they hire and promote be leaders, team players, change agents, entrepreneurs, coaches—all ways of saying that their high-potential employees must understand the "people" side of management and be able to take effective action in the organizations of today and tomorrow. This chorus of demands for organizational skills is rooted in the widespread perception that we are in an era of organizational transformation, when new forms of enterprise are emerging and old forms are changing radically, often in ways that make it more difficult for individuals to act effectively, at least in the ways they have been accustomed to taking action. This module introduces you to the models of organization that dominated management thinking for many decades as well as those that are emerging today, describes the major drivers behind their development, provides a sampling of the controversies over the scale and significance of the so-called new model, and presents some of the challenges in taking effective action in the new organization. In addition, in working through this module, you will begin to build your capabilities in experiential learning; that is, learning by reflective analysis of your own experience and that of your classmates and from interactive class exercises.

The module begins with an extended Class Note on "Changing Organizational Models," which examines the key features of traditional and emerging models of organization and through which we weigh the "old" organizational model (often called "bureaucracy") against the "new" networked, flat, flexible, diverse, and global organization. The Class Note points out that the early excitement about the new model that was ubiquitous in the business press in the early 1990s has been replaced by a growing recognition of how difficult it can be to shift to the new forms, and how challenging it can be for those trying to take action in the new work context. It then provides an introduction to some of the individual skills and organizational features required by the new model.

The Class Note is followed by a sampling of comments by leading academics on the new model, some from those who believe that a major organizational transformation is taking place today, and some from those who take a much more skeptical view, but who also differ from each other on what matters about organizational trends in today's society. The purpose of these brief quotations is to hone your own ability to reflect critically on what you read and what you have experienced concerning today's organizations.

Finally, the module ends with a one-page questionnaire, "Mapping Your Organization," which asks you to characterize an organization in which you have worked in terms of how well it fits the model of the new organization. Fill out the questionnaire prior to class, and come prepared to discuss the following questions:

1. What specific structures or processes in your organization led you to rate it as you did on each of the five features of the new organization?
2. What skills and knowledge were most important for you in working effectively in that organization? What skills do you think were most important for the person who was your manager?

The module also includes two elective readings on the new organization from the business press, one from the early 1990s and one more recent. The 1992 article gives you a sense of the excitement that pervaded writing on the emergence of the new organizational model. The second reading, taken from *Business Week*'s special 2002 issue on the twenty-first-century corporation, was written at the height of the Internet boom, when optimism about an economic and organizational revolution was pervasive, and where Enron was widely seen as an exemplar of the twenty-first-century corporation (rather than the prototype of the excesses of the late twentieth-century that it is today). As you read these two pieces, reflect on what they have in common and where they differ. These readings are preceded by a second Class Note on "Reading the Business Press," which is intended to provide some perspective on the articles, and to encourage you to develop your critical skills as you read popular business journals and the business section of the newspaper.

Additional Exercises

You can expand your learning about the issues raised in this module in several ways. One is to go through current issues of the business press, such as *Business Week, Fortune, Forbes, The Wall Street Journal, The Economist, Management Today, The Asian Wall Street Journal,* and the *Far Eastern Economic Review,* and look for stories on individual organizations that are held up as models or for general trends in management and organization.

See how many of the themes from the readings and discussions in this module also loom large in these articles. What is the viewpoint of the story? Is it admiring? Skeptical of the extent of change? Does it focus on successes, or difficulties, or both? On what kind of information sources does it draw?

Another way of learning more about what kinds of changes might be occurring in today's organizations is to talk with individuals from your parents' generation about the changes they have seen in their workplaces over the last decade. You might also look more closely at the organization in which you now find yourself (or your business school or college) and try to assess the extent to which it is facing some of the same pressures for change—changes in technology, pressures to become more efficient, competitive forces toward greater innovation—that are seen as the drivers of the move to the new organization.

Finally, you can draw on more systematic frameworks and analysis through the readings cited in the footnotes for the Class Note, or in articles in recent issues of the more reader-friendly management research journals such as the *California Management Review*, the *Harvard Business Review*, and the *Sloan Management Review*.

The "New Organization: Taking Action in an Era of Organizational Transformation

CORE

Module

Changing Organizational Models

In the 1990s, a rapidly growing stream of articles in the business press proclaimed that a major organizational transformation was taking place in the United States. The organization of the twenty-first-century was already emerging, according to these writers, and it was radically different from what had gone before: it was customer-focused; team-based; networked in alliances with suppliers, customers, and even competitors; flat, flexible and innovative, diverse, and global. Its workforce was empowered and committed; its managers acted as coaches, not bosses; it was a "learning organization," constantly striving to improve and innovate. The rapid expansion of the Internet in the late 1990s, a development not foreseen when the new model first developed, only reinforced these trends. Organization theorists, some of whom had long predicted that the shift to the "knowledge-based society" would bring about a major change in organizations, provided a more academic perspective on the new era of the "post-modern," "post-bureaucratic," "post-Fordist" organization (see for example Clegg, 1990; Heckscher and Donnellon, 1994; Kaysen, 1996; Capelli et al., 1997; Powell, 2001).

U.S. corporations were not the only organizations to respond to the drumbeat of organizational change. The U.S. administration picked up the theme of organizational transformation, vowing to re-invent government to make it leaner, more responsive, and more flexible. Government organizations from the postal service to the Internal Revenue Service organized teams and task forces, moved to more flexible labor practices, and looked to the corporate world for models of effective new organizational practices. Private nonprofit organizations, from public broadcasting to universities, adopted and adapted the language and the models of the new organization. The robust U.S. economy, whose successes in generating employment, growth, new industries, and global competitiveness were widely associated with organizational transformation, legitimated the "cutting-edge" models espoused by American management and organizations in much of the rest of the world.

A survey of Asian business in 1993 portrayed leading companies in Japan, Korea, Taiwan, and Southeast Asia as "becoming less bureaucratic and more customer focused, decentralising responsibility, motivating staff, continually improving quality, enhancing efficiency, and speeding up decision making . . . exploring management buzz concepts such as 'downsizing' and 'business process re-engineering' that have hitherto seemed irrelevant to Asian companies enjoying double-digit growth" (Selwyn, 1993, 22–23). The 1997 Asian economic crisis only intensified these efforts, doing much to discredit the large, hierarchical diversified business groups that dominated most of these economies before the crisis.

Some European firms such as Nokia could convincingly claim to have been leaders rather than followers in the transition to the new organizational form, and provided local models of the new organization for other European firms. Business leaders in the emerging market economies of Latin America, Eastern Europe, and Russia had hopes of "leap-frogging" rapidly from their more traditional organizational forms of family business groups or state-owned enterprise to the models of the next century. Throughout the world, subsidiaries of U.S. multinational corporations tried, with varying degrees of success, to implement abroad at least some of the changes they were undergoing at home, thereby disseminating at least the rhetoric of the new organization.

By the early twenty-first-century, the early sense of excitement and liberation from the "old," stodgy ways of doing things that characterized writings about the "new organization" in the late 1980s and early 1990s has given way to a recognition of the enormous challenges involved in the transformation. Not only is it often extraordinarily difficult to shift organizations from the "old" to the "new," but as the "new" is established in some companies, it often presents problems and challenges of its own. Working and managing in the old organization may have been boring, constricting, and frustratingly slow. But working and managing in a networked, team-based, flat, flexible, diverse, and global organization often involves long hours, high levels of uncertainty, and rapid personnel turnover that get in the way of developing the networks needed to make an organization work. Stress and burnout take their toll, and many people quit in search of less stressful work. Involuntary departures have also increased, as down-sizing becomes a way of life in many companies: according to one source, in the United States downsizing eliminated more jobs in 1999, a year of record corporate profit levels and impressive economic growth, than in any previous year in that decade (Powell, 2001, 34). The expectations of the 1960s that technological advances would produce a wealthy leisure society proved to be sadly misplaced: Americans are working longer hours, and individual incomes overall are not rising (although household incomes tended to rise as women joined the labor force), except for top executives. The wage gap between the highest and lowest paid worker in a company has been rising steadily. In the early 1970s, U.S. CEO salaries were 35 times those of the entry-level worker (Thurow, 1996, 405); by 2002, they were 400 times the salary of the average employee (*Financial Times*, 2002, 11).

Analysts are divided on whether these developments are only a temporary by-product of the shift to the new organizational model, or whether they are intrinsically linked to the flat, flexible, networked features of the new organization. They do agree on two things, however: first, for organizations that grew up with the old model it can be difficult to move to the new model and, second, it can be hard to work in it when you get there. Moreover, the certainty of the early 1990s that every organization would move to the new model has given way to a recognition that not only will we see a number of variants of the new organization, but that for many organizations the old model has shown considerable resiliency. We see today some organizations that continue to follow the old model, and many more that exhibit features of the old in combination with aspects of the new. In a recent interview, for example, a manager in a major hotel chain proudly described his company's new team-based, customer-focused organization, and in the next breath revealed that their management experts were training maids in the 60 steps to follow in making a bed, which according to intensive study had proved to be the fastest and most efficient way to make a bed. Such rigidity in standard operating procedures, characteristic of the old organization, can be seen in a wide range of successful organizations today, from McDonald's production of burgers and fries to software developers.

Nevertheless, the model of the new organization has transformed the organizational landscape in which we work and try to take effective action, whether as employees, as managers, as customers, as suppliers, or as citizens and stakeholders struggling to come to terms with the effects of the new organizational forms on our societies and our communities. Business schools are increasingly required to change their curricula to produce managers who can act effectively in organizations that are more team-based, more closely linked to customers and suppliers, flatter, quicker to respond to change, more diverse in the composition of their workforce, and more effective at operating in an increasingly global economy. Organizations in both the private and public sectors want managers with the people skills and the understanding of organizations to help them move toward what many of their leaders see as the organizational model of the twenty-first century. The strong emphasis on "developing leaders" in business schools and in many companies reflects the extent to which organizations desperately need people who can take effective action in the complex world of the new organization. To understand more clearly what these needs mean, we must examine more closely the key features of the old model and the new.

Key Features of the "Old" Model of the Organization

The German sociologist Max Weber (1864–1920) was the first to identify systematically a set of features shared by modern large-scale organization in both the private and the public sectors. For Weber, writing at the turn of the century, the model of "rational-legal bureaucracy" that he developed was the new organization of his era, the quintessential modern organizational form. This organizational form provided the base for the expansion in scale and the predictability of the large industrial enterprise and the administrative apparatus of the nation-state that were to dominate the organizational landscape of the new twentieth century.

Today, when we take for granted the idea that such different organizations as General Motors, Citibank, UPS, Harvard University, the Army, and state government are fundamentally the same kind of social system and that they can "benchmark" their practices and learn from each other, the concept of an "organization" as a basic category of social systems is hardly surprising. This recognition is a relatively recent phenomenon, however, and Max Weber can be seen as its originator, even though his identification of the bureaucratic model occurred much earlier than its widespread application in the study of organizations. Weber's work was first translated into English in the late 1940s, at a time when the expansion of the social sciences in U.S. universities and the rapid expansion of U.S. industrial enterprise opened up new opportunities for behavioral scientists to pursue research into the behavior of people in organizations and the behavior of organizations of a wide range of types. Weber's model of bureaucracy provided a conceptual framework for generalizing beyond the study of any one particular type of organization. Subsequent generations of organizational theorists expanded Weber's model of "bureaucracy," moving beyond his focus on the organization's internal features to include an analysis of its relationships with its external environment.

The classic model of formal organization or bureaucracy, which in the 1950s and the 1960s defined the modern organization, included the following features:

1. Clearly delineated specialized individual positions and jobs, with careful and detailed specification of the qualifications required to fill the position, the responsibilities and performance requirements of that position, and the assignment to it of the resources required to do the job
2. A formal hierarchy of these positions, with a clear line of authority that sets out clearly the powers—and limitations of those powers—for each position or office, in a detailed "chain of command" (hence the reference to the classic model is often called a command-and-control system)
3. Formal rules and standard operating procedures that govern activities, specified in written documents and files (the feature of the old organization that has given bureaucracy such a negative image as a social system that too often seems to make following the correct rules and procedures more important than accomplishing the ultimate goals)
4. Set boundaries for each department and subunit, and clear boundaries between the organization itself and its environment, with relationships that cross those internal and external boundaries assigned to formal "boundary-spanners," which are offices that specialize in handling various elements in the environment and protecting the rest of the organization from "disturbances" from the outside
5. Standardized training and training requirements, career paths, and reward systems, based on the development of expertise and creating a predictable and stable career for those who fulfilled dutifully the requirements of their positions

In most organizational analyses, the organization's environment was assumed to be a single country. Even in multinational corporations, this assumption was rarely challenged. Such companies were usually organized into country subsidiaries responsive to their local environment, and linked to the rest of the corporation through specified boundary-spanning departments, such as the international division, or through top-level expatriate managers who served as key boundary-spanners in the multinational system.

The classic model of the organization had many strengths. Its virtues included:

1. *Predictability and Reliability:* The emphasis on following rules and standard procedures that so exasperates the critics of bureaucracy ensures, at its best, that outcomes are predictable and reliable. Organizations as diverse as the traditional local bank branch and IBM in its heyday had, in common with a reputation for being bureaucratic, the ability to offer customers reliable, standard, predictable products and services, time after time.
2. *Impartiality:* One of the main reasons for the bureaucratic emphasis on rules, standard procedures, and clearly specified arenas of responsibility is to produce what Max Weber called an "impersonal" system that does not differentiate its outcomes and procedures according to individual differences or favoritism. This contrast to the family-based enterprise and the personalized state systems of feudalism was long seen as one of the strengths of bureaucracy and one of its peculiarly modern characteristics.
3. *Expertise:* The specialization of jobs and positions allows individuals and departments to deepen their expertise in a particular task, making for levels of experience-based and knowledge-based capabilities that exceed those of less specialized systems.
4. *Clear Lines of Control:* The hierarchy of offices makes it clear who has the authority to make decisions and to receive information on which to base those decisions. In the classic model, information flows up and decisions flow down.

The very strengths of the old bureaucratic model can become weaknesses, however, if the environment changes so that these virtues are no longer a source of advantage. Analysts of organizations have long known that not all parts of the organization are equally bureaucratic: those parts of the organization that had to be more innovative (research laboratories, for example) usually exhibited fewer bureaucratic features, including much less reliance on rules, less standardization, and flatter hierarchies. For many years, a more "organic" and less "mechanical" version of organization was seen as a necessary corrective to the dominant bureaucratic model in certain parts of the organization (such as R&D laboratories, or in new high-growth businesses, for example). Increasingly, as organizations found themselves having to respond to intensifying competition by becoming more innovative in more areas such as customer service, continuous improvement in manufacturing, and greater diversity of products and services, the virtues of bureaucracy in terms of stability and predictability often came to be seen as liabilities. The business process reengineering efforts of the 1990s revealed to many organizations that deeply entrenched specializations and internal "walls" between departments could get in the way of the cross-departmental and cross-functional cooperation needed to implement change and improve customer service. New information technologies changed the nature of the "files" and information channels so central to the concept of bureaucracy. For many companies, international competition and expanding global markets widened the cross-border dimension of activity beyond the group of specialized international managers whose preserve it had been for so long.

Gradually, over the 1990s, the changes necessary to make organizations work more effectively came to be seen by many managers and management scholars as constituting a new model of organization, whose key features were in sharp contrast to those that had long been central to the classic model of organization.

Key Features of the "New" Model of the Organization

The "new" organization can be defined in terms of five complex, interacting features: networked, flat, flexible, diverse, and global. Let us take each in turn, and look more closely at the elements that make up each feature and the factors in the business environment that are widely seen as drivers of the new features.

Networked

U.S. management theory and practice long emphasized the need for clear lines of individual authority and responsibility, for managerial autonomy, and for protecting the organization's core activities from the uncertainties and volatility of its environment. In contrast, the new model sees the organization as based on interdependence across individuals, groups, and subunits within the organization and with key elements of its environment. The boundaries of the new model are permeable or semipermeable, allowing the much more frequent movement of people and information across them.

Within the organization, this permeability translates into several specific subfeatures:

1. Emphasizing teams as fundamental units of activity within each organizational arena of activity, rather than individual jobs
2. Using cross-functional teams that bring together people from different departments or sections of the organization
3. Creating systems for sharing information widely in the organization, horizontally and in both directions vertically (as opposed to the old model in which information travels up and decisions travel down)

In the organization's relations with its environment, it means:

1. Building close relationships with suppliers, rather than buffering the effects of their behavior (or misbehavior) through inventories and arm's-length contracts and control systems. The just-in-time delivery systems popularized by the quality movement, for example, mean that suppliers are closely integrated into the manufacturing process, delivering small lots of parts as they are needed for production. The growing outsourcing of components and subsystems in manufacturing and support activities in service industries means sharing much more information with suppliers, and developing much higher levels of interdependence with them. The largest supplier of networking systems, Cisco Systems, for example, owns only two factories; most of its "value added" in manufacturing comes from its extensive network of closely linked suppliers.
2. Putting people in functional areas such as production and R&D directly in contact with certain customers, rather than relying on specialized boundary-spanning departments like marketing or customer service to mediate between the customer and those parts of the organization that develop and produce products or services.
3. Building coalitions to work together with key stakeholders, such as local community groups or government agencies over environmental issues or with labor unions over the organization of work, rather than adopting a confrontational or defensive posture.
4. Building alliances and cooperative networks with other companies, so that another firm may be a "3-C" company—one that is simultaneously a competitor, a customer, and a collaborator, or partner.

One version of the networked organization is what has been called the *virtual company*. It seems close to what in the 1980s was called the *hollow corporation*; that is, a small cluster of managers who contract out all or nearly all of the tasks involved in producing the company's product or service. One example of the "virtual organization" is the independent movie project, where the producer contracts for the duration of the production with the writer, director, actors, camera operators, and so on. Some of the more dramatic scenarios of organizational transformation posit that more and more organizations in the twenty-first-century will be virtual companies, linking workers, suppliers, and customers around the globe through advanced communications technologies.

Many complex factors drive the growing recognition of the importance of networks, including the following:

1. The availability of new telecommunications and information technologies vastly increases

the range of possibilities for connecting people and organizational units across distance and across formal organizational boundaries.
2. The competitive need for rapid response to customer needs, changing environments, and demands for innovation means that specialized individual jobs and "islands" of expertise can no longer provide the integration of knowledge needed to create value for customers.
3. The need for increasingly complex and diverse resources to develop and deliver value to customers means that companies can no longer hope to rely wholly on internally generated resources and capabilities, but must draw on external sources as efficiently and effectively as possible.
4. The old model of dealing with a rapidly shifting environment by trying to insulate the core activities of the firm from the sources of change too often meant that a company followed its routines long after they proved inadequate. Instead, organizations have found that it is more effective and efficient to deal with volatility (that is, rapid shifts) in the environment by building networks between the source of that volatility (the customer, the supplier, the regulator) and the part of the organization most directly affected by it: for example, by putting product development engineers into direct contact with key customers, or linking suppliers directly into the production process with Internet-based reordering and just-in-time delivery systems.

Flat

Perhaps the broadest consensus on the organization of the twenty-first-century (and on what constitutes a best practice today) is that the company is much leaner and has far few layers of management than the old model. Many large companies such as IBM, Procter & Gamble, and even Toyota removed several layers of middle management in the past decade. As companies grow in sales but reduce their number of employees, productivity improves significantly.

Flattening the hierarchy is not simply a matter of reducing layers of management. The "flat" organization is also one that seeks "empowerment" of the operating levels of the organization, pushing decision making down to the "front line" of the company so that the unit of the organization responsible for implementing any decision also has the power to make it, or at least participate in making it. This flattening of the hierarchy becomes both possible and necessary because of the following factors:

1. Organizations need to respond more rapidly and more flexibly to changes in their markets and technology and to engage their people in continuous improvement of operations, and therefore to eliminate the delays caused by a tall, control-oriented hierarchy.
2. Changes in information technology remove the need for layers of middle managers whose main tasks centered on organizing and transmitting information, which allows organizations to monitor activities more quickly and adjust accordingly. It removes the long-standing justification for more hierarchical systems of control—that people at the front line of the organization had to be prevented from taking unapproved initiatives that might take weeks or months to correct if they were wrong.
3. Organizations face intense competitive pressures to cut costs. Some attribute these pressures to competition from firms in other countries in an increasingly global economy; others stress instead the intense competition among U.S. firms to increase their appeal to stock analysts and investors by steadily improving their bottom line—and cutting costs is a proven way of looking good to these constituencies. Fewer managers mean a smaller payroll, and firms have finally discovered that getting rid of a manager cuts costs more significantly than getting rid of a low-level employee.

Flexible

Many companies are finding it difficult to rely on the well-codified but rigid rules, routines, and structures that have been the key characteristics of the models of bureaucracy and formal organization in the past. The great strengths of "going by the rules" have been predictability, control, and fairness. Today, however, companies are increasingly called to respond flexibly to diverse needs of employees, customers, and other stakeholders (that is, those who have a "stake" in the survival and success of the organization, including shareholders and local communities), in ways that allow a variety of responses without giving rise to serious accusations of injustice and unfairness. Individuals must turn their hands to whatever activity will help to solve a problem or satisfy the customer, without being restrained by formal procedures or job descriptions. Many manufacturing firms, for example, have moved to flexible production or customized mass production systems that enable a factory to adjust quickly to a wide variety of changing market demands. Many service firms emphasize tailoring their services to the specific needs of particular customers or groups of customers, rather than following a one-size-fits-all approach. More difficult, perhaps, they must develop systems that encourage innovation and creativity, instead of blocking change because it might cause unpredictability and instability.

Part of this flexibility is the growing use of temporary structures such as projects, task forces, and informal "communities of practice" that do not affect an individual's formal position or the formal organizational structure, but that allow the speedy reconfiguration of people and resources to address certain problems. It also involves the use of temporary or contingent workers. Microsoft, for example, had 39,000 employees at the beginning of 2001; it also employed an additional 5,000 temporary workers (programmers, code testers, secretaries, etc.) who were mostly supplied by outside staffing agencies.

The need for flexibility is driven by the following factors:

1. Intensifying competition, so that capabilities for tailoring products and services to a range of customer needs are increasingly a source of competitive advantage
2. An increasingly diverse labor force, with needs that differ over the life cycle as well as across workers
3. An increasingly complex and unpredictable external environment, with which the organization is more and more interdependent, as we saw in the discussion of the externally networked organization

Diverse

The three previous features of the new model reinforce the fourth: the need for the new organization to accommodate a diversity of perspectives and approaches, career paths and incentive systems, people and policies within its boundaries, and to respond to an increasingly diverse array of external constituencies and stakeholders. The old model, in retrospect, is exemplified by the "organization man" of the 1950s—a male executive, committed to serving the interests of the firm in return for a secure, predictable, and long-term career and social identity, and usually with a wife who does not work outside the home—and by a managing-by-the-rules approach that treats every employee and every situation by a predefined, standardized set of rules. The new model presents a diverse array of possible career trajectories, including part-time work, home-based telecommuting (where employees are linked to the office through a home computer), different "tracks" that people can choose depending on their interests and family situations, and increasing levels of exits from the firm. It includes an array of people who are in the firm but have a nontraditional relationship to it: full-time contract workers, for example, or former employees hired on as independent consultants. It is open to people from a wide variety of backgrounds and provides avenues for them to let the organization know whether older systems of communication and traditional expectations of managers are creating a difficult or stressful work environment.

An organization that values diversity is preferred in today's world based on the following reasons:

1. The growing diversity of the workforce in demographic terms (more women, greater ethnic diversity, more international scope, more people entering and leaving the organization at different points in their life cycle)
2. A greater need for innovation and creative approaches to solving problems, which seem to benefit from diverse approaches and viewpoints
3. Growing volatility (that is, unpatterned and unpredictable change) in the business environment
4. "Requisite variety," or the diversity that matches the diversity of key elements of the environment

Flat, flexible, and networked organizations that are linked closely to other organizations with different systems and cultures, and with customers who have a variety of needs and approaches, often find that they need to muster comparable diversity internally. Functioning effectively in this environment requires not only an ability to recognize and tolerate diversity but a willingness to value it.

Global

Many companies in the past were international, but not global: that is, they operated in many countries, but they kept operations in each country quite separate, with little interdependence or interaction across the organizations in different countries. To be "global" means to be involved in interactions across borders. For example, in the past the Japanese subsidiary of a company such as IBM or Procter & Gamble focused primarily on developing and producing products for the Japanese market. Today, it will have a "global mandate" for certain product lines for markets around the world. The products developed in its technical centers will often be transferred to the company's subsidiaries elsewhere for manufacture. Even products assembled in Japan will have components or ingredients manufactured elsewhere in the company.

Relatively few companies are now insulated from international interactions with suppliers, customers, or competitors from outside their home country. Even firms in those industries that remain quite strongly focused on their home market must often deal with competitors from another country and with the need to learn from a best practice developed outside that market. In consequence, more and more of the networks that characterize the new organization stretch across borders. Some of these networks are internal to the company, as the firm extends itself across borders by setting up its own marketing offices or factories outside its home country. Other networks are external. Companies build international links with foreign customers and suppliers, expanding their markets by export or by marketing alliances with foreign firms and reducing their costs by finding low-cost sources for parts and subsystems. More and more, we see that value chains (that is, the steps involved in producing a final product or service), which tended to be located within one country in the "old" model, are crossing borders.

We are also seeing that linking across countries, which used to be the job of specialist international managers, increasingly involves a much greater number of individuals at middle and even lower levels of the company. Blue-collar workers go from the American or Asian auto plants in which they are employed to the Japanese factories of their parent company to learn core skills. Junior engineers travel internationally to solve problems for customers or to work on international technology development projects. More and more people in the organization are required to develop an international or global way of thinking about their business.

Some of the key factors that underlie the growing importance of the global dimension of the new organization follow:

1. Greatly reduced costs of international transportation and communications, such that products and parts can be made in one location and sold at competitive prices in many locations. For example, cars made in Japan and Korea and car parts from Germany and Taiwan are sold throughout the world.
2. The growing equalization across advanced industrial and emerging market societies of what Michael Porter calls "advanced factor endowments," including workforce education levels, technological and managerial capabilities, telecommunications, and transportation infrastructure. This equalization increases the number of firms that can pick up and apply new product or process technologies. Components for consumer electronics or telecommunications equipment, for example, are made by companies based in countries all around the world. This equalization both intensifies international competition and increases the range of strategic options that any firm has in purchasing components or finding markets for its products.
3. The globalization of markets, as living standards become more similar across countries and as the consuming class becomes larger and more oriented to the international market in many countries. Although many markets remain local and distinctive, others increasingly offer firms the opportunity to expand their markets with only modest tailoring of their products or services.
4. Continuing differences in cost structures across countries, such that firms trying to lower their costs can identify high-capability but lower-cost locations for support activities (such as the growing use by U.S. companies of software engineering centers in India or data-processing centers in Ireland) or for production (such as manufacturing operations in the export processing zones of Asia).
5. The potential for expanding the capabilities of the firm by cross-border learning, especially by building networks into leading markets or centers of technology. Formerly, companies expanded internationally by exploiting the advanced capabilities they had developed in their home markets. Today, however, we see that long-established multinationals from the "Triad" (North America, Japan, and Western Europe) and new multinationals from emerging market countries are both expanding into the most advanced markets in order to improve (rather than exploit) their competitive advantage. Japanese and European pharmaceutical firms enter the United States to gain biotechnology capabilities, for example; U.S. firms go to Japan to set up business units in advanced display technologies; Korean and Taiwanese electronics firms set up research centers in Silicon Valley; Indian software firms set up development centers in the United States.
6. The growing role of international nongovernmental organizations (NGOs) in pressuring companies worldwide to reduce pollution and to adopt corporate codes of conduct and social responsibility.

Figure 1.1 provides a summary of the contrasts between old and new organization.

The model of the networked, flat, flexible, diverse, and global "new" organization presented here, which you will continue to encounter in many of your readings about organizations today and in the business press, is an "ideal type" in the sense used by Max Weber. It is a construct or mental model that is useful in identifying the key elements of a complex social phenomenon. Few if any real organizations completely embody all the features of the model. Moreover, an "ideal type" is not an "ideal" in the popular sense of being intrinsically good and desirable. Weber's model of bureaucracy was an ideal type, but Weber himself

Figure 1.1 Summary of Contrasting Features of the Old and New Models of Organization

Old Model	New Model
Individual position/job as basic unit of organization	Team as a basic unit
Relations with environment handled by specialist boundary-spanners	Densely networked with environment
Vertical flows of information	Horizontal and vertical flows of information
Decisions come down, information flows up	Decisions made where information resides
Tall (many layers of management)	Flat (few layers of management)
Emphasis on structures	Emphasis on processes
Emphasis on rules and standard procedures	Emphasis on results and outcomes
Fixed hours	Flexible workday, part-time workers
Career paths upward, linear	Career paths lateral, flexible
Standardized evaluation and reward systems	Customized evaluation and reward systems
Single strong culture with strong expectations of homogeneous behavior	Diversity viewpoints and behaviors
Ethnocentric mindset	International/global mindset
Specialist international managers	Boundary-crossers at all levels
Local value chains	Value chains crossing borders
Environment defined in terms of country of location	Environment seen as global

was far from considering it ideal. He referred to the "iron cage" of bureaucracy and worried about its effects on the quality of modern work life. Similarly, the "new" organizational model is an ideal type that is useful in analyzing the trends of change in organizations today, but it is also a model that exerts great pressure on organizations today to think about changing to become more networked, flat, flexible, diverse, and global. Three reasons explain this pressure. First, this model seems to be more effective and more efficient for organizing certain kinds of economic, political, and social activities in an information-based world. Second, it has become so widely accepted in today's society that an organization that does not present itself as networked, flat, flexible, diverse, and global runs the risk of being seen as stodgy, old-fashioned, and unattractive to prospective employees and investors. A third reason is that many managers and writers regard the features of the new model not just as an ideal type but as a set of ideals. They believe strongly that organizing by teams, for example, is not just more effective than organizing by individual positions, but that it is better in terms of what is good and even morally right, or in terms of the great wave of history. They believe that flat is better than tall, flexible is better than predictable, diverse is better than homogeneous, and global is better than than domestic, regardless of the organization's context. You may choose to believe likewise, but the model of the new organization we have presented here does not make this assumption. It is meant as a Weberian "ideal type" that helps you understand and categorize certain aspects of today's organizations. We encourage you to question and assess critically the idealization of the new model, even as you wrestle with the challenges of taking effective action in organizations that have adopted, or are in the process of adopting, its elements.

Taking Action in the New Model

These and other features of the new organization involve major changes in the roles and careers of individual managers, the kinds of organizational capabilities needed by the organization, and the relationships that the organization has with its environment. For example, the fact that firms are simultaneously calling for high commitment and effort from employees and moving to a flexible workforce requires rethinking the relationship between the individual and the organization. In a flat, networked organization, managers cannot rely on formal authority to accomplish their goals; they must negotiate with other key players, build trust, and work across the boundaries of their assigned roles. Most of the analyses of the new organization agree that it changes the skills that individuals need in order to take action, and changes the kinds of tools that the organization must make available to employees.

This change is not easy. Rosabeth Kanter, a pioneer in analyzing the challenges facing the old organizations trying to change to the new model, has identified a set of contradictory demands that the "new game," as she calls it, generates for individual managers:

Think strategically and invest in the future—but keep the numbers up today.

Be entrepreneurial and take risks—but don't cost the business anything by failing.

Continue to do everything you're currently doing even better—and spend more time communicating with employees, serving on teams, and launching new projects.

Know every detail of your business—but delegate more responsibility to others.

Become passionately dedicated to "visions" and fanatically committed to carrying them out—but be flexible, responsive, and able to change direction quickly.

Speak up, be a leader, set the direction—but be participative, listen well, cooperate.

Throw yourself wholeheartedly into the entrepreneurial game and the long hours it takes—and stay fit.

Succeed, succeed, succeed—and raise terrific children. (Kanter, 1989, 20–21)

Obviously, taking action in the new organization and shifting organizations from the old to the new model both have wide-ranging implications on three levels: (1) for the skills and knowledge of the individual manager, (2) for the capabilities of the organization, and (3) for the organization's relationships with its environment. Let us turn to a brief examination of some of these challenges.

One way to think about what the new organization means for the kinds of skills needed by individual managers, the challenges of managing the organization, and the challenges of managing the organization's interactions with its environment is to take each of the five characteristics of the new model and look at its implications for each of these levels. A complete analysis would take a book rather than a short survey, but the following section gives one example for each level and each feature. You yourself can and should think of others. The examples also show how difficult it can be to isolate any one feature of the new organization and discuss it separately from the rest. Each feature is related to the others in important ways.

Networked

For individual managers, the increasing reliance on teams as a basic building block of the organization means that they must develop their capabilities at teamwork, that is, their skills as team members as well as team leaders. (Far more managers are eager to develop their skills at leadership rather than at membership.) Too often we assume that "being a good team player" is a matter of personality. Although some people do find teams a more congenial setting than others, being a good team member and a good team leader involves a wide range of skills that can be learned and steadily improved. These skills include understanding the dynamics of team interactions and how they are likely to develop over time, developing better observation skills to enable you to see those dynamics at work in your teams, and learning how to diagnose and address team problems.

At the level of the organization, moving to teams requires processes within the organization for putting effective teams together and for setting the conditions under which they can work well. It requires developing team structures that are clearly understood within the organization and that enable people to assimilate quickly to a new team. It does not mean that an organization can have only one kind of team. It can have several kinds of teams, but action will be most efficient when each type of team has a clear and widely shared model of its structure and process ("If this team is cross-functional and tasked with addressing quality issues, it means that we have people from each key function, shared formal responsibility, etc.").

At the level of the organization's interactions with its environment, networks with outside organizations involve alliances with other organizations. Often these alliances require a delicate balancing of current cooperation and potential competition, so that an organization needs to develop systems to manage information flows with its "allies" and to maximize its learning from the alliance. Long-term alliances covering many related projects (with a supplier firm, for example, or a key customer) require different systems for management than short-term, single-project alliances. Developing and continuously adapting these systems is one of the major challenges of operating in an external alliance network.

Flat

In a flat organization, managers can rely far less on getting things done by simple commands and a reference to the authority of the managers above them. Often they must work with people in departments who report to different bosses, and follow a different set of priorities and incentives. In this kind of organization, managers must develop negotiation skills that enable them to identify the interests and needs of the people whose cooperation they must have, and to work through to a win-win situation in which all those involved are better off because of the cooperation. Again, we too often think that a good negotiator is someone with a certain kind of personality. Like teamwork, however, negotiation skills can—and in the new model of the organization, must—be learned.

A flat organization offers fewer opportunities for moving up a career ladder than the old, tall organizational hierarchy. Therefore one of the traditional incentives for good performance—promotion—is much scarcer in the new model. Organizations therefore need to develop new incentive systems, and new concepts of the career that involve more horizontal movement than vertical movement.

In a flat organization that is also increasingly networked with its environment, relationships with the "outside" are no longer monopolized by a small number of specialized boundary-spanners or by top management. More and more people in the organization are working across its external boundaries and interacting with customers, with suppliers, with other stakeholders. In this context, it can be difficult to maintain the sense of "boundaries"—of being committed first and foremost to one's own organization, and of being cooperative but not coopted (not, that is, substituting the needs and agendas of the other organization for one's own). The flat organization needs to develop ways of simultaneously maintaining effective cooperative links across the boundaries of the firm and the commitment of the employees to the long-term interests of their own organization.

Flexible

One of the features of the flexible organization is that managers are often working on several projects or teams simultaneously. Developing the skills of multitasking—of managing one's time and commitments so as to be able to work efficiently at several tasks—can be crucial to survival in the firm.

One of the major challenges in the flexible organization is workforce management. In the bureaucratic model, workforce management is, ideally, simply a matter of figuring out which rule applies in a particular case and then applying it. In the flexible organization, a multitude of different practices makes for much more uncertainty. For example, being responsive to the customer can mean that someone from the organization must travel to that customer and fix a problem. How is that extra time compensated? Can the person take extra time off later? If someone is particularly good at handling this kind of situation, and gets sent out a lot, thereby accumulating extra compensatory time off, does that create perceptions of unfairness among others in that person's group? If so, how should they be addressed? If that person is working in a team and is suddenly called away to cope with unexpected customer demands, how can the team cope? In the flexible organization, these issues can rarely be addressed by developing a set of rigid rules. Instead, they require active management and perhaps contingent rules that apply in certain situations.

In the interactions between the flexible organization and its environment, one of the key management challenges is to maintain learning. One of the reasons for becoming more networked with other organizations is to keep the organization innovative and responsive to change. The relations with those other organizations must involve systems for capturing what the organization learns from that relationship and sharing it with other parts of the organization for whom it may be relevant. For example, a group of engineers may find in working with one of their suppliers that a certain set of supplier incentives creates serious problems, and they may work out with that supplier a much more effective set. The organization will benefit most from that learning if it can be spread from that particular group to other groups that are working with suppliers, to see whether the new approach works better in other settings as well.

Diverse

In an organization with an increasingly diverse workforce and increasingly differentiated teams and sets of activities, managers need to develop better listening skills and the capacity for empathy, which means understanding how something looks and feels to the other person. Listening skills can and must be cultivated. Many managers think they are being good listeners when instead they are dedicated talkers. Others think they are being empathetic when they ask themselves, "What would I do if I were in this person's position?" when instead they should be asking, "What does this person's position feel like to him/her?" In a diverse organization, managers cannot assume that their own background and experience give them the bases for understanding how things are seen by others.

In an organization characterized by diversity, conflicts are inevitable, and if well-handled they can provide opportunities for the organization to become more flexible and more innovative. This kind of climate requires systems for conflict resolution and an organizational culture that recognizes the inevitability of conflict and believes it can be resolved.

Managing the environment in the diverse organizations involves an increasingly diverse set of stakeholders. For U.S. companies, for example, increasingly demanding institutional investors (pension funds, mutual funds) may pull the firm in the direction of emphasizing current returns, while local communities, employees, and unions may pull the firm in entirely different directions. Environmental groups are employing an array of tactics, from legislation to lawsuits, to influence company policies. As organizations become more international, they increase the range of stakeholders they have and also increase the potential for contradictory pressures from them. As organizations become more externally networked, they increase their interdependence with key external stakeholders, including suppliers and customers. Managing the diverse stakeholders of the new model is a major organizational challenge.

Global

As more activities of the organization stretch across country borders, managers need to develop their skills in cross-cultural communication. In many ways these skills build on and even contribute to the skills of listening and empathy that managers need to cultivate to respond to diversity. Cross-cultural communication, however, often involves specific understanding of the particular context of the organization in other societies. The knowledge required reaches from the minutiae of what constitutes a courteous way to introduce oneself in a business setting to the complexities of how customers and other stakeholders expect to be treated in that country in that particular industry segment.

At the level of the organization, stretching activities across countries involves major challenges in cross-border integration, that is, in coordinating activities taking place in different locations and in very different contexts. A U.S. company producing subassemblies in a subsidiary in Singapore, for example, needs to integrate the production schedules of the subsidiary with the final assembly at home, and make sure it develops a rapid feedback system to resolve any problems that emerge either with the schedule or with the subassembly itself.

Organizations operating outside their home country must decide on the extent of local responsiveness they want to develop in their activities. For example, many Japanese companies set up manufacturing plants in the United States. Often they feel that in order to maintain their competitive advantage, they must introduce work systems and practices with which U.S. workers are not familiar and which are not in any sense "local." To compensate for bringing in unfamiliar expectations, these companies have tried to be more locally responsive to the communities in which their U.S. plants are located, encouraging their executives to get involved with a variety of community activities in which they would never be involved in Japan. Deciding on the degree of local responsiveness to the established organizational patterns of each country is a major challenge for organizations operating across country borders.

These five factors and the related actions necessary for the new organization are summarized in Figure 1.2. As we have seen, the new model of the organization can be challenging as a workplace. Moreover, the transition to the new model—or even to certain elements of it—is itself often besieged by paradox. Much of the writing in the business press today assumes that the major challenge facing managers is to "get everyone on board" in moving to the new model. Yet more thoughtful analysts identify some apparent contradictions in the march to the new organization:

1. "Downsizing" and "flattening" the organization, thereby increasing insecurity among employees about whether they have any future with the organization—and at the same time demanding greater effort, commitment, and involvement from employees
2. Moving an organization to a team-oriented empowered organization—but at the top-down command of a strong leader
3. Trying to build the new organizational capabilities of the new model in the expectation that this format will enable the firm to perform well over the long term, while facing intense competitive pressures for immediate improvement in financial performance
4. Increasingly recognizing that firms depend on the resources and the dynamism of their environments to build competitive advantage—even as they pursue strategies that are good for the firm but have negative consequences for their environment. Some of those strategies include the move to a smaller but more highly

Figure 1.2 — Framework for Taking Action in the New Organization

Organizational Characteristics	Requisites for Taking Effective Action		
	Individual Skills	Organizational Features	Managing the Environment
• Networked	Teamwork	Building team structures	Developing alliances
• Flat	Negotiation	Developing incentive systems	Boundary management
• Flexible	Multitasking	Workforce management	Learning
• Diverse	Listening/empathy	Conflict resolution systems	Stakeholder relationship building
• Global	Cross-cultural communication	Cross-border integration	Local responsiveness

rewarded core of high commitment employees, and a growing auxiliary workforce of part-time and contract employees. This shift may increase unemployment and lead to an increasingly unequal distribution of income in the society, and in the long run affect the size of the market for the firm's products. In other words, an implicit tension exists between the recognition that what is good for the firm may not be good for the system as a whole, and the recognition that the competitiveness of the firm is closely related to the comparative advantage of the economic and social system in which it is embedded.

Yet for more and more organizations, the new organization is an "ideal" in the popular sense: a model to strive towards, a vision of where the organization is going, and a source of inspiration and motivation (a "rhetorical device"). Taking action in today's organization increasingly demands an understanding of the networked, flat, flexible, diverse, and global model and of the kinds of individual skills and organizational capabilities needed to work more effectively in this context.

"This context"—the new model of organization—remains more clearly defined in theory than in practice. One reason is that we are realizing how much variation there is across different versions of the "new," such as how many different variants of "networked" are possible, for example, and how even a simpler element like "flat" can be manifested in a variety of structures and empowerment. The most likely scenario for the twenty-first century is a wide variety of forms of new organizations, which can best be understood as different versions of the basic model. "Diverse" is likely to be a feature not only of the new organization itself, but also of the emerging population of networked, flat, flexible, diverse, and global organizations.

References

Capelli, Peter, et al. 1997. *Change at Work.* New York: Oxford University Press.

Clegg, S. R. 1990. *Modern Organizations: Organization Studies in the Postmodern World.* London: Sage Publications.

Heckscher, C., A. Donnellon, A. (Eds.). 1994. *The Post-Bureaucratic Organization: New Perspectives on Organizational Change.* Thousand Oaks, CA: Sage Publications.

Kanter, Rosabeth Moss. 1989. *When Giants Learn to Dance.* New York: Simon and Schuster.

Kaysen, Carl (Ed.). 1996. *The American Corporation Today.* New York: Oxford University Press.

Powell, Walter W. 2001. "The Capitalist Firm in the Twenty-first Century: Emerging Patterns in Western Enterprise." In Paul DiMaggio (Ed.), *The Twenty-First Century Firm: Changing Economic Organization in International Perspective* (pp. 33–68). Princeton: Princeton University Press.

Scott, W. Richard. 1992. *Organizations: Rational, Natural, and Open Systems*, 3rd ed. Englewood Cliffs, NJ: Prentice Hall.

Selwyn, Michael. 1993. "Radical Departures: Revolutionary Strategies Are Separating Asia's Leaders from the Followers." *Asian Business* (August 1993), 22–25.

Thurow, Lester. 1996. "Almost Everywhere: Surging Inequality and Falling Real Wages." In Carl Kaysen (Ed.), *The American Corporation Today* (pp. 383–412). New York: Oxford University Press.

A Sampling of Analyses of the New Organization

The Coming of the New Organization

The typical large business 20 years hence will have fewer than half the levels of management of its counterpart today, and no more than one-third the managers. In its structure, and in its management problems and concerns, it will bear little resemblance to the typical manufacturing company, circa 1950, which our textbooks still consider the norm. Instead it is far more likely to resemble organizations that neither the practicing manager nor the management scholar pays much attention to today: the hospital, the university, the symphony orchestra. For like them, the typical business will be knowledge-based, an organization composed largely of specialists who direct and discipline their own performance through organized feedback from colleagues, customers, and headquarters. For this reason, it will be what I call an information-based organization. Businesses, especially large ones, have little choice but to become information-based. . . . A good deal of work will be done differently in the information-based organization. Traditional departments will serve as guardians of standards, as centers for training and the assignment of specialists; they won't be where the work gets done. That will happen largely in task-focused teams.

Source: Reprinted by permission of *Harvard Business Review*, from "The Coming of the New Organization" by Peter F. Drucker. Jan/Feb 1988. Copyright © 1988 by the Harvard Business School Publishing Corporation; all rights reserved.

The New Managerial Work

Managerial work is undergoing such enormous and rapid change that many managers are reinventing their profession as they go. With little precedent to guide them, they are watching hierarchy fade away and the clear distinctions of title, task, department, even corporation, blur. Faced with extraordinary levels of complexity and interdependency, they watch traditional sources of power erode and the old motivational tools lose their magic...

Leaders in the new organization do not lack motivational tools, but the tools are different from those of traditional corporate bureaucrats. The new rewards are not based on status but on contribution, and they consist not of regular promotion and automatic pay raises but of excitement about mission and a share of the glory and the gains of success. The new security is not employment security (a guaranteed job no matter what) but employability security—increased value in the internal and external labor markets. . . . The new loyalty is not to the boss or to the company but to projects that actualize a mission and offer challenge, growth, and credit for results. . . .

The new managerial work consists of looking outside a defined area of responsibility to sense opportunities and of forming project teams drawn from any relevant sphere to address them. It involves communication and collaboration across functions, across divisions, and across companies whose activities and resources overlap. Thus rank, title, or official charter will be less important factors in success at the new managerial work than having the knowledge, skills, and sensitivity to mobilize people and motivate them to do their best.

Source: Reprinted by permission of *Harvard Business Review*, from "The New Managerial Work" by Rosabeth Moss Kanter. Nov/Dec 1989. Copyright © 1989 by the Harvard Business School Publishing Corporation; all rights reserved.

The American Corporation as an Employer

By the beginning of the twenty-first century, the organization men [and women] of the 1950s will be gone, and so, too, will many of the attributes that dominated their corporate lives. Upward mobility within a clearly defined job or function, conformity to the cultural and social norms of the top executives, strict lines of demarcation between work and family activities and obligations, geographic transfer and job choice based on one partner's career needs or demands, and loyalty to the corporation may all be part of corporate history. Hourly workers will no longer be able to count on seniority to produce increased wages, fringe benefits, promotion opportunities, and job security. Unions and collective bargaining will find it more difficult to move those with limited education or training into the middle class.

To do well in the corporation of the future, individual employees will need to enter the labor market with a solid technical and analytic educational foundation, gain access on the job to experiences in decision making, problem solving, and teamwork, commit to a lifetime process of learning and updating of one's skills, and organize into collective networks and organizations capable of bargaining and influencing their employers from the workplace up to the strategic levels of corporate decision making.

To be competitive and prosper in this environment, corporations will need to attract high-quality workers, design work systems that fully utilize their skills, encourage employees to stay long enough to appropriate the benefits of training investments, share power and cooperate with workers and their representatives, and release employees into the external labor market with marketable skills. For the overall economy and society to prosper in this new environment will require significant reforms of labor and employment policies that provide the education, training, and social insurance foundations needed to promote labor market mobility and effective negotiations, dispute resolution, and cooperation among stakeholders within and across organizations.

Source: Thomas A. Kochan, "The American Corporation as an Employer: Past, Present, and Future Possibilities" in *The American Corporation Today* edited by Carl Kaysen. Copyright © 1996 by the Alfred P. Sloan Foundation. Used by permission of Oxford University Press, Inc.

Designing Effective Organizations

Putting together the trends we have discussed . . . the twenty-first century organization begins to take shape. It is best summarized as a network organization. The network is multi-dimensional and dis-aggregated, consisting of many different units, each with its own focus. It is populated by entrepreneurial managers, who interact spontaneously and flexibly to share knowledge, achieve competitive advantage, and implement the corporate strategy. It supports learning and collaboration through open personal contacts between the units. It has minimal hierarchy and strong empowerment of the units, which are largely self-managing and self-motivated to drive for high performance. And renewal is possible through flexibility in network relationships and redefinition of unit boundaries. . . . In a network, much depends on the motivation, flexibility, and cooperativeness of individual managers. Traditional organization man, who follows instructions, sticks to rules, and is suspicious about collaboration with sister units, guarantees that networks will fail. Fortunately, a new generation of managers seems to be emerging who relish empowerment, expect to adapt to changing circumstances, and find it natural to collaborate with others to realize corporate objectives. Often in our research we heard about the difficulties faced by older managers in adapting to the demands of network structures and about the comparative ease with which younger managers handle the requirements. Twenty-first century organizational cultures, and the attitudes of the "new managers" who work in them, seem to be in tune with network organizations.

Source: Michael Goold and Andrew Campbell, excerpt from *Designing Effective Organizations*. Jossey-Bass, 2002. This material is used by permission of John Wiley & Sons, Inc.

The Mind of the CEO

In the business world, technology and globalization have created a level of competition that will lead to new categories of winners and losers and force a transformation in how companies are organized and led. The impact of these changes will spill over into the workplace and the economy. It will also spread to the political realm as citizens and governments search for new regulatory systems for both the national and global economies.

This is not the first time in modern history that the world has witnessed such a profound and complex interaction between business and society while both were reeling from all manner of new pressures. If you examine the past two industrial revolutions—England between 1750 and 1840, and America between the late 1860s and the 1920s—you can see many of the same phenomena that we are experiencing today. Then as now, new forms of business and work patterns emerged. . . . Nevertheless, it is likely that the business and societal challenges of the late twentieth and early twenty-first centuries will be seen as even greater than in previous epochs.

Source: Jeffrey E. Garten, *The Mind of the CEO* (Perseus Publishing/Basic Books 2002), pp. 19–20. Reprinted by permission.

. . . and Some Skeptical Voices

Beyond the Hype

Regardless of when Drucker is writing (and this is not to deny that his work has contained some very valuable insights), the present is always an exciting, challenging time to be contrasted with a stable past. These same stirring announcements of impending change can be found repeated in nearly all of his writings from the 1950s to the present. . . . Every generation believes itself to be on the forefront of a new managerial frontier and posits the coming of a new organization that will revolutionize the way people work and interact. . . . To see these claims about revolutionary newness only in regard to an underlying truth or falsehood is ultimately to miss the point. What is more important to understand is the rhetorical nature of management discourse and practice—now and then. To view management from a rhetorical perspective is to recognize that the way people talk about the world has everything to do with the way the world is ultimately understood and acted in, and that the concept of revolutionary change depends to a great deal on how the world is framed by our language. Viewing management in this way is also to realize that the primary concern of managers—as well as other players in the field of management—is, or at least should be, mobilizing action among individuals rather than endless quibbling about "the way the world really is."

Source: Reprinted by permission of Harvard Business School Press. From Robert G. Eccles and Nitin Nohria, with James D. Berkley, *Beyond the Hype: Rediscovering the Essence of Management.* Boston, MA, 1992, pp. 25, 29. Copyright © 1992 by the Harvard Business School Publishing Corporation; all rights reserved.

Will the Organization of the Future Make the Mistakes of the Past?

Americans often don't know or pay much attention to history. American business writers seem to know even less. Today we are bombarded with breathless descriptions of the virtual organization, the networked organization, and the boundaryless organization. We are told about the "new employment contract," a nice way of saying that long-term careers in a single organization are a thing of the past and that we are all contingent workers now. . . . A big problem exists with all of this—namely that the "new" organizational forms aren't all that new at all. In fact, this was how enterprise was organized more than one hundred years ago. . . . There are several enduring truths about organizations and management. One is the norm of reciprocity, which exists in all nationalities and cultures. We cannot expect dedication and loyalty from employees unless we are willing to make some reciprocal commitment to them. Another truth is the idea of core competence or capability. Contracting out core tasks has often been a recipe for disaster, in the 1890s as well as in the 1990s. This is because contracting out leaves the foundation of competitive success in the open market. A third truth is that to succeed you must understand the basic forces and ideas that shape modern economic life, reject trends if they don't make sense, and never substitute rhetoric for judgment.

Source: From Jeffrey Pfeffer, "Will the Organization of the Future Make the Mistakes of the Past?" in *The Organization of the Future* edited by Frances Hesselbein, et al. Copyright © 1997 The Peter F. Drucker Foundation for Nonprofit Management. This material is used by permission of John Wiley & Sons, Inc.

Coda to the New Organization

One of the first problems faced by advocates of the New Organization is that if its benefits are so obvious, why aren't there far more textbook examples available? . . . Our daily experience is perhaps mostly with organizations that seem to rationalize their operations in tune with the long-established principles of efficiency, predictability, quantification, and control, including the substitution of nonhuman for human technologies. Chains of command are obvious and the divisions of labor intense. The exemplar of the service industry seems to be McDonald's, where homogenous products, rigid technologies, standardized work routines, close supervision, and highly centralized control systems are clearly in place. To be sure, it is an organizational form that has a few elements of the new organization in place—an increasingly global presence (i.e. more McDonald's outlets now operate outside the United States than inside), tightly networked to suppliers (e.g., frozen potato vendors) and marketing partners (i.e., the Walt Disney Company), diverse in the social characteristics of its entry-level (but low-paid) workforce, and chock full of cross-functional teams and task forces at headquarters. In the main, however, McDonald's looks and feels far closer to the old form of organization based on assembly line production and bureaucratic rules and regulations. The principles of Frederick Taylor's scientific management are alive and well and thriving at McDonald's. Order and prescribed choice are enforced norms for both customers and employees. On your next visit, try ordering a Big Mac cooked medium rare.

More importantly, such forms of organization seem to be spreading—an imitative process that sociologist George Ritzer calls "the aggressive McDonaldization of society." Going or gone are the idiosyncratic, local family-run businesses of the past emphasizing personal, highly differentiated products and services. The look-alike chain stores of the suburban malls drive out the family-owned enterprises of Main Street. Wal-Marts open up and local pharmacies and hardware stores close. Corner gas stations and local garages lose work to AAMCO Transmissions and Midas Muffler and Brake Shops. KinderCare provides a stable of bonded contract babysitters in almost identical facilities located coast to coast. 7-Elevens and Circle Ks replace mom-and-pop markets. Au Bon Pain bakery cafes turn up in Paris. Kentucky Fried Chicken outlets appear in Beijing. Drive-in clinics provide McDoctors and McDentists. Century 21 sells real estate from interchangeable offices across the country (and beyond). None of these organizations embody the supposedly innovative and novel spirit that animates the flat, flexible, networked, diverse, and global characteristics of our rather idealized new organization, yet all are expanding rapidly. If Henry Ford were alive he'd probable be delighted: eating at McDonald's, having his taxes done at H&R Block, servicing his car at Jiffy Lube, buying gifts for his grandchildren at Toys 'R' Us and losing weight at Nutri/Systems."

Source: John Van Maanen, "Coda to the New Organization," MIT Sloan School Working Paper, 1997. Reprinted by permission of the author.

The Twenty-first Century Firm

How much autonomy can project groups be given before they begin to pursue interests other than those of the company's top management? Students of network forms of organization and, even more so, advocates of workplace reform, at times appear to neglect the truism that nearly everyone involved with organizations tries to use them for their own ends. . . . On the one hand, well-designed task forces and project teams enhance control by removing work from contexts in which departmental agendas can subvert corporate goals. . . . On the other hand, the dissolution of formal rules, and the accountability that is built into them, deprives management of a critical basis for evaluating employee performance, especially when the results of a project cannot be judged until long after the project group has been dissolved. Organizations are not very good at measuring complex task performance under the best of conditions, much less when individuals work in interdepartmental teams. . . . Moreover, we cannot assume that project-based systems of work *will* be properly designed, for large corporations often design and implement systems poorly. It seems likely that work-process redesign that relaxes rules and blurs interunit boundaries and responsibilities can be highly effective if well executed. But such systems may raise the stakes of failure, by eliminating the safety net of accountability that formal job descriptions and well-defined roles and responsibilities provide when things go wrong. Studies of popular workplace innovations often find a substantial difference between models and their implementation. . . . These observations suggest the importance, first, of constructive skepticism as to the potential for wide diffusion of organizational models that require exceptional selflessness and dedication from managers and technical professionals; and, second, of research into the circumstances under which such models *are* implemented successfully. . . .

Management consultants have always been in the business of distilling management wisdom into packages that can be sold to clients in digestible portions, a trade that makes them chronically susceptible to herdlike enthusiasms. Consultants are particularly taken with the network conception of the firm, I suspect, because it resonates so neatly with their own experience. Their work takes place in temporary project teams, often assembled from several geographically disparate offices, increasingly in collaboration with other firms. Their own organizational structures are flat and flexible, and their key staff routinely penetrate the boundaries of other large companies. Their success is governed by their principals' effectiveness at establishing and maintaining dense cooperative networks with both clients and collaborators. In effect, the network conception elevates their own experience into a paradigm for business writ large.

Source: Paul DiMaggio, "Conclusion," in DiMaggio (Ed.), *The Twenty-First Century Firm: Changing Economic Organization in International Perspective*. Copyright © 2001 by Princeton University Press. Reprinted by permission of Princeton University Press.

Mapping Your Organization

Your organization/company:
　　　　ORG/COMPANY NAME _____
　　　　TYPE OF BUSINESS/ACTIVITY _____
　　　　APPROXIMATE SIZE (Number of employees) _____

Which of the following statements best describes this organization?
　　_____ It fits the model of the "new" organization.
　　_____ It is trying to move toward the model of the "new" organization, but still has some features of the old.
　　_____ It fits the model of the "old" organization, without many signs that it is trying to change.
　　_____ It seems to be a fairly stable hybrid, combining features of the old and the new.

How would you rate that organization on each of the following five features of the "new" organization?

FLAT:

Very tall				Very flat
1	2	3	4	5

FLEXIBLE:

Very inflexible				Very flexible
1	2	3	4	5

NETWORKED:

Internally

Individual as key unit, few horizontal internal links				Teams as basic units, dense horizontal links
1	2	3	4	5

Externally

Very limited external links				Very extensive external links
1	2	3	4	5

DIVERSE:

Very homogeneous				Very diverse
1	2	3	4	5

GLOBAL:

Very locally focused				Extensive cross-border linking
1	2	3	4	5

Questionnaire

NOTES ON YOUR OWN ORGANIZATION
(Use this space to make any brief notes on your organization that you wish.)

The "New" Organization: Taking Action in an Era of Organizational Transformation

ELECTIVE

Module 1

Reading the Business Press

Much of the information about trends in management that you have and will acquire in your life as a manager comes from the business press. It is important to learn how to read this material quickly and critically. You can help enhance these skills by asking the following questions:

What is the "story" that this article is telling? Is the article advocating a certain point of view, or is it balancing different points of view? How has the author organized the "story"? What is the tone of the beginning paragraphs, and is it maintained consistently throughout, or does the author shift perspectives (for example, beginning with the bright side and then ending with the "dark underside," or starting with a hyperbolic "everyone believes that . . ." storyline and then switching to "but if you look closely the reality is that . . .")?

What kind of evidence does the article use? If it relies heavily on quotations from "authorities," who are they and how are these sources likely to influence the kind of information the article presents? If it presents "mini-cases," or specific company examples, what companies does it use and how diverse are they (for example, what industries are represented, and are any foreign examples used)? Does the article present any counterexamples?

What implicit assumptions underlie the story? Does the article have an explicit or an implicit causal model, that is, a set of assumptions about what drivers produce what effects?

Let's take the first article, "The Search for the Organization of the Future," as an example. Its storyline is signaled in the first paragraph: a major change is underway, and companies are rushing to change the way they organize. Like most business press articles, it relies heavily on quotations from authorities and on vivid short examples from specific companies. It has an explicit causal model: it argues strongly that changes in organization and management are necessary, given intensifying international competition and changing information technology. It also builds on the strong assumption that the change is inevitable and that companies that don't follow the search for the organization of tomorrow will be left behind by more alert competitors.

Let's look more closely at the evidence used in this article. Who are the authorities it invokes? The short table that follows (Figure 1.3) presents a list of those whose views are quoted directly or cited indirectly in the article. The largest group is managers, and they are overwhelmingly senior executives: three CEOs, three vice presidents, and two middle managers. The other sources are consultants and academics. On the surface, this group of authorities appears diverse. But think how the nature of the sources might color the portrayal of the "new organization." The authorities tend to be people with a strong stake in having the changes viewed as successful. The company managers want their organizations to be viewed as successful and as leaders in the shift to the new organization. The consultants (and perhaps some of the academics) want to establish themselves as important sources of knowledge and expertise on the new organization. It does not mean that their viewpoint is not useful; it means that the reader must look carefully beyond the specific examples to ask, "What would it take to convince me that the model underlying these stories is valid and useful?"

At the time the article was written, one of the "new new things" in the world of consulting was business process reengineering, an approach to organization that promised to make full use of the potential of information technology by rethinking organizational boundaries and reorganizing by processes rather than by functions. Much of the focus was on production processes in the factory and on back-office processes of the supply chain. Therefore two of the mini-cases in the article are from the factory (a Puerto Rico factory of GE; the factory for Kodak's black and white film) and one focuses on support processes (Xerox's customer operations). The exceptions are Hallmark greeting cards, an early client of CSC Index and a "poster child" for business process reengineering, and the San Diego Zoo. Do you think the addition of the Zoo adds or detracts from the argument of the story? One view is that the inclusion of such an unusual case reinforces the message: "If even a zoo is reorganizing. . . ."

One of the most useful skills you can develop is the ability to read critically—not in the sense of debunking everything you read, but in the sense of becoming a discriminating consumer who can recognize the underlying structure of an article or story, see its strengths and weaknesses, and learn from it judiciously.

Figure 1.3 The Search for the Organization of Tomorrow

Sources/Authorities	Number of Quotes
Managers:	
Lawrence Bossidy, CEO, Allied Signal	5
H. James Maxmin, CEO, Laura Ashley	1
Philip Jarrosiak, Manager HRM, GE's capacitor and power protection operations	2
Herman Simon, plant manager, Gaines	1
William Buehler, Senior VP, Xerox	1
Richard Palermo, VP, Xerox	1
Don Fletcher, VP, Hallmark	1
Paul Allaire, CEO, Xerox	1
Consultants:	
David Nadler, Delta Consulting	2
Doug Smith, McKinsey	5
Frank Ostroff	3
Mike Hammer, CSC Index	2
James Champy, CSC Index	2
Academics/Researchers:	
Peter Drucker	1
Marvin Weisbord	1
Shoshanna Zuboff	1
Quinn Mills	1
Robert Reich	1
Workers:	
Robert Brookhouse, Kodak "Zebra"	1

The Search for the Organization of Tomorrow

by Thomas A. Stewart

Lawrence Bossidy, CEO of Allied-Signal, predicts "organizational revolution" for corporate America. Says David Nadler, president of Delta Consulting Group, who works with the chiefs of AT&T, Corning, and Xerox, among others: "CEOs feel that companies need to be structured in dramatically different ways." In outfits as diverse as Eastman Kodak, Hallmark Cards, and General Electric—even the San Diego Zoo—the search for the organization perfectly designed for the 21st century is going ahead with the urgency of a scavenger hunt.

Source: Thomas A. Stewart, "The Search for the Organization of Tomorrow," *Fortune* (May 18, 1992), pp. 92–98. Copyright © 1992 Time Inc. All rights reserved. Reprinted by permission.

From many quarters we hear that hierarchical organization must wither away. In this view of the future middle managers have the life expectancy of fruit flies. Those who survive will not be straw bosses but Dutch uncles, dispensing resources and wisdom to an empowered labor force that designs its own jobs. Enabled, to use a trendy term, by information technology and propelled by the need to gain speed and shed unnecessary work, this flat, information-based organization won't look like the Pharaonic pyramid of yore but like—well, like what? Like a symphony orchestra, Peter Drucker suggests. No, a jazz combo, some say. More like a spider web, others offer.

Hamlet: Or like a whale?

Polonius: Very like a whale.

Gee, thanks. But where's my desk? What do I do eight hours a day—or ten, or twelve? Who gives me my annual review? When do we start?

Good questions, which as yet have not had good answers. Says H. James Maxmin, the CEO of Laura Ashley Holdings: "We're just beginning to explore the post-hierarchical organization. We don't know what it looks like yet." Some hints, however, are emerging.

The 21st-century organization arises at the confluence of three streams. One is described by the term "high-involvement workplace," meaning operations with self-managing teams and other devices for empowering employees. Novelties once, these participative mechanisms have proved they can consistently deliver jaw-dropping gains in productivity, quality, and job satisfaction. A second productivity turbocharger is a new emphasis on managing business processes—materials handling, say—rather than functional departments like purchasing and manufacturing. Third is the evolution of information technology to the point where knowledge, accountability, and results can be distributed rapidly anywhere in the organization. The trick is to put them together into a coherent, practical design. Then you have the company yours may become, and the one your sons and daughters will work for.

At the end of this rainbow, say those who have peeked, is a whole kettleful of gold. Advises Bossidy, who until last summer was vice chairman of General Electric: "Look at GE Appliances." In that $5.4-billion-a-year business, redesign brought with it a $200 million drop in average inventory. McKinsey & Co. principal Douglas Smith, one of the blue-chip consulting firm's experts on organization, figures that a company applying the new principles of organization design can cut its cost base by a third or more. Smith bases his claim on results from companies that have already reorganized parts of their operations: an industrial goods manufacturer that cut costs and raised productivity more than 50%, a financial service company where costs fell 34%, and others.

Results like that come from changing a company in profound ways, not just tinkering with the boxes on an organization chart. For years, Smith says, the basic questions about how best to arrange people and jobs stayed the same: "Do we centralize or decentralize—and where do we stick international?" The answer was never satisfactory. Companies were set up by product, or by customer, or by territory, and then switched when those arrangements stopped working. All that rejiggering missed the point, says Smith: "It mattered only to the top people in the company. Below them you found the same functional, vertical organization. For the 90% of the people who serve customers and make product, all that changed was the boss's name."

No longer. The Kodaks, GEs, and their ilk have first retailored the work people do, then management structures, with startling results. To make sense out of the rush of experimentation, McKinsey's Smith and his colleague Frank Ostroff are polishing a paper that lays out what Ostroff calls "perhaps the first real, fundamentally different, robust alternative" to the functional organization (see Figure 1.4). In the months since Ostroff released an early draft to his consulting colleagues, it has proved the document most often requested inside the firm.

There's nothing new about self-managing teams—they were "discovered" 43 years ago at the bottom of a coal mine in Yorkshire by a researcher from the Tavistock Institute of Human Relations in London. Since then, forms of worker self-management have been adopted at countless sites. Marvin Weisbord, an expert on organizational development, notes that all rely on one basic idea: "The people who do the work should have in their hands the means to change to suit the customer." That means workers should have the incentive and the power to respond to whoever buys their output—at times someone else within their organization—not just whoever cuts their paychecks. Weisbord adds that self-management *typically* delivers 40% increases in output per man-hour.

To see how it's done, skip the blackjack table next time you're in Puerto Rico and pay a visit to Bayamón, outside San Juan, where a new General Electric factory has been running for a year and a half. The place makes arresters, which are surge protectors that guard power stations and transmission lines against lightning strikes.

Figure 1.4 A New View of Organization

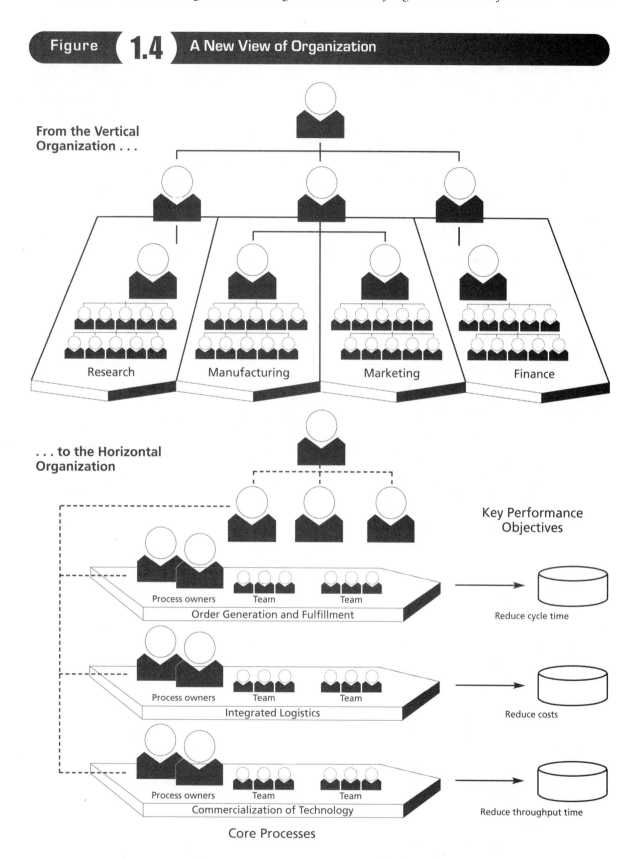

A new view of organization by McKinsey consultants Frank Ostroff and Doug Smith is meant to help clients hung up by the old template. Says Ostroff: "They needed a clear architecture" to show how a functional pyramid (top) could become a process-oriented, horizontal organization.

Bayamón is a godchild of Philip Jarrosiak, manager of human resources for GE's capacitor and power protection operations. Once a minor-league infielder, Jarrosiak joined GE when he was 20, landing an hourly job making aircraft engines in Rutland, Vermont. In the 32 years since, he put himself through college at night and worked his way into management ranks, where he specializes in designing high-performance workplaces at both greenfield and established sites. Bayamón is his newest and, Jarrosiak says, "an opportunity to put in everything I know."

The facility employs 172 hourly workers and just 15 salaried "advisers," plus manager R. Clayton Crum. That's it: three layers, no supervisors, no staff. A conventional plant, Jarrosiak says, would have about twice as many salaried people. Every hourly worker is on a team with ten or so others; they meet weekly. Each team "owns" part of the work—assembly, shipping and receiving, etc. But team members come from all areas of the plant, so that each group has representatives from both upstream and downstream operations. An adviser sits in the back of the room and speaks up only if the team needs help.

What vaults Bayamón into the next century is the way it teaches its workers. Says Harvard professor Shoshanna Zuboff, author of *In the Age of the Smart Machine*: "The 21st-century company has to promote and nurture the capacity to improve and to innovate. That idea has radical implications. It means learning becomes the axial principle of organizations. It replaces control as the fundamental job of management."

Bayamón is a perpetual-learning machine. Hourly workers change jobs every six months, rotating through the factory's four main work areas. In six months they'll begin their second circuit of the plant, and everyone on the floor will know his job and how it affects the next person in line. The reward for learning is a triple-scoop compensation plan that pays for skill, knowledge, and business performance. The first time around, workers get a 25-cent-an-hour pay raise at each rotation; thereafter they can nearly double their pay by "declaring a major," so to speak, and learning a skill like machine maintenance or quality control. More pay comes from passing courses in English, business practices, and other subjects. Toss in bonuses—$225 a quarter or more—for meeting plantwide performance goals and having perfect attendance. Promotions and layoffs will be decided by skill level, not seniority. In just a year the work force became 20% more productive than its nearest company equivalent on the mainland, and Jarrosiak predicts productivity will rise 20% more by the end of 1993.

For years plants like Bayamón existed barely connected to the organizations of which they are a part. Some Procter & Gamble factories were worker-run as long ago as 1968, a fact concealed from competitors—and sometimes from headquarters. The Gaines pet food plant in Topeka, Kansas, just celebrated 20 years of self-management. For two decades, under three owners—Anderson Clayton, General Foods, and Quaker Oats—Topeka has always placed first when its labor productivity was compared with that of other pet food plants within its company. According to Herman Simon, plant manager for 17 years, higher-ups who saw the numbers vowed never to mess with the plant. But they rarely went away determined to make their other factories over in its image.

Says a frustrated William Buehler, senior vice president at Xerox: "You can see a high-performance factory or office, but it just doesn't spread. I don't know why." One reason is that nervous executives experiment where failure won't be fatal, and thereby contain the gains too. Says Jarrosiak: "I hate pilot programs off in a corner of a plant. You need commitment."

You also need to be able to envision how such operations fit into a large-scale enterprise. Says McKinsey's Ostroff: "Executives know what teams can do. But they need a picture that links the high-performance team to the whole organization and multiplies the gains." It's relatively easy to oversee one of these operations when it's confined within one function, like manufacturing. For self-directed management to spread, a company must lay goals, responsibilities, and measurements across functions. Ostroff argues: "Senior managers need to be able to say 'empowerment' and 'accountability' in the same sentence."

Business processes—almost sure to become a term you will hear lots of—can form the link between high-performance work teams and the corporation at large. Organizing around processes, as opposed to functions, permits greater self-management and allows companies to dismantle unneeded supervisory structures.

It's a management axiom that crab grass grows in the cracks between departments. Purchasing buys parts cheap, but manufacturing needs them strong. Shipping moves goods in bulk, but sales promised them fast. "I call it Palermo's law," says Richard Palermo, a vice president for quality and transition at Xerox. "If a problem has been bothering your company and your customers for years and won't yield, that problem is the result of a cross-functional dispute, where nobody has total control of the whole process." And here's Palermo's corollary: People who work in different functions hate each other.

Upon this fratricidal scene, enter the process doctor. Depending on which consulting firm he's coming from, he may describe his work as "reengineering" or "core process redesign" or "process innovation." Michael Hammer, a consultant in Cambridge, Massachusetts, defines, though not exactly lyrically, what the doctor is up to: "Reengineering is the fundamental analysis and radical redesign of business processes to achieve dramatic improvements in critical measures of performance."

Process management differs from managing a function in three ways. First, it uses external objectives. Old-line manufacturing departments, for example, tend to be measured on unit costs, an intradepartmental number that can lead to overlong production runs and stacks of unsold goods. By contrast, an integrated manufacturing and shipping process might be rated by how often it turns over its inventory—a process-wide measurement that reveals how all are working together to keep costs down. Second, in process management employees with different skills are grouped to accomplish a complete piece of work. Mortgage loan officer, title searcher, and credit checker sit and work together, not in series. Third, information moves straight to where it's needed, unfiltered by a hierarchy. If you have a problem with people upstream from you, you deal with them directly, rather than asking your boss to talk to theirs.

Reengineered processes have been in place at Kodak for more than two years. The 1,500 employees who make black and white film—inevitably called Zebras—work not in departments but in what's called "the flow." (Black and white is big business: about $2 billion a year from sales of 7,000 products used in printing, X-rays, even spy satellites.) Headed by Richard Malloy, a 25-member leadership team watches the flow. They measure it with end-of-process tallies like productivity. Within the flow are streams defined by "customers"—Kodak business units—and scored on customer satisfaction measures such as on-time delivery. One stream, for example, is charged with making hundreds of types of film for the Health Sciences Division and works closely with it to schedule production and to develop new products, a Zebra specialty. In the streams most employees work in self-directed teams. A few functions—accounting and human resources—remain outside the streams.

When the flow began in 1989, the black and white film operation was running 15% over budgeted cost, took up to 42 days to fill an order, was late a third of the time, and scored worst in Kodak's morale surveys. Last year the group came in 15% under budget cost, had cut response time in half, was late one time out of 20, and wore the biggest smiles in Rochester, New York. Why? Says Zebra Robert Brookhouse: "When you create a flow and a flow chart, you find where you're wasting time, doing things twice. And because we own our entire process, we can change it."

Organizing around a process seems to yield sterling results as consistently as high-involvement factories do. Privately held Hallmark (1991 sales: $2.9 billion) expects big gains now that Steven Stanton of CSC Index, a Cambridge, Massachusetts, consulting firm, has helped the company reengineer its new-product process. The greeting-card maker lives or dies on new stuff—some 40,000 cards and other items a year, the work of 700 writers, artists, and designers on what Hallmark boasts is the world's largest creative staff. The process of developing a new card had become grotesque; it took two years—longer than the road from Gettysburg to Appomattox Court House. The company was choking on sketches, approvals, cost estimates, and proofs. Says Hallmark's Don Fletcher: "We needed a lot of people just to check items in and out of departments."

Fletcher's title, vice president for business process redesign, pretty much tells what happened. Starting this spring, about half the staff will be put to work on cards for particular holidays like Valentine's Day or Christmas. The birthday and get-well card folks will follow. A team of artists, writers, lithographers, merchandisers, bean counters, and so on will be assigned to each holiday. Team members are moving from all over a two-million-square-foot office building in Kansas City so they can sit together. Like a canoe on a lake, a card will flow directly from one part of the process to the next within, say, the Mother's Day team; before, it had to be portaged from one vast department to the next. This should cut cycle time in half, which will not only save money but will also make the company more responsive to changing tastes.

Hallmark hasn't eradicated departments. There will be "centers of excellence" to which workers will return between projects for training and brief, special stints, a bit like homerooms in high school. For now, department heads remain the senior managers of the business. But the head of graphic arts, which makes separations and proofs, has told Fletcher that he hopes the department infrastructure will eventually dissolve in the flow.

That's the right idea, say hard-core process managers. If you reengineer a process, pocket a one-time gain, and return to your desk, says McKinsey's Smith, "the barnacles you scrape off will just grow back." The way to keep them off, says Hammer, is to obliterate the functions: "In the future, executive positions will not be defined in terms of collections of people, like head of the sales department, but in terms of process, like senior-VP-of-getting-stuff-to-customers, which is sales, shipping, billing. You'll no longer have a box on an organization chart. You'll own part of a process map."

Can a whole company literally lie on its side and organize horizontally, by process? You got it, says Allied-Signal's Bossidy: "Every business has maybe six basic processes. We'll organize around them. The people who run them will be the leaders of the business."

An industrial company might select processes like new-product development, flow of materials (purchasing, receiving, manufacturing), and the order-delivery billing cycle. Into these process flows will go management teams to tend subprocesses and teams of workers to carry out tasks. Whoever is needed will be there: The materials-flow group might have finance folks but no marketers—but the marketers will be plentiful in the new-product process. There are no departments in Bossidy's 21st-century corporation: "You might have a CEO, but he won't have many people who report to him."

If metallurgists and actuaries are taken out of departments and clumped around processes, what happens to their specialized skills? A minor problem, argues James Champy, CEO of CSC Index: "State-of-the-art knowledge comes from a small group of people. Most people in a function don't contribute expertise. They execute." Put the innovators in a stafflike or lablike group. Create a house Yellow Pages so functional expertise is easy to find even though dispersed. Link experts in a real or electronic network where they can keep each other up to date and can get training and career development help.

McKinsey's Plan

It's hot stuff at McKinsey & Co. these days: a ten-point blueprint for a horizontal company prepared by Frank Ostroff and Doug Smith, consultants in the firm's organization-performance group.

1. *Organize primarily around process, not task.* Base performance objectives on customer needs, such as low cost or fast service. Identify the processes that meet (or don't meet) those needs—order generation and fulfillment, say, or new-product development. These processes—not departments, such as sales or manufacturing—become the company's main components.
2. *Flatten the hierarchy by minimizing subdivision of processes.* It's better to arrange teams in parallel, with each doing lots of steps in a process, than to have a series of teams, each doing fewer steps.
3. *Give senior leaders charge of processes and process performance.*
4. *Link performance objectives and evaluation of all activities to customer satisfaction.*
5. *Make teams, not individuals, the focus of organization performance and design.* Individuals acting alone don't have the capacity to continuously improve work flows.
6. *Combine managerial and non-managerial activities as often as possible.* Let workers' teams take on hiring, evaluating, and scheduling.
7. *Emphasize that each employee should develop several competencies.* You need only a few specialists.
8. *Inform and train people on a just-in-time, need-to-perform basis.* Raw numbers go straight to those who need them in their jobs, with no managerial spin, because you have trained front-line workers—salesmen, machinists—how to use them.
9. *Maximize supplier and customer contact with everyone in the organization.* that means field trips and slots on joint problem-solving teams for all employees all the time.
10. *Reward individual skill development and team performance instead of individual performance alone.*

"That's okay," says Bossidy. "The engineers can have a club. But they can't work in the same room, and they can't sit at the same table at the company banquet." His vision is somewhat radical, he admits, understating the case. "So corporations will first try to make the matrix work. Boy, that will drive employees and managers nuts."

One trouble with breaking down the walls: In most companies functional and hierarchical walls are load bearing. Remove them and the roof caves in. A big burden they bear is to collect, evaluate, and pass on information. Another is to determine employees' career paths—to define ambition, reward, and sycophancy. In a flat shop of teams and processes, both information flow and careers will have to be different.

Walk around futuristic companies and you see odd sights: suppliers who work in their customers' offices; widely available, easy-to-read charts tracking scrap, on-time delivery, and other data that rivals would kill for; hourly workers logged onto PCs reading their E-mail. They're all part of an effort to put information where it can be used at the moment it's needed. Says Delta Consulting's David Nadler: "In the organization of the future, information technology will be a load-bearing material—as hierarchy is now. You can't have self-management without it." That is, computer networks and the information they carry will help define your corporate structure. Let information flow wherever it's needed, and a horizontal self-managed company is not only possible, it's inescapable.

Building computer highways that can transport cost and other data sideways within a process, as well as vertically to top management, is a step in this direction. Other steps include training that teaches workers how their actions affect overall business performance and measurements that direct tasks at optimum outcomes, such as rewarding salespeople for gross margin, not gross sales.

You have to transport power as well as knowledge. In a hierarchy, rank defines authority: A manager can okay deals up to $50,000, his boss to $100,000, her boss to $250,000. . . . That's obsolete, in Harvard business school professor Quinn Mills's view. The question isn't how high the money gets; it's how high your customer's blood pressure gets. "Does he need an answer immediately? Do you have to be able to be flexible? If so, you have to empower the person who talks to the customer." If you can't entrust such matters to the folks in the field, maybe you should switch places with them. They can have your desk, where the decisions, obviously, are less important.

What happens to the career ladder? CSC Index Chief Executive Champy suggests that law firms, with only three levels of hierarchy—associate, partner, and senior partner—might provide the very model of a modern career path. Says Champy: "A lawyer's career is a progression to more complex work—tougher cases, more important clients. Titles don't change, but everyone knows who has the highest status."

The oldest art in organization design—carving out strategic business units—will still matter in this new world. The goal, as Nadler sees it, is to create "enterprises with clear customers, markets, and measures, and few internal boundaries." That means letting sets of customers or customer needs define business units, and grouping into businesses the people and processes necessary to serve them.

That's how Xerox designed its new horizontal organization. Until this year, Xerox was set up in the usual functions—R&D, manufacturing, sales, and the like. The new design creates nine businesses aimed at markets such as small businesses and individuals, office document systems, and engineering systems. Each business will have an income statement and a balance sheet, and an identifiable set of competitors. New manufacturing layouts will permit so-called focused factories dedicated to specific businesses.

Most of the businesses will sell through a new Customer Operations Group, a mingling of sales, shipping, installation, service, and billing, created so customers can keep just one phone number on their Rolodexes. In fact, the businesses will see to Customer Operations—that is, negotiate contracts—so that market forces extend deeply into the company. Teams lead the businesses, whose building blocks are what CEO Paul Allaire calls "microenterprise units": complete work processes or subprocesses. Says Allaire: "We've given everyone in the company a direct line of sight to the customer."

In a functional hierarchy, job descriptions, career paths, and information flow are all geared toward control—of work, workers, and knowledge. Compare that with the evolving 21st-century company, where work is lined up with customers, not toward bosses. Senior executives have charge of the handful of processes that are critical to satisfying customers. Self-directed, the work force does most of the hiring, scheduling, and other managerial tasks that once ate up kazillions in indirect labor costs. The few people left between the executives and the work teams spend their time trying to change the organization, not to control it: They are reaching out to grab a new technology or a new customer, or to respond to a new demand from an old one. Jobs, careers, and knowledge shift constantly.

The boundaries of the company will be fluid too. The growing number of strategic alliances suggests as much. So do the actions of companies like Wal-Mart Stores and Procter & Gamble, which have interwoven their order-and-fulfillment process so that the bells of Wal-Mart's cash registers in effect ring in P&G warehouses, telling them to ship a new box of Tide to replace the one you just bought.

In the view of Harvard economist Robert Reich, the boundaries will become so fluid that corporations will become temporary arrangements among entrepreneurial cadres. Except for high-volume, capital-intensive work, says Reich, "Every big company will be a confederation of small ones.

What a Zoo Can Teach You

The Zoological Society of San Diego has done more than most businesses to transform itself into a 21st-century organization. It deserves to be seen for its management as well as for its spectacular collection of beasts and birds.

With 1,200 year-round employees, $75 million in revenues, and five million visitors a year, the San Diego Zoo and its Wild Animal Park make a sizable outfit whose competitors—among them Walt Disney and Anheuser-Busch, owner of nearby Sea World—are real gorillas. Also, as a world-renowned scientific and conservation organization, the zoo must maintain high technical standards and a Caesar's wife-purity on environmental and other issues.

The zoo is steadily remodeling to show its animals by bioclimactic zone (an African rain forest called Gorilla Tropics, or Tiger River, an Asian jungle environment) rather than by taxonomy (pachyderms, primates). As displays open—three out of ten are finished—they're fundamentally altering the way the zoo is run.

The old zoo was managed through its 50 departments—animal keeping, horticulture, maintenance, food service, fund raising, education, and others. It had all the traits of functional management, says David Glines, head of employee development. Glines started out as a groundsman, responsible for keeping paths clear of trash. If he was tired or rushed, Glines remembers, "Sometimes I'd sweep a cigarette butt under a bush. Then it was the gardener's problem, not mine."

The departments are invisible in the redesigned parts of the zoo. Tiger River, for instance, is run by a team of mammal and bird specialists, horticulturists, and maintenance and construction workers. The four-year-old team, led by keeper John Turner, tracks its own budget on a PC that isn't hooked up to the zoo's mainframe. Members are jointly responsible for the display, and it's hard to tell who comes from which department. When the path in front of an aviary needed fixing last autumn, the horticulturist and the construction man did it.

Seven people run Tiger River. When it started there were 11, but as team members learned one another's skills, they decided they didn't need to replace workers who left. (P.S.: They're all Teamsters union members.) Freed from managerial chores now handled by teams, executives can go out and drum up more interest in the zoo.

Any effect on business? Southern California tourism took some hits in 1991—first from the Gulf war, then from the recession—but the San Diego Zoo enjoyed a 20% increase in attendance. Part of the reason is price: At $12 it costs less than half as much to enter the zoo gates as it does to get into Disneyland.

Zoo director Douglas Myers credits employees' sense of ownership. Says he: "I told them recession is coming; we're going to target our marketing on the local area alone, and we're going to ask all our visitors to come back five times—so each time they'd better have more fun that the time before. The employees came through.

All small organizations will be constantly in the process of linking up into big ones."

That may be more fluidity than most people can accept, at least as long as mortgage applications ask, "How long have you been with your current employer?" But the new flexible organization will be a powerful competitor. Smith finds a metaphor in *Terminator II*, the movie where Arnold Schwarzenegger faces a metal monster that liquifies, then hardens again in a new shape—now a man, now a machine, now a knife. Says Smith: "I call it the *Terminator II* company." How'd you like to have to compete with one of those?

Management by Web

By John A. Byrne

To thrive in this new century, companies are going to need a whole new set of rules

What advice would Alfred P. Sloan Jr., the legendary architect of the 20th century corporation, offer to today's leaders? If he proved to be as farsighted about the coming century as he was about the last, the former chairman of General Motors Corp. and author of *My Years with General Motors* would advise them to leave his tome on the shelf, understanding that it's as outdated as a '26 Le Salle.

Sparked by new technologies, particularly the Internet, the corporation is undergoing a radical transformation that is nothing less than a new Industrial Revolution. This time around, the revolution is reaching every corner of the globe and in the process, rewriting the rules laid down by Sloan, Henry Ford, and other Industrial Age giants. The 21st century corporation that emerges will in many ways be the polar opposite of the organizations they helped shape.

Indeed, if you've worked as a manager for at least a decade, you can forget much of what you've learned so far. Prepare to toss out your business-school case studies and set aside many of the time-honored principles that have guided generations of managers. The vast changes reshaping the world's business terrain are that far-reaching, that fundamental, and that profound. "We're not witnessing just a little change in our economy," David Ticoll, chief executive of Digital 4Sight Systems & Consulting Ltd., a business think tank and consulting firm. "This is an epochal change in the history of production."

Ephemeral

To survive and thrive in this century, managers will need to hard-wire a new set of rules and guideposts into their brains. Not so long ago, for example, leaders believed that building assets over the long haul guaranteed competitive advantage. In this new century, success will go to the companies that partner their way to a new future, not those that put heavy assets onto their balance sheets. Leaders once thought that creating intense rivalries among competitors motivated their employees and assured success. But in the days to come, a company's fiercest competitor might also be its most important collaborator. Since the dawn of trade, every business leader has wanted to build an enduring enterprise. In the new century, though, many companies will be intentionally ephemeral, formed to create new technologies or products only to be absorbed by sponsor companies when their missions are accomplished.

Many factors, from the need to expand beyond national borders to the inexorable shift toward intellectual capital, are driving change, but none is more important than the rise of Internet technologies. Like the steam engine or the assembly line, the Net has already become an advance with revolutionary consequences, most of which we have only begun to feel.

The Net gives everyone in the organization, from the lowliest clerk to the chairman of the board, the ability to access a mind-boggling array of information—instantaneously, from anywhere. Instead of seeping out over months or years, ideas can be zapped around the globe in the blink of an eye. That means that the 21st century corporation must adapt itself to management via the Web. It must be predicated on constant change, not stability, organized around networks, not rigid hierarchies, built on shifting partnerships and alliances, not self-sufficiency, and constructed on technological advantages, not bricks and mortar. Already, old business models that emphasized fixed assets, working capital, and economies of scale have become increasingly vulnerable to

Source: John A. Byrne, "The 21st Century Corporation—Management by Web," *Business Week* (August 28, 2000), pp. 84–96. Copyright © 2000 by Time, Inc. Reprinted with permisson.

nimbler organizations that employ new technologies to reduce costs.

Leading-edge technology will enable workers on the bottom rungs of the organization to seize opportunity as it arises. Employees will increasingly feel the pressure to get breakthrough ideas to market first. Thus, the corporation will need to nurture an array of formal and informal networks to ensure that these ideas can speed into development. In the near future, companies will call on outside contractors to assemble teams of designers, prototype producers, manufacturers, and distributors to get the job done. Emerging technologies will allow employees and freelancers anywhere in the world to converse in numerous languages online without the need for a translator. "The gap between what we can imagine and what we can achieve has never been smaller," says Gary Hamel, a consultant and author of *Leading the Revolution*.

That rapid flow of information will permeate the organization. Orders will be fulfilled electronically without a single phone call or piece of paper. The "virtual financial close" will put real-time sales and profit figures at every manager's fingertips via the click of a wireless phone or a spoken command to a computer. "We don't have science-fiction writers who have seen and written this future," says Lowell Bryan, a consultant who leads McKinsey & Co.'s Global New Economy practice. "Everything we see leads to greater diversity, greater choice, a far more integrative economy, yet more individualism."

How, exactly, will these forces reshape the 21st century corporation? The organizations that flourish will have several defining features.

- *It's management by Web.* That means not just Web as in Internet but the web-like shape of successful organizations in the future. If there are a pair of images that symbolize the vast changes at work, they are the pyramid and the web. The organizational chart of large-scale enterprise had long been defined as a pyramid of ever-shrinking layers leading to an omnipotent CEO at its apex. The 21st century corporation, in contrast, is far more likely to look like a web: a flat, intricately woven form that

Table One — What a Difference a Century Can Make

Contrasting Views of the Corporation

CHARACTERISTIC	20TH CENTURY	21ST CENTURY
ORGANIZATION	The Pyramid	The Web or Network
FOCUS	Internal	External
STYLE	Structured	Flexible
SOURCE OF STRENGTH	Stability	Change
STRUCTURE	Self-sufficiency	Interdependencies
RESOURCES	Atoms—physical assets	Bits—information
OPERATIONS	Vertical integration	Virtual integration
PRODUCTS	Mass production	Mass customization
REACH	Domestic	Global
FINANCIALS	Quarterly	Real-time
INVENTORIES	Months	Hours
STRATEGY	Top-down	Bottom-up
LEADERSHIP	Dogmatic	Inspirational
WORKERS	Employees	Employees and free agents
JOB EXPECTATIONS	Security	Personal growth
MOTIVATION	To compete	To build
IMPROVEMENTS	Incremental	Revolutionary
QUALITY	Affordable best	No compromise

Data: *Business Week.*

links partners, employees, external contractors, suppliers, and customers in various collaborations. The players will grow more and more interdependent. Fewer companies will try to master all the disciplines necessary to produce and market their goods but will instead outsource skills—from research and development to manufacturing—to outsiders who can perform those functions with greater efficiency.

Managing this intricate network of partners, spin-off enterprises, contractors, and freelancers will be as important as managing internal operations. Indeed, it will be hard to tell the difference. All of these constituents will be directly linked in ways that will make it nearly impossible for outsiders to know where an individual firm begins and where it ends. "Companies will be much more molecular and fluid," predicts Don Tapscott, co-author of *Digital Capital*. "They will be autonomous business units connected not necessarily by a big building but across geographies all based on networks. The boundaries of the firm will be not only fluid or blurred but in some cases hard to define."

- *It's more about bits, less about atoms.* The most profitable enterprises will manage bits, or information, instead of focusing solely on managing atoms (the corporation's physical assets). Sheer size will no longer be the hallmark of success; instead, the market will prize the ability to efficiently deploy assets. Good bit management can allow an upstart to beat an established player; it can also give an incumbent vast advantages. By using information to manage themselves and better serve their customers, companies will be able to do things cheaper, faster, and with far less waste.
- *It's mass customization.* The previous 100 years were marked by mass production and mass consumption. Companies sought economies of scale to build large factories that produced cookie-cutter products, which they then sold to the largest numbers of people in as many markets as possible. The company of the future will tailor its products to each individual by turning customers into partners and giving them the technology to design and demand exactly what they want. Mass customization will result in waves of individualized products and services, as well as huge savings for companies, which will no longer have to guess what and how much customers want.
- *It's dependent on intellectual capital.* The advantage of bringing breakthrough products to market first will be shorter-lived than ever, because technology will let competitors match or exceed them almost instantly. To keep ahead of the steep new-product curve, it will be crucial for businesses to attract and retain the best thinkers. Companies will need to build a deep reservoir of talent—including both employees and free agents—to succeed in this new era. But attracting and retaining an elite workforce will require more than huge paychecks. Corporations will need to create the kind of cultures and reward systems that keep the best minds engaged. The old command-and-control hierarchies, with their civil-service-like wages, are fast crumbling in favor of organizations that empower vast numbers of people and reward the best of them as if they were owners of the enterprise.
- *It's global.* In the beginning, the global company was defined as one that simply sold its goods in overseas markets. Later, global companies assumed a manufacturing presence in numerous countries. The company of the future will call on talent and resources—especially intellectual capital—wherever they can be found around the globe, just as it will sell its goods and services around the globe. Indeed, the very notion of a headquarters country may no longer apply, as companies migrate to places of greatest advantage. The new global corporation might be based in the U.S. but do its software programming in Sri Lanka, its engineering in Germany, and its manufacturing in China. Every outpost will be seamlessly connected by the Net so that far-flung employees and freelancers can work together in real time.
- *It's about speed.* All this work will be done in an instant. "The Internet is a tool, and the biggest impact of that tool is speed," says Andrew S. Grove, chairman of Intel Corp. "The speed of actions, the speed of deliberations, and the speed of information has increased, and it will continue to increase." That means the old, process-oriented corporation must radically revamp. With everything from product cycles to employee turnover on fast-forward, there is simply not enough time for deliberation or bureaucracy.

The 21st century corporation will not have one ideal form. Some will be completely virtual, wholly dependent on a network of suppliers, manufacturers, and distributors for their survival. Others, less so. Some of the most successful companies will be very small and very specialized; others will be gargantuan in size, scope, and complexity.

Some enterprises will last no longer than the time it takes for a new product or technology to reach the market. Once it does, these temporary organizations will pass their innovations on to host companies that can leverage them more quickly and at less expense. The reason: Every company has capabilities but also disabilities, as Harvard Business School's Clayton M. Christensen puts it. The disabilities—things like deeply held beliefs, rituals, and traditions—often smother radical thinking. Some biotech upstarts, for example, have already served as external labs for large, powerful pharmaceutical companies. Some technology ventures have drawn seed capital from Cisco Systems Inc., only to be acquired by the network giant once the technology has been proven.

Digitization

Just as the smaller companies will use technology to gain economies of scale, larger companies will harness technology to reduce the costs of complexity. McKinsey's Bryan points out that technology allows Bank of America to manage a continent-wide bank of $700 billion in assets as effectively as it once managed a single-state bank with $7 billion.

At the very core of the 21st century corporation is technology, or what most people today call digitization. Put simply, digitization means removing human minds and hands from an organization's most routine tasks and replacing them with computers and networks. Digitizing everything from employee benefits to accounts receivables to product design cuts time, cost, and people from operations, resulting in huge savings and vast improvements in speed. Everything a company does involves what Bryan calls "interaction costs," the expenses incurred to get different people and companies to work together to create and sell products. In the U.S. alone, Bryan surmises, such interaction fees account for over half of all labor costs. Digitization lowers these expenses dramatically. "You are going to see unbelievable speed and efficiencies," says John T. Chambers, Cisco's CEO. "Truly efficient companies, particularly in the first couple of waves of change, will be able to drive [overall] productivity at 20% to 40% a year."

Think of it this way: A typical bank transaction costs $1.25 when handled by a teller, 54¢ when done by phone, or 24¢ at an ATM. But the same transaction processed over the Internet, without the hefty capital and real estate costs of ATMs, costs a mere 2¢. The productivity improvement isn't incremental. It's revolutionary—on the order of more than 60 times. Similar examples already abound. Not long ago, for instance, Corning Inc. spent an average of $140 to procure the parts and supplies needed to make a single product. Simply switching to a Net-based catalog system reduced procurement costs to one-twentieth of that amount. Humana Inc., the health-care provider, reduced the average cost of handling a job application and résumé from $128 to 6¢ by digitizing the process, largely by eliminating labor costs. "The truly great businesses of today and especially tomorrow have powerful bit engines, digital systems for capturing, managing, and leveraging information both inside and outside the company," says Mercer Management Consulting Inc. partner Adrian J. Slywotzky.

Cultural Change

The potential for productivity gains is everywhere, in every process, in every industry. The bigger the company and the larger its costs, the greater the opportunity to see tremendous efficiencies. In the years to come, large incumbent corporations that get it will be the greatest beneficiaries of the Net, not the dot-com insurgents that once garnered all the publicity and market valuations.

Despite a handful of leading-edge companies, the true 21st century corporation, at least as it will eventually emerge, does not yet exist. John F. Welch Jr. of General Electric Co. may have created the archetypal "learning organization," a highly diverse company that shares ideas across its many boundaries. Chambers of Cisco Systems may boast the most networked organization in the world, a company in which nearly all its administrative functions are conducted over the Internet. Michael Dell may have built the most efficient supply-chain network ever, a model that requires virtually no inventory. But there is no one company today that embodies all the possibilities and promise of the superefficient 21st century corporation.

For companies that have begun to grasp the possibilities, the payoff can be enormous. Enron Corp., a onetime natural-gas pipeline company, is a good example. The Houston business employed the Net to make itself into a highly profitable energy and telecommunications service. Enron's Web-based trading platform, EnronOnline, now trades some 900 contracts per day for commodities including oil, natural gas, electricity, and even broadband telecommunications capacity. Earnings—up 30% in the second quarter—are skyrocketing, along with the company's stock price. Enron has created for itself an entirely new core competence: Web-based trading that could bring the company into financial products, chemicals, and data storage.

Many view Enron's transformation through the narrow lens of technology. The lesson for 21st century leaders, however, isn't just about clever application of the latest software. It's about culture and mind-set. By refusing to limit itself to the traditional notions of what an energy company should do, Enron has pioneered completely new businesses. And it's not just the bosses who are thinking up all the good ideas. Enron is a company of risk-taking entrepreneurs who share a broad definition of the businesses' boundaries.

The truly great 21st century companies will recognize that the real power of technology is not just the ability to make a business more efficient but also its potential to spark transformative changes. Much of that change will involve the company's relationship with its customers. In an era of unprecedented choice, in which prices and product specs for almost anything are only a click away, companies will have to offer a lot more than bargain prices.

By shifting corporate think from delivering a product to serving the customer, even long established companies can find ways to drive new business. Exxon Mobil Corp.'s Speedpass, a cylinder-shaped credit card that users can swipe against the gas tank before they fill up, is a good example. The simple device, which fits on a keychain, lets customers gas up and leave without trudging inside to pay or waiting for an attendant. "Mobil scientists spent an inordinate amount of time studying the molecules in gasoline in an effort to make better fuel," says Michael J. Clearly, president of WingspanBank.com, the online offshoot of Bank One Corp., who studies how companies achieve great service. "But it's not about whether Mobil's 89-octane is better than Exxon's. It's all about speed and customer relationships." By figuring out a way to offer a new level of convenience, Mobil significantly boosted revenues and customer loyalty.

Clearly is applying the same strategy to his online bank. "It's not about having a better CD rate," he says. "It's about customer service." From the start, Wingspan has been focused first and foremost on the customer, even adding an iBoard of Directors made up of customers who offer advice on products and strategy. The emphasis on service is pervasive. Applicants for home equity loans get answers in 60 seconds. The customer call center runs 24 hours a day, seven days a week. Every employee is required to listen to customer calls for at least 1½ hours a month, and the top executive team reads at least 20 customer emails a day. There are even "customer experience" departments and "customer advocacy teams" to quickly address complaints and suggestions.

Feedback

High-tech bells and whistles aside, how does this differ from previous efforts to "delight" customers? Wingspan invites customers to refine the bank's offerings. "Our customers have a great desire to improve the bank, and we act on their ideas," says Clearly. Customer feedback led to software changes that allowed users to access all their accounts at once, with a single sign-on. In response to customer suggestions, the bank is working on a way to allow deposits at ATMs and to improve downloads of financial data from Wingspan servers to customers' Quicken software.

The best-of-breed companies will go even further. They'll invite customers in as collaborators, binding them even tighter to the corporation. Procter & Gamble Co. spin-off reflect.com LLC, an online cosmetics merchant, is a harbinger of what's possible. By answering a series of queries ranging from color preferences to skin type, consumers can custom-design up to 50,000 different formulations of cosmetics and perfumes. When they're done, they can even design the packaging for the products. Procter & Gamble charges a premium price for the custom-blended blushers and lipsticks, and why not? Customers mixing their own shades aren't likely to try comparison shopping.

Reflect.com is one of many efforts to create enduring relationships with customers in an age of commoditization. "The next level up is where the consumer is really designing from scratch," says Ticoll of Digital 4Sight. "Organizations will learn from these new opportunities."

Applied correctly, this kind of mass customization can yield remarkable efficiencies. Already, Dell Computer Inc. generates more working capital than it consumes because its customers specify and pay for product before Dell has to pay suppliers. In contrast, Honeywell International Inc. has $3.5 billion of working capital tied up at any given time. The key to Dell's remarkable feat lies in the company's made-to-order business model, which greatly limits inventory. Already, the company turns over its tiny inventory 60 times a year, a tenfold improvement from 1994. The result is obvious. Dell's customers finance the company's growth so it does not have to take on debt. Mass customization also allows Dell to make only the products it will sell. So there are no write-downs or discounts to move unwanted or outdated merchandise.

Delivering the Goods

In the hands of a creative leader, even the most prosaic Industrial Age enterprises can reap quantum efficiencies by applying the new management principles of the 21st century corporation. No company proves that better than Cemex, which operates in one of the most mundane, commodity-driven businesses in the world: cement. Based in Monterrey, Mexico, Cemex was a modestly profitable business in 1985 when Lorenzo H. Zambrano, a Stanford University MBA whose grandfather founded the company, became chief executive. Cemex' biggest problem in an asset-intensive, low-efficiency business was unpredictable demand. Roughly half of its orders were changed by customers, often just hours before delivery. Dispatchers took orders for 8,000 grades of mixed concrete and forwarded them to six plants. The phones were often jammed with calls from customers, truckers, and dispatchers, resulting in lost orders and frustrated customers.

Then Cemex went digital, vastly reducing delivery and production problems. More important, the makeover helped management refocus efforts from managing assets to managing information. "Technology allows you to do business in a much different fashion than before," says Zambrano. "We used it not only to deliver a product but to sell a service."

For starters, Zambrano linked the company's delivery trucks to a global positioning satellite system so dispatchers could monitor the location, direction, and speed of every vehicle. That means Cemex can quickly send the right truck to pick up and deliver a specific grade of cement, or reroute trucks around congested traffic, or redirect deliveries as last-minute changes occur. It reduced average delivery times from three hours to 20 minutes. Zambrano reaped huge savings in fuel, maintenance, and payroll, since Cemex now uses 35% fewer trucks to deliver the same amount of cement. And because it can guarantee delivery of a perishable commodity product within minutes of an order, it can charge a premium for it.

By digitizing, Zambrano also eliminated a lot of the friction that slowed down the company and added costs at every step. The company's customers, distributors, and suppliers can use the Internet to place orders, find out when shipments will arrive, and check payment records—without having to speak to a customer-service rep. That allows employees to shift from low-value repetitive work to improving services that build stronger customer relationships. Zambrano and his executives, moreover, now have access to every conceivable detail about the company's operations within 24 hours, compared with the more typical month-old data generated by competitors; they can now better respond to customers and rivals. "They were able to substitute the management of information for the deployment of costly assets such as trucks, ships, and employees," says Slywotzky, who puts Cemex in a league with Dell and Cisco as one of the world's leading digital re-inventors.

Connections

True 21st century corporations will also learn to manage an elaborate network of external relationships. That far-reaching ecosystem of suppliers, partners, and contractors will allow them to focus on what they do best and farm everything else out. And it will let them quickly take advantage of fleeting opportunities without having to tie up vast amounts of capital. Outsourcing and partnering, of course, are hardly new. But in the coming century, such alliances will become more crucial.

Cisco Systems has taken the concept to an extreme. It owns only two of the 34 plants that produce its product. Roughly 90% of the orders come into the company without ever being touched by human hands, and 52% of them are fulfilled without a Cisco employee being involved. "To my customers, it looks like one big virtual plant where my suppliers and inventory systems are directly tied into an ecosystem," says Chambers. "That will be the norm in the future. Everything will be completely connected, both within a company and between companies. The people who get that will have a huge competitive advantage."

For some companies, the ecosystem represents not merely the outsourcing of a function or two to save a few bucks. It goes, instead, to the very heart of a company's ability to exist and compete. If not for its dozens of alliances and partnerships, Juno Online Services Inc. in New York, the Internet service provider, could not survive—at least not without hundreds of millions of dollars in additional capital and thousands of extra employees. "If we had to do it all ourselves, it would be prohibitively expensive," says CEO Charles Ardai, who spends 25% of his time on alliances. "For our customers, it's an invisible experience because of the technology. The coordination among the partners allows for real-time communication and makes it feel more like a single company."

Juno, though still unprofitable, is an example of an opportunistic insurgent in a new industry. It was formed in 1994 when investment banker David E. Shaw asked two of his managers to come up with ideas about how to exploit the Net. Jeff Bezos dreamed up the idea of an online bookseller and left D.E. Shaw & Co. to found Amazon.com Inc. Ardai, backed by Shaw, created Juno, the first provider of free Internet access, and challenged America Online Inc. Today, Juno is the third-largest ISP.

From the start, Ardai's focus was speed to market. "You start out with the premise that you don't have much time, so you build the core competency and partner for the rest," he says. Juno designed an easy-to-use e-mail service and user interface and then contracted out for just about everything else. It leased phone lines from a dozen companies. It hired out customer service, immediately gaining hundreds of call-center representatives. It partnered with an upstart advertising agency for ad sales. It aligned with dozens of content partners for news, weather, sports, movie reviews, health information, and travel advice. It even outsourced some programming and customer support in Hyderabad, India. "The partnerships allowed us to get started without huge capital expenditures," explains Ardai.

Talent Hunt

They also gave a small upstart immediate scale and reach. Juno, for instance, boasts fewer than 300 direct employees yet has nearly 700 technicians in customer service alone because of its alliance. "If we did all of this stuff ourselves, we would have to have at least 1,000 people to work on content alone," estimates Ardai.

Vast changes in technical and organizational structure, however, will only get leaders so far on their journey toward 21st century leadership. Nearly everyone agrees it still comes down to that most precious commodity: talented people. Attracting, cultivating, and retaining them will be the indispensable ingredient that will drive the ideas, products, and growth of all companies like never before. As management guru Gary Hamel puts it: "We have moved from an economy of hands to an economy of heads. Therefore, the price of imagination, the premium for it, will go up." Increasingly, companies will need to scour the world for the best intellectual capital, then create the kinds of challenging environments that will allow stars to flourish.

Few organizations have worked harder at this or with greater creativity than Trilogy Software Inc., the Austin (Tex.) producer of economic-commerce software. A private company with more than $200 million in revenues, Trilogy devotes an extraordinary amount of attention to recruiting the best engineers directly from campus. The Trilogy proposition: Rather than work in a huge organization like Microsoft Corp. as product managers, they could have a major impact at Trilogy in driving the company to the next level of competition.

Once hired, candidates attend a three-month-long intensive training program that co-founder and President Joe Liemandt calls Trilogy University. All the top executives show up to teach. "The same way people look at customers, we look at our jobs," says Liemandt. "We ask how you make the job compelling for employees. If you don't get the steel into the factory, there is no product. If you don't get the best people into the company, there is no product."

Incubator

As a private company, Trilogy can't offer stock options. Instead, it offers the chance to create and run new businesses. Liemandt throws out a daunting challenge to every incoming class: Within two years, the students will be responsible for the creation of at least 20% of new revenues. "They treat the university as an R&D incubator," says Noel M. Tichy, a University of Michigan management professor. Trilogy, for example, has spun out six companies, including one that's selling hundreds of millions of dollars' worth of cars online annually.

To make sure he doesn't lose touch with his employees, Liemandt uses the Net to establish one-on-one conversations with them. Trilogy's 1,500 employees go online to read—and respond to—the mission statements of top managers. Periodically, they're asked to assess managers online. "Energy and excitement is why people do startups," says Liemandt. "But as the company gets larger, people don't feel as engaged. They feel as if they are spoken to instead of being engaged in a collaboration. The net provides a ten-to-twenty-fold increase in the level of interaction you can have."

The 21st century corporation will require an array of new skills, all of which must be mastered for leaders to gain the upper competitive hand. Globalization has opened new markets. Deregulation has broken down industry boundaries. Venture capital has funded thousands of new tech-savvy insurgents who now threaten incumbents. And the ever-ubiquitous Web has brought the potential for remarkable gains in productivity—but also for frightening deflationary pressures. All these forces are fast propelling the creation of new business models in the 21st century, models that will look nothing like the once-healthy and seemingly invincible enterprises of an earlier age.

Index

advance factor endowments, 16
Allaire, Paul, 31, 37
alliances, inter-company, 13, 18–19
"The American Corporation as an Employer" (Kochan), 23
Ardai, Charles, 44–45
Asia, 10
authority, 12, 37

banking, 42
Bayamón, Puerto Rico, 32, 34
"Beyond the Hype" (Eccles and Nohria), 24
Bezos, Jeff, 44
bits vs. atoms, 41
Bossidy, Lawrence, 31, 32, 36, 37
boundaries and boundary-spanning, 12, 13, 19
Brookhouse, Robert, 31, 35
Bryan, Lowell, 40, 42
Buehler, William, 31, 34
bureaucracy. *See* old (bureaucratic) model
business press. *See* press, business
business process reengineering. *See* reengineering
business schools, 11

capability, core, 24
Cemex, 43–44
chain of command, 12
chain stores, 25
Chambers, John T., 42, 44
Champy, James, 31, 36, 37
Cisco Systems, 44
classic model of formal organization, 11–12
Clearly, Michael J., 43
"Coda to the New Organization" (Van Maanen), 24–25
"The Coming of the New Organization" (Drucker), 22
command-and-control system, 12
communication, cross-cultural, 20
communications, reduced costs of, 16
competition, 13, 14, 15
cooperative networks, 13
core capability, 24
core process redesign, 35
cross-border integration, 20
cross-cultural communication, 20
Crum, R. Clayton, 34
customer needs
    flexibility and, 15, 19
    management by Web and, 41, 43
    in process management, 37
    worker self-management and, 32
customization, mass, 41

decisionmaking, 14
delivery systems, and technology improvements, 43–44
delivery systems, just-in-time, 13
Dell, Michael, 42
Dell Computer, 43
demographic diversity, 15
departments, 12, 13, 34, 35–37
"Designing Effective Organizations" (Goold and Campbell), 23
digitization, 42
diversity
    of labor force, 15
    management implications, 19–20
    in new organization model, 15
downsizing, 10
Drucker, Peter, 31, 32

"ecosystem" of suppliers, partners, and contractors, 44–45
empathy, 19–20
Enron Corporation, 42–43
environment, external
    boundaries with, in bureaucratic model, 12
    diversity and, 15
    "ecosystem" of suppliers, partners, and contractors, 44–45
    flat organizations and, 19
    flexibility of an organization and, 15, 19
    global vs. international approach, 15–16
    national emphasis, 12, 15
    networked organization's relations with, 13, 18–19
    outsourcing, 13
equalization, 16
Europe, 10
expertise, management of, 12, 36

flat organizations
    horizontal structures, 33, 36, 37
    management implications, 19
    in new organization model, 14
Fletcher, Don, 31, 35
flexibility, 14–15, 19
Ford, Henry, 39

General Electric (GE), 32, 34
global dimension of new organizations, 15–16, 20, 41
government, reinvention of, 10
Grove, Andrew S., 41

Hallmark, 35
Hamel, Gary, 45

Hammer, Mike, 31, 35
headquarters, 41
hierarchical structure, 12, 14, 37
high-involvement workplace, 32
hollow corporations, 13
horizontal organizations, 33, 36, 37. *See also* reengineering

ideal types, 16–17
impartiality, 12
incentives, 19, 45
information, sharing of, 13
information-based organizations, 22
information bits, vs. atoms, 41
information technology (IT)
    digitization, 42
    flattening of hierarchy and, 14
    "Management by Web" (Byrne), 39–45
    networking and, 13–14
    process reengineering and, 37
innovation, 12, 14–15
intellectual capital and talent, 12, 36, 41, 45
interdependent networks, 13
international business, 10, 15. *See also* global dimension of new organizations
Internet. *See* information technology (IT)
In the Age of the Machine (Zuboff), 34
IT. *See* information technology

Jarrosiak, Philip, 31, 34
jobs, specialized, 12
journals, business. *See* press, business
Juno Online Services, 44–45
just-in-time delivery systems, 13

Kodak, 35

labor force, 15, 19
law firms, 37
learning in organizations, 19, 34
Liemandt, Joe, 45
listening skills, 19–20
local responsiveness, 20

magazines, business. *See* press, business
Malloy, Richard, 35
"Management by Web" (Byrne), 39–45
management consultants, 25–26
management implications of new model, 18–21. *See also* flat organizations
mapping your organization, 27–28
markets, globalization of, 16
mass customization, 41
Maxmin, H. James, 31, 32
McDonald's, 25
McKinsey & Co., 36
Microsoft Corporation, 15
Mills, Quinn, 31, 37

"The Mind of the CEO" (Garten), 23–24
multitasking, 19
Myers, Douglas, 38

Nadler, David, 31
national context, emphasis on, 12
negotiation and conflict resolution, 19, 20
networking
    global approach, 16
    "Management by Web" (Byrne), 39–45
    management consultants and concept of, 25–26
    management implications, 18–19
    in new organization model, 13–14, 23
    outsourcing and, 13, 44–45
    virtual companies, 13
"The New Managerial Work" (Kanter), 22–23
new organization model. *See also* old (bureaucratic) model
    overview, 6–7
    appeal of, 17
    assessments in business press, 22–26
    challenges in shifting to, 10–11, 18, 20–21
    characteristics of, 10
    diverse aspect, 15
    flat aspect, 14, 19
    flexible aspect, 14–15, 19–20
    global dimension, 15–16, 20
    as ideal type, 16–17, 21
    in international business, 10
    "Management by Web" (Byrne), 39–45
    management implications, 18–21
    mapping your organization, 27–28
    networked aspect, 13–14, 18–19, 23
    old model, contrasts with, 17
    "The Search for the Organization of Tomorrow (Stewart), 31–39
    skepticism about, 24–26
    society-business interactions, 23–24
    in U.S. government, 10
    vertical vs. horizontal structure, 33
    workforce management in, 19
NGOs (nongovernmental organizations), 16

old (bureaucratic) model
    characteristics of, 11–13
    diversity, lack of, 15
    hierarchical structure, 12, 14, 37
    innovative subunits within, 12
    new model contrasted with, 17
    resiliency of, 11, 12
    Weber's model of bureaucracy, 11, 16–17
    workforce management in, 19
operating procedures, flexible vs. rigid, 11, 12, 14–15
organization, concept of, 11
organization model, new. *See* new organization model

organization model, old. *See* old (bureaucratic) model
Ostroff, Frank, 31, 32, 34, 36
outsourcing, 13, 44–45

Palermo, Richard, 31, 34
perpetual learning, 34
Porter, Michael, 16
positions (jobs), specialized and hierarchical, 12
predictability, 12
press, business
    new organization in, 10
    prominent journals, 6
    reading critically, 30–31
problem-solving, and flexibility, 14–15
process management, 35
process reengineering. *See* reengineering
Procter & Gamble, 34, 38
promotion, 19
Puerto Rico, 32, 34

rational-legal bureaucracy, 11
reading critically, 30–31
reciprocity, 24
reengineering
    definition of, 30, 35
    "The Search for the Organization of Tomorrow (Stewart), 31–39
    vertical vs. horizontal structure, 33
Reich, Robert, 31, 38
reliability, 12
resources, and networking, 14
Ritzer, George, 25
rules, 12, 14–15

San Diego Zoo, 38
"The Search for the Organization of Tomorrow (Stewart), 31–39
self-management, 32
Shaw, David E., 44
Simon, Herman, 31, 34
skills
    listening and empathy, 19–20
    negotiation, 19
    teamwork, 18
Sloan, Alfred P., Jr., 39

Slywotzky, Adrian J., 42, 44
Smith, Douglas, 31, 32, 35–36, 39
society-business interactions, 23–24
specialization, 12, 36
stakeholders, 13, 20
Stanton, Steven, 35
suppliers, relationships with, 13

talent and intellectual capital, 12, 36, 41, 45
Tapscott, Don, 41
Taylor, Frederick, 25
teams, 13, 15
telecommunications technologies, 13–14
temporary workers, 15
Tichy, Noel M., 45
Ticoll, David, 39, 43
training, 12
transportation costs, international, 16
Trilogy Software, 45
"The Twenty-first Century Firm" (DiMaggio), 25–26

value chains, 16
vertical organizations, 33
virtual company, 13
volatility, 14, 15

wage gap, 11
Wal-Mart, 38
Weber, Max, 11, 16–17
Web technology. *See* information technology (IT)
Weisbord, Marvin, 31, 32
Welch, John F., Jr., 42
"Will the Organization of the Future Make the Mistakes of the Past" (Pfeffer), 24
worker self-management, 32
workforce, 15, 19
World Wide Web. *See* information technology (IT)

Xerox, 37

Zambrano, Lorenzo H., 43–44
Zoological Society of San Diego, 38
Zuboff, Shoshanna, 31, 34

MANAGING FOR THE FUTURE

Organizational Behavior & Processes

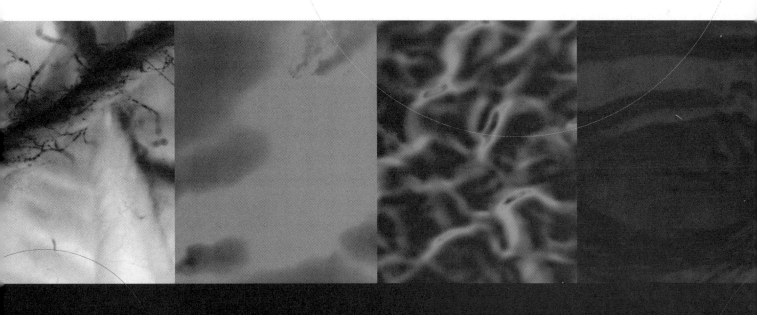

Three Lenses on Organizational Analysis and Action

Module 2

MANAGING FOR THE FUTURE
Organizational Behavior & Processes, Third Edition

Deborah Ancona
Sloan School of Management
Massachusetts Institute of Technology

John Van Maanen
Sloan School of Management
Massachusetts Institute of Technology

Thomas A. Kochan
Sloan School of Management
Massachusetts Institute of Technology

D. Eleanor Westney
Sloan School of Management
Massachusetts Institute of Technology

Maureen Scully
Graduate School of Management
Simmons College

Dedicated to those who have inspired us to try to be better students and teachers.
Special thanks to: Professor Jack Barbash • Professor Arthur H. Gladstein • Professor Marius B. Jansen • Professor Joanne Martin • Professor Edgar H. Schein

---

VP/Editorial Director
Jack W. Calhoun

VP/Editor-in-Chief
Michael P. Roche

Senior Publisher
Melissa S. Acuña

Executive Editor
John Szilagyi

Senior Developmental Editor
Judith O'Neill

Marketing Manager
Jacquelyn Carrillo

Production Editor
Emily Gross

Manufacturing Coordinator
Rhonda Utley

Compositor
Trejo Production

Printer
Von Hoffmann Press, Inc.
Frederick, MD

Internal Designer
Bethany Casey

Cover Designer
Bethany Casey

Photographs
©PhotoDisc

Design Project Manager
Bethany Casey

COPYRIGHT ©2005
by South-Western, a division of Thomson Learning. Thomson Learning™ is a trademark used herein under license.

Printed in the United States of America
1 2 3 4 5 07 06 05 04 03

For more information contact
South-Western College Publishing,
5191 Natorp Boulevard,
Mason, Ohio, 45040
Or you can visit our Internet site at:
http://www.swlearning.com

ALL RIGHTS RESERVED
No part of this work covered by the copyright hereon may be reproduced or used in any form or by any means—graphic, electronic, or mechanical, including photocopying, recording, taping, Web distribution or information storage and retrieval systems—without the written permission of the publisher.

For permission to use material from this text or product, contact us by
Tel: (800) 730-2214
Fax: (800) 730-2215
http://www.thomsonrights.com

Library of Congress Control Number: 2003113908
ISBN 0-324-05575-7

Contents

Three Lenses on Organizational Analysis and Action

Overview		4

Core

Class Note	Introduction	8
Class Note	The Strategic Design Lens	13
Case	Strategic Design at Dynacorp	28
Class Note	The Political Lens	33
The Press	Informal Network: The Company Behind the Chart	47
Class Note	The Cultural Lens	57
The Press	Organizational Culture	67
Class Note	Applying the Three Lenses	83
Case	Dynacorp Revisited: The Front/Back Organization	85

Index

Overview

This module introduces three lenses with organizational analysis and action. The lenses have been developed over the years by researchers, teachers, consultants, and practitioners who study and participate in organizations. Ours is a behavioral science perspective that differs both from the economic realm, with its bundles of contracts and utility-maximizing individuals, and from the decision-modeling realm, where all decisions can be programmed. The behavioral science perspective builds on psychology, sociology, political science, and anthropology. From these disciplines we developed *strategic design, political,* and *cultural lenses.*

You can think of these lenses as three different levels of magnification that you could put on your mental camera in order to get different views of an organization you are trying to understand and change. Through each lens, you can direct your attention to observe slightly different features; for example, the structure of the firm, key stakeholders and their interests, or organizational artifacts and assumptions, respectively. Each lens reveals a distinctive view from the others. An organization chart will represent a system of grouping and linking critical tasks in one lens, a picture of the current power structure and dominant coalition in the second, and a symbol to be interpreted in the third. As a manager taking action, the strategic design lens sets you up as an "organizational architect" improving the fit between strategy and organization across organizational components. The political lens casts you as a forger of coalitions and negotiator leveraging varying interests. The cultural lens defines your role as articulating a vision and creating symbols and stories. When all lenses are applied in analyzing an organization, your perspective becomes more rich and more complex than if you chose to view an organization solely through a strategic fiat.

The Structure of this Module

This module is divided into five Class Notes. The first Class Note provides an introduction and motivation for using the three lenses by way of the concept of cognitive schema. The second Class Note introduces the strategic design lens and calls for its application to a case on Dynacorp. The third introduces the political lens and uses the Rosewell role play to practice stakeholder analysis and action. The fourth provides readings on the cultural lens and provides an exercise that allows students to do a cultural analysis of their own institution. Finally, the fifth Class Note revisits the Dynacorp case and illustrates how all three lenses can be used to develop an integrated plan for analysis and managerial action.

Additional Activities

1. Find an article in the business press about a particular organization. Assess whether the article is using (implicitly or explicitly) the strategic design, political, or cultural perspective, or some combination thereof.

    For example, the business press was abuzz in 2001 about the appointment of Terry Semel to resuscitate Yahoo! Semel, largely viewed at the time as the by-the-numbers antithesis of departing CEO Tim Koogle, raised a huge cloud of conjecture over possible new directions for the firm. Some articles discussed who, among the old Yahoo! guard, would occupy the key roles after Semel's ascendancy and which services might be retained or eliminated (a strategic design perspective). Some articles discussed the interests of employees as both stockholders and knowledge workers with some power to leverage if they threatened to leave (a political perspective). After all, Koogle was much loved and had cultivated quite a loyal following of Yahooligans. Some articles discussed the implications of mixing such seemingly diverse corporate cultures as Silicon Valley and Hollywood (a cultural perspective).
2. Write a brief essay explaining which of the three perspectives you are most naturally comfortable with and why.

Additional Suggested Readings

The importance of looking at organizations from multiple perspectives is one of the hallmarks of a behavioral approach to organizations. The behavioral approach recognizes that individuals make sense of work in many ways, that behaviors in organizations can have numerous ramifications, and that multiple paths can be taken to a variety of organizational outcomes (from job satisfaction to corporate performance). The behavioral approach is, therefore, different from a more traditionally economic approach to organizations, which has tended to look for one best way to optimize profitability. The following books each present different clusters of approaches to organizational behavior and processes that overlap with or supplement the perspectives presented in this module.

Bolman, Lee G., and Terrence E. Deal. 1991. *Reframing Organizations: Artistry, Choice, and Leadership*. San Francisco: Jossey-Bass.

Morgan, Gareth. 1986. *Images of Organization*. Newbury Park, CA: Sage Publications.

Three Lenses on Organizational Analysis and Action

CORE

Module

Introduction

In order to solve an organizational problem or take advantage of an organizational opportunity, it is helpful to have a rich understanding of the organization and the issues. A good picture of an organization is useful for probing more thoroughly into the possible nature and sources of the issues and the range of approaches. It is easy to skip this analysis in favor of familiar approaches. People often summarize an organizational problem in a way that suggests a singular source, such as, "The main problem we have here is a delay in manufacturing." They leap into that line of inquiry: "OK, let's see what we can do to speed up the manufacturing process." In fact, if they had a richer picture of the organization, they might learn that the problem is elsewhere, perhaps to do with the design-manufacturing interface, or the relationship with suppliers, or the way that overtime compensation is handled. It is helpful to understand that one can look at an organization in many ways and many illuminating features that can be observed. Different individuals will tend to focus on one set of problems or issues over others.

An often-told parable about three blind men and an elephant reminds us of the importance of an individual's viewpoint:

> *Three blind men were asked to describe what an elephant is like. One blind man felt the elephant's tail and observed, "An elephant is very much like a piece of rope." The second blind man felt the elephant's side and observed, "An elephant is very much like a wall." The third blind man felt the elephant's trunk and observed, "An elephant is very much like a pipe." Each was right. And each was incomplete and partly misguided.*

Our informal diagnoses of organizations, based on bits and pieces of our experiences, are often partly right but somewhat incomplete and misguided. This module presents some more formal and complete models for looking at organizations that have been developed in the social sciences. Of course, none of these models is a complete theory of the world either. Rather, the challenge is for you to understand whether you tend to adopt certain approaches to organizations more naturally, whether you tend to overlook certain potentially useful approaches, and whether these two tendencies can be balanced and integrated to provide a more complete analysis.

This module introduces three classic perspectives on organizations. These three perspectives can be thought of as lenses, each of which presents a distinctive view of the organization. Before reading about how these three perspectives have developed, it is helpful to think about how each of us brings our own personal views to organizations.

Our Personal "Schemas"

Each of us has certain ways of looking at the world. We have what social psychologists call *schemas*, which we use every day to navigate through complex situations. "A schema is a cognitive structure that represents organized knowledge about a given concept or type of stimulus. A schema contains both the attributes of the concept and the relationship among the attributes" (Fiske and Taylor, 1984, p. 140). Social psychologists developed this idea upon observing that individuals construct their own maps of the social world.

What Is Helpful About Schemas?

Schemas help people function in cognitively efficient ways. As certain kinds of situations or data become familiar, it is easier to rely on a tried and true model of how to react than to rethink the situation anew. For example, someone who drives a crowded freeway to work every morning may always jump into the leftmost lane on approaching the toll plaza; it is her schema for dealing with traffic. She hardly has to think about it—she just does it. When she started driving that route, she may have taken different approaches and arrived at this one after trial and error. Even if it isn't the fastest lane each morning, overall it may reduce stress to have this taken-for-granted strategy, leaving her mind a little freer to focus on the radio news. Schemas give us an approach to repeated situations and free up our minds for other more complex and highly varying activities.

It is particularly helpful to develop schemas about organizations in which we work. It is the essence of becoming an "old hand." The value of employees with seniority is that they have worked out a number of their own unwritten schemas for how to get things done. (In more formal terms, they have developed specialized human capital or tacit knowledge that makes them particularly valuable and difficult to replace.) Without schemas, every task would be a monumental new project.

Most organizations provide complex and noisy informational environments in which organizational participants gather information about other individuals and relevant work tasks, which they must then integrate with their own thoughts, feelings, and work behaviors. To manage these multiple information-processing demands, people accomplish many cognitive activities without conscious awareness, attention, or much forethought. In other words people rely on highly structured, pre-existing knowledge systems to interpret their organizational world and generate appropriate behaviors. Such a knowledge system . . . is often called a schema. (Lord and Foti, 1986, pp. 20–21)

This cognitive processing is helpful because it helps individuals find recurring patterns in complex everyday data. But schemas are not meant to be hard and fast rules. Without some conscious examination of them, we might be led astray.

How Do Our Schemas Lead Us Astray?

Schemas Become Outdated Although our personal schemas may initially seem efficient, they can become outdated. People can be stubbornly attached to their schemas. Schemas need updating. Our schemas derive from our experiences, but over time they can also come to shape our experiences in self-fulfilling ways.

For example, in the past, textbooks included mostly examples of men in professional roles. On the one hand, these pictures were a fairly accurate representation, statistically, of who was most likely to occupy professional roles some years ago. A person with a schema that "you should ask for *Mister* so-and-so if phoning the manager" may have had an accurate, time-saving schema. On the other hand, schemas do not just reflect organizational life, they help to shape it. It has been difficult for women to move into traditionally male professional roles precisely because most people's schemas have not included a picture of women in those roles.

The entrance of women into professional roles may help some people change these particular schemas. At the same time, changing schemas may make it easier for women to enter professional roles. People who do not update their schemas may find themselves in embarrassing situations, such as the students who asked the woman standing in the department office for some help with photocopying, thinking she must be the secretary, only to discover they had just asked the chair of the department to photocopy their assignments.

Schemas Are Resistant to Change It is both a beauty and a weakness of schemas that they become familiar and difficult to change. Even if we know our old schemas are not perfect—the leftmost lane is not always the fastest moving in the morning commute—sometimes it is easier to stay with them than to experiment; it may be enough to have a schema that works out pretty well on average.

People may especially need to change their schemas in times of organizational change, but may be reluctant to do so. Resistance to organizational change usually does not come from a failure to come up with the right blueprint for future practices. It more often comes from people's reluctance to give up their comfortable old approaches. A familiar refrain in organizations is "But we've *always* done it that way." People may not simply be saying that the old way was wonderful. They may be saying that they had come up with ways of coping with the old system—some schemas for getting around the bugs, the red tape, and the obstacles—so that they could function in the old system without having to reinvent everything every day and get a headache from the stress. A new system requires building new schemas; it takes a lot of energy and thoughtfulness to update old schemas.

Schemas Become Universal Rules Schemas encourage us to react to types of situations or types of people in certain ways. Because it is difficult to collect additional, thorough data as each situation or person comes along, the universal rules embodied in our schemas save time. They are helpful to overworked people. However, much of organizational life is not universal ("always do X to make a business travel reservation"), but instead is contingent ("do X to make domestic travel arrangements and Y to make international travel arrangements"). What you do depends on some more specific, distinguishing information about the situation.

Consider a busy manager who was stressed about writing performance evaluations for his employees and documenting aspects of their performance. He came up with a simplifying schema to determine who his strongest employees were, a rule of thumb that he thought had been fairly accurate: "The people who are here the latest at night are the best workers." He began to worry, however, that his performance evaluations were demoralizing some excellent workers and praising some less productive workers. His schema was leading him astray. Employees who worked very efficiently and creatively but had families were rarely in the office until late at night. People who chatted and took long lunches during the day or people who had trouble grasping the more complex projects were often still there until late at night. When he saw someone either leave early or stay late, he needed to understand the contingencies that affected their work hours and not to make universal judgments.

Schemas Are Incomplete We develop schemas in line with our ongoing experiences, but we may miss some important features. Consider the new engineer who observed that the other engineers always spoke loudly and slowly when phoning down to the production floor. It became his schema too—always speak loudly and slowly to production. He inferred that the reason was because the people in production were not too bright. This assumption got him into trouble when he bumped into production people in the hallways and spoke to them loudly and slowly. The information that he was missing was that the engineers spoke loudly and slowly on the phone because the machinery running in the background was noisy.

As is often the case with schemas, his schema included some implicit causal reasoning about why something was done. Lacking complete information, his schema had faulty causal reasoning and encoded a stereotypical bias that was misguided and left him embarrassed. Schemas can be helpful to us, but it is useful also to be aware of our assumptions and to seek additional richer information about organizational life. Understanding multiple perspectives on organizations helps us become better organizational members, decision makers, and change agents.

Building More Complete Models

Despite their shortcomings, our personal schemas are pretty good as informal starting points for understanding and coping with how the world works. However, sometimes we would like to look at more formal models and data about how the world works, in order to check our own understandings. Social scientists look for patterns and insights about the social world, drawing on previous research, adding their own hypotheses, and collecting data that challenge, test, or expand their ideas in a systematic way. This wealth of social scientific data can expand our informal schemas.

For example, a marketing manager's schema may be to check and see what her major competitor is doing in the market as a convenient way of assessing her options. However, a more formal model built by a researcher with a large database could be used to assess where innovation in the market comes from. Perhaps the data show that it comes from small innovators on the margin, not from central competitors. The findings from a more formal model might help this manager to update her schema. She may read about networks to understand her company's environment better and how ideas travel among researchers of this environment.

Of course, social scientists have their own favorite personal schemas for how to study the social world and how to construct a research project. Therefore, the insights and findings that we gain from social scientific research can be clustered into different types. The approaches in economics, psychology, anthropology, sociology, and political science are each distinctive.

This module focuses on three classic perspectives—strategic design, political, cultural—that weave together colorful strands from different social science disciplines. Each perspective embodies certain assumptions about human nature, about the meaning of organizing, about the relative power of different actors, and about how to collect and analyze data. Each perspective developed from its own array of studies and models, like the preceding simple example of a study of market innovation. This research history makes the perspective a distinctive whole.

Three Classic Lenses on Organizations

Three Class Notes follow that describe the three classic perspectives. Think of each perspective as a different lens through which you can view the organization. These approaches reflect years of studies, interviews, observations, and participation in organizations. The Class Notes highlight the important features of each lens, the history of the development of that lens, and the kinds of questions about organizational processes that each lens might guide you to ask in order to get a richer picture of an organization or to conduct an organizational analysis. The three lenses are:

- The Strategic Design Lens
- The Political Lens
- The Cultural Lens

The Strategic Design Lens

People who take this perspective look at how the flow of tasks and information is designed, how people are sorted into roles, how these roles are related, and how the organization can be rationally optimized to achieve its goals. What if you considered the problem mentioned in the opening paragraph of this introduction, about delays in manufacturing, from this perspective? Just one possibility is that you might decide that looking at the design-manufacturing interface is a good place to start to chart the flow of information and detect any disconnections between roles.

The Political Lens

People who take this perspective look at how power and influence are distributed and wielded, how multiple stakeholders express their different preferences and get involved in (or excluded from) decisions, and how conflicts can be resolved. What if you considered delays in manufacturing from this perspective? Just one possibility is that you might decide that suppliers are critical stakeholders who must be considered, and you might explore whether they are influencing the delays to display their control over a crucial resource and gain influence in pricing.

The Cultural Lens

People who take this perspective look at how history has shaped the assumptions and meanings of different people, how certain practices take on special meaningfulness and even become rituals, and how stories and other artifacts shape the feel of an organization. What if you considered delays in manufacturing from this perspective? Just one possibility is that you might decide that overtime pay has a symbolic meaning to workers, that norms about who gets how much overtime have developed over the years, and that what look like delays might be attempts to spread out the overtime in ways that are valued as being more fair.

What Lens Do You Favor?

As you read about these lenses, try to surface your own implicit views of organizations. You might see whether you instinctively align with one of these three lenses. Compare and contrast what they say about organizational processes with what you have come to believe about organizational processes based on your own experiences.

The Three Lenses in Action

Think about how you might use the three lenses differently to understand some of the changes that are taking place—or being thwarted—in organizations today.

Analyzing Organizations

An organizational analysis often begins with an intuitive sense of where to look to understand an organization and describe its character to others. An organizational analysis is guided by an idea of how organizations work. Each of us has schemas that affect what we pay attention to and what we ignore. The three lenses provide a number of possible ways to expand your views of organizations and enrich your organizational analysis.

Balancing Multiple Perspectives

You will have a chance to use all three lenses as you conduct the organizational analysis that is described in the last Class Note in this module, which begins on page 83. At the same time, it is important to understand that sometimes these lenses suggest contradictory, not complementary, approaches or actions.

Throughout the term, you will have opportunities to work with other people who look at organizations differently or prefer a different perspective than you do, based on their different organizational experiences and standpoints.

We emphasize that problems don't have a single clear, correct, optimal solution. It does not mean that any analysis is a good analysis. Some analyses are better than others—more thoughtful, more complete, more attentive to contingencies and trade-offs, or more able to balance and integrate multiple perspectives. A failure to consider multiple perspectives represents an incomplete analysis.

References

Fiske, Susan T., and Shelley E. Taylor. 1984. *Social Cognition*. New York: Random House.

Lord, Robert G., and Roseanne J. Foti. 1986. "Schema Theories, Information Processing, and Organizational Behavior." In H. P. Sims, Jr., and D. A. Gioia (eds.), *The Thinking Organization* (pp. 20–48). San Francisco: Jossey-Bass.

The Strategic Design Lens

Overview

This section of the module introduces you to the strategic design perspective on organizations. It is the first of the three "lenses," ways of looking at and understanding organizations, which you will learn about in this module. Each provides invaluable insights for those who are are trying to take more effective action in organizations, but the strategic design perspective is probably the one that managers find most congenial. It sees an organization as a system deliberately constructed to achieve strategic goals. Its fundamental assumption is that the appropriate design, given an organization's strategy and environment, can maximize organizational efficiency and effectiveness. This module introduces you to the way this perspective "sees" an organization through a strategic design and provides an overview of the basic elements of organization design.

Organization design is a fundamental task of organizational life. It operates at all levels, from the design of the organization as a whole to the design of teams and work groups, right down to the design of individual tasks and jobs. You yourself are—or should be—engaged in designing an organization when you decide how to operate in teams in your classes. Understanding and working with the basic design principles introduced in this module can not only help you understand how complex organizations work, it can also have immediate application in your current activities.

This part of the module looks closely at the strategic design perspective. This Class Note provides you with the fundamentals of how the world looks through this particular "lens" and introduces the basic principles of organization design. It is followed by a case study of Dynacorp, an organization that has always had a functional structure but is experiencing problems and is considering adopting a new design. It sets out the choices that the organization confronts, and invites you to weigh the strengths and weaknesses of each in order to decide what choice you would make if you were managing in this company.

The purposes of this section of the module are the following:

- To introduce the basic concepts and approaches of the strategic design perspective on organizations.
- To provide an overview of the fundamental principles of organization design at all levels of the organization.
- To exercise your understanding of those concepts and principles by asking you to apply them to a company that confronts the challenge of whether it needs to change fundamentally its basic structure.

Assignment Summary

Come to class prepared to discuss the following questions related to your analysis of the Dynacorp case:

1. If you were on the Dynacorp task force, what would be your first choice for an alternative design? What would be your second choice?
2. Which of the problems of the current design would your chosen design address? What problems (if any) would it not address? Are there any new problems to which it might lead?
3. What linking and alignment mechanisms would you propose to make the "grouping" of your first choice design more effective?

It is also possible that your instructor may ask you to prepare written responses to one or more of these questions or ask you to prepare an organizational analysis of an organization you are familiar with.

Additional Suggested Readings

Galbraith, Jay. 2002. *Designing Organizations: An Executive Guide to Strategy, Structure, and Process*. San Francisco: Jossey-Bass. *The most recent work of one of the leading figures in the field of organization design.*

Goold, Michael and Andrew Campbell. 2002. *Designing Effective Organizations: How to Create Structured Networks*. San Francisco: Jossey-Bass. *A practical guide to designing large, complex organizations, providing a set of design tests to guide the design process. Most useful for experienced managers.*

This Class Note owes much to Nancy Staudemeyer and Michael Tushman. Michael Tushman graciously permitted us to draw heavily on his work with David Nadler, published in 1997 by Oxford University Press, entitled *Competing by Design: The Power of Organizational Architecture*.

Nadler, David A. and Michael L. Tushman. 1997. *Competing by Design: The Power of Organizational Architecture.* New York: Oxford University Press. *A comprehensive and detailed guide to organization design, with many rich examples.*

Miles, R. and C. Snow. 1994. *Fit, Failure, and the Hall of Fame.* New York: Free Press. *A much-cited book that links strategy and strategic organizational design.*

The Organization as Strategic Design

From Max Weber's discussion of "machine bureaucracy" at the turn of the century to the customer-oriented designs of the early twenty-first century, the dominant perspective on organizations has viewed them as *strategic designs*; that is, as systems deliberately constructed to achieve certain strategic goals. This perspective asserts that by understanding basic principles of organization design, by aligning the organization's design with its strategy, and by making sure that both strategy and design fit the environment in which the organization is operating, managers can make their organizations successful. The strategic design perspective emphasizes the efficiency and effectiveness of the organization. *Efficiency* involves accomplishing strategic goals with the least possible expenditure of resources; *effectiveness* involves ensuring that goals are accomplished to the standard necessary for the organization to succeed.

As the term *strategic design* implies, this perspective on organization is built on the assumption that the organization has a strategy for creating that provides the test for generating and assessing the organization's design. This *value* proposition, or *distinctive competitive advantage*, establishes what activities the organization must carry out to achieve success in its strategies, for example, providing speedy and reliable servicing of products to customers, getting products from R&D to the market quickly, or continuously driving down production costs through continuous improvement. But the activities at which the organization excels can (and should) influence the strategy. For example, an organization with an extensive marketing organization might be better off using that organization to get fast and detailed information on customer needs in order to adopt a strategy of providing premium-priced products and after-sales service, rather than adopting a low-cost strategy that involves cutting back on its full-time marketing personnel.

People working with this perspective often use metaphors of the organization as a mechanism or system, of "engineering" or "reengineering" the organization, of organization-building and "organizational architecture," of the organization as a complex organism that can be "diagnosed" like a medical patient. Like engineering, architecture, or medicine, management is seen as a matter of understanding and applying basic principles and processes, and adapting them to the context in which one is operating.

Key Elements of Organization Design

One way to think about the strategic design perspective is that it involves simultaneously drawing boundaries around clusters of tasks or activities (to define jobs, departments, processes) in the form of *strategic grouping* (differentiation), and then creating links across those boundaries through *strategic linking* (integration). In addition, it involves *aligning* other elements of the organization (such as rewards and incentives) so that each part of the organization has the resources and the incentives to do the tasks it is assigned by the grouping and linking. The basic assumption of the strategic design perspective is that an organization is most effective when its strategy fits the conditions of its environment and when the organizational components are aligned with the strategy and with each other.

The basic element of organization design is often seen as the *task*: the smallest unit of the activities that need to be performed if the organization is to realize its strategic goals. Tasks vary in *complexity,* from the relatively simple, like inserting circuit boards into the CPU of a personal computer on an assembly line, to more complex, such as reprogramming an industrial robot on an assembly line, to the extremely complex, like setting up a new business division to develop, produce, and sell industrial robots. Tasks also vary in the level of *routinization,* that is, the extent to which the activity can be specified and programmed. Usually simple tasks are more routine, but even complex tasks can also be routinized. For example, the analysis of how software is designed and the breaking of what had been seen as a complex "art" or task into discrete programming steps led to the creation of "software factories" with high levels of efficiency in producing certain kinds of software programs.

In addition, tasks vary in the nature of their interdependence. Some tasks are highly independent of other tasks, and can be performed quite separately from others, with little linking across them. Most tasks that are incorporated into an organization, however, involve some level of interdependency. *Task interdependence* at its simplest varies from low to high, but it can also be seen in terms of the *kind* of interdependence. James Thompson (1967) developed a highly influential typology of task interdependence, identifying three different types: *sequential interdependence,* when one task is completed and then handed off for the next stage; *pooled interdependence,* when interdependent tasks are undertaken at the same time, and the final results are put together or pooled; and *reciprocal interdependence,* when tasks are conducted in repeated interaction with each other (see Figure 2.1). To turn once again to software engineering for illustrations, *sequential interdependence* can be seen when the development of a software program is divided into distinct stages or phases, with "milestones" to mark the completion of one stage and the hand-off to the next. Pooled interdependence occurs when different groups work on modules of a program that are then put together to form the final program. Reciprocal interdependence characterizes complex programs in which the different tasks involved in developing the program are carried on in dense interaction with each other, because the solutions to problems in one element of the program affect the solutions that can be implemented in others. Pooled interdependence is the easiest to manage: once the task assignments are defined, each unit can proceed without detailed information exchange with other units. Sequential interdependence is harder to manage than pooled, because information flows are quite dense at the point of transfer. Both pooled and sequential are easier to manage than reciprocal interdependence, which involves sustained and interactive linkages across the boundaries of the units.

As these examples show, many complex tasks can be taken apart into simpler activities. Nearly a century ago Frederick Taylor developed what came to be called "Scientific Management," using time and motion studies to analyze the most efficient set of movements needed to perform industrial tasks, such as shoveling coal in a steel mill. Then he reaggregated the movements into a standard operating procedure that defined the job. Nearly 100 years later, this same approach of the disaggregation and careful analysis of tasks underpins total quality management and business process reengineering. TQM analyzes each step in a process to identify and correct the sources of problems. BPR analyzes the steps in delivering a product or service to the customer to eliminate unnecessary activities and then recombines tasks into more effective and efficient jobs and subunits.

Organizational design choices begin with *strategic grouping,* which involves the differentiation of clusters of activities, positions, and individuals into work units. Once activities are divided into "boxes," however, the units must be linked according to the nature and level of interdependence in their tasks to ensure that information and other needed resources flow effectively and efficiently between the activities or groups separated by group boundaries (*linking*). In other words, creating boundaries in organizations also creates the need for linking across boundaries. Finally, the design must use a variety of *alignment* mechanisms (incentive systems, information systems, etc.) to ensure that people have the resources and the incentives to carry out the tasks assigned.

Strategic grouping, linking, and alignment are relevant at every level of the organization, from the design of teams or departments to the overall design of the organization.

Figure 2.1 Forms of Interdependence

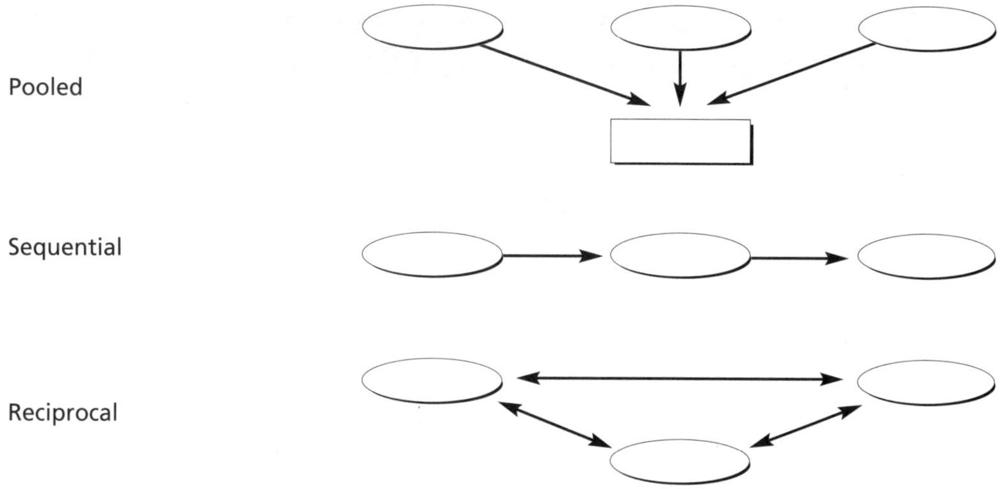

Pooled

Sequential

Reciprocal

Strategic Grouping

Grouping decisions dictate the basic framework within which all other organizational design decisions are made. Grouping gathers together some tasks, functions, or disciplines, and separates them from others. It is (or ought to be) a direct outgrowth of the strategy of the organization as a whole and the associated strategy of the particular organizational unit. A fundamental assumption of organization design is that coordination and communication are easier and denser within a unit than across units. This assumption means that sharing information and building and adding to a common knowledge base are easier within than across units. Therefore the most important areas of interdependence should be under a unified reporting structure. The strategy should guide the design by identifying the most strategically important parameters of coordination, interdependence, and knowledge sharing.

Strategic grouping focuses on questions of how to cluster tasks and activities. Should people performing the same kinds of tasks in similar ways be clustered together, or should people performing complementary tasks be grouped together? How many subgroups should be created, and in how many layers? Grouping can be seen as "drawing the boxes" of the organization design. The three basic forms or "ideal types" of grouping each comes with a distinct set of strengths and weaknesses.

Basic Structures

Grouping by Expertise/Function Grouping by function (or more broadly, by expertise) brings together individuals who share similar functions, disciplines, skills, and work processes. At the level of the organization, grouping by activity gives rise to *functional organizations*, the oldest form of business enterprise and one that is still often the form first adopted in new organizations. In the functional organization, all the activities concerned with a particular function are grouped into separate divisions, as shown in Figure 2.2.

Grouping by function has three major strengths. First, it allows the development of deep functional expertise and a high degree of specialization of knowledge within each function. These organizations can be extremely innovative in specific technologies or functions. The second strength is what economists call "economies of scope"; that is, the functional organization makes it relatively easy to transfer resources across activities within functions. If sales of one product decline, for example, the manufacturing division can switch a production line or a factory to a product that is in greater demand; engineers can be switched across projects; marketing divisions can reallocate their sales and support efforts. Finally, a functional organization allows each group to create separate incentive and control systems suited to its needs and to reinforcing its strengths.

However, these advantages come at the cost of integration across functions. This model often assumes a sequential interdependence across the functions, from upstream (R&D) to downstream (marketing). Functional organizations are often not very responsive to changes in markets or customers. Moreover, as their level of specialization increases, individuals tend to develop narrower perspectives, and have difficulty in solving problems that require joint efforts with other groups. It can be difficult in this kind of organization to

Figure 2.2 Functional Grouping Structure

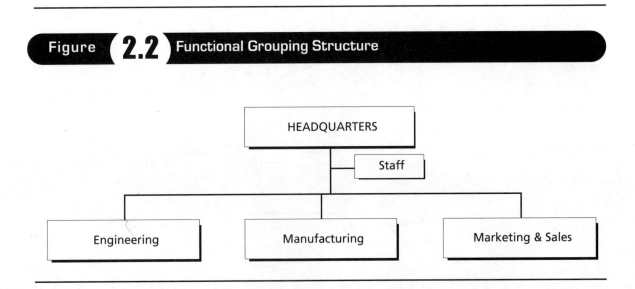

assess costs clearly, especially on a product line basis, and to assign accountability for the overall performance of the organization. Finally, because career ladders are primarily within functions and the number of functions is limited, the tendency is for the number of levels of management in each function to expand over time. Large functional organizations often have tall hierarchies that can inhibit speedy and effective information flows. Moreover, because few opportunities are available for managers to gain experience outside their functional areas as they move up the career ladder, the functional organization does not develop a large supply of general managers who can see the organization as a whole and make decisions that serve the organization's strategy instead of following a specifically functional logic.

A functional organization is frequently adopted by new organizations and maintained over time by organizations that have a single major business, or several businesses that share the same technologies and have similar markets.

Grouping by Output/Product This structure organizes on the basis of the service or product provided. The people within the group perform a variety of different tasks and activities, but they are all contributors to the same final output (a product or set of closely related products or services). For example, firms with a range of product lines and markets usually find the functional organization too inflexible and instead adopt a *product line* or *multidivisional* structure. In this design, pioneered in the United States by DuPont and General Motors (Chandler, 1962) and in Japan by Matsushita, the functions are distributed across the business or product line they support, as shown in Figure 2.3.

The product division structure has two major advantages. First is transparency of performance: it makes the costs and profits of each business much clearer than does the functional structure. Second is the clear strategic focus it provides for the managers of the product division. These strengths made the multidivisional structure the dominant form of business enterprise for most large American corporations in the 1980s.

On the other hand, it is not without disadvantages. Making each business unit accountable for its own profit and loss statement (P&L) can make it difficult for units to share resources and can lead to duplication of activities (each unit wants its own accounting staff, its own training staff, and so on).

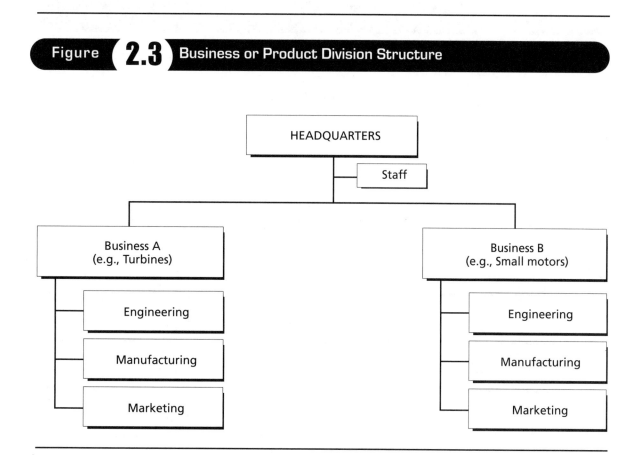

Figure 2.3 Business or Product Division Structure

It can also make new business creation difficult: in some cases business units focus exclusively on expanding their existing business, instead of finding new opportunities; in others, units compete to "own" new business. And because functional specialists are spread across different groups, they can lose their professional focus and become less attuned to breakthrough innovations in their own fields (and this point holds true across functions, from R&D to accounting). Distributing activities across business units can also lead to missed learning opportunities in core functions (e.g., factories in one business unit may be unaware of potentially useful innovations in another business unit's factories). Many companies spent the 1990s trying to break down their "functional silos" by setting up business divisions only to discover that they had created "business unit silos" that were just as internally competitive and resistant to developing potential cross-boundary synergies as the old functional organization had been.

Grouping by Market (Geography or Customer) Market-oriented companies often adopted this structure, which gathers together people who perform different activities and tasks and produce different outputs but who serve the same customers or market segments. The most common dimension is geography. Large multinational companies operating around the world, for example, historically favored a geographic organization, grouping by geographic region and country (see Figure 2.4).

Even domestic companies have often grouped by geography—by sales territories, for example. But grouping by the type of customers rather than their location is also a variant of this form. Publishers, for example, are often organized on the basis of what customer group the division serves: textbooks (often subdivided by educational level—primary, secondary, college), business and professional books, mass market, and so on.

The strength of this structure is its capacity for developing deep customer knowledge and close customer relationships, and therefore it is often found in service industries. It allows the organiza-

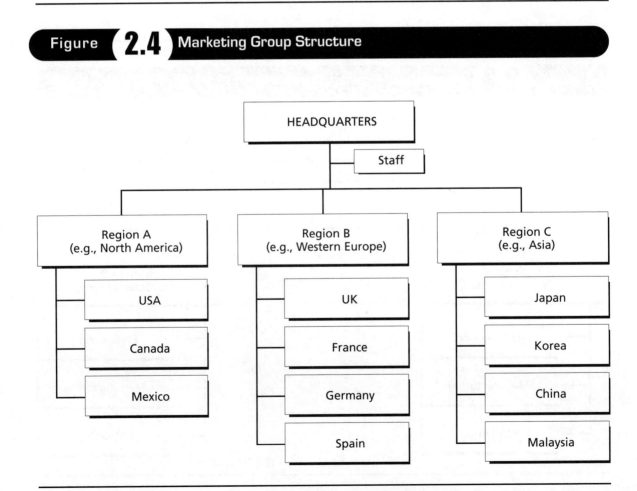

Figure 2.4 Marketing Group Structure

tion to tailor its products and services to differentiated customer needs. The weaknesses are similar to those of the product division structure: the duplication of activities and resources, the erosion of deep technical expertise, missed opportunities for synergies and learning.

No universally ideal choice emerges for a grouping pattern. Each strategic grouping option comes with its own set of strengths and weaknesses. Every organization design must address all three elements of activity/function, business/product, and geography/customer. The critical grouping question is which dimension will be primary, and how the others will be nested at the next levels: function within business within geography, for example, or function within geography within business.

Hybrid Structures

Some companies have found that grouping on any single dimension—function, business, geography— is inadequate. Corporate strategies frequently require attention to multiple priorities simultaneously (e.g., product and function or customers and technical expertise). Many organizations turn to hybrid or multidimensional grouping structures in an attempt to break out of the constraints imposed by a single mode of strategic grouping. Two of the most common hybrids today are matrix organizations and the somewhat awkwardly named "front/back" structure.

Matrix Organization A matrix structure is an organizational form that picks two strategic grouping dimensions and gives them equal weight in the organization structure, so that the manager of each operating unit reports to two "bosses," one for each dimension. In a business/functional matrix, for example, such as the one illustrated in Figure 2.5, the right side of the matrix contains the traditional functional departments (engineering, manufacturing, marketing), which are responsible for maintaining state-of-the-art expertise in each function. The left side is composed of product groups, with a product manager coordinating the functional activities involved in developing and producing the product and getting it to the market.

Figure 2.5 Functional/Product Matrix

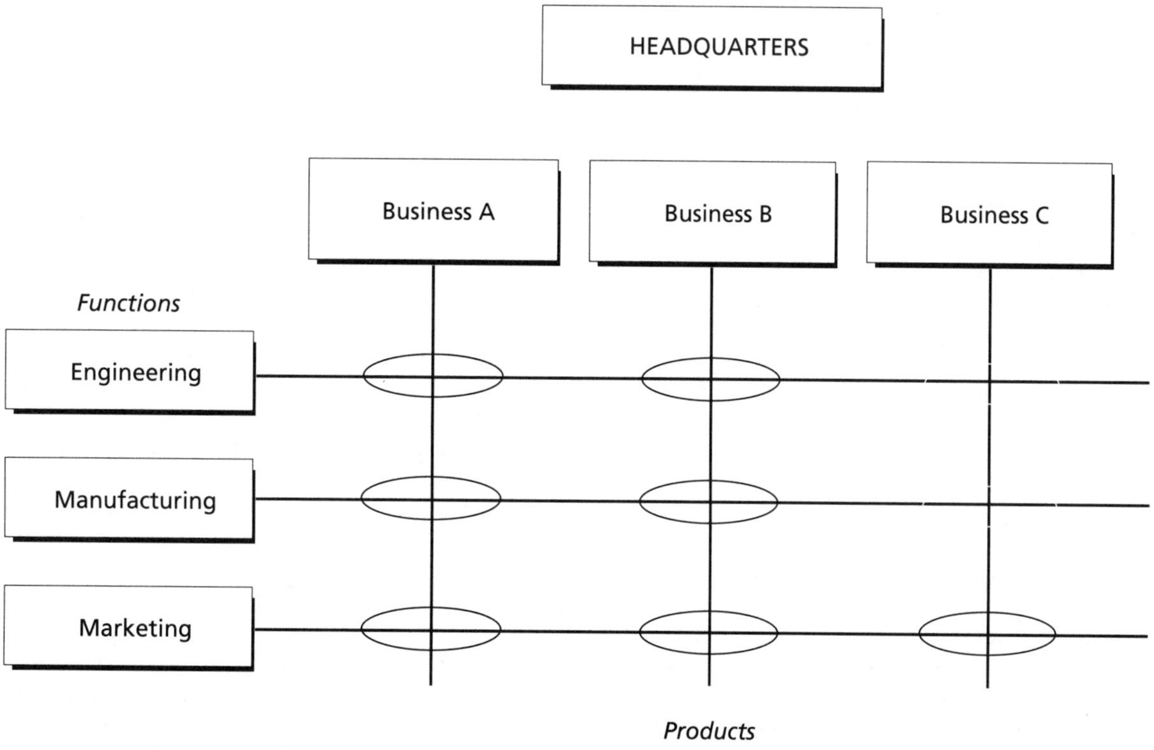

Thus, an engineering manager within an operating unit would report to two bosses: the head of engineering and the product line manager. Matrix structures vary in the number of people who report equally to two bosses. In some, the matrix penetrates deeply into the organization, so that every engineer, for example, would have both an engineering manager and a product manager; in others, only those in relatively high-level management positions have two bosses. The global electrical engineering firm ABB, for example, had a business/geography matrix, in which only the head of each local operating unit reported to two managers (a country manager and a business manager); employees of the local operating companies had only one boss, the local operating unit head.

Matrix organizations were popular in the 1980s because they seemed to provide a way of balancing two equally important grouping dimensions. However, from every perspective they are more complicated than single-dimension organizations: they require dual systems, roles, controls, and rewards that reflect both dimensions of the matrix. Along with this complexity can come confusion, higher costs, delays in reaching decisions, and a heightened potential for conflict. Often, organizations that adopted a matrix structure found that despite the formal effort at balancing the two, one dimension tended to be more powerful than the other, negating the potential advantages of the matrix structure. Even when the balance was fairly even, many people found it extremely difficult to have two "bosses." Finally, a growing number of companies found that they needed to make their organizations responsive to more than two dimensions (e.g., product, geography, and customer segment). As a result, many companies abandoned the matrix in favor of simpler structures that relied on linking mechanisms rather than grouping to make the organization responsive to multiple strategic dimensions.

Front/Back Structure This structure gets its somewhat awkward name because the organization is divided into two parts, both multifunctional but each with a different grouping dimension. The front end faces the customer and is organized by market (either geography or customer segment). It includes the functions that directly relate with the customer: marketing, sales, distribution, service and support. The back end is organized by product and takes the form of business units that include technology development (product development and process engineering), production, and logistics (including the management of outsourcing relationships). Basically, the back end is responsible for developing and producing products; the front end is responsible for selling them to the customer and providing service and after-sales support (see Figure 2.6). The front/back form became popular in the late 1990s in information and telecommunications companies that found themselves producing an array of products with different technologies that were combined into "systems" or "solutions" and sold to customers who wanted a "single point of contact" with a company divided into multiple business units (Galbraith, 2000, pp. 238–269).

The structure has become popular well beyond the industry in which it originated because it seems to combine some of the key advantages of the product division, the market structure, and the functional structure. It has the potential for facilitating, in the back end, the close integration of technology development and production that was one of the strengths of the product division structure, and for building in the front end the close customer relationships and deep knowledge of the market characteristic of market-based or functional structures. It does this without the complexity of the matrix structure. However, the front/back structure can also exhibit some of the key weaknesses of these other structures: fragmentation of technical expertise in the back end, and the poor integration between market needs and technology development that we sometimes see in functional or market-based structures. In addition, ensuring adequate integration and synergy between the front and back ends can be a challenge. For example, if both the front end and the back end units are treated as profit centers, then the internal transfer pricing between the two can become extremely difficult and contentious.

Obviously no single structure is ideal in all respects, and the choice of structure depends heavily on the organization's strategy. Even though matching the strategic grouping to the organization's strategy is crucially important, however, it alone does not constitute an organizational design. Matching strategic linking to the grouping and to the strategy is equally, if not more, important.

Strategic Linking

Linking involves designing formal and informal structures and processes to connect and coordinate organizational units and subunits whose tasks are interdependent but that have been separated by strategic grouping decisions. The level of interdependence across groups depends in part on the tasks they perform. We saw earlier that task interdependence can take three forms: pooled, sequential, and reciprocal. These tend to involve different needs for linking and integration. Each type of interdependence benefits from different types and intensity of linking mechanisms: to be effective, reciprocal interdependence demands more intense coordination than does sequential interdependence, which in turn demands greater coordination than pooled interdependence (Nadler and Tushman, 1997, p. 94).

Figure 2.6 Front/Back Structure

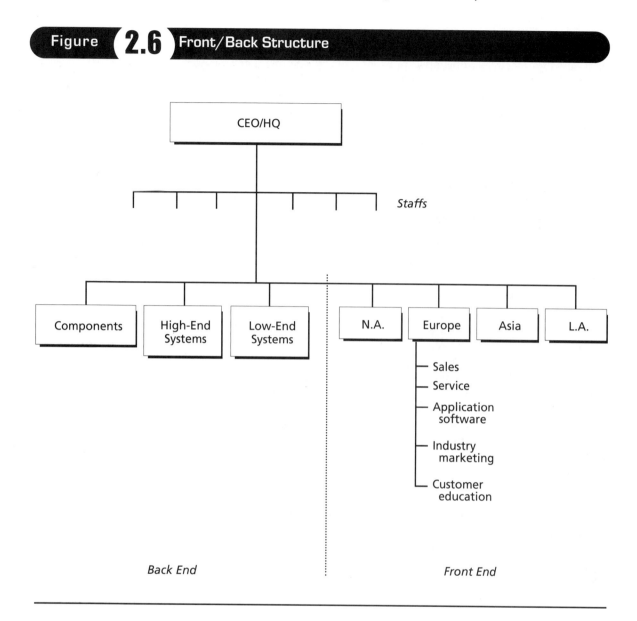

Routinized task interdependence is not the only determinant of linking that is important for organizations, however. Professional scientists and engineers working in technical organizations need to maintain contact with their peers inside and outside the company in order to keep abreast of changes in a particular discipline. Different parts of the organization may draw on common resources (e.g., training facilities or corporate services). Temporary and abnormally high degrees of interdependence can also arise during emergencies, crises, or one-time efforts aimed at solving certain problems. In the aftermath of the collapse of the World Trade Center on September 11, 2001, for example, some companies with operations there, such as Cantor Fitzgerald, were extremely successful in mobilizing their remaining employees to deal with customers, support the bereaved families of employees, and get their operations back on line.

A growing challenge for organizations is the need to develop and maintain linking mechanisms that extend beyond the traditional external boundaries of the company, reflecting growing interdependence with customers, suppliers, and partners. The same basic linking patterns, however, are applicable to external as well as internal linking.

Organizations can draw on a range of linking mechanisms, which are listed and described next. As the need for coordination increases, organizations tend to resort to more and more of these mechanisms to connect the different parts of their structures.

Formal Reporting Structures: Hierarchy and "Dotted Line" Relationships The strategic grouping structure, with its formal assignment of responsibility for coordinating activities to specific positions in the hierarchy, obviously provides the fundamental pattern of linking. In this regard, the organization chart is not simply a "map" of strategic grouping; it is also a map showing who must keep whom informed and who has responsibility for linking which activities. For example, in a divisional grouping structure, functional managers report to their respective divisional general managers who, in turn, report to their respective divisional general managers who, in turn, report to the company president. Managers in different divisions at the same level coordinate their group's activities via their common boss, who channels information, controls the type and quantity of information that moves among groups, and adjudicates conflicts.

Often formal direct reporting structures include what is commonly called a *dotted line* hierarchical relationship, indicating that the lower-ranking person is formally responsible for supplying all relevant information to the higher-ranked person, but that the latter has no formal authority over the former beyond the information flow.

The formal hierarchy and reporting structures are the simplest and most pervasive of the formal linking mechanisms, but they are also quite limited. In particular, individual managers can quickly become overloaded as the number and complexity of coordination issues requiring their attention rises. As a result, key decisions may be delayed. The risk of message distortion also arises when orders and information pass up and down in a hierarchy. People at the top may be shielded from critical or negative information, while people at the bottom are sometimes excluded from information that could help them in their work. Formal reporting structures are therefore often inadequate when conditions change rapidly.

Liaison Roles When the coordination requirements involving two or more groups expand, the organization frequently assigns responsibility for coordinating across the groups to specific individuals, who serve as conduits for information and expertise, and as contacts and advisors on the work involving their groups. Their roles are primarily information-focused; they rarely have the authority to impose decisions on others, especially those in other groups. One example might be the engineering liaison in a manufacturing plant, who is a member of the engineering organization but who is physically located in the plant to link the two units. The liaison role is often not a full-time responsibility, but is combined with other activities.

Integrator Roles Some situations may require a more general management perspective and swifter resolution of problems or issues involving several units than is offered by liaison roles, and in such cases organizations will sometimes assign to an individual the responsibility for acting as an integrator. The integrator has some "carrots and sticks" with which to reinforce the role, such as the integrator's having a role in the performance evaluation of other actors involved or a budget line to provide resources, etc. Product, brand, geographic, program, and account managers are all examples of formal integrator roles. In each case, the task of the integrator is not to do the work but to coordinate the activities and the decision processes. In effect, the integrator serves as a "little general manager" with responsibility for a particular decision process. Research from the auto industry found that, in some of the most successful Japanese automakers, the "heavyweight project manager" is a key element of the remarkable speed of their new model development process. The heavyweight project manager plays an integrator role, coordinating the activities of a product development team on the one hand, and working with senior management to create an overarching product concept on the other.

Permanent Cross-Unit Groups These groups bring together representatives of different task or work groups, with a formal mandate to pool their expertise and coordinate the efforts of their respective groups with respect to particular products, clients, markets, or problems. Examples include technology planning boards, with representatives from engineering, manufacturing, various business units that share a base in certain core technologies, and even outside technical experts; strategic partnership teams, which have the responsibility for coordinating relationships with a particular strategic partner who has an array of relationships with the organization; and standing committees on various cross-unit issues such as environmental policy or diversity. Lucent Technologies, for example, relies on standing, cross-functional, cross-business committees called Process Improvement Teams (PMTs) to improve the quality of its software development processes on an ongoing basis. Membership on these groups is often combined with other activities, and is often not a full-time assignment.

Temporary Cross-Unit Groups These often resemble permanent cross-unit groups in their composition and bring together representatives from various groupings in the organizations, but they are problem-focused and exist only until the particular problem is solved or the assigned task is accomplished. Cross-functional project teams are a common example in today's organizations: they bring together a team of people from different functions to accomplish a task (such as developing a new product and getting it to market). The task force is another increasingly common example of this form of cross-unit group: it represents a temporary patchwork on the formal structure, used to intensify communications links in times of high uncertainty or great pressure. For example, we see companies pull together task forces to analyze problems in customer satisfaction and to make recommendations for improvement, or even to analyze the organization's grouping and linking mechanisms and to make recommendations for changes in organizational design. Membership on these groups is more often a full-time assignment than is the case for the permanent cross-unit groups; members return to their original groups after the completion of the assigned task. However, many task forces are composed of people whose primary tasks lie elsewhere, just like the more permanent cross-unit groups.

Some companies (such as consulting firms) rely so heavily on project teams to organize work that it often seems that the project *is* the grouping dimension. However, such organizations usually do have an identifiable formal grouping criterion, which is often less salient to their members than the projects in which they spend their time. Some consulting firms use geography as their basic grouping criterion, and everyone formally belongs to an office in a particular location. Others use expertise-based grouping: everyone reports to the head of a particular practice (such as strategic consulting, logistics, IT). The heads of project teams play *integrator roles* in the project-based organization, and the linking mechanisms actually assume primacy over the grouping structures that are so important in other kinds of organizations.

Information Technology Systems Computer and advanced telecommunications technologies have rapidly increased the linking and coordinating alternatives open to organizations, and they are profoundly influencing the way companies organize and manage work. Computer networks, electronic mail, digital scanning and printing, desktop video conferencing, and collaborative software allow organizations to push back the constraints imposed by time and distance, disseminate information more broadly and quickly, and facilitate collaboration and teamwork. Salespeople in the field can communicate instantly with their office, feeding in the latest information on their customers and their activities and drawing on shared databases on products and sales options. E-mail bulletin boards foster the cultivation of informal networks across departments. Technology-focused organizations such as HP, Apple, and Microsoft and consulting firms such as McKinsey maintain online databases that codify knowledge and identify technical and customer "experts" within the firm. Decision-making and decision support systems also increasingly extend outside the company, creating links with customers and suppliers. Wal-Mart relies on an extensive information technology system for automatic order fulfillment by its suppliers. Increasingly, information and communications technology systems provide not only enhanced support for the linking and coordinating mechanisms chosen in an organization; they can be seen as linking mechanisms in their own right.

Planning Processes At the peak of the era of strategic planning groups in the 1970s and early 1980s, hundreds of people were employed in corporate strategic planning offices, whose mandate was to generate a plan for each major grouping in the company. The focus was on the plan as roadmap for the organization. In the years since then, strategic planning offices have fallen out of favor, but strategic planning remains important. Its importance for most organizations, however, lies less in the output—the plan—than in the planning process itself, as a linking mechanism for bringing people from different groups to work together to identify major challenges and develop jointly a set of goals for a certain time horizon.

Linking mechanisms connect people and units separated by strategic grouping and coordinate their activities as needed to achieve the organization's strategic goals. The flow of information is a critically important element of their role, and the challenge for managers is "to design the appropriate pattern of linkages that will create the clearest channels of information with the minimum commitment of people, time, money, and other organizational resources" (Nadler and Tushman, 1997). In other words, the challenge is to construct linking mechanisms that are both effective and efficient. The easiest linking mechanisms to design and maintain are those whose coordination benefits are readily recognized by the units involved. Most grouping structures also entail what Goold and Campbell (2002, pp. 61–71) call "difficult linkages," which are strategically important for achieving the organization's strategic goals but whose coordination benefits are not easily recognized by the units involved. Designing the linkages is in such cases only the first step; making them work involves *alignment*, the third element of organization design.

Alignment

The third strategic design process is *alignment,* which means ensuring that the units and individuals assigned certain tasks and activities by the grouping and linking patterns have the resources and the motivation to carry them out effectively. One of the reasons for the failure of so many organizational redesign efforts, according to this perspective, is *a lack of organizational congruence,* or misaligned supporting systems and processes. This problem with congruence includes organizational patterns that pull groups and individuals into behaviors that undermine the strategic intent or that pull different groups in opposing directions. Consider, for example, a company in which the manufacturing division is rewarded on the basis of gross margins while the sales division is rewarded for volume. No amount of linking mechanisms can prevent the two groups from working at cross purposes: sales will do everything possible to reduce the unit price in order to sell as much as possible, which hurts the manufacturing margin. Manufacturing may then respond by cutting corners in order to cut costs, thereby diminishing the product's quality or features and reducing its appeal to customers. What the organization design requires in this case is the alignment of performance measurement systems and incentives for the divisions.

Although evaluation and incentives are the two aspects of alignment that most managers recognize most readily, there are others that are equally, if not more, important. The main alignment systems include organizational performance measurement systems, individual rewards and incentives, resource allocation, human resource development, and informal systems and processes, which are discussed next.

Organizational Performance Measurement Systems How will the organization's leaders know whether the strategic intent underlying the grouping and linking patterns is being realized? The system for measuring organizational performance should provide crucially important information that signals to an organization whether its design is effective. That system should also be aligned with the strategic intent. Some organizations redesign their organizations to improve responsiveness to customers, for example, but then continue to rely on older performance measures such as return on assets, sales growth, and market share, without adding measures of customer satisfaction. The growing popularity of the "balanced scorecard" as a system for measuring overall organizational performance reflects the need for organizations to align their measurement systems with their strategic intent.

Organizations also need to align the measurement systems used for different strategic groupings, so that they do not pull groups in incompatible directions that undercut linking mechanisms, as in the preceding example of manufacturing and sales.

Individual Rewards and Incentives Most of us have experienced how powerful individual rewards and incentives can be as a tool for changing behavior. In most organizational change efforts, aligning individual rewards and incentives with the strategic grouping and linking patterns is regarded as one of the most important factors in the success or failure of the organization design. Bonuses, raises, and promotions have traditionally been the primary reward mechanisms in organizations. In flatter organizations, assignment to interesting projects, training opportunities, and greater choice in assignments often replace the more traditional incentives of promotions and large raises.

In their recent book on organization design, David Nadler and Michael Tushman set out the following general principles for reward and incentive systems:

- Incentives should clearly link performance to pay and should directly link performance to specific standards and objectives. If a team's objective is customer satisfaction, that should be the measure of performance, rather than volume or duration of service calls, which may bear little relation to whether the customer's needs were actually met.
- Rewards should relate directly to the nature of performance required at each level of the organization. At Corning, for example, in order to develop a true team perspective among top executives, the bonus plan for each member of the senior team is based largely on the entire company's success in meeting certain specific financial goals, such as stock price. In other situations, such as fund managers in an investment firm, it's more appropriate to base rewards on each person's individual performance.
- Rewards should be directly linked to objectives that are within the group's or individual's power to control.
- Incentive plans should match measurement periods for rewards to relevant performance periods; some goals can be assessed after three months, while it might not be practical to evaluate others in less than a year. Some incentive programs recognize that fact by containing both short- and long-term goals.
- Reward systems should be guided by the principle of equity, not equality. (Nadler and Tushman, 1997, p. 107)

In the literature on individual rewards and incentives, we can observe two somewhat different sets of assumptions about the alignment of individual rewards. One view, sometimes called Theory X, views individuals as oriented to material rewards and prone to "free ride" on the efforts of others, such that the behaviors that the organization wants must be carefully measured and rewarded, while unproductive behavior brings down negative sanctions. The other, called Theory Y, rests on the belief that most individuals basically want to do a good job, and that the main challenge in designing reward systems is to avoid misalignment that rewards behavior that does not meet the requirements of the organization's strategic intent and the demands of its grouping and linking systems (which economists call "perverse incentives" or "hoping for A while paying for B"). A common example of such misalignment is reorganizing work into teams, but continuing to base evaluations and rewards solely on individual accomplishments.

Resource Allocation Do the units created by the strategic grouping process have the resources they need to achieve their goals? Are the linking mechanisms accompanied by the allocation of adequate resources to be effective? Resources in this context include people, money, things (equipment, office space, etc.), and—most importantly—information and expertise. Assessing the adequacy of resource to carry out the assigned tasks can be the most demanding and difficult task in implementing an organizational design.

Human Resource Development By strict logic, human resource development could be considered a subset of resource allocation: one of the primary activities of human resource management is the assignment of people to positions, jobs, and tasks. However, its importance is so great, and the distinction between *allocating* resources and *developing* or *creating* them so valuable, that it deserves separate consideration. Many organizational redesigns fail because they do not recognize the need to align human resources and skills and expertise with the new design. Often people need training in new ways of doing things—in team processes, for example. A change in design often needs a change in the way careers are designed. For example, moving from a functional to a business unit organization often works best if the organization fosters cross-functional mobility as part of the career structure of high-potential managers. Training, personnel transfers, and career planning are among the key alignment mechanisms.

Informal Systems and Processes The most elusive and challenging element of alignment involves the informal processes in the organization. No formal blueprint for organizational design can ever capture fully the processes and interactions that make the organization work. These systems emerge over time as people adapt to the organization and to the demands of their jobs and their environments. Often an organizational redesign is less effective initially than its designers expect, or it initially seems to work but then runs into unexpected snags and glitches. The reason may be that the redesign wrenched apart the formal and the informal organization; indeed, it often has been deliberately designed to break established patterns and habits. From the strategic design perspective, the informal systems constitute a somewhat difficult design element that can be structured through various alignment mechanisms, such as the creation of various arenas in which people can form new networks, discuss problems, and form new patterns. Sometimes this possibility can be designed into training programs or incorporated into linking mechanisms. Sometimes the worst problems of misalignment of the previous structure and the new design can be anticipated, and steps taken to counteract them: for example, by rotating personnel into different positions, or providing extra linking mechanisms early in the adjustment process. But overall, although this perspective recognizes that the realignment of formal and informal processes takes time, it assumes that such realignment is fundamentally a design challenge that can be solved.

The Strategic Organizational Design Process

Design changes, once fairly rare events in an organization, are becoming a normal, ongoing process in many enterprises. In fact, the ability to adapt organizational structure to respond quickly and effectively to new conditions in the business environment and changing strategies, not merely to react but to anticipate change and design and implement new architectures may be among the most valuable organizational capabilities in today's competitive environment.

To some extent, managers are making design decisions all the time. Every time a specific job is designed, a procedure created, a process altered, or a task moved, the organization design is being changed. Yet we know that the very process of redesign, and especially the major redesigns of the organization that seem to be increasingly common in many companies, involve inherent and significant costs.

Disruption of the Normal Flow of Business Redesign efforts obviously occupy the time and attention of managers and tie up organizational resources. People throughout the organization tend to focus on the implications of the redesign for themselves and their part of the organization, sometimes at the cost of their immediate tasks.

Risk to Long-Term Relationships with Key Customers and Suppliers Established communications patterns are often severed, either temporarily or permanently, during redesign efforts, leaving customers and suppliers with no idea of whom to talk to in the company. Unfortunately, competitors will be more than ready to seize the opportunity and satisfy those unmet needs.

Stress and Anxiety Endless waves of restructuring can lead to enormous anxiety, a loss of continuity, the departure of key people, and may seriously damage the core competences that made the company successful. People worry about losing their jobs, friends, status, or day-to-day routine. Anxiety often leads to a number of predictable reactions ranging from panic or withdrawal to outright resistance.

A careful process of organization design is one way to develop the organizational capability for proactive change or for rapid reactive response, and can minimize the costs of change, although it can never expect to eliminate them entirely. Nadler and Tushman provide some general "ground rules" that underpin a good design process:

> *First, the best designs are those that emerge from consideration of the widest possible range of alternatives. Second, the best design processes involve people who fully understand the organization and its work; in large corporations, third- and fourth-level managers are positioned better than either the senior team or outside consultants to understand the way the organization works, both formally and informally. Third, the best designs are developed with implementation in mind. And design—like any organizational change—will have significantly better chance of success if the people responsible for making it work feel they were a part of shaping the change.* (Nadler and Tushman, 1997, p. 179)

No matter how successful a company may be at any point in time, powerful forces are at work, both within an organization and in its external environment, which make redesign inevitable. Sometimes redesign is a response to the growth, evolution, and maturation of an organization and of its products. As organizations grow, for example, they become more complex, and simply multiplying existing units does not suffice to cope with the broader range of customers, employees, and products. Sometimes management succession provides the stimulus for change efforts, as a new CEO or division head seeks to put a personal stamp on the organization or to take advantage of the change in leadership to address some long-standing organizational problems. At other times, redesign is necessary because of internal problems, such as lack of coordination, excessive conflict, unclear roles, poor work flows, or a proliferation of ad hoc organizational units such as task forces, committees, and special project teams.

The most frequent stimulus to design changes, however, is that the current design no longer fits the pressures from the external business environment. The organization is, in this perspective, seen as a "throughout-put" system that takes inputs from the environment, adds value to them through various internal processes, and then distributes them to users outside the organization; accordingly, the environment is primarily seen as a source of inputs and a market for outputs (the input-set and the output-set). Shifts in the firm's environment can make the established design inadequate: new competitors, technical innovations that affect either the nature of potential inputs or ways of distributing outputs (an example of the latter would be the rise of Internet marketing and sales), changes in markets and the customer base, changes in the supplier base or in the labor markets that supply personnel, and regulatory changes that affect what inputs an organization can use (e.g., "green" restrictions on certain chemicals or labor legislation affecting the use of part-time labor). As the environment changes, the organization must adjust its design to "fit" the environmental pressures.

What Do You Look for in Understanding an Organization?

In order to understand an organization from the strategic design perspective, you need first to know its *strategy*: What is the organization trying to accomplish? How is it trying to differentiate itself from other organizations trying to accomplish the same things? What is it trying to do better than those other organizations?

Second, you need to map its *design*. Design questions include:

- What is the formal *grouping* structure, that is, what is the organization chart for this organization?
- How are the units created by the grouping structure linked and coordinated?
- Are the basic systems—performance measurement, incentives and rewards, resource allocation, human resource development, and informal systems and processes—aligned with each other and with the tasks required by the grouping structure and the linking mechanisms? Do they positively reinforce each other or do they pull people's behavior in different and incompatible directions?
- Does the organization design fit the demands of its environment and of the organization's strategy? Is it getting the kinds of inputs it needs? Meeting the requirements of customers? Effectively competing with other firms trying to achieve similar goals?

Summary

The strategic design lens sees organizations as fundamentally rational, in the sense that, in a well-designed organization, each person and each unit in the organization can and should be oriented to accomplishing its goals. The major impediments to realizing this situation are that people do not adequately understand the goals or tasks (inadequate information), that they do not have the resources necessary to accomplish their assigned tasks, or that an inadequate organizational design is directing their efforts to subunit goals that get in the way of the overall goals. Strategic grouping, linking, and alignment are the key processes for ensuring that the organization does indeed build the right foundations for realizing its strategic goals (see Figure 2.7).

Figure 2.7 — Strategic Organizational Design Process: Specific Decision-Making Steps

Steps	Objectives
1. Generate design criteria	Create a series of statements that can serve as criteria for assessing different designs
2. Generate grouping alternatives	Create a large number of different grouping alternatives designed to meet the design criteria
3. Evaluate grouping alternatives	Assess grouping alternatives in terms of design criteria; eliminate, modify, and refine alternatives
4. Identify coordination requirements	For each grouping alternative, identify the information-processing needs, working from the design criteria
5. Generate structural linking mechanisms	For each grouping alternative, create a set of structural linking mechanisms that will be responsive to the coordination requirements and will enhance the extent to which the design meets the design criteria
6. Evaluate structural linking mechanisms	Assess each alternative in terms of the design criteria; eliminate, modify, and refine alternatives; combine alternatives if necessary.
7. Conduct impact analysis	Assess each surviving design alternative in terms of predicted impact on or fit with other organizational components, especially alignment systems
8. Refine and eliminate designs	Based on the impact analysis, eliminate designs, resulting in a first choice design recommendation, and refine designs as appropriate
9. Identify issues for operational design and alignment	Based on impact analysis, identify where operational design needs to be done and the alignment systems to be addressed by the design
10. Identify issues for implementation	Based on impact analysis, identify key issues to be considered in planning implementation of the design

Source: From *Competing by Design: The Power of Organizational Architecture* by David A. Nadler, Michael L. Tushman, and Mark B. Nadler, copyright © 1997 Oxford University Press. Used by permission of Oxford University Press, Inc.

References

Chandler, Alfred D. Jr. 1962. *Strategy and Structure*. Cambridge, MA: MIT Press.

Galbraith, Jay R. 2000. *Designing the Global Corporation*. San Francisco: Jossey-Bass.

Galbraith, Jay R., and Lawler, Edward E. 1993. *Organizing for the Future: The New Logic for Managing Complex Organizations*. San Francisco: Jossey-Bass.

Goold, Michael, and Andrew Campbell. 2002. *Designing Effective Organizations: How to Create Structured Networks*. San Francisco: Jossey-Bass.

Nadler, David A., and Michael L. Tushman. 1997. *Competing by Design: The Power of Organizational Architecture*. New York: Oxford University Press.

Thompson, James D. 1967. *Organizations in Action*. New York: McGraw-Hill.

Strategic Design at Dynacorp

"We're too slow, too unresponsive to the market, and too undisciplined about costs. And the main reason is how we're organized—it just isn't working any more. We've outgrown the old design in so many ways, but we're still trying to manage with the same structure we had when we started the company."
—Dynacorp product manager

"There's a lot of talk now about changing our organization design. But we should be careful that we're not throwing the baby out with the bathwater. We're fixating on what's wrong with the organization instead of thinking about how to make it work better."
—Dynacorp engineering manager

The Dyna Corporation, known in the industry as Dynacorp, is a major global information systems and communications company. Originating in an office equipment company that moved into high-technology applications in the 1960s and 1970s, Dynacorp had, by the 1980s, established a position as an industry leader, known for its technological innovation. Dynacorp was first to the market with innovative and high-quality products that were significant advances on anything its competitors were offering. Customers would gladly wait months, and even a year or so, to take delivery of products bearing the Dynacorp logo. The customers were typically sophisticated users who were willing to do some of their own applications work and to figure out how to integrate Dynacorp's new products with the rest of their operations. During this period, the company grew at a very fast rate, and expanded its market to Europe, Asia, and Latin America.

The 1990s were a much more difficult period for the company. It continued to grow, but at a slower rate, and experienced periods of significantly reduced earnings. Critics both inside and outside the company attributed Dynacorp's difficulties to a loss of leadership in getting new products to market, costs that were too high, and changes in the marketplace that Dynacorp was slow to recognize. Competitors were closing the technology gap, and were often faster getting products to market. In a growing number of product areas, Dynacorp had been surprised by competitors who, although they had started working on a new product much later than Dynacorp, were faster at getting the product to the customer at an attractive price. In addition, a growing number of information technology and communications (ITC) consulting firms were capturing the relationship with the large customer by offering "value-added services and solutions." The consulting firms acted as intermediaries, supervising the purchase of ITC hardware and software, providing integration services, and capturing much of the high-margin business.

A growing number of executives in Dynacorp were coming to believe that the problems could not be addressed effectively with Dynacorp's current organizational structure. Like most companies, Dynacorp had been established with a functional organization. As the company expanded its activities across five continents and greatly increased its product range, top management began to ask whether Dynacorp needed a major redesign.

As a first step, the CEO appointed a small internal task force to make preliminary recommendations on organization design to the top management team. The CEO personally launched the task force with a company-wide communication listing the challenges Dynacorp was facing: high costs, being too slow to get new products to the market, and a need to increase the value created for customers. The CEO emphasized that the current task force's mandate was driven by Dynacorp's commitment to maintaining its leadership position in its industry, and asked all Dynacorp employees to cooperate fully and frankly with the task force's inquiries.

A number of the task force members traveled around the company conducting interviews with managers at multiple levels across the three major divisions of the company, while others embarked on an "external benchmarking" exercise to look at how other companies in the industry were organized. As they consolidated their findings, they found themselves in agreement that Dynacorp's current organization had serious shortcomings, but they disagreed vehemently on what the best design solution might be. The CEO had made it clear, however, that he did not want a simple listing of alternatives; he wanted the task force, at the very least, to provide a ranking of the alternative choices.

Dynacorp's Design: The Functional Organization

Since its earliest days of operation, Dynacorp had been organized functionally. The three line divi-

---

Source: From *Competing by Design: The Power of Organizational Architecture* by David A. Nadler, Michael L. Tushman, and Mark B. Nadler, copyright © 1997 Oxford University Press. Used by permission of Oxford University Press, Inc.

sions, each led by an executive vice president, were engineering, manufacturing, and marketing. These were supported by a number of corporate staff divisions, including finance, human resource management, and corporate affairs.

The engineering division was organized by technical area into 10 groups. The advanced technology group worked on developing the next generation of technology, often in close collaborations with university labs and independent research institutes. In addition, eight groups were based on technical specialty (devices, storage systems, software, etc.). Finally, a process technology group had been set up relatively recently to work on the development of advanced computer-aided manufacturing systems.

Originally, the personnel of the engineering division were clustered in one location. Over time, however, both constraints on space and the recognition of the need to have a presence in key technology "hot spots" meant that the engineering division eventually spread across sites in three regions of the United States, including the two coasts. Recently discussions were held about setting up engineering centers in Europe and Asia, where sales were growing rapidly, but no decision had been made, although the marketing organizations in those regions strongly advocated the internationalization of engineering.

Dynacorp was one of the few American companies that had successfully implemented a dual career ladder in its engineering division, whereby outstanding engineers and scientists could continue to advance in salary and status without leaving the "bench" or the lab. Instead of moving into engineering management positions, they could rise on a ladder of positions that paralleled the management career steps. Many companies tried to implement such a system, but as a rule the technical ladder does not begin to match the prestige and pay of the management ladder. In Dynacorp, however, a significant number of outstanding technical people rose to top positions on the technical ladder. Most engineers, however, advanced into management positions in the engineering division. Over time the number of rungs on both the technical and the management ladders had increased, allowing for advancement opportunities within the division.

The manufacturing division was organized by location; the basic unit was the factory, which was a cost center, measured on overall costs, productivity (which was strongly shaped by capacity utilization), and quality. Some of the factories had begun by manufacturing one particular product line, but over time, as some products were phased out and new product lines introduced, most factories had come to produce a range of products. This production variety made it somewhat difficult for factory managers to calculate clear production costs for any one product line, because of the shared factory overheads.

Dynacorp had a higher percentage of its products manufactured in its own factories than most of its U.S. competitors. The company had been an early American adopter of total quality control and was a lead user of new process technology. The career ladder in manufacturing had originally been quite short (Dynacorp had prided itself on its flat organization), but as the size of the plants grew, the number of management grades increased over time. The most coveted position in the function was that of general manager of a manufacturing plant.

Like engineering, manufacturing had begun in one location, but it expanded earlier into different locations within the United States, in search of lower costs and proximity to growing markets. The company had plants in 12 states in the United States and two countries in Europe. Production had not yet been set up in the Asia-Pacific region, but the company was increasingly drawing on suppliers located in that region, and some managers advocated setting up manufacturing operations there in order to take advantage of its local manufacturing expertise and lower costs. Some of the marketing people who had been pushing hard for this option blamed the company's slowness to move on the reluctance of manufacturing to lose domestic production. They also criticized manufacturing for being unwilling to outsource more of its production, because this would affect the promotion possibilities within the function. Manufacturing executives denied this accusation vehemently, and asserted that their overriding concern was to ensure the continuation of Dynacorp's reputation for production quality.

The marketing division was also organized by geography, but the geographic divisions differed from those of the manufacturing division. Six regions in the United States were in turn divided into sales territories or branches. Marketing and sales outside the United States were handled by an international group that was organized by country. Marketing people cultivated close ties with their customers, so close that junior recruits often complained that their managers "owned" customers and were reluctant to involve them deeply in serving existing clients. The marketing division prided itself on the continuity of its customer relationships and on the depth of its people's knowledge of and fierce loyalty to Dynacorp products.

The marketing division's tasks had changed considerably over time. In its early years and well into the company's high-growth era, Dynacorp had targeted the sale of its products to technical specialists in customer companies. These customers recognized the technical superiority of Dynacorp's products and were happy to work with its technical support people to work out any problems. However, more and more companies were taking system purchasing out of the hands of their technical enthusiasts, and Dynacorp's marketing people increasingly found themselves selling to business unit purchasing groups—often backed up by, or even represented by, consulting firms with special practices in ITC. This shift meant a high demand for technical support, lower customer tolerance of early stage problems with new product lines, the need to integrate Dynacorp products with other systems to provide solutions, and more polished marketing pitches. It also meant that it became more difficult to cultivate the close personal relationships with buyers that had been a long-standing element of Dynacorp's marketing strategy.

Dynacorp's top management was justifiably proud of what their functional organization had accomplished. Its engineering division had an excellent technical reputation and was able to attract top technical talent and to develop the close working relationships with leading scientists and engineers at major research universities that enabled it to stay on the cutting edge of new technology. Its manufacturing division had built strong capabilities in quality manufacturing at a time when U.S. industry overall was widely criticized for falling behind in production systems. It could also boast of a dedicated and knowledgeable marketing function whose people had built close working relationships with customers who were fiercely loyal to Dynacorp products.

Top management recognized that the competitive environment was changing, and that Dynacorp's high costs, slow pace of getting new products to market, and the need to generate value-added services for customers made the company vulnerable. Dynacorp was not facing an immediate crisis—it was still profitable, growing, and highly respected in its industry. But the industry was changing, and Dynacorp's top management believed that they had a window of a year or two to address the problems before the current trends led to really serious problems.

Internal Investigation: Diagnosing the Organizational Problems

The task force found widespread agreement on the importance of the problems that Dynacorp was facing, but considerable variation of opinion on what was causing them or on how to fix them. The engineering division's managers were convinced that the primary responsibility for high costs and delays in getting products to market lay with manufacturing. One senior engineering manager said that even though his people tried to hand the manufacturing site a detailed and complete set of specifications, the manufacturing manager kept coming back with questions or objections; he wanted to substitute standard parts that would mean reconfiguring the design or lowering the product functionality, or to change elements of the design to make it easier to produce, or to clarify things simply because his people didn't understand something about the design. Each iteration took time, because the engineers on the project had by that time gone on to other activities and had to be hauled back "kicking and screaming" to work on something they thought they'd finished.

Manufacturing managers recognized the problem, but they believed it was due to the fact that engineering cared more about the design than the product. They complained that engineering liked to design "from the ground up," instead of using standard components that could considerably lower the product cost. One complained that "if a few engineers get really good at designing widgets, then they want to design a better, cooler widget for every product they work on, instead of accepting that some other engineer's widget would do the job just fine." But one manufacturing manager put the problem in the context of Dynacorp's growth:

When I first joined the company, we were all still basically in the same town, and we got to know each other. So if I had a problem with the design, I'd just walk over to engineering and grab one of the guys to give me a hand. Of course he'd grumble about us manufacturing guys being a bunch of idiots, but he'd either sit down with us or find one of the engineering team who would help out—and half the time they'd realize that we had a point, and we'd work things out. Now I'm in a plant that's in a different state and I don't really know any of the bench engineers the same way. They hand us a spec [specifications] file that's hundreds of pages long, and they think their job's finished. By the time we've identified a problem, they're all off on new projects, and finding the ones responsible for that part of the design, getting their attention, convincing them that we aren't numbskulls and that there really is a problem—well, that all takes a lot of time. And changing the specs is a big deal, because everyone has signed off on them, so even a minor change becomes a major time sink.

The only thing on which engineering and manufacturing people unanimously agreed was that one reason for falling profits was marketing's eagerness to cut prices to make a sale. The view that "those [marketing] guys are measured on sales volume, and to make their targets they'll let the customer squeeze the margins" was widespread. Several engineers also expressed the view that marketing also bore some of the responsibility for products coming late to market, because they kept trying to add features or functions during the development process, even in the late stages, when changes were increasingly difficult and costly. According to one engineer, "They come in when we're nearly at the last gate to say, 'Hey, we've talked about this product to one of our best customers and they think it would be cool if we had a model that would yodel the Star-Spangled Banner on the Fourth of July' or some other crazy idea. We can usually talk them out of it, but it can sure slow things down while we sort them out. The problem is that those marketing guys have no idea of how much engineering is needed to change the functionality even by a small increment."

To meet the challenge of linking the functions in product development, Dynacorp relied heavily on two linking mechanisms: *cross-functional product development teams*, with representatives from manufacturing and marketing as well as engineering, and the position of *product manager*, who had the formal responsibility of overseeing the entire process from initial conception to product launch.

In their interviews inside the company, the design task force members heard widespread complaints about the cross-functional teams, especially from manufacturing and marketing. One manufacturing manager put his misgivings this way:

We don't really have cross-functional product development teams; we have cross-functional product development meetings. But everyone is sitting there wearing their functional hats, and no one really listens to anyone else. They close ranks against the other functions. Even if the design engineers disagree among themselves, they'd never bring the issue to the team to discuss and resolve; they'd work it out among themselves and then present a united front in support of "the engineering solution" at the next meeting.

Another manager pointed out that the company did not have an easy time identifying and developing good product managers:

Ideally, a product manager would have some experience in each function. But here at Dynacorp we all move up within a function, and very few people move across the functional boundaries in their careers. So the product managers come to the job with a fairly narrow experience base. They've all been on cross-functional teams, but in a functional role. They have to learn on the job—fast. The few really good product managers that we have are in high demand, and are too busy managing product teams to train anybody else. We burn out a lot of good functional people who get promoted to be product managers and then find they aren't up to the job.

As one product manager (who was widely regarded as very successful) pointed out, the job itself was a very difficult one.

I don't have much in the way of carrots and sticks to influence the behavior of the team members. I have an input into their evaluations, but the evaluations themselves are done by their functional managers, and it's the quality of their functional expertise that determines how they are valued, not their ability to subordinate functional criteria to product success. And because each engineer works on anywhere from six to twenty projects in a year, my input is only a small piece of the overall evaluation of the engineering project members. It gets even more complicated: if I give someone who is seen as a really good engineer a poor evaluation because he's a bad team player, word gets around, and then I'm going to have trouble getting good people onto my teams. Furthermore, the budget allocations for the project are controlled by the senior functional managers, not by me or by the project leaders from each function. If the project needs more resources, I have to coax them out of the functions. So I have a lot of responsibility without the formal authority to back it up.

The internal investigation also collected a number of more general criticisms of Dynacorp's organization design. Younger members of the organization complained that the organization had too many layers of managers, and even some of the older managers who had benefited by the proliferation of steps in the career ladder looked back nostalgically on the flat, speedy organization of their early years in the company. Information seemed to take a long time to travel up and down the company. Several managers complained of a growing tendency to push problems up the hierarchy for resolution, instead of tackling problems when and where they arose. One relatively junior marketing manager said that he had grown discouraged by the amount of time it took to get a response to his suggestions for ways of improving the customer database:

I went to my manager with a proposal, and she sent it on to her manager, and I don't know where it went from there. Ideas and suggestions go up, and nothing ever seems to come down, or if anything comes down it's a request for further study. I've given up trying to change anything around here.

On the other hand, many of the employees expressed some apprehension about the mandate of the task force, fearing that a major redesign of Dynacorp would damage rather than improve the company. As one engineer said,

We all complain about the organization. But I have friends who work in other high-tech compa-

nies, and their problems are even worse than ours. One friend's company has a product division structure, and they can't seem to transfer engineers or manufacturing capacity across product lines without huge fights about who's going to pay for it and how much. If we're running late on one product development project, for example, senior engineering management can shunt in good engineers from other less important projects at a moment's notice. Or if one product is in unexpectedly high demand, a plant manager can switch lines quickly to get the product volumes out the door. I wouldn't want to see us lose that.

A marketing executive who had been hired from the outside made a similar point:

My old company was organized by product divisions, and we were stepping all over each other selling different product lines to the same customers. Sometimes we were our own fiercest competitor: the small systems customer representatives were pushing one solution, the large systems people a different one. That was one reason I left, and I don't want to see Dynacorp get into the same dilemma.

External Investigation: Identifying Alternative Designs

Some members of the task force focused on the search for alternative organization designs. They surveyed the leading companies in information technology and communications (ITC) industry, talked with executives in some of those companies, and interviewed a set of consultants who specialized in organization design (and who were eager to sell Dynacorp their services). They also talked with some of Dynacorp's own managers who had been hired out of other companies in the industry, to get their views on the strengths and weaknesses of the organization design at their previous employer compared to Dynacorp's. From these investigations, task force members identified five models that they felt were viable alternatives for the company.

- *Product division structure:* This design would divide Dynacorp's functional divisions into product-based multifunctional product divisions based on the product technology, with a general manager in charge of the entire value chain (from technology development through after-sales service) for each major product line. Related product divisions would be grouped into business divisions (e.g., large systems) headed by an executive vice president. Shared corporate services would include not only the current set of activities but also advanced technology development, which would be in effect a corporate R&D center providing cutting-edge technology for future product lines.

- *Customer division structure:* Dynacorp's functional divisions would be divided into multifunctional divisions, but the criteria for creating the divisions would be primarily the customer segment they served (e.g., small business division), rather than the technology of the product.

- *Functional/product matrix:* This structure would matrix the existing functional structure with a product division structure, so that individuals would report both to a functional manager and a product manager. Only one company in the industry was using this structure successfully, and several companies that had adopted this structure had abandoned it after a few years. However, rather than regarding it as a failure, two or three had employed it as a transitional structure to develop the people and the systems to move more easily from a functional to a product-based organization design.

- *Front/back:* This newest structure, adopted by a very small number of companies, was strongly advocated by several of the consultants as the "cutting edge" of organization design in the ITC field. The structure would keep the marketing division as a separate front-end structure, responsible for selling the entire range of Dynacorp products and systems. However, it would enhance its technical support capabilities to enable it to deliver systems and solutions more effectively to customers. Engineering and manufacturing would be divided into product-based business units that would be responsible for design and production.

- *Functional structure with stronger linking mechanisms:* This most conservative alternative would keep Dynacorp's functional structure, but would set up a much stronger array of cross-functional linking mechanisms and alignment systems to support cross-functional linkage.

None of the designs seemed to have been successful in every company that tried it; each had success and failure cases within the industry. The front/back structure was so new that no obvious "failure" cases had yet arisen, but even some of its strongest advocates in the industry admitted that it had proved more challenging to implement than they had initially expected.

After the task force had digested both the information on the problems of Dynacorp's current structure and the mapping of the five design alternatives, the task force began the discussion with a quick show of hands on each member's first and second choice for a new design. The result showed a wide distribution across the five alternatives, and it was clear that no quick consensus would point to the best way forward for the company.

The Political Lens

Overview

The political lens brings into sharp focus some aspects of the organization that are distinctly different from those we see using the strategic design lens. Where the strategic design lens sees the organization as a social system, deliberately constructed to achieve overarching strategic goals, the political lens sees it as an arena for competition and conflict among individuals, groups, and other organizations whose interests and goals differ and even clash dramatically. In the strategic design perspective, the roots of any conflict lie in different analyses of problems and opportunities; more data and better analysis can resolve any disagreements through a shared rationality. In the political perspective, the roots of conflict lie in different and competing interests, and disagreements require political action, including negotiation, coalition building, and the exercise of power and influence, all of which recognize that rationality is local. The strategic design perspective asks, "What is the problem? What solution is best suited to the strategic environment and the capabilities of the organization?" The political perspective asks, "Who's defining the problem, and what gives them the power to define it? Who's advocating what solution, and why? How can I get an outcome that serves the interests of my group and me?"

The political aspects of an organization are simultaneously the focus of much of the attention (and even more of the gossip) of those working in and leading the organization, and the least accepted. When people say, "That was a political decision," they are usually implying that it was a bad decision made on the wrong criteria. If decisions are to be effective, however, they must be political—good decisions as well as bad. They must have the buy-in of those who have the power to implement or to block action. Power and interests, coalition building and negotiation, conflict and conflict resolution are essential aspects of organizational life. If the formal design of the organization is the equivalent of the skeleton of the organization, the political system is the musculature. It is essential to action.

This part of the module provides an overview of the basic concepts of the political lens as well as some tools for using these concepts effectively. It also contains an elective reading on informal networks that looks at organization through the political lens. In their article, originally published in the *Harvard Business Review*, Krackhardt and Hanson show the importance of the multiple informal networks that link individuals and subunits in organizations and constitute a key element of the political system of any organization. They provide some useful concepts for understanding them better than most managers apparently do.

Assignment Summary

1. Think about the organizations in which you have worked. Who were the most powerful individuals and groups, and why? Come to class prepared to discuss this issue.
2. Think about your own class. Who are the individuals or groups that have the strongest influence, and why? What are the key indicators of influence?

Suggested Further Readings

Burt, Ronald S. 1992. "The Social Structure of Competition." In Nitin Nohria and Robert G. Eccles (Eds.), *Networks and Organizations: Structure, Form, and Action* (pp. 57–91). Boston: Harvard Business School Press. A succinct and clear explanation of social networks and their effect on intraorganizational competition, by one of the most influential network theorists.

Kanter, Rosabeth. 1977. *Men and Women of the Corporation.* New York: Basic Books. A classic study of power dynamics in U.S. corporations, whose insights are still widely cited and applied today.

Kets de Vries, Manfred F. R. 1993. *Leaders, Fools, and Imposters: Essays on the Psychology of Leadership.* San Francisco: Jossey-Bass. A psychological analysis by a leading European researcher of the dynamics of the use and abuse of power by top executives.

Meyerson, Deborah E. 2001. *Tempered Radicals: How People Use Difference to Inspire Change at Work.* Boston: Harvard Business School Press. A study of political activism in organizations, building on the tradition of social movement analysis.

Morrill, Calvin. 1995. *The Executive Way: Conflict Management in Corporations.* Chicago: University of Chicago Press. A fascinating study of conflict among high-level executives and how it is handled, based on intensive observation of 13 U.S. companies.

Pfeffer, Jeffrey. 1992. *Managing with Power: Politics and Influence in Organizations.* Boston: Harvard Business School Press. A thorough and extremely readable analysis of power and its sources and use in organizations.

Porter, Lyman W., Harold L. Angle, and Robert E. Allen (Eds.). 2003. *Organizational Influence Processes*, 2nd ed. Armonk, NY: M.E. Sharpe. A useful compendium of writings on power and influence in organizations, organized by the direction of influence (downward, lateral, and upward).

Useem, Michael. 2001. *Leading Up: How to Lead Your Boss So You Both Win*. New York: Three Rivers Press. An interesting guide to exerting influence upward in the organization, built on detailed historical and contemporary case studies.

The Organization as a Political System

Organizations are strategic designs to accomplish shared goals, but they are not *only* strategic designs. Organizations are also political systems. When we think of political systems, we usually think first of political parties, elections, governments, and interest groups. The key elements of power and politics, however, are interests, conflict, competition, coalition building, and negotiation. These elements are not unique to political parties or to governments, but are essential to all organizations, even the smallest and most egalitarian.

For many people, including many successful and powerful executives, politics constitutes the dark side of the organization, an aspect created by the selfishness and dishonesty of others. "Playing politics" is something other people do. An inability or an unwillingness to deal with the political aspects of organizations, however, is a serious handicap for anyone trying to take effective action in an organizational setting. Jeffrey Pfeffer, who is one of the most widely recognized contributors to the analysis of power and politics in organizations, has observed:

> *I have seen, all too often, otherwise intelligent and successful managers have problems because they did not recognize the political nature of the situation, or because they were blindsided by someone whose position and strength they had not anticipated. (Pfeffer, 30).*

Pfeffer's reference to "position and strength" is another way of saying "interests and power." They are the core concepts of a political perspective on organizations. *Interests* refer to what people want—what's at stake for them in a decision or course of action. Depending on how an action affects their interests, people will support or oppose it. Managers often run into trouble because they fail to recognize what's at stake for other units or for other individuals in their proposed course of action. The effectiveness of the support or opposition of others depends on the amount and nature of the *power* held by those units or individuals. Understanding how to leverage interests and power is an essential base for taking effective action in organizations.

Interests

In the political perspective, organizational behavior is grounded in interests. The political lens shares with economics the fundamental assumption that people act rationally to serve their own interests. Where the two approaches differ is in their analysis of "interests." The classic economic model of *homo economicus* ("economic man") is an individual acting in his own personal interests, which, however numerous and varied they may be, are reducible to a common economic currency that allows that individual to compare the relative value or "utility" of meeting each interest. The political lens acknowledges the importance of individual interests, but it broadens their scope beyond what can be calculated in terms of some dollar or net present value amount to include a variety of interests (such as autonomy and status) that are difficult to reduce to economic terms. It also devotes equal or even greater attention to collective interests.

Collective interests are those shared by others who belong to the same group or category, and center on the welfare and maintenance of the group. The most obvious collective interests are those defined by the organization design. Seen through the political lens, the boundaries between the "boxes" or units in the formal design define not only responsibilities and roles but also the borders of interest groups that compete with each other for resources and for the attention and approval of top management. Ed Schein, in a recent analysis of Digital Equipment Corporation, provides an example of the power of collective interests:

> *When DEC was small these political battles [over setting priorities] were among individuals fighting for their individual points of view in a climate of rational debate and problem solving reminiscent of academia. With growth and success, those same managers now "owned" organizational units with many employees for whom they felt increasingly responsible. To give in to an argument now meant letting your organization down. (Schein, 157)*

This example also illustrates how strongly individual interests come to be identified with collective interests.

Groups defined by the formal structure are, however, only one of an array of possible collective interest groups within an organization. Demographic groups—those defined by population variables such as age, gender, ethnicity, or marital status—also share collective interests that can affect certain kinds of organizational action. For example, many U.S. companies today face challenges from older employees who are fighting their companies' efforts to improve the bottom line by switching from traditional "defined benefits" plans (where the employee gets a set amount per month after retirement, based on salary) to "defined contributions" plans. These plans center on individual retirement accounts, to which both the employee and company contribute, and which younger workers value because they can are portable across employers. Older workers, however, found that in switching to the new plans in the middle of their careers they would receive much lower postretirement incomes and benefits than they had been expecting.

Other potential bases for collective interests include the following:

- Position in the division of labor (such as full-time or part-time employees, salaried or hourly workers, blue-collar or white-collar or managerial employees)
- Location (country in the case of multinational corporations, or site in the case of domestic companies)
- Profession/occupational category (engineers, accountants, MBAs, skilled workers, etc.)

An increasingly common approach to understanding collective interests is the *stakeholder* perspective. The term stakeholders identifies groups that have a shared "stake" (i.e., a set of collective interests) that is affected by what the organization is and how it carries out its activities. Each stakeholder group not only has common interests but shares an awareness of those interests and a willingness to act to further them. The stakeholder perspective identifies both internal stakeholders (those within the organization) and external stakeholders (including suppliers, customers, communities, and shareholders).

Internal stakeholders vary considerably both in the extent to which they themselves are organized and in the kind of ties they construct with external stakeholder groups. In many manufacturing companies, for example, blue-collar workers belong to unions. In Britain, unions are organized by craft, so that one company will contain members of a number of different unions. In the United States, the dominant form of union is the industrial union, which incorporates employees in the industry regardless of their specific craft (e.g., the United Automobile Workers). In Japan, most unions are company unions (Toyota and Honda each have their own union, instead of a single industrial union or multiple craft unions that cut across company boundaries). These different patterns of organization strongly affect the interests of different categories of workers and the alignment—or lack of it—between the interests of management and union. Other examples of organized stakeholder groups include the well-known Black Caucus in Xerox, which emerged to provide advice and mentoring for African-American employees (mostly in the managerial ranks), and technical "communities of practice" (which have as a primary purpose the sharing of knowledge and "best practice" but which also give a voice to the needs and interests of their members).

Simply recognizing that interests are important is the first step in developing an ability to use the political lens to take more effective action in organizations. The next step is much harder: analyzing what those interests are and what priority they have for key individual and collective actors. Interests are both complex and dynamic. People have multiple interests at the individual level. They have, for example, both short-term goals and long-term ambitions. They want both autonomy and cooperative relations with others. They want to develop a reputation for dedication to their work, and to meet personal quality of life aspirations. They are also members of multiple stakeholder groups that have different and sometimes competing interests. One person can simultaneously be a member of a particular division of the company, a particular occupational group, a particular demographic group (such as single parents), a particular site or facility that is competing with other sites in the company for new activities, and the community in which that site is located.

To complicate the analysis further, collectivities also have multiple interests. To give just one example, a business division in a diversified corporation may be struggling to try simultaneously to reduce costs and speed up its response to a changing marketplace. Sharing support services with other divisions may be a way to reduce costs. On the other hand, the difficulties of moving to a new shared services structure and the potential loss of control over access to those services may undermine the division's ability to respond rapidly to current market changes. It will also reduce the control of the division's executives over the service activities. Rarely is a clear, data-grounded base evident for making a choice, especially when it is much easier to assign a dollar value to cost savings than to loss of control—even though both may have an equal effect on competitive position in the marketplace. The decision process in such a case is heavily "political"; that is, it depends on how the key decision makers see and assign weight to their interests.

Furthermore, interests at both the individual and collective levels are *dynamic*: that is, they change in content and in relative importance over time and as context changes. For example, as a younger single employee I may not feel my interests are strongly affected by a company's efforts to change its benefits plans, including medical coverage. However, if I develop a chronic health problem, the company's benefits plan may suddenly assume much greater salience among my various interests. This example illustrates another factor in the complexity and dynamic nature of interests. Interests may be latent; I may not realize I have a certain stakeholder interest until it is evoked by circumstances or by someone trying to mobilize my support for a certain course of action.

Individuals and groups will support, be indifferent to, or try to block organizational actions based on how those actions affect their interests. To carry an action forward, its initiator needs to understand what interests will be affected by it. In deciding how to proceed, however, one further element of a political analysis is needed: how much power those individuals and groups have to affect the course of the action.

Power

Power has always been a difficult concept to define in the context of organizations, although most people, if asked to identify the most powerful units or individuals in their organization, have no difficulty answering. Pfeffer's definition of organizational power will serve as a useful base for our discussion: "the potential ability to influence behavior, to change the course of events, to overcome resistance, and to get people to do things that they would not otherwise do" (Pfeffer, 1992, 30). A recent issue of *Fortune* magazine that focused on power used an abbreviated version of this same definition: "Our definition of power was straightforward: the ability to affect the behavior of other people" (*Fortune*, August 11, 2003, 58). From this perspective, getting things done in organizations requires power. Its use is inevitable, and the more you have, the more you can accomplish.

Many people in today's organizations are uncomfortable talking about power, particularly their own. They often prefer to talk about influence, especially when their own power is at issue, or about authority when their boss's power is the topic, and about power only when they are talking about coercion or domination. These three variants of power—influence, authority, and coercion—are well recognized in research on power and organizations. Authority is a classic concept in the study of organizational power, and refers to power that is defined as legitimate by those who are subject to it. Authority in organizations is most commonly associated with formal positions in the organizational hierarchy: the head of a division has authority over those who work in that division. One of the common political strategies for dealing with conflict in organizations is to "push it up"—that is, to ask someone higher in the organization with formal authority over the contending parties to resolve the issue. Influence connotes informality and is often used in interactions where someone does not have formal authority but develops the ability to induce or persuade others to act in ways they would not act in the absence of that influence. Coercion (often called "domination") has been defined as "the control of the behavior of one individual by another who can offer or restrict benefit or inflict punishment" (Powell and Smith-Doerr, 1993, 376). Coercion is rarely seen as legitimate, and although it can indeed force people to behave in ways that they otherwise would not, it breeds resentment and a desire to get even.

Power is fundamentally based in control over or access to valued resources, and has a number of sources, including personal characteristics, expertise, track record, formal hierarchical position, and informal network position. The following discussion explains each in greater detail.

Personal Characteristics

Research on personal characteristics and the effective use of power has often been linked to the concept of "charisma." Max Weber, one of the pioneers of sociology and of the study of power, drew the concept from the field of religion. Charisma means "the gift of grace," and Weber used it for the kind of power that derives from a deep emotional connection between leader and followers based on the distinctive personal qualities of the charismatic leader and on the distress or tension experienced by the followers, which the leader promises to alleviate (Gerth and Mills, 1958, 52). Although this concept has become increasingly generalized, Weber saw the personalized and emotional nature of charisma, which transcends rules and routines, as potentially disruptive in established organizational settings. Moreover, charisma is, for Weber, inherently unstable, both because it requires constant proof of the unique gifts and vision of the leader and because it is difficult to transfer from one context to another or from one leader to another (Weber, 1958, 52–53).[1] In contemporary business, a visionary founder of an entrepreneurial firm would potentially embody both the strengths and weaknesses of Weberian charismatic authority.

Personal characteristics do, however, play a role as a source of power in established formal organizations. Jeffrey Pfeffer, for example, provided a list of personal characteristics used for effective political action in organizations:

- Energy and physical stamina
- Focus (the ability to set priorities and concentrate on the most important things)
- Sensitivity to others and an ability to understand how they see their interests
- Flexibility (based on concentrating on ultimate objectives and adjusting to what is possible in a particular context)
- Ability to tolerate conflict
- Submerging one's ego and getting along

Pfeffer is the first to admit that the role of each trait in building power has not been systematically tested; the list is based on his extensive work on power in organizations. The first two features, energy and focus, are common in portrayals in the business press of powerful executives, and their role is easy to understand. The third—sensitivity to the interests of others—does not, as Pfeffer quickly points out, mean acting in the interests of others. "Sensitivity simply means understanding who they are, their position on the issues, and how best to communicate with and influence them" (Pfeffer, 1992, 172). As Pfeffer points out, sensitivity to other's interests is not worth much if one is not prepared to adjust one's behavior to use that understanding ("flexibility"). Because conflict is unavoidable in organizations, a willingness to engage in conflict to further one's individual and collective interests is a source of power, particularly if others are conflict-avoidant. Finally, Pfeffer argues that because interdependence is an unavoidable feature of action in organizations, a willingness to put one's ego aside in order to listen and expand one's information and understanding, build alliances, share credit, and get buy-in from others is an essential personal quality in today's organizational settings.

Scarce and Valued Expertise

The mastery of a skill or body of knowledge that is both valued by the organization and relatively scarce can be a significant source of power. A particularly gifted innovator in an R&D organization, a software engineer with exceptional ability at diagnosing problems, a skilled mediator in an organization facing politically crippling labor problems—these individuals can become significantly more powerful than their less-skilled counterparts. They also become central in the task and advice networks that are part of organizational networks of power and influence.

At various organizational levels, groups or subunits with scarce and valuable expertise can gain significant power in the organization. Michel Crozier's classic study of power in organizations included a much-cited case study of a manufacturing firm where one of the most powerful groups was the maintenance engineering department. The factory was highly capital-intensive, which meant that if the complex machinery broke down, the performance of the factory suffered until it came back on-line. The maintenance engineers had a monopoly of the expertise required for diagnosing and fixing the machinery, and therefore the factory manager deferred to their demands and interests much more attentively than to those of any other unit or subgroup in the plant (Crozier, 1964). In U.S. corporations, the finance department steadily gained influence as the firm diversified, because financial analysis and access to financial markets came to be crucially important elements of the control systems and strategies of multibusiness firms (Fligstein, 1987).

Past Performance/Track Record

A third source of power for both individuals and subunits is past performance or "track record." Individuals who have a history of successful achievement in their assignments generally have greater power than those with less outstanding records. One reason is that they are often identified as "high fliers"—people who are likely to rise higher in the organization. Others are therefore usually more eager to cooperate with them, in expectation of future valuable relationships. People are also more likely to be eager to interact with them, and therefore they are often better able to expand their access to information, which is one of the most important organizational resources. In addition, they are usually able to elicit a higher level of effort and commitment from those who work for them. As Rosabeth Kanter pointed out:

When employees perceive their manager as influential upward and outward, their status is enhanced by association and they generally have

---

1 Weber's key writings were produced in Germany during the first quarter of the 20th century, but were not well-known to English-speaking social scientists until after World War II, when translations made them widely available. They were extremely influential in the emerging field of organization theory.

high morale and feel less critical or resistant to their boss. (Kanter, 1979).

Similar patterns hold at the subunit level. A division or department that has a record of outstanding past performance (e.g., the most consistently profitable division, or the plant with the highest quality rating) usually has more power in the organization than similar units without such strong performance records. Successful divisions can often claim higher levels of resources, and they attract skilled and ambitious employees.

Sociologists dubbed the concept of success as a source of power that breeds further success as "the Matthew effect," based on the verse in the Gospel according to St. Matthew: "Unto every one that hath shall be given, and he shall have abundance: but from him that hath not shall be taken away even that which he hath." (Matt. 25:29).

Formal Position as a Source of Power

From the political perspective, the organization chart is more than a design that specifies reporting responsibilities; it is also a rudimentary political map of the organization—rudimentary because, although it provides a good guide to the vertical power system of the organization, it is not an accurate guide to the horizontal system. In other words, equivalence of position on the formal organization chart is not a good indicator of relative power. The executive vice presidents of a company may occupy equivalent positions on the organization chart, but they usually differ significantly in their power relative to each other, both because of the factors described in the preceding paragraphs and because of the network position factors described in the following section.

The organization chart does, however, provide a good guide to the vertical power system. Individuals who occupy positions at the top of sub-units have formal power over employees below them in that unit, based on their control over several processes:

- Resource allocation (for example, whether someone gets a new computer or an enhanced travel budget)
- Information flows (subordinates have the formal obligation to share information with the person to whom they report)
- Evaluation of the employee's performance, which affects both current rewards and future job possibilities
- Task assignment (who gets the interesting and high-profile tasks, and who gets stuck with the unrewarding or unpleasant tasks)
- Conflict resolution (disputes between subordinates are usually decided by the formal superior, although most organizations have some avenues of appeal for certain kinds of conflicts, such as those that involve discrimination or unfair process)

One of the paradoxes of power based on position in the organizational hierarchy, however, is that excessive reliance on the control processes just listed can undermine that power. The classic definition of authority is power that is accepted as legitimate by those who are subject to it and therefore is not resisted. When a boss encounters resistance from subordinates, heavy reliance on sanctions can transform authority into coercion. Coercion is rarely accepted as legitimate, either by those subject to it or by those who are merely observing it. When people talk in negative terms about power in their organizations, they are often thinking about the coercive use of formally conferred power to control behavior (e.g., the boss who tells a subordinate, "Unless you stop objecting and work on this project, I'll see to it that you never get another promotion in this company"). Coercion often backfires, because it breeds resentment and a desire to get even somehow; the compliance that results is seldom wholehearted, and often conceals covert resistance and even sabotage.

Informal Network Position as a Source of Power

Both company gossip and social research have long recognized that "know-who" is as important as "know-how" in any organization. In today's flat, interdependent organizations, the kind of influence that comes from social networks is often much more significant than the authority that derives from formal hierarchical position.

In the popular view, the size of your network—the number of names in your PDA—and the number of powerful people in it are key factors to power. One of the oldest strategies for gaining power is to do favors for others, thereby building up an extensive network of obligations that can be redeemed later to serve your own interests or the interests of another person in order to expand your obligation network. This "Godfather" strategy rests on the premise that doing something for others, as a giver rather than a taker, builds a sense of obligation, even if at the time no expectation of an immediate return is expressed. The tacit expectation, however, is that someday, in some way, the favor will be reciprocated.

The growing body of research on social networks in organizations demonstrates, however, that although the *size* of your network is indeed important, your *position* in the network is even more important. The key concept that researchers use to identify powerful individual positions in a social network is *centrality*. Centrality, as used in network analysis, is a multidimensional concept, quantified using a number of measures. These measures include how many people you communicate with directly and indirectly, closeness (how many contact steps away you are from powerful individuals),[2] and "between-ness" (the number of pairs or clusters for whom you are the link).

A related measurable feature of a personal social network is *efficiency*. Two people can have similar numbers of contacts and differ greatly in their influence, because one has a highly redundant network, in which the people he or she knows also know each other, and the other has an efficient network, which includes one person from each of a large number of network clusters (see Figure 2.8).

The two actors in Figure 2.8, Lee and Leslie, have an identical number of contacts in their network. Lee, however, has a dense network in which everyone to whom Lee is connected is connected with the others in Lee's network. In such a network, information travels extremely quickly, and Lee has the same information as everyone else. Leslie, however, has contacts with a number of separate groups, and the links are efficient because they are not redundant. Leslie can obtain information quickly from Groups B, C, D, and F, and the information from those groups is likely different. Leslie therefore has information from each group that can be used to exchange for information from the other groups. These exchanges keep the information flowing to Leslie and can enhance Leslie's centrality in the overall network.

Network position is a source of influence in organization for two principal reasons. The first is the information advantage it can confer. Leslie gets a variety of information that can be integrated to identify opportunities and potential problems that are not evident to people who have less centrality and less efficient networks. Leslie also gets information earlier (the Leslies of the organization are usually the first to know what's going on). In addition, Leslie's information resources have advantages in "referrals," which provides opportunities for others in the organization (e.g., Leslie will know which project or task force needs another member, and which person from Group C would fit that assignment). The second reason that network position is a source of influence is its potential for building coalitions. Lee may be able to

Figure 2.8 Redundant vs. Efficient Networks

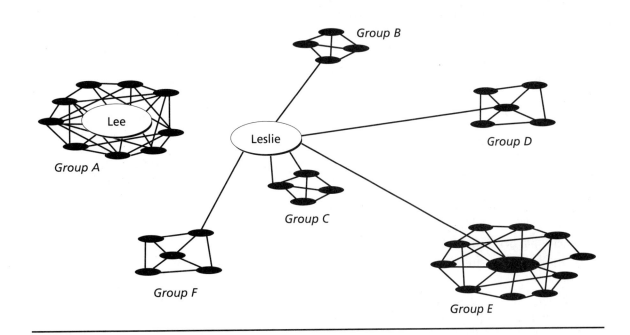

---

[2] *Closeness* or *degree* is a term made famous in "six degrees of separation"—the idea that everyone is connected to everyone else through six contact steps. See Duncan Watts (2003) for one of the best recent treatments of social networks.

mobilize Group A to support a certain set of interests, but Leslie is in a much better position to mobilize broad support, from more groups (Groups B, C, D, and F). However, Lee may be better able to keep Group A committed once it is mobilized.

Much of the recent research on social networks in organizations has focused on *structural holes*. Holes in an organizational network occur where no direct link exists between individuals or subunits that could benefit from being linked (i.e., they have real or potential interdependencies). Finding a structural hole and acting as the informal bridge or broker connecting the individuals or units is potentially a significant source of power.[3] As Ron Burt, the architect of "structural hole theory," pointed out, someone who bridges subunits that aren't linked either in the formal hierarchy or through other social networks has several sources of power:

The information benefits make Robert [Robert being someone acting as a bridge across structural holes] more likely to know when it would be valuable to bring together certain disconnected contacts, and this knowledge gives him disproportionate say in whose interests are served when the contacts do come together. In addition, the holes between his contacts enable him to broker communication while displaying different beliefs and identities to each contact. (Burt, 2002, 157)

Individuals who bridge structural holes have the opportunity to become entrepreneurs within an organization, developing new opportunities and adding value for the organization, as well as increasing their own power and rewards.

Given the complexity of social networks, we should not be surprised by the finding in a number of network studies that most managers do not have an accurate picture of the social networks of those who work for and with them. One reason is that, of the many different kinds of networks, each has its own structure and dynamics, including the following:

- Task-related networks (with whom people communicate to solve work-related problems)
- Friendship networks
- Advice networks (including mentoring relationships)

Networks are also dynamic: task-related networks change as people take on different tasks, advice networks change as career paths evolve, and even friendship networks change over time as people enter and exit groups and organizations. Just because you understand the network at one point in time does not mean you have a solid grasp of what it looks like a year later.

As more and more activities in today's organizations assign responsibilities without formal authority, however, the importance of informal network position as a source of influence has increased, and social network analysis has attracted growing attention from researchers and managers. Companies are even buying social network analysis packages from consulting firms in order to analyze their organization's networks. The amount of data required for a thorough analysis of the social networks that produce influence is large, however, even if people trust the motives of the analysis enough to answer the lengthy surveys candidly and completely. Statistical formal network analysis can be a useful tool for solving particular problems, but given the short life of the accuracy of a network map, its greatest value may lie in sensitizing managers to the complexity and importance of informal networks in their organization's capacity for getting things done.

This sensitivity to the importance of social networks and a rudimentary understanding of who the key players are in a given network can be an important resource for anyone trying to get something done in an organization.

Summary

Power in organizations derives from a number of sources (see Figure 2.9). Obviously, the more sources of power an individual has, the more power they potentially command, although the accumulation of power across sources is never simple and linear.

As Pfeffer pointed out, "An important source of power is the match between style, skills, and capacities and what is required by the context and the formal position" (Pfeffer, 1992, 77). It is true not only of the fit between personal sources of power and context, but of each potential source of power. Some sources are more important in a particular organization or context than others. In a flat, flexible, networked "new" organization, for example, influence based on informal networking is often the most important source of power, especially if it is reinforced with control of scarce resources and expertise. In a strongly hierarchical "traditional" organization, on the other hand, people in formal positions of authority are the ones best able to

---

[3] "Structural hole theory defines organizational power in terms of the information and control advantages of being the broker in relationships between actors otherwise disconnected in social networks," (Occasio, 2002, 371).

Figure 2.9 Sources of Power

Personal Characteristics

- Energy and physical stamina
- Focus
- Sensitivity to interests of others
- Flexibility
- Ability to tolerate conflict
- Ability to submerge one's ego in order to get something accomplished

Scarce and Value Expertise

Track Record

Formal Position in Organizational Hierarchy

Informal Network Position

Source: Jeffrey Pfeffer, *Managing with Power: Politics and Influence in Organizations* (Boston: Harvard Business School Press, 1992), 165–185.

---

enhance their influence through expanding their informal networks. Someone without formal authority who tries to enhance his or her influence through informal networking is apt to be punished for trying to circumvent established channels.

How can you identify who has power in an organization? Pfeffer (1992, 67–68) identified four ways to assess power:

- *Reputation:* Ask different people in the organization who has power in the organization.
- *Representational indicators:* Identify which units or groups are relatively overrepresented in important organizational roles (such as influential committees, promotions to top executive positions, etc.).
- *Observation of consequences:* Observe which units, groups, or individuals benefit most from decision making and resource allocation (on such measures as salaries, for example, or budget increases). Just as important, ask which units, groups, or individuals can keep certain issues or problems from getting attention.
- *Symbols of power:* See which units, groups, or individuals enjoy the symbolic accoutrements of power (such as spacious, attractive offices close to the center of power; outward deference from those they come in contact with; special "perks" such as memberships in the same golf club as the company CEO).

Although the specifics of any one of these categories may differ widely across organization (the symbols of power, for example, are very different in a global financial institution and a neighborhood not-for-profit organization), the categories themselves are useful and revealing. The challenge for anyone trying to take more effective action in any given organization is to match a political strategy based on an understanding of power to the organizational context and to the interests and goals that guide individual and organizational behavior. Let us look at some specific examples.

Using the Political Lens to Take More Effective Action in Organizations

1. Mapping Interests and Power

The first step in using the political lens is understanding clearly who is affected by what you want to do, what their interests are, and how much power they have to facilitate or to block what you propose to do. Jeffrey Pfeffer set out four basic questions that you need to ask:

- *Supporters:* Whose cooperation do you need to carry out your proposed action? Whose support will be necessary to get the appropriate decisions made and implemented?
- *Blockers:* Whose opposition could delay or derail what you are trying to do?
- *Potential stakeholders:* Who will be affected by what you are trying to do (e.g., in terms of how they do their work, how they are rewarded, and their power or status)?
- *Existing coalitions:* Who are the friends and allies of the people you have identified as potential supporters and blockers, and what potential interests are at stake for them?[4]

Two of the tools available to help you focus your answers are the commitment chart (Beckhart and Harris, 1987, 93–95) and the stakeholder map.

The commitment chart (see Figure 2.10) addresses the first two questions in Pfeffer's list, about supporters and blockers. It is a complete listing of the key individuals ("players") who will be involved in approving and implementing the action you want to take. It maps their current position with regard to your proposed action on a continuum from opposition ("keep it from happening") through neutrality ("let it happen") to support on two levels: assistance ("help it happen") and championing ("make it happen" by putting the full weight of their power and resources behind it). The commitment chart also indicates whether you need to change their position if your efforts are to succeed.

The second mapping tool, *stakeholder mapping*, helps you to develop an effective strategy for moving them from their current position to where you want them to be (Figure 2.11).

Stakeholder mapping helps you to identify the interests of those who will be affected by your action and how salient those interests are for them (i.e., which interests have the greatest priority for them). It also pushes you to identify more than one interest for each major stakeholder. This approach is a useful corrective to a common tendency to oversimplify the motivations of others, and to attribute to them a single-mindedness that we know would be impossible for us. It also alerts us to latent interests, or interests that stakeholders might have but of which they are not yet explicitly aware. For example, if a new CEO arrives who proclaims a new customer-focused strategy, the product design groups might be slow to recognize that they now have an interest in obtaining—or being seen to obtain—expanded customer data.

Mapping stakeholder interests provides guidance on how to convince key stakeholders that your initiative serves their interests, and then how to tailor your initiative so that it incorporates or accommodates key stakeholder interests.

2. Getting "Buy-In"

The phrases getting buy-in and sharing ownership are common in organizations, though the people who use them rarely recognize that they are talking about political processes. Getting buy-in means getting people to commit themselves to

Figure 2.10 Commitment Chart

Key Players	Keep It from Happening	Let It Happen	Help It Happen	Make It Happen
Jones		●		◆
Messier	●		◆	
Tanaka	●	◆		
Lin		●	◆	
Schmidt		●◆		

● Current position (where key player is now)

◆ Desired future position (where you want the key player to be)

---

4 These four questions are adapted from Jeffrey Pfeffer, *Managing with Power: Politics and Influence in Organizations* (Boston: Harvard Business School Press, 1992), 67–68.

Figure 2.11 Stakeholder Mapping Tool

Stakeholder	Highest Priority Interest	2nd Priority Interest	3rd Priority Interest	Late Interests (If any)
A				
B				
C				
D				

supporting or participating in a course of action begun by someone else. The most obvious path to getting buy-in is to persuade others that supporting your initiative will serve their interests, but it is not the only way. Among the additional techniques for getting buy-in are two important strategies grounded on research in social psychology: escalation of commitment and perceptions of influence.

The concept of "escalation of commitment" comes out of research on decision-making processes. Experimental studies found that people were much more likely to persist in supporting or carrying out a course of action once they committed resources (including time and attention) to it. Once they made such a commitment, they were more likely to continue their support, and even to increase it, than they were to draw back and consider alternative courses of action. In the literature on decision making, the escalation of commitment is often treated as a distortion of rational decision making that should be avoided. Its pervasiveness, however, indicates that if you can get potential supporters or stakeholders to commit even a small amount of resources to your initiative, they will be more likely to persevere in supporting you. Moreover, if you can manage to continue their allocation of resources over time, and even to increase it slightly, they are even more likely to "buy in" and sustain their commitment. Finally, if they make this commitment publicly, so that others in the organization are aware of it, they will be less likely to backslide or withdraw their support.

The second technique, perception of influence, centers on giving key stakeholders a chance to provide feedback and input on the development of an initiative. A recent study by Pfeffer and Cioldini (1998) demonstrated what they called "the illusion of influence" in a carefully constructed experiment that involved the creation of an advertisement. The subjects were divided into three groups, and given a first draft of the ad, on which they were asked to provide feedback, and then a second draft, which they were asked to evaluate. The first group was told that the team preparing the ad would not have access to the feedback on the first draft; the second group was told that they would see it but would not have time to incorporate the suggestions for improvement, and the third group was told that the second draft would reflect their suggestions. In fact, the second draft was prepared in advance and was identical for all three groups. As you might expect, the third group evaluated the ad more highly than the other two. The inescapable inference is that one way to increase the "buy-in" of stakeholders is to give them, in reality or in gesture, the feeling that they have an influence on the content or process of the course of action.

Neither of these techniques is without risk, of course. By asking for a commitment of resources, however small, you may cause a potential supporter to back off. By providing the opportunity to have some influence on a course of action, you run the risk of losing control of the initiative. Even more dangerous is the possibility that others suspect your openness to their ideas is simply a ploy to hook them into your agenda, rather than a sincere desire for their input. In such a case, their resistance to your initiative is likely to increase significantly. As with any action using the political lens, the effectiveness of your approach will depend on the accuracy and completeness of your understanding of the interests and power of those with whom you need to interact.

3. Finding Allies and Building a Coalition

Finding allies is a crucial element of a successful political strategy. A coalition is a set of allies who act together to support certain policies and activities. A coalition can be built to support a specific course of action, such as a proposal to allow business units to contract out certain support activities that are currently being performed by a corporate shared services group, or a proposal to set up a day-care center at a particular site. A more long-lasting coalition can form around common interests, such as an interest in cost reduction through outsourcing or an interest in advancing family-friendly policies. Finally, it is possible to construct general coalitions of allies who provide reciprocal support for each other's interests. One of the most common examples of a general coalition is the "dominant coalition" in an organization, which is composed of a set of upper-level executives. Each member can expect the support of the other members for his or her initiatives on the understanding that he or she will support those of the others. For example, a dominant coalition may support the family-friendly policies advocated by one of its members in exchange for a tacit agreement that this individual will not raise other contentious social responsibility issues.

The challenge in building a coalition around a specific issue is identifying potential allies whose interests will benefit from your proposed course of action, and then making them aware of your initiative and of how it will serve their interests. Both the commitment chart and stakeholder mapping can provide you with guidance in identifying potential allies and in finding out what interests are potentially compatible with your initiative. All too often, someone will initiate a course of action thinking that its virtues and advantages will be obvious to everyone, which is rarely the case in organizations. The advantages of a course of action need to be articulated, often in informal settings where frank discussions of interests and outcomes are possible. Finding allies in advance of formal decision points is an important success factor in a good political strategy.

Building longer-lasting interest-based or general coalitions requires a greater investment of attention and resources than the construction of issue-based coalitions. General coalitions are based on long-standing patterns of *reciprocity*, that is, of exchanges that over time maintain a roughly equal balance. The exchange of information and resources, mutual willingness to do favors for allies, and an agreement (tacit or explicit) not to take actions that seriously damage the interests of allies are key elements of successful coalitions.

4. Building a Network

Your informal networks are potentially your most important source of influence, both because of the resources you can mobilize by using them and because they can provide you with direct knowledge of the interests of individuals and groups elsewhere in the organization. You can greatly enhance your capacity to take action if you put time, effort, and thought into constructing and maintaining an effective network.

An effective network extends in three directions: upward, to those who are in higher positions of formal authority; horizontally, to those in adjacent units who are similar in formal position; and downward, to those who are working for you or who are engaged in tasks that have important consequences for your own work. The strategic design of the organization provides you with a set of networks in each position you occupy, through its grouping and linking systems: you have a boss to whom you report, and subordinates who report to you, and you participate in task forces and projects. You can decide, however, whether to reach beyond the links handed to you by the organization design, and whether to maintain those networks when you move to a new position. We all know people who stay in touch with key individuals they encountered on task forces, projects, and committee assignments, and who maintain a connection with their former bosses and co-workers when they move on to new positions. We also know people who take the time to seek out and build networks with people to whom they have no formal ties (e.g., their boss's administrative assistant. Some people spend time and effort identifying and bridging structural holes. The key challenge is *how* to go about effectively expanding and improving your network once you identify the opportunities.

Much of the advice on constructing effective networks adopts a set of economic metaphors: you invest in your networks through processes of exchange in multiple currencies that are traded in an organization. The exchange perspective on power and social networks has a long history (e.g., Blau, 1964), and has traditionally emphasized the importance of *reciprocity* and *trust*. Reciprocity means the shared expectation that if you do something for me, I have an obligation to return that service by doing something of importance for you. In some cases this reciprocity is direct: you do something for me, and I do something equivalent for you. In some contexts, however, the reciprocity is indirect, as in mentoring relationships: I play the role of mentor to you, and you in turn honor my efforts by being a mentor in your turn to someone more junior. As you and I establish a reputation for honoring social obligations, others will trust both of us to do the same with them.

The economic metaphor puts exchange into the context of multiple "currencies" that people value, including:

- Reward-related (including salary, bonus, promotion, assignment to interesting projects)
- Task-related (assistance, information, cooperation, and resources relevant to assigned tasks)
- Relationship-related (acceptance, inclusion, support, understanding)

- Status-related (recognition of importance, deference, "perks" that confer prestige)

You can improve your networks by understanding which currencies have most value for which actors in the organization, and taking advantage of the fact that different currencies are valued differently by different individuals and by different groups and units in the organization. For example, status-related currencies may be highly important to one unit: Whose offices host the meeting? Who presents the agenda? Another unit may place a higher value on task-related currencies, and be willing to exchange status-related currency for access to task-related information. Understanding these differences enables you to build effective exchange relationships with both groups and between them.

5. Building Your Negotiation Skills

One of the most popular courses for business school students today is negotiation. Its popularity reflects the recognition that negotiation is a central element of managerial capability in an increasingly networked organizational world. The editors of a recent volume on influence processes go so far as to assert that "an organization is essentially a negotiated relationship among many participants" (Porter, Angle, and Allen, 2003, 416–417). Negotiation skills can be developed through courses and training, through watching and learning from skills role models, and through practice.

Conclusion

The ability to analyze an organization's political system and to take effective political action—get buy-in, find allies, build a network, negotiate—is essential to getting things done in organizations. The most effective political action, however, avoids the political label. People with the best political skills rarely get defined as political "operators." Instead, their colleagues praise them as having good people skills, an ability to work with the system, and a capacity to overcome obstacles and opposition. The fundamental insights for gaining such a reputation, however, are drawn from an understanding of the political perspective on organizations. It is the least widely respected and yet perhaps the most important of the three lenses on organization.

References

Beckhard, Richard, and Reuben T. Harris. 1977. *Organizational Transitions: Managing Complex Change*. Reading, MA: Addison-Wesley Publishing Company.

Blau, Peter. 1964. *Exchange and Power in Social Life*. New York: John Wiley.

Burt, Ronald. 1992. *Structural Holes: The Social Structure of Competition*. Cambridge, MA: Harvard University Press.

Burt, Ronald. 2002. "The Social Capital of Structural Holes." In Mauro F. Guillen, Randall Collins, Paula England, and Marshall Meyer (Eds.), *The New Economic Sociology: Developments in an Emerging Field* (pp. 148–190). New York: Russell Sage Foundation.

Crozier, Michel. 1964. *The Bureaucratic Phenomenon*. Chicago: University of Chicago Press.

Fligstein, Neil. 1987. "The Intraorganizational Power Struggle: Rise of Finance Personnel to Top Leadership in Large Corporations 1919–1979." *American Sociological Review* 52, no. 1: 44–58.

Fortune. 2003. "The Power Issue," August 11.

Kanter, Rosabeth. 1979. "Power Failure in Management Circuits." *Harvard Business Review*, July–August, 65–75.

Occasio, William. 2002. "Organizational Power and Dependence." In Joel A.C. Baum (Ed.), *The Blackwell Companion to Organizations* (pp. 363–385). Oxford: Blackwell Publishers.

Pfeffer, Jeffrey. 1992. *Managing with Power: Politics and Influence in Organizations*. Boston: Harvard Business School Press.

Pfeffer, Jeffrey, and Robert D. Cioldini. 1998. "Illusions of Influence." In Robert M. Kramer and Margaret A. Neale (Eds.), *Power and Influence in Organizations*. Thousand Oaks, CA: Sage Publications.

Porter, Lyman W., Harold L. Angle, and Robert E. Allen (Eds.). 2003. *Organizational Influence Processes*, 2nd ed. Armonk, NY: M. E. Sharpe.

Powell, Walter W., and Laurel Smith-Doerr. 1993. "Networks and Economic Life." In N. Smelser and A. Hedberg (Eds.), *The Handbook of Economic Sociology* (pp. 368–402). Princeton, NJ: Princeton University Press.

Schein, Edgar H. 2003. *DEC Is Dead, Long Live DEC* (with Peter S. DeLisi, Paul J. Kampas, and Michael M. Sonduck). San Francisco: Berrett-Koehler.

Watts, Duncan. 2003. *Six Degrees: The Science of a Connected Age*. New York: W.W. Norton.

Weber, Max. 1958. "The Sociology of Charismatic Authority." In H.H. Gerth and C. Wright Mills (Eds.), *From Max Weber: Essays in Sociology* (pp. 245–252). New York: Oxford University Press.

Informal Network

The company behind the chart

by David Krackhardt and
Jeffrey R. Hanson

Many executives invest considerable resources in restructuring their companies, drawing and redrawing organizational charts only to be disappointed by the results. That's because much of the real work of companies happens despite the formal organization. Often what needs attention is the *informal* organization, the networks of relationships that employees form across functions and divisions to accomplish tasks fast. These informal networks can cut through formal reporting procedures to jump start stalled initiatives and meet extraordinary deadlines. But informal networks can just as easily sabotage companies' best laid plans by blocking communication and fomenting opposition to change unless managers know how to identify and direct them. Learning how to map these social links can help managers harness the real power in their companies and revamp their formal organizations to let the informal ones thrive.

If the formal organization is the skeleton of a company, the informal is the central nervous system driving the collective thought processes, actions, and reactions of its business units. Designed to facilitate standard modes of production, the formal organization is set up to handle easily anticipated problems. But when unexpected problems arise, the informal organization kicks in. Its complex webs of social ties form every time colleagues communicate and solidify over time into surprisingly stable networks. Highly adaptive, informal networks move diagonally and elliptically, skipping entire functions to get work done.

Managers often pride themselves on understanding how these networks operate. They will readily tell you who confers on what technical matters and who discusses office politics over lunch. What's startling is how often they are wrong. Although they may be able to diagram accurately the social links of the five or six people closest to them, their assumptions about employees outside their immediate circle are usually off the mark. Even the most psychologically shrewd managers lack critical information about how employees spend their days and how they feel about their peers. Managers simply can't be everywhere at once, nor can they read people's minds. So they're left to draw conclusions based on superficial observations, without the tools to test their perceptions.

Armed with faulty information, managers often rely on traditional techniques to control these networks. Some managers hope that the authority inherent in their titles will override the power of informal links. Fearful of any groups they can't command, they create rigid rules that will hamper the work of the informal networks. Other managers try to recruit "moles" to provide intelligence. More enlightened managers run focus groups and host retreats to "get in touch" with their employees. But such approaches won't rein in these freewheeling networks, nor will they give managers an accurate picture of what they look like.

Using network analysis, managers can translate a myriad of relationship ties into maps that show how the informal organization gets work done. Managers can get a good overall picture by diagramming three types of relationship networks:

- The advice network shows the prominent players in an organization on whom others depend to solve problems and provide technical information.

- The trust network tells which employees share political information and back one another in a crisis.

- The communication network reveals the employees who talk about work-related matters on a regular basis.

Maps of these relationships can help managers understand the networks that once eluded them and leverage these networks to solve organizational problems. Case studies using fictional

Source: Reprinted by permission of Harvard Business Review from "Informal Networks: The Company Behind the Chart," by David Krackhardt and Jeffrey R. Hanson, *Harvard Business Review*, July–August 1993. Copyright © 1993 by the Harvard Business School Publishing Corporation; all rights reserved. **David Krackhardt** is associate professor of organizations and public policy at the H. John Heinz III School of Public Policy and Management at Carnegie Mellon University. Jeffrey R. Hanson is president of J. R. Hanson & Company, a management consulting firm in Bronxville, New York.

names, based on companies with which we have worked, show how managers can bring out the strengths in their networks, restructure their formal organizations to complement the informal, and "rewire" faulty networks to work with company goals.

The Steps of Network Analysis

We learned the significance of the informal network 12 years ago while conducting research at a bank that had an 80% turnover rate among its tellers. Interviews revealed that the tellers' reasons for leaving had less to do with the bank's formal organization that with the tellers' relationships to key players in their trust networks. When these players left, the others followed in droves.

Much research had already established the influence of central figures in informal networks. Our subsequent studies of public and private companies showed that understanding these networks could increase the influence of managers outside the inner circle. If they learned who wielded power in networks and how carious coalitions functioned, they could work with the informal organizations to solve problems and improve performance.

Mapping advice networks, our research showed, can uncover the source of political conflicts and failure to achieve strategic objectives. Because these networks show the most influential players in the day-to-day operations of a company, they are useful to examine when a company is considering routine charges. Trust networks often reveal the causes of nonroutine problems such as poor performance by temporary teams. Companies should examine trust networks when implementing a major change or experiencing a crisis. The communication network can help identify gaps in information flow, the inefficient use of resources, and the failure to generate new ideas. They should be examined when productivity is low.

Managers can analyze informal networks in three steps. Step one is conducting a network survey using employee questionnaires. The survey is designed to solicit responses about who talks to whom about work, who trusts whom, and who advises whom on technical matters. It is important to pretest the survey on a small group of employ-

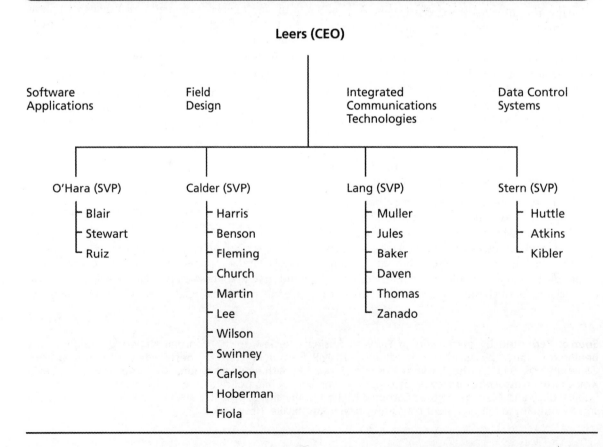

The Formal Chart Shows Who's on Top

ees to see if any questions are ambiguous or meet with resistance. In some companies, for example, employees are comfortable answering questions about friendship; others they deem such questions too personal and intrusive. The following are among the questions often asked:

- Whom do you talk to every day?
- Whom do you go to for help or advice at least once a week?
- With one day of training whose job could you step into?
- Whom would you recruit to support a proposal of yours that could be unpopular?
- Whom would you trust to keep in confidence your concerns about a work-related issue?

Some companies also find it useful to conduct surveys to determine managers' *impressions* of informal networks so that these can be compared with the actual networks revealed by the employee questionnaires. In such surveys, questions are posed like this:

- Whom do you think Steve goes to for work-related issues?
- Whom would Susan trust to keep her confidence about work-related concerns?

The key to eliciting honest answers from employees is to earn their trust. They must be assured that managers will not use their answers against them or the employees mentioned in their responses and that their immediate colleagues will not have access to the information. In general, respondents are comfortable if upper-level managers not mentioned in the surveys see the results.

After questionnaires are completed, the second step is cross-checking the answers. Some employees, worried about offending their colleagues, say that talk to everyone in the department on a daily basis. If Judy Smith says she regularly talks to Bill Johnson about work, make sure that Johnson says he talks to Smith. Managers should discount any answers not confirmed by both parties. The final map should not be based on the impressions of one employee but on the consensus of the group.

The third step is processing the information using one of several commercially available computer programs that generate detailed network maps. (Drawing maps is a laborious process that tends to result in curved lines that are difficult to read.) Maps in hand, a skilled managers can devise a strategy that plays on the strengths of the informal organization, as David Leers, the founder and CEO of a California-based computer company, found out.

Whom Do You Trust?

David Leers thought he knew his employees well. In 15 years, the company had trained a cadre of loyal professionals who had built a strong regional reputation for delivering customized office information systems (see "The Formal Chart Shows Who's on Top"). The field design group, responsible for designing and installing the systems, generated the largest block of revenues. For years it has been the linchpin of the operation, led by the company's technical superstars, with whom Leers kept in close contact.

But Leers feared that the company was losing its competitive edge by shortchanging its other divisions, such as software applications and integrated communications technologies. When members of field design saw Leers start pumping more money into these divisions, they worried about losing their privileged positions. Key employees started voicing dissatisfaction about their compensation, and Leers knew he had the makings of a morale problem that could result in defections.

To persuade employees to support a new direction for the company, Leers decided to involve them in the planning process. He formed a strategic task force composed of members of all divisions and led by a member of field design to signal his continuing commitment to the group. He wanted a leader who had credibility with his peers and was a proven performer. Eight-year company veteran Tom Harris seemed obvious for the job.

Leers was optimistic after the first meeting. Members generated good discussion about key competitive dilemmas. A month later, however, he found that the group had made little progress. Within two months, the group was completely deadlocked by members championing their own agendas. Although a highly effective manager, Leers lacked the necessary distance to identify the source of his problem.

An analysis of the company's trust and advice networks helped him get a clearer picture of the dynamics at work in the task force. The trust map turned out to be most revealing. Task force leader Tom Harris held a central position in the advice network—meaning that many employees relied on him for technical advice (see "The Advice Network Reveals the Experts"). But he had only *one* trust link with a colleague (see "But When It Comes to Trust . . ."). Leers concluded that Harris's weak position in the trust network was a main reason for the task force's inability to produce results.

In his job, Harris was able to leverage his position in the advice network to get work done quickly. As a task force leader, however, his techni-

The Advice Network Reveals the Experts

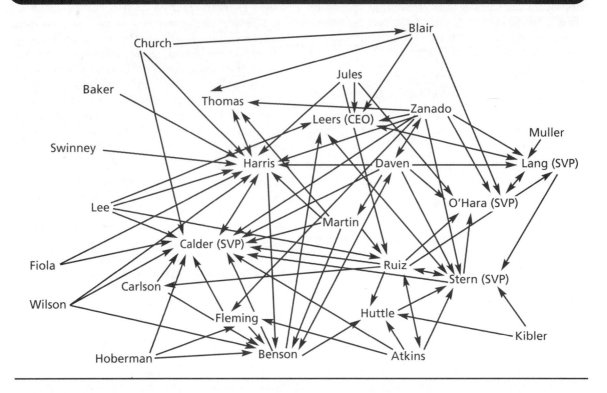

But When It Comes to Trust...

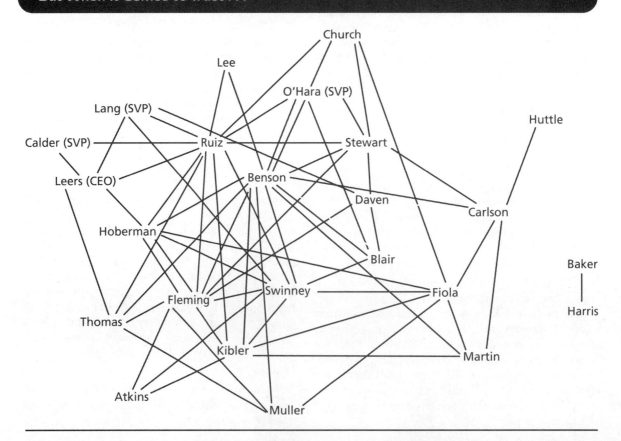

cal expertise was less important than his ability to moderate conflicting views, focus the group's thinking, and win the commitment of task force members to mutually agreed-upon strategies. Because he was a loner who took more interest in computer games than in colleagues' opinions, task force members didn't trust him to take their ideas seriously or look out for their interests. So they focused instead on defending their turf.

With this critical piece of information, the CEO crafted a solution. He did not want to undermine the original rationale of the task force by declaring it a failure. Nor did he want to embarrass a valued employee by summarily removing him as task force head. Any response, he concluded, had to run with the natural grain of the informal organization. He decided to redesign the team to reflect the inherent strengths of the trust network.

Referring to the map, Leers looked for someone in the trust network who could share responsibility with Harris. He chose Bill Benson, a warm, amiable person who occupied a central position in the network and with whom Harris had already established a solid working relationship. He publicly justified his decision to name two task force heads as necessary, given the time pressures and scope of the problem.

Within three weeks, Leers could see changes in the group's dynamics. Because task force members trusted Benson to act in the best interest of the entire group, people talked more openly and let go of their fixed positions. During the next two months, the task force made significant progress in proposing a strategic direction for the company. And in the process of working together, the task force helped integrate the company's divisions.

A further look at the company's advice and trust networks uncovered another serious problem, this time with the head of field design, Jim Calder.

The CEO had appointed Calder manager because his colleagues respected him as the most technically accomplished person in the division. Leers thought Calder would have the professional credibility to lead a diverse group of very specialized design consultants. This is a common practice in professional service organizations: make your best producer the manager. Calder, however, turned out to be a very marginal figure in the trust network. His managerial ability and skills were

How the CEO Views the Trust Network

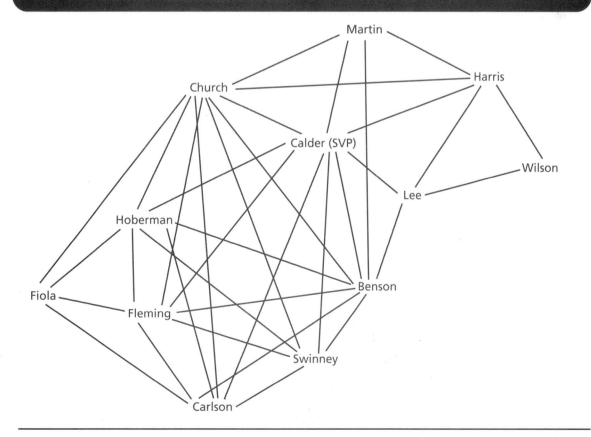

The Trust Network According to Calder

Fleming ——————————————————— Hoberman

sorely lacking, which proved to be a deficit that outweighed the positive effects derived from his technical expertise. He regularly told people they were stupid and paid little attention to their professional concerns.

Leers knew that Calder was no diplomat, but he had no idea to what extent the performance and morale of the group were suffering as a result of Calder's tyrannical management style. In fact, a map based on Leers's initial perceptions of the trust network put Calder in the central position (see "How the CEO Views the Trust Network"). Leers took for granted that Calder had good personal relationships with the people on his team. His assumption was not unusual. Frequently, senior managers presume that formal work ties will yield good relationships over time, and they assume that if *they* trust someone, others will too.

The map of Calder's perceptions was also surprising (see "The Trust Network According to Calder"). He saw almost no trust links in his group at all. Calder was oblivious to *any* of the trust dependencies emerging around him—a worrisome characteristic for a manager.

The information in these maps helped Leers formulate a solution. Again, he concluded that he needed to change the formal organization to reflect the structure of the informal network. Rather than promoting or demoting Calder, Leers cross-promoted him to an elite "special solutions team," reporting directly to the CEO. His job involved working with highly sophisticated clients on specialized problems. The position took better advantage of Calder's technical skills and turned out to be good for him socially as well. Calder, Leers learned, hated dealing with the formal management responsibilities and the pressure of running a group.

Leers was now free to promote John Fleming, a tactful, even-tempered employee, to the head of field design. A central player in the trust network, Fleming was also influential in the advice network. The field group's performance improved significantly over the next quarter, and the company was able to create a highly profitable revenue stream through the activities of Calder's new team.

Whom Do You Talk To?

When it comes to communication, more is not always better, as the top management of a large East Coast bank discovered. A survey showed that customers were dissatisfied with the information they were receiving about bank services. Branch managers, top managers realized, were not communicating critical information about available services to tellers. As a result, customers' questions were not answered in a timely fashion.

Management was convinced that more talking among parties would improve customer service and increase profits. A memo was circulated ordering branch managers to "increase communication flow and coordination within and across branches and to make a personal effort to increase the amount and effectiveness of their own interpersonal communications with their staffs."

A study of the communication networks of 24 branches, however, showed the error of this thinking. *More* communication ties did not distinguish the most profitable branches; the *quality* of communication determined their success. Nonhierarchical branches, those with two-way communication between people of all levels, were 70% more profitable than branches with one-way communication patterns between "superiors" and staff.

The communication networks of two branches located in the same city illustrated this point. Branch 1 had a central figure, a supervisor, with whom many tellers reported communicating about their work on a daily basis. The supervisor confirmed that employees talked to her, but she reported communicating with only half of these tellers about work-related matters by the end of the day. The tellers, we later learned, resented this one-way communication flow. Information they viewed as critical to their success flowed up the organization but not down. They complained that the supervisor was cold and remote and failed to keep them informed. As a result, productivity suffered.

In contrast, Branch 2 had very few one-way communication lines but many mutual, two-way lines. Tellers in this branch said they were well-informed about the normal course of work flow and reported greater satisfaction with their jobs.

After viewing the communication map, top management abandoned the more-is-better strategy and began exploring ways of fostering mutual communication in all the branches. In this case, management did not recast the formal structure of the branches. Instead, it opted to improve relationships within the established framework. The bank sponsored mini-seminars in the branches, in which the problems revealed by the maps were openly discussed. These consciousness-raising sessions spurred many supervisors to communicate more substantive information to tellers. District managers were charged with coming up with their own strategies for improving communication. The bank surveyed employees at regular intervals to see if their supervisors were informed of the results.

The communication network of a third branch surfaced another management challenge: the branch had divided itself into two distinct groups, each with its own culture and mode of operation. The network map showed that one group had evolved into the "main branch," consisting of tellers, loan officers, and administrative staff. The other group was kind of a "sub-branch," made up primarily of tellers and administrators. It turned out that the sub-branch staff worked during non-peak and Saturday hours, while main-branch employees worked during the peak and weekday hours. The two cultures never clashed because they rarely interacted.

The groups might have coexisted peacefully if customers had not begun complaining about the sub-branch. The main-branch staff, they reported, was responsive to their needs, while the sub-branch staff was often indifferent and even rude. Sub-branch employees, it turned out, felt little loyalty to the bank because they didn't feel part of the organization. They were excluded from staff meetings, which were scheduled in the morning, and they had little contact with the branch manager, who worked a normal weekday shift.

The manager, who was embedded in the main branch, was not even aware that this distinct culture existed until he saw the communication network map. His challenge was to unify the two groups. He decided not to revamp the formal structure, nor did he mount a major public-relations campaign to integrate the two cultures, fearing that each group would reject the other because the existing ties among its members were so strong. Instead, he opted for a stealth approach. He exposed people from one group to people from the other in the hopes of expanding the informal network. Although such forced interaction does not guarantee the emergence of stable networks, more contact increases the likelihood that some new ties will stick.

Previously planned technical training programs for tellers presented the opportunity to initiate change. The manager altered his original plans for on-site training and opted instead for an off-site facility, even though it was more expensive. He sent mixed groups of sub-branch and main-branch employees to programs to promote gradual, neutral interaction and communication. Then he followed up with a series of selective "staff swaps" whereby he shifted work schedules temporarily. When someone from the main branch called in sick or was about to go on vacation, he elected a substitute from the sub-branch. And he rescheduled the staff meetings so that all employees could attend.

This approach helped unify the two cultures, which improved levels of customer satisfaction with the branch as a whole over a six-month period. By increasing his own interaction with the sub-branch, the manager discovered critical information about customers, procedures, and data systems. Without even realizing it, he had been making key decisions based on incomplete data.

Network Holes and Other Problems

As managers become more sophisticated in analyzing their communication networks, they can use them to spot five common configurations. None of these are inherently good or bad, functional or dysfunctional. What matters is the *fit*, whether networks are in sync with company goals. When the two are at odds, managers can attempt to broaden or reshape the informal networks using a variety of tactics.

Imploded relationships. Communication maps often show departments that have few links to other groups. In these situations, employees in a department spend all their time talking among themselves and neglect to cultivate relationships with the rest of their colleagues. Frequently, in such cases, only the most senior employees have ties with people outside their areas. And they may hoard these contracts by failing to introduce these people to junior colleagues.

To counter this behavior, one manager implemented a mentor system in which the senior employees were responsible for introducing their apprentices to people in other groups who could help them do their jobs. Another manager instituted a policy of picking up the tab for "power breakfasts," as long as the employees were from different departments.

Irregular communication patterns. The opposite pattern can be just as troubling. Sometimes employees communicate only with members of other groups and not among themselves. To foster camaraderie, one manager sponsored seasonal sporting events with members of the "problem group" assigned to the same team. Staff meetings can also be helpful if they're really used to share the resources and exchange important information about work.

A lack of cohesion resulting in factionalism suggests a more serious underlying problem that requires bridge building. Initiating discussions among peripheral players in each faction can help uncover the root of the problem and suggest solutions. These parties will be much less resistant to compromise than the faction leaders, who will feel more impassioned about their positions.

Fragile structures. Sometimes group members communicate only among themselves and with employees in one other division. This can be problematic when the contribution of several areas is necessary to accomplish work quickly and spawn creativity. One insurance company manager, a naturally gregarious fellow, tried to broaden employees' contracts by organizing meetings and cocktail parties for members of several divisions. Whenever possible, he introduced employees he thought should be cultivating working relationships. Because of his warm, easygoing manner, they didn't find his methods intrusive. In fact, they appreciated his personal interest in their careers.

Holes in the network. A map may reveal obvious network holes, places you would expect to find relationship ties but don't. In a large corporate law firm, for example, a group of litigators was not talking to the firm's criminal lawyers, a state of affairs that startled the senior partner. To begin tackling this problem, the partner posed complex problems to criminal lawyers that only regular consultations with litigators could solve. Again, arranging such interactions will not ensure the formation of enduring relationships, but continuous exposure increases the possibility.

"Bow ties." Another common trouble spot is the bow tie, a network in which many players are dependent on a single employee but not on each other. Individuals at the center knot of a bow tie have tremendous power and control within the network, much more than would be granted them on a formal organizational chart. If the person at the knot leaves, connections between isolated groups can collapse. If the person remains, organizational processes tend to become rigid and slow, and the individual is often torn between the demands of several groups. To undo such a knot, one manager self-consciously cultivated a stronger relationship with the person at the center. It took the pressure off the employee, who was no longer a lone operative, and it helped to diffuse some of his power.

In general, managers should help employees develop relationships within the informal structure that will enable them to make valuable contributions to the company. Managers need to guide employees to cultivate the right mix of relationships. Employees can leverage the power of informal relationships by building both strong ties, relationships with a high frequency of interaction, and weak ties, those with a lower frequency. They can call on the latter at key junctures to solve organizational problems and generate new ideas.

Testing the solution. Managers can anticipate how a strategic decision will affect the informal organization by simulating network maps. This is particularly valuable when a company wants to anticipate reactions to change. A company that wants to form a strategic SWAT team that would remove key employees from the day-to-day operations of a division, for example, can design a map of the area without those players. If removing the central advice person from the network leaves the division without a group of isolates, the manager should reconsider the strategy.

Failure to test solutions can lead to unfortunate results. When the trust network map of a bank showed a loan officer to be an isolate, the manager jumped to the conclusion that the officer was expendable. The manager was convinced that he could replace the employee, a veteran of the company, with a younger, less expensive person who was more of a team player.

What the manager had neglected to consider was how important this officer was to the company's day-to-day operations. He might not have been a prime candidate for a high-level strategy team that demanded excellent social skills, but his expertise, honed by years of experience, would have been impossible to replace. In addition, he had cultivated a close relationship with the bank's largest client—something an in-house network map would never have revealed. Pictures don't tell the whole story; network maps are just one tool among many.

The most important change for a company to anticipate is a complete overhaul of its formal structure. Too many companies fail to consider how such a restructuring will affect their informal organizations. Managers assume that if a company eliminates layers of bureaucracy, the informal organization will simply adjust. It will adjust all right, but there's no guarantee that it will benefit the company. Managers would do well to consider what type of redesign will play on the inherent strengths of key players and give them the freedom to thrive. Policies should allow all employees easy access to colleagues who can help them carry out tasks quickly and efficiently, regardless of their status or area of jurisdiction.

Experienced network managers who can use maps to identify, leverage, and revamp informal networks will become increasingly valuable as companies continue to flatten and rely on teams. As organizations abandon hierarchical structures, managers will have to rely less on the authority inherent in their title and more on their relationships with players in their informal networks. They will need to focus less on overseeing employees "below" them and more on managing people across functions and disciplines. Understanding relationships will be the key to managerial success.

The Cultural Lens

Overview

The cultural perspective on organizations takes issue with a good deal of conventional managerial thought on how to run a business. It is a complex perspective that emphasizes the inherent limitations of managerial authority and influence and rejects claims that strictly structural, rational, or interest factors best describe or explain human behavior. A cultural perspective focuses on social and personal identities carried by people, the cognitive or mental maps they utilize to come to terms with the requirements and difficulties they face in their day-to-day activities, and the moral precepts and normative standards they take for granted but nonetheless bring to bear on the world and those around them. Attention is directed to such matters as the ideas and skills individuals and groups hold, display, and value; the reasons or motives people accept as legitimate accounts for their actions and thus enact in their ordinary affairs; the special languages and expressions they cultivate and use; the boundaries they recognize to mark membership in various social groupings and the networks of trust to which they belong that wax and wane within, across; and often beyond work organizations. Cultural understandings are collectively shaped and rooted in the past and, as a result, are often difficult to surface and articulate because they are so taken-for-granted as natural, obvious, habituated, and unquestionable by organizational members.

The cultural perspective emphasizes what it is that people must learn to become fully functioning and accepted organizational members. Underlying such an emphasis is an appreciation for the situationally specific character of individual and collective action—that people take action only on the basis of what a specific situation means to them. Assigning meaning is of course an interpretive act and therefore rests on cultural understandings because the terms, labels, concepts, and languages we have available to us to make sense of the world come from the social and not physical or biological world. The cultural perspective on organizations focuses then on the meanings people assign to their respective work experiences. People are thus more than cogs in a machine, nodes in a network, sources of intellectual capital or self-interested political actors. They are more importantly meaning makers, identity carriers, moral actors, symbol users, storytellers who are actively engaged in organizational life and, through interaction with one another, they continually create, sustain and modify organizational events, processes and products.

Assignment Summary

1. Come to class having read and fully digested the Class Note on the cultural lens and Shein's article, "Organizational Culture."
2. Be prepared to participate in a cultural diagnostic exercise of a particular organizational culture. Your instructor will identify the targeted culture, most likely your school culture, and direct you to assemble some artifacts of that culture.

The Centrality of Symbolism

The concern for meaning in organizations focuses attention on such matters as values, languages, beliefs, founding legends, social norms, myths, rituals, mental frameworks or maps, metaphors, superstitions and ideologies shared by a few, many or all organizational members. Meanings guide behavior. The key to the cultural perspective is not meaning *per se* but the symbol—a more or less arbitrary but conventionalized sign that stands for something else. Symbols are vehicles for meaning. A symbol such as a corporate logo or a marketing slogan may stand for a particular company or a public claim of quality. They may also invoke notions of personal identification and honor to some and alienation and distrust to others. The symbol is the unit on which the cultural perspective rests and decoding what a given symbol or set of symbols means to a specific group of people is what cultural analysis is all about.

Symbols carry both denotative and connotative meanings. *Denotative meanings* refer to the direct, instrumental uses of a symbol, such as an annual report as standing for the performance of a given firm. *Connotative meanings* refer to the expressive, more general, and broader uses of a symbol, as in the annual report standing for a firm's meticulous record keeping and its concern for the financial well-being of its stockholders. The two are not unrelated or necessarily stable, however. Take, for example, the financial reporting practices of major U.S. companies. Up to, say, the year 2000, those companies such as Intel who apparently always met or exceeded their projected quarterly or annual revenue and profit goals were the darlings of Wall Street. Yet when the false reporting scandals shook the investment community, those firms who never missed their paper targets were under closer scrutiny and the meaning of financial reports began to shift. What had been viewed as superlative came to assume new and more problematic meaning. To take a cultural perspective on organizations is to treat symbolism seriously and learn how meanings are created, communicated, enforced, contested, and sometimes changed by individuals and groups interacting both inside and outside the organization.

At least four interconnected areas need to be explored when the workings of a given symbol are at issue. First, symbols—both material (e.g., buildings, products, machines) and ideational (e.g., values, norms, ideologies)—are cultural objects or artifacts whose form, appearance, logic, and type can be categorized (although category systems differ and some differ spectacularly). Second, symbols are produced and used by identified (and self-identifying) people and groups within (and beyond) organizations for certain purposes and thus the intentions of the symbol creators and users must be understood. Third, symbols are always put forth within a particular historical period and social context, which severely shapes and limits the possible meanings a symbol may carry. Finally, symbols typically mean different things to different groups of people so the receptive competencies and expectations of those who come into contact with given symbols must be examined. Because each domain plays off the others, the interpretation of symbols—even simple ones—can be complicated.

Take, for example, the Big Mac as a symbol of interest. Consider the audience first. To some McDonald's patrons, the Big Mac is the quintessential American meal, a popular and desirable hamburger served up in a timely and tasty fashion. To others, the Big Mac is food without nourishment, a travesty of a healthy meal and a cause of obesity. To still others, the Big Mac is a sterile and unappetizing sign of the McDonaldization of society in which vast capital resources, advanced technologies, and those rapacious fast-food principles of efficiency, calculability, and predictability serve to drive out competition and homogenize services and products well beyond the local hamburger stand. But social context is of considerable importance too. A Big Mac in Jerusalem is simply not the same cultural object as a Big Mac in Boston. Nor is the history of the Big Mac irrelevant to its current meaning because this more or less edible symbol has been around for some 50 years and comes packed with consumer myths, production rules, social standing, snappy advertising, and associated symbols all cross-referenced to an uncountable number of life's little pleasures: "We love to make you smile" and "You deserve a break today." Some of this symbolism is by design, some accidental, and some highly circumstantial and fleeting. A cultural perspective directs attention to how context helps shape meaning; how symbols are created, packaged and, in a variety of ways, understood; how connotative meanings grow from denotative ones, and vice versa; and, centrally, how various audiences receive and decode symbols and then act on the basis of the meaning the symbols hold for them.

The interpretation of symbols is at the heart of the cultural perspective on organizations—whether the organization of interest is a small and relatively autonomous work group within a corporation or a huge multinational firm operating in diverse social, linguistic, and political contexts around the world. Symbolism is also central to any concern for communication in organizations because communication itself rests on a coding framework that is shared by at least some if not all organizational members. Symbolism reaches into all aspects of organizational behavior because it is the process by which all organizational activities, ceremonies, objects, products, stories, services, roles, goals, strategies, and so on are made sensible and hence logical and perhaps desirable to given audiences both inside and outside recognized organizational boundaries. Leadership can therefore be seen as symbolic action as can other organizational influence attempts such as selection practices, training rituals, and distribution of rewards. From a cultural perspective, symbolism is the elementary or fundamental process that makes organizational behavior both possible and meaningful.

Toward a Working Definition of Culture

Culture is to social scientists as the concept of life is to biologists, or force is to physicists, or god is to theologians. It is without doubt one of the most complex and contentious concepts at play in everyday and scholarly life. In its broadest anthropological sense, culture refers to a way of life shared by members of a given society and includes knowledge, belief, art, morals, law, custom, and any other abilities and habits acquired by members of that society. Viewing culture generally as a "way of life" passed from one generation to the next avoids the ethnocentrism and elitism associated with definitions that flow from the arts and humanities (i.e., "culture as the best that has been thought, known, and produced"). But, alas, such a broad definition lacks precision and focus.

The current trend is toward trimming the culture concept down and making explicit distinctions about what exactly is to be the object of cultural analysis. Take the useful distinction between cultural *products* and cultural *processes* as an illustration. Cultural products are tangible social constructions, symbolic goods, or commodities that are explicitly produced—business cards, TV sit-coms, or a raise and promotion handed out in a corporate setting. Cultural processes are more general, implicit features of social life itself that underlie and prefigure such products, such as the ways Japanese and Americans handle business cards, the ways gender roles are constructed and understood within a society, or the ways performance appraisals are conducted, interpreted, and used in different companies. The distinction between product and process helps not because one conception of culture is somehow deeper or more real than another but because the distinction itself helps sort out the many ways to approach culture.

It is important also to distinguish culture from structure although the two are intricately related. Structure represents those institutional conditions—both social and material—that characterize and more or less direct the communal, economic and political life of a given society (organization or group). Culture represents the values, beliefs, norms, and so forth that provide meaning and legitimacy—albeit, imperfectly—to such patterns. The fit between structure and culture is, in theory, a close one. Harmony, not opposition, is ordinarily the rule, at least in settled times. Societies (organizations or groups) that persist are those in which structure and culture are more or less aligned and something of a balance is maintained over time through a process of mutual accommodation. As culture shifts, so too does structure. The reverse is true as well because structural change implies, however slow, cultural change. One without the other is incomplete and usually a recipe for trouble.

Does culture lead or follow structural shifts? A good deal of ink has been spent on this question, but the best answer seems to be a timid one: "It all depends." In some cases, structural changes precede cultural ones, creating the proverbial cultural lag. Work redesign projects that rely heavily on "virtual forms of organization" provide a convenient example in this regard. Rapid technological improvements and massive capital investments have made high-speed, high-power and, to varying degrees, user-friendly computers accessible to vast numbers of people in organizations. In theory, communications across individuals and groups in the organization have been vastly enhanced such that geographically separate units within the organization are far better able to plan, coordinate and accomplish their work, and increased productivity and performance result. But the everyday use of virtual systems to organize the work of dispersed individuals and groups has typically lagged far behind their availability and presumed economic value. For many workers and managers alike, computers and the virtual worlds they promise seemingly threaten to obliterate established and comfortable cultural meanings, routines, and relationships in the workplace.

On the other hand, examples of culture leading structure are not hard to find. Perhaps the most famous example is Max Weber's analysis of the role of the Protestant Ethic as the foundational "spirit" of capitalism. Consider too cultural sources of organizational innovation of the ideational sort pushed by charismatic business figures ("gurus") such as Jack Welch and Tom Peters; or popular business school programs that offer state-of-the-art MBA and executive education programs; or bands of true-believers that form social movements devoted to advancing such ideas as business reengineering or e-business models in organizations; or those in highly visible and expensive consulting firms who sell similar (re)organization analysis and advice across organizational boundaries. These cultural innovations emerge and (arguably) prosper without any obvious structural push. Of course, the pull is not always apparent either. Take, for instance, the widespread belief in the United States that women deserve equal pay for equal work. Even though the culture has seemingly shifted, the wage structure and institutional arrangements that would support such a structure are slow to catch up; women continue to earn far less than their male counterparts. The connection between structure and culture is not one to be reduced to formula.

Culture is indeed a multidimensional concept and can be used in a number of ways. The term covers much ground and takes on many different shades of meaning. Precisely because it is such an all-purpose label, however, any discussion of culture must be definitionally clear. As a working definition for the sections that follow, *culture* refers to the symbolic or expressive side of human life—actions, objects, and ideas that carry specific meanings to particular people and groups and hence stand for something. In short, culture provides a template on which meanings are read and actions are based. It is attached to both the material and immaterial, to words and deeds and it shapes and reflects social and material conditions. To take a cultural perspective is to consider the historically grounded pattern of meanings that guide the thinking, feeling, and behavior of the members of some identified group.

Organizational Culture

How does culture affect the way people deal with one another at work or the way organizations, *writ* large, manage to get things done in a world that is increasingly interconnected? People who work for profit-seeking firms ordinarily think of themselves as serious, practical types who are trying only to get the job done, beef up the bottom line or, more often than not, fix this or that problem so the organization as they know it will function more smoothly. Yet, even as practical types, men and women of the corporation must inevitably deal with the symbolic and expressive side of organizational life. Making deals, establishing or meeting goals and standards, and getting products out the door are complicated everywhere and always by the fact that these activities must be accomplished collectively. Business organizations are social systems in which people must do things together and therefore the management of meaning is as central to this collective task as is the management of money, production, and sales.

Organizations are positioned within and across cultures, but they also produce cultures of their own. Owners, workers, managers, customers, suppliers, legislators, and so on all participate in the creation and consumption of cultural products and processes that both help and hinder the workings of an organization. Moreover, culturally specific meanings are constructed within and across many levels of potential organizational analysis (e.g., individual and small work groups; larger clusters of employees such as departments, divisions, functional units, project teams, unions, and various other associational groups; and the organization as a whole as it is nested within sets of other organizations at home and abroad). Each conceptual level raises distinct questions of cultural relevance. Consider, first, the face-to-face or so-called micro levels of organizational culture.

Culture and Control

How does a boss get people to work hard, to coordinate what they do with others, to put themselves out for the good of the group or, in general, to do things they might not otherwise do if left to themselves? These quintessential top-down problems are faced by all organizations, from the Mom-and-Pop convenience store to the multinational corporation. Coercive theories hold that most people will respond accordingly only when management holds a (symbolic) whip over their backs. The exercise of raw force is, of course, more than a little inefficient not to mention inhumane and illegal. Running an organization as a forced labor camp or maximum-security prison is simply not an option for most business organizations.

Exchange theories hold that most people work for tangible rewards like money and the things that money will buy. Desire usually outstrips the means people possess so they will work harder for more pay. Still, however plausible these economic incentive or material reward theories appear on the surface (countless varieties of them), they do not seem to work very well. Numerous studies of work units have shown, for example, that groups develop their own standards for appropriate and reasonable behavior and, over time, manage to set and enforce their own internal rates of production—ones that are considered just and comfortable by most members of a work group. Regardless of what management might do to try to increase production, group members stick to their rates and ordinarily resist change. Group members who overproduce are shunned as rate busters; those who underproduce are usually aided by other members of the group to keep production rates at reasonable levels (from the perspective of the work group) even though it is often not in the self-interest of individual group members to do so.

From a cultural perspective, what occurs in such situations is the creation of highly specific work norms and practices at odds with managerial ideals. Such cultural inventions may be highly unstable or relatively fixed. Members of a given work unit may share a good many norms and practices with others in the organization or very few, but subversion of managerial objectives by small groups of employees occurs virtually everywhere in the world. If sheer economic incentives or the coercive imposition of rules and regulations cannot be used to predictably move people in managerially desired directions, what does work? Managers in organizations have tried a variety of methods and, at root, all involve attempts to forge a type of organizational culture (at various levels and segments of the organization) that values hard work and respect for managerially approved objectives.

One way to deal with motivational issues is to try to alter organizational structure in the hope that the culture will follow. Changing the organizational chart from one that is tall and thin to one that is short and fat is an illustration of trying to build a managerial approved work culture that conceivably might increase communications across the organization and reduce status differences among employees. Local rationalities might then give way to an organizational rationality. It might also bring the average employee closer to the centers of control and decision making in the organization thus, in the language of the day, "empowering" them. The greater influence employees have over what happens in the firm or, more critically, in their own segments of the firm, the more employees will presumably identify with and contribute to the goals of the organization.

Another way of tackling motivational problems is to try to create a preferred kind of organizational culture directly by recruitment, selection, training, placement, and long-term career development programs and promises. These tactics seems particularly favored by many Japanese companies noted—in Western eyes—for their intense, within-firm socialization practices and their surprisingly robust lifetime employment practices that persist despite economic downturns. Similar practices are not unknown elsewhere of course. Indeed many variants of Japanese practices can be seen in U.S. organizations, and vice versa, although few if any adopt a full version of the Japanese system. Disneyland is an example of an organization that relies heavily on trying to select ride operators for the park who are viewed by their peers as cheerful and extroverted and then training them both formally and informally to perform their "on-stage" work roles with as much enthusiasm as they can muster so that the explicit corporate goal of generating happy customers can be met. When service is the product that is, in fact, being sold, building a concern—real or faked—among employees for the customers' comfort and pleasure is quite likely to be at the core of an organization's culture.

A third way to motivate employees in managerially approved directions is to promote conceptual models of thought and action for employees to follow. Lobbies of corporate offices may be decorated with pictures of "employees of the month" or sales organizations may publicly honor those high performers who exceed their quotas for the year. If such ceremonial events and ritualized rewards are not overused, honored employees may become models of desirable behavior for other members of the organization to emulate. Other models for behavior come from the stories repeatedly told on formal occasions (e.g., orientation sessions, company training events, reward ceremonies, etc.) or conveyed, usually more effectively, by the informal exchanges that occur among employees in and out of the workplace about exemplary behavior—the telephone lineman who braved a flood to restore service to an isolated community or the computer technician who worked through the night to discover and rectify a bug in a system for an important client. Such tales, managers often assume, help create organizational loyalties and motivate employees in the proper direction.

It is the case of course that not all stories are exemplars in the eyes of either management or the workforce. Tales about insensitive bosses, managerial stupidities, troublesome co-workers and customers from hell (and what to do about them) are also common in organizations and they too play a role in shaping organizational cultures. Many stories circulate in organizations. Some filter up from the bottom, some ooze from the middle, and some trickle down from the top. Censorship is virtually impossible in this domain and the would-be culture shapers of the organization can only do so much to encourage what from their (varied) perspective(s) are appropriate lines of behavior. In this sense, organizational culture can be venerated or berated, loved or blamed. It is quite possible for members of an organization at all levels to be quite unhappy with the work culture of which they are a part but feel powerless to alter. Culture need not always be popular.

Perhaps most critical in terms of building organizational culture at the face-to-face level is what employees—particularly managers—pay attention to in their day-to-day dealings with others in the organization. An obsessive focus on quarterly returns (and reports) may produce a culture with little concern for long-run profitability. A sales or marketing driven company is distinguishable from one geared to manufacturing. What is consistently encouraged (or discouraged) as "the way we do things around here" can be expected to become the norm. Some actions may become so taken-for-granted as the "natural" way to go about one's work that members of the organization no longer consider alternative actions. Culture is thus habit and it is in this sense that culture is a blueprint for behavior.

All the preceding means for motivating organizational members are usually in operation simultaneously. Many high-tech companies, for example, favor an organizational structure that is decentralized, project-centered, rather vague as to who is to do what, and continually in flux. Such a structure is more or less compatible with a faith in professional independence and self-management (i.e., the chain of command is not considered to be important), with norms encouraging information sharing and consensual decision making (i.e., positions and functions are not believed to be necessarily aligned with needed expertise), and a strong emphasis on profit-oriented creativity and entrepreneurial advocacy (i.e., too much bureaucracy is thought to stifle innovation). Control in such contexts is primarily normative and put in place by selection, socialization, stories, rewards of many sorts beyond the monetary, models of exemplary behavior, rituals of solidarity, and everyday routines. To a large degree, managers in such contexts tend to be quite aware of the norms they wish to foster in the organization and thus self-consciously promote an organizational culture to serve what they take to be the firm's best interest.

Subculture and Segmentation

Moving beyond managerially influenced work units and cultures, consider now the presence of subcultures within and across organizations. Subcultures are groups of people who share common identities based on characteristics that often transcend or override their organizationally prescribed roles and relationships. Subcultures emerge more or less autonomously in all organizational settings and influence the behavior of organizational members in a variety of ways. As noted, groups of people who work together produce their own cultural understandings but cultural production in organizations is not confined strictly to fixed work positions and units. The larger social context in which people live beyond the organization can be expected to play a role, and here is where the idea of subculture is most relevant. For example, even though ethnicity is not supposed to count when performing a particular job, it certainly counts in the external world and members of different groups bring different cultures with them to work. Employee subcultures may then form along class or ethnic lines because cultural similarities are strongly felt and people are drawn to others who share their meaning systems.

One of the most powerful divisions influencing subcultural development in organizations occurs between management and labor. Like non-commissioned soldiers and officers in the army, business firms usually draw clear lines between workers and managers. Symbolism reinforces the divide: the executive lounge, the worker's cafeteria; the manager's monthly salary, the worker's hourly wage; the suit and tie, the work shirt and hardhat; and so forth. The labor/management divide is also dependent on the larger social context within which a firm is located. In a relatively homogeneous society like Japan, company unions and worker-manager socializing may help bridge the gap. In Britain, class consciousness may sustain and harden the gap that is bridged, if at all, primarily by institutional means lodged outside the organization—in law, by labor negotiations, by religious beliefs, through education. In a relatively healthy and highly individualized society like the United States where most working people—regardless of their position—view themselves as middle class, ethnicity may help bridge the gap in some cases and amplify it in other cases.

Subcultural groupings may also emerge from occupational interests and education backgrounds. Often these reflect functional boundaries in organizations—accountants working with other accountants, machinists with machinists, programmers with programmers, carpenters with carpenters, and so forth. Subcultural ties and interests are thus deepened. Some organizations may represent rather loose coalitions of occupational communities whose members share little sense of belonging to the same organizational culture but nonetheless display a fierce loyalty and commitment to their own vocational enclave. Managers too may develop their own sense of culture beyond that of their employing organization. Such a subculture is based on class interests, common work experiences, similar management training and, importantly, opportunities for interaction and exchange across internal and external organizational boundaries. Even among managers, though, different cultures are possible. Top corporate executives may focus primarily on their fiduciary responsibilities to shareholders and thus emphasize their fiscal duties whereas line managers may regard day-to-day operations of greatest concern and worry most about "moving product" through the organization. Engineering managers may regard their tasks as primarily technical and take their notions of management from professional (and external) role models. Thus even within management circles multiple cultures may appear.

In general, a focus on subcultures emphasizes a segmentalist or cleavage model of organizational culture. The classic fault line is between labor and management but gender, religion, ethnicity, age, occupation, organizational function (e.g., engineering versus marketing), and so on can foster comparable subcultures of conflicting perspectives and actions. Subcultures, however, may be less stable and predictable these days than in times past. Fragmentation seems to be on the move. Many firms today are riddled with shifting and inconsistent goals and strategies. Work procedures and policies are often up for grabs. Many if not most firms are in the midst of responding to the rapid structural, technical, environmental, and even cultural changes taking place in the social and economic spheres that surround them. Internal shake-ups, downsizings, reorganizations, mergers, and acquisitions (with their persistent absorption dilemmas) are common. Employees in many organizations move continually from one collaborative, perhaps cross-functional, work unit to another. Projects, not departments, define work identities. People come and go in organizations making attachments to any given work unit uncertain at best. In such settings, one will undoubtedly find numerous and competing versions of what constitutes appropriate lines of action.

Some observers of organizational life—particularly in the West—argue that the increased fragmentation at work and the understandably diminished loyalty employees offer to their respective organizations reflect a radical cultural shift in the meaning of the organization itself. The argument suggests that we have moved from viewing the work organization as a bounded, corporate entity, a collective "body" akin to a small yet sacrosanct society, to viewing the organization as hollow fiction, having no natural or fixed boundaries and consisting of nothing more than a "bundle of contracts" among individuals each subject to rapid revision or termination. Talk about an embracing or unifying organizational culture in this context becomes highly suspect.

Less speculatively and perhaps more to the point, people within organizations—fragmented or not—are capable of taking multiple perspectives on what they do. A single employee is not so much an organization type (an IBM, BMW, or Mitsubishi man or woman) or a member of a single identity group within the organization (a saleswoman, financial analyst, or engineer) as the individual is a repository for different cultural perspectives Take, for instance, a married, politically liberal, African American woman with three young children who is a practicing Catholic and is currently working in the equity trading division of a large, multinational bank. Different issues that arise in the workplace tap different identities. A dispute over a particular stock issue may find her lined up with analysts in her work group arguing vigorously that the firm should move quickly in a specific manner against higher-ups in the company who push for caution and further study. On a question of company-sponsored childcare, she may line up with others who share her family interests and liberal leanings. Or, if the bank suddenly flounders in the market place, she may be willing to take a less desirable position in the firm or a salary freeze and try to ride out the economic downturn as a quiet and conforming company woman. The cultural perspective suggests that rather than try to find a single organizational culture (or most salient subculture) to explain individual or group behavior, the best approach may be to look for the kinds of issues that call up different meaning systems or cultures for the person or collectivity involved.

Organizations and Cultural Contexts

Thus far, we have considered culture as played out within membership boundaries of organizations. What then of the relationship between an organization as a whole and the cultural context in which it operates? Some organizational scholars and practitioners have suggested that large business firms in modern industrial states are inevitably converging toward a more or less singular and highly rationalized bureaucratic model that is based primarily on efficiency considerations. Yet, other scholars and practitioners are intrigued by the variations—modest to massive—in the bureaucratic model that occur in different societies. Coming to terms with such differences means examining closely the relationship between organizations and their surrounding cultures. For the moment, at least, it appears that pronouncements about the inevitable convergence toward a singular organizational form—be it the bureaucratic "iron cage" or the flexible "horizontal network"—are a trifle premature.

Indeed, since the early 1970s, interest in the cross-cultural context of organizational life has been intense. The increasing globalization of the economy is perhaps the central reason behind this interest. Numerous firms that once operated within a restricted local or national context have now expanded internationally in terms of finance, production, and sales. For many organizations, rapid growth across country boundaries means that they must become knowledgeable about cultural differences from the slight to the enormous if they are to be successful. Moreover, the global economy is itself being reshaped both structurally through the use of new communication technologies and changes in legal and monetary systems as well as culturally through the intensified cross-national migrations of people and ideas. Little wonder that culture has become a hot topic.

Of considerable interest here are questions surrounding the applicability of certain organizational forms and work methods in different cultural contexts. On this matter, we have some evidence generated by a good deal of research devoted to understanding the economic success of Japanese organizations in the 1980s and the success of the so-called Four Little Dragons of Taiwan, Singapore, South Korea, and Hong Kong throughout most of the 1990s. Do, for instance, Japanese practices work in the United States as they do in Japan? The answer it seems is complicated: some do and some don't. Certain practices such as guarantees of job security, concentrated labor/management cooperation on quality issues and a (relatively) high degree of worker participation in local decision making seem to increase worker commitment and satisfaction wherever they are applied. Japanese firms tend to engage in more of such practices but the same relationships should, in principle, hold in virtually all organizations. Other practices such as intense socialization to work, elaborate and frequent corporate rituals, and routine social contacts between workers and managers do not appear to travel as well—at least to the United States and Europe.

These kinds of research findings apparently reflect broad cultural differences across societies (although numerous exceptions to the rule always emerge within societies). The Japanese, for example, seem to favor close relations with supervisors and working in groups while Americans press for individual autonomy and independence. These differences influence work attitudes and behavior yet do not wash out the effects of other organizational matters such as participation in decision making. Other cross-cultural comparisons will no doubt produce different stories depending on the work practices and societies involved. In other words, one can expect particular cultural differences to influence employee behavior in a firm but such differences are subtle and specific, less sweeping and general than often portrayed by cultural chauvinists of various stripes.

A useful way to think of the links between cultural contexts and organizational forms or practices is to recognize the powerful role the former plays in legitimizing the latter. Enterprise groups in Taiwan and South Korea, akin to the *keiretsu* organizational form in Japan, provide an example in this regard. An enterprise group is a set of separate firms bound together by common ownership. They engage in mutual financial exchanges and, in general, are highly interdependent. Exact counterparts do not seem to exist in the United States. In South Korea, enterprise groups are quite centralized and vertically dominated by a founding company. In Taiwan, enterprise groups are typically smaller, less centralized with more horizontal connections to noncompeting firms and backed by powerful single families. What is most interesting, however, is that in each country, enterprise groups take shape in a fashion that mirrors the way other institutions in that society are organized and managed—schools, families, government agencies, the legal system (itself a cultural product), and so on. Thus, specific organizational forms and practices reflect unique cultural patterns—"patrimonialism" in South Korea and "familialism" in Taiwan.

In this regard, it is instructive to recall that the root word for organization is the Greek term *organon*, which means tool or instrument. English-speaking countries seem most comfortable with the highly utilitarian sense of the word, "to serve collective purposes." As a cultural contrast, consider that the two Chinese characters for organization mean "grouping" and "weaving." The Chinese notion of organization also implies collectivity and patterning, of course, but it lacks the direct sense of instrumentality that is present in the English term. It is not entirely fanciful then to wonder just what such a difference might mean to those who invent, manage, and work for organizations in such distinctive cultural contexts.

It is one thing, however, to recognize that cultural differences have an effect on how organizations are put together and operate in various parts of the world, and another thing entirely to come to terms with such differences by having to actively coordinate business operations within a variety of cultures. This distinction is as true for a company in Los Angeles attempting to manage a Mexican, Vietnamese, Arabic, and American workforce as it is for a multinational firm trying to manage its production flow in four different nations. In both cases, multiple cultural systems interact, and the pitfalls of dealing with such cultural differences are legendary. To take just one example, consider the comic but costly General Motors promotion of its economy-sized Chevy Nova in Mexico. Apparently, no one involved in the doomed project had recognized (or taken seriously) that *No va* translates to "it doesn't go" in Spanish.

The pitfalls of cultural differences go deeper of course than simply misunderstanding the relationship between words and referents. Because culture concerns shared meanings (however localized they may be), working with some success in different cultural contexts means understanding the assumptions and nuances on which different meaning systems rest. Knowing that *hai* is the Japanese equivalent of yes is a start but it is of little value unless one is also familiar with the culturally tuned uses to which *hai* can be put. To wit, it may mean that the speaker has heard what was said and is now thinking about a proper response; it may mean simple agreement; or it may mean that the speaker has heard what was said but unfortunately cannot grant the request. Matters such as these are hardly to be taken lightly when doing business across cultural boundaries. General rules are difficult if not impossible to promote in this domain. Obvious dangers lie in both underestimating and overestimating the degree of meaning overlap. Perhaps the best advice to be offered to both individuals and organizations when engaged in cross-cultural exchanges is to be alert at all times for colliding meaning constructions, because incompatibilities at either the denotative or connotative level carry significant potential for disruption in both the short and the long run.

Toward a Cultural Diagnosis of Organizations

It seems the case that we now live in fast times. The world is increasingly interconnected and new communication, production, and transportation technologies alter the way business is conducted at home and around the world. The international flows of people, information, goods, images, and entertainment suggest that all organizations must contend with cultural multiplicity and all the potential misunderstanding and injury such multiplicity implies. Taking a cultural perspective on organizations helps predict areas of potential trouble and can help reduce such conflict if possible or at least help manage it more effectively—and, presumably, more empathically—where and when it does arise. Then again, as this rather breathless essay suggests, the perspective is a broad one and covers much territory. In summary form, six features of the cultural lens on organizations stand out as particularly crucial.

1. *Symbols and meaning.* Taking a cultural perspective means trying to decipher what things mean to particular people and groups in organizations. Strategies, goals, rewards, and so forth may well mean different things to different people, and discovering where and why such differences arise is a matter of considerable diagnostic and ultimately practical importance for the understanding and running of an organization.

2. *Identity.* In many ways, culture and identity are interchangeable concepts because one implies the other. Both are in principle fluid and alterable, but both typically display remarkable stability over time and account for

what economists regard as the inexplicable "stickiness" of entrenched ways of thinking and doing that persist in the face of the most compelling and ostensibly rational argument. Once identity is established in the workplace, the pressure is on to live it even if it means sacrificing one's individuality to do so. Even though we carry a variety of potentially relevant identities, those that are valued, endure and, brought into continual play in the workplace, carry heartfelt moral precepts on which our actions are based. Identities are powerful because they build up interests, values, projects, and experiences and refuse to dissolve by virtue of the tight and special connection they have with geography, religion, education, family background, supportive others, and the specific character of given work tasks.

3. *Social control.* Organizations must develop the means to ensure that employees act in ways that are more or less beneficial to the goals of the enterprise. Both individuals and groups may follow norms and standards that disrupt or otherwise interfere with managerially approved objectives. Identifying the ways in which satisfying and productive work cultures are created (or not created) in organizational settings is a crucial diagnostic task for managers and one that requires paying close attention to such matters as recruitment practices, socialization and training programs, reward policies (both formal and informal), corporate rituals, exemplary role models, and the stories that are frequently told in and around a company.

4. *Subcultures.* Homogeneous organizational cultures are probably quite rare and, when present, are typically found in relatively small, closely held, and highly focused firms. As organizations grow in size, subcultures emerge more or less naturally and on occasion challenge and resist managerial direction. Within a given organization, subcultures provide alternative identities for employees and allow meanings that flow from groups outside the firm's boundaries to find internal expression. Understanding subcultures is often a most practical matter for it means being able to anticipate the different meanings that new policies or programs may take in various segments of the organization.

5. *Cultural relativity.* Strong cultural models claim that national, local, or firm-specific culture (or some combination) fully explains organizational behavior. The counterpoint is taken up by either strong power or structural models that discount the potential lead culture takes in promoting or thwarting organizational change or ignore the mediating and legitimating roles culture plays when stability is desired. The cultural perspective presented here rejects an either/or approach for a more complicated mutual accommodation idea stressing the cultural influences on power and structure and the need to always interpret both in light of a specific cultural lens. Such an approach is particularly helpful when an organization operates in more than one country or several cultural groups must work together in a single operational setting. Managers cannot control the cultural frameworks that make their operations (or products) meaningful in such settings but they can appreciate their lack of control and inability to impose unitary meanings. Given such inherent limitations, managers can perhaps understand just when cultural incompatibilities will seriously challenge what they would like to do and thus act sensibly and respectfully in light of such understanding.

6. *Habits and history.* Culture emerges slowly and unevenly. It is dependent on what worked in the past to sustain group endeavors and is consequently built on traditions and the experience of success. Culture thus displays a good deal of continuity over time. As people move into new work settings they ordinarily find social worlds and the identities they offer waiting for them that are already organized and understood in historically dependent ways. What is often referred to as the "bounded rationality" of organizational members is in fact a kind of human cleverness that allows individual decisions and behavior to be handed over to habits of thought and action. This form of institutional thought and behavior not only conserves effort but also provides a way of tapping into the collective experience of others because habits and ideas are learned. Their strength turns on the question of the strength of the institutions in which an idea or habit is lodged. Take, for example, the notion of loyalty to the firm. Field reports in the United States reveal a somewhat surprising and tenacious level of employee support, commitment, and identification with large firms despite a decade or more of layoffs and downsizing. Advocates, such as self-identifying IBMers or Motorolans, promote loyalty as an end in its own right, a virtue that when collectively honored stands for the presence of enthusiasm and solidarity within the firm, the desire to remain in rough times, the willingness to put in a hard day's work, and the prideful representation of the organization to outsiders. All this loyalty may eventually change, of course. Indeed, those who have suffered from layoffs report severe culture shock that comes not only from experiencing

the alien reality of unemployment but from the loss produced by the interruption of one's close relationships and familiar patterns of work (and often love). In this sense, taking a cultural perspective on organizations offers far more than what dismissive critics might regard as a softhearted descriptive fantasy of the "soulful corporation" but offers rather an explanation for why change and the ritualized arguments that are designed to legitimate such change are so often unpersuasive.

Postscript: The "New" Organization

The "new" organization is essentially a structural description for the form business organizations seem to be moving toward at the moment in advanced capitalistic societies. Flattened hierarchies, greater workplace diversity, global scope, increased lateral communication and cooperation (within and across organizational boundaries), and increased flexibility are the definitional elements. As argued here, each element is not only complex but must be defined relative to historical trends and always local circumstances. As a result, each element is quite likely to take on a variety of meanings—each to a degree specific to a given cultural context. What diversity means in parts of eastern Europe where the terror of ethnic cleansing has so recently been an ugly fact of death is most assuredly distinct from the meaning of diversity in the eastern United States.

Even within particular cultural contexts, the structural elements of an organization may be less critical than the relatively ignored cultural processes that must support the outcomes presumably fostered by "new" organizational forms. Flattened hierarchies are, for example, intended to encourage unbiased information flows up and down the chain of command. Yet unbiased information flows may have less to do with the number of people involved in a communication chain than with the degree to which people involved in such chains know and trust one another. Similarly, operating on a global scale for large consumer product firms that were founded in, say, small market European nations may be far less troublesome than for similarly sized firms that originated in large home market countries who, by contrast, have relatively little experience operating on foreign soil. In short, the different dimensions of the "new" organization are subject to numerous cultural qualifications.

Perhaps the most important and general qualification recalls our earlier discussion about cultural and structural lags. On the cultural side, it seems apparent that managers are becoming increasingly aware of the conserving nature of culture and the protective and defensive reactions of people when their customary and sometimes cherished ways and identities are threatened. Culture probably buries more planned (and unplanned) changes than it ever advances. On the structural side, cautionary wisdom can be advanced as well. Redesigning an organization in the form of the "new" is perhaps not so great a challenge as that of bringing social practices in line with what the design is intended to accomplish. Culture may eventually follow design but it is unlikely to do so swiftly. The question a culturally sophisticated manager is likely to pose to advocates of the "new" organization is what guarantees that the structure the organization is currently pointed for is the one that will prove effective if and when the destination is reached? If all organizations assume the "new" organizational form, where will competitive advantages derive? From this angle, we should keep in mind that organizations and the environments in which they sit are changing all the time. What such changes mean is far from transparent. The "new" organization is therefore likely to be a never-ending story.

Recommended Further Reading

DiMaggio, Paul (Ed.). 2001. *The Twenty-First Century Firm: Changing Economic Organization in International Perspective*. Princeton, NJ: Princeton University Press. A convenient set of well-turned essays summarizing what knowledgeable members of the academic organizational research culture have to say on the origins and future of the so-called "new organization."

Griswold, Wendy. 1992. *Cultures and Societies in a Changing World*. Thousand Oaks, CA: Pine Forge Press. A broad sociological treatment of culture in a rapidly changing world including a number of illuminating examples of the interaction between structure and culture.

Hannerz, Ulf. 1992. *Cultural Complexity: Studies in the Social Organization of Meaning*. New York: Columbia University Press. A useful and quite accessible anthropological reworking of the culture concept in the context of a postmodern, information-intensive, and shrinking world.

Schein, Edgar H. 2004. *Organizational Culture and Leadership, 3rd ed*. San Francisco: Jossey-Bass. A highly practical but careful, psychologically oriented look at the creation, maintenance, and alteration of organizational culture.

Van Maanen, John. 1988. *Tales of the Field: On Writing Ethnography*. Chicago: University of Chicago Press. A general but quick glance at the ways culture has been diagnosed and captured in print by anthropologists and sociologists over the past 100 or so years.

Watson, James (Ed.). 1997. *Golden Arches East: McDonald's in East Asia*. Palo Alto, CA: Stanford University Press. An engaging and highly informative set of studies of how a distinctly American firm and global product have been received and localized in five East Asian cities.

Weeks, John. 2004. *Unpopular Culture: The Ritual of Complaint in a British Bank*. Chicago: University of Chicago Press. A lucid ethnography of a large British bank (circa 2000) focused on the culture of complaint that characterized the organization and paradoxically obstructed change.

Organizational Culture

by Edgar H. Schein

Abstract: *The concept of organizational culture has received increasing attention in recent years both from academics and practitioners. This article presents the author's view of how culture should be defined and analyzed if it is to be of use in the field of organizational psychology. Other concepts are reviewed, a brief history is provided, and case materials are presented to illustrate how to analyze culture and how to think about culture change.*

To write a review article about the concept of organizational culture poses a dilemma because there is presently little agreement on what the concept does and should mean, how it should be observed and measured, how it relates to more traditional industrial and organizational psychology theories, and how it should be used in our efforts to help organizations. The popular use of the concept has further muddied the waters by hanging the label of "culture" on everything from common behavioral patterns to espoused new corporate values that senior management wishes to inculcate (e.g., Deal and Kennedy, 1982; Peters and Waterman, 1982).

Serious students of organizational culture point out that each culture researcher develops explicit or implicit paradigms that bias not only the definitions of key concepts but the whole approach to the study of the phenomenon (Barley, Meyer, and Gash, 1988; Martin and Meyerson, 1988; Ott, 1989; Smircich and Calas, 1987; Van Maanen, 1988). One probable reason for this diversity of approaches is that culture, like role, lies at the intersection of several social sciences and reflects some of the biases of each—specifically, those of anthropology, sociology, social psychology, and organizational behavior.

A complete review of the various paradigms and their implications is far beyond the scope of this article. Instead I will provide a brief historical overview leading to the major approaches currently in use and then describe in greater detail one paradigm, firmly anchored in social psychology and anthropology, that is somewhat integrative in that it allows one to position other paradigms in a common conceptual space.

This line of thinking will push us conceptually into territory left insufficiently explored by such concepts as "climate," "norm," and "attitude." Many of the research methods of industrial/organizational psychology have weaknesses when applied to the concept of culture. If we are to take culture seriously, we must first adopt a more clinical and ethnographic approach to identify clearly the kinds of dimensions and variables that can usefully lend themselves to more precise empirical measurement and hypothesis testing. Though there have been many efforts to be empirically precise about cultural phenomena, there is still insufficient linkage of theory with observed data. We are still operating in the context of discovery and are seeking hypotheses rather than testing specific theoretical formulations.

A Historical Note

Organizational culture as a concept has a fairly recent origin. Although the concepts of "group norms" and "climate" have been used by psychologists for a long time (e.g., Lewin, Lippitt, and White, 1939), the concept of "culture" has been explicitly used only in the last few decades. Katz and Kahn (1978), in their second edition of *The Social Psychology of Organizations*, referred to roles, norms, and values but presented neither climate nor culture as explicit concepts.

Source: Edgar H. Schein, "Organizational Culture," *American Psychologist*, February, 1990. Copyright © 1990 by the American Psychological Association. Reprinted with permission.

Organizational "climate," by virtue of being a more salient cultural phenomenon, lent itself to direct observation and measurement and thus has had a longer research tradition (Hellriegel and Slocum, 1974; A. P. Jones and James, 1979; Litwin and Stringer, 1968; Schneider, 1975; Schneider and Reichers, 1983; Tagiuri and Litwin, 1968). But climate is only a surface manifestation of culture, and thus research on climate has not enabled us to delve into the deeper causal aspects of how organizations function. We need explanations for variations in climate and norms, and it is this need that ultimately drives us to "deeper" concepts such as culture.

In the late 1940s social psychologists interested in Lewinian "action research" and leadership training freely used the concept of "cultural island" to indicate that the training setting was in some fundamental way different from the trainees' "back home" setting. We knew from the leadership training studies of the 1940s and 1950s that foremen who changed significantly during training would revert to their former attitudes once they were back at work in a different setting (Bradford, Gibb, and Benne, 1964; Fleishman, 1953, 1973; Lewin, 1952; Schein and Bennis, 1965). But the concept of "group norms," heavily documented in the Hawthorne studies of the 1920s, seemed sufficient to explain this phenomenon (Homans, 1950; Roethlisberger and Dickson, 1939).

In the 1950s and 1960s, the field of organizational psychology began to differentiate itself from industrial psychology by focusing on units larger than individuals (Bass, 1965; Schein, 1965). With a growing emphasis on work groups and whole organizations came a greater need for concepts such as "system" that could describe what could be thought of as a *pattern* of norms and attitudes that cut across a whole social unit. The researchers and clinicians at the Tavistock Institute developed the concept of "socio-technical systems" (Jaques, 1951; Rice, 1963; Trist, Higgin, Murray, and Pollock, 1963), and Likert (1961, 1967) developed his "Systems 1 through 4" to describe integrated sets of organizational norms and attitudes. Katz and Kahn (1966) built their entire analysis of organizations around systems theory and systems dynamics, thus laying the most important theoretical foundation for later culture studies.

The field of organizational psychology grew with the growth of business and management schools. As concerns with understanding organizations and interorganizational relationships grew, concepts from sociology and anthropology began to influence the field. Cross-cultural psychology had, of course, existed for a long time (Werner, 1940), but the application of the concept of culture to organizations *within* a given society came only recently as more investigators interested in organizational phenomena found themselves needing the concept to explain (a) variations in patterns of organizational behavior, and (b) levels of stability in group and organizational behavior that had not previously been highlighted (e.g., Ouchi, 1981).

What has really thrust the concept into the forefront is the recent emphasis on trying to explain why U.S. companies do not perform as well as some of their counterpart companies in other societies, notably Japan. In observing the differences, it has been noted that national culture is not a sufficient explanation (Ouchi, 1981; Pascale and Athos, 1981). One needs concepts that permit one to differentiate between organizations within a society, especially in relation to different levels of effectiveness, and the concept of organizational culture has served this purpose well (e.g., O'Toole, 1979; Pettigrew, 1979; Wilkins and Ouchi, 1983).

As more investigators and theoreticians have begun to examine organizational culture, the normative thrust has been balanced by more descriptive and clinical research (Barley, 1983; Frost, Moore, Louis, Lundberg, and Martin, 1985; Louis, 1981, 1983; Martin, 1982; Martin, Feldman, Hatch, and Sitkin, 1983; Martin and Powers, 1983; Martin and Siehl, 1983; Schein, 1985a; Van Maanen and Barley, 1984). We need to find out what is actually going on in organizations before we rush in to tell managers what to do about their culture.

I will summarize this quick historical overview by identifying several different research streams that today influence how we perceive the concept of organizational culture.

Survey Research

From this perspective, culture has been viewed as a property of groups that can be measured by questionnaires leading to Likert-type profiles (Hofstede, 1980; Hofstede and Bond, 1988; Kilmann, 1984; Likert, 1967). The problem with this approach is that it assumes knowledge of the relevant dimensions to be studied. Even if these are statistically derived from large samples of items, it is not clear whether the initial item set is broad enough or relevant enough to capture what may for any given organization be its critical cultural themes. Furthermore, it is not clear whether something as abstract as culture can be measured with survey instruments at all.

Analytical Descriptive

In this type of research, culture is viewed as a concept for which empirical measures must be developed, even if that means breaking down the concept into smaller units so that it can be analyzed and measured (e.g., Harris and Sutton, 1986; Martin and Siehl, 1983; Schall, 1983; Trice and Beyer, 1984; Wilkins, 1983). Thus, organizational stories, rituals and rites, symbolic manifestations, and other cultural elements come to be taken as valid surrogates for the cultural whole. The problem with this approach is that it fractionates a concept whose primary theoretical utility is in drawing attention to the holistic aspect of group and organizational phenomena.

Ethnographic

In this approach, concepts and methods developed in sociology and anthropology are applied to the study of organizations in order to illuminate descriptively, and thus provide a richer understanding of certain organizational phenomena that had previously not been documented fully enough (Barley, 1983; Van Maanen, 1988; Van Maanen and Barley, 1984). This approach helps to build better theory but is time consuming and expensive. A great many more cases are needed before generalizations can be made across various types of organizations.

Historical

Though historians have rarely applied the concept of culture in their work, it is clearly viewed as a legitimate aspect of an organization to be analyzed along with other factors (Chandler, 1977; Dyer, 1986; Pettigrew, 1979; Westney, 1987). The weaknesses of the historical method are similar to those pointed out for the ethnographic approach, but these are often offset by the insights that historical and longitudinal analyses can provide.

Clinical Descriptive

With the growth of organizational consulting has come the opportunity to observe in areas from which researchers have traditionally been barred, such as the higher levels of management where policies originate and where reward and control systems are formulated. When consultants observe organizational phenomena as a by-product of their services for clients, we can think of this as "clinical" research even though the client is defining the domain of observation (Schein, 1987a). Such work is increasingly being done by consultants with groups and organizations, and it allows consultants to observe some of the systemic effects of interventions over time. This approach has been labeled "organization development" (Beckhard, 1969; Beckhard and Harris, 1977, 1987; Bennis, 1966, 1969; French and Bell, 1984; Schein, 1969) and has begun to be widely utilized in many kinds of organizations.

The essential characteristic of this method is that the data are gathered while the consultant is actively helping the client system work on problems defined by the client on the client's initiative. Whereas the researcher has to gain access, the consultant/clinician is provided access because it is in the client's best interest to open up categories of information that might ordinarily be concealed from the researcher (Schein, 1985a, 1987a).

The empirical knowledge gained from such observations provides a much needed balance to the data obtained by other methods because cultural origins and dynamics can sometimes be observed only in the power centers where elements of the culture are created and changed by founders, leaders, and powerful managers (Hirschhorn, 1987; Jaques, 1951; Kets de Vries and Miller, 1984, 1986; Schein, 1983). The problem with this method is that it does not provide the descriptive breadth of an ethnography nor the methodological rigor of quantitative hypothesis testing. However, at this stage of the evolution of the field, a combination of ethnographic and clinical research seems to be the most appropriate basis for trying to understand the concept of culture.

Definition of Organizational Culture

The problem of defining organizational culture derives from the fact that the concept of organization is itself ambiguous. We cannot start with some "cultural phenomena" and then use their existence as evidence for the existence of a group. We must first specify that a given set of people has had enough stability and common history to have allowed a culture to form. This means that some organizations will have no overarching culture because they have no common history or have frequent turnover of members. Other organizations can be presumed to have "strong" cultures because of a long shared history or because they have shared important intense experiences (as in a combat unit). But the content and strength of a culture have to be empirically determined. They cannot be presumed from observing surface cultural phenomena.

Culture is what a group learns over a period of time as that group solves its problems of survival in an external environment and its problems of internal integration. Such learning is simultaneously a behavioral, cognitive, and an emotional process. Extrapolating further from a functionalist anthropological view, the deepest level of culture will be the cognitive in that the perceptions, language, and thought processes that a group comes to share will be the ultimate causal determinant of feelings, attitudes, espoused values, and overt behavior.

From systems theory, Lewinian field theory, and cognitive theory comes one other theoretical premise—namely, that systems tend toward some kind of equilibrium, attempt to reduce dissonance, and thus bring basic categories or assumptions into alignment with each other (Durkin, 1981; Festinger, 1957; Hebb, 1954; Heider, 1958; Hirschhorn, 1987; Lewin, 1952). There is a conceptual problem, however, because systems contain subsystems, organizations contain groups and units within them, and it is not clear over what range the tendency toward equilibrium will exist in any given complex total system.

For our purposes it is enough to specify that any definable group with a shared history can have a culture and that within an organization there can therefore be many subcultures. If the organization as a whole has had shared experiences, there will also be a total organizational culture. Within any given unit, the tendency for integration and consistency will be assumed to be present, but it is perfectly possible for coexisting units of a larger system to have cultures that are independent and even in conflict with each other.

Culture can now be defined as (a) a pattern of basic assumptions, (b) invented, discovered, or developed by a given group, (c) as it learns to cope with its problems of external adaptation and internal integration, (d) that has worked well enough to be considered valid and, therefore (e) is to be taught to new members as the (f) correct way to perceive, think, and feel in relation to those problems.

The strength and degree of internal consistency of a culture are, therefore, a function of the stability of the group, the length of time the group has existed, the intensity of the group's experiences of learning, the mechanisms by which the learning has taken place (i.e., positive reinforcement or avoidance conditioning), and the strength and clarity of the assumptions held by the founders and leaders of the group.

Once a group has learned to hold common assumptions, the resulting automatic patterns of perceiving, thinking, feeling, and behaving provide meaning, stability, and comfort; the anxiety that results from the inability to understand or predict events happening around the group is reduced by the shared learning. The strength and tenacity of culture derive, in part, from this anxiety-reduction function. One can think of some aspects of culture as being for the group what defense mechanisms are for the individual (Hirschhorn, 1987; Menzies, 1960; Schein, 1985b).

The Levels of Culture

In analyzing the culture of a particular group or organization it is desirable to distinguish three fundamental levels at which culture manifests itself: (a) observable artifacts, (b) values, and (c) basic underlying assumptions.

When one enters an organization one observes and feels its *artifacts*. This category includes everything from the physical layout, the dress code, the manner in which people address each other, the smell and feel of the place, its emotional intensity, and other phenomena, to the more permanent archival manifestations such as company records, products, statements of philosophy, and annual reports.

The problem with artifacts is that they are palpable but hard to decipher accurately. We know how we react to them, but that is not necessarily a reliable indicator of how members of the organization react. We can see and feel that one company is much more formal and bureaucratic than another, but that does not tell us anything about why this is so or what meaning it has to the members.

For example, one of the flaws of studying organizational symbols, stories, myths, and other such artifacts is that we may make incorrect inferences from them if we do not know how they connect to underlying assumptions (Pondy, Boland, and Thomas, 1988; Pondy, Frost, Morgan, and Dandridge, 1983; Wilkins, 1983). Organizational stories are especially problematic in this regard because the "lesson" of the story is not clear if one does not understand the underlying assumptions behind it.

Through interviews, questionnaires, or survey instruments one can study a culture's espoused and documented *values*, norms, ideologies, chargers, and philosophies. This is comparable to the ethnographer's asking special "informants" why certain observed phenomena happen the way they do. Open-ended interviews can be very useful in getting at this level of how people feel and think, but questionnaires and survey instruments are generally less useful because they prejudge the dimensions to be studied. There is no way of knowing whether the dimensions one is asking about are relevant or salient in that culture until one has examined the deeper levels of the culture.

Through more intensive observation, through more focused questions, and through involving motivated members of the group in intensive self-analysis, one can seek out and decipher the taken-for-granted, underlying, and usually unconscious *assumptions* that determine perceptions, thought processes, feeling, and behavior. Once one understands some of these assumptions, it becomes much easier to decipher the meanings implicit in the various behavioral and artifactual phenomena one observes. Furthermore, once one understands the underlying taken-for-granted assumptions, one can better understand how cultures can seem to be ambiguous or even self-contradictory (Martin and Meyerson, 1988).

As two case examples I present later will show, it is quite possible for a group to hold conflicting values that manifest themselves in inconsistent behavior while having complete consensus on underlying assumptions. It is equally possible for a group to reach consensus on the level of values and behavior and yet develop serious conflict later because there was no consensus on critical underlying assumptions.

This latter phenomenon is frequently observed in mergers or acquisitions where initial synergy is gradually replaced by conflict, leading ultimately to divestitures. When one analyzes these examples historically one often finds that there was insufficient agreement on certain basic assumptions, or, in our terms, that the cultures were basically in conflict with each other.

Deeply held assumptions often start out historically as values but, as they stand the test of time, gradually come to be taken for granted and then take on the character of assumptions. They are no longer questioned and they become less and less open to discussion. Such avoidance behavior occurs particularly if the learning was based on traumatic experiences in the organization's history, which leads to the group counterpart of what would be repression in the individual. If one understands culture in this way, it becomes obvious why it is so difficult to change culture.

Deciphering the "Content" of Culture

Culture is ubiquitous. It covers all areas of group life. A simplifying typology is always dangerous because one may not have the right variables in it, but if one distills from small group theory the dimensions that recur in group studies, one can identify a set of major external and internal tasks that all groups face and with which they must learn to cope (Ancona, 1988; Bales, 1950; Bales and Cohen, 1979; Benne and Sheats, 1948; Bennis and Shepard, 1956; Bion, 1959; Schein, 1988). The group's culture can then be seen as the learned response to each of these tasks (see Table 2.1).

Another approach to understanding the "content" of a culture is to draw on anthropological typologies of universal issues faced by all societies. Again there is a danger of overgeneralizing these dimensions (see Table 2.2), but the comparative studies of Kluckhohn and Strodtbeck (1961) are a reasonable start in this direction.

If one wants to decipher what is really going on in a particular organization, one has to start more inductively to find out which of these dimensions is the most pertinent on the basis of that organization's history. If one has access to the organization one will note its *artifacts* readily but will not really

Table 2.1 The External and Internal Tasks Facing All Groups

External Adaptation Tasks	Internal Integration Tasks
Developing consensus on:	Developing consensus on:
1. The core mission, functions, and primary tasks of the organization vis-à-vis its environments	1. The common language and conceptual system to be used, including basic concepts of time and space
2. The specific goals to be pursued by the organization	2. The group boundaries and criteria for inclusion
3. The basic means to be used in accomplishing the goals	3. The criteria for the allocation of status, power, and authority
4. The criteria to be used for measuring results	4. The criteria for intimacy, friendship, and love in different work and family settings
5. The remedial or repair strategies if goals are not achieved	5. The criteria for the allocation of rewards and punishments
	6. Concepts for managing the unmanageable—ideology and religion

Source: Tables adapted from Edgar H. Schein, *Organizational Culture and Leadership.* Copyright © 1985 by Jossey-Bass, Inc., Publishers. Used with permission.

| Table 2.2 | Some Underlying Dimensions of Organizational Culture |

Dimension	Questions to be Answered
1. The organization's relationship to its environment	Does the organization perceive itself to be dominant, submissive, harmonizing, searching out a niche?
2. The nature of human activity	Is the "correct" way for humans to behave to be dominant/proactive, harmonizing, or passive/fatalistic?
3. The nature of reality and truth	How do we define what is true and what is not true; and how is truth ultimately determined both in the physical and social world? By pragmatic test, reliance on wisdom, or social consensus?
4. The nature of time	What is our basic orientation in terms of past, present, and future, and what kinds of time units are most relevant for the conduct of daily affairs?
5. The nature of human nature	Are humans basically good, neutral, or evil, and is human nature perfectible or fixed?
6. The nature of human relationships	What is the "correct" way for people to relate to each other, to distribute power and affection? Is life competitive or cooperative? Is the best way to organize society on the basis of individualism or groupism? Is the best authority system autocratic/paternalistic or collegial/participative?
7. Homogeneity vs. diversity	Is the group best off if it is highly diverse or if it is highly homogenous, and should individuals in a group be encouraged to innovate or conform?

Source: Tables adapted from Edgar H. Schein, *Organizational Culture and Leadership.* Copyright © 1985 by Jossey-Bass, Inc., Publishers. Used with permission.

know what they mean. Of most value in this process will be noting *anomalies* and things that seem different, upsetting, or difficult to understand.

If one has access to members of the organization one can interview them about the issues in Table 2.1 and thereby get a good roadmap of what is going on. Such an interview will begin to reveal *espoused values*, and, as these surface, the investigator will begin to notice inconsistencies between what is claimed and what has been observed. These inconsistencies and the anomalies observed or felt now form the basis for the next layer of investigation.

Pushing past the layer of espoused values into underlying *assumptions* can be done by the ethnographer once trust has been established or by the clinician if the organizational client wishes to be helped. Working with motivated insiders is essential because only they can bring to the surface their own underlying assumptions and articulate how they basically perceive the world around them.

To summarize, if we combine insider knowledge with outsider questions, assumptions can be brought to the surface, but the process of inquiry has to be interactive, with the outsider continuing to probe until assumptions have really been teased out and have led to a feeling of greater understanding on the part of both the outsider and the insiders.

Two Case Examples

It is not possible to provide cultural descriptions in a short article, but some extracts from cases can be summarized to illustrate particularly the distinctions between artifacts, values, and assumptions. The "Action Company" is a rapidly growing high-technology manufacturing concern still managed by its founder roughly 30 years after its founding. Because of its low turnover and intense history, one would expect to find an overall organizational culture as well as functional and geographic subcultures.

A visitor to the company would note the open office landscape architecture; a high degree of informality; frenetic activity all around; a high degree of confrontation, conflict, and fighting in meetings; an obvious lack of status symbols such as parking spaces or executive dining rooms; and a sense of high energy and emotional involvement, of people staying late and expressing excitement about the importance of their work.

If one asks about these various behaviors, one is told that the company is in a rapidly growing high-technology field where hard work, innovation, and rapid solutions to things are important and where it is essential for everyone to contribute at their maximum capacity. New employees are carefully screened, and when an employee fails, he or she is simply assigned to another task, not fired or punished in any personal way.

If one discusses this further and pushes to the level of assumptions, one elicits a pattern or paradigm such as that shown in Figure 2.1. Because of the kind of technology the company manufactures, and because of the strongly held beliefs and values of its founder, the company operates on several critical and coordinated assumptions: (a) Individuals are assumed to be the source of all innovation and productivity. (b) It is assumed that truth can only be determined by pitting fully involved individuals against each other to debate ideas until only one idea survives, and it is further assumed that ideas will not be implemented unless everyone involved in implementation has been convinced through the debate of the validity of the idea. (c) Paradoxically, it is also assumed that every individual must think for himself or herself and "do the right thing" even if that means disobeying one's boss or violating a policy. (d) What makes it possible for people to live in this high-conflict environment is the assumption that the company members are one big family who will take care of each other and protect each other even if some members make mistakes or have bad ideas.

Once one understands this paradigm, one can understand all of the different observed artifacts such as the ability of the organization to tolerate extremely high degrees of conflict without seeming to destroy or even demotivate its employees. The value of the cultural analysis is that it provides insight, understanding, and a roadmap for future action. For example, as the company grows, the decision process may prove to be too slow, the individual autonomy that members are expected to exercise may become destructive and have to be replaced by more disciplined behavior, and the notion of a family may break down because too many people no longer know each other personally. The cultural analysis thus permits one to focus on those areas in which the organization will experience stresses and strains as it continues to grow and in which cultural evolution and change will occur.

By way of contrast, in the "Multi Company," a 100-year-old multidivisional, multinational chemical firm, one finds at the artifact level a high degree of formality; an architecture that puts great emphasis on privacy; a proliferation of status symbols and deference rituals such as addressing people by their titles; a high degree of politeness in group meetings; an emphasis on carefully thinking things out and then implementing them firmly through the hierarchy; a formal code of dress; and an emphasis on working hours, punctuality, and so on. One also finds a total absence of cross-divisional or cross-functional meetings and an almost total lack of lateral communication. Memos left in one department by an outside consultant with instructions to be given to others are almost never delivered.

The paradigm that surfaces, if one works with insiders to try to decipher what is going on, can best be depicted by the assumptions shown in Figure 2.2. The company is science based and has always derived its success from its research and

Figure 2.1 The Action Company Paradigm

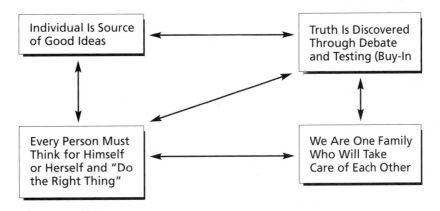

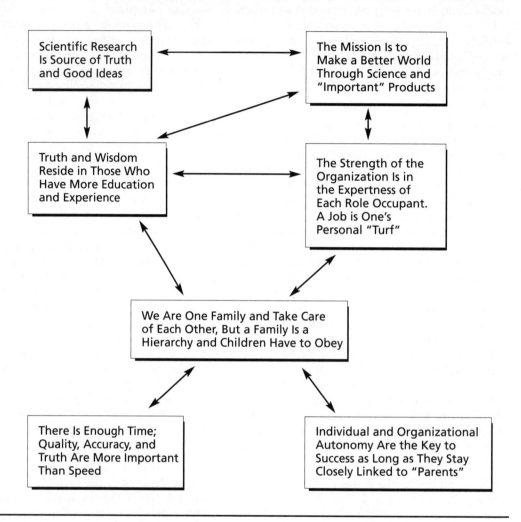

Figure 2.2 The Multi-Company Paradigm

development activities. Whereas "truth" in the Action Company is derived through debate and conflict and employees down the line are expected to think for themselves, in the Multi Company truth is derived from senior, wiser heads and employees are expected to go along like good soldiers once a decision is reached.

The Multi Company also sees itself as a family, but its concept of a family is completely different. Whereas in the Action Company, the family is a kind of safety net and an assurance of membership, in the Multi Company, it is an authoritarian/paternalistic system of eliciting loyalty and compliance in exchange for economic security. The paradoxical absence of lateral communication is explained by the deeply held assumption that a job is a person's private turf and that the unsolicited providing of information to that person is an invasion of privacy and a potential threat to his or her self-esteem. Multi Company managers are very much on top of their jobs and pride themselves on that fact. If they ask for information they get it, but it is rarely volunteered by peers.

This cultural analysis highlights what is for the Multi Company a potential problem. Its future success may depend much more on its ability to become effective in marketing and manufacturing, yet it still treats research and development as a sacred cow and assumes that new products will be the key to its future success. Increasingly the company finds itself in a world that requires rapid decision making, yet its systems and procedures are slow and cumbersome. To be more innovative in marketing it needs to share ideas more, yet it undermines lateral communication.

Both companies reflect the larger cultures within which they exist in that the Action Company is an American firm whereas the Multi Company is European, but each also is different from its competitors within the same country, thus highlighting the importance of understanding organizational culture.

Cultural Dynamics: How Is Culture Created?

Culture is learned; hence learning models should help us to understand culture creation. Unfortunately, there are not many good models of how groups learn—how norms, beliefs, and assumptions are created initially. Once these exist, we can see clearly how leaders and powerful members embed them in group activity, but the process of learning something that becomes shared is still only partially understood.

Norm Formation Around Critical Incidents

One line of analysis comes from the study of training groups (Bennis and Shepard, 1956; Bion, 1959; Schein, 1985a). One can see in such groups how norms and beliefs arise around the way members respond to critical incidents. Something emotionally charged or anxiety producing may happen, such as an attack by a member on the leader. Because everyone witnesses it and because tension is high when the attack occurs, the immediate next set of behaviors tend to create a norm.

Suppose, for example, that the leader counterattacks, that the group members "concur" with silence or approval, and that the offending member indicates with an apology that he or she accepts his or her "mistake." In those few moments a bit of culture has begun to be created—the norm that "we do not attack the leader in this group; authority is sacred." The norm may eventually become a belief and then an assumption if the same pattern recurs. If the leader and the group consistently respond differently to attacks, a different norm will arise. By reconstructing the history of critical incidents in the group and how members dealt with them, one can get a good indication of the important cultural elements in that group.

Identification with Leaders

A second mechanism of culture creation is the modeling by leader figures that permits group members to identify with them and internalize their values and assumptions. When groups or organizations first form, there are usually dominant figures or "founders" whose own beliefs, values, and assumptions provide a visible and articulated model for how the group should be structured and how it should function (Schein, 1983). As these beliefs are put into practice, some work out and some do not. The group then learns from its own experience what parts of the "founder's" belief system work for the group as a whole. The joint learning then gradually creates shared assumptions.

Founders and subsequent leaders continue to attempt to embed their own assumptions, but increasingly they find that other parts of the organization have their own experiences to draw on and, thus, cannot be changed. Increasingly the learning process is shared, and the resulting cultural assumptions reflect the total group's experience, not only the leader's initial assumptions. But leaders continue to try to embed their own views of how things should be, and, if they are powerful enough, they will continue to have a dominant effect on the emerging culture.

Primary embedding mechanisms are (a) what leaders pay attention to, measure, and control; (b) how leaders react to critical incidents and organization crises; (c) deliberate role modeling and coaching; (d) operational criteria for the allocation of rewards and status; and (e) operational criteria for recruitment, selection, promotion, retirement, and excommunication. *Secondary articulation and reinforcement mechanisms* are (a) the organization's design and structure; (b) organizational systems and procedures; (c) the design of physical space, facades, and buildings; (d) stories, legends, myths, and symbols; and (e) formal statements of organizational philosophy, creeds, and charters.

One can hypothesize that as cultures evolve and grow, two processes will occur simultaneously; a process of differentiation into various kinds of subcultures that will create diversity, and a process of integration, or a tendency for the various deeper elements of the culture to become congruent with each other because of the human need for consistency.

Cultural Dynamics: Preservation Through Socialization

Culture perpetuates and reproduces itself through the socialization of new members entering the group. The socialization process really begins with recruitment and selection in that the organization is likely to look for new members who already have the "right" set of assumptions, beliefs, and values. If the organization can find such presocialized members, it needs to do less formal socialization. More typically, however, new members do not "know the ropes" well enough to be able to take and enact their organizational roles, and thus they need to be trained and "acculturated" (Feldman, 1988; Ritti and Funkhouser, 1987; Schein, 1968, 1978; Van Maanen, 1976, 1977).

The socialization process has been analyzed from a variety of perspectives and can best be conceptualized in terms of a set of dimensions that highlight variations in how different organizations approach the process (Van Maanen, 1978; Van Maanen and Schein, 1979). Van Maanen identified seven dimensions along with socialization processes can vary:

1. *Group versus individual:* the degree to which the organization processes recruits in batches, as in boot camp, or individually, as in professional offices.
2. *Formal versus informal:* the degree to which the process is formalized, as in set training programs, or is handled informally through apprenticeships, individual coaching by the immediate superior, or the like.
3. *Self-destructive and reconstructing versus self-enhancing:* the degree to which the process destroys aspects of the self and replaces them as in boot camp, or enhances aspects of the self, as in professional development programs.
4. *Serial versus random:* the degree to which role models are provided, as in apprenticeship or mentoring programs, or are deliberately withheld, as in sink-or-swim kinds of initiations in which the recruit is expected to figure out his or her own solutions.
5. *Sequential versus disjunctive:* the degree to which the process consists of guiding the recruit through a series of discrete steps and roles versus being open-ended and never letting the recruit predict what organizational role will come next.
6. *Fixed versus variable:* the degree to which stages of the training process have fixed timetables for each stage, as in military academies, boot camps, or rotational training programs, or are open-ended, as in typical promotional systems where one is not advanced to the next stage until one is "ready."
7. *Tournament versus contest:* the degree to which each stage is an "elimination tournament" where one is out of the organization if one fails or a "contest" in which one builds up a track record and batting average.

Socialization Consequences

Though the goal of socialization is to perpetuate the culture, it is clear that the process does not have uniform effects. Individuals respond differently to the same treatment, and, even more important, different combinations of socialization tactics can be hypothesized to produce somewhat different outcomes for the organization (Van Maanen and Schein, 1979).

For example, from the point of view of the organization, one can specify three kinds of outcomes: (a) a *custodial orientation,* or total conformity to all norms and complete learning of all assumptions; (b) *creative individualism,* which implies that the trainee learns all of the central and pivotal assumptions of the culture but rejects all peripheral ones, thus permitting the individual to be creative both with respect to the organization's tasks and in how the organization performs them (role innovation); and (c) *rebellion,* or the total rejection of all assumptions. If the rebellious individual is constrained by external circumstances from leaving the organization, he or she will subvert, sabotage, and ultimately foment revolution.

We can hypothesize that the combination of socialization techniques most likely to produce a custodial orientation is (1) formal, (2) self-reconstructing, (3) serial, (4) sequential, (5) variable, and (6) tournament-like. Hence if one wants new members to be more creative in the use of their talents, one should use socialization techniques that are informal, self-enhancing, random, disjunctive, fixed in terms of timetables, and contest-like.

The individual versus group dimension can go in either direction in that group socialization methods can produce loyal custodially oriented cohorts or can produce disloyal rebels if countercultural norms are formed during the socialization process. Similarly, in the individual apprenticeship the direction of socialization will depend on the orientation of the mentor or coach.

Efforts to measure these socialization dimensions have been made, and some preliminary support for the above hypotheses has been forthcoming (Feldman, 1976, 1988; G. R. Jones, 1986). Insofar as cultural evolution is a function of innovative and creative efforts on the part of new members, this line of investigation is especially important.

Cultural Dynamics: Natural Evolution

Every group and organization is an open system that exists in multiple environments. Changes in the environment will produce stresses and strains inside the group, forcing new learning and adaption. At the same time, new members coming into the group will bring in new beliefs and assumptions that will influence currently held assumptions. To some degree, then, there is constant pressure on any given culture to evolve and grow. But just as individuals do not easily give up the elements of their identity or their defense mechanisms, so groups do not easily give up some of their basic underlying assumptions merely because external events or new members disconfirm them.

An illustration of "forced" evolution can be seen in the case of the aerospace company that prided itself on its high level of trust in its employees, which was reflected in flexible working hours, systems of self-monitoring and self-control, and the absence of time clocks. When a number of other companies in the industry were discovered to have overcharged their government clients, the government legislated a system of controls for all of its contractors, forcing this company to install time clocks and other control mechanisms that undermined the climate of trust that had been built up over 30 years. It remains to be seen whether the company's basic assumption that people can be trusted will gradually change or whether the company will find a way to discount the effects of an artifact that is in fundamental conflict with one of its basic assumptions.

Differentiation

As organizations grow and evolve they divide the labor and form functional, geographical, and other kinds of units, each of which exists in its own specific environment. Thus organizations begin to build their own subcultures. A natural evolutionary mechanism, therefore, is the differentiation that inevitably occurs with age and size. Once a group has many subcultures, its total culture increasingly becomes a negotiated outcome of the interaction of its subgroups. Organizations then evolve either by special efforts to impose their overall culture or by allowing dominant subcultures that may be better adapted to changing environmental circumstances to become more influential.

Cultural Dynamics: Guided Evolution And Managed Change

One of the major roles of the field of organization development has been to help organizations guide the direction of their evolution, that is, to enhance cultural elements that are viewed as critical to maintaining identity and to promote the "unlearning" of cultural elements that are viewed as increasingly dysfunctional (Argyris, Putnam, and Smith, 1985; Argyris and Schon, 1978; Beckhard and Harris, 1987; Hanna, 1988; Lippitt, 1982; Walton, 1987). This process in organizations is analogous to the process of therapy in individuals, although the actual tactics are more complicated when multiple clients are involved and when some of the clients are groups and subsystems.

Leaders of organizations sometimes are able to overcome their own cultural biases and to perceive that elements of an organization's culture are dysfunctional for survival and growth in a changing environment. They may feel either that they do not have the time to let evolution occur naturally or that evolution is heading the organization in the wrong direction. In such a situation one can observe leaders doing a number of different things, usually in combination, to produce the desired cultural changes:

1. Leaders may unfreeze the present system by highlighting the threats to the organization if no change occurs, and, at the same time, encourage the organization to believe that change is possible and desirable.
2. They may articulate a new direction and a new set of assumptions, thus providing a clear and new role model.
3. Key positions in the organization may be filled with new incumbents who hold the new assumptions because they are either hybrids, mutants, or brought in from the outside.
4. Leaders systematically may reward the adoption of new directions and punish adherence to the old direction.
5. Organization members may be seduced or coerced into adopting new behaviors that are more consistent with new assumptions.
6. Visible scandals may be created to discredit sacred cows, to explode myths that preserve dysfunctional traditions, and destroy symbolically the artifacts associated with them.
7. Leaders may create new emotionally charged rituals and develop new symbols and artifacts around the new assumptions to be embraced, using the embedding mechanisms described earlier.

Such cultural change efforts are generally more characteristic of "midlife" organizations that have become complacent and ill adapted to rapidly changing environmental conditions (Schein, 1985a). The fact that such organizations have strong subcultures aids the change process in that one can draw the new leaders from those subcultures that most represent the direction in which the organization needs to go.

In cases where organizations become extremely maladapted, one sees more severe change efforts. These may take the form of destroying the group that is the primary cultural carrier and reconstructing it around new people, thereby allowing a new learning process to occur and a new culture to form. When organizations go bankrupt or are turned over to "turnaround managers," one often sees such extreme measures. What is important to note about such cases is that they invariably involve the replacement of large numbers of people because the members who have grown up in the organization find it difficult to change their basic assumptions.

Mergers and Acquisitions

One of the most obvious forces toward culture change is the bringing together of two or more cultures. Unfortunately, in many mergers and acquisitions, the culture compatibility issue is not raised until after the deal has been consummated, which leads, in many cases, to cultural "indigestion" and the eventual divestiture of units that cannot become culturally integrated.

To avoid such problems, organizations must either engage in more premerger diagnosis to determine cultural compatibility or conduct training and integration workshops to help the meshing process. Such workshops have to take into account the deeper assumption layers of culture to avoid the trap of reaching consensus at the level of artifacts and values while remaining in conflict at the level of underlying assumptions.

The Role of the Organizational Psychologist

Culture will become an increasingly important concept for organizational psychology. Without such a concept we cannot really understand change or resistance to change. The more we get involved with helping organizations to design their fundamental strategies, particularly in the human resources area, the more important it will be to be able to help organizations decipher their own cultures.

All of the activities that revolve around recruitment, selection, training, socialization, the design of reward systems, the design and description of jobs, and broader issues of organization design require an understanding of how organizational culture influences present functioning. Many organizational change programs that failed probably did so because they ignored cultural forces in the organizations in which they were to be installed.

Inasmuch as culture is a dynamic process within organizations, it is probably studied best by action research methods, that is, methods that get "insiders" involved in the research and that work through attempts to "intervene" (Argyris et al., 1985; French and Bell, 1984; Lewin, 1952; Schein, 1987b). Until we have a better understanding of how culture works, it is probably best to work with qualitative research approaches that combine field work methods from ethnography with interview and observation methods from clinical and consulting work (Schein, 1987a).

I do not see a unique role for the traditional industrial/organizational psychologist, but I see great potential for the psychologist to work as a team member with colleagues who are more ethnographically oriented. The particular skill that will be needed on the part of the psychologist will be knowledge of organizations and of how to work with them, especially in a consulting relationship. Organizational culture is a complex phenomenon, and we should not rush to measure things until we understand better what we are measuring.

References

Ancona, D. G. 1988. Groups in organizations; Extending laboratory models. In C. Hendrick ed., *Annual Review of Personality and Social Psychology: Group and Intergroup Processes.* Beverly Hills, CA: Sage.

Argyris, C., R. Putnam, and D. M. Smith. 1985. *Action Science.* San Francisco: Jossey-Bass.

Argyris, C., and D. A. Schon. 1978. *Organizational Learning: A Theory of Action Perspective.* Reading, MA: Addison-Wesley.

Bales, R. F. 1950. *Interaction Process Analysis.* Chicago: University of Chicago Press.

Bales, R. F., and S. P. Cohen. 1979. *SYMLOG: A System for the Multiple Level Observation of Groups.* New York: Free Press.

Barley, S. R. 1983. Semiotics and the Study of Occupational and Organizational Cultures. *Administrative Science Quarterly* 28, pp. 393–413.

Barley, S. R., C. W. Meyer, and D. C. Gash. 1988. Culture of Cultures: Academics, Practitioners and the Pragmatics of Normative Control. *Administrative Science Quarterly* 33, pp. 24–60.

Bass, B. M. 1965. *Organizational Psychology.* Boston: Allyn & Bacon.

Beckhard, R. 1969. *Organization Development: Strategies and Models.* Reading, MA: Addison-Wesley.

Beckhard, R., and R. T. Harris. 1977. *Organizational Transitions: Managing Complex Change.* Reading, MA: Addison-Wesley.

Beckhard, R., and R. T. Harris. 1987. *Organizational Transitions: Managing Complex Change,* 2nd ed. Reading, MA: Addison-Wesley.

Benne, K., and P. Sheats. 1948. "Functional Roles of Group Members." *Journal of Social Issues* 2, pp. 42–47.

Bennis, W. G. 1966. *Changing Organizations.* New York: McGraw-Hill.

Bennis, W. G. 1969. *Organization Development: Its Nature, Origins, and Prospects.* Reading, MA: Addison-Wesley.

Bennis, W. G., and H. A. Shephard. 1956. "A Theory of Group Development." *Human Relations* 9, pp. 415–437.

Bion, W. R. 1959. *Experiences in Groups.* London: Tavistock.

Bradford, L. P., J. R. Gibb, and K. D. Benne (Eds.). 1964. *T-Group Theory and Laboratory Method.* New York: Wiley.

Chandler, A. P. 1977. *The Visible Hand.* Cambridge, MA: Harvard University Press.

Deal, T. W., and A. A. Kennedy. 1982. *Corporate Cultures.* Reading, MA: Addison-Wesley.

Durkin, J. E. (Ed.). 1981. *Living Groups: Group Psychotherapy and General Systems Theory.* New York: Brunner/Mazel.

Dyer, W. G., Jr. 1986. *Cultural Change in Family Firms.* San Francisco: Jossey-Bass.

Feldman, D. C. 1976. A Contingency Theory of Socialization. *Administrative Science Quarterly,* 21, pp. 433–452.

Feldman, D. C. 1988. *Managing Careers in Organizations.* Glenview, IL: Scott, Foresman.

Festinger, L. 1957. *A Theory of Cognitive Dissonance.* New York: Harper and Row.

Fleishman, E. A. 1953. Leadership Climate, Human Relations Training, and Supervisory Behavior. *Personnel Psychology* 6, pp. 205–222.

Fleishman, E. A. 1973. Twenty Years of Consideration and Structure. In E. A. Fleishman and J. G. Hunt Eds.). *Current Developments in the Study of Leadership.* Carbondale, IL: Southern Illinois University Press, pp. 1–39.

French, W. L., and C. H. Bell. 1984. *Organization Development,* 3rd ed. Englewood Cliffs, NJ: Prentice Hall.

Frost, P. J., L. F. Moore, M. R. Louis, C. C. Lundberg, and J. Martin (Eds.). 1985. *Organizational Culture.* Beverly Hills, CA: Sage.

Hanna, D. P. 1988. *Designing Organizations for High Performance.* Reading, MA: Addison-Wesley.

Harris, S. G., and R. I. Sutton. 1986. Functions of Parting Ceremonies in Dying Organizations. *Academy of Management Journal* 29, pp. 5–30.

Hebb, D. 1954. The Social Significance of Animal Studies. In G. Lindzey (Ed.). *Handbook of Social Psychology,* Vol. 2. Reading, MA: Addison-Wesley, pp. 532–561.

Heider, F. 1958. *The Psychology of Interpersonal Relations.* New York: Wiley.

Hellriegel, D., and J. W. Slocum, Jr. 1974. Organizational Climate: Measures, Research, and Contingencies. *Academy of Management Journal* 17, pp. 255–280.

Hirschhorn, L. 1987. *The Workplace Within*. Cambridge, MA: MIT Press.

Hofstede, G. 1980. *Culture's Consequences*. Beverly Hills, CA: Sage.

Hofstede, G., and M. H. Bond. 1988. The Confucius Connection: From Cultural Roots to Economic Growth. *Organizational Dynamics* 16(4), pp. 4–21.

Homans, G. 1950. *The Human Group*. New York: Harcourt, Brace, Jovanovich.

Jaques, E. 1951. *The Changing Culture of a Factory*. London: Tavistock.

Jones, A. P., and L. R. James. 1979. Psychological Climate: Dimensions and Relationships of Individual and Aggre-gated Work Environment Perceptions. *Organizational Behavior and Human Performance*, 23, pp. 201–250.

Jones, G. R. 1986. Socialization Tactics, Self-Efficacy, and Newcomers' Adjustments to Organizations. *Academy of Management Journal*, 29, pp. 262–279.

Katz, D., and R. L. Kahn. 1966. *The Social Psychology of Organizations*. New York: Wiley.

Katz, D., and R. L. Kahn. 1978. *The Social Psychology of Organizations*, 2nd ed. New York: Wiley.

Kets de Vries, M. F. R., and D. Miller. 1984. *The Neurotic Organization*. San Francisco: Jossey-Bass.

Kets de Vries, M. F. R., and D. Miller. 1986. Personality, Culture, and Organization. *Academy of Management Review*, 11, pp. 266–279.

Kilmann, R. H. 1984. *Beyond the Quick Fix*. San Francisco: Jossey-Bass.

Kluckhohn, F. R., and F. L. Strodtbeck. 1961. *Variations in Value Orientations*. New York: Harper & Row.

Lewin, K. 1952. Group Decision and Social Change. In G. E. Swanson, T. N. Newcomb, and E. L. Hartley (Eds.). *Readings in Social Psychology*, rev. ed. New York: Holt, Rinehard, and Winston, pp. 459–473.

Lewin, K., R. Lippitt, and R. K. White. 1939. Patterns of Aggressive Behavior in Experimentally Created "Social Climates." *Journal of Social Psychology*, 10, pp. 271–299.

Likert, R. 1961. *New Patterns of Management*. New York: McGraw-Hill.

Likert, R. 1967. *The Human Organization*. New York: McGraw-Hill.

Lippitt, G. 1982. *Organizational Renewal*, 2nd ed. Englewood Cliffs, NJ: Prentice Hall.

Litwin, G. H., and R. A. Stringer. 1968. *Motivation and Organizational Climate*. Boston: Harvard Business School, Division of Research.

Louis, M. R. 1981. A Cultural Perspective on Organizations. *Human Systems Management* 2, pp. 246–258.

Louis, M. R. 1983. Organizations as Culture Bearing Milieux. In L. R. Pondy, P. J. Frost, G. Morgan, and T. C. Dandridge (Eds.). *Organizational Symbolism*. Greenwich, CT: JAI Press, pp. 39–54.

Martin, J. 1982. Stories and Scripts in Organizational Settings. In A. Hastorf and A. Isen (Eds.). *Cognitive Social Psychology*. New York: Elsevier.

Martin, J., M. S. Feldman, M. J. Hatch, and S. Sitkin. 1983. The Uniqueness Paradox in Organizational Stories. *Administrative Science Quarterly*, 28, pp. 438–454.

Martin, J., and D. Meyerson. 1988. Organizational Cultures and the Denial, Channeling, and Acknowledgement of Ambiguity. In L. R. Pondy, R. J. Boland, and H. Thomas (Eds.), *Managing Ambiguity and Change*. New York: Wiley.

Martin, J. and M. E. Powers. 1983. Truth or Corporate Propaganda: The Value of a Good War Story. In L. R. Pondy, P. J. Frost, G. Morgan, and T. C. Dandridge (Eds.), *Organizational Symbolism*. Greenwich, CT: JAI Press, 93–108.

Martin, J. and C. Siehl. 1983. Organizational Culture and Counter-Culture: An Uneasy Symbiosis. *Organizational Dynamics*, 12, 52–64.

Menzies, I. E. P. 1960. A Case Study in the Functioning of Social Systems as a Defense Against Anxiety. *Human Relations*, 13, 95–121.

O'Toole, J. J. 1979. Corporate and Managerial Cultures. In C. L. Cooper (Ed.), *Behavioral Problems in Organizations*. Englewood Cliffs, NJ: Prentice Hall.

Ott, J. S. 1989. *The Organizational Culture Perspective*. Chicago: Dorsey Press.

Ouchi, W. G. 1981. *Theory Z*. Reading, MA: Addison-Wesley.

Pascale, R. T., and A. G. Athos. 1981. *The Art of Japanese Management*. New York: Simon & Schuster.

Peters, T. J., and R. H. Waterman, Jr. 1982. *In Search of Excellence*. New York: Simon & Schuster.

Pettigrew, A. M. 1979. On Studying Organizational Cultures. *Administrative Science Quarterly* 24, 570–581.

Pondy, L. R., R. J. Boland, and H. Thomas. 1988. *Managing Ambiguity and Change*. New York: Wiley.

Pondy, L. R., P. J. Frost, G. Morgan, and T. C. Dandridge (Eds.). 1983. *Organizational Symbolism*. Greenwich, CT: JAI Press.

Rice, A. K. 1963. *The Enterprise and Its Environment*. London: Tavistock.

Ritti, R. R., and G. R. Funkhouser. 1987. *The Ropes to Skip and the Ropes to Know*, 3rd ed. New York: Wiley.

Roethlisberger, F. J., and W. J. Dickson. 1939. *Management and the Worker*. Cambridge, MA: Harvard University Press.

Schall, M. S. 1983. A Communication-Rules Approach to Organizational Culture. *Administrative Science Quarterly*, 28, 557–581.

Schein, E. H. 1965. *Organizational Psychology*. Englewood Cliffs, NJ: Prentice Hall.

Schein, E. H. 1968. Organizational Socialization and the Profession of Management. *Industrial Management Review* (MIT) 9, 1–15.

Schein, E. H. 1969. *Process Consultation*. Reading, MA: Addison-Wesley.

Schein, E. H. 1978. *Career Dynamics*. Reading, MA: Addison-Wesley.

Schein, E. H. 1983. The Role of the Founder in Creating Organizational Culture. *Organizational Dynamics* 12, 13–28.

Schein, E. H. 1985a. *Organizational Culture and Leadership*. San Francisco: Jossey-Bass.

Schein, E. H. 1985b. Organizational Culture: Skill, Defense Mechanism or Addiction? In F. R. Brush and J. B. Overmier (Eds.), *Affect, Conditioning, and Cognition.* Hillsdale, NJ: Erlbaum, pp. 315–323.

Schein, E. H. 1987a. *The Clinical Perspective in Fieldwork.* Beverly Hills, CA: Sage.

Schein, E. H. 1987b. *Process Consultation,* Vol. 2. Reading, MA: Addison-Wesley.

Schein, E. H. 1988. *Process Consultation,* rev. ed. Reading, MA: Addison-Wesley.

Schein, E. H., and W. G. Bennis. 1965. *Personal and Organizational Change Through Group Methods.* New York: Wiley.

Schneider, B. 1975. Organizational Climate: An Essay. *Personnel Psychology* 28, 447–479.

Schneider, B., and A. E. Reichers. 1983. On the Etiology of Climates. *Personnel Psychology* 36, 19–46.

Smircich, L., and M. B. Calas. 1987. Organizational Culture: A Critical Assessment. In F. M. Jablin, L. L. Putnam, K. H. Roberts, and L. W. Porter (Eds.), *Handbook of Organizational Communication.* Beverly Hills, CA: Sage, pp. 228–263.

Tagiuri, R., and G. H. Litwin (Eds.). 1968. *Organizational Climate: Exploration of a Concept.* Boston: Harvard Business School, Division of Research.

Trice, H., and J. Beyer. 1984. Studying Organizational Cultures Through Rites and Ceremonials. *Academy of Management Review* 9, 653–669.

Trist, E. L., G. W. Higgin, H. Murray, and A. B. Pollock. 1963. *Organizational Choice.* London: Tavistock.

Van Maanen, J. 1976. Breaking In: Socialization to Work. In R. Dubin (Ed.), *Handbook of Work, Organization and Society.* Chicago: Randy McNally, 67–130.

Van Maanen, J. 1977. Experiencing Organizations. In J. Van Maanen (Ed.), *Organizational Careers: Some New Perspectives.* New York: Wiley, 15–45.

Van Maanen, J. 1978. People Processing: Strategies of Organizational Socialization. *Organizational Dynamics* 7, 18–36.

Van Maanen, J. 1988. *Tales of the Field.* Chicago: University of Chicago Press.

Van Maanen, J., and S. R. Barley. 1984. Occupational Communities: Culture and Control in Organizations. In B. M. Staw and L. L. Cummings (Eds.), *Research in Organizational Behavior,* Vol. 6. Greenwich, CT: JAI Press.

Van Maanen, J., and E. H. Schein. 1979. Toward a Theory of Organizational Socialization. In B. M. Staw and L. L. Cummings (Eds.), *Research in Organizational Behavior,* Vol 1. Greenwich, CT: JAI Press, pp. 204–264.

Walton, R. 1987. *Innovating to Compete.* San Francisco: Jossey-Bass.

Werner, H. 1940. *Comparative Psychology of Mental Development.* New York: Follett.

Westney, D. E. 1987. *Imitation and Innovation.* Cambridge, MA: Harvard University Press.

Wilkins, A. L. 1983. Organizational Stories as Symbols Which Control the Organization. In L. R. Pondy, P. J. Frost, G. Morgan, and T. C. Dandridge (Eds.), *Organizational Symbolism.* Greenwich, CT: JAI Press, pp. 81–91.

Wilkins, A. L., and W. G. Ouchi. 1983. Efficient Cultures: Exploring the Relationship Between Culture and Organizational Performance. *Administrative Science Quarterly* 28, 468–481.

Applying the Three Lenses

Academic researchers have the luxury of focusing on one of the three lenses and becoming an expert on it: strategic design, political, or cultural. One expert may analyze the organization chart primarily as a map of information flows and formal roles and responsibilities, for example, and assess it in terms of how well its formal structure meets the strategic needs of the organization. Another may regard it as one piece of data in analyzing the political system of the organization, as a map of who has formal authority over whom. Another may see it as a cultural artifact, viewing its significance in terms of how often the chart is reproduced and in what contexts, and whether members of the organization refer to the "org chart" when they try to explain their organization to outsiders or whether they assert that no one can understand the organization by looking at the chart.

Taking effective action in organizations, however, requires an ability to see the organization through all three lenses, not just one, and to integrate the insights derived from each into action steps that will work on all three dimensions. This part of the module asks you to practice your skills in the context of a single case, which follows up the case on Dynacorp presented earlier in the strategic design section of the module. In order to prepare for the class discussion on integrating the perspectives, you should go back and review each of the three lenses: the strategic design, political, and cultural lenses. Please also read the additional background material on the Dynacorp organization that begins on page 85. This material also includes a transcript of the Dynacorp video that you will see in class. The video itself provides much richer information than the transcript alone, but you might want to read through the written version before class to enable you to focus more attention on the nonverbal cues in the video.

To help you prepare to do the analysis, here are a few questions posed from each of the three perspectives, that can guide your thinking. This list is suggestive, not exhaustive. Try to think of additional questions to consider under each category.

Strategic Design Lens

- What is the strategy of the organization as a whole? How well is it understood and implemented by the members of the organization at various levels?
- What is the basis for the formal grouping structure? Are roles and responsibilities clearly defined and understood? On what activities does the structure focus attention?
- What are important interdependencies across the formal units represented by the "boxes" in the organization design (i.e., with what other units does any one unit need to interact on a regular basis to carry out its assigned activities)? Are adequate linking mechanisms in place? What are they, and how well are they working?
- How is the performance of the organization and its members being measured? What is the incentive system and is it recognizing and rewarding strategically valuable behaviors and activities? Are there "perverse incentives" that are rewarding dysfunctional behavior (i.e., behavior that is impeding the achievement of desired goals)?
- Do people in the organization have the resources and the motivation they need in order to carry out the tasks assigned to them? If not, why not? What are the barriers that are getting in the way?

Political Lens

- Who has power and status in the organization? What is the basis of their influence? Is power concentrated (at the top, or elsewhere), or are there multiple power centers?
- What are the key arenas of conflict? Who are the key actors in this conflict (individuals, groups, subunits), and what are the basic causes of the disagreements? What are the interests of the key actors?
- What, if any, mechanisms of conflict resolution exist, and how effectively are they working? If they are not working effectively, why not?
- Who benefits most from the current patterns in the organization, and why?
- Who gets credit in the organization when things are going well and performance goals are met? Who gets blamed when the organization does not meet its goals? Do those who get blamed have the power to make changes that will improve performance?
- How well do information about problems and requests for help move up the hierarchy? How open are those in positions of formal authority to suggestions and initiatives from below?

Cultural Lens

- What artifacts, stories, symbols, and observed behaviors provide important clues to the culture of the organization? How much uniformity or variety do you observe?

- What are the espoused values of the organization and how are they transmitted? How widely are these shared?
- Are there any inconsistencies between the behavior observed and the espoused values? What basic assumptions do these reveal? What other basic assumptions can you uncover in the language and stories people repeat?
- Do those at the top of the organization have the same perceptions and beliefs about the organization as those at the bottom? Do different units or groups share these beliefs and perceptions, or are there significant differences?
- What messages are those at the top of the organization hearing from those in positions of authority? How are they interpreting them? Are they hearing the message that the senders intend?
- What individuals are held up as exemplars? Who is identified as a good manager or a good worker? What does this reveal about the basic cultural assumptions?
- What is the emotional atmosphere in the organization (confident, anxious, contentious, etc.)?

Taking Effective Action Steps

In order to help you practice using the analytical skills that you are developing by using the three lenses, the class discussion will ask you to recommend action steps for one of the key actors in the case, based on your analysis. Here are some of the features of a good action step.

- *Specific and concrete:* It is an *action* that you can take and that will have an observable outcome, not a general prescription such as, "Show confidence in your team." An action step spells how what you could actually do to show confidence in your team.
- *Comprehensive:* It demonstrates an ability to think through the immediate action step to include subsequent action steps that will be needed if the first is to have any positive impact. For example, you might start with a recommendation such as, "Conduct a survey of employees." This step would not only need more detail to make it *specific and concrete* (e.g., what topics would it cover? how would you administer it?), but would also address the necessary follow-up steps (e.g., what will you do with the data when you get it? with whom will you share it?).
- *Effective on all three lenses:* You need to think through whether an action that might seem appealing using one lens is consistent with what you are trying to accomplish using the other lenses. For example, to pursue the example of the employee survey, it might be tempting, using a political lens, to have a cover letter or introductory message from the CEO on the survey, in order to show that it has significant support in the company and to increase the eagerness of people to respond. If the survey is part of an effort to get employees to take more responsibility for improving the organization, however, the cover letter may send a signal of top-down "ownership" of the improvement program that contradicts the goals of the initiative.
- *Consistency with your analysis:* Make sure that your recommended action steps actually build on your analysis. Many of us have "recipes" to which we resort in times of pressure, especially if those recipes have worked in the past (e.g., "change the incentive system" or "ensure that you have the support of top management"). Many of the failures in organizations occur because a manager comes into an organization and applies recipes that worked for him or her in the past, but are not justified by the context in which they are now operating.

Remember that in making recommendations, as in real life, it is much better to have a small number of specific, comprehensive, well-thought-out action steps that form a coherent sequence than it is to have a large number of steps that take you, in the immortal words of Stephen Leacock, riding madly off in all directions.

Assignment Summary

Review the materials on each of the three lenses to make sure you understand their key features. Come to class prepared to do further analysis of the Dynacorp case using each of the three lenses.

1. For each lens, what are the key indicators you would look for?
2. What are action steps that you might take in an organization, in terms of each lens?
3. Read "Dynacorp Revisited" and be sure that you understand the key elements of its organization design described in the *first four pages* of the case. Reading the transcript of the video that you will see is optional but recommended.
4. [*Optional*] What are the key sources of Dynacorp's problems in implementing its new customer organization in terms of the strategic design lens? the political lens? the cultural lens?

Dynacorp Revisited

The front/back organization

The Dyna Corporation, known in the industry as Dynacorp, is a major global information systems and communications company. Originating in an office equipment company that moved into high-technology applications in the 1960s and 1970s, Dynacorp had, by the 1980s, established a position as an industry leader, known for its technological innovation. Dynacorp was first to the market with innovative and high-quality products that were significant advances on anything its competitors were offering. Customers would gladly wait months, and even a year or so, to take delivery of products bearing the Dynacorp logo. The customers were typically sophisticated users who were willing to do some of their own applications work and to figure out how to integrate Dynacorp's new products with the rest of their operations. During this period, the company grew at a very fast rate, and expanded its market to Europe, Asia, and Latin America.

The 1990s were a much more difficult period for the company. It continued to grow, but at a slower rate, and experienced periods of significantly reduced earnings. Critics both inside and outside the company attributed Dynacorp's difficulties to a loss of leadership in getting new products to market, costs that were too high, and changes in the marketplace that Dynacorp was slow to recognize. Competitors were closing the technology gap, and were often faster getting products to market. In a growing number of product areas, Dynacorp had been surprised by competitors who, although they had started working on a new product much later than Dynacorp, were faster at getting the product to the customer at an attractive price. In addition, a growing number of information technology and communications (ITC) consulting firms were capturing the relationship with the large customer by offering "value-added services and solutions." The consulting firms acted as intermediaries, supervising the purchase of ITC hardware and software, providing integration services, and capturing much of the high-margin business.

Since its founding, Dynacorp had a functional structure, with the principal line divisions being engineering, manufacturing, and marketing. Believing that this structure no longer served the company's strategic needs, the CEO set up an internal task force to make recommendations on how the company should organize to meet the growing challenges it faced. Worried that the task force was moving too slowly, however, the CEO hired an external consulting firm to work with the task force to generate recommendations. The consultants, who had worked with a number of companies in the ITC industry, strongly believed that the front/back organization design provided the quickest and most effective way to meet Dynacorp's needs, and they persuaded both the task force and the CEO to share this view. Based on the task force's report, the CEO mandated Dynacorp's change to the front/back structure.

The Front/Back Design at Dynacorp

In the old Dynacorp, the engineering division had been the strongest and most prestigious area of the company, and most of the top management team had begun their careers in engineering. Dynacorp's manufacturing division had also built strong capabilities and an excellent reputation for quality. However, because of the difficulties in moving new product designs across the divisional boundary between engineering and manufacturing, Dynacorp had been slow in getting its products to market, and a number of the company's highly anticipated new product introductions had been delayed long past their original announced launch date, alienating customers and giving competitors a chance to introduce competing products.

The new design created a "back end" that put the engineering and manufacturing functions together in a set of business units (BUs), each focusing on a particular product category (e.g., large systems, peripherals, small systems). In addition, a small number of people from the old marketing division were assigned to each BU to deal with market strategy and product positioning. Some scientists and engineers from the old engineering division stayed in a separate research and advanced development group, reporting directly to the CEO and working on new technologies with product horizons three to ten years in the future.

Source: From Competing by Design: The Power of Organizational Architecture by David A. Nadler, Michael L. Tushman, and Mark B. Nadler, copyright © 1997 Oxford University Press. Used by permission of Oxford University Press, Inc.

The overwhelming majority of the engineers, however, found themselves in cross-functional business units that combined product development, manufacturing, and market strategy. Most of the heads of the new BUs came from the old engineering division and had been leaders in the development of the products around which the BU was organized.

Most of the old marketing division was relabeled "customer operations" and, reflecting the growing importance of international markets, organized into three large geographic divisions, of which the largest was U.S. customer operations. Each division was in turn organized by geography: by country in Europe and Latin America/Asia, by region in the United States. At first glance, it might seem that the front/back design had less impact on the marketing function than on the old engineering and manufacturing divisions. In reality, however, the daily activities of employees in marketing, sales, and service changed more profoundly than those of the engineers and production workers in the new BUs in the back end. In the past, each of the eight U.S. regions had been organized by geographic branches with a specific sales territory: for example, the Northeast Region had eight branches located in major urban centers, Boston being the largest in terms of sales. The new design kept the terms *branch* and *branch manager*, but each of ten branches now covered the entire Northeast region for a particular set of industries or sectors, such as state and local government, process industries, or health services. In the old organization, each customer had a designated individual account manager, who cultivated close personal relationships with key individuals responsible for IT purchasing. As Dynacorp's product range increased, it became harder for a single individual to have real expertise on all the possible solutions for a customer's requirements. The new design created account teams, which had collective responsibility for a customer.

Support services, including sales support, technical support, customer administration (which handled order processing), and a new industry solutions development group, was a shared services organization reporting directly to the executive vice president of U.S. customer operations. The importance of critical mass in developing the expertise involved in these activities justified concentrating them into a nationally organized structure, even though individual sections were dispersed geographically into the regions. In the past, individual account managers had developed informal networks into sales and technical support groups to gain access to information and resources, but over time, some newer account managers experienced difficulties in making the right contacts. In the new design, therefore, each customer account team had a member from each of the relevant shared service groups formally assigned to the team. In many cases teams included "virtual" team members: that is, each person was a member of several teams and participated in team meetings through distance hookups.

Given the scale of these changes and the ongoing competitive pressures in the marketplace, the U.S. customer operations division has been struggling to meet its targets since the reorganization. Top management remains confident, however, that the company has put the right organization design into place and that it is only a matter of time—and effort—for the changes to pay off in renewed growth and profitability.

Your Role

You are a member of a student research team that is conducting an organizational analysis of a change initiative in a company of their choice for their class project in their organizational processes course. Carl Greystone, the current executive vice president for U.S. customer operations in Dynacorp, is an alumnus of your school, and he has agreed to provide your team with access to his organization for your project. Customer operations just reorganized its regions into industry-focused branches to improve customer responsiveness and better support the business units. The Northeast region headquarters is located in the same building as the corporate center.

You told Mr. Greystone that you would like to talk with people at each level of his customer operations group, and he agreed to select key informants for you to interview. Your team wants to develop an analysis of the current state of the change process in Dynacorp, to look at what is facilitating and what has been hindering the change, and to practice your analytical skills by identifying action steps that might make the change process work more effectively.

The Situation

Mr. Greystone suggested that your team focus on the recent change initiative in the U.S. customer operations group that reorganized the salesforce in each region into account teams. Each account team focuses on customers in a particular market segment, defined by their industry (e.g., financial services).

In your initial discussions, Mr. Greystone admitted that for the past year and a half, the U.S. customer operations group has consistently been behind plan in both revenue and profit, and that the business unit presidents have expressed some frustration with the performance of his group. But he is confident that the recent change initiative will turn the situation around. He tells you, "Recently, we've made a tremendous amount of progress. If

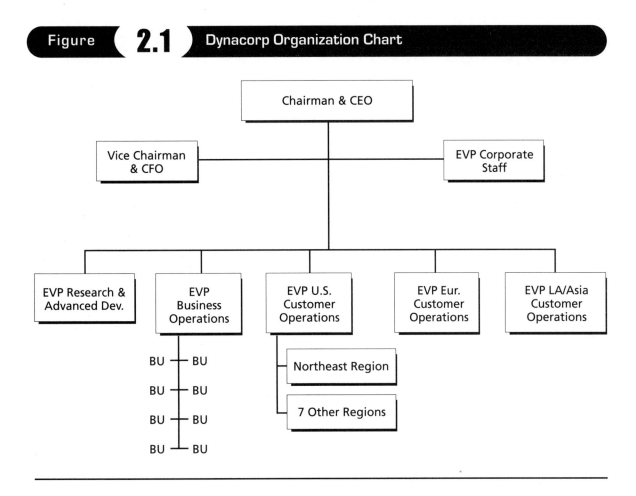

Figure 2.1 Dynacorp Organization Chart

you could have seen this place two years ago, when the company first created the business units, you would have been horrified. We've made the big changes—we've reorganized into regions and customer teams, and we have our people thinking about the business in new terms. I think we're beginning to see the light at the end of the tunnel."

Mr. Greystone has agreed to talk with you himself, to provide an overview of the change initiative and its background, and then has arranged for you to meet with Ben Walker, the vice president for the Northeast region. Ben Walker in turn will give you his perspective on the change, and will then introduce you to one of his branch managers, to whom the account teams report. You also hope to sit in on an account team meeting, to get a clearer sense of how the teams are really working.

The Visits and Discussions

You spend the day at the Dynacorp building, and are successful in getting time with people at each of the levels of the organization you wanted to talk with. (These visits are shown on the accompanying videotape. A transcript of the dialogue is included on the following pages.) It is now the following day, and your team is trying to make sense of what it has seen and heard.

Dynacorp Video Transcript
Northeast Region

C. Greystone (EVP U.S. Customer Operations Group): . . . So the past few years have not been easy. As you know, both foreign and domestic competitors have been cutting into our market share, and our gross margins are way down. There was a time when our customers would pay high prices for our state-of-the-art technology. But now, they are looking for systems solutions, more customized software, and more value-added services. We've been forced to develop a strategy that more closely matches with the current marketplace. Customer teams must now function as consultants by helping the customers identify their needs and providing high-quality products, integrated solutions, and customized services to

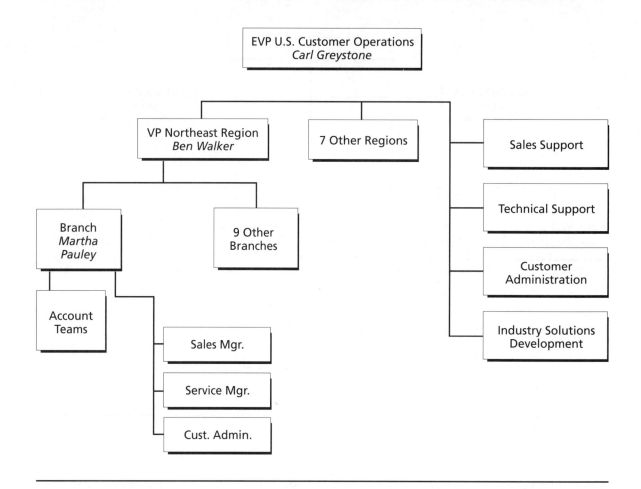

Figure 2.2 Dynacorp U.S. Customer Operations

fit those needs. To support the new plan, we've restructured the U.S. customer operations group into regions and a new customer team structure.

Now the way we go about that is to assign multifunction and multiproduct account teams to specific customers in specific industries instead of having them cover a mixed bag of clients in the sales territory. That way, our people are industry specialists, not just product knowledgeable. In addition, we are focusing the salesforce on selling customized solutions based on integrating our products, rather than on selling fancy hardware. You see, we feel that by targeting our investments toward growth of sales in specific industries and developing solutions to fit their needs, we'll rebuild our market share and increase margins.

I'd like you to talk to Ben Walker, my most experienced general manager. I'll have my secretary call Ben and tell him that you'll be over to visit after we have lunch. Ben can fill you in on some of the details in his area.

B. Walker (VP Northeast Region): Carl outlined the new strategy. I think it's a move in the right direction. Finally we're able to compete with the foreign and domestic competitors that are grabbing the market with their emphasis on customized solutions. Our short-term problem is that we have a new structure, but the same people to fill the slots. There are too many people who know how to sell products but not solutions. Right now we have the customer teams functioning under new guidelines that force them to collect information on customer needs and develop solutions. But too many team members are still operating under the old attitude that the equipment sells itself and the customers will do the work of integrating our products into their operations. The notion of helping the customer from initial call through implementation and use of the system is still quite alien to many of our people. In fact, the skills and attitudes on many levels are mismatched with our current needs. Let me give you an example. Instead of focusing on the customer teams and making sure that they are being more responsive to customer needs, some branch managers seem to spend most of their time worrying about the new performance measurement system. You see, under our new structure, branch managers and product managers in the business units are compensated on performance against revenue and margin goals.

This causes considerable friction because no one in these jobs has the skills to be a team player. Honestly, I feel that with the help of early retirements, downsizing, and the addition of appropriately retrained staff, we'll be able to profit soon from our new approach. Unfortunately, we project that at least 25 percent of the current staff needs to be replaced. Hopefully, that will show everyone that we are serious about change. It's not an easy answer, but I guess it's the price we pay for success in this new world. The market and the customers are very unforgiving.

One of the industry-focused branches is on the fourteenth floor. Let's go down and I'll introduce you to Martha Pauley, the branch manager. She's one of our best, and she'll show you the setup.

M. Pauley (Branch Manager): Excuse me for just one minute. I'll get back to you with that information later this afternoon.

Well, first let me tell you how we're set up. I work for Ben Walker and manage the six sales teams that handle financial institutions, insurance, and education in the Northeast region. I share revenue goals for my teams with the product team's general managers in the business units. My teams are made up of account managers, product specialists, solution consultants, service technicians, customer administration specialists, and systems specialists. I haven't had a chance to develop a cohesive sales plan to show you. Everyone has been so busy trying to understand their new responsibilities while still keeping up with our customers that we have communicated only through e-mail messages. We haven't had time for the off-site meeting that I had planned. Anyway, we're still getting modifications on the job guidelines from the staff group. You see, moving from a product salesperson to a provider of solutions is a big change. It involves knowledge of the industry and the company, the full line of products, our various software applications, and concepts of systems integration. Exactly who handles all the pieces of a sale like this is still unclear. In addition, different product team leaders in the business units are pushing different types of sales, depending on their particular product lines.

Another big issue is our ability to compete. Our prices are still higher than our competitors', and technical support services are way too slow. The new plant in Indonesia was supposed to help bring prices down, but they're having problems getting the factory up and running. Since I have no control over unit manufacturing costs or the availability of technical support resources, I can't help the team's effectiveness in these areas.

There is an account team meeting going on in the conference room down the hall. Under the current guidelines, they meet as a team once every two weeks. Let's take a quick look and then you can see some of how a team functions.

M. Pauley: Hi, how would you feel about having an overseas guest and me sit in on your meeting for a few minutes?

Sales Team Member 1 (Team Leader): It's fine with me. How do the rest of you feel? [Others nod and say fine.]

M. Pauley: Great, thanks a lot. What happened to the rest of your team? It looks like about half of you are missing.

Sales Team Member 1: It's true. Jim Davis, the head of the large systems business unit, is having a big meeting for the field to introduce his new product line. We thought we ought to send a few representatives.

M. Pauley: Oh yes, now I remember. Well, I guess we have to be responsive to them. I didn't mean to get you off track by my question.

Sales Team Member 1: No problem, Martha. Listen, did the Boston bank make a decision yet on their system?

Sales Team Member 2: Yes they did. We didn't get the contract. National Systems won the bid. They had lower prices and a much more comprehensive package. They were able to link their machines to the systems network. Plus, they have a partnership with a software applications company that is going to come in and customize their interface and provide training to all the employees. It's a pretty impressive package, even though their products are not as good as ours.

Sales Team Member 3: This situation is getting very depressing. We have to figure out a new strategy pretty quickly or we are not going to make our quarterly targets.

Sales Team Member 1: What about the Thompson account? Has that system been installed yet?

Sales Team Member 3: We are still waiting on technical support. This is one of those custom systems that they just can't seem to gear up for. I'm meeting with our support person tomorrow and we are going to try to work out a schedule so that we don't miss the deadline.

Sales Team Member 2: Well, anyway, Judy Brown called me yesterday. She's great. She's been a good customer of mine for years. I'm having lunch with her on Tuesday. She'll tell me exactly what she wants, and it looks like a whole set of standard off-the-shelf equipment for her bank. If only we had more customers like Judy.

M. Pauley: As I said earlier, there are some bugs to work out. But I think some training will do the trick once the guidelines are in place.

Index

"Action Company" paradigm, 71, 73
action steps, in organizational analysis, 84
adaptation tasks, external, 72
advice networks, 40, 47–52
African American caucus groups, 35
alignment, 14, 15, 23–25, 26
allies and coalitions, 43–44
analysis, organizational, 8, 11. *See also* organizational analysis and action, lenses on
analytical descriptive research, 68–69
anxiety, 25
artifacts, 70
assumptions, 70–71, 73, 78
authority, 36, 38

behavioral science, 4
benefits, 35
Big Mac, as symbol, 58
Black Caucus at Xerox, 35
blockers and supporters, mapping, 42, 43
boundaries, and collective interests, 34
bounded rationality, 65
"bow ties," 54
Burt, Ron, 40
business division structure, 17–18
business/functional matrix, 19
business process reengineering (BPR), 15
business units (BUs), 85–86
business unit solos, 18
"buy-in," getting, 42–43

caucus groups, 35
centrality, 38–39
charisma, 36–37
cleavage model of organizational culture, 62
climate, organizational, 68
clinical descriptive research, 69
coalitions, 39–40, 43–44
coercion as power, 36, 38
coercive theories, 60
cognitive processing, 8–9
collective interests, 34–35
commitment, escalation of, 42
commitment chart, 42, 43
communication networks, 47, 48, 52–55
competitive advantage, 14
complexity of tasks, 14
conflict, 33, 36, 37
congruence, 23
connotative meanings, 57
consequences, observation of, 41
control and motivation, 60–61, 65
creation of culture, 75
creative individualism, 76
critical incidents, 75

cross-functional teams, 31, 85–86
cross-unit groups, 22–23
Crozier, Michel, 37
cultural island, 68
cultural lens/perspective. *See also* organizational culture
  overview, 4, 11, 57
  definition of culture, 58–59
  diagnosis of organizations, 64–66
  external cultural context, 63–64
  habits and history, 65
  identity and, 63, 64–65
  motivation and control, 60–61, 65
  "new" organization and, 66
  relativity, cultural, 65
  structure and culture, 59
  subcultures, 61–63, 65
  symbolism and meaning, 57–58, 64
cultural processes and products, 58–59
culture, organizational. *See* organizational culture
cultures, national, 63–64
"currencies," and network construction, 44–45
custodial orientation, 76
customer division structure, 18–19, 32

defined benefits vs. defined contribution plans, 35
demographic groups, and collective interests, 35
denotative meanings, 57
design, strategic. *See* strategic design lens/perspective
development of human capital, 25
differentiation, 14, 77
difficult linkages, 23
Digital Equipment Corporation, 34
Disneyland, 61
distinctive competitive advantage, 14
dominant coalition, 44
dotted line hierarchical structure, 22
dual career ladder, 29
Dynacorp case, 28–32, 85–90
dynamics, cultural, 75–78

"economic man," 34
economies of scope, 16
effectiveness, 14
efficiency, 14
efficient networks, 39
ego, submersion of, 37
energy, and power, 37
enterprise groups, 63–64
environment, external, 21, 26
escalation of commitment, 42
espoused values, 71
ethnography, 69

evolution, cultural, 76–78
exchange perspective, 44–45
exchange theories, 60
expertise, 16–17, 37
external adaptation tasks, 72
external environment, 21, 26
external stakeholders, 35

factionalism in networks, 54
flat organizations
    communication networks and, 52
    incentives, 24
    social networks, and influence, 38
    unbiased information flows in, 66
flexibility, as power source, 37
focus, and power, 37
formal reporting structures, 21–22
formal vs. informal organization, 47
fragmentation, 62
friendship networks, 40
front/back structure, 20, 21, 32, 85–86
functional grouping structure, 16–17, 28–30, 32
functional/product matrix, 19, 32

gender, 9
General Motors (GM), 64
geographic grouping structure, 18–19, 29
getting "buy-in," 42
globalization, 63, 66
"Godfather" strategy, 38
grouping, strategic, 14, 15, 16–20, 26

hierarchical structure
    communication networks and, 52
    in functional organizations, 17
    as strategic grouping, 21–22
    vertical power systems and, 38
high fliers, 37
historical method, 69
holes in networks, 40, 54
homo economicus ("economic man"), 34
horizontal power systems, 38
human assets, development of, 25
hybrid grouping structures, 19–20

identification with leaders, 75
identity, 63, 64–65
illusion of influence, 42–43
imploded relationships in networks, 53
incentives and rewards, 24–25
individualism, 76
individual retirement accounts, 35
influence. *See also* power
    negotiation skills and, 45
    network-building and, 44–45
    perception and illusion of, 42–43
    as power, 36
informal networks, 38–40, 47–55

informal systems and processes, 25
information, 22, 39, 40, 66
information technology (IT), 23
innovation, ideational, 59
integration (strategic linking), 14, 15, 20–23
integration tasks, internal, 72
integrator roles, 22, 23
interactions, organizational. *See* political lens/perspective
interdependence of tasks, 14–15, 16, 20–21
interests
    coalitions of allies, 43–44
    collective, 34–35
    definition of, 34
    dynamic nature of, 36
    mapping, 41–42
    multiple and competing, 35
    political perspective and, 34–36
internal integration tasks, 72
internal stakeholders, 35
international business, 18–19, 63–64

Japan, 63, 64

Kanter, Rosabeth, 37–38
Koogle, Tim, 4

labor/management divide, 62
language, and cultural context, 64
leadership, 75, 77
learning as culture, 69
Leers, David, 49–52
lenses. *See* organizational analysis and action, lenses on
liaison roles, 22
linking, strategic, 14, 15, 20–23
loyalty, 62, 65
Lucent Technologies, 22

management/labor divide, 62
mapping of interests and power, 41–42
mapping of networks, 47–55
market, grouping by, 18–19
matrix structure, 19–20
the Matthew effect, 38
McDonald's, 58
meaning, cultural, 57–58
mechanism, organization as, 14
mergers and acquisitions, 71, 77–78
models, formal, 10
motivation and control, 60–61, 65
"Multi Company" paradigm, 73–74
multidimensional grouping structures, 19–20
multidivisional structure, 17–18

Nadler, David, 24, 26
negotiation skills, and influence, 45
networks

advice, 40, 47–52
analysis of social networks, 40
"bow ties," 54
communication, 47, 48, 52–55
construction of, 44–45
efficient vs. redundant, 39
factionalism in, 54
fragile structures, 54
friendship networks, 40
holes in, 40, 54
imploded relationships, 53
informal, 38–40, 47–55
mapping and analysis of, 47–55
power, and network position, 38–40
relationship networks, 47–52
size of, 38
solution testing, 54–55
structural hole theory, 40
task-related, 40
trust, 47–52
new organization model, 66
norms, 60, 75

observation of consequences, 41
organizational analysis and action, lenses on, 4–5, 83–84. *See also* cultural lens/perspective; political lens/perspective; strategic design lens/perspective
organizational behavior, 68
organizational charts
Dynacorp, 87, 88
grouping structures, 16–20, 26
and power systems, vertical and horizontal, 38
organizational congruence, 23
organizational culture. *See also* cultural lens/perspective
overview, 59–60, 67
"Action Company" paradigm, 71, 73
artifacts, values, and assumptions, 70–71
content of, 71, 72
definition of, 69–70
dynamics, cultural, 75–78
evolution, cultural, 76–78
external cultural context, 63–64
historical and theoretic background, 67–69
"Multi Company" paradigm, 73–74
research methods, 68–69, 78
segmentalist model of, 62
socialization, 75–76
stories, circulation of, 61
"Organizational culture" (Schein), 67–82
organizational psychology, 68, 78
organizational structure and design. *See* strategic design lens/perspective
organization development, 69
output, grouping by, 17–18
ownership, sharing, 42

past performance, and power, 37–38
paternalism, 74
perception of influence, 42–43
performance evaluations, 9
performance measurement systems, 24
performance record, and power, 37–38
permanent cross-unit groups, 22
personal characteristics, as source of power, 36–37
personal schemas, 8–10
perspectives. *See* organizational analysis and action, lenses on
Pfeffer, Jeffrey, 34, 36, 40, 41–42
political lens/perspective. *See also* power
overview, 4, 10–11, 33
effective action and, 41–45
informal networks, analysis of, 47–55
interests, 34–36
political systems, 34
power sources, 36–41
pooled interdependence, 15, 20
position, in networks, 38–40
power. *See also* political lens/perspective
assessment of, 41
authority as, 36, 38
"bow ties," 54
coercion as, 36, 38
definitions of, 36
influence, 36, 42–43, 44–45
sources of, 36–41
and support or opposition, 34
symbols of, 41
vertical vs. horizontal, 38
primary embedding mechanisms, 75
processes, cultural, 58–59
Process Improvement Teams (PMTs), 22
product division structure, 17–18, 32
product manager position, 31
products, cultural, 58–59
psychology, organizational, 68

questionnaires, for network analysis, 48–49

rationality, 26, 65
rebellion, 76
reciprocal interdependence, 15, 20
reciprocity, 44
recruitment, 75
redesign. *See* strategic design lens/perspective
redundant networks, 39
relationship networks, 47–52
relativity, cultural, 65
reporting structures, formal, 21–22
representational indicators of power, 41
reputation, 41
research methods, 68–69, 78
resource allocation, 25
resources, human, 25

restructuring, effect on informal organization, 54
retirement plans, 35
rewards and incentives, 24–25
routinization of tasks, 14
rules, 9

scarce expertise, 37
Schein, Ed, 34
schemas, 8–10
"scientific management," 15
scope, economies of, 16
secondary articulation and reinforcement mechanisms, 75
segmentalist model of organizational culture, 62
Semel, Terry, 4
sensitivity, and power, 37
sequential interdependence, 14–15, 15, 16, 20
sharing ownership, 42
socialization, 60–61, 75–76
social networks, 38–40. *See also* networks
software for network mapping, 49
South Korea, 63–64
specialization, 16
stakeholders, 35, 42, 43
stories, 61, 70
strategic design lens/perspective
    overview, 4, 10, 13–14
    alignment, 14, 15, 23–25, 26
    costs of redesign, 25–26
    definitions, 14
    design process, 25–26, 27
    Dynacorp case, 28–32, 85–90
    environment, demands of, 26
    grouping, 14, 15, 16–20, 26
    key elements, 14–15
    linking, 14, 15, 20–23
    network construction and, 44
    political lens compared to, 33
    rationality and, 26
    understanding an organization from, 26
strategic planning groups, 23
structural hole theory, 40
structure and culture, 59
structures of organizations. *See* strategic design lens/perspective
subcultures and segmentation, 61–63, 65, 70, 77
success, as source of power, 37–38
supporters and blockers, mapping, 42, 43
survey research, 48–49, 68
symbols, and cultural lens, 57–58, 64
symbols of power, 41
systems approach, 14, 68

Taiwan, 63–64
task, as unit of activity, 14
task forces, 22–23, 28, 30–32
task interdependence, 14–15, 16, 20–21
task-related networks, 40
Taylor, Frederick, 15
teams, 22–23, 31, 85–86. *See also* grouping, strategic; task forces
temporary cross-unit groups, 22–23
Theory X and Theory Y, 24
Thompson, James, 14–15
throughout-put systems, 26
total quality management (TQM), 15
track record, and power, 37–38
training, 68, 75
trust, and exchange perspective, 44
trust networks, 47–52
Tushman, Michael, 24, 26

unions, 35
universal rules, 9

valued expertise, 37
values, as level of culture, 70, 71
values, espoused, 71
vertical power systems, 38
virtual systems, 59

Weber, Max, 14, 36–37, 59
"who you know," and power, 38
women, 9
work methods, 63

Xerox, 35

MANAGING FOR THE FUTURE

Organizational Behavior & Processes

TEAMS

Module 3
Making Teams Work

Module 4
Diverse Cognitive Styles in Teams

Module 5
Team Processes

Module 6
Teams in Organizations

Ancona • Kochan • Scully
Van Maanen • Westney

MANAGING FOR THE FUTURE

Organizational Behavior & Processes

MANAGING FOR THE FUTURE
Organizational Behavior & Processes, Third Edition

Deborah Ancona
Sloan School of Management
Massachusetts Institute of Technology

Thomas A. Kochan
Sloan School of Management
Massachusetts Institute of Technology

Maureen Scully
Graduate School of Management
Simmons College

John Van Maanen
Sloan School of Management
Massachusetts Institute of Technology

D. Eleanor Westney
Sloan School of Management
Massachusetts Institute of Technology

Dedicated to those who have inspired us to try to be better students and teachers.
Special thanks to: Professor Jack Barbash • Professor Arthur H. Gladstein • Professor Marius B. Jansen • Professor Joanne Martin • Professor Edgar H. Schein

---

VP/Editorial Director
Jack W. Calhoun

VP/Editor-in-Chief
Michael P. Roche

Senior Publisher
Melissa S. Acuña

Executive Editor
John Szilagyi

Senior Developmental Editor
Judith O'Neill

Marketing Manager
Jacquelyn Carrillo

Production Editor
Emily Gross

Manufacturing Coordinator
Rhonda Utley

Compositor
Trejo Production

Printer
Von Hoffmann Press, Inc.
Frederick, MD

Internal Designer
Bethany Casey

Cover Designer
Bethany Casey

Photographs
©PhotoDisc

Design Project Manager
Bethany Casey

COPYRIGHT ©2005
by South-Western, a division of Thomson Learning.
Thomson Learning™ is a trademark used herein under license.

Printed in the United States of America
1 2 3 4 5 07 06 05 04 03

For more information contact
South-Western College Publishing,
5191 Natorp Boulevard,
Mason, Ohio, 45040
Or you can visit our Internet site at:
http://www.swlearning.com

ALL RIGHTS RESERVED
No part of this work covered by the copyright hereon may be reproduced or used in any form or by any means—graphic, electronic, or mechanical, including photocopying, recording, taping, Web distribution or information storage and retrieval systems—without the written permission of the publisher.

For permission to use material from this text or product, contact us by
Tel: (800) 730-2214
Fax: (800) 730-2215
http://www.thomsonrights.com

Library of Congress Control Number: 2003113908
ISBN 0-324-05575-7

Contents

Making Teams Work

    Overview   6

Core

    Class Note   **A Team Primer**   10
                            Key Terms 10
                            Types of Teams 11
                                  Quality Circles 11
                                  Cross-Functional Teams 11
                                  Self-Managed Teams 11
                                  Office of the President 11
                                  Transnational Teams 12
                                  Virtual Teams 12
                            Teams versus Individuals 12
                            A Team Effectiveness Model 13
                            References 15

    Assessment   **Team Assessment Survey**   17

Index

Overview

Unlike other modules, this one does not correspond to a class. This module is designed to provide you with a shared vocabulary and model of teams, team performance, and teamwork, and to give you the tools to make your teams more effective. As you work through this module, you will not only learn about teams conceptually, but will also have the opportunity to practice creating, monitoring, and improving an ongoing team effort.

Our emphasis on learning skills in setting up teams, making them work, and improving their performance over time comes in response to an increased use of teams in today's organizations. This trend of giving more and more tasks to teams, as opposed to individuals, is predicted to continue well into the future as work becomes more complex, cross-functional, and subject to time constraints. In organizations that move to a more networked form, teams provide a primary vehicle for coordinating people with the various skills and expertise needed for a particular job. As organizational structures become flatter and more flexible, teams are often configured and reconfigured as demands change. Managers must be able to quickly pull a set of individuals together to carry out a specific assignment. Increasingly, as organizations become more global and diverse, that set of individuals will be more heterogeneous in age, gender, race, functional background, priorities, and nationality. Thus, this module focuses primarily on the individual skills needed to promote effective teamwork in the organization of the future.

Unfortunately teams are complex entities that are often difficult to manage. Team members often complain of meetings that are a waste of time, of decisions that never get made, and of conflicts that never get resolved. This module provides pragmatic advice about how to make teams work in an effort to head off problems before they arise.

The module consists of three parts: a Class Note, a Team Handbook, and a Team Assessment Survey. The Class Note provides an introduction to the basic terminology of teams, the types of teams in organizations today, when to choose a team versus an individual structure, and a model of team effectiveness. This "Team Primer" is meant to provide some basic level of knowledge about teams so that you begin work with a common vocabulary and an understanding of what teams are all about. The model of team effectiveness is meant to show you the primary levers that can be used to improve effectiveness.

The **Team Handbook** is a workbook designed to help you jump-start your work as a team, to avoid common problems, and to continually improve over time. The handbook presents concrete suggestions about what team members can do to make their time together more productive, and it contains tips and barriers to point out potential pitfalls and what to do about them. You can use the handbook as a resource when needed, or you can work your way through the entire handbook. It is probably a good idea to skim through the entire handbook before the team meets to give you a sense of which parts of the handbook might be most useful to you.

The handbook is organized around five questions that your team will try to answer over the course of the term.

1. Who are we? (i.e., understanding team composition)
2. What do we want to accomplish? (i.e., establishing team goals)
3. How can we organize ourselves to meet our goals? (i.e., setting a team structure)
4. How will we operate? (i.e., defining team operations)
5. How can we continuously learn and improve?

The **Team Assessment Survey** is a questionnaire designed to evaluate how well teams are doing in answering the five questions posed in the Team Handbook. You will complete the Team Assessment Survey midway through the term as a gauge of how well your team is operating and performing, which will help you chart a course for improvement. Team members are not graded on the team assessment survey scores, but you may be graded on how well you use the information from the survey to take stock of the team and plan for the future.

Working on a team can be both a challenging and a rewarding experience. Good luck.

Additional Activities

The materials in this module represent a first step in making teams work. Other activities that would enhance learning in this area include the following:

1. Meet with your teammates to discuss prior team experiences. Each member can relate what worked and what did not work in these other experiences and what he or she learned that can transfer to future team experiences. Then pool those lessons and make some

decisions about how to integrate them into the ongoing processes of your own team.

2. Call the human resource departments of some local companies to find out how they help teams to get started. Telephone interviews or actual visits might help you learn how team building is done in these companies and what resources are available when teams are first formed. This information can then be pooled and the team can decide whether any of these organizational practices can be applied to your own team.

3. Try to obtain access to teams in local companies, in your university, or in volunteer agencies in your community. Through telephone or personal interviews, learn what particular early steps helped and hindered the work of these teams. Ask questions about what structures, activities, and decisions helped teams to move ahead and be productive, and which ones interfered with team progress. Again, this information can then be pooled and the team can decide whether any of these organizational practices can be applied to your own team.

4. Take some time to think about your vision of the perfect team. In some detail, describe such things as how often the team would meet, the type of leadership that would exist, how members would handle conflict, how work would be allocated, and so on. Then meet with your team to exchange visions. Discuss the similarities and differences across visions. Negotiate among yourselves as to which aspects of each vision you will try to incorporate into your own team.

5. Once the team members begin to work together, they can put together a team contract. A team contract consists of all the commitments that each of the members agrees to fulfill. Commitments might include how often to meet, how to treat one another, or how much time to devote to the team. Even though contracts may have to be renegotiated over time, the act of writing down agreed-upon rules and making a public commitment to follow them goes a long way in ensuring that those commitments are honored.

6. Additional reading material might provide an even better sense of how to build an effective team. Suggested readings include the following:

    Duarte, D., and N. Snyder. 2001. *Mastering Virtual Teams.* San Francisco: Jossey-Bass.

    Hackman, J. 1990. *Groups That Work (and Those That Don't).* San Francisco: Jossey-Bass.

    Hanson, P. G. and B. Lubin. 1986. Characteristics of an Effective Work Team. *Organization Development Journal* (Spring).

    Hirschhorn, L. 1991. *Managing the New Team Environment. Reading,* MA: Addison-Wesley.

    Lipman-Blumen, J., and H. J. Leavitt. 1999. *Hot Groups.* Oxford, England: Oxford University Press.

    Schein, E. 1969. *Process Consultation: Its Role in Organization Development.* Reading, MA: Addison-Wesley.

    Thompson, L. 2002. *Making the Team: A Guide for Managers.* Upper Saddle River, NJ: Prentice Hall.

Making Teams Work

CORE

Module 3

A Team Primer

Teams. They are a critical component of organizational life in the 21st century. Everyone's talking about virtual and geographically distributed teams, about teamwork, and being a team player. Teams are a central element in the "new" organization and a mechanism to cope with downsizing and decentralized decision making. We discuss team processes and team structures. But what does it all mean?

Many of these words are so common that we all assume we know what each other is talking about. In reality, these terms mean different things in different organizations. Even team researchers do not agree on definitions. To make certain that we have a common understanding of the words and concepts all of us use in discussing teams, we offer this primer. We start by defining some key terms and types of teams, then discuss under what circumstances a team might be formed, and then provide an overall model of team performance, in which we define key terms and relationships.

Key Terms

One of the major distinctions that creates some order out of the chaos is to distinguish between a working group and a team.

A **working group** is defined as a small set of individuals (three to about twenty-five) who are aware of each other, interact with one another, and who have a sense of themselves together as a unit (Schein, 1992). A working group's performance is a function of what each member does as an individual because members do not work interdependently and do not share responsibility for each other's results. Successful working groups get together to share information, perspectives, and best practices; make decisions that help each member do his or her job better; and reinforce individual performance standards (Katzenbach and Smith, 1993). Many top management teams are really working groups in which members get together to help each functional or divisional manager do a better job. The firm's performance is the sum of each member's contribution, and each individual's performance has little to do with how the others are doing.

A **team** includes all of the characteristics of a working group but adds several others, including members working interdependently and being jointly accountable for performance goals. Thus, team members work both as individuals and jointly. Although it is easy for working groups to point to what each member did and accomplished, teams meld member efforts to produce a "collective work product" (Katzenbach & Smith, 1993). When you read a team report, it reflects members building on each other's contributions and communicating in a unified voice. Thus, all members are accountable for their joint products. Top management teams that really function as a team take joint responsibility and work together to create and meet the strategic and operational goals of the firm. Members of these teams are measured on how well the firm does and members' performance is a function of how well they work together.

The distinguishing characteristics of teams are intensity and interdependence. The team's effectiveness depends on how members work together. A team has more power and potential than a working group, but it requires more investment by members to realize that potential. A team is not better than a group; it is simply more effective when the task at hand requires interdependence and joint accountability. Teams may also be chosen over working groups when members want the greater intensity of the team experience, the opportunity to learn about how to work in a team, or the sense of belonging that comes from working so closely with others.

High-performing teams excel in several categories of team effectiveness. Team effectiveness can be broken down into four components:

1. Performance (how well team members produce output, measured in terms of quality, quantity, timeliness, efficiency, and innovation)
2. Member satisfaction (how well team members create a positive experience through commitment, trust, and meeting individual needs)
3. Team learning (how well team members can acquire new skills, perspectives, and behaviors as needed by changing circumstances)
4. Outsider satisfaction (how well team members meet the needs of outside constituencies such as customers and suppliers)

High-performing teams somehow manage to do their jobs better than others thought possible by setting difficult and clear performance goals, structuring themselves to get the work done, taking into account member and outsider needs, and changing as circumstances warrant. These teams are often held up as exemplars throughout the organization.

Hot groups refers to a state of mind that exists in groups or teams whose members are obsessed about their task and full of passion (Lipman-Blumen & Leavitt, 1999). Hot group members are spirited and intensely motivated, they stretch themselves to new levels. Examples of hot group experiences follow:

> *"We even walked differently than anybody else. We felt we were way out there, ahead of the whole world."* —*aerospace executive reflecting on a project team (p. 9)*

> *"Everybody was involved in that show. . . . We actors didn't just read our lines. We worked on the whole show with the writers and directors. . . . We knew we were doing something wonderful, something innovative and important."* —*Barbara Babcock on her experience with* Hill Street Blues

Hot groups can result in high levels of motivation and task accomplishment, but they are also often short-lived, falling prey to the hierarchy and bureaucracy in their organizations. In order to create and support such teams, managers need to support and champion the people who are committed to a course of action they believe in.

Teamwork, a word often confused with teams, represents a set of values whereby members of some collective (a group, team, division, or organization) are encouraged to help one another, to listen and give feedback to others, and to provide support and recognition to others. Teamwork values can exist even if a team does not.

A **team player** is a member of some collective (a group, team, division, or organization) who embodies teamwork values. He or she is known for putting group or team needs above personal ambition and for being encouraging, being a good listener, and providing support and recognition to others. A team player works hard to make the collective meet its goals. In some organizations where teams and teamwork are widely used, employees are evaluated on how well they carry out the team player role.

Types of Teams

As teams proliferate in organizations, they take many forms. Some of the more common types of teams are described next.

Quality Circles

Quality circles became popular as a result of the total quality programs that swept through Japan, the United States, and parts of Europe. Quality circles (QCs) are small groups of employees who get together to solve quality-related problems such as quality control, cost reduction, and production planning. Quality circle members get training in problem-solving techniques, meet together about once a week on company time, and report in to management on problems that are outside of their control (Nelson & Quick, 1994).

Quality circles first became popular in Japan after World War II as the Japanese imported and embraced the teachings of W. Edward Deming. Their use has also been widespread in Sweden, as companies like Volvo incorporated them and as workers demanded more involvement, and later in the United States when companies like Ford, Xerox, and Hewlett-Packard began to think of quality as part of a competitive strategy. Now the quality movement extends beyond production to product development, sales, and even human resources management. The key is to understand the key work processes and to continuously find ways to improve them.

Cross-Functional Teams

Cross-functional teams consist of members that represent multiple functions within the firm, such as manufacturing, engineering, finance, marketing, and sales. These teams are formed to improve the coordination among functions in such areas as product development, process improvement, and allocation of resources. Cross-functional teams are thought to better link upstream and downstream organizational activity (so that, for example, manufacturing considerations can be designed into a product rather than being discovered after prototypes already exist), to push decision making down to those who have the real expertise, and to speed coordination. These teams bring the necessary expertise together but members often need time to learn how to bring their diverse views together.

Self-Managed Teams

Self-managed teams (also known as autonomous work groups) make decisions that were once restricted to management. These teams may be given the responsibility to hire members, allocate tasks and roles to members, determine work schedules and work flow, and handle disputes. As companies move to create self-managed teams, they are said to be empowering employees by moving power and decision making downward in the organizational hierarchy. Members of these teams often receive training in problem solving and negotiation. Because these teams can be threatening to middle managers, a move to this type of structure needs to include appropriate change-management tools.

Office of the President

The office of the president is the term often given to the set of executives who run a corporation. The dominant model of firm leadership still involves a COO (chief operating officer) reporting to a CEO (chief executive officer), with functional or divisional managers reporting to the COO, but many organizations are moving to team leadership. Under this model the COO is eliminated and the functional or divisional managers report directly to the CEO. This set of executives is given the title of Office of the President and it collectively assumes the role of the COO in managing internal operations and helps the CEO formulate strategy and manage external relations. In order to carry out this task the executives need to shift their focus from their function or division to the corporation (Ancona & Nadler, 1989).

Transnational Teams

A transnational team is composed of people from different countries whose activities cross multiple borders. For example, at one advertising firm, members from ten different country groups got together to create a global ad for a new car. As organizations become more global in their operations, a corresponding increase in the number of transnational teams, including joint venture teams where the sponsoring companies are from different countries, is evident. Transnational teams pose a particular type of challenge: nationality has been shown to influence individuals' cognitive schema, values, nonverbal behavior, and language, all of which influence behavior in teams. As Linda Hill (2001) points out, cross-national differences occur on the individual-collective dimension (Erez & Earley, 1993). In individualistic cultures such as the United States and the Netherlands, people tend to use personal achievements to define themselves, view relationships as more short-term, and value the individual more than the team. Collectivist cultures such as Japan and Brazil, however, are characterized by high commitment to, and identification with, the team, and group harmony, unity, and loyalty are valued more than individual gain (Hill, 2001).

These observations are generalizations, however, and do not hold for all individuals. Furthermore, organizational culture can reinforce or reduce the impact of national culture on an individual. In addition, some evidence shows that the more people are exposed to multiple nationalities, the less likely they are to conform to the customs and beliefs of their own (Hambrick, et al., 1994). Nonetheless, most transnational teams must work to break through the barriers of different fundamental values, cultural assumptions, and stereotypes (Kozlowski & Bell, 2001).

Virtual Teams

A virtual team differs from a traditional face-to-face team in that its members are dispersed in space and members communicate through technological mediation (Kozlowski & Bell, 2001). Thus, in virtual teams members rely on electronic tools such as e-mail, fax, voice mail, videoconferencing, and "virtual workspaces" to communicate with each other. Even though virtual teams enable people from many different locations and time zones to work together, members are also less likely to share information and more likely to escalate conflict than in face-to-face teams. Members are also less likely to share background information, which is a key antecedent of trust (Hill, 2001; Jarvenpaa, Knoll, & Leidner, 2001).

To overcome these problems, several strategies can be effective. If possible, team members should have some short, face-to-face experience early in the tenure of the team. If these meetings are not possible, then a one-day videoconference where members get to know each other a little bit is helpful. When such interventions are not possible early in the team's tenure, later meetings help to cement ties among members. Besides meetings members should be encouraged to share background information and personal data such as hobbies. Finally, members might want to include in their electronic communications information about their context that is often missing. One example would be explaining that an e-mail had to be cut short due to a fire alarm. Such information helps teams to avoid misinterpretation and misunderstandings that increase conflict.

Teams versus Individuals

Even though teams became widespread in the 1990s, it is clear that not all team initiatives have been successful. Teams may create the promise of greater competitiveness, faster decision making, fewer levels of hierarchy, greater commitment and quality, and greater employee satisfaction, but they can also be difficult to manage, evaluate, and support. Creating teams requires an investment in training and organizational design. It often means making changes in existing reward systems and in the corporate culture that surrounds the team. Therefore, one should not jump into team designs unless the potential advantages outweigh the costs.

Work structured for individuals offers a number of advantages for both the individuals and the company. In such a context, work often takes less time and individuals feel a greater sense of control over their work. Under this mode individual accountability is high, and limiting the involvement of others can lessen their ability to interfere or obstruct work. It is easier to measure and reward good performance, without incurring the costs involved in getting people to learn how to work together.

Teams also offer advantages. A team design usually results in greater ownership of the final product and high levels of commitment to implementing the team's ideas. Teams provide a vehicle to pool diverse views and perspectives as well as a place for refining raw ideas. Teams foster innovation and allow for coordination across individuals and departments. Finally, teams offer many social rewards to individuals seeking support, camaraderie, and assistance in their work.

So, how can one determine whether to use a team approach? The following conditions should be present:

- The work requires a range of different skills, views, or expertise.
- The different components of the work are highly interdependent.
- Sufficient time is available to organize and structure team effort.
- The organizational reward structure and culture support a team approach.
- A need is identified to build commitment to a course of action or set of decisions.
- The issues being worked on require refinement.
- Needs are high for innovation and coordination.
- Members can be trusted not to purposefully obstruct the team's efforts.
- Individuals desire a team experience.

(This list is based on those contained in *Developing Effective Work Teams*, by the Delta Consulting Group.)

A Team Effectiveness Model

Once a team is formed, what factors are likely to contribute to its success? Figure 3.1 presents a model of team effectiveness. The model shows the organizational culture, team design, and rewards leading to a set of team operations that contribute to team effectiveness. A feedback loop from effectiveness back to team operations shows that these two components interact over time.

As mentioned earlier **team effectiveness** is thought to have four components (see Sundstrom & McIntyre, 1994):

1. *Performance* (how well team members produce output, measured in terms of quality, quantity, timeliness, efficiency, and innovation)
2. *Member satisfaction* (how well team members create a positive experience through commitment, trust, and meeting individual needs)
3. *Team learning* (how well team members acquire new skills, perspectives, and behaviors as needed by changing circumstances)
4. *Outsider satisfaction* (how well team members meet the needs of outside constituencies such as customers and suppliers)

In turn, team effectiveness is a function of **team operations**, which have two components:

1. *Internal team processes* evolve from the way in which team members interact with each other to accomplish the task and to keep themselves together as a team. Key processes include communication, influence, task and maintenance functions, decision making, conflict management, atmosphere, and emotional issues (see

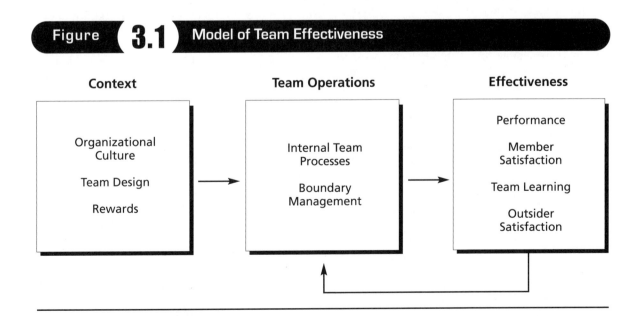

Figure 3.1 Model of Team Effectiveness

Module 5, Team Processes, for more detail about these processes).
2. *Boundary management* consists of the way in which teams define their boundaries, identify key external constituencies, and interact with those outsiders. Key boundary management activities include buffering the team from political infighting, persuading top management to support the team's work, and coordinating and negotiating with other groups on work deadlines (see Module 6, Teams in Organizations, for more detail about these processes).

Team operations are the product of the **context** in which the team is created. Context includes the organizational culture in which the team resides, the way in which the team is designed, and the rewards given to the individuals that make up the team:

- *Organizational culture* influences and is influenced by the values and underlying assumptions about teams and teamwork as communicated through symbols, stories, and rituals. Attempts at creating teams often may fail because the underlying culture is essentially individualistic, despite the rhetoric of teams. Organizational cultures that emphasize cooperation, mutual responsibility, and the exchange of information are more supportive of teams than those that emphasize barriers and distinctions (Orlikowski, 1994). Other authors stress the importance of egalitarian cultures (Gittell, 1995) and those in which individualism and teamwork are both truly held up as the ideal.
- *Team design* refers to the way in which teams are put together, including their composition, the nature of their task, and their structure. Composition refers to the makeup of the team. The mix of skills, backgrounds, experience, and personalities found among team members profoundly affects the team's ability to work effectively on different tasks. In addition, the extent to which team members share values and perspectives affects members' ability to cohere and work together. The nature of the task refers to whether the team's task is designed to encourage interdependence. For example, two companies designed their computer repair units in different ways. One firm gave each engineer a given geographic territory and held him or her responsible for it. The other firm gave a team of engineers several geographic territories and let them jointly determine how best to service those areas. The first company provided individual-level feedback on customer satisfaction and average time to customer, while the second provided this data at the team level. Obviously some tasks lend themselves more easily to a team design, so the nature of the task needs to be considered when a team is formed. Structure includes the size of the team, the way in which members organize the work (e.g., when to work in subgroups, deadlines, what approaches to take for different tasks, and who will be responsible for what), the formal roles that members are given (e.g., facilitator or project manager), the goals of the team, and the norms—or expectations about how to behave—that team members bring to the team.
- *Rewards*, both formal and informal, act as a key determinant of how team members will interact with one another and those outside the team. Cross-functional teams whose members are evaluated by functional bosses often demonstrate higher levels of conflict than those whose members are evaluated by the team leader. Similarly, managers who promote employees based solely on individual achievement are sending a double message when they say that teams are important. Thus, the rewards need to support the type of teamwork that is desired in the organization.

Although the model shown in Figure 3.1 identifies some key elements that affect team effectiveness, we shied away from identifying universal characteristics of a good team. Teams may be effective in any number of different ways, and teams in different environments need to be configured differently. Teams that exist in an environment with greater external demands, due to how threatening the environment is, its pace of change, its complexity, and its interconnectedness, must pay more attention to external boundary processes. Teams that have greater interdependence, more divergent membership, and a more complex task must work harder on their internal team processes, such as communication and conflict resolution. Similarly, different team designs may work for different types of teams and different organizational cultures.

Although no one best way even exists, as organizations experiment in their quest to become the organizations of the future we learn more about how the key elements can be configured to produce effective teams. Consider, for example, Southwest Airlines, the fastest-growing airline of the 1990s, with the best record for reliability, safety, and customer satisfaction. Southwest achieved these outcomes using fewer resources as it broke through the cost/quality boundary that was taken for granted in the airline industry, much as Toyota did with its lean production strategy in the auto industry (Gittell, 1995, 2000).

According to Gittell, Southwest's strategy relies on quick turnaround time. Airplanes arrive at the gate, are unloaded, serviced, reloaded, and depart in an average of 17 minutes, compared with the industry average of 43 minutes. Behind this strategy are cross-functional teams that coordinate up to 10 distinct functional groups, from pilots to cabin cleaners. Rather than add costly buffers between these different functional groups and have decisions made further up the hierarchy, Southwest gives its front-line workers more decision-making responsibilities. These sets of cross-functional workers communicate often, work at improving their ability to work together rather than trying to blame one another for failures, and engage in rapid decision making as planes arrive at the gate. Team members keep each other informed of what is going on in other parts of the airport and about weather conditions. Thus, both internal and boundary management work are taking place. This interdependence is fostered by a project manager, shared accountability for outcomes across functional lines, an egalitarian organizational culture, shared monetary rewards, training and selection for teamwork skills, and flexible work rules. As Gittell notes, "Together this set of practices offers the means for employees to transfer information across functional lines, the incentive to do so, and a means to strengthen the underlying relationships" (1995, p. 4).

The Southwest example shows how specific contextual factors create teams that are able to engage in complex internal and boundary management processes. The key for using the model is creating the culture, design, and reward system that will best facilitate the processes that are needed for a given task. Under these conditions team effectiveness results. In turn, the effectiveness feeds back to enhance the motivation of the team and its ability to carry out the appropriate processes. Teams can then enter a positive cycle in which their processes and their effectiveness continue to improve. Unfortunately, many teams are not designed well enough nor do they exist in cultures that are supportive. Under these conditions teams can enter into negative cycles in which team operations are not adequately carried out, resulting in low levels of effectiveness, which, in turn, create additional conflict and confusion in the team, further eroding effectiveness.

The team effectiveness model acts as a guide to team management. Once the team context is set, the model suggests a series of questions that act as a guide for effective team management. These questions include:

1. Who are we? (i.e., understanding team composition)
2. What do we want to accomplish? (i.e., establishing team goals)
3. How can we organize ourselves to meet our goals? (i.e., setting a team structure)
4. How will we operate? (i.e., defining team operations)
5. How can we continuously learn and improve?

In attempting to answer these questions we believe that teams will enhance their effectiveness. The Team Handbook that follows takes team members through some specific suggestions, tips, and barriers that will help them to jump-start their work together, avoid common problems, and continually improve over time.

The management of teams is fraught with difficulties. The terminology is often ambiguous, the decision to use teams involves many costs and benefits, and multiple roads lead to either success or failure. This primer has attempted to clarify the terminology, outline the trade-offs between individuals and teams, and present a model of team effectiveness. With this primer as background we hope that you can go on to make your own team experience a successful one.

References

Ancona, D. G., and D. Nadler. 1989. Top Hats and Executive Tales: Designing the Senior Team. *Sloan Management Review* 19, 19–28.

Delta Consulting Group, Inc. 1996. *Developing Effective Work Teams.*

Earley, P. C., and M. Erez (Eds.). 1997. *New Perspectives on International Industrial/Organizational Psychology.* San Francisco: The New Lexington Press.

Erez, M., and P. C. Earley. 1993. *Culture, Self-Identity, and Work.* New York: Oxford University Press.

Gittell, J. H. 1995. *Cross-functional Coordination and Human Resource Systems: Evidence from the Airline Industry.* Dissertation, Massachusetts Institute of Technology, Sloan School of Management.

Gladstein, D. 1984. Groups in Context: A Model of Task Group Effectiveness. *Administrative Science Quarterly* 29, 499–517.

Hambrick, D. C., S. C. Davison, S. A. Snell, and C. C. Snow. 1994. *When Groups Consist of Multiple Nationalities: Toward a New Understanding of the Implications*. Lexington, MA: International Consortium for Executive Development.

Hill, L. 2001. *A Note on Team Process*. Harvard Business School, N9-402-032.

Jarvenpaa, S. I., K. Knoll, and D. E. Leidner. 2001. Is Anybody Out There? Antecedents of Trust in Global Virtual Teams. *Journal of Management Information Systems* 14 (4), 29–64.

Katzenbach, J. R., and D. K. Smith. 1993. The Discipline of Teams. *Harvard Business Review*, March–April 1993, 111–124.

Kozlowski, S. W. J., and B. S. Bell. 2001. Work Groups and Teams in Organizations. In *Comprehensive Handbook of Psychology (Volume 12): Industrial and Organizational Psychology*. New York: Wiley.

Lipman-Blumen, J., and H. J. Leavitt. 1999. *Hot Groups*. Oxford, England: Oxford University Press.

Nelson, D. L., and J. C. Quick. 1994. *Organizational Behavior: Foundations, Realities, and Challenges*. St. Paul, MN: West Publishing Company.

Orlikowski, W. J. 1994. *Information Technologies as Integrative Mechanisms: Insights from Practice*. Submission to the Academy of Management, Organization and Management Theory Division.

Schein, E. 1992. *Organizational Culture and Leadership*, 2nd ed. San Francisco: Jossey-Bass.

Sundstrom, E., and M. McIntyre. 1994. *Measuring Work-Group Effectiveness: Practices, Issues, and Prospects*. Working paper. Knoxville, TN: University of Tennessee, Department of Psychology.

Thompson, L. 2000. *Making the Team: A Guide for Managers*. Upper Saddle River, NJ: Prentice Hall.

MANAGING FOR THE FUTURE

Organizational Behavior & Processes

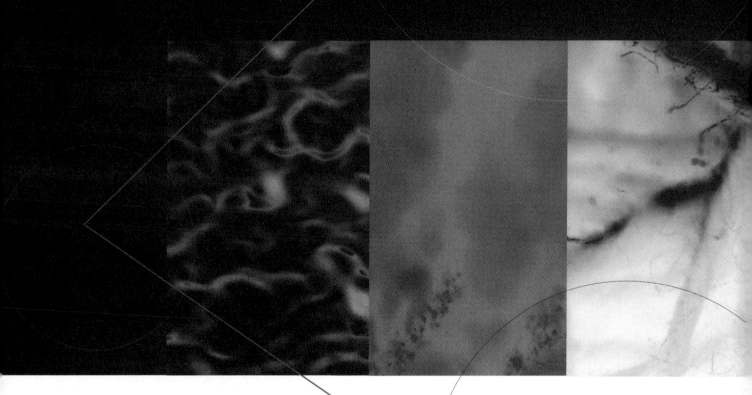

HANDBOOK

**Ancona • Kochan • Scully
Van Maanen • Westney**

Contents

Overview	3
I. Who Are We?	3
• Description	3
• Suggestions	4
II. What Do We Want to Accomplish?	5
• Description	5
• Suggestions	5
III. How Can We Organize Ourselves to Meet Our Goals?	6
• Description	6
• Suggestions—Work Structure	7
• Suggestions—The Facilitator Role	7
• Suggestions—The Project Manager Role	8
• Suggestions—The Boundary Manager Role	8
• Suggestions—Agreeing Upon Norms	9
IV. How Will We Operate?	10
• Discussion	10
• Suggestions—Planning an Agenda	10
• Suggestions—Brainstorming	11
• Suggestions—Multivoting	11
• Suggestions—Communicating Cross-culturally	12
V. How Can We Continuously Learn and Improve?	13
• Suggestions—Giving Feedback	13
• Suggestions—Assessing Yourself and the Team	14

Overview

This handbook outlines a set of tools to enhance team effectiveness. It is designed to help team members (managers, students, consultants, etc.) to jump-start their work together, to avoid common problems, and to continually improve over time. The handbook can be used in its entirety to guide a team along its development, or it can be used in pieces to deal with specific issues as they arise.

The basic assumption of this handbook is that team effectiveness is enhanced when team members explicitly try to answer five important questions:

1. Who are we?
2. What do we want to accomplish?
3. How can we organize ourselves to meet our goals?
4. How will we operate?
5. How can we continuously learn and improve?

For each question, a brief *description* of what the team is meant to address is presented. Then a series of *suggestions* follows, including *tips* and alerts to *barriers*, which ought to help the team as it works to answer the question. The suggestions included in the handbook are just that, suggestions, so feel free to be creative in designing your own method of answering the questions posed. Hopefully, this handbook will help your team experience to be both rewarding and fun.

A Note About Getting Started

The start-up of any team is a unique time and opportunity to set core modes of operation. As Edgar Schein, professor of Organization Studies at MIT, points out, it is also a time when four issues are raised for individuals: those related to identity (who am I in this team?); power/control (who will have it and what will that mean for me?); goals (which of mine will be met in this team?); and acceptance/intimacy (will people like me?). These questions play out over the life of the team, but are especially influential in the beginning stages. Stay aware of your own and others' expectations, and be aware that finding tentative answers to these questions is as important as getting other work done. Teams are dynamic, fascinating entities. Follow the old adage as you work to make this team a whole that is greater than the sum of its parts.

I. Who Are We?

Description

The team should begin by coming to terms with its composition (i.e., understanding the makeup of the team). Individuals approaching a team task each bring their own "baggage"—positive and negative—reflecting their backgrounds, experiences, personalities, and prejudices. Members represent different races, genders, and religions, as well as different hierarchical levels and functional backgrounds. Members bring different expectations, needs, and abilities to contribute to any particular task. Only through a process of mutual discovery can the team come to understand how to harness these differences toward the team's goals. By candidly exploring who is best suited to each task and each role, the team can configure itself to operate most effectively.

Before the team meets to start this process of mutual discovery, it is useful for each team member to think about what he or she brings in terms of expectations, needs, preferences, skills, experiences, biases, and commitment level. This information can then form the basis of initial discussions among members.

Plan to hold these initial discussions in a setting in which a comfortable atmosphere can be created. Members should try to listen carefully to one another, and try to put themselves in the shoes of the other person to understand what each team member needs and how those needs might be met. Some general discussion about how the team might best capitalize on the similarities and differences that exist is helpful. This discussion isn't a one-time event; it needs to be ongoing as member needs, preferences, and skills shift. Remember that the more individuals feel that their own needs are met, the more committed and productive they can be for the team as a whole.

Suggestions

To begin the process of getting to know each other:

1. Go around the team several times and ask members to convey the following:
    - Birthplace, previous places lived, education
    - Hobbies and interests
    - Work experiences
    - Unique skills and areas of expertise
    - An adjective that best describes each member's personality
    - Prior team experiences—the best and the worst
    - What you most want to accomplish in this team

    Alternative: Break up into pairs. Have each member of the pair interview the other using the preceding questions. Then have the pairs introduce each other to the rest of the team.
2. Discuss your responses as a team.
3. Discuss how you can capitalize on the similarities and differences that exist.

Tips

- Determine how much time you have for this activity and pace yourselves accordingly.
- Distribute addresses and phone numbers to aid communication.
- Hold the initial discussion in an informal setting, such as over dinner, at the beach, or at someone's apartment.
- Don't be too serious; humor helps everyone relax, and getting to know each other should be as much fun as it is work.

Barriers

- Some people have a harder time opening up than others.
- Be aware of cultural differences in participation.

(Be patient and respectful, and consider using the suggested alternative.)

II. What Do We Want to Accomplish?

Description

Before a team can organize itself to work effectively members need to agree upon goals. Goals serve to focus team member activity on specific tasks and motivate members toward a similar endpoint. They also enable the team to set milestones and measure their progress. Clarity and specificity are important, because when goals are ambiguous they often create confusion and conflict. Team goals come in four categories:

- *Performance* refers to team output. Specific goals for the quality, quantity, timeliness, efficiency, and innovation levels that the team would like to produce will determine the work that members need to carry out. For example, new product development teams set goals related to budgets, schedules, technical specifications, and product innovation. Student teams need to determine the grades they want, the level of preparation for each class, the standards for assignments and the time they want to devote to the class.
- *Member satisfaction* involves providing team members with a positive experience. It is often related to the level of commitment and trust created within the team. Satisfaction is also related to meeting personal goals, such as having a good time, getting to know other team members, or establishing a supportive environment. Personal goals also include the time and commitment that members wish to offer.
- *Team learning* refers to the team's ability to survive, improve, and adapt to changing circumstances. Learning goals include finding innovative approaches to problems, becoming more efficient over time, acquiring new skills, and changing norms and procedures when external circumstances warrant change.
- *Outsider satisfaction* has to do with meeting the demands of, and pleasing, outside constituencies, such as customers, suppliers, clients, government agencies, or community groups. For example, if a product development team has a high-quality product but they cannot convince the marketing group and the customers of its appeal, then they face a problem. Similarly a student team may work many hours on a project, but unless the professor is satisfied, they may not reap the rewards of their labor.

Suggestions

To begin the process of establishing goals:

1. Brainstorm a list of goals that members have the for team. Some examples might be:
    - Getting an A on our team project
    - Being well prepared for class and for team assignments
    - Having a high level of camaraderie in the team
    - Having a good time
    - Having efficient meetings
    - Learning a lot about organizational behavior and how to manage a team
    - Satisfying the professor and other student teams
2. Ask each member to indicate his or her three top choices. Tally up the results of the ratings. Then discuss the ratings, negotiate, and agree upon a preliminary set of team goals.

Tips

- Identify some smaller goals that you can accomplish in the short term. Examples might be finding a firm for the course project within two weeks or finding a set time and place to meet every week.
- More challenging goals may give you more direction and a greater sense of purpose but require more commitment by all members.
- Continually test people's ongoing commitment to goals and level of agreement. As deadlines approach and team norms settle, you may need to explicitly renegotiate.
- In cases of conflict think about trades—I'll help you study if you do this part of the analysis.

Barriers

- Conflicting goals can be a major barrier to a team's progress.
- Teams struggle without a definition of goals.

(Don't assume that others will share goals. Getting an A and having fun may seem obvious to you, but to others they may not be worth the time or energy they demand. All goals need to be negotiable at the start.)

III. How Can We Organize Ourselves to Meet Our Goals?

Description

Once goals have been set, the team needs to organize itself to meet those goals. Teams will develop different levels of structure depending upon their tasks and makeups. Detailed and predictable work is better suited to high levels of structure than is abstract and ambiguous work. Some people enjoy structure and clarity, while others like the free and easy approach. Your team can be creative in the way in which it structures its activities.

Three major aspects are involved in organizing a team:

- *Creating a work structure* requires that the team move from the goals to the work that needs to be done to achieve those goals. For example, if a new product team wants to be innovative, it has to spend time brainstorming, looking at what the competition is doing, and experimenting with new materials. A student team that must analyze an organization needs to contact the organization, develop interview questions, analyze its data, and write up a report. Once the work has been identified, the team decides how it will organize itself to do the work. One key issue is determining when members will work alone and when they will work in subgroups or as a whole. Also important are when work must be done, what approaches will be taken, and who will be responsible.
- *Roles* are specific activities taken on by particular individuals. Many different role typologies are available, but here we focus on the roles of facilitator, project manager, and boundary manager. The **facilitator** focuses on task and maintenance functions during meetings. Task functions help the team to do its work, while maintenance functions hold the team together so that members can continue to get along with one another and even have some fun. The **project manager** organizes the work plan and sees that it is implemented. The **boundary manager** determines

how the team will deal with key stakeholders such as clients, other teams, and upper management. As a team comes to understand its task and members better, additional roles will develop.
- *Norms* refer to expectations of acceptable behavior. They are unwritten rules enforced by team members. Norms can cover all aspects of team behavior. Norms that seem to cause the most disruption to team behavior if they are not discussed include when and how often to meet, who will lead the team, what will the leader do, how will work be distributed and how will members treat each other.

Suggestions—Work Structure

Follow these steps in structuring your work to help you manage it more effectively:
1. List the goals that need to be accomplished.
2. List the major pieces of work that need to get done to meet the goals.
3. Work backwards from final deadlines to define the due dates by which each piece of work must be completed. Set milestones to measure progress.
4. Decide whether each piece of work will be done by an individual, a subgroup, or the entire team and then assign people to responsibilities.
5. Clarify which members have primary responsibility for the task versus those who will contribute to the effort.
6. Prepare and build in time for contingencies, problems, and emerging issues.

Tips

- Ensure that each member buys into his or her responsibilities as outlined.
- Use a responsibility chart as part of your plan. Include who is responsible for which pieces of work and their due dates.
- Distribute the plan and use it to measure progress.
- Use the plan as a picture of current agreements among members, and change it as circumstances warrant.
- Celebrate when milestones are reached and people have met deadlines.

Barriers

- Initial enthusiasm may lead to commitments that are not kept.
- Inadequate preparation can lead to a poorly written plan.
- A plan that is too structured can harm creativity.
- Changes in the plan may result in members resenting those who have not followed through on their commitments.

Suggestions—The Facilitator Role

A *facilitator* role is to:
1. Focus the team toward the task.
2. Engage participation from all members.
3. Protect individuals from personal attack.
4. Suggest alternative procedures when the team is stalled.
5. Summarize and clarify the team's decisions.

Tips

- Be neutral, do not interject your views.
- Keep the team to its agreed time frame.
- Express out loud what you think is happening (e.g., "everybody seems to be very tense since John spoke").
- Don't be afraid to confront problems openly—that's your job.
- Listen carefully and test for understanding.
- Allow members to be silent if they do not wish to speak.

Barriers

- People often feel personal discomfort with conflict.
- People often fear that being an active facilitator will look like power grabbing.

(Just take a stab at the role; be prepared to discuss with others what you did well and what you did poorly.)

Suggestions—The Project Manager Role

The *project manager* role is to:

1. Develop the project plan.
2. Remind members of upcoming deadlines and commitments.
3. Bring up issues that may mean a plan revision is needed.
4. Confront the team when the plan is not followed.

Tips

- Get everyone involved in developing and reevaluating the project plan. It should be a team, not an individual project.
- Do not delegate all work to individuals. Without joint work, you are just a collection of individuals, not a real team.

Barriers

- Some people will volunteer for too much work and others will not want to do anything.
- All the work that needs to be done will not be clear when the team is starting out.

(The project plan, like other aspects of the team's work, is an area for discussion and negotiation. Don't be afraid to confront problems and to push for clarification.)

Suggestions—The Boundary Manager Role

The *boundary manager* role is to:

1. Identify key stakeholders, people or groups who will influence, or be influenced by, the work you are doing.

2. Decide what to do with each stakeholder:
   - Influence
   - Inform
   - Involve
   - Get information
   - Coordinate
   - Get permission
3. Assign responsibility for each outsider to a specific team member.

Tips

- Begin early and keep up the relationship with each stakeholder.
- Ensure that team members do not overlap or send mixed signals.
- Look in all directions, not just up.

Barriers

- It is not always easy to recognize who will affect the team.
- High levels of interaction with outsiders can make it harder to integrate across team members.

Suggestions—Agreeing Upon Norms

Meet and discuss your team's norms. Include the following categories:

1. *Meeting norms.* Expectations include when, where, and how often to have meetings. What is expected of members with regard to attendance, timeliness, and preparation? Also, what is the balance between work and fun?
2. *Working norms.* Expectations involve standards, deadlines, how equally effort and work should be distributed, how work will be reviewed, and what to do if people do not follow through on commitments.
3. *Communication norms.* Expectations center on when communication should take place, who is responsible, how it should be done (phone, e-mail, etc.), and how to discuss feelings about the team or members.
4. *Leadership norms.* Expectations include whether a leader is needed, if leadership is rotated, responsibilities, and how to keep the leader from doing all the work.
5. *Consideration norms.* Expectations center on being considerate of members' comfort with things like smoking, swearing, and so on, and their ability to change norms if they are uncomfortable with what is going on in the team.

Tips

- Spend time discussing norms in order to agree upon a common approach.
- Keep norms simple and consistent (e.g., meeting every Friday at 1:00 P.M. is easier than picking a new time each week).

Barriers

- Subjects that are difficult to talk about often remain undiscussed.
- Members often shy away from responsibilities or team needs for leadership. (The facilitator should push to see that all categories of team norms are discussed, especially when problems arise.)

IV. How Will We Operate?

Discussion

One of the most interesting and exciting aspects of teams is the way their dynamics unfold. The interaction among team members is often unpredictable and different from what was anticipated when the team began. This interaction among team members is called *team process*. As team process unfolds it often reshapes the team's structure, which, in turn, creates a new process. Thus, structure and process remain interrelated throughout the life of the team.

Team process includes communication, influence, task and maintenance functions, decision making, atmosphere, and conflict resolution; that is, who talks to whom, how often, who is influencing decisions, how the team organizes itself, how conflict is handled, and what happens in and between meetings (see Module 5, Group Process Observation Guide, for more detail.) The previous section outlined the plans for how the team will operate; here, however, team process focuses on the behaviors that actually take place among members. For example, even though the plan may give responsibility for a certain activity to one member, influence on decisions may come entirely from another.

A number of tools have been developed to help harness the potential of team process. Here we include agenda setting, brainstorming, multivoting, and tips on cross-cultural communication. Agenda setting helps to organize meetings and improve efficiency. Brainstorming is a tool for generating a lot of creative ideas. Multivoting enhances the team's ability to reach consensus. Consensus means reaching a solution that is acceptable to all, not necessarily the top strategy or preference of any or all. It is achieved by negotiating key requirements among the parties so that everyone can "live with" the outcome. The suggestions for cross-cultural communication help communication among diverse team members.

Suggestions—Planning an Agenda

When planning an agenda:

1. Write down the major items that the team wishes to tackle.
2. Ensure that all team members have the opportunity to contribute.
3. Clarify what the team wants to accomplish for each item—discussion, brainstorming, making a decision, taking action, etc.
4. Prioritize items and allocate time to each.
5. Leave time at the end to discuss how the meeting went.

Tips

- The first item on the agenda should be a "check-in," in which each person spends a minute or so telling other members what is currently on his or her mind. This activity legitimizes air time for everyone.
- Make the agenda available to members before the meeting.
- Assign a timekeeper to keep the team on track.
- Leave time to discuss the team process, not just the task.

Barriers

- An agenda that is too structured can stifle creativity and an open atmosphere.
- An agenda that is not followed can frustrate team members.

Suggestions—Brainstorming

When brainstorming:

1. Clearly define the subject or problem to be discussed.
2. Give people time to think and write responses individually.
3. Invite everyone to call out their ideas (or go around the team).
4. Write down all ideas.

Tips

- Don't evaluate. Something that sounds unrealistic or off the mark initially may spark a great new idea. (Beginning ideas aren't perfect solutions, they are just beginning ideas.)
- Encourage creative and different thinking. Assure people that sometimes wacky ideas are the best. (Many creativity tools are available for this task.)
- Encourage people to hitchhike, or build on others' ideas.
- Some people take longer than others to form their ideas. Allow some silence to get everyone's ideas out.
- Do not stop too soon. Eventually people will come up with more ideas.

Barriers

- People are sometimes afraid that their beginning ideas will be "wrong" or sound stupid, which is why it's essential to avoid evaluating too early and to set up an uninhibited atmosphere.
- Once you have generated a number of ideas, their quantity and lack of realism may be overwhelming. (It is essential to set up a nonthreatening way to select and build on those ideas with the most promise for a new but workable solution.)

Suggestions—Multivoting

To multivote you should:

1. Brainstorm ideas.
2. Discuss what each idea means and how it will solve the problem at hand.
3. Have each person vote on the top four choices. You can split your votes any way you want to across the set.
4. Choose three to five ideas that are the highest priorities.
5. Identify similarities and differences among ideas, then positive and negative aspects of each idea, then what is really important to each person.
6. Rework the top priorities as needed, and have each person vote on his or her top two priorities.

Tips

- Sometimes ideas are similar and votes are split. Consolidate ideas so that strong support is not watered down.
- Try to be open to the ideas of others. You are trying to come to a team decision, not to win at all costs.

Barriers

- Some members will find this method too structured.

Suggestions—Communicating Cross-culturally

Members of cross-cultural teams generated this list of suggestions based on their experiences over several months together:

1. Recognize the different cultures and languages represented in the team.
2. Meet in areas with minimal noise and distraction.
3. Have adequate time for meetings.
4. Start meetings with a check-in, in which each member spends a minute or so telling other members what is on his or her mind. This exercise forces everyone to contribute equally at the start of the meeting.
5. Record main points on a chalkboard or similar display. Distribute meeting notes.
6. Check frequently to make sure all members are in agreement with what the team has decided.
7. Get to know each other personally.
8. Assign buddy pairs: one buddy from the host country and one from a foreign country.
9. Do not use slang or complex language.
10. Be aware that behavior is viewed differently in different countries. Check on what it means to interrupt, to resolve conflict, to discuss feelings, to disagree.

Be patient! Remember, the relationships you build in this team are not just for now, they can also bring great rewards in the future. Cross-cultural communication can demand a great deal of time and energy. Yet the relationships forged provide a network that bridges people, companies, and countries.

The story of one international team illustrates these ideas. In this student team one member from another country was very quiet and no one tried to learn about her background and skills. Several other team members complained about how she did not know anything and was of no help to the team. She felt as if no one was interested in what she had to say.

The following semester the school planned a trip to this student's home country. When the students on the trip arrived, they received a red-carpet welcome. To the surprise of her fellow team members it turned out that this "quiet" student was the daughter of the Minister of Finance. During the trip she was poised and outgoing and took on a leadership role. All the team members lamented the missed opportunities for learning and their inability to "see" what this quiet team member had to offer. Try to make sure that this kind of situation is not what happens in your team.

V. How Can We Continuously Learn and Improve?

Description

In addition to goals, structure, and process, an essential component in a team's health is its ability to learn from experience. This learning comes in the form of additional skills, enhanced ability to play the roles required of the task, and the team's willingness and ability to build a climate that encourages change and learning. A team's ability to be flexible in the face of obstacles and to learn about its own strengths and weaknesses is the core to keeping energy and motivation high and to achieving high performance results. Researchers note that teams have different degrees of "reflexivity."[1] Reflexivity refers to the extent that members discuss and reflect upon their objectives and processes and then adapt to new environmental challenges (West, 1996). In essence, reflexivity is about learning.

Two critical tools are required for reflexivity and team learning. The first is *assessment*—both of oneself and the team. Self-assessment is an internal observation and reflection on what is working or not working about one's own behavior in pursuit of identified goals. Team assessment is the team's picture of the same issues, looking not only at individual behaviors, but at the team norms, processes, and climate, among other key areas.

The second key tool for team learning is *feedback*. Feedback is the nonjudgmental observation that others offer. It is a picture of how effectively one's behavior or action is helping to move the person or team toward the desired outcome or goal.

Feedback and assessment should be ongoing activities in any team. Learning itself becomes an increasingly honed skill, and the team's evolution is dependent upon it.

Suggestions—Giving Feedback

In giving feedback to others, you should describe the problem and how it affects you and the team. State how you feel, and describe what you'd like instead. It is important that feedback:

1. Be specific, not general.
2. Describe behavior, not judge the person.
3. Start with the word *I*, not the word *you* (to avoid blaming).
4. Be timely.

---

[1] West, M. A. 1996. "Reflexivity and Work Group Effectiveness: A Conceptual Integration." In M. A. West (Ed.), *Handbook of Work Group Psychology* (pp. 555–579). Chichester, U.K.: John Wiley.

Tips

- When giving feedback, you can ask and expect people to change their behavior, not their feelings or attitudes.
- The more you give feedback, the easier it gets. It should not be focused only on one or a few people, but be a part of the whole team's norm of dealing with issues.
- Positive feedback about what is going well in the team is as important as negative feedback.

Barriers

- Initially, it is hard to give feedback. Take a deep breath and give it a try.
- Sometimes people do get angry or take negative feedback personally. A negative reaction shouldn't stop you from giving feedback, but makes it essential that you follow the guidelines on not being judgmental in tone.

Suggestions—Assessing Yourself and the Team

In assessing yourself or the team, ask the following questions:

1. *Goals*: Are my and our goals being met?
2. *Roles and structure*: What are our roles? How effectively are they being carried out? What works or doesn't work about our team structure?
3. *Process*: How effectively do we make decisions and resolve conflict? How do we communicate? What is the atmosphere in our meetings?
4. *Plans to change*: How can we improve any of these areas? What actions or ideas should we take?

Tips

- To make team assessment a regular part of your routine, you might try a three-minute "check-out" at the end of every meeting to ensure that issues or problems are identified quickly.
- At key milestones (i.e., the midpoint, the delivery of the product, or concluding a major project phase), take the time to do a more structured team assessment covering all of the preceding questions.

Barriers

- Assessment can be time- and energy-consuming.

Team Assessment Survey

Please indicate the extent to which you, individually, think that your team exhibits the following characteristics and behaviors.

QUESTIONS

	To a very small extext		To some extent		To a very great extent
1. Team members understand the range of backgrounds, skills, preferences, and perspectives in the team.	1	2	3	4	5
2. Team member differences and similarities have been effectively harnessed toward achieving team goals.	1	2	3	4	5
3. The team cannot integrate diverse viewpoints.	1	2	3	4	5
4. Members view themselves as a team (e.g., they work interdependently, have joint accountability, and are committed to joint goals), not a collection of individuals who have their own particular jobs to do.	1	2	3	4	5
5. Team members have articulated a clear set of goals.	1	2	3	4	5
6. The team's goals are not motivating to members.	1	2	3	4	5
7. Team members agree on what goals and objectives are most important.	1	2	3	4	5
8. The team has an effective work structure (i.e., an understanding of what work needs to be done, when work needs to be completed, and who is responsible for each piece of work).	1	2	3	4	5
9. It is not clear what each person in the team is supposed to do.	1	2	3	4	5
10. Team members have devised effective timetables and deadlines.	1	2	3	4	5
11. Team members have a clear set of norms that cover most aspects of how to function.	1	2	3	4	5
12. Team members often disagree about ideas, procedures, and priorities.	1	2	3	4	5
13. Members take arguments personally and get angry with one another.	1	2	3	4	5
14. Every member does his or her fair share of the work.	1	2	3	4	5

	To a very small extext		To some extent		To a very great extent
15. A few members do most of the work.	1	2	3	4	5
16. A few people shirk responsibility or hold the team back.	1	2	3	4	5
17. Team members are imaginative in thinking about new or better ways to perform our tasks.	1	2	3	4	5
18. All team members participate in decision making.	1	2	3	4	5
19. Team members have the resources, information, and support they need from people outside team boundaries.	1	2	3	4	5
20. The team has a clear leader.	1	2	3	4	5
21. Team members take turns performing leadership roles.	1	2	3	4	5
22. Team meetings are well organized.	1	2	3	4	5
23. Team meetings are not productive.	1	2	3	4	5
24. Coordination among members is a problem: people seem not to know what to do and when to do it for smooth team functioning.	1	2	3	4	5
25. Members express their feelings freely in the team.	1	2	3	4	5
26. Team members support each other.	1	2	3	4	5
27. Team members are not effective at making decisions.	1	2	3	4	5
28. The quality of our work is superior.	1	2	3	4	5
29. The quantity of our work is superior.	1	2	3	4	5
30. All in all, I am satisfied with being a member of this team.	1	2	3	4	5
31. This team keeps getting more effective all the time.	1	2	3	4	5
32. A lot of learning goes on in this team.	1	2	3	4	5
34. We have met the needs of our "clients."	1	2	3	4	5

Note: This survey instrument was based on questions from the following sources:
Ancona, D., and D. Caldwell. 1992. "Bridging the Boundary: External Activity and Performance in Organizational Teams." *Administrative Science Quarterly* 37, 634–665.
Gladstein, D. L. 1984. "Groups in Context: A Model of Task Group Effectiveness." *Administrative Science Quarterly* 29, 499–517.
Hackman, J. R. 1983. *A Normative Model of Work Team Effectiveness.* Technical Report #2. New Haven, CT: Yale University, School of Organization and Management, Research Program on Group Effectiveness.

Index

accountability, joint, 10

boundary management, 14

chief operating officer (COO), 11–12
collectivist vs. individualistic cultures, 12
context of teams, 14
cross-functional teams, 11, 15
culture, organizational, 14
cultures, and transnational teams, 12

Deming, W. Edward, 11
design of teams, 14

effectiveness model, for teams, 13–15
executives, 11–12

Gitell, J. H., 14–15
globalization, and transnational teams, 12

high-performing teams, 10
hot groups, 11

incentives, 14
individualistic vs. collectivist cultures, 12
individual work, compared to teams, 12–13
interdependence, 10
internal team process, 13–14

Japan, 11

learning, in teams, 10

management of teams, 15

networking, 6

Office of the President, 11–12
operations, team, 13–14

performance of teams, 10

quality circles, 11

rewards, 14

self-managed teams, 11
Southwest Airlines, 14–15

teams
    overview, 6–7
    definition of key terms, 10–11
    effectiveness model, 13–15
    individual work compared to, 12–13
    at Southwest Airlines, 14–15
types of, 11–12
transnational teams, 12

virtual teams, 12

working groups, 10

MANAGING FOR THE FUTURE

Organizational Behavior & Processes

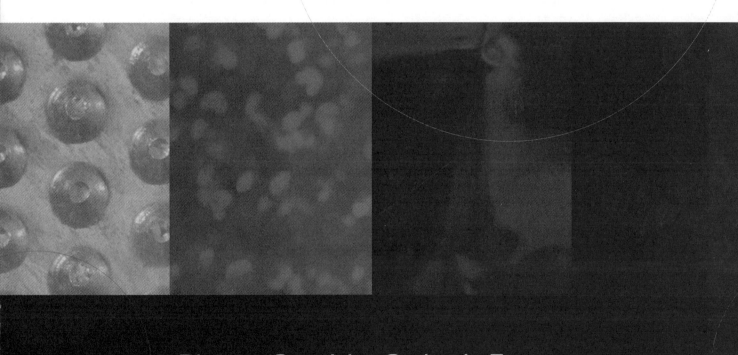

Diverse Cognitive Styles in Teams

Module 4

MANAGING FOR THE FUTURE
Organizational Behavior & Processes, Third Edition

Deborah Ancona
Sloan School of Management
Massachusetts Institute of Technology

Thomas A. Kochan
Sloan School of Management
Massachusetts Institute of Technology

Maureen Scully
Graduate School of Management
Simmons College

John Van Maanen
Sloan School of Management
Massachusetts Institute of Technology

D. Eleanor Westney
Sloan School of Management
Massachusetts Institute of Technology

Dedicated to those who have inspired us to try to be better students and teachers.
Special thanks to: Professor Jack Barbash • Professor Arthur H. Gladstein • Professor Marius B. Jansen • Professor Joanne Martin • Professor Edgar H. Schein

VP/Editorial Director
Jack W. Calhoun

VP/Editor-in-Chief
Michael P. Roche

Senior Publisher
Melissa S. Acuña

Executive Editor
John Szilagyi

Senior Developmental Editor
Judith O'Neill

Marketing Manager
Jacquelyn Carrillo

Production Editor
Emily Gross

Manufacturing Coordinator
Rhonda Utley

Compositor
Trejo Production

Printer
Von Hoffmann Press, Inc.

Frederick, MD
Internal Designer
Bethany Casey

Cover Designer
Bethany Casey

Photographs
©PhotoDisc

Design Project Manager
Bethany Casey

COPYRIGHT ©2005
by South-Western, a division of Thomson Learning.
Thomson Learning™ is a trademark used herein under license.

Printed in the United States of America
1 2 3 4 5 07 06 05 04 03

For more information contact
South-Western College Publishing,
5191 Natorp Boulevard,
Mason, Ohio, 45040
Or you can visit our Internet site at:
http://www.swlearning.com

ALL RIGHTS RESERVED
No part of this work covered by the copyright hereon may be reproduced or used in any form or by any means—graphic, electronic, or mechanical, including photocopying, recording, taping, Web distribution or information storage and retrieval systems—without the written permission of the publisher.

For permission to use material from this text or product, contact us by
Tel: (800) 730-2214
Fax: (800) 730-2215
http://www.thomsonrights.com

Library of Congress Control Number: 2003113908
ISBN 0-324-05575-7

Contents

Diverse Cognitive Styles in Teams

Overview		4

Core

Assessment	**Cognitive Style Self-Assessment**	6
	Scoring Scheme 8	
	Summary Score 9	
Class Note	**Mapping Multiple Perspectives**	11
The Press	**Mapping Managerial Styles**	13

Managerial Mapping 13
Personal Work Styles 15
    Meeting with Others 15
    Generating Information 15
    Making Decisions 15
    Choosing Priorities 15
Work Preferences 15
    Establishing Relationships: Extrovert Approach 16
    Establishing Relationships: Introvert Approach 16
    Generating Data: The Sensing Approach 17
    Generating Data: The Intuitive Approach 17
    Making Decisions: The Thinking Approach 18
    Making Decisions: The Feelings Approach 19
    Establishing Priorities: The Judging Approach 19
    Establishing Priorities: The Perceptive Approach 20
    Overall Profiles 20
A Basis for Self-Understanding 21
    Managerial Style and Decision Making 22
    Organization Structures 22
    Approaches to Change 23
    Creativity and Innovation 24
    Career Development, Appraisal, and Training 24

Elective

The Press	Give Me an E. Give Me an S.	28

Index

Overview

This module on **Diverse Cognitive Styles in Teams** looks closely at the different ways individuals selectively absorb and use information. The phrase *cognitive style* refers to the general way a person approaches and attempts to solve problems encountered in the world at large, including, of course, problems faced by teams in the workplace. Cognitive style represents a way of seeing and thinking—a perspective. The module is built around a consideration of cognitive style and makes use of a short self-assessment (see the Cognitive Style Self-Assessment on page 6). You are to fill out this instrument and score it. An in-class group learning task will follow (including a presentation by each group), and then the self-assessment will be discussed. *The readings assigned for this module should not be read until the group learning task and class presentations have been completed.* For class, then, all you need to do is complete the self-assessment and turn it in at the assigned time.

The instrument itself—called the **Cognitive Style Self-Assessment**—is based on the psychological-type theory developed by Carl Jung. This quick paper-and-pencil instrument is a loose variant of the much longer and more rigorously designed diagnostic inventory first developed by Isabel Myers and Katheryn Briggs in the 1940s and 1950s (and much refined since then by many researchers who follow the general Myers-Briggs approach to personality assessment). Our instrument is intended to give you a rough idea of your own cognitive style and just how your style might operate in team and organizational settings. A way to interpret your answers and summary scores on the various dimensions of the instrument (and based on the readings included in the module) will be provided in class.

Assignment Summary

1. Complete the **Cognitive Style Self-Assessment** on page 6. The summary of your scores (page 9) is to be handed in to your instructor sometime before class.
2. Come to class and take part in the group learning task for the session. Be sure to bring to class your Cognitive Style Self-Assessment answer sheet (page 8). All other information regarding this task will be provided to you by your instructor.
3. Following the class session devoted to interpreting the self-assessment, read the Class Note and the two articles included in this module.
   a. Class Note: Mapping Multiple Perspectives.
   b. Margerison, Charles, and Ralph Lewis. 1981. "Mapping Managerial Styles." *International Journal of Manpower* 2, 1 (1981).
   c. Golden, Daniel. "Give Me an E. Give Me an S." *The Boston Globe* (January 8, 1990).

Again, do not read these articles or the Class Note until the self-assessment has been discussed in class. This sequence is important because the readings are likely to make a good deal more sense to you after the group learning task and in-class debriefing. The first reading elaborates the concepts covered in the class discussion. Read it first. The second reading, which is optional, addresses various ways organizations use (and sometimes abuse) personality-based testing. Read it second. The third reading is a brief Class Note written to summarize some of the key learning points advanced in this module. Read it last.

Diverse Cognitive Styles in Teams

CORE

Module 4

Cognitive Style Self-Assessment

This set of questions is designed to indicate your cognitive style. The answer you choose to any question is neither "right" nor "wrong." It simply points out where your cognitive preferences lie. You will find a number of paired statements and words. Please give every statement a score so that the pair adds up to 5 on a scale from 0 to 5 with 0 being minimum and 5 being maximum. For example:

In describing my work, I would say it is:

> a. Challenging and exciting   4
> b. Routine and dull   + 1
>   = 5

Clearly, work can sometimes be challenging and sometimes dull. In the preceding example we weight the job four parts challenging and one part dull. The score could, in your case, be 3 + 2 or 5 + 0 or another combination.

Please choose your scores, one against another, from the following scale:

Minimum				Maximum
0 1	2	3	5

1. Are you influenced more by:
   a. Values   ___
   b. Logic   + ___
              = 5

2. When you have to meet strangers, do you find it:
   a. Something that takes a good deal of effort   ___
   b. Pleasant, or at least easy   + ___
              = 5

3. Does following a plan:
   a. Appeal to you   ___
   b. Constrain you   + ___
              = 5

4. Do you get along better with people who are:
   a. Creative and speculative   ___
   b. Realistic and "down to earth"   + ___
              = 5

5. Are you naturally:
   a. Somewhat quiet and reticent around others   ___
   b. Talkative and easy to approach   + ___
              = 5

6. Is it harder for you to adjust to:
   a. Standard procedures   ___
   b. Frequent changes   + ___
              = 5

7. Is it better to be:
   a. A person of compassion   ___
   b. A person who is always fair   + ___
              = 5

8. At a party, do you usually:
   a. Try to meet many new people   ___
   b. Stick with the people you know   + ___
              = 5

9. When you learn something new, do you:
   a. Try to do it like everyone else does   ___
   b. Try to devise a way of your own   + ___
              = 5

10. Are you at your best:
    a. When following a carefully worked out plan   ___
    b. When dealing with the unexpected   + ___
               = 5

11. Do you get more annoyed at:
    a. Fancy theories ___
    b. People who don't like theories + ___
    = 5

12. Is it better to be regarded by others as a person with a:
    a. Visionary outlook ___
    b. Practical outlook + ___
    = 5

13. Are you more often:
    a. Soft-hearted ___
    b. Hard-headed + ___
    = 5

14. When you buy a gift, are you:
    a. Spontaneous and impulsive ___
    b. Deliberate and careful + ___
    = 5

15. Do you find talking to people you don't know:
    a. Usually easy ___
    b. Often taxing + ___
    = 5

16. Do you think it is a worse mistake to:
    a. Show too much emotion ___
    b. Try to be too rational + ___
    = 5

17. Do you prefer people who have:
    a. Vivid imaginations ___
    b. Good common sense + ___
    = 5

18. Do you usually:
    a. Organize and plan things in advance ___
    b. Allow things to just happen and then adapt + ___
    = 5

19. Do people get to know you:
    a. Quickly ___
    b. Slowly + ___
    = 5

20. At work, would you rather:
    a. Encounter an unscheduled problem that must be solved right away ___
    b. Try to schedule your work so you won't be up against the clock + ___
    = 5

21. When you are with people you don't know, do you usually:
    a. Start conversations on your own ___
    b. Wait to be introduced by others + ___
    = 5

Please allocate scores to the following pairs of words to indicate your preferences.

22. a. Personal ___
    b. Objective + ___
    = 5

23. a. Timely ___
    b. Casual + ___
    = 5

24. a. Reason ___
    b. Feeling + ___
    = 5

25. a. Make ___
    b. Design + ___
    = 5

26. a. Easy ___
    b. Hard + ___
    = 5

27. a. Unjudgmental ___
    b. Judgmental + ___
    = 5

28. a. Composed ___
    b. Lively + ___
    = 5

29. a. Facts ___
    b. Theories + ___
    = 5

30. a. Imaginative ___
    b. Practical + ___
    = 5

Scoring Scheme

Look back at the scores you allocated to each of the questions. Add up the scores as indicated in the following categories.

Dimension E		Dimension I		Dimension S		Dimension N	
Question	Score Given	Question	Score Given	Question	Score Given	Question	Score Given
2b	4	2a	1	4b	3	4a	2
5b	2	5a	3	9a	3	9b	2
8a	4	8b	1	11a	3	11b	2
15a	3	15b	2	12b	2	12a	3
19a	2	19b	3	17b	3	17a	2
21a	3	21b	2	25a	2	25b	3
28b	2	28a	2	29a	4	29b	1
Total:	20	Total:	14	30b	2	30a	3
				Total:	22	Total:	18

Dimension T		Dimension F		Dimension J		Dimension P	
Question	Score Given	Question	Score Given	Question	Score Given	Question	Score Given
1b	2.5	1a	2.5	3a	3	3b	2
7b	2	7a	3	6b	3	6a	2
13b	1	13a	4	10a	2	10b	3
16a	3	16b	2	14b	3	14a	2
22b	2	22a	3	18a	2	18b	3
24a	3	24b	2	20b	2	20a	3
26b	3	26a	2	23a	2	23b	3
27b	2	27a	3	Total:	17	Total:	18
Total:	18.5	Total:	16.5				

Now transfer each of the Total Scores to the Summary Score sheet that follows. Thus, your total score under Dimension E should be placed next to the E, the total score under Dimension I should be placed next to the I, and so on.

Summary Score (to be turned in to your instructor)

	Total		Total
E	20	I	14
S	22	N	18
T	18.5	F	16.5
J	17	P	18

NAME: _____

Mapping Multiple Perspectives

The articles in this module span a broad opinion spectrum. The writers of the first article, Charles Margerison and Ralph Lewis, believe strongly in personality testing, which is not surprising because it is what they do for a living. Daniel Golden, the author of the second article, is at best skeptical (again, not surprising because he is a journalist trained to be suspicious of grand claims). We fall somewhere in between these poles. The use and abuse of personality testing is too large a topic to take up here, but in this Class Note we quickly summarize our position on personality testing after first looking at why we think it is important to take seriously the role cognitive style plays in teams specifically and organizational life generally.

This module focuses on individual differences and the role they so often play in the functioning of teams, groups, and organizations. Of the many ways to classify and conceptualize individual differences, some are obvious and quite visible, such as gender, race, language, national origin, social background, and class. Other ways rest on less visible but nonetheless influential distinctions, such as cultural and educational differences. Here we are concerned with personality-based differences, in particular, differences in the manner in which individuals absorb and selectively use information available to them.

The phrase *cognitive style* refers to the way a person approaches and attempts to solve problems encountered in the world at large, including the problems faced at work. Viewed most broadly, cognitive style is a way of seeing and thinking—a perspective. Its origins are deep and diffuse. Family origins, childhood socialization, schooling, higher education, work experience, and patterns of past success and failure all play a role. It can perhaps best be thought of as a fairly stable, though certainly not fixed, part of each individual's personality or character. Differences in cognitive style are often most apparent in organizations when individuals come together to jointly solve problems, negotiate agreements, or work together for extended periods of time in teams. Integrating multiple perspectives is then predominantly an interactive, not a structural, task. It requires a good deal of listening to others, empathy, and mutual give and take. It requires also an appreciation for what contrasting cognitive styles can offer a team, group, and organization.

To illustrate cognitive style and the role individual differences play in organizational life, we use the Cognitive Style Self-Assessment, which is a short, altered, and rough variant of the much-used (and approximated) Myers-Briggs Type Indicator (MBTI™) as discussed in the Margerison and Lewis reading. The instrument rests on Carl Jung's approach to personality.[1] Certainly other personality theories and measuring devices are available, but the Jungian approach we selected offers several advantages.

First, the Jungian approach to personality is enormously popular at the moment. Many business, educational, and governmental organizations make use of the Myers-Briggs approach in their management training and executive development efforts. Also, voluminous research literature devoted to both Jungian theory and its Myers-Briggs variant is available. Moreover, it is likely that a few students in any given class will already be familiar with the Myers-Briggs approach (or similar personality inventory) and can thus speak to the class about their past experiences—how accurate the assessment seemed at the time, how it was used, and how it compares with the Cognitive Style Self-Assessment. Part of the popularity of the Myers-Briggs approach and theory is perhaps that, unlike many other conceptual models of personality type, the Jungian model classifies individuals in positive terms, by what people like rather than what people lack.

Second, the emphasis of Jung's personality theory on the things people pay attention to and ways they make decisions matches up nicely with the key features of most managerial jobs. The Sensing/

---

[1] The Myers-Briggs Type Indicator (MBTI) is available from the Consulting Psychologists Press, Inc. at 577 College Avenue, Palo Alto, CA 94306. Sandra Krebs Hirsh and Jean M. Kummerow provide a useful interpretive guide to the MBTI called *Introduction to Type in Organizations,* 2nd ed. (1990), available also from the Consulting Psychologists Press. Another useful guide is David Keirsey and Marilyn Bates's popular book called *Please Understand Me* (1984). The book is distributed by Prometheus Nemesis Book Company, Box 2748, Del Mar, CA 92014. This book contains a 70-item self-assessment instrument, called the Keirsey Temperament Sorter. In general, many instruments (and items, scoring schemes, interpretive standards, and so forth), found in the psychological literature, follow the Myers-Briggs approach and are basically consistent with Jungian theory. Those students interested in taking the MBTI test itself can attend a workshop on the Myers-Briggs types or go to a counselor or psychologist authorized to administer the test. Information about workshops and consultation can be obtained by contacting the Center for Applications of Psychological Type (CAPT) at 2720 NW 6th Street, Gainesville, FL 32609.

iNtuitive and Thinking/Feeling dimensions translate well to the interactionally dependent and informationally intensive world of managerial work. Jung's theory has a relevance not currently found in many other personality theories (although it shares a good deal of overlap with other personality measures on several dimensions; notably, **S-N** and **T-F**). Jung's work brings to the surface matters that can be seen and felt in familiar circumstances and thus gives order to the seemingly limitless variations of managerial thought and behavior.

Third, and perhaps most important, making use of individual differences benefits the organization whereas ignoring or merely tolerating such differences does not. If the structural characteristics of organizations shift in accordance with a model of the "new" organization as outlined in Module 1—networked, flat, diverse, flexible, and global in orientation—differing cognitive styles are likely to be of vital importance. The challenges facing organizations are increasingly complex. The application of multiple perspectives is necessary if these challenges are to be addressed adequately. Relying on our own perspective or, more generally, on a single and, within the team, group, or organization, dominant and (for most) comfortable perspective is quite limiting.

At the individual level, cognitive style is a way of ordering preferences for thought and action. As these preferences are incorporated into our personalities, we take them for granted as natural, normal, even proper ways to think and behave. Others with different cognitive styles may then be regarded as odd, improper, perhaps out of sync with the way the world really works. Bridging these differing perspectives requires a common language and a genuine appreciation for those individuals whose cognitive styles differ from our own. But multiple perspectives cannot be integrated until they are understood.

Important qualifications are to be made, however. Personality typing is everywhere and always problematic. It is far from an exact science, and inordinate care, sensitivity, and restraint must be taken when characterizing individuals by the use of virtually any diagnostic device. One of the attractions of Jung's theorizing is his principled hesitation to classify individual personality in a static or timeless way. Personal growth and balance are inherent in Jungian approaches, and breaking from type is an important developmental task.

Nonetheless, a danger is always present of flattening and pigeonholing individuals and thus stereotyping them in unjustified and ignorant ways. Cognitive style is but a small part of personality. Its functioning and measurement are imperfectly understood. It is theoretically and empirically made up of a complicated and shifting mix of analytically distinct preferences. And, most critically, it is difficult if not impossible to make strong behavioral predictions on the basis of cognitive style—simply too many influences are at work in the calculus of human behavior to isolate single causes.

Using personality typing, then, to select (or deselect) individuals for particular jobs or membership in a particular work team is, we think, inappropriate, both practically and ethically. Measures are at best primitive, and, even when positive correlations can be drawn among particular types and job performance, such correlations are not guaranteed to be stable. Job demands change, markets shift, new tasks replace old tasks. The modern work environment is simply too volatile to neatly locate the "right" person for the job by means of personality testing.

Using personality typing loosely and discursively is, however, a different matter. It can provide a set of terms and concepts for talking about the role individual differences play in teams and the workplace. It can also provide a way of considering comparatively one's own perspective on the world. A good deal of personal insight, mutual understanding, and increased respect for one another can be fostered by collective discussion prompted by well-designed and thoughtful personality inventories. Differences in cognitive style may, for example, provide a relatively sound and nonjudgmental hypothesis to account for some, although certainly not all, of the personal misunderstandings and conflicts that characterize team and organizational activity.

Teams are about people doing things together: the better individuals are able to get along with one another, the better the products of their interaction are likely to be. Such practical wisdom is often played out in organizations as individuals with similar ways of thinking and acting cluster together in groups, divisions, departments, and so forth. Homogeneity seems to increase as one moves up the hierarchy in most organizations. Bosses naturally favor subordinates who think along similar lines and, thus, promote the interests and careers of like-minded subordinates. Homogeneity smoothes interaction, increases comfort levels, and, in general, eases the strains or tensions involved in doing things together. When the source of homogeneity is more or less invisible, as it is with cognitive style, the heightened similarity of thought and action among individuals may go unnoticed by them—although surely noticed by those not sharing the dominant mode.

Homogeneity has a price. In the classroom assignment of this module, for instance, groups are assigned the task of developing a new work arrangement for a few technical employees of an organization. These task groups were designed to be as homogeneous as possible, given the data that were collected on individual cognitive style. Although most of these groups were comfortable, they were also restricted in range in terms of the possibilities considered for making the new arrangement work. The "best solution," it seemed, would be one that combined the insights of all the groups.

The point here is that cognitive diversity adds value to an organization and increases the likelihood that innovative solutions to work problems will arise. Making effective use of diverse cognitive styles does not come easy though. The forces of homogeneity must be countered time and time again. Understanding diverse cognitive styles and recognizing the need for integration is only part of the answer. Ways of operating effectively in teams made up of diverse individuals must be developed and sustained. And, in many respects, this is a never-ending task. Not only are we growing, developing, and changing in a variety of ways that reflect the teams of which we are a part and the tasks to which we put our efforts, so too are the others who surround us in these teams and on our tasks.

Mapping Managerial Styles

by Charles Margerison and Ralph Lewis

Managerial Mapping

We wish to produce a new way in which managers can look at how they manage themselves and their teams. We have called the approach Mapping Managerial Styles because it is possible for each person to assess his or her own approach to work and look at how it compares with other people's. This is particularly important for every manager.

The job of managing essentially involves motivating and leading other people. To do this a manager is required to have a good understanding of people's approach to work.

Indeed, it is common to hear managers complain that they need to know more about "what makes people tick" or what motivates people. People who are promoted to managerial positions have usually done well at the technical aspect of their jobs. They are usually intelligent. They are invariably people who are concerned about achieving things. They usually have quite a number of good ideas which they want to put into practice. The one issue which they commonly confront, which causes a lot of heart-searching, is how to get the energies of the people for whom they are accountable mobilized in such a way that they work together.

It is vital, therefore, that managers do have a theory which can govern their relationships with other people at work, particularly in the areas of selection, training, appraisal, work allocation and, probably above all, in building a successful team.

Up to now there have been very few theories which can help managers on an overall basis make the right kinds of decisions in these areas. The ones that have been put forward are in our view far too simple. They have concentrated on such things as having a high concern for production and a high concern for task, or being more democratic rather than autocratic. More recently we have moved towards what have been called contingency theories but these again have not provided a clear basis for managers to understand people's work preferences and motivations in depth.

And yet, this is the area that managers spend most of their time upon. There are numerous research studies which show that well over 70 percent and often 80 and 90 percent of managerial time is spent working with other people. Of all this time, perhaps the most important is the time spent in selection. Peter Drucker, reporting a conversation with Alfred Sloan, who was head of General Motors, had asked him why he spent as much as four hours of his personal time as committee chairman selecting a master mechanic in a small division of the company. Sloan replied, "Tell me what more important decision is there than that about the management of people who do the job. If that master mechanic is the wrong man our decision here on the 14th floor might as well be written on water." Sloan prided himself on the trouble he spent in making the right judgment when it came to people. As he said, "If we didn't spend four

Source: Charles Margerison and Ralph Lewis, "Mapping Managerial Style," *International Journal of Manpower, Special Issue*, 2, no. 1 (1981), pp. 2–20. Reprinted by permission of MCB University Press.

hours on placing a man right, we'd spend 400 hours cleaning up after our mistake."

Most managers would empathize with those words and recognize in their own decisions key points when they had not read the situation correctly. However, making the right decision in itself is not the answer. Once people have been appointed the manager really needs to understand them as individuals and enable them to contribute their best. This means understanding their strengths and enabling them to work in a way which maximizes their abilities. Moreover, it means developing a team of people who can work together.

In this we believe that it is vitally important that a manager understands his own style and motivational pattern and in doing so will more easily understand those of his team. To this end the current monograph outlines a very powerful explanatory theory of human behavior. It was originally developed by Carl Jung[1] in his book *Psychological Types*. Jung is better known as a psychiatrist and philosopher. However, he had a number of important insights and contributions to managerial thought which have long been ignored.

Our own work shows how the original theory can be applied to a number of areas of business life. In particular, we shall look at the relationships between the five key aspects of any work situation shown in Figure 4.1.

Each of these areas interacts with the other, within the constraints and opportunities of the market place. A key influence, however, in the internal working of the organizations are the motivational interests and styles that the individual members bring with them.

We have therefore adapted Jung's theory of personal (motivational) preferences and applied it to industrial and commercial organizations. This is based on a lot of research. In particular 849 managers contributed to the generation of information used in the mapping procedures.

The mapping process enables each person to identify the core values and ideas that he or she brings with them to the work situation. Now these core values relate to the way in which each person wishes to run his or her life. While the particular values may be religious, humanistic, political or utilitarian there is an overall pattern which can be identified and mapped. We are concerned with the underlying patterns which have also been well described recently by Myers.[2]

The competitive nature of organizational life and the day-to-day pressures mean that we often find it difficult to live life in the way we prefer. Therefore, there is usually a fair degree of stress between one's own personal preferences and the job and the task to be done. Add to this the other pressures from other people who have different work patterns, the constraints about doing jobs on time and a host of other factors, then each person has to adapt his or her behavior accordingly. However, as we shall show, people rarely change their core values and basic motivational styles. Wherever possible they will revert to type and play the game in the way they

Figure 4.1 Five Key Aspects of Work Situations

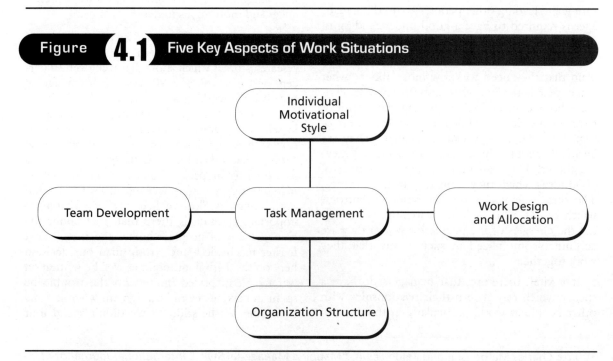

1 Jung, C. G. 1923. *Psychological Types*. London: Kegan Paul.
2 Myers, J. B. 1962. *The Myers-Briggs Type Indicator*. Princeton: Educational Testing Service.

know best. This will mean that people will try to reorganize their jobs and indeed the work of others to fit into their preferred pattern of working.

It is important that we understand these motivational style patterns which come from basic core values and preferences that people bring to work. The next section sets out how this can be done by using Jung's theory and method of application.

Personal Work Styles

While work is a set of complicated activities there are four major things that everyone has to do each day. These four activities are:

1. Meeting with others
2. Generating information
3. Making decisions
4. Choosing priorities

Let us look briefly at each of these activities, all of which have two opposite dimensions.

Meeting with Others

In essence this is the way we prefer to relate and the sort of relationships we like to have. We shall therefore call this activity *managing relationships*.

According to Jung's theory there are two major ways in which this can be done. One approach he called *extroverted*. The other approach he called *introverted*. These terms have become widely acknowledged and used, even though they are not always fully understood.

As we shall illustrate, no one is totally introverted, nor is anyone totally extroverted. We all have the ability to behave either way at various times. However, we all have preferences on how we wish to relate with others and when, where and what we will relate about. It is these issues that require explanation.

Generating Information

Gathering information is crucial in all aspects of life, but particularly so at work. In order to make a contribution you have to find out a lot of information or explore a range of ideas.

There are two major aspects to this. One dimension is called *sensing* and the other *intuition*.

People who prefer sensing usually emphasize, among other things, getting the facts. They are good on detail and prefer information that is based on some form of measurement that can be done using one or more of the senses.

In contrast, other people prefer to generate information by intuition. This means developing data through the use of one's imagination and creative insight, as, for example, a novelist does.

Again the preferences are not totally independent of each other. Most of us gather facts and also express ideas. However, we all tend to prefer one of these more than the other when it comes to doing a job.

Making Decisions

Once the information has been gathered there is usually a requirement to do something with it. Here again there are two major options, one of which Jung called *thinking*, the other *feeling*.

Some people prefer to make decisions using a thinking or analytical approach. Others prefer to make decisions using a feeling, or decisions based upon personal convictions or beliefs, approach. As before, there is no right or wrong way; it is just a matter of motivational preferences. Most of us decide some things by thinking, and some things through feeling. However, we do usually have an overall preference for one or the other and will revert to this when free from other pressures.

Choosing Priorities

Finally, all of us have to make a choice in how we allocate our time. The priorities referred to here are those of either:

1. Getting more facts (sensing) or ideas (intuition)
2. Making decisions (thinking) or (feeling)

The more you are oriented towards generating data, the higher you will be on what the theory calls *perceiving*. The higher you are on making decisions, then the more likely you are to be *judgmental*. These are the two options associated with the priorities for time allocation. Again, neither is right or wrong, but choices usually have to be made. Moreover, most people tend to prefer one to the other.

The theory is not a hard and fast set of rules, but rather a set of guidelines within which people can assess their own preferences and those of others. The model below outlines the options from the factors mentioned above.

Extrovert ———— Establishing Relations ———— Introvert
Sensing ———— Generating Information ———— Intuitive
Thinking ———— Making Decisions ———— Feeling
Judgmental ———— Choosing Priorities ———— Perceptive

Work Preferences

In this section we will look at the main dimensions in more detail, especially with respect to the way work is approached. Most emphasis will be placed on generating and using information with a briefer look at establishing relationships and priorities.

Establishing Relationships: Extrovert Approach

Extroverts require variety and stimulation. They can become easily bored. Their sociability may be just one facet of their desire to obtain stimulation. They often, therefore, try to keep a number of balls in the air at the same time and will take on a number of jobs which they try to do in parallel. Their interests are essentially those of going out and looking for new situations.

Because they talk a lot (in order to stimulate others) they are often seen to be influential although in reality this may not be so. Introverts can also be extremely influential, though they typically talk far less. Extroverts do, however, seem to be far less inhibited. They are more likely to put forward an idea before they have thought it through sufficiently and argue their way through to a conclusion. They will usually take the initiative in making new friends and establishing relationships. At business gatherings they will typically come up and introduce themselves rather than wait to be introduced. They will initiate the subject of conversation and feel quite at home in exchanging observations, views and ideas.

Extroverts, however, are not easily organized. It is difficult for an extrovert to fit into a set of rules in a structured and a planned way of doing things. This is because typically they will be somewhat impulsive and do what they feel is required even if it does not conform to the plan.

An extrovert manager may well have an open door policy. That is, he might deliberately keep his door open so that he is in touch and stimulated by events going on in the office. He will probably actually enjoy people coming in and interrupting him from time to time so that he can get going on another problem. The telephone ringing is really not a major difficulty for the extrovert—it is stimulating!

The more extroverted a person is the more he will feel at ease in meeting with people he does not know, contributing to meetings, making an after-dinner speech, representing the company in negotiations and generally entering into situations that have high demands for interpersonal relationships. In this sense the caricature of the salesman who is the hail-fellow-well-met extrovert does in fact have some bearing in reality. However, it is unwise to take this too far. Everyone in business requires some degree of extroversion but, like most things, it can become a weakness rather than a strength if overplayed. People get bored with too many funny stories and want to get away from the high-pressure conversation.

If you have a boss who approaches work in an extroverted way then he will probably like a lot of meetings and try to get his information by going out into the world. If you have subordinates who are extroverts they will, no doubt, exert quite considerable pressure upon you as they will continually want to relate with you on a personal basis. They will have ideas, very often bubbling over with enthusiasm, and you will have to try and encourage them while at the same time making sure that they do not take up too much of your time.

Establishing Relationships: Introvert Approach

Introverts, on the other hand, like to take time to think things through clearly before they communicate. They may become overstimulated by too much variety and consequently they spend their time trying to reduce the number and length of their contacts. One of the reasons they may not talk as much as extroverts is that this stimulates others to reply and perhaps gives the introvert too much information to work on in too short a space of time.

It must be remembered that the introvert is very open to information. He or she can pick up very subtle points of information or feeling and may well grasp ideas from very little information. Hence the need to switch off and to sit and think it through. This, of course, is a major strength. However, it can also be a weakness. Because of his sensitivity he may assume that others also understand the issues in the same way. The result is that the introvert may not communicate his understanding as he feels it is obvious. While it is obvious to himself, it is not always so for others. Therefore introverts are often accused of not being good at letting people know what they know or think. This is not entirely true. Introverts will communicate well with those they trust or when the situation demands it. Many an introvert makes a fine conference speech or presentation to a meeting but it is usually more of a strain than it is for the extrovert.

An interesting point is that although introverts and extroverts are equal in terms of intelligence, introverts predominate in the higher levels of the education system. This is because they can adjust to the routine and isolation of study more easily than extroverts. If organizations promote on qualifications rather than merit, they may end up with more introverts at the top. And introverts, as indicated earlier, may find it more difficult to communicate to the rest of the organization. Hence, the complaints of some employees about being kept in the dark!

Another point about introverts is that they will work at a problem in a concentrated way for quite a period of time. They will pursue an issue in depth. By doing so they feel that they can get in command and control of the situation so that when they do put forward an opinion or a proposition it is well founded.

Some introverts, however, get upset when their propositions in a meeting are met with rejection or doubt. Because they have thought them through so well, they find it hard to believe that anyone else cannot see the validity of their point of view.

If you have a boss who has an introverted approach, it may take a long time for you to get to know her. You may feel that she does not communicate as well as you would wish. However, she is likely to do so in her own way. For example, she is more likely to use memos rather than call informal meetings. To this extent you may well have to use the same form of communication if you are to get through to her.

If you have a subordinate who adopts an introverted approach, then likewise you may find him or her hard to understand at times. Introverts may seem to live in a world of their own. To a certain extent, this is true, in that they do put more credence upon their own ideas rather than going out and searching for other people's. However, to get communication at its best then one perhaps has to talk through quietly and on a confidential basis with these people on their own view. Perhaps it is best to ask them to write down their thoughts prior to a discussion. Certainly they appreciate the opportunity to think issues through before sounding off an opinion, and giving them forewarning of issues is very helpful. They are particularly good at looking at things in depth, providing you can organize sufficient time and freedom from successive interruptions.

The danger is that introverted people can often be overlooked. Indeed, they themselves can often be their own worst enemies and they do not go out and seek company. They will stick with the people they know even at coffee breaks and informal meetings. Their list of acquaintances, therefore, is often more limited than those of extroverts and, as a consequence, their opportunities for influence are likely to be less.

Extrovert Approach	Introvert Approach
Will often think things out by talking them through	Prefers to think things out before speaking
Enjoys meeting other people and often seeks social gatherings	Does not have a high need to meet regularly with others
Enjoys a variety of tasks and activities	Likes to concentrate on a few tasks at a time
Stimulated by unanticipated interruptions	Dislikes unanticipated interruptions
When speaking publicly will often talk impromptu	When speaking publicly will prepare in depth and speak to a plan
Likely to contribute a lot at meetings	May be more quiet at meetings
Can be impulsive	More likely to consider things before acting

Generating Data: The Sensing Approach

People who use the sensing approach are usually very much matter of fact. They do not trust things unless they can touch them, weigh them, move them or in some way assess their worth through practical means. They like clear tasks with specific things to do. They enjoy developing and using their skills, and essentially are more interested in doing things where they can see that they have had an effect. These people are usually good at gathering information on mechanical methods, working on particular jobs which require manipulating physical materials, or assessing the practical implications of change, which involves the reorganization of physical things.

However, they tend to dislike problems unless there are standard ways of solving them. Problems must be approached logically or sequentially. Frustration occurs with ambiguous or complex situations which do not have tangible outcomes such as philosophical questions. Their concern is to deal with practical issues and generate information which can have a bearing upon the specific outcome. Such people enjoy the present and deal with the practicalities of life, rather than theorizing or developing grand ideas of how life should be.

If you are the manager of people who have a strong practical base, then it is important to give them work which does have some tangible aspect to it. It is no good bringing such a group together to develop radical new ways of working. They will not necessarily be very successful in generating new ideas or brainstorming. However, they will be extremely valuable in applying their minds to a specific problem and utilizing their experience. Such people can be very effective when asked to develop a more effective way of organizing the work process or mending or rectifying situations which are getting out of control. They can be as clever as anyone else, but they like to use their abilities to deal with practical problems, particularly in the here-and-now situation.

Generating Data: The Intuitive Approach

People who use the intuitive approach tend to stress more the imaginative side of their personalities. They are like the novelist who perhaps sees two people fighting in the street and then goes home and writes a novel about urban violence and the breakdown of law and order. The novel emerges out of a specific incident which the writer then develops according to his insight. They often do not know themselves what is happening and why. Nevertheless they do come up with ideas and possibilities, some of which may be worthwhile, some not!

The characteristics of the intuitive person would include the following points. First of all, she concentrates on the whole field, rather than specifics. This means that she can be poor in attending to detail. Such people do not like routine. They get impatient, frustrated and show anxiety when they have to engage in such work. The effect of this is that they may sometimes take shortcuts and play hunches. Such people are often difficult to talk with. Their minds are racing ahead, looking for the consequences and the implications.

It is of no use putting people who have the high capacity for intuition into jobs which demand repetitive behavior over a period of time. Such people enjoy tackling new jobs and are extremely good on project work. They love learning a new skill. Indeed, having learned a new skill they may not then want to use it but instead go quickly to the next interesting assignment.

Often such people work in quick and energetic spells. They may seem to be lazy at times and not be applying themselves. However, as Andrew Carnegie, the great industrialist, used to say, "I've got the flash," and would then rush off to tackle a new project.

Such people can be exciting individuals to have alongside you. However, they are not easy to understand. It is necessary, though, if we are to develop an effective team or organization, to harness the talents of such people. Typically this is difficult to do because of their dislike of routine, and their enjoyment of complexity.

Examples of such teams are the research and development laboratories of major organizations. Many of these are separated away from the operational side of work, such as manufacturing or refining. Many of the researchers will often come in late in the morning and work till all hours of the evening if they are pursuing something that they feel has value. In one sense the creative process cannot be tied down to time, and the nine-to-five day has little meaning for someone who is extremely creative.

We have distinguished here between two ends of a continuum. We have referred to people as having either more of a sensing or more of an *intuitive* approach to gathering information. In reality all of us have some degree of both. Therefore, what we are talking about is the emphasis that we place on one in contrast to the other. This is a matter of preferences. Clearly we develop over a period of time and gather strength in one or both of the dimensions. Therefore we will move towards using our strengths and often reinforce them.

This is usually manifested in the fact that we choose certain jobs which play to our strengths. Therefore, if you find a person who likes practical detail, precision, and specific task working in a creative situation of ambiguity it is likely he or she will be dissatisfied. Equally, if you find a creative person working in a situation where he is tied down to specific work which has to be done in a specific time, he is also likely to get frustrated and leave the job. The task of the manager, therefore, is to identify the strengths of the people he has around him and be able to place them in jobs which best suit their work preferences.

The following summary gives the main elements of the sensing and the intuitive approaches.

Sensing Approach	Intuitive Approach
Prefers practical problems	Enjoys ambiguous problems
Prefers systems and methods	Gets bored with routine problems
Likes to work with tested ideas	Regularly floats new ideas
Likes to work with real things	Sees possibilities and implications
Patient with routine detail	Frequently jumps beyond the facts
Will test established facts	May get facts wrong
Pays attention to facts and detail	Has creative vision and insight
Wants to see detailed parts	Follows inspirations
Likes schedule of working	Searches for the new; innovation
Searches for standard problem-solving approach	Likes complexity and searches for creative approaches

Making Decisions: The Thinking Approach

People who use the thinking approach subject information to a careful process of analysis before deciding. That is, they look, stand back and weigh the facts rather than give way to their feelings.

Such people will try to bring whatever analytical aids there are to help assess the situation. In the world of business they will like to use decision analysis, linear programming, cost benefit analysis, extrapolative forecasting, and other methods for cutting down the risk.

The emphasis on analytical reasoning sounds like a hard, cold, and logical process. However, for many people it is an exciting challenge. They like working with figures and assessing the conclusions of particular lines of action. They treat forecasting as a science. Their development of budgets and the preparation of plans are a fundamental part of the analytical approach. The use of statistical methods to work out probabilities is a key aspect. The aim is not to eliminate risk but to reduce it. Such methods can only work, however, where there are clear objectives. It is the objective-setting process which is perhaps the most difficult part of the thinking approach.

Those who favor the thinking approach often take a detached view of the decision-making process. They talk about markets rather than people. They talk about products rather than processes. They like to have clear criteria for assessing the decision to be taken.

If you have a boss who has a strong thinking approach, it is best to give him evidence. He will want to be convinced by data. Likewise, if you have subordinates who decide on a basis of analytical reasoning it is important that they see the factual basis upon which you come to a decision if they are to be motivated. Trying to get them to act on purely personal conviction will rarely be sufficient.

People who prefer a thinking and analytical approach to decision making may hurt other people's feelings without being aware of it. Because their concern is to do what "the situation" demands they may ignore people's concerns and emotions. Increasingly, managers are being made to comply with laws and codes which demand a cold analytical decision. For example, staff now have to be warned at least three times before they can be dismissed for inadequate work performance. No longer can the manager just make people redundant without giving thought to the social and legal aspects as well as the basic profit and loss aspects.

Making Decisions: The Feelings Approach

Most of us have strong beliefs, whether it be on how to bring up a family or the way in which society should be run or, indeed, the way in which business should be conducted. The question that we have to consider is how far these beliefs dominate our decision-making process.

People who have strong beliefs usually ask whether the decision that is to be taken will be congruent with their values. They will, therefore, look at things very much in terms of their own personal standpoints rather than sit back and decide things on the basis of cold analysis. People with strong religious, political or humanitarian views will therefore look very much at the extent to which the decision is related to their own perspectives on life.

People who have strong feelings can be enormously helpful to those whom they feel could be converted to support their own views. They are often very friendly people who like to see that there is a great deal of commonality in the way people see the world.

However, if other people do not see the world in their terms equally they can be fierce opponents. They will polarize the issues as being for or against.

This can be seen in various facets of the business. At one level the shop steward is often a person with very strong convictions. He judges the decisions of management as to whether or not they accord with his views on the way in which a business should be run. Likewise the businessman can be equally strong in his convictions. He may well ignore the logic of the situation to press for what he believes is right. Indeed, Henry Ford did this producing the original Model T car. However, when other competitors developed their cars, Ford was still insisting on the standard Model T. It nearly ruined his business. Eventually he had to face the cold hard facts and make his decisions upon an analytical basis. However, by that time he had lost millions and it took a long time to get the organization profitable again.

Beliefs are therefore critical. It is very important that people do have standards and ideals against which they can measure their facts. It is not a question of just deciding everything according to conviction or, alternatively, deciding everything according to the facts. There must be a mixture of both.

Thinking Approach	Feeling Approach
Tries to establish objective decision criteria	Has personal subjective decision criteria
Measures decisions against payoffs	Measures decisions against beliefs
Can be seen as detached and cold	Can be seen as overcommitted to a point of view
Believes in deciding according to situation	Believes in deciding on personal considerations
Is likely to be flexible depending on situation	Is likely to be nostalgic, holding to traditional ways
Negotiates on the evidence	Negotiates on rights and wrongs of the issues
Has concern for fairness based on the rules	Believes fairness relates to values and beliefs
Likes analysis and clarity	Likes harmony based on common values
Sets objectives and beliefs follow	Objectives emerge from beliefs
Task orientated	Principles orientated

Establishing Priorities: The Judging Approach

We all have an inclination to get into action or wait until we have information. These priorities considerably influence our overall preferences.

People who are high on judging like to have issues clarified and resolved. They will often come across as detached, impersonal decision makers. They will, however, be more open to change, providing people can convince them with hard evidence that has been subject to careful review. They do essentially respect the logic of problem solving, but do not like to spend too much time before getting into action.

Judging is clearly a vital aspect of any manager's role. The higher the manager gets in the organization, the more he has to balance the considerable information required for decision making with the need for clarity and order. Those concerned with judging will put more weight on the decision process of either thinking or feeling as described above. In short, the judgmental process leads towards decision making. The opposite is true for the perceptive approach.

Establishing Priorities: The Perceptive Approach

People who prefer the perceptive approach will put a priority on getting as much information as possible. Therefore, perceptive people put more weight on either the sensing or intuitive factors. The perceptive sensing person will focus heavily on in-depth investigations to dig up the facts associated with the problem. They will put pressure on others for "hard" data and they will not be easily put off with generalizations, hearsay, or other circumstantial evidence. They may even demand information way beyond what you feel is necessary in order to make the decision. That is not seen as important by perceptive persons. It is their concern to know and understand that dominates. They can frustrate their colleagues, subordinates and boss by not taking decisions. Of course, this can also upset others who do not wish to be bothered by more inquiries.

If the person is high on perceiving and also on intuition, then it may be more difficult to observe the process that goes on. The reason for this is that the intuitive process is based on insight, imagination and developing new ideas. So, rather than going outside of herself to generate data, the perceptive intuitive person may sit around doodling, scribbling and waiting for the inspiration. In short, such people are waiting for the great idea to strike them, or trying to link a set of ideas into a coherent whole. The perceptive person, therefore, does not mind letting things hang loose. Although maybe frustrated that he does not have enough information, he is usually prepared to hang on till he does.

It is also noticeable that some perceptive people tend to take on a number of projects simultaneously and never do justice to any. However, it satisfies their concern to be involved in a lot of activities, and to be aware and knowledgeable. Therefore, in summary, the perceptive person has a lot to contribute but needs to be focused towards time schedules, output quotas, and commitments if he is to make the best use of his abilities.

Judging Approach	Perceptive Approach
Likes clarity and order	Enjoys searching and finding
Concerned with resolving matters	May procrastinate in search of even better information
Dislikes ambiguity	Can tolerate ambiguity
Very orderly	Concerned to know, not organized
May rush to quick decisions	Takes in lots of data—maybe too much
Can be somewhat inflexible once judgment is made	Open minded and curious
Concerned to work to a plan	Works according to the requirements of the data
Emphasizes decision making over information getting	Emphasis on diagnosing over concluding and resolving
Concerned with implementation	Concerned with knowledge
Likes to get things resolved and operating	Likes to find out as much as possible before action

Overall Profiles

In summary, each person has a personal way of working and living which is influenced considerably by a number of important factors. These, of course, are not by any means the only factors. However, they are very influential in the way a person organizes his or her work.

We can summarize these preferences in the following way:

E Extrovert Preference or I Introvert Preference

Prefers to live in contact with others and things	Prefers to be more self-contained and work things out personally

S Sensing Preference or N Intuition Preference

Puts emphasis on fact, details, and concrete knowledge	Puts emphasis on possibilities, imagination, creativity, and seeing things as a whole

T Thinking Preference or F Feeling Preference

Puts emphasis on analysis using logic and rationality	Puts emphasis on human values, establishing personal friendships; decisions mainly on beliefs and dislikes

J Judging Preference or P Perceiving Preference

Puts emphasis on order through reaching decisions and resolving issues	Puts emphasis on gathering information and obtaining as much data as possible

The initial letter of each preference provides a shorthand reference to the factor for understanding and discussion. Each one carries the initial letter of the factor except for intuition which is coded N, so that it does not conflict with I for introvert.

We shall use these letters to describe the factors and make up the maps to describe managerial styles and teamwork. This will be based upon the research we have conducted and this we shall not describe.

A Basis for Self-Understanding

The individual descriptions, while valuable, are insufficient. It is the combination of the various preferences that gives us a better indication of how a person will manage.

There are 16 combinations from the alternatives outlined. These can be seen from the following model, which builds upon the shorthand letters that have been adopted for each factor. Therefore:

    E = Extrovert ——————— I = Introvert
    S = Sensing ——————— N = Intuitive
    T = Thinking ——————— F = Feeling
    J = Judgment ——————— P = Perceiving

The range of options that emerges is shown in Figure 4.2.

Each combination has detailed explanations of its views and values in the Myers-Briggs Handbook. The resulting descriptions make fascinating reading. For example, the "INTP" type is often considered to be the most "academic" of all the types, whilst the "ESFP" is seen as the most sociable. Clearly, however, it is impossible for us to go into depth here. Our concern will be the relation of the types to managerial roles.

Our research, based on 849 managers attending business school short courses, showed the following breakdown.

	Percentages			
	Extrovert	Total	Introvert	
ESTJ	20.7	44.5	23.8	ISTJ
ESFJ	5.9	12.4	6.5	ISFJ
ENTJ	8.8	15.3	6.5	INTJ
ENFJ	1.6	4.0	2.4	INFJ
ESTP	3.9	8.2	4.4	ISTP
ESFP	1.2	2.4	1.2	ISFP
ENTP	4.2	7.1	2.9	INTP
ENFP	2.9	6.0	3.1	INFP

It can be seen that the STJ's form by far the largest chunk of the senior and middle managerial ranks. This suggests that not only are there certain types of people who are attracted to managerial roles, but also that they are selected more often than not. Also of interest, is the low proportion of SFP's—the most "sociable" of the types. Does this mean that managers are not "sociable" or at least that they find it difficult to maintain relationships with others? This is one of the issues to be explored later. For the moment we shall use the four basic conceptual types that were outlined earlier.

The percentage breakdown for these in our sample are as shown:

	Total	ST	SF	NF	NT
Managers	849	52.8%	14.8%	10%	22.4%

The implications of these figures will be discussed in the next section on applications.

The preceding sections have discussed the basic model of work preferences and have shown that different preferences lead to different ways of working. However, of more interest is that application to managerial and organizational issues. The ones we shall comment on are:

1. Managerial style and decision making
2. Organization structure

Figure 4.2 Combinations of Preference Alternatives

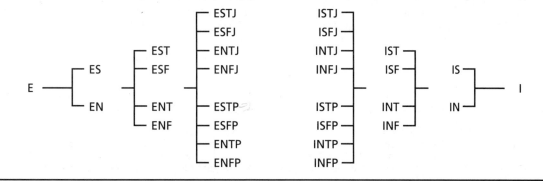

3. Approaches to change
4. Creativity and innovation
5. Career development, appraisal, and training

Managerial Style and Decision Making

A number of authors have discussed the need for different types of conceptual skill and style within the managerial context. For example, Mintzberg[3] in his article "Planning on the Left Side, and Managing on the Right" describes the implications of research on the human brain. It has been suggested that the human brain is specialized with logical, linear functions occurring in the left hemisphere and holistic, rational functions occurring in the right. Managers with the left hemisphere more developed would, Mintzberg suggests, be much better at planning and analytical work, which managers with the right hemisphere developed would be better at imaginative overall control. This appears to reflect the sensing/intuitive dimension postulated by Jung.

Leavitt[4] also contrasts the analytical approach to management as exemplified in America by the MBA student with that of a more imaginative integrated approach based upon "consciousness raising." He comes to the conclusion that "we need to integrate wisdom and feeling with analysis." Again one can see some parallels with the typology through the need to integrate the thinking and feeling functions. McKenney and Keen[5] have also developed research on cognitive styles concerned with the differences between management scientists and general managers. They said management scientists were more logical and analytical than general managers who operate by the seat of their pants.

By far the majority of the work in this context has been done by Kilmann and Mitroff[6] using the four conceptual types outlined earlier. Their work has a tremendous number of applications. One of these is the preference of the different types for certain stages in decision making. Essentially:

1. The NF type prefers ambiguity, creating, feeling, problems/opportunities.
2. The NT type prefers defining problems/opportunities, identifying basic objectives and policies, establishing criteria for success.
3. The ST prefers defining solutions and planning their implementation.
4. The SF type prefers to be practical but work on the basis of what he feels to be the right way to go.

This suggests that cognitive styles will be different between staff and line managers, as each has to concentrate on different parts of the decision-making process. Kilmann and Mitroff go slightly further; not only do they postulate the existence of these different types of managers but they make three further propositions.

1. All types are necessary for an effective balanced solution that is implemented.
2. The views of each type, being so essentially different, will lead to difficulties in communication between them.
3. Not only their way of working will be different, but also their long-term goals.

What therefore are the implications for managers based on our sample?

If we consider the sample of managers, we can see that managers are predominantly the ST type. They will be concerned first and foremost with practical and logical problems. They will also prefer problems that are concrete and specific rather than ambiguous and abstract, hence, their impatience and distrust of issues that to them seem nebulous and not based on tangible factors. This is not to say that some managers do not prefer problem exploration and definition. As can be seen from the table, all the basic types are represented. However, it is also of interest to note that the types most concerned with people problems are outnumbered 3:1 by those most concerned with technical problems. Perhaps this explains the need for "interpersonal" skills courses for managers. The SF's are a low proportion—these are the types which act as "lubricant" to the social mechanism of management and again perhaps their low proportion explains some of the industrial relations problems that occur in organizations.

Organization Structures

One of the constant themes of our work has been that people see and organize their world, including the world of work, in very different ways. This is why we are concerned with the mapping of personal spaces. Following the preferences given earlier it might be expected that the types of organizational structures set up will reflect these preferences. Again Kilmann and Mitroff have investigated this aspect. Table 4.1 gives a summary of some of their findings.

---

[3] Mintzberg, H. 1976. "Planning on the Left Side and Managing on the Right," *Harvard Business Review* (July–August), pp. 49–58.
[4a] Leavitt, H. J. 1975. "Beyond the Analytic Manager," *California Management Review,* XVII, no. 3, pp. 5–12.
[4b] Leavitt, H. J. 1975. "Beyond the Analytic Manager: Part II," *California Management Review,* XVII, no. 4, pp. 11–21.
[5] McKenney, J. L. and P. G. W. Keen. 1974. "How Managers' Minds Work," *Harvard Business Review,* pp. 79–80.
[6] Mitroff, I. I. and R. H. Kilmann. 1975. "Stories Managers Tell: A New Tool for Organizational Problem Solving," *Management Review,* pp. 18–28.

Table 4.1 Organizational Preferences of Different Types

Areas	Types			
	Practical (ST)	**Social (SF)**	**Idealistic (NF)**	**Theoretical (NT)**
Structure	Practical bureaucratic, well-defined hierarchy, central leader	Friendly, hierarchical but open	Completely decentralized, no clear lines of authority, no central leader	Complex organization, flexibility, changing authority, task forces
Emphasis in interactions	Task orientation, complete control, specificity, fixed rules	Human qualities of people doing work as individuals	Humanitarian, general concern for development of employees	Goals, clients, effect of environment
Organizational goals	Productivity work flow	Good interpersonal relations	Personal and humanitarian	Macroeconomic theoretical

It can be seen that NFs prefer an organizational structure which is decentralized, which has no clear line of authority and no central leader. On the other hand, STs prefer an authoritarian and bureaucratic organization with a well defined hierarchy and central leadership. The reasons for this stem from the nature of the work preference types. The NF person requires a high degree of autonomy and freedom in order to exercise his preferences and feeling. He prefers making contact with people regardless of their level and organization before he can work effectively. The ST type, on the other hand, prefers a well defined structure because this enables him to get on with what he enjoys doing—practical, everyday matters at hand. Discussions with people about feelings and intuition are often seen by ST people to be a waste of time and barriers to getting the task done.

Richek[7] found that sensing types had more positive attitudes to authority than intuitives. He also found that reality was perceived in different ways ranging from tangible material reality to intangible imaginative reality. One of the findings of the Aston studies was that the organizational structure of the company studied and the data collected were very much dependent on the attitudes of managers in each function. For example, the accountants often saw the organization very differently from the marketing people and also had different wishes for the type of structure they wanted. Handy[8] also examines this link between structure and individual most amusingly and instructively in *Gods of Management*.

Most managers are STs and NTs with the thinking-judgmental style predominating. Organizations in which they worked, therefore, would be expected to follow a hierarchical principle, and this appears to be true of most industrial organizations. On the other hand, there exist organizations such as the theatre, or to a certain extent, academic institutions, in which there is relatively little hierarchy. Our own work[9] examined the preferences of academics in a business school and shows that their dominating preference was intuition, which accords with a loose form of organization.

What is being said, therefore, is that as people perceive organizations in different ways they will tend to try and reinforce this perception by creating organizational structures that will leave them free to work in the way they most prefer. *This is one of the main motivating forces behind the action of individuals in organizations. It has major implications for top manager selection and development—when people select others in their own image.*

Approaches to Change

One of the major issues of importance in behavior is the individual's responsiveness to change. This is reflected in his or her attitude towards time.

It had been suggested by Mann et al.[10] that the different Jungian types react to time and change very differently; that is:

---

7 Richek, H. G. and O. H. Brown. 1968. "Phenomenological Correlates of Jung's Typology." *Journal of Analytical Psychology,* 13, pp. 57–65.
8 Handy, C. 1978. *Gods of Management,* Souvenir Press.
9 Margerison, C. J. and R. Lewis. 1979. Management Educators and Their Clients. In Beck, J. and C. Cox, eds. *Advances in Management Education.* New York: John Wiley.
10 Mann, H., M. Siegler, and H. Osmond. 1965. "The Many Worlds of Time," *Journal of Analytical Psychology,* 13, pp. 33–56.

Sensation types ———— present orientation

Intuitive types ———— future orientation

Feeling types ———— past orientation

Thinking types ———— time as a linear continuum

These approaches appear to have been borne out by some of the work that Kilmann and Mitroff[11] did in getting some groups within the American Bureau of Census to plan ahead to the year 2000. They concluded that:

To summarize, STs can be characterized as real-time, operational-technical, problem-solvers; NTs are future-time, strategic-technical problem generators; and SFs are real-time operational-people problem solvers related to intuitives; the planning horizon of sensing people is extreme; however the extreme sensing people are not interested in planning at all. They do not believe that one can talk sensibly about the future because one cannot sense it directly.

Again, if we look at the distribution of managers we can see that the majority (the sensing-thinking types) will be concerned with the present here-and-now. They will not be interested in long-term theoretical issues but those of immediate value. Hence, from a study of the types, it would be expected that for management educators to try to get managers to concentrate on theoretical ideas of general interest will not work. There is a reluctance to examine issues that are not directly pertinent to the current job.

Creativity and Innovation

It might be expected from the preceding section that innovators would essentially be the intuitive types. However, this must depend on how creativity and innovation are viewed. Certainly, intuitive types predominate in creativity that involves redefinition of the problem with new and different ideas. The work of McKinnon[12] has shown a preponderance of intuitives in "creative" professions such as architecture and novel writing. However, creativity can and does also involve coming up with many different solutions and alternatives rather than redefining the problem area. Kirton[13] defines these two different types of creativity as adaptor-innovator. The adaptor can find many different ways of solving a problem but within the context of the rules and system—the innovator goes outside the accepted system and comes up with one or two radical proposals. Thus all types may be said to be creative but in different ways.

It is also in order to look at the prime areas in which the various types usually operate well and show their strengths.

Sensing—Thinking	ST	Practicality
Sensing—Feeling	SF	Social Relations
Intuitive—Feeling	NF	Idealism
Intuitive—Thinking	NT	Theory

Creativity to an ST, for example, may well be in redesigning or building machinery, a brick wall, or sewing a dress, etc. Creativity for the SF could be selling, or making people happy. For the NT, it could be developing a new model or concept and for the NF in creative writing, or communication. This is fine as long as each type recognizes the creativity implicit in each other's chosen personal space.

From our sample we can see that the majority of managers would find it easiest operating within a system and working to rules and regulations. They will not want to continually question the basic framework within which they would be operating. Hence, again with some exceptions, because of the different types, managers would be uncomfortable with radical and drastic changes coming about through innovation. They would prefer "adaption," and gradual change.

Career Development, Appraisal, and Training

The model of work preferences that we have been discussing is based on the original theories and ideas of Jung. In essence, he was interested in a developmental guide to the path or career that an individual follows throughout his life. This aspect has recently been examined by Sheehy,[14] for example. In this context the ideas of Jung are well worth following up as they do appear to facilitate the understanding of problems of career change and development. They are extremely complex ideas if considered only in theory, but when related to individual life patterns develop clarity and simplicity.

One such idea is that of the shadow. This is the "opposite" of the preferred type of orientation and as such is an area in which the individual prefers not to work. He or she also would find it very difficult to understand others of the shadow type. For example, logical thinking types would have as their shadows feeling types. How often have "thinkers" dismissed with scorn the "softness" of feeling types—and in return the feeling types characterized thinkers as cold and heartless.

---

11 Mitroff, I. I., V .P. Barabba, and R. H. Kilmann. 1977. "The Application of Behavioral and Philosophical Technologies to Strategic Planning: A Case Study of a Large Federal Agency," *Management Science*, 24, no. 1 (September).
12 McKinnon, D. W. 1962. "The Nature and Nurture of Creative Talent," *American Psychologist*, pp. 484–95.
13 Kirton, M. J. 1977. *Kirton Adaptation-Innovation Inventory*. National Foundation for Educational Research.
14 Sheehy, G. 1978. *Passages: Predictable Crisis of Adult Life*. Corgi.

The dilemma is, however, that whilst there may be misunderstanding or even hostility towards "shadow" in other people, it also exists within our personalities. In order to end up a balanced, mature individual Jung believed we must develop this "shadow" self. If we do not, he argued, it will develop itself—either in the form of a breakdown or overcompensation. Careers can be seen in this light.

What we are suggesting, and in fact have used, is that this concept of "shadow" is of great use in appraisal and training. The majority of managers would have their shadow in the area of "theory" if our sample is a guide. There would also seem to be from our sample a considerable need for interpersonal skills development to help understand and improve relations with others. The dilemma is that this type of training, whilst absolutely necessary for balance, may be rejected because it is in the shadow—the hidden and feared part! This may well be the cause of the unease that some managers feel with regard to participation. A knowledge of type can therefore be of immense use to the trainer.

Other Readings by the Authors

Lewis, R., and C. Hibbert. 1980. Career Development: Meeting Individual and Organizational Needs, *Journal of European Industrial Training*, 4, no. 4.

Margerison, C. J., R. Lewis, and C. Hibbert. 1978. Training Implications of Work Preferences, *Journal of European Industrial Training*, 2, no. 3, pp. 2–4.

Margerison, C. J. 1950. Leadership Paths and Profiles, *Leadership and Organization Development Journal*, 1, no. 1.

The Centre for Applications of Psychological Types acts as a reference centre for Myers-Briggs Type Indicator. Their address is 1221 Norwest 6th Street, Suite B 400, Gainesville, Florida 32609, USA.

Diverse Cognitive Styles in Teams

ELECTIVE

Module 4

Give Me an E. Give Me an S.

Or How About an I or a P? Or a Left-Brained Type? Sound Like Gibberish? It's the Language of Personality Testing, Corporate America's Hot New Tool.

by Daniel Golden

Author's apology to detail-oriented, random, quantitative readers: The personality tests I have taken over the past few months indicate that I am intuitive, sequential, and abstract—in other words, just the opposite of you.

Although I've tried to flex my less dominant sides in this article, I'm afraid it will bore you. Please try to learn my language, and remember that differences enhance team-building. As Rocky Balboa once said about his girlfriend, Adrian: "I've got gaps. Together we fill gaps." If a left-brained extrovert like the Italian Stallion and a right-brained introvert like Adrian can hit it off, so can we.

After a mutual friend introduced them this past August, it wasn't long before psychologist Otto Kroeger was offering to pump up morale and improve communication at Ralph Jacobson's troubled company.

Jacobson, the chief executive officer of Draper Laboratory in Cambridge, was intrigued. Draper had long specialized in guidance systems for underwater missiles, but much of that research had been torpedoed by glasnost, and the company had undertaken a variety of smaller projects. This shift required a reorganization. In August 1988, employees who had worked together for years were divided into specialized teams. Not surprisingly, some were unhappy with the change, and tensions ensued between teams responsible for scheduling deadlines and those in charge of engineering. This past July, the firm laid off 60 employees.

So Jacobson listened to the ebullient Kroeger and then read his book, *Type Talk*, an introduction to the Myers-Briggs Type Inventory, one of the world's most frequently used personality tests. At his office in Fairfax, Virginia, Kroeger trains more than 500 people a year to administer the MBTI. He also does "interventions" at U.S. and foreign companies.

In September the psychologist flew to Cambridge and gave the MBTI to Jacobson and six of his top aides. The seven executives answered 126 questions, including, "In your way of living, do you prefer to be original or conventional?" and "Do you prefer to arrange dates, parties, etc., well in advance or be free to do whatever looks like fun when the time comes?"

On the basis of their responses, the test-takers were categorized as Introverts (I) or Extroverts (E), Sensors (S) or Intuitives (N), Thinkers (T) or Feelers (F), and Judgers (J) or Perceivers (P). Then they discussed their types. Although Kroeger and Jacobson are reluctant to talk about the test results, Kroeger does say, "Sixty percent of the managers of any company are TJs." Top executives tend to be Is; Es are too indiscreet to advance that far.

Jacobson found the discussion so helpful that he brought Kroeger back in November to give the test to 40 more managers. "The experience and outcome of the day produced better understanding," says Joseph O'Connor, Draper's vice president for human resources and administration, who took the test in September. "The instrument was an amazingly accurate predictor of my own personality, and the others felt the same way."

Reflecting the values of the baby boom generation and the influence of the Japanese model of corporation-as-family, more and more American businesses are recognizing that their success may depend not on technological innovation but on human factors such as teamwork, communication, and leadership—elusive goals that in the end boil down to the interaction of personalities. And, for an inexpensive but supposedly accurate reading on the personalities of job applicants and employees, U.S. firms increasingly rely on personality testing.

Long used by career counselors and government agencies but disdained by most companies out of skepticism or fear of bad publicity, personality testing is becoming a mainstay of the corporate world. Advocates believe that testing can help companies ease the pain of layoffs, build support for affirmative-action policies, and make the transition from entrepreneurial start-up to established

Source: Golden, Daniel (1990, January 8). "Give Me an E. Give Me an S." *Boston Globe Magazine*. Reprinted courtesy of *The Boston Globe*.

institution. Wayne Camara, director of scientific affairs for the American Psychological Association, estimates that in the past five years the number of tests available to industry has tripled. Major corporations such as Digital Equipment Corp. have behavioral psychologists on staff who develop tests for in-house use.

In many offices, guessing your personality type is the hottest fad since the team decision-making technique known as quality circles. Members of this cult of personality have Myers-Briggs four-letter type designations inscribed on their license plates or nameplates. Or they pin schematic diagrams of their brains on their bulletin boards to identify themselves as predominantly right- or left-brained.

Ideally, personality tests match employees to tasks, teams, and environments that suit their temperaments, thereby raising productivity. One nationwide trucking firm recently hired University of Tulsa psychology professor Robert Hogan, developer of the Hogan Personality Inventory, to analyze the personalities of its drivers. The local delivery men were alienating customers, while long-distance truckers complained of boredom. The test showed that most of the local drivers were introverts uncomfortable with personal contact, while the long-distance ones were extroverts who needed stimulation. The company switched their assignments, and the complaints decreased.

Test-testing carries risks as well. The field is largely unregulated by the government. It is perfectly legal to sell or administer a bogus test as long as it does not discriminate against protected groups such as minorities and women. Most tests do not have to be administered by psychologists, which reduces their price but makes it harder for organizations such as the APA to monitor them. "We have no good gauge on test misuse in employment," Camara says.

Although the association and its division of industrial psychologists publish professional guidelines, many test developers refuse to show their questions and scoring systems to the APA or *Buros' Mental Measurements Yearbook*, the leading review publication. Test developers say they are worried about plagiarism. "Psychologists steal from each other all the time," says Arnold Daniels, chairman of Praendex Inc. in Wellesley, which markets the Predictive Index. Daniels' company has never submitted the index to the yearbook, although it did commission two Harvard Medical School staffers to analyze the test's reliability.

Some academic psychologists contend that test developers are simply afraid of scrutiny and test business customers aren't interested in spending the time or money necessary to learn about what they're buying. Seymour Epstein, a University of Massachusetts at Amherst psychology professor who developed the Constructive Thinking Inventory several years ago, says several companies contacted him about using it. But when he responded that he would not let them use the test until research showed how it applied to their companies, they lost interest. Even when he told some companies that he would compare his test—for free—with the ones they were already using, there were no takers. "It's become not a scientific thing, it's a business thing," Epstein says. "There's a lot of black magic and mumbo jumbo."

According to Camara, companies often find themselves deluged with test offers, without the sophistication to choose the best one for their needs. "Organizations that have no expertise are trying to make a decision from 10 different salesmen all pushing their own test," he says. "They're exposed to a lot of hype, and they're at an extreme disadvantage."

There is also the risk of oversimplification. People enjoy knowing about their personality type as much as they like reading their horoscope—it's a conversation piece, a way to connect. Yet personalities may be too varied to be easily categorized, and many people don't fall into any one type. If they are shoehorned by co-workers or bosses into a type that doesn't fit them, or if they're regarded as misfits because they won't play the game, personality typing can turn into a dangerous kind of stereotyping.

"A lot of management tests put you in categories that aren't justified statistically," says Boston psychologist Kenneth Kraft, who favors administering several different tests to avoid pigeonholing employees. "They want you to walk away with a label, 'I'm a this or I'm a that.'"

Personality typing, of course, is nothing new. Medieval philosophers divided humanity into four humors, or temperaments—phlegm, melancholy, blood, and cholera. Victorian phrenologists analyzed personality by feeling bumps on the skull. The advent per modern psychiatry spurred more scientific testing starting with the Rorschach, or ink-blot, test, a staple of clinical treatment for half a century.

The grandfather of modern personality indicators is the Minnesota Multi-Phasic Inventory. Designed as a clinical measurement of neurosis, it is also used by many government agencies and private employers to weed out unstable applicants. Because it includes such true-false questions as "I am very strongly attracted by members of my own sex" and "I believe in the second coming of Christ," the MMPI remains controversial. Most recently, a California department store that administers the MMPI was sued on invasion of privacy grounds by an applicant for a security guard job. The case is pending.

Today, the MMPI is just one of hundreds of tests. They are not proliferating because psychologists are discovering new aspects of personality. Quite the contrary. An increasingly accepted theory among academic psychologists synthesizes personality traits into five spectrums, nicknamed the "Big Five": abstract to concrete, self-confident to depressed, prudent to impulsive, outgoing to shy, and empathic to hostile.

What's happening, instead, is that consultants design tests just original enough to call their own. Most of the tests on the market try to assess one or more of the Big Five dimensions and many of them ask similar questions. Only the interpretive jargon changes. What the Myers-Briggs calls intuitive, for example, overlaps considerably with what other tests label as abstract, conceptual, or right-brained.

Once consultants develop a test, they try it out on executives in the industries they want as customers until they can show that patterns of answers correlate with behavior on the job. Then they translate these patterns into management personas: inspirer, perfectionist, assimilator, accommodate, implementer, experimenter.

Even the most ardent proponents of personality testing concede there is a lack of statistics or studies showing that it improves productivity or lowers attention. Yet tests steadily gain ground in the workplace. Because their results are couched in terms of style and preference rather than aptitude and intelligence, they seem unthreatening to most employees. And for employers who are trying to hire, they come at a time when other sources of information are drying up.

For example, intelligence and aptitude tests are more likely than personality tests to discriminate on the basis of race—which makes them more vulnerable to legal challenge. Another traditional tool, checking an applicant's references, has lost its usefulness because many past employers won't speak frankly for fear of being sued. Since Congress outlawed the lie detector test for private employment in 1988, many companies have turned to pen-and-pencil honesty tests.

Changes in the corporate world trigger demand for testing. Many firms, including *The Boston Globe*, use tests to ease tensions associated with affirmative action and drive home the lesson that personality types know no race or gender. If a white male and a black female discover at a workshop that they are both introverted judgers, perhaps that bond will erase any mutual suspicion.

With deregulation of financial services, many banks want customer-service workers to change from being passive order-takers to aggressive salespeople. Testing may show which workers can adapt most easily. Other companies have shifted from a hierarchical organization to a structure based on equal and interdependent teams. That structure delegates more responsibility to midlevel employees and makes chemistry more crucial. In choosing team members, again, personality testing often plays a role.

A few companies, though, are disillusioned. The Knight-Ridder newspaper chain, long a proponent of personality tests, still gives them to managerial candidates and uses them for [hiring decisions but they no longer use] them for prospective reporters because it could not demonstrate any link between personality traits such as high levels of energy and the ability to write on deadline. "Tests are not to be used as an excuse to throw brains out the window," says Ivan Jones, assistant vice president of personnel research and development for Knight-Ridder. "That's the trouble with tests. They're quick, they're easy, their value is easy to overemphasize, so hiring managers rely on them."

Just for fun, let's divide companies that use personality tests into two types: communicators and evaluators. Communicators test employees at workshops in which participation is usually voluntary. Employees often score their own tests and do not have to share the results with their bosses. The tests, then, are used not to assess performance or potential but to spark conversation about morale or team-building. While this approach reduces concerns about privacy and stereotyping, its benefits are often limited because of a lack of follow-up.

Says one therapist who used to give the Myers-Briggs at businesses: "It's hard to change patterns that have been going on for a long time unless a structure is set up, such as a process time to discuss communication before each meeting. When things get stressed out, when your profits go down, that's when you most need this stuff, and it's not there."

Unlike communicators, evaluators have enough faith in testing to rely on it for hiring and promotion. And while communicators boast about their trendy workshops, evaluators sound defensive. They decline comment or describe their questionnaire as a tool, an instrument, an indicator—anything but a test. They realize that many people agree with the Boston woman who withdrew her application for a management job in the Sheraton hotel chain after being asked to take a battery of personality [tests].

"When you accept a job, it should be based on your skills," she says. "If a psychologist is making the decision, you don't need to work there. My interpretation of dots, or whatever they use, is nobody's business."

Tobias Fleishman Shapiro and Co., a Cambridge accounting firm, is one of the few companies willing to discuss its personality testing for prospective employees. For the past five years, TFS has required most applicants to take the Predictive Index, which has been available since 1955. Praendex chairman Arnold Daniels based the index on his work in World War II with a psychologist who studied Air Force bomber crews. The corporations using the test range from banks to fast-food chains, and their number has more than doubled in a decade, from 800 in 1979 to 1,700. The index lists two identical sets of adjectives—"eloquent," "conscientious," "life of the party," etc.—on either side of a sheet of paper. On one side, applicants check the adjectives that describe their behavior; on the other, they mark the ones that describe how others expect them to act. According to Daniels, the self-description indicates personality traits, and comparing it with the perceived expectations suggests the individual's pattern of adjustment.

The total number of adjectives checked is supposed to reflect the individual's energy level. But that seemed dubious in one case. A highly respected *Globe* writer who took the PI anonymously for the purposes of this article was surprised to be told that, according to Daniels' analysis of his responses, he held a subordinate position and was frustrated by the routine nature of his job. When Daniels was asked how he had reached his conclusion, he said it was because the writer checked only a few adjectives.

In a world where recruitment agencies charge $10,000 to find an entry-level accountant, TFS executives regard the Predictive Index as insurance against making an expensive hiring mistake. The additional cost of personality testing for TFS is minuscule: $1,400 to train recruiting director Laura Share to administer the index, plus a $400 annual licensing fee.

Share says that the ideal entry-level accountant is a detail-oriented extrovert, equally at ease with numbers and clients. If the results signal introversion or inattention to detail, TFS executives probe those areas in interviewing the applicant and calling references. "If we see someone who's opposite to everyone here, we want to make sure they'd be happy here," Share says. "Otherwise, chances are they won't stay long."

TFS executives recognize that using the Predictive Index could drive away potentially valuable employees. Occasionally, they waive the test for especially desirable applicants. After praising the index for the better part of an hour, Tracy Gallagher, director of administration, concedes that he decided not to give it to Lawrence Kaye, for fear of alienating him. Kaye is now manager of training and education.

On the other hand, since an important part of happiness at the office is getting along with the boss, TFS often tests not only the job applicant but also the supervisor for that position, to see if their personalities would be compatible. Share says, "If the supervisors say they want someone who is independent, and they're dominant themselves, you ask, 'Are you sure? Do you really want someone like yourself?'"

It doesn't take long to realize that Manny Elkind is artistic, visionary, turned off by sequences and numbers—in a word, right-brained. When a reporter interrupts Elkind's fluid exposition of the left-brained personality ("You like to think it through, then you say, 'Okay, let's get it done'") to ask permission to accompany him to a workshop, Elkind agrees. Checking his calendar, he says he will lead a session on brain dominance technology at an insurance company the following Monday. Elkind calls the company and informs an answering machine of the reporter's wish: "I've got a good feeling about this guy," he tells the machine. Only after hanging up the phone does he realize that he has the date wrong. He conducted the workshop the previous week.

Like a cat in a dog pound, Elkind worked for years as an operations manager in the left-brained milieu of Polaroid. There, he says, he saw promising innovations, such as a plan for cameras to be put together by small teams rather than on assembly lines, thwarted by supervisors reluctant to give up control. Realizing that managers need to understand themselves to work effectively with others, he began attending workshops on self-awareness—including est, the controversial California-based movement that flourished in the late 1970s. In 1979, Elkind became Polaroid's senior manager of experimental projects, with an opportunity to implement what he had learned.

Ned Herrmann, developer of the Herrmann Brain Dominance Instrument, visited Polaroid in 1983 and gave a seminar on left- and right-brained personalities. According to Herrmann, everyone prefers one or more of four styles: cerebral left (analytical, mathematical); cerebral right (creative, holistic); limbic left (controlled, conservative); and limbic right (interpersonal, emotional). "This technology was the best combination of most valuable and least threatening," Elkind says. "It's a whole-brain concept. It appeals to everyone. I had an immediate vision of what I could do with it."

The following year, Elkind began using Herrmann's test for workshops he conducted at Polaroid. They were so popular that he invited other corporations to send their employees. The number of people enrolled in his seminars increased from 300 in 1984 to 4,000 in 1988. Then Elkind became concerned about Polaroid's future after a takeover attempt, and he grew frustrated because, as he puts it, the company would not support "the more intensive training people need to move into." He left to start Mind-Tech Inc. in Stoughton. His workshop remains popular with Massachusetts companies: It is required for loan officers at Bank of Boston and for senior managers at John Hancock Mutual Life Insurance Co.

Among his other activities, Elkind gives a daylong workshop every month at Bentley College in Waltham, open to anyone. This past November about 30 people paid either $215 apiece, the corporate rate, or $125, the rate for employees of nonprofit enterprises, to attend the session. The group, which had twice as many women as men, included a dozen employees from Bank of Boston's customer relations division, a Bank of New England employee who was evaluating the workshop for use in the bank's training program, and four employees of a Texas Air subsidiary that has suffered from high turnover and low morale.

Elkind's genial manner makes the group feel at home. He encourages its members to change seats every 45 minutes: By the afternoon, everyone has met everybody else. The activities are a fast-paced melange of lecture, films, discussion, and exercises. Asked to draw a flower, left-brainers depict no-frills stems and petals of mathematical exactness, while right-brainers, emptying their crayon boxes, scrawl impressionistic blossoms.

"The thinking preferences affect you at every level of your life," Elkind says. "The way you choose cars, the way you choose clothes, the way you choose careers."

At one point, Elkind tells the group that Herrmann's theory does not depict the brain's actual division of labor. It is just a schematic, a metaphor, with no more claim to a physiological basis than other models of personality. He urges his audience to explore other typologies, such as the distinction between matchers and mismatchers. Matchers, he says notice similarities, while mismatchers see differences.

"I'm a matcher, and my wife is a mismatcher," Elkind says. "I'd suggest going out to dinner, and she'd say, 'I can't do it either Tuesday or Thursday.' I'd get angry, thinking she was negative. I'd tell her, 'Don't tell me when you can't do it. Tell me when you can do it.' I finally realized that her mind worked by process of elimination. She was telling me that she could do it Monday, Wednesday, and Friday."

Before his first workshop in 1984, Elkind gave Herrmann's questionnaire to the Polaroid executives who had volunteered to participate. When he graded the tests, he was distressed to find that everyone in the group was left-brained. Since the workshop needed a mix of personalities, he asked the executives to invite the most creative, freewheeling people they knew to take the test. Any right-brainers, he said, could come for free.

Miriam Kronish, an elementary school principal in Needham, heard about Elkind's offer from a school media specialist who was married to a Polaroid manager. Kronish had wondered for years if she was unsuited to her job because she was bored by budgets and schedules. Intrigued by the concept of personality types, she took the test, which showed that she was very right-brained. Then she went to the workshop. It was an "epiphany," she says. "It changed my way of looking at myself professionally."

Since then, Kronish has matched wits with the *New York Times* crossword puzzle every day to develop her left brain. Along with other Needham teachers and administrators who had been impressed by Elkind, she attended workshops that applied personality types to the classroom. Today, the Needham elementary school curriculum is not only divided into right- and left-brained activities but is tailored to four learning styles: innovative, analytic, common sense, and dynamic.

At the John Eliot School, where Kronish is principal, a recent unit on the physically impaired appealed to all four styles. A concert by a band of physically impaired people at a school assembly, which culminated in teachers and students dancing in the aisles, gave innovative learners the emotional reason they need to study a topic. Analytic learners, who used to be called bookworms, absorbed facts galore. Common sense learners, seeking sensory experience, tried on crutches and braces. And dynamic learners designed a better wheelchair.

Unlike many corporations, which have neglected to transfer the lessons of the workshop to the office, school systems such as Needham's have woven personality theory into everyday interaction. Since teachers rather than students take the tests, there is less danger of stereotyping children.

Every teacher in Newburyport is required to take a workshop about Anthony Gregorc's theory, which divides learners into four "mindstyles"; abstract-random, abstract-sequential, concrete-sequential, and concrete-random. (They correspond roughly to Needham's innovative, analytic, common sense, and dynamic learners.) The school system also paid for several teachers to receive advanced training. They act in their spare time as peer coaches, helping their colleagues to implement the theory.

One peer coach is Nancy Duclos, a geometry teacher at Newburyport High School. Giving a lesson on congruent triangles to her class of sophomores and juniors one recent afternoon, Duclos, like an expert fisherman, floated a lure for each type of learner. She reviewed the textbook for sequential learners and enticed randoms with a freewheeling discussion. Then she divided students into groups to draw their own triangles, pleasing concretes as well as abstract-randoms, who enjoy collaborating.

"When I learned this, I didn't want to put a label on kids," Duclos says afterward, still holding her yardstick and chalk-tipped compass. "All I know is that when I'm at the front of the room, it's possible that I have at least one kid of every learning style in my classroom. It's my job to do something that each of those kids would like.

"I could have gotten up there and given it to them from the book. Two days later, I'd have to give it to them again, because they'd forget it. This way, they've discussed it, they've experienced it, and they'll remember it."

After a 1988 federal law banned the use of lie detector tests for job applicants in private industry, Wackenhut Corp. had to find a substitute. The international security firm based in Coral Gables, Florida, chose the Phase 2 Profile Integrity Status Inventory, a questionnaire that claims to measure, among other things, "Basic Dishonest Attitudes," "Ability to Measure Dishonesty," and "How Often a Person Thinks or Plans About Doing Something Dishonest."

Today, Wackenhut officials say that the Phase 2 is more accurate than the polygraph. They boast that only 10 percent of employees who passed the test turn out to be dishonest, although a skeptic might wonder whether other Phase 2-approved workers, might be stealing undetected. The firm uses it in every state except Massachusetts, where honesty testing has been prohibited since 1986. Without the test, Boston-area manager James Healey complains, he has to conduct in-depth background checks, which are both more expensive and less reliable.

Honesty tests are the fastest-growing type of personality test in the United States, and the most controversial. Desperate to arrest employee theft, which costs American business an estimated $40 billion per year, 10,000 companies now administer the tests to 3 million people annually. Test marketers do not guarantee that an applicant with a passing score is honest or that one with a failing score is crooked, but they do claim that failing applicants represent a higher risk to the employer.

Critics of the tests contend that they are meaningless and that even if they are valid in the aggregate, it is unfair to reject an individual because he or she has a 30 percent or 40 percent probability of stealing on the job. Both the APA and the U.S. Office of Technology Assessment are now studying the issue.

"The use of so-called honesty tests to make hiring or promotion decisions is on the same shaky ground as are the polygraphs . . . and is the equivalent of a random procedure," wrote University of Illinois psychology professor Benjamin Kleinmuntz in a review of the Phase 2 in *Buros' Mental Measurements Yearbook*. "They are themselves dishonest devices. They are dishonest toward employers because they reject many potentially productive workers, hence causing greater costs than savings. And they are dishonest toward prospective employees because they constitute an unfair method of screening."

Kleinmuntz and other critics point out that such testing rests on a paradox: It relies on dishonest people to make honest admissions of dishonest acts. Yet marketers say that no matter how strange it seems, many applicants confess to crimes. Of 10,000 applicants in 1988 who took a test developed by Reid Psychological Systems of Chicago, 7 percent admitted stealing money or merchandise from an employer, and 5.6 percent admitted using marijuana, amphetamines, or cocaine at work.

The reason for these admissions, according to test marketers, is that dishonest people rationalize their behavior by convincing themselves that the rest of mankind is more corrupt than they are. If they don't acknowledge a few bad acts, they think, they will look like liars. That is why, besides directly asking about criminal behavior, most tests probe the applicant's view of human morality. Anyone who answers "No" to "Do you think police officers are usually honest?" is off to a bad start.

The flaw in this approach is that workers in certain world-weary professions tend to believe, regardless of their own conduct, that other people are crooks. Reporters usually fail honesty tests—unless they take the Phase 2, which has a built-in cynicism factor, according to its designer, Gregory Lousig-Nont.

Another assumption underlying the tests is that honest people want harsher penalties for crime than dishonest people do. There are exceptions to this rule as well, the best known being a nun who sought a job in a Minneapolis bookstore and was given an honesty test. As a believer in Christian mercy, she favored leniency for thieving employees. She flunked.

Your wife will die of cancer tomorrow unless she takes a new miracle drug. It costs $2,000, but you only have $1,000. Should you steal it from the drugstore?

In a cozy Prudential Center apartment, its window shades half-drawn to keep out the light, 10 managers from *The Boston Globe* ponder this hypothetical question. Some say they would do anything to save their spouses' lives. Others object, asking what would happen if everyone broke the law when it suited their needs.

There is no right answer, organizational consultant Emily Souvaine tells the group. The differing responses reflect personality types. Fs—feelers—make decisions subjectively. Ts—thinkers—make them objectively. In the business world there is pressure to be a T. "This is a way of honoring the F side of decision-making, as well as the T side," Souvaine says.

Like their cohorts at Draper Laboratory, all managers at the Globe have attended these workshops to learn about themselves and their co-workers. Based on the work of Carl Jung, the Myers-Briggs Type Indicator theorizes that there are 16 different personalities, derived from four pairs of contrasting types. ISTJs (or introverted, sensing, thinking judgers), for example, are serious and quiet and succeed by concentration and thoroughness. Among their most popular careers is pollution control, and their least favorite is dental hygiene.

Developed from 1945 to 1962 by a mother-and-daughter team, the MBTI was available only for research until 1975. During the next decade it was mainly used in religious organizations, government, and higher education. In 1980 the University of Maine at Orono began giving the test to all incoming freshmen. As often as possible, it matched roommates who shared two of their four types so that they would support each other while leaving room for understanding differences. The university found that roommates selected with the MBTI had higher grade point averages and lower dropout rates.

The indicator proved equally helpful in explaining a rash of vandalism in one dormitory. By studying the types of residents, university officials found that the dorm contained more than its share of EPs—extroverted perceivers, who need lots of stimulation and physical activity. The university started a health club and aerobics classes in the dorm, and vandalism returned to normal levels.

Now corporations are supplanting universities as leading users of the MBTI. Of the nearly 2 million MBTI answer sheets sold each year in the United States, 30 percent go to private industry. (Until 1985, the Japanese were the world's largest users of the MBTI, and they still rank second.) *The Type Reporter*, a promotional newsletter, has devoted several recent issues to the MBTI's role in the workplace, using headlines such as, "How to Keep Ss from Getting Stuck on Specifics," "How to Keep Ps from Procrastinating," and "How to Keep Js from Jumping to Conclusions."

A study by Jean Kummerow, co-author of *Introduction to Type in Organizational Settings*, found that 62 percent of workers who took the MBTI in one study felt that it assessed their types correctly. Of the 10 people in the *Globe's* workshop, five agreed with their MBTI results, and four said that it had identified three of their four types. One person said that only two types were correct.

For those who disagree with their type, a frequent comment is that the MBTI has no middle ground: You must be either E or I, S or N, and so on. Yet some people lack a strong preference in at least one dimension. This analysis applies to most personality tests. They tend to be more vindicating for people with strongly defined personalities, such as Manny Elkind or Miriam Kronish. Those in the middle of the spectrum—call them well-balanced or, in MBTI jargon, "undifferentiated"—may find their results more perplexing than revealing. "People come to me and say, 'Shall I answer this the way I am at home or at work?'" says Caroline Weaver, a consultant who uses the MBTI for corporate team building.

The MBTI is not recommended for hiring, mainly because it is rather transparent, and takers could skew answers to fit the job description. Computer Sciences Corp., a high-tech company with 21,000 employees, uses the indicator to improve its hiring indirectly: Its instructors take the MBTI before training managers to interview job applicants. At the *San Jose Mercury News*, a group of editors used to interview each job applicant together. After being exposed to the MBTI, they realized that this process felt threatening to introverts, and they considered switching to one-on-one interviews.

The workshops at the *Globe* indicate that 70 percent of its managers are introverted—a surprising finding, since 70 percent of Americans are extroverted. Dolly King, *The Charlotte Observer*'s director of organizational development, says most editors in the Knight-Ridder newspaper chain are ENTJs—"hearty, frank, decisive leaders."

Back at the Prudential Center, Souvaine poses another stumper: You are vacationing in Paris, and this morning you plan to visit the Louvre. On your way, you pass a lively street fair. Do you stick to your schedule or postpone the museum to enjoy the fair?

If you head straight for the "Mona Lisa," you must be a judger, Souvaine says. If you veer off to eat a croissant or watch a juggler, you are a perceiver.

"Are you still a J if you plan to be a P?" one member of the group asks.

"That's a totally J question," Souvaine answers. "How can you plan to be spontaneous?"

To tell you the truth, I'm still a bit confused about my personality. On the Myers-Briggs, I come out as an INTJ—skeptical, critical, independent, stubborn, most likely to become an architect and least likely to become a food-counter worker. The Predictive Index concurs: I am analytical, quick-thinking, tense, and driven, although I'm trying to conform to demands made by an organization or leader and be more patient than I really am. "When we're out selling our program people like you are among our toughest prospects," says Arnold Daniels who developed the PI.

But the Herrmann Brain Dominance Instrument sees me differently. Like "the clear majority of women, I'm creative holistic, interpersonal and feeling—right-brained to the max." I'm suited to be a teacher, social worker, or nurse.

So what's the true me?

Guess I'd better take some more tests.

Index

American Psychological Association (APA), 29
analytic reasoning, 18

Boston Globe, 33–34
brain dominance, left and right, 22, 31–32
Briggs, Katheryn, 4

Camara, Wayne, 29
career development, 24–25
cognitive style
    overview, 4
    brain dominance, left and right, 22, 31–32
    composite types (Myers-Briggs), 20–21
    decision-making style (thinking/feeling), 15, 18–19
    definition, 4, 11
    hiring and promotion based on, 12, 30–31, 34
    homogeneity and cognitive diversity, 12–13
    honesty tests, 33–34
    information generation style (sensing/intuition), 15, 17–18
    Jungian approach, advantages of, 11–12
    learning styles and schools, 32–33
    management and, 13–15, 21–25
    Minnesota Multi-Phasic Inventory (MMPI), 29–30
    organizational issues, 11
    organizational structure and, 22–23
    popularity of, 28–29, 30
    Predictive Index, 29, 31
    priorities style (perceiving/judging), 15, 19–20
    problems with approach, 12, 29–31
    relationship style (extrovert/introvert), 15, 16–17
    self-assessment test, 6–9, 11
    shadow type, 24–25
    universities and, 34
core values and preferences, 14–15
creativity, 24

Daniels, Arnold, 29, 31
decision making, 15, 18–19, 22
discrimination, 12, 30
Draper Laboratory, 28
Drucker, Peter, 13
Duclos, Nancy, 32–33

Elkind, Manny, 31–32
Epstein, Seymour, 29
extroversion. *see* Myers-Briggs Type Indicator (MBTI)

"Give Me an E. Give Me an S." (Golden), 28–35
Golden, Daniel, 28
Gregorc, Anthony, 32

Herrmann, Ned, 31
Herrmann Brain Dominance Instrument, 31–32
hiring and promotion, 12
Hogan, Robert, 29
homogeneity among personnel, 12–13
honesty tests, 33–34

information gathering, 15, 17–18
innovation, 24
introversion. *see* Myers-Briggs Type Indicator (MBTI)
intuition. *see* Myers-Briggs Type Indicator (MBTI)

Jacobson, Ralph, 28
Jones, Ivan, 30
Jung, Carl, 4, 14
Jungian approach to personality type, 11–12

Keen, P. G. W., 22
Kilmann, R. H., 22–23, 24
Kirton, M. J., 24
Kleinmuntz, Benjamin, 33
Knight-Ridder newspaper chain, 30, 34
Kraft, Kenneth, 29
Kroeger, Otto, 28
Kronish, Miriam, 32
Kummerow, Jean, 34

learning styles, and schools, 32–33
Leavitt, H. J., 22
Lewis, Ralph, 13
logical thinking, 18

management, and cognitive style, 13–15, 21–25
"Mapping Managerial Styles" (Margerison and Lewis), 13–25
Margerison, Charles, 13
MBTI. *see* Myers-Briggs Type Indicator
McKenney, J. L., 22
McKinnon, D. W., 24
Minnesota Multi-Phasic Inventory (MMPI), 29–30
Mintzberg, H, 22
Mitroff, I.I., 22–23, 24
Myers, Isabel, 4
Myers-Briggs Type Indicator (MBTI)
    career development and, 24–25
    change, approaches to, 23–24
    Cognitive Style Self-Assessment, 6–9, 11

composite types, 20–21
corporate use examples, 28, 34
creativity and innovation and, 24
extrovert/introvert (relationships), 16–17
hiring decisions and, 34
managerial style and decision making, 22
organizational structure and, 22–23
perceiving/judging (priority-setting), 15, 19–20
relationship management and, 15
sensing/intuition (information generation), 15, 17–18
shadow type, 24–25
thinking/feeling (decision making), 15, 18–19
in universities, 34

"new" organization model, 12

O'Connor, Joseph, 28
organizations, structures, 22–23

personality type. *see* cognitive style; Myers-Briggs Type Indicator (MBTI)
Phase 2 Profile Integrity Status Inventory, 33

Polaroid Corp., 31–32
Predictive Index, 29, 31
preferences and personality. *see* cognitive style
priority-setting, 15, 19–20

relationships, 15, 16–17
Richek, H. G., 23

schools, and learning styles, 32–33
"shadow" personality type, 24–25
Share, Laura, 31
Sloan, Alfred, 13–14
Souvaine, Emily, 34
stereotyping, 12
structures of organizations, 22–23

Tobias Fleishman Shapiro and Co. (TFS), 30–31

universities, and personality testing, 34

values, 14–15, 19

Wackenhut Corp., 33
work styles. *see* cognitive styles

MANAGING FOR THE FUTURE

Organizational Behavior & Processes

MANAGING FOR THE FUTURE
Organizational Behavior & Processes, Third Edition

Deborah Ancona
Sloan School of Management
Massachusetts Institute of Technology

John Van Maanen
Sloan School of Management
Massachusetts Institute of Technology

Thomas A. Kochan
Sloan School of Management
Massachusetts Institute of Technology

D. Eleanor Westney
Sloan School of Management
Massachusetts Institute of Technology

Maureen Scully
Graduate School of Management
Simmons College

Dedicated to those who have inspired us to try to be better students and teachers.
Special thanks to: Professor Jack Barbash • Professor Arthur H. Gladstein • Professor Marius B. Jansen • Professor Joanne Martin • Professor Edgar H. Schein

VP/Editorial Director
Jack W. Calhoun

VP/Editor-in-Chief
Michael P. Roche

Senior Publisher
Melissa S. Acuña

Executive Editor
John Szilagyi

Senior Developmental Editor
Judith O'Neill

Marketing Manager
Jacquelyn Carrillo

Production Editor
Emily Gross

Manufacturing Coordinator
Rhonda Utley

Compositor
Trejo Production

Printer
Von Hoffmann Press, Inc.
Frederick, MD

Internal Designer
Bethany Casey

Cover Designer
Bethany Casey

Photographs
©PhotoDisc

Design Project Manager
Bethany Casey

COPYRIGHT ©2005
by South-Western, a division of Thomson Learning. Thomson Learning™ is a trademark used herein under license.

Printed in the United States of America
1 2 3 4 5 07 06 05 04 03

For more information contact
South-Western College Publishing,
5191 Natorp Boulevard,
Mason, Ohio, 45040
Or you can visit our Internet site at:
http://www.swlearning.com

ALL RIGHTS RESERVED
No part of this work covered by the copyright hereon may be reproduced or used in any form or by any means—graphic, electronic, or mechanical, including photocopying, recording, taping, Web distribution or information storage and retrieval systems—without the written permission of the publisher.

For permission to use material from this text or product, contact us by
Tel: (800) 730-2214
Fax: (800) 730-2215
http://www.thomsonrights.com

Library of Congress Control Number: 2003113908
ISBN 0-324-05575-7

Contents

Team Processes

Overview		4

Core

Class Note	**Team Process Observation Guide**	8
	Membership 8	
	Organizational Context 8	
	Team Processes 8	
	Task and Maintenance Functions 9	
	Task Functions 9	
	Maintenance Functions 9	
	Decision Making 9	
	Communication 11	
	Influence 12	
	Conflict 13	
	Atmosphere 13	
	Emotional Issues 14	
	Taking Action 14	
	References 15	
The Press	**Virtually There?**	16
	Doctors: Not Just Cheaper, Smarter 17	
	Developers: Even Better Than the Real Thing? 18	
	Consultants: New Behaviors for New Technologies 20	
	Bankers: Less Paper Means More Backers 20	
	The Trouble with Teams	21

Index

Overview

This module is designed to help you learn about and practice observing ongoing internal team processes. It is also geared to help you think about how to manage and change existing processes. Internal team processes refer to the ways in which team members interact with one another. The major categories of team processes are (1) task and maintenance functions, (2) decision making, (3) communication, (4) influence, (5) conflict, (6) atmosphere, and (7) emotional issues. All groups and teams exhibit team processes that shift over time in response to changes in membership, task, external influences, or the growth that members exhibit as they work together. In this module you will have the opportunity to analyze your own team processes or those of a decision-making group.

Internal team processes, although only one determinant of team effectiveness (see Figure 5.1, Model of Team Effectiveness—a model covered more fully in Module 3, Making Teams Work), constitute the aspect of teams over which members have the most control and that most influences team member satisfaction. The amount of learning that takes place in teams is also influenced by team processes. Once you learn more about what team processes are and how to observe them, you should be better able to manage them to achieve better team effectiveness.

It is predicted that the understanding and management of team processes will be important skills in the organization of the future. As the work of teams becomes more complex, cross-functional, virtual, and varied, more demands are placed on the members of those teams. As organizations become more diverse and global, team membership becomes more heterogeneous, and the possibilities for conflict and poor communication increase. All of these issues occur in a competitive setting in which the demands for high performance are ever increasing. Managers must be able to create smooth team processes in the face of these challenges if they are to succeed.

This module consists of three readings (two of which are designated as elective) and an exercise. The core reading, the Class Note: Team Process Observation Guide, provides some detail about each of the major categories of internal team processes, why each category is important, and hints about how to carefully observe the category in an ongoing team. This Class Note points out that, although most of us have participated in many different teams, we seldom take the time to systematically observe and analyze them. Observation and analysis are, however, precursors to understanding and managing teams. As you read through the Class Note you should try to think about how you can use the concepts to better understand your own team or a team that you might observe. What aspects of the team will you monitor? Why? How will you go about monitoring how the team members are interacting with one another? What conclusions will you be able to draw from your observations?

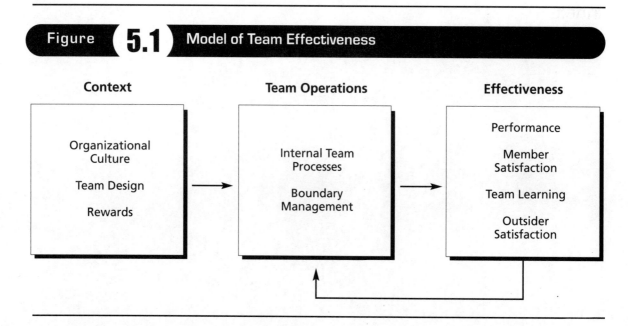

Figure 5.1 Model of Team Effectiveness

The first elective reading, "Virtually There," comes from the popular business periodical, *Fast-Company*. This article examines where the future may take us as new technologies enable virtual and transnational teams to communicate in a variety of new ways. It challenges the traditional idea that teams need to meet together face-to-face in order to be more productive and suggests new modes in which teams may work together.

The second elective reading, excerpts from *Fortune* magazine's article, "The Trouble with Teams," takes us beyond the hype to investigate the myth that everybody loves teams. Instead, it focuses on the difficulties that people and companies encounter as they try to implement team designs. Teams require a lot of work, a different type of reward system, and cannot be used as a smokescreen to downsize the organization. The article emphasizes the need to create the right types of teams and the context that will support them.

Conceptual understanding of internal team processes is essential, but this module also emphasizes the application of those concepts. Therefore, you will be asked to participate in an exercise in which you have to observe and analyze team processes and think about how to improve them. You might be asked to observe a film of a decision-making group or to work with other team members to create a new product. (Your instructor will provide additional details regarding the exercise at a later date.) In either case, you will be called upon to use the readings to interpret what goes on in a team meeting and to suggest how the dynamics among members might be reshaped. Team processes are complex and exciting; they should be more comprehensible after you complete this module.

Additional Activities

You can expand your learning about internal team processes in several ways. One is to start to keep a journal documenting what is occurring on a team of which you are a part. This team might be a student team, an athletic team, or even your family. As you write your entries, try to cover all the categories of team processes that are discussed in the readings. What insights occur as you systematically observe what is going on? How are communication, influence, decision making, and conflict handled? Who takes care of task and maintenance activities? What does your analysis suggest about what you wish to do on this team?

Another way to learn more about team processes is to get permission to observe a team in a local company or in your school. You might want to create an observation form that helps you to organize the data you collect while you are observing. When you enter the team, your presence may seem to interfere with its regular work, but over time your presence will become quite natural. After you finish your observations you might want to offer to share your reactions with the team members, or you may be more comfortable simply thanking them for their participation.

Finally, you can think back over the team experiences you have had in the past. Try to figure out which aspects of team processes were most satisfactory to you and which ones were most distressing. How did these processes come about? What could you have done to make your bad experiences better? What can you do in the future to create the types of processes that work best for you?

For those who wish to learn more about internal team processes the following references are suggested.

References

Donnellon, A. 1996. *Team Talk: The Power of Language in Team Dynamics.* Boston: Harvard Business School Press.

Eisenhardt, K. M., J. L. Kahwajy, and J. L. Bourgeois. 1997. How Management Teams Can Have a Good Fight. *Harvard Business Review* 75 (4), 77–85.

Gabarro, J. J., and A. Harlan. 1983. "Process Observation." In L. Schlesinger, R. Eccles, and J. J. Gabarro (Eds.). *Managing Behavior in Organizations* (pp. 57–66). New York: McGraw Hill.

Guzzo, R. A., and M. W. Dickson. 1996. Teams in Organizations: Recent Research on Performance and Effectiveness. *Annual Review of Psychology* 47, 307–338.

Hackman, J. R. (Ed.). 1990. *Groups That Work and Those That Don't.* San Francisco: Jossey-Bass.

Janis, I. 1972. *Victims of Groupthink.* Boston: Houghton-Mifflin.

Lipman-Blumen, J., and H. J. Leavitt. 1999. *Hot Groups*. New York: Oxford University Press.

Marks, M. A., S. J. Zaccaro, and J. E. Mathieu. 2000. Performance Implications of Leader Briefings and Team Interaction Training for Team Adaptation to Novel Environments. *Journal of Applied Psychology* 85, 971–986.

Nadler, D. A., and J. L. Spencer, Delta Consulting Group. 1998. *Executive Teams*. San Francisco: Jossey-Bass.

Patton, R., K. Giffin, and E. Patton. 1989. *Decision-Making Team Interaction*. New York: Harper & Row.

Schein, E. 1988. *Process Consultation: Its Role in Organization Development*, 2nd ed. Reading, MA: Addison-Wesley.

Thompson, L. 2000. *Making the Team: A Guide for Managers*. Upper Saddle River: Prentice Hall.

Team Processes

CORE

Module 5

Team Process Observation Guide

Although most of us have been in various kinds of teams throughout our lives, we seldom take time to systematically observe and analyze how they function.[1] Yet observation and analysis are the first steps in understanding teams, shaping their dynamics, and, ultimately, improving their performance. Every team, be it a family, sports team, task force, or platoon, can be characterized as a set of individuals who depend on each other to reach certain goals. Team process observation focuses on these individuals and the ways in which they interact with one another.

Membership

Before observing a team it is useful to understand something about the individuals who comprise it. Differences in personality, style, race, and gender often play a role in team dynamics. Within organizations, differences in hierarchical level, functional background, and commitment to team goals also contribute to the level of cohesion or conflict within a team. In addition, length of association among members affects team functions. Teams in which members are familiar or strongly tied to each other are better at sharing the unique information that each member has, while groups of strangers outperform familiar teams when members possess redundant knowledge (Gruenfeld, Mannix, Williams, & Neale, 1996).

Another aspect of membership is knowing who knows what. A key aspect of making a team effective is to have what is called a "transactive memory system" (Mohammed & Dumville, 2001). In a transactive memory system, each member works to keep current on what other members know, channels incoming information to the appropriate person, and seeks out the best form of expertise when a problem arises. All of these efforts help the team to work efficiently.

Key questions concerning membership include the following:

- Do team members have the required expertise and authority to carry out the task? Are all individuals who have a stake in the team's decisions included in the team?
- What are the personalities and styles of team members? How does this combination affect the team?
- What is the racial and gender mix within the team? How does this combination affect the team?
- How committed are individual members to the team? In what ways are conflicts over different levels of commitment resolved?
- Which hierarchical levels and functional teams are represented? How do they affect the team?
- Is the team made up of strangers or members who know each other well? With what effect?
- How well can members identify and use the particular expertise of other members?

Organizational Context

The larger organization in which a team operates also contributes to its success or failure. Groups need appropriate institutional direction, information, and resources (Hackman, 1990). Problems occur when the organizational mission is unclear, tasks are poorly defined, teams are not allowed sufficient autonomy, or rewards are granted to individuals rather than to teams.

Key questions regarding a team's organizational context include the following:

- Have the goals and tasks of the team been clearly identified?
- Are team members rewarded for individual rather than team performance?
- Has management granted the team enough autonomy to accomplish its task?
- Does the team have access to the information and resources needed to perform its task?

Team Processes

Process observation focuses on the process, not the content, of team discussion; that is, it is less concerned with what the team is doing or discussing than in how the team is going about its task. For example, it does not focus on the specific details of the new car that a product development team is designing, but on who is talking to whom, who is influencing decisions, how the team organizes itself, how conflict is handled, and what happens in and between meetings. The seven major categories of team process are (1) task and maintenance functions, (2) decision making, (3) communication, (4) influence, (5) conflict, (6) atmosphere, and (7) emotional issues.

---

1 This reading builds heavily on the chapter "Process Observation," pp. 57–68 in Gabarro and Harlan (1983), and on Schein, (1988).

Task and Maintenance Functions

In order for teams to operate effectively, they must engage in task and maintenance functions. Task functions help the team members to organize themselves to get the work done. They include activities such as setting team agendas, keeping the team on target, prioritizing tasks, structuring the way the team makes decisions, and proposing alternative ways to solve problems. Maintenance functions hold the team together so that members can continue to get along with one another and even have some fun. Figure 5.2 outlines the task and maintenance functions identified by Benne and Sheats (reported in Schein, 1988). Questions associated with task and maintenance functions follow.

Task Functions

- Do team members make suggestions as to the best way to proceed? How frequently?
- Do members give or ask for information, opinions, feelings, and feedback, or indicate that they are searching for alternatives?
- How is the team kept on target?
- Are all ideas presented given adequate discussion before evaluation begins?
- Does the team summarize what has been covered? Does the team review who is responsible for doing what, when team member inputs are due, or when the team will meet again? How?

Maintenance Functions

- Are all team members encouraged to enter into the discussion?
- Are attempts made by any team members to help others clarify their ideas?
- Are team members careful to reject ideas, and not people? In what way?
- Are conflicts among members ignored or addressed in some way?
- Are all team members treated respectfully?
- If a member is insulted or put down, do other members step in to help?

Decision Making

Groups make decisions all the time, both consciously and subconsciously. Those decisions may concern the task at hand, team procedures, norms or standards of behavior, or how much work the team will take on. Many key decisions that subsequently shape the team are made early—sometimes at the first meeting—and are notoriously difficult to reverse. Therefore, understanding how decisions are made is key to team functioning.

The four key steps in decision making are (1) identifying the problem or opportunity, (2) analyzing the problem, (3) proposing and evaluating solutions, and (4) implementing the decision. Teams often need to cycle through these steps several times as new information and changing circumstances shift decision premises. Decision making seldom evolves smoothly; poor organization, interpersonal conflicts, bias, and even subconscious processes can work to distract the process. Too often the multiple steps of decision making are ignored as team members rush toward a quick decision and implementation. This *solution mindedness* relieves the anxiety of not having a solution to a problem, but often results in decisions needing to be revisited later. Team members should try to avoid the impulse to rush to a solution and take the time to go through the four steps.

Within teams, members often feel pressure to conform to the majority opinion. Subtle and not so subtle pressures from the majority often push those with differing opinions to remain silent. The chances of a minority being able to shift the majority rise dramatically when more than one person presents the minority opinion. Even when a minority opinion is not able to shift the decision, however, it serves a useful function. It forces the team to think about alternative views, to justify the majority opinion, or to find creative ways to alter the decision to meet a broader set of criteria. Thus it is important to set a norm of communicating doubts and divergent viewpoints. Members should be encouraged to play the devil's advocate role and force the team to look at the possible negative consequences of their chosen option (Nemeth, 1986).

Consensus decision making allows all team members to feel that they are a part of the decision-making process and increases their commitment to a chosen course of action. However, consensus decision making can be time-consuming. Many corporate decision teams, in particular, are finding that consensus decision making takes too long. In a study of top management teams in the fast-paced mini-computer market, Eisenhardt (1990) found that although teams strive for consensus, they also have fall-back plans (e.g., they let the leader decide or they vote) if consensus is not easily forthcoming.

In general it is helpful for the team to be clear about how they will make decisions. Will they use consensus, consult to the leader and let her make the decision, let the leader make the decision, or try consensus and if that doesn't work let the leader decide? Different types of decisions may require different modes of decision making (Vroom & Yetton, 1973).

Figure 5.2 Functions Required for Effective Group Functions

	Function	Description	Example
Functions that build task accomplishment	Initiating	Stating the goal or problem, making proposals about how to work on it, setting time limits.	"Let's set up an agenda for discussing each of the problems we have to consider."
	Seeking Information and Opinions	Asking group members for specific factual information related to the task or problem or for their opinions about it.	"What do you think would be the best approach to this, Jack?"
	Providing Information and Opinions	Sharing information or opinions related to the task or problem.	"I worked on a similar problem last year and found . . ."
	Clarifying	Helping one another understand ideas and suggestions that come up in the group.	"What you mean, Sue, is that we could . . . ?"
	Elaborating	Building on one another's ideas and suggestions.	"Building on Dan's idea, I think we could . . ."
	Summarizing	Reviewing the points covered by the group and the different ideas states so that decisions can be based on full information.	Appointing a recorder to take notes on a blackboard.
	Consensus Testing	Periodic testing about whether the group is nearing a decision or needs to continue discussion.	"Is the group ready to decide about this?"
Functions that build and maintain a group	Harmonizing	Mediating conflict between other members, reconciling disagreements, relieving tensions.	"Don, I don't think you and Sue really see the question that differently."
	Compromising	Admitting error at times of group conflict.	"Well, I'd be willing to change if you provided some help on . . ."
	Gatekeeping	Making sure all members have a chance to express their ideas and feelings and preventing members from being interrupted.	"Sue, we haven't heard from you on this issue."
	Encouraging	Helping a group member make his or her point. Establishing a climate of acceptance in the group.	"I think what you started to say is important, Jack. Please continue."

Questions concerning decision making include the following:

- Does the team follow the four steps of decision making? With what consequences?
- Does the team move too quickly toward a solution?
- Does the team encourage minority opinion?
- Which form of decision making does the team use: consensus, consultative, or leader decides? Does this form "fit" the decision?
- Can the team change its form of decision making if circumstances warrant a change?

Communication

Communication patterns offer clues as to who is influencing the team, which subgroups and coalitions exist, how well the team is progressing, and how members are feeling. Those who participate most frequently are often, but not always, the most influential individuals. Influence often falls to aggressive and highly articulate team members who are able to sway the team discussion in their favor. In addition, ideas that are repeated over and over are usually adopted more readily than those that are mentioned only once. Team members need to learn to listen for content as well as excess enthusiasm.

Where coalitions exist, members will "trigger" each other to support a particular alternative (e.g., "John's idea to have customers pay for this service is a great one!") or oppose another (e.g., "I think we're better off with Debbie's suggestion of trying to cut costs."). Quiet members may be content just to listen, or may be angry or disconnected from the team. A team facilitator should occasionally query quiet members to see whether they want to make a contribution.

Team communication patterns can easily be measured by use of a sociogram (see Figure 5.3 below). In a sociogram each team member is represented by his or her initials. Directional arrows run between the sets of initials, indicating a verbal exchange between individuals, and from the initials to the center of the diagram, indicating a communication to the team as a whole. Each time a member of the team talks to another individual or to the team as a whole, the observer puts a mark on the appropriate arrow. Each time a team member interrupts another, the observer places an "i" above his or her initials; each time a member encourages another, the observer places an "e." For example, the sociogram shows that AD has the highest number of communications with other team members (two to WE, six to MVJ, five to SM, and five to KT). MVJ has the fewest communications (two to

Figure 5.3 Sociogram of Group Communication

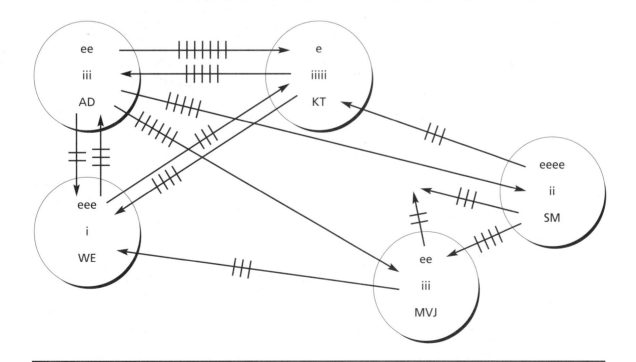

the whole team and three to WE). KT interrupted others five times, and WE interrupted only once. SM was the most encouraging.

The sociogram presents a map of communication patterns that the team may want to analyze to better understand who is playing what role in the decision-making process. If some members are dominating, the team may ask each member to state his/her position. If the domination continues then several members may have to be asked to remain silent for part of the meeting (Hill, 2001).

Sociograms can help provide clues to the following questions:

- Who are the most frequent participants? Why? What is the effect of their participation?
- Who are the least frequent participators? Why? What is the effect of their lack of participation?
- Are there shifts in participation? What causes these?
- Who talks to whom? Who responds to whom? Who triggers whom?
- How are "silent" and "noisy" members handled?
- Are team members with the requisite information contributing?

Influence

Although the formal leader often has the most power and influence in the team, it is common for influence to shift throughout a team's history. Influence, like communication, is often related to a member's status within the organizational hierarchy, level of experience, and personality. It is also a function of an individual's ability to argue articulately and persuasively for his or her position. The most effective arguments are those that are vivid, offer new information, and reflect team rather than individual goals.

Team members can also influence one another through the use of "influence tactics" (see Figure 5.4 for a listing of these tactics). Team leaders typically exert the most influence by using a combination of these tactics. The choice of tactics, for leaders and members alike, depends on the situation at hand and the individual's preferences. If certain team members are unable to influence team outcomes they may want to practice different influence tactics.

Early on, power struggles may occur in any team. As individuals vie with one another for

---

Figure 5.4 Influence Tactics

Rational Persuasion: The agent uses logical arguments and factual evidence to persuade the target that a proposal or request is viable and likely to result in the attainments of task objectives.

Inspirational Appeals: The agent makes a request or proposal that arouses target enthusiasm by appealing to target values, ideals, and aspirations, or by increasing target self-confidence.

Consultation: The agent seeks target participation in planning a strategy, activity, or change for which target support and assistance are desired, or is willing to modify a proposal to deal with target concerns and suggestions.

Ingratiation: The agent uses praise, flattery, friendly behavior, or helpful behavior to get the target in a good mood or to think favorably of him or her before asking for something.

Personal Appeals: The agent appeals to target feelings of loyalty and friendship toward himself or herself when asking for something.

Exchange: The agent offers an exchange of favors, indicates willingness to reciprocate at a later time, or promises a share of the benefits if the target helps to accomplish a task.

Coalition Tactics: The agent seeks the aid of others to persuade the target to do something, or uses the support of others as a reason for the target to agree also.

Legitimating Tactics: The agent seeks to establish the legitimacy of a request by claiming the authority or right to make it, by verifying that it is consistent with organizational policies, rules, practices, or traditions.

Pressure: The agent uses demands, threats, frequent checking, or persistent reminders to influence the target to do what he or she wants.

Source: This material was taken from Yukl. 1994. *Leadership in Organizations*, 3rd ed. Upper Saddle River, NJ: Prentice Hall, p. 225.

leadership, they may impede team progress if they push for their suggestions and ideas regardless of appropriateness. Early power struggles are normal, but if they persist and become a normal part of team operations, team effectiveness can suffer.

Helpful questions in observing influence patterns include the following:

- Who has the most impact on the team's actions and decisions?
- Whose ideas are ignored? What is the result?
- What tactics do members use to influence one another?
- Is there rivalry in the team? What effect does it have?
- How does the formal leader exert his/her influence?

Conflict

Opinions about conflict in teams range from "it encourages innovation and creativity" to "it hampers a team's ability to implement decisions." Recent research on conflict (see Jehn, 1995; Pelled, 1994) suggests that conflict can be advantageous or problematic, depending on what type of conflict it is. The "good" kind of conflict is called *substantive conflict*, which consists of differences of opinion about the team task and how it should be carried out. The "bad" kind of conflict is called *affective conflict*, which consists of interpersonal clashes due to personality or perceived differences in style, background, or values.

Substantive conflict may help a team by pushing members to exchange more task-related information, explore alternative positions, and examine issues in more depth. This type of conflict may also energize team members to get more involved in team activities. Affective conflict is problematic in that relations among members become characterized by frustration and hostility. These emotions disrupt work, lower team performance, and cause members to withdraw from team activity.

A frequent problem in cohesive teams is a phenomenon called *groupthink* (Janis, 1972). Here, team members avoid all types of conflict and shy away from deviating from what appears to be the team consensus. Despite doubts, fears, and personal disagreement, team members remain silent, feeling compelled to avoid creating dissension. Under these conditions, team members need to find ways to create the opportunity for substantive conflict.

The key for teams is to find ways to encourage substantive conflict while taking time out to improve relations among members when affective conflict is apparent. Teams can engage in proactive strategies aimed at avoiding affective conflict before it starts, as well as reactive strategies that deal with conflict as it arises in the team. Proactive strategies include team-building activities, stressing team goals over individual interests, and discussion of similarities as well as differences among members. Reactive strategies include pointing out when team members violate key norms of how to treat others, and suspending task activities to focus on how team members are working together.

Key questions regarding team conflict include the following:

- How often do members disagree about the work to be done? Is this conflict useful?
- To what extent do people take the arguments in the team personally? How can this conflict be managed?
- How often do members get angry with one another while working?
- Do team members feel free to disagree?

Atmosphere

Team members bring with them many assumptions about how teams should function. These expectations may not be shared by all team members. One member may feel that team meetings are "strictly business," whereas another may want to include many social activities; one member may prefer that the team have a single leader, whereas another may want to share leadership; or one member may have high standards for the team, whereas another is satisfied if the team just finishes the job. The way in which these expectations and assumptions are expressed and resolved often determines what the climate or atmosphere in the team will be. If members have been able to air their differences and find common ground, the team will operate differently than if they have been unable to do so.

The key to creating a trusting, supportive, team is "psychological safety"—a shared belief that the team is safe for interpersonal risk taking (Edmonson, 1999). This psychological safety enables the team to seek feedback, share information, experiment with new ways of operating, and talk about mistakes. These behaviors help the team by allowing it to shift direction if circumstances change and to discover unanticipated consequences of their actions.

Thus, teams can evolve into trusting, supportive units or tense, conflict-ridden environments. Figure 5.5 lists characteristics of both.

Questions that help to characterize the atmosphere in a team include the following:

- Are people friendly and open or formal with one another?

> **Figure 5.5   Supportive and Defensive Environments**
>
> **Characteristics of a supportive environment**
>
> **Provisionalism:** Members encourage flexibility, experimentation, and creativity.
>
> **Empathy:** Members attempt to listen and to understand each other's views and values.
>
> **Equality:** Members respect the positions of others and no one is made to feel inferior.
>
> **Spontaneity:** Members express ideas freely and honestly without hidden motives.
>
> **Problem Orientation:** Members openly discuss mutual problems without rushing to give solutions or insist on agreement.
>
> **Clear Description:** Communications are clear and describe situations fairly. Members share perceptions without necessarily implying a need for change.
>
> **Characteristics for a defensive environment**
>
> **Evaluation:** Members' manner of speech, tone of voice, or verbal content is perceived as critical or judgmental of others in the team.
>
> **Control:** Communication is perceived as an attempt to manipulate or dominate the recipient.
>
> **Strategems:** Members are seen as operating from hidden motives, playing games, feigning emotion, withholding information, or having private access to sources of data.
>
> **Superiority:** Members convey an attitude of condescension toward others.
>
> **Dogmatism:** Members insist that their own points are best and try to foist them on the team.
>
> Source: Patton, Giffin, and Patton. 1989. *Decision-Making Team Interaction*. New York: Harper & Row.

- Are people involved and interested? Is there an atmosphere of work? Play? Competition?
- Are people in constant conflict or disagreement?
- Is any attempt made to avoid unpleasantness by ignoring tough issues?
- Do people feel safe enough to take interpersonal risks?

Emotional Issues

In certain cases, individual members may become disruptive as they deal with some of the basic problems and emotional issues associated with teams. Groups tend to ignore such behavior, to the detriment of the unit and the member who is having difficulty.

The main issues that individuals may face in teams concern the following (Schein, 1982; 1988):

Identity: Who am I in this team? Where do I fit in? What role should I play?

Goals and Needs: What do I want from this team? What do I have to offer? Can the team's goals be made consistent with mine?

Power and Control: Who will control what we do? How much power and influence do I have?

Intimacy: How close will we get to each other? How much trust exists among us?

Group members may react to these issues in different ways and at different times. The disruptive behaviors they may exhibit in response to these problems include the following:

Fighting and Controlling: Asserting personal dominance; attempting to get their own way regardless of others

Withdrawing: Trying to reduce discomfort by psychologically leaving the team

Dependency and Counterdependency: Waiting passively for a leader to emerge who will solve the problem or, contrarily, opposing or resisting anyone in the team who represents authority

Taking Action

These seven categories of team process, combined with membership and context, provide the building blocks for analyzing team dynamics, and also the cues for managing and changing that process. If a team is not producing as required, is mired in conflict, or is not meeting member needs, then these categories suggest a range of interventions. The key is to do a careful analysis of the problem so that the appropriate intervention is found.

The seven categories can actually be mapped onto the three lenses that are introduced in earlier modules. The strategic design lens focuses on how the team task should be structured. Key categories here would be task functions, effective communications, and decision making. Of course, some of these categories can be seen through other lenses as well. For example, even though the team members can try to structure their decision making to be as effective as possible, political and cultural forces may be at work to deter the team from following that process. Key categories for the political lens are participation, influence, and conflict. For the cultural lens atmosphere, emotional issues, and maintenance functions play a big role in determining the culture that emerges. Each lens suggests different ways of examining the team process and different interventions to help the team to be more effective.

A team might require a structural intervention, such as assigning task functions, appointing a devil's advocate, imposing an agenda and allocating time for each phase of decision making, or setting norms with negative consequences for noncompliance. Team issues can also be addressed through shifting the power and influence in the team. Team members and leaders can empower other members, form new coalitions and break up existing ones, negotiate new norms, and work to resolve affective conflicts. Simply finding a new way to bring silent members into team discussion can alter existing patterns of dominance.

Finally, team issues can be addressed by interventions aimed at shifting a team's underlying culture. Members can point out aspects of the team that create a defensive environment and try to model the empathy, spontaneity, and equality of a supportive environment. Members can work hard to produce an atmosphere of psychological safety. Members can also observe other teams and note how their values and assumptions differ, and how they might want to change. Often all three types of interventions, structural, political, and cultural, are needed to create significant changes within a team.

References

Edmonson, A. C. 1999. Psychological Safety and Learning Behavior in Work Teams. *Administrative Science Quarterly* 44, 350–383.

Eisenhardt, K. M. 1990. Speed and Strategic Choice: How Managers Accelerate Decision Making. *California Management Review* 32(3), 1–16.

Gabarro, J. J., and A. Harlan. 1983. Process Observation. In L. Schlesinger, R. Eccles, and J. J. Gabarro (Eds.), *Managing Behavior in Organizations* (pp. 57–66). New York: McGraw Hill.

Gruenfeld, D. H., E. A. Mannix, K. Y. Williams, and M. A. Neale. 1996. Group Composition and Decision Making: How Member Familiarity and Information Distribution Affect Process and Performance. *Organizational Behavior and Human Decision Processes* 67, 1–15.

Hill, L. 2001. A Note on Team Process. Harvard Business School, N9-402-032.

Janis, I. 1972. *Victims of Groupthink*. Boston: Houghton-Mifflin.

Jehn, K. A. 1995. A Multimethod Examination of the Benefits and Detriments of Intragroup Conflict. *Administrative Science Quarterly* 40, 256–282.

Kozlowski, W. J., and B. S. Bell. 2001. Work Groups and Teams in Organizations. *Comprehensive Handbook of Psychology*, Vol. 12. New York: Wiley.

Mohammed, S., and B. C. Dumville. 2001. Team Mental Models in a Team Knowledge Framework: Expanding Theory and Measurement Across Disciplinary Boundaries. *Journal of Organizational Behavior* 22, 89–106.

Nemeth, C. J. 1986. "Differential Contributions of Minority and Majority Influence." *Psychology Review* 93, 23–32.

Patton, R., K. Giffin, and E. Patton. 1989. *Decision-Making Team Interaction.* New York: Harper & Row.

Pelled, L. H. 1994. Team Diversity and Conflict: A Multivariate Analysis. *Academy of Management Best Paper Proceedings.* Madison, WI: Omni Press.

Schein, E. 1982. What to Observe in a Team. In *NTL Reading Book for Human Relations Training* (pp. 72–74), Bethel, ME: NTL Institute.

Schein, E. 1988. *Process Consultation: Its Role in Organization Development,* 2nd ed. Reading, MA: Addison-Wesley.

Vroom, V., and P. Yetton, 1973. *Leadership and Decision Making.* Pittsburgh, PA: University Press.

Yukl, G. 1994. *Leadership in Organizations,* 3rd ed. Englewood Cliffs, NJ: Prentice Hall.

Virtually There?

Ideas need to move faster than ever. Global teams have to cooperate more closely than ever. Nonstop travel seems less appealing than ever. The solution: an ever-growing collection of tools for electronic collaboration. Can it be that when it comes to doing real work across long distances, we are . . . virtually there?

by Alison Overholt

Dr. Laura Esserman leans forward and speaks with conviction, making broad gestures with her hands. "Over the past couple of decades, I've watched industries be transformed by the use of information systems and incredible visual displays," she says. "What we could do is to completely change the way we work—just by changing the way we collect and share information."

Sounds familiar, right? But Esserman isn't championing yet another overzealous Silicon Valley startup—she's envisioning how cancer patients will interact with their doctors. If Esserman, a Stanford-trained surgeon and MBA, has her way, patients won't sit passively on an exam table, listening to impenetrable diagnoses and memorizing treatment instructions. Instead, they'll have access to a multimedia treasure chest of real-time diagnosis, treatment, and success-rate data from thousands of cases like their own. Better still, they won't meet with just one doctor. There will be other doctors on the case—some from the other side of the hospital and some, perhaps, from the other side of the world.

Esserman and her colleagues at the University of California San Francisco's Carol Franc Buck Breast Care Center are pioneers in the new world of virtual teams and virtual tools, a world in which there will be real change in the way highly trained people whose work depends on intense collaboration get things done. After years of grand promises about the power of high-quality videoconferencing, high-speed Internet connections, and well-designed collaboration software, it may finally be time for virtual work to become a business reality.

Part of the good news is, of course, rooted in bad news: In a period of war and recession, fewer people relish a life of nonstop travel, and fewer companies want to pay for it. But there's more to it than that: The tools are better than they used to be. "The technology has really evolved," says Leon Navickas, chairman and CEO of Centra Software, based in suburban Boston, whose Web-enabled collaboration and e-learning platform is used by more than 1.7 million people. "We're capable of a high degree of interactivity, of developing a very rich media environment through an ordinary computer, even with those who are connected to the Internet at low speeds. And we're able to get through proxy servers and firewalls without compromising the security of the Internet or a corporate intranet."

Meanwhile, companies are beginning to understand the uses (and limitations) of the technology. Accenture is a classic power user. The giant consulting firm, long famous for its fanatical commitment to training and development, uses Centra software, along with all kinds of other virtual tools, as part of its strategy to help people collaborate more and travel less. The company's online-learning portal, myLearning.com, has become a major piece of its knowledge infrastructure. (The

Source: Alison Overholt, "Virtually There," *FastCompany* (March 2002). Copyright 2002 by Bus Innovator Group Resources/Inc. Reproduced with permission of Bus Innovator Group Resources/Inc. in the format Textbook via Copyright Clearance Center.

firm expects that up to 70% of all of its courses will be offered via e-learning rather than in person.) But the goal, says Reinhard Zeigler, global lead partner for Accenture's eLearning and Knowledge Management group, is "blended learning—a careful mix of virtual and physical learning experiences. We'll never go completely virtual."

What follows, then, is a real-world guide to the promise and perils of electronic collaboration. To answer the most basic questions about virtual work, *FastCompany* spoke to a broad group of technology suppliers and leading-edge users, from doctors and developers to consultants and engineers. Their conclusion: When it comes to delivering on the real promise of electronic work, we are virtually there.

Doctors: Not Just Cheaper, Smarter

Be honest. Most companies look to virtual technologies to work cheaper—to save money on airfare and hotels. But that cost-cutting mindset underestimates the real potential of the tools available. Electronic collaboration can help people work smarter; it can bring more brains to bear more quickly on more-important problems.

That's why Laura Esserman is so passionate about fully collaborative health care. Her goal at the Buck Breast Care Center is to use virtual tools to bring more useful information (and more doctors) into the exam room. Why? Because two heads really are better than one. She explains that when patients see their doctors after a breast-cancer diagnosis, for example, they are handed a recommended course of treatment that involves serious choices and trade-offs. Of course, most patients don't know enough about the merits of, say, a lumpectomy versus a mastectomy to make an informed choice, so they trust their doctors to tell them what to do.

But a single doctor isn't always equipped to make the best decision, especially since different procedures can have very different long-term physical and emotional impacts—but may not be all that different in their short-term medical

A (Virtually) Perfect Close

Talk to almost any sales manager in almost any company, and you'll hear the same refrain: To close a big deal, you've got to meet your customer face-to-face. Michael Nelson, cofounder and CEO of emWare Inc., sings a different tune. He manages to close business without the hassles of long-distance travel. In part, that's because Nelson's company, which provides software and services that add remote-management capabilities to electronic devices, is ideally suited to doing business over the Web. But in large part, it's because emWare has been clever about making the virtual-sales process attractive to its customers.

Before the economic downturn, Nelson's company maintained a large sales force that was always on the road. Now, however, with his team scaled down to an eight-member sales-and-business-development team, virtual sales calls have become a necessity. And they've turned out to be enormously successful.

Previously, for example, a favorite sales technique was to bring a potential corporate customer to Salt Lake City, where emWare is based, for a technology demo. The signature gambit: Let the customer drop a Coke from a soda machine using the Web-based controls on a computer across the room. Today, using emWare's technology, the same demo can be performed from anywhere. EmWare's remote-device-management technology allows customers to take control of the soda machine and drop the Coke from Boston or Boise. A Webcam and a telephone audio hookup allow the customer to see and hear when it happens.

We tried the demo ourselves, and the next day, a can of Coke appeared at Fast Company's San Francisco offices. "It sounds hokey, I know," says Nelson. "But you'd be shocked to know how often that soda on the desk seals the deal." And there you have it—a virtually perfect close.

outcomes. "Very often," Esserman says, "doctors recommend a particular treatment because they're more familiar with it. But we should be advocates for our patients, rather than our specialties."

Although her full-blown program is a long way off, Esserman has run a pilot project with 24 patients. She worked with both Oracle, the Silicon Valley database giant, and MAYA Viz, a Pittsburgh company that develops "decision community" software, to allow doctors across the country to collaborate virtually. Through Esserman's approach, when a patient arrives at the doctor's office to receive treatment instructions, instead of listening to a physician's monologue, she's handed a printout. On the top left side of the page is the diagnosis, followed by patient-specific data: the size and spread of the tumor, when it was discovered, and the name of the treating doctor. Below that is statistical information generated from clinical-research databases, such as the number of similar cases treated each year and details about survival rates.

A set of arrows point to treatment options. Next, the patient reads the risks and benefits associated with each treatment. She can follow along as the doctor explains the chances that the cancer will recur after each option and the likelihood that a particular treatment will require follow-up procedures, as well as a comparison of survival rates for each one.

At this point, the patient has an opportunity to voice concerns about treatment options, and the physician can explain her experiences with each one. "When you share this kind of information, patients and doctors can make decisions together according to the patient's values," Esserman says. This is where the network tools come into play. Drawing from stored databases of both clinical trials and patient-treatment histories local to the hospital, the physician can compare courses of action and results far beyond her own personal experience. "A medical opinion is really just one physician's synthesis of the information," notes Esserman. "So you need a way to calibrate yourself—a way to continually ask, Are there variations among the group of doctors that I work with? Am I subjecting people to procedures that turn out not to be useful?"

With a real-time, shared-data network, these questions can be answered at the touch of a button instead of after hours, weeks, or months of research. But that's just the beginning. A real-time network also presents the possibility of seeking help from other specialists on puzzling cases, even if those specialists are on the other side of the world.

Ultimately, says Esserman, the questions that might be answered by this new way of practicing medicine are fundamental to the field. "Who's doing something different, and how do we learn? With tools like these, we have the opportunity to bring learning back in real time to the practice of medicine," she explains. And patients have the opportunity to get a second—and even a third and a fourth—opinion while their primary doctor stands by.

Developers: Even Better Than the Real Thing?

Most people who consider using virtual-collaboration tools assume that, even at their best, they are a second-best solution. If companies had unlimited travel budgets and if teams had endless amounts of time, then face-to-face meetings would be the best way to work, right? Not so fast. A team of product developers at Texas Instruments has discovered that virtual meetings work better than their face-to-face alternative.

A case in point: TI's efforts to develop the next generation of wireless communications devices. The company's Dallas-based mobility and collaboration team recently delivered a crucial strategy presentation to employees and business partners in Europe, Japan, and the United States. The format was pretty standard: 45 minutes of PowerPoint slides followed by an extended Q&A. Not so long ago, TI would have flown in participants from all over the globe. This time, managers conducted the meeting over WebEx, the Internet-based virtual-meeting platform. Participants followed the slides using their laptops and instant-messaged their questions and comments throughout the presentation.

The virtual meeting reduced travel costs and saved time. But over the course of the session, the team discovered that the virtual presentation was also more effective at soliciting feedback from attendees than any of the face-to-face meetings that they had conducted with international participants. "So many of our international partners are not comfortable with English," says Evan Miller, team manager. "On a conference call, or even in person, accents can be tricky—especially when you gather a group from Europe, Japan, and the United States. With WebEx's chat feature, we found that many people could type English better than they could speak it. It made everything so much smoother."

Smoother, even, for meeting participants who were already in Dallas. During the same presentation, Miller's colleague Lisa Maestas was connected via WebEx from TI's South Campus, about five miles across the traffic-choked city. Says Maestas: "I got to stay at my desk, listen in, and participate, but I could still keep an eye on my other projects."

> ## 4 Real Tools for Virtual Work
>
> The fast-growing world of electronic collaboration is filled with helpful tools—as well stuff that promises more than it delivers. These are a few of our favorite things.
>
> **1. PlaceWare's "Question Manager" feature** (http://www.placeware.com): Most online-meeting programs allow you to "raise your hand" by clicking an icon, signifying a question for the entire online group. Most software also allows you to instant-message a question or comment directly to the meeting host. But only PlaceWare has the panel-of-experts feature—a direct instant-messaging capability that allows users to ask spontaneous questions of a designated group of experts throughout a meeting session. By directing on-the-spot queries to the panel, meeting attendees don't have to confess ignorance to the whole group. Nor do they bother everyone else in the middle of a presentation. The panel can also keep a record of issues raised throughout the session—and the questioners actually learn what they need to know when they need to know it.
>
> **2. WebEx's desktop control-sharing capability** (http://www.webex.com): This feature is the reason why WebEx isn't just an online meeting facilitator—it's the way teams work together across vast distances. By allowing someone other than the meeting host to take control of the desktop and annotate a document, this feature makes it possible for engineers, designers, or anyone else to virtually grab the document at hand and say, "No, wait! I've got it! What if we tried it this way?"
>
> **3. Centra's flexible configurations** (http://www.centra.com): Big group conference? Individual workspace? Centra is remarkably flexible. Unlike many collaboration tools that have a single mode of operation (presentation mode), Centra's service allows users to customize their views for group meetings, for one-on-one work sessions—even for individual learning environments. Quick links to the different views mean that users can even change modes midsession. During a CEO presentation to the entire company, for example, a Centra user can switch over midsession for a quick breakout meeting with her department and still rejoin the larger session with her group's questions and ideas before the presentation ends.
>
> **4. The Tandberg 1000 wireless videoconferencing unit** (http://www.tandberg.net): In a field of high-tech gadgetry sexy enough to make any geek swoon, this device is in a class by itself (and not just because of its $5,490 price tag). The Tandberg 1000 is the first videoconferencing product capable of running on a wireless LAN, which means that the executive boardroom is no longer the only place equipped for a videoconference. Wherever you are is where your next videoconference will be. No wires. No permanent hardware installations. No hassle. Unless, of course, your colleagues grab it first.

In fact, local group interaction is quickly becoming one of the most valuable uses of WebEx for this TI team—even among people who are sitting in the same room. Portions of both of the company's Dallas facilities are outfitted for wireless network connectivity. So these days, when Miller, Maestas, and other local members of the mobility team gather for a meeting, they bring their laptops, make their wireless connections, power up WebEx, and take a personal view of the document under discussion. "It's usually so hard to crowd around a screen to see what people are talking about," says Maestas. "With four laptops, everyone can see the screen. We can share control of the screen and annotate as we go along. At the end of the meeting, everyone has the same version of what we worked on. There's no more confusion."

Consultants: New Behaviors for New Technologies

Some of the the most advanced users of learning and collaboration tools are at the top consulting firms. At Accenture, for example, employees have become virtual maestros of virtual work. They use Centra along with videoconferencing, eRoom online work-flow software, the company's corporate intranet, and their myLearning.com portal. The technology is impressive, but what's most impressive is the way that Accenture's power users have devised small social cues to make sure that virtual work goes as smoothly as face-to-face sessions. They've figured out what it takes to smile, to interrupt, even to yawn online—which is why the technology works as well as it does.

Joanne McMorrow is someone who has had to think about how she works in order to make technology work. Three years ago, she transitioned from consulting with clients to working on internal knowledge-management projects. "I went from being 100% face-to-face on the consulting side to being 100% virtual in the knowledge-management practice," McMorrow says. Accustomed to jumping on a plane every Sunday night to be at client sites by Monday morning, she had to adjust her habits to join a new team that was spread across multiple cities; face-to-face meetings were a rarity. "It was a drastic change," she says. "You have to be more explicit with colleagues about certain things when you're working virtually."

Now, after changing roles a second time to become a marketing manager in Accenture's human-performance group, McMorrow says she has the virtual routine down pat. She uses Accenture's Knowledge eXchange to share documents and track progress of her group projects, NetMeetings and her telephone to participate in team meetings, and myLearning.com to take courses and track her personal-learning budget. Throughout her workday, McMorrow makes sure to verbalize to colleagues when she's shifting mental gears, when she's stepping away from her desk during a long virtual meeting, and when she needs more feedback. Once a quarter, McMorrow attends an in-person meeting of the entire "people enablement" practice in order to solidify personal connections.

McMorrow's work-style transition is a good illustration of what's involved in successful long-distance collaboration, says Accenture's Zeigler. "There are two important questions," he says. "Who's going to collaborate and for what purpose? And how does the collaborative environment fit into the way people do their work?" According to Zeigler, these are the same issues that companies face when they roll out a virtual strategy enterprisewide. "Take our e-learning strategy," he explains. "MyLearning.com allows employees to sign up for, track, and take courses online. They can also sign up for in-person courses at various locations around the world. Which one they choose depends on the business purpose of the course."

When Accenture consultants search the portal for a course, they can search by service line to view recommendations for the industries in which they consult or by career level to see what courses other consultants are taking. If consultants choose a service-line course, they're likely looking for content-specific knowledge—which means that they're likely to take the course online. But if they choose a course according to career level, perhaps they are searching for tools that their peers find most useful in their own jobs or for the types of assignments that have been most enriching to their careers—which would be best translated face-to-face. "In this particular case, the teaming and interpersonal skills learned by taking the course in person are as important as the content gained," explains Zeigler.

Bankers: Less Paper Means More Backers

Any new technology has its share of skeptics. And when that technology shapes how people work, resistance can be intense. With virtual work, one way to overcome resistance is to focus on everyone's favorite enemy: paperwork. More electronic collaboration means less paper documentation.

At Fleet Securities Inc., for example, the loan-syndications team has embraced Web-based tools for some of its most sensitive operations. New England bankers aren't famous for their digital enthusiasms. But in this case, virtual work has meant dramatic reductions in paperwork and improved service to corporate investors—which means that the bankers are on board.

Jeff McLane, a senior associate in Fleet's loan-syndications team, remembers what it was like before his group started using a secure online service to post materials for investors. "The worst was the time we went to the printer and discovered that someone had accidentally shredded our deal books. We ended up sending people to five different printers to make the deadline. But today, when you finish compiling material on a deal, you post them directly to the Web. You've eliminated the entire printing process."

McLane and his Fleet colleagues use a service called IntraLinks. Common to the banking and legal industries, IntraLinks allows companies to create secure Web sites for each deal. Team leaders determine which individuals can view which materials, and each time new material is posted, notifications go to the people who need to read or respond to it. Lawyers can even post due-diligence materials.

"Once the site is up, you can see who looked at which document," says McLane. "I can call up John Smith and say, 'You downloaded the book this morning. Do you have any questions or problems with it?'" Never mind that these virtual features save time and money—they also buy peace of mind. No more worries about whether a FedEx package reached an investor who's on vacation. "It takes out the guesswork," says McLane.

William Maag, managing director of Fleet Securities, reports that virtual tools are figuring prominently in the final stage of the deal-making process: the close. Maag says that more and more investors—sometimes up to 60%—are participating via conference call, rather than making a trip. "We'll do a PowerPoint presentation, but the nice thing is that now, if you are on the phone, we can post the presentation to the IntraLinks site and people can follow along," says Maag. It's just one more piece of evidence that such tools for virtual collaboration are becoming reliable enough for businesspeople to bank on.

The Trouble with Teams

by Brian Dumaine

Corporate America is having a hot love affair with teams. And why not? When teams work, there's nothing like them for turbocharging productivity. Beguiling examples abound: Scores of service companies like Federal Express and IDS have boosted productivity up to 40% by adopting self-managed work teams; Boeing used teams to cut the number of engineering hang-ups on its new 777 passenger jet by more than half. Says Boeing President Philip Condit: "Your competitiveness is your ability to use the skills and knowledge of people most effectively, and teams are the best way to do that."

But wait a minute. Forget all the swooning over teams for a moment. Listen carefully and you'll sense a growing unease, a worry that these things are more hassle than their fans let on—that they might even turn around and bite you. Says Eileen Appelbaum, author of *The New American Workplace:* "It's not that teams don't work. It's that there are lots of obstacles."

That may explain why the use of high-performance teams like the ones that got the results mentioned above hasn't spread as fast as you might have expected. The Center for Effective Organizations at the University of Southern California recently conducted a survey of *Fortune* 1,000 companies showing that 68% use self-managed or high-performance teams. Sounds like a lot—but the study also shows that only 10% of workers are in such teams, hardly a number betokening a managerial revolution. "People are very naive about how easy it is to create a team," says USC's Edward Lawler, the management professor who oversaw the study. "Teams are the Ferraris of work design. They're high performance, but high maintenance and expensive."

The most common trouble with teams: Many companies rush out and form the wrong kind for the job. Quality circles, primitive types in which people take a few hours off each week to discuss problems, didn't die in the 1980s, though they declined. While they may provide incremental gains in productivity, they'll never give you high-octane boosts. Those come from self-managed or high-performance teams, whose members are truly empowered to organize their work and make decisions. What often happens is that a company afraid to let go of control will create a humdrum quality circle where what's really needed is a dynamic self-managed team, and then wonder why its teams don't work.

To compound the problem, teams often get launched in a vacuum, with little or no training or support, no changes in the design of their work, and no new systems like e-mail to help communication between teams. Frustrations mount, and people wind up in endless meetings trying to figure out why they're in a team and what they're expected to do. Says Paul Osterman, a professor of management at MIT's Sloan School: "When teams are introduced in combination with other organization changes, they work. When they're introduced as an isolated practice, they fail. My gut feeling is most are introduced in isolation."

Source: Brian Dumaine, excerpt from "The Trouble with Teams," *Fortune* (September 5, 1994), pp. 86–92. Copyright © 1994 by Time, Inc. All rights reserved. Reprinted by permission.

Boeing's Condit identifies another problem: "Teams are overused." Remarkably, many companies will create teams where they're not really needed. What they don't realize is that workers who are lone wolves or creative types aren't necessarily better off in a team. Making them sit in a team meeting waiting to reach a consensus can even stifle creativity. The key is to analyze the work before you form a team. Does the task really require that people interact with each other? Can the work be done faster by a single person? After all, teams take a lot of time and energy to set up. Says Henry Sims, a management professor at the Maryland business school and author of *Business Without Bosses*: "You don't use teams with insurance salesmen and long-haul truckers."

When it comes to paying teams, most managers still throw up their hand-held computers in despair. Pay the team as a group? Then won't your star performers feel slighted? Pay for individual performance? What does that do to encourage teamwork? Companies that use teams best generally still pay members individually, but with a significant difference: They make teamwork—a sharing attitude, the ability to deal well with others—a key issue in an individual's annual performance review.

The reengineering craze is also taking its toll on teams. Executed ruthlessly, reengineering can corrode the esprit de corps vital to teamwork. Listen to US West's Jerry Miller, whose team of billing clerks in Duluth, Minnesota, got downsized out of existence last month: "When we first formed our teams, the company came in talking teamwork and empowerment and promised we wouldn't lose any jobs. It turns out all this was a big cover. The company had us all set up for reengineering. We showed them how to streamline the work, and now 9,000 people are gone. It was cut-your-own-throat. It makes you feel used." US West, which argues that in the long run reengineering will enhance teamwork, admits that for now, "People's stress levels will be high, and some people will be sad and angry."

For all the trickiness entailed in getting them right, corporate America obviously shouldn't give up on teams. Used correctly, they still increase productivity, raise morale, and in some cases spur innovation. Smart companies like Textron, Nynex, Boeing, and Allina navigated the bumps and potholes of team building. Their stories offer compelling examples of how to overcome the troubles with teams. Here's what they've learned.

• **Use the Right Team for the Right Job.** A common mistake among managers is to think a team is a team is a team. To the contrary, a more accurate taxonomy reads like Homer's catalogue of ships in the *Illiad*: problem-solving teams, product-development teams, self-managed teams, and virtual teams, to name just a few. Too often a CEO will get excited about the idea of teams and order them up as if only one type existed. That kind of unthinking, one-tool-for-all-jobs application is bound to send tremors through the ranks. The CEO of a Western manufacturing company suddenly announced that from now on everybody was going to be in a team. The next day absenteeism soared.

The teams most popular today are of two broad types: work teams, which include high-performance or self-managed teams, and special-purpose problem-solving teams. Problem-solving teams have specific missions, which can be broad (find out why our customers hate us) or narrow (figure out why the No. 3 pump keeps overheating). Once the job is done, such teams usually disband. The USC survey found that 91% of American companies use problem-solving teams, about a third more than seven years ago. And on average, about 20% of a company's employees are beavering away at any given time on such teams.

While problem-solving teams are temporary, work teams, used by about two-thirds of U.S. companies, tend to be permanent. Rather than attack specific problems, a work team does day-to-day work. A team of Boeing engineers helping to build a jet would be a work team. If a work team has the authority to make decisions about how the daily work gets done, it's properly described as a self-managed or high-performance team. Common tests for a self-managed team are: Can it change the order of tasks? Does it have budgets?

• **Create a Hierarchy of Teams.** Time and again teams fall short of their promise because companies don't know how to make them work together with other teams. If you don't get your teams into the right constellations, the whole organization can stall.

Boeing has an organizational structure that encourages teams to work together and seize initiative. Says Henry Shomber, a Boeing chief engineer: "We have the no-messenger rule. Team members must make decisions on the spot. They can't run back to their functions for permission." This kind of freedom allowed Boeing to use teams to build its new 777 passenger jet, which flew its first successful test flight this summer with fewer than half the number of design glitches of earlier programs.

When the Seattle aerospace giant set out to design the 777, a massive project eventually involving 10,000 employees and more than 500 suppliers, it knew it wanted an entirely team-based organization but wasn't sure how to make it all work. In the end the company created a hierarchy of teams, a structure meant to get all Boeing's work teams pulling in the same direction. "Our goal," says Boeing's Condit, "is a barrier-free enterprise where all are working to satisfy the customer."

Boeing's 777 project looks like a traditional organizational pyramid, but instead of layers of management, it has three layers of teams. In all there are over 200 cross-functional teams, each made up of people from departments like engineering, manufacturing, and finance. At the top of the pyramid is a management team of the five or six top managers from each discipline who, as a group, have responsibility for the plane's being built correctly and on time. Underneath this management group is a large group of the 50 or so leaders—half each from engineering and operations, set up in 25 to 30 two-person teams—who oversee the 200-plus work teams that have responsibility for specific parts of the plane. These work teams are typically cross-functional groups of five to 15 workers. Examples: a wing team, a flap team, a tail team, and so on.

The top management team holds a weekly meeting. The members of the second tier communicate with the top team through their leaders in engineering and operations, and also hold meetings in which they handle major issues like schedule delays or quality problems with suppliers. The group of 50 then returns to the work teams with solutions to big problems. While this team structure worked well to move information quickly up the organization, Boeing realized near the end of the 777 project that information wasn't moving well horizontally. In other words, the wing teams weren't necessarily communicating as well with the cockpit team as Boeing would have liked, causing design glitches. To solve the problem, the company added a fourth layer of what it calls airplane integration teams—five groups, each with 12 to 15 people drawn from the work teams.

These teams act like the corpus callosum, the part of the brain that transfers information back and forth between the left and right hemispheres. Top management makes sure the integration teams have access to everyone in the organization. Says Scott Forster, an integration team leader: "We can go and get any information now. I can go to the chief engineer. Before, it was unusual just to see the chief engineer."

A few months ago, two Boeing work teams discovered a conflict: one had designed the passengers' oxygen system in the same spot that the other had put the system for the gasper, the little nozzle that shoots fresh air toward the passenger. One of the teams, noticing the conflict, called in an integration team, which got everyone thinking about what was best for the airplane. Within hours the three teams, working together, came up with an ingenious solution: a special clamp that holds both systems. At the old Boeing a problem like that probably wouldn't have been caught until the plane was being manufactured.

• **You Can't Have Teams Without Trust.** Reengineering presents a devilish paradox for teams. As a company reengineers, it cuts out layers of middle management, pushing work down. Employees, forced to find new ways to do more work, naturally gravitate toward teams. But the very thing that often gives rise to teams—reengineering—can have a devastating effect on team spirit.

Nynex, the Baby Bell for New York and New England, must restructure itself to prosper in the Information Age. That means shedding 17,000 workers, 30% of its work force, most of whom work in local telephone operations, the company's traditional business. To keep team morale high, Nynex in April signed a landmark labor agreement. Instead of wholesale layoffs, Nynex and the Communications Workers of America, a tough union that conducted a bitter four-month strike against the company in 1989, have a new contract that virtually guarantees no involuntary layoffs. For workers near retirement it adds six years to the person's age, plus six years of service, and supplements Social Security payments. (It didn't hurt that Nynex's pension fund was overfunded.) For those who either can't or don't want to retire, the contract guarantees training for a new job inside Nynex or one with another company. The training provision is particularly generous: A worker can take two years off and receive $10,000 a year for tuition or can work four days a week and go to school for the fifth, again for two years. Says CEO Ferguson: "It costs in the short term, but I believe we'll build shareholder value in the future by doing this."

• **Tackle the People Issues Head-on.** So you've created the right types of teams, built an atmosphere of trust, and changed your organizational structure—and your teams still seem to be misfiring. What's the rub? Most likely it's clashing personalities. Asks Robert Baugh, a workplace specialist at the A.F.L.-C.I.O.: "How do you get people who have been at each other's throats for years to start to cooperate?"

Companies must train managers and workers to deal openly and frankly with other team members. While this sounds elementary, most companies don't do an adequate job. There's no secret or magic formula. While a motivational consultant or two may help loosen people up, most team members pick up new behavior by watching closely how management acts.

A company that set a good example for teamwork is Allina, which runs 17 nonprofit hospitals in

Minnesota. The company tried to form teams through the 1980s but always failed. It had the kind of hostile relations with labor unions that could make a World Cup match look genteel. A nurses' strike in 1984 basically shut a hospital for six weeks. Some Allina managers who had been working there for as long as 20 years had never even met a union official. The unions weren't blameless either. A worker remembers being taught by union officials that all you need to know is that boss spelled backward is double SOB. Says Jack Dobier, Allina's labor-management coordinator: "You'll fail with teams if you don't change people's attitude."

Allina did this by forming a team of management and union officials and giving it the power to make a difference. For instance, it found a way to close one of Allina's hospitals without leaving employees stranded. The team set up an employment center that placed 95% of the closing hospital's employees elsewhere in Allina or in other companies.

Not only did this gesture raise morale generally and save the company $8 million in severance costs, but more important, it also showed that management was serious about working with labor. Allina has since created worker-management teams in 11 of its 17 hospitals, with stunning results. One of these problem-solving teams saved the company $200,000 a year by suggesting that maintenance on some hospital equipment, such as emergency electrical generators and operating room lights, be done by the company's own staff.

Ellen Lord, a team leader at Davidson Interiors, a division of Textron in Dover, New Hampshire, found that to keep teams happy, managers must have the patience and presence of mind to act like a parent, teacher, and referee all at once. Lord's product-development team in 1992 created a new product called Flexible Bright—a high-tech coating that makes plastic for cars look exactly like chrome but won't rust, scratch, or crack. The grille of Ford's new Lincoln Mark VIII contains this new material, and the auto maker plans to use it in other lines.

But that success followed an emphatically unpromising start. Team members in the early days sometimes got into fights. A neatnik sitting next to a slob lost his cool. People were becoming emotional about what kind of coffee was brewing in the pot. The manufacturing types thought the engineering members were focused on trivia and bluntly let them know this.

Lord argues that no matter how bad it gets, you must keep people together and talking until they feel comfortable, a process that can take months. Says she: "We threw all the people in one room and forced them to work together. If people from different functions don't get to know each other, they can't ask favors, and teamwork stalls." Lord believes the infighting would have been much worse if she hadn't carefully screened team members before inviting them to join: "As long as all of them were doers who had a depth of knowledge they could apply, I knew the personalities would work themselves out."

Yes, teams have troubles. They consume gallons of sweat and discouragement before yielding a penny of benefit. Companies make the investment only because they've realized that in a fast-moving, brutally competitive economy, the one thing sure to be harder than operating with teams is operating without them.

Index

Accenture, 16–17
affective conflict, 13
Allina, 23–24
analysis and observation of teams, 8, 14–15
appeals, personal and inspirational, 12
Appelbaum, Eileen, 21
atmosphere, in teams, 13–14

banking, 20–21
Baugh, Robert, 23
Boeing, 20–21
Buck Breast Care Center, 16, 17

Center for Effective Organization (USC), 21
Centra Software, 16, 19
clarifying function, 10
coalitions, 11, 12
collaboration, electronic. *See* electronic collaboration
communication, 11–12, 14
Communications Workers of America, 23
compromising function, 10
condescension, 14
Condit, Philip, 20, 21, 23
conflict, 13, 23–24
consensus-building, 9
consensus testing, 10
consultation, as influence tactic, 12
consulting firms, 20
context of teams, 8
criticism within teams, 14

Davidson Interiors, 24
dealmaking, and virtual sales, 17, 21
decision community software, 18
decision making, 9, 11
defensive environments, 14
dependency and counterdependence, 14
description, clear, 14
Dobier, Jack, 24
doctors, in virtual teams, 16, 17–18
dogmatism, 14
downsizing, 23

effectiveness, and team members, 8
effectiveness model, 14
elaborating function, 10
electronic collaboration and virtual teams
    overview, 16–17
    banking, 20–21
    consulting firms, 20
    medical, 16, 17–18
    meetings, virtual, 18–19
    sales, 17

emotional issues, 14
empathy, 14
emWare Inc., 17
encouraging function, 10
equality in teams, 14
Esserman, Laura, 16, 17–18
exchange, as influence tactic, 12

fighting among team members, 14
Fleet Securities, 20–21
Flexible Bright, 24
Forster, Scott, 23

gatekeeping function, 10
goals, 14
groupthink, 13

harmonizing function, 10
hierarchy of teams, 20–21
high-performing teams, 21

identity, as team issue, 14
individual member characteristics, 8
influence and power, 12–13, 14
information-seeking function, 10
information technology (IT). *See* electronic collaboration
ingratiation, 12
initiating function, 10
inspirational appeals, 12
integration teams, 23
Internet. *See* electronic collaboration
interventions, 15
intimacy as team issue, 14
IntraLinks, 20–21
IT (information technology). *See* electronic collaboration

journal-writing, 5
judgmentalism, 14

labor unions, 23, 24
Lawler, Edward, 21
legitimating tactics, 12
long-distance collaboration. *See* electronic collaboration
Lord, Ellen, 24

Maag, William, 21
Maestas, Lisa, 18
maintenance functions, 9, 10
majority opinion, power of, 9
management consultants, 20
management issues, 4

McLane, Jeff, 20–21
McMorrow, Joanne, 20
medical industry, 16, 17–18
meetings, virtual, 18–19. *See also* electronic collaboration
member characteristics in a team, 8
memory system, transactive, 8
Miller, Evan, 18
Miller, Jerry, 20
minority opinion, 9, 11
MyLearning.com, 20

Navickas, Leon, 16
Nynex, 23

observation and analysis of teams, 8, 14–15
opinions, majority and minority, 9, 11
opinions, sharing of, 10
Osterman, Paul, 21

panel of experts, in virtual meetings, 19
personal appeals, 12
persuasion, rational, 12
PlaceWare, 19
power and influence, 12–13, 14
pressure, as influence tactic, 12
problem orientation, 14
problem-solving teams, 20
problems with teams, 21–24
provisionalism, 14
psychological safety, 13

quality circles, 21
"Question Manager" (PlaceWare), 19

rational persuasion, 12
reengineering, 20, 23
remote-device technology, 17

safety, psychological, 13
sales, virtual, 17
Shomber, Henry, 20
Sims, Henry, 20
sociograms, 11–12
software for electronic collaboration, 19
solution mindedness, 9

spontaneity, in teams, 14
stratagems, 14
strategic design, 15
substantive conflict, 13
summarizing function, 10
supportive environments, in teams, 14

Tandberg software, 19
task functions, for teams, 9, 10
team effectiveness model, 14
team processes, internal
    overview, 4–5
    categories of, 4, 8
    communication patterns, 11–12, 14
    conflict, 13, 23–24
    decision making, 9, 11
    electronic collaboration, 16–21
    emotional issues, 14
    hierarchy of teams, 20–21
    individual members, 8
    influence and power, 12–13
    maintenance functions, 9, 10
    management issues, 4, 15
    observation and analysis, 8, 14–15
    organizational context, 8
    problems with, 21–24
    reengineering and, 20, 23
    supportive vs. defensive atmosphere, 13–14
    task functions, 9, 10
    types of teams, choosing, 20
    working with other teams, 20–21
Texas Instruments (TI), 18–19
transactive memory system, 8
"The Trouble with Teams" (Dumaine), 21–24
types of teams, choosing, 20

videoconferencing. *See* electronic collaboration
"Virtually There" (Overholt), 16–21
virtual sales, 17
virtual teams. *See* electronic collaboration and virtual teams

WebEx, 18–19, 19
withdrawing, in teams, 14

Zeigler, Reinhard, 17, 20

MANAGING FOR THE FUTURE

Organizational Behavior & Processes

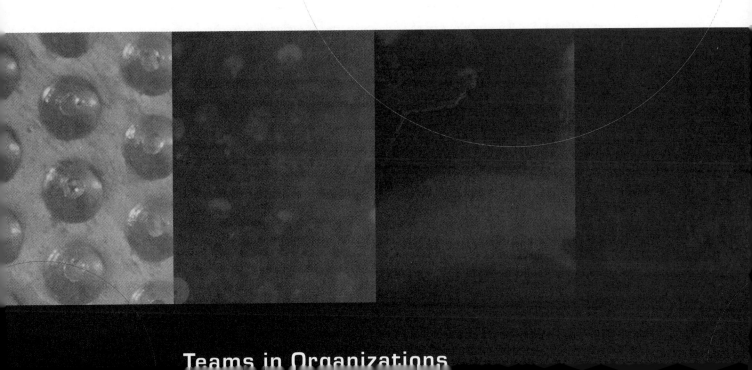

Teams in Organizations

MANAGING FOR THE FUTURE
Organizational Behavior & Processes, Third Edition

Deborah Ancona
Sloan School of Management
Massachusetts Institute of Technology

John Van Maanen
Sloan School of Management
Massachusetts Institute of Technology

Thomas A. Kochan
Sloan School of Management
Massachusetts Institute of Technology

D. Eleanor Westney
Sloan School of Management
Massachusetts Institute of Technology

Maureen Scully
Graduate School of Management
Simmons College

Dedicated to those who have inspired us to try to be better students and teachers.
Special thanks to: Professor Jack Barbash • Professor Arthur H. Gladstein • Professor Marius B. Jansen • Professor Joanne Martin • Professor Edgar H. Schein

---

VP/Editorial Director
Jack W. Calhoun

VP/Editor-in-Chief
Michael P. Roche

Senior Publisher
Melissa S. Acuña

Executive Editor
John Szilagyi

Senior Developmental Editor
Judith O'Neill

Marketing Manager
Jacquelyn Carrillo

Production Editor
Emily Gross

Manufacturing Coordinator
Rhonda Utley

Compositor
Trejo Production

Printer
Von Hoffmann Press, Inc.
Frederick, MD

Internal Designer
Bethany Casey

Cover Designer
Bethany Casey

Photographs
©PhotoDisc

Design Project Manager
Bethany Casey

COPYRIGHT ©2005
by South-Western, a division of Thomson Learning. Thomson Learning™ is a trademark used herein under license.

Printed in the United States of America
1 2 3 4 5 07 06 05 04 03

For more information contact
South-Western College Publishing,
5191 Natorp Boulevard,
Mason, Ohio, 45040
Or you can visit our Internet site at:
http://www.swlearning.com

ALL RIGHTS RESERVED
No part of this work covered by the copyright hereon may be reproduced or used in any form or by any means—graphic, electronic, or mechanical, including photocopying, recording, taping, Web distribution or information storage and retrieval systems—without the written permission of the publisher.

For permission to use material from this text or product, contact us by
Tel: (800) 730-2214
Fax: (800) 730-2215
http://www.thomsonrights.com

Library of Congress Control Number: 2003113908
ISBN 0-324-05575-7

Contents

Teams in Organizations

Overview		4

Core

Class Note	**Outward Bound: Linking Teams to Their Organization**	8
	Team Effectiveness 9	
	Moving Outward 9	
	Analyzing and Managing the External Environment Using the Three Lenses 9	
	References 10	
Case	**Aston-Blair, Inc.**	11
	Company Background 11	
	Formation of the Task Force 12	
	Initial Meeting of the Task Force 12	
	Preparation of the Task Force Report 14	
	The August 4 Report of the Task Force 15	

Elective

The Press	**The Comparative Advantage of X-Teams**	22
	Five Components That Make X-Teams Successful 22	
	Is the X-Team for Your Company? 29	

Index

Overview

This module is designed to allow you to apply some of the key concepts of team processes and boundary management to real teams in organizations. Through a case analysis you will examine how one team leader and those assigned to work with him set up a temporary team, got the team started, worked with others in the organization, presented the team's recommendations, and ended the team. Analyzing this team in depth will help you develop an understanding of how concepts such as participation, goal setting, conflict management, and boundary management can be used to comprehend why some teams work and others do not. You should also come away with a greater understanding of the dynamics of task forces with diverse membership.

As organizations become more networked, both literally through the use of information technology and structurally through the implementation of networked forms of organization, the use of temporary teams is on the rise. These teams are created for a short time to deal with an immediate problem or issue that cannot be solved through standard practices. A diverse membership often characterizes temporary teams, which must also deal with many people and groups outside of the team. Their short-term nature and diverse composition provide flexibility to the organization and an ability to learn new things. Unfortunately, their diversity, short-term nature, and challenge to the status quo also pose unique management challenges. Finding ways to meet these challenges is critical because management theorists predict that the organization of the future will be built around such temporary teams.

This module contains a short Class Note, a case, and one elective reading. The Class Note, "Outward Bound: Linking Teams to Their Organizations," introduces the concept of boundary management. Boundary management refers to the way in which a team handles interactions with those outside its boundary. It is one of the major categories of team operations and plays a key role in creating and maintaining team effectiveness (see Figure 6.1 for a model of team effectiveness, which is introduced in Module 3—Making Teams Work). Although most managers and researchers focus their attention on internal team processes, boundary management is actually more predictive of team performance. In today's business environment, teams can no longer work in isolation. Members must learn to interact effectively with top management, other functions, and units within the organization, as well as with suppliers, customers, and distributors outside the firm. This boundary management function is critical to achieving cross-functional coordination, the speedy delivery of new products, and integration across nations and firms. The first reading provides concrete suggestions as to how to carry out boundary management effectively.

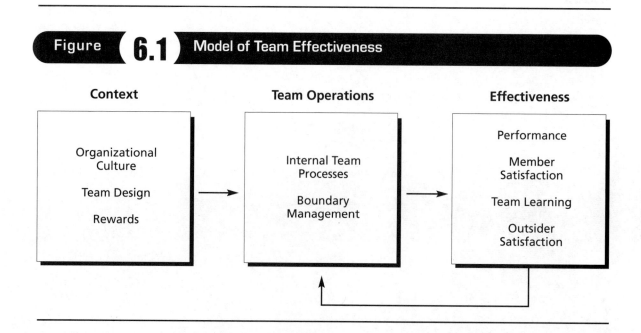

Figure 6.1 Model of Team Effectiveness

The elective reading, "The Comparative Advantage of X-Teams," builds on the core Class Note by describing a type of team that uses both internal and boundary management extensively. This type of flexible and adaptive team seems to be well suited to today's fast-changing world. The article describes these X-teams and offers guidelines for how to create them. X-teams are not for every situation, but when they are needed they help the organization to link to markets and technologies outside the organization and effectively to use external information for tasks within the firm.

In the case in this module, "Aston-Blair, Inc.," you will follow the struggles of one team leader who tries to handle the many challenges of running a temporary team. Through his example you will be able to monitor the complexities inherent in blending the management of internal team processes and external boundary management. You will see how quickly a team culture forms and how politics often plays a major role in cross-functional teams. By putting yourself in the team leader's place, you can think through how you would meet the challenges he faces. What would your first steps be? How would you plan the first team meeting? How would you monitor progress? How would you handle boundary management? How would you prepare for your major presentation? How could you construct an X-team? Through trying to answer these questions, applying the concepts in the readings, comparing your responses to those of your classmates, and engaging in class discussion, you should be better prepared to be an effective team leader and member.

Also included in this module are some case work materials (pages 17–19) that should be taken with you to class. These materials will help you to keep track of all of the different people in the case and to think about what the team needs to do to be successful. "Tips on Task Force Management" lists the things that a manager needs to do to manage such a team. A task force is a short-term team that is put in charge of a particular project. The list moves through the various stages of a task force, from getting started, through the first meeting, work, and bringing the project to completion. The list demonstrates that internal team-building skills need to be paired with external boundary management in order for this type of team to succeed.

Assignment Summary

1. Come to class prepared to discuss the Ashton-Blair case in depth. Use the Class Note reading to back up your analysis and focus on these questions:
   a. What are the problems facing Bacon at the end of the case?
   b. How did those problems evolve?
   c. What actions would you take at the end of the case? Why?
2. Be sure to bring all case work materials to class on the day the case will be discussed.
3. If assigned, the elective reading on the comparative advantage of X-teams, originally published in the *MIT Sloan Management Review*, provides a comparative twist on boundary management (one that builds out from the Class Note and focuses on a new form of externally oriented team).

Additional Exercises

You can expand your learning about boundary management in several ways. First, you can analyze the boundary issues for a team in which you are currently a member, or one in which you were a member, or one that you have read about. What are the key interdependencies for this team? Who, besides the team members, has resources or information that can impact the team? Who can aid or sabotage the work of the team? What would be the best way to deal with outsiders? Who must be influenced? Who must be provided with information? With whom must negotiations take place?

Second, you can interview someone who was recently part of a task force. Ask that person what boundary management issues arose and how they were handled. Find out how the organizational context helped and hindered the work of the team. Find out how the team member would handle boundary management activity in the future. By conducting several of these interviews, you can learn more about how boundary management is handled in real task forces.

Finally, you can read up on boundary management and related concepts. The following references serve as a guide for further reading.

References

Allen, T. J. 1984. *Managing the Flow of Technology: Technology Transfer and the Dissemination of Technological Information Within the R & D Organization*. Cambridge, MA: MIT Press.

Ancona, D. G. 1990. Outward Bound: Strategies for Team Survival in the Organization. *Academy of Management Journal* 33, 334–365.

Ancona, D. G., and D. Caldwell. 1992. Bridging the Boundary: External Activity and Performance in Organizational Teams. *Administrative Science Quarterly* 37, 634–665.

Ancona, D. G., and D. Caldwell. 2000. Compose Teams to Assure Successful Boundary Activity. In E. A. Locke (Ed.), *The Blackwell Handbook of Principles of Organizational Behavior,* Oxford: Blackwell.

Hackman, J. R. 1999. Thinking differently about context. In R. Wageman (Ed.), *Research on Managing Groups and Teams* (pp. 233–247). Stamford, CT: JAI Press.

Hansen, M. T. 1999. The search-transfer problem: The role of weak ties in sharing knowledge across organizational subunits. *Administrative Science Quarterly* 44, 82–111.

Nohria, N., and R. G. Eccles (Eds.). 1992. *Networks and Organizations: Structure, Form, and Action.* Boston: Harvard Business School Press.

Reagans, R., and J. Galaskiewicz. 2000. Distribution of knowledge, group network structure, and group performance. *Management Science* 46(5), 612–625.

Sutton, R., and A. B. Hargadon. 1996. Brainstorming groups in context: Effectiveness in a product design firm. *Administrative Science Quarterly* 41 (December), 685–718.

Wheelwright, S. C., and K. B. Clark. 1992. *Revolutionizing Product Development.* New York: Free Press.

Teams in Organizations

CORE

Module 6

Outward Bound:

Linking teams to their organization

The new computer project was a grand success. The cross-functional team was stellar, turning out an amazing new system that worked faster than anyone thought possible. Then management killed the project. No team is an island.

It is not enough anymore to work well around a conference table or in the laboratory; it is not enough to know how to build internal consensus and effective team decision making; it is not even enough to work well as a cross-functional team on concurrent engineering or horizontal processes. Unless you know how to manage within and across the new organization, you lose. The only way to survive is to manage the external environment: boundary management.

Teams need to manage their boundaries, to protect their territory, and also to build bridges. The new product is now part of a "family" of products. The new service must interface with the computer and accounting systems. All innovation must fit into a strategic direction that is changing at a rate faster than ever before. All these activities are set within a context in which the competition is trying to do the exact same thing. The need for new information, feedback, and coordination with outsiders means that teams must have dense linkages within and outside the firm. Here we focus on those within the firm.

Most researchers tended to concentrate their efforts on understanding internal group dynamics. Others looked at how teams function in the larger environment of corporate realities and how their external strategies and styles affect performance. In studies of project teams, product development teams, R&D groups, sales teams, consulting teams, and management teams, clear patterns begin to emerge. Here we concentrate on the work of Ancona and Caldwell (1992) in their exploration of team boundary management.

The external strategies of teams are a complex matter. The team leader or project manager may play a key role in managing outside relations, or the work may be distributed across several team members. Teams need to manage various interfaces and interconnections with numerous parts of the organization. These interactions can be examined across several dimensions: influence, task coordination, and information.

The *influence dimension* is vertical. The important external connections in this dimension are upward. Few teams become high performers without learning to "manage up." They need ambassadorial activities, whereby individuals who are skilled in diplomacy and know how to play organizational politics work the power structure, effectively marketing the project and the team as well as building and maintaining a good reputation through their representation of the team and its interests. Whether for good or bad, public relations can greatly affect team success. A team's reputation can become a self-fulfilling prophecy: "good" teams get the pick of projects and people and priority access to shared resources, whereas no one returns phone calls to those thought to be failing. Upward communication can also help a team to align its goals with that of top management.

Key to ambassadorial activity is the need to identify secure, effective sponsorship within upper management, which can protect the team from the shifting winds of influence and interests as divisions are sold, companies are acquired, middle managers move, or projects are canceled. It is also important to identify potential threats to the team so that damage can be limited.

Task coordination is essentially a horizontal matter, involving lateral connections across functions and managing a team's work interdependence with other units. Teams that excel at this activity bargain with other groups, trade services or essential resources, and get feedback from others as to how their work meets expectations. These teams coordinate with other groups, pushing them to meet deadlines and to come through on commitments made to the team. They keep the work flowing in and out of the team, joining together upstream and downstream activity so that work moves quickly through the firm, not back and forth between warring functions or divisions.

The *information*, or scouting, *activity* is also largely lateral. Liaison here involves investigating markets, technologies, and competition, gathering information on what is going on in other parts of the organization, and bringing large amounts of data to the team.

Just as teams develop distinctive styles of working internally, specializing in different aspects, they

Source: This Class Note is based on Larry Constantine, "People-Ware, Team Politics," *Software Development* (August 1993), 96–97.

also seem to develop characteristic ways of managing their boundaries and interacting with the rest of the organization. Some teams remain isolated and members almost never stray beyond the team boundaries, other teams focus on a particular type of boundary activity like ambassadorial or scouting, while still others take on a more comprehensive strategy. This comprehensive strategy combines multiple types of boundary activity at once.

Team Effectiveness

How do these various styles fare in the real world? In the short term, the isolated teams and those that specialized in ambassadorial activity are the most satisfied. Members of these teams do not have to deal with the complexity of the external world or the difficulties of trying to coordinate with others. Here team members can come together, set goals, and agree on working procedures among themselves. The trouble is that the rest of the organization is not onboard. Even though a few of the isolationist teams manage to create innovative products and get support from the top, this scenario is the exception rather than the rule.

For true team effectiveness over the long haul, the comprehensive strategy is the best. The comprehensive teams, with their well-orchestrated and diversified strategies, prove to be the corporate winners. Such teams balance internal performance with external demands. They get the information they need but do not get stuck in perpetual research. They work the system in terms of the power structure and work flow to meet their goals. Although the early history of these teams can be a bit rough, as they attempt to tackle internal and external issues, over time they become the high-performing teams. As external groups show their support, internal operations become smoother and a positive cycle is produced. In short, the winning strategy is outward bound.

Moving Outward

The notion of managing beyond one's borders is counterintuitive to many team managers. We are all taught that team building begins with setting goals and priorities and having team members get to know one another. Nothing is said about checking those goals against management objectives or getting feedback from other parts of the organization. Thus, the first move to successfully carrying out boundary activity is to educate team members about its importance.

Next, team members need to organize themselves to carry out a comprehensive strategy. The team might begin by listing those individuals and groups within the organization that have information, expertise, control, or resources that the team might need. Members might also list those whose support will help the work of the team, and those who may be antagonistic to the team or its work. Then the team must decide how to allocate the work of managing all of these liaisons. The team leader might manage more of the vertical communication, whereas lateral communication is more distributed within the group.

Team members might begin by interviewing key outsiders about what they expect from the team, what they would really like the team to produce, and how the team's product affects them and their group. This information can help to shape the way the team defines its task and its output. Outsiders need to be informed all along of the history of the team. Those who may do damage need to be courted or controlled; those who have expertise and a stake in the team's output need to be brought into team decision making at the appropriate times. The team may also need to limit its exposure to those who would influence it in negative ways. Thus, a delicate balance is required between too much and too little interaction with those beyond the team's border. Team members often need to spend a lot of time explaining and "talking up" what they are doing, as well as pushing others to come through on earlier commitments.

Changes in organizations mean that the new flat, flexible, networked, diverse, global organization is often team-based. These teams cannot work as they did in the past. Success depends on linking up with other organizational members to get the job done. Previously, success was more a function of human capital, which are the skills and abilities of team members. Now it is a function of social capital, or the value that members add to their teams through their external ties to others (Coleman, 1988; Burt, 1992). Social capital is the "value that comes from knowing who, when, and how to coordinate through various contacts within and beyond the firm" (Thompson, 2000, p. 175). The teams that can best pull together the expertise of the firm and move their ideas and products quickly through the organization are those that will succeed. Members of these teams rely on a set of strong connections with others throughout the firm and outside it, as well as weak ties with disparate groups that are not usually connected. Through these connections, team members can gain commitment for their work as well as access to new ideas and opportunities (Bert, 1992; Thompson, 2000).

Analyzing and Managing the External Environment Using the Three Lenses

Another way to think about external boundary spanning is through three analytic lenses (see

Module 2): strategic design, political, and cultural. From a strategic design perspective, team members need to analyze those providing inputs and accepting outputs from the team in order to improve efficiency and effectiveness. From this view of the world, ambassadorial activity is important in getting key resources from top management; task coordinator activity is key to ensuring a smooth work flow to and from the team; and scouting assures the input of accurate and up-to-date information. Improving the flow of resources, work, and information is the major goal here.

From a political perspective, team members need to identify the key "stakeholders" external to the team. Stakeholders play a role in the survival and success of the team and are affected by its activities—they have a stake in its operations. Here the focus is on assessing the environment's influence and potential influence on the team and the team's bargaining power vis-à-vis that environment.

In the stakeholder model the focus is on stakeholders' interests (what do they want?), their power and influence (how much do they have and what form does it take?), the negotiations that take place between them and team members, and the coalition building used by team members with outsiders to spread their agendas. From this perspective, ambassadorial activity is aimed at influencing top management, a major stakeholder. Here the goal is to align firm and team interests and to garner support for team interests from this powerful group. Task coordination activity is aimed at negotiating with the groups and divisions that members represent, as well as those that are not represented in the team. Special interest groups, professional groups, customers, suppliers, and employee groups might also have a stake in team outcomes and require ambassadorial and task coordinator activity. Scouting activity involves identifying the interests of other professional groups and divisions, customers, and suppliers.

The cultural perspective focuses on the artifacts, norms, values, and assumptions of the organization in which the team resides, as well as the overall societal view of teams in general. Here we look at the pressures on team members to design their teams in particular ways and to act according to standard scripts. High-performance teams, virtual teams, and transnational teams are all models of appropriate behavior that are currently being imposed on many teams. We also look at the team members' attempts to change the cultural expectations that limit and constrain behavior.

Ambassadorial, task coordinator, and scouting behavior can be used to learn more about the expectations facing the team, the "rules of the game," and what happens when those rules are broken. For example, one member of a product development team who often took on ambassadorial activity, fought long and hard to gain acceptance for allowing his team members to talk directly to customers. The "rules" in the organization made customer interaction solely a marketing activity.

Thus, external boundary activity is essential to team performance. Ambassadorial, task coordinator, and scouting activity allow the team to improve the efficiency of receiving inputs and exporting outputs, to negotiate and build coalitions with key external stakeholders, and to understand and possibly change cultural expectations.

References

Ancona, D. G. 1990. Outward Bound: Strategies for Team Survival in the Organization. *Academy of Management Journal* 33, 334–365.

Ancona, D. G., and D. Caldwell. 1992. Bridging the Boundary: External Activity and Performance in Organizational Teams. *Administrative Science Quarterly* 37, 634–665.

Ancona, D. G., and D. Caldwell. 2000. Compose Teams to Assure Successful Boundary Activity. In E. A. Locke (Ed.), *The Blackwell Handbook of Principles of Organizational Behavior*, Oxford: Blackwell.

Burt, R. S. 1992. *The Social Structure of Competition*. Cambridge, MA: Harvard University Press.

Coleman, J. S. 1988. Social Capital in the Creation of Human Capital. *American Journal of Sociology* 94, S95–S120.

Constantine, Larry. 1993. People-Ware, Team Politics. *Software Development* (August), 96–97.

Thompson, L. 2000. *Making the Team: A Guide for Managers*. Upper Saddle River, NJ: Prentice Hall.

Aston-Blair, Inc.

Bringing Aston-Blair's June 12 executive committee meeting to a close Wynn Aston, III, chief executive officer and chairman of the board, asked Peter Casey, vice president of marketing, and Chris Trott, vice president of corporate planning, to seriously reexamine the company's procedures for forecasting sales. Aston hoped that improved product demand projections would lead to better inventory control, financial planning, and production scheduling. Aston-Blair had suffered significant losses in the first quarter of 1991 and expected even greater losses in the second quarter (the first losses the company had experienced since 1975). Aston felt that poor forecasting was one of several underlying factors contributing to the firm's poor performance.

Casey and Trott subsequently met with Richard Pack, president and chief operating officer, to briefly discuss his ideas on the subject. The two men then decided to form a task force to investigate the forecasting problem. Casey and Trott agreed to put Michael Bacon, a recent graduate of Stanford's Graduate School of Business, in charge of the task force. Bacon had been with Aston-Blair for two years and was currently a special assistant to Chris Trott. Prior to his present assignment, Bacon had worked as a financial analyst in Trott's financial planning group, and he was now assigned to Trott's market planning group. The assignment to market planning was an intentional move on Trott's part to broaden Bacon's exposure to different aspects of Aston-Blair's business. Bacon was regarded by both Trott and Casey as an especially promising and capable individual.

Company Background

Aston-Blair was the third largest U.S. producer of precious metal alloys and other specialized alloys for commercial and industrial use. The medium-sized company was headquartered in Chicago and had four major sales offices and five plants throughout the United States. Its products included alloys of silver, gold, platinum, and other precious or rare metals. The company sold its alloys in the form of ingots, bars, coil, strip, and wire. Most of its raw material was purchased from abroad. Aston-Blair sold its products to a wide range of customers including dealers in precious metals, jewelry manufacturers, scientific firms, and electronic and other industrial companies, which used precious metals or other alloys in the manufacture of instruments and other devices.

The company's present difficulties were precipitated by two sets of related events. The first was the economic slowdown in the early 1990s, which had affected the company's sales to both industrial customers and jewelry manufacturers. The second factor was the declining price of gold beginning in 1991. On the day President Bush announced the air strike against Iraq, the price of gold fell $27 an ounce, and the price continued to decline throughout 1991. The combination of the declining price of gold and Aston-Blair's overly optimistic sales forecasts for the first two quarters of 1991 had resulted in excessive inventories of overvalued gold, silver, and platinum, and sizable losses.

Aston-Blair's current problems stood in dramatic contrast with the company's recent record of outstanding growth and profitability. The company had been founded by Aston's great-grandfather in 1881, and it had always enjoyed a reputation for being a premiere supplier of precious metals. During Aston's 10-year stewardship as chief executive officer, the firm had quadrupled in size and had become the most profitable firm in the industry. Aston attributed this recent success to the company's aggressive marketing efforts and to its ability to identify potential users of precious metal alloys and to work with them in developing products tailored to their requirements. Under Aston and Pack's direction, the company was the first firm in the precious metals industry to develop a marketing organization where market managers and product managers were responsible for focusing on specific market segments and applications areas. (Pack had been vice president of marketing prior to his promotion to president in 1989.)

Despite his family's obvious influence in the company, Aston had come up through the ranks and had a solid grounding in the business. Himself an MBA, Aston had made a concerted effort to hire business school-trained managers since becoming chief executive officer and had hired a

---

Source: "Aston-Blair, Inc." Copyright © 1993 by the President and Fellows of Harvard College. Harvard Business School Case 9-494-015. This case was prepared by Prof. John J. Gabarro with the assistance of Prof. Deborah Ancona as the basis for class discussion rather than to illustrate either effective or ineffective handling of an administration situation. Reprinted by permission of the Harvard Business School.

number of MBA's from Columbia, Dartmouth, Harvard, MIT, Stanford, and Wharton. It was generally acknowledged that many of these MBAs were received with some resistance from industry old-timers, although several of them had gained considerable influence and success within the company, including Casey (a Harvard MBA) and Trott (an Amos Tuck MBA), both of whom were now vice presidents.

Formation of the Task Force

After some discussion, Trott and Casey concluded that the major area for the task force to study should be the Marketing Division, because it was the four market managers who made the final forecasts for product demand. The market managers based their forecasts on information they received from their product managers, the vice president of sales, the vice president of manufacturing, and the macroeconomic forecasts made by the vice president of economic analysis and forecasting (see Exhibit 1 for company organization chart).

Having decided on the task force's mandate, Casey and Trott met with Bacon and described the problem as they saw it. Casey said that he would appoint three product managers to the task force to represent the Marketing Division. He suggested that it would not be necessary to involve the market managers (to whom the product managers reported), since they were very busy and had been resistant to similar changes in procedures in the past. Trott, in turn, said that he would ask Jed Burns, vice president of Sales, to appoint a representative from Sales to the task force. He also suggested that two others, in addition to Bacon, be assigned from Corporate Planning. The first was Vicki Reiss, a young Harvard MBA, whom Trott felt would add analytic strength to the group; and the second was Robert Holt, a man in his middle 50s, whom Trott thought would add balance because he was an old-timer and would be able to relate well to the product managers. Trott also added that he would ask Dr. Russell Cornelius, vice president of economic analysis, to appoint a representative from his group.

The three then agreed that the task force would report back to Trott, Casey, and the market managers on August 4. After the August 4 presentation, Trott would arrange for a subsequent presentation to the president and chairman of the board later in the month.

Initial Meeting of the Task Force

A week after his discussion with Trott and Casey, Bacon had his first meeting with the newly appointed task force. In addition to himself, Vicki Reiss, and Robert Holt, it included the three product managers from the Marketing Division, Randy Meir, an economic analyst from Dr. Cornelius' group, and Emile Bodin, a special assistant to the vice president of Sales. (See Exhibit 2 for the names and positions of the task force members.)

The three product managers were all men in their middle to late 40s; all were obviously uneasy at the beginning of the meeting. Bacon had had few prior contacts with them and did not know them well. By contrast, he knew Vicki Reiss and Robert Holt fairly well because they also worked for Trott in Corporate Planning. Bacon had previously worked with Reiss and had come to admire her analytic ability, quickness, and perceptiveness. Although he had never worked directly with Holt, he knew that Holt was widely respected within the company for his competence, knowledge, and thoughtfulness.

Randy Meir, the representative from the Economic Analysis and Forecasting group, was a Wharton MBA and a contemporary of Bacon and Reiss. Bacon had once worked with Meir on a project before Meir had been transferred from Corporate Planning to Cornelius' group. Bacon had found this experience to be less than satisfying, and he and Meir disagreed over several issues while working together.

Emile Bodin, the representative from the Sales Division, was in his late 50s and had spent almost all his career in sales. His last five years had been as a troubleshooter, and special assistant to the vice president of Sales. Bodin, like Holt, was well-liked and widely respected within the company.

The meeting had a slow and awkward beginning, with Emile Bodin, Vicki Reiss, and the three product managers saying almost nothing. In contrast, Randy Meir was quite vocal and emphatic about the need to develop a model for the internal forecasting process. Meir argued that it was essential for the task force to identify the basic assumptions on which the present product demand forecasts were based, and then to make a model of the entire process. Reiss finally interrupted Meir to say that although she agreed a forecasting model might be useful in the future, she thought the creation of such a model should not be the task force's purpose. Rather, it might be one of the recommendations that the task force might make based on what they found. She also added that it was much more difficult to develop a single-firm forecasting model than it was to develop the macroeconomic models that Dr. Cornelius and his group worked with.

After a long pause, Robert Holt suggested that the task force divide up its work so that he and the three product managers could concentrate on the

Exhibit 1 Simplified Organization Chart

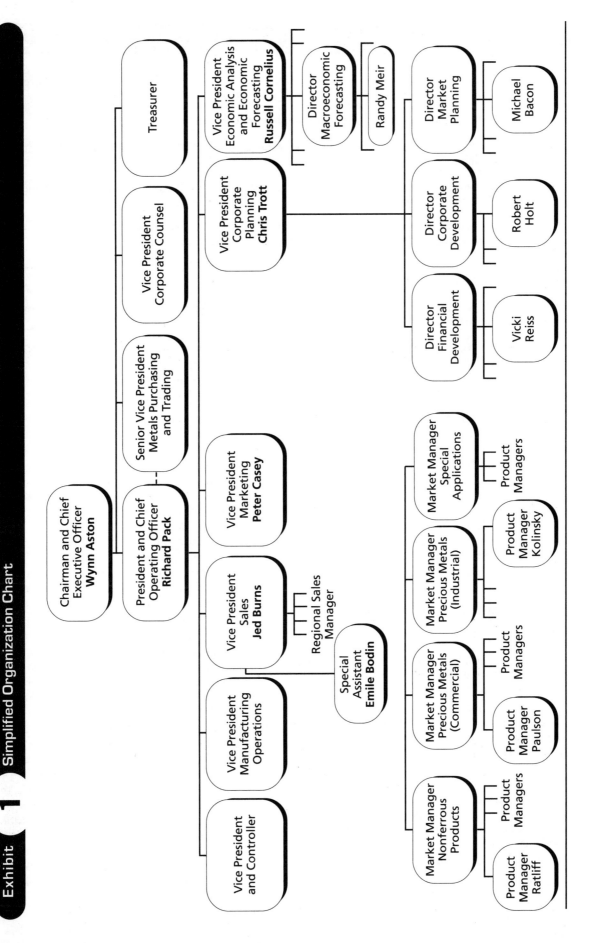

Exhibit 2: Members of the Forecasting Task Force

Michael Bacon, 28, chairman: Market planning analyst and assistant to the vice president of Corporate Planning; (Stanford MBA).

Vicki Reiss, 27: Financial planning analyst; representative of Corporate Planning; (Harvard MBA).

Robert Holt, 54: Corporate development specialist; representative of Corporate Planning; (B.S., Missouri School of Mines, Rolla).

Peter Ratliff, 47: Product manager (Nonferrous Products Market Group); representative of Marketing Division; (B.S., Wayne State).

Charles Paulson, 43: Product manager (Precious Metals, Commercial Applications Market Group); representative of Marketing Division; (B.S., Illinois Institute of Technology).

David Kolinsky, 48: Product manager (Precious Metals, Industrial Applications Market Group); representative of Marketing Division; (M.S., City University of New York).

Emile Bodin, 58: Special assistant to the vice president of Sales; representative of the Sales Division; (B.M.S., Massachusetts Maritime Academy).

Randy Meir, 29: Economic analyst; representative of the Economic Analysis and Economic Forecasting Group; (Wharton MBA).

Marketing Division and Meir could concentrate on gathering whatever hard data he felt were necessary for a model. Bacon thought that this was a good idea. He then asked Vicki Reiss and Emile Bodin if they would be willing to concentrate on the Sales Division's inputs into the forecast. Reiss and Bodin exchanged ideas briefly and then agreed to take responsibility for this part of the project. Shortly thereafter the meeting adjourned, the consensus being that individual subgroups would stay in contact with Bacon.

Preparation of the Task Force Report

In the following five weeks, Bacon spent much of his time working with Holt and the three product managers on the Marketing Division's part of the study and with Reiss and Emile Bodin on the Sales Division's part. Holt and the product managers worked well together and Bacon found his meetings with them to be enjoyable and at times exciting. He also found that he, Reiss, and Bodin enjoyed working together and that the three of them were making considerable progress in identifying how the regional sales managers prepared the sales estimates for the vice president of Sales (which in turn constituted the Sales Division's inputs to the market managers).

Meir, on the other hand, spent most of his time traveling to the various sales offices gathering data on historic sales trends, as well as interviewing all of the product managers in the company headquarters. Bacon's exchanges with Meir were brief and infrequent and occasionally strained. Bacon suspected that Meir resented Bacon's more rapid progress within the company. He had also heard through the grapevine that Meir's boss, Dr. Cornelius, was disturbed that he had not been asked by Aston to look at the forecasting problem, or by Trott and Casey to head the task force. Several of Meir's comments reinforced Bacon's suspicions, since Meir made it clear that the internal product demand forecasting should be done by Cornelius' group instead of the market managers.

By July 23, Bacon felt that the group had made enough progress to report back to Trott, Casey, and the market managers. The next day, he called the members of the task force together to share their findings and to discuss a strategy for presenting their recommendations to Casey and Trott on August 4. All of the task force members attended, except Meir who was in New York City gathering sales data and could not make the meeting. Holt and the three product managers were quite enthusiastic about several recommendations that they were sure would improve the quality of the product-demand forecasts. Bodin and Reiss also reported that they had found what they described as some systematic biases in the Sales Division's inputs into the forecast. They felt that they needed more time, however, before they could make any specific recommendations. They did think that they could make some recommendations of a general nature at the August 4 presentation.

After the meeting ended, Emile Bodin took Bacon aside and explained that the information he had on how the regional managers made their sales estimates was quite sensitive, and that he needed to discuss it with Jed Burns, the vice president of Sales, before proceeding further. Bodin said that he would first prepare a report of his findings for only Bacon and Reiss to look at; then, after the three had discussed it, he would take the report to Burns. He said that he did not yet have all the information necessary and that the report would probably not be ready before the August 4 presentation. He also added that it would take several discussions with Burns before his findings could be presented to the rest of the task force since he thought his report would place the Sales Division in an embarrassing situation. He expected, however, that once Burns understood the report and its implications, some significant changes could be made to improve the Sales Division's inputs into the market manager's forecasts. He also felt that Burns would support these recommendations. Reiss joined Bodin and Bacon partway through their conversation, and she concurred that all of this work could not possibly be completed by August 4. She suggested that their general recommendations be followed up at a later date with more specific recommendations after Bodin had discussed his report with Burns.

During the following week Robert Holt and the product managers spent most of their time preparing for the presentation, while Emile Bodin worked as rapidly as he could on his report for Burns. Vicki Reiss, in addition to consulting with Bodin on the report, concentrated on preparing some general recommendations about the Sales Division's input into the forecast.

Bacon had spoken with Meir as soon as he returned from New York and briefed him on the results of the earlier meeting. Meir agreed to outline a proposal for the development of an internal planning model as his part of the August 4 presentation. Meir added that gathering his data had been a frustrating experience, and that he suspected that the regional sales managers were hiding information from him.

The August 4 Report of the Task Force

Prior to the task force's oral presentation on August 4, Bacon, Holt, and the three product managers agreed that Holt should be the one to report his subgroup's findings and recommendations. The three product managers felt that if they made the presentation, it would put them in an awkward position with their bosses, the market managers, because several of their conclusions were critical in nature. Bacon agreed with this strategy; he also decided (with the approval of the other members of the task force) on a tentative agenda. The plan was for Bacon to begin the oral report with a 15-minute summary of the group's purpose, what they saw as the general problems, and their major recommendations. He was to be followed by Meir, who would recommend that an internal forecasting model be developed to assist the market managers in making their individual product-demand forecasts. Meir would also report on the historic sales data and on what he thought were the critical, underlying assumptions that needed to be clarified in developing an internal forecasting model. Then, Holt would report his subgroup's findings on how the Marketing Division should restructure its procedures for making future product-demand forecasts. After Holt's report was completed, Reiss would present her general recommendations concerning the Sales Division's inputs into the product-demand forecasts.

The presentation was scheduled to last from 10:00 A.M. to 1:00 P.M. in Peter Casey's office. Bacon arrived at his own office at 8:00 A.M. to go over his notes and slides. Shortly after 9:00 A.M., Emile Bodin came into Bacon's office with a copy of the report he had been working on all week. Bodin had stayed up most of the night typing it himself so that Bacon could see it before going into the meeting. Bacon skimmed the six summary statements on the first page and was indeed surprised by what they said. It was clear that the regional sales managers were consistently overstating their sales estimates in order to insure adequate inventory and rapid delivery. He called Reiss on the telephone and the three decided to discuss Bodin's report the next day, but not to report any of its findings at the presentation.

The presentation began promptly at 10:00 A.M. Everyone seemed very much at ease, except for the three product managers. The meeting went smoothly until Meir finished his portion of the presentation. Meir asked if there were any questions, and one of the market managers said he hoped that what the others had to say would be more relevant than Meir's recommendations. He added, "You guys in Cornelius' group can't even forecast what the economy is going to do; how the hell are your models going to tell me what our customers are going to do?" The other market managers laughed at this remark, and to save Meir further embarrassment, Bacon said that Meir's recommendations would make more sense after the market managers heard the other reports.

Holt then presented the report on the Marketing Division's procedures for forecasting product demand and the task force's recommendations on how they should be changed. During Holt's presentation, the product managers asked him several questions of a clarifying nature, which Bacon felt were useful in getting certain points across to the market managers. At the conclusion of Holt's presentation, Paulson, one of the product managers, said that all three of them felt that the conclusions and recommendations were sound, and that they were prepared as individuals to stand solidly behind them and take personal responsibility for their consequences.

Following this remark, Casey, the vice president of Marketing, asked his market managers what they thought of Holt's presentation. One of them said he thought the recommendations might improve the forecasts, while the other three said that the recommendations could not possibly work. Their comments included such arguments as the recommendations would not allow enough room for necessary subjective factors, and that the new procedures would involve too much red tape. The discussion became quite heated, with most of the questions being addressed to Holt. Several times the product managers were cut off by their bosses, in their attempts to answer the questions or clarify certain points. Finally, one of the marketing managers said to Holt, "Robert, frankly, I'm amazed that this kind of nonsense could come from you. I would expect it from a tenderfoot like Bacon or Reiss or Meir, but from you? You've been around here long enough to know our business better than to come up with this nonsense." A second market manager added, "Look, I'm just getting things under control again so we won't lose money next quarter. The last thing I need is this garbage." He then turned to Casey and said, "In no way am I going to swallow this stuff." Casey began to respond, when Trott interrupted to say that he thought tempers were hot and that the recommendations were not as controversial as they might first appear to be. He suggested that the meeting be adjourned until 3:00 P.M. to give everyone a chance to cool off and think things over. Casey agreed that the suggestion was a good one and the meeting ended at 11:30 A.M.

Trott asked Bacon to remain after everyone else had left. Trott then closed the door and said to Bacon, "We've got one hell of a mess here, and you better figure out what you're going to do at 3:00. In the meantime, Casey and I will put our heads together and see what we can come up with." Bacon picked up his notes and left.

When Bacon returned to his own office, he found Meir sitting at his desk thumbing through the report that Emile Bodin had left for him earlier in the morning. Bacon explained that the report had been loaned confidentially to Bacon for study purposes only, and that Bodin had to discuss the report with his boss before presenting it to the full task force. Bacon added that none of the report data would be presented in the afternoon meeting, except in the most general terms. He said that it was important to respect Bodin's wishes and that the report would be shared with the task force when the time was right. Meir responded by saying that Bodin's data would certainly have made his own task much easier; he suspected all along that the regional sales managers had been withholding information from him. Meir added that he was angry that he had not received more support from Bacon and Reiss when the market managers had attacked him during the morning meeting. Bacon explained his rationale for wanting to move the discussion on to another topic—one of his reasons for doing so was to get Meir out of the tough spot that he was in. He said he was sorry that Meir had interpreted it as a lack of support. Meir accepted his apology and left.

A few moments later, Reiss came in to ask Bacon to join her for lunch. The two spent most of their lunch discussing what Bacon should do when the meeting reconvened at 3:00 P.M. After lunch, Reiss accompanied Bacon back to his office where they found Dr. Cornelius waiting at Bacon's door. Cornelius said that he wanted some information on two of the points that Bodin had made on the first page of his report. Bacon noticed that Cornelius was holding a piece of yellow lined paper with Bodin's six major points written on it. Cornelius stated that he needed this information for a meeting that he had scheduled for 4:00 P.M. with Jed Burns, the Sales vice president (and Bodin's boss), to get "some real progress going on the forecasting problem." Bacon replied that it was impossible to give him that data, and that the report was considered confidential. Cornelius smiled and asked how company information could be thought of as confidential when it was a corporate vice president who was asking for it. Cornelius left by saying that he would get the information he needed from Burns himself when they met at 4:00 P.M.

Reiss who had overheard Bacon's exchange with Cornelius, seemed incredulous at what had transpired. Bacon explained that Meir had seen the report before lunch and that he had explained its confidentiality to him. Meir had presumably understood the situation, although he had not actually said that he would keep it confidential. Reiss was by now quite angry, and said that if Emile Bodin was in any way hurt or compromised by this turn of events, it would be Bacon's responsibility. She said that Bodin had taken a personal risk in sharing the information with them and that if Bodin ended up in trouble because of it, Bacon's word would not be "worth a plugged nickel" in the future. Bacon attempted to again explain what had happened, but Reiss cut him off by saying, "You've got a problem, man, which you'd better fix in a hurry."

6.1 Major Players in the Case

Wynn Aston III—CEO and Chairman of the Board
Peter Casey—VP Marketing
Chris Trott—VP Corporate Planning
Richard Pack—President and COO
Jed Burns—VP Sales
Russell Cornelius—VP Economic Analysis
Michael Bacon, Task Force Leader—Corporate Planning
Vicki Reiss, Harvard MBA—Corporate Planning
Robert Holt, old-timer—Corporate Planning
Randy Meir, Wharton MBA—Economic Analyst
Emile Bodin, old-timer—Special Assistant to the VP Sales
Peter Ratliff, Charles Paulson, David Kolinsky—Product Managers

Source: This material has been adapted from James Ware. 1983. Managing a Task Force. In L. A. Schlesinger, R. G. Eccles, and J. J. Gabarro (eds.), *Managing Behavior in Organizations: Texts, Cases, and Readings* (pp. 16–126). New York: McGraw-Hill.

6.2 Tips on Task Force Management

I. **Getting Started**
   A. Think strategically about whether a task force is needed to carry out the assignment.
   B. Clarify the task, the objectives, and the output of the task force. Is the task force to conduct a preliminary investigation, engage in problem solving, or implement an agreed-upon change?
   C. Meet with management to go over goals, purpose, and final products. To follow up, write a memo summarizing project objectives and ask the managers to react to it.
   D. Meet with management to determine task force resources and operating guidelines.
      - How many members? Full- or part-time?
      - When should the task be completed?
      - How often will the team leader meet with management?
      - What information will be available to the team?
      - How much decision-making power has been delegated to the team?
      - What will the team's budget be?
   E. Select task force members carefully. Members should have:
      - Task knowledge

- Problem-solving and decision-making skills
- Interpersonal and team skills
- Organizational influence and credibility
- Ability to represent all areas that will be affected by the team's work
- Time to devote to the team and an interest in the problem

F. Manage boundary processes.
- Clarify who will evaluate and receive the team's proposals.
- Do a political environmental scan—whose interests are at stake and how much power does each interest have to block or support proposals?
- Meet with the major interests to get their expectations and suggestions for the task force.
- Scan for needed resources and begin to negotiate for them.

G. Prepare for the first meeting.
- Ask the commissioning managers to attend.
- Review all that you know about the problem, resources, members, and outside interests.
- If possible meet with team members to determine initial reactions.
- Take a first pass at defining the often ill-structured problem.

II. Conducting the First Meeting

A. Start with commissioning managers to discuss the importance of the task force and its work.

B. Get members to introduce themselves.

C. Reach a common understanding of the team's task and goals.
- Encourage everyone to participate.
- Achieve general agreement on the nature of the problem.
- Prevent a premature consensus on a solution.
- Test the team's view of the problem with key outsiders.
- Develop a sense of joint responsibility and appropriate next steps.

D. Define working procedures and relationships.
- The frequency and nature of full task force meetings
- The need for subgroups and, if needed, their structure
- Ground rules for communication and decision making between meetings
- Decision-making and conflict-resolution norms
- Schedules and deadlines
- Ground rules for dealing with sensitive issues
- Procedures for monitoring and reporting progress
- A process to critique and modify processes and procedures
- A procedure for boundary management

III. Running the Task Force

A. Manage internal team dynamics.
- Hold full task force meetings often enough to keep all members informed and up-to-date on team progress.
- Meet with all subgroups and encourage appropriate team process principles.
- Do not align yourself with any one position or subgroup too early.
- Set interim project deadlines.
- Be sensitive to conflicting loyalties created by task force membership.
- Bring in new information and challenge team assumptions.
- Spend part of every meeting assessing how well the team is carrying out its task.

B. Manage external dynamics.
- Keep externals informed; use them to deal with other key outside constituencies to clarify or negotiate conflicts.
- Appraise key external interests beforehand of what will be presented in public meetings; get their reactions and help them to understand who might be opposed, and see if they are willing to go to bat for your recommendations in the face of expected opposition.
- Offer to help team members with their boundary or constituency problems—a letter of support, joint visits, take the blame, "side payments."

IV. Bringing the Project to Completion

- Prepare a tentative outline of the report and circulate it among team members.
- Try to reach team consensus before presenting any recommendations.
- Carefully plan and organize the final presentation.
- Rehearse the presentation to obtain feedback and fine-tune key points.
- Brief key managers and other constituencies before the final presentation to prevent defensive reactions and rejection of the proposal. If necessary, negotiate changes to make the proposal more acceptable.
- Plan two meetings: one to summarize findings and recommendations and one to decide upon action.
- Remember to praise and reward team members and outsiders who have put a lot of time and energy into the report.

Source: This material has been adapted from James Ware. 1983. Managing a Task Force. In L. A. Schlesinger, R. G. Eccles, and J. J. Gabarro (eds.), *Managing Behavior in Organizations: Texts, Cases, and Readings* (pp. 16–126). New York: McGraw-Hill.

Teams in Organizations

ELECTIVE

Module 6

The Comparative Advantage of X-Teams

by Deborah Ancona, Henrik Bresman and Katrin Kaeufer

The current environment demands a new brand of team—one that emphasizes outreach to stakeholders and adapts easily to flatter organizational structures, changing information and increasing complexity.

Often teams that seem to be doing everything right—establishing clear roles and responsibilities, building trust among members, defining goals—nevertheless see their projects fail or get axed. We know one such team that had a highly promising product. But because team members failed to get buy-in from division managers, they saw their project starve for lack of resources. Another group worked well as a team but didn't gather important competitive information; its product was obsolete before launch.

Why do bad things happen to good teams? Our research suggests that they are too inwardly focused and lacking in flexibility. Successful teams emphasize outreach to stakeholders both inside and outside their companies. Their entrepreneurial focus helps them respond more nimbly than traditional teams to the rapidly changing characteristics of work, technology and customer demands.

These new, externally oriented, adaptive teams, which we call *X-teams*, are seeing positive results across a wide variety of functions and industries. One such team in the oil business has done an exceptional job of disseminating an innovative method of oil exploration throughout the organization. Sales teams have brought in more revenue. Drug-development teams have been more adept at getting external technology into their companies. Product development teams have been more innovative—and have been more often on time and on budget.

The current environment—with its flatter organizational structures, interdependence of tasks and teams, constantly revised information and increasing complexity—requires a networked approach. X-teams have emerged to meet that need. In some cases, they appear spontaneously. In other cases, forward-looking companies have established specific organizational incentives to support X-teams and their high performance levels.

Our studies all support the notion that the rules handed down by best-selling books on high-performing teams need to be revised. (See "About the Research.") Teams that succeed today don't merely work well around a conference table or create team spirit. In fact, too much focus inside the team can be fatal. Instead, teams must be able to adapt to the new competitive landscape, as X-teams do. X-teams manage across boundaries—lobbying for resources, connecting to new change initiatives, seeking up-to-date information and linking to other groups inside and outside the company. Research shows that X-teams often outperform their traditional counterparts.[1]

Five Components That Make X-Teams Successful

X-teams are set apart from traditional teams by five hallmarks: external activity, extensive ties, expandable structures, flexible membership and internal mechanisms for execution.

External Activity

The first hallmark of the X-team is members' external activity.[2] Members manage across boundaries, reaching into the political, informational and task-specific

---

Source: Reprinted from "The Comparative Advantage of X-Teams" by Deborah Ancona, Henrik Bresman, and Katrin Kaeufer, *MIT Sloan Management Review*, Spring, 2002, pp. 3–39, by permission of the publisher. Copyright © 2002 by Massachusetts Institute of Technology. All rights reserved. **Deborah Ancona** is the Seley Distinguished Professor in Management at MIT Sloan School of Management, where **Henrik Bresman** is a doctoral candidate and **Katrin Kaeufer** is a visiting scholar. Contact the authors at ancona@mit.edu, hbresman@mit.edu and kaeufer@mit.edu.

1 D.L. Gladstein, "Groups in Context: A Model of Task Group Effectiveness," *Administrative Science Quarterly* 29 (December 1984): 499–517; D.G. Ancona and D.F. Caldwell, "Bridging the Boundary: External Activity and Performance in Organizational Teams," *Administrative Science Quarterly* 37 (December 1992): 634–665; D.G. Ancona and D.F. Caldwell, "Demography and Design: Predictors of New Product Team Performance," *Organization Science* 33 (August 1992): 321–341; D.G. Ancona, "Outward Bound: Strategies for Team Survival in an Organization," *Academy of Management Journal* 33 (June 1990): 334-365; D.G. Ancona and D.F. Caldwell, "Compose Teams to Assure Successful Boundary Activity," in *The Blackwell Handbook of Principles of Organizational Behavior*, ed. E.A. Locke (Oxford: Blackwell, 2000), 199–210; D.G. Ancona and K. Kaeufer, "The Outer-Net Team," working paper, MIT Sloan School of Management, Cambridge, Massachusetts, 2001; and H.M. Bresman, "External Sourcing of Core Technologies and the Architectural Dependency of Teams," working paper 4215-01, MIT Sloan School of Management, Cambridge, Massachusetts, November 2001.

2 Ancona, "Bridging the Boundary," 634–665.

About the Research

Our research occurred over many years and with many types of teams and industries. The bottom line is that certain team characteristics coincided with better performance. We call the high-performing teams X-teams.

When we asked some managers with responsibility for consulting teams to rate teams with X-team characteristics, they ranked them high—1 or 2 on a 5-point scale, with 1 being the best performer. But they ranked more-traditional teams 3, 4 or 5.* In another study, 37% of X-team customers said that the teams were meeting customer needs better than in the past, compared with 23% of more traditional teams' customers.†

Teams in two companies we call Zeus and Pharma Inc. are of particular interest.

Zeus. Swallow is a product-development team at Zeus, a multidivisional company developing proprietary hardware and software products. It is especially illustrative of X-team activity. Zeus has since been acquired by one of the world's largest computer makers.

Pharma Inc. Pharma is a large international pharmaceuticals enterprise. At the time of our research, it had experienced a string of mergers and acquisitions that resulted in drugs being developed by different organizational units, each of which had a distinctly different management approach. The unit with the best-performing teams illustrates organizational characteristics conducive to X-team behavior.

Type of Company	Number of Teams	Length of Times Studied	Methodology
One telecommunications company	100	4 months	Interviews, survey
One educational-consulting company	5	1 year	Interviews, surveys, logs, observation
Five high-tech, product-development companies	45	2 years	Interviews, surveys, logs, observation
One multinational, integrated oil company	2	Life of the teams	Project reports
One computer manufacturer	5	2 years	Interviews, observation
One large pharmaceuticals company, 3 units	12	2 years	Interviews, survey, observation, project reports

* D.G. Ancona, "Outward Bound: Strategies for Team Survival in an Organization," *Academy of Management Journal* 33 (June 1990): 334–365.

† For the product-development teams, using X-team characteristics as predictors of adherence to budget and schedule—and innovation, as rated by managers—yielded statistically significant results at greater than .01.

structures around them. In some cases, the team leader takes on the outreach; in other cases, it is shared by everyone. High levels of external activity are key, but effectiveness depends on knowing when to use the particular kind called for: ambassadorship, scouting or task coordination.

It doesn't matter how technically competent a team is if the most relevant competency is the ability to lobby for resources with top management. And even resources mean little without an ability to reach outsiders who have the knowledge and information to help team members apply the resources effectively. Thus at any given time, any X-team member may be conducting one or more of the three external activities.

Ambassadorial activity. Ambassadorial activity is aimed at managing upward—that is, marketing the project and the team to the company power structure, maintaining the team's reputation, lobbying for resources, and keeping track of allies and competitors. Ambassadorial activity helps the team link its work to key strategic initiatives; and it alerts team members to shifting organizational strategies and political upheaval so that potential threats can be identified and the damage limited.

For example, the leader of what we call the Swallow team wanted to manufacture a new computer using a revolutionary design. The company's operating committee, however, wanted only a product upgrade. The team leader worked with a key decision maker on the operating committee to portray the benefits of the product to the organization—and eventually got permission for the design. He continued to provide updates on the team's progress, while keeping tabs on the committee's key resource-allocation decisions.

Scouting. Scouting activity helps a team gather information located throughout the company and the industry. It involves lateral and downward searches through the organization to understand who has knowledge and expertise. It also means investigating markets, new technologies and competitor activities. Team members in our studies used many different modes of scouting, from the ambitious and expensive (hiring consultants) to the quick and cheap (having a cup of coffee with an old college professor or spending an hour surfing the Internet).

Effective teams monitor how much information they need—for some, extensive scouting early on to get the lay of the land is all that's needed. For others, scouting continues throughout the life of the team. In particular, teams working with technologies created by outsiders can never relax their scouting activities.

Task coordination. Task-coordinator activity is much more focused than scouting. It's for managing the lateral connections across functions and the interdependencies with other units. Team members negotiate with other groups, trade their services and get feedback on how well their work meets expectations. Task-coordinator activity involves cajoling and pushing other groups to follow through on commitments so that the team can meet its deadlines and keep work flowing. When the Swallow team needed to check some new components quickly and learned that the testing machine was booked, team members explored swapping times with another team, using the machine at night or using machines elsewhere—whatever it took to keep the work on track.

Extensive Ties

In order to engage in such external activity, team members need to have extensive ties with outsiders. Ties that academic researchers call *weak ties* are good for certain purposes—for example, when teams need to round up handy knowledge and expertise within the company. One team we studied gave a senior position to a new hire straight out of graduate school because of his ties to important experts at prestigious academic institutions. The ties were weak but extensive and contributed immensely to the success of the team's project.

Strong ties, however, facilitate higher levels of cooperation and the transfer of complex knowledge. Strong ties are most likely to be forged when relationships are critical to both sides and built over long periods of time.[3] In the case of Swallow, the team leader's prior relationship with the operating-committee member helped snare funding for the revolutionary computer design. And the three team members from manufacturing had ties that smoothed the transition from design to production.

Expandable Tiers

But how to structure a large, complex team? How to combine the identity and separateness of a team with the dense ties and external interactions needed to accomplish today's work? Our research

---

[3] M.S. Granovetter, "The Strength of Weak Ties," *American Journal of Sociology* 78 (May 1973): 360–380; D. Krackhardt, "The Strength of Strong Ties: The Importance of Philos in Organizations," in *Networks and Organizations: Structure, Form and Action*, eds. N. Nohria and R.G. Eccles (Boston: Harvard Business School Press, 1992), 216–239; and M.T. Hansen, "The Search-Transfer Problem: The Role of Weak Ties in Sharing Knowledge Across Organization Subunits," *Administrative Science Quarterly* 44 (March 1999): 82–111.

shows that X-teams operate through three distinct tiers that create differentiated types of team membership—the core tier, operational tier and outernet tier—and that members may perform duties within more than one tier.

The core members. The core of the X-team is often, but not always, present at the start of the team. Core members carry the team's history and identity. While simultaneously coordinating the multiple parts of the team, they create the team strategy and make key decisions. They understand why early decisions were made and can offer a rationale for current decisions and structures. The core is not a management level, however. Core members frequently work beside other members of equal or higher rank, and serve on other X-teams as operational or outer-net members.

The first core member of the Swallow team was the leader; then two senior engineers joined and helped to create the original product design and to choose more members. The core members were committed to the revolutionary computer concept and accepted its risks. They understood how quickly they had to act in order to make an impact on the market. The core members chose more engineers for the team, helped coordinate the work across subgroups, and kept in touch with the company's operating committee and other groups. They decided when to get feedback from outsiders, and they set up a process to make the critical decisions about how compatible with industry standards to make the design. They organized team social events—and when members had to work long hours to make a deadline, they even brought in beds.

Having multiple people in the core helps keep the team going when one or two core members leave, and it allows a core member who gets involved with operational work to hand off core tasks. Teams that lose all their core members at once take many months to get back on track.

The operational members. The team's operational members do the ongoing work. Whether that's designing a computer, creating an academic course or deciding where to drill for oil, the operational members get the job done. They often are tightly connected to one another and to the core (and may include some core members). In the Swallow group, 15 engineers were brought into the operational layer to work on the preliminary design. They made key technical decisions, but each focused on one part of the design and left oversight of the whole to the core.

The outer-net members. Outer-net members often join the team to handle some task that is separable from ongoing work. They may be part-time or part-cycle members, tied barely at all to one another but strongly to the operational or core members. Outer-net members bring specialized expertise, and different individuals may participate in the outer net as the task of the team changes.

For example, when the Swallow team wanted to ensure its initial design made sense to others, it brought in outer-net people from other parts of R&D. For two weeks, the enlarged team met to discuss the design, its potential problems, ideas for changes and solutions for problems that operational members had identified. Then those new members left. Meanwhile, designated members of the core group met weekly with different outer-net members—people from purchasing, diagnostics and marketing—for information sharing, feedback and smoothing the flow of work across groups. Some X-teams' outer nets also include people from other companies.

The three-tier structure is currently in use at a small, entrepreneurial startup we know—except that the employees there say "pigs," "chickens" and "cows" to refer to core, operational and outer-net team members. Think about a bacon-and-eggs breakfast. The pig is committed (he's given his life), the chicken is involved, and the cow provides milk that enhances the meal. The startup's terms are handy for discussing roles and responsibilities. A person might say, "You don't need to do that; you're only a chicken" or "We need this cow to graze here for at least two weeks."

Flexible Membership

X-team membership is fluid.[4] People may move in and out of the team during its life or move across layers. In a product-development team similar to Swallow, there was a manufacturing member who shifted from outer-net member to operational member to core member. At first, he was an adviser about components; next he worked on the actual product; then he organized the whole team when it needed to move the product into manufacturing. He became team leader and managed the transition of team members back into engineering as more manufacturing members were brought in.

Mechanisms for Execution

An increasing focus on the external context does not mean that the internal team processes are unimportant. In fact, traditional coordination

---

[4] D.G. Ancona and D.F. Caldwell, "Rethinking Team Composition From the Outside In," in *Research on Managing Groups and Teams*, ed. D.H. Gruenfeld (Stamford, Connecticut: JAI Press, 1998).

mechanisms such as clear roles and goals may be even more important when team members are communicating externally, membership is changing, and there are different versions of membership. The trick is to avoid getting so internally focused and tied to other team members that external outreach is ignored. X-teams find three different coordination mechanisms especially useful: integrative meetings, transparent decision making and scheduling tools such as shared timelines.

First, through integrative meetings, team members share the external information each has obtained. That helps keep everyone informed and increases the information's value by making it widely available. The meetings ensure that decisions are based on real-time data from combinations of task-coordinator, scouting and ambassadorial activity.

Second, transparent decision making, which keeps people informed about the reasons behind choices, is good for nudging everyone in the same direction and for maintaining motivation. Even when team members are frustrated that a component they have worked on has been dropped, they appreciate knowing about the change and why it has been made. Finally, measures such as clearly communicated but flexible deadlines allow members to pace themselves and to coordinate work with others. The just-in-time flexibility allows for deadline shifts and adjustment. If external circumstances change, then work changes and new deadlines are established.

Putting the Pieces Together

X-team components form a self-reinforcing system. To engage in high levels of external activity, team members bring to the table outside ties forged in past professional experience. To be responsive to new information and new coordination needs, X-teams have flexible membership and a structure featuring multiple tiers and roles. To handle information and multiple activities, they have coordination mechanisms and a strong core. The five components cannot work in isolation. They complement one another. Although small or new teams may not have all five components, fully developed X-teams usually do.

Supporting X-Teams

The more dependent a team is on knowledge and resources in its external environment, the more critical is the organizational context. Companies that want high-performing X-teams can create a supportive organizational context—with three-tier structures mandated for teams, explicit decision rules, accessible information and a learning culture. Within a company, it's generally the organizational unit that sets those parameters, provides resources and lays down rules. (See "Creating an X-Team.")

A large pharmaceuticals company that we call Pharma Inc. illustrates the importance of such support. One of the authors was asked to investigate a dramatic performance variation among drug-development teams that were working on molecules from external sources. (Such projects are known as in-licensing projects.) A performance assessment showed that the teams of one unit were doing well, the teams of a second unit showed varying results, and the teams of a third unit were doing poorly. To probe the differences, we picked a chronological sequence of three teams at the best-performing site (the Alpha site) and three teams at the worst-performing site (the Omega site) for a careful study.

The story that emerged seemed almost implausibly black-and-white: All the central steps the three Alpha teams took seemed to contribute to positive performance, whereas the opposite was true for the Omega teams. It appeared that despite fluctuating external circumstances, the Omega teams were sticking to a traditional approach that had served them well enough when they worked on internally developed molecules. The Alpha teams, however, were adapting to the changing environment by using an X-team approach, although they didn't call it that. In the wake of the molecular biology revolution, which has led to increased use of in-licensed molecules, they saw the importance of external activity and extensive ties, and they adapted.

Three-Tier Structure

Organizational structure has a profound effect on team behavior. All Alpha-unit teams used a mandated three-tier structure that gave core members oversight of the activities of operational and outer-net team members. Importantly, the roles were not a reflection of organizational hierarchy. Often a core-team member was junior in the organizational structure to an outer-net member.

Having the core team tied to the outer net was particularly helpful when much external technical knowledge was needed quickly. With links already established, a core member could get information from an outer-net member at short notice. The brief time commitment for serving on the outer net gave X-teams access to some of the company's most sought-after and overbooked functional experts.

The Omega-unit teams, however, used a traditional one-tier structure. In X-team terminology, the Omega teams had only core members. Although that worked well for coordination, it hampered team members' ability to adapt to changing external demands.

Explicit Decision Rules

X-teams favor decision rules that adapt to new circumstances. The Alpha unit's X-teams, like most

X-Teams Versus Traditional Teams: Five Components

Traditional Teams	X-teams
Internal Focus — Focus on trust, cohesion and effective work processes	**External Activity** — Combination of internal and external activity
Ties to Other Members — Efforts to build close ties and strong identity	**Extensive Ties** — Internal ties supplemented with both strong and weak ties outside the team (and inside and outside the company)
One Tier — One structural tier: team versus environment	**Expandable Tiers** — Core, operational and outer-net tiers
Stable Membership — Leaders and members	**Flexible Membership** — Movement across tiers—and in and out of the team
Mechanism for Execution — Coordination among individuals	**Mechanism for Execution** — Coordination among tiers

product development teams, used traditional flow charts, but they constantly updated them. Also, they complemented flow charts with decision rules that allowed the charts to become evolving tools rather than constraints. One such rule was that, all things being equal, the search for solid information was more important than speed. It wasn't that the teams tolerated slackers. In fact, at times speed had to take precedence over information, but it was the team leader's responsibility to identify when that should occur.

Another rule mandated that whenever important expertise was not available in the time allotted, a team member would be free to bring in additional outer-net members. Such rules allowed for flexibility but spared team members any ambiguity about what to do at important crossroads. Furthermore, the rules gave them the confidence to act on their own and to raise issues needing discussion. For example, it was never wrong for a team member to suggest that a process be stopped because of a lack of important information in that member's area. Even if the team overruled the request, speaking up on the basis of an explicit decision rule was definitely appropriate.

The Omega unit's teams, by contrast, used process flow charts quite rigidly and without complementary decision rules. Team members had to stick to the planned process and were allowed little latitude for tweaking the process even when they saw the need. There was no mechanism for making adjustments.

Creating an X-Team

Staffing the Team
- Before staffing the team, understand the external context
- Change team members as needed
- Treat a team member's connections as a key competency

Building the Team
- Map the external domain, including key stakeholders
- Create mechanisms for internal *and* external communication
- Set team goals, knowing what external constituencies want

Create a Supportive Organizational Environment
- Design and support a three-tier team structure
- Formulate decision rules for an unambiguous yet flexible process
- Maintain a rich information infrastructure
- Establish a learning culture

X-Team

Accessible Information

Access to valid, up-to-date information is always critical, but when knowledge is widely dispersed, the information infrastructure becomes even more important. The Alpha unit had processes that supported teams' need for accessible data. After every project, a report was written detailing important issues and the lessons learned. The store of reports increased over time. In addition, the Alpha unit maintained a "know-who" database, which provided names of experts in various fields and explained the unit's historical relationship with those experts.

Unfortunately, at Omega, project reports were written only occasionally and contained mainly the results of internal lab tests. And Omega did not have a know-who database at all.

A Learning Culture

A useful information infrastructure cannot be established instantly. It has to be nurtured. That's why Alpha insisted on project reports whether or not the project was considered a success and regardless of time pressures on team members. Alpha also saw to it that past team members conferred with ongoing teams.

Strong recognition from top management at the Alpha unit reinforced the information infrastructure. The relentlessly communicated learning culture not only generated positive performance for any given team, but helped make every team perform better than the previous one.

The Omega unit had no such practices. As a consequence, new teams in that unit generally had to reinvent the wheel.

Is the X-Team for Your Company?

X-teams are particularly valuable in today's world (many companies already deploy X-teams without calling them that), but they are not for every situation. Their very nature as tools for responding to change makes them hard to manage. The membership of the X-team, the size of the team, the goals and so on keep fluctuating.

In a traditional team, coordination is mostly internal to the team. It involves a clear task and the interaction of a limited number of members. In an X-team, coordination requirements are multiplied severalfold. The X-team's internal coordination involves more members, more information and more diversity. On top of that are the external-coordination concerns. Executives considering X-teams must be sure the potential benefits are great enough for them to justify the extra challenges.

The IDEO product-development consulting firm thinks they are. IDEO, based in Palo Alto, California, is an example of a company that depends on the innovativeness and agility of its teams. During brainstorming, experts from multiple industries serve as outer-net members soliciting unique information. Team members go forth as "anthropologists" to observe how customers use their products and how the products might be improved. Employees at IDEO also have been busy creating a knowledge-distribution system they call Tool Box, which uses lively demonstrations to communicate learned knowledge and expertise.[5]

We recommend using an X-team when one or more of three conditions hold true. X-teams are appropriate, first, when organizational structures are flat, spread-out systems with numerous alliances rather than multilevel, centralized hierarchies. Flat organizations force teams to become more entrepreneurial in getting resources and in seeking and maintaining buy-in from stakeholders.[6]

Second, X-teams are advised when teams are dependent on information that is complex, externally dispersed and rapidly changing. In such cases, it is critical to base decisions on realtime data.[7]

Third, use X-teams when a team's task is interwoven with tasks undertaken outside the team. For example, if every new product that a team works on is part of a family of products that others are working on too, teams need to coordinate their activities with what is going on around them.[8]

Increasingly, modern society is moving in a direction in which all three conditions are routinely true. That's why we believe that, ready or not, more organizations will have to adopt the X-team as their modus operandi.

---

5 R. Sutton and A.B. Hargadon, "Brainstorming Groups in Context: Effectiveness in a Product Design Firm," *Administrative Science Quarterly* 41 (December 1996): 685–718.
6 For a recent interpretation of power dynamics in organizations, see G. Yukl, "Use Power Effectively," in *The Blackwell Handbook of Principles of Organization Behavior*, ed. E.A. Locke (Oxford: Blackwell, 2000), 241–256.
7 Consistent with this logic, John Austin convincingly demonstrated how team members' knowledge of the location of distributed information has a positive impact on performance. See J.R. Austin, "Knowing What and Whom Other People Know: Linking Transactive Memory with External Connections in Organizational Groups" (Academy of Management Best Paper Proceedings, Toronto, August 2000).
8 For an insightful account of how different tasks require different models of team management, see K.M. Eisenhardt and B. Tabrizi, "Accelerating Adaptive Processes: Product Innovation in the Global Computer Industry," *Administrative Science Quarterly* 40 (March 1995): 84–110.

Index

ambassadorial activities, 8, 9, 10, 24
Aston, Wynn III, 11–12, 14
Aston-Blair case study, 11–17

Bacon, Michael, 11–17
Bodin, Emile, 12–17
boundary management
    overview, 4–5
    activities and processes of, 8–10
    Aston-Blair case study, 11–17
    definition of, 4
    importance of, 4, 8, 9, 10
    rules of the game, 10
    styles of, 8–9
    task force management tips, 17–19
    X-teams, 22–29
boundary-spanning, by X-teams, 22, 24
Burns, Jed, 12–17

capital, social, 9
Casey, Peter, 11–17
"The Comparative Advantage of X-Teams"
    (Ancona, Bresman, and Kaeufer), 22–29
comprehensive strategy, 9
coordination mechanisms, in X-teams, 25–26
core members, in X-teams, 25
Cornelius, Russell, 12–17
cultural perspective, 10
culture, learning, 28–29

decision making, transparent, 26
decision rules, 26–27
definition of boundary management, 4

economic forecasting, 12, 15
effectiveness model, 4
effectiveness of teams, 9
extensive ties, in X-teams, 24
external activities of X-teams, 22, 24

flat organizations, and X-teams, 29
flexibility in X-team membership, 25
fluid membership, in X-teams, 25
forecasting, economic, 12, 15
forecasting, sales, 11–17

gold, price of, 11

high-performing teams. See X-teams
Holt, Robert, 12–17

IDEO, 29
influence dimension, 8, 10
information, 28–29
information activity, 8, 9, 10

innovation, 8, 22
interviewing, 9
isolationist teams, 9

learning culture, 28–29

macroeconomic forecasting, 12
mechanisms for coordination, in X-teams, 25–26
Meir, Randy, 12–17
membership of X-teams, flexible, 25

networking, and X-teams, 22
new organization model, 9

operational members, of X-teams, 25
organization, team relations with. See boundary
    management
organization of teams, 9
outer-net members, of X-teams, 25

Pack, Richard, 11
Pharma Inc., 23, 26–29
political perspective, 10

Reiss, Vicki, 12–17
relationship of team with organization. See
    boundary management
reputation of teams, 8
rules, decision, 26–27
rules of the game, 10

sales forecasting, 11–17
satisfaction, 9
scheduling tools, in X-teams, 26
scouting activity, 8, 9, 10, 24
social capital, 9
sponsorship, 8
stakeholders, 9, 10
stakeholders model, 10
strategic design, 10
strategy, comprehensive, 9
strong ties, 24
styles of boundary management, 8–9
Swallow team, 23–25

task coordination, 8, 10, 24
task forces
    Aston-Blair case study, 11–17
    definition of, 5
    management tips, 17–19
    nature of, 4
team effectiveness, 4, 9
temporary teams. See task forces
tiers, in X-teams, 24–25, 26
ties, extensive, 24

tips on task force management, 17–19
transparent decision making, 26
Trott, Chris, 11–17

weak ties, 24

X-teams
    overview, 22
    components of, 22, 24–26, 27
    creating, 28
    research parameters, 23
    suitability of, 29
    supporting, 26–29

MANAGING FOR THE FUTURE

Organizational Behavior & Processes

ORGANIZATIONS

Module 7
Workforce Management:
Employment Relationships in
Changing Organizations

Module 8
Managing Change in Organizations

Module 9
Organizational Actions in Complex
Environments

Module 10
Learning Across Borders:
Disneyland on the Move

Ancona • Kochan • Scully
Van Maanen • Westney

MANAGING FOR THE FUTURE

Organizational Behavior & Processes

**Workforce Management:
Employment Relationships in
Changing Organizations**

MANAGING FOR THE FUTURE
Organizational Behavior & Processes, Third Edition

Deborah Ancona
Sloan School of Management
Massachusetts Institute of Technology

John Van Maanen
Sloan School of Management
Massachusetts Institute of Technology

Thomas A. Kochan
Sloan School of Management
Massachusetts Institute of Technology

D. Eleanor Westney
Sloan School of Management
Massachusetts Institute of Technology

Maureen Scully
Graduate School of Management
Simmons College

Dedicated to those who have inspired us to try to be better students and teachers.
Special thanks to: Professor Jack Barbash • Professor Arthur H. Gladstein • Professor Marius B. Jansen • Professor Joanne Martin • Professor Edgar H. Schein

VP/Editorial Director
Jack W. Calhoun

VP/Editor-in-Chief
Michael P. Roche

Senior Publisher
Melissa S. Acuña

Executive Editor
John Szilagyi

Senior Developmental Editor
Judith O'Neill

Marketing Manager
Jacquelyn Carrillo

Production Editor
Emily Gross

Manufacturing Coordinator
Rhonda Utley

Compositor
Trejo Production

Printer
Von Hoffmann Press, Inc.
Frederick, MD

Internal Designer
Bethany Casey

Cover Designer
Bethany Casey

Photographs
©PhotoDisc

Design Project Manager
Bethany Casey

COPYRIGHT ©2005
by South-Western, a division of Thomson Learning. Thomson Learning™ is a trademark used herein under license.

Printed in the United States of America
1 2 3 4 5 07 06 05 04 03

For more information contact
South-Western College Publishing,
5191 Natorp Boulevard,
Mason, Ohio, 45040
Or you can visit our Internet site at:
http://www.swlearning.com

ALL RIGHTS RESERVED
No part of this work covered by the copyright hereon may be reproduced or used in any form or by any means—graphic, electronic, or mechanical, including photocopying, recording, taping, Web distribution or information storage and retrieval systems—without the written permission of the publisher.

For permission to use material from this text or product, contact us by
Tel: (800) 730-2214
Fax: (800) 730-2215
http://www.thomsonrights.com

Library of Congress Control Number: 2003113908
ISBN 0-324-05575-7

Contents

Workforce Management: Employment Relationships in Changing Organizations

	Overview	6

Core

Class Note	Managing a Changing Workforce in Turbulent Times	12
The Press	The Changing Social Contract for White-Collar Workers	25
	Building Competitive Advantage Through People	29
	What's Wrong with Management Practices in Silicon Valley? A Lot.	36
	In Silicon Valley, Loyalty Means Paying a High Price; Cultural Strengths Help Offset Loss of Paper Wealth	38

Elective

Case	The Part-Time Partner (A)	44
	The Part-Time Partner Redux: So We Solved the Problem, Didn't We? (B)	52
The Press	Integrating Work and Family Life: A Holistic Approach	54
	Addressing the Crisis in Confidence in Corporations: Root Causes, Victims, and Strategies for Reform	58

Index

Overview

Workforce management is a significant part of a manager's job. You can understand its many dimensions by using the three lenses that guide our analysis of organizations. From the strategic design perspective, managers determine where and how employees work, establish human resource policies and rules governing job duties, compensation, and promotion paths, deploy employees onto one or more teams, and provide incentives. The workforce is viewed as both a major cost and an increasingly important asset and source of competitive advantage to an organization. The manager must therefore find the right balance between investing in this asset for competitive advantage and controlling labor costs.

Employees are more than commodities, however—as everyone from Karl Marx to Peter Drucker has stressed. Workers have their own interests. They generally want the firm to succeed and also want a share of that success. Many want a life that balances work with interests outside of work. In deciding how to work, they take into account their labor market alternatives and bring to bear their personal values, experience, and ideas. When workers take a job, they are investing and putting at risk a portion of their human capital, just as shareholders put at risk their financial capital when investing in a firm. As human capital or knowledge becomes a more important source of value to the firm, we can expect employees to want more information and perhaps a voice in how their interests are reflected, not only in their immediate jobs but in the overall strategy and governance of the firm. From a political perspective, then, the manager's job is to find ways of integrating employees' personal interests and aspirations with the needs of the organization to produce "mutual gains." Managers must negotiate equitable compromises when interests or expectations conflict.

As people work together, the organizational culture evolves, gets passed along, and is sometimes changed. From a cultural perspective, therefore, the art of managing the workforce lies in understanding how a given request, decision, or proposal for change will affect the cherished cultural norms that the workforce has created or the particular norms of a subgroup. All these factors determine how loyal, secure, empowered, and motivated employees will feel—and, ultimately, whether a manager can mobilize his or her group to get the work done.

We approach workforce management through the study of the "employment relationship." The employment relationship is the set of practices that govern the exchange between employees and employers. In its simplest form, employees provide effort toward the achievement of employers' goals and receive compensation in return. In more developed forms of the employment relationship, employees may provide loyalty and extra commitment in exchange for long-term employment, career development, and a sense of belonging. Employees may develop special firm-specific skills and receive a wage premium for remaining with their employer to use and further develop these skills.

Instead of the usual approach, which looks at loyalty and motivation as individual personality traits that a manager works around, this module considers the broader system in which workforce management occurs. Employees' loyalty, commitment, and sense of fairness arise from the structures and incentives that are part of their work world. From a more systemic perspective, we can see how managers must regard the pieces of workforce management as parts of a larger whole.

This module presents historical and international comparative examples. Knowing more about history helps the smart manager to think ahead and see how trends are cyclical. Today's solutions sometimes breed tomorrow's problems. Consider the many corporations that are now scrambling to rehire and rebuild loyalty in the wake of layoffs that were justified not so long ago. The crisis in corporate confidence that has arisen in the aftermath of scandals at Enron, WorldCom, and other highly visible firms is likely to leave a lasting imprint on employees who put their trust in the top executives and managers of their firms and have experienced severe losses in job security, retirement savings, and perhaps personal identity. How this crisis will affect the attitudes and behavior of workers toward future employers and therefore how it will change the task of managing the workforce remain open questions. Resolving those questions and rebuilding trust and confidence in managers and in the firm as an institution in society will be a major challenge and responsibility facing managers and other leaders of American corporations in the twenty-first century.

Knowing more about other countries' arrangements helps the smart manager understand that no single right model or policy is available for structuring employment relations and managing the workforce as determined by technology and markets. Many varieties are on the menu. Managers can try other options more in line with their analyses of situations, their understanding of the broader implications and possible future ramifications, and their values about which stakeholders must be respected.

The larger context for workforce management is characterized by an ongoing but incomplete transformation from old to new organizational forms. During this transformation, managers face special challenges. They must create a committed group of employees in the midst of the insecurity caused by layoffs. They must encourage people to share information and build trust as team members, even as team membership keeps changing in the face of rapidly shifting assignments and downsizing. They have to encourage people with rewards, even as the promise of upward advancement is diminishing, and new lateral moves and broad job titles are still vague and not as highly valued as promotions.

How can you, as a manager, take action in this context? The first step toward wisely guided action is to understand the system in which you work and how its many components go together (or sometimes, contradict one another). You may not be able to change your company's policies overnight, but you can be aware of how they are affecting your employees and your performance. You can serve as an agent of change, either individually or by coalescing with other employees and managers experiencing similar problems. Most significant innovations in employment practices, such as the introduction of modern fringe benefits, flexible hours, and other practices to integrate work and family responsibilities came from ideas and pressures exerted from the workforce itself (and sometimes from its representative bodies, such as unions). Thus, managers need to be attentive and responsive to ideas for improving workforce relations from wherever they come from, and, indeed, the manager of the twenty-first century may need to be entreprenuerial by inventing new solutions to better meet the needs of the firm and its employees.

Taking action may sometimes involve pushing back on corporate policies with which you do not agree. You can pick your battles. If you have a broader understanding of the system, you will have better grounds for registering your concerns about negative repercussions and unintended consequences.

If you have read Module 1 on the "new" organization—or if you read the business press and keep up with the coverage of real, and sometimes exaggerated, trends—you are aware that a new model of employment appears to be emerging to replace the old. The old was bounded, hierarchical, fixed, homogeneous, and local, but the new promises to be networked, flat, flexible, diverse, and global. These promises, whether hype or real, affect the way that corporations plan and justify their policies. They shape the context for workforce management.

The following are a few examples of how each of these changing dimensions pose some exciting opportunities that may motivate and empower employees (+), some problems and uncertainties that will make workforce management more difficult (−), and some questions that remain unsolved but that today's manager must understand in order to take well-considered action (?):

- As organizations move from **bounded to networked**:
  + Interesting opportunities will arise for collaboration with new colleagues across boundaries, making work stimulating and providing new opportunities for learning.
  − Careers will involve a patchwork of jobs in different organizations, with some measure of uncertainty and stress, and authority and responsibility for supervision must be shared among managers of different units or even of different organizations.
  ? How can managers maintain loyalty between employees and companies and between employees and teams as memberships are in flux? How can managers ensure that employees' fundamental concerns, such as safety, training and development, and fairness, are attended to when authority is shared among them?

- As organizations move from **hierarchical to flat**:
  + More employees at all levels will have access to decision-critical information and may be involved in projects that were formerly restricted to higher levels.
  − Fewer vertical promotion paths and some confusion about what "career success" means are more evident. And power is more widely dispersed and likely to give rise to more use of influence and power from the bottom up to challenge top-down dictates.
  ? How can managers motivate employees without the traditional promise of promotions (will the promise of more stimulating work become a meaningful reward)? How can managers translate workforce knowledge, motivation, and ideas into a competitive asset?

- As organizations move from **fixed to flexible**:
  + Employees will have a range of ways to organize the time and space in which they work.
  − It may be difficult to coordinate the efforts of employees working under different arrangements.

? How can managers balance flexibility and coordination?
- As organizations move from **homogeneous to diverse**:
  + A range of new approaches to work will be stimulated as new groups are increasingly included.
  - Differences may breed contests between groups over what is fair and who should get what considerations (such as who gets special hours to balance work and family, who gets invited to be in the mentoring program, etc.).
  ? How can managers be responsive to diverse constituencies in ways that respect differences but are also fair and consistent?
- As organizations move from **local to global**:
  + New ways to include multiple stakeholders will be added to the menu (e.g., different national approaches to temporary workers or to employer-provided training or to labor/management relations).
  - The range of choices will make it more challenging to present any one choice as legitimate (e.g., it may be difficult to argue that temporary workers should not get benefits if they are known to in other countries).
  ? How can managers learn from different global examples?

Readings

Core

This module begins with an extended Class Note on the changing employment relationship and the changing workforce, which presents our views of restoring employee loyalty and of defining a new social contract between employers and employees in turbulent times.

Four readings follow the Class Note and expand the discussion, adding contrast and additional perspective. The first reading, "The Changing Social Contract for White-Collar Workers," by Charles Heckscher, addresses what happens as more employees try to redefine themselves as "free agents." The social contract is the moral underpinning of the employment relationship; it is a deep set of assumptions about what is right, reasonable, and fair in the exchange between employees and employers. Lifelong employment was once regarded as a "best practice." The dismantling of lifelong employment options is a breach of the social contract, and a new social contract has not yet emerged.

The second reading, "Building Competitive Advantage Through People," discusses what two leading business strategy professors, Charles Bartlett of Harvard and Sumantra Ghoshal of the London School of Economics, believe organizations need to do to treat human capital as a strategic resource in the twenty-first century, equivalent to the role of financial capital in the twentieth century corporation. It reflects the view that rebuilding the social contract is possible by returning to the basics of good human resource policy and practice. Do you agree?

The third and fourth readings are short articles that discuss employment practices in the heart of the entrepreneurial Silicon Valley. First, Jeffrey Pfeffer critiques a number of prevailing practices found in Silicon Valley firms in "What's Wrong with Management Practices in Silicon Valley? A Lot." Then an article by Alex Berenson from the New York Times describes the practices of Calico Commerce, a company trying to manage through the ups and downs of the high-tech economy.

Elective

In addition to the Core readings, this module includes an optional case that your instructor might ask you to prepare along with some additional readings. The case, "The Part-Time Partner" (Part A) and "The Part-Time Partner Redux" (Part B), grapple with some of the issues managers face with employees' new, flexible arrangements, which create a variety of responses from employees who are affected differently.

To prepare for Part A of this case, consider this scenario:

Imagine that you are a partner at this firm and you have to vote YES or NO in each partnership decision. Analyze the arguments about the partnership decisions in the case and come to class prepared to defend your votes. A vote will be taken at the start of class.

- *Would you vote to make Julie partner? Why or why not?*
- *Would you vote to make Tim partner? Why or why not?*

To prepare for Part B, ask: Haven't we already solved this problem with the policies implemented in response to the issues raised in Part A? What is the problem now? Is this new issue a "solvable" problem?

The first elective reading is a useful complement to "The Part-Time Partner" case. "Integrating Work and Family Life: A Holistic Approach" is a summary of a larger report by a group of work-family researchers and calls for a coordinated effort to address work and family issues. It suggests that this problem cannot be addressed successfully by individuals, families, firms, unions, community groups, or government each acting alone. Instead, by working together to complement each other's efforts, significant progress can be made. As you read it, see whether you agree with this expert group's analysis of the problem and the priorities set in their "Call to Action." Then ask what it would take to get this coordinated approach to happen.

The second elective reading is a short essay that outlines some of the root causes of the crisis in corporate confidence caused by recent scandals and presents ideas on what might be done to better protect workers from bearing the costs of corporate misconduct in the future. It poses some strong public policy recommendations aimed at rebalancing power in corporate governance and employment relations. By staking out a strong position, it seeks to generate a debate. What do you think should be done to reform corporations in light of recent developments? Should employees be given a voice in corporate governance? Should they sit on the boards of their pension funds? Perhaps this debate is worth having with your fellow students—even with your professor!

Assignment Summary

1. Come to class prepared to discuss all assigned readings.
2. If "The Part-Time Partner" (Part A) has been assigned, be prepared to defend your for-partnership or against-partnership vote.
3. If "The Part-Time Partner Redux" (Part B) has also been assigned, be prepared to discuss your responses to the What-is-the-problem-now? and the Is-this-problem-solvable? questions.
4. Come to class and take part in an experiential exercise entitled "Redeployment Meets Teamwork." All information regarding this exercise will be provided to you by your instructor on the day set aside for running it.

Additional Suggested Readings

- On background data on the changing workforce, from a widely quoted report commissioned by the U.S. Department of Labor, which has influenced managers' and policy makers' perceptions and approaches:
Workforce 2000: Work and Workers for the 21st Century. Indianapolis: Hudson Institute, 1987.

- On analyzing changes in employment, grounded in the empirical evidence about changes in work and the employment relationship:
Capelli, Peter (with Laurie Bassi, Harry Katz, David Knoke, Paul Osterman, Michael Useem). 1997. *Change at Work*. New York: Oxford University Press.

- On the changing nature of jobs, employment relationships, and work, from two books receiving popular attention:
Bridges, William. 1994. *Job Shift: How to Prosper in a Workplace Without Jobs*. Wesley, MA: Addison-Wesley.
Rifkin, Jeremy. 1995. *The End of Work: The Decline of the Global Labor Force and the Dawn of the Post-Market Era*. New York: G.P. Putnam's Sons.

- On several aspects of managing workers, teams, projects, empowerment, fast cycle times, and shifting loyalties in the new organizational form, by two sets of leading academics:
Donnellon, Anne, and Charles Heckscher, eds. 1994. *The Post-Bureaucratic Organization: New Perspectives on Organizational Change*. Newbury Park, CA: Sage.
Galbraith, Jay R. and Edward E. Lawler, eds. 1993. *Organizing for the Future: The New Logic for Managing Complex Organizations*. San Francisco: Jossey-Bass.
Pfeffer, Jeffrey. 1998. *The Human Equation*. Cambridge, MA: Harvard Business School Press.

- On how one innovative Brazilian company is approaching jobs and subcontracting differently:
Semler, Ricardo. 1993. *Maverick: The Success Story Behind the World's Most Unusual Workplace*. New York: Warner Books.

- On how labor. management, government, and community groups can play different kinds of roles in updating employment practices to meet the needs of the modern workforce, employers, and the economy:
Osterman, Paul, Thomas A. Kochan, Richard Locke, and Michael Piore, *Working in America: A Blueprint for the New Labor Market*. Cambridge, MA: MIT Press, 2001.

Workforce Management: Employment Relationships in Changing Organizations

CORE

Module 7

Managing a Changing Workforce in Turbulent Times

Mobility. Empowerment. Teams. Cross-training. Virtual offices. Telecommuting. Reengineering. Restructuring. Delayering. Outsourcing. Contingency. If the buzzwords don't sound familiar, they should: They are changing your life. In the past decade, perhaps more than any other time since the advent of mass production, we witnessed a profound redefinition of the way we work (*Business Week*, 1994, p. 86). These buzzwords dominated the business press discussion of work in the mid-1990s. Then, as the dot.com boom occurred, new terms were added: *talent wars, knowledge workers, signing bonuses, confidentiality* and *non-compete agreements,* and *stock options.* More recently, in the wake of the dot.com bubble and corporate accounting and related financial scandals, still new words entered public discussions: *transparency, conflicts of interest, trust* and *confidence* (or lack of), *globalization, voice,* and *governance.* But how do you make sense of them? Where is work going? For employees, is the buzz good, with its promises of increased flexibility and opportunity? Or is the buzz all bad news, with lurking threats of downsizing, longer hours, and greater stress and insecurity? For organizations, do the ups and downs of business and the economy mean that managers have little or no control over how they manage the workforce? Can managers establish a set of enduring principles for building effective organizations and employment practices that will withstand the economic ups and downs and breakdowns in trust and confidence in institutions? Or are both managers and workers doomed to be victims of short-sighted fads that generate as many unintended problems as solutions?

This Class Note will give you a context for assessing how the employment relationship is changing and ways that you, as a manager and as an employee, might gain greater control over your destiny and the performance of your work unit and organization.

The employment relationship is the set of arrangements and work practices that describe and govern the relationship between employee and employer. This relationship runs deeper than an economic arrangement. A "social contract" (or "psychological contract") exists between employees and employers—a shared cultural understanding of what is right, good, and fair about the ongoing exchange. The social contract that evolved up until the past few years specified a longer-term, substantive relationship between employee and employer for their mutual benefit. Employees not only contributed their skills but were often encouraged to bring their whole selves to work, contributing their loyalty, commitment, ingenuity, and extra effort. Employers not only paid a wage, but provided job security, offered additional benefits ranging from health care to on-site child care to substance abuse counseling, and even promoted the image of the company as a big family.

This employment relationship and the social contract that bolstered it are changing. Two distinctly different stories—the good news and the bad news from the employee's perspective—accompany these changes. First, the good news story sings the praises of flexible arrangements that allow employees to balance work and family time better. Images abound of telecommuters sitting at home working with their laptops in their pajamas ("working naked" as one recent book put it). Instead of job insecurity, employees are encouraged to look at the bright side and all the new avenues they can pursue when they become free agents managing their own careers. Managers, in turn, can attract and retain valued employees whose family responsibilities otherwise would not allow for traditional full-time work in the office. And managers can keep in touch while they are traveling or at home and reach employees 24/7 through their cell phones, computers, and related technologies. Second, the bad news story points to the harsh realities of downsizing, job insecurity, and the constant hustle for the next assignment or contract. Temporary jobs can be associated with difficult conditions, low pay, and no benefits. Managers are finding it hard to balance the equities among those who must remain in the office while others work at home or on flexible schedules and get frustrated when the flexibility offered by company policies is underutilized. They wonder why it is so hard to make flexibility work for them, for their employees, and for their organization.

Companies once praised for their "best practices" in forging long-term employment relationships have made headlines over the past few years for their "restructuring" and elimination of positions. In some more recent cases, companies that may have gone too far in wielding the axe are trying to hire employees back and cajole loyalty from them again. The overly optimistic and rapid rise of the dot.coms in the late 1990s sent shock waves through labor markets creating a so-called "talent war." When the dot.com bubble burst, many MBAs and other professionals had job offers rescinded and held stock options that were worthless These changing conditions serve to remind us that no "trend" is permanent. At the same time, neither are they totally driven by forces outside the control of good managers. To be effective as a manager and credible to employees requires gaining control over these ups and downs and fashioning a work culture and environment that works for both one's organization and its employees. In the pages that follow we assess these trends and their implications for managers in following sections:

- **The "Old" Versus "New" Employment Relationship**—looks at five features of work and how they are shifting and considers the challenges accompanying the changes.
- **Flexibility: What Kind, What Is Changing, and For Whom?**—considers the different types of flexibility and their positive and negative implications for employers and employees.
- **Putting More Options on the Menu for the New Employment Relationship**—considers alternative approaches to the emerging need for flexibility, including debates about traditional and alternative forms of worker voice and their effects on organizational performance.
- **Treating Worker Knowledge as an Asset**—examines the implications for the role of management and the design of the twenty-first century organization.
- **Attending to Perceived Inconsistencies and Unintended Consequences**—discusses the implications for management during a time of turbulence and change, emphasizing the need to think about the coherence of employment practices and their perceived legitimacy to different constituencies.

The "Old" Versus "New" Employment Relationship

As you examine this material, you might ask yourself some questions asked in numerous articles and debates about the changes in employment relations:

- Has the implicit social or psychological contract in employment relationships broken down or changed for the better?
- Have the terms of the exchange between employees and employers shifted to create a new set of "winners" and "losers"?
- What can you as a manager do to both gain value for the organization from your employees' knowledge and motivation and, in return,

create a rewarding and fair work culture and an environment that fosters further learning, development, and loyalty?

A common historical picture leads us to the present-day debates. From the end of World War II through the 1970s, workers and firms enjoyed a sustained period of shared prosperity, with real wages and personal income rising in tandem with increases in productivity in the American economy. Employee loyalty (especially for white-collar, managerial, and professional employees) and long tenure, generally, were rewarded by increased employment security and a rising level of income. Many employees worked in "internal labor markets" characterized by a constellation of features: long-term employment with one employer, internal advancement up a company job ladder, well-defined jobs linked in a progression that defined a career, and individual compensation based on merit, seniority, or some combination thereof. This system was called an "internal labor market," because in general, neither employees nor managers went back to the "open" market to apply or hire for openings above entry level, but instead counted on the promotion of trained, talented people from within. These features worked together as a system, because collectively they made sense and reinforced one another. They were the consistent pieces of a firm's overall human resource strategy (Osterman et al., 1999).

From the mid-1970s to the mid-1990s, however, productivity growth slowed down, real wages stagnated for all employees except those at the very top of the occupational and income distribution (senior executives and the highly educated and mobile professionals), and inequality in income distribution greatly increased. The late 1990s saw improvements in earnings for all employees as labor markets tightened and expectations were fueled by the seemingly permanent economic boom. Still, through this period, restructuring continued to produce a significant number of white-collar and managerial layoffs. But the layoffs were counterbalanced by the new jobs being created. Labor shortages created abundant opportunities for well-educated, skilled professionals. More jobs were also created in the lower half of the income distribution, but many of these failed to provide "living" wages or benefits. The phenomenon of "the working poor"—people employed in full-time jobs that do not pay a living wage—clashed with the image of prosperous American employment from preceding decades. A popular book, *Nickeled and Dimed* (Ehrenreich, 2001), chronicled the human challenges faced by individuals unable to support themselves or their families by working in low-level service jobs.

Today more jobs are filled by turning to the external market rather than promoting from within, especially in firms facing changing technologies and rapidly changing product markets. Peter Cappelli (1998) describes the new employment relationship as "market mediated" rather than an internal labor market process.

Keep this broad characterization of recent changes in mind as you examine the material in this module. Ask yourself: Given this up-and-down history, and the vastly different worlds of work experienced by highly educated professionals with marketable skills and those with less human capital and fewer good labor market alternatives, what can I as a manager do to gain greater control over the conditions of work I offer my employees? What can I do to ensure that my organization treats people fairly with dignity, and gains fair value in return for their knowledge, skill, and effort? In short, how might we redefine the social contract to do what a social contract is expected to do: to meet "the broad expectations and obligations that employees, employers, and society have for work and employment relationships?

In thinking about these questions, consider that all employment relationships are composed of interrelated features that function as a system. It is difficult to change particular features in a piecemeal fashion. However, piecemeal change typically occurs in a time of transition. As some features change more rapidly and others more slowly, contradictions and inconsistencies may appear that make managing more difficult, as discussed in the final section.

Employment Security: Long Term Versus Short Term

From the 1950s to the 1970s, many employees and employers in the United States expected the employment relationship to be long term. They enjoyed employment security, while the company gained the benefits of the "firm-specific skills" their employees acquired. Of course, jobs were always available in the "periphery" of the economy, jobs that were disproportionately held by women and racial minorities and that offered low wages and no security nor advancement opportunities. Despite these counterexamples, the dominant model that infused the management press was that of the long-term employment relationship. "The images that best characterize the American corporation as an employer in the 1950s are ones of stability and uniformity, shared gains among multiple stakeholders, and world model" (Kochan, 1994).

The 1980s brought a change in this "implicit contract" between employees and employers. Large companies long known for lifelong careers and promises of employment security began to lay off employees. For example, IBM, once 406,000 employees strong, cut some 170,000 employees from 1986 to 1994 and then steadily rebuilt itself and its workforce as a full-service information systems company. By 2002 it once again employed more than 300,000 and an extended array of contractors doing work deemed to be outside the company's core competencies (including much of its routine human resource and information systems service work). In recent years, companies with household names such as Xerox, AT&T, Boeing, Cisco Systems, Lucent, Intel, and others all announced large-scale layoffs as part of restructuring processes despite the fact that some of these firms were earning profits at the time. Each firm was also hiring new employees at the same time it was displacing others. In fact, during this same time, the U.S. economy was viewed worldwide for its ability to create new jobs at a high rate—outstripping the job losses experienced in these organizational downswings and restructuring.

A number of forces and rationales drove these changes in the United States, including the following:

- Globalization and international competition prompted companies to look for work that could be done more cheaply in developing countries or that needed to be moved to countries or geographic areas where products are being marketed.
- Changing technologies were producing demand for employees with new skills.
- Companies found it easier to hire workers on the external labor market with the skills needed for the current technologies and markets than to retrain employees whose skills had become outmoded.
- The wage bill often appeared to be the obvious choice to slash first.
- It was time to get rid of "dead wood"—whether because some employees were regarded as complacent in the face of lifelong employment or because longer-term employees, with more skills and more deferred compensation due to them, were more expensive.
- Competition over quality and faster cycle time prompted companies to find ways to "do more with fewer people."
- The power of unions declined, making it difficult for employees to exercise a collective voice and bargain for employment security.
- Companies began to find it more economically appealing and socially legitimate to use subcontractors and temporary workers, whether by hiring cheaper labor through temporary agencies domestically or sourcing work abroad to areas where labor was cheaper.

The increase in anxiety over job security is happening around the globe. European workers experienced a decade of unemployment averaging 10 percent or more. New markets opened in some countries, such as Mexico, Brazil, and India, which produced new jobs in new industries but were accompanied by precariousness and restructuring from instability in currencies and elimination of jobs in industries previously protected by import restrictions or state subsidies. In Japan, long considered the paragon of lifetime employment, this institution is being reconsidered in the wake of prolonged economic stagnation. Unemployment is now a persistent problem in Japan for the first time since Japan recovered from the effects of World War II. The deep financial crises that hit South Korea, Indonesia, Thailand, and then Brazil, Argentina, and other developing Asian countries in recent years forced a number of multinational firms to close facilities or scale back investment plans, and forced many local firms to likewise abandon long-standing employment security practices.

The "old" employment relationship was sometimes criticized as too paternalistic. Perhaps the new employment relationship corrects this tendency to an extreme. Employees have been empowered and are now expected to shoulder the responsibility for their own employment. The phrase "lifetime employment" (provided by the employer) has been replaced by the phrase "lifetime employability" (traits that are supposed to be polished continuously by the employee). One of the questions that remains is whether employers will provide training and "lifelong learning" needed to help employees stay current, continue to learn new skills, and remain employable. New arrangements that form the overall system that bolsters the new employment relationship are still evolving.

Advancement: Climbing the Ladder Versus Moving in Circles

Traditionally, employees spent a career advancing within a company, a classic feature of the bureaucracy. The "flattening" of job ladders resulted in fewer or different types of advancement opportunities for those employees who remain with an employer. Lateral advancement or advancement up the levels of a skill set relevant to one's own job (often called pay-for-skills plans) are common substitutes. The expectation of a promotion every few years has changed radically. Thus, flattening of the organization may be greeted with ambivalence. On the one hand, employees may enjoy greater decision-making authority. On the other hand, they see fewer opportunities for promotion, ironically just at a time when employees are shouldering more of the responsibilities that used to signal readiness for promotion. The challenge to managers in flattened organizations is to provide opportunities for learning and development and ways of rewarding employees without the visible status and financial signals that accompanied moving up the old hierarchy.

Jobs and Compensation: Fixed and Individualistic Versus Multidimensional and Team-Based

The prototypical organizational chart contained boxes with distinct job titles and showed the reporting links among jobs. The new division of labor in organizations may defy a two-dimensional chart. Tasks and relationships connect in every which way to form a complex web. A number of features of the new employment relationship are breaking the boundaries of the old job and creating opportunities for managers to value (through pay or symbolic rewards) employees who effectively manage their horizontal relationships and responsibilities—the multiskilled employee who works well in cross-functional teams and organizational networks.

What other changes in the work system are required to manage multitasked or multidimensional jobs? First, individual jobs are increasingly defined as "multiskilled," getting away from the tradition of tightly and narrowly defined job descriptions or functional specialization. Employees are encouraged to "cross-train" and learn a variety of tasks, in order to "job rotate." Job rotation provides flexibility in that the same group of people, if they are multiskilled, can be employed in a number of different configurations to accomplish a number of different tasks. Opportunities for learning and development are thereby created. Finally, the reward system needs to be adjusted to ensure that these broader skills and capabilities are appropriately valued. This adjustment often requires sharing performance appraisal responsibilities among two or more managers or between a team leader and a functional supervisor. And finally, it requires periodic refresher training and education in one's home discipline or function to ensure that basic knowledge and skills are kept current.

Even though some employees express enthusiasm at the prospect of making their jobs more interesting by learning new tasks, others express ambivalence, fearing that job rotation can also be a path to being "forgotten" in one's home unit, caught between loyalty to one's function and the cross-functional team, longer hours as one does "two jobs" rather than one, and greater stress (Scully and Preuss, 1994). Ideally, multiskilling makes a workforce more productive, and increased productivity allows the creation of jobs with more reasonable hours, as a result of working smarter.

The scenario that many fear is that, instead, many people will be laid off and those who remain must work harder, faster, and longer at a more complex chain of tasks. Managing to gain the benefits and avoiding having these fears realized is a central requirement for making these new organizational forms both productive in the short run and sustainable in the longer term.

Second, the very notion of a job itself, as a discrete bundle of tasks, is being questioned:

> *The job is a social artifact, though it is so deeply embedded in our consciousness that most of us have forgotten its artificiality or the fact that most societies since the beginning of time have done just fine without jobs. The job is an idea that emerged early in the 19th century to package the work that needed doing in the growing factories and bureaucracies of the industrializing nations. Before people had jobs, they worked just as hard but on shifting clusters of tasks, in a variety of locations, on a schedule set by the sun and the weather and the needs of the day. The modern job was a startling new idea—and to many, an unpleasant and perhaps socially dangerous one. Critics claimed it was an unnatural and even inhuman way to work. They believed that most people wouldn't be able to live with its demands. It is ironic that what started as a controversial concept ended up becoming the ultimate orthodoxy—and that we're hooked on jobs. (Bridges, 1994)*

Third, compensation systems need to shift from individual incentives tied to specific job titles and duties to rewards for learning new skills and working effectively in teams and across organizational boundaries (Donnellon and Scully, 1994), which is easier said than done. Companies are experimenting with various team-based pay systems and group rewards but challenges remain over issues such as who decides on how well a team has performed (the team leader, the functional manager, or someone above both?), who sets the budgets for rewarding teams and teamwork (human resources or line managers?), and who decides how rewards are to be distributed among team members (share equally, allocated by the team leader or supervisor, allocated by team members through peer reviews?). Resolving all these questions are central tasks for the contemporary manager of flexible, multi-dimensional work systems.

Thus, these types of changes do not happen in a vacuum and must be supported by other related changes in employment and social systems. Although some of these changes are within the control of individual managers, others require changes in an organization's overall human resource system (e.g., compensation rules, training and development policies, etc.). Managers therefore must be advocates and change agents to ensure these internal policies are adjusted and aligned to support teamwork and flexible job assignments. And, some changes are needed in external employment policies and institutions as well. For example, unemployment insurance might be provided, not just for people who are not working at all, but for people who are working fewer hours while between assignments or back at school to update their skills. Managers need to therefore also advocate changes needed to update these external rules, policies, and institutions to fit the new realities of work.

Building New "Knowledge Based" or "High Performance" Work Systems

The old set of features described previously made sense as a system. The new features, when taken together and functioning cohesively, are sometimes referred to as "knowledge-based" (Nonaka and Takeuchi, 1995; Cutcher Gershenfeld et al., 1998) or "high performance" (Ichniowski et al., 1996) work systems. Firms struggling to achieve a knowledge-based or high-performance work system and its benefits seek to get all the pieces in place in a way that produces mutually beneficial results for employers and employees. It requires, as the preceding section suggested, starting with reconceptualizing employees not mainly as a cost to be controlled but as a potential source of value to the organization. To generate that value requires bundling together policies regarding selection for the ability to learn and to work together as well as for technical skills, job and work designs that promote teamwork and multiskilling, training and development to support ongoing learning, employee voice and input into decision making and problem solving to make full use of their knowledge, compensation rules that reinforce teamwork and skill acquisition, and employment security and career opportunities to maintain trust in the system.

Firms in a wide array of industries from autos and steel to airlines and telecommunications have experimented with these new work systems. The evidence is quite strong that, when implemented together in a systemic way, these workplace changes outperform more traditional work systems, producing significantly higher quality, productivity, and profitability (Ichniowski et al., 1996). Not surprisingly, these practices spread steadily in the past decade, especially in those industries and firms facing increased competitive pressures to upgrade the quality of their products and services. Sustaining this momentum and maintaining both organizational and workforce commitment to these new systems is a critical challenge and responsibility of managers today.

Flexibility: What Kind, What Is Changing, and for Whom?

The demand for flexibility in work arrangements is often traced to the entrance of women into the paid workforce in increasing numbers. (The contribution of women's unpaid work at home to national productivity is a separate issue.) In 1950, 32 percent of women were in the labor force compared to about 60 percent today. The latest data, presented in Figure 7.1, show significant changes in the sex and race composition of the U.S. workforce.

Much attention has been given to the increasing numbers of women entering the workforce. At the same time, it is important to remember that women have been in the workforce for a long time (32 percent in 1950, as already cited) and have long faced issues of balancing work and family. Women of color in particular have had a long history of workforce participation, in disproportionately greater numbers than white women. Much can be learned from their experiences of balancing work and family before any broader societal dialogue and some corporate support for the issue occurred.

It is interesting, though not surprising, that it is the rise of white, middle-class women into higher positions in organizations that prompted new dialogues about ways to balance work and family. These women may have had somewhat more capacity to bargain for new conditions of work, even though it is risky to raise the issue or deviate from career norms. The dialogue gradually expanded from "just a women's issue" to include fathers taking leave, "parental leave time" more generally, leave time for adopting children, and flexible time arrangements for caring for elderly parents or ill family members. As a result, the number of firms offering "family friendly" benefits

Figure 7.1 Changes in the Distribution of the U.S. Labor Force by Subgroup, 1994–2005, (number in thousands, percent in parentheses)

Labor Force Subgroup	1994	New Entrants	Leavers	2005	Net Additions	Change in %
Non-Hispanic White Men	54,306 (41.4)	12,937 (32.9)	10,814 (46.4)	56,429 (38.4)	2,123 (13.2)	–3.0
Non-Hispanic White Women	46,157 (35.2)	13,122 (33.4)	7,363 (31.6)	51,916 (35.3)	5,759 (35.9)	0.1
Non-Hispanic African American Men	6,981 (5.3)	2,314 (5.9)	1,512 (6.5)	7,783 (5.3)	802 (5.0)	0.0
Non-Hispanic African American Women	7,323 (5.6)	2,557 (6.5)	1,271 (5.5)	8,609 (5.9)	1,286 (8.0)	0.3
Hispanic Men	7,210 (5.5)	3,321 (8.4)	1,039 (4.5)	9,492 (6.5)	2,282 (14.2)	1.0
Hispanic Women	4,764 (3.6)	2,765 (7.0)	690 (3.0)	6,838 (4.6)	2,074 (12.9)	1.0
Asian and Other Men	2,317 (1.8)	1,148 (2.9)	326 (1.4)	3,139 (2.1)	822 (5.1)	0.3
Asian and Other Women	1,994 (1.5)	1,180 (3.0)	274 (1.2)	2,900 (2.0)	906 (5.6)	0.5
Totals	131,051 (99.9)	39,343 (100)	23,289 (100.1)	147,106 (100.1)	16,054 (99.9)	0.0*

* Does not add up to zero due to rounding error.

Source: From Judith Friedman and Nancy DiTomaso, "Myths About Diversity: What Managers Need to Know About Changes in the U.S. Labor Force." Copyright © 1996, by The Regents of the University of California. Reprinted from the *California Management Review*, vol. 38, no. 4. By permission of the Regents.

and policies continues to expand. As we will see, however, these policies are often underutilized. The question is why. What can managers do to make flexibility work for both their employees and their organization?

Flexibility: Choices, Balance, Varied Work

It is important to understand what features of employment are being made flexible in each of the various trends that appear under the umbrella of "flexibility." Analyzing the different types of flexible arrangements in this way is helpful for understanding just what and how much is changing. Some kinds of flexibility will pose greater challenges to workplaces and managers than to others.

Flexible Space. Telecommuting allows employees to work at home, at distant sites, or on the road. Usually these employees are linked electronically to the main site by computer modem and fax machine and are often expected to be available at certain regular hours or to report to work in person at specified times. They may do the same job, and even work longer hours, just in a different place. Systems for ensuring their accountability are evolving. They range from those based on strict monitoring to those based on high trust.

One corporate approach to reducing costs is to weaken employees' link to a single physical space by establishing a "virtual office." The number of square feet maintained per employee is an indicator to which corporations are paying greater attention, but square feet per employee may be decreasing. A virtual office can be like a hotel, where employees check in at scheduled times in a certain cubicle, and a "concierge" helps put the right files into cubicles for that day's occupant. Flexible space must fit with other elements of the new employment system; for example, employees will need to work effectively as teams over electronic links, and learn when face-to-face contact needs to be scheduled.

Flexible Time and Allocation of Tasks. In its simplest form, flexibility in the hours of work came in the form of "flex time," where employees had some choice in their start and end times. The basic nature of the job was unchanged. Part-time work and job sharing involve different partitioning of work. Part-time work may involve a schedule that is reduced on a weekly basis (e.g., five half days or three full days) or an annual basis (seasonal employment). Job sharing involves two employees sharing the responsibilities that were typically associated with one job description, devising ways to communicate across their roles.

As the preceding section suggests, the notion of what set of tasks constitutes "the job" is being reconsidered. Discussions of flexible time and tasks have evolved from "flex time" to much more fundamental questions about work. Thinking about the flexibility of time and tasks now involves more than thinking about how to carve up traditional 40-hour jobs into different start and end times or into two 20-hour jobs. The promise of technology used to be that it would reduce the working week to about 30 hours and generate more time for leisure pursuits. Instead, the number of hours of work is increasing, not just for individuals, but also for family units that have more than one person employed for pay. As long as jobs are conceptualized as 40—or more—hours per week, an imbalance is likely to continue between people who are overworked and stressed out, on the one hand, and people who are underemployed and unable to generate a sufficient salary from 30 hours or fewer of work, on the other hand. Again, from a holistic perspective, reducing the number of hours of work will require thinking concomitantly about a variety of changes, such as changes in pay systems to provide sufficient wages and benefits for employees who work fewer or more highly variable hours.

Flexible Career Paths. Career paths in the "old" employment relationship were more linear—employees climbed a job ladder within a company. They were implicitly designed for the "organization man" (i.e., a male breadwinner who would work full time in the labor force from the time he entered after completing school until retirement). This arrangement was possible because he was supported by a wife at home taking care of family and community responsibilities. Of course, this view of the typical or "ideal" worker (Williams, 2000) no longer fits today's diverse workforce or families.

New models of careers are needed but slow in developing. Some firms are offering part-time or reduced hour options for parents (men or women) who need time to care for children or elders. As we will see in the article "The Part-Time Partner," this model requires changing compensation criteria, rules governing promotions, and most importantly assumptions and norms about what constitutes a "good" worker. Is commitment to long hours still to be taken as a signal of high productivity and dedication or are more actual performance or project-based indicators called for? Can part-time employees be given challenging assignments and become eligible for promotions without creating a sense of inequity among those who remain full time? Can the workplace culture be modified to overcome the fear that using these options will hinder one's career or forever put one behind one's peers? The evidence consistently shows that these are the constraining factors that leave flexible career opportunities, part-time options, and other family-friendly benefits underutilized (Bailyn et al., 2001). Studies of leading law firms have shown, for example, that even though more than 90 percent of firms offer flexible career paths, less than 5 percent of lawyers take advantage of these option. A clue to why this pattern persists is that one third of lawyers fear doing so will jeopardize their careers (Women's Bar Association of Massachusetts, 2000).

Yet despite the overall pattern, countless examples exist where managers and employees have worked out solutions and created a workplace culture that supports and encourages use of flexible hours and career opportunities. The key to these success stories is that the parties worked out local solutions to redesign work to achieve what our colleague Lotte Bailyn called the "dual agenda," namely designing work for both high performance and work-family integration (Rappaport et al., 2002). This challenge then, is the responsibility facing managers of the contemporary workforce and organizations.

Flexible Workforce Size and Firm Boundaries. The so-called "virtual" corporation is one in which multiple activities are spun off to subcontractors, an arrangement that might at once allow flexible adaptability to changing market conditions and create tenuous employment relationships. These relationships cause anxiety and are prompting people to ask normative questions about the severing of the bond between employer and employee, as in the following passage from *Business Week*:

> *In computerese, a virtual disk exists only in the computer's memory; when the computer is turned off, the virtual disk is obliterated. By analogy, I suppose, people who work for the new virtual corporations can be called virtual employees. What happens to these people when the power is turned off and their virtual employer disappears? Do they vanish along with the electrons? Are they put together again somewhere when some chief executive loads another virtual corporation into memory? (Patterson, 1994, p. 86)*

In recent years, more firms have turned to temporary workers as a way to cope with variations in markets and demand for work. Manpower, Inc., which not only provides temporary workers to large firms but also carefully screens and sometimes trains them, became one of the largest employers in the United States, with some 600,000 workers on its rolls in 2002. Many other temporary help firms or employee leasing firms joined Manpower in supplying skilled professionals such as graphic artists, Web designers, and other high-technology specialists.

Working in these temporary assignments, and managing temporary or contract employees is clearly a double-edged sword. On the one hand, the evidence is clear that many independent contractors prefer the flexibility and freedom from the old bureaucratic world of the large firm and internal labor markets and career ladders. They learn from each new assignment and have (at least theoretically) more control over when and for whom they work. Studies of these high-level contractors in Silicon Valley and elsewhere (Kunda, Barley, and Evans, 1999) indeed document high levels of satisfaction among these workers. Also, studies of managers responsible for staffing and overseeing projects that employ contract workers alongside permanent workers show that with proper planning, training, and supervision, the work gets done efficiently (Lautsch, 2002). Clearly, therefore, temporary work is here to stay, as is the need to learn how to manage it effectively.

A dark side of temporary work is also evident, however. For example, some cases received a lot of publicity where large employers laid off their permanent employees, claiming that changing markets and competitive measures reduced their need for a large workforce, only to rehire almost the same number of employees through temporary agencies. Some so-called "temporary" workers remain with an employer for years. These cases highlight the fact that a principal motive of employers for flexing the number of permanent employees may be the savings in wages and benefits. Other cases highlight major safety risks associated with use of temporary workers in industries such as petrochemical plants, where contractors are called in to do some of the most dangerous maintenance and repair work and managers are told to leave their supervision to the contracting firm for fear of being held liable for being a "co-employer" should an accident or other violation of an employment law occur (Kochan et al., 1994). The same set of safety issues are prominent in health care as hospitals seek to cope with nursing shortages by hiring temporary nurses and other employees who often lack specific knowledge of a given hospital's procedures or familiarity with their patients.

The hidden costs of downsizing and increased use of temporary workers can include loss of employee loyalty and commitment, which are increasingly important if teamwork and shared decision making are to be implemented effectively, the loss of "firm-specific skills" that permanent employees develop over a longer-term relationship, and increased stress and conflict at work. Management of these potentially negative consequences requires both careful thought about the costs and benefits of when and what to outsource and a clear strategy and consistent implementation of a plan for supervising work and building a positive culture among those working side by side in these settings.

Putting More Options on the Menu for the New Employment Relationship

The weakening of the employee/employer bond was only one solution to the competitive, technological, and social pressures facing companies in the United States. It is important to bear in mind that this response was but one choice from a menu of possible responses. Sometimes, both the research literature and the business press convey a sense that the current changes in the employment relationship, such as downsizing and the increasing use of temporary employees, are an inevitable and unfortunate new development, rather than a choice. These developments are portrayed as the necessary outcome of market and technological changes, such as faster cycle time and an increasing demand for high quality standards. However, one could imagine, for example, that the increased demand for quality could result in the hiring of more workers and an increased reliance upon employee loyalty to a single firm.

Downsizing is sometimes bemoaned as the unfortunate but inevitable outcome of market and technological changes. However, it has not proven to be a panacea for companies. In a 1993 Conference Board survey of human resource executives, many reported lowered morale among layoff "survivors" and greater need for training as costly and sometimes unanticipated consequences of downsizing. "An American Management Association (AMA) survey of companies that had made 'major staff cuts' between 1987 and 1992 found that, despite the reduced labor costs, less than half improved their operating earnings—while one in four saw earnings drop. More ominously, said the AMA's report, 'these figures were even worse for companies that undertook a second or third round of downsizing.' Many companies that fail to get their expected results with the first round of cuts simply repeat the process" (Bridges, 1994, p. 64).

It is difficult to discern the causal relationship between downsizing and poor performance, but this cycle of crises and cuts may be an example of the kind of negative feedback loop that systems dynamics theorists warn companies about. Given the complexity of restructuring, it makes sense to look for other solutions, rather than simply to make cuts. Ideas for other solutions may come not just from abroad but from a deeper analysis and understanding of what exactly is changing, what is at stake and for whom, and how a new system of arrangements will hold together in a fashion that makes sense.

Global Comparisons

One of the best ways to understand what other choices exist for relating how work is structured and managed to other aspects of an organization is to think globally and look at the responses of a variety of industrialized nations. Faced with the same international and technological pressures, for example, Japan and Germany made different choices. These countries developed different institutional arrangements, which embed different historical choices and shape different approaches to similar challenges. Both countries emphasized and maintained longer-term employment relationships. When this relationship is threatened, their alternative approaches include maintaining a greater number of employees and having them work shorter hours (an example of one kind of flexibility discussed previously), having top managers and executives take pay reductions, moving work back inside the firm from outside contractors, and at a societal level, requiring substantial severance or early retirement payments to those laid off.

For example, one of the questions raised earlier was whether employers will provide ongoing training for employees, particularly if they will not have a long-term relationship with these employees. Ideas for alternative approaches to training may come from countries such as Germany, which has an elaborate apprentice system that provides the highly skilled technicians that will be in increasing demand with new technologies. In Germany and Japan, work-related practices fit into an organizational setting that expects firms to weigh employee and community responsibilities in addition to maximizing shareholder value. It is interesting that as of this writing, the appropriate weight to give shareholder value vis-à-vis other "stakeholder" interests is a matter of debate in a variety of settings. Japan and Germany are both under pressure to give greater weight to shareholders and to loosen some of the traditions or laws that protect employees or give them a voice in corporate governance. In the United States the corporate scandals of recent years reenergized a debate over whether corporations give too much weight to maximizing shareholder value at the expense of employee and broader societal interests. We included a short essay on this subject to allow you to consider and join this debate. How it is resolved will have a substantial effect on how workforce management fits into the portfolio of responsibilities of managers and will help shape the organizations of the future.

Human Assets and Twenty-First Century Organizational Forms

Because labor costs are normally the largest variable cost in most firms, employees are traditionally viewed as a cost that needs to be tightly controlled. But human resources are also an important asset in many firms, particularly those in which employee knowledge is a critical competitive resource. In consulting, law, and other professional service firms, for example, employees who leave take significant portions of the firm's assets (their knowledge and sometimes their clients) with them. The organizational forms adopted in these situations often reflect this risk by creating partnerships in which crucial employees share in the ownership, profits, and governance processes of the firm. We might wonder, therefore, whether other organizations will begin to take on more of these features as knowledge becomes a more important strategic asset (Blair, 1995). The organization of the future may therefore need to find new ways to bind these critical knowledge workers to the firm or risk losing significant capital.

Indeed, economists as politically different as Lester Thurow and Gary Becker or management and organizational analysts as different as Peter Drucker and Jeffrey Pfeffer all seem to agree that human capital and knowledge are becoming as important a source of competitive value to the twenty-first-century firm as financial capital was to the twentieth-century firm. The question then is: How can human capital and knowledge be translated into real value to the organization and what changes in managerial mindsets and organizational practices will be needed to fully capitalize on this human potential? We believe this issue is the perhaps the biggest challenge and opportunity facing management today.

But in some ways, it is not a new challenge. Fifty year ago MIT's Douglas McGregor posed this same question by challenging managers to assess their assumptions about employees and their motivations. Were employees reluctant contributors to organizations, costs to be controlled and monitored to assure compliance with management-initiated directions, or were they motivated to work and contribute to the mission of their organization and work unit?

McGregor raised good questions for his time. Today, perhaps more profound questions have to be raised that challenge managers to not only reassess their assumptions about employee motivation but to also question how they view the nature of work, technology, leadership, and the goals of organizations. Figure 7.2 poses contrasting assumptions for each of these components of an organization. Each individually, but more importantly, how they are combined and fit together as a system of management and organizational governance, will determine whether twenty-first-century organizations meet the challenge of generating value from their human assets.

Attending to Perceived Inconsistencies and Unintended Consequences

Managers need to keep in mind how the policies they are implementing hold together. If employees perceive inconsistencies, they may well become cynical or accuse management of hypocrisy, which is what occurred in the wake of the various corporate scandals that surfaced in recent years. Employees saw top executives taking care of their personal

Figure 7.2 Contrasting Assumptions in Twentieth- and Twenty-First-Century Organizations

	Assumptions Characterizing Twentieth-Century Organizations	Assumptions That May Characterize Twenty-First-Century Organizations
People	Theory X: People are a cost that must be monitored and controlled.	Theory Y: People are an asset that should be valued and developed.
Work	Segmented, industrially based and individual tasks	Collaborative, knowledge-based projects
Technology	Design technology to control work and minimize human error	Integrate technology with social systems to enable knowledge-based work
Leadership	Senior managers and technical experts	Distributed leadership at all levels
Goals	Unitary focus on returns to shareholders	Multidimensional focus on value for multiple stakeholders

Source: Thomas A. Kochan, Wanda Orlikowski, and Joel Cutcher Gershenfeld, "Beyond McGregor's Theory Y: Human Capital and Knowledge Work in the 21st Century Organization," MIT Sloan School of Management, 2002.

interests (sometimes legally and sometimes illegally), and, at the same time, that other managers and employees of the organization were losing part or all of their retirement savings, and in some cases, their jobs. This example is just the extreme case of a broader challenge to management. Employees eventually respond to inconsistencies between rhetoric and reality by losing trust in and abandoning a sense of loyalty to their organizations. Calls for teamwork and statements that employees are valued assets will only have their desired effects when backed up by a coherent system of organizational policies and practices and managerial values and behaviors that can sustain trust. Moreover, each generation of managers inherits the sins (or virtues) of their fathers and mothers. One member of a group of engineers described this process in a classroom discussion as follows:

> *Companies are now paying for their past sins. They showed no loyalty to us and so now we have to take care of ourselves and move to where we get the best offers. Today the most talented people in our companies can do this without even uprooting their families and so they ask themselves: Why would I stay here?*

It is in this context that the management of today's workforce takes place—a context in which the loyalty and commitment of both firms and employees to each other has been weakened by the memory of past and recurring downsizings and restructurings.

Past and Future Models of Employee Representation

Consider one final challenge for managing the workforce of the future. One of the biggest labor market developments of recent years has been the decline in union representation. In the United States, unions declined from their peak of representing about 35 percent of the private sector labor force in the mid-1950s to representing about 9 percent of private sector workers (14 percent of all private and public sector workers) in 2002. This trend, while less dramatic in magnitude, is visible in most other highly industrialized countries around the world. Britain, Japan, Australia, and even some of the European countries with strong labor-social democratic traditions such as Sweden experienced significant declines in union membership in the past two decades (International Labour Organization, 1997).

Are we witnessing the end of unionism? Will unions rebound in response to the anxieties many workers are experiencing today? Or, will new organizations emphasizing new strategies arise to provide workers with a voice on their jobs and the assistance needed to move across firms as job opportunities come and go? These questions are difficult to answer. However, history teaches us that no democratic country has existed for long periods of time without some significant independent force advocating and representing employee interests. Perhaps this century will witness the creation of new organizational forms for representing employees that are better matched to the nature of the new economy, the new organization, and the contemporary workforce. Some are already emerging. An organization called Working Today provides health benefits and social networking opportunities for highly mobile media workers in New York City. One important question will be how will—and how should—managers react to these organizations? Should they resist and undermine them? Share power with them? Attempt to work with them and shape them in ways that fit the needs of employees and the organization? Managers of the future are likely to encounter these questions. For this reason we include as the next reading an essay by Charles Heckscher speculating about these issues.

Summary

This Class Note focused on the issues that arise in managing employees during a time of transition and increasing flexibility and uncertainty. It highlighted some of the potential advantages and disadvantages of flexibility from the perspectives of varied constituencies of employees. The impact on employees should be of concern to you as a manager, because successful performance is affected by employee recruitment, retention, motivation, and, in particular, the willing contribution of effort and skill where self-managing and shared decision making are increasingly important.

The enthusiasm in the business press for flexible and virtual organizations comes from their ability to enhance the focus on "core competencies" and allow the organization to adapt quickly to a changing environment. At the same time, some reservation about these practices is evident because they seem to create a world of chaos and insecurity, at least in the short run, during the transition to new organizational forms. In the longer run, new practices may be devised that take into account employees' concerns for balancing work in their lives, that provide institutional supports at both the organizational and societal levels for flexible working arrangements, and that help to resolve some of the unexpected consequences and perceived contradictions that arise during the transition.

This Class Note was designed to make you aware of the tensions that can arise so that you are not taken by surprise, to urge you to think analytically about what it is that is changing when "change" is so broadly discussed, and to inspire you to think more broadly and creatively about some of the options and changes that can be devised.

In conclusion, here are some things to keep in mind:

- The overall coherence of the multiple pieces of your approach—*the old system was indeed a system and new pieces need to make sense together and to be bolstered by a new social contract.*
- The possible negative consequences of a "mismatch" of practices—*for example, teamwork and downsizing do not go together well, nor do teamwork and individualistic, competitive rewards.*
- The occasional positive consequences of a "mismatch" of practices—*for example, the realization that teamwork requires a new reward system is pushing companies to innovate.*
- The perceived legitimacy of practices to multiple stakeholders—*for example, some people will feel pleased and motivated and some will feel cheated if companies begin to change the shape of career paths, and it is difficult to assess the net impact on motivation, withheld effort, and ultimately, productivity.*
- The need to think of creative alternative ways to get work done—*for example, how staffing needs can be met flexibly in a way that creates jobs that people want to have and that recognizes the role that business plays in shaping the quality of life in societies.*
- The need to understand how human assets relate to the mission and goals of the organization and its search for competitive advantage.
- The need to consider how firms fit into a broader network of labor market and product and community institutions that together are responsible for developing a highly skilled and fairly treated workforce.
- The need to repair the broken promises and trust some employees experienced in the turbulent ups and downs of the economy and of individual organizations in recent years.

References

Bailyn, Lotte. 1993. Patterned Chaos in Human Resource Management. *Sloan Management Review* 34, 77–83.

Bailyn, Lotte, Robert Drago, and Thomas Kochan. 2001. *Integrating Work and Family Life: A Holistic Approach.* Cambridge, MA: MIT Sloan School of Management.

Bane, Mary Jo, and David Elliott. 1993. Is American Business Working for the Poor? *Harvard Business Review.*

Blair, Margaret. 1995. *Ownership and Control.* Washington, DC: The Brookings Institution.

Bridges, William. 1994. The End of the Job. *Fortune* (September 19, 1994), 64.

Business Week. The New World of Work. (October 17, 1994), 76.

Cutcher Gershenfeld, Joel, et al. 1998. *Knowledge Driven Work Systems.* New York: Oxford University Press.

Deming, W. E. 1986. *Out of the Crisis.* Cambridge, MA: Massachusetts Institute of Technology Center for Advanced Engineering Technology.

Donnellon, Anne, and Maureen Scully. 1994. Teams, Merit, and Rewards: Will the Post-Bureaucratic Organization Be a Post-Meritocratic Organization? In Anne Donnellon and Charles Heckscher (eds.), *The Post-Bureaucratic Organization: New Perspectives on Organizational Change.* Thousand Oaks, CA: Sage Publications.

Ehrenreich, Barbara. 2001. *Nickeled and Dimed: On Not Making It in America.* New York: Holt.

Ichniowski, Casey, Thomas Kochan, David Levine, Craig Olsen, and George Strauss. 1996. What Works at Work. *Industrial Relations* 35, 299–333.

International Labour Organization. 1997. *World Labor Report: Industrial Relations, Democracy, and Social Stability*. Geneva: International Labour Organization.

Kochan, Thomas A. 1994. The American Corporation as an Employer: Past, Present, and Future Possibilities. Unpublished paper. Sloan School of Management, Massachusetts Institute of Technology, p. 4.

Kochan, Thomas A., Michal Smith, John C. Wells, and James B. Rebitzer. 1994. Human Resource Strategies and Contingent Workers: The Case of Safety and Health in the Petrochemical Industry. *Human Resource Management* 33, 255–278.

Kochan, Thomas, and Paul Osterman. 1994. *The Mutual Gains Enterprise: Human Resource Strategies and National Policy*. Boston: Harvard Business School Press.

Kohn, Alfie. 1993. *Punished by Rewards: The Trouble with Gold Stars, Incentive Plans, A's, Praise, and Other Bribes*. Boston: Houghton Mifflin.

Kunda, Gideon, Stephen Barley, and James Evans. 1999. "Why Do Contractors Contract? Working Paper No. 4, MIT Task Force on Reconstructing Labor Markets, available at http://www.mit.edu/iwer.

Lautsch, Brenda. 2002. Uncovering and Explaining Variance in the Features and Outcomes of Contingent Work. *Industrial and Labor Relations Review* 56, 23–43.

National Research Council. 1991. *Pay for Performance: Evaluating Performance Appraisal and Merit Pay*. Washington, DC: National Academy Press.

Nonaka, Ikujiro and Hirotaka Takeuchi. 1995. *The Knowledge-Creating Company: How Japanese Companies Create the Dynamics of Innovation*. New York: Oxford University Press.

Osterman, Paul. 1988. *Employment Futures: Reorganization, Dislocation, and Public Policy*. New York: Oxford University Press.

Osterman, Paul. 1992. *Securing Prosperity*. New York: Russel Sage.

Osterman, Paul, Thomas A. Kochan, Richard Locke, and Michael Piore. 1999. *Working in America: A Blueprint for the New Labor Market*. Cambridge, MA: MIT Press.

Patterson, Jack. 1994. Welcome to the Company That Isn't There. *Business Week* (October 17), 86.

Rappaport, Rona, Lotte Bailyn, Joyce K. Fletcher, and Betty H. Pruitt. 2002. *Beyond Work-Family Balance: Advancing Gender Equity and Workplace Performance*. San Francisco: Jossey-Bass.

Scully, Maureen. 1993. The Imperfect Legitimation of Inequality in Internal Labor Markets. Working Paper #3520-93. Cambridge, MA: Sloan School of Management, Massachusetts Institute of Technology.

Scully, Maureen, and Gil Preuss. 1994. The Dual Character of Trust During Workplace Transformation. *Proceedings of the Industrial Relations Research Association*. Madison, WI: Industrial Relations Research Association.

Williams, Joan. 2000. *Unbending Gender: Why Family and Work Conflict and What to Do about It*. New York: Oxford University Press.

Women's Bar Association of Massachusetts. 2000. *More than Part Time*. Boston: Boston Bar Association.

Workforce 2000: Work and Workers for the 21st Century. 1987. Indianapolis: Hudson Institute.

The Changing Social Contract for White-Collar Workers

by Charles Heckscher

The unprecedented attack on middle management during the past decade creates a new theoretical and moral challenge to our employment relations system. The impact goes far beyond numerical body counts from corporate layoffs; what has been shaken is not just individual lives, but an implied social contract that has long governed employment relations at the management level. The disruption of expectations has profoundly affected much of the workforce, undermining the sense that one can predict and understand the future and resulting in a dangerous sense of drift and confusion.

The Theoretical Challenge

The theoretical challenge for our field stems from the fact that much of the industrial relations system is based on a model of stable hierarchical companies. At the white-collar level, managers have long been treated as part of a corporate "family" protected from market fluctuations; this is part of the reason why they have been exempted from the Wagner Act protections and located instead within a legal framework positing a need for loyalty. At the blue-collar level, too, periodic contracts have sought to "lock in" a system that can provide reliable benefits to employees; and a sense of loyalty, of lifelong relation to a large employer, has been a crucial part of the "good life" built by unionized workers. If employees, after the current wave of restructurings, are less tied to a single employer, and if middle managers are in the same boat as blue-collar employees, then the current system of representation falls to the ground: neither contracts nor paternalistic family-feeling provide protection.

The moral issue is still more profound: the layoffs undermine the contract that has helped managers make sense of the world. As I have talked to middle managers and professional employees in large corporations, I have been struck by the sense of moral violation they have experienced. Their life as employees has been governed by a relatively simple rule of loyalty: as one expressed it,

> *My basic mindset was, there's an implicit contract. I expect that the company will provide me a career, development opportunities, and reasonable pay and benefits; and they, in turn, should expect from me that I'm willing to work very hard for them. When either one of us is unhappy with that situation, the contract is broken. And up until the past two years, as a corporation I had faith that that would occur.*[1]

> *But when downsizings reached these ranks, the whole world-view began to come apart: Loyalty comes with trust and believing, and this has been cast out across the whole company as being not the way to run things. And then when you look around you see takeovers and the crumbling of everything in the whole economy.*

With "the crumbling of everything" people begin to cast about to make sense of the world. Many of them simply put their heads down and try to block out the reality of the change, hoping that they can make it through to retirement; others brush up their resumes and in a more-or-less meandering way test out their prospects in the outside world. No one gains much by these moves: not the companies, who find their employees acting more timid and bureaucratic and less entrepreneurial than before; and certainly not the employees themselves.

A Return to the Past? The Limits of Loyalty

One major response has, not surprisingly, been to lament the passing of the old ethic and to wish for its return: hardly a day passes without a newspaper article decrying the unfeeling heartlessness of corporate downsizings. From there it is only a short and common step to proposing that managers be

---

Source: Heckscher, Charles. 1997. "The Changing Social Contract for White-Collar Workers." *Perspectives on Work* pp. 18–21. Reprinted by permission of the Industrial Relations Research Association. **Charles Heckscher** is a professor at Rutgers University and chair of the Labor Studies and Employment Relations Department. His research explores alternatives to bureaucratic systems of management. He has worked for many years as a consultant on organizational transformation, especially in joint union-management settings.

1 This and other quotes are drawn from my book *White-Collar Blue: Management Loyalties in an Age of Corporate Restructuring.* NY: Basic Books, 1995.

forced to maintain the familiar system through bargaining or government regulation. It seems like a highly reasonable idea: it would bring us back to an order that we know how to deal with, that makes sense, and that has provided to a reasonable degree for many people the main things we look for from society: happiness, wealth, order.

The last forty years of political history, however, should make us wary of trying to engineer the social order. Loyalty in its heyday was not forced or engineered—few regulations *before* the '80s tried to guarantee employment security. Security for the core labor force arose naturally, as it were, out of the economic system, as a way of promoting needed cooperation within large oligopolistic bureaucracies. Chester Barnard, a former president of New Jersey Bell, said without equivocation in the '30s, "The most important single contribution required of the executive . . . is loyalty."

Today Barnard's counterparts say no such thing. As they chop at the previously accepted obligations of loyalty, many have tried to stop them. Plant-closing legislation and security clauses as a center of collective bargaining are recent phenomena, countering a shift already in motion. But unless we understand *why* business leaders have shifted their grounds—what are the underlying forces that have eroded an order that previously seemed "natural"—we should be cautious about attempts to hold that order in place.

Put that way, it should be obvious what has happened. Building a long-term culture of trust within an organization was eminently sensible in Barnard's era: it was a period in which the economy hit a stride, with a dominant group of large companies producing a relatively stable group of products. But today we are in the midst of instabilities of quite a different magnitude. The list of transformative pressures is familiar but worth repeating in order to take stock of how deeply the new employment relation is bound to overwhelming social change: information technology, scrambling entire industries and changing methods of work in almost every corner of the economy; the opening of international competition, forcing a reconfiguration of production patterns; the maturing of the consumer economy, creating new demands for innovation and customization; and the rising educational level of the workforce, generating a reserve of intelligence never used by traditional bureaucracies.

With all that, the long-term and hierarchical pattern of loyalty just doesn't fit. The problem is not that today's corporate leaders are somehow more callous than their predecessors. It is that the conditions of the existing moral contract no longer hold.

If we wanted to go back to a stable system of loyalty, we would also have to recreate some elements that are perhaps more controversial: a lower level of technology; a less capable and independent workforce; less demanding consumers; and closed borders. This is not only impractical, it is on the whole undesirable from a *moral* point of view. For in our nostalgia for employment stability and the ethic of loyalty, we often forget the less pleasant side.

The condition of security in the contract of loyalty, as Barnard understood, was a kind of paternalistic domination. Consider, for instance, the conclusion of his dictum just cited: "The most important single contribution required of the executive . . . is loyalty"—and here the part I omitted—"and *domination by the organization personality*."[2] The traditional corporation was a closed world and managers were expected to keep within it. They might be taken care of, but they were not to question the care. Women and minorities, as Rosabeth Kanter notably documented,[3] were not welcomed into this tight informal world; on the contrary, as wives they were expected to support their husbands, following wherever corporate needs took them. Executives were expected to follow a dress code, join the right clubs, and speak an internally coded language.

So if we want to go back to loyalty, we would also have to give up what I would consider significant moral advances of recent years. In an increasingly international world, executives have to be more mobile than ever—how could this be possible without submissive wives to follow along? Loyalty demands a high level of conformity—how could it incorporate the demands of an increasingly diverse workforce? The demands of paternalistic corporations extend deep into the private lives of their employees, and we have only begun to make progress in separating private choices in things like political or sexual orientation from the demands of work. Loyalty demands subordination, acceptance of what one is told. We are just beginning to move to greater "empowerment," participation, and sharing of information in corporations. Let us not be too quick with our condemnation of change.

Moving On: Free Agency and Professionalism

If loyalty is gone, many assume that there is only one alternative: a cold logic (as one manager

---

2 Barnard, Chester I. 1938. *The Functions of the Executive*. Cambridge, MA: Harvard University Press. Italics added.
3 *Men and Women of the Corporation*. NY: Basic Books, 1977.

expressed it to me) of "give and get, give and get," watching out only for oneself—a vision of free agency, conjuring up images of spoiled, high-paid baseball players and investment bankers, entailing no moral obligations.

This attitude—I can't call it an ethic, because it is really nothing other than the absence of a moral contract—is almost universally unpopular: none of the managers I have interviewed, nor (as far as I can remember) any of my business students, embrace such an approach. Sometimes those who have been made cynical by the violation of prior obligations *say* they are going to go over to an attitude of pure self-interest; but if you push them at all they immediately express their distaste for the whole idea.

The absence of a moral alternative is one powerful factor that makes so many hold on to traditional loyalty. The fact is—and this would not have surprised Adam Smith, though it might surprise Milton Friedman—that few people are willing to leap into an abyss of amoral self-interest. But the traditional ethic of loyalty, with its flaws, is not the only alternative to this doom. Many managers are developing a new ethic, or a new vision of a social contract, that accommodates a more flexible and less paternalistic relationship. I have called it "professional," though it is rather different from the professionalism of closed societies like doctors and lawyers. It entails centrally an *open negotiation of obligations between employee and employer.*

Where loyalty is diffuse and eternal, the professional ethic is relatively specific and time-limited. Its core assumption is that the employment relation is a meshing of interests between parties who are independent and changing. That assumption both reflects the real world and allows far more moral autonomy to the employee than the traditional relationship. It does not, however, lead to an atomized concept of self-interested individuals: the employment relation does create *obligations* that cannot legitimately be ignored.

The first obligation is honesty:

> *What's the psychological contract? The main thing is to keep things open. We have agreed to have open agendas, nothing hidden, no hidden agendas, to be open and honest with each other.*

Thus, as these managers view it, they have both a right and an obligation to make known their personal agendas—what they hope to accomplish, what limits they set on their willingness to obey, and whether they are looking for other opportunities. The company, for its part, has an obligation to be open about its business prospects, what it expects for the employee, and what challenges it can provide in the future.

Both sides of this obligation, it should be stressed, are unfamiliar in a relationship of loyalty. The loyal employee is not expected to set limits—to say, for instance, that family obligations prevent a major move is seen as a violation of loyalty and therefore a "career killer." And the company is not expected to reveal its plan—business information flows less freely, and evaluations of career prospects are largely hidden for fear of "demotivating" people.

The second key obligation is for each party to work for the health of the other. If a company's business plans change—a financial crisis, a change in strategy, a takeover—"professional" managers do not expect to be taken care of permanently, but they do expect the company to do all it can to put them in a position of strength for the future. This means, among other things, that the company should constantly encourage and help employees to develop generalized skills that can be transferred to the world outside.

Again, those of a loyalist perspective see this as madness, and it drives many HR leaders crazy—they reason that if you want people to remain loyal you certainly don't want to encourage them to leave. The professional logic, by contrast, is that if you want people to contribute with their full intelligence you want them to stay only as long as *they* want to.

On the other side of this obligation, "professional" employees do not feel justified in leaving at a moment's notice or merely for money. If some circumstance causes them to leave—and a major new career challenge counts as a legitimate reason—they feel obligated to finish the projects they are working on and to assist the company in replacing their skills and knowledge.

In the best of circumstances, this relationship escapes paternalism by establishing a kind of equality between the organization and the individuals—an exchange of abilities for challenge, in place of the loyalty bargain of effort for security. It accepts the reality of downsizing and restructuring, as well as of career change and growth, without tossing everything into the pit of naked self-interest. This is, I would emphasize, not merely a theorist's ideal-type, but a real construction of certain managers faced with the "crumbling of everything" from the familiar world of loyalty.

The Conditions for Professionalism

There is just one flaw in this picture: though the professional ethic exists in some people's minds, it does not exist in the society at large. A new ethic must develop not just an abstract concept of obligations, but an employment relations *system* that provides the conditions for fair negotiation and enforcement of obligations.

The existing system supports instead the old pattern of long-term loyalty. The legal order, for instance, takes it as a given that the manager's obligation of loyalty supersedes almost everything else, including (in many cases) the duty to obey the law. The educational system is set up to set people on the path of occupational life, and then withdraw to allow companies to take over training and career formation throughout adulthood. Prestige is heavily tied to one's employer. There are few kinds of certification that enable someone to carry a reputation from one firm to another. And, of course—most concretely—health care and retirement benefits are still generally tied to tenure with a single company.

Thus those who take the ethic of professionalism seriously—who take seriously the widespread rhetoric about "shaping your own career" and "maintaining employability"—find themselves naked and alone. There are still very few employers that encourage the development of generalized skills; few educational mechanisms for gaining certification for new careers in adulthood; only the beginnings of portable health insurance; and very poor mechanisms of information about available jobs.

There is still a need for institutions of employment relations, but redesigned to encourage the new contract rather than the old. Collective bargaining will surely not disappear, but is becoming a special case of the broader process of negotiation.

Many levels of innovation are needed, but I would stress two. The first is collective action, or association. Though negotiation around the professional ethic is more individualized than the centralized contracts of industrial relations, group support is still essential. The burden of negotiating the professional relation is far too much for anyone to handle alone. Managers find a constant need to establish networks and get information and advice from others in similar situations.

Thus support groups and associations are acquiring increasing significance in helping people navigate unpredictable career shoals. And many are beginning, in a tentative way, to act also as pressure groups, using publicity and mobilization of internal networks to hold management to its own rhetoric of empowerment and openness. This is the logic behind the formation of Working Today—an organization that aims to represent employees under the new social contract.

Nor is this need restricted to managers and true professionals: more and more blue-collar and service workers see themselves as similarly "on their own" in the work world, unable to depend on a company. Unions have been slowly but increasingly looking for ways to support them through services of "associate membership" and representation outside a collective bargaining contract.

The second major innovation involves the role of government. Though associations can do a great deal, they need a foundation of obligations embodied in law. The existing governmental role, of regulating organizing and bargaining processes under the Wagner Act, seems ineffectual and beside the point for many employees today—but that doesn't mean there is no needed government role. A century's worth of law, affirming (in the words of one key decision) that "there is no more elemental cause for discharge of an employee than disloyalty to his employer," needs to be recast on a different foundation. A labor relations system conceived around a balance of power between stable bureaucracies must give way to one that facilitates individual mobility within a collective vision of fairness—the obligations of the new social contract have to find their way into enforceable law. There is also a critical role for government in developing portability of benefits and various kinds of "disaster insurance" in an increasingly risky world—either by directly providing these benefits or by backing up private insurance mechanisms.

A social contract is both far simpler and far deeper than contracts bargained on the open market or through shows of force: it shapes daily lives and expectations through a huge range of different roles in a society. The wave of downsizings, driven by forces that are only partly understood, has left a void that is easily filled with individualistic cynicism or backwards-looking reaction.

Our field has, I believe, a major role to play in revitalizing the employment relation, as it led the way once before in the creation of the industrial relations system. But it has to start from a clear acceptance of (as the old prayer has it) "what cannot be changed" in the current developments—that business organizations are becoming more flexible and responsive to rapid environmental change and therefore less stable and protective. Our problem is to conceptualize fairness, and a way to enforce it, within that context.

Building Competitive Advantage Through People

By Christopher A. Bartlett and Sumantra Ghoshal

Most managers today understand the strategic implications of the information-based, knowledge-driven, service-intensive economy. They know what the new game requires: speed, flexibility and continuous self-renewal. They even are recognizing that skilled and motivated people are central to the operations of any company that wishes to flourish in the new age.

And yet, a decade of organizational delayering, destaffing, restructuring and reengineering has produced employees who are more exhausted than empowered, more cynical than self-renewing. Worse still, in many companies only marginal managerial attention—if that—is focused on the problems of employee capability and motivation. Somewhere between theory and practice, precious human capital is being misused, wasted or lost.

Having studied more than 20 companies in the process of trying to transform themselves, we have concluded that although structure is undoubtedly an impediment to the process, an even bigger barrier is managers' outdated understanding of strategy. (See the table "The Evolving Focus of Strategy.") At the heart of the problem is a failure to recognize that although the past three decades have brought dramatic changes in both external strategic imperatives and internal strategic resources, many companies continue to have outmoded strategic perspectives.

In the competitive-strategy model in which many of today's leaders were trained, sophisticated strategic-planning systems were supposed to help senior managers decide which businesses to grow and which to harvest.[1] Unfortunately, all the planning and investment were unable to stop the competition from imitating or leapfrogging their carefully developed product-market positions.

In the late 1980s, the search for more dynamic, adaptive and sustainable advantage led many to supplement their analysis of external competition with an internal-competency assessment. They recognized that development of resources and capabilities would be more difficult to imitate: The core-competency perspective focused attention on the importance of knowledge creation and building learning processes for competitive advantage.[2] But this approach, too, faced limits as companies recognized that their people were not equal to the new knowledge-intensive tasks. By definition, competency-based strategies are dependent on people: Scarce knowledge and expertise drive new-product development, and personal relationships with key clients are at the core of flexible market responsiveness. In short, people are the key strategic resource, and strategy must be built on a human-resource foundation. As more and more companies come to that conclusion, competition for scarce human resources heats up.

The Role of the Executive in the "War for Talent" Era

Senior managers at most traditional companies have been left gasping for air at the breadth and rapidity of change during the past two decades. Hierarchy has to be replaced by networks, bureaucratic systems transformed into flexible processes, and control-based management roles must evolve into relationships featuring empowerment and coaching. In observing companies going through such change, we have come to the conclusion that as difficult as the strategic challenges may be, they are acted on faster than the organizational transformation needed to sustain them. And however hard it is to change the organization, it is even harder to change the orientation and mind-set of its senior managers. Hence today's managers are

---

Source: Reprinted from "Building Competitive Advantage Through People" by Christopher A. Bartlett and Sumantra Ghoshal, *MIT Sloan Management Review*, Winter, 2002, pp. 34–41 by permission of the publisher. Copyright © 2002 by Massachusetts Institute of Technology. All rights reserved. **Christopher A. Bartlett** is a professor of business administration at Harvard Business School, and Sumantra Ghoshal is a professor of strategic leadership at London Business School.

1 For a review of such approaches, see C. Hofer and Dan Schendel, *Strategy Formulation: Analytical Concepts* (St. Paul, Minnesota: West Publishing, 1978), 69–100.
2 The core-competence model is elaborated in G. Hamel an C.K. Prahalad, *Competing for the Future* (Boston: Harvard Business School Press, 1994).

The Evolving Focus of Strategy

	Competition for Products and Markets	Competition for Resources and Competencies	Competition for Talent and Dreams
Strategic Objective	Defensible product-market positions	Sustainable competitive advantage	Continuous self-renewal
Major Tools, Perspectives	• Industry analysis: competitor analysis	• Core competencies	• Vision and values
	• Market segmentation and positioning	• Resource-based strategy	• Flexibility and innovation
	• Strategic planning	• Networked organization	• Front-line entrepreneurship and experimentation
Key Strategic Resource	Financial capital	Organizational capability	Human and intellectual capital

trying to implement third-generation strategies through second-generation organizations with first-generation management.

In an earlier study we analyzed the evolution of CEO Jack Welch's thinking at General Electric Co. and the simultaneous adjustment of his leadership role during the company's two decade transformation.[3] In many ways, however, Welch is an exception: Very few top executives have been able to transform themselves from being analytically driven strategy directors to people-oriented strategy framers. Yet for a traditional company to make the transition into the New Economy, that transformation is vital. In our ongoing research, we have identified three important changes the CEO must make.

A Changing View of Strategic Resources

The hardest mind-set to alter is the longstanding, deeply embedded belief that capital is the critical strategic resource to be managed and that senior managers' key responsibilities should center around its acquisition, allocation and effective use.

For the vast majority of companies, that assumption simply is no longer true. Without denying the need for prudent use of financial resources, we believe that, for most companies today, capital is not the resource that constrains growth. Global capital markets have opened up the supply side, while widespread excess industry capacity has reduced the demand side. The recent reversals in some sectors notwithstanding, most companies are awash in capital. Of them, many cannot even generate sufficient high-quality capital-budget projects to use the available resources—and therefore go on merger-and-acquisition expeditions.

The stock market is telling managers what the scarce strategic resource is. When it values a mature, capital-intensive company like GE at 10 times its book value, it is seeing something of greater worth than the physical assets recorded in financial accounts. Though the dot-com bubble burst, the exuberant and often irrational funding of technology-savvy entrepreneurs pointed to the same lesson: There is a surplus of capital chasing a scarcity of talented people and the knowledge they possess. In today's economy, that is the constraining—and therefore strategic—resource.

The implications for top management are profound. First, human-resources issues must move up near the top of the agenda in discussions of the company's strategic priorities. That means that a first-class human-resources executive must be at the CEO's right hand. Eventually, traditional strategic-planning processes will need to be overhauled and the financially calibrated measurement and reward systems will have to be redesigned to recognize the strategic importance of human as well as financial resources.

---

[3] S. Ghoshal and C.A. Bartlett, *The Individualized Corporation* (New York: HarperCollins, 1997), 243–270. An overview of GE's transformation is also contained in our article "Rebuilding Behavioral Context: A Blueprint for Corporate Renewal," *Sloan Management Review* 34 (Winter 1996), 11–23.

A Changing View of Value

Recognizing that the company's scarce resource is knowledgeable people means a shift in the whole concept of value management within the corporation.

In the early 1980s, competitive strategy was seen as a zero-sum game. Michael E. Porter, for example, saw the company surrounded by its suppliers, customers, competitors and substitutes, engaged in a battle with them to capture the maximum economic value possible.

The subsequent interest in building and leveraging unique internal capabilities caused a gradual shift in emphasis from value appropriation to value creation. As information and knowledge came to provide competitive advantage, the game shifted. Unlike capital, knowledge actually increases when shared, thus eliminating the zero-sum game. Clearly, the focus on value creation demands a different approach than a focus on value appropriation.[4]

One of the most basic issues is how the value that the company creates should be distributed. Most companies operate under the assumption that shareholders, as contributors of capital, have the primary claim. But recruiting difficulties that large traditional companies face, employees' eroding sense of loyalty and cynicism over the growing gap between the compensation of those at the top and those on the front lines all indicate that value distribution must change. The rapid spread of stock options as a form of compensation shows that companies have begun to recognize that the owners of the scarce resources are no longer only the shareholders but also the employees.

The implications are profound. Top management must begin renegotiating both implicit and explicit contracts with key stakeholders, particularly with employees. Unless those who contribute their human and intellectual capital are given the opportunity to enjoy the fruits of the value creation they are driving, they will go where they have that opportunity—typically to newer, less tradition-bound companies.

A Changing View of Senior Managers' Roles

Unlike capital, scarce knowledge and expertise cannot be accumulated at the top of the company and distributed to those projects or programs in which it will yield the greatest strategic advantage. It resides in the heads of individuals at all levels and is embedded in the relationships of work groups—those closest to the customers, the competitors and the technology. Therefore, rather than allocate capital to competing projects (the zero-sum game), senior managers must nurture individual expertise and initiative, then leverage it through cross-unit sharing (the positive-sum game).

Already we have seen downsizing of corporate planning departments, simplification of strategic-planning and capital-budgeting processes, and massive overhauls of corporate structures and processes—all in an effort both to shift initiative to those deep in the organization who possess valued expertise and to break down the barriers to effective sharing of that expertise.

But senior managers also must rethink their role in shaping strategic direction. Their main contribution has shifted from deciding the strategic content to framing the organizational context. That means creating a sense of purpose that not only provides an integrating framework for bottom-up strategic initiatives, but also injects meaning into individual effort. It means articulating company values that not only align organizational effort with the overall enterprise objectives, but also define a community to which individuals want to belong. And it means developing organizational processes that not only get work done effectively, but also ensure the empowerment, development and commitment of all members of the organization. The philosophical shift requires executives to expand beyond strategy, structure and systems to a simultaneous focus on the company's purpose, process and people.

Implications for HR Professionals

In many companies the transition process is becoming an important proving ground for the human-resources function, with many old-school HR executives finding that neither their training nor their experience has prepared them for a leading strategic role. In the 1980s era of competitive-strategy analysis, their function was typically supportive and administrative. Once line managers had translated top management's strategic objectives into specific operational priorities, the role of HR staff was to ensure that recruitment, training, benefits administration and the like supported the well-defined strategic and operational agenda.

When strategic priorities became more organizationally focused in the 1990s, human-resources managers increasingly were included in the strategic conversation, often to help define and develop the company's core competencies—and almost

---

4 For a richer elaboration of that argument, see S. Ghoshal, C.A. Bartlett and P. Moran, "A New Manifesto for Management" in *Strategic Thinking for the Next Economy,* ed. M.A. Cusumano and C.C. Markides (San Francisco: Jossey-Bass, 2001), 9–32.

always to align the organizational design and management skills to support those strategic assets.

Now, as companies move into the war for talent and as individuals with specialized knowledge, skills and expertise are recognized as the scarce strategic resource, HR professionals must become key players in the design, development and delivery of a company's strategy. (See the table "The Evolving Role of Human Resources.")

Unfortunately, many top-level human-resources managers view the new task through old lenses. They continue to treat employees as raw materials to be acquired and then made useful through training and development, or at best they acknowledge employees to be valuable assets on whom expenditures in the form of development and generous compensation are worthwhile investments. In response to the demands resulting from the growing importance of human capital, they develop more aggressive approaches to recruitment, create more innovative training programs, and experiment with more-sophisticated compensation packages. The problem is twofold: They are tackling a strategic task with old, functional tools, and they are trying to bring about major systemic change with incremental, programmatic solutions. Human-resources managers must see employees as "talent investors," to be treated as partners and rewarded the way other investors are.

We have identified three core tasks that align the human-resources function with the strategic challenge of developing the company's human capital for sustainable competitive advantage: building, linking and bonding.

The Building Challenge

Many companies claim that their people are their most important asset, but few have built the human-resources systems, processes or cultures that can even offset, let alone challenge, the deeply embedded bias toward financial assets. For example, in almost any company, decisions relating to capital expenditures are subjected to well-documented capital-budgeting procedures. Typically, guidelines define approval levels (for example, division presidents may approve expenditures up to $1 million, the CEO up to $5 million, and the board above that level), require clear evaluation processes (for example, positive discounted-cash-flow returns above the weighted cost of capital) and set specific benchmarks (for example, payback on new equipment in three years).

When it comes to hiring a district sales manager or a shift foreman, however, decisions are routinely made by front-line managers who choose the best available among three or four marginal applicants to address a short-term difficulty. Yet that is at least a $2 million decision if one calculates recruiting costs, training costs and a discounted cash flow of the expected future stream of salary and benefits payments over the average tenure of such employees. But by recruiting a merely average individual, the company loses the opportunity to gain competitive advantage through a hiring decision. If the company were to make the decision strategic, it would have to set standards, monitor activities and measure recruiting outcomes in a way that made the decision as precise and rigorous as those guiding capital allocation.

Converting recruitment into a strategic task means making an ongoing commitment to locating and attracting the best of the best at every level and from every source. Microsoft Corp. is unusually thorough in its recruitment process, annually scanning the entire pool of 25,000 U.S. computer-science graduates in order to identify the 8,000 in whom it has an interest. After further screening, it targets 2,600 for on-campus interviews and invites just 800 of those to visit the company's Redmond,

The Evolving Role of Human Resources

	Competition for Products and Markets	Competition for Resources and Competencies	Competition for Talent and Dreams
Perspectives on Employees	People viewed as factors of production	People viewed as valuable resources	People viewed as "talent investors"
HR's Role in Strategy	Implementation, support	Contributory	Central
Key HR Activity	Administering of recruitment, training and benefits	Aligning resources and capabilities to achieve strategic intent	Building human capital as a core source of competitive advantage

Washington, headquarters. Of them, 500 receive offers, and 400—the top 2% of that year's graduates—typically accept. Yet that massive college-recruiting effort provides less than 20% of the company's new-people needs. To locate the rest, the company maintains a team of more than 300 recruiting experts whose full-time job is to locate the best and brightest in the industry. That strike force builds a relationship with literally thousands of the most capable systems designers, software engineers and program managers, often courting them for years. In the late 1990s, the effort resulted in more than 2,000 of the most talented people in the industry joining Microsoft annually.

After a company has acquired top talent, the building challenge also requires the human-resources function to lead company efforts in constantly developing those talented individuals. That requires more than traditional training programs provide. Today development must be embedded in the company's bloodstream, with all managers responsible for giving their team members on-going feedback and coaching. That is something McKinsey does unusually well, which helps to explain why MBAs worldwide are more likely to seek employment there than at any other employer. (See the boxed feature "One Company's Way of Valuing People.")

There is one other aspect of building human capital that is grossly undermanaged at most companies. As any good gardener knows, to promote healthy growth, in addition to fertilizing and watering you also must prune and weed. That is a metaphor Jack Welch used often in describing the performance-ranking process he introduced to cull chronic underperformers at GE. Yet in most companies, the human-resources department focuses considerable effort on planting, staking, watering and fertilizing—and practically none on cutting out deadwood or growth-inhibiting underbrush.

Culling is no longer confined to hard-driving U.S. industrial companies. South Korea's LG, traditionally a cradle-to-grave employer, uses a "vitality index" as a critical performance measure. All managers have to rank their direct reports on a 1-to-5 scale (with 1 equal to the bottom 10% and 5 representing the top 10%). The vitality index is the ratio of new recruits who are ranked at 4 or 5 to employees of rank 1 or 2, who are counseled to move on.

One Company's Way of Valuing People

The global management-consulting firm McKinsey & Co. is an example of a company that truly values its employees, as it demonstrates through its commitment to their development. Although formal training plays an important role, by far the most critical development tools are intensive individual feedback and coaching.

Such activities absorb 15% to 20% of the average partner's time. Every consultant receives a formal performance review from his or her office's partner group twice a year, with the individual's designated development director offering detailed feedback, counseling and career advice. The input for that biannual review comes from reports prepared by each of the client-engagement managers, senior-level consultants who are responsible for the day-to-day management of the team to which the individual belongs and who have supervised the individual's work. The engagement managers also provide the consultant with feedback, evaluation, and development advice after each of the four or five engagements that span a typical year's assignment. During each engagement, the consultant also has dozens of additional one-on-one feedback and coaching sessions with the more senior people managing and directing the project. In total, each consultant receives scores of specific, detailed coaching sessions per year. The company maintains that its in-depth approach to development is one of the main reasons why people join McKinsey—and why they stay.

The Linking Task

Just as there is value in attracting and developing individuals who hold specialized knowledge, there is value in the social networks that enable sharing of that knowledge. Indeed, unless a company actively links, leverages and embeds the pockets of individual-based knowledge and expertise, it risks underutilizing it or, worse, losing it. As companies seek the best ways to convert individual expertise into embedded intellectual capital, the classic response is to give the task to the chief information officer—along with the faddish title of chief knowledge officer.

Not surprisingly, people with information-systems background immediately focus on the task of mapping, modeling and codifying knowledge. Under their leadership, companies have developed databases, expert systems and intranets to help capture and make accessible the company's most valuable information. Yet in many companies, managers do not take full advantage of those elegant new knowledge-management systems.

At the heart of the problem is a widespread failure to recognize that although knowledge management can be supported by an efficient technical infrastructure, it is operated through a social network. Information technologists may help in organizing data and making it accessible, but they must be teamed up with—and operate in support of—those who understand human motivation and social interaction. Only then can individual roles and organizational processes be designed to ensure the delicate conversion from available information to embedded knowledge.

Thus, the second core strategic role of the top HR executive is to take the lead in developing the social networks that are vital to the capture and transfer of knowledge. Because that requires an understanding of organization design, process management, interpersonal relationships and trust-based culture, it calls for leadership from sophisticated human-resources professionals who also have a strong understanding of the business.

The most obvious challenge is to build on the process reengineering that most companies implemented during the 1990s to break down bureaucracy and unlock core competencies. The re-engineered processes (whether at a micro level, as in order entry, or a macro level, as in new-product development) had two major objectives: breaking down hierarchical barriers to rapid decision making, and opening up new horizontal channels and forums for cross-unit communication and collaboration. Those activities are precisely what will link isolated individuals and organizational units into dynamic social networks.

In the early 1990s, British Petroleum built such networks under the leadership of John Browne, who at the time was overseeing the development of BP's prototype knowledge management and organizational-learning program as head of BP Exploration. Transferring the approach to the whole company when he became CEO in 1995, Browne avoided installing a new set of information systems, focusing instead on a practice he described as "peer assists." The assist was a small-scale project that encouraged those on the front line in one business unit (operators on a drilling platform in the North Sea, for example) to contact other BP operations (offshore drillers in the Gulf of Mexico, for instance) that had the expertise to help solve particular problems. Cutting through formal layers and complex procedures, the process became an accepted way of doing business, and managers soon recognized that it was not acceptable to refuse a request for help.

The process was supplemented by "peer groups" of business units engaged in similar activities at similar stages of their life cycle (for example, all start-up oil fields, all mature oil fields or all declining-yield oil fields) and facing similar strategic and technical challenges. The idea was to create a way that managers of BP's newly decentralized operations could compare experiences and share ideas. In recent years "peer assist" has been expanded into "peer challenge' in which peers not only review one another's goals and business plans, but the best performers are formally made responsible for improving the performance of the worst performers.

In a third major element of the program, technology was introduced—but only as the transmission pipeline and storage system for ideas that were already flowing. Rejecting the notion of trying to capture and encode the company's knowledge, the virtual teams built networks to give those with problems access to those with expertise.

Although the initiative involved a major investment in hardware and software, including multimedia e-mail, document scanners, videoclip encoders, desktop videoconferencing and chat rooms with chalkboards, the IT function took responsibility only for installing the equipment. The project was driven by the Virtual Teamwork group and its subteams. About one-third of the Virtual Teamwork budget was allocated for coaches to help managers use the new tools to achieve their business objectives. In the end, it was the ability to change individual behavior and to shape group interaction using the powerful IT tools that allowed BP's process change to succeed.

BP has created processes and a supportive culture to link and leverage the expertise of individual employees, embedding knowledge within the organization. Its social networking is strategic because it drives innovation, responsiveness and flexibility yet is extremely difficult for competitors to imitate.

The Bonding Process

The third major strategic task HR must undertake is to help management develop the engaging, motivating and bonding culture necessary to attract and keep talented employees. In such a culture, the potential in competent individuals and fully functioning networks can be converted into engaged, committed action. Companies must reject the notion that loyalty among today's employees is dead and accept the challenge of creating an environment that will attract and energize people so that they commit to the organization. Such advice flies in the face of conventional wisdom, which maintains loyalty has been replaced by a free-agent talent market that requires companies to convert their long-term trust-based relationships with employees to short-term contracts. Higher employee turnover, the use of temporary help and the expansion of outsourcing are all part of the envisioned future.

But if a company can outsource services or hire temporary expertise, so can its competitors. Such actions, therefore, are unlikely to lead to any competitive advantage. And if recruitment and retention are based primarily on the compensation package, the person lured by a big offer will almost certainly leave for a bigger one.

Consider SAS Institute, a billion-dollar software company based in Cary, North Carolina, which rejects the use of contract programmers and other outsourcing yet still attracts people to work without stock options and maintains turnover below 5%. How is that possible? CEO Jim Goodnight explains that what has consistently given his company a prominent place in *Fortune*'s survey of the best U.S. companies to work for is not stock-option programs, which he calls Ponzi schemes, but rather, competitive salaries and generous bonuses based on the company's performance and the individual's contribution.

In an industry featuring high pressure and burnout as the norm, SAS Institute has created an island of common sense. Actions and decisions are based on four simple principles: to treat everyone equally and fairly, to trust people to do a good job, to think long term and to practice bottom-up decision making. Then there are the hours. The software-industry joke may be generally apt (flex time means the company doesn't care which 15 hours you work each day), but company policy at SAS Institute is to work 35 hours per week. Exceptional benefits also reflect the value SAS puts on its people: There is a free, on-site medical facility for employees and family members, a subsidized on-site day-care facility, a gymnasium free to employees and their families, subsidized restaurants and cafes, and so on. That environment makes employees feel like valued members of a community, not replaceable gunslingers for hire. And for these self-selected individuals, that is reason enough to want to spend their career at SAS.

But the bonding process involves more than creating a sense of identity and belonging. It also must lead to an engaging and energizing feeling of commitment to the organization and its goals. But the visioning exercises and values cards many companies have developed in response to that need often fall short. The role of the HR professional is to get senior managers to move beyond hollow, slogan-driven communications, which are more likely to lead to detached cynicism than to engaged motivation, and to help them develop a clear personal commitment to an organizational purpose. Commitment implies a strongly held set of beliefs that not only are articulated in clear human terms, but also are reflected in managers' daily actions and decisions.

Henri Termeer, CEO of Genzyme, a biotechnology firm based in Cambridge, Massachusetts, regularly meets with people suffering from the diseases on which his researchers are working. He wants to feel angry about the pain and loss the disease is causing and passionate about the need to help. And he wants to transmit that passion to those working at Genzyme. Equally important, Termeer backs his words with actions. Because the company focuses on therapies for rare diseases, the cost of treatment is high. But the company refuses to let economics get in the way of its commitment to treat the afflicted and literally searches them out in Third World countries to provide free treatment. By acting on the company's beliefs, Termeer stirs the passion and engages the energy of Genzyme's employees.

The bonding process can succeed only when senior management realizes that the company is more than a mere economic entity; it is also a social institution through which people acting together can achieve meaningful purpose. In the war for talent, organizations are engaged in what one senior executive describes as "a competition for dreams."

The Heart of Strategy

The arrival of the information-based, knowledge-intensive, service-driven economy has forced massive change on companies worldwide, most dramatically in the way they must redefine their relationship with their employees. The shift in strategic imperatives over the past 25 years has necessitated new battle plans. The competition remains intense for strategic market positions and for scarce organizational resources and capabilities, but the war for talent has shifted the locus of the battle front. Today managers must compete not just for product markets or technical expertise, but for the hearts and minds of talented and capable people. And after persuading them to join the enterprise, management also must ensure that those valuable individuals become engaged in the organization's ongoing learning processes and stay committed to the company's aspirations.

It was this recognition that led McKinsey's partners to reexamine their long-established mission "to serve clients superbly well." After much debate, the partners decided that the changes occurring in the world of business were significant enough for them to reconsider the core purpose of their firm. Now McKinsey has a dual mission: "to help our clients make distinctive, substantial and lasting improvements in their performance and to attract, develop, excite and retain exceptional people." McKinsey and other organizations making the change have found new meaning in the term *competitive strategy* as they compete for the hearts, minds and dreams of exceptional people.

What's Wrong with Management Practices in Silicon Valley? A Lot.

To prevent high turnover, burnout and loss of employee commitment, learn to avoid four practices that are undermining some high-profile companies.

by Jeffrey Pfeffer

Everyone seems enamored of Silicon Valley. It has certainly spawned much new technology and created vast wealth. As a consequence, many executives visit Silicon Valley companies, read books about them and seek to copy the Valley's approach to management. But as high-tech commentator Esther Dyson has perceptively noted, although Silicon Valley is good at generating new technologies quickly, it has been much less successful in building sustainable organizations or in using sound management practices. So, before you rush to copy the Silicon Valley approach to management, a word or two of caution seems in order.

Silicon Valley's Approach to Management

What is Silicon Valley's approach to management? In general, it encompasses four practices. First is the free-agency model of employment, featuring relatively little commitment on the part of companies to their people or vice versa. Individuals are expected to watch out for themselves (the term at Sun Microsystems is "career resilience") and move on at a moment's notice. Labor mobility and limited attachments are expected and accepted.

Second is the extensive use of outside contractors, even for hardware and software development. The Valley may be the home of the virtual or almost virtual company.

Third is the use of stock options as an important form of compensation. Stock options are used even by companies in relatively staid industries, such as the manufacture of tamper-evident bottle caps. If the company is located in San Jose, California, it feels obliged to offer options as part of the pay package.

Finally, long working hours are typical. Indeed, they seem to be a badge of honor. The feeling is, if you aren't working constantly, you must not be essential to the success of your enterprise—a suspicion that is hard on the ego.

The Consequences

There are predictable and observable consequences for each of the four practices. The free-agent mentality, for instance, generates high turnover. Esti-

---

Source: Reprinted from "What's Wrong With Management Practices in Silicon Valley? A Lot." by Jeffrey Pfeffer, *MIT Sloan Management Review*, Spring, 2001, pp. 101–102, by permission of the publisher. Copyright © 2001 by Massachusetts Institute of Technology. All rights reserved. **Jeffrey Pfeffer** is a professor of organizational behavior at the Graduate School of Business at Stanford University. Contact him at pfeffer_jeffrey@gsb.stanford.edu.

mates range from 20% to more than 30% annually. The cost of recruiting and training replacements is enormous, particularly when combined with less direct costs: the productivity costs of positions going unfilled; the disruption to relationships with customers who must continually deal with employees in training; the costs to the product-design and development functions as knowledge walks out the door. And then there is the cost of building up one's competition, as former employees take positions with established competitors and startups.

But isn't high turnover inevitable in high-technology companies? In a word, no. SAS Institute, the largest privately owned software company in the world, with 1999 sales of more than $1 billion, had a turnover of less than 3% in the 12 months from June 1999 to June 2000 in its Cary, North Carolina, headquarters. MTW Corporation, a small, rapidly growing software- and computer-consulting company based in Kansas City, Kansas, has a turnover rate approaching 5% and falling. Cisco Systems has a turnover of about 8%, and there are some startups in Silicon Valley that have almost no turnover at all. If you tell people when they come to work for you that you don't expect them to stay, and if you treat them accordingly, they'll move on. Turnover has become an accepted way of life. It doesn't have to be.

Nor does contracting everything out and using lots of temporary help always make sense. What sustainable competitive advantage can a company have when much of its core technology is in the hands of people with little loyalty? What kind of service does a customer get when talking to people who don't even work for the company from which the customer has made a purchase?

The use of contractors has several predictable effects. First, contractors generally leave faster than permanent employees, exacerbating high turnover. In fact, in order to avoid problems with U.S. labor law and tax regulations defining who is a contractor, many companies now limit temporary and contract employees to a term of one year, necessarily guaranteeing 100% turnover in that portion of their labor force. Second, most contractors have less commitment to the company and its products and customers than employees do, with obvious implications for performance. Third, contracting out does not always save money. That's an illusion. Few companies, if any, evaluate the full cost of using contract labor or outside contractors. They see the direct cost savings, but they don't see the costs added through diminished customer retention, reduced productivity and fewer chances for developing internal intellectual capital.

Illustrating those problems is a recent study by Stanford University Ph.D. candidate Laura Castenada on the use of temporary help and contract labor at Applied Materials, a company based in Santa Clara, California. Most temporary employees there wanted to become permanent employees. When they knew they would not and saw their one-year term at the company drawing to a close, they held back from sharing their knowledge and skills with others, including their replacements—and spent many of their last days on the job looking for work. The loss in tacit knowledge and effort under such circumstances can be damaging.

Many of the Valley's compensation practices, particularly the use of signing bonuses and stock options, inadvertently help fuel the high turnover. Giving a signing bonus that vests over four years rewards people for leaving. After earning the bonus, they simply move to another company to collect another signing bonus.

And what about options? Employee ownership is a great thing—it helps employees think like owners. But options are not ownership. In real employee stock ownership, employees purchase shares and thus have, to use the colloquial phrase, "skin in the game." They are committed. Options are given to employees, not purchased. When the stock price goes down, the options are repriced or, now that repricing has become less acceptable to institutional investors, companies issue more options at the new, lower price, as Microsoft and Amazon.com have done. The potential dilution to earnings is enormous, even if accounting conventions do not yet fully capture the hit.

Moreover, as technology columnist and venture capitalist William Gurley has observed, options encourage a gambling mentality. Go for broke. If there's a big win, fine. If there's disaster, move on and try again. That is not the mentality of real ownership.

And finally, there are the long working hours. The practice of having people work until they are exhausted leads to both turnover and burnout. How many years or even months can you work 80-plus hours per week at the expense of friendships and social life? Why would free agents work endlessly for an institution for which they have little or no feeling? They won't. They're there because of the money or the network- and résumé-building—not because they care about the company or its customers, products and services. As soon as the money is earned or appears unlikely to materialize, they leave.

More fundamentally, there is a confused notion that being productive is the same thing as working long hours. It isn't. As Jim Goodnight, the wise co-founder and CEO of SAS Institute, has said, "If you've put in a full day, by 6 o'clock, you shouldn't have anything left, so go home." Amazingly for the software industry, SAS thrives on a 35-hour work week. Long hours also are partly responsible for the defect-filled products we have come to expect and accept. People who work when they are exhausted make mistakes. And as the quality movement taught us, it is more expensive to find and correct errors than it is to prevent them.

Silicon Valley's success has not repealed the basic rules of business. Your profits come from loyal customers who do business with you for reasons other than just price. Customer loyalty is a consequence of loyalty from employees who produce great products and offer great service. In the short run, with enough venture money and enough product demand, any business model may appear feasible. In the long run, those companies that actually run their businesses efficiently and produce sustainable results will be the ones you keep reading about.

In Silicon Valley, Loyalty Means Paying a High Price; Cultural Strengths Help Offset Loss of Paper Wealth

by Alex Berenson

In November, more than 100 employees of Calico Commerce were millionaires, at least on paper. Today only 20 are. As Calico's stock has fallen 80 percent from its November peak, the rest have watched their fleeting wealth burn away like fog in the California sun. In April alone, Calico shares lost nearly half their value. In Silicon Valley, where job hopping is a way of life and even robust companies regularly lose workers to start-ups dangling chances at instant wealth, a stock meltdown like Calico's might seem a recipe for disaster, prompting top employees to flee and crippling morale among those who remain.

But Calico, which makes software that helps companies sell products over the Internet, has weathered the storm so far, thanks to an intangible commodity that is supposedly even scarcer around here than out-of-work software engineers: the striking loyalty of its workers.

So far this year, only 15 of Calico's 330 workers have left the company. That translates into an annual rate of 12 percent, barely half the typical turnover at Silicon Valley companies, according to Steve Radford, who has surveyed salaries and turnover at high-technology companies for more than two decades. Calico's stability is no accident, employees say. While many Silicon Valley companies depend largely on the promise of riches to attract and retain workers, Calico has gone a different route, using more than money to keep employees happy. The company tries to combine the openness and workplace perks common in Silicon Valley companies with the very uncommon understanding that employees sometimes have lives outside the office.

So far, the mix seems to be working. From Alan Naumann, Calico's chief executive, to Aleida Kolodzieski, an administrative assistant, employees interviewed at Calico's headquarters in San Jose last month said they believed in their company, whatever the stock market might think.

Of course they say that, a cynic might interject. But many Calico employees have put their money where their mouths are.

In March, five months after the company went public, restrictions on insider stock sales expired and Calico workers were free to sell shares and turn their paper wealth into cash. Few did. In fact, Mr. Naumann actually spent more than $2 million in late April to buy 150,000 shares on the open market, building his total stake in the company to 1.65 million shares.

Joe Schwartz, a 29-year-old manager who was Calico's 13th employee and has been with the company since 1995, said he shared that confidence. With more than 5,000 options, Mr. Schwartz lost more than $300,000 in paper wealth

---

Source: "In Silicon Valley, Loyalty Means Paying a High Price; Cultural Strengths Help Offset Loss of Paper Wealth" by Alex Berenson, *The New York Times*, May 28, 2000. Copyright © 2000 by The New York Times Co. Reprinted with permission.

as Calico's stock price shriveled. Yet he remains a believer. "I would encourage my parents to buy, my best friends to buy," he said.

A strong company culture only goes so far, and even Mr. Naumann admits that his company will eventually start losing people if the stock price remains depressed. And it is hard to forecast what the immediate future holds for the company. Its products compete in a hotly contested market niche against offerings from specialists like Fire-Pond and giants like Oracle. Though Calico's sales have grown steadily at 70 percent annually or better, reaching $35.6 million in the year ended March 31, its losses have widened as well, to $27.8 million—a new-economy story that investors used to shrug off but now have little patience for.

Still, Calico's efforts to make its employees feel like partners seem for the moment to have cushioned the blow of the stock slump.

"The difference between good and bad management teams in the valley is their ability to manage through the natural ebb and flow of the business," said Roger McNamee, a venture capitalist whose investment funds own more than 5 percent of Calico. "This is a management team that understands the business that they're in. They made a conscious choice to run the business for the long term."

That choice makes Calico unusual—and could help the company prosper over time, management consultants said.

The notion that employees and companies have a social contract with each other that goes beyond a paycheck has largely vanished in United States business. In its place is a free-agent culture where workers are expected to look out for themselves and switching jobs regularly is seen as normal.

But a few big companies, like Cisco Systems, Southwest Airlines and Men's Wearhouse, have found success by going out of their way to make employees feel valued, according to Charles O'Reilly, a Harvard professor who is writing a book about the cultures of successful companies.

"The average point of view is that loyalty is for chumps, that the longer you stay on the job, the stupider you are," said Fred Reichheld, a fellow at Bain Consulting who is writing a book about loyalty. "Most business leaders cannot tell you why their people should be loyal. They get it confused with obedience, or just staying there, or fear."

Instead, companies often try to combat turnover with big salaries and option grants. But Mr. Reichheld said that approach is self-defeating, because it works only as long as times are good and an organization can afford to pay a fairly small roster of stars above-market salaries.

Being honest with employees and giving them a chance to grow at their jobs builds loyalty in a way that money cannot, he said.

Mr. Naumann appears to have taken that lesson to heart. He shares lots of information with employees, holding monthly company-wide meetings to discuss where Calico stands relative to its competitors and internal goals. In addition, he hosts a monthly group breakfast for employees whose birthdays have fallen that month and solicits feedback from the group. That level of disclosure and communication is vital to building loyalty, Mr. O'Reilly said.

"The all-too-typical M.B.A. response is that people can't be trusted, and they're not very smart, so why would you give them this information?" he said. But companies that keep workers well informed find that employees come to feel they have a stake in the company, even if they own only a little stock. "Then people feel like owners, and they stick around even if the stock price dips," Mr. O'Reilly said.

Of course, Calico is not alone in fostering an atmosphere of openness. Young companies often share more information with their employees than bigger, older businesses; the gulf between management and the rank and file tends to widen over time. And some of Calico's other perks, like allowing employees to telecommute twice a week, are typical at young Silicon Valley companies where employees put in long hours.

But Calico does differ from its young cousins in some crucial ways. With weak or nonexistent human resources departments and a culture that puts work first, many young companies stumble when dealing with employees having personal crises. Not at Calico, said Rob Devine, a 32-year-old consultant who joined the company in June, six months before his wife died of ovarian cancer.

"Leadership two and three levels above was completely fair" in its treatment of him, Mr. Devine said. As his wife's health worsened, he said, the company arranged his work to minimize travel and offered him extra time off, an offer he declined because, he said, "it's important when you're in a situation like that to have something where you feel you're contributing."

Shelly Begun, Calico's vice president for human resources, said the company allowed an employee whose wife gave birth prematurely more than two months' leave to help care for the baby. "It is a huge deal for people that, when they have these types of situations, Calico will help to deal with them," Ms. Begun said.

Nancy McDermand, a manager whose grant of more than 10,000 options has just begun to vest, said she had recently turned down a job at a start-up that offered her "lots of shares" and more money, preferring to remain at Calico for its collegial atmosphere. "If it weren't like that, I could leave tomorrow," she said.

To maintain that spirit, Calico has made a concerted effort to seek out employees considered likely to fit into its culture, placing a premium on recruiting graduates directly from college or business school.

Hewlett-Packard and other successful technology companies "do superaggressive college hiring, because it's the only way to get people who fit in," said Mr. Naumann, an Iowa native who worked for Hewlett-Packard for five years after graduating from college. "We're trying to do the same thing."

Make no mistake, though, this is still Silicon Valley, the overnight-millionaire factory. Most Calico employees acknowledge forthrightly that tantalizing stock windfalls like those that were briefly within their grasp are a large part of what brought them to Calico to begin with.

"The potential money that could be made getting into a company pre-I.P.O. really was a big consideration," said John Driver, Calico's director of field marketing.

So too, for many people in Silicon Valley, are bragging rights, and Calico's stock no longer yields employees much of those. "There is a gold rush mentality" in the new economy, said Barry Obrand, managing director of Russell Reynolds Associates, the executive recruiting firm. "For people who haven't made it in some way, shape or form, there's a sense that you haven't done as well for yourself or your family."

Yuri Smirov, an engineer who joined Calico last year after two years at a privately held start-up, looks at Calico's prospects through that lens. Working for a company that does not succeed is extremely costly in Silicon Valley, he said, because "time is becoming the most expensive resource."

"Time is something you lose and it doesn't come back," Mr. Smirov said.

Mr. Smirov, who emigrated to the United States from Russia in 1992 and earned a doctorate in computer science at Carnegie Mellon University in Pittsburgh, said moving from Russia to Pennsylvania was a smaller adjustment for him than moving from Pennsylvania to Silicon Valley. The people he met in Pittsburgh were white and middle-class, with "the same income, with the same interests," he said. "Here, people are stratified much more."

As for the stock, he said, "the hardest part is mismatching your expectations." Mr. Smirov, who will receive more than 25,000 options between now and 2003, used to think he would be able to buy a house large enough for his two children to have separate bedrooms. That prospect is now remote, but Mr. Smirov remains hopeful.

Housing is on the mind of Ms. Kolodzieski, the administrator with only "a couple of thousand shares," as well. She and her husband hope one day to move out of the condominium apartment they rent. "We want to have a family, and part of that equals buying a home," she said.

Mr. Naumann knows his staff's patience will not last forever. "Our total compensation packages have to be competitive, or we won't retain people," he said. But for now, the stock woes have, if anything, pulled the company closer together, he said. "The market's got it wrong, and we're just going to have to prove them wrong."

For a New Insider, It Was a Risk Worth Taking

Of Calico Commerce's 330 employees, John Driver might have the best reason to be upset with the company's plunging stock price.

Mr. Driver joined the San Jose-based software company as director of field marketing two weeks before it became a public company last October, scrapping a thriving business as an independent consultant. His take-home pay at Calico came to only half what he had been making in fees; to compensate, Calico promised him more than 25,000 stock options, a potentially huge payoff. (Typically for Silicon Valley, Mr. Driver will receive his options over four years—one-quarter of the grant on his first anniversary with the company and the rest in equal monthly installments thereafter.)

When Calico shares soared to $75 in November, Mr. Driver's decision to join the company looked brilliantly lucrative. Even if the stock failed to rise any farther before 2003, he stood to reap more than $1.5 million from his options.

Not so now that Calico's stock has plunged by 80 percent, right back to the initial offering price of $14 a share. At that price Mr. Driver's options are worthless. So does Mr. Driver, who has an 18-month-old daughter and another child on the way, regret his career decision now?

No, he said, for lots of reasons. First off, his stock wealth does not yet really exist, even on paper; it will only accumulate over time as his options vest. "I have a very practical view of the stock," he said. "Even if the stock was trading at 100 today, I don't vest until September."

Mr. Driver, who said he is a fan of Warren E. Buffett, invests for the long haul and has "actually never sold a stock," is optimistic that by the time the options are actually his to exercise, Calico shares will have rebounded.

"I think Calico at the moment is actually undervalued," he said. "We have a good strategy, a good management team. There's a market there, and Calico is going to get some of it."

Even if the stock does not recover, Mr. Driver said, he is glad he joined the company. He enjoys working there, and even on half his former pay he and his wife will be able to support their family, he said. And the chance to be a part of the action, instead of on the outside looking in, was too exciting to pass up. "It was a gamble," he said. "It was a risk, and if things don't work out, you've really got to be okay with the outcome. I have a great life the way it is—I have a great house, I have a little kid, another on the way. If I wind up making millions of dollars, it's a bonus. If it doesn't happen, I have a really good life."

Workforce Management: Employment Relationships in Changing Organizations

ELECTIVE

The Part-Time Partner (A)

by Gary W. Loveman

Meeker, Needham & Ames, a long-established metropolitan law firm, employs 100 associates and 20 partners and is preeminent in corporate litigation. Each year, the promotions committee nominates associates for promotion. This year, the partner nominations carried particular weight; MN&A's overall billings and partner incomes were stagnating, showing the effects of intensified competition and in-house corporate counsel. The three associates under consideration had all worked for the firm seven years, meeting the minimum requirement for partner.

Chairing the meeting was George Hartwig, 53, for three years the managing partner. Also on the committee were Maury Davidson, 62, a senior partner and managing partner for seven years before Hartwig; Pamela Fisher, 44, a tax law specialist and the only female partner; and Jim Welch, 47, director of litigation.

The day after the meeting, Hartwig circulated the minutes. Memos from Fisher and Davidson appeared on Hartwig's desk the same day.

Meeker, Needham & Ames
Minutes of the Promotions Committee
Meeting September 1, 1990

Present: George Hartwig, chair, Maury Davidson, Pamela Fisher, Jim Welch; Absent: None

Mr. Hartwig called the meeting to order at noon. He began by reminding the committee that, although there was no fixed number of slots available for partners, the committee must consider carefully who it decided to recommend for promotion. Given the severe competition facing the firm, he said, the decision carried with it both risk to the incomes of existing partners and opportunities for new and increased billings. He also stated that the committee should nominate all worthy candidates but should carefully evaluate merit in terms of client service and the ability to generate revenues. He then asked Mr. Davidson to begin the consideration of Rick Stewart.

Mr. Davidson said that he believed that Mr. Stewart should not be promoted to partner. "While Rick has done well in this firm," said Mr. Davidson, "he hasn't really distinguished himself. Nor has he developed a practice that will generate new clients."

Mr. Welch supported Mr. Davidson's position. "Rick's work as a litigator has been solid, as his file indicates. But I don't think he'll become the kind of attorney who can capture the confidence of the high-level executives we want to represent."

Mr. Hartwig asked if anyone wished to support Mr. Stewart. Hearing no one, he declared Mr. Stewart's candidacy dropped and asked Mr. Welch to speak to Tim Brower's candidacy.

Source: Reprinted by permission of *Harvard Business Review*, "The Case of the Part-Time Partner," by Gary W. Loveman (September–October 1990). Copyright © 1990 by the President and Fellows of Harvard College; all rights reserved. **Gary W. Loveman** is an assistant professor at the Harvard Business School, where he teaches organizational behavior and human resource management. HBR's cases are derived from the experiences of real companies and real people. As written, they are hypothetical, and the names used are fictitious.

Mr. Welch stated that, in his opinion, Mr. Brower could serve as a model for the young, hard-working, committed attorneys the firm would need to attract in the future. "Tim has distinguished himself in virtually every way possible," said Mr. Welch. "He has consistently handled difficult cases with exceptional results and has earned praise from clients. He volunteers for more work and can be found at the office nights and weekends. And he has more than once proposed new legal avenues for us to pursue, based on his expertise in some of the more technical areas of our practice."

Mr. Hartwig asked if there were any reservations to Mr. Brower's candidacy.

Mr. Davidson responded that his only concern was that Mr. Brower seemed more interested in legal technicalities than in pursuing new clients.

Ms. Fisher remarked that his file clearly indicated a lack of new-client development.

Mr. Welch responded that Mr. Brower's networking and client-development abilities were definitely weak but that the rest of his performance was so outstanding that he was certain Mr. Brower could improve in these areas.

Mr. Hartwig asked for the sense of the committee. It unanimously supported Mr. Brower's candidacy for partner.

Mr. Hartwig said that he would introduce the candidacy of Julie Ross. He reminded the committee members that they all had firsthand knowledge of Ms. Ross's capabilities since she had worked for each of them at various times. Her file indicated that they had found her performance exemplary. Her work had ranked among the best in the firm, displaying both keen insight into legal issues and top-notch courtroom litigation. Moreover, Mr. Hartwig stated, in the past two years Ms. Ross had shown a growing capability for attracting new business. In most cases, she had received additional work from existing clients, but in two instances, satisfied clients had given her name to other companies that had then engaged MN&A as their main counsel.

Mr. Hartwig said that the main issue the committee needed to address was Ms. Ross's part-time status. "When Julie had her baby three years ago," he said, "she requested and was given a reduction in her client load. We should consider her promotion in light of how it will affect firm perceptions and policy on part-time status in general."

Mr. Welch asked Mr. Hartwig to review the agreement made with Ms. Ross as well as the firm's other part-time arrangements.

Mr. Hartwig responded that Ms. Ross had negotiated a flexible schedule that permitted her to work "as necessary" to meet the needs of her clients. She and the firm understood that this would require approximately 50% of the billable hours of her colleagues, with salary and benefits reduced accordingly. Mr. Hartwig recalled that there had been much debate about the agreement and that many senior partners had been adamantly opposed to part-time work. Nevertheless, Mr. Hartwig had agreed to the proposal, making MN&A the first firm of its size in the city to implement part-time schedules for its attorneys.

Mr. Hartwig said that after negotiating the agreement with Ms. Ross, he had issued a memorandum stating that the firm would entertain similar requests from other attorneys, would have no general policy on part-time professional work, and would work out decisions and details case by case. Since that time, two other female junior associates had been granted part-time status. Both had negotiated fixed schedules of three days per week.

Ms. Fisher stated that although Ms. Ross exhibited outstanding skills, she was not qualified for promotion. "We all had these skills when we were up for partner. But what distinguished us from the others was our dedication to the firm and to our clients through years of exceptionally hard work and long hours." Ms.

Fisher said that as an associate, she had worked a minimum of 70 hours per week, as had most associates who made partner. These long hours were not only evidence of commitment but had also been invaluable in giving her a feel for the firm's distinctive culture and an understanding of its needs. "We have all just agreed that Mr. Brower should be made partner, in part because of his demonstrated commitment to the firm. Skills alone are not enough," she concluded.

Mr. Welch stated that he agreed with Ms. Fisher that Ms. Ross should not be nominated. "Julie's performance may have been excellent, but it has been based on a less-than-equal standard," Mr. Welch said. He noted that partners had refrained from assigning Ms. Ross the most complex and demanding work because of her limited schedule and her inability to go on lengthy trips. He concluded that he could not support her candidacy unless she returned to work full-time on the same kinds of cases and under the same conditions as her peers.

Ms. Fisher pointed out that the committee needed to address the issue of establishing precedent. "If we promote Julie without demanding an equal commitment to the firm," she stated, "we will be telling all of our associates that we no longer value motivation and dedication."

Mr. Hartwig agreed with Ms. Fisher that Ms. Ross's case would affect the firm's future direction, but he disagreed with her conclusion. He said that the proportion of female law school graduates was increasing each year and with it the number of female associates joining the firm. He pointed out that 40% of new hires in the past five years had been female, yet the firm still had only one female partner. "Our best female associates aren't staying around long enough even to be considered for partner," he stated. "Unless we establish a more flexible environment, we'll continue losing them. Julie is the only promising female candidate we'll have for the next two years. Promoting her will help us attract and retain the best people." Mr. Hartwig concluded that it was in the firm's best interest to balance the costs of nontraditional work schedules against the benefit of keeping people like Ms. Ross.

Mr. Davidson stated that establishing a flexible environment was important to men as well as women. Although no men had yet shifted to part-time schedules, he noted, the firm had recently lost several outstanding male associates who had left to pursue careers that gave them more time with their families. "This is not purely an issue of gender," Mr. Davidson said. "It is an issue of how we structure our work and the demands we place on all of our people. When I came up through the ranks, I expected to work and to do little else. All of us in the partnership paid a very high price in our home and family life, including separation and divorce. Today many of our best associates are unwilling to live as we did, and I can't say I blame them." Mr. Davidson concluded that the firm would have to make some changes in order to keep the best attorneys, and that included promoting Ms. Ross.

Mr. Welch reminded Mr. Hartwig of the debate that had ensued when Ms. Ross was given part-time status as an associate. He predicted that making Ms. Ross a part-time partner would produce an even greater crisis. Mr. Welch said, "I am not convinced that the threat of losing Julie and people like her is worth putting this firm through the convulsions that would follow her promotion. We can always attract enough people like Pam Fisher, Tim Brower, and ourselves among the many associates we hire each year to keep this firm growing and prosperous."

Mr. Hartwig stated that the committee was clearly divided on Ms. Ross's candidacy. Mr. Hartwig said that he would recommend Tim Brower for promotion and would draft a report describing each committee member's arguments regarding Ms. Ross's candidacy. He would circulate the report among the partners and schedule a meeting of the partnership for an open discussion.

Mr. Hartwig adjourned the meeting of the promotions committee at 3:30.

Memo from Pam Fisher

September 2, 1990

To: **George Hartwig**

From: **Pam Fisher**

I've just looked over the minutes of the promotions committee meeting, and there are two things I'd like to add.

First, I have to point out, George, that the entire discussion wouldn't have been necessary if, at the time you made the part-time agreement with Julie, you had been explicit about how it would affect her chances of making partner. I don't understand why the issue wasn't clarified from the beginning.

Second, I see an important distinction between part-time associates and part-time partners. I respect Julie's decision to spend time at home with her young child. As an associate, I probably would have made the same decision if I'd had children. But I would not have expected to make partner. Associates can cover for other associates, but nobody can cover for a partner; we are the critical link to the client. I need not remind you that this firm is in trouble. I don't think we should consider making someone a partner who would not be working full-time to help us out of this situation.

Memo from Maury Davidson

9/2/90

George—

Nice job handling the discussion at the meeting. You've got a tough assignment ahead of you outlining for the partners the committee's divergent positions on Julie.

I don't mean to complicate the matter, but to me the issue isn't simply about making Julie a partner. Her case will effectively establish the firm's policy on part-time work. The relevant issues here include flexible work schedules, motivation of both male and female associates, the reaction of the firm's clients, and the concerns of the existing partners.

But even more important, our decision will reflect our beliefs as an organization about how the quality of one's personal life affects one's work at the firm.

I think you know my position on this. I intend to spend more time with my family—I don't want to wait until retirement to begin enjoying my grandkids. Furthermore, I'm convinced that doing this will make the time I spend at the firm more productive.

Maury

Should Meeker, Needham & Ames Make Julie Ross a Partner?

Five experts from both inside and outside the law profession consider this question.

Sally C. Landauer *is a partner at Ball, Janik & Novack, a Portland, Oregon, law firm, where she has worked a four-day week for the past eight years. At a previous firm, she was one of the first part-time partners on the West Coast.*

Meeker, Needham & Ames is a law firm in trouble. It is an associate mill, grinding out young lawyers so rapidly that by the seventh year, only 3 of its 100 associates are left to be considered for partnership.

This should be an economic disaster for the firm. It means that each year it must hire some two to three dozen new associates. Even its second-year associate load must be very heavy. John P. Weil, an Orinda, California, law firm consultant, warns that the first-year cost of hiring an associate fresh from law school is $100,000. That includes capital costs, but it also takes into consideration revenue generated. If MN&A hires 30 new associates, it will spend $3,000,000. MN&A cannot afford to lose Julie Ross—despite her part-time status—because she is, by admission of the partnership committee, a client getter.

The committee, however, focused on how Ross's partnership would affect firm perceptions and policies on part-time work in general. The two partners arguing against Ross focused only on her lack of "dedication" to the firm. Pam Fisher, in particular, confuses Ross's part-time schedule with a lack of motivation and dedication. As a mother of three who tried for four years to be a full-time lawyer and an adequate mother, I can assure Fisher that motivation and dedication are not the problem. Despite my present four-day-a-week schedule, I have developed sufficient expertise and enough clients to be asked to join three firms as a partner.

What are the firm's options? Having made the initial mistake of not establishing Julie Ross's position on or off the partnership track at the time she requested part-time status, there are still a number of ways the firm can make Ross a partner. It can:

1. Delay her partnership by an amount of time equivalent to her reduced number of hours. A delay of a year and a half (50% of the three years of part-time work) would enable Ross to re-assess whether to stay on a part-time basis at the end of that time or return to full-time work.
2. Establish an income partnership. This option is becoming more common in law firms around the country as competition squeezes profits and as more lawyers reject the 70-hour-a-week work schedule that has traditionally aided partnership entry. With this kind of partnership, Ross would be entitled to partnership status, a guaranteed income rather than points and profit sharing, and the right to vote on all matters except points (compensation) for partners and mergers. She would have no equity investment. She would not share in upside potential, but she would not be exposed to risk, either.
3. Establish a nonequity partnership in which part-time partners participate in profit and loss but make no capital investment and share in none of the firm's assets.
4. Make Ross an equity partner, but establish her level of compensation and investment at 50% of the lowest level of the average compensation of the partners who entered the class ahead of her, her class, and the class behind her. Her points would be determined in the same manner. She would always be compensated less than others similarly situated, but this is the price she must pay for the privilege of part-time status.
5. Make her a nonequity partner for five years, with a move up to equity after that time.

One final note. A litigation-only firm will have more difficulty with part-time associates and part-time partners than a business or transactional firm; court appearances, depositions, and trials frequently cannot be arranged around a part-time schedule. A transactional attorney, on the other hand, can often arrange his or her practice around the part-time schedule.

To be competitive in today's recruiting marketplace, MN&A must change its policies. It is throwing years of investment down the hole if it rejects Julie Ross as a partner. She will have no choice but to seek employment elsewhere, taking her considerable skills and her obviously growing practice with her. MN&A cannot afford to lose Julie Ross or to set a precedent that part-time is a career dead end.

Marsha E. Simms *is a partner at Weil, Gotshal & Manges, a New York City law firm.*

"Julie Ross wants a job—not a career."

My gut reaction as a woman was that of course Julie Ross should become a partner at MN&A. But when I considered the issue in light of the realities of today's law firms and businesses, I concluded that she should not. A partner in any professional firm has to have made a conscious decision to have a career. Julie Ross has decided she wants a job—not a career.

Part-time partnership raises important issues for clients, peers (male and female), and other women in the firm.

The Firm's Clients

While there will be some clients who can work within a part-time partner's time constraints, most clients expect a partner to be available whenever needed. A partner also has to be willing to work to expand the client base and to work with any client of the firm who needs that person's expertise. Julie Ross wants to limit her practice to meeting the needs of only *her* clients (so long as those needs are not full-time), not the firm's.

The Part-Time Partner's Peers

Without a doubt, making someone a partner who has not "suffered" as much as his or her peers creates resentment in the partnership. While most lawyers have reached a point where they accept "stepping out" for a limited period of whatever reason (maternity leave or a sabbatical, for instance), they expect their partners to be the people who have made and are willing to continue to make the same commitment as they have to the firm over an extended period. If someone is not willing to make that commitment, then peers will question whether that person should be given a status that symbolizes the commitment.

Other Women in the Firm

Most women who have attained a level of professional success have done so by consciously sacrificing other aspects of their lives—whether it be marriage, children, or community involvement. They have discovered that they *can't* have it all and have had to choose what they want most. Creating a new set of partnership criteria for part-time associates, most of whom will be women, risks alienating women who have earned their status in the traditional way and have made the sacrifices Julie Ross was unwilling to make. Such a policy might also imply that women should be judged by a different, less demanding set of criteria, which brings into question the competency and commitment of all professional women.

I am not suggesting, however, that MN&A reject for all time the possibility of making Julie Ross a partner. If she ever returns to work full-time, then she should be considered for partnership. If at that time she is still performing at the same level that she is now, she should be made a partner.

MN&A could have avoided its dilemma by discussing with Julie Ross (and then making it a part of its announced policy) at what point, if any, an associate who works part-time would be considered for partnership. Unfortunately, most firms have no policy on part-time employment or other nontraditional work roles and instead treat each case on an ad hoc basis. This approach makes it difficult for those who are contemplating a part-time arrangement to evaluate how it might affect their futures. Also, the resulting disparate treatment of different part-time requests creates its own set of problems.

The most workable policy in a law firm, therefore, is one in which associates are permitted to take leaves of absence or work part-time schedules with the understanding that they will have to return to work full-time before they can be considered for partnership. For those who do not want to be considered for partnership, the firm should try to work out a mutually satisfactory schedule. As one MN&A partner mentioned, the firm cannot afford to lose intelligent lawyers because of its unwillingness to be flexible.

Walter R. Trosin *is vice president of strategy and development for Merck & Co., Inc., where he oversees personnel and human resources planning, strategy, policy, and development activities worldwide.*

"The issue goes beyond partnership to the whole question of work and families."

This case raises an important question: Given that most employees who are parents have a spouse who also works, how can companies address the needs of employees who have dual obligations?

In Julie Ross's case, MN&A could not begin to answer this question because it did not think through the implications of her part-time arrangement at the time it was made. George Hartwig should have, for instance, asked Ross what kinds of expectations she had from the firm and whether she would be willing to make child-care arrangements when emergencies arose at work. And he should have let her know the extent of the firm's commitment to her and what chance she had for partnership.

At this point, the firm can at least revisit the terms of the agreement it made with Ross. For instance, did a part-time schedule mean she would be working 25 hours a week or 40? This will also force the firm to examine its requirements for partner. Given the reality of pressures from an increasingly stressful world outside the office, including but not limited to family obligations, is MN&A (and other businesses) really benefiting from a tradition of working its employees 70 hours a week?

Within MN&A's present culture of "hit the ground running and keep your nose to the grindstone," I would be very reluctant to make Ross a full-time partner. In such a firm, it would send a signal that hard work is not necessary to move forward. Still, MN&A should discuss with Ross the possibility of granting her a limited partnership status or allowing her to share her partnership with another person who has a similar arrangement.

At Merck, we base promotion decisions on how well individuals perform and on our judgment of their ability to perform at a higher level. We expect people to work hard and to be dedicated—but we do not expect them to give up their families. In fact, I believe (as Maury Davidson implies in his memo) that workers are most effective when they do *not* work constantly.

As in the case with a growing number of companies, Merck has part-time work policies—and we have found that they have unexpected payoffs: for example, part-time employees frequently focus more on task completion and getting jobs done rather than simply on attendance. And doing the job, after all, is what we pay employees for.

Nevertheless, it is only nonmanagers that work part-time at Merck; we don't have managerial part-time work. It would be very difficult for a senior manager to work part-time because, let's face it, supervising is a full-time job. The only possible way managers could work part-time is on a job-sharing basis. The rules here are still emerging; Merck, for instance, has not yet dealt with this. Given the increasing need in our diverse workforce for more flexible approaches, however, we may have to address this sooner rather than later.

Barbara Mendel Mayden *practices law in New York City and is a member of the American Bar Association Commission on Women in the Profession.*

"Never mind hours worked; what about talent, efficiency, and values?"

Let me get this straight. Julie Ross has displayed exemplary performance as a lawyer, and unlike her colleague Tim Brower who is being nominated for promotion, she has demonstrated revenue-generation skills. She passes the tests articulated by the firm.

Why should the number of hours Ross works, an arrangement approved by the firm, determine whether she should be made a partner? Is it some sort of initiation rite? While a firm may decide that the attributes it is looking for in a partner may take longer to attain working part-time, when those criteria are met, what does a threshold number of hours add to the equation?

Experience, expertise, and other effects of tenure that Ross gained while working an alternative schedule should not fall into a black hole. She is a lawyer who has attained skills, has garnered firm and client respect, and has presumably done her *pro rata* share of *pro bono*, community service, and firm administration. She should accordingly be promoted.

Yet Pam Fisher argues that because she and her colleagues worked 70-hour weeks, so should anyone who comes up behind them. Fisher's memory may be a little clouded by fatigue; legal management firms tell us that the billable-hour spiral is much higher than this. In the late 1970s, average annual billables for associates hovered around 1,700 hours, which today would be considered "part-time" compared with the more than 2,000 billable hours associates now average.

So should Ross, who bills, say, 1,500 hours a year working part-time, take home the same amount of money as Brower, who bills 3,000 hours? Of course not. (After all, the 3,000-hour-a-year lawyer will likely have alimony and child support to pay.) Hours worked may be relevant to the size of Ross's piece of the pie but not to her ability to sit down at the table.

Jim Welch believes that the firm needs a young, hard-working, committed attorney for a model. But maybe the focus of that model ought instead to be talent, efficiency, and values. Reporter Marilyn Goldstein, in an article appearing last year in *New York Newsday*, wrote:

> *The question should not be what's wrong with a woman who doesn't want to work 12-hour days but what's wrong with a man who does—and a culture that . . . applauds, glorifies, promotes people who put their jobs before their families. . . . This penchant for promotions via . . . overtime reflects an assumption that those willing to work long hours are the best and brightest [but] maybe the ones willing to work long hours are just the ones willing to work long hours. . . . What if we discover the answer to moving American commerce and industry ahead is finding those smart enough not to work 12-hour days and turning the reins of business over to them? Who knows, we might come up with a mother lode of talent.*

Implicit in the discussion about whether to make Ross a partner is that it is uneconomic to do so. Some of the most successful law firms in the country, however, have shown that, alternative work schedules that don't "mommy track" women into pink-collar, no-room-for-advancement ghettos can be profitable. Those firms report that their reduced-schedule lawyers—both partners and associates—demonstrate increased productivity with a higher ratio of billable hours to hours worked. Fixed costs relating to such lawyers can be reduced. Fears about part-time partners being unable to supervise or to deal with client concerns have not been borne out; more often than not, the partner on an alternative work schedule is more accessible than the 2,500-hour-a-year workaholic juggling too many matters.

Firms that don't provide a work environment where family and professional responsibilities can be reconciled will lose their most valuable resources—many of their best people—to firms that are more "family friendly." Retention of valued, experienced professionals produces distinct value. Firm costs escalate with lawyer turnover. When firms don't offer options, they lose lawyers just when they have become profitable. (It has been noted that a woman professional's most productive years are also her reproductive years.) Clients become frustrated finding their matters constantly being shifted to new lawyers unfamiliar with their circumstances.

How firms deal with balancing family and work responsibilities is not just a women's issue, as Maury Davidson points out in the case. Perhaps women were the first to notice these issues, but what is becoming increasingly evident is that men are now leaving firms in greater numbers. No longer is the prototypical new lawyer a man who was put through school by a working wife who remains at home after her husband becomes a lawyer and devotes herself to providing her husband and children with a well-organized home life. Today both women and men are dealing with more responsibilities at home, in addition to those at the office. Men are increasingly opting out of those firms that cultivate an obvious "bottom-line only" environment. The managing partner of a major New York law firm recently noted that even men who don't intend to work part-time or take parental leave look for these kinds of policies in firms because they reveal how much importance a firm places on family issues.

Jim Welch is naive to think that without flexible policies, MN&A will continue to attract young lawyers of the quality of Fisher and Brower. While the lure of the big money was once all-powerful, law students are now becoming aware of the downside of a law firm environment where a 2,500-hour-billable-year expectation is not uncommon. In evaluating law firms, they are looking beyond the highest bidder and at the importance of lifestyle and family issues.

Pam Fisher is concerned about the message the firm will send by making Julie Ross a partner. With proper guidance from the top (and a written policy clearly articulating the firm's reasoning and the parameters of the policy), the other associates and potential recruits will see that Ross is a hard-working lawyer who has excelled in her field and who has traded the extra hours demanded of others for a significant cut in pay and benefits. And they will see MN&A as an organization that has responded to the demographics of the 1990s and that understands the importance of maintaining human values in a busy, successful legal practice.

D. Timothy Hall *is a professor of organizational behavior and associate dean for faculty development in the school of management at Boston University. He is the author of several books on career management.*

"The rules must change because the game has changed."

It is crucial at this point in MN&A's history that it take innovative action: it should promote Julie Ross.

First, let's look at the state of affairs for law firms and businesses alike. The emergence of global marketing and technological innovations means that our world has never been more competitive. And the most competitive assets for any business, as the saying goes, leave the building each night (however late the departure might be!). The only way to grow a business in these uncertain times is through a clear strategy of recruiting and grooming the finest talent available.

MN&A's three central criteria in evaluating partner candidates are: (1) legal performance, (2) commitment to the firm's work, and (3) client service and ability to generate new business. There is no doubt that Ross's performance is outstanding on the first and third criteria. But she has also been outstanding in the second area—when measured against the expected commitment level the firm negotiated with her. Furthermore, based on what George Hartwig says, Ross is the kind of lawyer who is committed to do whatever it takes to serve a given client, regardless of the number of hours a week she has agreed to work.

MN&A has to redefine the word "commitment" to mean whatever it takes to meet client needs—not a particular number of hours spent at the office each week. It must then let everyone at the firm know that this new commitment to *service* (rather than *hours*) will be its major strategic advantage. In effect, this will create a new psychological contract between the firm and its staff: if an employee performs well, shows commitment and flexibility, and opens up new areas of business, the firm will provide financial rewards, professional growth opportunities, a long-term relationship, and flexible work options.

For MN&A's current partners, this means new rules. MN&A acknowledged that the rules had changed when it implemented flexible work for associates. The rules have had to change because the game has changed: employees in all business realms are needing and insisting on more flexibility.

The most important thing is to make changes discussable. MN&A employees need information about what to expect under the new contract. For example, employees working part-time may need to modify their career goals and expect to be promoted more slowly than their full-time counterparts.

As part of this communication process, MN&A will also need to give suitable recognition to its current partners who made family trade-offs so they could serve the firm full-time. George Hartwig needs to let people like Pam Fisher and Tim Brower know how much he values their contributions and that he realizes that they had fewer options. As MN&A communicates its new career contract more widely, inside and outside the firm, not only will it retain and develop key assets like Julie Ross but it will also be better able to attract other women and men of her caliber who want a work-family balance that other firms aren't yet offering.

This kind of new contract is an opportunity for a business to create a strategic human-resource-development plan. This would entail examining future needs for skills and experience, the extent to which those needs are already being met, what gaps exist, and a plan for addressing those gaps by recruiting, selecting, developing, retaining, and rewarding future staff.

A staff task force could be appointed to work on this plan. It could survey clients to assess their future needs, and it could survey staff at all levels to assess career and personal needs. The task force could then develop an overall plan with policy recommendations addressing issues like flexible work arrangements, career timetables, compensation and benefit policies, career coaching and mentoring, and dependent care. The plan could be communicated and discussed with all staff in a variety of settings—regular staff meetings, a company newsletter, partner meetings, or "brown bag" lunch seminars.

Included in such a plan could be a lengthened timetable for part-timers. If a major objection to Ross's candidacy is that she has not yet done the same volume of work as her full-time peers, MN&A might require her to work additional years until she has.

Similarly, it might establish different levels of partnership to deal with the compensation issue and the concern that part-time partners might bring in less new business. One level would be fully participating partners who would share in the profits of the firm. A second level would be salaried partners who would not share in firm profits. Salaried partners would be either part-timers or technical specialists who would not generate business; in addition to lower financial return, they would have the advantage of lower risk since they would not sign firm loans or otherwise participate in the firm's investments. A few Boston law firms have already adopted this structure, and public accounting firms have implemented comparable structures.

Another option might be to allow employees to move from one level to another as their circumstances change. In addition to keeping the full-partner role open for part-timers, this could also be a way for older, fully participating partners to phase gradually into retirement or to continue working longer than they otherwise would—without the pressures of full-profit participation and contribution.

Regardless of what the new plan includes, the key is to make it discussable. This should be easy in a firm the size of MN&A. George Hartwig should act quickly to meet the needs of both the staff and the firm and use this opportunity to gain a strategic advantage over competitors.

The Part-Time Partner Redux

So we solved the problem, didn't we? (b)

My husband's first law firm, one of the most prestigious in the city, offered a three-month paid parental leave to anyone who had just adopted or had a baby. When Jacob was born my husband took his full leave because it coincided with the term during which I was finishing my PhD dissertation and lecturing for the first time in the Sociology Department. There is no way I could have accomplished these things without him at home. It allowed me the maximum amount of time to devote to my writing and teaching. But it is so unusual for men actually to take advantage of the leave policy that it hurt him professionally and he eventually realized that he was going to have to leave the firm if he was going to advance.

He was at a new firm (equally well known and prestigious) when June was born. This time he did not dare to take advantage of their equally generous leave policy.

I faced a different type of problem when I was still planning an academic career. After Jacob was born, it became clear to me that I was only going to be able to devote a typical work day (9 to 5) to my profession if I wanted to live up to my own standards of parenthood. But those who are most successful in academia are the ones who have the freedom to read, think, and work from the moment they get up until they go to bed. This is not going to change, even if it becomes more acceptable to split one's time between work and family. My guess is the same could be said of careers in business and medicine. It is certainly true in the world of law, where one bills by the hour. I find it hard to envision a world where entire fields reduce their standards of excellence when even a fraction of its practitioners are willing to make that extra effort.

By the turn of the century, nearly 90 percent of law firms had implemented formal part-time policies for associates and partners. Most thought they had solved the problem encountered in the part-time partner case. Formal policies regarding time and criteria for promotion, part-time compensation arrangements, and related human resource policies were in place to support individuals choosing reduced hours option.

But the reality was something else. A study by the Women's Bar Association of Massachusetts[1] found that:

1. Consistent with the national pattern, over 90% of major Boston firms offered a part-time or reduced hours option;
2. Less than 5% of associates took advantage of it; less than 2% of all partners used it.
3. One third of those that used it (and an equal number who did not use it) believed that it hurt the careers of those using this option because they were perceived as being less committed to either the firm or their profession than those who continued to work full time, long hours;
4. The biggest barrier to use reported in both surveys and focus groups of lawyers was the stigma attached to breaking the norms of the profession; and,
5. Women constitute 28% of the attorneys in Boston law firms but account for 40% of attorneys leaving these firms. Approximately 40% of those who left their firm reported the attitudes toward the reduced hours arrangements affected their decision to leave.

The quote above, written to us in response to a work family report[2] we had prepared, captured the real experiences of those who took the option. The problem was far from solved. The formal policies failed to overcome the informal norms or culture that penalized professionals for deviating from what was engrained in the minds of senior partners and perhaps in the minds of others in the profession as the "ideal worker."

Yet there continues to be evidence that a substantial proportion of lawyers would individually prefer to work shorter hours. But as one study demonstrated, no individual is likely to take this action as long as others do not follow suit.[3] Thus there is a collective action problem at work here. And, if we take the last point in the quote seriously, even those who would prefer shorter hours worry that by promoting use of this policy, standards of excellence in one's profession may erode.

This is the state of affairs today. Most organizations offer reduced hours options for family reasons; few people take it, and both those who take it and those who would like to but don't take it worry about the negative career stigma it connotes. Meanwhile, the inability to manage these policies effectively appears to induce high rates of turnover and all its associated costs of recruitment, training, and lost productivity.

Clearly, this is a problem with multiple stakeholders—employees who, given their family needs, would prefer shorter hours; managing partners who are concerned about attracting and retaining talented professionals; clients who want high-quality services when they need them; family members who bear the costs of unusable policies or policies that add more stress to those who use them. Or, is it an unsolvable trade-off, as the last sentence of the letter seems to imply?

The Question

What, if anything, can or should be done to solve this problem? In developing a strategy, consider both what the different stakeholders might do individually or separately and what they might do if they worked together in a coordinated fashion.

---

1 *More Than Part-Time.* 2000. A report of the Employment Issues Committee of the Women's Bar Association of Massachusetts, Boston, MA.
2 Lotte Bailyn, Robet Drago, and Thomas Kochan. 2001. *Integrating Work and Family Life: A Holistic Approach,* MIT Sloan School of Management.
3 R. Landers, J. Rebitzer, and L. Taylor. 1996. "Rat Race Redux: Adverse Selection in the Determination of Work Hours in Law Firms," *American Economic Review* 86, 329–348.

Integrating Work and Family Life

A holistic approach

by Lotte Bailyn, Robert Drago, and Thomas A. Kochan

Executive Summary: Reframing the Debate

The challenge of integrating work and family life is part of everyday reality for the majority of American working families. While the particulars may vary depending on income, occupation, and stage in life, this challenge cuts across all socioeconomic levels and is felt directly by both women and men. For many these challenges are experienced as:

- *An increasing time squeeze.* Many working adults, particularly single parents and those in dual-earner families, have difficulty providing the ordinary daily attention needed for the well-being of family members, including themselves. Between 1970 and 1997, the percentage of employed women working more than 50 hours per week rose from 4.5 to 9.6, and the figure for men rose from 21.0 to 25.2 percent.
- *Financial pressures.* Women who are mothers as well as employees earn less than other women, and the family incomes of single mothers are particularly low, leaving the U.S. with the highest poverty rate for children among developed countries. Two-parent families in poverty also face difficulties, since parents at work must often leave children alone, with serious consequences for their safety, health, learning, supervision, and nurturance. Well into the middle class, working parents have insufficient income to pay for the care they cannot provide themselves; and even those who can afford it, often have difficulty locating the stable, quality care they would like.
- *A low wage ceiling for paid care providers.* Because of these limitations on family resources and the historical devaluing of care work, many paid care workers do not earn a living wage, resulting in hardships for these workers and their families and, in turn, in an unstable and inadequately trained care labor force. In the late 1990s, the starting salary for child-care employees with college degrees was $15,000 to $16,000 per year and, predictably, turnover at child-care centers averages around 30 percent each year in the U.S.
- *Spillover of stresses to other social and community institutions.* Family stresses inevitably spill over into places not designed nor sufficiently funded to deal with them—schools, social service agencies, police, courts, religious institutions—creating institutional overload and additional stressors for their employees. The fastest-growing program in American schools for the last few years has been before- and afterschool care programs, but these remain of limited availability.
- *High costs of turnover, absenteeism, and lost investments in human resources.* Employers with workers facing difficulties at home experience the costs of losing valued workers as workers seek more accommodating arrangements or even leave the workforce altogether. Ultimately, the economy and society pay the price of this underutilization of human resources in both a lower standard of living and a reduced quality of life.

These problems are manifestations of a deeper, often unstated but outdated image of work and of the "ideal worker." Workplaces continue to be structured around the image of an ideal worker who starts to work in early adulthood and continues for forty years uninterrupted, taking no time off for child bearing or child rearing, supported by a spouse or family member who takes primary responsibility for family and community. In the last half century, however, we have moved from a division of labor depending generally on men as breadwinners and women as family caregivers to a way of life in which both men and women are breadwinners. But we have done so without redesigning work or occupational career paths and without making new provisions for family care. The result is a policy and institutional lag that has produced a care crisis and a career dilemma.

Unfortunately, American society is not addressing the underlying assumptions that give rise to these problems. Yet the problems this mismatch

---

Source: "Integrating Work and Family Life: A Holistic Approach" (Executive Summary) by Lotte Bailyn, Robert Drago, and Thomas Kochan. Reprinted by permission of Sloan Work-Family Policy Network, MIT Sloan School of Management.

causes working families and the economy will not go away, nor will they be solved if each of the key institutions that share responsibilities for addressing them continue the current pattern of working separately, on sometimes parallel and sometimes conflicting paths.

This report, commissioned by the Alfred P. Sloan Foundation and prepared by a group of work and family researchers, offers a different and, we believe, more productive, holistic approach to the challenge of integrating work and family life. Our basic premise is straightforward: Integrating work and family life today requires a well-informed collaborative effort on the part of all the key actors that share interests and responsibilities for these issues. *Employers, families, worker and family advocacy groups, government, and communities all have roles to play in integrating work and family life, but none of them can solve this problem acting alone.* Each must reexamine the implicit assumptions of what constitutes an "ideal worker" in today's economy and society, and then engage other groups and institutions in an ongoing dialogue over how to close the gap between today's work and family realities and the policies and practices that govern their interrelationships.

Now is the time for change. What is needed is the public discourse, leadership, and collective will to get on with the task.

Responses of the Different Actors

Though most public discourse still frames these issues as private troubles, that is, logistical or "balance" problems that individuals or families should solve on their own, there have been a range of proposals for change. So far, however, such efforts have produced only piecemeal or patchwork solutions, each moving on its own, sometimes in parallel and sometimes down conflicting paths. Few question the existing organization of paid work or the fundamental proposition that paid work is the only "work" that matters. Examples of the contributions and limitations of the individual efforts of the different actors include:

- *Family advocates*, assuming unchanged work structures, seek new systems of paid care for the children of working parents and have been successful in getting the federal government to allow states to experiment with different ways to fund paid parental leave. But these efforts take little account of how some businesses already provide paid leave as part of their benefit packages. Business groups, therefore, tend to oppose these efforts as yet another federal or state government mandate that adds costs and administrative burdens without being responsive to their specific business realities, organizational practices, or workforce needs.

- Many *employers* are offering "family-friendly" policies designed to recruit and retain valued workers in tight labor markets, and make it easier for them to work the hours that businesses seemingly require. But without changing the cultural definition of career success or explicitly designing work systems to meet dual workplace and family concerns, they do not address the fundamental issue of the inability of ideal workers to make time for family commitments. Moreover, not all employees feel free to use these policies, and those who do often feel they send a signal that hurts their careers.

- Some *civil-rights lawyers* point out that if you define the ideal worker around men's traditional life patterns, the result, legally, is discrimination against women.

- *Politicians and policy analysts* tend to propose piecemeal solutions that reflect particular ideological views or institutional perspectives. Some would leave work-family problems to the market to solve. Others see them largely as poverty issues and focus on the need to assist low-wage parents to provide for the health, education, and development of their children. Still others propose specific legislation or regulations to address particular problems, such as the need for paid leave or more flexible working hours and overtime rules. This stance focuses the debate on symptoms rather than on the underlying causes and holistic strategies or solutions.

- Some *unions* have begun to address these issues by negotiating and funding various leave and child-care provisions, complementing the traditional union emphasis on providing health-care and pension coverage, but their contribution is limited, given current union-management relations.

- *Community groups* are becoming more active in attempting to provide supports for families and children. For example, they have built coalitions at the grassroots level around "livability initiatives" that link economic development, environmental protection, and the care and health of children and families. But these efforts cannot be developed and sustained without resources from business, philanthropy, and/or government.

Each of these approaches addresses only parts of the larger problem and, if implemented, would benefit only select segments of the broad population. In the end, they leave in place the default solution of unchanged reliance on the care work of women—as if their work days had not changed. And they leave most workers and families stressed by the incompatibility of workplace requirements and the needs of family care.

We believe U.S. society is ready to take a different, more holistic approach. Men and women are ready to step up to meet the problem if given the necessary resources and institutional supports. They recognize that this is a societal issue, one they cannot solve on their own by simply changing the division of labor at home or ending discriminatory practices at work. What is required is a comprehensive effort at reenvisioning paid work, careers, and care work, bringing together scattered structural "leads" from across the country into a blueprint for change.

Putting the Pieces Together

What is needed to reach this goal is for each of the actors to work together and complement each other's efforts. The total combined impact could indeed be significantly greater than the sum of the parts. In this section we suggest steps that each of these parties might take to energize a collaborative, systemic effort, and end by suggesting specific steps for jump-starting this type of effort.

First, what changes by each of the actors are needed for a systemic approach to be put in motion?

Employers. Clearly, firms should continue to act in their self-interest by expanding the array and reach of "family-friendly" benefits and practices to better enable workers to contribute to their business objectives and meet their family and personal responsibilities. But firm-initiated benefits will inevitably be limited to those with labor market power, will not reframe the objectives of these efforts around the dual agenda of strengthening work *and* family outcomes, and will continue to be underutilized. To both increase the utilization and effectiveness of their own policies and to contribute to a more collaborative, systemic effort, we believe employers need to (1) focus on work design, (2) share control and responsibility for designing and implementing organizational policies with employees, and (3) work collaboratively with other actors.

1. *Focus on Work Design.* Work design is a root cause of many of the problems associated with work-family integration as well as a key lever and opportunity for making progress. The problem, however, should not be framed as how can organizations design high-performance work systems, but as how can work practices be redesigned to achieve both high performance at work and a more satisfying personal and family life.
2. *Share Control and Responsibility with Employees.* Research on the underutilization of family-friendly policies documents several reasons why sharing control over these policies and practices is critical for this effort. First, front-line employees and supervisors know their work practices best. Their inputs, therefore, are critical to any effort at work redesign. Second, only by engaging employees in efforts to change the prevailing workplace culture will fear be overcome that use of part-time or flexible work options will hurt one's career prospects. Further, the culture must allow men as well as women to participate in these options. Unless this happens, flexible policies will continue to be underutilized. Third, dialogue among people in a work group is critical to overcoming both subtle resistance among supervisors and resentment of peers to benefits seen as favoring one group (e.g., young parents) over others.
3. *Move More Women into High-Level Corporate Positions.* The fastest way of elevating the priorities assigned to work and family issues is for corporate leaders to reflect the demographic profile of their staff. While work and family are not simply women's issues, the reality is that women often have more personal experience than men in dealing with these issues and are more likely than men to make them a priority.
4. *Engage Other Actors in a Systemic Approach.* The traditional tendency of managers to protect their organizational autonomy has to be overcome for a holistic approach to succeed. Employers will need not only to work together as a cohesive and responsible business community, but also to participate constructively in community, state, and national dialogues that involve unions, professional associations and other worker advocates, women and family advocates, and government agencies.

Unions and Professional Associations. Unions and professional groups also need to (1) give work and family issues a higher priority in their organizing, recruitment, negotiation, coalition building, and joint efforts, (2) move more women into leadership positions, and (3) expand coalitions with other groups that share a commitment to better integrating work and family life.

1. *Organize for Work and Family.* Just as we urge employers to accept a dual agenda, we urge unions and professional groups to organize for both work and family benefits and concerns. This means seeing potential members as both employees and as citizens, parents, and members of households with varying needs.
2. *Move More Women into Leadership Positions.* As is true of corporations, a larger cadre of women leaders in unions and professional associations is more likely to place issues of equal pay for equal work as well as the expansion of negotiated health care, paid leave, flexible hours, quality part-time work, and other family benefits higher on their agendas than men would.

3. *Build Lasting Coalitions with Other Actors.* The power of recent living-wage campaigns illustrates the value of coalition-building efforts of unions and community groups. Joint union-management child-care and educational programs in the health-care, hotel, and other industries demonstrate the innovative potential and staying power of shared ownership and stable funding. Such partnerships represent an opportunity both to build new institutions and processes for dialogue, and to make substantive progress in diffusing benefits to broader segments of the population in ways that build on rather than conflict with or limit what already is being done.

Governments. We envision a key but very different role for government agencies as complementary participants in a systemic approach to advancing work and family integration. The role of government needs to be recast as a catalyst for private actions, addressing the needs of workers and families that private actors will not or cannot reach on their own. While we emphasize a recasting of the perspective and processes by which government influences private efforts, government must also be the force to ensure that basic minimum standards for work and family life are available to all. We feel that the government agenda should deal with (1) issues of care, (2) flexible employment relations, and (3) national and local work-family councils.

1. *Paid Time for Care and Quality Care Work.* A strong case can be made in support of efforts to provide more paid time off for family responsibilities to more workers and family members. Steps must also be taken to ensure that care workers have the skills needed to provide quality care and are compensated a living wage for doing so.
2. *Work Hours, Quality Part-Time Jobs, and Portable Benefits.* Following the historical trend, the long-term goal of policy should be to reduce gradually the length of the workweek and work year, consistent with growth in productivity. Further, given the substantial numbers of individuals who prefer part-time work at particular stages in life, a key policy objective should also be to improve the quality of part-time jobs. This implies providing proportionate income, benefits, and promotional opportunities and ensuring that individuals can move between part-time and full-time work without fear of discrimination or career retribution. Finally, health-care and pension benefits tied to specific employers should become portable.
3. *National and Local Work and Family Councils.* Finally, we suggest the need to establish broadly representative work and family councils at the national and local levels to promote, coordinate, and evaluate the types of systemic efforts called for in this report. The councils should have the authority and resources to promote experimentation, evaluation, and learning and should issue annual reports assessing progress toward goals laid out in this report.

Communities and Families. Two effects of implementing a holistic approach would be to stop assuming that families can take care of themselves under present conditions or hoping that voluntary community institutions will fill the gaps left by government and other private-sector efforts. This does not, however, mean that families and communities do not have important roles to play as part of a holistic effort. But like the other institutions, some changes in their traditional roles would be needed.

1. *Build Coalitions Across the Actors.* Community groups derive most of their strength and legitimacy from their membership and leadership base. A key role these groups play in the holistic model envisioned here is one of bringing together and coordinating the efforts of the diverse players—business, labor, governments, and families. The broader the base of support that groups can build, the more sustainable their efforts are likely to be.
2. *Organize Cooperative Family Programs.* Children, elders, and others in need of care benefit from the services of schools, daycare centers, libraries, and various supportive programs in their communities, and from the participation of family members in such services. But few working adults have time to volunteer their labor. Working together with each other and with employers, unions, and professional associations, community institutions could promote such efforts as sustained paid leave time for volunteering, as well as networks of cooperative family care. At the same time employers need to make it possible for their employees to become clients and participants in such cooperative arrangements.

A Call to Action

The conditions leading to our current situation will not go away. Indeed, we believe the problems will continue to deepen as the population ages. Therefore, all of the institutions needed to create a successful result, one that will lead to coherent, coordinated, and systemic efforts to address the problems, have and will continue to have a strong incentive to be involved. The opportunity is there for the taking.

To jump start this approach, we suggest the parties begin working together to achieve five high-priority objectives:

- **Work Design.** Managers, employees, and employee representatives should work together to redesign work systems, processes, and schedules to meet the dual agenda of improving work and organization performance, and personal and family life.
- **Paid Leave for Family Caregiving.** American families need access to a universal paid leave policy to meet different needs over their life course. But the specific forms and means of financing paid leave should build on what leading firms and union agreements already provide some workers. State-level experimentation with alternative financing arrangements and options that build on private sector practices must be encouraged.
- **Reduced Hours and Hours Flexibility.** The historic trend of reduced hours of work in tandem with economic growth has been reversed in recent decades for many Americans. More options for working reduced hours while simultaneously increasing flexibility and responsiveness to employer and customer requirements need to be available to working families. Experiments are needed to allow employers and employees to negotiate arrangements that better suit their varying needs, to administer them together in ways that are mutually beneficial, and to prevent and reduce overwork.
- **Women in Leadership Positions.** Research shows that women in positions of leadership in corporations, unions, and government organizations give work and family issues a higher priority in decision-making. All these institutions therefore need to accelerate the pace of moving women into top-level positions.
- **Worker Voice.** These policies will only be effective if all the parties share in their design and administration and experiment with different ways to fit them to their varied work and family circumstances. This requires updating and strengthening labor law to ensure workers have their own voice in shaping workplace policies and practices.
- **Community Empowerment.** We need to recognize the importance of community-based institutions by fostering greater investment in their services, and by facilitating volunteerism in their programs. These groups are diverse, and they must have a seat at the table when work-family problems are defined and work-family solutions are created.
- **Work-Family Councils and Summit.** To foster and learn from policies and practices of employers and unions, government at all levels, communities, and others, and to keep these issues on the national agenda, we suggest creating a set of broad-based regional Work-Family Councils whose members would come together annually for a national-level Working Families Summit.

Addressing the Crisis in Confidence in Corporations

Root causes, victims, and strategies for reform

by Thomas A. Kochan

Root Causes

The place to begin is to correctly identify the root cause of the current corporate scandals. Failure to get this right means the solutions chosen will be at worst wrong or at best inadequate. My view is that most analysts to date have danced around or avoided identifying the real root cause, namely the overemphasis American corporations have been forced to give in recent years to maximizing shareholder value without regard for the effects of its actions on other stakeholders.

A brief historical review is needed to understand how these forces grew and reinforced each other over the past two decades. As pressures from Wall

Source: "Addressing the Crisis in Confidence in Corporations: Root Causes, Victims, and Strategies for Reform" by Thomas A. Kochan. *From Academy of Management Executive: The Thinking Manager's Source* by Thomas A. Kochan. Copyright 2002 by Academy of Management. Reproduced with permission of Academy of Management in the format Textbook via Copyright Clearance Center.

Street grew in the aftermath of the contests for corporate control in the 1980s, executives turned more and more of their attention to meeting analysts short-term expectations and to restructuring operations to boost earnings (Useem, 1996). Board committees and compensation consultants restructured executive contracts to better align management incentives with investor interests. Boards likewise turned to CEOs who could best manage relations with the financial community and project an image of confidence. The era of the charismatic CEO was born (Khurana, forthcoming). Wall Street, the business media and press, and business school case writers alike reinforced these trends by committing a classic attribution error—they attributed the successes of organizations to the leadership and vision of the CEO and his (mostly his) top executive team. This served to increase the perceived value of CEOs. The self-reinforcing escalation of executive compensation that ensued eventually led to a 400 to 1 ratio of CEO compensation to the average worker. Power became highly concentrated at the top of organizations and the adage that "power corrupts and absolute power corrupts absolutely" once again has proven true.

This view is not yet part of the public or political discourse today. Instead it is easier to focus on personal ethical failures of executives, accountants, and others in the inner circles of power in corporations and financial market institutions. Clearly there have been ethical failures. But simply punishing a few "bad apples," imposing stiffer penalties to deter similar misconduct in the future, or imploring executives to be more responsible will fail to get at the conditions that created the incentives for misconduct and that, if not addressed, will likely do so again in the future. To stop here means we will rely on lawyers to be the guardians of ethical behavior. This is not my idea of an adequate solution.

The Victims

Not only have the root causes been too narrowly construed, so too have the range of victims of these developments. Clearly investors and pension holders are major victims. One estimate puts the loss in the value of pension and 401(k) plans since 2000 at $7 trillion (Siebert, 2002). That's roughly $28,000 for every man, woman, and child in America! So investors and current and future pensioners deserve better protections. Reforms limiting conflicts of interests among auditors, consultants, stock analysts, investment bankers, and corporate executives, requiring personal affirmation of the accuracy of financial statements, and stiffening penalties, enforcement procedures, and oversight authority of the SEC are all appropriate.

But another major class of victims has been eerily silent in these debates to date. Workers and their families are also paying a huge price for trusting business executives to protect their interests. But current proposals fail to protect employees against the corporate actions that have led to dramatic losses in jobs, retirement income, professional and personal identity, and voice in the workplace. The past two decades have witnessed a precipitous decline in the power and voice of workers in American corporations. As the labor movement declined and the favored business model shifted to focus on core competencies, American executives discovered they could turn to layoffs not as a strategy of last resort but as a preemptive strike to ensure future earnings would not be compromised. For a short period of time, those that did so were actually rewarded with a spike in their stock price. This led to a breakdown in the old social contract that traded employee loyalty and good performance for employment, career, and retirement security. Over this same period, retirement risks shifted from corporations to individuals as defined benefit pension plans were replaced with defined contribution, cash balance, and 401(k) savings plans. And the disparities in income and wealth that future historians will mark as the signal feature of the past two decades continued throughout the booming 1990s.

Addressing the losses absorbed by this generation of workers and providing the next generation with the tools to avoid a similar fate requires not only rebalancing power to protect investors; it requires revisiting the very purposes of corporations. American corporations and their executives must be accountable to the workers, families, and communities that share their risks.

It is ironic that policy makers are not yet considering how workers can contribute to corporate reform since economists, organization theorists, and management writers all are recognizing that worker knowledge, skills, and commitment are at least as important sources of competitive advantage to the twenty-first-century corporations as financial capital was to the twentieth-century firm. Through their knowledge and effort, workers add value to the firm, but in joining, and more importantly, in staying with a given firm, they also put a significant part of their human capital at risk (Blair, 1995). Employees who are forced to find new jobs frequently lose between 15 to 20 percent in wages plus the value of the benefits that don't move with them (Osterman, 1999). So like investors of financial capital, employees absorb significant risk—but unlike financial investors, they have no legal rights to a voice in how their corporation is run, and unless specifically protected by a collective bargaining or individual contract, workers can be fired or laid off at will.

Remedies

The last time America recognized the need to rein in the power of executives was in the 1930s. At that time, corporate reform, via the Security and Exchange Commission, was directly followed by passage of the National Labor Relations Act. Today's Congress should finish the job, as did their New Deal counterparts and follow reforms designed to protect investors with actions that address the legitimate stake workers and their families have in the modern corporation. This will require a major overhaul and update of the labor laws that were designed for the world of work of the 1930s, not the knowledge driven organizations, fluid labor markets, and diverse workforce and families of today.

The first step is to finally fix well-documented flaws in labor law by restoring workers' right to control whether and how they are represented at the workplace. Today, one in 20 workers who vote for a union can expect to be fired. This is illegal, but the penalties are so delayed and weak that many employers violate the letter or spirit of the law anyway.

Steps to fix federal labor law include making the financial penalties for violating the rights guaranteed by labor law equal to those that apply to other forms of discrimination; placing tight time limits on union election campaigns to eliminate delaying tactics; and providing a right to arbitration if employers stonewall efforts to negotiate a first collective bargaining agreement. A presidential commission endorsed such proposals nearly a decade ago—the current corporate crisis makes their enactment even more overdue.

Reforming labor law is not enough. All workers, union or not, need the right to elect representatives who meet periodically to review their company's human resource policies from top to bottom, including executive compensation policies, training and development strategies, pensions, leave benefits and layoff provisions. Just as investors need fuller access to information, workers need such transparency to ensure that corporate policies are fair across the board. American labor law now prohibits this type of representation, even though surveys find that more than 70 percent of the workforce wants it.

Another necessary reform is to grant loyal employees who invest and put at risk their human capital a right to sit on the boards of their corporations and pension funds just as these rights are granted to investors of financial capital. Opening these boards to worker representatives is not unprecedented. Workers already elect representatives to most public sector pension funds and share in the governance of multi-employer plans such as those found in the construction industry and in TIAA-CREF, the largest pension fund covering college professors. The same is true for corporate boards of directors. The steel, trucking, and airline industries invited employee representatives onto their boards in recent years in exchange for major worker concessions to save their companies. But why should employees only get a voice in governance in failing companies? Their voice should be heard in all firms, not just the basket cases of corporate America. Elected employee representatives will give workers a say in decision making that directly affects them while also providing investors with an additional, independent check and balance on executive actions. Having employees serve on the board committees that set executive compensation would add a fairness and transparency test needed to ensure there is someone on the "other side of the table" in these deliberations.

Also like investors, employees have learned that they cannot put all their eggs in one basket—in today's labor market, workers must be ready and able to move to new jobs. This requires weaning employment benefits away from their individual corporate focus; as a long-term objective, pensions, health insurance, training and development, and all other benefits must become fully portable.

For too long politicians, business school faculty, and the general public have accepted as a matter of faith the view that the corporation exists only to enrich its shareholders. It is time to once again call this issue into question and ask to whom and how should corporations and their executives be held accountable? Corporate failure to similarly value other objectives—including the well-being of employees and their community—has helped produce today's scandals. Greater protections for investors and more regulatory oversight are important pieces of a cure. But employees offer in-place, frontline protection against corporate abuse. Any reform package that fails to rebalance power by addressing the legitimate needs and rights of employees to monitor executive behavior and protect their human capital investments fails to complete the job.

Finally, not all remedies can come from Washington, from a rebuilding of the labor movement, or from internal corporate reforms. As management educators and researchers we must also examine our role in allowing the conditions that gave rise to these behaviors to develop on our watch and ask what changes in our personal research agendas and our teaching programs are needed to learn from these experiences and ensure the next generation of managers and educators do not allow similar scandals to emerge on their watch.

References

Blair, Margaret. 1995. *Ownership and Control.* Washington, DC: The Brookings Institution.

Khurana, Rakesh. Forthcoming. *Searching for a Corporate Savior: The Irrational Quest for Charismatic CEOs.* Princeton, NJ: Princeton University Press.

Osterman, Paul. 1999. *Securing Prosperity.* Princeton, NJ: Princeton University Press.

Siebert, Muriel. 2002. "To Encourage Recovery, Encourage Investors," *The New York Times* (August 6), A19.

Useem, Michael. 1996. *Investor Capitalism.* New York: Basic Books.

Index

"Addressing the Crisis in Confidence in Corporations" (Kochan), 58–61
advocacy groups, 55
anxiety, 15, 19
Applied Materials, 39
apprentice system, 20
assets, human. *See* human assets
associations, and professionalism, 28

Bailyn, Lotte, 19
Barnard, Chester, 26
Begun, Shelly, 39
benefits, portability of, 60
boards of directors, 60
bonding process, 35
bounded organizations, 7
British Petroleum (BP), 34–35
Brower, Tim, 44–45, 46, 50
Browne, John, 34
budgeting, of capital vs. talent, 32
"Building Competitive Advantage Through People" (Bartell and Ghoshal), 29–36
building human capital, 32–33
buzzwords, 12

Calico Commerce, 38–41
capital, 30, 32
capital, human. *See* human assets
Cappelli, Peter, 14
career development, 7, 18, 27, 28
CEOs, corporate scandals and, 59
"The Changing Social Contract for White-Collar Workers" (Heckscher), 25–28
childcare, 54, 57
Cisco Systems, 37
civil rights, and work-family integration, 55
coaching sessions, 33
coalition-building, 57
collaborative relationships, 7
commitment. *See* loyalty and commitment
community empowerment, 58
community groups, 55, 57
compensation
    benefits, portability of, 60
    bonding process and, 35
    boundary crossing and, 16
    executive, 59
    part-time partners and, 48, 52
    restructuring, and loss of living wage, 13
    Silicon Valley practices, 39
    teams and, 16
competency-based strategies, 29, 30
competition for human capital
    business growth and, 51
    contract workers and, 35
    restructuring and, 14
    strategy of, 29, 30, 36
competitive-strategy model, 29, 30, 36
confidence, corporate, 6, 58–61. *See also* loyalty and commitment
contracts, social, 39. *See* social contracts
contract workers, 14, 35, 36–37
cooperative family programs, 57
core-competency strategy, 29, 30
corporate confidence, 6, 58–61. *See also* loyalty and commitment
corporate paternalism, 25–26
councils, work and family, 57, 58
cross-training, 15
culling of human resources, 33
cultural perspective, 6
culture, organizational, 6, 35
customer loyalty, 38

Davidson, Maury, 44–47
development, career, 7, 18, 27, 28
development of human capital, 32–33
Devine, Rob, 39
discrimination against women, 55
diversity, 8, 17
domination, corporate, 26
dot.com bubble, 13
downsizing. *See* restructuring and downsizing
Driver, John, 40
dual agenda, 19

employability, lifetime, 15
employees. *See also* workforce management
    as assets vs. costs, 16, 21
    corporate scandals and, 59–60
    "ideal worker," 54, 55
    labor reforms and, 60
    multi-skilled, 15–16
    as stakeholders
    as talent investors, 32
    virtual, 19
employment, lifelong, 8, 14, 15
employment relationship. *See also* workforce management
    alternatives, 20
    changes in, 12–13
    definition of, 6, 12
    flexibility and, 12, 17–19
    free agency, 26–27, 35, 36, 39
    knowledge-based, 16, 20–21
    lifelong employment, 8, 14, 15
    long-term vs. short-term, 12, 14, 20
    market-mediated, 14
    negotiation of, 28
    old vs. new, 13–16

policy inconsistencies and, 21–22
social contracts, 8, 12, 14, 25–28, 39
employment security, 6, 15, 26. *See also* lifelong employment
equity partnerships, 48
executive compensation, 59
external labor markets, 13–14

family advocates, 55
family-friendly policies, 17–18, 55, 56
family leave, 49–51, 52–53, 58
family-work balance. *See* work-family integration
feedback, and talent development, 33
financial pressures, and work-family integration, 54
Fisher, Pamela, 44–47, 48, 50, 51
flat organizations, 7, 15
flexibility
    job rotation, 15
    part-time partner case, 44–53
    types of arrangements, 18–19
    work-family integration and, 58
    workforce diversity and, 17
    workforce management issues, 7–8, 12
flex time, 18
free agency, 26–27, 35, 36, 39

Genzyme, 35
Germany, 20
globalization, 8, 14, 15
goals, and changing assumptions, 21
Goldstein, Marilyn, 50
Goodnight, Jim, 35, 37
governments, 28, 57

Hall, D. Timothy, 51–52
Hartwig, George, 44–47, 51, 52
Hewlett-Packard, 40
hierarchical structure, 7, 25–28
high-performance work systems, 16
holistic approach to work-family integration, 54–58
home, balancing with work. *See* work-family integration
honesty, 39
honesty with employees, 27
hours of work
    impact of long hours, 36, 37
    trends in, 18
    work-family integration and, 57, 58
human assets
    competition for, 14, 29, 30, 36, 51
    knowledge-based work systems and, 16, 20–21
    recruitment and development of, 32–33
    restructuring, and risk distribution, 59–60
    scarcity as resource, 30
    strategy based on, 29–36

human resources management, evolving role of, 31–32
human resources managers, and human-capital strategy, 31–36

"ideal worker," 54, 55
income partnerships, 48
independent contractors, 14, 19, 35, 36–37
information, sharing with workers, 39
information technology (IT), 34
innovation, 7, 28
"In Silicon Valley, Loyalty Means Paying a High Price" (Berenson), 38–41
"Integrating Work and Family Life: A Holistic Approach" (Bailyn, Drago, and Kochan), 54–58
intellectual capital. *See* human assets
interests of workers, 6
internal labor markets, 13–14
investors, 59

Japan, 15, 20
job ladder, 18
job rotation, 15
jobs, multitasked or multidimensional, 15–16
jobs, notion of, 16
job security, 6, 15, 26. *See also* lifelong employment
job sharing, 18

knowledge-based work systems, 16, 20–21
knowledge management, and social networks, 34–35
Kolodzieski, Aleida, 38, 40

labor laws, reform of, 60
labor markets, internal vs. external, 13–14
labor unions
    changed employment relationships and, 28
    decline of power, 14, 22, 59
    work-family integration and, 55, 56–57
Landauer, Sally C., 48
layoffs. *See* restructuring and downsizing
leadership, changing assumptions of, 21
leadership, women in, 56, 58
leave policy, 49–51, 52–53, 58
LG, 33
lifelong employment, 8, 14, 15
lifetime employability, 15
linking, and knowledge management, 34–35
long-term employment relationships, 12, 14, 20
loyalty and commitment
    bonding process, 35
    Calico Commerce case, 38–41
    customer loyalty, 38
    downsizing and, 19
    honesty with employees and, 27, 39
    networking and, 7

policy consistency and, 21–22
professionalism vs. loyalism, 25–28
Silicon Valley practices and, 38
workforce management and, 6

managers, 25, 29–36
Manpower, Inc., 19
market-mediated employment relationship, 14
Mayden, Barbara Mendel, 50–51
McDermand, Nancy, 39–40
McGregor, Douglas, 21
McKinsey & Co., 33, 36
McNamee, Roger, 39
Meeker, Needham & Ames (MN&A), 44–52
Merck & Co., Inc., 50
Microsoft Corporation, 32–33
middle management, 25
moral issue, in downsizing, 25
motivation, 6, 7. *See also* loyalty and commitment
MTW Corporation, 37
multitasking, 15–16
mutual gains, and workforce management, 6

Naumann, Alan, 38
negative feedback loop, in downsizing, 20
networking, 7, 34–35
new organization model, 7–8, 13–16, 21
nonequity partnerships, 48

obligations, under professional ethic, 27
Obrand, Barry, 40
office, virtual, 18
old (bureaucratic) model, 7–8, 13, 18
organizational charts, 15
"organization man," 18
outsourcing, and competition for talent, 35.
    See also contract workers; temporary workers

parental leave, 49–51, 52–53, 58
partnerships, and human capital, 21
partnerships, part-time, 44–53
"The Part-Time Partner" (Loveman), 44–52
part-time workers, 18, 44–53, 57
paternalism, 25–26
peer assists, 34
pension funds, 59, 60
performance ranking, 33
policies, consistency in, 21–22
policies, effecting change in, 7, 16, 51–52
policy analysts, and work-family problems, 55
political perspective, 6
politicians, and work-family problems, 55
positive-sum game, 31
power, in flat organizations, 7
productivity, and hours of work, 38
professional associations, 56–57
professional ethic, 27–28

promotion, 7, 15, 44–53
psychological contracts, 12. *See also* social contracts

quality, of part-time jobs, 57

race, in workforce composition, 17
recruitment as strategic task, 32–33
reengineering, 34
Reichheld, Fred, 39
resource-based strategy, 30
resources. *See* human assets
restructuring and downsizing
    costs of, 19–20, 20
    history of, 13
    human capital risks, 59–60
    long-term employment and, 14
    loyalty and, 25–28
    moral issue, 25
rights, labor, 60
Ross, Julie, 45–52

safety issues, with temporary workers, 19
SAS Institute, 35, 37–38
satisfaction, 19. *See also* loyalty and commitment
scandals, corporate, 58–61
Schwartz, Joe, 38–39
security, employment, 6, 15, 26. *See also* lifelong employment
self-interest, amoral, 27
shareholder value vs. societal interests, 20
Silicon Valley, 36–40
Simms, Marsha E., 48–49
skills, generalized, 27, 28
Smirov, Yuri, 40
social contracts
    definition and history of, 12
    disappearance of, 39
    employment relationship and, 8
    professionalism vs. loyalism, 25–28
    redefining, 14
social networks, 34–35
societal interests vs. shareholder value, 20
space flexible, 18
staffing. *See* workforce management
stakeholders, 8, 31
Stewart, Rick, 44
stock options, 31, 36, 37, 38–41
strategic design perspective, 6
strategy, evolving focus of, 29–31
strategy, talent-based, 29–36
stresses, family, 54
subcontractors, and flexibility, 19. *See also* contract workers
success, conception of, in flat organizations, 7
systemic approach to work-family integration, 56, 57
systems perspective, 7, 14

talent-based strategy, 29–36. *See also* human assets
talent investors, employees as, 32
teams, 15, 16
technology, changing assumptions of, 21
telecommuting, 18
temporary workers, 14, 19, 35
Termeer, Henri, 35
time flexibility, 18, 44–53. *See also* hours of work
time squeeze, in dual-earner families, 54
training
    alternative approaches, 20
    generalized skill development, 27, 28
    lifetime employability and, 15
    shorter-term employment and, 20
Trosin, Walter R., 49–50
trust, 6, 22, 26. *See also* loyalty and commitment
turnover, 36–37

unions. *See* labor unions
universal paid leave policy, 58

value management, 31
virtual corporation, 19
virtual employees, 19
virtual office, 18
vitality index, 33
voice, worker, 58

wages, 13, 54. *See also* compensation
Wagner Act, 25, 28
Welch, Jim, 44–46, 50, 51
Welch, John F., Jr. (Jack), 33
"What's Wrong with Management Practices in Silicon Valley? A Lot" (Pfeffer), 36–38
women. *See also* work-family integration
    discrimination against, 55
    in leadership positions, 56, 58
work-family integration and, 55, 56, 58
    in the workforce, 17
Women's Bar Association of Massachusetts, 53
work, nature of, 21
work design, 56, 58
work-family integration
    costs of, 54
    dual agenda, 19
    holistic approach, 54–58
    part-time partner case, 49–51
workforce diversity and, 17
workforce, sex and race composition of, 17
workforce management. *See also* employment relationship
    alternative responses, 20
    assumptions, 21
    dimensions of, 6
    employee representation models, 22
    flexibility and, 12, 17–19
human capital and knowledge, 16, 20–21
    interests of workers, 6
    in old and new models, 7–8, 13–16
    options, 20
    policy inconsistencies, 21–22
    systems perspective, 7, 14
work hours. *See* hours of work
Working Family Summit, 58
working poor, 13
Working Today, 22, 28
work systems, knowledge-based or high-performance, 16

zero-sum game, 31

MANAGING FOR THE FUTURE

Organizational Behavior & Processes

Managing Change in Organizations

Module 8

MANAGING FOR THE FUTURE
Organizational Behavior & Processes, Third Edition

Deborah Ancona
Sloan School of Management
Massachusetts Institute of Technology

John Van Maanen
Sloan School of Management
Massachusetts Institute of Technology

Thomas A. Kochan
Sloan School of Management
Massachusetts Institute of Technology

D. Eleanor Westney
Sloan School of Management
Massachusetts Institute of Technology

Maureen Scully
Graduate School of Management
Simmons College

Dedicated to those who have inspired us to try to be better students and teachers.
Special thanks to: Professor Jack Barbash • Professor Arthur H. Gladstein • Professor Marius B. Jansen • Professor Joanne Martin • Professor Edgar H. Schein

---

VP/Editorial Director
Jack W. Calhoun

VP/Editor-in-Chief
Michael P. Roche

Senior Publisher
Melissa S. Acuña

Executive Editor
John Szilagyi

Senior Developmental Editor
Judith O'Neill

Marketing Manager
Jacquelyn Carrillo

Production Editor
Emily Gross

Manufacturing Coordinator
Rhonda Utley

Compositor
Trejo Production

Printer
Von Hoffmann Press, Inc.
Frederick, MD

Internal Designer
Bethany Casey

Cover Designer
Bethany Casey

Photographs
©PhotoDisc

Design Project Manager
Bethany Casey

COPYRIGHT ©2005
by South-Western, a division of Thomson Learning. Thomson Learning™ is a trademark used herein under license.

Printed in the United States of America
1 2 3 4 5 07 06 05 04 03

For more information contact
South-Western College Publishing,
5191 Natorp Boulevard,
Mason, Ohio, 45040
Or you can visit our Internet site at:
http://www.swlearning.com

ALL RIGHTS RESERVED
No part of this work covered by the copyright hereon may be reproduced or used in any form or by any means—graphic, electronic, or mechanical, including photocopying, recording, taping, Web distribution or information storage and retrieval systems—without the written permission of the publisher.

For permission to use material from this text or product, contact us by
Tel: (800) 730-2214
Fax: (800) 730-2215
http://www.thomsonrights.com

Library of Congress Control Number: 2003113908
ISBN 0-324-05575-7

Contents

Managing Change in Organizations

Overview		4

Core

Class Note	**Organizational Change: An Overview**	6
	Why Is Organizational Change So Difficult? 6	
	Organizational Change at Procter & Gamble: Organization 2005 *8*	
	Stage Models of Change Processes 11	
	Dimensions of Change 15	
	Being a More Effective Change Agent 18	
	References 21	
Case	**The Strategy That Wouldn't Travel**	22
	Inside Wichita 23	
	Cookie-Cutter Conundrum 24	

Elective

Readings	**The Life Cycle of Typical Change Initiatives**	28
	The Leadership of Profound Change	32
	The Myth of the Hero-CEO 32	
	A Different View of Executive Leadership 33	
	What Is Leadership and Who Are the Leaders? 35	
	Culture Change at General Electric	38
	Stage One: Work-Outs and the "RAMMP" Matrix 38	
	The Payoff Matrix 40	
	Stage Two: Best Practices 40	
	Stage Three: Process Maps 41	
	Stage Four: Change Acceleration 41	
	Stage Five: Strategic Initiatives 42	
	Stage Six: Making Customers Winners 42	
	Stage Seven: Six Sigma Quality 42	
	The Integrated Learning Process 42	

Index

Overview

Organizations increasingly look to their employees to be "change agents" who can make the organization more flexible, more productive, more responsive to customers, more innovative, more competitive—in short, more successful. But changing an organization is no easy task. By their very nature, as generations of theorists have emphasized, organizations are characterized by inertia. After all, they are defined by patterned behavior based on routines, established ways of doing things, standard operating procedures, and complex interdependencies across activities. Given these powerful inertial forces, even change initiatives that initially appear to be successful often have unanticipated consequences that undermine the desired change. Indeed, several studies of organizational change initiatives indicate that most do not achieve their goals. But few organizations stop to consider the reasons for the lack of success. Instead, they turn to new change initiatives, in—to borrow a phrase from Oscar Wilde—a continuing triumph of hope over experience.

This module will give you some important keys to being more effective in the organizational change initiatives in which you will be a participant and a leader during the course of your career. The Class Note, "Changing Organizations: An Overview" provides a basic framework for understanding organizational change and is an introduction to the fundamentals of taking effective action in change initiatives. It looks at change through three lenses on organization—strategic design, political, and cultural—and anchors each perspective in a major and widely publicized corporate change initiative: Procter & Gamble's move from a geographic to a product grouping structure. The Class Note then turns to five stage models of change initiatives. These models provide a set of different but complementary perspectives on how a change initiative unfolds over time. The Class Note then presents four dimensions of change initiatives: top-down vs. bottom-up, radical vs. incremental, discontinuous vs. continuous, and planned vs. emergent. Finally, the Class Note provides guidance on how the frameworks can help you become a more effective change agent.

The case that follows, "The Strategy That Wouldn't Travel," gives you an opportunity to test and hone this ability. This case looks at a change initiative that succeeds in one location but runs into serious problems when the "change agent" attempts to replicate it in a second site.

The Readings section contains several excerpts from *The Dance of Change*, a recent book by Peter Senge and a number of colleagues about the challenges of building an organization that meets the aspirations of today's organizations for a change capability. Senge calls it "the learning organization." The last excerpted reading, "Culture Change at GE," was written by a GE manager and provides a concrete example of an approach to change that differs considerably from the example of Procter & Gamble discussed in the Class Note. Both companies are trying to change their cultures, but P&G undertakes a radical, planned transformation and GE introduces a series of incremental, emergent change initiatives. The differences illustrate some fundamental distinctions in organizational change patterns.

The purposes of this module include the following:

- To provide frameworks for understanding the complexity of organizational change and to see why so many change initiatives fail.
- To improve your ability to analyze the dynamics of change initiatives.
- To help you take more effective action in change initiatives in organizations.

Assignment

Come to class prepared to discuss the following questions related to "The Strategy That Wouldn't Travel" case:

1. Where would you place the Wichita change initiative on the four dimensions of change initiatives described in the Class Note, "Organizational Change: An Overview" (i.e., scope, source, pacing, and process)?
2. What were the main problems at the Wichita facility that Jimenez's change initiative addressed? Why was the initiative successful at Wichita?
3. What are the problems at Lubbock? Why is the change initiative not as successful at the Lubbock facility?
4. What actions should Jimenez take immediately? If you were brought in to advise Jimenez, what actions would you recommend to her to move the change initiative forward at Lubbock? Within the company as a whole?

Managing Change in Organizations

CORE

Module

Organizational Change

An overview

Over the past two decades, organizations in nearly every sector of society faced strong pressures not only to change but also to become flexible enough to change continuously—to "make change the one constant in our organization," in the words used by more than one senior executive. North American, European, Asian, and Latin American organizations have all experienced the pressures of rapidly changing technologies, the globalization of markets and competition, and dramatic variability in growth and profitability in a wide range of markets and sectors—external changes to which they believe they cannot respond effectively without major changes in their organizations. Established organizations strive to become flatter, more flexible, increasingly networked internally and externally, more diverse, and more global; young entrepreneurial organizations struggle to develop more stable systems and processes as they face cycles of rapid expansion and unpredicted slowdown. Moreover, increasingly dense networks between suppliers and customers and across business partners create pressures for mutual organizational change and adaptation. The result has been a stream of change initiatives in most organizations.

The success rate of these change initiatives, however, remains startlingly low. A 1999 survey of 300 European executives found that they believed only 20 percent of the change initiatives undertaken in their organizations had been successful, whereas 63 percent had produced some change at the time but had not been sustained, and 17 percent had no result at all (Cairncross, 2002, p. 179). Similar studies of U.S. companies revealed comparably unsatisfactory outcomes. Surprisingly, many organizations often seem to be uninterested in assessing the results of their change initiatives in any systematic way, often replacing one faltering initiative with a new program instead of trying to understand why the first one failed to meet expectations. The cynicism generated in the rank and file of the organization by an apparently unending series of unrelated change programs can seriously hamper further change initiatives, and adds to the already formidable inertia of large organizations.

The extent to which organizations can change has been the subject of considerable debate in the study of organizations over the past two decades. Much of the management-oriented writing has focused on how to change organizations, portraying the key to major transformation as a clear strategic vision of what the organization should be, and sometimes implying that a sufficiently determined change agent who communicates the vision effectively can easily overcome any obstacles. Much of the analysis in organization theory, in contrast, focused on inertia and the constraints on change. One of the most influential paradigms during this period, population ecology, built its approach on the assumption that organizations faced such formidable internal and external constraints on change that any major transformation could only occur through the replacement of one kind of organizational form by another, through the elimination of the older organizations.

By the end of the 1990s, however, both sides of the debate recognized the value of the other perspective. As one of the leading writers on organizational evolution, Howard Aldrich, put it, "After almost two decades of research, even ecologists are willing to admit that organizations can and often do change, sometimes in quite radical ways. Advocates of strategic choice, in turn, have noted that organizations often face formidable obstacles to their own transformation" (Aldrich, 1999, p. 172).

Why Is Organizational Change So Difficult?

In his book on the turnaround at IBM after he became CEO in 1993, Lou Gerstner states unambiguously, "Nobody likes change. Whether you are a senior executive or an entry-level employee, change represents uncertainty and, potentially, pain" (Gerstner, 2002, p. 77). Many CEOs and even more mid-level managers would strongly agree with this view: change is difficult because resistance to change is a basic feature of *human nature*.

At the organizational level of analysis, a similar explanation—that resistance to change is fundamental—invokes the concept of *organizational inertia*. Organizations are, by definition, systems of patterned behaviors, designed to produce predictable and repeatable outputs. Stability is an inherent feature of organizations, in this view, and is actively maintained by the organizational systems and cultures, and by the interests of the organization's members and of external social actors (customers, regulators, stakeholders) with which it interacts (Scott, 1995, pp. 79–81). Resistance to change, in this view, is embedded in the very nature of organizations.

A third explanation focuses instead on the *unanticipated consequences* of organizational change initiatives. Organizations are complex social structures, and changes even in the simplest organizational design can have effects on other parts of the design and on its political and cultural systems that are difficult to predict in advance. Change initiatives can have a better chance of succeeding when these unanticipated consequences are identified early and appropriate responses are developed, but in many cases these unanticipated consequences can change the speed and direction of change, and even derail the initiative entirely.

What do we mean by *organizational change*? The term can conjure up a wide array of images. For many of those who study organizations, organizational change means change in design. When Procter & Gamble replaces its long-standing geographic structure based on countries with a global product design, or when ABB abandons its famous product/geography matrix for a front/back structure, few would argue that they present examples of significant organizational change. When the U.S. government establishes a new Department of Homeland Security that incorporates 22 agencies from 12 different government departments (including the Coast Guard, the Immigration and Naturalization Service, the Customs Service, and the Lawrence Livermore National Laboratory), it is seen as the most far-reaching organizational change in the federal government since the end of World War II. For those working in organizations, however, organizational design change is often much more modest in scope: for example, a new set of liaison or integrator positions (such as Global Account Managers); new cross-functional teams to monitor customer feedback; a change in the reporting system that requires different or more frequent data inputs; a new incentive system.

In both types of examples, however, organizational change means a change in design: in the organization chart (*grouping*), in integration mechanisms (*linking*), or in the systems for motivating people and ensuring that they have the resources they need to carry out the activities required by grouping and linking (*alignment*). This design change is what comes to mind for most people when they hear the term *organizational change*, but it is by no means the only one.

Another important dimension of organizational change is change in the power structure. For those who see organizations primarily as political systems, significant organizational change centers on changes in who makes decisions, which individuals and groups influence those decisions and how, and what interests are served by the actions of the organization. One recent example of the political dimension of organizational change is the postmerger power struggle at AOL-Time Warner, after the Internet company AOL and the diversified media conglomerate Time Warner merged in January 2001. Although the "merger" was formally an acquisition by AOL of Time Warner, from the beginning the company seemed to be caught in a struggle between the Internet-oriented executives from AOL and the established media managers from Time Warner. During the first two years after the merger, the business press closely watched who was being promoted, who was "in" and who was "out," who was getting support from key shareholders, such as Ted Turner, who was out of favor, and whose views of strategy were reflected in corporate announcements. When Steve Case, the former CEO of AOL, resigned from his position as chairman of AOL-Time-Warner, the business press saw the power struggle as having been won by the Time Warner side, a victory that would set the direction and organization of the company for the foreseeable future.

The political side of organizational change is most easily observed in the aftermath of mergers and acquisitions, when it is relatively easy to identify coalitions and shifting influence networks and to attribute interests to various actors. It is not the only context in which politics matters. Often the political dimensions of change are underestimated because they are difficult to see from outside the organization. Many major design changes in organizations, for example, are driven as much by a new CEO's desire to change the top management team of the company as by urgent strategic needs (eliminating top executives' positions is a face-saving way of encouraging them to retire), but no CEO would ever announce this motivation.

Most cases of political change in organizations never reach the business press. Who gets promoted, for example, and which subordinates get taken along in such promotions? Is the new head of the division a potential candidate for the CEO's position, or not? Do the managers of a newly created department share a set of similar networks with other parts of the organization or are their networks different, and do these differences affect the structure and actions of the new department? Does the rapid growth of a new business unit change the relative influence of the managers of older units on the company's resource allocation? When a new technology is introduced into a plant, does the power of the maintenance engineers rise or fall? For those inside the organization, changes in the political system have as much or more impact on their work, their careers, and the organization as a whole as do changes in design.

A third way of thinking about organizational change is in terms of culture: change in norms, values, mental models, and shared assumptions about the organization and the world in which it operates. When *Business Week* asserts that Ericsson, the Swedish telecommunications equipment giant, requires "a huge cultural shakeup" if it is to succeed in shifting its strategy from manufacturing equipment to developing new telecommunications-related services, it is taking a cultural approach to the challenges of organizational change (Reinhart, 2002). So is Lou Gerstner, when he asserts that the most important aspect of IBM's turnaround in the 1990s was its transformation from an inward-looking culture based on the shared assumption that "anything important started inside the company" (Gerstner, 2002, p. 189) to an outward-looking culture focused on serving customers and beating the competition. Gerstner went so far as to declare, "I came to see, in my time at IBM, that culture isn't just one aspect of the game—it *is* the game" (p. 182).

What does a cultural change in an organization mean? Fundamentally, it means changing not only people's behaviors and how they carry out their activities, but the ways they think about those activities and about their own roles and identities. For example, Carlos Ghosn, the French executive who was sent from Renault to manage the turnaround at Nissan in 1999, said that one problem the company faced was "a culture of blame." "If the company did poorly, it was always someone else's fault. Sales blamed product planning, product planning blamed engineering, and engineering blamed finance. Tokyo blamed Europe, and Europe blamed Tokyo" (Ghosn, 2002, p. 40). Turning around the company meant encouraging people to take responsibility for fixing problems, which involved both a change in behavior and roles of top management (so that they took personal responsibility for clearly defined sets of activities), eliminating positions that lacked clear role responsibilities (which meant the dismissal of some highly paid senior positions and individuals), and changes in design (such as clarifying job responsibilities, including responsibility for linking across different parts of the organization). All these changes, however, were directed at changing culture, that is, the way individuals defined their own roles in the organization and their basic assumptions about what kinds of behavior the company valued and needed. The Nissan example illustrates how initiatives to change culture often involve changes in the strategic design and political systems of the organization, just as changes in the political system often involve changes in design and can challenge the established culture, and design changes have effects on the political and cultural systems of the organization.

People are therefore justified in being wary of change initiatives. Even the best-planned initiatives cannot anticipate all their consequences, and therefore every change initiative will have unanticipated consequences. Too often, the initiators of change are so focused on driving their change programs that they do not realize that resistance to change can be an important signal of real problems that must be addressed if the change effort is to succeed, rather than some fundamental resistance to change embedded deeply in human nature or organizational inertia.

To understand more clearly the complex interactions of the design, political, and cultural aspects of organizational change, let us look at one case study of a major organizational change effort, Procter & Gamble's *Organization 2005* program.

Organizational Change at Procter & Gamble: *Organization 2005*

In 1996, Procter & Gamble's CEO committed the company to doubling its worldwide sales by the year 2006, to $70 billion. Two years later, P&G had barely managed 3% annual growth and its share price was falling dramatically. The CEO, John Pepper, and the COO, Durk Jager, together embarked on a personal study mission to twelve top companies, including GE, H-P, and 3M, to gain a broader perspective on how they might go about making P&G more innovative, faster to market, and more efficient. They concluded that P&G's problems were deeply embedded in its organization, in a culture that was risk-averse and skeptical of innovation, and a political system that focused power on country general managers, each of whom had the right to decide which P&G products would be sold in that country and whether those products would be manufactured locally or sourced from other P&G units.

Their solution was a change program called "Organization 2005," and the task of carrying it out passed to Jager, a lifelong P&G manager who became CEO in January 1999. "Organization 2005" tackled the challenges of cultural and political change by redesigning the organizational structure. It replaced the long-standing geographic design with a product divisional structure, composed of seven global business units—GBUs.[1] *Each GBU had worldwide responsibility for the entire value chain of the products in the division, from new product development and production to marketing and distribution. Because it also had responsibility for support functions such as IT and personnel, most of P&G's corporate functional staff moved into the GBUs, although a Global Business Services organization was set up to centralize the*

---

1 The divisions were Baby Care, Beauty Care, Fabric and Home Care, Feminine Protection, Food and Beverages, Health Care and Corporate New Ventures, and Tissue and Towels.

previously geographically distributed functions of accounting, payroll, and order management. This GBS organization was to provide support not only for the GBUs but for another set of units: the Marketing Development Organizations (MDOs). These were eight regional market development organizations, whose mandate was to develop business strategies for their geographic regions and provide consumer and market information to the GBUs and to bring all regional markets up to the level of the best current performers. Product managers within the old country organizations would now report directly to a GBU; country managers would have a narrower range of responsibility and report to their MDO Vice President.

Even for those within P&G who welcomed the new structure, the scale of the changes was formidable. The new head of worldwide marketing for the Food and Beverage GBU, for example, was the former head of the Latin American region. He took on the position of head of the new Latin American MDO as well as his new GBU position, and persuaded the company to base his new organization, which developed the worldwide marketing strategy for brands such as Jif peanut butter, Folger's coffee, and Pringles potato chips, in his home city of Caracas. P&G saw large numbers of its managers moving physically as well as organizationally, to fit into their new organizational roles. One account claimed that by June 2000, only 20% of P&G's top 200–300 managers were doing the same job they had 18 months earlier. According to another account, "P&G's staff lost their 'feel' for the company; so many found themselves in new roles that senior management admitted that they no longer had that crucial instinctive understanding of how the company was operating."(Rees, 2000)

Initial press coverage was favorable, although there were many skeptics who cautioned that seeing clear results from the change processes would take time. Sales did not grow quickly, however, and profits actually fell. The few new products that emerged, although they were introduced with a speed that was impressive by traditional P&G standards, were not seen as home runs (they included, for example, the Swiffer electrostatic broom). A couple of highly publicized attempts at acquisitions failed to materialize. Rumors began to emerge that there was strong internal resistance to the changes, and a number of managers—nearly a quarter of P&G's brand managers, according to one report—quit the company. Complaints began to surface of a growing gap between Jager's optimism about the company's progress and the growing unhappiness and confusion within P&G's ranks. All of this resulted in a fall in the share price that halved the value of the company between January and June 2001. Jager resigned in June 2001, barely 18 months into his tenure.

Analysis in the business press spanned a wide range of opinion. At one extreme was the judgment of the Lex columnist in the Financial Times, *who commented that: "Things have come to a pretty pass when a company has to restructure its way out of its previous restructuring. Procter & Gamble's 1999 revamp—'Organization 2005'—is only 50% complete but already 100% a disaster. It has neither boosted innovation and sales growth nor reduced costs. Revenues in the fiscal year to June will be flat at best; operating profits have fallen for the past four quarters; and administrative costs, at 30% of sales, are 300 basis points higher now than in 1998" (Lex, 2001). Other commentators blamed P&G's board for not giving Jager enough time to deliver on his program: "'They hanged the wrong guy,' says Burt Flickinger III of Reach Marketing. 'He was just what was needed in a culture that had gotten far too complacent. Durk was a take-no-prisoners, win-dammit-win CEO.' Flickinger points out that former P&G chief John Smale gave Jack Smith nearly a decade to reverse the decline of General Motors. 'At P&G, the board did not give the CEO sufficient time to turn the company around'"(Farrell, 2000).*

In their conversations with the business press, which was eagerly covering the P&G situation, the Board of Directors gave three reasons for moving to replace Jager so quickly. One was of course the fall in the share price. Underlying the fall, however, was the second factor: perceived failures in the reorganization effort, especially the changes in reporting responsibility and systems. As one source pointed out, "P&G, a model of fiscal conservatism, overpromised on its numbers for the past two quarters because accurate numbers about profit and loss were not getting to headquarters in Cincinnati"(Farrell, 2000). Finally, the Chairman of the Board criticized Jager for a political failure: having moved "too far, too fast" and failing to carry the company with him. "Jager's inability to win over the majority of his key subordinates contributed to the board's loss of confidence in him"(Farrell, 2000).

P&G's employees welcomed the announcement that Jager's successor as CEO would be Alan G. Lafley, a P&G senior manager known for his superb "people skills." The analysts and the business press were far more skeptical. In fact, the share price fell when his appointment was announced, and Business Week *carried a critical article entitled "Warm and Fuzzy won't save P&G."[2] Lafley*

---

[2] Ellen Neuborne and Robert Berner, "Warm and fuzzy won't save Procter & Gamble," *Business Week,* June 26, 2000, p. 48.

refocused P&G's strategy on its existing brands and tackled the cost increases that accompanied Organization 2005 by cutting 9,600 jobs and ending some of Jager's cherished product innovation projects. He did, however, keep the new organization design of GBUs and MDOs and GBS, either because he thought it was an improvement on the old structures or because he believed that the company would not cope well with another radical restructuring, even one that returned it to its former design. Just over two years later, Lafley was hailed by Fortune *magazine for turning P&G around in 27 months and held up as a example of "the new breed of turnaround specialist" who leads by listening rather than by making speeches about vision and by a focus on building upon established strengths rather than on initiating aggressive change programs (Brooker, 2002).*

Procter & Gamble provides an excellent example of what first comes to mind with the term *organizational change:* a radical, top-down change program intended to break with the established patterns of the organization in terms of its design, its political system, and its culture. It also illustrates, even in the brief account given here, some of the major reasons why organizational change is so difficult.

Even in relatively small organizations, changing the organization design usually has unanticipated consequences, because the complex interdependencies across the grouping structures, linking mechanisms, and alignment systems mean that changing some elements of the design has effects on others. In a large multibusiness multinational company like P&G, the interdependencies are so complex that even the best-informed organizational architects cannot design solutions in advance to all the problems that may arise. A period of transition, during which emerging problems can be identified and addressed, is inevitable. Take as just one example P&G's problem in maintaining accurate flows of financial information to headquarters during the move from a country-based to a product-based and shared services model. The challenges in making an IT system, which is a key linking mechanism, serve the needs of a new organization design are never purely technical. In Organization 2005, the new design simultaneously redrew the boundaries of the units on which performance data were collected and shifted the responsibility for collecting and analyzing the data to a new shared services unit (Global Business Services). Figuring out how to allocate costs and returns across the new units, recalculating transfer prices, and allocating clear responsibilities for gathering and analyzing the data undoubtedly took time. That the performance data sent to headquarters was less accurate for the first two quarters of the transition than it had been under the old design is hardly surprising. What is more surprising is that P&G top management seemed unprepared for the transition period, and therefore apparently was unable to manage expectations effectively.

Another significant problem in a major redesign is the challenge of learning new roles. When an individual—let's say Jo Smith—moves into a position in an established organization, she is taking on a role that is new to her but not to the organization. She has multiple ways of learning the role: advice from the previous incumbent, coaching from her immediate supervisor, informal help from others who occupy similar positions, and signals from subordinates who provide cues to the expected behaviors. Compare that with Jo Smith's challenges when she takes up a new role in a new organization design—in the case of P&G, a role as head of one of the units in Global Business Services or in one of the Marketing Development Organizations. No previous incumbents exist to call on for advice. Her immediate supervisors and those in similar roles in the new design are themselves learning new roles, and may have little time for coaching and indeed may well lack a clear idea of what her role should be. Subordinates are looking to Jo for clarity on their roles as well as on hers, and Jo is more likely to see their expectations as a burden than as a source of guidance to the specifics of her job. In a major redesign, as P&G found, most people not only find themselves in new jobs, they find that they no longer know who's doing what in the organization, and the informal networks that are a key element of the alignment system of any organization are therefore in disarray.

New designs usually provide the most detailed information on the responsibilities of the major new structures and on the roles of those who manage them. Middle managers—those who are not themselves in charge of one of the major new units but who report to one of the new unit heads and supervise the next layer of management (which is usually the layer that directly supervises the frontline workers)—often find that their roles and responsibilities are the least clearly spelled out in the new design. It is not surprising, therefore, that top executives often identify middle managers as the bottleneck in a major change process—blaming the individuals rather than the challenges in the redesign and transition processes, and not recognizing the need for the organization to provide the resources (including time) for them to develop and adjust to new roles.

The design challenges are therefore formidable in themselves, but the difficulties of any major organizational restructuring are further complicated by the political and cultural aspects of the transformation. As in P&G, a structural design change is often a tool for achieving broader political and cultural change. Organization 2005, for example, aimed to transform P&G's culture from one that was risk-averse and slow-moving to one that was innovative and quick to respond to changes in customers and markets. Jager believed that to achieve this goal, he had to shift the power in the company away from the long-serving and established country managers. The centrality of a cultural and political change agenda in major organizational restructuring is far from unusual. Radically and rapidly changing the political systems and cultures of large, complex organizations is a formidable challenge, and even those at the top of the organization do not have many effective tools at their command. Changing the design is one of the most dramatic ways to begin transforming the power structure and the culture.

One of the most common approaches to changing the political system, for example, is for CEOs to put their own allies into key positions, but it often does not work as well as the top executives expect. Powerful organizational subunits exert a strong influence on anyone who joins them, at the top as well as at the bottom, and the new manager often "goes native" and takes on the interests of the subunit that is, after all, a personal power base. Moreover, subunits often resist anyone who takes over the unit but does not defend subunit interests and identity. CEOs therefore often find either that a supposedly loyal ally becomes less responsive to the change agenda when he or she is put in charge of a powerful subunit or that the ally's ability to bring the subunit into line with the change agenda is compromised by conflict and resistance. Redrawing the subunit boundaries through a change in the organization design (e.g., reallocating many of the responsibilities of the country managers to global product managers as in the case of P&G) is therefore an appealing prospect for top executives trying to drive a major political change. Doing so, however, can create resistance from managers who have knowledge that is essential for making the new systems work.

Changing the culture of an organization is even more difficult than changing the political system. As former IBM CEO Lew Gerstner pointed out, "In the end, management doesn't change culture. Management invites the workforce to change the culture." (Gerstner, 2002, p. 187) Issuing the invitation is sometimes difficult, however, and a radical restructuring is one way to send a strong signal to the organization that change is necessary and inevitable. It also holds out the possibility of shaking up deeply established subcultures. Reconfiguring a function such as finance or human resource management so that it reports to a global shared function instead of a country manager, as Organization 2005 did, can be a step in "inviting" its people to redefine their identity more in terms of their expertise than their citizenship.

Appealing though a CEO may find it to drive a political and cultural transformation through a major change in the organization design, the complex interdependencies of the strategic design and the interactions of the design, political, and cultural elements of the change process make unanticipated consequences inevitable. How change leaders recognize and respond to these consequences is one of the major factors shaping the outcomes of organizational change initiatives.

The case of P&G also illustrates another feature of change processes: shifts that occur over time in the focus and nature of change activities and the challenges encountered by change advocates. "Organization 2005" began with great energy and optimism, encountered unexpected and seemingly increasing problems over time, and finally saw the departure of the person most widely identified as the change leader, followed by the consolidation of the initiative under a new chief executive, who focused more on what would be retained than on what still needed to change. The temporal course of change initiatives has long been a focus of research and analysis in the study of organizational change, and some of the most widely used frameworks for understanding change initiatives have been stage models that focus on how change processes vary over the course of a change initiative. The following section examines some of the most influential of these models.

Stage Models of Change Processes

One of the earliest and most enduring models of change is Kurt Lewin's portrayal of the change process as a three-stage sequence of unfreezing–change–refreezing (Lewin, 1947). Developed more than 50 years ago, it is still a touchstone in the debates over the nature of organizational change.[3] Lewin participated in a number of planned change initiatives in a variety of settings, including factories, communities, and

---

[3] See for example Karl Weick (2000, p. 235): "If people want to change a system in which they feel inertia runs deep, then their best bet is to start with Kurt Lewin's prescription for change: unfreeze–change–refreeze."

public bureaucracies, and made two observations. First, the change initiatives encountered strong resistance, even when there was general agreement on the desirability of the goals of the initiatives. Second, even initiatives that appeared to overcome resistance and get implemented successfully were often short-lived, with the system returning to its previous state in a matter of months.

These experiences led Lewin to see organizations as social systems that are highly resistant to change, both because of "human nature"—individual-level habits, patterned behaviors, and acceptance of group norms—and because of organizational inertia. The inertia is created by a "force field" in which the organization maintains a state of "quasi-equilibrium." The force field consists of social structures and processes (including interest groups, communications networks, and external organizations) that exert pressures for change, while others create counterbalancing forces for stability. To succeed in the long run, organizational change initiatives must first disrupt the equilibrium (the process Lewin called "unfreezing") before the change initiative begins, and then has to create a new equilibrium state that maintains the new conditions (refreezing). One of Lewin's much-cited insights is that "unfreezing" is more successful if it is directed to reducing the forces that block change, rather than to increasing the forces for change. As he pointed out, increasing the pressures for change often generates countervailing resistance, both at the individual and organizational levels, and it increases the anxiety and tension in the organization. Removing or mitigating blocking forces often proves to be more effective in unfreezing an organization and opening the way for change initiatives.

Lewin's work on change laid the foundations of the field of organizational development (OD), defined by one of its founding figures as the use of behavioral science knowledge to increase organizational effectiveness and health through planned interventions (Beckhard, 1969). From the 1960s into the 1980s, OD dominated managerially oriented approaches to organizational change in the United States, both in business schools and in corporations.[4] Many firms set up their own OD departments, and even more engaged as consultants the leading academics in the field (including Dick Beckhard, Warren Bennis, Douglas McGregor, Ed Schein, and Noel Tichy). In its early years, OD was often associated primarily with small-group activities (such as T-groups or sensitivity training) aimed at "unfreezing" organizations by helping people to develop greater mutual trust and openness to change. Just as important in the OD field, however, were large-scale change initiatives based on data-driven organizational diagnosis and led from the top of the organization. Much of today's work on leadership and organizational learning rests on the frameworks and analyses of OD.[5]

Some of the key insights of the OD approach to change are captured in a three-stage model developed by Beckhard and Harris (1977). They point out that change initiatives often focus primarily on the *future state* of the organization—on what the organization will look like, how things will work, and what people will do when the change is completed. Developing an explicit model of the future state of the organization is an essential part of a successful change initiative, but it is not sufficient. Effective change also requires both a diagnosis of the *present state* of the organization and proactive management of the *transition state*, when people are leaving behind the old system and learning how to make the new system work (see Figure 8.1).

Many change initiatives fail, according to Beckhard and Harris, because managers make erroneous assumptions about how the organization currently operates and about what groups and subunits will be most affected by the change, the attitudes of the managers and their people toward the change, and each unit's capacity to make the proposed changes in the proposed time frame. A good diagnosis of the *present state* of the organization specifically addresses all these issues by gathering and analyzing data through a variety of means (including interviews, surveys, informal conversations, and meetings). Such data gathering is never a neutral exercise. As Schein emphasized, data gathering is itself an intervention (Schein, 1996). Its very occurrence signals to the organization that some initiative is being planned, and the kinds of questions asked, the nature of feedback from the data gathering (or its absence), and the perceived leadership of the data gathering (e.g., an external consultant, a top executive, a staff group) all send cultural and political signals, set expectations, and focus attention in ways that often have unanticipated consequences. For example, the appearance of an external consulting group conducting interviews or surveys about whether the technical services group is providing effective system support can get people thinking about and discussing a set of issues on which they haven't previously focused,

---

4 In the United Kingdom and Europe, the sociotechnical paradigm focused on similar issues, but paid more attention to the interactions (especially the potential conflict) between the technocratic and technological aspects of organizations on the one hand and organizations as social systems on the other.
5 Even today, one of the largest divisions of the Academy of Management, the main professional association of business school faculty, is Organizational Development and Change (ODC), established in 1971.

and perhaps developing a shared view of who is to blame for any problems they have experienced, and who has the responsibility for fixing them. This shared view can be completely different from the premises of the proposed change initiative, and can be difficult to dislodge.

Beckhard and Harris also point out that effective change initiatives recognize that the *transition* to the desired future state often requires special-purpose structures (e.g., task forces, pilot projects, and training courses), processes (such as problem identification), and governance roles that are not part of the current organization and will likely fade away as the goal of the change is achieved. The organization often needs to develop a transition team to manage the transition state. Simply making current managers responsible for transition activities is often a recipe for failure. After all, the world doesn't stop while the organization changes, and managers are often fully stretched with the tasks of current operations. One of the major challenges of the transition state is getting the commitment of key individuals and their units to the change plan, and therefore any transition team needs people who can mobilize the necessary resources, maintain the respect of both the current operating managers and the advocates of change, and have effective interpersonal skills (Beckhard and Harris, 1977, p. 46).

Another approach that is also grounded in the OD perspective is a stage model in two senses: it identifies three distinct stages in the sequencing of organizational change, and it uses the metaphor of the theater to focus attention on the role of the change leader. Noel Tichy and Mary Anne Devanna (1986, 1990) portray the evolving role of the "transformational leader" in three acts:

- Act I: Recognizing the need for revitalization (creating a felt need for change, overcoming political and cultural resistance to change)
- Act II: Creating a new vision: (diagnosing the problem, creating a motivating vision, mobilizing commitment)
- Act III: Institutionalizing change

None of these "acts" involve concepts that are unfamiliar to those who know the earlier models of Lewin, Beckhard, and others in the OD tradition, but they draw particular attention to the role of the leader. In the stage metaphor, leaders play a highly visible role in the drama of change, and they must always bear this role in mind. What they do is seen and interpreted by the rest of the cast (the other actors in the change process) and by the audience (the rest of the organization and key external constituencies). Leaders who act inconsistently when they are "on stage" and "off stage"—who extol the importance of a major change initiative in all their public speeches but who never find time to get to the meetings about it, for example—are quickly seen by their audience and the rest of the cast as insincere, and they quickly lose their ability to play an effective leading role. Tichy and Devanna believe that successful leaders place a strong emphasis on symbolism and ritual and on the dramatic gesture that seizes attention and focuses it on the required changes.

A different approach to the temporal sequencing of change comes from applying the classic evolutionary model of "variation–selection–retention" to organizations. In its simplest form, evolutionary biology portrays change as a process of natural selection, in which a member of a species can develop a variation in form in response to a change in its environment or even random genetic mutation. If that particular organism is more successful in obtaining scarce resources than its standard counterparts, it will survive, reproduce, and outcompete less effective varieties, eventually dominating its environmental niche, at least until a more successful variant appears.

In the field of organization studies, both population ecology and evolutionary theory have applied this model, both at the level of populations of organizations (e.g., Hannan and Freeman, 1989) and at the level of individual organizations (e.g., Aldrich, 1999). In this perspective, variation within organizations may be frequent, but it is usually local and short-lived. Efforts to solve problems generate innovations, but these rarely spread, because the selection regime (both in the competitive environment and within the organization) is based on selecting for "the tried and true," or predictability and stability. Occasionally, however, a local innovation is picked up and tried out elsewhere in the organization, recognized as successful, and retained.

This three-stage model embodies several valuable insights. First, organizational inertia is not the same as a lack of change. Change is occurring all the time in organizations, as people solve problems, bend the rules, and try out new ideas; however, organizations usually do not allow these changes to spread, and they either remain purely local or are "selected out" and eliminated. Second, the model reminds us of the systemic forces that shape the fate of change initiatives, particularly the role of the larger external environment, so that even the strongest commitment to change and the most gifted leadership may not succeed in the face of an adverse selection regime. Sometimes, these systemic forces may be potentially short-lived; for example, an innovation in logistics can cause problems with suppliers and reduce the efficiency of the organization. Even if the problems are potentially temporary, however, they can trigger the "corporate immune system" to reject the innovation that caused them, even if persistence would be rewarded by better performance if the interface with suppliers is improved. Third, successful change is not always the result of planned change initiatives generated by the top management. It can also be produced by local initiatives and experiments directed at problems that may seem to be local but which are in fact widespread in the organization. Too often, the organization, however, fails to recognize and select for these changes.

In managerial terms, the evolutionary approach highlights the need for organizations to develop a capability for increasing the level of local initiatives in problem solving and experimentation (increasing variation) and to develop systems for identifying and disseminating the most successful initiatives (modifying the selection regime away from selecting for stability toward selecting for innovation). The total quality movement of the late 1980s and early 1990s demonstrated to U.S. managers the value of fostering local problem solving on the factory floor, and paved the way for the widespread interest in the "learning organization" in the 1990s.

The concept of the learning organization provided a concrete translation of the abstract models of the evolutionary perspective into more specific organizational terms. One of the leading figures in the work on the learning organization has been Peter Senge, who draws both on the OD tradition and on systems dynamics to develop insights on how to improve an organization's capacity to improve its work practices. The learning organization approach advocates "starting small" with a small pilot team whose members share a recognition that a particular problem cannot be "fixed" easily because it is a symptom of deeper issues. They agree that these issues must be addressed if performance is to improve. Once the pilot project has demonstrated the value of its approach, the larger organization faces the challenges of changing its selection regime so that it can build on and diffuse the learning from the pilot project—not in terms of selecting for a particular solution to a problem or a codified recipe for specific changes, but in terms of expanding the organization's capacity to encourage more pilot projects and build a learning capability.

In contrast to Lewin's pioneering model, the learning organization approach focuses on building a capacity for continuing change and learning rather than on "refreezing" the organization. It shares with Lewin's model, however, the systems-based view of the organization as a quasi-equilibrium and the view that identifying and mitigating blocking or limiting factors are essential strategies for change. In *The Dance of Change* (1999), Senge and his colleagues organize their treatment of change around the challenges of change in three stages: initiating the change effort, sustaining it, and redesigning and rethinking the larger system so that the learning from the pilot project is diffused to the rest of the organization.

- The challenges of initiating:
  — No time: people can't find the time to work on the initiative.
  — No help: people feel isolated and ill-equipped to tackle the challenge, and find it difficult to identify or access the experience and the coaching that would help them.
  — Not relevant: people don't see a business case for expending the time and effort on the change initiative.
  — Not walking the talk: even the champions of change act in ways that undercut their espoused values and goals, which leads people to dismiss their sincerity or their commitment.
- The challenges of sustaining:
  — Fear and anxiety: as the initiative proceeds, it triggers the classic resistance to change in those not directly involved.
  — Assessment and measurement: the gap between the change initiative's results and the organization's established ways of measuring results.
  — True believers and nonbelievers: the more profound the change in behavior involved in the change initiative, the more risk its participants face in being defined as "deviants" or "cultists" by those grounded in the current dominant culture.
- The challenges of redesigning and rethinking:
  — Governance: how to develop systems that both encourage and support local initiatives and maintain the coordination necessary for systems with high levels of interdependence.
  — Diffusion: how the organization can learn from the experience of local initiatives, thereby avoiding reinventing the wheel, without imposing "solutions" that inhibit the initiatives of other local groups.
  — Strategy and purpose: how pilot groups can influence the larger strategies of the organization.

Senge and his colleagues identify challenges that are common across organizations, but they assert that the most effective ways to address them are highly local and context-specific. For example, what constitutes a convincing business case for a change initiative in one organization may be very different from what is effective in another setting, or even at a different point in time in that same organization. A convincing business case for an e-commerce initiative in a company in the year 1999 might not be at all convincing in 2004. In this approach, the keys to effective action are identifying the challenges or limiting factors, and analyzing a variety of ways that different groups have addressed them. The goal of looking at the experience of others is not to generate "recipes" or generic solutions, but to open minds to the array of possible approaches, in a way that leads to more creative, context-specific solutions effective in that particular setting.

The five stage models are summarized in Figure 8.1. They offer different insights and different but complementary ways to frame the complexities of organizational change. They highlight different aspects of change: processes (Lewin, Senge et al.), states (Beckhard and Harris), the role of the individual leader (Tichy and Devanna), the role of pilot teams (Senge et al.), the role of systemic forces (Aldrich). They share, however, the insight that the focus of activity in a change initiative alters over time. They also share the view that what most people think of as "organizational change" is bracketed by a period of preparing the organization for change and a period of ensuring that the change will be embedded in the organization.

Dimensions of Change

The kind of change that Peter Senge and his colleagues portray seems quite different from the kind of change that is the focus of Tichy and Devanna's model of the transformational leader. The dramatic changes at P&G also seem to belong to a different category of change initiative from those involved in developing a learning organization, or even from the changes at P&G under Jager's successor. Change initiatives come in an enormous variety of forms. In the innumerable analyses of organizational change that have been produced over time, four dimensions emerge as particularly useful ways to think about different kinds of change.

One dimension is the *scope* of change. Change efforts such as the transformation of P&G involve every aspect of the organization: how work is done and by whom, who makes decisions and controls resources, what activities and resources have status and value, what the company should be and how it should be seen. Such change is *radical* in scope, involving fundamental changes in the organization's strategic design, political system, and culture. Other change efforts are *incremental*: they are local rather than systemwide and involve modifications to the established strategic design, political system, and culture, or they involve changes in only one aspect of the organization (e.g., changing the culture to one that values being more open about problems, rather than concealing them). Like all dichotomies that are fundamentally the poles of a continuum, the distinction between radical and incremental change can sometimes be easier to make conceptually than empirically. CEOs are fond of proclaiming that their organizations are undergoing a radical transformation, but on close examination the change looks far less radical than their rhetoric of change proclaims. On the other hand, a series of incremental change initiatives carried out over time can eventually produce an organization that has changed significantly—even radically—from its original state.

Another dimension of change is the *pacing*. Change can be *punctuated*; that is, it has a clear beginning and an end, when the change efforts cease. Lewin's model of unfreezing–change–refreezing is the epitome of a punctuated change process. In other approaches, change can be *continuous*: it proceeds over time, and one change leads to another. The model of the learning organization entails developing continuous change processes of ongoing experimentation and improvement.

Figure 8.1 Stage Models of Organizational Change

Author	Model		
(1) Lewin (1947)	Unfreezing	Change	Refreezing
(2) Beckhard and Harris (1977)	Present State	Transition State	Future State
(3) Tichy and Devanna (1986)	Act I Awakening	Act II Mobilizing	Act III Reinforcing
(4) Aldrich (1979, 1999)	Variation	Selection	Retention
(5) Senge et al. (1999)	Initiating	Sustaining	Redesigning & Rethinking

A third dimension is the *source* of the change initiative. Is it driven by top management (*top-down*), or is the center of the change initiative broader and located farther down the organization (*bottom-up*)? Like the other dichotomies, this one can blur in practice. Still, the difference is obvious between a CEO like Durk Jager presenting the organization with a vision and a model of the *future state* of the organization (to use the Beckhard and Harris term) and a CEO saying to the organization, as Jack Welch did with the Work-Out Program in GE, "I'm providing a forum for you to figure out how to address problems." Although the CEO is a major figure in both cases, the P&G case would be close to the "top-down" end of the continuum, and GE would be much farther along the "bottom-up" end. "Bottom-up" does not necessarily mean the bottom rungs of the organization. The Japanese management scholar Ikujiro Nonaka points out that most of the change initiatives in Japanese organizations have a "middle-up-down" pattern of change: the middle levels of the organization identify a problem or an issue, the top provides the middle with a mandate to solve it and a general "vision" to serve as a goal, and the middle works with the lower levels to solve the problem and operationalize the vision (Nonaka, 1988). In Japan, the total quality movement was developed and driven by middle-level engineers working on the factory floor; in contrast, in the United States, it did not succeed until top management "took ownership" and drove the commitment to quality throughout the organization. The key distinction is that the critical role in driving change can either be played by the top management (or in some heroic models of change, a single top executive), or it can rest at the middle or lower levels of the organization.

Finally, change efforts differ in terms of their *process*. Some change initiatives are carefully *planned*. Beckhard and Harris advocate this kind of change, in which the fundamental problems of the organization are clearly diagnosed, an explicit model of the future state toward which the change effort is directed is provided, and a clear transition plan formulated to get from the present to the future state. In other kinds of change initiatives, the process is *emergent*: that is, the change initiative starts with no explicit map of how it should proceed, but develops over time as one action leads to another. Emergent change initiatives are often unforeseen and unexpected, driven forward by experiments rather than plans. Emergent initiatives are at the heart of the learning organization model developed by Peter Senge and his colleagues.

Figure 8.2 summarizes the four dimensions of change. The profiles of specific change initiatives can vary considerably across the four dimensions. For example, initiatives in a number of U.S. factories in the 1980s and 1990s involved workers, unions, and plant managers working together in unprecedented ways to change work processes and factory organization in pursuit of the dramatic improvements in productivity and quality that would enable them to survive in competition with foreign factories. Many of these initiatives were radical and punctuated, but also bottom-up and emergent. Change initiatives do tend, however, to cluster on one side of the four continua or the other—to be either radical, top-down, punctuated, and planned (like the P&G reorganization) or incremental, bottom-up, continuous, and emergent like many of the initiatives that make up the model of the learning organization.

The reasons for this clustering are evident in the change models discussed in the previous section. Radical change is extremely difficult, and it is usually triggered either by a significant change in strategy or by a major crisis, or both. Especially when a strategic shift is the trigger for the organizational change initiative, top management is likely to drive the change and see its leadership as indispensable to its success. Because radical change is so demanding of attention, energy, and resources, most experts on organizational change have insisted, like Lewin, that organizations need a period of consolidation and stability once the initiative ends before they embark on another radical initiative. In addition, another radical change initiative would by definition undo much of the work of the first, which would undercut any success

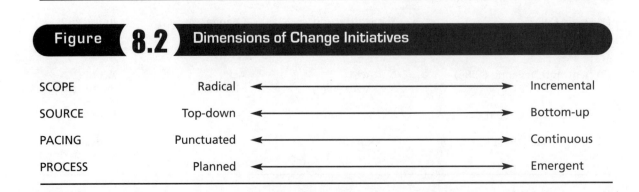

Figure 8.2 Dimensions of Change Initiatives

SCOPE	Radical	←——————————→	Incremental
SOURCE	Top-down	←——————————→	Bottom-up
PACING	Punctuated	←——————————→	Continuous
PROCESS	Planned	←——————————→	Emergent

achieved by the first and breed cynicism and distrust concerning the next round of radical change. As we saw, this reason explains in part why P&G's new top management decided not to embark on a major change program to redress the problems of Jager's transformation initiative, preferring instead to focus on consolidation and smaller-scale adjustments. Finally, it is easier to win support for radical change that is accomplished by a clear plan for the transformation, as Beckhard and Harris pointed out.[6] On the other hand, incremental change is likely to be a more politically realistic strategy for bottom-up initiatives, and continuous pacing and emergent processes are more feasible with incremental than with radical change.

Change initiatives on the two extremes of the continuum have different strengths and weaknesses. A radical, top-down, punctuated, planned change initiative is often the only feasible alternative when current patterns of work and organization are no longer able to meet the demands of the environment and both the strategy and the organization as a whole have to change significantly and quickly. It is also the preferred way to deal with major organizational disruptions, such as a merger or a large acquisition, again because it can embrace the entire organization with at least the appearance of speed. Furthermore, when a crisis hits, this kind of change focuses the attention and resources of many in the organization and sends powerful signals to outside stakeholders and anxious organizational members that the situation is under control and decisive steps are underway to deal with the problems.

On the other hand, critics have long noted the weaknesses of radical, top-down, planned change. Karl Weick, a leading organizational theorist who has contributed greatly to understanding sensemaking and emergent change, provides a succinct summary of its disadvantages:

The liabilities of planned change include a high probability of relapse; uneven diffusion among units; large short-term losses that are difficult to recover; less suitability for opportunity-driven than for threat-driven alterations; unanticipated consequences due to limited foresight; temptations toward hypocrisy (when people talk the talk of revolution but walk the walk of resistance); adoption of best practices that work best elsewhere because of a different context; ignorance among top management regarding key contingencies and capabilities at the front line; and lags in implementation that make the change outdated before it is even finished. (Weick 2000, p. 227)

Although Weick sees emergent change as having strengths that are "the mirror image" of these weaknesses, he also provides a similar list of the disadvantages of emergent change:

Emergent changes can be slow to cumulate; too small to affect outputs or outcomes; less well suited for responding to threats than for exploiting opportunities; limited by preexisting culture and technology; deficient when competitors are wedded to transformation; better suited to implementation in operations, plants, and stores than to strategy, firm-level, or corporate change; diffuse rather than focused; insufficiently bold or visionary . . . and unlikely to generate a shift from one frame of reference to a totally different one. (Weick, 2000, p. 227)

Increasingly, however, experts in organizational change assert that in today's flat, flexible, networked, complex organizations, the four dimensions of change describe modalities that are complementary rather than mutually exclusive (e.g., Tushman and O'Reilly, 1996). Weick, for example, suggests that radical, top-down, planned change initiatives are more likely to succeed in organizations that have fostered incremental, bottom-up, emergent patterns of change. The capacity to make local adaptations and adjustments will help a large-scale radical initiative work in the widely varying local contexts that exist in today's differentiated organizations. A top-down, planned initiative will work more effectively if those in the lower levels of the organization come to "own" it, and not only adapt it to the local context but feed information on what works and what doesn't back up to the top managers driving the change. Conversely, a bottom-up change initiative will have more impact if its value is recognized and championed by someone at the top of the organization.

In other words, the temporal sequencing of any *single* change initiative, as described by the stage models of change, is only one aspect of understanding change. In addition, both change agents and change theorists must recognize the importance of the temporal sequencing of the *multiple* change initiatives that occur in any organization over a longer time span. The study of organizational change has long focused on single change initiatives and how they unfold over time. This focus reflects the preoccupations of change agents within organizations, who naturally are preoccupied with the particular change project in which they are currently engaged. The outcome of any single initiative, however, is strongly affected by previous initiatives—their frequency, their perceived success, the capabilities they

---

[6] Indeed, Beckhard and Harris dismiss the idea of emergent change processes with the remark, "We will not pursue the obvious fact that a planned [transition] activity program tends to be better than an unplanned one." (1977, p. 52). Their focus throughout the book is on radical, top-down change initiatives.

have developed (or stifled) in the organization. One view asserts that a series of change initiatives has a better chance of succeeding if the different efforts are *consistent*. GE, for example, attributed much of its well-publicized success in organizational change in the 1990s to consistency across seven change initiatives introduced over a seven-year period, beginning with Work-Out in 1989. Each initiative was consistent with its predecessor in terms of framing, values, leadership, coordination, and control, and each built on and reinforced the previous initiative instead of displacing it (see "Cultural Change at GE" in the Readings section, p. 38–42).

Fundamentally, all organizational change is local. Even the revolutionary changes of top-down, planned change need to be "localized," accepted and adapted in units that are operating in different settings within the organization. The aspirations of today's top executives to develop organizations that have a "change capability" require both change agents who can carry out individual change initiatives effectively and a deeper capacity to foster simultaneously different and complementary patterns of change.

Being a More Effective Change Agent

How do frameworks like those just presented help you to be a more effective change agent? First, they can expand your repertoire of actions so that you are not limited to only a few tactics for intervention. Second, they can help you avoid serious mistakes. Third, they can sensitize you to the importance of temporal sequencing. Finally, they can help you to be a much more sophisticated user of the stream of advice on change purveyed by consultants and published in the business press.

Expanding Your Repertoire of Actions

Most managers, confronted with a need to change their organization, think first about redesigning role responsibilities and accountabilities and changing the incentive system. These tools for change are powerful, but too many managers stop there. They should not be the only ones in your repertoire. Even within the strategic design perspective, the set of tools is much broader and includes a variety of linking mechanisms (e.g., planning processes) and alignment systems (e.g., education and training, resource allocation, and informal systems and processes).

The political and cultural lenses expand the action repertoire much further. The political perspective reminds us that no one can change an organization single-handedly. One of the first actions in a change initiative should be building a coalition of allies who share a commitment to the change program. It is also useful to develop a larger political strategy at an early stage of the initiative. As one leading researcher in the field of organizational change, Andrew Pettigrew, has stated, "All change processes are influence processes. All influence processes require awareness of, if not action in, the political processes of the organization. Change and politics are inextricably linked" (Pettigrew, 2000, pp. 249–250). One way to proceed is to draw up a "political map" that identifies key actors in the organization in terms of several categories: those whose active support is necessary if the initiative is to succeed, those whose acceptance of it is essential, those who can remain neutral without affecting the outcome, and those likely to oppose it. The next step is to assess both the current position of each individual on the map and the position required for success in the change effort (e.g., someone may be currently opposed, but the initiative can only work if they are neutral or accepting). Finally, the change agent and his or her coalition need to devise plans for getting each individual from the current to the desired position. Both the coalition itself and the political map are likely to change over time and should be reassessed as the initiative proceeds.

One example is the Rosewell case (from Module 2), in which the CEO of this diversified corporation had been embarrassed in a Board meeting by his inability to respond to detailed questions about the relative performance of the various divisions and product lines. As a result he charged the vice president of management information systems (MIS) to find a way to get rapid information on the company by division and product line to the president's office. Unless the VP of MIS could get the VPs of the two most powerful divisions in the company to be active supporters of his new information system, his initiative would fail. Both currently opposed the initiative, one because in some of his product lines he was facing serious short-term cost escalations that he wanted to fix before any detailed information reached the CEO's office, the other because his division was investing heavily in growth and showing few profits. To get these two individuals to support his proposal, the VP of MIS had to identify specific benefits that each would get from the new information system, additional services that the proposed system could provide to each if they came on board (e.g., improvements in expediting and tracking shipments for the growth division), and modifications to the change plan to allow the required time lag for the first division to fix its short-term problems.

In addition, many change initiatives require a shift in the locus of decision making. Front-line teams may have to take immediate actions that in the past needed the authorization of much higher-level management, for example. The current holders of the decision rights are often reluctant to give them up, and the potential new holders may not believe that their managers are really willing to surrender them. As a result, decisions continue to be pushed up even when the formal responsibility shifts. A combination of political actions, strategic design changes, and culturally based actions is often necessary. For example, changing the resource allocation system so that teams can directly carry out changes involving expenditures under a certain level is a frequently used way both to shift the formal responsibility and to provide a powerful symbolic gesture signaling the direction of change. If the managers formerly responsible for making the decisions also provide strong positive recognition for early initiatives under the new system, they will reinforce the message of change.

As this example suggests, drawing on the cultural perspective for action steps highlights the importance of symbolic actions, that is, dramatic gestures that capture attention, challenge basic assumptions, and provide memorable representations of change goals or concepts. John Kotter and Dan Cohen provide one vivid example. In one manufacturing company they studied, a manager in the procurement department believed that the company could save large amounts of money by standardizing and coordinating purchasing for its various factories. Despite several detailed presentations to top management, however, he had not been able to get active support for his plan, largely because it would mean reducing the authority of the powerful individual plant managers. He decided to provide a demonstration of the scale of the company's procurement problems by hiring a summer intern to study the procurement of safety gloves in the factories. She found that the company was placing 424 different orders for gloves, purchased from different suppliers and at different prices. The procurement manager had her collect a sample of every glove order and tag it with the price paid and the factory that ordered it. He then spread the 424 pairs of gloves on the boardroom table and invited the vice presidents of the divisions to take a look. They were so impressed with this dramatic demonstration that they sent the exhibit on a "road show" to every factory in the country—and then they authorized the change in procurement policy (Cotter and Cohen, 2002, pp. 29–31).

According to an old Chinese proverb, "I hear and I forget. I see and I remember. I do and I understand." The cultural perspective emphasizes the challenges of changing how people view the world, what they value, and how they feel about their work and their company. A major theme of much of the work on organizational change is the ineffectiveness of "change by exhortation," of expecting people to change because someone in a position of authority asks for or insists on change. Vivid symbols of change, dramatic actions, and personal experience have much greater impact. For example, if a CEO wants her company to be more customer-oriented she can send out a companywide message calling for greater attention to customers. This approach is less effective than her going around the company giving speeches about customer responsiveness. And giving speeches is less effective than her going out to visit customers and reporting back on her experiences. And even this activity is less effective than her going out to visit customers and insisting that every member of the top management team do the same, sometimes with her and sometimes on their own, and that those top managers demand that their immediate subordinates also get out into the field.

Constantly remembering that organizational change is a political and cultural process as well as a strategic necessity is an invaluable way to become more creative and more effective in developing action steps that will advance the change process.

Avoiding Mistakes

Organizational change is such a complex process that some mistakes and missteps are inevitable. However, many of the disappointing outcomes of change initiatives are the result of a key change agent taking an action step that seems valid in one perspective but undercuts the desired effect in terms of another.

For example, the strategic design perspective highlights the importance of information and sees change as a rational process driven by strategic or operating needs. The implication is that if you give people the information about why the change is needed and what has to change, they'll "get the message" and get involved in the change effort. The advice from so many effective change leaders to "communicate, communicate, communicate" is excellent, but it is not sufficient. The style and the setting for the communication matter enormously, in political and cultural terms. Take, for example, a large meeting of employees called by a CEO or a divisional vice president to launch an initiative to stimulate bottom-up, emergent problem solving. The executive gives a lengthy PowerPoint presentation on the drivers of change, the framework of the initiative, and the expected results. He then asks for questions, and proceeds, as each one is asked, to give a lengthy reply, and then to ask, "Does anyone have a different question?" He then closes the meeting with the reminder that everyone's participation in the initiative is valued and important—the overt theme of the meeting. The political message, however, is clearly that he is in firm control of the process (and therefore that the power structure is not going to change) and the cultural signal is that, whatever he might say, the organization is still management-centric and management has the answers.

Contrast that effect with the potential impact of a meeting where the CEO did not make a detailed presentation, but instead made a brief statement of the goals of the change initiative and asked for comments and examples of problems that could be addressed at the local level. Instead of answering or commenting on each issue raised, he could turn to the audience and say, "Does anyone else have a similar issue or experience? Anyone have a comment?" As people spoke, he could take notes on their comments, showing that he really was listening. Such behavior would actually begin to model the kind of change that the organization was trying to initiate. Note, however, that if the intent of the meeting was to set out a radical, top-down, planned change initiative to deal with a major crisis, the more participative style might well send the wrong signal: that management was not in control, that the plan was incomplete and fuzzy, and that no one was really in charge. The result would be heightened anxiety and disaffection. Effective actions are always highly context-specific, and what works well in one context may be disastrous in another.

Failed change initiatives are full of examples of action steps that undercut the intended effects. The widespread criticism that the change agent or the organization's leaders aren't "walking the walk" means that what they do isn't supporting what they say, or that what they do at one point in time undercuts what they do at another. When these examples are examined closely, they usually prove to be cases where something that makes sense from one perspective fails to be effective from another. Being able to assess a proposed action step through all three lenses—strategic design, political, and cultural—can be a capability that reduces the inconsistencies and mistakes that undermine so many change initiatives.

Working with Temporal Sequencing

The stage models of change do not provide a single unified road map for change. They provide something more valuable if they are studied carefully: an awareness of the temporal sequencing of change, why it occurs, and why it matters. This awareness in turn helps the change agent make useful shifts in focus over time. Politically, for example, building a coalition is an essential step in the early stages of a change initiative. As the change proceeds, however, the focus of effort should shift to extending commitment and "ownership" of the initiative much more broadly. Often, in order to broaden commitment, the change agents need to broaden the coalition itself. This task is not always easy; the initiating coalition may have built up a strong sense of identity and may resist incorporating "latecomers" to their ranks. If the initiative is seen as owned by a small group that is unwilling to open itself to broader participation as the initiative proceeds, however, it will encounter strong resistance in its middle stage on political grounds alone, regardless of its merits. Finally, as the change initiative achieves "success" and moves into the consolidation and institutionalization phase, the change agents need to be vigilant that key supporters are in positions to ensure that it is not quietly buried or overwhelmed as attention moves on.

Culturally, the key challenge in the early stage of a change initiative is generating shared recognition of the need to change. Once this recognition becomes more general, however, the focus of activity needs to shift from dramatic gestures that challenge basic assumptions to activities that highlight the desired behaviors and provide exemplars and models. This focus includes celebrating both successes and exceptional efforts that did not achieve their goals but that generated valuable learning. Finally, once the goals are accomplished, the change agents need to shift their efforts to identifying symbols and artifacts that embody the basic assumptions that will ground the new patterns of behavior in the organizational culture.

Becoming a Sophisticated Consumer of Advice on Change

Because organizational change is so difficult, management consultants and the business press provide a steady stream of advice about how to do it. The best of them provide useful frameworks for change and build on the insights of the research and analysis of the last half-century. The worst promise quick fixes and "one-two-three" no-fail recipes for change. The insights of the theories and frameworks discussed here will help you to understand what you can use and what you need to take with a grain of salt in your particular change context.

Generic advice, such as "create a sense of urgency," for example, must be tempered with the realization that ratcheting the urgency message up too high can (as Lewin pointed out more than 50 years ago) generate either countervailing forces that resist the pressure or lead to dysfunctional levels of anxiety that make it hard for people to turn their attention to the change agenda. Advice like "create a convincing vision" resonates with decades of OD experience and has been offered by many change experts. The best of them warn, however, as do Beckhard and Harris, that the vision of the future must be balanced with a solidly based understanding of the present and careful attention to what must be done to get the organization from its present state to the envisioned future state. The widespread prescription to target and celebrate small wins in the early stages of a change initiative is good advice, but a sophisticated change agent knows that too heavy an emphasis on quick wins too early in the process can send the message that the desired changes are easy and painless, and can cause people to hide problems and fudge outcomes that fall short of expectations.

Good advice on change incorporates all three perspectives on the organization (strategic design, political, and cultural); it recognizes the temporal sequencing of change initiatives; it acknowledges that change initiatives can have different dimensions, and how the advice is applied in a radical planned change may be distinctly different from its application in an incremental emergent change; it recognizes that each change initiative is affected by the unique history of the organization and by the outcomes of previous change initiatives; and it recognizes foolproof simple recipes for successful organizational change do not exist.

References

Aldrich, Howard. 1999. *Organizations Evolving*. London: Sage Publications.

Beckhard, Richard, and Reuben T. Harris. 1977. *Organizational Transitions: Managing Complex Change*. Reading, MA: Addison-Wesley Publishing Company.

Beer, Michael, and Nitin Nohria (Eds.). 2000. *Breaking the Code of Change*. Boston, MA: Harvard Business School Press.

Brooker, Katrina. 2002. "The Un-CEO." *Fortune*, September 16, 88–96.

Cairncross, Frances. 2002. *The Company of the Future*. Boston, MA: Harvard Business School Press.

Farrell, Gary. 2000. Impatient P&G Ousts Jager. *USA Today*, June 9, p. 1B.

Gerstner, Louis V. 2002. *Who Says Elephants Can't Dance? Inside IBM's Historic Turnaround*. New York: Harper Collins.

Hannan, Michael T., and John Freeman. 1989. *Organizational Ecology*. Cambridge, MA: Harvard University Press.

Kanter, Rosabeth Moss, Barry A. Stein, and Todd D. Jick. 1992. *The Challenge of Organizational Change*. New York: Free Press.

Kotter, John, and Dan S. Cohen. 2002. *The Heart of Change*. Boston, MA: Harvard Business School Press.

Lewin, Kurt. 1947. Frontiers in Group Dynamics—Concept, Method, and Reality in Social Science: Social Equilibria and Social Change. *Human Relations* 1, 5–41.

Lex Column. 2001. *Financial Times*. March 23, 24.

Nonaka, Ikujiro. 1988. Toward Middle-Up-Down Management: Accelerating Information Creation. *Sloan Management Review* 29(3), 9–18.

Pettigrew, Andrew. 2000. Linking Change Processes to Outcomes: A Commentary on Ghoshal, Bartlett, and Weick. In Michael Beer and Nitin Nohria (Eds.), *Breaking the Code of Change*. Boston, MA: Harvard Business School Press, pp. 243–265.

Reinhardt, Andy, with Karim Djemai. 2002. Saving Ericsson. *Business Week*, November 11, 64–8.

Scott, W. Richard. 1995. *Institutions and Organizations*. Thousand Oaks, CA: Sage Publications.

Senge, Peter, Art Kleiner, Charlotte Roberts, Richard Ross, George Roth, and Bryan Smith. 1999. *The Dance of Change*. New York: Doubleday.

Tichy, Noel, and Mary Anne Devanna. 1986. *The Transformational Leader*. New York: Wiley and Sons (2nd ed., 1990).

Tushman, Michael L., and Charles A. O'Reilly. 1996. The Ambidextrous Organization. *California Management Review*, 38(4), 1–23.

Weick, Karl. 2000. Emergent Change as a Universal in Organizations. In Michael Beer and Nitin Nohria (Eds.), *Breaking the Code of Change*. Boston, MA: Harvard Business School Press, pp. 223–241.

The Strategy That Wouldn't Travel

by Michael C. Beer

It was 6:45 P.M. Karen Jimenez was reviewing the notes on her team-based productivity project for what seemed like the hundredth time. In two days, she was scheduled to present a report to the senior management group on the project's progress. She wasn't at all sure what she was going to say.

The project was designed to improve productivity and morale at each plant owned and operated by Acme Minerals Extraction Company. Phase one—implemented in early 1995 at the site in Wichita, Kansas—looked like a stunning success by the middle of 1996. Productivity and morale soared, and operating and maintenance costs decreased significantly. But four months ago, Jimenez tried to duplicate the results at the project's second target—the plant in Lubbock, Texas—and something went wrong. The techniques that had worked so well in Wichita met with only moderate success in Lubbock. Productivity improved marginally and costs went down a bit, but morale actually seemed to deteriorate slightly. Jimenez was stumped.

She tried to "helicopter up" and think about the problem in the broad context of the company's history. A few years ago, Acme had been in bad financial shape, but what had really brought things to a head—and had led to her current dilemma—was a labor relations problem. Acme had a wide variety of labor requirements for its operations. The company used highly sophisticated technology, employing geologists, geophysicists, and engineers on what was referred to as the "brains" side of the business, as well as skilled and semi-skilled labor on the "brawn" side to run the extraction operations. And in the summer of 1994, brains and brawn clashed in an embarrassingly public way. A number of engineers at the Wichita plant locked several union workers out of the offices in 100-degree heat. Although most Acme employees now felt that the incident had been blown out of proportion by the press, the board of directors had used the bad publicity as an excuse to push out an aging chief executive and bring in new blood in the form of Bill Daniels.

The board had asked Daniels to lead the company in part because he came from a prominent management consulting firm that was noted for its approach to teamwork and change. As it turned out, he had proved a good choice. Daniels was a hands-on, high-energy, charismatic businessman who seemed to enjoy media attention. Within his first year as CEO, he had pretty much righted the floundering company by selling off some unrelated lines of business. He had also created the share-services department—an internal consulting organization providing change management, reengineering, total quality management, and other services—and had tapped Jimenez to head the group. Her first priority, Daniels told her, would be to improve productivity and morale at the company's five extraction sites. None of them were meeting their projections. And although Wichita was the only site at which the labor-management conflict was painfully apparent, Daniels and Jimenez both thought that morale needed an all-around boost. Hence the team-based productivity project.

At the time, Jimenez felt up to the task. She had joined Acme in her late twenties with an MBA and a few years at a well-known consulting firm under her belt. She had been at the helm of more than a few successful change efforts. And in the ten years since she joined Acme, she had gained experience in a number of midlevel positions.

With a hardworking team of her own in tow, Jimenez commenced work. First, she decided on a battle plan. For several reasons, Wichita seemed ideal as an inaugural site. Under the former CEO, the site had spent long periods of time on the market. The plant consistently underperformed, and the old regime wanted to be rid of it. Periodically, frustrated by the lack of what he considered serious offers, the former CEO ordered improvement programs, which were always abandoned after a short time. Jimenez believed that the failures of those change programs were predictable: expectations had been unrealistic, there had been little commitment from management, and the improvement-project team members had been given little authority to implement changes. As she considered her mission at Wichita, Jimenez was certain that her new political clout combined with her experience as a consultant would make the project manageable. Moreover, she reasoned that because many previous efforts had failed, her efforts would look doubly good if the project succeeded. If it

---

Source: Reprinted by permission of *Harvard Business Review*, "The Strategy That Wouldn't Travel," by Michael C. Beers, Harvard Business Review, November–December, 1996. Copyright © 1996 by the Harvard Business School Publishing Corporation; all rights reserved.

failed, the situation could be positioned with the proper spin as an intractable set of problems that no one could solve.

The biggest problem at Wichita was clearly that labor and management didn't get along. As a result, costs to maintain the heavy equipment were significantly out of line with those incurred by other operations. Wichita's high fixed costs and razor-thin margins meant that every dollar saved in maintenance was a dollar for profit. While operating costs were high, too, they weren't nearly as high as maintenance costs.

Jimenez set about fixing the labor relations problem. And although things hadn't improved as smoothly or as quickly as she had hoped, Wichita was a great success. The problem was, Daniels had wasted no time in touting the early successes to stakeholders. In fact, not long after the Wichita project had gotten under way, he described it at great length in a speech to the Financial Analysts' Society on Wall Street. With characteristic embellishment, he cited the project as a vision for the future of Acme—indeed, he called it *the* organization for the twenty-first century. He all but told the analysts that the Wichita model would soon be rolled out through the entire enterprise.

Jimenez had been furious—and more than a little frightened. She didn't want her feet held to the fire like that; she knew that reproducing Wichita's success might not be possible and that even if it were, it might not be accomplished in a cookie-cutter fashion. In fact, she had tried to let Daniels know of her feelings on more than a few occasions, long before he spouted off to Wall Street. She had met with him and sent him reports, e-mail, and memos. The message, it seemed, had fallen on deaf ears.

Inside Wichita

Jimenez looked at the clock again: it was now 7:30. The $75 million project that could bring Acme into the twenty-first century was listing, she mused, and so was her career. She looked at her computer screen for inspiration, but it was blank. Maybe if she reviewed the success story once more. She opened the file marked "Wichita" and studied the work-process flowchart. The site had been unexceptional in almost every way. There were three functional groups: operations, which consisted of hourly workers who operated and maintained the extraction equipment; "below ground," a group composed of engineers, geologists, and geophysicists who determined where and how to drill for the desired minerals; and "above ground," a group of engineers in charge of cursory refinement and transportation of the minerals. Before the team project had been put in motion, Wichita had shown little coordination or communication among these groups.

Jimenez knew that she had at least one stroke of good luck in Wichita in the form of David Keller. Keller, a 39-year Acme veteran, had been looking for one last job before he retired, and he wanted it to be in Wichita, where his family had lived for eight years earlier in his career. He wanted to retire there. Keller was widely respected in the company and Jimenez genuinely liked him. So, with the blessing of Daniels and the other senior managers, she had appointed him project leader.

She smiled as she thought about Keller. He was a Korean War vet who had relocated several times for Acme, serving in just about every possible line and staff position. He joined the company in 1957 and was immediately baptized in the dust and heat of North Africa, where the company had set up operations soon after World War II. Keller was a link to Acme's heady past, when it had thought nothing of clearing Allied land mines planted in the desert in its drive to expand. It struck Jimenez that Keller had joined the company before she was born.

Jimenez thought about the Wichita project's rough spots. One of them had been the institution of a monthly "problem chat," an optional meting open to all staff to discuss unresolved problems. No one attended the first one. She and Keller sat there nervously, together eating six doughnuts before she called a secretary and had them carted away.

But over time, people began to show up. After about four months, the meetings were well-attended, lively problem-solving discussions that actually produced some improvements. In one case, a maintenance worker explained to a facilities engineer that one of the standard equipment configurations was failing as a result of high levels of heat and sand contamination, resulting in occasional downtime. With Keller mediating, the complaint had been taken well, without the usual friction. The engineer easily fabricated a new configuration more suitable to the conditions, and downtime was virtually eliminated. Such insights were common at the problem chats. Previously no organizational mechanism had existed for capturing solutions or transferring them to other parts of the operation.

Jimenez and Keller then introduced teams to "select a problem and implement a tailored solution," or SPITS. These were ad-hoc groups made up of members from each of the functional areas. The groups were formed to work on a specific project identified in a problem chat; they were disbanded when the problem was solved. It was the implementation of SPITS teams that led some eight months later to a wholesale reorganization of the Wichita work site. Jimenez believed that SPITS had been a breakthrough that had shown her how to boost productivity and morale—the goal that Daniels had set for her. The program had given cross-functional teams of 12 to 15 people from operations, above ground, and below ground the responsibility and authority to address problems as they occurred without seeking the approval of management.

Jimenez reminded herself that even after SPITS, there were still some rocky moments in Wichita. Some engineers resented having to work alongside operations personnel. They told Keller, "These miners don't understand why we do what we do." Likewise, some operations staff balked at having to work with engineers who "knew how to mine only on a computer screen."

But one year into the pilot, things began to hum. People weren't just working together, they were socializing together. At one of the problem chats, an operations worker jokingly suggested that the brains and the brawn duke it out once a week to get rid of the tensions. Keller jumped on the joke and had T-shirts made that said BRAINS AND BRAWN; he then challenged the groups to square off weekly in a softball game. Early into the first game, a 200-pound miner slammed into a thin, wiry engineer at home plate, and Jimenez, watching from the sidelines, was sure that her corporate change plan had just been called out. But the engineer simply dusted himself off, laughing and swearing at the same time. At the next game, the engineer showed up wearing knee and shoulder pads, and Jimenez heard both his colleagues and the operations guys laughing. She knew something had changed. Later that night at a bar, the beer flowed in massive quantities, but she happily picked up the check. Her BRAINS AND BRAWN shirt now hung on her office all—a symbol of everything that was wrong and everything was possible.

Cookie-Cutter Conundrum

Jimenez again came back to the present. She closed the file, got up abruptly, and grabbed her coat. She needed some air and some food and decided to walk the two blocks to the local sandwich joint. She felt a little like an inventor who had just developed a great new invention that is certain to make the company tons of money. "That's great!" and imaginary boss replies. "Now give me another 50 just like it!"

As she walked, she tried to think objectively about the Lubbock site. Lubbock was in better shape than Wichita to begin with, but not by much. Operating costs there were too high, and the plant rarely met its production goals. Acme had considered divesting itself of Lubbock on more than one occasion. When Jimenez initially planned the team-based productivity rollout, she had thought of Lubbock as a beta site; kinks from Wichita would be worked out there, and then the plan would be rolled out to the rest of the company over a two-year period. The shared-services department didn't have the staff to oversee Wichita's fine-tuning and concentrate on Lubbock as well, so Jimenez assigned only one of her top internal consultants, Jennifer Peterson, and two of Peterson's staff to the Lubbock project. She then engaged Daniels' former consulting firm and assigned Dave Matthews, a vice president of the firm, on-site responsibility.

Bad news seemed to dog Jimenez at every turn. For example, Keller declined to be a part of the team. Mystified and a little hurt, Jimenez turned up the pressure a bit, hinting that it might look bad for him not to work on the Lubbock site. Keller was resolute.

"Look, Karen," he had said. "I'm 63 years old. My kids are all out of the house. I've relocated ten times for the company, but I plan to retire soon. I don't want to spend the next three years burning myself out traveling all over the country. I'm staying in Wichita. If I have to, I'll take early retirement and walk." Although Jimenez thought he might be bluffing, she couldn't afford to call his hand. Keller had many powerful allies in the company and was viewed as the prototypical Acme man; his latest success with the Wichita turnaround was seen as yet another in a series of impressive achievements. Jimenez knew she couldn't afford to lose his experience and knowledge; if she couldn't get him full time, she would do her best to pick his brain and transfer his knowledge to a project team.

Keller had promised full access to his entire staff; the consultants could interview and brainstorm and strategize all they wanted. Jimenez, Peterson, and Matthews took advantage of that opportunity, but even extensive interviews with Keller and his staff hadn't yielded any truly valuable insights. No matter how carefully Jimenez and her group tried to recreate the circumstances and techniques that had worked so well in Wichita, they made very little progress. The Lubbock employees just didn't seem to react with the same enthusiasm as the Wichita workers had. Because no one was showing up for the problem chats—despite the "selling" of the meetings' benefits by Jimenez, Peterson, and Matthews—attendance was made mandatory. It was true that Jimenez's team had attempted to reduce the cycle time and "total time to investment recovery" of the project, but that goal hadn't seemed unreasonable. Jimenez thought that there would be fewer mistakes in Lubbock and that the project would need less time and fewer resources than Wichita had.

If anything, just the opposite occurred. Problems never encountered in the Wichita project created havoc at Lubbock. One particularly vexing to Jimenez was that the Lubbock workers refused to engage in any of the team-building exercises and events developed for them by the project team. The softball games that had been played with enthusiasm in Wichita were skipped by the Lubbock crowd until the project team finally offered to spring for food and beer. Even then, there was more eating than playing. I felt like I was bribing prison inmates, Jimenez remembered.

There had been some improvements. The site had begun to meet its weekly goals more consistently and had seen some reduction in operations and maintenance costs. Normally, Jimenez would have been complimented on a job well done, but in the context of what had gone before and what was expected, the improvements weren't enough—and Jimenez knew it.

She returned to her office, still without an answer. Full and generous funding had been approved for the team-based productivity project by the steering committee at the personal request of Bill Daniels; this level of funding was not easily come by at Acme. How could she convince him—without looking like a failure—that the project couldn't be rolled out with the speed and grace he envisioned? What's more, it was clear that stalling the implementation would dull some of the project's luster and in all likelihood jeopardize funding. She *did* think that the project would work, given time. But she wasn't exactly sure how. And any waffling might get her crucified by her colleagues.

The meeting with the senior managers was rapidly approaching. What could she say to them?

Managing Change in Organizations

ELECTIVE

Module 8

The Life Cycle of Typical Change Initiatives

by Peter Senge

Most change initiatives fail. Two independent studies in the early 1990s, one published by Arthur D. Little and one by McKinsey & Co., found that out of the hundreds of corporate Total Quality Management (TQM) programs studied, about two thirds "grind to a halt because of their failure to produce hoped-for results." Reengineering has fared no better; a number of articles, including some by reengineering's founders, place the failure rate somewhere around 70 percent.

Harvard's John Kotter, in a study of one hundred top management-driven "corporate transformation" efforts, concluded that more than half did not survive the initial phases. He found a few that were "very successful," and a few that were "utter failures." The vast majority lay ". . . somewhere in between, with a distinct tilt toward the lower end of the scale" Clearly, businesses do not have a very good track record in sustaining significant change. There is little to suggest that schools, healthcare institutions, governmental, and nonprofit organizations fare any better.

> The many, many references about these failures include *The Economist*, April 18, 1992 (describing the Arthur D. Little and McKinsey studies); "Why Do Employees Resist Change?" by Paul Strebel, *Harvard Business Review*, May/June 1996, p. 86 (cites a 20–50% reengineering success rate); "Leading Change: Why Transformation Efforts Fail," by John P. Kotter, *Harvard Business Review*, Mar/Apr 1995, p. 59; and "Reengineering: A Light That Failed," by James Champy, *Across the Board*, vol. 32, no. 3, pp. 27–31, March 1995.

Even without knowing the statistics, most of us know firsthand that change programs fail. We've seen enough "flavor of the month" programs "rolled out" from top management to last a lifetime. We know the cynicism they engender. We have watched ourselves and others around us "salute the flag" and then say privately, "Here we go again," and "This will never work." Some companies even create their own jargon to laugh a bit at their skepticism: At Harley-Davidson, management's latest great ideas are greeted with the phrase "AFP," which is translated publicly as "Another Fine Program."

This failure to sustain significant change recurs again and again despite substantial resources committed to the change effort (many are bankrolled by top management), talented and committed people "driving the change, " and high stakes. In fact, executives feeling an urgent need for change are right; companies that fail to sustain significant change end up facing crises. By then, their options are greatly reduced, and even after heroic efforts they often decline.

Our core premise in writing this book is that the sources of these problems cannot be remedied by more expert advice, better consultants, or more committed managers. The sources lie in our most basic ways of thinking. If these do not change, any new "input" will end up producing the same fundamentally unproductive types of actions.

To understand why sustaining significant change is so elusive, we need to think less like managers and more like biologists. We can start by seeing that, over time, most change initiatives follow a generic life cycle that looks something like the diagram on the following page.

The innovative practices advocated by the initiative—be it total quality management, process redesign, or "building a learning organization"—grow for a while and then stop growing. Maybe they cease altogether. Maybe the initiative persists at a low level, the religion of a small group of "true believers." Either way, the initial growth fails to realize its potential. It is understandable that many innovative new practices do not spread because they turn out never to generate sufficient benefits. But what about those that do demonstrate significant benefits and still do not spread, as occurs with a great many promising innovations that "die on

---

Source: From *The Dance of Change* by Peter M. Senge, Kleiner, Roberts and Ross, copyright © 1999 by Peter Senge, Art Kleiner, Charlotte Roberts and Richard Ross. Used by permission of Doubleday, a division of Random House, Inc.

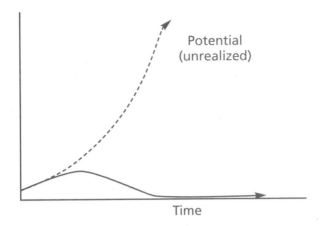

the vine" in large corporations? The dash curve on the diagram indicates the potential growth that the innovative practice could have enjoyed. Why, if the new ideas or tools or processes had real potential, did they only penetrate to 1 percent of the organization? Why was only 5 percent improvement in new product development rate achieved when there might have been a 100 percent improvement? Why did the momentum die out?

As any biologist would immediately say, the curve in the diagram is not idiosyncratic to organizational change efforts. It traces the pattern followed by anything that grows in nature, even something that grows and dies "prematurely." In fact, the s-shaped growth pattern occurs so consistently in biology that it has its own name: "sigmoidal" growth. All individual organisms, from humans to beetles, likewise grow according to the same pattern: accelerating, then gradually slowing until "full" adult size is reached. Biological populations grow the same way: accelerating for a time, then gradually slowing. This pattern recurs again and again in nature because of the way nature generates and controls growth.

> For examples of change initiatives and innovations that did not realize their potential (even though they eventually became highly influential), see *The Age of Heretics*, by Art Kleiner (New York: Doubleday, 1996) or *Failure in Organization Development and Change: Cases and Essays for Learning*, by Philip H. Mirvis and David N. Berg, editors (New York: John Wiley and Sons, 1977).

All growth in nature arises out of an interplay between reinforcing growth processes and limiting processes. The seed contains the possibility for a tree, but it realizes that possibility through an emergent reinforcing growth process. The seed sends out small feelers. These primitive roots draw in water and nutrients. This leads the roots to expand farther, drawing in more water and nutrients, leading to further expansion—more water, nutrients, and so on. The initial growth process is under way. But how far it progresses depends on a host of limits: water, nutrients in the soil, space for the roots to expand, warmth. Eventually, as the tree begins to extend beyond the surface, other limits will come into play: sunlight, space for the tree's branches to spread, insects that destroy the tree's leaves.

When growth stops "prematurely," before the organism reaches its potential, it is because the growth has encountered constraints that could be avoided, that are not inevitable. Other members of the species will grow more because they do not encounter the same constraints. Any particular limit mentioned above—not enough water, nutrients, or space for the root system—could potentially keep the seed from growing.

What, then, can biology teach us about the growth and premature death of organizational change initiatives?

First, it immediately suggests that most leadership strategies are often doomed at the outset. Leaders instigating change are often like gardeners standing over their plants, imploring them: "Grow! Try harder! You can do it!" No gardener tries to convince a plant to "want" to grow: If the seed does not have the potential to grow, there's nothing anyone can do to make a difference.

Second, it suggests that leaders should especially focus on understanding the limiting processes that could slow or arrest change. Above all else, the gardener must understand the constraints that can limit growth and attend to these constraints. Why should this be any different for leaders seeking to sustain significant change? Entreating people to try harder, to become more committed, to be more passionate cannot possibly have much lasting effect. The biological world teaches that sustaining change requires understanding the reinforcing growth processes and what is needed to catalyze them, and addressing the limits that keep change from occurring.

So, what types of limits might these be? What are some of the constraints that all efforts to sustain significant change encounter? One insight may lie in a phrase that became common in the heyday of TQM. I remember sitting in a meeting in the mid-1980s with a group of managers on the vanguard of TQM at a leading U.S. manufacturer. "We've picked all the low-hanging fruit," one stated. When I asked what he meant, he said, "We've done all the easy things. In truth, things were so bad in many of our production facilities that it was enough just to give people a little bit of authority to fix practices that many had known needed to be changed for a long time. Now we're up against much tougher problems and the rate of improvement is declining. Now we're up against problems where the real problem is us, the management. We're pretty good at directing others to change, but not so great at changing ourselves."

Most serious change initiatives eventually come up against issues embedded in our prevailing system of management. These include managers' commitment to change as long as it doesn't affect them; "undiscussable" topics that feel risky to talk about; and the ingrained habit of attacking symptoms and ignoring deeper, systemic causes of problems.

> The capabilities referred to here are embodied in the five "learning disciplines" of *The Fifth Discipline*: personal mastery and shared vision (aspiration), mental models and team learning (reflection and inquiry), and systems thinking.

We are limited in dealing with such issues by our collective learning capabilities. Shared ability to change develops only with collective capability to build shared aspirations. People start discussing "undiscussable" subjects only when they develop the reflection and inquiry skills that enable them to talk openly about complex, conflictive issues without invoking defensiveness. People start seeing and dealing with interdependencies and deeper causes of problems only as they develop the skills of systems thinking. In my experience, if basic learning capabilities like these are deficient, then they represent a fundamental limit to sustaining change.

> I am indebted to Nitin Nohria of Harvard for pointing out how inadequate learning capabilities limit change initiatives. —Peter Senge

Most advocates of change initiatives, be they CEOs or internal staff, focus on the changes they are trying to produce and fail to recognize the importance of learning capabilities. This is like trying to make a plant grow, rather than understanding and addressing the constraints that are keeping it from growing. Consequently, their initiatives are doomed from the start to achieve less than their potential—until building learning capabilities becomes part of the change strategy.

But . . . there remains a problem. For the past ten years and longer, many people have been doing just that—building learning capabilities as an essential part of producing more effective work practices. We often call these "learning initiatives." Many have had great success. But just as many have failed. And, where success has been achieved, innovators continue to struggle to sustain momentum. Obviously, building learning capabilities is necessary but not sufficient.

I have come to the conclusion that what is missing is more subtle. In practice, most learning initiatives do not reflect any deep understanding of nature's growth dynamics. In effect, they deal only with the growth processes and not with the limiting processes. Developing learning capabilities in the context of working groups and real business goals can lead to powerful reinforcing growth processes. This has been the focus of most of the "learning organization work" for the past twenty years. Activating the self-energizing commitment and energy of people around changes they deeply care about has been the key to the many successes that have been achieved. But, nothing in nature grows in the absence of limiting processes. And, we have given these limiting processes much too little attention. This is why so many learning initiatives, like so many other change initiatives, ultimately fail to sustain momentum.

> The quote from Humberto Maturana is from "Biosphere, Homosphere, and Robosphere: What has that to do with business?," a presentation at the Society for Organizational Learning (SoL), June 23–24, 1998, re-created by Pille Bunnell. An edited transcript by Maturana and Bunnell is available through SoL; for access, see *http://www.fieldbook.com/sol.html*. Also see *The Tree of Knowledge*, by Humberto Maturana and Francisco Varela (Boston: Shambala/Random House, 1987, 1992); *Autopoiesis and Cognition: The Realization of the Living*, by H. R. Maturana and Francisco Varela, (Boston: D. Reidel Publishing Co., 1980); the Observer Web site, dedicated to Maturana and Vaerla's work: *http://www.informatik.umu.se/~rwhit/AT.html* and the Fieldbook referrals to Maturana's work at *http://www.fieldbook.com/maturana.html*.

Sustaining any profound change processes requires a fundamental shift in thinking. We need to understand the nature of growth processes (forces that aid our efforts) and how to catalyze them. But we also need to understand the forces and challenges that impede progress, and to develop strategies for dealing with these challenges. We need to appreciate the "dance of change," the inevitable interplay between growth processes and limiting processes. As Chilean biologist Humberto Maturana puts it, "Every movement is being inhibited as it occurs." This is nature's way. We can either work with it, or work against it.

This requires us to think of sustaining change more biologically and less mechanistically. It requires patience as well as urgency. It requires a real sense of inquiry, a genuine curiosity about limiting forces. It requires seeing how significant change invariably starts locally, and how it grows over time. And it requires recognizing the diverse array of people who play key roles in sustaining change—people who are "leaders."

The Leadership of Profound Change
Toward an ecology of leadership

by Peter Senge

The Myth of the Hero-CEO

"Significant change only occurs when it is driven from the top."

"There is no point in going forward unless the CEO is on board."

"Nothing will happen without top management buy-in."

How many times have we all heard these familiar refrains, and simply accepted them as "the way things are"? Probably many times, and yet there are good reasons to challenge these hoary truisms. The evidence for top management's power to direct large organizations to change is thin at best. Everywhere one hears of CEO's needing to "transform" their organizations, yet the examples of successful, sustained transformation are few. Moreover, in this "age of empowerment," doesn't it all seem a bit strange that we are asked to accept the singular power of top executives so unquestionably? How can we hope to bring about less hierarchical, authoritarian organizations solely through recourse to hierarchical authority?

In fact, the myth of the omnipotent CEO is merely a special case of a deeper cultural icon, the myth of the hero-leader. According to this shared story, leaders are the few special people blessed with the capability for command and influence. They have become leaders precisely because of their unique mix of skill, ambition, visions, charisma, and no small amount of hubris. They can overcome the blocks that stymie everyone else. They make great things happen. The implication is clear: If you too want to make a difference, you had better be one of these special people.

In the world of today's organizations, this idealization of great leadership leads to an endless search for heroic figures who can come in to rescue the rest of us from recalcitrant, noncompetitive institutions. But might this very thinking be a key reason such institutions prevail? Might not the continual search for the hero-leader be a critical factor in itself, diverting our attention away from building institutions that, by their very nature, continually adapt and reinvent themselves, with leadership coming from many people in many places, not just from the top?

I have come to see our obsession with the hero-CEO as a type of cultural addiction. Faced with the practical needs for significant change, we opt for the hero-leader rather than eliciting and developing leadership capacity throughout the organization. A new hero-CEO arrives to pump new life into the organization's suffering fortunes. Typically, today, the new leader cuts costs (and usually people), and boosts productivity and profit. But the improvements do not last. Many of the leader's grand strategies never get implemented; instead, people cling to habitual ways of doing things. New ideas do not spring forth from people at the front lines because they are too intimidated to stick their neck out. Energies are not released to create new products or new ways to meet customer needs because people are too busy competing with one another to please their bosses. Sooner or later, new crises ensue, giving rise to the search for new hero-leaders. In effect, the myth of the hero-leader creates a reinforcing vicious spiral of dramatic changes imposed from the top, and diminished leadership capacity in the organization, leading eventually to new crises and yet more heroic leaders.

Worshipping the cult of the hero-leader is a surefire way to maintain change-averse institutions. In fact, one can hardly think of a better strategy to achieve precisely this goal. The price that we all pay, in the long run, is incalculable: institutions that lurch from crisis to crisis, continual stress on the members of those institutions, mediocre (at best) long-term financial performance, and a subtle, pervasive point of view that the "common people" are powerless to change things.

In the business world, the vicious addictive spiral extends into the investment community. Investor pressures for improved short-term financial performance lead to calls for more aggressive top management. New hero-leaders come forward who can boost short-term performance. But their strategies typically preclude long-term investments in developing collective capacities to innovate, thereby guaranteeing long-term mediocre finan-

Source: From *The Dance of Change* by Peter M. Senge, Kleiner, Roberts and Ross, copyright © 1999 by Peter Senge, Art Kleiner, Charlotte Roberts and Richard Ross. Used by permission of Doubleday, a division of Random House, Inc.

cial results. This, in turn, leads to more pressures from investors and more hero-leaders. In other words, the investment community paradoxically colludes in sustaining a system guaranteed to undermine creation of wealth in the long run.

A Different View of Executive Leadership

Now consider a different set of statements:

"Little significant change can occur if it is driven only from the top."

"CEO proclamations and programs rolled out from corporate headquarters are a great way to foster cynicism and distract everyone from real efforts to change."

"Top management buy-in is a poor substitute for genuine commitment and learning capabilities at all levels in an organization. In fact, if management authority is used unwisely, it can make commitment and capability less likely to develop."

These views are not just heard at lower levels in the hierarchy; they are echoed by senior executives in organizations that have achieved some sustained success.

"When I first came in as CEO," Shell Oil's Phil Carroll has said, "everyone thought, 'Phil will tell us what to do.' But I didn't have the answer, thank goodness. If I had, it would have been a disaster."

Harley-Davidson chairman Rich Teerlink has commented: "Anyone who thinks a CEO can drive this kind of change is wrong."

And Charles Szulak, former President of Visteon Automotive Systems at Ford Motor Company, has said, "Carrying significant change through an organization of eighty-two thousand people cannot possibly be done by a handful of people at the top."

There are good reasons why these executives, and others like them, have come to hold more humble views about the powers of executive leadership. First, they know that people, especially in large organizations, have become cynical about "flavor of the month" management fads.

Second, they appreciate the fundamental differences between compliance and commitment. The word "commitment" has become fashionable because it is widely believed that "high commitment" work environments are more productive, and probably also because many managers feel uncomfortable telling people to "comply" with management's directives. But the simple fact is that most management-driven change efforts do not require commitment. They are built around compliance. Either people comply with the new reorganization, or they know they will be at odds with their bosses. Knowing that it is difficult to discern visions from commands when they travel down the hierarchy, savvy senior managers use the power of their position with great care—because they seek to foster more than just compliance.

> For more information about the relationship between "commitment" and "compliance," see *The Fifth Discipline*, p. 218.

Deep changes—in how people think, what they believe, how they see the world—are difficult, if not impossible, to achieve through compliance. Reflecting on twenty years of leading change toward more value-based work environments, retired Hanover Insurance CEO Bill O'Brien says, "What people pressuring for management to 'drive' cultural change don't understand is: A value is only a value when it is voluntarily chosen."

Last, thoughtful executives know that many top management initiatives are not just ineffective, they often make matters worse. This is not just true for short-term financially driven changes that increase fear and internal competitiveness. It is equally true for many management efforts to improve organizational effectiveness. For example, Harvard's Chris Argyris has shown how management efforts to improve internal communications—like employee surveys, focus groups, and "360 feedback"— can give people anonymous ways to "tell management what is wrong" without assuming any responsibility for improving matters. The feedback process thereby subtly reinforces the view that management is the source of problems and only management has the power to fix them.

If the power of top management is in fact limited, why then do people in organizations continue to cling to the belief that only the top can drive change? As Argyris suggests, this belief allows us all to continue to hold the top responsible for whether or not change happens. While that view might be disempowering on one level, it provides a convenient strategy if our real goal is to preserve the status quo. Moreover, there are different types of change, some of which—like reorganizing or creating new corporate strategy—can only be brought about by top management. Such top-driven changes are familiar to most of us—but they do not reduce fear and distrust, nor unleash imagination and creativity, nor enhance the quality of thinking in the organization. When people confuse top-driven change and profound change, it's easy to hold an exaggerated view of the power of top management, a confusion that no doubt persists among some top managers as well. Finally, we simply have no strategy for escaping cultural addition to the myth of the hero-leader. In the U.S., especially, it seems to be part of our cultural DNA.

> See "Good Communication that Blocks Learning," by Chris Argyris, *Harvard Business Review*, July/August 1994, p. 77.

What Is Leadership and Who Are the Leaders?

In business today, the word "leader" has become a synonym for top manager. When people talk about "developing leaders" they mean developing prospective top managers. When they ask, "What do the leaders think?" they are asking about the views of top managers.

There are two problems with this. First, it implies that those who are not in top management positions are not leaders. They might aspire to "become" leaders, but they don't "get there" until they reach a senior management position of authority. Second, it leaves us with no real definition of leadership. If leadership is simply a position in the hierarchy, then, in effect, there is no independent definition of leadership. A person is either an executive or is not. There's nothing more to say about leadership. End of story.

We look at leadership differently.

We view leadership as the capacity of a human community to shape its future, and specifically to sustain the significant processes of change required to do so. This is an unusual definition of leadership today, but actually not a new one. It is a definition that we think comes closer to most people's actual experience of leadership.

We believe, specifically, that leadership actually grows from the capacity to hold creative tension, the energy generated when people articulate a vision and tell the truth (to the best of their ability) about current reality. This also is not a new idea. "Leadership is vision," says Peter Drucker. Or, as expressed in Proverbs 29:18, "Where there is no vision, people perish."

Most great leaders intuitively appreciate the principle of creative tension. Martin Luther King, Jr. expressed the idea beautifully in his famous "letter from the Birmingham jail": "Just as Socrates felt that it was necessary to create a tension in the mind, so that individuals could rise from the bondage of myths and half-truths . . . so must we . . . create the kind of tension in society that will help men rise from the dark depths of prejudice and racism." While Dr. King is famous for his "dream," his leadership practice centered around "dramatizing the present situation" so that people could see the current reality of racism.

> "Letter from a Birmingham Jail," by Martin Luther King, Jr., written April 16, 1963, published at http://www.ai.mit.edu/-isbell/HFh/black/eventsandpeople/008.letter from jail.

By this definition, any organization has many leaders because there are many people at many levels in the hierarchy who play critical roles in generating and sustaining creative tension. Consequently, we will focus on leadership communities rather than hero-leaders. This view of leadership communities has arisen gradually over the past ten years, as we have seen again and again, diverse people in diverse positions contribute vitally to the way that an enterprise shapes it future.

In particular, we have come to appreciate the interplay between three types of leaders:

> ## Change, Transformation, and Profound Change
>
> The original meaning of the old French word *changer* was "bend," or "turn," like a tree or vine searching for the sun. The idea that "the only constant is change" has been a truism of life since at least the time of Heracleitus, circa 500 B.C.
>
> Today, in business and organizations, the word "change" means several often-contradictory things. It sometimes refers to external changes in technology, customers, competitors, market structure, or the social and political environment. ("We know our world will change, and we have to adapt along with it.") "Change" also refers to internal changes; how the organization adapts to changes in the environment. The timeless concern is whether these internal changes—in practices, views, and strategies—will keep pace with external change.
>
> Concerns over the pace of internal change lead executives to intervene. Hence today, "change" can also mean top-down programs like reorganizing, reengineering, and many other "re's." Because these change programs are typically imposed from the top, many in the organization feel threatened or manipulated by them—even if they support in principle the intent or rationale behind the management change agenda. As organizational change pioneer Richard Beckhard once put it, "People do not resist change; people resist being changed."
>
> Today, some managers use the word "transformation" to describe comprehensive organizational change initiatives, such as those at General Electric and Shell Oil. We chose not to do that in this book. We recognize that transformation can mean many things to many people. As W. Edwards Deming said, "Nothing changes without personal transformation." Yet, perhaps because of the tradition of top-down change programs, we worry a bit about "corporate transformation" coming to mean "really large changes" imposed from top management. (The original Latin word *transformare* simply means "to change shape.") We also worry about the word's connotation of a singular episode of change, "transforming" the organization from one state to another. (Inventor Joseph Henry chose the term in 1830 to name his device for changing the voltage of electric current from one steady-state to another.)
>
> We use the term "profound change" to describe organizational change that combines inner shifts in people's values, aspirations, and behaviors with "outer" shifts in processes, strategies, practices, and systems. The word "profound" stems from the Latin *fundus*, a base of foundation. It means, literally, "moving toward the fundamental." In profound change there is learning. The organization doesn't just do something new: it builds its capacity for ongoing change. The emphasis on inner *and* outer changes gets to the heart of the issues that large industrial-age institutions are wrestling with today. It is not enough to change strategies, structures, and systems, unless the thinking that produced those strategies, structures, and systems also changes.

- **Local line leaders:** We have rarely seen any successful change initiatives that did not involve imaginative, committed local line leaders. By "local line leaders," we mean people with accountability for results and sufficient authority to undertake changes in the way that work is organized and conducted at their local level. This local level may be limited to a few people or involve a few thousand people. Local line leaders can be plant managers, heads of product development teams, or sales managers. They can also be teachers or principals, or nurse shift managers. Local line leaders are vital because only they and their colleagues, not executives, can undertake meaningful organizational experiments to test the practical impact of new ideas and approaches.

- **Internal networkers, "network leaders," or community builders:** Likewise, we have never seen any examples of broad diffusion of new learning practices without the enthusiastic participation of effective internal networkers. Indeed, many studies of the diffusion of innovative practices show the importance of the informal networks through which new ideas and innovative practices spread organically in and across organizations. Internal networkers may be internal staff people, such as internal consultants or people in training or executive development departments. They may also be front line people—salespeople, manufacturing supervisors, or engineers who participate in ongoing "communities of practice."

> See, for example, *Communities of Practice: Learning, Meaning, and Identity*, by Etienne Wenger (New York: Cambridge University Press, 1998).

Internal networkers are a natural counterpart to local line leaders. The great strength of local line leaders is their passion for creating better results within their unit; their limitation is that they often have limited contact beyond their unit. Internal networkers complement the provincialism of local line leaders. Their strength is their ability to move about the larger organization, to participate in and nurture broad networks of alliances with other, like-minded individuals, and to help local leaders, both by assisting directly and by putting them in contact with others who share their passions and from whom they can learn. They are the natural "seed carriers" of new ideas and new practices. Because they carry ideas, support, and stories through the organization, internal networkers can also help make executive leaders more aware of the support that change initiatives in the company need from them.

The role of internal networkers or community builders is tangible, but difficult to specify; because it belongs much more to the informal social networks of the company than it does to the hierarchy. In some ways, paradoxically, their lack of hierarchical authority makes them effective. When a "boss" calls a meeting, everyone has to show up. When a boss visits a local operation, everyone reacts. The boss may ask: "Who is committed to the new plan?" Everyone will respond affirmatively. By contrast, when someone without hierarchical authority organizes a meeting, only those who are interested show up. When she or he asks who wants to learn more, only those who are genuinely interested respond affirmatively.

> The three types of leaders were originally discussed in "Leading Learning Organizations; The Bold, the Powerful, and the Invisible," in The Drucker Foundation's *The Leader of the Future,* by F. Hesselbein, M. Goldsmith, R. Beckhard, eds. (San Francisco: Jossey-Bass, 1996).

- **Executive leaders:** None of the above implies that effective executive management is unimportant. If anything, it is more necessary today than ever, because the changes that institutions confront are long-term and "deep," in the sense of entailing shifts in hitherto taken-for-granted assumptions and norms, and in traditional organizational structures and practices. Effective executive leadership is probably more challenging today than ever before, especially because of the combination of the demands of the profound change and extraordinary external pressures, like the investor pressures discussed above.

This role of executive leaders is complicated by the fact that they are one step removed from the organization's direct value-producing activities. They have overall accountability for organizational performance but less ability to directly influence actual work processes. They may be corporate presidents, vice presidents and directors, school superintendents, or hospital CEOs. They are vital to profound change through their efforts to create an organizational environment for continual innovation and knowledge generation.

They do this in many ways: through investing in new infrastructure for learning, through support and inquiry, and ultimately through "leadership by example," establishing new norms and behaviors within their own teams. They become mentors, coaches, and stewards. They focus on design more than on making key decisions. They work to push decisions down to more local levels, unless they are the only ones who can make those decisions.

We have found that the most effective leaders start by recognizing that "this is a new ballgame," and many of their own most trusted traditional skills and behaviors may be their biggest obstacles. To foster a more learning-oriented culture, they must give up feeling that they have to have all of the answers. They must become more comfortable with, and capable of, asking questions that do not have easy answers. And they must realize that they cannot do this alone, that they need partners, that becoming isolated heroes will cut them off from the support and assistance that they must have to be effective.

Undoubtedly, this simple tripartite categorization of different types of leaders oversimplifies the reality of leadership communities. But at least it heads us in a direction away from isolated hero-leaders and toward a view of different people leading change in different ways, who need each other to sustain significant change. In essence, leaders are people who "walk ahead," people genuinely committed to deep changes, in themselves and in their organization. They naturally influence others through their credibility, capability, and commitment. And they come in many shapes, sizes, and positions.

This taxonomy of "three leaders" has been influenced by Edgar Schein's analysis of the complementary role of executives, engineers, and operators in corporations. See Edgar H. Schein, "The Three Cultures of Management," *Sloan Management Review,* Fall 1996.

Culture Change at General Electric

The evolution of productivity and effectiveness increases, from "Work-Out" to Six Sigma

by Jacquie Vierling-Huang, Manager of Work-Out and Change Acceleration, GE Crotonville

General Electric is renowned for its pioneering approaches to organizational change—and for recognizing that significant change requires profound shifts in people's attitudes and beliefs. Herein, a senior leader from GE's famous "corporate university" at Crotonville, New York, describes how the problem of "not enough time" led to a comprehensive and thoroughly innovative initiative for organizational learning. Some readers may notice the reference to crisis and heroic leadership, and wonder if GE's approach is based more on compliance than on commitment, with a sense of urgency handed down by charismatic leaders like Chairman Jack Welch. GE seems to rely on both compliance and commitment, in ways that overlap within each person and team. Wherever your organization is coming from, there's much to learn from the GE experience.

In the 1970s, General Electric was known for its strategic planning. Some say we defined the practice. In the faster-moving 1980s and 1990s, we've learned that even the most detailed plans can be blown away by a single unanticipated event—such as the fall of the Berlin Wall, the Gulf War, or the current Asian economic difficulties.

Instead of being a company governed by planning, GE is working to become an organization that values change. When a surprise occurs—when customers make new demands, or competitors enter the marketplace—our people might not predict it. But they should be able to recognize and respond quickly, for the benefit of the whole company.

[The name "Work-Out" is a trademark of the General Electric Corporation. It is used here only to describe the particular programs managed and marketed by General Electric. Any reference in these pages to "Work-Out" refers to that trademark.]

Work-Out, which was launched in 1989, was named for the idea of taking excess "work out" of the system, thus eliminating bureaucracy and freeing up people's time. It was deliberately designed to focus on the cultural side of change: helping people change their attitudes about their work and the ways they approached their jobs. We needed to involve our employees in the task of improving productivity across GE. They needed to learn how to translate companywide imperatives (such as the need to increase operating margins) into their individual actions.

Over the years, as the diagram on the next page shows, our learning effort has evolved through seven stages, from basic Work-Out to Six Sigma Quality. We draw upon all of these in everything we do today. All of GE's formal training programs play a key role in enabling employees to respond rapidly and effectively to change.

Stage One: Work-Outs and the "RAMMP" Matrix

We started, back in 1989, with one- to three-day "town meetings"—gatherings of people focused on ending the bureaucratic, hierarchical wastes of time and productivity. We grouped people in "diagonal slice teams," including people who worked together across functions and levels, because we knew that wastes of time and effort

---

Source: From *The Dance of Change* by Peter M. Senge, Kleiner, Roberts and Ross, copyright © 1999 by Peter Senge, Art Kleiner, Charlotte Roberts and Richard Ross. Used by permission of Doubleday, a division of Random House, Inc.

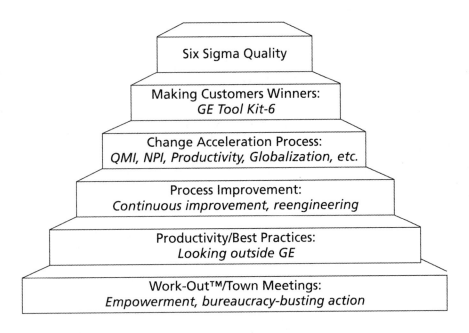

often developed at the boundary points between functions, departments, and levels. Our teams followed a framework called RAMMP:

- **Reports:** "Is this report really necessary?" Teams noted the time it took to create and read reports, versus the number of people who valued them. There were cases where leaders routinely demanded reports, without any idea that they took three person-weeks to develop. Other reports circulated unread, every year across dozens of desks. After RAMMP sessions, people could say to their bosses, "You asked for such-and-such a document, but if you changed the requirements slightly, we could do it in half the time."
- **Approvals:** "Does this decision need to be approved by so many people?" People found purchase orders needing twelve signatures for approval; scientists trusted with enormously complex experiments, for example, were not allowed to order rubber gloves on their own.
- **Meetings:** "Do we need to have this meeting?" Participants asked each other whether time-consuming meetings actually accomplished anything. Was the time allotted too long? Could they be set up in a better way? Could they use videoconferencing or teleconferencing to avoid costly and time-consuming travel?
- **Measures:** Participants listed all the behaviors that they wanted to see more of, and then drew a line between their existing measures and these behaviors.
- **Policies and procedures:** Did the compensation plans, incentives, appraisal methods, and other policies help people get work done more effectively? Or did they get in the way?

All the RAMMP conversations essentially focused on one question: "Do we really need to keep doing these things the same way?" These meetings encouraged a mind-set for continual questioning. At the end, in a full house session with all the subteams present, participants demonstrated their ideas for change directly to the business leaders.

We encouraged business leaders to say "yes" most of the time. We wanted them to involve and engage our employees, because we knew that the people closest to the work had the best ideas for productivity improvement. If people saw that business leaders listened to, and implemented, their ideas, they would behave differently. Partly for that reason, we started with the "low-hanging fruit"—the safe and easy changes, which business leaders could accept and which would yield quick and comfortable success.

At one manufacturing plant, for instance, when people took portable computers home, they needed elaborate security clearance requests—until 6 P.M., when the security guard went home, and they could freely take their computers home. This inconsistency had bothered many people in the plant for years, but no one had ever felt safe bringing it up. Now they finally told the plant manager, "You don't have a security system, since we can walk out after 6 P.M. with the equipment. So let's eliminate the paperwork."

There's a natural temptation to blame people: "Who instituted that security system in the first place?" But that doesn't help anyone change. Instead, we tried deliberately to talk about the original security needs. Could we remove the system without side effects—or would some other old problem reappear? Once Work-Out removed bureaucratic artifacts like that ineffective security system, we used newsletters to let everyone know what we had accomplished. This helped pave the way for further innovation.

An old GE model had told us: "Ask your manager and learn." This new model suggested: "Look everywhere—above you, below you, beside you, and outside. Your manager may be learning from you."

When we need to cut cycle time, we now go to the workers who manage a particular process. We don't tell them how to do it. We give them a goal, such as cutting their cycle time by fifty percent. Then we say: "Do a Work-Out, do whatever you need to do, and come up with an answer. Their ideas are generally better than the plant managers' ideas, because they know the situation better.

The Payoff Matrix

One of the most valuable conversational tools at RAMMP meetings was a single matrix.

People posted their suggestions for improving "reports, approvals, meetings, measures, policies, and procedures" on this four-block grid. We wanted to identify ideas that would be easy to implement and have a big impact (Block 1). The results might show, for instance, that implementing a whole new computer system would be relatively easy, and produce the highest impact on the work.

After a session with this four-block grid, even if they disagreed with the final choice of priorities, everybody fully understood why the group picked the projects. We still use this matrix today, generally applying it to far more challenging issues.

Over time, we have learned to use all of the Work-Out tools, techniques, and processes in joint ventures and with major customers, to raise critical challenges for working together. Formerly, we had excluded key customers (like the railroads who purchase our locomotives) from these no-holds-barred sessions because we didn't want them to see all of our mistakes and problems. But we soon discovered that our customers already knew about those. So we began inviting them to attend Work-Out with us and talk about our problems together. This openness is a plus: I've heard large customers say, "That's exactly the kind of partner we want."

After the first couple of years of Work-Out, word began to get around within GE about its effectiveness. Now if there was a problem, people would say, "We ought to do Work-Out on this," instead of waiting for the manager to initiate a solution.

Stage Two: Best Practices

Work-Out's second phase began in 1990, when, to wring "NIH" (not invented here) from our culture, we began sending people outside our businesses, and outside the company, to find the best ideas. We changed incentives to reward people for sharing ideas instead of hoarding them.

Every time we launch anything new, we study what others are doing, and we keep our antennae up. We host numerous visits from customers, partners, and other outside organizations at Crotonville. We ask about their best practices. And we listen.

We introduced the exchange of best practices at key business meetings—starting with the most sen-

	Easy to accomplish	Difficult to accomplish
High impact on the organization	1	2
Low impact on the organization	3	4

ior executives of the company, who meet quarterly in the Corporate Executive Council, convened by GE CEO Jack Welch. At one session, a Wal-Mart manager described their seven-day learning cycle. Wal-Mart sends key sales managers out in the field every week, visiting their own stores and competitors' stores. They regroup at Benton, Arkansas, corporate headquarters every Friday night to compare notes. If they learn that a competitor is coming out with a new promotion, they can make the necessary decisions and announce a companywide countermove on Saturday.

"If Wal-Mart can do that," our people said, "why can't GE?" So the company instituted weekly "Quick Market Intelligence" (QMI) conferences on various topics. Some highlight critical sales issues; others deal with technology changes. People from Latin America, Asia, and Europe participate through tele- or videoconference.

Stage Three: Process Maps

By 1991, we focused on the fact that the companies that continually increased productivity had learned to pay attention to processes. This was new for GE, whose people traditionally focused on immediate goals (like getting product out the door by the end of the month). So we began to bring multifunctional teams together to learn process mapping techniques. These techniques revealed that, in our processes (like those of most businesses), as little as 5 to 15 percent of our activities added value to our products or services. Authorizations waited for two weeks in someone's in box. Contracts languished because someone was on vacation with no backup.

So the Work-Out sessions started bringing the people who affect a process together to ask: "How would we love our processes to work? And how can we get there?" As with RAMMP, we involved customers, adding their needs and priorities to the maps. When engineers predicted, "The customers will love this new feature," we wanted to hear what the customers actually thought—and not through the filter of a focus group.

Process mapping uncovered more subtle, pervasive bottlenecks, where (unlike RAMMP) people did not already perceive blockages. No one person or group has the full perspective. People are often stunned when they find out what happens after they hand a project over to the next part of the process.

We instituted "stretch goals" in process mapping: goals big enough to force people to think differently. For instance, we might say, "Cut your cycle time by fifty percent." People feel stunned at first: "How will I ever get there?" Then they see that they'll need to think differently. They may not reach the goal you've set, but they'll get much farther than if it were an incremental goal. Most people will not change unless they feel a sense of crisis. A leader must create that sense of urgency, so there is time to change before it's too late. But it's not enough to give employees the sense of crisis. You have to provide them with the tools, techniques, and processes to deal with it.

Stage Four: Change Acceleration

When I joined Work-Out as a team leader in 1991, we knew that our senior leaders had not been given enough tools and techniques to initiate, lead, and manage change. Work-Out was increasing our productivity, but we felt that by training senior leaders, we could move even more quickly toward our goals.

> Other key members of the Change Acceleration Process design team included Cathy Frierson and Amy Howard of the Crotonville team, plus Dave Ulrich of the University of Michigan, Ann Arbor, Mary Anne Devanna of Columbia University, and Jon Biel, Ron Gager, and Craig Schneier.

My first assignment was to develop a change management program. We pulled together a design team that included the Work-Out team, Steve Kerr, now the head of Crotonville, and several other outside consultants. We started, in 1992, with seven in-depth workshops for the four hundred most senior people in the company. In this Change Acceleration Process (CAP) we tried to demystify the subject of organizational change by providing a framework or model along with a series of tools or lenses that could be used to analyze an organization.

We asked these executive leaders to come in prepared to talk about an existing strategic, "must-do" change project in their organization, where even improvements of 1 percent would pay for the training. We included material on the importance of cultural change, and the power of new ways of thinking. We coached them to become champions for change, to articulate the case for change, to develop a vision for fundamental improvement, and to shape the vision in a way that helped everybody understand it and connect it to his or her own job.

We also shared several key tools that could be used to drive successful change. For instance, in one exercise, the leaders identified all the key stakeholders who must be on board for a change process to succeed. Then they had to analyze the list: "How much does each stakeholder support this idea today? And why? Where do they need to be? What's our plan for leading them in the right direction?"

Over the years, as new CAP courses continued, we developed a cadre of "follow-through" coaches for CAP graduates. These "super facilitators," trained in CAP techniques, were charged to work with teams on an ongoing basis. Around 1994, we began bringing customers into CAP sessions. Now, when many industrial customers buy from GE, they share in our own training. Our salespeople have explicitly become facilitators to our customers' success, sometimes taking on the role that a management consultant might fill elsewhere.

Stage Five: Strategic Initiatives

Having come this far, we set up a series of in-depth initiatives, focusing on highly significant issues: developing new competence or dealing with intractable problems. For instance, we had learned from our original best-practices work that successful companies need to continually introduce new products. GE's Corporate Initiatives Group focused on identifying and sharing the best practices for new product information (NPI).

Stage Six: Making Customers Winners

We began to share some of our integrated learning techniques with customers. Several GE businesses have "customer productivity programs," working with customers to increase the productivity of their operations. In some cases, we provide enough extra service to bill; otherwise, we are rewarded by better relationships and more capable business partners.

Stage Seven: Six Sigma Quality

In 1995, Jack Welch gave GE a major stretch goal: to be a "Six Sigma" company by the year 2000. GE's interest was stimulated after Larry Bossidy (CEO of Allied Signal and an ex-GE vice chairman) suggested it. Six Sigma Quality had been developed at Motorola; it's an integrated quality process that aims at achieving no more than 3.4 defects per million opportunities. The potential advantages are enormous. Customers are demanding higher quality. Competitors have already moved in this direction. And the cost savings for GE could be billions of dollars per year.

The Six Sigma methodology, known as DMAIC (Define, Measure, Analyze, Improve, and Control) brings a rigor to identifying defects, correcting them, and controlling work processes as a whole. One key component is training. Every professional in GE will go through Six Sigma training, covering the DMAIC processes, along with statistical and change management tools. Each GE business has a quality leader; a quality control council that meets quarterly to share best practices; and our measures and rewards include quality objectives. We're building on everything we've learned to make Six Sigma work.

The Integrated Learning Process

We have not discarded any earlier activities. If the original Work-Out felt like weeding a garden, we've learned that weeds grow back. There are always processes to be mapped, best practices to learn, and new applications for our CAP.

Some visitors say they hope to duplicate our integrated learning process within a year or two. We wish them luck. Cultural change takes twice as long as you expect. In a sense, our learning effort started in 1981, when Jack Welch became chairman of GE. Twenty years from now, our approach will still be evolving.

If people from another company asked me how to duplicate our programs, I would not advise them to copy our approach verbatim. Instead, I would emphasize four key lessons that have emerged from our integrated learning experience, and that guide everything we do:

- Involve and engage all your employees, as well as customers, partners, and suppliers. Be boundaryless in this engagement; work to develop win-win solutions across levels, functions, businesses, and companies.
- Identify and transfer best practices from inside and outside the company. Keep your antennae tuned to anyone who can help you be more productive and successful.
- Integrate these initiatives with key human resource practices. You need to ensure that you staff, train, measure, and reward consistently with your business objectives.
- Set "stretch goals." Once employees are forced to let go of the existing conventional wisdom, they can be creative and innovative, as they design new approaches. We are constantly raising the bar.

Index

Acme Minerals Extraction Co. case, 22–25
action steps, 18–19, 20
advice, 20–21
Aldrich, Howard, 6
AOL-Time Warner, 7
approvals, in RAMMP matrix, 39

Beckhard, Richard, 12–13
behavioral science, 12
best practices, 40–41, 42
blame, culture of, 8
Bossidy, Lawrence, 42
bottom-up change, 16, 17

capabilities, learning, 30–31
change
    overview, 4
    Acme Minerals Extraction Co. case, 22–25
    action steps, 18–19, 20
    advice on, 20–21
    communication about, 19–20
    compliance vs. commitment, 33
    consistency of, 18
    cultural perspective, 7–8, 11, 19
    dimensions of, 15–18
    GE productivity case, 38–42
    inertia, organizational, 4, 6, 12, 13
    leadership and, 32–37
    learning new roles, 10
    limiting processes, 29–31
    localization of, 18
    meaning of, 7, 34–35
    mistakes, avoiding, 19–20
    pacing of, 15
    political perspective, 7, 10–11
    power structure and, 11
    pressures to, 6
    processes of, 16
    Proctor & Gamble case, 8–11, 16, 17
    profound, 34–35
    resistance to, 4, 6, 8, 12, 34
    Rosewell case, 18
    scope of, 15
    sources of, 16
    stage models of, 11–15
    strategic design perspective, 7, 10–11, 18, 19
    success and failure of initiatives, 6, 28–29
    temporal sequencing of, 17–18, 20
    unanticipated consequences, 6–7, 10
Change Acceleration Process (CAP), 41–42
coalition-building, 20
commitment vs. compliance, 33, 38
communication of change initiatives, 19–20
community builders, 36
compliance vs. commitment, 33, 38
consistency of change, 18
continuous change, 14, 15
Corporate Initiatives Group (GE), 42
cross-functional teams, 23–24
cultural lens/perspective, 7–8, 11, 19
customer productivity programs, 42

The Dance of Change (Senge), 14
Daniels, Bill, 22–25
data gathering, and change, 12
Devanna, Mary Anne, 13
dimensions of change, 15–18
DMAIC (Define, Measure, Analyze, Improve, Control), 42

emergent change, 16, 17
equilibrium, 12
evolutionary model, 13–14
executive leaders, role of, 36–37
exhortation, change by, 19

failure of change initiatives, 6, 28–29
Flickinger, Burt, III, 9
force field, 12
future state, 12, 16

General Electric (GE), 38–42
geographic grouping structure, 8–9
Gerstner, Lou, 6, 8, 11
Ghasn, Carlos, 8
global business units (GBUs), 8–9
goals, stretch, 42
growth patterns, 29

Harris, Reuben T., 12–13
hero-CEO, myth of, 32–33
hierarchical authority, 36

IBM, 8
incremental change, 15, 17
inertia, organizational, 4, 6, 12, 13
information gathering, 12
initiating-sustaining-redesigning model, 14–15
innovation, 13, 36
integrated learning process, 42
interests of subunits, 11
internal networkers, 36

Jager, Durk, 8, 9, 11, 16
Japan, 16
Jimenez, Karen, 22–25

Keller, David, 23–24
King, Martin Luther, Jr., 35

Kotter, John, 28

labor/management divide, 22–25
Lafley, Alan G., 9–10
leadership, 13, 32–37
"The Leadership of Profound Change" (Senge), 32–37
learning capabilities, 30–31
learning organization approach, 14, 30–31
learning process, integrated, 42
Lewin, Kurt, 11–12, 14
"The Life Cycle of Typical Change Initiatives" (Senge), 28–31
limiting processes, in change initiatives, 29–31
localization of change, 18
local line leaders, 35–36

Marketing Development Organizations (MDOs), 9
matrix, payoff, 40
matrix, RAMMP, 38–40
Matthews, Dave, 24
Maturana, Humberto, 31
measures, in RAMMP matrix, 39
meetings, in RAMMP matrix, 39
mergers and acquisitions, 7
middle management, 10
middle-up-down change pattern, 16
mistakes, avoiding, 19–20
Motorola, 42

networkers, internal, 36
network leaders, 36
Nissan, 8
Nonaka, Ikujiro, 16

"Organization 2005" change initiative, 8–11
organizational culture, changing, 7–8, 11
organizational development (OD), 12
organizational inertia, 4, 6, 12, 13

pacing of change, 15
payoff matrix, 40
Pepper, John, 8
Peterson, Jennifer, 24
Pettigrew, Andrew, 18
pilot teams, 14
planned change, 16, 17
policies and procedures, in RAMMP matrix, 39
political lens/perspective, 7, 11
population ecology paradigm, 6, 13
power structures, and change, 7, 11
present state, 12–13
processes of change, 16
process maps, 41
Proctor & Gamble, 8–11, 16, 17
procurement policy, 19
product division structure, 8–9
productivity, 41, 42
profound change, 34–35
punctuated change, 15

Quick Market Intelligence (QMI), 41

radical change, 15, 16–17
RAMMP matrix, 38–40
redesigning, 14–15
reengineering, failure of, 28
refreezing, 11–12
reinforcing growth processes, 29
reports, in RAMMP matrix, 38–39
resistance to change, 4, 6, 8, 12, 34
retention, 13
rethinking, 14–15
Rosewell case, 18

scope of change, 15
selection, 13
Senge, Peter, 14, 16
sigmoidal growth patterns, 29
Six Sigma Quality, 42
sources of change, 16
SPITS ("select a problem and implement a tailored solution"), 23–24
stage metaphor, 13
stage models of change, 11–15
stakeholders, 41–42
strategic design lens/perspective, 7, 11, 18, 19
"The Strategy That Wouldn't Travel" (Beer), 22–25
stretch goals, 42
subunit interests, 11
success and failure of change initiatives, 6, 28–29
sustaining, in change model, 14–15
systemic forces, and change initiatives, 13
systems perspective, 14

teams, cross-functional, 23–24
teams, pilot, 14
temporal sequencing of change, 17–18, 20
theater metaphor, 13
Tichy, Noel M., 13
Time Warner, 7
top-down change, 16, 17
total quality management (TQM), 28
training, at GE, 38–42
"transformation," 34
transformational leader, 13
transition state, 12–13

unanticipated consequences, 6–7, 10
unfreezing-change-refreezing model, 11–12

variation-selection-retention model, 13

Wal-Mart, 40–41
Weick, Karl, 17
Welch, John F., Jr. (Jack), 16, 42
Work-Outs program, 38–40

MANAGING FOR THE FUTURE

Organizational Behavior & Processes

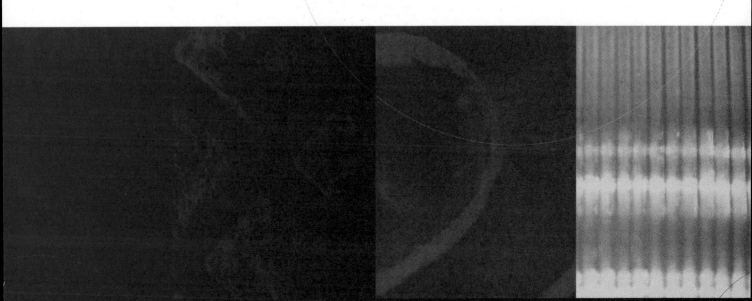

MANAGING FOR THE FUTURE
Organizational Behavior & Processes, Third Edition

Deborah Ancona
Sloan School of Management
Massachusetts Institute of Technology

John Van Maanen
Sloan School of Management
Massachusetts Institute of Technology

Thomas A. Kochan
Sloan School of Management
Massachusetts Institute of Technology

D. Eleanor Westney
Sloan School of Management
Massachusetts Institute of Technology

Maureen Scully
Graduate School of Management
Simmons College

Dedicated to those who have inspired us to try to be better students and teachers.
Special thanks to: Professor Jack Barbash • Professor Arthur H. Gladstein • Professor Marius B. Jansen • Professor Joanne Martin • Professor Edgar H. Schein

---

VP/Editorial Director
Jack W. Calhoun

VP/Editor-in-Chief
Michael P. Roche

Senior Publisher
Melissa S. Acuña

Executive Editor
John Szilagyi

Senior Developmental Editor
Judith O'Neill

Marketing Manager
Jacquelyn Carrillo

Production Editor
Emily Gross

Manufacturing Coordinator
Rhonda Utley

Compositor
Trejo Production

Printer
Von Hoffmann Press, Inc.
Frederick, MD

Internal Designer
Bethany Casey

Cover Designer
Bethany Casey

Photographs
©PhotoDisc

Design Project Manager
Bethany Casey

COPYRIGHT ©2005
by South-Western, a division of Thomson Learning.
Thomson Learning™ is a trademark used herein under license.

Printed in the United States of America
1 2 3 4 5 07 06 05 04 03

For more information contact
South-Western College Publishing,
5191 Natorp Boulevard,
Mason, Ohio, 45040
Or you can visit our Internet site at:
http://www.swlearning.com

ALL RIGHTS RESERVED
No part of this work covered by the copyright hereon may be reproduced or used in any form or by any means—graphic, electronic, or mechanical, including photocopying, recording, taping, Web distribution or information storage and retrieval systems—without the written permission of the publisher.

For permission to use material from this text or product, contact us by
Tel: (800) 730-2214
Fax: (800) 730-2215
http://www.thomsonrights.com

Library of Congress Control Number: 2003113908
ISBN 0-324-05575-7

Contents

Organizational Action in Complex Environments

Overview		4

Core

Class Note	**Organizations and Their Environments:** **Sets, Stakeholders, and Organizational Fields**	8
	The Strategic Design Perspective: The "Organization Set" 8	
	The Political Perspective: The Stakeholders Model 13	
	The Cultural Perspective: Institutional Fields 17	
	Integrating Perspectives: Seeing the Environment Through Three Lenses 22	
	References 22	
Case	**RU-486: The Handling by Roussel-Uclaf of a Double Dilemma**	23
	The Company 23	
	The Product 23	
	Discovery 23	
	How It Works 23	
	Testing RU-486 24	
	Its Medical Advantages 24	
	The French Government's Authorization 24	
	The Debate: Proceed to Market, or Not? 25	
	The Ethical Issues 25	
	Public Opinion and Advocacy Groups 25	
	The Position of Hoechst 26	
	Potential Internal Problems from the Sale of RU-486 26	
	Issues in Worldwide Distribution Strategy 26	
	The Decision 27	
	Reactions 28	
	The Government's Order 28	
	Reactions 28	
	RU-486 in the Rest of Europe 29	
	RU-486 in Asia 30	
	RU-486 in the United States 30	

Index

Overview

This module takes us into complex organizational terrain: the organization's external environment, which potentially means everything outside the organization's boundaries that could affect it in some way. Finding one's way in such an extensive and complex landscape requires a map or, more accurately, a set of maps. Just as the three lenses allow different but complementary views of the organization itself, so each lens provides a distinctive map of the environment and a different set of tools for interacting with it.

With the strategic design lens, we look outside the organization and see a resource environment composed of organizations that supply needed inputs and constitute a market for its outputs, that have the formal power to regulate its resource environment, and that compete with it for inputs and for output markets (the organization set model). The political lens provides a view of an environment of external stakeholders that have their own interests to serve and that have a stake in the organization's actions. And the cultural lens focuses on an institutional environment of values, norms, shared beliefs and mindsets, and perceptions. As the case we use in this module illustrates, using all three lenses provides a much richer analysis of the complex interactions between an organization and its environment than does any single lens used alone and a broader set of tools to help you take effective action in the complex environments that organizations face today.

Such tools are increasingly important. Interacting effectively with entities outside its formal boundaries demands an organization's managerial attention to a greater extent each year and is likely to become even more important in the future. The outsourcing of an expanding range of activities and the trends toward closer relationships with customers continue to increase the number and, in many cases, the intensity of networks with external social actors. In addition, a growing number of companies are working to expand their external networking in the context of "nonmarket strategies," that is, strategies for influencing the regulatory and institutional environment. This effort includes alliances with competitors to establish product standards, cooperation with nongovernmental organizations (NGOs) on "greening" and on sustainable development, and the establishment or expansion of units dedicated to influencing regulators (Microsoft, for example, greatly expanded its activities in Washington, D.C., in the aftermath of the antitrust suit brought against it by the Department of Justice). Finally, the globalization of business means not only that more and more firms are operating in multiple national environments but also that a growing number of the external organizations with which they deal are themselves also multinational in nature.

The Class Note in this module, "Organizations and Their Environments: Sets, Stakeholders, and Organizational Fields," provides an overview of the three models of the environment and a concrete illustration of each in the expansion of a Japanese automobile manufacturer into a new environment, the United States. The Case, "RU-486," gives you an opportunity to use these frameworks and explore their implications for action. The case is about the dilemma facing the company that developed RU-486, the abortion-inducing drug that provides an alternative to surgical abortion. The issue of abortion is a difficult and emotional one for many people, and the external environment has polarized on one side into groups and organizations that believe that the company has an ethical obligation to suppress the product and on the other side into those that are convinced of the company's ethical obligation to bring the product to market. The company faces a difficult environment, which seems to hold negative consequences, whatever it decides to do. Its decision is complicated by the fact that the company, Roussel-Uclaf, has sold more than half its shares to the giant international chemical corporation, Hoechst, which is headquartered in Germany and is worried about the potential impact of Roussel's decision on its subsidiaries throughout the world. How Roussel's managers analyze their environment and how much ability they have to influence it are both crucial to the actions they can take. The case looks at the environment first in France, the company's home country, as the company faces the initial decision about whether to bring the drug to market, and then at the environment in the United States, as Roussel faces the challenge of whether to take RU-486 into markets outside its home country. One of the key issues for discussion in the case is how effectively you think the top management of Roussel analyzes and manages in this difficult environmental context.

The purposes of this module are therefore:

- To develop an understanding of the organization's environment as a critically important aspect of management—as a source of

resources for organizational action, constraints on it, and shared interpretations and evaluations of action.
- To understand both how managers can make the environment work for them in solving complex problems, *and* how the environment limits the scope of managerial action.
- To understand and develop an ability to use models of the organizational environment that go beyond the usual strategic design model of the resource environment to include the political perspective's stakeholders model and the cultural perspective's institutional field model.
- To apply the three models of the environment to a particularly complex case, and thereby learn how to work with them and explore their action implications.
- To realize how environments in the same industry and for the same organization can differ across countries.

Assignment Summary

Come to class prepared to discuss the following questions regarding the case:

1. Do you think that Edouard Sakiz (chair of the Roussel-Uclaf group) did a good job or a poor job of handling the decision about marketing RU-486 in France? Do you see him as effective or ineffective in this environmental context?
2. What aspects of the environment do you think were (and should have been) the most important in making the decision about RU-486 in France?
3. Is the environment for RU-486 in the United States significantly different from what it faced in France? Can the company's leaders "manage" this environment?
4. What general "lessons" can you draw from this case? Give other examples of complex and contradictory pressures an organization might experience.

Organizational Action in Complex Environments

CORE

Module 9

Organizations and Their Environments

Sets, stakeholders, and organizational fields

What lies outside an organization is often just as important for managers as what is going on inside. Indeed, it is impossible to understand an organization well without understanding the environment in which it operates. Taking effective action in organizations therefore often involves managing the organization's interactions with its *organizational environment*—that is, with external social actors, especially other organizations, that are important for its survival and success. But just as different perspectives bring focus to organizations, so different but complementary perspectives help in assessing the organizational environment.

Each of the three perspectives on organizations—the strategic design, political, and cultural perspectives—offers a distinctive way of analyzing the organizational environment. Each highlights different elements of the environment; each provides useful insights on how managers can "manage" the environment, the limits to managing it, and how understanding the environment can help in dealing with change and the lack of change in the organization.

The Strategic Design Perspective: The "Organization Set"

When we look out at the organizational environment through the strategic design lens, we see a *resource environment*. The strategic design perspective sees the organization as an "input/throughput/output system" that takes inputs from the environment, adds value to them in some way, and conveys the resulting product or service to clients or customers so that it gains the resources to continue the process. The environment, therefore, is seen primarily as the source for needed inputs and the market for outputs. One approach to mapping this resource environment is in terms of its attributes, especially its stability and predictability. Organizations in uncertain, unstable, or resource-poor environments require more flexible designs and need to devote more of their internal resources to monitoring the environment than do organizations that enjoy more stable, predictable, or munificent conditions. One criticism of this approach, however, is its deterministic nature: it treats the environment as a set of given conditions that managers have virtually no means of altering. The major managerial task in terms of the environment, in this context, is to understand the constraints environment imposes on the organization.

Therefore, we shall adopt another approach to mapping the resource environment, one that focuses on the organizations and other social actors that populate it and engage in direct transactions with one's own organization, especially the organizations that supply required inputs and provide and support a market for its outputs. The chief managerial task in terms of the environment then becomes designing relationships and interactions with key external actors that efficiently and effectively enable the organization to achieve its strategic goals. Such an approach has the potential for enabling managers to be far more proactive in their approach to the environment than does a model that portrays the resource environment as high or low on a set of attributes.

But which organizations are the "key" external actors in the resource environment? One useful tool for mapping the environment is the *organization set model*, which maps the resource environment primarily in terms of the input set and the output set (Evan, 1966). The input set includes the organizations that provide required inputs (materials, components, human resources, financial resources, technology, and knowledge). The output set includes not only the customers for the organization's output of goods and services but also the distributors, retailers, service organizations, transport and logistics organizations, and so on that provide whatever infrastructure is required for getting the output to the customer. In many cases the output set also includes those businesses that get payments from the customer to the organization (e.g., banks, credit card companies, collection agencies, etc.).

Two additional elements make up the organization set. One is the regulatory set, which includes the organizations with formal authority to regulate the organization's own internal processes (such as the agencies that oversee employee health and safety, or financial reporting) and those that affect the size of the input and output sets (such as the agencies that issue operating licenses) and the kind of relationships that the organization is allowed to build with them (such as fair trade and antitrust agencies). The other is the set of competitors. Because the strategic design perspective focuses primarily on the relationships that the organization builds with the social actors in its environment, the organization set model looks at competitors and potential competitors with whom the organization interacts (for example, through industry associations or through strategic alliances). Increasingly, large corporations in particular have complex, multidimensional relationships with other large companies. Canon, for example, is simultaneously an important part of Hewlett-Packard's input set, supplying engines for most HP printers, and a leading competitor. Each firm devotes considerable resources to monitoring and managing the relationship between them.

Figure 9.1 portrays a simple organization set for an organization that sends its products primarily to distributors and to a few large direct-sales customer organizations. Little overlap exists between the input and output sets. If we were to look inside such an organization, we would probably find that each relationship is managed by a specialized organizational unit: a procurement department deals with suppliers, a subunit of the personnel department deals with relationships with business schools, executive search or "head-hunter" firms, and any other sources of employees with which the organization develops direct relationships. The financial inputs are handled by the corporate treasurer's office, and the technology inputs are handled by a department of the research and development laboratory. One of the strategic tasks of each of these units is to be alert to changes in the part of the environment with which they deal—the rise of new organizations, the decline of current members of the set—and to be prepared to respond quickly to such changes. But a more important, and more difficult, task is to improve the relationships and interactions in ways that help the strategic goals of the organization. For example, in dealing with regulatory agencies, an organization may set up a specialized department in an organization to interact with a regulatory agency on compliance. (In Figure 9.1, government agency A, which we'll assume, regulates working conditions and worker safety, such as the U.S. Occupational Health and Safety Agency, would interact with a health, safety, and environment department in the company that has responsibility for ensuring compliance with such regulations.) The company might also set up a lobbying unit in the national or state capital to interact with government agencies and to shape proactively the legislation and regulations that affect its activities and its input and output sets, in order to obtain more favorable tax treatment of certain kinds of expenditures on worker health and safety, for example, or to broaden the range of steps that are accepted as compliant with regulations.

In traditional models of the organization, analysts assumed that the organization tried to shield itself from uncertainties and instability in its environment by protecting its core activities through the use of "distancing" mechanisms such as buffering, stockpiling of inventories, and specialized boundary-spanning personnel whose job was to stand between the organization set and the people in the organization carrying out key functions (see Scott, 1992, chap. 8). In the "new model" of the organization, internal activities are more directly linked to important elements of the organization set—more densely "networked"—as key suppliers are integrated into manufacturing processes, for example, and "lead users" are drawn into product design. The quest for autonomy of the older model gives way to the recognition of interdependence and to the challenges of managing interdependent networks effectively.

What tools does this perspective provide for managing networks with external actors? They are the same basic tools that the strategic design perspective provides for internal organization design: grouping, linking, and aligning. The principal grouping tool is of course the establishment of a specialized unit or department responsible for managing a particular relationship or set of relationships. For example, in terms of suppliers, it could be a supplier logistics unit or a procurement department, with subunits that handle particular components or deal with specific supplier companies.

As in the case of internal organization design, it is important to look beyond the obvious formal structure of grouping tools. Creating specialized units is only one way of dealing with external actors; linking mechanisms are also extremely important tools. The array of linking mechanisms include the following:

- Liaison or integrator positions (for example, an individual designated to work with widget suppliers, or, in the case of a particularly important supplier, an individual charged with managing the relationship with the Acme Widget Company)
- Temporary boundary-spanning groups (for example, a joint task force with a supplier or set of suppliers to implement a joint quality program, or co-development teams with suppliers to develop a new component or system)
- Permanent boundary-spanning groups (for example, a suppliers association like that organized by Toyota or Nissan, to which all regular suppliers belong and that holds regular information-sharing meetings)
- IT systems (such as computer-aided design, or CAD, systems that are shared with suppliers, or shared production tracking systems that enable suppliers to provide inputs in a timely fashion)

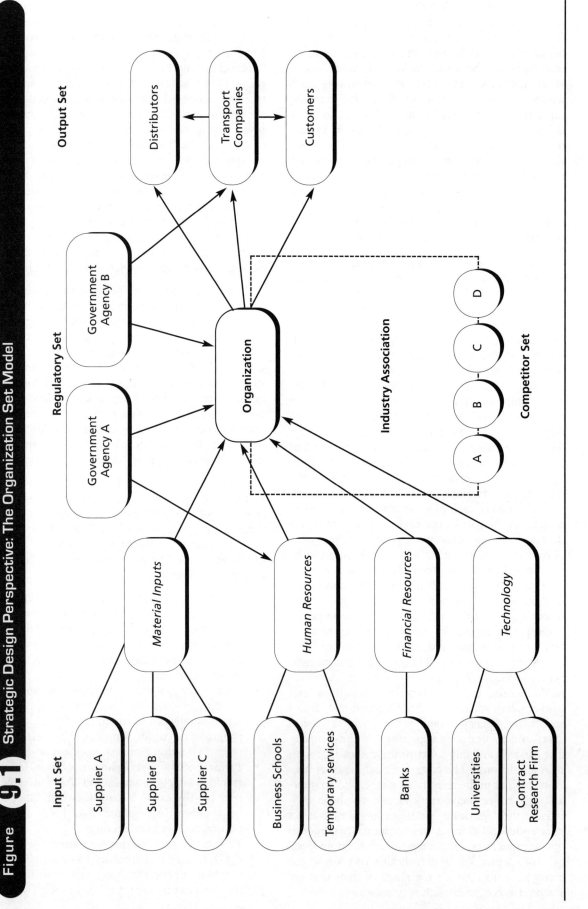

Figure 9.1 Strategic Design Perspective: The Organization Set Model

In addition, several of the alignment mechanisms that work inside an organization are also useful for developing effective relationships with key organizations in the environment, including:

- Performance measurement systems (shared ways of measuring the quality of the relationship, such as defect ratios for suppliers or service quality measures shared with customers)
- Incentive systems (ways of sharing additional returns generated by extra efforts and commitment of resources from organizations in the input or output sets—for example, agreements for higher-volume purchases or exclusive supply contracts with a supplier who reaches certain quality and cost targets)
- Resource allocation (commitment of additional resources in the form of personnel, technology, and even financial resources to help "strategic partners" achieve certain performance targets or to survive unexpected crises—for example, Toyota often helps key suppliers to get access to preferential financing for investments in new capital equipment)
- Human resource development (shared training programs, as when the company's key suppliers and customers attend courses together)

Proactive management of an organization set is often most observable when an organization enters a new environment, as a result either of entering a new business or of expanding internationally. This type of change forces managers to ask the following questions: Is the input set already in place? If not, what role should our company play in trying to develop it? Is the output set in place? Can we manage this input set and output set with the same kinds of systems that we use for our current set? What, if any, changes in our design should we make to develop the most efficient and effective relationships with the key social actors in the organization set? The following example of Nissan's establishment of manufacturing operations in the United States provides a concrete example of the strategic design perspective on the environment.

Nissan's Establishment of an Automobile Factory in the United States: An Organization Set Approach

By the late 1970s, Japanese auto firms faced rising protectionist pressures in the United States, their largest single export market. The Japanese and U.S. governments negotiated a set of so-called voluntary export restrictions, holding Japanese auto manufacturers to the share of the U.S. market that they held at the time of negotiation. Honda, the number three auto company in Japan in terms of domestic market share, was the first to decide on a strategy of producing automobiles in the United States, and it opened a plant at the site of its existing motorcycle plant in Marysville, Ohio, in 1982. Nissan was the second firm to commit itself to local production, deciding on a site in Tennessee in 1980 and beginning production of trucks there in 1983 and autos in 1985.

Once Nissan decided on a strategy of local U.S. production, it faced several organizational challenges in transferring its production capabilities to a new location so as to maintain the quality and reliability of the vehicles it produced. Several of these involved its organization set. The output set—distribution and sales organizations—had already been built up over two decades of sales in the United States. The challenges it faced fell within the other parts of the organization set: the regulatory set, and especially the input set:

(a) *Regulatory Agencies:* For Nissan a key set of regulatory agencies included the federal Environmental Protection Agency and related state-level agencies engaged in setting emission standards and pollution control standards.

(b) *Source of Managers:* Nissan needed managers who could understand and transfer the key elements of Nissan's production system to the United States, could work effectively with U.S. suppliers, and manage a U.S. labor force.

(c) *Supplier Network:* Nissan, like other Japanese producers, produced a relatively low proportion of its components and subsystems in-house. In Japan it relied on a network of suppliers with which it worked closely in new product design (in a system of "simultaneous engineering" whereby suppliers worked on new components simultaneously with Nissan's design of a new model) and in inventory management (suppliers shipped parts to Nissan plants on an "as-needed" or "just-in-time" basis, which contributed both to holding down inventory costs and to ensuring quality).

(d) *Source of Workers:* Nissan's system of building in quality required workers who could analyze problems using fairly sophisticated methods of statistical quality control and who could work in teams, doing a variety of tasks, rather than in a single individual position in a factory where quality control was the domain of engineers.

Nissan chose to deal with these issues as follows:

(a) *Regulatory Agencies:* Nissan set up a research and development (R&D) organization in 1983 in Michigan to provide Nissan engineers with a better linkage to U.S. regulatory agencies and a better capacity for working with those agencies and finding out what changes were contemplated in U.S. environmental and emissions requirements. It chose to establish this center in Michigan because the concentration of the U.S. auto firms there produced a large number of experienced engineers who understood the industry, had good networks with regulatory authorities, and who, due to the down-sizing of U.S. auto firms, were often eager to find good employment in their field.

(b) *Managers:* Nissan hired a former Ford executive who had risen through the manufacturing side of Ford to become its vice president for body and assembly by the time he retired from the company. He brought with him a number of former Ford executives to form the core of his management team.

(c) *Supplier Network:* Nissan embarked on a major campaign to identify and work with American suppliers who were willing and able to meet Nissan requirements. In addition, a number of Japanese suppliers to Nissan set up their own branch plants in the United States. Finally, the supplier network of Nissan in the United States stretched across borders to include some suppliers in Japan who shipped components to Tennessee. By the late 1980s, as production expanded in the Tennessee plant, Nissan realized that its U.S. suppliers faced great difficulties in working closely with Nissan design engineers back in Tokyo in order to improve the coordination between component development and new car design. Therefore in 1988 Nissan expanded the mandate of its Michigan R&D center to include working with U.S. suppliers in the development of components and subsystems. Nissan planned eventually to build an R&D organization in the United States that could design new vehicles for the U.S. market and coordinate the production links with the factory and with suppliers.

(d) *Workers:* Nissan set up a system whereby job applicants had to undergo unpaid preemployment training in a specially design external training program, funded in cooperation with the state government of Tennessee, before being considered for a job at Nissan. This training was part time, so that it could be combined with other jobs. This training both built up the skills of new recruits before they entered the company and enabled Nissan to be extremely selective in the quality and commitment of its workforce.

Nissan's recognition of the critical role of its organization set in maintaining its competitive advantage in its new setting and its skill in developing the organizational systems for managing that set were critical elements of its success in its U.S. setting.

The Political Perspective: The Stakeholders Model

The political perspective's focus on power, interests, influence, coalition-building, and negotiation can be extended beyond the formal boundaries of the organization with the concept of *external stakeholders*. The term *stakeholders*, which today has entered the basic vocabulary of businesspeople, lies at the core of a political perspective on the organizational environment. Stakeholders are the social actors (meaning groups of individuals, or other organizations) who are affected by an organization's activities; that is, they have a *stake* in its operations.

Often a distinction is made between internal stakeholders—those who are formally members of the firm—and external stakeholders. This distinction is extremely useful in many ways, but it can be hard to maintain rigorously, because many internal stakeholders hold multiple stakeholder identities. Employees, for example, are internal stakeholders, but as residents of their local community they also have other and potentially conflicting interests as external stakeholders. For example, as employees they may have a strong stake in the expansion of the production facilities of their company, but if plant expansion means the company builds on green space or parks enjoyed by community residents, even employees may feel a conflict of interest between their roles. Some employees may also have external stakeholder identities as members of a union; others (especially top managers) may be shareholders. It is not only the internal stakeholder who can have multiple identities. Some external organizations also play multiple stakeholder roles. For example, in enterprises that are wholly or partly state-owned (such as Roussel-Uclaf of France in the RU-486 case that follows), government may be simultaneously an important customer, a shareholder, and a regulator. It may also have a strong stake in the survival, if not the profitability, of the enterprise, because its leaders want to maintain a national presence in an industry.

In the stakeholder model, analyses tend to focus on the following key variables:

- Interests (What does each set of stakeholders want? How clearly defined are those interests? What are the priorities assigned to those interests, and can priorities be altered?);
- Power and influence (What is the basis of power or influence of each set of stakeholders over the organization?)

External stakeholders can include unions, shareholders, creditors such as banks, governments, local communities, customers and suppliers, and even the general public. Figure 9.2 presents a simple stakeholders model of an organization, but it should not be taken as a generic template applicable in all settings. Different organizations have different sets of external stakeholders. The external stakeholders of a family firm, for example, often include family members, even if they are not formal owners (for example, the children of the owner of a family firm may be external stakeholders, even if they neither have an ownership share nor hold positions in the firm). In a town that has one or two large companies that make up the main part of the tax and employment base, both the local community and the local government may be major stakeholders in those companies. If those same companies have operations in a large city with a diversified employment base, however, it may well be that neither local community nor the city government has a significant stake in their operations.

The list of external stakeholders sometimes includes the same categories of organizations (suppliers and customers) as mapped into the organization set model of the strategic design perspective. Even when the categories populating the map of the external environment in the two perspectives overlap considerably, however, both the focus and the modes of taking effective action with regard to them differ. The organization set model focuses on resource flows; the stakeholders model focuses on interests and influence. A supplier of an important component may be an important member of the organization set, for example, but it may not be a stakeholder if it supplies that component to many firms and has little stake in whether the organization continues to buy from it. Similarly, customers may also be stakeholders if few other providers of the particular goods or services produced by a firm are available, but if they have many alternatives for the good or service, they may have no stake at all in that particular firm.

One of the major contributions of the political perspective on the environment is to draw attention to how internal stakeholders can involve external stakeholders in organizational decisions and actions. The key tools for action in organization-environment relations, highlighted in this model, include the following:

- *Mobilization* of the interests of external stakeholders
- *Coalition-building* between internal and external stakeholders and among external stakeholders
- *Cooptation*, as one stakeholder or set of stakeholders gets others to accept its own agenda, either through persuasion or through offering to further their interests in some way

In general, external stakeholders have a lower stake in the organization than do its internal

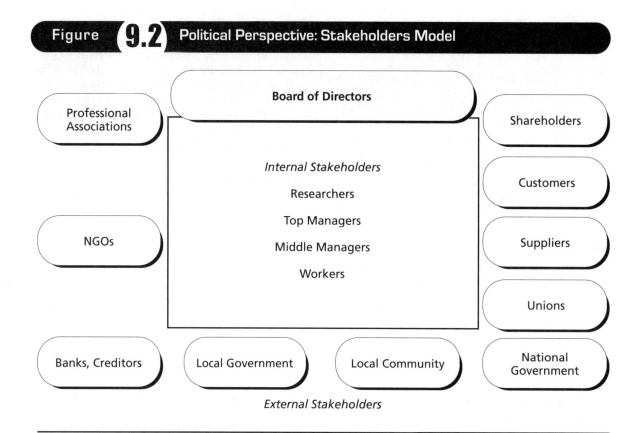

Figure 9.2 Political Perspective: Stakeholders Model

stakeholders (though exceptions would pertain to specific issues or actions of the organization). However, because they have potential influence over the organization, external stakeholders can use that influence to obtain outcomes desired by a particular set of internal stakeholders. This occasion can be as simple as the case of a marketing group inviting a lead customer to voice complaints about a product directly to the engineering group, in order to influence the features of the next generation of products (an example of mobilization). It might also be as complex as the case in which a local plant manager, alarmed by a company decision to close her plant, carefully passes the information along to local government officials and local activists, who thereupon build a coalition to pressure the company to keep the plant open. Another kind of action is to change the scale and nature of the stake that a particular external stakeholder holds in the organization. For example, defense contractors that manufacture complex weapons systems often routinely hire senior military officers and Defense Department officials for lucrative management positions after they retire from public service. Strategic design reasons explain why companies recruit these individuals; such people have deep knowledge of key elements of the organization set. Political reasons are also involved, however; the prospect of getting a good postretirement job creates an additional interest for public service officials and officers in seeing that the company prospers (cooptation).

The stake held by external stakeholders in an organization can involve a number of specific interests. A local government, for instance, has multiple interests in a large manufacturing company's plant located in its jurisdiction. Economic interests are obvious: the plant provides jobs and contributes to the tax base. The local government is also interested in the plant's being a "good" employer, treating its employees well, and encouraging them to participate in local activities.

It will be concerned with the plant not causing deterioration in the physical environment through effluents, noise pollution, or traffic congestion. Local government officials may also have an interest in the plant's managers boosting the municipality as a great location in which to do business, thereby contributing to the town's ability to attract investment from other companies.

These interests may have different priorities at different times. In an economic downturn, for example, the municipality may put a higher priority on the company's role as an employer than on what it is doing to the physical environment. Even stakeholders with a much narrower range of interests, such as shareholders, may still have more than one interest that can be mobilized. They may value both short-term gains in the share price and investments in future growth, and they may also value good corporate citizenship and ethical conduct. Internal stakeholders can leverage these multiple interests by trying to increase the priority that the external stakeholders assign to one particular interest.

When an external stakeholder wants to influence an organization, of course, it can use these same tactics: mobilizing a particular set of internal stakeholders, building a coalition with other external stakeholders with similar interests, or coopting key internal stakeholders. In today's organization, stakeholders are becoming more diverse and often draw the members of the organization more aggressively into recognizing and identifying with their interests. In other words, stakeholders are becoming more densely networked across the boundaries of the organization. They are also crossing boundaries in another sense. As firms become more global, their stakeholders also become more international. In some cases rivalries emerge between parallel sets of stakeholders in different countries (in discussions of whether the Canadian or the Brazilian factory gets closed, for example, or which government has jurisdiction over what activities). In other cases, such as environmental and pollution issues, stakeholders are themselves forming global coalitions. For example, in June 1995, Shell UK, a subsidiary of Royal Dutch Shell, one of the world's largest oil companies, announced that it would dispose of one of its obsolete oil rigs in the North Sea by sinking it in deeper waters. Greenpeace and other environmental groups organized large-scale protests in Europe, especially in Germany, where concerns about the pollution of the North Sea are strong. German consumers began to boycott Shell gas stations, to a point where Shell gas station owners in that country began to talk of suing Shell for damages in lost business. After insisting for weeks that sinking the oil rig did not threaten the environment, Shell suddenly announced that it would instead remove the rig to land and dispose of it there.

An organization set approach to a management issue, such as entering a new business or market or making a major change in the organizational structure, would ask questions similar to the following: Who are the key stakeholders who will be affected by this decision? What is their reaction likely to be? Can/should we make efforts to increase the involvement of the stakeholders favorably disposed to this move? How will it affect the relative power of current stakeholders? The Nissan example that we examined earlier through the strategic design lens of the organization set, also gives us an opportunity to see what can be added to our understanding by using the political lens of the stakeholders model.

Nissan's Establishment of an Automobile Factory in the United States: A Stakeholder's Approach

When Nissan decided to set up manufacturing in the United States in 1980, it was a time of considerable tension between Japan and the United States, especially in the auto industry, given the steady inroads Japanese producers had made on the Big Three (GM, Ford, and Chrysler) share of the market and the consequent loss of American jobs.

Nissan therefore set out to cultivate potential stakeholders in the United States. It began this approach early in its decision-making process, sending teams of its managers to the United States to negotiate with governors and investment offices in various states to find a favorable setting. It picked Tennessee for a number of reasons, but among them was the strong commitment of the governor to developing a good relationship with Nissan and to providing state support for the plant, and the fact that Tennessee was a state in which the labor force was not strongly unionized and that was distant both physically and culturally from the heartland of the auto industry. The local stakeholders—the local community, and the local and state governments—had a strong interest in the employment opportunities offered by the plant, the prospect that supporting industries would be attracted to Tennessee as a result of Nissan's location there, and the long-term improvement of the local tax base. They also had no competing direct stakes in U.S. auto plants, which were located in other states.

Nissan stated from the beginning that it did not want to have a unionized workforce on the grounds that unions introduced rigidities into the organization of work and fostered conflict between management and workers. Its preference for recruiting workers who had no previous auto industry experience was explained by Nissan as the company's desire to have workers with no preconceptions about how work should be carried out, but critics saw it as a way to screen out union members. In 1988, however, the United Automobile Workers (UAW) announced an organizing drive at Nissan in Tennessee, and in a six-month campaign closely watched by the media and by the government's Labor Relations Board, tried to persuade Nissan employees that their interests would be better served with the support of a union that would serve their interests by:

(a) Ensuring better safety conditions in the plant
(b) Protesting against line speed-ups and extended working hours
(c) Ensuring orderly promotions and equal opportunities within the plant

Nissan responded with a vigorous countercampaign, saying that the union was more interested in winning a victory against Nissan than in the interests of the workers themselves, and arguing that with an "open-door" policy whereby workers were encouraged to bring any grievances to management, workers did not need a union. Nissan argued that the union's efforts would lower productivity and make the plant less competitive. At the same time, Nissan announced plans for a major plant expansion. The proposal to join the union was defeated.

Nissan was able to reassure key stakeholders back in Japan that jobs would not be lost there because of production in the United States. Cars would still be exported to North America from Japan, but the limits set by the voluntary export restrictions meant that the only way the company could increase sales in the United States was to produce there. The fact that Japanese workers' interests were not negatively affected by the U.S. plant was significant for getting their cooperation in training American workers, and played a role in the success of the technology transfer from Japan to the United States.

Nissan also made great efforts to ensure that its distributors and customers received vehicles that met all the quality standards to which they were accustomed, with the added appeal of a locally produced vehicle, an appeal Nissan used in its advertising.

The interests of suppliers were more complicated to handle, and Nissan devoted much attention to negotiating with its suppliers. Some of Nissan's existing base of Japanese suppliers had a sufficient stake in Nissan that they were willing to set up subsidiaries in the United States to supply the Tennessee plant. But if Nissan worked exclusively with Japanese suppliers, even those who were providing jobs for Americans in their subsidiaries, the firm could lose credibility with other local stakeholders. Nissan also needed to build a set of U.S. suppliers, and it needed to persuade Japanese suppliers to share some of their know-how with U.S. counterparts. In some cases, Japanese suppliers set up joint ventures with U.S. partners (in steel, for example). In other cases, Japanese supplier companies were persuaded to engage in alliances with U.S. component manufacturers. Nissan was able to get extensive cooperation from key Japanese suppliers in part because there were no immediate plans to cut back procurement in Japan (a parallel with its ability to get cooperation from its Japanese workers in training Americans), and because Japanese suppliers realized that maintaining their long-term relationship with Nissan meant helping it succeed in its U.S. operations.

In short, Nissan made great efforts to build and maintain good relations with key external stakeholders, and to ensure that its stakeholders did not include organizations with interests that challenged Nissan's own interests significantly.

The Cultural Perspective: Institutional Fields

The cultural perspective of organizations insists that the shared ways in which people see and interpret their social context are as important to understanding organizations as resources and power. This perspective views organizations as embedded in a social system of expectations, taken-for-granted ways of doing things, status, and legitimacy, which exert a powerful influence on organizations and actors in organizations. The environment is a source of beliefs and values, rules of the game, interpretations and mindsets, fads and fashions shared across organizations that occupy the same social space.

Often when we want to understand and take action in a particular organization, we focus our attention exclusively on that organization. However, it is often more difficult than we realize to understand any single organization without looking at other organizations engaged in the same kinds of activities and occupy similar places in the environment. Managers and employees may try to differentiate their organization from others engaged in similar activities, and yet act on widely shared beliefs about what makes an organization successful. These beliefs lead them to accepted recipes, ways of doing things, and "fads," so that their organizations become more similar to others, rather than distinctive. In the last two decades, organizational researchers developed the concept of the *institutional field* to analyze the interactions between organizations and their environments, with a focus on shared beliefs, values, and mindsets.

The institutional field has been defined in one influential paper as "those organizations that, in the aggregate, constitute a recognized area of institutional life: key suppliers, resource and product consumers, regulatory agencies, and other organizations that produce similar services or products" (DiMaggio and Powell, 1983, p. 147). These organizations constitute a "social reference group" analogous to the social actors who act as a reference set for the individual, against whom individuals assess their own behavior and status and who serve as models. Organizations also have a reference group of other organizations against whom they measure their own performance and status and who serve as models of "best practice." Often these organizations are competitors, but they may also be members of the organization set (key suppliers or customers). The concept of the institutional field also includes the analogue of the "socializing agents" that we observe in cultural models of the organization: external agencies that propagate, disseminate, and pass along shared values and assumptions and that often impose some kind of sanctions on violators of norms and expectations. These cultural agents or "structuring agencies," as they are sometimes called in the context of the institutional field, include the business press and the business media, business schools, analysts, consultants, and professional, business, and industrial associations. The parallels with the categories of organizations in the organization set and the stakeholders models are striking, but as with the overlap between the maps of those two perspectives, the similarities are more apparent than real. Like the organization set, the institutional field includes suppliers, customers, regulators, and competitors. Like the stakeholder model, it includes unions and professional and industry associations. The field approach, however, focuses not on resource flows or on the interests and power of the external organizational actors but on their role in shaping perceptions about organizational behaviors and patterns. It adds the structuring agencies such as the business media and analysts that have no role in the other models of the environment but loom so large in the concerns of many top executives, because they play an important role in shaping how the organization is "seen" and evaluated by key external actors, by the general public, and even by the members of the organization itself. Reading a favorable story in the press about one's organization, or learning that it has been listed as one of the top ten "excellent companies to work for," or as one of the top ten business schools, can have a powerful impact on one's commitment and motivation.

Figure 9.3 presents a simple mapping of an organizational field. As with the stakeholders model, it is difficult to map a field in the abstract, because considerable variation can be found across fields in the identity of the organizations that play the key roles of the structuring agencies. In some fields, the movie industry for example, the trade press plays a significant role; in other fields, the general business media and stock market analysts are far more important.

The term *institutional field* is taken from the much older concept of institutionalization: the process by which certain organizational patterns come to be accepted as legitimate, as the right way to do things, or even as the only way to do things (taken for granted). Institutionalization, as Richard Scott pointed out, can have a normative component (the "right" way to do this) and a cognitive component (the only way we've ever considered to do this). Organizational patterns and actions in an institutional field come to have considerable similarities across the organizations in the field, a process that institutional theorists call *isomorphism*. Isomorphism means structural similarity, and refers to the processes by which organizations become similar to others in their field. Organizations adopt prevailing patterns of structure and action for several reasons:

Figure 9.3 Cultural Perspective: Institutional Field Model

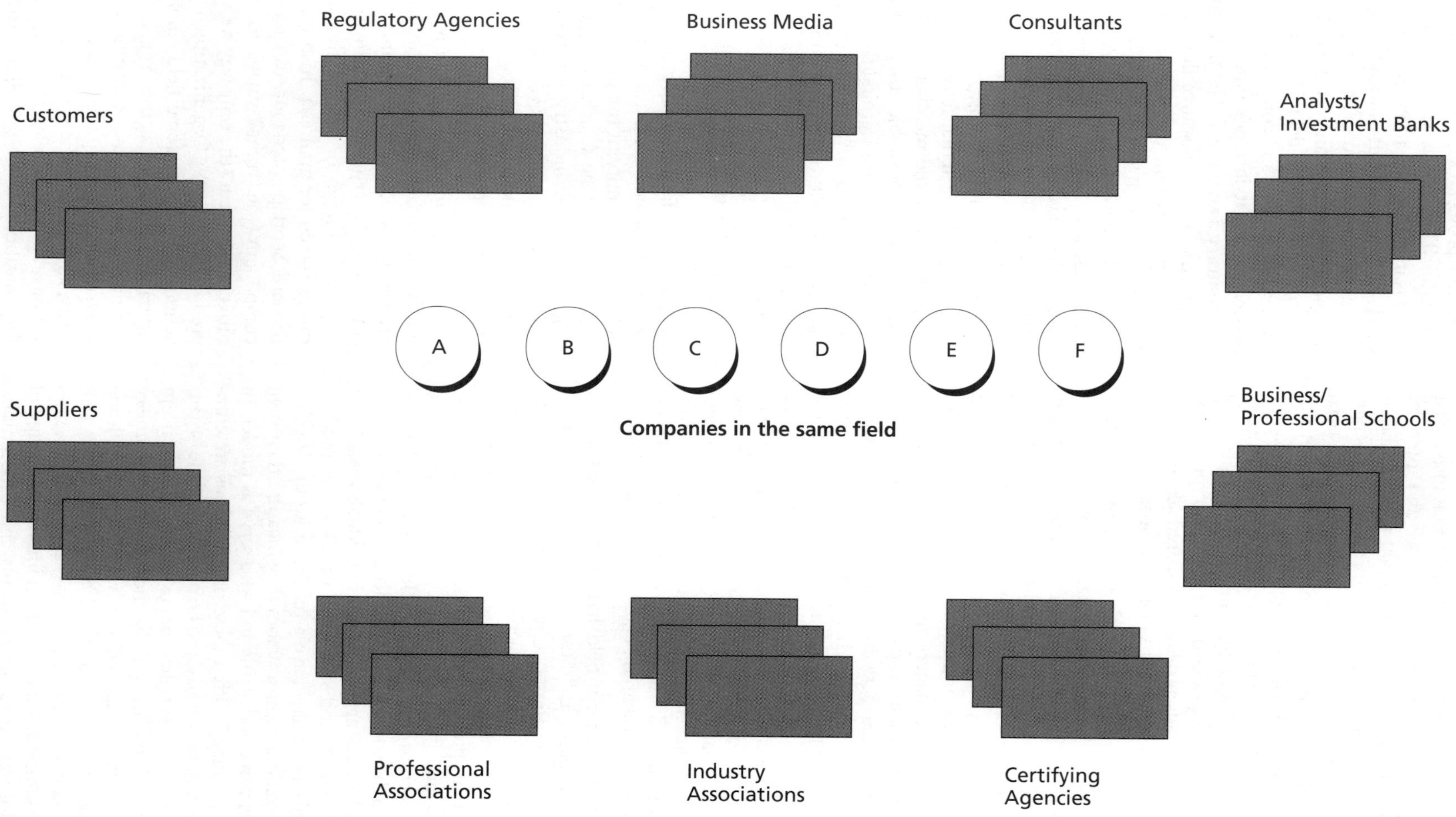

Analysts/Investment Banks

Business/Professional Schools

Consultants

Certifying Agencies

Business Media

Industry Associations

Regulatory Agencies

Professional Associations

Customers

Suppliers

A B C D E F

Companies in the same field

- A powerful organization in their field demands that they do so: *coercive isomorphism*—for example, when a government imposes certain personnel procedures, or an important customer demands that its suppliers adopt quality control programs
- Professional or interest groups insist that such patterns are the "right" way to do things: *normative isomorphism*—for example, when doctors shape hospital management systems or professors shape research universities
- Organizations take successful organizations as models: *mimetic isomorphism*, the most common of the three isomorphic processes in business firms

The imitation of mimetic isomorphism is most common when organizations really don't know what makes a management system work or fail—that is, under conditions of uncertainty—or when an organization in trouble tries to win credibility by changing its structures and processes to match those used by successful organizations. A CEO returning from a conference on organizational culture, for example, and calling in the top management team to tell them, "I want a program in place by next week to build a strong corporate culture," is an example of isomorphism in action.

Institutional fields can vary in the strength of their effects on the organizations in the field. The effects are often stronger when organizations share a location as well as a set of activities, for example, the concentration of the U.S. auto industry in Detroit or the garment trade in New York city (Uzzi, 1997). In such cases, many of the structuring agencies, such as the trade press, specialized consultants, and associations and training schools, also share the same location, and the easy flow of people and information across the field reinforces the development of isomorphic processes and a shared "field culture."

Although the institutional field model tends to emphasize the constraints on organizations from the field, it also provides some useful tools for organizational action. A key challenge in organizational change is gaining acceptance of the change initiative. One set of tools for facilitating change is political—appealing to the interests of key internal and external stakeholders. Another set of tools is institutional or cultural: invoking the example of the social reference group in the form of admired organizations, for example. Often managers react to a proposed innovation by asking, "Who else has tried it?" If the answer is "No one, yet," they may well be reluctant to proceed. After all, if it were a really good idea, surely someone else would already have done it. If the answer is that some organization that they have never heard of—or worse, an organization that has a poor reputation has tried it—they will be even more reluctant. However, if the answer invokes a high-status, highly respected "excellent company," then they are likely to be much more open to the idea. This response is not an irrational one: following the example of a highly respected firm may well have reputation benefits, and it will increase the chances of success if the initiative is seen both outside and inside the organization as legitimate and promising. Identifying acceptable organizational models is a good way to legitimate a proposed action. Appealing to established norms and values is another. For example, in the health care field, appealing to professional standards and the well-being of customers can have greater legitimacy than appealing to profits, and therefore initiatives aimed at increasing profits are more likely to be successful if they are clothed in the rhetoric of "efficiencies that benefit the patient." And a third set of tools parallels the mobilization of external stakeholders in the political perspective: an action or an initiative (or opposition to an initiative) can be strengthened by attracting the attention of external "structuring agencies." It is not uncommon for a group struggling to maintain a program in a company to invite the attention of a reporter in order to get a favorable story into the press, which will be read by executives and influence their perceptions of the program. One human resources department in a Boston company, for example, learned that the company was considering closing the employee daycare center as part of a drive to cut costs. The department invited a group of reporters to tour the center and as a result got favorable stories into the Boston press about the center and the way its existence both demonstrated the commitment of the company to its female employees and gave it an advantage over other employers in a tight high-tech labor market. Top executives read the stories, and vetoed the closing of the center.

The use of the concept of the institutional field to analyze the cultural or the social construction aspects of the organizational environment has tended to displace an older concept: national culture. National culture has been—and indeed remains—a powerful concept in analyzing the cultural environment of an organization. One criticism of national culture models, however, is that they don't allow either for the considerable variation within countries across corporate cultures (across industries or sectors in particular) or for the changes that can occur in organizational patterns over time. The institutional field model addresses both these points, because it focuses more narrowly on particular organizational sectors and because it addresses the role of structuring agencies in disseminating and legitimating patterns.

This approach puts the concept of the institutional field at the center of the debates over globalization. In today's global economy, organizational fields increasingly cross boundaries, and involve companies with "homes" in different countries. The leading companies network with each other in international alliances and cooperative agreements; cross-border mergers create large multinational corporations. These firms share suppliers and compete for the same customers; increasingly, their executives read the same newspapers (*The Wall Street Journal* and *Financial Times*) and graduate from the same business schools (or at least from business schools whose faculty have graduated from the same business schools). Each watches carefully what the other is doing, in competitive benchmarking efforts and mutual learning. Powerful isomorphic pressures are operating in these "global" organizational fields. The critics of globalization fear "global capitalism" primarily because they see it as producing managers who, whatever passport they hold, share the same mindsets, values, beliefs, and behaviors, who then populate companies that increasingly use similar structures and processes and take similar actions, overriding national cultures and differences. Whether this form of isomorphism actually occurs—and which industries and institutional fields most strongly feel its global effects—will be a focus of debate and research in the coming decade.

A cultural approach to a business issue such as entering a new business or market would ask questions like the following: What other organizations are involved in this "field" and what are the established ways of doing business? How different are the expectations from what we are used to? What would be the reaction if we do not follow the "established" ways? Can we improve our chances of success by following the established (or institutionalized) patterns? We can use Nissan again as an example of how to use this perspective to understand organizational action.

The Japanese Auto Plants in the United States: An Organizational Field Approach

It is difficult to understand Nissan's entry into the United States—or that of Honda or any of the other Japanese auto firms—without examining what was happening in the organizational field as a whole. Nissan's establishment of production facilities in Tennessee, which we examined in the context of the organization set model and the stakeholders model, took place at a time when the organizational field of the U.S. auto industry was being transformed by the entries of a steady stream of Japanese companies. Honda was the first, in 1982; Nissan began production of trucks in 1983 and cars in 1985; Toyota undertook a joint venture in California with General Motors (NUMMI), which began production in 1984. Mazda followed in 1987 in Flat Rock, Michigan; Toyota built a wholly owned plant in Kentucky that opened in 1988; Subaru-Isuzu began production in Lafayette, Indiana, in 1989.

These entries took place at a time when the U.S. auto producers had lost credibility with the American public for being arrogant and unresponsive to customer needs, and for producing high-cost and low-quality vehicles. The early responses of the American Big Three (General Motors, Ford, and Chrysler) to Japanese export competition made their image worse. They complained about the low quality of American labor, made large investments in automation to replace that labor, and insisted that the Japanese enjoyed unfair cost advantages because they produced in Japan. By producing vehicles in the United States, the Japanese were saying implicitly as well as explicitly that the problem with the U.S. auto industry was not American labor but American management. The popular and business press picked up this theme, and portrayed the early Japanese plants in extremely favorable terms, in part as a way of criticizing the U.S. companies and spurring them to change. Honda in particular, as the first entrant, was extremely careful to maintain a favorable public image, and it paved the way for later entrants. The Japanese firms all made strong statements about the importance they assigned to employment stability and job security, combined with a commitment on the part of workers to work hard, to work in teams, and to use their intelligence as well as their hands—all statements that fit well with the values prevailing in much of the popular press and among academic analysts. The fact that the Japanese were able to produce cars in the United States with an American labor force and maintain their quality and cost advantages seemed to legitimate their organization and management systems. This legitimation was reinforced when U.S. producers themselves began to adopt and adapt several of their systems.

The fact that so many Japanese companies were coming to the United States and the extremely favorable press coverage they received gave legitimacy to the efforts of any one company to change what had been standard practices in the auto industry in labor relations, supplier relations, and customer relations (minimizing the number of options, reducing the amount of bargaining between the distributors and the customers, providing long-term warranties). U.S. management scholars and consultants and the business press contributed to this process by portraying many of these innovations not as "Japanese" but as "post-Fordist," as the next wave of industrial innovation.

The entry of several producers and the move of U.S. producers to emulate such supplier-related practices as just-in-time inventory management and total quality management (shared quality programs undertaken jointly with suppliers) increased the strength of any individual company in convincing suppliers to adopt the new patterns. Moreover, a supplier that could adapt to Japanese transplant demands could expand sales to other Japanese producers, to U.S. producers, and perhaps even to Japanese plants back in Japan. The extensive entry of Japanese producers also attracted leading Japanese supplier companies to the United States. For example, Bridgestone in tires, several Japanese steel companies, and large component producers like Nippon Denso and Yazaki all entered production in the United States, either by acquisition (Bridgestone acquired Firestone, the Japanese steel companies entered joint ventures with U.S. producers or acquired shares in U.S. companies) or by setting up new plants. These new entrants not only reinforced the competitive pressure on U.S. suppliers to adapt to the new rules of competition; they also provided them with models of those new rules in action in their own territory.

The U.S. auto firms were not alone in losing legitimacy at the time of Japanese entry into the United States. The U.S. labor unions faced steadily eroding membership and increasing criticism for outdated approaches to labor-management relations and inflexibility. The determination of Honda, Nissan, and Toyota in its wholly owned plant in Kentucky to build nonunion plants was met with less determined resistance from American workers than might have been the case a decade or so earlier. They also all selected sites that were in nonindustrial, nonunionized communities, where unions had even less legitimacy and acceptance than in the industrial heartland.

The large-scale entry of the Japanese auto producers transformed the field. This transformation smoothed the path for individual firms, and made possible a degree of technology and management transfers from Japan that would have been much more difficult, if not impossible, for any single firm operating alone. When we contrast the success of Nissan's establishment of production facilities in the United States with Volkswagen's unsuccessful entry in the 1970s, we realize the importance of the field level of analysis.

Integrating Perspectives: Seeing the Environment Through Three Lenses

Like the three models of the organization on which they build, the three models of the environment are complementary rather than competing. Although some key social actors in the environment appear in all three (suppliers and customers in particular), each model constructs a somewhat different map of the external organizational landscape. In addition, even for the social actors that are common to all three models, each model highlights a different aspect of their relations with, and affect on, the organization.

The strategic design-based model of the organization set is the most focused of the three, with its input set, output set, regulatory set, and competitor set. The political stakeholders model broadens the view of the environment to include a range of social actors that do not have direct resource transactions with the organization but have some stake in its actions. It also reminds us that some of the organizations in the organization set may be stakeholders who have distinct interests. They too have their own internal stakeholders whose interests might differ, which may provide opportunities for the organization to shape its interactions with those stakeholders to serve its own interests and strategies. The institutional field model draws a still more extensive map of the environment: it includes a much wider set of social actors that do not themselves engage in direct transactions with the organization or have any direct stake in it but which powerfully affect the range of acceptable, legitimate actions and behaviors in which the organization can engage. It also points out that the members of the organization set have expectations of the organization as well as resource flows, and that stakeholders have values and assumptions as well as interests. Those expectations and values are socially constructed and reinforced by influential external agencies in the field, and while they are hard for the organization to change, they can, if they are well understood, be selectively leveraged to influence both the interactions with external actors and actions and processes within the organization.

Actions to deal with the organizational environment are most effective when they take all three models into account. The organization set model focuses on how the tools of organization design (grouping, linking, and alignment) can be used to improve interorganizational relationships—not simply the efficiency and effectiveness of resource flows on which this perspective focuses, but also the interactions with external stakeholders. For example, growing numbers of multinational companies that incorporate sustainable development into their codes of corporate conduct also set up specialized departments and liaison positions to work with NGOs and external interest groups to get information about best practices and to ensure that the company is seen to be "walking the talk" in this arena. The stakeholders model directs attention to how external stakeholders can be mobilized and coalitions formed in order to influence the outcomes of decision making inside the organization (including decisions about organization design). The institutional field perspective highlights the importance of external models, legitimation, and attention from external structuring agencies in managing the organization and the environment, and managing the organization set and external stakeholders as well as members of the organization itself.

Managing for the twenty-first century will demand growing sophistication about the complex and demanding environments in which organizations must operate. The analytical and action tools provided by the three models of the environment are invaluable in expanding the capabilities of managers and of organizations in taking effective action in these complex environments.

References

DiMaggio, Paul, and Walter W. Powell. 1983. "The Iron Cage Revisited: Institutional Isomorphism and Collective Rationality in Organizational Fields." *American Sociological Review*, 48.

Evan, William M. 1966. "The Organization-Set: Toward a Theory of Interorganizational Relations." In James D. Thompson (Ed.). *Approaches to Organization Design*. Pittsburgh: University of Pittsburgh Press.

Scott, W. Richard. 1992. *Organizations: Rational, Natural, and Open Systems*. Englewood Cliffs, NJ: Prentice Hall.

Thompson, James D. 1967. *Organizations in Action*. New York: McGraw-Hill.

Uzzi, Brian. 1997. "Social Structure and Competition in Firm Networks: The Paradox of Embeddedness." *Administrative Science Quarterly*, 42, 35–67.

RU-486

The handling by Roussel-Uclaf of a double dilemma

In October 1988, the French pharmaceutical firm Roussel-Uclaf faced an extremely difficult decision: whether to go ahead with marketing RU-486, an abortion-inducer, also incorrectly known as the "morning-after pill." It found itself under pressure from powerful but contradictory forces in the environment, some strongly urging the company to keep the drug off the market, and others insisting that firm should make it available. The pressures were internal as well as external, not only within Roussel-Uclaf itself but also within its parent firm (at that time Roussel-Uclaf was 56 percent owned by the global chemical giant Hoechst of West Germany). The company seemed caught in a situation where any decision that its top management team made would lead to problems.

The Company

The French scientist Gaston Roussel founded the pharmaceutical firm named after him at the beginning of the century. When he died in 1947, he left a well-structured group to his son, Jean-Claude Roussel, who gave the company a more international outlook and diversified its activities to include animal health and plant care. Roussel-Uclaf became a leader of the French pharmaceutical industry and developed an important presence worldwide, especially in the fields of endocrinology, cardiovasculars, and antibiotics. Its research strengths and leading position in the French pharmaceutical market attracted the interest of the giant German chemical and pharmaceutical company Hoechst, which acquired a 56 percent stake in the company (the other 44 percent was held by the French government). Roussel-Uclaf's profits rose steadily between 1978 and 1988, and by the end of the 1980s international sales had grown to more than two-thirds of company revenues. In 1989 Roussel-Uclaf employed 15,637 people (8,619 in France and 7,018 abroad); its annual sales reached FF 12,369 million.

Roussel-Uclaf was proud of the importance it attached to research and development activities (in 1989 the R&D budget amounted to 11 percent of the groups' consolidated turnover). Roussel-Uclaf had established cooperative R&D agreements with leading French universities and research organizations. From 1981 to the end of 1993, Roussel-Uclaf was presided over by Dr. Edouard Sakiz. Sakiz, born in Istanbul to an Armenian family, was a medical doctor, biologist, and first-rank researcher in the field of steroids.

The Product

Discovery

Researchers at Roussel-Uclaf had synthesized the RU-486 antihormone in 1980. Dr. Sakiz explained the discovery of the product to the *Pharmaceutical Executive*: "This compound came out from research we started ten years ago into antihormones. There were no real antihormones, and what was used instead were the weak hormones. We said, it would be beautiful one day if we had a compound that gets into the receptor and has no action at all. There was no such compound available before RU-486. It was the first real antihormone."

It had not been the intention of Roussel-Uclaf researchers to create an abortion inducer, and no top executive could have predicted the turmoil the product would cause. The drug's abortion-provoking—or "contragestive"—effects had been discovered subsequently by Prof. Etienne-Emile Baulieu's team. Professor Baulieu was a researcher at INSERM, one of France's leading research institutes. Contracting out certain aspects of drug development—including the application research for a newly discovered compound—has become an increasingly common practice in the pharmaceutical industry, and companies carefully cultivate their relationships with the best research organizations. Not only was INSERM one of the best in Europe, but Baulieu himself was a star of French medical research and a prominent figure in the world medical research community. He had been working in close collaboration with Roussel-Uclaf for over twenty-five years, and it was he who had introduced Dr. Sakiz to Roussel-Uclaf. The two men remained close personal friends.

How It Works

RU-486 is an "antihormone" that works by blocking the action of the hormone progesterone, which

Source: This case was originally developed at INSEAD by Gilda Villaran under the direction of Prof. Henri-Claude de Bettignies with financial support from the INSEAD Alumni Fund European Case Programme, and adapted for this text by D. Eleanor Westney.

is essential to maintain a pregnancy. The administration of the product was established as follows: women in the early stages of pregnancy take a 600 mg. dose of RU-486 (three pills of 200 mg. each) in front of the doctor in an abortion clinic; they then go home. Two days later, the effectiveness of the product is complemented by the administration of *prostaglandins* (which work on the muscles of the uterus, producing contractions that facilitate the expulsion of the fetus) either in the form of an injection or a vaginal pessary. Roussel-Uclaf does not produce prostaglandins, but they are available in France. The only pharmaceutical firms that produced them in the late 1980s were Schering, and the Japanese laboratory Ono, which had licensed the product in France to Rhone Poulenc. RU-486 is only effective when the pregnancy is between 21 and 35 days old.

Testing RU-486

Extensive clinical testing proved the safety of the product. The drug was administered to 20,000 volunteers with a 96 percent success rate with the supplementary administration of prostaglandins. (The success rate had been only 80 percent in previous tests, when RU-486 alone was taken.) In none of the 4% of the cases in which RU-486 failed was there a threat to the woman's health; "failure" constituted either incomplete abortions (3 percent of the cases) or no response at all to the drug (1 percent of the cases). However, since there was no absolute certainty that the fetus had not been damaged, these women then underwent surgical abortions. During testing in England a small number of women on whom RU-486 had had no effect, although informed of the risks, decided not to undergo surgical abortion. All gave birth to healthy babies.

The World Health Organization (WHO) had an important role in testing the substance. Following an agreement signed in 1982, WHO conducted testing and development programs in fifteen countries, some of which were developing countries. WHO included in the agreement a clause that stipulated that, in the event of Roussel-Uclaf deciding not to continue the development of RU-486, the company should provide WHO (if it was still interested) with the product, or transfer its rights to another company that would continue its development. The U.S. Population Council also endorsed the use of RU-486, although testing in the United States was limited due to the controversial nature of abortion.

Its Medical Advantages

Abortion with RU-486 has some clear advantages over surgical abortion (suction). It avoids the administration of general anesthesia (surgical abortion, even under local anesthesia, is painful; therefore in France it is mainly done under general anesthesia); it eliminated the risks of uterus perforation and laceration of the uterus neck; it does not require hospitalization (needed because of the administration of general anesthesia) and so its costs are lower. Studies quoted by the Population Crisis Committee (Washington, D.C.) have shown that most women prefer a nonsurgical method of abortion because it provides greater privacy, is less invasive, and avoids anesthesia.

The disadvantages of RU-486 are: it requires the patient to revisit the doctor, and its effectiveness is limited to a very short period of time, unlike surgical abortion.

The French Government's Authorization

On October 9, 1987, the Laboratoires Roussel (in charge of marketing the pharmaceutical products of the Roussel-Uclaf group) applied for government authorization of the commercial use of mifepristone, which is the name of RU-486 (the commercial brand name in France is Mifegyne).

Roussel's application for the commercial use of RU-486 rekindled the whole discussion on abortion, despite the fact that the issue had been more or less dormant in France since 1975, which had legalized the voluntary interruption of pregnancy. The law allowed abortion to be carried out before the end of the tenth week of pregnancy, and required a prior discussion with a psychologist or a family counsellor and a period of reflection of one week.

In the RU-486 decision, the Government solicited the opinion of the French National Committee on Ethics, presided over by Professor Jean Bernard. The Committee delivered its opinion on December 15, 1987. In spite of the somewhat reluctant tone of the statement, the Committee approved RU-486 and recommended its use with the same legal limitations under which surgical abortions are performed. More precisely, the committee advised that the substance be administered by authorized abortion clinics only and not sold in drugstores.

Responding to these restrictions, the French press saw the committee's opinion as a warning light to RU-486: *Le Monde* reported in big type, "Feu Orange a la Pillule IVG" and *Le Figaro* said "Oui, mais . . . au RU-486." However, Roussel had always maintained that RU-486 should only be used under these strict conditions.

The French government finally approved the commercial use of RU-486. The other government that promptly authorized the drug was the Chinese, which approved the use of RU-486 even before France did. In the 1980s, China had the world's biggest abortion service: 11.5 million abortions were performed every year, legally and mostly safely. It also conducted the largest number of clinical trials of RU-486 outside France (more than 1,600 pill-induced abortions were carried out).

The Debate: Proceed to Market, or Not?

As Roussel came to the decision point of whether to take RU-486 to the market, the company faced a much more complex environment than it usually encountered in launching a new product, and managers' assessments of that environment affected virtually every approach to the decision. Deciding whether to proceed to market or not generated great differences of opinion internally and externally.

The Ethical Issues

The fundamental values involved in the abortion issue made discussion as well as decision difficult. Even among those who agreed that the right to life is the fundamental right of human beings, the fact that neither scientists nor religious leaders had reached agreement on when human life starts raised the contentious issue of weighing a woman's right to free choice against a fetus's right to be born. Many people felt strongly that while the law might tolerate it, abortion was still morally wrong, and that to facilitate abortion was therefore unacceptable. Others argued that a company had no right to place limits on the exercise of legally enforceable rights, and that personal beliefs on abortion were irrelevant: the decision to condemn or accept abortion was made by society, and French society, through its parliament, had already decided that abortion was, if not exactly desirable, at least tolerable and that its exercise was, under certain constraints, legal.

The ethical issue was critical to an assessment of the implications of the marketing of RU-486 for the firm's image. The pill's proponents emphasized the prestige that the marketing of such an original and innovative product would give the company. RU-486 foes might counter that Roussel-Uclaf's company slogan, "at the service of life," would become paradoxical if it sold a product that ended human life at the very outset. RU-486 defenders in turn could argue that the product was a saver of lives: WHO has estimated that out of 500,000 women per year dying from pregnancy-related complications (99 percent of whom were Third World women), 200,000 deaths were due to improperly performed abortions.

Public Opinion and Advocacy Groups

Although public opinion was divided, those opposing RU-486 had expressed their views more vigorously than those in favor of it. The Catholic Church condemned RU-486, a ruling consistent with its rejection of both contraception and any form of abortion. Archbishop Jacques Julien, head of the Family Commission of the French Episcopate, raised the argument of the "banalization" of abortion. The "Laissez-les-vivre" (France's anti-abortion movement) used Archbishop Julien's argument several times, contending that if abortion procedures were made too easy and commonplace, the abortion decision would be obscured. Moreover, members of the movement claimed that RU-486 would encourage sexual permissiveness by reducing the number of unwanted pregnancies.

Several other French organizations, like the "Association for Conscientious Objectors to all Participation in Abortion" and international organizations such as the "Association of Medical Doctors for the Respect for Life" actively campaigned against RU-486. Forming a committee called "Save the Unborn Children," they organized a press conference on December 7, 1987, and alerted the public to the threat posed by RU-486. The powerful International Right to Life Federation, presided over by Dr. John Willke, initiated its own crusade against RU-486. In June and December 1987, Dr. Willke sent letters to the then Prime Minister of France, Jacques Chirac, warning against the risks posed by RU-486, including the risk of fetus toxicity.

The moral condemnation and emotive slogans (such as calling the drug the "death pill" and "human pesticide") contained in these and other letters had been accompanied by a threat of a boycott, not only of Roussel-Uclaf products but also of the products of the parent company Hoechst. Threats made in the United States had already alarmed Hoechst-Roussel Pharmaceuticals Incorporated (HRPI), the pharmaceutical division of Hoechst-Celanese (the American subsidiary of Hoechst).

As Dr. Willke was prompt to remind Roussel-Uclaf, American anti-abortion groups had already defeated at least one pharmaceutical company: Upjohn had stopped research in this field in 1985 because of a hostile campaign against Proston, a drug able to induce abortion. In fact, the large American pharmaceutical companies had abandoned birth-control-related research. Although right-to-life organizations claimed the credit for this, one of the main causes of the reluctance of American firms to continue research was the relatively small size of the market. According to *Technology Review*, the estimated U.S. demand was 400,000 doses a year. And while estimates made by the consulting firm of Intercare (of Flemington, New Jersey) determined that the worldwide market for contraceptives and abortifacient substances was worth $1 billion, the market for cardiovascular drugs in the United States alone was worth $2.5 billion. Rising liability costs were another and perhaps more important reason for the cessation of research in this field.

On the other hand, the importance of the American market for Hoechst was indisputable: a quarter of the giant's U.S.$ 25 billion came from the U.S. market. HRPI had a sales of $485 million, which represented 8 percent of Hoechst-Celanese's sales and 11 percent of Hoechst's total pharmaceutical sales. Hoechst-Celanese had a sales volume two-and-a-half times larger than Roussel-Uclaf's.

The Position of Hoechst

Hoechst was plainly against the sale of the product. Wolfgang Hilger, its president, was known to be personally opposed to abortion and had always declared: "It is simply not company policy to sell an abortifacient."

The position of the company's executives with respect to marketing an abortifacient substance reflected the fact that, in general, West Germans have more conservative views on abortion than the French. However, religious and moral beliefs did not seem to be the most decisive reason for Hoechst's opposition. Several of Hoechst's executives, in discussions with Roussel-Uclaf's marketing people, made the same basic point: let us put aside the moral, philosophical and religious implications of the decision and see if the international marketing of the pill makes sound business sense. What Hoechst might lose in the face of a full boycott of its products would be economically much more important than the potential profits from the sale of the pill. Profits would never be very great, given that sales of RU-486 were not expected to be high in Western Europe, where abortion had decreased in the past few years, and that sales in developing countries, following the agreement signed with WHO, would be at cost value. Considering the credibility of the boycott threat, many of Hoechst's managers concluded that the product was not worth the risk. Some Roussel managers agreed.

Lastly, the possibility of conflict with the parent company Hoechst had to be evaluated. So far, differences between Hoechst and Roussel had not amounted to open controversy and both continued to agree on major issues. However, there remained the question of whether overinsistence on the sale of RU-486 might not lead to Roussel being excluded from future major decision making. There was a distinct possibility that Hoechst, considering the huge economic factors at stake, might decide to handle the issue itself.

Potential Internal Problems from the Sale of RU-486

Executives and employees were themselves divided about the ethics of marketing RU-486, and were also under considerable pressure from anti-abortion groups. The "Association for Conscientious Objectors to all Participation in Abortion" had been distributing letters at Roussel-Uclaf's front gate, urging employees to refuse to participate in the research and production of RU-486. Whether employees would respond to this kind of appeal and whether such an "internal boycott" of RU-486 would lead to open conflicts were difficult to assess. It was not easy to predict whether marketing RU-486 would divide the organization's members into hostile groups. Several executives had made clear their open disagreement with the sale of an abortifacient and expressed their surprise at Roussel-Uclaf's role in its development. A few decades ago, the firm had the opportunity to enter the contraceptive market at an early stage; it had refused to do so because of conservative concerns; now the firm was in the vanguard of innovative abortion methods. On the other hand, deciding not to market RU-486 might alienate the researchers who were so important to continuing product development at Roussel. They were not happy at the idea of suppressing the first major product to come out of their antihormone research.

The issue of abortion divides societies; it could well divide the company, and not only in France. The same kind of controversy could arise between Roussel and its subsidiaries: subsidiaries that were predominantly anti-RU-486 might refuse to follow instructions issued by the Paris headquarters. Finally, Edouard Sakiz had expressed fears about the security of the company's employees. Sakiz did not want to jeopardize the safety of company employees by provoking the anger of extremists.

Issues in Worldwide Distribution Strategy

The first decision was whether to proceed with marketing in France. The Health Division suggested a step-by-step strategy for worldwide marketing: having gained solid experience in France, the company would then move to market the product in other European countries. Five conditions would have to be met before the pill was marketed: (1) abortion must be legal; (2) abortion must be accepted by political, public, and medical opinion; (3) synthetic prostaglandins (which Roussel-Uclaf did not produce) must be available; (4) distribution channels must be strictly controlled; (5) patients must sign a consent form, agreeing to undergo surgical abortion if RU-486 failed.

After France, sales were projected to follow in England, the Scandinavian countries, and Holland. Not many other countries would fulfill the conditions. Eastern European countries, which constituted an important potential market, did not meet the third and fourth requirements.

With regard to the distribution of the pill in the Third World, Roussel-Uclaf knew it had to move cautiously. Here the firm anticipated several problems. First, it was by no means sure that the governments of many developing countries would allow use of the pill. Latin American laws, for instance, make abortion a criminal offense. But even assuming that WHO (which would be in charge of the distribution of the product in the Third World) could break down the barriers imposed by governments, those countries would still not be in a position to fulfill all the conditions required by Roussel-Uclaf. Above all, fears centered on the fact that the product could pose a risk if it was badly administered. Roussel was aware that the medical environment of less developed countries would not provide guarantees for the safe use of the product.

An additional fear was the possibility that a black market for the product would emerge. Entrepreneurial traders could benefit from the fact that RU-486 would be sold at lower prices in the Third World and Eastern Europe. By transporting the product back to Western Europe, they could make illicit profits. More important, the main risk of a black market is the misuse of the pill (insufficient doses, late administration, lack of adequate medical supervision, etc.). Thus the day when RU-486 would be widely available in the Third World appeared remote, which was, in a certain way, contradictory given the aims of the product. As one Roussel-Uclaf employee put it, "RU-486 represented significant progress not as an alternative to surgical abortion, which is almost as safe as RU-486, although more painful and traumatizing, but as an alternative to knitting needles." However, it was in countries where such methods were commonplace that the product would not be available, at least not in the foreseeable future.

The Decision

Announcement:

Taking into account the feelings expressed by some French and foreign members of the public, together with the debate fired by the possibility of marketing the antihormone mifepristone (RU-486), which causes the voluntary interruption of pregnancy, the Roussel-Uclaf group has decided to suspend distribution of this product as a medical alternative to surgical abortion in France and abroad as of today. The Roussel-Uclaf group is considered to be a pioneer in endocrinology. After having developed numerous hormones (sexual steroids and corticosteroids), it has oriented the research towards the field of hormones and antihormones and their application. The nilutamide (anti-androgen) has recently been released to the medical community as a therapy for prostate cancer. The Roussel-Uclaf group, convinced of the therapeutic effect of antihormones, intends to continue its research and development efforts and to maintain its world leadership in that field.

This was the communique by which the management of Roussel-Uclaf announced its decision on Friday, October 21, 1988 to suspend distribution of RU-486. Until that time, distribution had been done free of charge and for testing purposes only. By a show of hands vote of sixteen to four, members of the executive office and the Board of Directors of Roussel-Uclaf had decided, after a one-hour debate during a meeting on October 21, not to market the product.

Those who voted for the suspension gave as their main reason the risk of boycott of their other products, and not only those of Roussel-Uclaf, but also those of Hoechst. "The prospect of significant economic gains had never been a motive for developing the product, but a fear of economic losses was a reason for taking it off the market," said Madame Mouttet, Roussel-Uclaf's International group manager for hormonal products.

On the other hand, a minority had maintained that the firm should not give in to blackmail, and that the withdrawal of a first-rate medical product would deprive women of a safe and relatively painless means of ending unwanted pregnancy. Catherine Euvrard, communications director and the only woman present at that meeting, had insisted on a woman's right to free choice.

Michel Delage, CEO of Roussel-France, declared to the press that "under these circumstances, we finally decided that we did not have the right to put on one side of the scales the firm's development, and, on the other, the improvement of our group's corporate image in the medical community, which would result from the sale of such an interesting and original product." Pierre Joly, vice president of Roussel-Uclaf, further explained that the firm did not want to take responsibility for cases in which, due to a "hostile religious or moral environment," women would fail to complete their treatment using the drug. To be sure, the laboratories had decided that, in addition to complying with the requirements set by French law, women considering taking RU-486 should sign a consent form agreeing to undergo surgical abortion in the event of failure of the product. However, Roussel-Uclaf would not be able to enforce this agreement. Obviously, the vice president was afraid that the firm's responsibility did not end with the signing of the consent form.

Edouard Sakiz, the group's chairman and CEO, justified the decision by saying to the press: "Imagine your workers going back on the evening train and their children saying, 'Father, is it true you are an assassin?'" He was also quoted by *The New York Times* as saying: "We have a responsibility for managing a company; but if I were a lone scientist, I would have acted differently." And Professor Etienne-Emile Baulieu, the "discoverer" of RU-486, relates in his book that, in a private meeting following the decision to suspend distribution, his good friend Dr. Sakiz had expressed the distress that this affair had caused him. He referred to the pressure exerted by the American subsidiary, Hoechst-Roussel Products Incorporated, and his responsibility vis-à-vis Roussel-Uclaf's personnel. However, he gave Professor Baulieu the green light to react as strongly as he wanted. "Your position is completely different from mine; you are free to act as you see fit," Sakiz had said.

Reactions

Until the decision, public pressure had come mainly from the anti-abortion side. After the decision to withhold the product was made public, pressure from the "pro-choice" lobby mounted. The firm was caught in an unusual situation: it was subject to strong pressure from opposing sides, one emphasizing the firm's moral obligation not to sell, the other emphasizing the firm's moral duty to sell the product.

The French Archbishops, in plenary session in Lourdes on October 26, were relieved by the announcement, and greeted it with long applause. Monseigneur Jacques Julien congratulated Roussel-Uclaf for its "courageous decision" and "constructive attitude."

Meanwhile, commentators in the French press debated whether the firm had the right to withdraw a pharmaceutical product whose sale had been authorized because of its usefulness, for fear of economic sanctions. Researchers at Roussel-Uclaf characterized the withdrawal of the drug as "morally scandalous" and Professor Baulieu declared: "The firm has given way to intolerance."

The world's medical community protested strongly against the cessation of sales. Three days after Roussel-Uclaf decided to withdraw RU-486, the 1988 World Congress of Gynecology and Obstetrics was opened in Rio de Janeiro, Brazil. Two thousand of its participants, mainly physicians, university professors, representatives of the World Health Organization (WHO), the Rockefeller Foundation, and the World Bank, sent a petition to Edouard Sakiz asking him to reconsider the decision. In addition, the directors of the International Federation of Gynecology and Obstetrics, which had organized the Rio Congress, sent a letter to Wolfgang Hilger, President of Hoechst. Apparently, in his reply, Hilger wrote that abortion was morally condemnable, and that the sale of RU-486 was against the firm's philosophy.

The Government's Order

Only a week after Roussel-Uclaf's top management had decided to withdraw RU-486 from the market, Claude Evin, France's health minister, invited Pierre Joly, vice president of Roussel-Uclaf, to a meeting. Arguing "in the interests of public health," he ordered the company to reverse its decision and start selling the product. The French Government's reasoning was straightforward. The sober "communiqué" that reported the meeting did not deal with the issue of a woman's right to choose; rather, it emphasized the law. The Minister stressed the legal right of women to undergo abortion, and the government's authority to require companies to market drugs deemed to be in the public interest. He said that RU-486 should be sold to avoid the trauma and pain that surgical abortions cause women. Later, Evin made a comment to the press that was to become the slogan of pro-choice activists in the United States: "RU-486 is the moral property of women."

Reactions

The government's order was unprecedented: no one in Roussel-Uclaf could recall an occasion when the Health Ministry had used its legal right to force a pharmaceutical firm to sell a product that it deemed to be in the interests of public health. The Ministry of Health was legally empowered to give the order, under threat of taking away the license of the product from the firm (in application of articles 37, 38, and following the law of January 2, 1968, on patents). However, there was no certainty as to how the government could oblige the laboratories to provide the information on testing that only they possessed. Therefore, it would not have been easy for the Health Ministry to enforce the order.

However, no one at Roussel even insinuated that the firm should refuse to abide by it. "The Government has settled the issue: I do not see why I would search for legal quibbles to resist the order," Pierre Joly told the press. Moreover, Dr. Sakiz, Roussel-Uclaf's CEO, described the Health Minister's mandate as "beautiful help." Indeed the Government's order was a great relief to the company.

The Confederation of Associations of Catholic Families declared that they were outraged and described the minister's intervention as a flagrant abuse of power. The committee "Save the Unborn Children" said that this whole affair was a tragicomedy that discredited both Roussel-Uclaf and the French Government. Across the Atlantic, participants in the World Congress of Gynecology and Obstetrics applauded the determination and involvement of the French Government. Jose Pinotti, President of the International Federation of Gynecology and Obstetrics, stated: "This courageous decision proves that the course of science cannot be blocked by political considerations."

On December 7, 1988, Roussel-Uclaf's Board of Management decided on the policy for the commercialization of RU-486 abroad. A number of options were open to them. The option chosen was to consider France as a test market. "It is, in effect, important—the Board said—to be able to judge from an adequate distance the satisfactory working and the viability of the distribution channels, as well as the acceptability and the understanding of the product, by both doctors and patients." While waiting for confirmation of the success of the drug, the Board decided not to make RU-486 available to foreign orthogenic centers. As a result, it decided the following: (a) to withdraw the registration file submitted in Holland; (b) to suspend the submissions that were about to be made in Great Britain and Sweden; (c) to continue the clinical trials in progress, but not to accept new protocols for the indication of pregnancy termination; (d) to continue studies into the product's other indications (cancer, endometriosis, obstetrics, etc.).

The many organizations that believed RU-486 constituted a major progress in reproductive medicine resented what they saw as the overly cautious and slow strategy of Roussel-Uclaf. For example, the International Planned Parenthood Federation passed, in November 1989, a resolution expressing "deep concern over the lack of progress in making the product RU-486 (mifepristone), a revolutionary breakthrough in fertility regulation, available to women in the world who could benefit greatly from using this drug."

In September 1989, Dr. Baulieu received the 1989 Albert Lasker Award for Research in Clinical Medicine for his contribution to the knowledge of steroid hormones. The development of RU-486 was mentioned in the attribution of the award, presented in New York. As was to be expected, giving this prestigious award to Dr. Baulieu provoked strong reactions and was followed by extensive press coverage.

After discussions on the price of the product, eventually set at 256 French francs, Roussel-Uclaf started selling the pill in France at the beginning of 1990 (before then, the product had been distributed free of charge). Roussel had proposed a price of at least FF 500, taking into account the high development costs of the product (not inferior to those incurred during the development of any other pharmaceutical product, like an antibiotic, for example) and the cost of alternative abortion methods. The French authorities proposed a price of less than 100 francs. Roussel-Uclaf decided not to insist on a high price because it feared being accused of wanting to make a profit out of abortion.

Over the next five years, RU-486 was administered in France without any disruption and under strict controls ("as if it were morphine," an executive has said). The laboratories had complete control over how many doses are administered, where they were administered (only in abortion clinics), and under what conditions.

In 1990, RU-486 was used in a quarter of the abortions performed in France; 50,000 patients used the drug to terminate unwanted pregnancies. The latest figures confirm the 96 percent success rate that was attained when the drug was first tested in combination with prostaglandins. French Social Security reimburses patients for 80 percent of the total cost of the medical pregnancy termination (Arrêté Ministériel, February 26, 1990).

Dr. Sakiz declared that, contrary to what the pill's foes anticipated, the number of abortions had not increased in France since RU-486 became available. This would be in accordance with Dr. Baulieu's contention that abortion is neither more frequent when it is legal—the number of abortions in Eastern Europe actually diminished when abortion was legalized—nor is there a correlation between the "easiness" of the abortion procedure and the number of abortions.

RU-486 in the Rest of Europe

By mid-1990, Roussel-Uclaf decided it could move to selling RU-486 in other countries of Western Europe. Roussel-Uclaf's subsidiary in England started discussions with the British Health Minister to get his assurance that distribution channels would be as efficient as they were in France, and that patients would also be required to sign a consent form in which they are informed that in case of failure, a surgical abortion is recommended. Once Roussel obtained a guarantee that it would be possible to meet all the requirements laid down by the laboratories, the firm filed an authorization request. RU-486 received approval in the United Kingdom in 1991, and Sweden shortly followed.

In Austria and the Catholic countries of Southern Europe, the situation remained on hold. In Italy, for example, RU-486 produced considerable controversy. In 1989, Elena Marinucci, undersecretary of state at the Health Ministry, asked Roussel Maestretti (Roussel-Uclaf's Italian subsidiary) to present the product registration dossier because "experience to date shows that it is the least traumatic and most economic way in which to terminate a pregnancy." Behind the 187,000 abortions in Italy every year "lies the lack of any real education in matters of responsible procreation and contraception," Ms. Marinucci said. "Unfortunately, recourse to abortion is a reality and it is to give women the chance to approach abortion in a less traumatic way that I have taken this initiative, of which the Minister has been informed." Nevertheless, the Health Minister, Francesco de Lorenzo, appeared to have distanced himself from his undersecretary's move, saying that he did not oppose it but neither did he support it. "I believe that it is not within our remit to ask a pharmaceutical company to begin the registration process for a drug. If a registration application is made, we will evaluate it with the usual technical and scientific objectivity. I am aware that this is a very sensitive case." Mr. De Lorenzo added that when the registration documentation was presented in Italy he would set up a special ethical committee to examine the moral aspects of the product.

Eastern Europe represents a market of enormous potential, of much greater importance than the U.S. market. Moreover, in Eastern Europe, abortion is "socially acceptable." However, these countries cannot guarantee distribution channels that would allow optimal control of the use of the product. Roussel executives did not find a solution to the possibility of black marketing (profiting from the different prices at which the pill would be sold in Eastern and Western Europe), and fear that women's health will be put in peril through misuse of the product.

RU-486 in Asia

China was the first country to approve the use of RU-486. However, it has not concluded a distribution agreement with Roussel-Uclaf. The firm did not get an assurance that distribution channels there would be effective enough. Although testing in China was impeccable, it is mostly a rural country, and the company feared that in the countryside the lack of adequate facilities meant that China could not ensure the safe distribution of the pill and its administration under close medical supervision. The Chinese government worked through the World Health Organization to develop plans for beginning the use of the pill in the major cities and moving into other regions as distribution channels developed. WHO itself was somewhat cautious, fearing to put at risk its U.S. funding, given the strong anti-abortion position taken in international population circles by the Reagan and Bush administrations.

Even in the more developed countries of Asia, RU-486 met with obstacles. For example, a Hoechst-Singapore spokesperson said that RU-486 would not be marketed in Singapore. Reportedly, there was pressure on the Health Ministry from two anti-abortion groups to prevent the introduction of the drug there; tests carried out on the product by WHO and the national university hospital were terminated.

RU-486 in the United States

Across the Atlantic, the situation was delicate. The issue of RU-486 quickly became politicized because of the intense conflict over abortion in the United States. Roussel-Uclaf, like most pharmaceutical firms, saw itself as a scientific and technical organization and did not want to get involved in the political debate on abortion. Sakiz said, "We had nothing to do with this discussion. We never said we are for abortion or we'd spread out the compound. . . .We said, instead of using aspiration, if a woman wants, she can take three tablets, that's all." But since many Americans do not see it that way, the company thought it prudent to adopt a wait-and-see attitude. However, it did not anticipate compliance with the "social approval" requisite that it set as a precondition for selling RU-486.

In addition, Roussel-Uclaf did not have immediate access to prostaglandins in the United States. Sakiz believed that RU-486 would have to be made available separately, as would prostaglandins. This would be a lengthy process. To start with, neither Schering nor Ono, the producers of prostaglandins, wanted to provoke the anger of the American pro-life lobby, and were reluctant to export the product to the United States.

However, Roussel-Uclaf felt growing pressure from both sides of the abortion debate. Abortion foes pledged to mount a boycott of all products of Hoechst if the drug was exported from France. Pro-choice groups retaliated with a threat to boycott Hoechst if the drug was not made available.

On December 7, 1989, Dr. Willke of the International Right to Life Federation addressed a long letter to Wolfgang Hilger explaining the position of his organization. In that letter, Willke held both Hoechst A.G. and Roussel-Uclaf directly responsible for the use of RU-486 as an abortifacient. He stated that Hoechst had been sending contradictory signals. On the one hand, Hoechst had attempted to distance itself from the abortion pill. Willke reported that in February 1988, Dr. Victor Bauer wrote to him to state that his company "will not become involved (in the abortion pill's) development, nor do we have any interest or intention whatsoever in marketing this compound." But on the other hand, Willke went on, Hoechst officials failed to take positive steps to prevent RU-486 from being put back onto the market and then later participated in setting Roussel-Uclaf's current policy on using the abortion pill. Also, neither Roussel-

Uclaf nor Hoechst challenged the legality of the Minister of Health's interpretation of French law.

Next, Willke explained the reasons for withdrawing RU-486: (a) Killing unborn babies is morally wrong and ethically indefensible. "Never in modern times has the state granted to one citizen the absolute legal right to have another killed in order to solve their own personal, social, or economic problems. And yet, abortion does all of these," he said. (b) The pill poses serious risks to women. Willke emphasized that the drug could be dangerous to Third World women who often suffered from anemia, malnutrition, and other health problems. "It borders on medical malpractice to send this death pill into the underdeveloped world." (c) Risk of fetal deformity. Willke offered as evidence the text of the consent release form that women who take RU-486 must sign: "I have been clearly warned that the child and/or I may be susceptible to risks, notably malformation of the fetus or the child." (d) Risk of psychological harm to women. He quoted studies that had identified a pattern of psychological problems, known as "post-abortion syndrome." Next he underscored that the long-term effects of RU-486 were completely unknown.

Finally, Willke threatened that right-to-life advocates could approach Hoechst Celanese's large customers and request that they turn to alternative sources for their materials. And, more precisely, he enumerated some of Hoechst's and Roussel's products that would be the target of a boycott, if the firms did not decide to withdraw the product from the market.

There was also pressure from the pro-choice side. In July 1990, a delegation made up of scientists and representatives of women's organizations went to Roussel-Uclaf's Paris headquarters with 400 kilos of petitions asking the firm to accelerate the process of making the product widely available in the United States. Also in July 1990, seventy members of the U.S. Congress, most of them Democrats, sent an open letter to Roussel-Uclaf urging the firm to allow American women to have access to the abortion pill.

However, those Americans who could have accelerated the process remained reluctant to do so. Hoechst-Roussel Pharmaceuticals Incorporated made it clear that it would not take the initiative for marketing the pill. No other large firm approached Roussel to get marketing rights.

Reluctance to become embroiled with the "pro-life" movement in the United States was clearly at work. But unsympathetic regulatory authorities were also a factor. The drug approval process in the United States is under the supervision of the FDA (Food and Drug Administration), whose top officials are appointed by the administration, which throughout the Reagan and Bush presidencies was strongly opposed to abortion. (One of the reasons that the World Health Organization was not more active in the testing and distribution of RU-486 in the poor countries of the developing world was the clearly expressed opposition of the Reagan and Bush administrations to funding any international organization that "promoted" abortion.) In 1989, the FDA put RU-486 on its "import alert" list, which meant that customs officials were instructed to confiscate it even from individuals bringing in the drug for their own use. In 1992, following the Supreme Court ruling upholding the legality of abortion, a Californian woman tried to bring a packet of RU-486 into the country for her own use, in a much-publicized effort to draw attention to the unavailability of the compound in the United States. As anticipated, it was confiscated on her entry into the country, and the Supreme Court upheld the legality of this action.

However, the election of the Democratic candidate for president in November 1992, changed the regulatory climate considerably. The abortion issue loomed large throughout the presidential and congressional campaigns of 1992, with the Bush-Quayle campaign seen as championing the anti-abortion cause, and the Democrats strongly supporting (and supported by) the pro-choice forces. The triumph of the Democrats in both the presidential and congressional elections signalled a major shift in the U.S. environment. Within days of his inauguration, President Clinton issued an executive order assigning the Secretary of Health and Human Services, Donna Shalala, the task of reversing the Bush ban on RU-486 and promoting the testing, licensing, and manufacturing of RU-486 in the United States. Abortion rights groups applauded the decision, believing that RU-486 could be administered by private physicians and could thereby reduce the vulnerability of doctors and abortion clinics to the increasingly assertive demonstrations by anti-abortion activists.

Roussel-Uclaf faced a major challenge in responding to this reversal of pressure in the regulatory environment. Although the administration was now strongly urging Roussel-Uclaf to move ahead with testing and preparing to produce and market the drug in the United States, abortion remained a highly charged political and social issue, with the anti-abortion forces vowing to step up their campaign against abortion clinics and continuing to threaten a boycott if Roussel-Uclaf went ahead with the testing and approval process in the United States. Observers speculated that the company might license RU-486 to a new company, created with venture capital for the sole purpose of marketing the drug in the United States. Others speculated that the company might resolve the problem in the same way the manufacturers of IUDs had done earlier: give the license for the technology to the nonprofit Population Council, and let it find smaller companies willing to manufacture it and aid in its distribution. A boycott threat would be powerless against a single-product firm or a nonprofit organization, and its lack of economic strength would make it less vulnerable to lawsuits.

On the other hand, the potential applications for RU-486 were expanding. The drug proved to be beneficial in therapeutic abortions (i.e., later in pregnancy, up to the third term, when a pregnancy must be ended because the fetus is significantly malformed or the health of the mother is at risk). It can also help to facilitate the expulsion of a fetus that has died in the uterus, and for aiding in normal deliveries, to induce labor at term (which may help to avoid some Caesarean deliveries). Test-tube studies indicated uses for RU-486 in fields other than reproduction (including the treatment of breast cancer and Cushing's syndrome). In addition, the U.S. pharmaceutical company, G.D. Searle, had begun producing prostaglandins in the United States for other applications.

The size of the market remained extremely difficult to estimate, even in the United States, because so much depended on how quickly RU-486 might displace surgical abortion, and that depended on how quickly it was made available in the distribution system and adopted by the professional community. In France, RU-486 was used in up to 80 percent of the abortions in some clinics, and was used in 200,000 abortions in the first two years after its introduction. In the United Kingdom in the first year it was approved, it was used in fewer than 3,000 of the 167,400 abortions. Pricing of drugs in the U.S. market was, however, unregulated, making it more feasible to set a price that would provide a satisfactory return.

The United States remains the world's largest single market for pharmaceutical products. Dr. Baulieu stated in an interview, "I believe the key to the future of RU-486 lies in the United States." Yet the U.S. subsidiary, Hoechst-Roussel, was far from eager to undertake marketing and distribution of the product in the United States, and a year after President Clinton's directive, in early 1994, Roussel had still not taken any steps to move toward testing and distribution. Indeed the shift in the regulatory climate under the Clinton administration seemed if anything to put Roussel-Uclaf, Hoechst, and their U.S. subsidiary in an even more difficult position than before, facing internal and external problems whatever they chose to do.

Chronology of RU486

1980	Roussel-Uclaf researchers synthesize RU-486 antihormone.
1980–1982	Dr. Baulieu of INSERM and his team discover abortion-provoking properties of RU-486, refine product.
1982	World Health Organization begins testing and development programs in 15 countries.
	WHO signs agreement with Roussel for right to distribute in developing countries if Roussel decides not to distribute.
	RU-486 endorsed by U.S. Population Council.
1987/ October 9	Marketing arm of Roussel applies for government approval of RU-486.
1987/October	French government asks National Committee on Ethics for opinion.
1987/ December 15	Committee gives go-ahead, citing legal right to abortion in France and desirability of safest possible methods.
1988/Spring	French government authorizes marketing and distribution of RU-486.
1988/ June 23	General Assembly of Roussel's shareholders discusses market strategy, divided on whether to go ahead, no decision.
1988/September	French anti-abortion group distributes letters at Roussel, urging employees to refuse participation in research and production for RU-486.
1988/ October 21	Executive Office and Board of Directors decide, 16 votes to 4, not to market RU-486.
	CEO of Roussel, Sakiz, meets with Baulieu of INSERM to tell him the decision.
1988/October 24–25	1988 World Congress of Gynecology and Obstetrics (meeting in Rio de Janeiro) publicly petitions Sakiz to reverse decision.
1988/ October 26	French Archbishops plenary session applauds announcement of no-go decision.
1988/ October 28	French Minister of Health orders Roussel to begin marketing in France, citing approval already given to the drug and the legal right to abortion.
1988/December 7	Roussel's Board of Management frames policy for commercialization abroad; withdraws registration file submitted in Holland, suspends submissions in Great Britain and Sweden.

Index

abortion. *See* RU-486 case
action. *See* tools for action
advocacy groups, 25–26
alignment mechanisms, 11
antihormones, 23
Asia, and RU-486, 24–25, 30
Association for Conscientious Objectors to all Participation in Abortion, 25, 26
automobile industry. *See* Nissan

Bauer, Victor, 30
Baulieu, Etienne-Emile, 23, 28, 29, 32
Bernard, Jean, 24
black marketing, 27, 30
boundary-spanning, 9
boycotts, 25, 26
Bridgestone, 21
Bush, George, 31

Catholic Church, and RU-486 case, 25, 28
China, and RU-486, 24–25, 30
Clinton, Bill, 31
coalition-building, 13
coercive isomorphism, 19
competitors, 9
Confederation of Associations of Catholic Families, 28–29
cooptation, 13
cultural perspective on environment, 4, 17–21, 22

Delage, Michel, 27
de Lorenzo, Francesco, 30
distancing mechanisms, 9

employees as stakeholders, 13
engineering, simultaneous, 12
environment, external
    overview, 1–5
    action tools, 9, 11, 13, 19, 22
    competitors, 9
    cultural perspective, and the institutional field model, 4, 17–21, 22
    importance of interactions, 8
    input set and output set, 8
    integrated perspectives, 22
    key external actors, 8
    national culture models, 19
    new organization model and, 9
    political perspective, and the stakeholders model, 4, 13–16, 22
    regulatory set, 8–9
    RU-486 case, 4, 23–32
    strategic design perspective, and the organizational set model, 4, 8–12, 15, 22

environmental issues, 15
ethical issues, for RU-486 and abortion, 4, 25, 30–31
Europe, and RU-486, 29–30
Euvrard, Catherine, 27
Evin, Claude, 28
external environment. *See* environment, external
external stakeholders, 13

France. *See* RU-486 case

globalization
    external environment and, 4
    global organizational fields, 19–20
    stakeholders and, 15
goals, and strategic design, 9
government, local, 14
grouping mechanisms, 9

Hilger, Wolfgang, 26, 28
Hoechst. *See* RU-486 case
Honda, 11, 20
human resources, 11

incentives, 11
influence, in stakeholder model, 13, 14
information technology (IT), 9
input/throughput/output system, 8–11
INSERM (Institut National de la Sante et de la Recherche Medicale), 23
institutional field model, 4, 17–21, 22
institutionalization, 17
interdependent networks, 9
interests, in stakeholder model, 13, 14–15, 16
internal boycott, 26
internal stakeholders, 13
International Federation of Gynecology and Obstetrics, 28
International Planned Parenthood Federation, 29
International Right to Life Federation, 25
isomorphism, 17, 19, 20
IT (information technology), 9
Italy, 29–30

Joly, Pierre, 27, 28
Julien, Jacques, 25, 28

key external actors, 8

Le Monde, 24
liaison positions, 9
linking mechanisms, 9
lobbying, 9
local government, 14
location, and institutional fields, 19

Marinucci, Elena, 29–30
media, in institutional fields, 17, 19
mifepristone, 24
mimetic isomorphism, 19
mobilization of interests, 13

national culture models, 19
networking
    interdependence and, 9
    outsourcing and, 4
    of stakeholders, 15
new organization model, 9
Nissan
    institutional field case, 20–21
    organizational set case, 11–12
    stakeholder model case, 15–16
nonmarket strategies, 4
normative isomorphism, 19

organizational environment. *See* environment, external
organizational set model, 4, 8–12, 15, 22
output set, 8–11
outsourcing, 4

performance measurement systems, 11
pharmaceuticals. *See* RU-486 case
Pinotti, Jose, 29
Planned Parenthood, 29
political perspective on environment, 4, 13–16, 22
post-Fordism, 21
power, in stakeholder model, 13
press. *See* media
pricing of RU-486, 29
pro-choice movement. *See* RU-486 case
pro-life movement. *See* RU-486 case
prostaglandins, 24, 30
Proston, 25
public opinion, in RU-486 case, 25–26, 28, 30–31

quality management, total, 21

Reagan, Ronald, 31
reference groups, 17
regulatory set, 8–12
relationships, in external environment, 8, 9, 22
resource allocation, 11
resource environment, 4, 8
Roussel, Gaston, 23
Roussel, Jean-Claude, 23

Roussel-Uclaf. *See* RU-486 case
Royal Dutch Shell, 15
RU-486 case
    overview, 4, 23
    in Asia, 24–25, 30
    chronology, 9-32
    debate on proceeding to market, 25–27
    decision not to distribute, and reaction, 27–28
    distribution in France, 29
    in Europe, 29–30
    French government and, 24–25, 28–29
    history of Roussel-Uclaf, 23
    potential applications, 32
    pricing, 29
    the product, 23–24
    in United States, 30–32

Sakiz, Edouard, 23, 26, 28, 29, 30
Scott, Richard, 17
Shalala, Donna, 31
simultaneous engineering, 12
Singapore, 30
social actors, 4. *See also* environment, external
social context, 17
socializing agents, 17
social reference group, 17
stakeholders model, 4, 13–16, 22
strategic design, 4, 8–12, 22
structuring agencies, 17, 19
suppliers, in Nissan case, 12, 21
suppliers, interests of, 16
sustainable development, 22

tools for action
    in institutional field model, 19
    integrating the environmental models, 22
    in organizational set model, 9, 11
    in stakeholder model, 13
total quality management, 21
Toyota, 20

UAW (United Automobile Workers), 16
unions, 16, 21
United Automobile Workers (UAW), 16
Upjohn, 25

Willke, John, 25, 30–31
World Congress of Gynecology and Obstetrics, 28, 29
World Health Organization (WHO), 24, 27, 30

MANAGING FOR THE FUTURE

Organizational Behavior & Processes

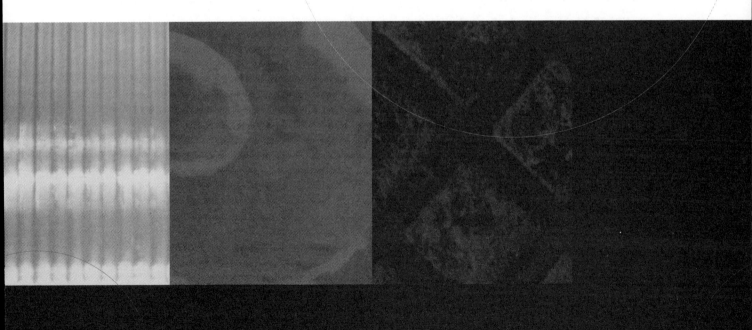

**Learning Across Borders:
Disneyland on the Move**

MANAGING FOR THE FUTURE
Organizational Behavior & Processes, Third Edition

Deborah Ancona
Sloan School of Management
Massachusetts Institute of Technology

Thomas A. Kochan
Sloan School of Management
Massachusetts Institute of Technology

Maureen Scully
Graduate School of Management
Simmons College

John Van Maanen
Sloan School of Management
Massachusetts Institute of Technology

D. Eleanor Westney
Sloan School of Management
Massachusetts Institute of Technology

Dedicated to those who have inspired us to try to be better students and teachers.
Special thanks to: Professor Jack Barbash • Professor Arthur H. Gladstein • Professor Marius B. Jansen • Professor Joanne Martin • Professor Edgar H. Schein

---

VP/Editorial Director
Jack W. Calhoun

VP/Editor-in-Chief
Michael P. Roche

Senior Publisher
Melissa S. Acuña

Executive Editor
John Szilagyi

Senior Developmental Editor
Judith O'Neill

Marketing Manager
Jacquelyn Carrillo

Production Editor
Emily Gross

Manufacturing Coordinator
Rhonda Utley

Compositor
Trejo Production

Printer
Von Hoffmann Press, Inc.
Frederick, MD

Internal Designer
Bethany Casey

Cover Designer
Bethany Casey

Photographs
©PhotoDisc

Design Project Manager
Bethany Casey

COPYRIGHT ©2005
by South-Western, a division of Thomson Learning. Thomson Learning™ is a trademark used herein under license.

Printed in the United States of America
1 2 3 4 5 07 06 05 04 03

For more information contact
South-Western College Publishing,
5191 Natorp Boulevard,
Mason, Ohio, 45040
Or you can visit our Internet site at:
http://www.swlearning.com

ALL RIGHTS RESERVED
No part of this work covered by the copyright hereon may be reproduced or used in any form or by any means—graphic, electronic, or mechanical, including photocopying, recording, taping, Web distribution or information storage and retrieval systems—without the written permission of the publisher.

For permission to use material from this text or product, contact us by
Tel: (800) 730-2214
Fax: (800) 730-2215
http://www.thomsonrights.com

Library of Congress Control Number: 2003113908
ISBN 0-324-05575-7

Contents

Learning Across Borders: Disneyland on the Move

Overview		4

Core

Class Note	**Disneyland in the US of A** *The Copy: Disneyland Goes to Florida 10* *References 13*	8
The Press	**The Smile Factory: Work at Disneyland** *It's a Small World 14* *The Disney Way 22* *References 23*	13
Class Note	**Disney Goes to Tokyo: Crossing the Pacific** *The Cultural Marketplace 26* *References 28*	25
The Press	**Displacing Disney: Some Notes on the Flow of Culture** *The Transformation 28* *Cultural Experience Revisited 32* *References 33*	28
Class Note	**Disney Goes to Paris: Crossing the Atlantic** *References 39*	35
The Press	**Mouse Trap** *Mickey's Misfires 40* *Disney Knows Best 40* *Tarnished Image 40* *Corporate Hubris 41* *Ballooning Costs 41* *Good Attendance 42* *High Prices 43*	39
Class Note	**Disney Goes to Hong Kong: An Uncertain Journey** *A World with Mouse Ears? 49* *References 49*	45
The Press	**The Ever-Expanding, Profit-Maximizing, Cultural-Imperialist, Wonderful World of Disney**	50

Index

Overview

When a company takes its operations abroad, its managers face an array of conscious decisions about what organizational patterns to adopt. The range is wide, from taking a few to taking most of its established ways of doing things across borders. However, the firm also enters a learning process because much of what it takes abroad is less the product of conscious choice than a consequence of the organization's current political structure and culture. And, quite often, the patterns associated with the power arrangements and taken-for-granted assumptions of the organization's leadership create unanticipated difficulties in the new environment. Rarely is a cross-border move unproblematic.

Moving organizational patterns from the social context in which they were developed to a different context always involves learning and change. Some of the change needed can be anticipated and planned for by managers who have a deep understanding of their organizations and of the similarities and differences across the environments in which they are working. But much is, of necessity, a product of learning by doing in the new environment. Flexibility and fast learning become extremely important in this setting.

This module offers a window into these change dynamics through the case of Disneyland. The popular theme park (now a "resort") has been an enormously successful organization in its home environments—Anaheim and Orlando. It was successful beyond all expectations in its first venture abroad, Tokyo Disneyland. Yet it was troubled beyond all expectations in its second global venture in France and the troubles continue today even though the amount of yearly park visitors makes Disneyland Paris far and away the number one tourist site in Europe. Now a fifth Disneyland park is under construction. Hong Kong Disneyland is slated to open in 2005. How will it fare in the land of one country, two systems? What lessons will Disney have learned as a result of its 20+ years in the cross-border amusement trade?

Disneyland is a rich case in the study of cross-border learning. It is, at home, an exemplar of the service industry where organization is not only key to its competitive advantage (in the current language of strategy) but the organization is itself part of its product. Successfully moving key elements of the organization abroad is therefore critical to the success of its internationalization. But service products are very much a product of their social context. How do services developed in one particular national context play out in another? Disneyland provides a case where services are tied closely to the cultural context of their provision. As Walt Disney remarked in 1957: "There's an American theme behind the whole park. And I believe in emphasizing the story of what made America great and what will keep it great" (quoted in Watts, 1997, p. 142). How does such an apparently tight connection between Disney and America play out in Japan, France, and Hong Kong?

The service industry setting for this case has another implication. Disneyland is in what might be called the "feeling business." Its elementary product is emotion—comfort, awe, pleasure, laughter, and well-being. Its corporate image is one in which the customers are happy, the workers good-looking, and the managers all above average. Yet, as the materials in this module make clear, whatever cheerful services Disney executives believe they are providing to the millions of visitors that flow through its park gates each year, employees at the bottom of the organization are the ones who must provide them. Thus the work-a-day practices that employees adopt to amplify or dampen customer spirits are crucial to the success of the organization. The happiness trade is, like all service-oriented businesses, an interactional one. It rests partly on the symbolic resources put into place by history, other corporate products (notably movies), and park design. But it also rests on the presence of a visibly enthusiastic and animated workforce more or less eager to greet the guests, pack the trams, push the buttons, deliver the food, dump the garbage, and, in general, marshal the will to meet and perhaps exceed customer expectations. Indifference, false moves, detected insincerity, rude words or glances, careless disregard for safety, cynicism, or simply a sleepy and bored expression on Pocahontas or Peter Pan can undermine the enterprise and ruin a sale. How Disney manages its production and cast of thousands each day (and year after year) in quite distinct national contexts is very much a matter of concern in this case.

Like many service companies, Disney is widely regarded as addressing this challenge through its explicit fostering of a strong organizational culture. Although Disney is consistently heralded as one of the best-run companies in the United States, a number of instructive anomalies are associated with its work policies and practices. For example, visitors to Disneyland are often quite taken by the seemingly effortless courtesy shown them by park operatives, by the energetic ways these operatives take on their work roles, and by their well-scrubbed faces, pleasant smiles, and apparent concern for maintaining order and cleanliness in the park. Yet Disney operatives work at odd times, for minimum wage, on jobs designed with little or no discretion, in stressful and crowded conditions, and under omnipresent if not draconian supervision. Most work part-time and have virtually no career opportunities nor is much choice allowed them as to personal appearance, demeanor, type of job, or working hours (which shift from week to week and sometimes day to day). A standard textbook in the field of organizational behavior would suggest that work designed in such a fashion would be most unattractive and unlikely to generate much employee interest, enthusiasm, or job commitment. However, Disney in the United States has historically attracted an educated, hard-working, well-groomed, loyal, rather charming, and altogether enviable workforce and continues to do so today (albeit with a bit more effort than in times past). What is going on here?

As suggested in this module, any answer to this question must take into account not only the organizational culture of Disneyland, as nurtured by management, but its various indigenous worker subcultures as well as the broader national and customer cultures within which it operates. It is a complex and ever-changing picture, for culture itself is continually changing. But taking a cultural perspective in this case means we must seriously consider the perspectives of those who are both "working for the Mouse" and those who are "guests of the Mouse." The aim here is to show just how, where, and why culture matters in the workplace. And looking at Disneyland across several cultural contexts—internal and external, national and transnational—provides an intriguing portrait of a sometimes wildly romanticized world of work and play that perhaps travels less well than we might expect.

In addition, Disneyland provides an interesting reversal of the usual internationalization process of U.S. firms. Most U.S. companies set up their first foreign operations in Canada, which is physically and culturally close, and then expand to Europe. Only after being successful in Canada and Europe does a company build on its experience in internationalization—what it has learned about crossing borders—to venture to Asia, which is much more distant physically and culturally and often proves to be a much more difficult organizational environment in which to succeed. Disneyland, in contrast, went first to Japan, a notoriously challenging environment for Western companies, where it was a smashing economic success; then, presumably having learned how to "go international," it went to Europe, where it came close to a spectacular failure and, even after more than 10 years of operational experience, is not yet out of financial hot waters. To further complicate matters, its next move will be into Hong Kong, where the post-1970s rise of a new class of highly educated, sophisticated, affluent consumers reside in a political and economic sphere characterized by a curious mix of socialist bureaucracy and bare-knuckled frontier capitalism.

The readings in this module are organized around a running set of four Class Notes that provide an overview of Disneyland in each of four contexts: the United States, Japan, France, and Hong Kong. Interspersed between these Class Notes are a series of more detailed analyses taken from the research literature or business press. The first Class Note on Disneyland in the United States is followed by "The Smile Factory," a close look at the social organization and work culture of ride operators at Disneyland. This ethnographic study by John Van Maanen focuses on managerial demands and worker responses at Disneyland. The second Class Note on Disneyland in Tokyo is followed by a brief analysis of the Japanese park. "Displacing Disney," also written by John Van Maanen, looks at how the Japanese have absorbed, modified, and otherwise made Tokyo Disneyland their own. The third Class Note, on Disneyland in France, is followed by a reading from *The Wall Street Journal*, by Peter Gumbel and Richard Turner. "Mouse Trap" explores the problems Disneyland was facing several years after the park opened outside Paris (and, to a lesser—but pressing—extent still faces today). The final Class Note takes up a few of the questions that Hong Kong poses for Disney. It is followed by a thoughtful analysis from *Wired* by Jonathan Weber, wonderfully titled in turn-of-the-century style "The Ever-Expanding, Profit-Maximizing, Cultural-Imperialist Wonderful World of Disney."

Assignment Summary

1. Come to class having read all four Class Notes and their accompanying articles and excerpts and be prepared to discuss the following issues:
   - How does Disneyland produce the "Disneyland Experience" in the United States?
   - What made Tokyo Disneyland so successful? What lessons did Disney learn from it?
   - Why was Disneyland Paris so troubled? What did Disney do to try to turn it around?
   - What problems do you expect Hong Kong Disneyland to face when it opens in 2005?

2. Your instructor may form in-class discussion groups to consider specific questions related to Disneyland on the move.

Additional Suggested Readings

On Disneyland

Fjellman, Stephen. 1992. *Vinyl Leaves: Walt Disney's World and America*. Boulder CO: Westview Press. A breathless tour of Disney World conducted by a witty anthropologist. The flip side of Steve Birnbaum's Official Disneyland guides.

Foglesong, Richard E. 2001. *Married to the Mouse: Walt Disney World and Orlando*. New Haven, CT: Yale University Press. An intriguing historical work tracing the co-evolution of Walt Disney World and the city of Orlando with an emphasis on the consequences of the enticements granted the organization for coming to Florida—among them the establishment of their own private government (what the author calls "the Vatican with Mouse ears").

Grover, Ron. 1997. *The Disney Touch: Disney, ABC, & the Quest for the World's Greatest Media Empire* (rev. ed.). Chicago: Irwin Professional Publishing. A journalist's account of the Disney corporation, with particular attention to the turnaround of the company in the mid-1980s led by Michael Eisner, and the company's recent acquisition of ABC.

Raz, Avid. 1999. *Riding the Black Ship: Japan and Tokyo Disneyland*. Boston: Harvard University Press. A cultural reading of the customer reactions to the rides, sites, and shows of Tokyo Disneyland combined with an analysis of their production by those who work in the park.

Wasko, Janet, Mark Phillips, and Eileen R. Meehan (Eds.). 2001. *Dazzled by Disney? The Global Disney Audiences Project*. New York: Leicester University Press. A smart reading of the results of an 18-country study of the Disney brand around the world undertaken by a small group of media researchers. Country profiles are developed to display and explain the reception of Disney products in specific national and cultural contexts.

Watts, Steven. 1997. *The Magic Kingdom: Walt Disney and the American Way of Life*. Boston: Houghton Mifflin Company. A scholarly but altogether readable account, by a historian, of the life of Walt Disney and the evolution of his company and vision.

On Organizational Culture and Internationalization Processes

Pells, Richard. 1997. *Not Like Us: How Europeans Have Loved, Hated, and Transformed American Culture Since World War II*. New York: Basic Books. An enjoyable and often surprising analysis by a cultural historian of the interactions between European and American culture.

Schein, Edgar. 2001. *Organizational Culture and Leadership*, 3rd ed. San Francisco: Jossey-Bass. A careful, psychologically oriented look at the role founders and managers play in the creation, maintenance, and alteration of organizational culture.

Watson, James L. (Ed.). 1997. *Golden Arches East: McDonald's in East Asia*. Palo Alto, CA: Stanford University Press. A wonderfully detailed and textured study of the reception McDonald's restaurants has had in five Asian cities plus a useful treatment of the often-voiced fear that a homogeneous, global culture is around the corner.

Zachary, G. Pascal. 2000. *The Global Me*. New York: Public Affairs Press. A lively and contemporary look at the staying power of identity ("hybrid identities" in particular) in a time in which traditional markers of identity are in decline (nations, religion, class) as global capitalism—and its presumed relentless opposition to local culture—works its way around the world.

Learning Across Borders: Disneyland on the Move

CORE

Module

Disneyland in the US of A

The amusement trade is big business. It is a cultural business whose goal, it seems, is to generate good feelings for a good price. At the top of the trade are the spinning turnstiles of Disneyland and Disney World whose yearly tourist traffic surpass that of the nation's capital, ranking fourth in the world (and closing fast) behind the great pilgrimage sites of Mecca, the Vatican, and Kyoto. If attendance figures and repeat visits are our guide, it would certainly seem that Disney has made good on its claim to have built "the happiest place on earth."

The concept of Disneyland took shape in the early 1950s when Walt Disney, the creator of Mickey Mouse and the founder of Hollywood's most successful animation studio (then and now), decided to construct an amusement park built around Disney films and characters. The legend of Disneyland tells how Walt's own brother Roy, the financial director of Walt Disney Productions, was one of many skeptics who thought the amusement park idea absurd and how Walt had to borrow on his life insurance for seed money for the venture (Grover, 1997). Apparently, those within the company are far less inclined to remember that Walt bolstered his famous creative instinct by hiring the Stanford Research Institute to conduct first an economic feasibility study of his plan and then commissioned a follow-up study to analyze area demographics, land use, traffic patterns, and so on to come up with a recommendation for construction on the site.

On the basis of SRI's recommendation, Disney acquired 160 acres of orange groves in Anaheim, California, in 1953. A few months later, he signed an agreement with ABC Television to provide financing to move ahead. Other television networks had been courting Disney, trying to lure him to the emerging medium, but only ABC, then a distant and struggling third among the three major networks, was willing to pay Walt's price: Not only generous payments for a weekly show, but also working capital for his new park. ABC became a partner in Disneyland (owning 34 percent of the shares, a proportion equal to that of Walt Disney Productions) and immediately put up half a million dollars to finance construction. It also guaranteed loans for a further $4.5 million.

The premiere of the "Disneyland" TV show, on October 27, 1954, drew 52 percent of the potential viewing audience (Brooks and Marsh, 1979). It was ABC's first hit show, and the network was delighted when the Disney studios followed it with the weekly "Mickey Mouse Club" (premiering in 1955). From the beginning, the Disneyland program was built around the park, whose five "lands," or areas, provided the framing for the weekly shows. In the nine months between the premiere of the show and the opening of the park, in July of 1955, several programs on the park's construction, ushering viewers behind the scenes of the building process to see the plans taking concrete shape and preparing them for the glories that the finished product would offer, were broadcast. The park's opening took place under the eyes of a platoon of television cameras beaming the opening to a television audience of millions.

The reality of opening day at what some close observers, to their future embarrassment, dubbed "Walt's Folly" was not as triumphant as it appeared on television. Social historian Steven Watts (1997, p. 387) described the day as follows:

> *While ABC cameras conveyed scenes of bustling joy and announcers pontificated about the historical significance of the event, the behind-the-scenes situation veered dangerously close to total collapse. Construction went on through the night until just moments before the ceremonies began, and Tomorrowland remained muffled in banners and balloons to hide its half-completed state. Near chaos ensued as traffic jams tangled up the Santa Ana freeway and the festivities prompted one disaster after another. A gas leak forced a temporary shutdown of Fantasyland, the park restaurants ran out of food, a paucity of bathrooms and drinking fountains made many guests grumpy, and the blazing heat melted freshly laid asphalt into sticky black goo that caught and broke many a lady's high heel. Jack Kinney, the studio animator and director, remembered that staff members and their families had been assigned to populate certain areas and they did their duty by smiling and waving when the television cameras turned on them.*

The recovery from these opening-act follies was swift and sure. Attendance quickly began streaming through the enchanted gates. More than a million customers visited Disneyland within six months and the park was well on its way to becoming something of a treasure, a symbol of American popular culture and a must-see for foreign visitors (and even foreign dignitaries). As a business, however, Disneyland provided an anchor for the growing Disney empire: creating what marketing gurus call "synergies" across Disneyland the park, Disneyland the TV show, Disney movies, Disney clothing, and Disney comics, records, books, and other products. It proved its worth. Excerpts from the movies provided fodder for the TV show, an assortment of theatrical productions, various themes for Disneyland "rides," as well as merchandising spin-offs from clothing to music. The television show also provided free advertising for the park and the movies. Steven Watts (1997, p. 391) provides some apt measures: "Its success quickly became evident. In 1955 [the year the park opened], Walt Disney Productions' gross income more than doubled from the year before, and it continued to grow by leaps and bounds, going from $11.6 million in 1954 to $58.4 million in 1959."

The enduring appeal of Disneyland is indeed remarkable. In 2002, Disneyland—along with the rest of what is now called the Disney Resort in Anaheim (including a "second gate," Disney's California Adventure)—drew just under 23 million visitors. Disney World in Florida attracts a far greater number, somewhere in the neighborhood of 40–50 million per year. Disneyland has become the icon of the service industry by delivering a "product" that is completely defined (and "consumed") by the customer's interaction with it. But, what explains the product's drawing—and staying—power?

Viewed as a product, Disneyland is part movie center, part carnival, part tourist site, part shopping mall, part museum, part state fair, part playground, part shrine, part ceremony, part family institution, part spectacle, part festival, and so on. In contemporary America, Disneyland seems to emerge as a calm and peaceful island in stressful and troubled times. Inside its boundaries, the forces of decay are arrested, sanity and safety prevail, sexual innuendoes are all but forbidden, liquor is taboo, evil is overcome, the innocent rule, disorder is tamed, the future is clarified, the past cleaned up, and, in general, the perverse world of doubt, fear, and unfair competition outside the gates is held at bay. One of the most striking features of Disneyland has been its celebration of America. In remarks made at the official opening of Disneyland in 1955, Walt Disney explicitly dedicated the park to "the ideals, the dreams, and the hard facts which have created America." Most observers would agree:

> *The park promoted an unproblematic celebration of the American people and their experience. . . . Functioning as a kind of three-dimensional movie, the park offered guests an ordered sequence of environments that began with the optimistic, nostalgic warmth of Main Street, USA, progressed to the innocent thrills of Adventureland, the patriotic history of Frontierland, the childlike sense of wonder in Fantasyland, and the confident futurism of Tomorrowland. Subtle psychological touches—a carousel where all of the horses are painted white, a haunted house where death is funny, a miniaturized automobile ride where order and safety prevail—combined to encourage feelings of security, harmony, and well-being.* (Watts, 1997, p. 437)

Disneyland has of course been subject to countless assessments by culture critics who, while not always impressed by its wonders, do manage to agree on a number of unifying themes standing behind the product, themes that apparently integrate and make meaningful a visit to the park. Most begin by noting the order, safety, and cleanliness at Disneyland and the marked contrast these features bear in relation to contemporary urban life in America. The rectangular grid of the city is replaced in the park by the graceful, curved walkways. Motorists become pedestrians. The drab, industrial, metropolitan landscape is replaced by brightly colored buildings done up in ebullient and whimsical forms and covered by sumptuous ornaments and the twinkling of lights that turn night into day. The crowded, disorderly, fear-inspiring city scenes of ordinary life are transformed within the park to obedient, friendly queues and the peaceful strolling of people kept secure by unarmed, unobtrusive yet ever-present and smiling park police ("security hosts" in Disney-speak). Work clothes give way to leisure garb. Adults take on the role of children while children take on adult roles by driving snarling miniature automobiles on toy freeways, exploring deep space, and making family choices about what to do next. The frontier towns of yesteryear are no longer dusty, dirty, and rather formless but become prim, tidy, and "what they should have been" by virtue of their scrubbed, freshly painted, simple, and sweet look.

In the American context, Disneyland is a topsy-turvy world that highlights in its physical and social design a long string of contrasts that set the park off as a sought-after cultural experience for patrons: work/play; adult/child; dirty/clean; poverty/wealth; dangerous/safe; rude/civil; cold/warm; routine/festive; and on and on. These contrasts of America/Disneyland create the differences on which the park's claim to be "the happiest place on earth" rests. To bring off such a claim is no trivial matter however and requires the banishment (or at least minimization) of all signs of decay, crime, confusion, discontent, pain, or struggle in the park's design and the reduction wherever possible of the social, stylistic, and ideological diversity on the part of customers and employees alike.

This image, as all Disneyland designers, planners, and managers would attest, rests on Disney's (near) total control of the environment to create a common and structured experience for the visitor alongside the clever concealment of this control. What the individual might regard as the experience of spontaneity, personal imagination, and communal intimacy are cast within a social context of directed flow, crowd control, the expertise of well-placed park attendants, designated picture-perfect photo sites and the presence of endless attractions and spectacles in which fun becomes consumption and memory is guaranteed by the purchase of souvenirs. Again, historian Watts (1997, p. 389) makes the point well:

> *A shrewd design and engineering scheme, for example, manipulated both the movements and emotions of the huge crowds. One essential principle emphasized what Walt liked to call "weenies," which caught the eye and drew people along preordained routes so that crowds flowed smoothly. This was augmented by another clever design ploy, which muted the frustration of waiting in long lines for the park's attractions. Disney planners came up with a unique system: first, a snakelike pattern masked the length of a line by running it back and forth in parallel lines; then a variety of visual and audio images kept those in line entertained; and finally, a cleverly engineered schedule kept visitors steadily embarking on the ride so the line would always appear to be moving forward.*

Three groups of people are largely responsible for the control that underpins Disneyland: the Imagineers, the Suits, and the Cast Members. The Imagineers are the designers. They represent the rather eclectic mix of engineers, programmers, artists, landscapers, robotics experts, sculptors, writers, machinists, and model builders that design and update the parks and the rides, script the presentations, and shape the physical and imaginative landscape of the park. Until Walt Disney's death in 1966, they worked directly under him as a separate organizational unit, and they still regard themselves as a rather special and insulated part of the company that is carrying on his tradition. The Suits are the finance, marketing, and management people who, among other duties, identify and exploit the synergies across Disney's businesses, manage costs, line up the corporate sponsors whose signed presence in and around Disneyland is ubiquitous, keep the Disney brand alive and well and, most generally, try to insure that the current strategic thrusts of the organization are carried out effectively.

Most crucial to the experience of Disneyland and most visible to the customers, however, are the Cast Members—the front-line staff at the park who control the traffic, sell the tickets, welcome the Guests (as customers are called), operate the rides, staff the shops, serve the food, bus the dishes, make the beds, manage and direct the crowds, play the Disney characters that so amuse children, and, critically, do so in such a way that conveys an air of spontaneous fun and delight essential to the Disneyland experience. Carefully selected, trained, and closely monitored in their jobs, Cast Members (in particular, ride operators) and the organization that shapes their work are described in detail later in this module.

The Copy: Disneyland Goes to Florida

By the late 1950s, Walt Disney, while proud of Disneyland where he kept an apartment over the firehouse on Main Street, USA, grew interested in adding to Disney revenues by tapping the larger American market. Only 2 percent of the average daily attendance at Disneyland during its first five years of operation came from the eastern portion of the United States. Moreover, having tasted the predictable and overflowing revenue streams generated by his new and improved West Coast version of the amusement park (now known to the trade as a "theme park"), Disney wanted to diversify his business away from what he called "the damn fickle motion picture industry" (Foglesong, 2001, p. 65). Adding to the motivation for growth, Disney was also bothered by the uncontrolled development that Disneyland had brought to Anaheim beyond the park gates. He saw the chain restaurants, no-tell motels, tacky tourist shops, and side-show amusements that sprang up around Disneyland—in cheap and unattractive buildings—as both an aesthetic affront to the attractiveness of his park and as allowing "a bunch of opportunists" to make money off his creation. Walt and his senior managers (armed again with numerous consulting reports) decided to build a second park to reach a new market and this time the guarantee of stronger Disney control of the park's surrounding environment and future opportunities would be a major criterion for site selection.

In 1964, Walt Disney Productions quietly began buying land in and around Orlando, Florida. The choice of location was based on Disney's desire to avoid coastlines and thus, like the park in Anaheim, disassociate the new park from earlier boardwalk amusement zones and also to allow 360 degree expansion within a well-buffered development space. A "tourist bubble" could thus be created within which no competing "weenies" (i.e., alternative tourist attractions) would exist. With considerable stealth, purchase and sale agreements were worked out surreptitiously to avoid a run-up in land prices. Eighteen months later, in 1965, when Disney's plans eventually leaked out, the company had acquired more than 27,000 acres—43 square miles, roughly the size of San Francisco.

As publicly announced, Walt Disney envisioned the creation on this land not only of a bigger Disneyland but also EPCOT, the Experimental Prototype Community of Tomorrow. While pitching the development in Florida, the Disney organization characterized EPCOT as a utopian "planned urban community" for some 20,000 initial residents complete with an industrial park, electric mass transit system, and housing and apartment complexes. Disney's sudden death in December 1966 meant that this larger vision was never achieved, although EPCOT Center, focusing on corporate-sponsored pavilions, exhibits, and attractions set in a World's Fair-like setting, provided the substitute. So goes the official story.

Foglesong (2001), however, suggests—with a good deal of evidence—that Disney never intended EPCOT to include permanent residents (who, after all, would not only require municipal services but might well also want a say and vote in the community). The original EPCOT "vision" is perhaps best seen as a negotiating ploy the company used to induce the City of Orlando and surrounding counties to provide long-term guarantees of Disney's sovereignty over the land they purchased thus allowing growth to take place unrestrained by any awkward external review process or uncooperative civic officials and to proceed at whatever pace suited the organization.

Whatever the truth of the matter, Disney soon became the envy of other land developers because the agreements worked out with local governing agencies left the company free to regulate the use of their land in whatever way they chose. As set up by the governance structure devised in 1967—the Reedy Creek Improvement District—Disney has near total control of their considerable land holdings. They can provide (or not provide) fire and police services. They can build roads and lay sewer lines. They can regulate the sale and manufacture of alcoholic beverages. They can even build an airport and nuclear power plant.

The Orlando deal was indeed a sweet one for the company. If nothing else, the structure put into place vividly displays the power a global corporation can exercise through its location decisions over eager local governments and community leaders. Seeking to attract a large, name brand business and the employment gains, status boosts, tax revenues, and urban development such a business is likely to advance, growth-oriented local officials are only too willing to enter into iron-clad, prenuptial-like agreements that disproportionately favor the long-term interests of one party (Disney) over the other (Orlando).

This arrangement is not to say that Orlando did not have much to gain by Disney's presence and growth over the years. What it did mean, however, is that the initial agreements carved out left Disney in the driver's seat and put the Disney World growth decisions outside the reach of voters and elected officials. It is arguably the case that initially the interests of Disney and Orlando were closely matched—a gain for one was a gain for the other. As the region developed and subsequently changed, the interests of the two drifted apart. Today, more than half the Orlando workforce is engaged in low-paying service and retail work, wages are stagnant and have been for a decade or more, roads are crowded and traffic congestion is a major problem, municipal services are stretched, education facilities are inadequate, and affordable housing is scarce. Most significantly, state and local agencies in charge of such matters are hard-pressed to bring Disney to task for what the company regards as external economic and social failings well beyond their control, concern and responsibility.

What the company did accomplish with its resources and power in the late 1960s was to build another theme park: "The Magic Kingdom." It opened in 1969 and now with its peripheral attractions—EPCOT center (1971) MGM-Disney Studios (1989), Animal Kingdom (1998) and an ever increasing number of Disney-owned and operated hotels and fun zones—the total complex in Orlando outdraws Disneyland by a wide margin. Walt Disney World has in fact grown so large that some liken it to "Mickey Mouse on Steroids." Yet, despite its size, variety of attractions, and popularity, it doesn't overwhelm its predecessor from the company's or customer's point of view simply because its very own construction sets Disneyland apart as an "original," giving it the measure of authenticity and dignity that only a copy can provide.

The copy is not, of course, perfect. The scale is larger and some attractions such as the Matterhorn bobsleds are still found only at Disneyland. The Magic Kingdom lacks some of the intimacy of Disneyland but when combined with the other tourist sites at Walt Disney World it becomes part of an activity menu that lengthens the average visitor stay to a matter of days rather than hours. Even though Disney greatly expanded its California operations in recent years (2000–2001) and now calls its Anaheim complex "The Disney Resort," the Orlando plant remains far larger and represents most successfully (and assertively) what those in the tourist trade call a "total destination site."

Other, more modest changes within the park are visible as well. Sleeping Beauty's Castle is replaced by a bigger, more photogenic and splendid version, Cinderella's Castle. Some of the rides like Big Thunder Mountain are longer and slightly more harrowing. Others, such as the Pirates of the Caribbean, which is much more elaborate and lengthy at Disneyland, are thin replicas. Still, despite small changes, the cultural experience for American visitors to the two theme parks must be much the same. The context does not shift radically nor do visitors seemingly notice much difference—beyond scale—in the two parks (Adams, 1991; Wasko, 2001). What the park in Walt Disney World provides however is a measure of choice for those about to build yet another copy of Disneyland.

Walt's brother Roy presided over the initial building of Disney World. Roy died in 1971, months after the reconstituted EPCOT opened. A rather conservative set of managers drawn from the top ranks of the organization succeeded the Disney brothers. Their approach was to play the role of guardians of the Disney legacy by avoiding risk taking and by trying to keep expenses down. Despite the fact that Orlando had, by 1982, become the most popular tourist destination in the world, they left the development of hotels on the property to others (contrary to Walt's original plans) and took what can only be called a caretaker's attitude toward the business. Attendance began to fall at both parks just as the audience for "The Wonderful World of Disney" fell. The show was eventually cancelled in the early 1980s. Movies made and distributed during this caretaking period were, with few exceptions, box office (and critical) failures. The loss of free advertising and the declining fortunes of the company were acutely felt. Yet the long tradition of not advertising Disneyland(s) continued until the advent of a new CEO, and new era, for Walt Disney Enterprises.

Michael Eisner came on board in 1984. He was an outsider to the company but had cut his managerial teeth in the entertainment industry and emerged to head Disney as an aggressive, innovative, and growth-oriented manager. Eisner quickly put together a new management group called TeamDisney, consisting of Eisner, Frank Wells, and Jeff Katzenbach. They immediately raised prices at the two parks, launched an extensive advertising campaign, and made major investments in refurbishing the parks, opening new rides and recreational areas, and building a number of massive hotels. Stockholders and Imagineers were delighted—stockholders because the investments brought about an immediate upturn in the business and Imagineers because they were now cut loose to get to work and no longer chaffed at the penny-pinching ways of the Suits.

By the late 1980s and throughout the 1990s, park attendance grew steadily. The hotels operated near full occupancy. A six-acre district of late-night entertainment opened at Walt Disney World in 1989 that attracted crowds looking for somewhat livelier entertainment than that provided in the theme park itself or at EPCOT. Pleasure Island included bars, restaurants, and a dance venue with 170 video screens. A similar development, Downtown Disney, opened in Anaheim in 2001. Disney, under Eisner, put forth a string of highly successful movies with adult themes and started producing and distributing modestly popular foreign films—using Touchstone, Miramax, and Merchant-Ivory production companies to distribute those films not associated with the family-oriented, PG-rated Disney brand. The animation studios (sometimes in partnership with other animation firms such as Pixar) cranked out blockbuster hit after blockbuster hit: *Beauty and the Beast, The Little Mermaid, The Lion King, The Hunchback of Notre Dame, Hercules, Aladdin, Toy Story, A Bug's Life, Finding Nemo,* and so on. As video players and tapes became available, affordable, and popular, a new market virtually tailored-made for Disney products opened up. It was this market that provided "free" advertising for Disneyland; most Disney videotapes opened with "trailers" touting the delights of a visit to a Disney park. Indeed, with only an occasional slip in Disney's financial performance (2000–2002), the business press for two decades gushed at the seeming Midas Touch of Michael Eisner and lavished much praise on the wonderful (corporate) world of Disney.

As of 2004, the synergies at Disney seem stronger than ever. A short list of the cross-fertilizing activities in the Disney empire (circa 2003)—as put together largely during the Eisner regime—include the making of films, videotapes, television, and radio programs (ABC, ESPN, cable channels), and a variety of theatrical shows. In addition to its theme parks, the company owns and runs cruise ships, hundreds of retail stores and a wide range of resort properties from rustic (but expensive) family campgrounds to five-star luxury hotels. Walt's dream of Disneyland seems downright humble when seen in light of the corporate riches Disney now holds—generating more than $25 billion of revenue in 2002.

Yet, it is worth noting that the theme parks of Walt's imagination in California and Florida still provide the fuel for both the growth and revenue stability of the Disney organization. Theme park revenues for Disney in the United States are rather consistent and provide on average about 40–50 percent of Disney profits from year to year, profits that support (and cover) other Disney ventures (Hirsch, 2000). At the heart of the theme park of course are the thousands of low-level employees

(15,000 in Anaheim and almost 55,000 in Orlando) who must put on the show day after day after day. The work of a highly visible subset of these Disneyland Cast Members—ride operators—are described in detail in the accompanying article, "The Smile Factory."

References

Adams, Judith A. 1991. *The American Amusement Park Industry: A History of Technology and Thrills*. Boston: Twayne Publishers.

Brooks, Tim, and Earle Marsh. 1979. *The Complete Directory to Prime Time Network TV Shows 1946–Present*. New York: Ballantine Books.

Hirsch, Jerry. 2000. It's the most profitable unit after all. *Los Angeles Times* (July 22).

Grover, Ron. 1997. *The Disney Touch: Disney, ABC, & the Quest for the World's Greatest Media Empire* (rev. ed.). Chicago: Irwin Professional Publishing.

Foglesong, Richard E. 2001. *Married to the Mouse: Walt Disney World and Orlando*. New Haven, CT: Yale University Press.

Wasko, Janet. 2001. *Understanding Disney: The Manufacture of Fantasy*. Oxford: Blackwell.

Watts, Steven. 1997. *The Magic Kingdom: Walt Disney and the American Way of Life*. Boston: Houghton Mifflin Company.

The Smile Factory

Work at Disneyland

by John Van Maanen

Author's Note: This paper has been cobbled together using three-penny nails of other writings. Parts come from a paper presented to the American Anthropological Association Annual Meetings in Washington, D.C., on November 16, 1989, called "Whistle While You Work." Other parts come from Van Maanen and Kunda (1989). In coming to this version, I've had a great deal of help from my friends Steve Barley, Nicole Biggart, Michael Owen Jones, Rosanna Hertz, Gideon Kunda, Joanne Martin, Maria Lydia Spinelli, Bob Sutton, and Bob Thomas.

Part of Walt Disney Enterprises includes the theme park Disneyland. In its pioneering form in Anaheim, California, this amusement center has been a consistent money maker since the gates were first opened in 1955. Apart from its sociological charm, it has, of late, become something of an exemplar for culture vultures and has been held up for public acclaim in several best-selling publications as one of America's top companies, most notably by Peters and Waterman (1982). To outsiders, the cheerful demeanor of its employees, the seemingly inexhaustible repeat business it generates from its customers, the immaculate condition of park grounds, and, more generally, the intricate physical and social order of the business itself appear wondrous.

Disneyland, as the self-proclaimed "Happiest Place on Earth," certainly occupies an enviable position in the amusement and entertainment worlds, as well as the commercial work in general.

Source: John Van Maanen, "The Smile Factory: Work at Disneyland," from *Reframing Organizational Culture*, edited by Peter J. Frost et al., pp. 58–76. Copyright © 1990 by Sage Publications, Inc. Reprinted by Permission of Sage Publications, Inc.

Its product, it seems, is emotion—"laughter and well being." Insiders are not bashful about promoting the product. Bill Ross, a Disneyland executive, summarizes the corporate position nicely by noting that "although we focus our attention on profit and loss, day-in and day-out we cannot lose sight of the fact that this is a feeling business and we make our profits from that."[1]

The "feeling business" does not operate, however, by management decree alone. Whatever services Disneyland executives believe they are providing to the 60 to 70 thousand visitors per day that flow through the park during its peak summer season, employees at the bottom of the organization are the ones who must provide them. The work-a-day practices that employees adopt to amplify or dampen customer spirits are therefore a core concern of this feeling business. The happiness trade is an interactional one. It rests partly on the symbolic resources put into place by history and park design but it also rests on an animated workforce that is more or less eager to greet the guests, pack the trams, push the bottoms, deliver the food, dump the garbage, clean the streets, and, in general, marshal the will to meet and perhaps exceed customer expectations. False moves, rude words, careless disregard, detected insincerity, or a sleepy and bored presence can all undermine the enterprise and ruin a sale. The smile factory has its rules.

It's a Small World

The writing that follows[2] represents Disneyland as a workplace. It is organized roughly as an old-fashioned realist ethnography that tells of a culture in native categories (Van Maanen, 1988). The culture of interest is the Disneyland culture but it is not necessarily the same one invented, authorized, codified, or otherwise approved by park management. Thus the culture I portray here is more of an occupational than a strictly organizational one (Van Maanen and Barley, 1985).

This rendition is of course abbreviated and selective. I focus primarily on such matters as the stock appearance (vanilla), status order (rigid), and social life (full), and swiftly learned codes of conduct (formal and informal) that are associated with Disneyland ride operators. These employees comprise the largest category of hourly workers on the payroll. During the summer months, they number close to four thousand and run the 60-odd rides and attractions in the park.

They are also a well-screened bunch. There is—among insiders and outsiders alike—a rather fixed view about the social attributes carried by the standard-make Disneyland ride operator. Single, white males and females in their early twenties, without facial blemish, of above average height and below average weight, with straight teeth, conservative grooming standards, and a chin-up, shoulder-back posture radiating the sort of good health suggestive of a recent history in sports are typical of these social identifiers. There are representative minorities on the payroll but because ethnic displays are sternly discouraged by management, minority employees are rather close copies of the standard model Disneylander, albeit in different colors.

This Disneyland look is often a source of some amusement to employees who delight in pointing out that even the patron saint, Walt himself, could not be hired today without shaving off his trademark pencil-thin mustache. But, to get a job in Disneyland and keep it means conforming to a rather exacting set of appearance rules. These rules are put forth in a handbook on the Disney image in which readers learn, for example, that facial hair or long hair is banned for men as are aviator glasses and earrings and that women must not tease their hair, wear fancy jewelry, or apply more than a modest dab of makeup. Both men and women are to look neat and prim, keep their uniforms fresh, polish their shoes, and maintain an upbeat countenance and light dignity to complement their appearance—no low spirits or cornball raffishness at Disneyland.

The legendary "people skills" of park employees, so often mentioned in Disneyland publicity and training materials, do not amount to very

---

1 The quote is drawn from a transcript of a speech made to senior managers of Hurrah's Club by Bill Ross, Vice President for Human Relations at Disneyland, in January 1988. Elsewhere in this account I draw on other in-house publications to document my tale. Of use in this regard are "Your Role in the Show" (1982), "Disneyland: The First Thirty Years" (1985), "The Disney Approach to Management" (1986), and Steven Birnbaum's semi-official travel guide to Disneyland (1988). The best tourist guide to the park I've read is Sehlinger's (1987) adamantly independent *The Unofficial Guide to Disneyland*.
2 This account is drawn primarily on my three-year work experience as a "permanent part-time" ride operator at Disneyland during the late 1960s. Sporadic contacts have been maintained with a few park employees and periodic visits, even with children in tow, have proved instructive. Also, lengthy, repeated beach interviews of a most informal sort have been conducted over the past few summers with ride operators (then) at the park. There is a good deal written about Disneyland, and I have drawn from these materials as indicated in the text. I must note finally that this is an unsponsored and unauthorized treatment of the Disneyland culture and is at odds on several points with the views set forth by management.

much according to ride operators. Most tasks require little interaction with customers and are physically designed to practically insure that is the case. The contact that does occur typically is fleeting and swift, a matter usually of only a few seconds. In the rare event sustained interaction with customers might be required, employees are taught to deflect potential exchanges to area supervisors or security. A training manual offers the proper procedure: "On misunderstandings, guests should be told to call City Hall. . . . In everything from damaged cameras to physical injuries, don't discuss anything with guests . . . there will always be one of us nearby." Employees learn quickly that security is hidden but everywhere. On Main Street, security cops are Keystone Kops; in Frontierland, they are Town Marshals; on Tom Sawyer's Island, they are Cavalry Officers, and so on.

Occasionally, what employees call "line talk" or "crowd control" is required of them to explain delays, answer direct questions, or provide directions that go beyond the endless stream of recorded messages coming from virtually every nook and cranny of the park. Because such tasks are so simple, consisting of little more than keeping the crowd informed and moving, it is perhaps obvious why management considers the sharp appearance and wide smile of employees so vital to park operations. There is little more they could ask of ride operators whose main interactive task with visitors consist of being, in their own terms, "information booths," "line signs," "pretty props," "shepherds," and "talking statues."

A few employees do go out of their way to initiate contact with Disneyland customers but, as a rule, most do not and consider those who do to be a bit odd. In general, one need do little more than exercise common courtesy while looking reasonably alert and pleasant. Interactive skills that are advanced by the job have less to do with making customers feel warm and welcome than they do with keeping each other amused and happy. This is, of course, a more complex matter.

Employees bring to the job personal badges of status that are of more than passing interest to peers. In rough order, these include: good looks, college affiliation, career aspirations, past achievement, age (directly related to status up to about age 23 or 24 and inversely related thereafter), and assorted other idiosyncratic matters. Nested closely alongside these imported status badges are organizational ones that are also of concern and value to employees.

Where one works in the park carries much social weight. Postings are consequential because the ride and area a person is assigned provide rewards and benefits beyond those of wages. In-the-park stature for ride operators turns partly on whether or not unique skills are required. Disneyland neatly complements labor market theorizing on this dimension because employees with the most differentiated skills find themselves at the top of the internal status ladder, thus making their loyalties to the organization more predictable.

Ride operators, as a large but distinctly middle-class group of hourly employees on the floor of the organization, compete for status not only with each other but also with other employee groupings whose members are hired for the season from the same applicant pool. A loose approximation of the rank ordering among these groups can be constructed as follows:

1. The upper-class prestigious Disneyland Ambassadors and Tour Guides (bilingual young women in charge of ushering—some say rushing—little bands of tourists through the park)
2. Ride operators performing coveted "skilled work" such as live narrations or tricky transportation tasks (like those who symbolically control customer access to the park and drive the costly entry vehicles, such as the antique trains, horse-drawn carriages, and Monorail)
3. All other ride operators
4. The proletarian Sweepers (keepers of the concrete grounds)
5. The sub-prole or peasant status Food and Concession workers (whose park sobriquets reflect their lowly social worth—"pancake ladies," "peanut pushers," "coke blokes," "suds divers," and the seemingly irreplaceable "soda jerks")

Pay differentials are slight among these employee groups. The collective status adheres, as it does internally for ride operators, to assignment or functional distinctions. As the rank order suggests, most employee status goes to these who work jobs that require higher degrees of special skill, relative freedom from constant and direct supervision, and provide the opportunity to organize and direct customer desires and behavior rather than to merely respond to them as spontaneously expressed.

The basis for sorting individuals into these various broad bands of job categories is often unknown to employees—a sort of deep, dark secret of the casting directors in personnel. When prospective employees are interviewed, they interview for "a job at Disneyland," not a specific one. Personnel decides what particular job they will eventually occupy. Personal contacts are considered by employees as crucial in this job-assignment process as they are in the hiring decision. Some employees, especially those who wind up in the lower ranking jobs, are quite disappointed with their assignments as is the case when, for example, a would-be Adventureland guide is posted to a New Orleans Square restaurant as a pot scrubber. Although many of the outside acquaintances of our pot scrubber may know only that he works at Disneyland, rest assured, insiders will know immediately where he works and judge him accordingly.

Uniforms are crucial in this regard for they provide instant communication about the social merits or demerits of the wearer within the little world of Disneyland workers. Uniforms also correspond to a wider status ranking that casts a significant shadow on employees of all types. Male ride operators on the Autopia wear, for example, untailored jump suits similar to pit mechanics and consequently generate about as much respect from peers as the grease-stained outfits worn by pump jockeys generate from real motorists in gas stations. The ill-fitting and homogeneous "whites" worn by Sweepers signify lowly institutional work tinged, perhaps, with a reminder of hospital orderlies rather than street cleanup crews. On the other hand, for males, the crisp, officer-like Monorail operator stands alongside the swashbuckling Pirate of the Caribbean, the casual cowpoke of Big Thunder Mountain, or the smartly vested Riverboat pilot as carrier of valued symbols in and outside the park. Employees lust for these higher status positions and the rights to small advantages such uniforms provide. A lively internal labor market exists wherein there is much scheming for the more prestigious assignments.

For women, a similar market exists, although the perceived "sexiness" of uniforms, rather than social rank, seems to play a larger role. To wit, the rather heated antagonisms that developed years ago when the ride "It's a Small World" first opened and began outfitting the ride operators with what were felt to be the shortest skirts and most revealing blouses in the park. Tour Guides, who traditionally headed the fashion vanguard at Disneyland in their above-the-knee kilts, knee socks, tailored vests, black English hats, and smart riding crops were apparently appalled at being upstaged by their social inferiors and lobbied actively (and, judging by the results, successfully) to lower the skirts, raise the necklines, and generally remake their Small World rivals.

Important, also, to ride operators are the break schedules followed on the various rides. The more the better. Work teams develop inventive ways to increase the number of "time-outs" they take during the work day. Most rides are organized on a rotational basis (e.g., the operator moving from a break, to queue monitor, to turnstile overseer, to unit loader, to traffic controller, to driver, and, again, to a break). The number of break men or women on a rotation (or ride) varies by the number of employees on duty and by the number of units on line. Supervisors, foremen, and operators also vary as to what they regard as appropriate break standards (and, more importantly, as to the value of the many situational factors that can enter the calculation of break rituals—crowd size, condition of ride, accidents, breakdowns, heat, operator absences, special occasions, and so forth). Self-monitoring teams with sleepy supervisors and lax (or savvy) foremen can sometimes manage a shift comprised of 15 minutes on and 45 minutes off each hour. They are envied by others and rides that have such a potential are eyed hungrily by others who feel trapped by their more rigid (and observed) circumstances.

Movement across jobs is not encouraged by park management but some does occur (mostly within an area and job category). Employees claim that a sort of "once a sweeper, always a sweeper" rule pertains but all know of at least a few exceptions to prove the rule. The exceptions offer some (not much) hope for those working at the social margins of the park and perhaps keep them on the job longer than might otherwise be expected. Dishwashers can dream of becoming Pirates, and with persistence and a little help from their friends, such dreams just might come true next season (or the next).

These examples are precious, perhaps, but they are also important. There is an intricate pecking order among very similar categories of employees. Attributes of reward and status tend to cluster, and there is intense concern about the cluster to which one belongs (or would like to belong). To a degree, form follows function in Disneyland because the jobs requiring the most abilities and offering the most interest also offer the most status and social reward. Interaction patterns reflect and sustain this order. Few Ambassadors or Tour Guides, for instance, will stoop to speak at length with Sweepers, who speak mostly among themselves, or to Food workers. Ride operators, between the poles, line up in ways referred to above with only ride proximity (i.e., sharing a break area) representing a potentially significant intervening variable in the interaction calculation.

These patterns are of more than slight concern because Disneyland, especially in the summer, can be compared quite usefully to a college mixer where across-sex pairing is of great concern (Schwartz and Lever, 1976). More to the point, what Waller (1937) so accurately called the "rating and dating complex" is in full bloom among park employees. The various modern forms of mating games are valued pastimes among Disneyland employees and are often played with corporate status marker in mind. Thus, when Yvone, the reigning Alice in Wonderland, moved in one summer with Ted, a lowly Sweeper, heads were scratched in puzzlement even though most knew that Yvone was, in her other life, a local junior college student and Ted was in premed at USC. The more general point is that romance flourishes in the park and, at least, if folklore is our guide, marriages made in Disneyland are not uncommon.

Even when not devoted strictly to pairing-off objectives, employee pastimes usually involve other employees. Disneyland's softball and volleyball leagues, its official picnics, canoe races, employee nights at the park, beach parties, and so on provide a busy little social scene for those interested. Areas and rides, too, offer social excitement and bonuses, such as when kegs of beer are rolled out at an off-site party after work crews break turnstile records ("We put 33,147 on the mountain today"). During the summer, some night crews routinely party in the early morning while day shift crews party at night. Sleep is not a commodity greatly valued by many employees caught up in a valued social whirl.

The so-called youth culture is indeed celebrated in and out of the park. Many employees, for example, live together in the large and cheap (by Los Angeles standards) apartment complexes that surround Disneyland. Employees sometimes refer to these sprawling, pastel, and slightly seedy structures as "the projects" or "worker housing." Yet the spirited attractiveness of the collective, low-rent lifestyle for those living it is easily grasped by a few landlords in the area who flatly refuse to rent to Disneyland employees during the summer as a matter of principle, and maybe, sorry experience because these short-term rentals serve as amusement parks for off-duty Disneylanders who, as they say, "know how to party."

A fusion of work and play is notable, however, even when play seems to be the order of the occasion. Certainly no Disneyland get-together would be complete without ride operators launching their special spiels practiced (or heard continuously on tape) at work:

Welcome aboard the African Queen, folks. My name is John and I'll be your guide and skipper for our trip down these rivers of adventure. As we pull away from the loading dock, turn around and take a last look at the people standing there, it may be the last time you ever see them. . . . Please keep your hands inside the boat as we go past these hungry alligators; they're always looking for a handout. . . . And now we return to civilization and the greatest danger of all, the California freeways.

The figurative parallel of this party is, of course, the atmosphere of a most collegial college. It has a literal parallel as well.

Paid employment at Disneyland begins with the much renowned University of Disneyland whose faculty runs a day-long orientation program (Traditions I) as part of a 40-hour apprenticeship program, most of which takes place on the rides. In the classroom, however, newly hired ride operators are given a very thorough introduction to matters of managerial concern and are tested on their absorption of famous Disneyland fact, lore, and procedure. Employee demeanor is governed, for example, by three rules:

First, we practice the friendly smile.

Second, we use only friendly and courteous phrases.

Third, we are not stuffy—the only Misters in Disneyland are Mr. Toad and Mr. Smee.

Employees learn too that the Disneyland culture is officially defined. The employee handbook put it in this format:

Dis-ney Cor-po-rate Cul-ture (diz'ne kor'pr'it kul cher) n 1. Of or pertaining to the Disney organization, as a: the philosophy underlying all business decisions; b: the commitment of top leadership and management to that philosophy; c: the actions taken by individual cast members that reinforce the image.

Language is also a central feature of university life and new employees are schooled in its proper use. Customers at Disneyland are, for instance, never referred to as such, they are "guests." There are no rides at Disneyland, only "attractions." Disneyland itself is a "park," not an amusement center, and it is divided into "back-stage," "on-stage," and "staging" regions. Law enforcement personnel hired by the park are not policemen, but "security hosts." Employees do not wear uniforms but check out fresh "costumes" each working day from "wardrobe." And, of course, there are no accidents at Disneyland, only "incidents."

So successful is such training that Smith and Eisenberg (1987) report that not a single Disneyland employee uttered the taboo and dread words "uniform," "customer," or "amusement park" during the 35 half-hour interviews they conducted as part of a study on organizational communication. *The Los Angeles Times* (July 28, 1988) also gives evidence on this matter, quoting a tour guide's reaction to the employees' annual canoe races. "It's a good release," she says, "it helps you see the other cast members (park employees) go through the same thing you do." Whether or not employees keep to such disciplined talk with one another is, of course, a moot point because the corporate manual is concerned only with how employees talk to customers or outsiders.

The university curriculum also anticipates probable questions ride operators may someday face from customers and they are taught the approved public response. A sample:

Question (posed by trainer): *What do you tell a guest who requests a rain check?*

Answer (in three parts): *We don't offer rain checks at Disneyland because (1) the main attractions are all indoors; (2) we would go broke if we offered passes; and (3) sunny days would be too crowded if we gave passes.*

Shrewd trainees readily note that such an answer blissfully disregards the fact that waiting areas of Disneyland are mostly outdoors and that there are no subways in the park to carry guests from land to land. Nor do they miss the economic assumption concerning the apparent frequency of Southern California rains. They discuss such matters together, of course, but rarely raise them in the training classroom. In most respects, these are recruits who easily take the role of good student.

Classes are organized and designed by professional Disneyland trainers who also instruct a well-screened group of representative hourly employees straight from park operations on the approved newcomer training methods and materials. New hires seldom see professional trainers in class but are brought on board by enthusiastic peers who concentrate their scripted lessons on those aspects of park procedure thought highly general matters to be learned by all employees. Particular skill training (and "reality shock") is reserved for the second wave of socialization occurring on the rides themselves, as operators are taught, for example, how and when to send a bobsled caroming down the track or, more delicately, the proper ways to stuff an obese adult customer into the midst of children riding the Monkey car on the Casey Jones Circus Train or, most problematically, what exactly to tell an irate customer standing in the rain who, in no uncertain terms, wants his or her money back and wants it back now.

During orientation, considerable concern is placed on particular values the Disney organization considers central to its operations. These values range from the "customer is king" verities to the more or less unique kind, of which "everyone is a child at heart when at Disneyland" is a decent example. This latter piety is one few employees fail to recognize as also attaching to everyone's minds as well after a few months of work experience. Elaborate checklists of appearance standards are learned and gone over in the classroom and great efforts are spent trying to bring employee emotional responses in line with such standards. Employees are told repeatedly that if they are happy and cheerful at work, so, too, will the guests at play. Inspirational films, hearty pep talks, family imagery, and exemplars of corporate performance are all representative of the strong symbolic stuff of these training rites.

Another example, perhaps extreme, concerns the symbolic role of the canonized founder in the corporate mythology. When Walt Disney was alive, newcomers and veterans alike were told how much he enjoyed coming to the park and just how exacting he was about the conditions he observed. For employees, the cautionary whoop, "Walt's in the park," could often bring forth additional energy and care for one's part in the production. Upon his death, trainers at the University were said to be telling recruits to mind their manners because, "Walt's in the park all the time now."

Yet, like employees everywhere, there is a limit to which such overt company propaganda can be effective. Students and trainers both seem to agree on where the line is drawn, for there is much satirical banter, mischievous winking, and playful exaggeration in the classroom. As young seasonal employees note, it is difficult to take seriously an organization that provides its retirees "Golden Ears" instead of gold watches after 20 or more years of service. All newcomers are aware that the label "Disneyland" has both an unserious and artificial connotation and that a full embrace of the Disneyland role would be as deviant as its full rejection. It does seem, however, because of the corporate imagery, the recruiting and selection devices, the goodwill trainees hold toward the organization at entry, the peer-based employment context, and the smooth fit with real student calendars, the job is considered by most ride operators to be a good one. The University of Disneyland, it appears, graduates students with a modest amount of pride and a considerable amount of fact and faith firmly ingrained as important things to know (if not always accept).

Matters become more interesting as new hires move into the various realms of the Disneyland enterprise. There are real customers "out there" and employees soon learn that these good folks do not always measure up to the typically well-mannered and grateful guest of the training classroom. Moreover, ride operators may find it difficult to utter the prescribed "Welcome Voyager" (or its equivalent) when it is to be given to the 20-thousandth human being passing through the Space Mountain turnstile on a crowded day in July. Other difficulties present themselves as well, but operators learn that there are others on-stage to assist or thwart them.

Employees learn quickly that supervisors and, to a lesser degree, foremen are not only on the premises to help them, but also to catch them when they slip over or brazenly violate set procedures or park policies. Because most rides are tightly designed to eliminate human judgment and minimize operational disasters, much of the supervisory monitoring is directed at activities ride operators consider trivial: taking too long a break; not wearing parts of one's official uniform, such as a hat, standard-issue belt, or correct shoes; rushing the ride (although more frequent violations seem to be detected for the provision of longer-than-usual rides for lucky customers); fraternizing with guests beyond the call of duty; talking back to quarrelsome or sometimes merely querisome customers; and so forth. All are matters covered quite explicitly in the codebooks ride operators are to be familiar with, and violations of such codes are often subject to instant and harsh discipline. The firing of what to supervisors are "malcontents," "trouble-makers," "bumblers," "attitude problems," or simply "jerks" is a frequent occasion at Disneyland, and among part-timers, who are most subject to degradation and being fired, the threat is omnipresent. There are few workers who have not witnessed firsthand the rapid disappearance of a co-worker for offenses they would regard as "Mickey Mouse." Moreover, there are few employees who themselves have not violated a good number of operational and demeanor standards and anticipate, with just cause, the violation of more in the future.[3]

In part, because of the punitive and what are widely held to be capricious supervisory practices in the park, foremen and ride operators are usually drawn close and shield one another from suspicious area supervisors. Throughout the year, each land is assigned a number of area supervisors who, dressed alike in short-sleeved white shirts and ties with walkie-talkies hitched to their belts, wander about their territories on the lookout for deviations from park procedures (and other signs of disorder). Occasionally, higher level supervisors pose in "plainclothes" and ghost-ride the various attractions just to be sure everything is up to snuff. Some area supervisors are well-known among park employees for the variety of surreptitious techniques they employ when going about their monitoring duties. Blind observation posts are legendary, almost sacred, sites within the park. ("This is where Old Man Weston hangs out. He can see Dumbo, Storybook, the Carousel, and the Tea Cups from here.") Supervisors in Tomorrowland are, for example, famous for their penchant of hiding in the bushes above the submarine caves, timing the arrivals and departures of the supposedly fully loaded boats making the 8½-minute cruise under the polar icecaps. That they might also catch a submarine captain furtively enjoying a cigarette (or worse) while inside the conning tower (his upper body out of view of the crowd on the vessel) might just make a supervisor's day—and unmake the employee's. In short, supervisors, if not firemen, are regarded by ride operators as sneaks and tricksters out to get them and representative of the dark side of park life. Their presence is, of course, an orchestrated one and does more than merely watch over the ride operators. It also draws operators together as cohesive little units who must look out for one another while they work (and shirk).

Supervisors are not the only villains who appear in the park. The treachery of co-workers, while rare, has its moments. Pointing out the code violations of colleagues to foremen and supervisors—usually in secret—provides one avenue of collegial duplicity. Finks, of all sorts, can be found among the peer ranks at Disneyland, and although their dirty deeds are uncommon, work teams on all rides go to some

---

3 The author serves as a case in point for I was fired from Disneyland for what I still consider a Mickey Mouse offense. The specific violation—one of many possible—involved hair growing over my ears, an offense I had been warned about more than once before the final cut was made. The form my dismissal took, however, deserves comment for it is easy to recall and follows a format familiar to an uncountable number of ex-Disneylanders. Dismissal began by being pulled off the ride after my work shift had begun by an area supervisor in full view of my cohorts. A forced march to the administration building followed where my employee card was turned over and a short statement read to me by a personnel officer as to the formal cause of termination. Security officers then walked me to the employee locker room where my work uniforms and equipment were collected and my personal belongings returned to me while an inspection of my locker was made. The next stop was the time shed where my employee's time card was removed from its slot, marked "terminated" across the top in red ink, and replaced in its customary position (presumably for Disneylanders to see when clocking on or off the job over the next few days). As now an ex-ride operator, I was escorted to the parking lot where two security officers scraped off the employee parking sticker attached to my car. All these little steps of status degradation in the Magic Kingdom were quite public and, as the reader might guess, the process still irks. This may provide the reader with an account for the tone of this narrative, although it shouldn't since I would also claim I was ready to quit anyway since I had been there far too long. At any rate, it may just be possible that I now derive as much a part of my identify from being fired from Disneyland as I gained from being employed there in the first place.

effort to determine just who they might be and, if possible, drive them from their midst. Although there is little overt hazing or playing of pranks on newcomers, they are nonetheless carefully scrutinized on matters of team (and ride) loyalty, and those who fail the test of "member in good standing" are subject to some very uncomfortable treatment. Innuendo and gossip are the primary tools in this regard, with ridicule and ostracism (the good old silent treatment) providing the backup. Since perhaps the greatest rewards working at Disneyland offers its ride operator personnel are those that come from belonging to a tight little network of like-minded and sociable peers where off-duty interaction is at least as vital and pleasurable as the on-duty sort, such mechanisms are quite effective. Here is where some of the most powerful and focused emotion work in the park is found, and those subject to negative sanction, rightly or wrongly, will grieve, but grieve alone.

Employees are also subject to what might be regarded as remote controls. These stem not from supervisors or peers but from thousands of paying guests who parade daily through the park. The public, for the most part, wants Disneyland employees to play only the roles for which they are hired and costumed. If, for instance, Judy of the Jets is feeling tired, grouchy, or bored, few customers want to know about it. Disneyland employees are expected to be sunny and helpful; and the job, with its limited opportunities for sustained interaction, is designed to support such a stance. Thus, if a ride operator's behavior drifts noticeably away from the norm, customers are sure to point it out—"Why aren't you smiling?" "What's wrong with you?" "Having a bad day?" "Did Goofy step on your foot?" Ride operators learn swiftly from constant hints, glances, glares, and tactful (and tactless) cues sent by their audience what their role in the park is to be, and as long as they keep to it, there will be no objections from those passing by.

> *I can remember being out on the river looking at the people on the Mark Twain looking down on the people in the Keel Boats who are looking up at them. I'd come by on my raft and they'd all turn and stare at me. If I gave them a little wave and a grin, they'd all wave back and smile; all ten thousand of them. I always wondered what would happen if I gave them the finger. (Ex-ride operator, 1988)*

Ride operators also learn how different categories of customers respond to them and the parts they are playing on stage. For example, infants and small children are generally timid, if not frightened, in their presence. School-age children are somewhat curious, aware that the operator is at work playing a role but sometimes in awe of the role itself. Nonetheless, these children can be quite critical of any flaw in the operator's performance. Teenagers, especially males in groups, present problems because they sometimes go to great lengths to embarrass, challenge, ridicule, or outwit an operator. Adults are generally appreciative and approving of an operator's conduct provided it meets their rather minimal standards, but they sometimes overreact to the part an operator is playing (positively) if accompanied by small children. A recent study of the Easter Bunny points out a similar sort of response on the part of adults to fantasy (Hickey, Thompson, and Foster, 1988). It is worth noting too that adults outnumber children in the park by a wide margin. One count reports an adult-to-children ratio of four-to-one (King, 1981).

The point here is that ride operators learn what the public (or, at least, their idealized version of the public) expects of their role and find it easier to conform to such expectations than not. Moreover, they discover that when they are bright and lively others respond to them in like ways. This Goffmanesque balancing of the emotional exchange is such that ride operators come to expect good treatment. They assume, with good cause, that most people will react to their little waves and smiles with some affection and perhaps joy. When they do not, it can ruin a ride operator's day.

With this interaction formula in mind, it is perhaps less difficult to see why ride operators detest and scorn the ill-mannered or unruly guest. At times, these grumpy, careless, or otherwise unresponsive characters insult the very role the operators play and have come to appreciate—"You can't treat the Captain of the USS Nautilus like that!" Such out-of-line visitors offer breaks from routine, some amusement, consternation, or the occasional job challenge that occurs when remedies are deemed necessary to restore employee and role dignity.

By and large, however, the people-processing tasks of ride operators pass good naturedly and smoothly, with operators hardly noticing much more than the bodies passing in front of view (special bodies, however, merit special attention as when crew members on the subs gather to assist a young lady in a revealing outfit on board and then linger over the hatch to admire the view as she descends the steep steps to take her seat on the boat). Yet, sometimes, more than a body becomes visible, as happens when customers overstep their roles and challenge employees' authority, insult an operator, or otherwise disrupt the routines of the job. In the process, guests become "duffesses," "ducks," and "a__holes" (just three of many derisive terms used by ride operators to label those customers they believe to have gone beyond the pale). Normally, these characters are brought to the attention of park security officers, ride foremen, or area supervisors who, in turn, decide how they are to be disciplined (usually expulsion from the park).

Occasionally, however, the alleged slight is too personal or simply too extraordinary for a ride operator to let it pass unnoticed or merely inform others and allow them to decide what, if anything, is to be done. Restoration of one's respect is called for and routine practices have been developed for these circumstances. For example, common remedies include: the "seatbelt squeeze," a small token of appreciation given to a deviant customer consisting of the rapid cinching-up of a required seatbelt such that the passenger is doubled-over at the point of departure and left gasping for the duration of the trip; the "break-toss," an acrobatic gesture of the Autopia trade whereby operators jump on the outside of a norm violator's car, stealthily unhitching the safety belt, then slamming on the brakes, bringing the car to an almost instant stop while the driver flies on the hood of the car (or beyond); the "seatbelt slap," an equally distinguished (if primitive) gesture by which an offending customer receives a sharp, quick snap of a hard plastic belt across the face (or other parts of the body) when entering or exiting a seat-belted ride; the "break-up-the-party" gambit, a queuing device put to use in officious fashion whereby bothersome pairs are separated at the last minute into different units, thus forcing on them the pain of strange companions for the duration of a ride through the Haunted Mansion or a ramble on Mr. Toad's Wild Ride; the "hatch-cover ploy," a much beloved practice of Submarine pilots who, in collusion with mates on the loading dock, are able to drench offensive guests with water as their units pass under a waterfall; and, lastly, the rather ignoble variants of the "Sorry-I-didn't-see-your-hand" tactic, a savage move designed to crunch a particularly irksome customer's hand (foot, finger, arm, leg, etc.) by bringing a piece of Disneyland property to bear on the appendage, such as the door of a Thunder Mountain railroad car or the starboard side of a Jungle Cruise boat. This latter remedy is, most often, a "near miss" designed to startle the little criminals of Disneyland.

All of these unofficial procedures (and many more) are learned on the job. Although they are used sparingly, they are used. Occasions of use provide a continual stream of sweet revenge talk to enliven and enrich colleague conversation at break time or after work. Too much, of course, can be made of these subversive practices and the rhetoric that surrounds their use. Ride operators are quite aware that there are limits beyond which they dare not pass. If they are caught, they know that restoration of corporate pride will be swift and clean.

In general, Disneyland employees are remarkable for their forbearance and polite good manners even under trying conditions. They are taught, and some come to believe, for a while at least, that they are really "on-stage" at work. And, as noted, surveillance by supervisory personnel certainly fades in light of the unceasing glances an employee receives from the paying guests who tromp daily through the park in the summer. Disneyland employees know well that they are part of the product being sold and learn to check their more discriminating manners in favor of the generalized countenance of a cheerful lad or lassie whose enthusiasm and dedication is obvious to all.

At times, the emotional resources of employees appear awesome. When the going gets tough and the park is jammed, the nerves of all employees are frayed and sorely tested by the crowd, din, sweltering sun, and eyeburning smog. Customers wait in what employees call "bullpens" (and park officials call "reception areas") for up to several hours for a 3½-minute ride that operators are sometimes hell-bent on cutting to 2½ minutes. Surely a monument to the human ability to suppress feelings has been created when both users and providers alike can maintain their composure and seeming regard for one another when in such a fix.

It is in this domain where corporate culture and the order it helps to sustain must be given its due. Perhaps the depth of a culture is visible only when its members are under the gun. The orderliness—a good part of the Disney formula for financial success—is an accomplishment based not only on physical design and elaborate procedures, but also on the low-level, part-time employees who, in the final analysis, must be willing, even eager, to keep the show afloat. The ease with which employees glide into their kindly and smiling roles is, in large measure, a feat of social engineering. Disneyland does not pay well; its supervision is arbitrary and skin-close; its working conditions are chaotic; its jobs require minimal amounts of intelligence or judgment; and it asks a kind of sacrifice and loyalty of its employees that is almost fanatical. Yet, it attracts a particularly able workforce whose personal backgrounds suggest abilities far exceeding those required of a Disneyland traffic cop, people stuffer, queue or line manager, and button pusher. As I have suggested, not all of Disneyland is covered by the culture put forth by management. There are numerous pockets of resistance and various degrees of autonomy maintained by employees. Nonetheless, adherence and support for the organization are remarkable. And, like swallows returning to Capistrano, many part-timers look forward to their migration back to the park for several seasons.

The Disney Way

Four features alluded to in this unofficial guide to Disneyland seem to account for a good deal of the social order that obtains within the park. First, socialization, although costly, is of a most selective, collective, intensive, serial, sequential, and closed sort.[4] These tactics are notable for their penetration into the private spheres of individual thought and feeling (Van Maanen and Schein, 1979). Incoming identities are not so much dismantled as they are set aside as employees are schooled in the use of new identities of the situational sort. Many of these are symbolically powerful and, for some, laden with social approval. It is hardly surprising that some of the more problematic positions in terms of turnover during the summer occur in the food and concession domains where employees apparently find little to identify with on the job. Cowpokes on Big Thunder Mountain, Jet Pilots, Storybook Princesses, Tour Guides, Space Cadets, Jungle Boat Skippers, or Southern Belles of New Orleans Square have less difficulty on this score. Disneyland, by design, bestows identity through a process carefully set up to strip away the job relevance of other sources of identity and learned response and replace them with others of organizational relevance. It works.

Second, this is a work culture whose designers have left little room for individual experimentation. Supervisors, as apparent in their focused wandering and attentive looks, keep very close tabs on what is going on at any moment in all the lands. Every bush, rock, and tree in Disneyland is numbered and checked continually as to the part it is playing in the park. So too are employees. Discretion of a personal sort is quite limited while employees are "on-stage." Even "back-stage" and certain "off-stage" domains have their corporate monitors. Employees are indeed aware that their "off-stage" life beyond the picnics, parties, and softball games is subject to some scrutiny, for police checks are made on potential and current employees. Nor do all employees discount the rumors that park officials make periodic inquiries on their own as to a person's habits concerning sex and drugs. Moreover, the sheer number of rules and regulations is striking, thus making the grounds for dismissal a matter of multiple choice for supervisors who discover a target for the use of such grounds. The feeling of being watched is, unsurprisingly, a rather prevalent complaint among Disneyland people and is one that employees must live with if they are to remain at Disneyland.

Third, emotional management occurs in the park in a number of quite distinct ways. From the instructors at the university who beseech recruits to "wish every guest a pleasant good day," to the foremen who plead with their charges to "say thank you when you herd them through the gate," to the impish customer who seductively licks her lips and asks, "what does Tom Sawyer want for Christmas?" appearance, demeanor, and etiquette have special meanings at Disneyland. Because these are prized personal attributes over which we normally feel in control, making them commodities can be unnerving. Much self-monitoring is involved, of course, but even here self-management has an organizational side. Consider ride operators who may complain of being "too tired to smile" but, at the same time, feel a little guilty for uttering such a confession. Ride operators who have worked an early morning shift on the Matterhorn (or other popular rides) tell of a queasy feeling they get when the park is opened for business and they suddenly feel the ground begin to shake under their feet and hear the low thunder of the hordes of customers coming at them, oblivious of civil restraint and the small children who might be among them. Consider, too, the discomforting pressures of being "on-stage" all day and the cumulative annoyance of having adults ask permission to leave a line to go to the bathroom, whether the water in the lagoon is real, where the well-marked entrances might be, where Walt Disney's cryogenic tomb is to be found,[5] or—the real clincher—whether or not one is "really real."

---

4 These tactics are covered in some depth in Van Maanen (1976, 1977) and Van Maanen and Schein (1979). When pulled together and used simultaneously, a people processing system of some force is created that tends to produce a good deal of conformity among recruits who, regardless of background, come to share very similar occupational identities, including just how they think and feel on the job. Such socialization practices are common whenever recruits are bunched together and processed as a batch and when role innovation is distinctly unwanted on the part of the agents of such socialization.

5 The unofficial answer to this little gem of a question is: "Under Sleeping Beauty's castle." Nobody knows for sure since the immediate circumstances surrounding Walt Disney's death are vague—even in the most careful accounts (Mosley, 1983; Schickel, 1985). Officially, his ashes are said to be peacefully at rest in Forest Lawn. But the deep freeze myth is too good to let go of because it so neatly complements all those fairy tales Disney expropriated and popularized when alive. What could be more appropriate than thinking of Walt on ice, waiting for technology's kiss to restore him to life in a hidden vault under his own castle in the Magic Kingdom?

The mere fact that so much operator discourse concerns the handling of bothersome guests suggests that these little emotional disturbances have costs. There are, for instance, times in all employee careers when they put themselves on "automatic pilot," "go robot," "can't feel a thing," "lapse into a dream," "go into a trance," or otherwise "check out" while still on duty. Despite a crafty supervisor's (or curious visitor's) attempt to measure the glimmer in an employee's eye, this sort of willed emotional numbness is common to many of the "on-stage" Disneyland personnel. Much of this numbness is, of course, beyond the knowledge of supervisors and guests because most employees have little trouble appearing as if they are present even when they are not. It is, in a sense, a passive form of resistance that suggests there is a sacred preserve of individuality left among employees in the park.

Finally, taking these three points together, it seems that even when people are trained, paid, and told to be nice, it is hard for them to do so all of the time. But, when efforts to be nice have succeeded to the degree that is true of Disneyland, it appears as a rather towering (if not always admirable) achievement. It works at the collective level by virtue of elaborate direction. Employees—at all ranks—are stage-managed by higher ranking employees who, having come through themselves, hire, train, and closely supervise those who have replaced them below. Expression rules are laid out in corporate manuals. Employee time-outs intensify work experience. Social exchanges are forced into narrow bands of interacting groups. Training and retraining programs are continual. Hiding places are few. Although little sore spots and irritations remain for each individual, it is difficult to imagine work roles being more defined (and accepted) than those at Disneyland. Here, it seems, is a work culture worthy of the name.

References

Birnbaum, S. 1988. *Steve Birnbaum Brings You the Best of Disneyland*. Los Angeles: Hearst Publications Magazines.

Hickey, J. V., W. E. Thompson, and D. L. Foster. 1988. Becoming the Easter Bunny: Socialization into a Fantasy Role. *Journal of Contemporary Ethnography* 17, 67–95.

King, M. J. 1981. Disneyland and Walt Disney World: Traditional Values in Futuristic Form. *Journal of Popular Culture* 15, 116–140.

Mosley, L. 1983. *Disney's World*. New York: Stein and Day.

Peters, T. J., and R. H. Waterman. 1982. *In Search of Excellence*. New York: Harper & Row.

Schickel, R. 1985. *The Disney Version* (rev. ed.). New York: Simon & Schuster. (Original work published 1968.)

Schwartz, P., and J. Lever. 1976. Fear and Loathing at a College Mixer. *Urban Life* 4, 413–432.

Sehlinger, B. 1987. *The Unofficial Guide to Disneyland*. New York: Prentice Hall.

Smith, R. C., and E. M. Eisenberg. 1987. Conflict at Disneyland: A Root Metaphor Analysis. *Communication Monographs* 54, 367–380.

Van Maanen, J. 1976. Breaking-in: Socialization to Work. In R. Dubin (Ed.), *Handbook of Work, Organization, and Society* (pp. 67–130). Chicago: Rand McNally.

Van Maanen, J. 1977. Experiencing Organization. In J. Van Maanen (Ed.), *Organizational Careers* (pp. 15–45). New York: John Wiley.

Van Maanen, J. 1988. *Tales of the Field: On Writing Ethnography*. Chicago: University of Chicago Press.

Van Maanen, J., and S. R. Barley. 1985. Cultural Organization: Fragments of a Theory. In P. J. Frost, L. F. Moore, M. R. Louis, C. C. Lundberg, and J. Martin (Eds.), *Organizational Culture*. Beverly Hills, CA: Sage.

Van Maanen, J., and G. Kunda. 1989. Real Feelings: Emotional Expressions and Organization Culture. In B. Staw and L. L. Cummings (Eds.), *Research in Organization Behavior* 11 (pp. 43–103). Greenwich, CT: JAI Press.

Van Maanen, J., and E. H. Schein. 1979. Toward a Theory of Organizational Socialization. In B. Staw and L. L. Cummings (Eds.), *Research in Organization Behavior* 1 (pp. 209–269). Greenwich, CT: JAI Press.

Waller, W. 1937. The Rating and Dating Complex. *American Sociological Review* 2, 727–734.

Disney Goes to Tokyo

Crossing the Pacific

In the mid-1970s, the Oriental Land Company, a Japanese development company that owned a large tract of landfill east of Tokyo zoned for public leisure activities, approached Disney with the idea of building a Disneyland in Japan. Six hundred acres were set aside for the project. But, in an era of conservative (caretaking) management at Walt Disney Productions, senior executives at Disney were hesitant. After all, Japan was far away, quite distant in terms of culture, and Tokyo not only had much colder winters than California or Florida but endured a lengthy rainy season in June and July. Yet, after exploring alternative options at some length (including other sites in Asia), Disney decided to go ahead. Nevertheless, it insisted on a deal that left Oriental Land with virtually all of the risk. Instead of taking an ownership position in Tokyo Disneyland, Disney demanded royalties of 10 percent of the revenues from admissions and rides, and 5 percent of the receipts from food, beverages, and souvenirs. Disney also asked for and more or less received artistic control of the park. Its partner, with its experience in development projects in Tokyo, looked after the complex relationships with local planning and regulatory authorities, financing, and adjacent development.

At first glance, Tokyo Disneyland seems to be a close physical and social copy of Disneyland in Southern California. Disney's Imagineers were interested at the outset in adapting some of their attractions to the Japanese context—Samurai-land instead of Frontierland, for example. But their Japanese partner strongly resisted efforts to "localize" Disneyland, and persuaded the Imagineers that what would best attract the Japanese was a park that replicated as closely as possible the American original (Brannen, 1992). They pointed out that Disney tales and characters were long familiar to Japanese—indeed, Japanese television had carried a highly popular dubbed version of the Mickey Mouse Club for many years and Disney movies and merchandise were wildly popular in Japan. Who is to say that Mickey Mouse is not Japanese, they claimed, since he was perhaps more familiar to local youngsters than the mythical characters of national folklore. The Japanese carried the day for they were, after all, the owners of the park.

Tokyo Disneyland opened in April 1983. The weather was cold and raw. Opening day drew fewer people than anticipated. But in August it drew 93,000 people in a single day, higher than the record one-day attendance records in the U.S. parks (Brannen and Wilson, 1996). By the late 1980s, it was drawing more than 15 million people a year, more at that time than either of the U.S. parks. The park was so popular that occasionally the admission gates were closed by mid-day to avoid overcrowding. By 1993, ten years after opening, Tokyo Disneyland had welcomed 125 million visitors, a number, as Brannen and Wilson pointed out, roughly equal to the population of Japan. By 2003, Tokyo Disneyland sat next to a second gate—Tokyo Disney Seas (opening in 2001). The attendance draw from the two parks is now nearing 25 million visitors per year and the employee count comes close to 20,000 (75 percent of whom are entry-level, part-time workers).

Critical to the business side of the organization, nine out of ten customers on any given day in Tokyo Disneyland are repeat visitors ("recidivists"). The park has become a favorite destination for the regular school trips that are a feature of Japanese school life. It is also a favorite family vacation destination in a land of extremely short vacations, and excellent train connections with Tokyo make it an ideal weekend outing for the family. Many young couples prefer it for special dates and honeymoon packages attract newlyweds from all over Japan.

Tokyo Disneyland has even co-opted traditional holidays in Japan: "Look, for example, at Tokyo Disneyland's celebration of New Year's Day—perhaps the most serious of Japanese holidays, when people customarily ring out the evils of the old year with 100 rings of a temple bell. Now there's an annual New Year's party at Tokyo Disneyland. This party is so popular that in 1991 it drew in 139,000 people, including a large percentage of young lovebirds who reserved a room at the Tokyo Disneyland Hotel over a year in advance" (Brannen and Wilson, 1996, p. 100). And the park's added size, fine hotels, and location, relatively close to Narita Airport, Japan's major international gateway, has drawn a growing number of visitors from other Asian countries.

Tokyo Disneyland's unprecedented success did not escape notice back at corporate headquarters in Burbank. Indeed, the new, Eisner-led management team at Walt Disney Company watched as their royalties provided a steadily growing income stream but their Japanese partner, which had borne virtually all of the risk of the venture, enjoyed far more of the profits. Oriental Land collected not only the lion's share of the park's revenues but also virtually all the profits from the hotels and adjacent developments around Tokyo Disneyland. The rapid success of the park seemed to prove that Disneyland was in fact a wondrous global product that could readily move across national and cultural boundaries. As John Van Maanen (1992, p. 9) puts it, in the article that follows this Class Note: "The company line is that Japanese customers experience a pure, undiluted Americana. All is a direct copy. This may, of course, be merely an official position, privately scoffed at back at Disney headquarters. But, if so, the public line is pervasive and consistent. One Disney official, blissfully ignoring the role their partner played in the story, told the *New York Times* (April 18, 1991): 'We really tried to avoid creating a Japanese version of Disneyland. . . . We wanted to create a real Disneyland." The cultural assumption at work here seems to be drawn straight from the movie *Field of Dreams*: "If we build it, they will come."

Why they came in such numbers and what customers took away from visit after visit seems not to have generated much analysis—or, perhaps more accurately—much public recognition on Disney's part. A closer analysis suggests that Tokyo Disneyland involved more departures from the original model than the corporate line indicates. Before looking at these matters in more depth, a quick look at some grounding ideas relevant to the management of the global enterprise is warranted. These examinations begin with the notion of "cultural flow."

The Cultural Marketplace

How culture moves from place to place, from group to group, depends in part on the channels in play to allow such movement. In commercial spheres, anthropologist Ulf Hannerz (1992) notes that markets are channels for cultural flow as the products of one cultural group are offered to members of another. This flow assumes of course that commodities and services sent forth by profit-seeking organizations hold value for those who purchase them beyond whatever function they perform and whatever labor value is tied to their production. That is, a part of the "added value" sticking to a given product or service derives from the cultural meaning customers attach to it. A hamburger, book, or plane ride carries more meaning than simply whatever nutrition, story, or transportation it offers.

Sometimes it appears that meaning is all that is being sold. McCannel (1976) provides some fine examples of this sort of cultural consumption. In his ethnographic account of the contemporary tourist, he argues that the objects of the world are increasingly invested with symbolic capital. So much so that even pure experience can be marketed as a culturally infused "product" that leaves no physical trace like the "warmth" of a hotel lobby, the "style" of a restaurant, the "thrill" of a perfume, the "feel" of a car, the "ambiance" of a resort or, more pointedly, the "fun" of a Disneyland. Products and services can then be sold on the "experience" they deliver.

If experience associated with basic services and products is marketable, so too is the experience associated with culture. In fact, cultural experience is a hot item in the marketplace today. Cultural experience implies the transformation of an original emptiness, vagueness, or skepticism on the part of an individual or group into a feeling or belief that is based on some sort of real or simulated involvement in a novel social world. Experience in no way conveys competence in or acceptance of the new world—confusion, rejection, distaste, embarrassment, befuddlement are all possible results. But, personal encounters do promote a kind of cultural awareness that was previously lacking.

Examples of such cultural experiences for a fee are not hard to locate. Attending a baseball game at Fenway Park might serve as an "authentic" cultural experience for tourists from Japan. The more vitriolic and loutish the fans (and argumentative the players) the better, because then the game might well appear "more American" to the visitors. Similarly, ordering a cherry Coke and large fries at the Hard Rock Café on the Champs-Elysées while enduring the thirteen-minute Jim Morrison version of "Light My Fire" might provide a welcome American experience for Madame Duvall and friends. Or, to reverse the flow, Americans gobbling up raw fish at the local sushi bar and bantering away with the resident Japanese chief might well come away thinking they had experienced a bit of real life in the Land of the Rising Sun. Certainly in most of the world today, such cultural experiences are not difficult to locate, but what are we to make of them?

Two rough answers can be sketched out. Both are conventional. One answer focuses on cultural transmission and the agents or initiators of cultural flows. At the limit, this approach suggests that, as market channels open up, powerful cultural influences begin to pound away on the sensibilities of people such that whatever bits and pieces of indigenous culture they hold are eventually ground down. Global homogenization results as the local character of exposed (and vulnerable) cultures are replaced by the appealing transnational symbolic forms, products, and services originating elsewhere. This process is cultural imperialism pure and simple. Homogenization results from a center-to-periphery flow bringing about something of a highly commercialized world culture. In this zero-sum game, the loss of culture shows itself most directly in the least organized and powerless communities while the more organized and powerful grow increasingly similar, coming in the end to shape, share, and signal world culture. In this view, the Great Wall of China is well on its way to becoming the Great Mall of China.

The other answer, however, looks to the cultural acquisition process and those on the receiving end of culture flows. This perspective suggests that those cultural experiences that do not fold easily into local patterns of everyday thought and action are (1) unmarked entirely and are thus without influence or appeal; (2) rejected out-of-hand as culturally insulting, inappropriate, or unattractive; or (3) eventually brought into line through transformations of one sort or the other. Culture may still flow from the center outward but it does not always penetrate. Change and alteration take place down the line, but the core of the target culture is left largely intact. The local core may even be recharged or reinvigorated, its representatives made more aware and assertive of their own values and perspectives as a result of such contact. Everyday life thus colonizes the center rather than vice versa, reshaping the imported culture to its own tastes and specifications. Here, the Great Wall remains just that.

The problem for global managers faced with cross-border operations is that both theoretical answers are far too simple. Homogenization scenarios commercialize and thus trivialize culture by reducing its relevance to something that is bought and sold and thought to be under the control of a few and exported to many. Resistance scenarios enshrine culture as local, beyond commercial reach, impenetrable, unique, unfathomable, and essentially timeless and omnipresent. Minimally, when looking at the culture flows that accompany cross-border learning, we must pay close attention to the meaning (and cultural experience) associated with a given product or service from the perspectives of both those who send it forth and those who (more or less) receive it. This view calls for a symbolic and almost circular double vision whereby the cultural assumptions of one group are brought to light by those of another and both may shift as a result.

It is important to note, however, that cross-border learning is less of an "ah-ha" occurrence than a slow process. The pace may well be glacial and intergenerational. Tokyo Disneyland moved from the exotic to the ordinary in Japan, but such a shift did not occur overnight. And the process—one essentially of localization of the global rather than globalization of the local—was a two-way street. Watson (1997) provides a marvelous example in this regard in his studies of how the McDonald's Corporation moved into East Asia in the 1970s. What he discovered was that while certain elements of McDonald's highly standardized system and supportive organization culture were accepted by Asian owners, employees, and customers (e.g., orderly queuing, self-provisioning of eating utensils and accoutrements, self-seating), other elements were rejected—notably those related to the time, space, demeanor, and menu. To take a single example, many if not most McDonald's restaurants in the region—from Beijing to Taipei—were turned into local leisure centers and after-school clubs for studious and social teenagers. Thus the meaning of "fast" in these settings referred only to the delivery of food, and not the consumption.

Watson's materials also display the power of children and young adults to further cultural learning and change. To illustrate, the most eager "early adopters" of McDonald's were largely young people who patronized the restaurants precisely because they weren't local or traditional. They were, for a time, attractive because they were exotic. Over the long term, of course, McDonald's grew less exotic both from frequent use and from modest but continued alterations taking place in the restaurants themselves as owners and managers made efforts to reconfigure their operations to fit comfortably (and successfully) into the local scene. And early customers (youth) taught later customers (adults) the ins and outs and small pleasures of eating at McDonald's, such that the restaurant's appeal broadened across generations. By the time the original customers had children to take to McDonald's, it was no longer seen as foreign. It had become absorbed and taken for granted as a fun and familiar place and enjoyed at this stage in cross-border cultural learning for just those reasons.

With these lessons in mind, we continue our story by looking at how Disneyland moved into new territory well beyond the social worlds of its origin. Tokyo Disneyland is, of course, an ongoing tale for Disney, which, like that of McDonald's, continues to change over time both at home and away. This constant evolution is important to keep in mind because the excerpts from John Van Maanen's research writing that follows, *Displacing Disney*, are but a glossy snapshot that invariably tries to freeze what cannot be frozen. Enter now the wonderful world of Tokyo Disneyland.

References

Brannen, Mary Yoko. 1992. B'wana Mickey: Constructing cultural consumption at Tokyo Disneyland. In J. J. Tobin (Ed.). *Re-Made in Japan*. New Haven, CT: Yale University Press.

Brannen, Mary Yoko, and J. M. Wilson III. 1996. "Recontextualization and Internationalization: Lessons in Transcultural Materialism from the Walt Disney Company." *CEMS (Community of European Management Schools) Business Review*, vol. 1, 1st ed.

Hannerz, Ulf. 1992. *Cultural Complexity: Studies in the Social Organization of Meaning*. New York: Columbia University Press.

McCannel, Dean. 1976. *The Tourist*. New York: Schocken Books.

Van Maanen, John. 1992. Displacing Disney: Some Notions of the Flow of Culture. *Qualitative Sociology* 15 (1), 5–35.

Watson, James L. 1997. *Golden Arches East: McDonald's in East Asia*. Palo Alto, CA: Stanford University Press.

Displacing Disney

Some notes on the flow of culture

by John Van Maanen

The Transformation

Disneyland went international in 1983 with the opening of its Tokyo operation. As noted on the surface, it claims to be a near perfect replica of the Disneyland production minus a few original attractions. There are some recognized modifications but these are imports selected from the Magic Kingdom instead of Disneyland (e.g., Cinderella's Castle and the Mickey Mouse Theater). In terms of organizational control, it is as decentralized as they come—the Oriental Land Company, a Japanese development and property management firm, took full control shortly after the park was built and now provides Walt Disney Enterprises with a rough ten-percent cut of Tokyo Disneyland's profits from admissions, food, and merchandise sales. A small American management team ("Disnoids") remains in Japan as advisors and consultants to keep the park in tune with Disney doctrine and the firm hires a handful of non-Japanese employees, mainly Americans, as "cast members" (entertainers, crafts people, and characters) strategically scattered throughout the park. The question I now raise concerns the flow of culture from the west to the east. To what extent does Tokyo Disneyland mean the same thing to its new patrons as it means to its old?

In a nutshell, Tokyo Disneyland does not work, indeed, cannot work, in the same way as its American counterpart. The cultural meaning of the park shifts significantly. This is not to say that the symbols and Disney narratives are meaningless in the Japanese context. Such a view could not begin to explain the popularity of the park which, in 1991, outdrew Disneyland by nearly five million customers (*European Elan*, October 18–20, 1991). But, what does appear to be happening is the recontextualization of the American signs so that the Japanese are able to make them their own. This process may be highly general and something of the norm for cultural transformations.

Source: Excerpted from John Van Maanen, 1992, "Displacing Disney: Some Notes on the Flow of Culture," *Qualitative Sociology* 5–35. Reprinted by permission of Plenum Publishing Corporation.

Most observers of modern Japan note the country's penchant for the importation of things foreign, from public bureaucracies (Westney, 1987) to fashion (Stuart, 1987); to language (Mirua, 1979; Kachru, 1982); to baseball (Whiting, 1977). In fact, Japan's widescale adoption of things American is now something of a universal cliché. The choice of imports is, however massive, highly selective. From this perspective, the consumption of foreign goods in Japan seems less an act of homage than a way of establishing a national identity of making such imports their own through combining them in a composite of all that the Japanese see as the "best" in the world. Some of this conspicuous consumption correlates with significant increases in per capita disposable income and what appears to be a new and more relaxed attitude among the Japanese toward leisure and play (Fallows, 1989; Emmott, 1989). But, whatever the source of this omnivorous appetite, the Japanese seem unworried that their cultural identity is compromised by such importation.

Not to be overlooked, however, are the subtle, sometimes hidden, ways alien forms are not merely imported across cultural boundaries but, in the very process, turned into something else again and the indigenous and foreign are combined into an idiom more consistent with the host culture than the home culture. Several features of the way Disneyland has been emulated and incorporated in the Japanese context bear mention. Each suggest that Tokyo Disneyland takes on a rather different meaning for workers and customers alike in its new setting.

Consider the way Tokyo Disneyland is made comfortable for the Japanese in ways that contrast with its California counterpart. In some ways, the fine tuning of the park's character follows a domestication principle familiar to anthropologists, whereby the exotic, alien aspects of foreign objects are set back and deemphasized, replaced by an intensified concern with the more familiar and culturally sensible aspects (Wallace, 1985; Douglas, 1966). Thus the safe, clean, courteous, efficient aspects of Disneyland fit snugly within the Japanese cultural system and can be highlighted. Disneyland as "the best of America" suits the Japanese customer with its underscored technological wizardry and corporate philosophy emphasizing high quality service. Providing happiness, harmony, and hospitality for guests by a staff that is as well-groomed as the tended gardens is certainly consistent with Japanese practices in other consumer locales (Vogel, 1979; Taylor, 1983; Dore, 1987). The legendary sotto voce, stylized gestures and scripted interaction patterns used by Japanese service providers in department stores, hotels, elevators, and shops is merely a slight step away from the "people specialist" of planned exuberance and deferential manners turned out by the University of Disneyland in the United States—at least in theory if not in practice (Van Maanen, 1990). And, "Imagineer-ing," a smart Disney term used to designate the department responsible for the design of park attractions ("the engineers of imagination"), is used for public purposes in Japan, as in the United States, without a touch of irony or awareness of contradiction.

If anything, the Japanese have intensified the orderly nature of Disneyland. If Disneyland is clean, Tokyo Disneyland is impeccably clean; if Disneyland is efficient, Tokyo Disneyland puts the original to shame by being absurdly efficient, or, at least, so says *Business Week* (March 12, 1990). While Disneyland is a version of order, sanitized, homogenized, and precise; Tokyo Disneyland is even more so, thus creating, in the words of one observer, "a perfect toy replica of the ideal tinkling, sugarcoated society around it, a perfect box within a box" (Iyer, 1988, p. 333). One of the charms of both Disneyland and Disney World to American visitors is the slight but noticeable friction between the seamless perfection of the place and the intractable, individualistic, irredeemable, and sometimes intolerable character of the crowd. In the midst of its glittering contraptions and mannerly operatives are customers strolling about wearing "shit happens" or "dirty old man" T-shirts. Tourists in enormous tent dresses, double-knit leisure suits and high-prep Brooks Brothers outfits share space in the monkey car of Casey Jones's Circus Train with tattooed bikers, skinheads, and Deadheads. Obese men and women wearing short shorts mingle and queue up with rambunctious teenagers on the make, all to be crammed onto hurling, clockwork bobsleds and sent on their way for a two-minute roller-coaster ride. Park police—dressed as U.S. Marshals or tinhorn cops—chase down the little criminals of Disneyland on Tom Sawyer's Island or Main Street as irate parents screech at their offspring to wipe the chocolate off their faces, keep their hands off the merchandise, and behave themselves. For the Disneyland patron, such contrasts give life to the park and provide a degree of narrative tension.

In Tokyo, the shadow between the ideal and reality is not so apparent. Adults and children bend more easily toward the desired harmonious state and out of order contrasts are few and far between inside (and perhaps, outside) the park. This is a society where the word for different means wrong and "the nail that sticks out is the nail that must be hammered down" (Bayley, 1976; Kamata, 1980, White, 1987). To the extent that there is order in Tokyo Disneyland is expected and largely taken-for-granted such that the park glides effortlessly rather than lurching self-consciously toward its fabled efficiency. Iyer (1988, p. 317–318) summarizes his visit to Tokyo Disneyland in the following way:

> *There was no disjunction between the perfect rides and their human riders. Each was as synchronized, as punctual, as clean as the other. Little girls in pretty bonnets, their eyes wide with wonder, stood in lines, as impassive as dolls, while their flawless mothers posed like mannequins under their umbrellas. (They) waited uncomplainingly for a sweet-voiced machine to break the silence and permit them to enter the pavilion—in regimented squads. All the while, another mechanized voice offered tips to ensure that the human element would be just as well planned as the man-made: Do not leave your shopping to the end, and try to leave the park before rush hour, and eat at a sensible hour, and do not, under any circumstances, fail to have a good time.*

Such failures to have a good time are rare partly because of the way Tokyo Disneyland has rearranged the model to suit its customers. Despite its claim as a duplicate, a number of quite specific changes have taken place and more are planned. The amusement park itself is considerably larger than Disneyland (124 acres to 74). As a result, it loses some of its uncharacteristic intimacy in a Southern California setting but gives off a feeling of conspicuous spaciousness rather unusual in greater Tokyo, where it seems every square inch is fully utilized. Disneyland's fleet of Nautilus-like submarines is missing perhaps because of Japan's deep sensitivity to all things nuclear. There are a few outdoor food vendors in the park but over forty sit-down restaurants, about twice the number in Disneyland. It is considered rude to eat while walking about in Japan—the munching of popcorn in the park being apparently the only exception.

Several new attractions have been added in Tokyo. Each are quite explicit about what culture is, in the final analysis, to be celebrated in the park. One, incongruously called "Meet the World," offers not only a history of Japan but an elaborate defense of the Japanese way. In this regard, it is not unlike Disneyland's "Meet Mr. Lincoln" where visitors are asked at one point to sing a passionate version of "America the Beautiful" along with the mechanical icon of Honest Abe. In "Meet the World," a sagacious crane guides a young boy and his sister through the past, pausing briefly along the way to make certain points such as the lessons learned by the Japanese cave dwellers ("the importance of banding together") or the significance of the Samurai warrior ("we never became a colony") or the importance of early foreign trade ("to carry the seeds offered from across the sea and cultivate them in our own Japanese garden"). Another site-specific attraction in Tokyo Disneyland is the Magic Journey movie trip across five continents which culminates, dramatically, in the adventure's return to "our beloved Japan where our hearts always remain."

Another singular attraction in Tokyo Disneyland is situated inside Cinderella's Castle and produced as a tightly packed mystery tour through a maze of dark tunnels, fearsome electronic tableaux, and narrow escapes. Groups of about 15 to 20 persons are escorted through this breathless 13-minute adventure in the castle by lively tour guides. Little passivity is apparent on this attraction as customers whoop and holler to one another and race wildly through the castle trailing their tour guide. The climactic moment of the tour takes place when the guide selects from the group a single representative to do battle with a menacing evil sorcerer. The chosen hero or heroine is provided a laser sword and, backed by nifty special effects and timely coaching from the tour guide, manages to slay the dark lord just in the nick of time. The group is thus spared, free again for further adventures in the park. The attraction ends with a mock-solemn presentation of a medal to the usually bashful group savior who then leads everyone out the exit after passing down an aisle formed by applauding fellow members of the mystery tour.

It is hard to imagine a similar attraction working in either Disneyland or Disney World. Not only would group discipline be lacking such to insure that all members of the tour would start and end together but selecting a sword bearer to do battle with the Evil One would quite likely prove to be a considerable test for the tour guides when meeting with the characteristic American chorus of "Me, Me, Me" coming from children and adults alike. The intimacy, proximity and physical, almost hands-on, interaction between customers and amusement sources found in Tokyo Disneyland are striking to a visitor accustomed to the invisible security and attention given to damage control so prevalent in the U.S. parks. Tokyo Disneyland puts its guests within touching distance of many of its attractions, such that a customer who wished to could easily deface a cheerful robot, steal a Small World doll, or behead the Mad Hatter. This blissful audience respect for the built environment at Tokyo Disneyland allows ride operators to take more of an exhibitory stance to their attraction than a custodial one, which is often the perspective of Disneyland operatives (Van Maanen and Kunda, 1989).

Other distinctly Japanese touches include the white gloves for drivers of the transportation vehicles in the park, a practice drawn from the taxi and bus drivers in Japan; name tags for employees featuring last names rather than first names; a small picnic area just outside the park for families bringing traditional box lunches to the park, a reminder of family customs in Japan and a compromise on the Disney tradition of allowing no food to be brought into the park. All ride soundtracks and spiels are, of course, in Japanese and one American visitor reports considerably more ad-libbing on the part of the Japanese ride operators compared to their American counterparts (Brannen, 1990). The sign boards are dominated by English titles (Romaji) but all have subtitles in Japanese. Such concessions to the Japanese guest contrast with the proclamation of a pure copy. One might argue that such changes are minor adjustments in keeping with the fundamental marketing techniques of both capitalistic societies, namely, tailoring the product to its audience. But, it is also important to keep in mind that even the notion of consumer capitalism in the two contexts varies systematically.

Main Street U.S.A., for example, has become in Tokyo, the World Bazaar. Little remains of the turn-of-the-century midwestern town of Walt's slippery memory. The World Bazaar is quite simply an enormous, modern, up-scale shopping mall where many of the products (and possibilities) of the five continents are brought together in a postmodern Disney collage that is distinctly Japanese. Few modest trinkets are on sale at the World Bazaar but instead costly, high status items are offered, all bearing an official Disney label and wrapped in Tokyo Disneyland paper suitable for the gift giving practices of the Japanese as outlined by Brannen (1990). Frontierland's presentation of the continental expansion of the United States has given way to Westernland, which is apparently understood only through the Japanese familiarity with the Wild West imagery of American movies, television, and pulp fiction. Thus, to the extent that nostalgia, patriotism and historical narratives provide the context of meaning for visitors to Disneyland, visitors to Tokyo Disneyland are made comfortable by devices of their own making. While the structure may appear quite similar, the meaning is not.

Take, for example, something as fundamental as the physical design of Tokyo Disneyland. The very layout of the park seems to be something of a mystery and cultural maze for many Japanese visitors. Far more customers in Tokyo are seen wandering hesitantly through the park with a map in hand than in the United States where customers, by contrast, appear quite confident and determined while strolling about the park. Certain attractions, too, are apparently decoded by the Japanese only with difficulty (and, perhaps, with the help of the guidebook passed out at the front gate). Notoji (1988) quotes some native informants in this regard. One, a middle-age and -class Japanese housewife says:

I went to see the Pirates of the Caribbean at Tokyo Disneyland because the guidebook said it was a must. I had no idea what to expect and I didn't quite understand why they had to have the Pirates of the Caribbean there. The word "the Caribbean" has no meaning to me except for the image of an expensive yacht cruise for some rich folks. I didn't know that pirates once lived there until I saw this attraction at Tokyo Disneyland. Yes, the pirate robots were very well made and their firing of cannon balls at the seaport town was realistic. But so what?

Another, an elderly Japanese woman, remarks:

I didn't understand what the whole thing was trying to say. What impressed me was that the fireflies were computerized. That Americans would go through such trouble to do such things. You know, we used to have Japanese pirates around the Inland Sea, but we are more familiar with those mountain bandits who raided and stripped the travelers naked. I would have understood it if they had these bandits on the show instead of the Caribbean pirates.

In these cases it seems that unless the park visitor is familiar with western-style pirate stories, the ride—as a symbol of exotic adventure, wicked deeds, and the pursuit of treasure and pleasure—simply fails to work. It may of course become something else again. Virtually all of Notoji's informants were taken by the mechanical gimmickry employed on the ride, impressed more by the "movements of the chicken robots and cat robots" than by the narrative. The pirates, to these visitors at least, are simply clever robots doing some incomprehensible things. This may well be the response generated by other attractions in Tokyo Disneyland, such as the Enchanted Tiki Room, the Haunted Mansion, and Bear Country Jamboree; attractions that on the surface at least seem to offer little symbolic worth to the Japanese.

Not all rides fall into this category. Many Japanese children and adults are quite familiar with other western stories and fairy tales. Moreover, Disney editions of some of these stories are so widely circulated that many Japanese children, like their American counterparts, believe Alice in Wonderland, Peter Pan, and Snow White are the products of Walt Disney's imagination. Those who know these tales have little trouble no doubt understanding and enjoying the attractions keyed to them in a way that the ride-designers would appreciate. But, even for the most well-versed of visitors, there remain crucial contextual differences that will not go away and produce for the Japanese in Tokyo Disneyland a rather different cultural experience than what most Americans expects and take away from their visits to the old parks at home.

This shift in meaning can perhaps best be appreciated by considering some aspects of the emulation process at Tokyo Disneyland that run counter to some of our more benign (or, at least, calming) beliefs about the workings of culture flows. Tokyo Disneyland serves as something of a shrine in Japan to Japan itself, an emblem of the self-validating beliefs as to the cultural values and superiority of the Japanese. Disneyland serves as such a shrine in America, of course, but it is America that is celebrated. How is it that a painstaking near-copy of what is undeniably an American institution—like baseball—can function to heighten the self-awareness of the Japanese?

The answer lies in the workings of culture itself, for culture is not only an integrating device, but a differentiating device as well, a way of marking boundaries. Tokyo Disneyland does so in a variety of ways. One already mentioned is the outdoing of Disneyland in the order-keeping domain. The message coming from Japan (for the Japanese) is simply "anything you can do, we can do as well (or better)." If one of the characteristic features of modern Japan is its drive toward perfection, it has built a Disneyland that surpasses its model in terms of courtesy, size, efficiency, cleanliness, and performance. Were the park built more specifically to Japanese tastes and cultural aesthetics, it would undercut any contrast to the original in this regard. While Disneyland is reproduced in considerable detail, it is never deferred to entirely, thus making the consumption of this cultural experience a way of marking the boundaries between Japan and the United States. Japan has taken in Disneyland only, it seems, to take it over.

Consider, also, another cultural flow analogous to the way Disneyland itself treats the foreign and exotic. Tokyo Disneyland maintains, indeed amplifies, Self and Other contrasts consistent with Japanese cultural rules. Only Japanese employees wear name tags in the park, the foreign (western) employees do not. Americans hired to play Disney characters such as Snow White, Cinderella, Prince Charming, Alice in Wonderland, Peter Pan, or the Fairy Godmother are nameless, thus merging whatever personalized identities they may project with that of their named character. Other western employees such as craftsmen (e.g., glass blowers, leather workers), dancers, magicians, musicians, and role-playing shopkeepers also remain tag-less. Musicians play only American songs—ranging from the Broadway production numbers put on the large stage settings of the park to the twangy country-western tunes played by a small combo in a fake saloon of Westernland. During the Christmas season, songs such as Rudolf the Red-Nosed Reindeer, Silent Night, and the Hallelujah Chorus of Handel's Messiah are piped throughout the appropriately festooned park as a portly American Santa Claus poses for snapshots with couples and families who wait patiently in long queues for such a photo opportunity. The gaijin (literally "outside person") ordinarily speak only English while in role which furthers their distinctiveness in the setting. Mary Yoki Brannen (1990) writes of these practices:

> . . . *rather than functioning as facilitators of the Disneyland experience like their Japanese counterparts, gaijin employees are put on display. Gaijin cast members are displayed daily in a group at the place of honor at the front of the Disneyland parade, and gaijin craftspersons are displayed throughout the day at their boxed-in work stations not unlike animals in cages at the zoo.*

The same general practice is followed at Disneyland where, of course, the roles are reversed and the "Others" are constructed out of different cultural building blocks. Just as blacks are more notable at Disneyland for their absence from the productions and the work force, Koreans are conspicuously absent in Tokyo Disneyland, victims, it seems, of the facial politics of Asia. Villains of the Disney narratives produced in the United States seem often to speak and act with vaguely foreign personae and accents, typically, but not always, Russian or German; evil in Tokyo Disneyland is represented by gaijin witches, goblins, and ghosts whose accents are distinctly non-Japanese. Such a practice of sharply separating gaijin from society mirrors other Japanese cultural productions such as the popular television shows devoted to portraying gaijin stupidities (Stuart, 1987) or the practice of limiting the number of baseball players on professional teams to two gaijin players per team (Whiting, 1989). The outsiders may be accorded respect but they are not to come too close for the culture provides no easy space for them.

Cultural Experience Revisited

These contrasts in meaning across the two parks could be extended considerably. The point, however, is not to enumerate all the amplifications, deflations, twists, or reversals in meaning but to note their pervasive presence. The Japanese cultural experience in Tokyo Disneyland is akin to a "foreign vacation" with a number of comforting homey touches built into a visit. The park is seen by the Japanese primarily as a simulated chunk of America put down by the Tokyo Bay. Passports are not required but guide books come in handy.

The perfect copy of Disneyland turns out therefore to be anything but perfect at the level of signification. If Disney is the merchant of nostalgia at home, he is the merchant of gimmickry, glitz, and gaijins in Tokyo. If Disneyland sucks the difference out of differences by presenting an altogether tamed and colonized version of the people of other lands who are, when all is said and done, just like the good folks living in Los Angeles or Des Moines, Tokyo Disneyland celebrates differences by treating the foreign as exotic, its peoples to be understood only in terms of the fact that they are not Japanese and not, most assuredly, like the good people of Osaka or Kyoto.

In this regard, both parks are isolated by a belief in their own cultural superiority. It would be asking too much perhaps of a commercial enterprise to question such a belief since the corporate aim in both settings is, in crude terms, to build and manage an amusement park such that people will come (and come again) to be run assembly-line fashion through its attractions and stripped of their money. But, in the cracks, Tokyo Disneyland offers some intriguing lessons in culture flow beyond the mere fact of its existence. I have three in mind.

First, the presentation of "the best in America" in Japan breaks some new ground and contributes modestly to what might be called post-modernism by combining cultural elements in new ways and then allowing customers and workers alike to develop the logic of the relationship. Thus, Mickey Mouse, a symbol of the infantile and plastic in America, can come to stand for what is fashionable and perky in Japan and used to sell adult apparel and money market accounts. This is not simply a matter of the Japanese appropriating Mickey but rather signals a process by which selected alien imports are reconstituted and given new meaning.

Second, not only are cultural meanings worked out rather differently in a new setting compared to the old and such adaptation takes time; but, as culture flows continue, people on both sides of the border become more aware of their own culture (and its contradictions). The traffic flow is messy but, as cultures move back and forth, people on both sides may discover new ways to do things and new things to do that might not have been apparent within either culture. People are not passive in relation to culture as if they merely receive it, transmit it, express it. They also create it and new meanings may eventually emerge as cultures interpenetrate one another. The notions of family entertainment, safe thrills, and urban leisure will surely never be the same in Japan since Tokyo Disneyland appeared on the scene. A recent poll in Japan, for example, reported that over fifty percent of Japanese adults when asked "where they experienced their happiest moment in the last year" responded by saying "Tokyo Disneyland" (Iyer, 1988).

Third, the view that cultural influences move easily along the tracks of massification—mass media, mass production, mass marketing, mass consumerism—ushering in a global culture which spells the eclipse of national and local cultures is certainly discredited by Tokyo Disneyland. This view is I think naive to the point of banality. While our understanding of cultural flows remains woefully inadequate, we do know that cultural acquisition is a slow, highly selective, and contextually dependent matter. Culture cannot be simply rammed down people's throats. As individual identity and membership distinctions become blurred, culture must be approached more as a rhetorical front than a felt reality. Thus, when a CEO of a multinational corporation refers to his firm as "a family" or when government leaders reach out and try to project the idea of a region as a culture, they may often be regarded as engaging in rhetoric or stating an aspiration that is all too obviously missing in practice. The trick in understanding culture flows would seem to be in finding the level where culture becomes more than an oratorical abstraction and begins to turn on experience, feeling, and consciousness. Here, then, is where meaning will be marked and cultural imports embraced, rejected, or perhaps most commonly, transformed.

All this is to say that cultural flows are loose, ongoing matters. Mickey Mouse has been hanging around Japan for along time and his cultural status has a history that is far from closed or complete. Working out the cultural meaning of Tokyo Disneyland is also a long-term project that is in all respects rather open. Many of the distinctive Japanese characteristics of the park were absent when the gates were first thrown back and more are surely to come.

References

Bayley, D. 1976. *Forces of Order*. Berkeley: University of California Press.

Brannen, M. Y. 1990. Bwana Mickey: Constructing Cultural Consumption at Tokyo Disneyland. Unpublished paper. School of Management, University of Massachusetts, Amherst.

Dore, R. 1987. *Taking Japan Seriously.* Stanford: Stanford University Press.

Douglas, M. 1966. *Purity and Danger.* London: Routledge and Kegan Paul.

Douglas, M. and B. Isherwood. 1980. *The World of Goods.* London: Penguin.

Emmott, B. 1989. *The Sun Also Sets.* New York: Simon & Schuster.

Fallows, J. 1989. *More Like Us.* Boston: Houghton Mifflin.

Iyer, P. 1988. *Video Nights in Kathmandu.* New York: Vintage.

Kachru, B. (Ed.). 1982. *The Other Tongue: English Across Cultures.* Urbana: University of Illinois Press.

Kamata, S. 1980. *Japan in the Passing Lane.* New York: Random House.

Miura, A. 1979. *English Loanwords in Japanese.* Tokyo: Charles Tuttle.

Notoji, M. 1988. Cultural Boundaries and Magic Kingdom: A comparative symbolic analysis of Disneyland and Tokyo Disneyland. Paper presented at the American Studies Association Annual Meetings, Miami Beach (October 27–30).

Stuart, P. M. 1987. *NihOnsense.* Tokyo: The Japan Times.

Taylor, J. 1983. *Shadows of the Rising Sun.* New York: Morrow.

Van Maanen, J., and G. Kunda. 1989. Real feelings: Emotional expression and organizational culture. In B. Staw and L. L. Cummings (Eds.), *Research in Organization Behavior* 11, pp. 43–103.

Van Maanen, J. 1990. The Smile Factory. In P. J. Frost et al. (Eds.), *Reframing Organizational Culture* (pp. 58–76). Newbury Park, CA: Sage.

Vogel, E. 1979. *Japan as Number One.* Cambridge: Harvard University Press.

Wallace, F. A. C. 1985. Rethinking technology "and" culture. Paper presented for the Mellon Seminar on Technology and Culture. University of Pennsylvania, Department of Anthropology.

Westney, E. 1987. *Imitation and Innovation.* Cambridge: Harvard University Press.

White, M. 1987. *The Japanese Educational Challenge.* New York: Free Press.

Whiting, R. 1977. *The Chrysanthemum and the Bat.* New York: Vintage.

Whiting, R. 1989. *You Gotta Have Wa.* New York: Vintage.

Disney Goes to Paris

Crossing the Atlantic

Euro Disney, now Disneyland Paris, opened to great fanfare in April 1992. It is located in Marne-la-Vallée, 32 kilometers east of Paris and, on the surface, is much less a duplicate of Disneyland in its design than Tokyo. Part of its differences are due to the insistence of the French government that the park have some "decided French touches" and partly to Disney's own market research and best guesses as to what would play well to the 310 million Europeans within a two-hours' flight of the park. In short, the kind of cultural sensibility operating in Disneyland Paris is different from in Tokyo Disneyland such that the cultural contrasts, blends, and conflicts are more noticeable in France than in Japan. This distraction is all rather ironic given the long and more or less peaceful, cooperative, and relatively close relations between the French and Americans.

The cultural sensibility on the part of both the French and the Americans is, however, anything but gentle or generous. Nor is it modest. The European Disney story is in fact still playing out, but a good part of the tale unfolds as a result of what can only be considered a rough beginning. The unprecedented success of Tokyo Disneyland led Disney's senior managers to believe they had a sure-fire global winner (a golden goose) on their hands, and Europe seemed the most appropriate and potentially most lucrative place to locate the next Disneyland. And this time Disney executives were determined not to let others reap most of the profits.

Following Walt's example of always trying to negotiate a deal with at least two parties at once (Foglesong, 2001, p. 46), Disney's management team played two country bidders off one another: Spain and France. The Spanish side put forth a site in Barcelona. Although it had weather better suited for an all-seasons resort, it was farther from the affluent population centers of northern Europe than Paris and less easily accessible to major transportation hubs. More critically however the French government, as eager as their Spanish counterparts to attract the jobs and the development spillovers of Disneyland, offered what the Suits at Disney took as a more attractive deal: 4,800 acres of land at below-market prices, land Disney could resell to other developers at any price it could command; major long-term property and employer tax breaks; low-interest loans from state-owned banks; major new construction for a high-speed highway, other traffic and local roadway improvements around the park; and an extension of the national high-speed rail network to a Disneyland station. All was to be accomplished at government expense (Toy et al., 1990).

The choice of the French site was announced in 1985. After extensive negotiations, the final contract for the $2 billion park—whose costs eventually ballooned to $5 billion—was signed in 1987 by Prime Minister Jacques Chirac and Disney CEO Michael Eisner. In anticipation of the implementation of the Maastricht Treaty, which was to formally change the European Community to the European Union in the year the park was to open, 1992, the highly visible development was named Euro Disney.

Although the Walt Disney Company was eager to reap the potential profits from the enterprise, the Suits were no more enthusiastic than they had ever been about assuming much of the risk. Therefore the structure for the new park was a complicated one. A finance company was set up as the owner of the park, in which Disney took a 17 percent stake (this arrangement is described in greater detail in the article "Mouse Trap" that appears at the end of this Class Note). A separate company, Euro Disney, was formed to operate the park, of which 49 percent was owned by the Walt Disney Company. The parent Disney made arrangements to collect royalties and licensing fees from Euro Disney on admissions, food, beverages, and souvenirs, similar to those of Tokyo Disneyland. To help raise capital, the rest of the shares of Euro Disney were listed on the Paris stock exchange and available to the public at an opening share price of $11.50 (quickly rising to its all-time high of $18). Disney paid about $1.50 for each of its shares, a fact that, when it became known in the wake of a falling share price in the 1990s, caused considerable public criticism (Solomon, 1994). Foreshadowing the discussion to follow, Euro Disney shares were selling on the Bourse in the summer of 2003 at about $0.60 a share (a level held for many years).

The business press began to carry stories about possible problems for Euro Disney as early as 1989 when the launch of Euro Disney shares in Paris was met by a group of egg-throwing protesters who managed to pelt Michael Eisner in full view of the press. Potato farmers and local residents in Marne-la-Vallée staged a number of well-attended protests and generated a good deal of public sympathy for what they claimed was a governmental giveaway of their lands and way of life. When Disney began hiring staff for the park, the press carried stories about the demanding conduct and dress code on which Disney insisted to the dismay of its employees. The company ran into some highly publicized disputes with 16 of its French contractors, which threatened to delay the scheduled opening and were sent to arbitration. Construction costs escalated, largely a result of Disney's desire to build an "architectural masterpiece" in Europe with no frills spared.

The eagerness of the French government to attract Disney was not matched however by French intellectuals. As cultural historian Richard Pells (1997, pp. 311–312) put it:

When the park opened in April 1992, writers competed with one another to see whose denunciations were the most hyperbolic. A "cultural Chernobyl" exclaimed the theater director Ariane Mnouchkine. "A terrifying giant's step toward world homogenization," the philosopher Alain Finkielkraut declared. To another commentator, Euro Disney was "a horror made of cardboard, plastic, and appalling colors, a construction of hardened chewing gum and idiotic folklore taken straight out of comic books written for obese Americans." According to the French intellectuals, Disney commercialized the fairy tales of children everywhere, thereby stifling their dreams and preparing them to become mere spectators and consumers. . . . Worst of all, Disneyland was no longer over there, across the ocean, in America, the home of mass culture. Now it was right here, in the heart of French civilization, practically within the boundaries of Paris itself.

Such criticisms were not abated by Disney's efforts to make the park more varied and "European" than its counterparts elsewhere. Several innovations in Disneyland traditions appear in the park. Tomorrowland is gone, replaced by Discoveryland (and later imported back to the original—without the name change—as part of the 1998 renovations in Anaheim). The shift was a result, in part, of Disney market surveys showing that Europeans hold an ambivalent and skeptical attitude toward the wonders of modern science and technology (Sassen, 1989). Discoveryland draws on the imagery of Jules Verne, Leonardo da Vinci, and H. G. Wells to find the future in the past and abandons the gleaming, crisp, militaristic Tomorrowland look of other parks. The Jungle Cruise is no longer around in the European park to remind visitors of their colonial past. Perhaps Disney surveys showed that Third World "natives" are less amusing to the French, English, or Dutch than to the Americans or Japanese. Identifications for the origins of the various narratives and fairy tales presented in the park, absent elsewhere, are prominent in Paris where the corporation agreed (reluctantly) to acknowledge the rightful authors—but not the imagery—of its expropriated children's tales (Glover, 1991, pp. 191–192). And, in Paris, Snow White now speaks German, Sleeping Beauty rests in her French chateau (Le Château de la Belle au Bois Dormant), Pinocchio reclaims his Italian heritage, and Peter Pan flies not from L.A. but from London again.

The critics have not been charmed or silenced by Disney's face work and expensive and sometimes rather elaborate revisions in the park design. Some still regard the project as a form of "creeping Americanism" and are disturbed less with the attractions and look of the park as with, for example, the tasteless fast food available on the grounds and having to eat it from tables and chairs bolted to the floor. In what has turned out to be altogether clairvoyant, local politicians and community leaders in the region voiced their concerns early on about "externalities" and the possible Orlando-ization of the region—the traffic and crowds the development would attract as well as the potential buildup of unwanted urban problems in the region.

The troubles inside the park seemed only to get worse after the opening. Although the expected number of paying guests came to the park (about 11 million the first year), they complained about the lack of restaurant space, the disorderly and lengthy queues, and the lack of the friendly service that the park's advertising and their experience of the Disney parks in the United States led many of them to expect. Vigilant and veteran Disney observers were not impressed either with the park's performance. Brannen and Wilson (1996, p. 104) were apparently shocked when they visited Disneyland Paris in 1995, almost three years after the opening.

On three out of five visits we noticed bathroom stall doors to be broken and the bathrooms themselves untidy, smiles from service people at restaurants on the park were not only uncommon but in one instance a food server got into a squabble with a customer over whether she had paid or not, and the grounds themselves were littered, with few sidewalk sweepers in sight (a notable fixture at other Disney parks).

The relative ease with which the Disney service culture of "the happiest place on earth" was transferred to Tokyo did not prepare the company for the challenges of implementing it in France. One early press story (Toy et al., 1990) carried the following revealing anecdote:

Disney University, a feature of all company parks, has launched the standard day-and-a-half course in Disney culture, plus job training that can last weeks. "*We have to do more explaining in class,*" admits David Kanally, director of the university's Paris branch. *Sessions often erupt into debates. One group of French students spent 20 minutes discussing how to define "efficiency."* Says Kanally: *"That wouldn't happen in Orlando."*

The angry employee reaction to the dress and conduct code and the public protests voiced in the press forced Disney to eventually relax some of its restrictions. But even so, in 1995, the park was charged with violating French labor law in its efforts to impose its dress code on its French employees. French labor law has thus far proved to be an unanticipated impediment for Disney in other ways for it contains far more limitations on the use of part-time and contingent workers than Disneyland is accustomed to in the United States or Japan. Of Disney's some 15,000 employees in the European park today, only about 3,000 are part-timers (close to a reversal of the full-time/part-time ratios of other parks). The French courts also consider illegal some of the major control tools much favored by American managers: the allocation of valued overtime work to the most effervescent and reliable workers and the speedy dismissal of those who fail to meet the Disney standards.

All has not been entirely antagonistic however. Although trade unions in France have often been difficult for Disney management, they do occasionally surprise. After the "storm of the century" blew through the Ile de France during the Christmas holidays in 1999 causing extensive damage, a bitter work stoppage involving 10,000 Disney employees was suspended by union leaders so that Cast Members could get back to work restoring the park. "Given the disastrous state of the park it would be unreasonable to continue the protest," said a union leader at the time (*International Herald Tribune*, December 31, 1999).

Customers are not unmindful of the on-stage (and backstage) debates occurring at the park. But it is doubtful that such matters are of overriding concern to them. Certainly, as noted, attendance targets have been met for most of the park's history. Indeed, Disneyland Paris is now—and has been for almost 10 years—the most popular European tourist destination by a large measure. But the company continues to lose money. Part of the problem is the accumulated debt that the company faces. In 2003, for example, reacting to a tourist slowdown from the Iraq war, the SARs scare, and the economic slump in Europe, Disney agreed to forgo licensing fees and royalties for the year and the company cautioned investors for the third time in the past decade that it might not have enough cash to pay debts owed to its banks (*New York Times*, August 1, 2003). Even though the little likelihood is small that Disney will ever face insolvency in France, given the continuous and strong political backing it gets at the national level in France and its role as an important employer in the Paris region; the company has yet to fully come to terms and manage its way out of the troubling conditions it faces.

Many of these difficulties reflect cultural mistakes and misunderstandings. Visitors do not spend as much time or money in the park as their counterparts in the United States or Japan. During the early years of the enterprise, they did not stay in the six (now seven) expensive themed hotels that Disney owned, primarily because people found few reasons to linger at a park that could easily be seen in a day or less. The crowds spent far less on souvenirs and food because many of them were "day-trippers" who preferred to spend their time and money in Paris or elsewhere. Americans and Japanese, it turns out, are willing to spend much more on their relatively short vacations than were Europeans, who enjoy much longer—and, for that reason, cheaper—vacations. Moreover, the French (and Europeans generally) and are much less willing to pull their children out of school for special vacation trips (as in the United States) or to see school trips to Disneyland as an appropriate educational experience (as in Japan).

Disney exacerbated these problems by its pricing policies. Staying at one of the Disney hotels was for years more expensive than staying at a comparable hotel in Paris. Souvenirs were of the low-quality, high-price variety. And admissions charges were for some time considerably higher than in the U.S. parks. It seems that Disney pricing policies were based initially on the costs of building and running a larger than necessary complex rather than based on what customers were willing to bear. The ambitions of Disney were, in retrospect, rather unattainable if not foolish. To wit, a company spokesperson said to the French press in 1991: "We aim to make Paris a side trip."

Almost from the beginning, it was clear Euro Disney was in quite serious trouble. Massive losses were costing the park about $1 million a day and few believed that the early-1990s recession was the sole cause. A new chief executive, Philippe Bourguignon, was appointed in 1994 to Euro Disney to stem the financial bleeding. The first rescue package proposed by the Suits from Walt Disney headquarters was indignantly rejected by the most important French stakeholders, the banks. A rescue package was finally approved, one that provided a moratorium on the royalties going to Disney as well as on the interest payments to the banks (*The Economist,* April 13, 1996, pp. 66–67). A step in Bourguignon's turnaround effort was taken when the ill-fated name *Euro Disney* was abandoned in favor of "Disneyland Paris." But, as most analysts pointed out, the rescue package and the new name would work only if the park was able to draw more customers, get them to spend more, and at the same time cut its operating costs.

The reorganization story in Paris is a continuing one. Disney is by no means out of hot water yet. Opening the second gate in 2002, Walt Disney Studios Park, certainly helped boost attendance some and pushed hotel revenues up due to more reasons for visitors to spend more time (and money) on the grounds. Disney has also been increasing the number of attractions in the park and trimming the workforce where possible. They have also been adding to the number of experienced French and European managers involved in running Disneyland Paris. This issue has been a problem for some time. Michael Eisner (1998, p. 176) alludes to the matter in his autobiography:

> *During the development of Euro Disney the company had trouble finding suitable executives for the project. Those who spoke French were not necessarily knowledgeable about the parks and those who were savvy about the parks refused to learn French.*

Eisner of course was looking for French-speaking American managers who would locate to France. Bourguignon solved the problem largely by hiring knowledgeable European managers who also spoke English. Slowly he and his successors have tried to Europeanize the management of the park, and relations with contractors, local residents, guests, and various employees groups have improved considerably.

Other small changes have occurred as Disneyland Paris continues to localize and hence learn across borders. Advertising, originally following the Euro Disney intention to "reach out to all of Europe" has increasingly focused on national markets. Features of the park that appeal, say, to Germans are not the same ones that draw Dutch or British visitors. This customization turned out to be vital because only about 40 percent of the park's visitors to date are from France, with 17 percent from Belgium, Luxembourg, and the Netherlands, 15 percent from Britain, and 10 percent from Germany. Wine was added to the menu, a much-remarked on omission that annoyed the French for its display of an apparent disregard for the country's taste and culture and its none-too-subtle assumption that whatever works in the United States would work in France.

Perhaps most important, ticket prices were reduced and discounts, special promotions, and events (e.g., Bastille Day, Christmas, and Oktoberfest celebrations) now play an important role in attracting customers. Seasonal fluctuations are more extreme at Disneyland Paris than at the other parks, so boosting attendance during slack winter months (or paring back operations) is crucial. The local population remains Disney's trump card and nurturing this customer base will make or break the park in the long run. Integrating a visit to Disneyland Paris into the leisure "routines" of French families within driving distance of the park will provide the repeat visitor foundation—"France first"—on which sizeable and predictable revenues depend. Experience, experiments, and a willingness to innovate are crucial here as is guidance from regional and community leaders in both public and private sectors.

The rise in occupancy rates at its big hotels in the late 1990s and early 2000s buoyed the company some. From the abysmal 40–50 percent rates in first few years of operation (when some hotels were shut down for months at a time) to what are now (typically) 70–80 percent rates, the park seems on its way to hard-won stability and economic gain. But, as has been historically the case at Disneyland Paris, there are flies even in this seemingly soothing ointment.

So successful has the park been at attracting crowds in the past few years (1999 onward) that a number of residents and local politicians in the Marne-la-Vallée region (and a few national figures as well) are now anxious and angry—intensifying public concerns that were raised over a decade ago. The company is in a growth period and is pushing hard to increase the returns on the land it bought in the early stages of the project. It opened, along with Walt Disney Studios Park, a mega-mall built by an outsider developer in Serris, the town next door to the resort. Highways leading to the park and mall are now frequently blocked off by traffic and continuous gridlock is a down-the-road possibility (*International Herald Tribune,* February 18, 2000). This issue, along with heightened concern for the "chewing gum jobs" the company provides (low pay, low skill, and rapid turnover) and the deeper penetration of American products and images in an environment already saturated with such commercial goods and symbols, will surely extract their toll on the company.

At the moment, it does seem that Disney has shrunk the size of its American flag a bit and tried with some success to put aside a few of its more homebound cultural assumptions. But much fine-tuning remains. It is also a tricky matter of degree, for certainly a part of Disneyland Paris's appeal remains its American look and feel, however loathe some Europeans may be to openly express such desire. In sum, cross-border learning at Disneyland

Paris has been slow and irregular, marked by peaks and valleys and associated more with the shifting mix of managerial personnel and their whims than with a gradual accumulation of useful organizational memory and culturally sensitive practices. The bottom-line is that some distance remains before Disneyland Paris and the people who visit and work there feel entirely comfortable and on their way to achieving the kind of success both the French and Americans who first entertained the project had imagined.

A litany of the problems the company faced in France several years after Disneyland's European debut follows. Importantly, as this Class Note emphasized, many of these difficulties are still troubling the company today. The article comes from *The Wall Street Journal* and nicely captures the way the Euro Disney to Disneyland Paris story was covered by the business and popular press in the United States. As one might expect, the press in Europe was generally far more mocking and dismissive. At times, the European press seemed downright elated with Disney's woes. Of course, whatever Disney does—good, bad or indifferent—never fails to attract attention. It is the company's curse as well as blessing.

References

Brannen, Mary Yoko, and J. M. Wilson III. 1996. "Recontextualization and Internationalization: Lessons in Transcultural Materialism from the Walt Disney Company." *CEMS (Community of European Management Schools) Business Review*, vol. 1, 1st ed.

Michael Eisner (with Tony Schertz). 1998. *Work in Progress.* New York: Random House.

Foglesong, Richard E. 2001. *Married to the Mouse: Walt Disney World and Orlando.* New Haven, CT: Yale University Press.

Grover, Ron. 1997. *The Disney Touch: Disney, ABC, & the Quest for the World's Greatest Media Empire* (rev. ed.). Chicago: Irwin Professional Publishing.

Pells, Richard. 1997. *Not Like Us: How Europeans Have Loved, Hated, and Transformed American Culture Since World War II.* New York: Basic Books.

Sassen, John. 1989. Mickey Mania. *International Management.* November, 32–4.

Solomon, Judy. 1994. Mickey's Trip to Trouble. *Newsweek* (February 14, 1994), pp. 34–38.

Toy, Stewart, Marc Marmot, and Ronald Grover. 1990. An American in Paris: Can Disney Work Its Magic in Europe? *Business Week* (March 12, 1990), pp. 34–38.

Mouse Trap

by Peter Gumbel and Richard Turner

Europe got its first taste of the management style of Walt Disney Co. when Joe Shapiro started kicking in a door at the luxury Hotel Bristol here.

It was 1986, and Disney was negotiating with the French government on plans to build a big resort and theme park on the outskirts of Paris. To the exasperation of the Disney team, headed by Mr. Shapiro, then the company's general counsel, the talks were taking far longer than expected. Jene-Rene Bernard, the chief French negotiator, says he was astonished when Mr. Shapiro, his patience ebbing, ran to the door of the room and

Source: "Mouse Trap" by Peter Gumbel and Richard Turner, *Wall Street Journal*, March 10, 1994. Copyright 1994 by Dow Jones & Co., Inc. Reproduced with permission of Dow Jones & Co., Inc. in the format Textbook via Copyright Clearance Center.

began kicking it repeatedly, shouting, "Get me something else to break!"

Mr. Shapiro says he doesn't remember the incident, though he adds with a laugh, "There were a lot of histrionics at the time." But Disney's kick-down-the-door attitude in the planning, building, and financing of Euro Disney accounts for many of the huge problems that plague the resort, which currently loses $1 million a day because of its sky-high overhead and interest payments on loans. The project is in danger less than two years after opening, as Disney and creditor banks try to work out a costly rescue. The sides are believed to be coming closer to an agreement by a deadline of March 31.

Mickey's Misfires

The irony is that even though some early French critics called the park an American cultural abomination, public acceptance hasn't been the problem. European visitors seem to love the place. The Magic Kingdom has attracted an average of just under a million visitors a month, in line with projections, and today it ranks as Europe's biggest paid tourist destination.

Euro Disney's troubles, instead, derive from a different type of culture clash. Europe may have embraced Mickey Mouse, but it hasn't taken to the brash, frequently insensitive and often overbearing style of Mickey's corporate parent. Overly ambitious, Disney made several strategic and financial miscalculations. It relied too heavily on debt—just as interest rates started to rise—and gambled, incorrectly, that the 1980s boom in real estate would continue, letting it sell off assets and pay down the debt quickly. It also made uncharacteristic slips in the park itself, from wrongly thinking Europeans don't eat breakfast to not providing enough toilets for the hundreds of bus drivers.

Disney Knows Best

Disney executives declined to comment for this article. In the past, the company has blamed its problems on external factors, including an unexpectedly severe European recession, high interest rates, and the devaluation of several currencies against the French franc. And Disney supporters note that many of the same people now complaining about Disney's aggressiveness were only too happy to sign on with Disney before conditions deteriorated. But Disney's contentious attitude exacerbated the difficulties it encountered by alienating people it needed to work with, say many people familiar with the situation. Its answer to doubts or suggestions invariably was: Do as we say, because we know best.

"They were always sure it would work because they were Disney," says Beatrice Descoffre, a French construction-industry official who dealt with the U.S. company.

If Euro Disney had been a financial success, few would have cared. In the project's early days, banks and private investors fell over one another to help finance the deal. S. G. Warburg & Co., a British investment bank that arranged Euro Disney's equity offering in the United Kingdom, put out a brochure describing the project as "relatively low-risk." As of December 31, Euro Disney, which opened in April 1992, had a cumulative loss of 6.04 billion francs, or $1.03 billion.

Tarnished Image

Now, just when it needs it most, Disney seems to have lost the goodwill it found when it first arrived in Europe—and along with it an unblemished reputation for success. "Tonya Harding just got her first endorsement," comedian Gary Shandling joked at this month's Grammy Awards, referring to the U.S. skater. "They go, 'Where are you going?' She says, 'I'm going to Euro Disney.'"

In practical terms, Disney's image problem could prove costly. To rescue its 49%-owned affiliate, Disney last October quietly proposed a $2 billion restructuring to the 60 creditor banks, and offered to pick up half the tab. People familiar with the proposal say Disney would have contributed three billion French francs ($520 million) in cash to a rights issue, and waived enough future management fees and royalties to bring its total contribution to $1 billion.

But the banks, feeling they were being steamrolled by Disney, rejected the offer. "They had a formidable image and convinced everyone that if we let them do it their way, we would all have a marvelous adventure," says a top French banker involved in the negotiations. "The Walt Disney group is making a major error in thinking it can impose its will once more."

People familiar with the debt negotiations say Disney and its banks have struck a much more conciliatory tone in just the past couple of weeks, raising hopes that a solution may be at hand.

If an agreement is reached, analysts say, Disney's cash-generating powers are such that it could absorb the blow of spending more than $1 billion in cash and deferred fees to save Euro Disney. More important will be to avoid more write-offs and losses in the future, so Disney can meet the ambitious growth targets it promises its shareholders, and preserve its future fee-earning power if Euro Disney turns around. The alternative for Disney—to walk away—likely would trigger a host of time-consuming lawsuits in France and cause an immeasurable loss of prestige.

Few believe Disney will allow the European resort to fall, even though it has threatened to cut off funding at the end of this month unless it can reach a deal with the banks. Too much rides on the future of Euro Disney for the U.S. company, the creditors, and the French government, which provided $750 million in loans at below-market rates, built road and rail networks to the park, and allowed Disney to buy up huge tracts of land at 1971 prices.

Already, Euro Disney has brought in new management and made other changes to save the project. Even detractors say they have been impressed by the way the company is changing tack, cutting prices, and reducing costs.

Corporate Hubris

The initial overconfidence of Disney, a company already known for corporate hubris, is perhaps understandable. The current management team of Chairman Michael Eisner and President Frank Wells arrived in late 1984 and immediately began tapping into the theme-park, film, and merchandising riches unmined by their predecessors. In the seven years before Euro Disney opened, they transformed Disney into a company with annual revenues of $8.5 billion—up from $1 billion—mainly through internal growth.

"From the time they came on, they had never made a single misstep, never a mistake, never a failure," says a former Disney executive. "There was a tendency to believe that everything they touched would be perfect."

Forged in the go-go culture of California and Florida, where growth seemed limitless, the new Disney team determined it wouldn't repeat two mistakes of years past: letting others build the lucrative hotels surrounding a park, as happened at Disneyland in Southern California, and letting another company own a Disney park, as in Tokyo, where Disney just collects royalties from the immensely profitable attraction.

But this determination exported poorly to Europe, particularly when combined with Mr. Eisner's vow to make Euro Disney the most lavish project Disney had ever built. Though tight with a buck in many ways, Mr. Eisner was almost obsessed with maintaining Disney's reputation for quality. And his designers—the "creative" people with whom he identified—convinced him that in Europe, home of great monuments and elaborate cathedrals, Euro Disney would have to brim with detail. Unlike the Japanese, Europeans wouldn't accept carbon copies of Disneyland and Florida's Walt Disney World, Disney reasoned.

Ballooning Costs

In argument after argument, executives say, Mr. Eisner sided with the designers and architects—who had direct access to the chairman's office—and piled on more detail. Even the centerpiece castle in the Magic Kingdom had to be bigger and fancier than in the other parks. So the cost of park construction, estimated at 14 billion francs ($2.37 billion) in 1989, rose by $340 million to 16 billion francs before the opening in April 1992. Construction of the hotels, estimated at 3.4 billion francs, rose to 5.7 billion.

One measure of Disney's overconfidence was a belief that it could predict future living patterns in Paris. Invited to the apartment of French negotiator Mr. Bernard in the western part of the city, where most of the French establishment has long lived, Mr. Eisner one evening boasted, "You live in the west of Paris, as do your friends, but your children and grandchildren will live in the east of Paris" near Euro Disney, Mr. Bernard says. Similarly, Disney executives believed, wrongly, that they could change certain European habits, such as a reluctance to yank their children from school in mid-session as Americans do, or their preference for longer holidays rather than short breaks.

With hindsight, some former executives, bankers, and other say Disney's biggest mistakes were its overambitious plans to develop the site, plus Euro Disney's financial structure itself, which depended on a highly optimistic financial scenario with little room for glitches. Both were creations of Gary Wilson, then the chief financial officer, a man known for his knack for creating financing packages that placed the risk for many Disney projects on outside investors while keeping much of the upside potential for the company. Mr. Wilson, now co-chairman of Northwest Airlines Corp. and still a Disney director, declined comment.

Mr. Wilson set up a finance company to own the park and lease it back to an operating company. This ownership vehicle, in which Disney kept just a 17% stake, was to provide tax losses and borrow huge sums at relatively low rates. Disney would manage the resort for hefty fees and royalties, while owning 49% of the equity in the operating company, Euro Disney SCA. The rest was sold to the public.

The park, moreover, was just the cornerstone of a huge and growing real-estate development by Disney in the area. The initial number of hotel rooms—at 5,200, more than in the entire city of Cannes, was expected to triple in a few years as Euro Disney opened a second theme park to keep visitors at the resort for a longer stay. There would also be office space, which would grow 20 times to a stunning 70,000 square meters, or just slightly smaller than France's biggest office complex, La Defense, in Paris. And the plan called for shopping malls, apartments, golf courses and vacation homes galore. Euro Disney would tightly control the design and build nearly everything itself, selling off the properties in due course at a big profit.

At first, all seemed to work beautifully. Disney's initial equity stake in Euro Disney was acquired for about $150 million, or 10 francs a share, compared with the initial price to investors of 72 francs a share. After the public offering, the value of the company's stake zoomed to $1 billion on the magic of the Disney name, and later to $2.3 billion when the stock peaked just before the park's opening. Today it is worth about $550 million. The company's shares closed at 36.15 francs yesterday on the Paris Stock Exchange.

Dozens of banks, led by France's Banque Nationale de Paris and Banque Indosuez, eagerly signed on to provide construction loans. Euro Disney's total debt stands at about 21 billion francs, or about $3.5 billion. Several European financial institutions, including Lazard Freres—Disney's own adviser—worried that the plan was too clever, according to people familiar with the financing.

"The company was overleveraged. The structure was dangerous," says one banker who saw the figures. The public offering price seemed high, and the proposed financing appeared risky because it relied on capital gains from future real estate transactions, critics charged.

But Disney's attitude, current and former executives say, was that those views reflected the cautious, Old-World thinking of Europeans who didn't understand U.S.-style free-market financing. Those who defend the deal point out that for more than two years after the offering, the stock price continued to swell, and that the initial loans were at a low rate. It was later cost overruns, they say, and the necessity for more borrowing, that handcuffed Euro Disney.

As the European recession started to bite, though, the French real-estate market tumbled, taking with it Disney's hopes that it could quickly sell many of the park's assets, especially the six big hotels. The company also passed up the chance to lessen its burden. "Disney at various points could have had partners to share the risk, or buy the hotels outright," says a Disney executive. "But it didn't want to give up the inside."

Good Attendance

Disney's early worries mainly concerned attendance. If Euro Disney could only meet its target of 11 million visitors in the first year, it reckoned, money would roll in. The target was met, but the reality turned out to be very different. And that helps explain why the park is doing reasonably well while Euro Disney is racking up huge losses.

The cost of building was simply too high. In his pursuit of perfection, Mr. Eisner himself ordered several last minute budget-breakers. For example, he removed two steel staircases in Discoveryland because they blocked a view of the Star Tours ride; that cost $200,000 to $300,00, a Disney official estimates. Disney built expensive trams along a lake to take guests from the hotels to the park. People preferred walking. Minibars were placed in economy hotel rooms; they lost money. Disney built an 18-hole golf course, then added nine holes, to adjoin 600 new homes. The homes haven't been built, and the golf courses, which cost $15 million to $20 million, are underused, says a former executive.

Disney and its advisers failed to see signs of the approaching European recession. "We were just trying to keep our heads above water," says one former executive. "Between the glamour and the pressure of opening and the intensity of the project itself, we didn't realize a major recession was coming."

European creditor banks feel they have been victimized by poor communications, too, and resent not being properly appraised of the resort's difficulties, some say. Until last July, Disney continued to say that plans for the development of a second theme park were on track. In November, Euro Disney reported a $905 million loss and Disney itself took a $350 million write-off, covering its initial investment and providing operating capital through March 31. Shortly afterward, Mr. Eisner gave an interview to a French news magazine in which he raised the possibility that Euro Disney could close. Disney advisers, however, say the banks were given regular, detailed financial statements and were just too slow to spot the problems.

Operational errors just made things worse. The policy of serving no alcohol in the park, since reversed, caused astonishment in a country where a glass of wine for lunch is a given. Disney thought Monday would be a light day for visitors, Friday a heavy one, and allocated staff accordingly; the reality was the reverse. The company still is struggling to find the right level of staffing at a park where the number of visitors per day in the high season can be 10 times the number in the low season. Disney, accustomed in Florida to telling an employee, "We don't need you today," has chafed under France's inflexible labor schedules.

The hotel breakfast debacle was another unpleasant surprise. "We were told that Europeans don't take breakfast, so we downsized the restaurants," recalls one executive. "And guess what?

Everybody showed up for breakfast. We were trying to serve 2,500 breakfasts in a 350-seat restaurant at [some of the hotels]. The lines were horrendous. And they didn't just want croissants and coffee. They wanted bacon and eggs." Disney reacted quickly, however, with prepackaged breakfasts delivered to rooms and satellite locations.

Another demand, from bus drivers, wasn't anticipated. "The parking space was much too small," says a former executive. "We built restrooms for 50 drivers, and on peak days there were 2,000."

From independent drivers to grumbling bankers, Disney stepped on toe after European toe. Former Disney executives shake their heads when they think about it, because much of Disney's attitude sprang, they say, from a relentless pursuit of quality, the same drive for perfection that has made the company so successful.

"We were arrogant," concedes one executive. "It was like, 'We're building the Taj Mahal and people will come—on our terms.'"

High Prices

So Disney priced the park and the hotels more to meet revenue targets than to meet demand. Park admission was set at $42.45 for adults, higher than at its U.S. theme parks. A room at the flagship Disneyland Hotel at the park's entrance cost about 2,000 francs, or about $340 a night, the same as a top hotel in Paris. The hotels have been just over half full on average, and guests haven't been staying as long or spending as much as expected on the fairly high-priced food and merchandise.

While visitors to Florida's Disney World tend to stay more than four days, Euro Disney—with one theme park, compared with Florida's three—is a two-day experience at most. Many guests arrive early in the morning, rush to the park, come back late at night, then check out the next morning before heading back to the park. There was so much checking-in and checking-out that additional computer stations had to be installed.

Disney executives have frantically lowered most prices in response, but high fixed costs and looming interest payments still are too great a burden without the addition of more development and a second theme park. Euro Disney is, in the words of one senior French banker familiar with the company, "a good theme park married to a bankrupt real-estate company—and the two can't be divorced."

If it didn't foresee all the potential financial pitfalls, Disney clearly realized at the outset that it might encounter cultural problems. It sought to head them off by choosing Robert Fitzpatrick as Euro Disney's president. He is an American who speaks French, knows Europe well and has a French wife. But he seemed caught in the middle, and quickly came to be regarded with suspicion by some on both sides.

Mr. Fitzpatrick, who was replaced last year by a French native but still does consulting for Disney, declines comment. Officials sympathetic to him say his warnings to Disney management that France shouldn't be approached as if it were Florida were ignored.

While Mr. Fitzpatrick was well acclimated, some of the American managers sent over to start up Euro Disney had their own culture shock. One French manager says he remembers being astonished when an American colleague complained about the cost of Evian bottled water, which is cheaper in France than in the U.S. It turns out the American was going through dozens of bottles per week because he was nervous about using French tap water for anything, including washing. One executive even had his own dog flown over, another manager says.

European executives felt they were in the shadow of Disney corporate types and almost always lost out when the interests of Euro Disney and Disney itself weren't the same. Disney, for example, refused in the early stages of development to renegotiate the management and royalty fees that it would be paid by Euro Disney; that might have lessened the financial burden on Euro Disney, these executives say.

Unfamiliar with the French market, Disney made mistakes in selecting contractors, French construction-industry officials say. Two general contractors filed for bankruptcy during construction, forcing Disney to pay twice for the work done by subcontractors, once to the failed general contractors and again to the 60 or so smaller firms that carried out the work. Euro Disney won't say how much the double payment cost, but French industry sources peg the amount at about 200 million francs, a number Disney has said is too high.

Bad press has dogged Euro Disney since the opening. Mr. Eisner and his management team dismissed early criticism by scornful French intellectuals as the ravings of an insignificant elite. But the mainstream press, too, described every Disney setback with glee. "There was a perceived arrogance on our part," concedes one former executive. The effect, he adds, was to demoralize the work force and cut down on initial French visitors. "Working for Euro Disney has a very pejorative connotation," says Patrick Roget, a union official at the park. "When I tell people that I work there, they say 'you poor thing.'"

Disney Goes to Hong Kong

An uncertain journey

In the United States, Mickey Mouse is rather soft and round, cuter and better behaved than in Tokyo where he is rather muscular, smart, and bratty. In Paris, he is cooler, thinner, and seemingly more urbane. Even in America, Mickey has changed over the years from a cruel and cocky mouse to a sweet, innocent, and more childlike mouse (Finch, 1979). How will he appear in China after Disney takes its next announced step and builds its fifth Disneyland at Penny's Bay on Lantau Island in Hong Kong?

Slated to open in 2005, Hong Kong Disneyland provides an opportunity to see what the Disney organization has learned about the design, export, and management of what they take to be their premier global product—the theme park. If the past provides lessons for the future, Disney has now more than 20 years of experience in the international theme park trade on which to draw that include both success and failure (big and small). What has it learned that will play well for the more than 6 million residents of Hong Kong, and what has it learned that will help move its organization assuredly and smoothly into this cosmopolitan gateway to (and from) mainland China?

While the project is far from completion as of this writing (2003), a good deal of background information is available that may shed light on further developments. The "deal" was first announced in 1999. It is, at least on the surface, another good one for Disney. The building of Hong Kong Disneyland is estimated to cost somewhere close to $4 billion, of which Disney is initially putting up only $300–400 million of their own funds. The remainder of the project is backed by the Hong Kong government who will be the majority stockholder (57%). Roughly $2 billion goes for land reclamation, road building, ferry connections, water treatment plants, artificial reefs, and other infrastructure necessary for the construction and operation of the new park. Disney, however, will control the design, manage the park and share—with 43 percent ownership—in the revenue stream generated by the enterprise. Put simply, the Disney organization has near total control of the show and property (about 300 acres).

As with Disney's entrance into France, two potential sites were in the running. Hong Kong, a sprawling city of towering apartment buildings, countless shopping malls and something of a modern citadel of commerce, won out over Shanghai in what was a lengthy series of tough negotiations. The city not only offered Disney more favorable terms than Shanghai but also appears from a business perspective to have the better mixture of per capita income, western-styled commercial infrastructure and culture, and an established tourist trade. In the recent past—before the 1998 Asian economic crisis and the SARs epidemic of 2003—some 10 million tourists visited Hong Kong yearly.

It is of course unclear as to whether Shanghai, itself a huge city seemingly eager to build its long dormant tourist trade, represented a viable and serious alternative for Disney. However, as pointed out in the reading that follows this Class Note, the company was asked by Hong Kong officials (as part of the agreement to bring the park to the region) to promise not to build on the coast of mainland China. Disney refused. It was not, however, a deal breaker for Hong Kong refused in kind to promise Disney theme park exclusivity in the territory.

The park under construction will be smaller than those in either Tokyo or Paris. The workforce required when Hong Kong Disneyland is up and running is estimated to be about 5,000 employees, and the company says it needs to attract only 5 or 6 million customers a year to break even—anticipated to grow to about 10 million by 2020. These figures represent about half the workforce and draw expected in the early stages of other Disneylands. One-third of the guests are likely to come from Hong Kong, one-third from China, and one-third from other Asian countries. In terms of park design, the buyers in Hong Kong ordered up the "original Disneyland" and were uninterested it seems in any unique Chinese touches beyond some of the cuisine served in the park and respect for local traditions. Ostensibly, these alterations will be no test for the Imagineers of Disneyland since the creative risks the company is undertaking appear to be slight.

Part of these prenuptial agreements on design and content may be because Disney products—including Disneyland—are rather well known in the area. Disney TV shows and cartoon characters have long been popular in Hong Kong and Disney has been beaming several much watched prime-time children's show throughout China since the late 1980s. Of course pirated versions of Disney movies and videotapes are everywhere in Asia thus providing another sort of "synergy" for marketing Disneyland (a synergy that may or may not be welcomed by Disney executives).

Wasko (2001) conducted a global survey of college students from 53 separate countries on the brand awareness of Disney products. It shows the Chinese no less than the Europeans or Japanese to be quite familiar with Disney characters, narratives, movies, and merchandise. Moreover, the broad meanings read into these cultural artifacts also appear quite similar across countries. Indeed the strongest findings in Wasko's survey were the near universal recognition of Disney products and the commonly shared understandings of what Disney means across the globe. For example, 93 percent of the respondents said Disney promoted "Fantasy and Fun"; 88 percent agreed on "Happiness," "Magic," and "Good over Evil"; and 80 percent thought Disney stood for "Family," "Imagination," and "Love/Romance." In short, Disney carries a set of core meanings and values that appear to be understood in the same way almost everywhere, and they are the same ubiquitous values that the organization itself emphasizes in its sales and marketing work.

This phenomenon seems to be something of a soft and cuddly form of globalization. Contact with Disney occurs for most in early childhood but is persistent, intense, and now intergenerational. Disney is accepted in part because its products and values appear friendly, innocent, and compatible with local culture such that watching a Disney videotape or carrying a Mickey Mouse pencil box does not feel like something that is being imposed from the outside but rather as something that people choose individually to fit comfortably into their patterns of everyday life. Seeing Disney products (including theme parks) as "natural" and somehow imbued with common and benign values does not however eliminate either ambiguity or criticism. Being seen as supportive of, say, "family values" does not specify what values in particular are to be furthered in a local context nor does the somewhat sacred status of Disney products and perceived content make criticism of its market saturation and business practices impossible.

It is in the domain of particulars that Disney's planned move to Hong Kong becomes most interesting. In this regard, the shift in family values that has more or less transformed East Asia over the past 20–30 years is relevant. In Hong Kong, a long economic boom began in the 1970s as the then-British territory moved from a low-wage, light industrial colonial outpost to a regional center for financial services and high-technology industries. A professionalized, white-collar middle class began to rapidly replace the postwar working class of Hong Kong. By the mid-1970s, the majority of residents were living in small, hard-working, nuclear families preoccupied with their own lives and children rather than a wider network of kin.

This shift produced what Watson (1997) calls a generation of "Little Emperors and Empresses"—children who grow up in small (striving) middle-class families rather isolated from their extended ties and hence garner a good deal of the attention, affection, and support of two parents (and sometimes four grandparents as well). Children in Hong Kong are not only much loved and fussed about as a rule but are regarded as independent decision makers and control substantial economic resources. A local study Watson cites from the *South China Morning Post* (December 2, 1995) notes that Hong Kong parents gave junior high school-aged children an average of more than $100 (US) a month to spend on snacks and entertainment. Surely such indulgence bodes well for Hong Kong Disneyland. Hong Kong is a relatively wealthy society, its families are small, and children clearly have spending power.

Next door to Hong Kong are 1.3 billion people in mainland China. Most of course cannot hope to visit Hong Kong Disneyland but residents just across the border in the Shenzhen Special Economic Zone are surely on the Disney map of potential paying guests. Shenzhen was one of the first regions in the People's Republic to benefit from Deng Xiaoping's economic reforms that began in the early 1980s, and the area has become something of a boom town where all the material products of the good life including luxury apartments, the latest fashions from New York and Paris, fine hotels and flashy discothèques are available to a few. China's single-child policy no doubt amplifies the "Little Emperors and Empresses" phenomenon in the area and recent policy changes at the national level now allow residents of the four largest cities in China—Beijing, Shanghai, Guangzhou, and Shenzhen—to travel to Hong Kong on their own as tourists instead of having to come only on officially approved business trips or with centrally approved and organized tours (*New York Times*, August 15, 2003). This policy change too should be good for Disney's theme park business.

Not all is rosy however. The Asian financial crisis of 1998 and beyond certainly slowed growth and the spread of prosperity in the region and its impact is keenly felt in Hong Kong. Residential mortgage failures are now at an all-time high and the middle classes have generally born the brunt of the economic slowdown. Moreover, Hong Kong's troubled ties with the mainland continue. The quasi-autonomy granted by the People's Republic to Hong Kong six years ago when the territory was returned to China– the "one country, two system" policy—remains controversial, its meaning and consequence still in the process of being worked out. Risking the ire of Beijing officials, pro-democracy street demonstrations, consisting mostly of college-educated, professionals, rocked Hong Kong in the summer of 2003 (*International Herald Tribune*, July 1, 2003). Political stability seems far from assured. Cross-strait relations are strained at the moment and this state of affairs is likely to continue for quite some time.

The Disney organization itself has occasionally run into trouble in China. Its 1999 film, *Mulan*, expected to be an artistic success, box office smash, and something of a cultural breakthrough in China, fell flat. When screened in China, the animated film, a westernized version of a much beloved Chinese folktale in which the key characters looked American and lived happily ever after, annoyed political leaders, the public, and critics alike. The movie did poorly among Chinese audiences in the United States as well. Trying to explain Disney's miscalculation of just how accepting the people and the country would be for the film, one culturally astute observer noted:

Every child in China grows up with the legend of Fa Mulan. But they couldn't identify with the movie and they couldn't recognize the characters because they were drawn for an international audience. Mulan looked more like Pocahontas than the average Chinese face. (International Herald Tribune, *June 16, 1999)*

Perhaps more serious and troubling are the difficulties Disney ran into in 1997 when releasing the Martin Scorsese film *Kundun* about the Dalai Lama, the exiled Buddhist monk who won the Nobel Peace Prize for his nonviolent efforts to liberate Tibet from Chinese occupational rule. Political leaders in Beijing objected to the film's content and distribution not in China (where, of course, it was not shown) but in the United States. Disney, to its credit, did not knuckle under and pull the film. Although the movie flopped at the box office and was rather quickly withdrawn from the market, Disney worried enough about offending the political sensitivities of the Chinese government (and being "blacklisted") that it hired the former U.S. Secretary of State, Henry Kissinger, to reestablish cordial relations for the firm in Beijing after the film ran its course. Shuttle diplomacy it seems is useful for more than peace-keeping missions among nations. Such diplomacy may well become a necessary part of Disney's operation in Hong Kong.

In terms of the local response to the building of Hong Kong Disneyland, most of the population appears pleased at present. Young people may well take to Disneyland as they took to McDonald's in the late 1970s and flock to the park precisely because it is foreign and distinctively not Chinese (Watson, 1997). To adults, Disneyland carries considerable symbolic value as a high-quality, safe, clean, modern, family-oriented, and desirable place to visit.

As true elsewhere, many in Hong Kong see the park as a high-profile and high-powered magnet that will draw visitors back to the region in numbers far greater than prior to 1998. It adds to the list of leisure options and potential pleasures available to residents of Hong Kong, one of the most tightly packed and stressful cities in the world in which to live. For some, the park is seen as a way to help preserve the novel and unique status of the former territory now in danger of losing its long-standing international flavor. Disneyland, many feel, will lift the appeal of Hong Kong as a tourist destination, particularly among families, teenagers, and honeymooners.

Not all in Hong Kong are quite so enamored with the park. Some local politicians have taken Disney (and the government) to task for not fully sharing information about the negotiated agreement and explaining the costs of the project to the public. Some cultural elites as well as some business leaders have expressed concern over the foreign influence Disney represents—a blatant example of cultural imperialism in their view—and argue that embracing yet another Disneyland sends the wrong message to the world. Hong Kong has its own vibrancy and heritage, they say, and bringing Disneyland to town is but a "pointless parody of American kitsch" (*International Herald Tribune*, June 16, 1999). Intellectuals, as always, have joined the fray suggesting that Hong Kong might be better served by offering tourists a taste of Tang Dynasty poetry, Sichuan cooking, and silk fashions than thrill rides, cartoon characters, and mouse ears. None of these Disneyland critics are likely to be disarmed either when reading that Michael Eisner's ebullient confidence in the project is based at least partly on his conviction that "the Chinese people love Mickey no less than Big Mac" (*Los Angeles Times*, June 6, 2002).

Popular culture thrives in Hong Kong as well and Disneyland may well fit nicely into this milieu. Like Tokyo, Hong Kong is itself a major center for the production of transnational culture. The Hong Kong fashion industry influences clothing in Los Angeles, Bangkok, and Paris. The "Cantotop" music that originates in Hong Kong is heard and enjoyed throughout Asia. Hong Kong is also the third-largest producer in the world of movies and the birthplace of the Kung Fu film genre. Most significantly perhaps is that Hong Kong is now emerging as a center for television production in Asia—surely a world that those in the Disney organization will know. They must learn to respect and appreciate it too because no institutional arrangement in Hong Kong will protect Disneyland from facing local competition from other entertainment options and venues. Given the small size of the region, holding an audience captive at Hong Kong Disneyland—unlike Walt Disney World—will be difficult if not impossible.

In terms of Disneyland's work-a-day operations, a few matters cause concern. However labor is probably not one of them. Not only is a talented and attractive young workforce available within the region, planners see few reasons to suspect that part-time labor will be frowned on. Moreover, a huge, well-educated, and hungry workforce is close at hand and the regime in Hong Kong that has bet on Disneyland's economic success might, if necessary, do away with some of the messy obstructions that organizations in more democratic societies must deal with as a matter of course—striking trade unions, active consumer movements, irksome property rights advocates, and so on. To date, however, labor problems are entirely speculative. Environmental and social problems are not and Disney is now facing a few of them in Hong Kong.

Construction of Disneyland Hong Kong has called for a good deal of landfill, earth moving, underwater dynamiting and dredging. Waters around the construction site are polluted. White dolphins are dying and fish stocks are dwindling (some say disappearing). It appears that, like the farmers in France who suffered when Disneyland Paris arrived, the livelihood of local fishermen is threatened. In 2001, a Disney spokeswoman said of the situation:

> *To date, there is no evidence that links the current issues the fishermen are raising to the reclamation at Penny's Bay. The government continues to monitor this. They've put measures in place on site to address this issue. They've assured us they are taking it seriously. (Reuters News Service, November 21, 2001)*

The response is familiar and strikingly reminiscent of Disney's corporate stance on social problems elsewhere—notably Orlando. The company's public position, which is ridiculed in environmental circles and in some Hong Kong newspapers as obdurate and obstructionist, is that such matters are external to the company and hence of little managerial concern ("Let the government take care of it.") Such a policy is no doubt cost-effective but may well have negative consequences in the long run, especially in the Hong Kong context where antagonism between the public and private sectors is less pronounced (or expected) than in the United States (or, for that matter, in France). Big Asian companies are expected by most to promote the general welfare of the communities in which they operate. Hong Kong now represents an odd mixture of socialism and capitalism, and Disney may have much to learn.

Some more modest lessons may be in store for Disney in terms of its service providing routines as well. As in France, the "grin-and-wave" approach to people processing within the park may strike some potential employees and customers as a bit over the top. Watson (1997) points out that consumers in Hong Kong are often suspicious of clerks or other service personnel who laugh and smile on the job. Hong Kong residents it seems place a high value on expressions of "seriousness" and workers are expected to assume a demeanor that conveys determination and unflappability that shows they are paying full attention to what they are doing. The result is apparently more frowning than smiling among service providers. Hence the congeniality and familiarity cast members are more or less famous for in other Disney parks may not be as well received in Hong Kong as will the projection of other qualities admired in the local culture—directness and competence.

All in all, however, the prospects for Hong Kong Disneyland appear fairly bright. Visiting the park from Hong Kong or mainland China will hardly be viewed as an act of cultural treason. A large and apt workforce is available and potential customers seem thrilled at the prospects of having their own Disneyland. Missteps and cultural misunderstandings will occur of course and one hopes learning on the part of the company, the government, the financial backers, and the consumers will be swift (and open-ended). The downside risks for Disney—less so for the region—appear to be well in hand. More problematic perhaps are the long-term consequences for both Disney and Hong Kong. If the formula of moving from the exotic to the ordinary works out, what will Disney have brought to the region? Will "chewing gum jobs" proliferate and create a drain on available social services as in Orlando? Will traffic congestion and pollution further strain an already-pressed metropolis as in Tokyo? Will cultural standards fall as Mickey Mouse ascends as many in Paris would argue? Will Hong Kong's valued contribution to an independent Asian entertainment industry be reduced as Disney with its seemingly unlimited financial resources enters into the scene? Will Hong Kong Disneyland prove to be a good corporate citizen or merely a greedy, rapacious ugly American? These and many more questions are all in play at present. Stay tuned for the continuing story.

A World with Mouse Ears?

At the limit, a global community is an impossible condition. It would prevail only if people the world over were to share a mutually intelligible and homogeneous culture. Even though the world is certainly shrinking as communication and transportation technologies proliferate and trade barriers are reduced, we are nowhere close to either mutual intelligibility or homogeneity. What we have seen of Disney and its travels around the world to date suggests as much.

What has occurred in the various parks and no doubt will occur in Hong Kong is more a process of localization than globalization. Some elements of the Disney way are accepted, some rejected, some changed, and some ignored. Moreover, it has been a slow and gradual, and, despite Disney's hopeful intentions and efforts, a thoroughly two-way process. Although the initial stages of cultural learning have for all parties been highly significant, they have not been fully determinative of the long-term success or failure of Disney's cross-border ventures. As we have seen, culture—as a set of ideas, reactions, assumptions, and expectations—is itself constantly changing as people and groups change.

Predictability in this domain is problematic at best. How Disneyland is used and what it means in Hong Kong will be different than how it is used and understood elsewhere. These differences are likely to grow rather than shrink with the passage of time as each park takes on its own special character as result of the constant interactions among managers, designers, employees, customers, environmentalists, politicians, policy makers, social critics, and the like. Although the ties of culture to place have been loosened in the late twentieth and early twenty-first centuries, they have not gone away and local identities are still highly valued. Businesses that forget about such matters are likely to pay a stiff price.

Culture is of course not a fixed condition and thus cultural learning is at best a most uncertain process, a continual flow of shifting ideas and things. Cultural products like Disneyland and the meanings we attach to them are at any moment the result of unremitting change coming from the interplay of the past and present, the familiar and strange, the local and distant. If this interplay intensifies, as the materials on Disney suggest, the consequences of moving cultural products and services developed in one land to another are probably less predictable than ever (and they have never been particularly predictable anyway). Someday, for example, we know that whatever magic draws crowds to the Disney parks will fade. Revenues will cease to cover costs and even the original, authentic, one-and-only Disneyland will close its gates (or, more likely, be declared a National Shrine and turned into a museum). We will not mourn its passage when this passing occurs for the happiness trade will have moved elsewhere. But, alas, exactly where this happiness business will go is as impossible to imagine right now as is a Disney-less world.

References

Finch, Charles. 1979. *Walt Disney's America*. New York: Academic.

Janet Wasko, Mark Phillips, and Eileen R. Meehan (Eds.). 2001. *Dazzled by Disney? The Global Disney Audiences Project*. New York: Leicester University Press.

Watson, James L. 1997. *Golden Arches East: McDonald's in East Asia*. Palo Alto, CA: Stanford University Press.

The Ever-Expanding, Profit-Maximizing, Cultural-Imperialist, Wonderful World of Disney

The serious business of selling all-American fun

by Jonathan Weber

It's a sunny afternoon at the Window on the World theme park in the southern Chinese city of Shenzhen, and Chen Ping and Wei Qing Hua are strolling the grounds. A cheerful young couple from China's Hubei province, Chen and Wei migrated to this city, a remarkable symbol of the new capitalist China, to make money—he's a taxi driver and she works in a factory. They've come to the park this Tuesday to, well, see the sights.

"It's nothing special," concludes Chen as he surveys cheesy small-scale replicas of the Roman Colosseum and the Arc de Triomphe that anchor the "Europe" section of the park. The sprawling grounds feature dioramas of tourist attractions from five continents—including the Sphinx, Mount Rushmore, and a life-size African village—but there aren't many people around. Bored vendors hawk cheap trinkets, without much success.

Just a half-hour train ride away, a rather more ambitious theme park is under construction. Slated to open in 2005, Hong Kong Disneyland will offer the sizzle, polish, and attention to detail that's woefully lacking in Shenzhen. Chen and Wei, already well acquainted with Mickey and Donald, say they'll certainly visit, visas permitting. "It would be very brilliant," says Chen. "If it comes from outside China, it's going to be better than what comes from inside. You just know it."

There could hardly be a better summation of the opportunity that American pop culture companies like Disney are enjoying overseas. With the end of the Cold War, the opening of China, and the worldwide triumph of American-style capitalism, the brand-name purveyors of American food, fashion, and entertainment have never had it so good. Hardly a city on the planet is without McDonald's and CNN and Levi's and MTV. American films are omnipresent and in some markets dominant, accounting for nearly three-quarters of movie admissions in Western Europe. *Who Wants to Be a Millionaire* is a hit in several Asian countries.

For many countries, especially in the developing world, the ever-growing presence of the U.S. culture industry is a mixed blessing. On the one hand, the pervasiveness of Americana can be seen as a sign of progress. U.S. brands are symbols of wealth and modernity and freedom. Drinking coffee at Starbucks or taking the family to Disneyland signals the rise of a worldly middle class. On a more concrete level, Western companies often bring a measure of quality and service that are both a boon for local consumers and a prod for domestic firms to raise their standards. At the same time, the enormous popularity of U.S. brands overseas can pose a threat not only to a nation's domestic industries but to its cultural traditions and sense of identity. For decades now, intellectuals in Europe have lamented the Americanization of their societies. Euro Disney, now known as Disneyland Paris, was once famously denounced by the French theater director Ariane Mnouchkine as a "cultural Chernobyl." In the developing world, cultural imperialism has long been seen as the handmaiden of political domination, another way for strong countries to take advantage of the weak.

Even champions of globalization increasingly fret that it may damage or destroy the diversity that makes the human race so fascinating, leaving nothing but homogenized, least-common-denominator forms of creativity. In the wake of September 11, there is a new urgency to these concerns. The fury of the terrorists—and of the alarming number of people around the world who viewed the attacks as a deserved comeuppance for an arrogant, out-of-control superpower—is sparked in part by a sense that America is imposing its lifestyle on countries that don't want it. And one needn't condone mass murder to believe that

---

Source: "The Ever-Expanding, Profit-Maximizing, Cultural-Imperialist, Wonderful World of Disney" by Jonathan Weber. Copyright © 2002 Conde Nast Publications. All rights reserved. Originally published in *Wired*, February 2002. Reprinted by permission. **Jonathan Weber** (jonathanweber@earthlink.net), the founding editor of *The Industry Standard*, is a visiting professor of journalism at the University of Montana. Joanne Lee-Young contributed to this story.

a new world order that leaves every place on the globe looking like a California strip mall will make us all poorer. No company conveys more powerfully the image of a conquering cultural army than Walt Disney. Its founder was a true-blue patriot who saw himself as a proselytizer for the values of the American heartland. The company's products and services—unlike, say, fast-food hamburgers or sugary soft drinks—are not merely symbolic of the American way of life, but contain as part of their essence a set of beliefs about good and evil and human aspiration. Disney, moreover, has throughout its history been extremely shrewd about building mutually reinforcing products across many different kinds of media, with theme parks and TV shows, movies and merchandise, all working together in service of the Disney way.

The company's drive for the China market shows how this machine can work overseas. Seen from the outside, the strategy seems quite savvy. It began with elemental Disney—its cartoons—which first aired on Chinese television in the mid-1980s, just as the country was opening up. Chinese entrepreneurs kicked in a flood of pirated videos and counterfeit merchandise, which did nothing for Disney's bottom line but had the effect of spreading its characters at viral speed.

In 1997, Disney's Miramax label released *Kundun*, a Martin Scorsese film about Tibet that angered the Chinese leadership. But behind the scenes the company was also working on *Mulan*, an animated blockbuster that brought a traditional Chinese fable to a global audience with classic Disney production values. In the wake of *Mulan's* warm reception, Disney cut a deal with Hong Kong to build a theme park, and attendance there will no doubt get a boost from a major new television agreement, announced in December, under which Mickey Mouse cartoons will appear daily, in kids' prime time, on China's biggest television channel.

Disney executives, including CEO Michael Eisner and COO Bob Iger, make regular trips to China, meeting with top leadership to pave the way for more deals. One possibility: a theme park in Shanghai. Meanwhile, China has become the world's largest producer of licensed Disney merchandise, which helps company executives when they push the government to crack down on the unlicensed variety. Despite all this, the image of Disney—and of America in general—as an unstoppable cultural juggernaut is misleading. The truth is that selling American culture overseas is a tricky business. Disney and other big global brands are driven not by grand plans to promote American values, but rather by incremental, pragmatic, financially oriented, market research-based business decisions—and even then, the companies struggle mightily to make their initiatives work. Success depends on some rather mundane factors: Have you selected good local partners? Do your executives understand local traditions and speak the language? Have you developed an organization that allows for strategic coordination across far-flung locations? Have you earned the goodwill of citizens groups and government officials?

In most countries, media-related industries in particular are still dominated by domestic firms, and there is little reason to think that will change in the near future. Disney gets less than 20 percent of its revenue from overseas, a share that's been stagnant even though management has long cited the international market as a major growth area. The company's experience abroad suggests that even in this age of interconnection, where the combination of technology and American hegemony makes a shallow global monoculture a possibility, that dull new world won't be arriving anytime soon.

The Burbank, California, headquarters of the Walt Disney Company sits on the impeccably manicured Disney Studios lot, surrounded by paths with names like Mickey Avenue and Dopey Drive and featuring a roof held aloft by 19-foot-high statues of the Seven Dwarfs. But as self-consciously cheery as it is on the outside, there's nothing lighthearted about what's happening inside. In the sprawling executive suites, the ambience is high corporate rather than California casual, reflecting the relentlessly competitive, hierarchical style of the CEO Eisner.

It is Eisner who can claim credit for transforming Disney from a drifting, dated icon of American middle-class entertainment into a global media superpower, one that trails only AOL Time Warner in scope and scale. The ghost of Walt, the creative genius who invented most of the famous characters as well as the concept of Disneyland, still inhabits many corners of the company. But as befits a huge, publicly traded corporation, the true guiding spirit today is the bottom line. When Eisner took over in 1984, Disney had $1.7 billion in revenue, hardly any profits, and a miserable reputation both in Hollywood and on Wall Street. Today, thanks to aggressive exploitation of the signature characters, continued success in developing new animated hits, the revival of the movie studio, and the 1996 acquisition of Capital Cities/ABC Inc., Disney boasts revenue of more than $25 billion and employs 120,000 people worldwide. With its global outlook and willingness to experiment in multiple media, Disney is a member of the *Wired* Index, the 40 businesses charting the future of the economy. The company certainly has its share of problems: Growth has slowed, the stock has sunk, and the advertising downturn and post-terrorism tourism slump have made bad conditions even worse. Still, no one questions its staying power as a dominant media brand.

Disney, in fact, can be a remarkable machine, and over the last decade it has been one of the few businesses of any kind that gives real meaning to the term *synergy*. Take a hit animated film like *The Lion King*. Released in 1994, it has grossed more than $765 million at the box office worldwide—and that's only the beginning. There was a bestselling record album, live stage shows (currently in four cities), cartoons on the Disney Channel, a Toontown attraction at Disneyland, a vast array of merchandise, and extraordinarily lucrative home video and DVD sales. In all, *The Lion King* franchise has contributed more than $1 billion to Disney's bottom line, says Sutro &Co. analyst Dave Miller.

What's more, much of the Disney empire is easy to export. The characters have long been popular overseas; Mickey Mouse is among the most recognized icons in the world. The animated feature films travel particularly well, since they can be seamlessly translated into other languages, and they are often big hits abroad. (*Tarzan*, for example, has cleared $449 million at the overseas box office since its release in 1999.) Disneyland Tokyo, opened in 1982, has been an unalloyed success, and the new Tokyo Disney Seas park, which debuted in September, appears poised to repeat that performance. Disneyland Paris had a terrible couple of years after opening in 1992, but it's now doing well enough that a Disney Studios park is about to move in next door. More than half of the sales of Disney merchandise come from outside the U.S. And because Disney stands for family entertainment and steers clear of political issues, it's even been mostly immune to a rising anti-American corporate backlash.

Yet with all of that, until a couple of years ago, the company had no real international strategy. "We had a couple hundred legal entities overseas that needed to be consolidated—we were not world class in that," says Michael Johnson, a cheery veteran of the home entertainment division who now heads up the entity called Walt Disney International. "We were spending a huge amount of money. We didn't have a grip on some of our characters and how they were performing. It was a legacy of these huge silos."

The silos Johnson is referring to are Disney's five lines of business: Media Networks, Parks and Resorts, Consumer Products, Studio Entertainment, and Internet. In principle, each business unit should constantly reinforce one another. In practice, each often goes its own way—especially overseas. To fix this problem, the company in 1999 created a system of country managers explicitly charged with coordinating brand strategy. That made a lot of sense. But so far it hasn't made a difference to the bottom line: International revenue inched from $4.2 billion in 1999 to $4.3 billion in 2001 even as domestic sales jumped by $1.7 billion.

• • •

With its massive population and emerging economies, Asia is the promised land for American culture merchants. And Japan, by far the richest country in Asia, is the logical first stop. Disneyland Tokyo has helped the company's animated movies and toys become staples for Japanese children. The new Disney Seas is one of the company's most innovative projects; aimed at adults as much as kids, it features beautifully crafted, self-contained environments such as the American Waterfront and the Mediterranean Harbor. A visit in November found both Tokyo parks mobbed, not just with families but with teens on dates, middle-aged couples, and even the occasional group of retirees. "We grew up with the Disney characters, so we feel comfortable with them," said repeat visitor Hideko Seki, a 36-year-old magazine designer from Kawasaki, Japan. The two Tokyo parks expect to draw some 25 million visitors in the first full year of Disney Seas operations.

That's the good news for Disney. The bad news is that it does not actually own these parks. In order to reduce the financial risk, Disney licensed construction and ownership of both Japanese parks to the Oriental Land Company. As a result, it earns only royalties and management fees. That's pure profit—Sutro analyst Miller estimates it at $200 million a year—but not the kind of windfall that would come with full or even partial ownership.

Japan is famous for its willingness to adopt Western culture even as it remains highly insular. One of Disney Internet's rare successes has been in the Japanese wireless market, where for reasons few understand, people are willing to pay to download cartoon characters onto their cell phones. But even here, Disney faces challenges. For one thing, Japan has its own strong tradition of animation. (Disney has even licensed the works of one top Japanese animator, *Princess Mononoke* creator Hayao Miyazaki, for international distribution.) It is also adept at creating its own pop culture characters: Think Pokémon and Power Rangers and Hello Kitty. Finally, there's the slumping Japanese economy. So while Japan remains Disney's biggest market outside the U.S., it's still a niche player with limited growth prospects beyond the new theme park.

Which explains why Disney's been looking farther west, to China. There could hardly be a more enticing market: a billion people, rapidly getting richer, who turn to foreign brands both for symbolic value and superior quality, and who are devoted to their families. Disney products, moreover, are seen by the Chinese authorities as politically innocuous—unlike, say, how they view AOL Time Warner's CNN. Chairman Mao once referred to Western movies and art as "sugar-coated bullets" and sought to eradicate them during the Cultural Revolution. But the pragmatists who run the Chinese Communist Party today have no such qualms about Disney. "We're a family entertainment company, and that is pretty well understood by the government officials," says Jun Tang, Disney's vice president for China affairs. The characters, especially Mickey and Donald, are part of the fabric of Chinese culture. A hip teen wandering the Window on the World park in Shenzhen says Disney is no longer cool—and yet there's a battered Mickey Mouse doll hanging from her backpack.

For Disney, as for most Western companies, the China strategy begins in Hong Kong. In this citadel of commerce, the countless shopping malls could be straight out of an American suburb, and people snap up Western goods without a second thought. Tai-Lok Lui, a professor of sociology at the Chinese University of Hong Kong, attributes this to the fact that Hong Kong is a society of migrants who chose to leave their culture behind in order to pursue a new beginning. America, he says, has always represented "high-tech, consumption, a comfortable way of life." Whether it was the moon landing or *Star Trek* or U.S. soldiers coming ashore on leave, the image of America is of a distant but powerful and glamorous place. "We would watch *Bewitched*, and we'd be bewitched by the modern American kitchen," says Lui.

Disney began eyeing Hong Kong as a possible theme park location in the mid-'90s, just after it opened the Paris park. Asia was the obvious next market, and Hong Kong had the right mix of high per-capita income, solid infrastructure, and knowledge of the tourism business. And it had the hunger. The Hong Kong economy fell into the doldrums following the departure of the British in 1997 and the Asian financial crisis in 1998; local leaders were terrified that it would be overwhelmed by a resurgent mainland China. Unemployment was rising, and tourism was hurting. Disney looked like a good fix for both of those things.

Just as it did in France, Disney squeezed a sweet deal out of the government—in part by threatening to build the park in Shanghai. Mike Rowse, the Hong Kong government's lead negotiator on the deal, quips: "They had the S-word and we had the U-word," referring to Disney's theme park rival Universal. It's not clear whether Shanghai was a real option; Steve Tight, a senior vice president in the Parks and Resorts group who leads Disney's Hong Kong project, says there still aren't enough people in China who can afford Disneyland. But sources say the deal almost collapsed when Disney insisted that Hong Kong promise it exclusivity—meaning no other foreign theme parks—but was unwilling to reciprocate with a promise not to build on the mainland. In the end, there is no exclusivity, and there may yet be a park in Shanghai someday.

If Disney erred in Japan by not having ownership—and erred in the other direction in Europe by assuming too much financial risk—in Hong Kong it's determined to find the right balance. In exchange for an investment of $314 million, Disney will own 43 percent of the park and earn royalties and management fees. The Hong Kong government, meanwhile, gets a majority stake in the park, but only after spending $1.7 billion on land reclamation, roads, and other infrastructure, plus $417 million for its majority equity stake. In addition, the government will lend the joint venture another $718 million. All in all, it's a good enough deal for Disney that some in Hong Kong have denounced it as a giveaway.

The park is a key Disney wedge into the region—even though it's just part of a larger Asian strategy. At Disney's Asia Pacific headquarters off Hong Kong's Times Square, more than 20 different Disney entities are trying to build the brand. Jon Niermann, an ebullient young marketing maven, is charged with "bringing everyone together at one Disney table," as he puts it, persuading, say, Buena Vista Entertainment Asia Pacific to work with Consumer Products. There's a weekly meeting with all the regional line-of-business managers. There's a weekly conference call with all the country managers. There's a "synergy calendar" on Niermann's wall, charting the major film and video releases and the marketing programs that will go along with them. On this day, Niermann is excited about an initiative to roll out a new line of merchandise based on Marie, a cat, in local Disney stores. "Asians love cats," says Niermann. "Music came to the table, and we pulled in a local canto-pop duo" to help launch the promotion. "TV got behind it by giving local TV exposures. The people who worked on this all wore two hats."

Niermann has high hopes for Disney's new China Central Television deal, under which 142 episodes of Mickey Mouse cartoons will be featured on the leading children's TV program on a major Chinese station. The arrangement is something of a coup because the channel reaches 75 percent of all Chinese TV sets—a cool 225 million households—while most foreign programming is still relegated to satellite channels with far less reach. Disney's Jun Tang says it's just one in a range of brand-building initiatives, from book publishing to animated films to shows like *Disney on Ice* and the Broadway version of *Beauty and the Beast,* both of which recently played in China.

But all the synergy Disney can muster in China doesn't guarantee success. Plenty of Western companies have discovered this promising market to be a mirage. For Disney, the theme park is close to a can't-miss proposition; it needs to draw only 5.5 million people a year—just one-third of what the Tokyo park gets—to meet company projections. (Disney predicts about one-third of the visitors will come from Hong Kong, one-third from the mainland, and one-third from elsewhere in Asia.) The market research shows that locals want the original Disneyland, not Sino-Disney, so there won't be a lot of execution risk on the creative side. Some wonder whether the impatient Chinese will put up with the lines, but if Americans are willing to wait two hours for a five-minute ride, the Chinese probably will be, too.

On other fronts, though, it's still an uphill battle. China Central Television has been making deals with most of the big Western broadcasters; Disney won't disclose the terms of its new arrangement, and it's not at all clear that it will be a significant moneymaker. "China has been very smart in the way it's done these deals," says Andrew Collier, Asian media analyst for Bear Stearns. "It's not going to let Western companies take a lot of profit." In the merchandising business, China has been home to so many counterfeit Disney goods for so long that it may be tough for the real thing—at Disney-style prices—to make inroads. And with movies, China retains strict caps on the number of Western films it will allow to be screened. Disney has enjoyed more than its share, but China is still a rounding error in overall box office statistics.

• • •

China's love-hate relationship with the West dates to the arrival of European colonialists in the 19th century. Even today, the increasingly pro-Western sentiment can quickly melt away. When NATO bombs accidentally hit the Chinese embassy in Belgrade during the Kosovo war, furious anti-American protests erupted throughout China. KFC franchises were stoned, and MTV was yanked off the air. "China is enthralled by America, and repelled by it, and at the same time overwhelmed by it," says Orville Schell, a China scholar who is now dean of the Graduate School of Journalism at Berkeley. "It's an absolute contradiction." Schell says the government tries from time to time to "curry popularity by surfing on anti-Western sentiment," but it's also eager to get the help of Western companies in building a more modern and prosperous country.

These contradictions exist in many countries; Islamic fundamentalists may denounce the Great Satan, but that doesn't stop them from drinking a Coke. In most industries, though, ambivalence about America doesn't much matter, because the products are basically value-neutral. A computer is a computer no matter who the manufacturer is, and while one might dislike modern multinationals, or believe that American computer imports are hurting local makers, IBM as a brand doesn't really represent anything other than good technology. Its machines don't speak any language other than binary.

But the culture industry is different. Disney and other media brands are fraught with emotional and psychological undercurrents. Disney represents certain ideas: fun, family, personal freedom, optimism about life and about the future, confidence that good will triumph over evil. These are in many respects universal Western Enlightenment values, rather than specifically American ones, and company executives say their market research shows that people are not drawn to Disney because of its connection to the United States. Yet analysts of global branding—as well as every Disney customer interviewed for this story—affirm that those who buy Disney products overseas are keenly aware that the items are foreign. Indeed that is part of the appeal.

"American brands are about anything being possible—the core value of all of them is optimism," says Martyn Straw, president of the consultancy Interbrand. "America is not a country, it's an idea; there is a distinction between America as a geopolitical entity and America as a concept, a place where you can be what you want to be. These themes play around the world, and the Disney brand is almost exclusively dependent on that."

The paradox, though, is that even as people are drawn to American brands as symbols, when it comes to actual cultural content, they are looking for something more. They want the production values they associate with modernity and technology, whether it takes the form of a state-of-the-art theme park or a fast-food restaurant that is clean, air-conditioned, and offers good service. At the same time, they want things tailored to their tastes. Disneyland Hong Kong, for all its loyalty to the original, will feature a broad selection of Asian food as well as shows and special events that are built around local holidays. Even McDonald's, a symbol of monoculture if ever there was one, insists that its success overseas is due to the creativity and innovation of its local franchisees, who can modify menus to suit local tastes.

In the TV business, the need to localize is especially evident. For one thing, most people want to watch television in their own language, even if they speak English, and dubbing imported programs goes only so far. "If you want to create things, they have to be of that culture," says James Murdoch, son of the Aussie magnate and head of the Asian satellite broadcaster Star Television. He cites the development of more local programming as the key factor in improving the performance of Star, whose original model was based on Pan-Asian English-language programming. In China and India, Star's Mandarin and Hindi channels outdraw its English ones by huge margins. Almost by definition, television programming in Mandarin or Hindi is going to be a local product, even if it carries the patina of an international brand.

The same is true over at MTV, another successful purveyor of American culture. "Our product changes dramatically from region to region," says Bill Roedy, head of MTV Networks International. "We're all about different languages, different VJs, different themes. We are the antithesis of homogeneity." He says MTV's 33 channels around the world tend to have 50 to 80 percent local content. Harry Hui—until recently head of MTV Asia and soon to move to Universal Music—says the glamour of MTV is what brings people in, but the quality of the programming is what keeps them.

Even in the Internet business, which ought to be intrinsically the most global, the trend is toward localization. In China, Disney handed over management of its Mandarin site to a local company, Sea Rainbow. AOL, which has a presence in 17 countries, doesn't use the America Online branding anywhere except in the U.S. and Latin America, and while the overseas operations piggyback on the mothership's technology, they are otherwise locally run, mostly with partners who own a substantial equity stake.

• • •

Iconic brands have enormous power, but they also impose constraints. Disney is so closely identified with family entertainment that it can be difficult for the company to get outside that box. To grab its share of the teen and adult movie markets, for example, Disney produces films under the Touchstone, Hollywood Pictures, and Miramax labels.

Likewise, Disney's biggest new international opportunity does not carry the Disney brand. Seeking to shore up its position in the fierce competition with the Cartoon Network and Nickelodeon, Disney recently spent $5.2 billion to buy the Fox Family Network from Rupert Murdoch. With 35 million viewers in Europe and Latin America, Fox Family has much greater penetration overseas than the Disney Channel. Its programming—edgier than Disney's, and thus in many ways more appealing to today's all-too-sophisticated kids—will be branded ABC Family, not Disney. Ironically, success with non-Disney brands, notably the ESPN sports network, will be a major factor in the long-term fortunes of the company's international operations.

Even more critical to Disney's success abroad is its performance in the U.S. After all, international customers are not going to be enamored of an American brand that's in decline at home. And Disney has had a tough few years. Network television is an increasingly difficult business as TV choices proliferate. The merchandising unit appears to be suffering from market saturation, and the company is closing about 100 of its roughly 750 Disney stores. Competitors are more powerful than ever, be they DreamWorks in animation or MGM/Universal in theme parks. The Internet business has been a fiasco—not only for Disney, to be sure, but it's been costly nonetheless. The setbacks have hurt Disney's stock price, which peaked in May 2000 at 43⅞ and this past December was trading at 22. The current downturn in advertising and tourism will reverse itself eventually, but not before it takes a big bite out of profits. Eisner says the brand has never been stronger. But some analysts suggest that "age compression"—essentially kids growing up faster—poses a long-term threat.

Disney's challenges both at home and abroad illustrate just how hard it is for even the biggest of American brands to keep growing—and give lie to many of the fears people have about cultural imperialism. Unlike other industries—oil, say, or agriculture, or even technology—culture businesses depend on giving people what they want, as opposed to what they need. It is true that the giant media conglomerates can sometimes suffocate competition and choice. But in television and theme parks in most of the world, there has never been much competition anyway, and in the sale of plush toys it is hardly an issue. For the most part, people will decide what elements of American culture they want. The Disneys of the world are slaves to the tastes of Chen Ping and Wei Qing Hua, not the other way around.

Index

ABC Television, 8
accents, at Tokyo Disneyland, 32
advertising, 38
Ambassadors, 15
American themes, 4, 9, 26, 32, 33
animation, 12, 52
appearance standards, 14, 18, 37
Asian financial crisis, 46
attendance, 25, 28, 36, 38, 42–43

Bourguignon, Philippe, 37
brands, American, 54–55
Brannen, Mary Yoki, 32
break schedules, 16

cast members, 10, 28, 32. *See also* worker subcultures
children, 27, 46
China, political factors in, 46. *See also* Hong Kong Disneyland
China Central Television, 53–54
Chirac, Jacques, 35
Cinderella's Castle, 11, 30
codes of conduct, 19–21, 37
Collier, Andrew, 54
conduct, codes of, 19–21, 37
contrasts, 9–10, 30
corporate operations, 51–52
cross-border cultural learning, 27, 38–39, 49
cross-marketing and synergies, 8–9, 12, 53, 53–54
cultural differentiation, 32
cultural flow, 26–27, 28, 32–33
cultural imperialism, 27, 47, 50–51
cultural perspective on Disneyland, 4–5
culture, corporate, 4–5, 17, 21. *See also* worker subcultures
customer expectations, 20, 28–33

dating among employees, 16–17
demeanor, standards of, 17, 48
development, land. *See* property development
differentiation, cultural, 32
Disney, as brand, 54–55
Disney, Roy, 12
Disney, Walt, 8, 9, 18, 51
Disneyland (California), 8–10
Disneyland, Hong Kong, 45–49, 50–55
Disneyland, Paris, 35–39, 39–45
Disneyland, University of, 17–18
Disney Sea (Japan), 52
Disney University, 36–37
Disney World (Florida), 10–13
"Displacing Disney: Some Notes on the Flow of Culture" (Van Maanen), 28–33

domestication, 29
dress code, 14, 18, 37

Eisner, Michael, 12, 35, 38, 41, 42, 51
emotional management, 14, 22
employee culture. *See* worker subcultures
employees, categories of, 10
employees, screening of, 14
environment, control of, 10
environmental issues, 48
EPCOT, 11
ethnography, 14
Euro Disney, 35–39, 39–45
"The Ever-Expanding, Profit-Maximizing, Cultural-Imperialist, Wonderful World of Disney" (Weber), 50–55
expectations, public, 20
experiences, cultural, 26–27, 32

fairy tales, 36
Family Network, 55
"feeling business," 4, 14
financial problems, at Euro Disney, 37–38, 39–45
financing, 35, 41–41, 45, 53
firings, 19
Fitzpatrick, Robert, 43
Florida, 10–13
flow, cultural, 26–27, 28, 32–33
food and concession workers, 15

gaijin ("outsider"), 32
globalization
    cultural imperialism, 26, 47, 50–51
    cultural meanings and, 46
    homogenization and, 26–27, 33, 49
guest misconduct, 20–21, 23

hands-on interaction, 30
"happiest place on earth," 9–10, 14, 36
happiness and orderliness, 4, 9–10, 14, 29
happiness trade, 4, 14
history and origins of Disneyland, 8–9
holidays, at Tokyo Disneyland, 25
homogenization, global, 26–27, 33, 49
Hong Kong Disneyland, 45–49, 50–55
hotel occupancy, 25, 37, 38, 43

identity, 22
image problem, 40–41
imagineers, 10, 12, 25
imperialism, cultural, 27, 47, 50–51
interaction, hands-on, 30
international business. *See also* globalization
    cross-border learning, 27, 38–39, 49
    cultural flow, 26–27, 28, 32–33

Euro Disney/Disneyland Paris, 35–39, 39–45
Hong Kong Disneyland, 45–49, 50–55
localization, 49, 56
organizational patterns and, 4
political factors in China, 46
Tokyo Disneyland, 25–26, 27, 28–33
internationalization, 4, 5
Internet, 55
"It's a Small World," 16

Japan
Disney Sea, 52
Tokyo Disneyland, 25–26, 27, 28–33, 52
Johnson, Michael, 52

Kanally, David, 37
Katzenbach, Jeff, 12
Kundun (film), 47, 51

land development. *See* property development
language, control of, 17
language barriers, 31, 32, 38
layout of park, 31
learning, cross-border, 27, 38–39, 49
lines, waiting in, 10
The Lion King (film), 52
"Little Emperors and Empresses," 46
localization, 49, 55
local opposition, 36–38, 45, 47, 48

Magic Kingdom, 11
management, 10, 12, 41
Marne-la-Vallée, France, 35, 38
massification, 33
McDonald's, 27
meaning, cultural, 28, 32, 46
"Meet the World," 30
Mickey Mouse
on Chinese television, 51, 53–54
cross-cultural variations, 33, 45
exportability of, 52
in Japan, 25, 33
minorities, 14
misconduct by guests, 20–21
"Mouse Trap" (Gumbel and Turner), 39–43
movies, Disney, 12, 47, 51
MTV, 55
Mulan (film), 47, 51
Murdoch, James, 55

name tags, 31, 32
Niermann, Jon, 53

occupational culture. *See* worker subcultures
opposition, local, 36–38, 45, 47, 48
orderliness, and happiness, 4, 9–10, 14, 29
organizational patterns, and internationalization, 4

organizational status, 15–16
Oriental Land Company, 25, 28, 52
Orlando, Florida, 10–13
Orlando, Florida, City of, 11
outsiders, at Tokyo Disneyland, 32
overconfidence, corporate, 41

Pells, Richard, 36
personnel, categories of, 10
"Pirates of the Caribbean," 31
popular culture, 47–48, 53. *See also* Disneyland
pricing policies, 37, 38, 43
product, Disneyland as, 9
promotion and advancement, 16
property development
Hong Kong, 45, 48
Orlando, 10–11
Paris, 35–36, 41–42
Tokyo, 25, 28
public expectations, 20

Reedy Creek Improvement District, 11
revenues, 12, 52
Rowse, Mike, 53

screening of employees, 14
security, 15, 21
self-other contrasts, at Tokyo Disneyland, 32
service industry, cultural context and, 4, 48
Shanghai, China, 45, 53
Shapiro, Joe, 39
Shenzen, China, 46, 50
"The Smile Factory: Work at Disneyland" (Van Maanen), 13–23
Spain, 35
staff, categories of, 10
Star Television, 55
status badges, 15
status rank ordering, 15–16
success and failure, 4, 27, 36–38
"Suits," 10, 35, 37
supervision, 19–20, 22
Sweepers, 15
synergies and cross-marketing, 8–9, 12, 52, 53–54

Tang, Jun, 53, 54
TeamDisney, 12
television
in China, 51, 53–54
localization and, 55
synergies with, 8, 12
terminations and dismissals, 19
terrorism, 50–51
time flexibility, 16
Tokyo Disneyland, 25–26, 27, 28–33, 52
Tour Guides, 15

training, 17–18, 29, 36–37

uniforms, 16, 17
unions, and Disneyland Paris, 37
University of Disneyland, 17–18, 29

values, 18

Walt Disney Company, 51–52, 55
Walt Disney Studios Park, 38
Walt Disney World (Florida), 10–13
Watts, Steven, 8, 9, 10
"weenies," 10
Wells, Frank, 12, 41
Western culture, opposition to, 54
Wilson, Gary, 41
Window on the World theme park, 50

"The Wonderful World of Disney" (TV), 12
worker subcultures
    appearance standards, 14, 18
    conduct codes, formal and informal, 19–21
    demeanor standards, 17
    emotional management, 14, 22
    guest misconduct and, 20–21, 23
    public interaction, 14–15, 18, 20–21
    socializing among workers, 16–17, 19–20
    status badges, personal, 15
    status rank ordering, 15–17
    supervisors and, 19–20, 22
    training and, 17–18
"World Bazaar," 31

young adults, 27
youth culture, 17

MANAGING FOR THE FUTURE

Organizational Behavior & Processes

SKILLS

Module 11
Managing Cultural Diversity

Module 12
Negotiation and Conflict Resolution

Module 13
Change from Within: Roads to Successful Issue Selling

Module 14
Leadership

Ancona • Kochan • Scully
Van Maanen • Westney

MANAGING FOR THE FUTURE

Organizational Behavior & Processes

Managing Cultural Diversity

Module 11

MANAGING FOR THE FUTURE
Organizational Behavior & Processes, Third Edition

Deborah Ancona
Sloan School of Management
Massachusetts Institute of Technology

Thomas A. Kochan
Sloan School of Management
Massachusetts Institute of Technology

Maureen Scully
Graduate School of Management
Simmons College

John Van Maanen
Sloan School of Management
Massachusetts Institute of Technology

D. Eleanor Westney
Sloan School of Management
Massachusetts Institute of Technology

Dedicated to those who have inspired us to try to be better students and teachers.
Special thanks to: Professor Jack Barbash • Professor Arthur H. Gladstein • Professor Marius B. Jansen • Professor Joanne Martin • Professor Edgar H. Schein

---

VP/Editorial Director
Jack W. Calhoun

VP/Editor-in-Chief
Michael P. Roche

Senior Publisher
Melissa S. Acuña

Executive Editor
John Szilagyi

Senior Developmental Editor
Judith O'Neill

Marketing Manager
Jacquelyn Carrillo

Production Editor
Emily Gross

Manufacturing Coordinator
Rhonda Utley

Compositor
Trejo Production

Printer
Von Hoffmann Press, Inc.
Frederick, MD

Internal Designer
Bethany Casey

Cover Designer
Bethany Casey

Photographs
©PhotoDisc

Design Project Manager
Bethany Casey

COPYRIGHT ©2005
by South-Western, a division of Thomson Learning.
Thomson Learning™ is a trademark used herein under license.

Printed in the United States of America
1 2 3 4 5 07 06 05 04 03

For more information contact
South-Western College Publishing,
5191 Natorp Boulevard,
Mason, Ohio, 45040
Or you can visit our Internet site at:
http://www.swlearning.com

ALL RIGHTS RESERVED
No part of this work covered by the copyright hereon may be reproduced or used in any form or by any means—graphic, electronic, or mechanical, including photocopying, recording, taping, Web distribution or information storage and retrieval systems—without the written permission of the publisher.

For permission to use material from this text or product, contact us by
Tel: (800) 730-2214
Fax: (800) 730-2215
http://www.thomsonrights.com

Library of Congress Control Number: 2003113908
ISBN 0-324-05575-7

Contents

Managing Cultural Diversity

	Overview	6

Core

Class Note	**Managing Cultural Diversity: From Understanding to Action**	10
	The Meaning of Diversity 10	
	Background: The U.S. Societal and Policy Context 13	
	Organizational Processes 14	
	Managing Diversity for High Performance 17	
	References and Additional Readings 17	
	Bystander Awareness: Skills for Effective Managers	20
	From Valuing Diversity to Taking Action 20	
	Historical and Conceptual Background 21	
	The Bystander in the Workplace 21	
	The Courage of One's Convictions 21	
	Collusion 22	
	Cultural Variation in Intervention Styles 22	
	Ideas for Bystanders 23	
	Structural Solutions 23	
	A Closing Thought 24	
Exercise	**Bystander Scenarios: What Would You Do?**	25
	Scenario 1: Introducing the Invisible Colleague 26	
	Scenario 2: Is It Really About Race? 26	
	Scenario 3: The Awkward Invitation 27	
	Scenario 4: Is It the Nature of the Project? 27	
	Scenario 5: Counting on a Colleague 28	
	Scenario 6: I Was Just Trying to Be Sensitive! 28	
	Scenario 7: You Just Weren't Listening 29	

Elective

The Press	**Making Differences Matter: A New Paradigm for Managing Diversity**	32
	The Discrimination-and-Fairness Paradigm 33	
	The Access-and-Legitimacy Paradigm 35	
	The Emerging Paradigm: Connecting Diversity to Work Perspectives 36	
	Eight Preconditions for Making the Paradigm Shift 37	
	First Interstate Bank: A Paradigm Shift in Progress 38	
	Shift Complete: Third-Paradigm Companies in Action 39	

Index

Overview

The diversity of the workforce is a present and future reality. Managers need to be skilled in managing cultural diversity in order to hire and retain people with a range of talents, to operate in a variety of markets within and across countries, and to draw upon diversity as a source of learning and enhanced organizational effectiveness. This module helps you to understand the meaning of diversity and its possible impacts in organizational contexts. Because diversity is such a complex topic, your work colleagues will likely have strong feelings about it. What can you do as a manager to foster an inclusive climate, where diversity is more than tolerated, but is fully tapped to expand the repertoires of how people accomplish work? The readings and exercises in the module present a way for you to be active in shaping a respectful workplace that brings out the best of people's talents. Acquiring specific skills in turning around awkward or offensive situations will help you create the kind of workplace in which you and others want to work.

This module begins with a two-part Class Note. The first reading, "Managing Cultural Diversity: From Understanding to Action," focuses on the dimensions of diversity and the multiple levels at which managers need to understand and address diversity (societal, organizational, and interpersonal). Data on changing workforce demographics in the United States are presented in an accompanying appendix. This introductory reading also presents the historical context of diversity in the United States and examines the meaning of affirmative action, often a contentious topic because it is misunderstood and involves conflicting interests. Although U.S. organizations may currently give the most attention to diversity, dimensions of diversity exist within every country and are certainly present in managing globally across countries.

Challenges remain in increasing diversity in the highest levels of organizations. More deeply, organizations need to tap diversity as a resource for ongoing learning and innovation. A true appreciation of diversity will reveal new ways of handling every aspect of organizational life and operations, from designing products to conducting performance evaluations to managing client relationships.

The next reading, "Bystander Awareness: Skills for Effective Managers," moves from understanding to action. So-called "bystanders" are active participants in the workplace who have a special role in signaling respect for diversity and helping to halt unprofessional behavior. This reading will explain who bystanders are and what they can do. We often admire the person who has the presence of mind to make a difference in a difficult situation and create the space for multiple viewpoints to be heard. With these skills and some opportunities to practice, you can be that person, a valued member of the team. At the same time, these individual actions exist in a broader organizational context that must provide support systems, policies, and resources for organizational level improvements.

Some specific "scenarios" are then presented so you can assess the actions and choices made by some sample bystanders. Finally, an elective reading by a noted organizational consultant on diversity introduces organizational level approaches to diversity.

Assignment Summary

1. Read the two-part Class Note, "Managing Cultural Diversity: From Understanding to Action," and "Bystander Awareness: Skills for Effective Managers," and come to class prepared to discuss the bystander scenarios, which begin on page 20.
2. Each bystander scenario has a videotaped counterpart. Your instructor may ask you to view one or more of the videos before class or may set aside classtime to show them to you as a group. Use the discussion questions provided for each scenario to guide your preparation and think about other bystander interventions you could also role-play.
3. Alternatively your instructor may ask you to develop and videotape either individually or as part of a group, an original bystander role play.

Additional Exercises

You can expand your learning about these issues in several ways. One way is to go through recent issues of the business press and look for examples of "the business case for diversity" (as summarized in Figure 11.1 and Figure 11.8 and elaborated in the supplementary reading by Thomas and Ely). How is the case for diversity expressed? Are there variations on these themes? Are other reasons for valuing diversity expressed (such as "It's the right thing to do" or "It helps us develop as human beings" or "It generates new ideas for effective ways to conduct business")? Who expresses the case for diversity and with what audience in mind?

Another way to learn more about different approaches is to ask your classmates or teammates about how diversity is understood and managed in their home countries, regions, or companies where they have worked. What dimensions of diversity were important? When was diversity valued or ignored and why?

Finally, this module shows you ways to develop specific skills for making a diverse workplace a great place to work. You can practice these skills by doing "role plays," similar to those in the scenarios in this module, drawing on your own experiences. Your instructor may direct you to try some specific kinds of role plays or to invent your own scenarios.

Managing Cultural Diversity

CORE

Module 11

Managing Cultural Diversity

From understanding to action

The Meaning of Diversity

The term *diversity* is used to describe many different features of contemporary and future organizations. Of the many dimensions of diversity, first and foremost, the concept refers to "social identities": personal characteristics (such as race, gender, nationality, sexual orientation, age, or disability) that are "social" in that they trigger others to treat people as members of a group rather than as individuals. These groups are products of layers of stereotypes and history, so the experiences of members and the reactions of others are quite culturally and politically complex.

In addition to these primary social identities, important secondary dimensions of diversity include additional personal characteristics (marital status, family background, educational level, cognitive style, leadership style, etc.) as well as aspects of organizational role (position, years of service, career employee or temporary worker or consultant, high-level executive or entry-level hourly employee, and so forth). The term *cultural diversity* refers specifically to the primary dimensions of diversity and the opportunities and challenges posed to work teams and departments that represent people from many groups.

Taylor Cox (1993, p. 6), a noted scholar of management science, defines cultural diversity as "the representation, in one social system, of people with distinctly different group affiliations of cultural significance."

Less than 10 years ago, *diversity* was a word used mostly to describe a stock portfolio or to indicate a variety of job functions. The topic of diversity has since catapulted to the forefront of organizational concerns. Organization leaders and management scholars believe that diversity management is an important tool for those organizations that want to achieve strategic advantage. Consequently, diversity and its management blossomed into a multimillion-dollar industry.

The diversity of the workforce is a present and future reality. Managers who want to hire and retain people with a range of talents and to tap a variety of markets will need to be skilled in managing diversity. The accompanying appendix on page 19 shows the demographic composition of the U.S. civilian labor force (broken down by sex, by race, and by Hispanic origin).

Diversity Within Nations and Around the Globe

Managers of the global organization of the future clearly must be sensitive to and skilled in leveraging the diversity they find in different parts of the world. Even though cross-cultural diversity across national boundaries is obvious, a great deal of diversity is also present within national boundaries. It may be commonplace to think of diversity as a U.S. phenomenon and preoccupation, but most nations have cultural differences—in ethnicity, language, gender, or class—that can be sources of division and tension as well as sources of creativity, learning, and value. For example, around the globe, women are underrepresented in top management positions—a mere 3 percent in many countries—but women's perspectives could shape new ways of doing business. The challenges for women's ascent are both similar and different across national contexts (Adler, 1997; Adler and Izraeli, 1994).

Historically and currently in the United States, race represents the most visible source of conflict. In the 1930s, Swedish observer Gunnar Myrdal dubbed racism "the American dilemma," because racism marred an otherwise exemplary experiment in democracy and equality that could be a worldwide model. The prescient writings of the African-American scholar W. E. B. DuBois (1903, 1968) on not only the hardships but also the essential talents and distinctly formed perspective of blacks in America still ring true today.

In Europe, historically and currently, ethnic and religious differences created the greatest conflicts (for example, the Bosnian, Serb, and Muslim conflicts in the former Yugoslavia or the long-simmering conflicts between Catholics and Protestants in Northern Ireland). Patterns of immigration also create tensions and inequalities (such as Turkish "guest workers" in Germany or Iranians in Sweden). In Asia, differences in national origin and immigration provide sources of division and prejudice (such as Japanese/Korean conflicts and the challenges for Korean workers in Japan or the hardships of Filipino domestic workers in Taiwan). In Latin America, the issues of indigenous peoples and the history of wide class differences continue to create tensions and challenges. Within any nation, gender differences affect the status, health, and opportunities of women.

All these issues will affect how organizations function internally and do business externally, and moreover, they affect whether business can deliver on its implicit promise (dating from Adam Smith) of using profit maximization to improve social welfare (or the "wealth of nations").

The Business Case for Diversity

As Lew Platt, former chairman and CEO of Hewlett-Packard once put it, managers are challenged to make the "business case" for diversity in their organizations (see Figure 11.1).

Despite the rhetoric in much of the business press about "valuing diversity" or that "diversity is just good business," the research evidence, accumulated in well over 100 studies conducted over many years, suggests that managers cannot expect that attracting and maintaining a diverse workforce is easy or a natural outgrowth of the changing demographics of labor markets (see Williams and O'Reilly, 1998; and Richard, Kochan, and McMillan-Capehart, 2002, for reviews of these studies). These researchers explain that diversity does not automatically translate into positive group or organizational performance. Instead, potential gains from greater diversity arise when training in communication and teamwork, and other work practices and cultural norms enable managers and employees to learn from diversity. As one comprehensive review recently concluded:

> *This review suggests we are not likely to see a simple direct relationship between diversity and performance, at least in the early stages of efforts to increase the representation of minorities in organizations. Instead, the effects are likely to be determined by how organizational leaders and participants respond to and manage diversity. We could posit two contrasting scenarios—a self-reinforcing vicious circle of negative effects, or a reinforcing circle of positive effects, depending on the actions taken as part of efforts to increase minority participation and representation in organizations. (Richard, Kochan, and McMillan-Capehart, 2002, pp. 280–281)*

And another set of research experts summarized the situation a bit more directly:

> *Diversity appears to be a double-edged sword, increasing the opportunity for creativity as well as the likelihood that group members will be dissatisfied and fail to identify with the group. (Milliken and Martins, 1996)*

These observations tell us that, if managed well, diverse groups and organizational units may have greater up-side performance potential; but if managed poorly, down-side performance risk may also be greater.

As Lew Platt pointed out (Figure 11.1), the desire is to have some data to convince skeptics about the value of diversity. But the business case for diversity will not be made conveniently with a single metric. Rather, the challenge of working with diversity—like almost any other business process from design to manufacturing to marketing—is to do the hard work and to learn along the way where the greatest improvements as well as pitfalls may lie.

What Managers Need to Understand and Do

To capture the benefits of diversity and avoid its potential pitfalls, managers need to understand how increased diversity affects group and organizational processes and how to manage these processes to produce positive results for the different stakeholders. Whatever the sources, managing diversity requires organizational leaders to be attentive to key stakeholders at three levels.

First, at the societal level, citizens and governments expect or legally require that organizations will provide equal opportunity and fair treatment

---

Figure 11.1 The Business Case for Diversity

"I see three main points to make the business case for diversity:
1. A talent shortage that requires us to seek out and use the full capabilities of all our employees.
2. The need to be like our customers, including the need to understand and communicate with them in terms that reflect their concerns.
3. Diverse teams produce better results.

This last point is not as easy to sell as the first two—especially to engineers who want data. What I need is the data, evidence that diverse groups do better."

Source: Lew Platt, [former] CEO, Hewlett-Packard. Informal comments to Diversity Research Network, Stanford Business School, March 18, 1998. Reproduced with permission of Hewlett-Packard Company.

Diversity and Organizational Learning

Some examples of how learning from diversity—in race, disability, sexual orientation, and gender—can enhance organizational processes.

1. **A better job posting system.** Black employees at Xerox were among the first to form an employee caucus group (in the 1970s) to represent their concerns about inclusion and fair treatment to the company and to coach each other to become better salespersons. The group discussed how it was difficult to advance in the company, because they often did not know when job openings arose, and positions were filled through informal contacts before the word got around. To address their concern, a more formal job posting system was created by the company, which benefited black employees but also redounded to the benefit of all employees as well as to the benefit of managers to whom a wider pool of talent was presented.

2. **Fuller utilization of groupware.** At an investment house, employees tended to leave informal Post-It notes on each other's desks to inform one another of "opinion changes" regarding specific stocks. The company installed a groupware system to facilitate wider information exchange online, better documentation of these opinion changes, and improved communication between U.S. and European offices. However, the informal culture of Post-It notes dominated, and no one really used the groupware. Then, the firm hired a blind employee. His colleagues realized that he could not read the flurry of Post-It notes and began to realize that it really was inefficient for everyone. People at last were inspired to use the groupware, with the general expectation that performance would improve.

3. **A new approach to design.** At the Ford Motor Company, a team of designers took a fresh approach to designing the Windstar. The team included more women than was typical in a group of engineers; they and men who were parents represented the point of view of what families (and specifically women who made car purchase decisions) might look for in a vehicle. The result was that the Windstar included new features such as control over lights and alarms so that a sleeping child would not be awakened when taken out of the car, larger cup holders for bottles (which also proved popular with a wider group of consumers as improved holders for sports drinks), and better sensors for people and objects when backing up. The new design showed how reflecting the potential market in the demographics of the design team could result in innovation.

4. **More relevant employee benefits for everyone.** At a large high-technology company, a group of gay, lesbian, bisexual, and transgendered (GLBT) employees lobbied for "domestic partner benefits" so that they could include their same-sex partners in the health and other benefits offered as part of the company's total compensation package. Their request triggered the human resources department to take a wider look at the benefits they were offering, and they learned that their health benefits package was geared to an employee with a non-working spouse (presumably a wife) and two children. This family situation characterized only about 10 percent of their workforce. Moreover, in addition to GLBT employees, other employees wanted to cover the people who they defined as their relevant family (e.g., many black and Hispanic employees wanted benefits for extended family members such as parents or siblings). The result of this analysis was that the company offered a more flexible benefits package to all employees (with the caveat that the IRS had not caught up to this model and that benefits beyond a traditional heterosexual nuclear family would be taxed as income). Employee response was overwhelmingly favorable and regarded as good for morale and retention.

Sources: 1. Black Caucus Groups at Xerox. Ray Friedman, HBS case; 2. and 3. Diversity training workshop at the MIT Sloan School of Management, 1999; 4. M. Scully and W.E.D. Creed, Annals of the American Association of Political Science, 1998.

to everyone at work. Where inequalities exist, many people believe that it is through work that groups can and should be able to overcome historic injustices and improve their welfare. Also at the societal level, shareholders may expect organizations to engage in diversity programs only to the extent that they improve performance, which is discussed next. Conflicts of interest may arise when some regard valuing diversity as a good end in itself or as a longer-term source of performance that is worth working patiently toward, while others see attention to diversity as a cost and a short-term drain.

Second, at the organizational level, employees have come to expect fair treatment and equal opportunity as part of the "social contract" (see Module 7), which connects them to their organization and motivates them to contribute their talent and energy.

Third, at the managerial level, it is increasingly every manager's job to translate diversity into positive organizational outcomes. Mission statements from top managers or boards of directors may give broad direction on diversity, while managers enact the vision and may even be formally evaluated on their efforts.

Background: The U.S. Societal and Policy Context

People bring strong feelings about diversity to the workplace. For you to act in an informed way as a manager and a colleague, you need to appreciate the historic background and the actual definition of currently loaded terms such as *affirmative action*.

The Civil Rights Movement

Equal opportunity and affirmative action requirements were born in a time of social crisis—in the midst of the upheavals and the civil rights movement of the 1960s led by Martin Luther King, Jr. A broad base of African Americans from all walks of life, and some white allies willing to take a stand against racism, united to contest the separate and unequal treatment of blacks throughout the United States. The legal prohibitions against discrimination and the proactive requirements for affirmative action were born in this time and reflect the U.S. government and American society's expectations for managerial practice and organizational policies.

Although modified over time through cases and experience, these policies continue to reflect American commitment to equality as a fundamental belief. Current debates echo differences of opinion over both the means of achieving equality and the degree to which inequality persists.

The 1960s delivered a wake-up call that social change was desperately needed. It is difficult today to keep in mind the intensity of the change and the need for visionary corporate leaders to play a role. Some people believe that much progress has been made since then. On the other hand, some people believe that the problems of racial division persist in the United States and that the clear and courageous language used to discuss racism in the past has been watered down by the contemporary language of "diversity." What do you think? On what important social issues would you take a bold stand?

Government Policies

Society outlines its broad expectations for managing diversity through the laws and regulations it enacts and the social norms and experiences that employees carry into their organizational roles. In 1964 the U.S. federal government enacted the first comprehensive law requiring firms to provide equal employment opportunities to all people regardless of race, color, religion, sex, or national origin. Later, other protected categories were added to the law, including age and disability. Sexual harassment was specifically prohibited. The law covers essentially all employment practices (hiring, promotion, discharge, and so forth). Moreover, in 1965 President Lyndon Johnson signed an Executive Order requiring all firms doing business with the government (virtually all large corporations and most small to medium-sized enterprises) to take affirmative action to hire and promote minorities and women in numbers proportionate to their availability in the external labor market.

To demonstrate compliance with the Executive Order, firms must have a plan with three components: (1) an analysis of the availability of minorities and women in the relevant labor markets in which the firm operates, (2) statistical data showing the utilization of these affected groups across the different job categories in the firm, and (3) a plan specifying targets and timetables for redressing underutilization of these covered workers.

Affirmative action does not, however, require hiring unqualified individuals, nor does it require or support choosing less-qualified members of a protected group over others who are more qualified. Instead, it requires organizations to make affirmative efforts to hire and promote members of the protected groups who are qualified for the positions involved. It does not require quotas, but does require proactive monitoring of numbers.

These policies prompted some positive effects, particularly in their early years as strong enforcement patterns interacted with strong rates of economic growth to expand opportunities. The best empirical studies showed that the combination of strong economic growth and the pressures of government enforcement improved the status of people of color from the late 1960s through the 1970s. The strongest gains were made by the better educated new entrants to the labor force. The enforcement efforts had their biggest effects on eliminating the most overt sources of discrimination in formal selection, promotion, training, and labor-management policies and practices (Leonard, 1983). These features are ones to which the strategic design perspective pays the most attention. Some of the remaining challenges are in resolving conflicts (important from the political perspective) and weaving an appreciation of diversity into the everyday practices of work (important from the cultural perspective).

Remaining Challenges

Despite overall progress, the report from the U.S. Department of Labor's Glass Ceiling Commission in 1995 puts these efforts in perspective and illustrates the significant challenges that remain for managers today. For instance, the report revealed that black men held only 2.3 percent of the executive, administrative, and managerial jobs in all private sector industries; they held 3.9 percent of these jobs in the public and private sectors combined. Black women held 2.2 percent of the executive, administrative, and managerial jobs in all private sector industries; they held 4.6 percent of these jobs in the public and private sectors.

Hispanics are not successfully progressing in the corporate ranks either. The 1990 census data reveal that the percentage of Hispanics who are managers and administrators in both the private and public sectors (Mexican-Americans, 6%; Puerto Ricans, 8%; Cuban-Americans, 7.5%; all other Hispanic-Americans, 7.5%) is far below the percentage of non-Hispanic whites (43%) who are managers and administrators. Eighty-six percent of the Hispanic senior executives were male, and more than 40 percent of these executives had been in their companies 16 years or more. Nationwide, Puerto Ricans account for only 0.7 percent of the managers in the manufacturing industry. Only 0.2 percent of the Cuban-American population is employed in the finance industry.

The story is also not good for Asian-Americans. Although members of this racial/ethnic group (Chinese, Filipino, Japanese, Asian Indian, Korean, Vietnamese, Cambodian, and Hawaiian) are stereotyped as being the "model minority," they lag behind whites in managerial and executive positions. Why? They are perceived as intelligent, hardworking, highly educated, polite, nonconfrontational, nonviolent, politically passive, culturally resourceful, and good at science. Consequently, they are perceived as not possessing the leadership skills to be effective managers. They often are trapped in technical jobs and denied access to management positions.

The question facing organizations in the future is not whether government policies promoting and regulating equal employment opportunity are still needed. The majority of Americans continue to support these policies, even while debating the relative merits of different approaches to affirmative action. The real question managers face is how to go beyond legal requirements or fairness arguments and come to a true appreciation of how diversity makes the integral aspects of business work in new and better ways (Thomas and Ely, 1996). We now turn to this question.

Organizational Processes

Recognition of the limits of government enforcement and legal compliance as a management strategy led throughout the 1980s and 1990s to a flurry of organizational interventions aimed at educating and socializing managers to "value diversity." Figure 11.2 lists the elements frequently included in diversity programs found in large U.S. corporations. The list comes from a survey of *Fortune* 500 companies published in 1995. Among these companies, fully 72 percent reported having formal diversity policy programs with some or all of the elements shown in this figure.

From a strategic design perspective, the focus is on aligning corporate policies to government regulations and other requirements from the corporate environment. The attention to compliance and the monitoring of numbers becomes an element of strategic design. Programs that focus on selecting qualified people, redefining the types of talents the organization needs, and matching people to jobs are all consistent with the concerns of a strategic design approach.

From a political perspective, the attention shifts to the underlying tensions and conflicts of interest that affect how diversity programs are perceived and carried out. The preceding statistics are one indication of why tensions over race and ethnicity continue to be visible in American society and politics. Because organizations are microcosms of the broader society, racial tensions and differences, not surprisingly, spill over into organizational life. On the one hand, some white males believe that *affirmative action* is a code word meaning incompetent minorities take jobs away from whites. And some people of color feel stigmatized from being beneficiaries of special treatment policies. On the other hand, in the face of evidence of persistent inequalities and stereotypes that continue to favor some groups over others in the final outcomes, other people feel strongly that affirmative action is still needed. A political perspective views the organization as an arena in which these political disputes must be mediated by policies and institutions that are updated as interests evolve.

Figure 11.2 Typical Elements in a Corporate Diversity Program

- A formal position or department dedicated to diversity management
- Training programs designed and conducted by employees
- Diversity advisory councils chaired by the CEO
- Mentoring programs open to all high-potential employees
- Participation in benchmarking studies of diversity programs in other companies
- Provision of electronic or printed diversity calendars and schedule of company-sponsored diversity events
- Formal employee networks, support groups, and task forces with direct access to top management that identify issues, explore solutions, and support implementation
- Awareness workshops with follow-up meetings and results
- Global video conferencing supported by a culturally sensitive manual

Source: Survey of *Fortune* 500 companies reported by the Society of Human Resource Management in *Mosaics* 1(1), March 1995, p. 5.

The more recent rise in valuing diversity programs comes at a time of resurgence of resistance from some who feel that people of color are receiving preferential treatment in the workplace. As part of a poll conducted by the *New York Times* and CBS News in 1995, Americans were asked:

Do you believe that where there has been job discrimination in the past, preference in hiring or promotion should be given to blacks today?

What do you think the responses were? What is your response? How might your classmates respond?

The results were that 58 percent of white people said, "No." In contrast, 24 percent of African Americans answered, "No."

From a cultural perspective, the important issues are how employees live out their approach to diversity and what norms they develop. Cultural beliefs about diversity are deeply embedded in the workplace and may even be taken for granted. Who eats lunch together, who golfs together, who invites one another over to their houses for dinner—in these deep ways, either exclusion or inclusion gets played out. The kinds of jokes that get told, and whether people laugh, are important data from the cultural perspective.

In the following sections, we consider three places in the organization where we see the complexities of diversity from a political and cultural perspective. First, we consider top leadership support for diversity. Second, we consider the grassroots efforts of employees who care about and are affected by diversity programs. Finally, we introduce a new approach—bystander awareness—which encourages you to think about how all employees might take ownership for a culture that values diversity.

Top Leadership Commitment

A key feature of diversity programs is that they are top-down, internally motivated initiatives. In the best examples, these efforts have the personal support of the CEO. They focus on education, awareness, and personal attitudes and behavior. Action strategies include one-on-one mentoring, discussion groups, training programs, and support for and exposure to multicultural events. The tone of these programs and the extent of their success reflect the organizational settings in which they are implemented.

Grassroots Employee Advocacy Groups

Some small groups of concerned employees have taken responsibility for improving their positions in and contributions to their organizations by forming various advocacy or self-help groups, which might be referred to as "networks" or "caucuses." The Black Caucus at Xerox is one of the most well-known and successful examples of this approach. It was created in response to the call from top management for a corporate commitment to social justice. One study finds that the links between top-down espousals of diversity and bottom-up employee efforts to make diversity real are a powerful combination (Scully and Segal, 1997).

Other groups of employees who share a "social identity" (and usually a history of discrimination) have formed networks. It is increasingly common to find a women's group, a Hispanic network, or a gay/lesbian/bisexual/transgender caucus in a corporation. These groups may coordinate their efforts through a Diversity Council, which brings representatives from each group into contact with top managers to address shared and specific concerns. One estimate is that about one-third of *Fortune* 500 corporations have such groups (Friedman and Carter, 1993). These groups are not motivated by any deep distrust of top management or by a rejection of diversity or affirmative action programs, but by the realization that it is up to them to help themselves and to sustain the commitment to diversity over time. Figure 11.3 provides several excerpts that convey these employees' beliefs.

At a recent meeting of high-level executives, nearly an even split occurred over whether such groups have been a positive or negative influence in their organizations. Several managers noted that they valued these groups highly for their networking and mentoring roles and indicated that these groups also helped by sharing responsibility for translating diversity into positive organizational results throughout the organization. They also provided a valuable upward communication channel to educate managers and top-level executives as to the real issues facing employees. In doing so, they helped sustain commitment to achieving further progress. Critics, on the other hand, stated their fear that these groups would proliferate in number, thereby making it difficult to integrate their diverse interests and concerns into coherent organizational policies.

What seemed to distinguish those managers with positive from those with negative experiences with employee advocacy groups was largely the organizational culture in which they were situated. Organizational cultures and top management styles that encouraged participation on a wide range of other matters were comfortable with diversity groups and saw them as adding considerable value to their firms. Those with more centralized, formal decision-making structures and cultures in which top executives managed in a more tightly controlled fashion reported more negative experiences. So, the organizational culture and structures have important effects on the viability, success, or failure of this approach to managing diversity. Once again, we are reminded to consider diversity programs—like any program—not as a stand-alone effort but instead to think holistically about how these programs fit into a broader array of organizational processes.

Bystander Training: A New Method for Broader Involvement

The previous sections discussed how top management and the employees most immediately concerned about diversity can play a role. A deep cultural change, however, requires broader involvement. Even where employees bring different political interests to bear, most want to work in a humanistic and inclusive environment and must learn to work across differences in their work teams in order to be effective.

The everyday issues that set the tone regarding diversity often pop up suddenly—an insensitive

---

Figure 11.3 Grassroots Employee Advocacy Groups

- "We formed because we feel it's important to have a voice, raise issues to senior management and help be proactive in the whole diversity effort."
- "The African-American Caucus evolved with a set of Black individuals coming together and just holding a meeting and saying we need to form an African-American Caucus because we don't feel that these issues are being addressed. To make sure that our agenda is heard and doesn't get swallowed up into this diversity stuff."
- "I see the diversity effort all as having come out of employee initiative, not senior management insight and benevolence . . . that's what gives it life and keeps it alive."
- "Usually there's some grassroots things going on. The people at the top have their heads in the clouds and awareness comes from, 'Oh God, there's an insurgency uprising out there. I mean we should listen to what the peasants are saying.'"
- "My feeling is that there are two routes toward those ends—one is grassroots and the other is sort of HR, top-down. I honestly . . . feel you need the action of grassroots sort of motivated people, who are motivated to make it happen." [Statement of an HR executive]
- "Well, the grassroots efforts that have happened are certainly all a result of people's frustration at things not happening sooner. They want to keep this whole idea out in front of people's faces."
- "I think it's easier for us now to just push—push to let ourselves be known that we're here to help facilitate the diversity effort, we're here to help support, but we're also going to start holding people accountable and to question the motives."

Source: From Maureen Scully and Amy Segal, "Passion with an Umbrella: Grassroots Activists Inside Organizations." Paper presented at the Academy of Management Meetings, Dallas, Texas, August 1994. Reprinted by permission.

comment, an inappropriate joke, a failure to listen to someone who is "different"—and require quick and informal "interventions."

The remaining readings and exercises in this module introduce you to *bystander awareness and skills*, a new approach to enacting diversity in organizations.

A bystander is anyone who is witness to an offensive or inappropriate remark or behavior and faces a choice; is he or she ready, able, and willing to do something about it? One's choices and skills in the moment will set the tone. Will people signal that diversity is valued? Or will they let these moments pass and, perhaps unintentionally, signal that diversity is not a strong, lived value?

What can you do to shape the culture regarding diversity, both as an organizational member and as a manager? The readings present ideas and ways to practice your skills.

Managing Diversity for High Performance

As a manager today, you will face different approaches to managing diversity in your organizations. You are required to comply with legal rules and expected as a responsible citizen to be fair in managing employment relations. Educational programs for valuing diversity and shaping the culture of the workplace will be available to you from outside consultants and often encouraged by senior executives. Employees will speak up individually and sometimes collectively and expect to have input into decisions affecting their work and careers. You will be held accountable for attracting and retaining a diverse workforce and translating diversity into positive performance results. So you will need to apply the tools of the different perspectives presented in the different modules of this book.

Our view of how to meet this challenge grows out of our organizational processes framework and is shared by knowledgeable researchers who have studied the effects of diversity on organizations. Figure 11.4 illustrates how this perspective has been mapped by one research group, the Diversity Research Network, a cross-university and industry consortium that is examining what leading companies are doing to translate diversity into positive business results. As shown in the figure, this group sees increased diversity affecting—and affected by—a wide array of organizational processes. Indeed, research conducted by members of this network in a set of large organizations known to be leaders in managing diversity found no consistent evidence of a direct relationship between either gender or racial diversity and business performance. (Kochan, et al., forthcoming). Instead the net effects of diversity on performance depends on how well teams, business units, and organizational processes respond to increased diversity and the the features of the larger organizational culture and strategies. For example, diverse teams performed better in cultures that stressed cooperation over competition and in settings where, as Thomas and Ely suggested, diversity was seen as an opportunity for integration and learning from each other.

All these findings suggest that the same skills emphasized throughout this book—aligning formal structures and policies to fit task and objectives, managing team dynamics, negotiating, resolving conflicts, assessing culture, and managing change—are also essential to managing diversity. In short, the future of managing diversity lies in working with legal and social pressures and expectations, ensuring that formal human resource and organizational policies are designed and implemented fairly, nurturing a culture that values differences, and supporting and managing self-help groups or caucuses if and when employees choose to form them. By doing so, you will manage in ways that produce the virtuous circle all stakeholders are looking for in organizations today and in the future.

References and Additional Readings

Adler, N. 1997. Global leadership: Women leaders. *Management International Review 37* (Special Issue 1): 171–196.

Adler, N. and Izraeli, D. N. 1994. Where in the World Are the Women Executives? *Business Quarterly* (Autumn): 89–94.

Cox, T. 1993. *Cultural Diversity in Organizations.* San Francisco: Berrett-Koehler Publishers.

DuBois, W. E. B. 1903. *The Souls of Black Folk.* Chicago: A. C. McClurg & Co.

Figure 11.4 Situating Diversity Within Multiple Organizational Processes

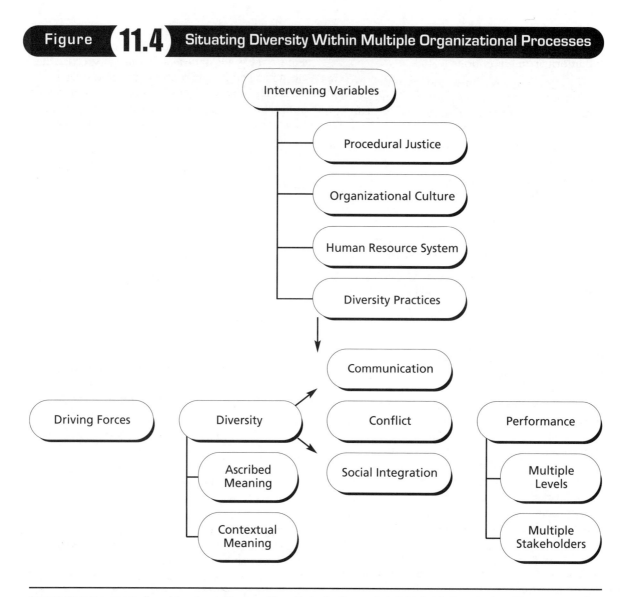

Source: From Maureen Scully and Amy Segal, "Passion with an Umbrella: Grassroots Activists Inside Organizations." Paper presented at the Academy of Management Meetings, Dallas, Texas, August 1994. Reprinted by permission.

DuBois, W. E. B. 1968. *The Gift of Black Folk: The Negros in the Making of America.* New York: Johnson Reprints.

The Glass Ceiling Commission. 1995. "Good for Business: Making Full Use of the Nation's Human Capital." A fact-finding report of the Federal Glass Ceiling Commission, Washington, DC.

Kochan, T., K. Bezrukova, R. Ely, S. Jackson, K. Jehn, A. Joshi, J. Leonard, D. Levine, and D. Thomas. Forthcoming. The Effects of Diversity on Business Performance: Results from the Diversity Research Network. *Human Resource Management Journal.*

Milliken, F., and L. Martins. 1996. Searching for Common Threads: Understanding the Multiple Effects of Diversity in Organizational Groups. *Academy of Management Review* 21, 402–433.

Myrdal, Gunnar. 1962. *The Negro Problem and Modern Democracy* (20th anniversary ed.). New York: Harper and Row.

Offerman, L., and M. Gowing. 1990. Organizations of the Future: Changes and Challenges. *American Psychologist* 45, 95–108.

Richard, O., T. Kochan, and A. McMillan-Capehart. 2002. The Impact of Visible Diversity on Organizational Effectiveness: Disclosing the Contents of Pandora's Box. *Journal of Business and* Management 8(3), 265–291.

Scully, M., and A. Segal. 1997. Passion with an Umbrella: Grassroots Activists in Organizations. Working Paper, MIT Sloan School of Management.

Thomas, D., and R. Ely. 1996. Making Differences Matter: A New Paradigm for Managing Diversity. *Harvard Business Review* (September–October), 79–91.

Williams, K., and C. O'Reilly. 1998. Demography and Diversity: A Review of 40 Years of Research. In B. Staw and R. Sutton (Eds.), *Research in Organizational* Behavior. Greenwich, CT: JAI Press.

Appendix: Composition of U.S. Labor Force

Levels and Percentages for 1990 and 2000; Projections for 2010 (Numbers in thousands)

Group	Level			Percent change		Percent distribution		
	1990	2000	2010	1990–2000	2000–10	1990	2000	2010
Total, 16 years and older	125,840	140,863	157,721	11.9	12.0	100.0	100.0	100.0
Men, Total	69,011	75,247	82,221	9.0	9.3	54.8	53.4	52.1
Women, Total	56,829	65,616	75,500	15.5	15.1	45.2	46.6	47.9
White, Total	107,447	117,574	128,043	9.4	8.9	85.4	83.5	81.2
Black, Total	13,740	16,603	20,041	20.8	20.7	10.9	11.8	12.7
Asian and other, Total*	4,653	6,687	9,636	43.7	44.1	3.7	4.7	6.1
Hispanic origin, Total	10,720	15,368	20,947	43.4	36.3	8.5	10.9	13.3
Other than Hispanic origin, Total	115,120	125,495	136,774	9.0	9.0	91.5	89.1	86.7
White non-Hispanic	97,818	102,963	109,118	5.3	6.0	77.7	73.1	69.2

*The "Asian and other" group includes (1) Asians and Pacific Islanders and (2) American Indians and Alaska Natives.

Note: The historical data are derived by subtracting "black" and "white" from the total; projections are made directly, not by subtraction.

Source: Bureau of Labor Statistics, U.S. Department of Labor, 2002. Visit http://www.bls.gov for additional information on the composition of the U.S. labor force.

Bystander Awareness

Skills for effective managers

A team calls for a break after a productive morning of work. Someone tells an offensive joke. Everyone is silent. A few people laugh quietly but nervously. One or two people may feel the sting of the joke especially sharply. Others worry about what to do and how to get back on track. The team's momentum is broken.

In this scenario, the "bystanders," those who witness offensive talk or inappropriate actions, could play a crucial role in signaling that the group values diversity and that offensive jokes are not appreciated. At best, they can help those who are offended understand that they are not alone and those who have given offense, intentionally or unintentionally, to back up, reconsider, and apologize and perhaps still save face. At least, bystanders can call for a halt and break the downward spiral of tension and misunderstanding that can destroy team cohesion.

Bystanders can uphold norms about the importance of valuing diversity. From the cultural perspective, we recognize the importance of norms in the workplace and the ways in which behavior over time can reinforce or erode a norm. If a norm is deeply held, its violation should provoke reactions. What sense can we make, then, of the silence of the bystanders?

Bystanders may very well appreciate that valuing diversity creates the kind of inclusive and culturally rich work world that they want to inhabit and that it encourages the contribution of talent from all people. They just may not know what to do.

From Valuing Diversity to Taking Action

Valuing diversity is an easy goal to espouse. But how do we practice and realize that goal? Diversity training is quite common in companies in the United States and has helped many organizations to find the "positive spiral" of diversity referenced in the Overview. However, the backlash against diversity training has also been significant. White men complain that they are demonized and misunderstood. Women and people of color complain that they are set up to speak for their entire group or to reveal their difficulties, only to have their candor come back to haunt them when the trainer goes away.

Diversity training too often delivers lectures to would-be "perpetrators," offers assertiveness hints for would-be "victims," or gives legal advice to worried managers. A new, alternative training approach has been designed at the MIT Sloan School of Management. A number of companies and other departments at MIT approached Sloan to learn more about this new approach. Instead of focusing on perpetrators, victims, or managers, it focuses on another crucial and often overlooked party: the bystander. A bystander is anyone who witnesses offensive or unprofessional behavior. With training, bystanders can have the understanding of how norms get shaped as well as the presence of mind and the needed skills to intervene.

It is easy to fall silent in an awkward situation. People rarely have a chance to rehearse how they might intervene effectively in a tense and awkward situation. But the actions of bystanders are often the most crucial for signaling that the norms of respect and inclusivity are to be taken seriously. A norm is empty if no one challenges its violation. Bystanders are concerned parties who take ownership for setting the tone.

The lack of support from bystanders often worsens the strains in work groups. Team members who are upset about mistreatment in a team setting do not just complain about the person who was offensive; they may expect to find "one in every crowd." Instead, the real hurt often comes from the silence of others, which appears as consent or indifference. People who are upset by stinging, prejudicial remarks will say things like "I can't believe no one jumped in to say anything—everyone just sat there," or "I was left out there alone without any support," or "Sure Joe is insensitive, but does everyone else agree?"

Practicing in advance helps bystanders know what to do; the word, gesture, or approach that

---

Acknowledgments: The bystander training program at the MIT Sloan School relied upon the research, expertise, and energy of many people. In particular, thanks for the material that informs this reading go to Laura Moorehead (of Joppa Consulting Partners), Bill Qualls, Rochelle Weichman, and especially Mary Rowe, who has observed the importance of bystanders in her experience as ombudsperson at MIT.

turns around the situation and reinforces a shared commitment to inclusivity and respect.

Historical and Conceptual Background

Research on bystanders comes from a number of areas of social science: the effects on children of watching someone getting hurt in abusive family settings, the motives of Good Samaritans in stopping to help someone in trouble, the reasons why some people join a social movement to improve conditions while others "free ride" on the collective benefits that may result, as a few examples.

Social psychologists in the United States addressed apparent bystander apathy following a disturbing and much-reported event. In 1965, a woman named Kitty Genovese was murdered on a street in New York City at night, while many people from adjacent apartment buildings watched. No one called the police or intervened. Why?

The first reaction of the press and the American public was that New York City was a heartless place and New Yorkers were cold and uncaring. But some researchers thought it was not quite so simple. The witnesses were horrified and upset. What is it that causes bystanders not to react?

They focused on two factors: uncertainty about what to do (people freeze when they do not have a well-rehearsed script in an unfamiliar situation) and diffusion of responsibility (everyone thinks that the situation is so serious that surely someone else, perhaps someone better qualified, will do something).

Other factors may affect bystanders' reluctance. Mary Rowe characterized reasons why complainants do not come forward or request that no further action be taken, reasons that apply as well to bystanders: fear of loss, including the loss of respect, ease, and comradeship with fellow employees; fear of silent disapproval; fear of vulnerability or invaded privacy in speaking from one's personal perspective; the risks of getting in the middle of things; the belief that they lack sufficient information about the situation; and concern they may be overreacting, as a few examples.

These insights about bystanders can be incorporated into diversity training. Bystander inaction can be reduced if people take the following steps:

- Practice some interventions in a safe space so they feel more ready.
- Think through various scenarios in advance.
- Expand their menu of possible responses.
- Understand cultural differences in appropriate interventions.
- Learn from others' experiments and discover new ways to act.
- Take personal ownership for the situation, instead of just sitting back.
- Become self-aware and understand the norms they want to uphold.
- Discuss options with one another and make bystander action more open, expected, and legitimate.

Consider emergency medical technicians who have to respond quickly in crises. They play out many scenarios in their training to gain the "situational awareness" they need to size up what is happening and intervene effectively.

The Bystander in the Workplace

A bystander reacts immediately in the moment. The first step is to be good enough at reading the political and cultural dynamics to know that trouble is brewing. Often the most important thing a bystander can do is just stop the situation from escalating. A simple call for a pause or clarification can help.

A bystander is not charged with dealing justice on the spot. It might be more appropriate to give feedback to individuals at a later time. Calling on institutional resources—such as a mediator or ombudsperson—can help.

To clarify the nature of the bystander, some images of what the bystander is and is not were generated. These descriptors are summarized in Figure 11.5.

The Courage of One's Convictions

Speaking up rather than remaining quiet requires some moral courage. You can speak from your own vantage point, about how uncomfortable the situation is making you or about your concern that the tone does not reflect the kind of organization in which you want to work. Or you can speak on behalf of another, which is more complex. In general, it is best to intervene just enough to let others have the chance to speak for themselves.

Speaking on behalf of another requires:

- *Tactfulness.* Quite simply, a bystander should not drown out or embarrass the person they're supporting or make them feel helpless or pathetic by jumping in too strongly.
- *Willingness to take risks.* Group backlash against the bystander is possible. Bystanders can become the target of the escalating anger in the group. They might be called "Pollyanna" or "bleeding heart liberal" or "knight in shining armor." They might be asked, "Who are you to say?" A bystander has to be prepared to take some heat.

Figure 11.5 What a Bystander Is and Is Not

A Bystander Is . . .

Witness	Observer	Onlooker	Eavesdropper
Concerned Party	Stakeholder		Advocate
Listener	Colleague	Peer	Audience
Mediator	Helper		Friend
Facilitator	Peacemaker	Humble Questioner	Learner

A Bystander Is *Not* . . .

Judge	Avenger	Enforcer	Fixer	Know-It-All
Rescuer	Hero/Heroine		Final Authority	

- *Awareness of one's own power or privilege.* Diversity training tends to focus on the experience of disadvantage by people who occupy solo roles in a group (e.g., the only older person in a young start-up) or who belong to historically oppressed social groups (e.g., African Americans in the United States). A true understanding of diversity adds the dynamics of privilege (what does it mean to be one of the "young fast-trackers"? What does it mean to be white in the United States?). It is emotionally exhausting for people in disadvantaged positions to keep presenting their perspective and advocating for their rights. Members of a privileged group can develop a sense of empathy and spend some of their "political capital" to speak out when they see injustice. It is powerful when white people speak out against racism, when men speak out against sexism, and when straight people speak out against homophobia.

Given the delicacy and risks, why should bystanders do anything? Aren't they giving away more than they're getting? Are the costs too great?

One benefit of playing an active bystander role is that you get to help create the kind of climate that you want in your organization and of which you may someday be a beneficiary. You can crystallize norms by exemplifying and defending them. Some bystanders who have taken heat from others say it is worth it to be true to themselves and what they believe. Another benefit is that you can demonstrate your group dynamics skills, which are increasingly listed as a factor in performance appraisals.

Collusion

Despite the advantages of playing an active bystander role, sometimes it is reasonable not to jump in. What are the costs and benefits of silence? One cost is a feeling of collusion with the offense. For example, sometimes women laugh at sexist jokes to signal that they're good sports, but afterwards they may wonder if they're just perpetuating a negative climate of sexism.

At the same time, some benefits may come from holding back. Sometimes it is necessary to "pick one's battles." Timing is important; waiting for "teachable moments" can make an important point. Speaking out too much can dilute one's message.

Another benefit of not speaking out in the moment is that sometimes it is best to pull people aside afterwards, to reduce embarrassment and wait until tempers cool to the point at which feedback can be heard and absorbed.

Cultural Variation in Intervention Styles

Whether bystanders act in the moment or wait, both the style and content of the intervention must be considered in cultural context. Cultures vary, for example, on one of the most delicate questions of intervention: whether to reprimand someone else's children when you see them misbehaving. It might be considered out of line to say something in one culture, or negligent *not* to say anything in another culture.

Survey your team members to see what kinds of interventions might work or fail in the countries or companies they come from. For example, is it better to stand up and leave than to say something? Is that considered dignified? Or would it be considered rude and awkward?

Bystanders just throw fuel on the fire if they fight one stereotype by invoking another. For example, a bystander intervenes on behalf of a woman on a team by saying, "You men from <wherever> are all so chauvinistic!" and potentially makes the situation worse.

Ideas for Bystanders

Some general types of interventions suggested by a range of participants in bystander training sessions are summarized in Figure 11.6.

Structural Solutions

The bystander's role during or just after an incident is important and can help shape cultural norms. However, it is an *ad hoc* response to issues that often require structural solutions. A successful bystander will interrupt unprofessional behavior, but systems must be in place that backup the norms and provide any subsequent support or

Figure 11.6 Some Tactics for Bystanders: Ideas from Workshop Participants

Inclusion:
Invite someone into the conversation
Solicit the opinions of people who have been quiet
Be an ally for someone taking a risk
Be gracious, help others save face

Discovery:
Ask questions
Give people a chance to clarify
Check assumptions
Consider the big picture, the broader context

Cooling things down:
Ask for a break
Use humor (but with care)
Suggest next steps, another meeting, off-line conversations

Heating things up:
Surface emotions
Say how the situation makes you feel
Point to the "unspeakable" issues that may be lurking

Body language/signaling:
Stand up
Turn away
Raise your hand
Bang the table
Say "ouch"
Laugh
Leave the room

action needed to prevent future incidents. Some examples of structural solutions, at both the local and corporate level, include the following:

- An organizational policy on harassment, distributed to everyone, periodically reviewed, systematically enforced
- A third party (mediator, ombudsperson, employee advocate) who can counsel individuals or groups, whose services are supported and publicized, and who keeps track of aggregate data on incidents
- Clear policies governing promotions, a mentoring program, and a review board that keeps track of who is promoted (or not) and why
- Regular sessions to discuss and consider the alternative ways in which people from different cultural backgrounds might approach the process and product of work (especially helpful for breaking free of taken-for-granted assumptions and "thinking outside the box")
- Training sessions on a variety of issues, such as giving culturally sensitive feedback, curbing sexual harassment, and recognizing different leadership styles.
- Celebrations of diversity, to recognize accomplishments and best practices from different teams or departments, to celebrate different heritages (e.g., a speaker or film during Black History Month in February)

Structural solutions should align with the organizational vision of how to embrace diversity. Organizations that plan to fundamentally reshape how work is done, based on more diverse inputs, will need more innovative structures to support that approach. Figure 11.7 shows an evolution of three approaches.

A Closing Thought

Jewish tradition gives us a Talmudic story that is relevant:

In the book of Proverbs, King Solomon said:
"A tongue can bring either life or death."
(Proverbs 18:21)

Why is a tongue mightier than a sword?
A sword can only kill one person at a time.
Hurtful words kill three people at once:
They hurt the one about whom they are spoken.
They hurt the one who said them.
They hurt the one who listened to them.
(Bereshit Rabbah 98)

Figure 11.7 Three Paradigms for Managing Diversity

Paradigm 1	*Paradigm 2*	*Emerging Paradigm 3*
Discrimination and Fairness	**Access and Legitimacy**	**Connecting Diversity to Work Perspectives**
Philosophy:		
Tolerate differences	Value differences	Learn from differences
Rationale:		
Increase numbers	Access market niches	Work in new ways
Sample action:		
Mentoring program	Employee networks	New processes

Source: David Thomas and Robin Ely. 1996. Making Differences Matter. *Harvard Business Review* (September–October).

Bystander Scenarios

What would you do?

This exercise describes eight scenarios (outlined in Figure 11.8) in which a bystander might want to take action. The scenarios have been videotaped. The videos feature real personnel, from the management department of a major university, role-playing the different parts. All the scenarios are based on real incidents that people from the school contributed. In this exercise, you read a brief introduction to each scenario, then view the videotape. A few questions are included for you to think about as you view the videotape. Note that your instructor might ask you to view the videotape as a basis for discussion, either in your class or within a team. You might also be asked to make up, and even to videotape, some scenarios of your own, based upon your own experiences and using the already-filmed scenarios as models.

In each scenario video, you will see three to five individuals in settings that should be familiar to you from everyday life in the university and in the workplace. You will notice a bystander (or two) who might remain silent or who might step in and try to do or say something.

Each of these scenarios has one to four "takes." Typically in Take One, the scene is set. Some offensive remark or behavior escalates unchecked. In subsequent takes, various more-or-less effective styles and strategies for bystanders are role-played. You can consider which of these strategies you like, as well as other approaches that you might try in a similar situation. In some cases, all the action happens in one take. (*Take Note!* The "actors" are role-playing. Their behaviors and remarks DO NOT reflect their real identities or beliefs.)

The actors, in discussions before each role play, agreed who would act—or overreact—in different ways and then they let the role play unfold improvisationally. The scenarios were not scripted. They allowed for some spontaneity. As a result, you'll hear some laughing sometimes at the end of a scenario, as the actors react to a surprising turn in the scene or just let out their nervous energy. The laughter is retained in the final edit, because it shows how intense, but enlightening, it was to do the role-playing. All the actors were incredibly good sports and willing to experiment and take risks. In our editing, we purposely left a bit of raw "MTV" feeling, which we think makes the scenarios more real and fun. You'll see the actors warm up a bit, hear the countdown, see the actual take, hear the "cut" instruction, and then some quips and unwinding.

As you read about the scenarios and watch the videotapes, be thinking at two levels. First of all, as a participant on a team or in an organization, you might encounter situations in which you could be an effective bystander. Think about approaches that might be comfortable for you.

Second, as a manager, you will need to find ways to signal to your employees that diversity is valued and to teach them the skills they need to advocate effectively for diversity. Being a bystander is one such way that employees can help uphold norms about diversity that you would like to see reinforced. These scenarios were used for training workshops at the university where they were created and were generally received quite positively. A mix of faculty, students, administrators, and staff

Figure 11.8 Eight Scenarios of Bystander Actions

Scenario Name	Some Dimensions of Diversity That Are Addressed
1. Introducing the Invisible Colleague	gender
2. Is It Really About Race?	race
3. The Awkward Invitation	sexual orientation
4. Is It the Nature of the Project?	nationality, language
5. Counting on a Colleague	invisible disability
6. I Was Just Trying to Be Sensitive	nationality, language, gender
7. You Just Weren't Listening	nationality, language, status
8. The Stapler	class/status/hierarchical level

participated in the training, and many commented on the special opportunity to discuss diversity issues with a mix of people from different positions and levels. The focus on everyday skills provided participants a way to really relate to the issues. A number of other universities and companies have become interested in these bystander training materials. As a manager, what kind of training programs will you sponsor?

In the videotape that accompanies this module, the eight scenarios address many dimensions of diversity. Your instructor might have you view all or just a few.

Scenario 1: Introducing the Invisible Colleague

Role Players: Gil, Ph.D. student
Jean, MBA student
Jim, MBA program administrator
Nils, Ph.D. student

Synopsis

A recruiter approaches a group of three students, two men and a woman. He pays attention only to the two men, even though the woman has the most interest in the company and the most relevant experience. How will she join the conversation?

Take One:

Jean, Gil, and Nils talk about the company presentation they just heard from Jim. Nils and Gil are lukewarm about it, confused about the issues, not really interested. Jean is clear, has experience in the area, and very interested. This information is an important setup for their differential treatment by Jim. Jim approaches the group and pays attention to Gil and Nils, while ignoring the enthusiastic Jean.

Gil interrupts Jean as she begins to ask questions of the recruiter. Nils takes Gil's lead to jump in with questions. Jean is rendered invisible to Jim as the men's excitement and enthusiasm develops.

Jean manages to give Jim her business card, but has not had a chance to talk about herself, so Jim pays no attention to her. Although he acknowledges that the two men don't have the background, he devotes his time and attention to them as potential candidates. Jean becomes increasingly frustrated.

Discussion Questions

- What are the issues here?
- Who stands to gain or lose?
- How is Jean responding to being rendered invisible? What other responses might we have seen in this situation?

Take Two:

In this replay of the situation, Nils tries to bring Jim's attention to Jean, however awkwardly. Gil takes over by asking about "Clone Corp.," the (fictitious) company where Jean had spent a summer. Nils is prodded by Jean to introduce her, and he does so by touching her shoulder and saying awkwardly, "She also has some background," but not introducing Jean by name. Jim is not interested yet.

Take Three:

Nils now recognizes that Jean should be in the conversation and does what he can to have Jim speak with Jean, rather than focus on Gil and Nils.

Take Four:

This time, Nils tries to tell Jim about Jean's experience, but Gil interrupts. Jean intervenes by suggesting that they all introduce themselves first as a way to be inclusive.

Discussion Questions

- What seemed like the best option among the multiple "takes"? Why?
- How did it feel when Jean was able to intervene successfully for herself? What does this take say for the role the bystander can play? What does it feel like when it doesn't happen?

Scenario 2: Is It Really About Race?

Role Players: Fred, Mid-career program student
John, MBA student
Wendy, Ph.D. student

Synopsis

Three students are discussing a class they've just attended. John is enthusiastic. Fred is less so, explaining that the problem with the class was that all the cases of business failures were about African American–owned businesses. He fears this pattern reinforces negative stereotypes about blacks in business. He wants to have a discussion about how race is a factor, but the others shut down the topic.

In the first take, Wendy is silent. In the second take, she jumps in and agrees that the choice of cases is a problem. In the third take, John and Wendy reverse roles.

Take One:

John is very excited about the class, and is unwilling to accept that Fred has a differing opinion. John denies vigorously that race is a factor and attempts to argue Fred out of his opinion. Fred quietly asserts himself, trying different ways to get through to John, but ends up discouraged. Wendy remains silent.

Discussion Questions

- What's going on for Fred?
- How could Fred have shifted the conversation?
- Is Wendy's silence awkward? Why?
- What strategies is John using?

Take Two:

Wendy now nods her head in agreement with Fred and joins in the discussion. With her support, Fred shows more energy. Their nonverbal cues and the rhythm of their conversation show connection and support.

Discussion Questions

- What does it mean for a bystander to be an ally versus taking over?

Take Three:

In this replay of the situation, Wendy and John switch roles. Now, Wendy is the person who is resistant to Fred's opinion, and John intervenes. Wendy struggles to find a reason why the professor may have selected these cases, as an alternative to the possibility that race is a factor. John supports Fred's disappointment, using a logical argument rather than responding to the emotion behind Fred's experience. Wendy comes around, Fred begins to take an educational stance, and John suggests they talk with the professor about the issue. The group moves to a proactive and collective action plan.

Discussion Questions

- How do the strategies of the two bystanders differ?
- Are there some gender dynamics that distinguish the bystander approaches in takes two and three?
- Why do white people seek attributions other than race when such incidents happen?

Scenario 3: The Awkward Invitation

Role Players: Jean, MBA student
                John, MBA student
                Maureen, professor
                Nils, Ph.D. student

Synopsis

The research team is having a final meeting after a successful presentation. The professor proposes a celebratory dinner. She invites people to bring their spouses, boyfriends, or girlfriends. The students all know that John would want to bring his partner, Mike, and they try to help him let the professor know about his partner, while also trying to help her recover from her awkwardness.

Take One:

The professor is very enthusiastic about her idea, and misinterprets John's reluctance to join them for dinner. Jean tries to provide an alternative for the group, that the four of them go to lunch instead.

Discussion Questions

- What is the dimension of diversity here?
- What is John's strategy? Why is Jean evasive?

Take Two:

Here Nils and Jean attempt casually to let the professor know about Mike, by telling her why she'll enjoy meeting him, and by speaking in glowing terms about him. However, they aren't direct, and because the professor is unprepared, she stumbles and is confused until John explains that Mike is his partner.

Discussion Questions

- What do the bystanders do? What is the effect of having two people share a bystander role?

Take Three:

In this take, Nils talks about Mike. The professor catches on quickly and bluntly blurts, "Oh, you're gay. . . ." She proceeds to make light of it, saying it's "no problem." However, she is so awkward that everyone becomes uncomfortable.

Discussion Questions

- What options do they have to reduce the awkwardness in the room?

Notice how the professor's preemptive assertion that there's no problem (when she clearly has one) makes it hard to find a wedge into the discussion.

Scenario 4: Is It the Nature of the Project?

Role Players: Benjamin (Yoong Il), MBA student
                Hyun, Ph.D. student
                Michael, professor
                Roy, MBA student
                Stephen, MBA student

Synopsis

The professor is concerned about the Staples team project. He has asked the team to meet with him after reading the last progress report. He asks what is going on, turning to the white, American men to respond first. Roy begins by complaining about Benjamin and Hyun's activities on the project. Stephen attempts to bring in another, more balanced perspective. The professor listens closely.

Hyun defends their contribution and says that the problem is that Stephen and Roy run the show without eliciting input from Benjamin and him. When Benjamin gets a chance to speak, he responds to Roy and Stephen's concerns, proposing that they try to understand the time pressure. He suggests that this dilemma may be less about culture differences than about the nature of the project. He proposes that they slow down and try to understand each other's strengths and weaknesses, and that they in essence "retreat from battle for awhile" to do so.

Stephen agrees to Benjamin's proposal. Roy goes along, but does not respond enthusiastically. The professor says to Roy, "Well, you say 'sure', but do you mean 'sure'?" Roy is unable to explain himself.

(*Note:* The layers of issues and the shifting bystander roles here are somewhat more complex than in preceding scenarios, but representative of the dynamics of cross-cultural teams at school and in the workplace.)

Discussion Questions

- Who plays the roles of the bystanders in this scenario? How do they intervene, and how are they effective?
- What types of effective mediation skills does the professor use?
- What else could the professor have done in this role? Does having a position of authority help or hinder a bystander?
- Where did you see cultural insensitivities?

Scenario 5: Counting on a Colleague

Role Players: Maura, career office administrator
Maureen, professor
Meg, marketing administrator

Synopsis

Maura, Meg, and Maureen are planning the logistics for a student educational trip to Cuba over spring break. All the details are in order, except for the concern that Maura has just raised. It seems that the co-leader, Josephine, has told Maura that she has epilepsy. Maura is unsettled about Josephine's ability to successfully lead the trip without a medical emergency.

Take One:

The discussion, starting with a straightforward concern, escalates. Their conversation conveys all their fantasies and fears about the trip being much more difficult to manage because of Josephine, not to mention that she might embarrass them in a public place or on a company visit. No one halts the heaping up of stereotypes.

Discussion Questions

- What are the issues here?
- Does Josephine have a responsibility to tell Maura, Meg, and Maureen?

Take Two:

Meg intervenes effectively, but Maura and Maureen nonetheless gang up on her for being sentimental and impractical. Meg experiences backlash against her intervention as a bystander.

Discussions Questions

- What are some of the risks for a bystander? How can they be handled?

Take Three:

Meg brings a sense of calm and logic to the conversation, in spite of the resistance, helping them understand how they can manage their concerns. The group resolves to talk to Josephine and hear her concerns directly.

Discussion Questions

- What works about Meg's intervention?
- How will the group rebuild its trust of Josephine?

Scenario 6: I Was Just Trying to Be Sensitive!

Role Players: Danielle, MBA student
Karen, Master's program administrator
Ken, Master's program staff member
Miguel, MBA student

Synopsis

The planning for the students' educational trip to Japan trip is going well. As they work into the evening on the final details, Miguel expresses concern that Danielle may need to leave, hinting at family obligations. With his question, the team interactions become stormy and confusing. Danielle is offended by Miguel's question, attributing his comments to chauvinism ("It's just like you Latin Americans. . . ."). Ken attempts to assist Miguel, but cannot quite turn the conversation around and adds new issues. Karen and Danielle resort to sarcasm to express their anger, exacerbating Miguel's embarrassment and confusion. Miguel, who was "just trying to be sensitive," doesn't understand their reactions, but apologizes.

Discussion Questions

- What are the various cross-cultural issues that arise?
- What was Miguel's intent?
- How might Danielle have reacted differently?
- What role does Karen play in the scenario?
- What about Ken's attempt to intervene as a bystander?
- Danielle suggests they "get back to work"—is this move possible at this point?

Scenario 7: You Just Weren't Listening

Role Players: Benjamin (Yoong Il), MBA student
Devra, MBA student
Hyun, Ph.D. student
Pete, professor
Stephen, MBA student

Synopsis

Devra and her team are meeting with their professor to convey the team's confusion about an accounting problem they are working on together. Benjamin attempts to clarify how they should be thinking about the problem, but the professor does not respond to him. Instead, he asks Stephen to translate ("Is that what he said?"). When Stephen repeats the same message, Benjamin insists that that was what he was saying. The professor responds by saying, "I didn't hear that." Benjamin tries to save face by muttering, "OK, sometimes that happens."

Discussion Questions

- Was Benjamin unclear? What was in the way of the professor's hearing Benjamin?
- Who took the bystander role?
- Why might Hyun have chosen not to intervene for Benjamin?
- How do you suppose Benjamin was feeling when he said, "OK, sometimes that happens"?

Scenario 8: The Stapler

Role Players: Molly, MBA program staff member
Stephen, MBA student
Tony, MBA program staff member

Synopsis

Molly and Tony are working on a scheduling issue, when Stephen, an MBA student shows up requesting to use Tony's stapler, a typical interruption in a day in the life of an administrative assistant. Stephen feels overworked and is anxious to get his paper turned in on time. Molly and Tony have a long list of tasks to handle that day.

Take One:

The interaction gets out of hand as the frustration level rises for everyone. How might it have been different if there had been another, less involved person who was willing to mediate?

Discussion Questions

- Have you seen this situation happen? What are the issues?

Take Two:

Molly intervenes, attempting to get Stephen to calm down and understand what might be happening for Tony. When Tony explains how he has to do his job, Stephen is more willing to step back and wait.

Discussion Questions

- In what ways did Molly successfully stop the interaction from spiraling further out of control?
- In what ways are class and power asserted?

Managing Cultural Diversity

ELECTIVE

Module 11

Making Differences Matter

A new paradigm for managing diversity

by David A. Thomas and Robin J. Ely

What will it take for organizations to reap the real and full benefits of a diverse workforce? A radically new understanding of the term, for starters.

Why should companies concern themselves with diversity? Until recently, many managers answered this question with the assertion that discrimination is wrong, both legally and morally. But today managers are voicing a second notion as well. A more diverse workforce, they say, will increase organizational effectiveness. It will lift morale, bring greater access to new segments of the marketplace, and enhance productivity. In short, they claim, diversity will be good for business.

Yet if this is true—and we believe it is—where are the positive impacts of diversity? Numerous and varied initiatives to increase diversity in corporate America have been under way for more than two decades. Rarely, however, have those efforts spurred leaps in organizational effectiveness. Instead, many attempts to increase diversity in the workplace have backfired, sometimes even heightening tensions among employees and hindering a company's performance.

This article offers an explanation for why diversity efforts are not fulfilling their promise and presents a new paradigm for understanding—and leveraging—diversity. It is our belief that there is a distinct way to unleash the powerful benefits of a diverse workforce. Although these benefits include increased profitability, they go beyond financial measures to encompass learning, creativity, flexibility, organizational and individual growth, and the ability of a company to adjust rapidly and successfully to market changes. The desired transformation, however, requires a fundamental change in the attitudes and behaviors of an organization's leadership. And that will come only when senior managers abandon an underlying and flawed assumption about diversity and replace it with a broader understanding.

Most people assume that workplace diversity is about increasing racial, national, gender, or class representation—in other words, recruiting and retaining more people from traditionally underrepresented "identity groups." Taking this commonly held assumption as a starting point, we set out six years ago to investigate its link to organizational effectiveness. We soon found that thinking of diversity simply in terms of identity-group representation inhibited effectiveness.

Organizations usually take one of two paths in managing diversity. In the name of equality and fairness, they encourage (and expect) women and people of color to blend in. Or they set them apart in jobs that relate specifically to their backgrounds, assigning them, for example, to areas that require them to interface with clients or customers of the same identity group. African American M.B.A.'s often find themselves marketing products to inner-city communities; Hispanics frequently market to Hispanics or work for Latin American subsidiaries. In those kinds of cases, companies are operating on the assumption that the main virtue of identity groups have to offer is a knowledge of their own people. This assumption is limited—and limiting—and detrimental to diversity efforts.

What we suggest here is that diversity goes beyond increasing the number of different identity-group affiliations on the payroll to recognizing that such an effort is merely the first step in managing a diverse workforce for the organization's utmost benefit. Diversity should be understood as the *varied perspectives and approaches to work* that members of different identity groups bring.

Women, Hispanics, Asian Americans, African Americans, Native Americans—these groups and others outside the mainstream of corporate America don't bring with them just their "insider information." They bring different, important, and competitively relevant knowledge and perspectives about how to actually *do work*—how to design processes, reach goals, frame tasks, create effective

---

Source: Reprinted by permission of *Harvard Business Review*, "Making Differences Matter: A New Paradigm for Managing Diversity," by David A. Thomas and Robin J. Ely, *Harvard Business Review*, September–October 1996. Copyright © 1996 by the Harvard Business School Publishing Corporation; all rights reserved. **David A. Thomas** is an associate professor at the Harvard Business School in Boston, Massachusetts. **Robin J. Ely** is an associate professor at Columbia University's School of International and Public Affairs in New York City. Their research and teaching focus on the influence of race, gender, and ethnicity on career dynamics and organizational effectiveness.

teams, communicate ideas, and lead. When allowed to, members of these groups can help companies grow and improve by challenging basic assumptions about an organization's functions, strategies, operations, practices, and procedures. And in doing so, they are able to bring more of their whole selves to the workplace and identify more fully with the work they do, setting in motion a virtuous circle. Certainly, individuals can be expected to contribute a company their first-hand familiarity with niche markets. But only when companies start thinking about diversity more holistically—as providing fresh and meaningful approaches to work—and stop assuming that diversity relates simply to how a person looks or where he or she comes from, will they be able to reap its full rewards.

Two perspectives have guided most diversity initiatives to date: the *discrimination-and-fairness paradigm* and the *access-and-legitimacy paradigm*. But we have identified a new, emerging approach to this complex management issue. This approach, which we will call the *learning-and-effectiveness paradigm,* incorporates aspects of the first two paradigms but goes beyond them by concretely connecting diversity to approaches to work. Our goal is to help business leaders see what their own approach to diversity currently is and how it may already have influenced their companies' diversity efforts. Managers can learn to assess whether they need to change their diversity initiatives and, if so, how to accomplish that change.

The following discussion will also cite several examples of how connecting the new definition of diversity to the actual *doing* of work has led some organizations to markedly better performance. The organizations differ in many ways—none are in the same industry, for instance—but they are united in one similarity: Their leaders realize that increasing demographic variation does not in itself increase organizational effectiveness. They realize that it is *how* a company defines diversity—and *what it does* with the experiences of being a diverse organization—that delivers on that promise.

The Discrimination-and-Fairness Paradigm

Using the discrimination-and-fairness paradigm is perhaps thus far the dominant way of understanding diversity. Leaders who look at diversity through this lens usually focus on equal opportunity, fair treatment, recruitment, and compliance with federal Equal Employment Opportunity requirements. The paradigm's underlying logic can be expressed as follows:

Prejudice has kept members of certain demographic groups out of organizations such as ours. As a matter of fairness to comply with federal mandates, we need to work toward restructuring the makeup of our organization to let it more closely reflect that of society. We need managerial processes that ensure that all our employees are treated equally and with respect and that some are not given unfair advantage over others.

Although it resembles the thinking behind traditional affirmative-action efforts, the discrimination-and-fairness paradigm does go beyond a simple concern with numbers. Companies that operate with this philosophical orientation often institute mentoring and career-development programs specifically for the women and people of color in their ranks and train other employees to respect cultural differences. Under this paradigm, nevertheless, progress in diversity is measured by how well the company achieves its recruitment and retention goals rather than by the degree to which conditions in the company allow employees to draw on their personal assets and perspectives to do their work more effectively. The staff, one might say, gets diversified, but the work does not.

What are some of the common characteristics of companies that have used the discrimination-and-fairness paradigm successfully to increase their demographic diversity? Our research indicates that they are usually run by leaders who value due process and equal treatment of all employees and who have the authority to use top-down directives to enforce initiatives based on those attitudes. Such companies are often bureaucratic in structure, with control processes in place for monitoring, measuring, and rewarding individual performance. And finally, they are often organizations with entrenched, easily observable cultures, in which values like fairness are widespread and deeply inculcated and codes of conduct are clear and unambiguous. (Perhaps the most extreme example of an organization in which all these factors are at work is the United States Army.)

Without doubt, there are benefits to this paradigm: it does tend to increase demographic diversity in an organization, and it often succeeds in promoting fair treatment. But it also has significant limitations. The first of these is that its color-blind, gender-blind, ideal is to some degree built on the implicit assumption that "we are all the same" or "we aspire to being all the same." Under this paradigm, it is not desirable for diversification of the workforce to influence the organization's work or culture. The company should operate as if every person were of the same race, gender, and nationality. It is unlikely that leaders who manage diversity under this paradigm will explore how people's differences generate a potential diversity of effective ways of working, leading, viewing the market, managing people, and learning.

Not only does the discrimination-and-fairness paradigm insist that everyone is the same, but, with its emphasis on equal treatment, it puts pressure on employees to make sure that important differences among them do not count. Genuine disagreements about work definition, therefore, are sometimes wrongly interpreted through this paradigm's fairness-unfairness lens—especially when honest disagreements are accompanied by tense debate. A female employee who insists, for example, that a company's advertising strategy is not appropriate for all ethnic segments in the marketplace might feel she is violating the code of assimilation upon which the paradigm is built. Moreover, if she were then to defend her opinion by citing, let us say, her personal knowledge of the ethnic group the company wanted to reach, she might risk being perceived as importing inappropriate attitudes into an organization that prides itself on being blind to cultural differences.

Workplace paradigms channel organizational thinking in powerful ways. By limiting the ability of employees to acknowledge openly their work-related but culturally based differences, the paradigm actually undermines the organization's capacity to learn about and improve its own strategies, processes, and practices. And it also keeps people from identifying strongly and personally with their work—a critical source of motivation and self-regulation in any business environment.

As an illustration of the paradigm's weaknesses, consider the case of Iversen Dunham, an international consulting firm that focuses on foreign and domestic economic-development policy. (Like all the examples in this article, the company is real, but its name is disguised.) Not long ago, the firm's managers asked us to help them understand why race relations had become a divisive issue precisely at a time when Iversen was receiving accolades for its diversity efforts. Indeed, other organizations had even begun to use the firm to benchmark their own diversity programs.

Iversen's diversity efforts had begun in the early 1970s, when senior managers decided to pursue greater racial and gender diversity in the firm's higher ranks. (The firm's leaders were strongly committed to the cause of social justice.) Women and people of color were hired and charted on career paths toward becoming project leaders. High performers among those who had left the firm were persuaded to return in senior roles. By 1989, about 50% of Iversen's project leaders and professionals were women, and 30% were people of color. The 13-member management committee, once exclusively white and male, included five women and four people of color. Additionally, Iversen had developed a strong contingent of foreign nationals.

It was at about this time, however, that tensions began to surface. Senior managers found it hard to believe that, after all the effort to create a fair and mutually respectful work community, some staff members could still be claiming that Iversen had racial discrimination problems. The management invited us to study the firm and deliver an outsider's assessment of its problem.

We had been inside the firm only a short time when it became clear that Iversen's leaders viewed the dynamics of diversity through the lens of the discrimination-and-fairness paradigm. But where they saw racial discord, we discerned clashing approaches to the actual work of consulting. Why? Our research showed that tensions were strongest among midlevel project leaders. Surveys and interviews indicated that white project leaders welcomed demographic diversity as a general sign of progress but that they also thought the new employees were somehow changing the company, pulling it away from its original culture and its mission. Common criticisms were that African American and Hispanic staff made problems too complex by linking issues the organization had traditionally regarded as unrelated and that they brought on projects that seemed to require greater cultural sensitivity. White male project leaders also complained that their peers who were women and people of color were undermining one of Iversen's traditional strengths: its hard-core quantitative orientation. For instance, minority project leaders had suggested that Iversen consultants collect information and seek input from others in the client company besides senior managers—that is, from the rank and file and from middle managers. Some had urged Iversen to expand its consulting approach to include the gathering and analysis of qualitative data through interviewing and observation. Indeed, these project leaders had even challenged one of Iversen's long-standing, core assumptions: that the firm's reports were objective. They urged Iversen Dunham to recognize and address the subjective aspect of its analyses; the firm could, for example, include in its reports to clients dissenting Iversen views, if any existed.

For their part, project leaders who were women and people of color felt that they were not accorded the same level of authority to carry out that work as their white male peers. Moreover, they sensed that those peers were skeptical of their opinions, and they resented that doubts were not voiced openly.

Meanwhile, there also was some concern expressed about tension between white managers and nonwhite subordinates, who claimed they were being treated unfairly. But our analysis suggested that the manager-subordinate conflicts were not numerous enough to warrant the attention they were drawing from top management. We believed it was significant that senior managers found it easier to focus on this second type of conflict than on mid-level conflicts about project choice definition. Indeed, Iversen Dunham's focus seemed to be a result of the firm's reliance on its particular diversity paradigm and the emphasis on fairness and equality. It was relatively easy to diagnose problems in light of those concepts and to devise a solution: just get managers to treat their subordinates more fairly.

In contrast, it was difficult to diagnose peer-to-peer tensions in the framework of this model. such conflicts were about the very nature of Iversen's work, not simply unfair treatment. Yes, they were related to identity-group affiliations, but they were not symptomatic of classic racism. It was Iversen's paradigm that led managers to interpret them as such. Remember, we were asked to assess what was supposed to be a racial discrimination problem. Iversen's discrimination-and-fairness paradigm had created a kind of cognitive blind spot; and, as a result, the company's leadership could not frame the problems accurately or solve it effectively. Instead, the company needed a cultural shift—needed to grasp what to do with its diversity once it had achieved the numbers. If all Iversen Dunham employees were to contribute to the fullest extent, the company would need a paradigm that would encourage open and explicit discussion of what identity-group differences really mean and how they can be used as sources of individual and organizational effectiveness.

Today, mainly because of senior managers' resistance to such cultural transformation, Iversen continues to struggle with the tensions arising from the diversity of its workforce.

The Access-and-Legitimacy Paradigm

In the competitive climate of of the 1980s and 1990s, a new rhetoric and rationale for managing diversity emerged. If the discrimination-and-fairness paradigm can be said to have idealized assimilation and color- and gender-blind conformism, the access-and-legitimacy paradigm was predicated on the acceptance and celebration of differences. The underlying motivation of the access-and-legitimacy paradigm can be expressed this way:

> *We are living in an increasingly multicultural country, and new ethnic groups are quickly gaining consumer power. Our company needs a demographically more diverse workforce to help us gain access to these differentiated segments. We need employees with multilingual skills in order to understand and serve our customers better and to gain legitimacy with them. Diversity isn't just fair; it makes business sense.*

Where this paradigm has taken hold, organizations have pushed for access to—and legitimacy with—a more diverse clientele by matching the demographics of the organization to those of critical consumer and constituent groups. In some cases, the effort has led to substantial increases in organizational diversity. In investment banks, for example, municipal finance departments have long led corporate finance departments in pursuing demographic diversity because of the typical makeup of the administration of city halls and county boards. Many consumer-products companies that have used market segmentation based on gender, racial, and other demographic differences have also frequently created dedicated marketing positions for each segment. The paradigm has therefore led to new professional and managerial opportunities for women and people of color.

What are the common characteristics of organizations that have successfully used the access-and-legitimacy paradigm to increase their demographic diversity? There is but one: such companies almost always operate in a business environment in which there is increased diversity among customers, clients, or the labor pool—and therefore a clear opportunity or an imminent threat to the company.

Again, the paradigm has its strengths. Its market-based motivation and the potential for competitive advantage that it suggests are often qualities an entire company can understand and therefore support. But the paradigm is perhaps more notable for its limitations. In their pursuit of niche markets, access-and-legitimacy organizations tend to emphasize the role of cultural differences in a company without really analyzing those differences to see how they actually affect the work that is done. Whereas discrimination-and-fairness leaders are too quick to subvert differences in the interest of preserving harmony, access-and-legitimacy leaders are too quick to push staff with niche capabilities into differentiated pigeonholes without trying to understand what those capabilities really are and how they could be integrated into the company's mainstream work. To illustrate our point, we present the case of Access Capital.

Access Capital International is a U.S. investment bank that in the early 1980s launched an aggressive plan to expand into Europe. Initially, however, Access encountered serious problems opening offices in international markets; the people from the United States who were installed abroad lacked credibility, were ignorant of local cultural norms and market conditions, and simply couldn't seem to connect with native clients. Access responded by hiring Europeans who had attended North American business schools and by assigning them in teams to the foreign offices. This strategy was a marked success. Before long, the leaders of Access could take enormous pride in the fact that their European operations were highly profitable and staffed by a truly international corps of professionals. They took to calling the company "the best investment bank in the world."

Several years passed. Access's foreign offices continued to thrive, but some leaders were beginning to sense that the company was not fully benefitting from its diversity efforts. Indeed, some even suspected that the bank had made itself vulnerable because of how it had chosen to manage diversity. A senior executive from the United States explains:

> *If the French team all resigned tomorrow, what would we do? I'm not sure what we could do! We've never attempted to learn what these differences and cultural competencies really are, how they change the process of doing business. What is the German country team actually doing? We don't know. We know they're good, but we don't know the subtleties of how they do what they do. We assumed—and I think correctly—that culture makes a difference, but that's about as far as we went. We hired Europeans with American M.B.A.s because we didn't know why we couldn't do business in Europe—we just assumed there was something cultural about why we couldn't connect. And ten years later, we still don't know what it is. If we knew, then perhaps we could take it and teach it. Which part of the investment banking process is universal and which part of it draws upon particular cultural competencies? What are the commonalities and differences? I may not be German, but maybe I could do better at understanding what it means to be an American doing business in Germany. Our company's biggest failing is that the department heads in London and the directors of the various country teams have never talked about these cultural identity issues openly. We knew enough to use people's cultural strengths, as it were, but we never seemed to learn from them.*

Access's story makes an important point about the main limitation of the access-and-legitimacy paradigm: under its influence, the motivation of diversity usually emerges from very immediate and often crisis-oriented needs for access and legitimacy—in this case, the need to broker deals in European markets. However, once the organization appears to be achieving its goal, the leaders seldom go on to identify and analyze the culturally based skills, beliefs, and practices that worked so well. Nor do they consider how the organization can incorporate and learn from those skills, beliefs, or practices in order to capitalize on diversity in the long run.

Under the access-and-legitimacy paradigm, it was as if the bank's country teams had become little spin-off companies in their own right, doing their own exotic, slightly mysterious cultural-diversity thing in a niche market of their own, using competencies that for some reason could not become more fully integrated into the larger organization's understanding of itself. Difference was valued within Access Capital—hence the development of country teams in the first place—but not valued enough that the organization would try to integrate it into the very core of its culture and into its business practices.

Finally, the access-and-legitimacy paradigm can leave some employees feeling exploited. Many organizations using this paradigm have diversified only in those areas in which they interact with particular niche-market segments. In time, many individuals recruited for this function have come to feel devalued and used as they begin to sense that opportunities in other parts of the organization are closed to them. Often the larger organization regards the experience of these employees as more limited or specialized, even though many of them in fact started their careers in the mainstream market before moving to special markets where their cultural backgrounds were a recognized asset. Also, many of these people say that when companies have needed to downsize or narrow their marketing focus, it is the special departments that are often the first to go. That situation creates tenuous and ultimately untenable career paths for employees in the special departments.

The Emerging Paradigm: Connecting Diversity to Work Perspectives

Recently, in the course of our research, we have encountered a small number of organizations that, having relied initially on one of the above paradigms to guide their diversity efforts, have come to believe that they are not making the most of their own pluralism. These organizations, like Access Capital, recognize that employees frequently make decisions and choices at work that draw upon their cultural background—choices made because of their identity-group affiliations. The companies have also developed an outlook on diversity that enables them to *incorporate* employees' perspectives into the main work of the organization and to enhance work by rethinking primary tasks and redefining markets, products, strategies, missions, business practices, and even cultures. Such companies are using the learning-and-effectiveness paradigm for managing diversity and, by doing so, are tapping diversity's true benefits.

A case in point is Dewey & Levin, a small public-interest law firm located in a northeastern U.S. city. Although Dewey & Levin had long been a profitable practice, by the mid-1980s its all-white legal staff had become concerned that the women they represented in employment-related disputes were exclusively white. The firm's attorneys viewed that fact as a deficiency in light of their mandate to advocate on behalf of all women. Using the thinking behind the access-and-legitimacy paradigm, they also saw it as bad for business.

Shortly thereafter, the firm hired a Hispanic female attorney. The partners' hope, simply put, was that she would bring clients from her own community and also demonstrate the firm's commitment to representing all women. But something even bigger than that happened. The new attorney introduced ideas to Dewey & Levin about what kinds of cases it should take on. Senior managers were open to those ideas and pursued them with great success. More women of color were hired, and they, too, brought fresh perspectives. The firm now pursues cases that its previously all-white legal staff would not have thought relevant or appropriate because the link between the firm's mission and the employment issues involved in the cases would not have been obvious to them. For example, the firm has pursued precedent-setting litigation that challenges English-only policies—an area that it once would have ignored because such policies did not fall under the purview of traditional affirmative-action work. Yet it now sees a link between English-only policies and employment issues for a large group of women—primarily recent immigrants—whom it had previously failed to serve adequately. As one of the white principals explains, the demographic composition of Dewey & Levin "has affected the work in terms of expanding notions of what are [relevant] issues and taking on issues and framing them in creative ways that would have never been done [with an all-white staff]. It's really changed the substance—and in that sense enhanced the quality—of our work."

Dewey & Levin's increased business success has reinforced its commitment to diversity. In addition, people of color at the firm uniformly report feeling respected, not simply "brought along as window dressing." Many of the new attorneys say their perspectives are heard with a kind of openness and interest they have never experienced before in a work setting. Not surprisingly, the firm has had little difficulty attracting and retaining a competent and diverse professional staff.

If the discrimination-and-fairness paradigm is organized around the theme of assimilation—in which the aim is to achieve a demographically representative workforce whose members treat one another exactly the same—then the access-and-legitimacy paradigm can be regarded as coalescing around an almost opposite concept: differentiation, in which the objective is to place different people where their demographic characteristics match those of important constituents and markets.

The emerging paradigm, in contrast to both, organizes itself around the overarching theme of integration. Assimilation goes too far in pursuing sameness. Differentiation, as we have shown, overshoots in the other direction. The new model for managing diversity transcends both. Like the fairness paradigm, it promotes equal opportunity for all individuals. And like the access paradigm, it acknowledges cultural differences among people and recognizes the value in those differences. Yet this new model for managing diversity lets the organization internalize differences among employees so that it learns and grows because of them. Indeed, with the model fully in place, members of the organization can say, We are all on the same team, *with* our differences—not *despite* them.

Eight Preconditions for Making the Paradigm Shift

Dewey & Levin may be atypical in its eagerness to open itself up to change and engage in a long-term transformation process. We remain convinced, however, that unless organizations that are currently in the grip of the other two paradigms can revise their view of diversity so as to avoid cognitive blind spots, opportunities will be missed, tensions will most likely be misdiagnosed, and companies will continue to find the potential benefits of diversity elusive.

Hence the question arises: What is it about the law firm of Dewey & Levin and other emerging third-paradigm companies that enables them to make the most of their diversity? Our research suggests that there are eight preconditions that help to position organizations to use identity-group differences in the service of organizational learning, growth, and renewal.

1. **The leadership must understand that a diverse workforce will embody different perspectives and approaches to work, and must truly value variety of opinion and insight.** We know of a financial services com-

pany that once assumed that the only successful sales model was one that utilized aggressive, rapid-fire cold calls. (Indeed, its incentive system rewarded salespeople in large part for the number of calls made.) An internal review of the company's diversity initiatives, however, showed that the company's first- and third-most-profitable employees were women who were most likely to use a sales technique based on the slow but sure building of relationships. The company's top management has now made the link between different identity groups and different approaches to how work gets done and has come to see that there is more than one right was to get positive results.

2. **The leadership must recognize both the learning opportunities and the challenges that the expression of different perspectives presents for an organization.** In other words, the second precondition is a leadership that is committed to persevering during the long process of learning and relearning that the new paradigm requires.

3. **The organizational culture must create an expectation of high standards of performance from everyone.** Such a culture isn't one that expects less from some employees than from others. Some organizations expect women and people of color to underperform—a negative assumption that too often becomes a self-fulfilling prophecy. To move to the third paradigm, a company must believe that all its members can and should contribute fully.

4. **The organizational culture must stimulate personal development.** Such a culture brings out people's full range of useful knowledge and skills—usually through the careful design of jobs that allow people to grow and develop but also through training and education programs.

5. **The organizational culture must encourage openness.** Such a culture instills a high tolerance for debate and supports constructive conflict on work-related matters.

6. **The culture must make workers feel valued.** If this precondition is met, workers feel committed to—and empowered within—the organization and therefore feel comfortable taking the initiative to apply their skills and experiences in new ways to enhance their job performance.

7. **The organization must have a well-articulated and widely understood mission.** Such a mission enables people to be clear about what the company is trying to accomplish. It grounds and guides discussions about work-related changes that staff members might suggest. Being clear about the company's mission helps keep discussions about work differences from degenerating into debates about the validity of people's perspectives. A clear mission provides a focal point that keeps the discussion centered on accomplishment of goals.

8. **The organization must have a relatively egalitarian, nonbureaucratic structure.** It's important to have a structure that promotes the exchange of ideas and welcomes constructive challenges to the usual way of doing things—from any employee with valuable experience. Forward-thinking leaders in bureaucratic organizations must retain the organization's efficiency-promoting control systems and chains of command while finding ways to reshape the change-resisting mind-set of the classic bureaucratic model. They need to separate the enabling elements of bureaucracy (the ability to get things done) from the disabling elements of bureaucracy (those that create resistance to experimentation).

First Interstate Bank: A Paradigm Shift in Progress

All eight preconditions do not have to be in place in order to begin a shift from the first or second diversity orientations toward the learning-and-effectiveness paradigm. But most should be. First Interstate Bank, a midsize bank operating in a midwestern city, illustrates this point.

First Interstate, admittedly, is not a typical bank. Its client base is a minority community, and its mission is expressly to serve that base through "the development of a highly talented workforce." The bank is unique in other ways: its leadership welcomes constructive criticism; its structure is relatively egalitarian and nonbureaucratic; and its culture is open-minded. Nevertheless, First Interstate had long enforced a policy that loan officers had to hold college degrees. Those without were hired only for support-staff jobs and were never promoted beyond or outside support functions.

Two years ago, however, the support staff began to challenge the policy. Many of them had been with First Interstate for many years and, with the company's active support, had improved their skills through training. Others had expanded their skills on the job, again with the bank's encouragement, learning to run credit checks, prepare presentations for clients, and even calculate the algorithms necessary for many loan decisions. As a result, some people on the support staff were doing many of the same tasks as loan officers. Why, then, they wondered, couldn't they receive commensurate rewards in title and compensation?

This questioning led to a series of contentious meetings between the support staff and the bank's senior managers. It soon became clear that the problem called for managing diversity—diversity based not on race or gender but on class. The support personnel were uniformly from lower socioeconomic communities than were the college-educated loan officers. Regardless, the principle was the same as for race- or gender-based diversity problems. The support staff had different ideas about how the work of the bank should be done. They argued that those among them with the requisite skills should be allowed to rise through the ranks to professional positions, and they believed their ideas were not being heard or accepted.

Their beliefs challenged assumptions that the company's leadership had long held about which employees should have the authority to deal with customers and about how much responsibility administrative employees should ultimately receive. In order to take up this challenge, the bank would have to be open to exploring the requirements that a new perspective would impose on it. It would need to consider the possibility of mapping out an educational and career path for people without degrees—a path that could put such workers on the road to becoming loan officers. In other words, the leadership would have to transform itself willingly and embrace fluidity in policies that in times past had been clearly stated and unquestioningly held.

Today the bank's leadership is undergoing just such a transformation. The going, however, is far from easy. The bank's senior managers now must look beyond the tensions and acrimony sparked by the debate over differing work perspectives and consider the bank's new direction an important learning and growth opportunity.

Shift Complete: Third-Paradigm Companies in Action

First Interstate is a shift in progress; but, in addition to Dewey & Levin, there are several organizations we know of for which the shift is complete. In these cases, company leaders have played a critical role as facilitators and tone setters. We have observed in particular that in organizations that have adopted the new perspective, leaders and managers—following in their tracks, employees in general—are taking four kinds of action.

They are making the mental connection. First, in organizations that have adopted the new perspective, the leaders are actively seeking opportunities to explore how identity-group differences affect relationships among workers and affect the way work gets done. They are investing considerable time and energy in understanding how identity-group memberships take on social meanings in the organization and how those meanings manifest themselves in the way work is defined, assigned, and accomplished. When there is no proactive search to understand, then learning from diversity, if it happens at all, can occur only reactively—that is, in response to diversity-related crises.

The situation at Iversen Dunham illustrates the missed opportunities resulting from that scenario. Rather than seeing differences in the way project leaders defined and approached their work as an opportunity to gain new insights and develop new approaches to achieving its mission, the firm remained entrenched in its traditional ways, able to arbitrate such differences only by thinking about what was fair and what was racist. With this quite limited view of the role race can play in an organization, discussions about the topic become fraught with fear and defensiveness, and everyone misses out on insights about how race might influence work in positive ways.

A second case, however, illustrates how some leaders using the new paradigm have been able to envision—and make—the connection between cultural diversity and the company's work. A vice president of Mastiff, a large national insurance company, received a complaint from one of the managers in her unit, an African American man. The manager wanted to demote an African American woman he had hired for a leadership position from another Mastiff division just three months before. He told the vice president he was profoundly disappointed with the performance of his new hire.

"I hired her because I was pretty certain she had tremendous leadership skill," he said. "I knew she had a management style that was very open and empowering. I was also sure she'd have a great impact on the rest of the management team. But she hasn't done any of that."

Surprised, the vice president tried to find out from him what he thought the problem was, but she was not getting any answers that she felt really defined or illuminated the root of the problem. Privately, it puzzled her that someone would decide to demote a 15-year veteran of the company—and a minority woman at that—so soon after bringing her to his unit.

The vice president probed further. In the course of the conversation, the manager happened to mention that he knew the new employee from church and was familiar with the way she had handled leadership there and in other community settings. In those less formal situations, he had seen her perform as an extremely effective, sensitive, and influential leader.

That is when the vice president made an interpretive leap. "If that is what you know about her," the vice president said to the manager, "then the question for us is, whey can't she bring those skills to work here?" The vice president decided to arrange a meeting with all three present to ask this very question directly. In the meeting, the African American woman explained, "I didn't think I would last long if I acted that way here. My personal style of leadership—that particular style—works well if you have the permission to do it fully; then you can just do it and not have to look over your shoulder."

Pointing to the manager who had planned to fire her, she added, "He's right. The style of leadership I use outside this company can definitely be effective. But I've been at Mastiff for 15 years. I know this organization, and I know if I brought that piece of myself—if I became that authentic—I just wouldn't survive here."

What this example illustrates is that the vice president's learning-and-effectiveness paradigm led her to explore and then make the link between cultural diversity and work style. What was occurring, she realized, was a mismatch between the cultural background of the recently promoted woman and the cultural environment of her work setting. It had little to do with private attitudes or feelings, or gender issues, or some inherent lack of leadership ability. The source of the underperformance was that the newly promoted woman had a certain style and the organization's culture did not support her in expressing it comfortably. The vice president's paradigm led her to ask new questions and to seek out new information, but, more important, it also led her to interpret existing information differently.

The two senior managers began to realize that part of the African American woman's inability to see herself as a leader at work was that she had for so long been undervalued in the organization. And, in a sense, she had become used to splitting herself off from who she was in her own community. In the 15 years she had been at Mastiff, she had done her job well as an individual contributor, but she had never received any signals that her bosses wanted her to draw on her cultural competencies in order to lead effectively.

They are legitimating open discussion. Leaders and managers who have adopted the new paradigm are taking the initiative to "green light" open discussion about how identity-group memberships inform and influence an employee's experience and the organization's behavior. They are encouraging people to make *explicit* use of background cultural experience and the pools of knowledge gained outside the organization to inform and enhance their work. Individuals often do use their cultural competencies at work, but in a closeted, almost embarrassed, way. The unfortunate result is that the opportunity for collective and organizational learning and improvement is lost.

The case of a Chinese woman who worked as a chemist at Torinno Food Company illustrates this point. Linda was part of a product development group at Torinno when a problem arose with the flavoring of a new soup. After the group had made a number of scientific attempts to correct the problem, Linda came up with a solution by "setting aside chemistry and drawing on my understanding of Chinese cooking." She did not, however, share with her colleagues—all of them white males—the real source of her inspiration for the solution for fear that it would set her apart or they might consider her unprofessional. Overlaid on the cultural issue, of course, was a gender issue (women cooking) as well as a work-family issue (women doing *home* cooking in a chemistry lab). All of these themes had erected unspoken boundaries that Linda knew could be career-damaging for her to cross. After solving the problem, she simply went back to the so-called scientific way of doing things.

Senior managers at Torinno Foods in fact had made a substantial commitment to diversifying the workforce through a program designed to teach employees to value the contributions of all its members. Yet Linda's perceptions indicate that, in the actual day-to-day context of work, the program had failed—and in precisely one of those areas where it would have been important for it to have worked. It had failed to affirm someone's identity-group experiences as a legitimate source of insight into her work. It is likely that this organization will miss future opportunities to take full advantage of the talent of employees such as Linda. When people believe that they must suggest and apply their ideas covertly, the organization also misses opportunities to discuss, debate, refine, and build on those ideas fully. In addition, because individuals like Linda will continue to think that they must hide parts of themselves in order to fit in, they will find it difficult to engage fully not only in their work but also in their workplace relationships. That kind of situation can breed resentment and misunderstanding, fueling tensions that can further obstruct productive work relationships.

They actively work against forms of dominance and subordination that inhibit full contribution. Companies in which the third paradigm is emerging have leaders and managers who take responsibility for removing barriers that block employees from using the full range of their competencies, cultural or otherwise. Racism, homophobia, sexism, and sexual harassment are the most obvious forms of dominance that decrease individual and organizational effectiveness—and third-paradigm leaders have zero tolerance for them. In addition, the leaders are aware that organizations can create their own unique patterns of dominance and subordination based on the presumed superiority and entitlement of some groups over others. It is not uncommon, for instance, to find organizations in which one functional area considers itself better than another. Members of the presumed inferior group frequently describe the organization in the very terms used by those who experience identity-group discrimination. Regardless of the source of the oppression, the result is diminished performance and commitment from employees.

What can leaders do to prevent those kinds of behaviors beyond explicitly forbidding any forms of dominance? They can and should test their own assumptions about the competencies of all members of the workforce because negative assumptions are often unconsciously communicated in powerful—albeit nonverbal—ways. For example, senior managers at Delta Manufacturing had for years allowed productivity and quality at their inner city plants to lag well behind the levels of other plants. When the company's chief executive officer began to question why the problem was never addressed, he came to realize that, in his heart, he had believed that inner-city workers, most of whom were African American or Hispanic, were not capable of doing better than subpar. In the end, the CEO and his senior management team were able to reverse their reasoning and take responsibility for improving the situation. The result was a sharp increase in the performance of the inner-city plants and a message to the entire organization about the capabilities of its entire workforce.

At Mastiff, the insurance company discussed earlier, the vice president and her manager decided to work with the recently promoted African American woman rather than demote her. They realized that their unit was really a pocket inside the larger organization: they did not have to wait for the rest of the organization to make a paradigm shift in order for their particular unit to change. So they met again to think about how to create conditions within their unit that would move the woman toward seeing her leadership position as encompassing all her skills. They assured her that her authentic style of leadership was precisely what they wanted her to bring to the job. They wanted her to be able to use whatever aspects of herself she thought would make her more effective in her work because the whole purpose was to do the job effectively, not to fit some preset traditional formula of how to behave. They let her know that, as a management team, they would try to adjust and change and support her. And they would deal with whatever consequences resulted from her exercising her decision rights in new ways.

Another example of this line of action—working against forms of dominance and subordination to enable full contribution—is the way the CEO of a major chemical company modified the attendance rules for his company's annual strategy conference. In the past, the conference had been attended only by senior executives, a relatively homogeneous group of white men. The company had been working hard on increasing representation of women and people of color in its ranks, and the CEO could have left it at that. But he reckoned that, unless steps were taken, it would be ten years before the conferences tapped into the insights and perspectives of his newly diverse workforce. So he took the bold step of opening the conference to people from across all levels of the hierarchy, bringing together a diagonal slice of the organization. He also asked the conference organizers to come up with specific interventions, such as small group meetings before the larger session, to ensure that the new attendees would be comfortable enough to enter discussions. The result was that strategy-conference participants heard a much broader, richer, and livelier discussion about future scenarios for the company.

They are making sure that organizational trust stays intact. Few things are faster at killing a shift to a new way of thinking about diversity than feelings of broken trust. Therefore, managers of organizations that are successfully shifting to the learning-and-effectiveness paradigm take one more step: they make sure organizations remain "safe" places for employees to be themselves. These managers recognize that tensions naturally arise as an organization begins to make room for diversity, starts to experiment with process and product ideas, and learns to reappraise its mission in light of suggestions from newly empowered constituents in the company. But as people put more of themselves out and open up about new feelings and ideas, the dynamics of the learning-and-effectiveness paradigm can produce temporary vulnerabilities. Managers who have helped their organizations make the change successfully have consistently demonstrated their commitment to the process and to all employees by setting a tone of honest discourse, by acknowledging tensions, and by resolving them sensitively and swiftly.

• • •

Our research over the past sixty years indicates that one cardinal limitation is at the root of companies' inability to attain the expected performance benefits of higher levels of diversity: the leadership's vision of the purpose of a diversified workforce. We have described the two most dominant orientations toward diversity and some of their consequences and limitations, together with a new framework for understanding and managing diversity. The learning-and-effectiveness paradigm we have outlined here is, undoubtedly, still in an emergent phase in those few organizations that embody it. We expect that as more organizations take on the challenge of truly engaging their diversity, new and unforeseen dilemmas will arise. Thus, perhaps more than anything else, a shift toward this paradigm requires a high-level commitment to learning more about the environment, structure, and tasks of one's organization, and giving improvement-generating change greater priority than the security of what is familiar. This is not an easy challenge, but we remain convinced that unless organizations take this step, any diversity initiative will fall short of fulfilling its rich promise.

About the Research

This article is based on a three-part research effort that began in 1990. Our subject was diversity; but, more specifically, we sought to understand three management challenges under that heading. First, how do organizations successfully achieve and sustain racial and gender diversity in their executive and middle-management ranks? Second, what is the impact of diversity on an organization's practices, processes, and performance? And, finally, how do leaders influence whether diversity becomes an enhancing or detracting element in the organization?

Over the following six years, we worked particularly closely with three organizations that had attained a high degree of demographic diversity: a small urban law firm, a community bank, and a 200-person consulting firm. In addition, we studied nine other companies in varying stages of diversifying their workforces. The group included two financial-services firms, three *Fortune* 500 manufacturing companies, two midsize high-technology companies, a private foundation, and a university medical center. In each case, we based our analysis on interviews, surveys, archival data, and observation. It is from this work that the third paradigm for managing diversity emerged and with it our belief that old and limiting assumptions about the meaning of diversity must be abandoned before its true potential can be realized as a powerful way to increase organizational effectiveness.

Index

access-and-legitimacy paradigm, 24, 35–36
Access Capital International case, 35–36
advocacy groups, 15–16
affirmative action, 13, 14. *See also* diversity
African Americans
    caucus groups, 12, 15, 16
    civil rights movement, 13
    corporate advancement, 14
Asian Americans, 14
assimilation, 34, 37
awareness, situational, 21
"The Awkward Invitation" scenario, 27

backlash, 20, 21
benefits, 12
body language, and bystanders, 23
business case for diversity, 11
bystander awareness and skills
    overview, 16–17
    backlash, 21
    cultural variation and, 22–23
    definition of bystander, 6
    inaction, reasons for, 21
    nature of the bystander, 21, 22
    risks and benefits, 21–22
    scenarios, 25–29
    structural support, 23–24
    tactics, 23
    value of, 20–21

caucus groups, 12, 15, 16
celebrations of diversity, 24, 35
civil rights, history of, 13
class, 39
college degree requirements, 38
collusion, and bystander awareness, 22
competencies, barriers to, 40–41
"cooling things down," 23
corporate diversity programs, elements of, 14–15
corporate ranks, diversity in, 14
"Counting on a Colleague" scenario, 28
Cox, Taylor, 10
cultural background, work perspectives and, 36–42
cultural diversity, defined, 10
cultural perspective on diversity, 15
cultural variation, and bystanders, 22–23
culture, organizational, 16, 38

Delta Manufacturing case, 41
demographics, workforce, 10, 19
design teams, and demographics, 12
Dewey & Levin case, 37
differentiation, 37
diffusion of responsibility, 21

discovery, as bystander tactic, 23
discrimination. *See also* diversity
    affirmative action and equal opportunity, 13–14
    dominance and subordination, 40–41
    remaining challenges, 14
discrimination-and-fairness paradigm, 24, 33–35
discussion, open, 40
diversity. *See also* bystander awareness and skills
    overview, 6–7
    access-and-legitimacy paradigm, 24, 35–36
    Access Capital International case, 35–36
    backlash, 20
    business case for, 11
    celebrations of, 24, 35
    in corporate ranks, 14
    cultural diversity, defined, 10
    definition and meaning of, 10
    Delta Manufacturing case, 41
    Dewey & Levin case, 37
    discrimination-and-fairness paradigm, 24, 33–35
    elements of corporate programs, 14–15
    First Interstate Bank case, 38–39
    grassroots employee advocacy programs, 15–16
    historical and policy context, 13–14
    Iversen Dunham case, 34–35, 39
    leadership commitment, 15
    learning and, 12, 38
    learning-and-effectiveness (work perspectives) paradigm, 24, 32–33, 36–37, 39–42
    Mastiff case, 39–40, 41
    organizational effectiveness and, 32, 33
    organizational processes and, 17, 18
    paradigm shift, 37–39
    performance, effects on, 17
    policy issues, 23–24
    societal, organizational, and managerial levels, 11, 13
    strategic design, political, and cultural perspectives on, 14–15
    structural solutions, 23–24
    Torinno Food Company case, 40
    training, 20
    "valuing," 14, 20
    workforce demographics, 10, 19
Diversity Council, 15
Diversity Research Network, 17
domestic partner benefits, 12
dominance and subordination, 40–41

effectiveness, 32, 33. *See also* learning-and-effectiveness (work perspectives) paradigm
employees, feelings of exploitation among, 36

employees, making feel valued, 38
English-only policies, 37
equal opportunity, 13, 33–35. *See also* diversity
executives, diversity among, 14
exploitation, employee feelings of, 36

fairness. *See* discrimination-and-fairness paradigm
First Interstate Bank case, 38–39
flat organizations, 38
flexibility, in benefits package, 12
Ford Motor Company, 12

gay, lesbian, bisexual, and transgendered (GLBT) employees, 12
global organizations, 10–11, 22–23, 35–36
grassroots employee advocacy programs, 15–16
groupware systems, 12

harassment policy, 24
"heating things up," 23
Hispanics, 14
historical context of diversity, 13–14

identity-group affiliations, 32–33, 35, 38, 39. *See also* diversity
immigration, 10
inclusion, as bystander tactic, 23
influence of grassroots advocacy groups, 16
integration, 37
international business, 10–11, 22–23, 35–36
"Introducing the Invisible Colleague" scenario, 26
"Is It Really About Race" scenario, 26–27
"Is It the Nature of the Project" scenario, 27–28
Iversen Dunham case, 34–35, 39
"I Was Just Trying to Be Sensitive!" scenario, 28–29

job posting, 12
jokes, offensive, 20

language, and English-only policies, 37
leadership, 14, 15, 41–42
learning, 12, 38
learning-and-effectiveness (work perspectives) paradigm, 24, 32–33, 36–37, 39–42
legitimacy. *See* access-and-legitimacy paradigm

"Making Differences Matter" (Thomas and Ely), 32–42
managerial level of diversity, 13
Mastiff case, 39–40, 41
mediation, 24
mission statements, 13, 38
multiculturalism, 35
Myrdal, Gunnar, 10

networking, 15
norms, and bystander action, 20, 23

offensive jokes, 20
organizational effectiveness, 32, 33. *See also* learning-and-effectiveness (work perspectives) paradigm
organizational level of diversity, 13
organizational processes, 17, 18

paradigms for managing diversity
  access-and-legitimacy, 24, 35–36
  discrimination-and-fairness, 24, 33–35
  evolution of, 24
  learning-and-effectiveness (work perspectives), 24, 32–33, 36–37, 39–42
paradigm shift, 37–39
performance, effects of diversity on, 17. *See also* effectiveness
performance standards, 38
"perpetrators," 20
Platt, Lew, 11
policy issues, 13–14, 23–24
political perspective on diversity, 14–15
Post-It® notes, 12
privileged group, 22
promotion, 24, 38

race, 10, 34–35. *See also* diversity
responsibility, diffusion of, 21

sexual orientation, 12
signaling, by bystanders, 23
situational awareness, 21
Sloan School of Management, MIT, 20
social contracts, 13
social identities, 10, 15
societal level of diversity, 11, 13
strategic design perspective on diversity, 14
structural solutions, 23–24

talent shortage, 11
team demographics, 12
"The Stapler" scenario, 29
third-party mediation, 24
Torinno Food Company case, 40
training, diversity, 20. *See also* bystander awareness and skills
trust, 41

uncertainty, and bystanders, 21

"valuing" diversity, 14, 20
"victims," 20

workforce demographics, 10, 19
work perspectives, connecting diversity to, 24, 36–42

Xerox, 12, 15

"You Just Weren't Listening" scenario, 29

MANAGING FOR THE FUTURE

Organizational Behavior & Processes

Negotiation and Conflict Resolution

Deborah M. Kolb
Simmons College

Module 12

MANAGING FOR THE FUTURE
Organizational Behavior & Processes, Third Edition

Deborah Ancona
Sloan School of Management
Massachusetts Institute of Technology

John Van Maanen
Sloan School of Management
Massachusetts Institute of Technology

Thomas A. Kochan
Sloan School of Management
Massachusetts Institute of Technology

D. Eleanor Westney
Sloan School of Management
Massachusetts Institute of Technology

Maureen Scully
Graduate School of Management
Simmons College

Dedicated to those who have inspired us to try to be better students and teachers.
Special thanks to: Professor Jack Barbash • Professor Arthur H. Gladstein • Professor Marius B. Jansen • Professor Joanne Martin • Professor Edgar H. Schein

VP/Editorial Director
Jack W. Calhoun

Marketing Manager
Jacquelyn Carrillo

Internal Designer
Bethany Casey

VP/Editor-in-Chief
Michael P. Roche

Production Editor
Emily Gross

Cover Designer
Bethany Casey

Senior Publisher
Melissa S. Acuña

Manufacturing Coordinator
Rhonda Utley

Photographs
©PhotoDisc

Executive Editor
John Szilagyi

Compositor
Trejo Production

Design Project Manager
Bethany Casey

Senior Developmental Editor
Judith O'Neill

Printer
Von Hoffmann Press, Inc.
Frederick, MD

COPYRIGHT ©2005
by South-Western, a division of Thomson Learning.
Thomson Learning™ is a trademark used herein under license.

Printed in the United States of America
1 2 3 4 5 07 06 05 04 03

For more information contact
South-Western College Publishing,
5191 Natorp Boulevard,
Mason, Ohio, 45040
Or you can visit our Internet site at:
http://www.swlearning.com

ALL RIGHTS RESERVED
No part of this work covered by the copyright hereon may be reproduced or used in any form or by any means—graphic, electronic, or mechanical, including photocopying, recording, taping, Web distribution or information storage and retrieval systems—without the written permission of the publisher.

For permission to use material from this text or product, contact us by
Tel: (800) 730-2214
Fax: (800) 730-2215
http://www.thomsonrights.com

Library of Congress Control Number: 2003113908
ISBN 0-324-05575-7

Contents

Negotiation and Conflict Resolution

Overview		4

Core

Class Note	**Negotiation and Conflict Resolution: An Introduction** *Purpose of This Module 7* *Negotiation as a Form of Conflict Management 7* *Dealmaking: The Building Blocks of Negotiation 8* *Conclusion 19* *References 19*	6

Elective

The Press	**Dealcrafting: The Substance of Three-Dimensional Negotiations** *Basic Dealcrafting Orientation 1: A Relentless Focus of Creating Maximum Value 24* *Basic Dealcrafting Orientation 2: A Relentless Focus on Differences as the Raw Material for Joint Gains 26* *Differences in Cost/Revenue Structure 26* *Differences in Capability 27* *Differences in Interest and Priority 27* *Implication: Agenda Management 28* *Differences in Forecast or Belief About the Future 28* *Contingent Agreements Based on Forecast Differences: A 3-D Extension 30* *Differences in Attitudes Toward Risk 30* *Differences in Attitudes Toward Time 32* *Differences in Tax Status 33* *Differences in Accounting Treatment and Reporting Sensitivity 33* *Crafting Value from a Variety of Differences 34* *Conclusion 35* *About the Authors 35* *References 35*	22
	Breakthrough Bargaining *Power Moves 36* *Process Moves 38* *Appreciative Moves 40* *About the Authors 42*	36

Index

Overview

The Negotiation and Conflict Resolution module is designed to help you become a more effective negotiator. In the past, you probably would need negotiation and conflict resolution skills only if your job entailed formal dealings with unions, suppliers, and customers. In other words, negotiation was a skill needed only by people who did it for a living, but all that has changed in the new organization.

When viewed through a political lens, all interactions both internal and external to the new organization, are basically negotiations. That means that as a manager, you are frequently operating in a situation where your responsibility exceeds your authority. You will need to negotiate with a range of internal and external stakeholders in order to get your job done. In network and team structures, you are but one voice among many. To accomplish your agenda, you will need to negotiate to build coalitions among different stakeholders and constituencies. As organizations become more diverse demographically and culturally, the potential for conflict increases, requiring even more attention to how we deal with it.

To be an effective negotiator in the new organization requires an understanding of the basic building blocks of the process. These activities include developing a stakeholder map of the parties, framing the issues, analyzing relative bargaining power, considering different models of negotiation, and planning and carrying through the process of agreement making. The Class Note presents these building blocks conceptually, and then translates them into a series of pragmatic preparation questions that can be used to get ready for a negotiation. At the same time as you are working out the substantive issues in a negotiation, you are also working out the terms of your relationship. In these shadow negotiations, you simultaneous position yourself to be an effective advocate for your interests as you strive to get buy-in from other parties. It is in the shadow negotiations, where gender, race, and cultural issues are most likely to surface. When negotiations reach an impasse, a person not directly involved in the process, a third party, can often assist. A third party can fulfill a variety of functions, but challenges lie in taking on this role in organizations.

The module is structured around a complex negotiation role-play—Mango Systems. Two senior managers from different divisions—Casey Roberts and Chris Mahoney—are under pressure from their respective bosses to work out an agreement on a significant organizational change. Each has different personal and organizational issues that play a part in the goals they set for the negotiation. Because it is set in an organization, the cultural, political, and strategic issues that inevitably influence negotiations play an important role in how the negotiations are framed and conducted. Your instructor will distribute role descriptions before you actually negotiate; they are not included in this module.

Two elective readings supplement the core materials. In **"Dealcrafting: The Substance of Three-Dimensional Negotiations,"** David Lax and James Sebenius focus on ways negotiators can create joint gains. Using case examples, they demonstrate how differences in risk, time, priorities, and beliefs about the future form the bases of deals that create value for all parties. In **"Breakthrough Bargaining,"** Deborah Kolb and Judith Williams suggest that more is involved in effective negotiation than just knowing how to craft deals. Negotiators also need to use strategic moves to get negotiations going and to shape the process so that dealcrafting is possible.

To be an effective negotiator requires practice and reflection. The materials in this module are only a beginning. The more you negotiate, the better you will become at it, but just negotiating is not enough. On a regular basis, you will want to reflect on your emerging expertise. Where are your areas of strength? Of weakness? What skills do you need to work on to become more effective? Becoming a reflective negotiator is a sure way to become more effective at this critical skill.

Assignment Summary

1. Read the Class Note, which provides (1) the conceptual building blocks for understanding the negotiation process and (2) a series of preparation questions that can be used in preparing for a negotiation.
2. On the assigned day, come to class prepared to participate in the Mango Systems role-play. Use the preparation questions in the Class Note to ready yourself for the negotiation.
3. If asked to do so, read the elective readings on dealcrafting and bargaining that begin on page 22.

Negotiation and Conflict Resolution

CORE

Module 12

Negotiation and Conflict Resolution

An introduction

Being able to deal with conflict effectively is a requirement for survival in the new organization. Even though conflict is certainly nothing new in organizations, in the past it was channeled into hierarchical structures, formal rules and procedures, and ideologies of cooperation that kept it more or less hidden. In times of stability, negotiation and conflict resolution are the primary responsibility of certain individuals (corporate counsel, labor negotiators, senior managers, among others). In the new organization, conflict is built into its very structure and fabric, and the capacity to deal with conflict is key to getting things done on an individual, managerial, and organizational level.

Consider the story of Sandy Max. Sandy is a marketing manager at a medical diagnostics firm. Her day began at 6 A.M. with a phone call from another mother in her carpool. The other mother was ill and wanted Sandy to pick up the children after school to take them to music lessons. Today is not a good day for this. The division president has invited Sandy to an important meeting this afternoon on new product design. She turns to her husband and asks what his day is like, and whether he can take over. His day is busy too, and so they negotiate over who will do what and when. The result is that he will pick up the children at school but Sandy will have to break away from her meeting early so she can take over after the music lesson, which will allow him to finish the report he needs to get out that day.

Sandy arrives at work at 8 A.M. for a meeting with the engineering group, which is developing a new product. She needs to get changes made in this product, based on trials with the customer. The engineers are already under pressure to get the project completed. She has taken one of the engineers to the customer site, and he now understands the issue and is willing to support her. They will stand together on the need for changes in the design, and hence a revised schedule. The outcome is that they agree to go to the vice president for research and development to see what can be done.

Her next meeting is with the division president and his other direct reports. They are doing their twice-yearly ranking of individual performance. It's one of those meetings where the managers put forth their people and argue for the rank they want. Although it's supposed to be based on objective criteria, it's a game of hanging tough and making trades.

Finally she returns to her office. The consultant she wants to bring in for negotiation training is on the phone to hear Sandy's reaction to her proposal. Sandy makes a few suggestions, and they agree on the price and deliverables. Her friend Laura comes in next for a brown bag lunch. Laura has just returned from maternity leave (her second child) and realizes that she needs to drop back to part-time. But her boss is not supportive and so she wants Sandy's advice on how to negotiate an agreement that will work for her but won't jeopardize her standing in the company. During lunch, Sandy gets a call from the director of marketing, who has just gotten off the phone with a distributor in Asia. The Asian distributor complained that the company must not value him as a strategic partner; if it did, he claimed, then the company would have sent a more senior person, and not a woman, to work out the agreement. It was a pretty standard contract, one that Sandy had negotiated all over the world. Under the circumstances, Sandy agrees that she and the director will handle this one together.

After lunch, Sandy prepares for an upcoming negotiation with Joe Green, an important customer. Last week, they had reached a tentative agreement on the level of services and the costs, with everything set to go. Yesterday, Joe called and told her he had just received the last quarter's results and a freeze on new spending was instigated companywide. He wants her to come back with a different proposal that is much lower than their tentative agreement. But Sandy is also under pressure to produce and tries to see what kind of deal she can put together, one that won't be too expensive but won't hurt her group's performance.

Some quiet time, and then it's off to the meeting to talk about the new product design process, which turns out to be interesting and full of good ideas. The division president asks Sandy to head the task force. Flattered, she agrees even though she has more work than she can accomplish. Now she must convince people to join the task force and help them find time and resources to do the work, not to mention what she will need to be successful in this endeavor. That's only the beginning: resistance to changing the process will be considerable. She needs to plan out a strategy to build support for whatever proposal the group pulls together.

Sandy says she will be in touch with all members of the task force via e-mail later that day to plan a meeting schedule, then excuses herself so she can pick up the children from music class at 5 P.M. After driving the other child home, she starts dinner, then gets on her home computer to send out e-mail messages regarding the meeting schedule and agenda for the first session. Her husband takes over dinner preparations at around 6 P.M., leaving Sandy time to continue working at her computer. The family eats together at 6:30. At 7 P.M., Sandy's seven-year-old is glued to the television and homework is yet to be done. The 12-year-old wants to go to a party on a school night. Negotiations ensue. Her husband, as he heads into their shared home office to go back to work, points out some brochures for the camping trip in the mountains he wants to take for summer vacation. All Sandy wants to think about right now is lying on the beach at a wonderful resort somewhere. Vacation destinations will come up for discussion, too.

A day in the life of Sandy in the new organization and in the new economy shows how much negotiation is required just to get through the day. In the flat organization in which Sandy works, her responsibility inevitably exceeds her authority to get things done so she must negotiate with the engineers and other groups in order to achieve her objectives. Sandy's function is networked both internally and externally: She carries out formal negotiations with key stakeholders (suppliers, customers, strategic partners) and informal ones with colleagues over compensation and commitment. Her organization is always changing and responding to meet the needs of individuals and of key stakeholders; negotiating is a way to deal with the resistances that inevitably accompany change. Her firm is diverse and learns from its diversity as individuals and groups negotiate for changes that make the company more inclusive and more sensitive to the blurred boundaries between work and family. Finally, the global nature of her function means that all negotiations take place in a context of cultural difference and diversity.

At one level, it is easy to distinguish negotiation from normal, everyday interactions. Certain negotiations are clearly demarcated events—for example, negotiating a contract with a supplier or customer, collective bargaining between union and management representatives, negotiating the terms and conditions of a job we are about to take. Although these events are common enough, they represent only a small segment of the negotiations that take place in the new organization. To recognize these other negotiations—and they are ubiquitous—we need to consider negotiation as an ongoing activity of social decision making where two or more interdependent people with some interests in common and some in conflict (mixed motive) engage in back-and-forth communication aimed at reaching a settlement (Strauss, 1978; Firth, 1995). In the new organization, we negotiate for resources, authority, time, products, and services. We negotiate to improve performance, solve problems, strive for equity and fairness, and foster learning and innovation, and create the conditions for our own success.

Purpose of This Module

- To introduce major concepts in negotiation.
- To compare and contrast negotiation processes and the tactics associated with them.
- To understand the various sources of bargaining power and how they are mobilized in different phases of a negotiation.
- To understand the ways in which organizational context—structure and systems, power and politics, and cultural assumptions—influence negotiations.
- To recognize the ways in which the interpersonal/interactional dynamics play out and influence consideration of substantive issues being negotiated.
- To develop a way to understand how diversity along gender, race, ethnic, and cultural lines plays out in negotiations.
- To see how outsiders to a particular conflict can facilitate its resolution.

Negotiation as a Form of Conflict Management

In the new organization, conflict is ubiquitous, but negotiation is only one of the many ways we have to deal with difference. Take a simple example from Sandy's organization. On a task force of engineers and marketers, conflicts erupt over the design of the prototype. Sandy wants the product that gives her customers flexibility while the engineers complain that what marketing wants will cost more and delay the product launch. Here are a few of the ways this situation could be handled:

- *Forcing behavior.* The division vice president could direct the squabbling group to produce the flexible system and instruct the engineers to do it in a timely fashion. If she's feeling generous, maybe she'll provide extra human or financial resources to help.
- *Smoothing.* Sandy and the engineers could gloss over their differences. In the meetings they appear collaborative. The engineers promise to make the changes and agree to keep to the schedule, but when they get to the next meeting the changes have not been made and the schedule has slipped.

- *Avoidance.* They all can decide not to deal with the issue and skip the meeting entirely.
- *Negotiating.* If they decide to *negotiate*, each party (the marketers and engineers) can put its issues on the table and work through a process to see whether they can come to an agreement. That agreement may involve engineering capitulating; or maybe it will be marketing that makes the concessions and bears the consequences with its customers; or maybe the two sides will creatively work together to fashion an agreement that meets both their interests.
- *Third-party assistance.* Finally, they could ask an outside person, one not directly involved in the disagreement, a *third party*, to help them figure out what to do. The plant manager, with an interest in moving the product into production, could help facilitate the process.

Dealmaking: The Building Blocks of Negotiation

Parties, issues, and interests, all in varying combinations, are the building blocks that structure the dealmaking or dealcrafting process. That process can resemble the prototypical market transaction where parties exclusively pursue their individual gain at the expense of the other. For example, Laura insists on a part-time schedule to accommodate family needs but her boss rejects her proposal. Laura threatens to quit, and the boss gives in. Or the process can be one where parties pursue mutual gain, looking to *expand the pie*, so that both can obtain more of what each wants—Laura figures out what she needs to deal with family issues and the boss determines his needs for the business. Together, they come up with a plan in which Laura gets a part-time office schedule but agrees to provisions that will ensure that her customers continue to receive good service. Or the process can have elements of both individual and mutual gain in it. Although Laura is able to get the part-time office schedule and her boss gets what he needs to justify this arrangement to his boss, Laura has to make a significant compromise to attend regular staff meetings at a time she would not necessarily be there.

Sometimes the process leads to a new framing of the problem with a different set of outcomes, ones not previously considered. As Laura pursues her negotiations over a flexible schedule, others in the group begin to think about how such an arrangement would help them integrate their work and personal life, and also start to see how telecommuting might actually make the total group effort more efficient. So other parties become part of the discussion and the negotiation shifts from being about one person's schedule to one about how the group can pursue a dual agenda of increasing business effectiveness and enabling people to integrate their work and family lives. It is these multiple ways in which parties deal with issues and interests in a particular context that shape what the negotiation process is like.

Parties

Negotiation takes place between and among parties. Parties can be two people negotiating on their own behalf: I sell my used car to you. Or parties can also be agents acting on behalf of somebody else—a client, or some institution, department, or group. When we negotiate on our own behalf, say, for a salary, psychological issues and considerations of self-esteem and self-worth become part of the picture. When we negotiate on behalf of others as an agent, these issues may be more or less prominent. As agents, we need to worry not only about what happens across the table, but also how we deal with constituent expectations—the challenge of intra-organizational negotiation or the "second table" problem (Walton & McKersie, 1965). So my group asks me to negotiate with the facilities manager over office space. As is usually the case, I am likely to come back with somewhat less than my group wants. Then I face the challenge of lowering their expectations so that I am not scapegoated for the deal I bring back. These scenarios suggest that in organizations, negotiations are likely to involve more than just two parties.

Relationships. Parties have different relationships with each other. In the prototypic market, we are strangers. What we negotiate and how we negotiate are seen as having little consequence in these encounters. However, most negotiations in the new organization, and across its boundaries, take place among parties who have ongoing relationships (Greenhalgh, 2001). Three primary consequences arise out of new organizational life. First, matters of relationship may be as important to the outcome we negotiate as the substantive issues that give rise to the process in the first place. Second, in ongoing relationships, negotiators develop their own mental models and scripts that constrain behavior on the one hand, but also help parties interpret and make sense of these strategic moves of each other (Valley & Keros, forthcoming). In labor negotiations, for example, a tendency to act adversarially and denounce the other party is not an indicator of how one feels about the issues, but rather is interpreted as a symbolic gesture, a performance for a constituent audience (Friedman, 1994). Finally, in ongoing relationships, linkage between a current negotiation and ones in the future are possible. So I might be willing to give you some slack at the moment, with the understanding that you will repay me as part of our next deal.

Number of Parties. Although we tend to think about negotiations as taking place between two parties, negotiations may involve multiple parties. Working on a team or task force, mobilizing an organization change effort, or pulling together an industry consortium are tasks that involve multiple parties. Once more than two parties are involved, the opportunities and possibilities for coalition formation become a key consideration. Coalition building entails mapping key stakeholders and their interests and concerns, and then implementing a sequencing strategy to bring them on board (Lax & Sebenius, 1986). Orchestrating decisions at meetings often involves building coalitions prior to the actual meeting.

Negotiator Characteristics. Part of the skill in negotiations is being able to "read" the other party, to make sense of their strategies and tactics. We can type negotiators by style and membership in particular groups. Anecdotally, we all know negotiators with certain styles they have honed over the years, which they believe serve them well. The *thug* is the negotiator who takes a position (and has the wherewithal to back it up) and never departs from it. The thug's intransigence means that others must organize their agreements with the thug's position as a constraint. The *conciliator* is the negotiator who wants to make sure that everybody feels good about the agreement and looks for ways to make that happen. Contemporary negotiation theory would have us become *rational analysts*, neither hard nor soft in our tactics. This negotiator constructs a decision tree before ever making a move. Then, the *intuitive* types simply let their experience be their guides. Research tends not to bear out our everyday experience. Consistent styles are more anecdotal than matters of empirical proof (Rubin & Brown, 1975; Bazerman et al., 2000).

Certain characteristics such as gender, race, and national culture are thought to influence how parties negotiate. The tendency is to see these characteristics as stable qualities of a person—that is, men will negotiate competitively, women collaboratively. Westerners will emphasize the terms of agreement, Asians will be more concerned with the relationship. Not surprisingly, research is equivocal on these issues. The belief, for example, that women are more collaborative than men is borne out in some studies but not in others (see Kolb & Coolidge, 1992). Although the wish to categorize parties in these terms is understandable, it ignores the importance of background, experience, and context in influencing how a negotiator negotiates. For example, people whose negotiating experience occurs primarily in situations where they lack power and influence will more likely be attentive to relationships and more collaborative, because that is the posture that has served them well in the past. Identifying that approach as more feminine than masculine appears to have more to do with how we code behaviors (Kolb & Williams, 2000) than what the approach actually is. Similarly, a negotiator new to the international business arena is more likely to display the characteristics of his or her national culture than an international negotiator who has done many deals. The professional and business culture, one that is shared across national boundaries, is more likely to minimize national differences (Rubin & Faure, 1993; Brett, 2001).

The focus on gender and cultural difference treats identities as more or less fixed. Rather than focus on individual differences, another approach looks to the interaction itself where expectations about gender, race, and culture are enacted. From this perspective, gender and other aspects of identity are continually socially being constructed, produced, and reproduced in interactions that occur in particular contexts. A focus on the interaction emphasizes the fluidity, flexibility, and variability of identity-related behaviors.

One way gender gets mobilized in negotiations, for example, has to do with identity and how salient gender is to an individual negotiator. So, at the individual level, one can consider the degree to which negotiators identify with the masculine and/or feminine sides of themselves and take up those roles or positions in the process. From this perspective, a man might choose, either consciously or unconsciously, to act in a stereotypically masculine way—shouting, bullying, acting competitively—because he believes that the context prompts him to behave in this way. By the same token, a woman might take up the role of helper or concentrate on the relationship, again because she perceives that the context calls for her to behave in that way. Negotiators, in other words, have some choice in the degree to which they take up gender roles in a negotiation.

Gender, race, and cultural expectations and stereotypes also influence how parties interpret others' actions in negotiation. In studies of car buying, for example, women and minorities fared considerably worse than white men did because of dealers' beliefs about the relative skill and knowledge about cars of these groups. Under these circumstances, the expectations of the dealers act as a hidden constraint in the negotiations. Similarly, cross-cultural stereotypes impact how we interpret tactics in negotiation. If we believe that a particular culture is exemplified by trustworthiness and honor, and another by shady dealing and manipulation, we will hear what parties say differently. Once into the negotiations, these expectations more often than not become self-fulfilling prophecies, where we find evidence to reinforce our expectations, but ignore cues that would disprove them (Rubin & Faure, 1994). In a sense, we create gender and cultural differences in negotiation rather than we discover them.

Organization Context. Organizational and other incentives can also shape parties' actions. Reward systems can set up competitive dynamics that encourage parties to act solely individualistically or collaboratively. In collective bargaining, for example, one company evaluated its plant managers on how minimal a wage increase they could achieve in negotiating with the local union representatives. Despite a rhetoric of "win-win" negotiations, the plant managers understandably took a hard line, and the union negotiators responded in kind. Where incentives promote interdependence, then parties often act more collaboratively. For example, in Sandy's organization, performance is judged on the product's performance, rather than on individual functional contribution. Thus, it is more likely for members of her organization to negotiate to solve problems that, under other conditions, they might avoid.

Similarly, culture within an organization can influence how parties negotiate. In cultures that promote competition among individuals and groups, negotiations will tend to be more like a zero-sum game. In one organization, for example, groups were given similar assignments and encouraged to fight it out, the idea being that truth would come through conflict. On occasions when these groups had to work together and negotiate their differences, they found it difficult to come to agreements. In another organization, where a culture of individualism and individual heroics reigned, even getting a sales group to sit down to negotiate over how to coordinate its customer promises with the operational realities was next to impossible. In sum, how parties act in negotiation is a complex combination of their individual styles, their experiences, our expectations and interactions with them, and the context in which the negotiations take place.

Preparation Questions

1. Who are the relevant parties? Who makes the decisions? Who will actually negotiate? Who are their relevant constituencies? What are the connections among them?
2. What do I want from the other party(ies)? How do they see their choices? What problems will meeting my needs create for them? Their boss(es)? Their colleagues? Other constituencies?
3. What organizational considerations are relevant? What negotiating behaviors are rewarded? How does the culture view negotiations? What organization constraints exist for them? For me?
4. What kinds of behaviors should I expect? How do they usually negotiate? How do I react to their negotiating style? What should I do to prepare myself? Should I expect that gender, race and/or culture will be issues in the negotiation?

Issues

Issues are the matters over which parties disagree and on which seek to reach agreement on. The most common distinction people make about issues concerns the number of them. When we negotiate over a single issue, such as price, negotiations inevitably become distributive, or zero sum (Raiffa, 1982), meaning that what one party gains comes at the expense of another, the so-called *fixed pie*, where we are splitting up shares or *claiming value*. When multiple issues are on the table, the possibilities for integrative or mutual gains bargaining increase because parties can make trade-offs among them. Under these circumstances, we are *creating value* (Lax & Sebenius, in this module).

Even though the number of issues has an important bearing on the type of negotiation process, it is not the only dimension that affects it. Issues can differ in terms of their specificity and clarity. Some issues are straightforward, such as what price I will pay for the red sports car I covet. In such situations, negotiations are a matter of finding an agreement that meets both parties' needs. Within organizations, however, issues are often more complex—how we will fulfill the mandate to reduce costs without loss in productivity. In these situations, defining the issues—how to structure a procedure for layoffs or figure out how to streamline processes—in many ways prefigures the agreement. The power to define the issues is a critical, yet often unrecognized source of influence in negotiations.

Finally, issues are not etched in stone. When we sit down to negotiate, we may think we are pretty clear on what the issues are, but find that the issues change and/or new ones emerge through the process. The manager of a major task force sits down to negotiate with her boss about the schedule for the final report. As they negotiate over the project, the charge changes, as do the force's members, all factors that impact the deadline. The fact that issues change during a negotiation means that we are never really in a domain where one form of negotiation is inevitable (Putnam & Kolb, 2000).

Preparation Questions

1. What are the issues we need to negotiate? Try to be as clear as possible.
2. Are the issues separate or can they be linked in the current situation or over time?
3. Are there other ways to frame the issues?

Interests

Interests are what parties seek to advance in negotiations. If the issues are the matters over which parties disagree, then interests are the wants, needs, goals, and desires parties have relative to the issues. In *Getting to YES* (Fisher, Ury, & Patton, 1991), an important distinction is drawn between positions and interests. Positions are the stands we take about an issue—I demand a 10 percent salary increase this year. Interests are the reasons we take a position. The idea is that if we focus on interests, there is more bargaining room to find agreement than if we just stick with a position. I might not be able to get that 10 percent increase in salary, but if we explore my interests—I want credit for a job well done; I feel I am not equitably compensated for my work; I need more childcare for my children—my firm can satisfy some of my interests even if they do not exactly meet my demands. I can get a bonus for a recent project, stock options, a new title and office, more time off, and so on. What happens when one focuses on interests is that they provide the means to convert single-issue negotiations with constrained definitions of the issues into possibilities for joint gain. Knowing your own interests and learning about those of the other party, and distinguishing them from positions, can potentially lead to more integrative outcomes. Whereas positions might be in direct conflict, interests offer the possibilities of compatibility and complementarity.

Types of Interests. We tend to think of interests primarily in monetary or substantive terms—what are the concerns and needs relative to the particular set of issues being negotiated. However, within organizations, interests are considerably more complex. Consider a negotiation between a systems group and a user group over a new system. Assume the parties have agreed on the scope of the project and are now negotiating over the cost and time frame. Substantive interests are those that relate directly to the issues being negotiated. They can cover the costs of a project (in human and financial terms), and the time and timing, among other interests. The systems group's substantive interests are in developing a good system and not being constrained too much in terms of cost and time. The user group is desperate for the system, wants it up and running as soon as possible, and does not want to pay too much for it.

Both groups have interests relative to the relationship. They want to maintain a good relationship, especially important to the systems group whose members see this project as the first of many. If they can get it done in a reasonable amount of time and for reasonable cost, they feel it is more likely that they will get a follow-up project. The two negotiators are also attentive to each other's constituencies—that they have to sell their agreements to their bosses and so they have to be defensible. Were one to have a potential agreement overturned, it would have negative consequences to both parties.

Organizational interests are involved as well. Both parties want to do what is best for their particular departments but recognize that, by pursuing this aim exclusively, consequences may affect the total organization or others who are not directly at the table. So, the systems group members have an interest in not setting a precedent that they underprice their services. At the same time, they do not want to price their services too high, or the user group might prefer an outside vendor, which would have negative consequences to the organization. Both negotiators might have career issues at stake. A successful negotiation (and a successful project) can help both parties, and the opposite can hold true as well. When these interests "kick in," they suggest that any agreement must be implementable if the parties are to realize the benefits of their negotiation.

Finally, each negotiator has personal interests at stake. Each wants to be seen by the other as competent and skilled. Often a mutual interest in saving the face of the other raises the incentive to find agreements that make each look good. The user group negotiator, for example, has not had much experience negotiating about systems, at least as compared with his counterpart who negotiates them both internally and externally. So the user wants to be known as a person who got a good deal and was not exploited. Reputation is also important in this regard. If the systems negotiator develops a reputation for inflexibility or exploitation, it will mean negative consequences for her, her career, and her group.

Several important points can be made about this process. First, it is helpful to be as specific as one can in articulating one's interests. Often people start with an interest such as "we want to do what is best for the organization." Such broad generalizations are of little help, and may actually work against understanding what each side really needs. One can start more generally and then continually unpack interests, pushing back on what people really think and feel they want or need. So, in our systems example, the user group wants the project done as soon as possible and the systems group needs time. In unpacking interests, it may become apparent that the users need certain functions quickly but have more flexibility on others. The systems group, it turns out, is worried about resources, because it is currently stretched by other projects. So its interests concerning time have to do with side issues to the negotiation. Understanding these different interests can lead to solutions that would work to the benefit of both.

Second, parties value interests and, indeed, issues differently. Understanding these differences constitutes the core of thinking about integrative and mutual gains negotiations. Because time is crucial to the user group and resources are crucial to the systems group, there are multiple opportunities to make creative deals. The user group might be willing to pay more in order to get the job done on time. These extra resources might be used either to put more engineers on this project or on the others the group is engaged in and/or to enable overtime work. Alternatively, the user group may be able to devote some of its human resources to the project to alleviate the burden on the systems group. The key is that once parties move away from their positions on time and money, they open up possibilities. Other priority interests that are less tangible (such as reputation and relationship) influence the degree to which the groups want to probe and unbundle interests.

How does one learn about interests? Preparation for a negotiation includes identifying interests and begins with an analysis of one's own and the other negotiators' interests relative to a given set of issues, and by working with the information one has to think through the consequences to each party of agreeing to different proposals. However, what one can know about the other in the absence of interaction is ultimately limited.

Talking About Interests. One of the major challenges in negotiation is to find ways to talk about interests. At one level, it is a pretty simple matter—one asks. Contextual questions about people's wants and needs can be directly posed: *What are your major areas of concern? What are the key things you need from an agreement?* Indeed, research suggests that if you seek information about others' preferences and provide information about your own, you are more likely to achieve mutual gain agreements (Thompson, 1997). However, learning about interests is considerably more complex for a number of reasons.

First, the naive ways that people frame negotiations, as a competitive zero-sum game, mean that they fear that revealing information will jeopardize their positions. It will be used to exploit them, to push for more concessions. So they tend to reveal information about their interests only reluctantly. If you ask directly about interests, you may be met with a hostile response—what business is it of yours?

Second, the structure of negotiation, with the possibilities both to create value in terms of joint gain and to claim the value that is created, adds incentives to withhold information. This phenomenon is referred to as the *negotiator's dilemma* (Lax & Sebenius, 1986; Walton & McKersie, 1965). In practice, what it means is that if negotiators are open and truthful about their interests, the opportunities to discover joint gains are increased. However, in sharing that information, they may cede advantage to the other side, who may be in a position to claim more of the value created. When both sides recognize this dilemma and act on it, then they conceal information about interests, which forecloses the possibility of joint gains. Further, when negotiators act from a value-claiming position, they often interpret the other's sharing of information about interests as a claiming tactic.

Third, in organizations, issues and interests are rarely clear-cut and fixed. In contrast to the clarity of our interests when we buy a car, our interests in complex negotiations are likely to be multiple and not always immediately obvious. Interests emerge and get constructed through the negotiation process itself (Kolb & Putnam, 1992). Thus, we want to create a space where parties can individually and collectively discover their interests, where they differ and where they dovetail. One way to do that is to gradually share information, testing the reaction of the other party. If that move is reciprocated, then more information about interests can be revealed. Another approach is to learn more about the circumstances or context that produced specific positions. So we want to ask questions about history, how we got to this point. We want to learn more about the conditions under which the issues arose. So rather than general questions about interests and what a person wants and why, we are more likely to elicit useful information by asking specific questions about causes, context, time, and conditions. Other indirect methods can also help elicit interests in complex situations. We can propose different scenarios and see how the other side responds. We can propose specific possibilities as a starting point. We can make multiple equivalent proposals to frame choices and learn from their reactions. All these approaches are useful in finding ways to talk about interests without giving away information that might be used against us.

Preparatory Questions

1. Why are the parties at the table?
2. What are my underlying concerns? What are theirs? What are their goals? Mine?
3. What interests are of higher priority? Are their differences in priorities?
4. What would they consider a good outcome? What would be in it for me?
5. What kinds of questions can I ask to learn about interests?

Bargaining Power

Henry Kissinger once said that the best you can ever hope to get in negotiations is the offer you open with, and it is generally downhill from there (Lax & Sebenius, 1986). The path from that opening offer to a place where agreement is reached involves the use of bargaining power. Bargaining power, in this sense, is the capacity to achieve agreement on one's own terms (Bacharach & Lawler, 1981). Although negotiators may come to the table with different sources of potential power, it is in how the parties position[1] themselves, both at and away from the table, in how power is mobilized to shape perceptions and expectations that ultimately affect what kinds of agreements are reached.

Sources of Power. A number of potential sources of power include the ability to reward or coerce another party to make particular concessions. If I am your boss or occupy a position of legitimate authority, I may be able to dictate terms that you are likely to accept because of this relationship. Similarly, if you identify with me or somehow see me as admirable, you may be more likely, though not always so, to find my ideas and proposals agreeable. If I have information or expertise that you credit, I might be able to use that to persuade you of a deal I want. Finally, if I have others who support me, strategic allies, they may intervene to convince you to go along with me.

Another important source of bargaining power is one's "best alternative to a negotiated agreement," or BATNA (Fisher, Ury, & Patton, 1991). Your BATNA is the answer to the questions, "What will I do if I cannot reach agreement? Do I have other courses of action?" BATNA is an indicator of dependence of one party on another. The more I need an agreement, because I have few alternatives, the more potential power you will have over me, and vice versa. If I have other viable alternatives, I might be able to take a stronger position in negotiation because I can walk away from the deal. Without such alternatives, I may be forced to accept terms that are not much to my liking.

Developing a BATNA. Evaluating one's BATNA can be pretty straightforward when the issues are simple—I can get prices on the same car from two dealers, for example. The currency is the same. More often, however, evaluating one's BATNA is more complicated. First, it may be difficult to compare two alternatives. I have two job offers, each with its own combination of desirable attributes and limiting drawbacks. Second, it may be difficult to identify an alternative: If the engineers simply will not agree to switch the schedule, identifying a substitute course of action is not easy. I would have to change the project definition, not a simple matter. Third, one's BATNA can escalate to difficult courses of action that might have high costs—going to court, quitting one's job. Fourth, one's BATNA can be a combination of actions that involve other parties whose impact is difficult to analyze precisely. Finally, it is rarely the case that one's BATNA is as good as one might hope to get from the agreement one is negotiating. If it were, you would not be negotiating, so it may be difficult to keep it in your mind as a viable alternative.

Even when it is difficult to develop a BATNA and evaluate it, doing so is a useful exercise for several reasons. In simple negotiations, it sets the reservation price, or bottom line, in a defensible way. If I know what price I can get for the car I covet down the street, I know then the maximum I am willing to pay. But even in the more common situations where one's BATNA is not exactly comparable, it makes sense to consider it because it helps define your position when you negotiate. It does so for two reasons. First, it helps you distinguish situations where you have potential bargaining power from those where you are lacking. If you have another job offer (even if it is not your first choice), you are not quite as dependent on the outcome of your negotiation than you would be if you were in a desperate situation with no other possibilities. Desperate situations (e.g., you're out of work, the mortgage and all the other bills are due, and you have no other job offers) generally mean that you go into negotiations in a weaker position than would be the case if you had a BATNA. Second, if you feel you have other choices, you are likely to be a more effective negotiator than if you see yourself in a weak, one-down situation, which is why it makes sense to try to improve one's BATNA going into a negotiation. Indeed, the research shows that negotiators who have alternatives do better both at creating value in negotiations and in claiming it (Thompson, 1997). It is also important to learn as much as you can about the other party's BATNA. Theirs may be worse than yours.

Mobilizing Power and Influence. Potential bargaining power is only part of the story. If power mattered absolutely, outcomes in a negotiation could be predicted by assessing the differential power and influence of the parties, but that is not always the case. Less powerful parties can often do well in negotiations. The key is how negotiators position themselves, at and away from the table,

---

[1] *Position*, as it is used here, is a verb that refers to how a negotiator is placed in the process relative to the other negotiator(s). This concept is to be distinguished from its more traditional usage in negotiation—as a demand, distinguished from interests.

how they use what resources they have to shape perceptions of themselves and of the agreement possibilities. Persuasion is perhaps what we think of first. We use our skill and knowledge to marshal defensible facts and figures to convince you of the merits of our sense of the deal. Of course, not all parties are equally well positioned to have access to relevant facts. Lower salary outcomes for women and minorities in negotiation may be more a function of access to critical social networks than of their situation in the immediate negotiation (Seidel, Polzer & Stewart, 2000). Thus, negotiators can use *strategic moves*, actions at and away from the table, to enhance their position and influence (see Kolb & Williams in this module).

Once into the negotiation, we use these moves to influence the negotiation. We might let you know subtly that we have a good BATNA and question yours. If you know our user group entertained an offer from an outside vendor, then you may be more flexible in giving us what we want. We might let it drop that other influential people support our ideas. We can structure the agenda so that it frames our interests to advantage. We can come prepared with options for agreement that anchor the deal in ways favorable to us. We can flatter and ingratiate ourselves so that you might be more tempted to go along with us.

In all these examples, mobilizing the power we have in the situations is intended to get us what we want; our actions are tactical and instrumental. Two important points need to be raised here. First, when our sources of power are mobilized in a negotiation, we are sending messages about the strength of our position, our position relative to the other party. At least some parity of positioning is required for parties to discover joint gains. If I come across as too weak, you are unlikely to want to accommodate my concerns. Likewise if I see you as weak relative to me, I have little incentive to work with you to create value. Thus, negotiators engage in some mutual posturing in order to move to a place where they can work toward joint gains.

Second, ethical issues always arise when we talk about managing impressions in the kinds of opportunistic situations that negotiations typically entail. The structure of negotiations can create incentives to exaggerate, distort, and otherwise misrepresent the situation. Often negotiators are blind to the egocentrism of their ethical judgments. They see themselves as more ethical than their counterparts and justify their actions as self-defense (Tenbrusel, 1998). What negotiators may overlook are the consequences. In organizations, one's reputation can be irreparably harmed by engaging in tactics that lead to short-term gains at the expense of long-term relationships.

Because negotiation is a two-way street, you use influence tactics at the same time they are used on you. One way to view negotiations is as an information game. Through moves and countermoves, through arguments and counterarguments, through proposals and counterproposals, negotiators seek to shape the negotiation in ways that will be to their advantage.

Preparatory Questions

1. What sources of power/influence does each party have?
2. What is your BATNA? Theirs? What ways exist to improve yours? Worsen theirs?
3. How well positioned are you relative to the other party?
4. What strategic moves can you use away from the table to influence the negotiation? How will you mobilize them once into the negotiations?

The Dealmaking Process

Dealmaking is the means by which parties work out their differences over issues and pursue their interests. It is typical in the field of negotiations to describe two basic processes: distributive and integrative negotiations. Each has a set of tactics, particularly around communication, associated with it that in some ways stand in marked contrast to each other. These contrasts capture the *mixed motive* quality of most negotiations; in other words, distributive and integrative potential are both present.

Distributive Negotiations. Bargainers in distributive (or win-lose) negotiations view each other as adversaries with interests that are in direct conflict over a single issue such as price.[2] These negotiations are called zero sum because what one party achieves comes directly at the expense of the other. The tactics used in distributive bargaining are intended to claim as much value as you can for yourself. Value claimers analyze their BATNAs and those of their opponents, seeking to enhance theirs and make the others worse. Claiming tactics begin with extreme opening offers that reveal as little information about true preferences as possible. One argues persuasively for one's own position and minimizes those made by the other side. Concessions are made slowly and grudgingly, all the time exaggerating the value of any concessions you make. Concessions made by the other side tend to be devalued and demeaned. Power tactics, such as bluffs and threats to leave the negotiation or com-

---

[2] For excellent discussions of distributive bargaining and claiming tactics, see David A. Lax and James K. Sebenius, *The Manager as Negotiator* (New York: Basic Books, 1986).

mitments to accept only certain deals, are common. Information about preferences is closely held.

The concessionary dance that marks these negotiations moves along a bargaining zone called the "zone of possible agreements" (ZOPA). The ZOPA is bounded by the reservation price (the least you'd be willing to accept or most you'd be willing to pay) of each party.[3] Parties make opening offers that anchor the negotiations and often become the focal point around which the negotiations pivot. A reliable advantage can be realized in making opening offers when you possess good information about the reservation price or bottom line of the other party. Absent such information, you risk giving away too much information. Advice from the experts cautions one to avoid opening offers without good information but, if forced to do so, make an offer that reveals as little as possible about one's bottom line. Opening offers lead to counteroffers and a series of concessions that typically get smaller as parties approach the point of compromise (Raiffa, 1982).

The communication tactics that mark these negotiations are intended to shape people's perceptions of what the bargaining zone is and where a likely agreement will be. The symbolic management of issues, alternatives to agreement, positions, and interests are critical elements in distributive negotiations. Think about purchasing a car. As a buyer, you might want to dress in something other than your designer suit and to mention good offers you have from another dealer, among other tactics. Such tactics are signals to suggest that you will not pay as much as the dealer might like. The salesperson likewise might ignore you for awhile, signaling her presumed lack of interest in a sale, then have trouble locating the model you want, and then make you wait while she checks with the dealer about price. These moves, in addition to the offers and counteroffers made are intended to make you think again about how much this car will cost you.

Integrative or Mutual Gains Negotiations. In integrative negotiations, the process is intended to be more open, making these symbolic and strategic communication gestures less prominent. Integrative negotiations are based on the premise (and observation) that it is possible, using a certain kind of problem-solving process, to find synergies and mutual gains in situations that look distributive.

The way to do that is to focus on interests, not positions, and then to be creative in searching for options that meet these interests (Fisher, Ury, & Patton, 1991). A story that is frequently used to describe this phenomenon deals with two sisters who both need the last orange in the house to bake a cake. One sister wants the orange for a fruit cake and the other for a chiffon cake. Neither sister can bake her cake with half an orange and so they appear at a stalemate. Through further dialogue, they discover that the first sister, who is making a fruitcake, needs the rind of the orange while the second sister needs the juice to make the chiffon cake. Both can get what they want from the single orange. The process operates based on a notion of *enlightened self-interest* (Breslin & Rubin, 1991): I can get what I want if I can find ways to help you get what you want.[4]

Sources of Mutual Gains. Identifying mutual gains is a process that requires some open sharing of interests, then a search for agreements that meet both parties' needs. Ways to meet these mutual needs include finding new resources, logrolling, nonspecific compensation, cost cutting, and bridging (Pruitt, 1981). In the systems group example, parties can expand the pie by *acquiring more resources*. Perhaps other interested groups could benefit from the system and might be willing to contribute to its development. *Logrolling* involves making trade-offs and exchanges based on differences. The user group, concerned about time, and the developers, concerned about costs, could make agreements that capitalize on these differences. The systems group would be willing to put more engineers on the project if the user group is willing to pay for overtime. Other dimensions along which parties can differ relative to their interests include differences in priority of issues, in expectations of uncertain events, in risk, in time preferences, among others. These differences can lead to trade-offs and contingent agreements that can leave both parties better off (Lax & Sebenius, this module). *Nonspecific compensation* means that one party gets what it wants and the other is paid in some unrelated coin. The developers get the additional funds and, in return, offer a training program at some later date. *Cost cutting* is when one party gets what it wants and the other side's costs are reduced. In order to get the project done on time, the user group devotes some of its human resources to the project to

---

[3] Establishing one's reservation price can be a simple matter or a complex process of assessing alternatives to agreement and the probabilities of reaching various outcomes. See Howard Raiffa, *The Art and Science of Negotiation* (Cambridge, MA: Harvard University Press, 1982); and David A. Lax and James K. Sebenius, *The Manager as Negotiator* (New York: Basic Books, 1986).

[4] This formulation of integrative negotiation is based on a set of assumptions about negotiations that do not always hold. For a discussion of these assumptions and the insights they yield in negotiations, see Deborah Kolb and Judith Williams, *Everyday Negotiations: Navigating the Hidden Agendas of Bargaining* (San Francisco: Jossey-Bass, 2003), Introduction.

alleviate the burden on the systems group. *Bridging* means coming up with a totally new option nobody else had thought about. In scoping out this project, both parties see that this project is really a template for others in the firm and so sell it to the executive committee as a means of developing more integration across units.

Several important points need to be mentioned about these approaches. First, the key to mutual gains agreements is to work from interests to find new issues, and to expand the range of possibilities for making trade-offs. Using *what if...?* questions gets people to think more expansively about the possibilities for mutual gain. Mutual gains can also come from defining a joint problem that both have a stake in solving and that minimizes conflict of interests and emphasizes those that are shared.

The key issue in mutual gains negotiation is to understand as much as you can about the interests of the other negotiator at ever-deeper levels and continue to come up with package deals that build on difference. A number of barriers block this creative process. They include seeing the negotiation exclusively as a distributive and adversarial process; focusing only on one's needs and interests; failing to take into account others' needs, or failing to assert one's interests effectively; working under a tight deadline; and lacking authority (Bazerman & Neale, 1992; Mnookin, 1993). Overcoming these barriers to creativity requires challenging assumptions, suspending judgment and evaluation about particular ideas, looking at the problem from different perspectives, and continuing to offer new options and/or alternative package deals if the first one is not a fit.

Negotiator's Dilemma. No matter how creative one is, the dilemma based in the mixed-motive structure of most negotiations remains. The *negotiator's dilemma* is inevitable in most situations. If we pursue distributive negotiation tactics—tactics to claim value for ourselves—we will be unlikely to move to a process of option creation that leads to mutual gain. If we pursue integrative negotiation tactics, that is, try to create value, we still face the issue of how we distribute the new value we have created. How much time for what level of compensation will always be an issue. Some argue that one can use objective, fair, or independent criteria to solve the distribution issue, but one's objective criteria may be seen as merely another bargaining position by the other (Fisher, Ury, & Patton, 1991).

Although it is theoretically possible to negotiate an agreement that maximizes potential value created with parties claiming equitable shares, it is typically not what happens in the real world nor is it necessarily desirable. The degree to which it matters, however, is variable. To the degree that the communicative contradictions of claiming and creating actually take place and leave possible mutual gains on the table, then a problem results. If in the interests of creating value, one party cedes all to another, the outcome is also probably less than desirable. Working around the negotiator's dilemma (one cannot really eliminate it) is best achieved in relationships that build over time, in situations where the value of creating outweighs incentives to claim. Process moves that increase the likelihood of creation include separating the inventing or creating process from the actual decisions, proposing multiple equivalent proposals, and making small incremental moves and then building on them either with the help of a third party or through improving them after the fact, with postsettlement settlements (Raiffa, 1982; Kolb & Williams, 2003).

Preparatory Questions

1. What assumptions does each party make about the type of negotiations? Is this likely to be distributive or integrative?
2. What arguments and tactics will I use to handle the distributive parts of the negotiation?
3. What options exist to satisfy mutual interests in the integrative parts of the negotiation? What trade-offs are possible based on differences in views regarding time, risk, resources, responsibilities, and needs? What package deals can I propose?
4. What kind of process should we agree to in order to come up with options that satisfy our mutual needs?
5. How will we manage the negotiator's dilemma?

Shadow Negotiations

Up to this point, we described the negotiation process primarily in terms of the substantive issues parties negotiate and what it takes to negotiate effective agreements. This focus on the agreement making is important, but it leaves out many of the features of negotiation that make effective negotiations possible. At the same time parties are negotiating the terms of their agreement, a parallel negotiation, a *shadow negotiation* is taking place, where parties position themselves and each other for the negotiation (Kolb & Williams, 2003). When parties negotiate with each other, they do more than argue for their proposals; they present themselves. The shadow negotiation is where negotiators work out the personal dynamic of their exchange. It is where they vie for control over who will set the terms of the discussion, or whose interests will be heard. It's where they size each other up, where they check for flexibility. The relational by-play in the shadow negotiations affects how issues and interests are seen, and what kind of agreement we get. Parties enter negotiations with certain predispositions and expectations about the other, which get played out as parties test and size each other up, looking for weakness or opportunity, to determine what kind of process will ensue. It makes a difference whether we believe the person speaks for the CEO or just herself.

In this shadow negotiation, negotiators are simultaneously advocating for themselves at the same time as they try to foster connection with the other party(s). Negotiators need to feel that they are in a legitimate position to effectively advocate for themselves. It means recognizing the ways they may undermine or disempower themselves by focusing on their own weakness, confusing toughness with effectiveness, and/or failing to recognize opportunities for negotiation. Negotiators need to be prepared to use strategic moves to deal with resistance, of either the passive or active sort. In these moves, negotiators seek to establish their own legitimacy and present themselves as parties the other side needs to negotiate seriously with. Managing these impressions is one of the ways we convince others to attend to us and our interests. When we negotiate our salary increase, it helps if we have just come off a big and successful project and start the conversation there.

Sometimes in a negotiation, moves are made that seriously undermine us. These *dirty tricks* of negotiation (Fisher, Ury, & Patton, 1991) may include giving you a seat with the sun directly in your eyes, the "good cop–bad cop" routine, or changing an agreement at the last minute, and are intended to place a negotiator in a one-down position. Sometimes, just recognizing these behaviors and the purpose they are intended to serve is sufficient. You can just ignore them. At other times, you can interrupt the moves, either by taking a break or shifting the conversation back to your issues (Fisher, Ury, & Patton, 1991; Kolb & Williams, 2003). Moves by the other seriously challenge our credibility, put us on the defensive, and need to be *turned* before they begin to define the situation in undermining ways. When the Asian distributor called Sandy's boss to complain about the partnership negotiations, for example, Sandy and her boss turned that move and so reinforced her legitimacy as the spokesperson for the firm. When they met with the distributor, Sandy's boss deferred to her regarding all questions. In this way, he demonstrated that Sandy has the authority to speak for the firm.

All these moves and countermoves are intended to preserve a position as a legitimate and savvy negotiator, so that the other side resists the temptation to take advantage. Shadow negotiation, however, also involves appreciative moves to build a more collaborative relationship. These efforts attempt to connect to the other person in order to build a bridge with them, to create relationships that foster norms of collaboration. Connection starts with a stance that recognizes and respects the legitimacy of the other. All too often, we place the other person in a negative and defensive position, making it difficult for them to work with us and for us to hear their concerns. Appreciative moves are intended to get them to participate actively. They include providing space for them to talk about the situation and their ideas, being open to hearing and holding multiple possibilities for solutions, and finding ways to help the other save face. These moves help parties understand each other's situation more deeply, more than just their interests. These understandings can lead to a form of mutual inquiry that results in agreements the parties could not anticipate on their own.

Preparatory Questions

1. How am I positioned in the organization to negotiate? Am I getting in my own way and what can I do about it?
2. Is the other party ready to negotiate with me? What strategic moves can I use to bring her to the table?
3. What kinds of moves can I expect that might put me on the defensive? How can I turn them?
4. Do I appreciate the other party's situation? What can I do to get him to open up more and talk about the problem?
5. What can I do to promote mutual inquiry in these negotiations?
6. What would be good mutual outcomes that we can work toward? Am I flexible and open enough to rethink my ideas about the outcome?

Assisted Negotiations

Negotiations do not always yield agreements. Sometimes, negotiations just stalemate or come to an impasse. Claiming tactics might drive out creative or even obscured potential areas of agreement. The issues may be difficult or of such a technical nature that it is hard to figure out where agreement might lie. Emotions may be running high, making it difficult for people to negotiate with each other. Power differentials might inhibit the kind of parity that is needed to engage in serious negotiations. Maybe relationships deteriorate so much that even the most basic of communication is impossible. In the waning days of Lehman Brothers, the two executive partners could not even be in the same room with each other and so an administrative partner served as go-between to run the firm by assisting their negotiations on a one-on-one basis (Auletta, 1986). Sometimes parties avoid conflict and need somebody to help make negotiations happen.

Third-Party Roles

Third parties can sometimes help. They can play many roles from process consultant to a binding decision maker, such as an arbitrator or judge. Postsettlement settlements are a variation in which the third party uses her expertise to enhance mutual gains (Raiffa, 1982). Assisted negotiation is more akin to mediation, a process that emphasizes intervention into the dispute but without the formal authority to render a decision. Mediators assist negotiators by helping the parties manage some of the dilemmas and difficulties of bilateral negotiations. In organizations, mediation is often employed as part of a formal complaint or grievance procedure and informally when managers and peers from the same or different departments become involved in some capacity.

Who plays this kind of role in organizations? Potentially, many people. Some positions are more likely to be drawn into disputes. In one organization, continual blaming behind the scenes but reluctance to confront differences kept the firm from moving ahead on a life-saving strategy. All sides took a human resources executive into their confidence and, based on the information she had, she was able to force issues out into the open, thereby creating the possibilities for confronting the issues directly through negotiation (Kolb & Bartunek, 1992). Other people develop a reputation for being good at it and so are sought out by colleagues. People come to their offices to discuss their situations and ask for help with the other. Sometimes another person is indirectly affected by a failure to resolve differences and so finds it in her best interests to assist the negotiations. Failure of engineering and operations, for example, to deal with a quality problem has negative implications for a marketing manager and so he decides to intervene. Although managers can assist negotiations with their subordinates, research suggests that they favor making a decision themselves over taking the time to assist the negotiations (Sheppard, 1984).

Functions

Informal mediators can perform a number of functions. Because they are not directly involved, they can cool things down and keep the other parties focused on the issues by building agendas and orchestrating the meetings. The structure of third-party involvement where a mediator can meet separately with each party means that she can explore for areas of flexibility without causing a party to make a public commitment to a deal that might be exploited. She might be able to be quite creative and invent options that the two parties have not been able to see. In other words, the presence of a third party might allow for public claiming but private creating and so contribute to finding a mutual gains agreement that had eluded the parties. Finally, the third party can help those directly involved explore the consequences of no agreement. Mediators call this process the *dose of reality*. Do you really want this disagreement to be aired to senior management? Do you really want the outside vendor to get this project? Have you considered the costs to your career of opting out of this project?

Challenges

Even though the potential contribution of a third party is significant, it is not an easy role to fulfill. Informal mediators face a number of challenges first. The tendency is to want to tell people what to do rather than assist them to resolve their own differences. Not surprisingly, such telling tends to breed resistance. In the beginning, parties might look to the mediator to suggest ideas, but once those ideas are suggested, their open stance often shifts to finding reasons to reject what is offered. After all, any solution will be less than the parties might actually prefer. Thus, any agreement that parties can accept requires some time for them to adjust. And of course, time is a rare commodity in the new organization.

A second key issue centers on the question of neutrality. Neutrality is basic to the ethic of most mediators; they need to keep their preferences under wraps. Although this advice might fit the role of professional mediators (and even this point is disputed), absolute neutrality is virtually impossible in organizations as the concept is generally understood. Given their knowledge of the organization and their own interests (no matter how tangential), informal mediators are rarely unbiased about outcomes. Typically, they would prefer certain outcomes over others. Existing relationships and career aspirations make it difficult to be absolutely indifferent among parties. However, even without being unbiased and impartial, it is still possible to be neutral, if one thinks about neutrality as a practice and not a state of being or individual characteristic (Cobb, 1993). A neutral practice means providing the space for each party to tell its story, and to argue its position on its own terms, not defensively in reaction to the first account of the situation. When mediators are neutral, parties feel heard, and are more likely to feel that the outcome is fair; hence, they are more committed to the outcome (Shapiro & Kolb, 1994).

When parties reach an impasse in negotiations, it is often difficult to help them come to an agreement. Not only might the problems themselves be difficult, but the parties may find it difficult to make concessions for a variety of reasons they think have merit. The informal third party can help in a number of ways. The first is to help the parties shift the way that they talk about the issues. Rather than blaming the other, for example, it helps to talk about the problem. Rather than dwelling on what happened, it helps to talk about the future, or what could be. Rather than make demands, it helps to talk about interests, to talk about what people want and are looking for from an agreement. Rather than make unilateral proposals, it helps to talk in terms of exchange, posing the "what if . . ." and "if then . . ." questions. A third party can help shift the conversation by restating what people say and asking questions that help the parties talk about the problem differently. If they talk about it differently, they may begin to see it differently (Kolb & Associates, 1994).

The second approach is to help the parties by framing the outlines of a possible agreement. Listening carefully and meeting in separate caucuses with them, the mediators begin to piece together elements of an agreement that might work. They might see obvious trade-offs, or they may come up with a creative idea to break a deadlock. Interestingly, however, how one introduces such ideas is as important as what the ideas are. It is often useful to introduce them as questions. Would this approach be possible? How would you improve on this idea? It is also important, research suggests, that mediators not become too vested in what they propose, because it is likely to undergo many changes before a final agreement is reached.

Finally, mediators can create explicit situations of choice. They can ask people to compare the current agreement to their BATNA, the alternative they would have to consider if agreement is not reached. One mediator describes this method as the *iron fist in the velvet glove* (Kolb & Associates, 1994). It is often difficult for people to make concessions or even to agree to deals that involve mutual gains. We tend to compare what is currently on the table with what we most want rather than what we will have to settle for if we don't reach an agreement. Pointing out the costs of delay, the costs to one's career and image, and the costs to the organization can often provide the extra push for parties to reconsider. It encourages parties to think more clearly about what would work for them and what they would be willing to accept.

Conclusion

The new organization is built on the capacity to deal with conflicts more productively, efficiently, and as close to the nexus of problems as possible. Forcing, smoothing, and avoiding, although still common responses to conflict, can undermine the virtues the new organization is meant to promote. Being able to confront differences productively through negotiation and/or with the assistance of a third party can turn conflict into a creative and innovative force.

References

Auletta, Ken. 1986. *Greed and Glory on Wall Street*. New York: Random House.

Bacharach, Samuel, and Edward Lawler. 1981. *Bargaining*. San Francisco: Jossey-Bass.

Bazerman, Max, and Margaret Neale. 1992. *Negotiating Rationally*. New York: Free Press.

Bazerman, Max, Jared Curhan, Don A. Moore, and Kathleen Valley. 2000. Negotiation. *The Annual Review of Psychology*, 51.

Breslin, J. William, and Jeffrey Z. Rubin. 1991. *Negotiation Theory and Practice*. Cambridge, MA: PON Books (Program on Negotiation at Harvard Law School).

Brett, Jeanne. 2001. *Negotiating Globally*. San Francisco: Jossey-Bass.

Cobb, Sara. 1993. "Empowerment and Mediation: A Narrative Perspective." *Negotiation Journal*, 9 (3), pp. 245–259.

Firth, Alan. 1995. *The Discourse of Negotiation*. New York: Elsevier.

Fisher, Roger, William Ury, and Bruce Patton. 1991. *Getting to YES: Negotiating Agreement Without Giving In*, 2nd ed. New York: Penguin.

Friedman, Raymond. 1994. *Front Stage, Backstage: The Dramatic Structure of Labor Negotiations*. Cambridge, MA: MIT Press.

Greenhalgh, Leonard. 2001. *Managing Strategic Relationships.* New York: The Free Press.

Kolb, D. M., and G. Coolidge. 1992. *Her Place at the Table.* In J. W. Breslin and J. Z. Rubin (Eds.), *Negotiation Theory and Practice* (pp. 261–277). Cambridge, MA: Program on Negotiation, Harvard Law School.

Kolb, Deborah M., and Linda L. Putnam. 1992. The Dialectics of Disputing. In Deborah M. Kolb and Jean Bartunek (Eds.), *Hidden Conflict in Organization.* Newbury Park, CA: Sage.

Kolb, Deborah M., and Jean Bartunek (Eds.). 1992. *Hidden Conflict in Organizations.* Newbury Park, CA: Sage.

Kolb, Deborah M., and Associates. 1994. *When Talk Works: Profiles of Mediators.* San Francisco: Jossey-Bass.

Kolb, Deborah, and Judith Williams. 2000. *The Shadow Negotiation: How Women Can Master the Hidden Agendas That Determine Bargaining Success.* New York: Simon and Schuster.

Kolb, Deborah, and Judith Williams, 2003. *Everyday Negotiations: Navigating the Hidden Agendas of Bargaining.* San Francisco: Jossey-Bass.

Lax, David A., and James K. Sebenius. 1986. *The Manager as Negotiator.* New York: Basic Books.

Mnookin, Robert M. 1993. "Why Negotiations Fail: An Exploration of Barriers to the Resolution of Conflict." *Ohio State Journal of Dispute Resolution* 8 (2), pp. 235–249.

Putnam, Linda L., and Deborah M. Kolb. 2000. Rethinking Negotiation: Feminist Views of Communication and Exchange. In P. Buzannell (Ed.), *Rethinking Organizational Communication from Feminist Perspectives.* Newbury Park, CA: Sage.

Pruitt, Dean. 1981. *Negotiation Behavior.* New York: Academic Press.

Raiffa, Howard. 1982. *The Art and Science of Negotiation.* Cambridge, MA: Harvard University Press.

Rubin, Jeffrey Z., and Bert R. Brown. 1975. *The Social Psychology of Bargaining and Negotiation.* New York: Academic Press.

Rubin, Jeffrey Z., and Guy Olivier Faure. 1993. *Culture and Negotiation.* Newbury Park, CA: Sage.

Seidel, Marc-David, Jeffrey Polzer, and Katherine Stewart. 2000. Friends in High Places: The Effects of Social Networks on Salary Negotiations. *Administrative Science Quarterly*, 45(1), 1–25.

Shapiro, Debra, and Deborah Kolb. 1994. Reducing the "Litigious Mentality" by Increasing Employees' Desire to Communicate Grievances. In S. Sitkin and B. Bies (Eds.), *The Litigious Organization.* Newbury Park, CA: Sage.

Sheppard, Blair. 1984. Third Party Conflict Intervention: A Procedural Framework. In B. M. Staw and L. L. Cummings (Eds). *Research in Organizational Behavior*, Vol. 6. Greenwich, CT: JAI Press.

Strauss, Anselm. 1978. *Negotiations.* San Francisco: Jossey-Bass.

Tenbrusel, Anne. 1998. Misrepresentation and Expectations of Misrepresentation in an Ethical Dilemma. *Academy of Management Journal*, 41, 330–339.

Thompson, Leigh. 1997. *The Mind and Heart of the Negotiator.* Upper Saddle River, NJ: Prentice Hall.

Valley, Kathleen, and Angela Keros. Forthcoming. It Takes Two: Interactively Determined Bargaining Scripts. *Administrative Science Quarterly.*

Walton, Richard, and Robert B. McKersie. 1965. *A Behavioral Theory of Labor Negotiations.* New York: McGraw-Hill.

Negotiation and Conflict Resolution

ELECTIVE

Module

Dealcrafting

The substance of three-dimensional negotiations

by David A. Lax and James K. Sebenius

Much of our understanding of negotiation focuses on the process at the table involving a complicated set of interpersonal dynamics and strategies, or a "one-dimensional" approach to the subject. Conceptually independent of one-dimensional process factors is a second dimension of negotiation, "dealcrafting," which focuses on substance in the effort to create joint value. A third dimension of negotiation, involving entrepreneurial moves "away from the table," includes the first two dimensions but offers ways in which negotiators can change the game advantageously. Within this overall 3-D perspective, the second dimension (dealcrafting) calls for a relentless focus on creating maximum value and an equally relentless focus on differences as means to create joint gains. Following their description of the overall 3-D approach, the authors use numerous case examples to illustrate how principles of dealcrafting work in practice.

Most people think of negotiation as an interpersonal *process at the table*, though the interplay could take place by phone, fax, e-mail or other means. Wherever it actually occurs, negotiation requires people to focus on a variety of important dynamics: communication, trust-building, cross-cultural perceptions, personalities, bargaining styles, and tactics such as crafting offers and counteroffers. Thus, a preoccupation with *process* underlies most analysis of negotiation among academics, whether economists, game theorists, or psychologists.

We use the shorthand "one-dimensional" to describe this focus on process, or the interpersonal behavior and tactics at the table dealing with a fixed game of parties, issues, no-deal options, and so forth. Indispensable as these process elements are, we argue that this common view can be partial and limiting. A primarily one-dimensional approach can weaken one's ability to analyze negotiating situations fully and to maximize one's potential outcomes.

"Two-dimensional negotiators" understand that an exclusively interpersonal process view can miss the underlying purpose of negotiation, which is substantive and should be driven by its value-creating potential. By joint action, the parties to a successful negotiation each seek to advance the full set of their interests relative to their no-agreement alternatives; thus the "pie" can be expanded or value created through agreement. Beyond process factors, therefore, two-dimensional negotiators tenaciously focus on the potential value latent in the situation and the "dealcrafting" principles for structuring agreements to realize that potential value for the parties. The concept of value in negotiation depends on the full set of the parties' interests, and these interests may be noneconomic as well as economic, intangible as well as tangible, altruistic as well as selfish, and group as well as individual. Since most important negotiations occur in the context of continuing relationships and since effective negotiators often look beyond single transactions, the key question thus is: How can parties create value on a sustainable basis? (Of course, that value must also be distributed or "claimed," often in tandem with its creation, but that is a subject for elsewhere.[1])

For effective two-dimensional (2-D for short) negotiators, deep understanding of substance and value should drive interpersonal process, not the reverse. In this view, process is the servant of substance, not its master. The goal of 2-D negotiators is to look relentlessly beyond interpersonal process to the underlying substance of the problem, seeking to figure out where potential value exists and how to embody it in sustainable agreements.

Our main purpose in this essay is to lay out the basic principles, independent of interpersonal process or tactics, for crafting value-creating deals in negotiation. What we refer to as "dealcrafting" involves the engineering of value in agreements; it is based in part on venerable economic theories of gains from trade, comparative advantage, and the design of optimal contracts.[2]

Consider, for example, a couple of deadlocked one-dimensional negotiators: an entrepreneur who is genuinely optimistic about the future prospects of her fast-growing company faces a potential buyer who truly likes the company but who is much more

---

Source: Lax, David A. and James K. Sebenius. "Dealcrafting: The Substance of Three-Dimensional Negotiations." *Negotiation Journal*, January 2002. Reprinted by permission of Plenum Publishing.

1 See Chapter Six of Lax and Sebenius (1986).
2 Standard economics texts deal with the first two bases of value creation; a modern example of the third can be found in Hart (1995).

skeptical about the company's future cash flow. While these parties have negotiated earnestly and in good faith, no unconditional price is acceptable to both sides. Informal meals together, joint trips to prime hockey games, earnest actions to build the relationship and trust, as well as actively listening for each side's real interests have been helpful but insufficient to bridge the fundamental gap between the high valuation of the seller and the sharply lower maximum of the prospective buyer. Unhappily, the gap has stubbornly resisted an array of tactical choices, such as starting high, agreeing to locking themselves in a room until an acceptable agreement emerges, and even the seller's feigning the existence of other interested buyers and an urgent deadline for the buyer to commit. At the end of the day, despite flip-chart and brainstorming virtuosity in the context of deep psychological insight, the interpersonal process at the table had failed: the two sides may simply disagree on the likely future of the company and, hence, a mutually acceptable unconditional price.

Of course, there is a promising dealcrafting solution that remained undiscovered: The two parties could bridge the value gap by structuring an agreement in which the buyer pays a fixed amount now, less than his current valuation of the company, and a contingent amount later based upon the performance of the company over a future period. Properly structured with adequate incentives and monitoring mechanisms in place, such a contingent payment, or earnout, will appear valuable to the optimistic seller but not particularly costly to the less optimistic buyer. Both sides may now find the deal attractive relative to walking away in the face of a process-resistant value gap.

While neither effective interpersonal behavior, process innovation, nor tactical skill could produce an acceptable agreement in this stylized example, knowledge of a basic principle of dealcrafting could have enabled the parties to create mutual expected benefits. In this case, given genuinely divergent beliefs about the future, the parties should explore a contingent contractual structure that gives to each side what it wants if the state of the world it believes to be most likely does, in fact, occur. The gain comes from substantive knowledge and is independent of process, though effective process may be necessary to discover the underlying differences of belief. Of course, this sort of agreement raises a number of complex design issues that we shall discuss later.

In many cases, the value that can be realized in interactions should be obvious. Two parties want the same thing and agree upon it. Or they come together to combine complementary capabilities: the technology manufacturer looks for someone who can sell the technology in new markets. Or the gains from potential economies of scale are captured by an acquisition and shared via the purchase price. Yet considerable experimental evidence, along with our own experience, suggests that significant and valuable joint gains often go unrealized.[3] There are many psychological and process barriers that result in potential value failing to be created.[4]

A unifying theory of the bases of value creation (or what we call dealcrafting) may be a useful antidote. By stressing the principles underlying value creation, we do not mean to minimize the potentially critical role of good process in crafting valuable agreements (see, for example, Susskind and Cruikshank 1987 or Ury 1991). And process itself can become a substantive interest of the parties (see Kim and Mauborgne 1997). Our premise in this introductory article, however, is that knowing the substantive underpinnings of what you are looking for while you work to create value can only enhance the effectiveness of various process and interpersonal suggestions.

The standard two-dimensional negotiation—balancing substance and process issues, no matter how cleverly—may not always be enough. We propose a third dimension of negotiation, negotiating away from the table, to change the perceived game itself. The great insight of 3-D negotiators is that, once the parties are engaged at the bargaining table in a face-to-face process of creating and claiming value over a given agenda, much of the die is cast. If single-dimensional players seek to resolve the issues under negotiation via the interpersonal process at the table, and 2-D negotiators think beyond process to the substance of potential value from cooperation, 3-D negotiators take entrepreneurial actions away from the table to set up and often reset the "table" to yield the best possible outcome. If 1-D and 2-D negotiators focus on the tactics of playing the game well at the table, 3-D negotiators focus on the strategy of designing the game and changing it advantageously, often away from the table. While the focus of this essay is on dealcrafting, the second dimension of negotiation, we shall nonetheless, in the following pages, offer examples in which the inclusion or exclusion of parties or the changing of the issues under discussion

---

3 See, for example, Thompson (1998: 49) for a summary of a number of standard papers on this subject.
4 The tension between creating and claiming value explored in Lax and Sebenius (1986) is one such barrier. A range of cognitive barriers is described in Baserman and Neale (1992). An even fuller review of psychological barriers can be found in Thompson (1998). The barriers perspective is also generally well treated in Arrow et al. (1995).

enables the parties to create additional value by changing the game that is being played.

Basic Dealcrafting Orientation 1: A Relentless Focus of Creating Maximum Value

Consider the case of a proposed joint venture between Lakeside Corp. and Tonicron Corp. to produce an improved custom chipset that could be sold to two classes of industrial customers. Either firm is capable of producing the chipset separately; the necessary capital cost would be $20 million. The different costs to each firm for making various contributions to the joint venture (debt, semi-finished chips, manufacturing) are summarized in Table One. As the last line of the table suggests, Lakeside is already selling an earlier version of this chipset to one class of industrial customers, while Tonicron is not.

How should this joint venture be structured? Which party should contribute what or carry out which activities? Several elements are obvious: The proposed joint venture would have the lowest net cost if Lakeside provides the semi-finished chips and Tonicron incurs the debt for capital expenditure and manufactures the chipset at its lower variable cost.[5] If each firm makes these contributions, overall cost and revenue sharing can be adjusted so there is a net benefit to both parties relative to other possible structures.

However (see the last line of Table One), notice that Lakeside wants to restrict the joint venture from selling to its existing class of customers to avoid cannibalizing its current business.[6] Tonicron wants complete marketing freedom for the joint venture to sell to all potential customers. This could play out as a classic positional battle in which Lakeside's preferred position in the negotiations was for full restrictions on new sales while Tonicron's position permitted complete marketing freedom. Clearly these individually preferred positions are incompatible.

The ordinary psychology of this kind of negotiation involves powerful and persistent images of a mythical fixed pie, meaning that one side's gain on this issue necessarily involves the other side's loss.[7] Indeed Leigh Thompson (1998) reviews a large series of experiments which show that the incompatibility bias—each side sees its interests fundamentally in conflict with the others—is so pervasive that large numbers of subjects in negotiating simulations failed to find resolutions in which their preferences were fully compatible. In short, it would be quite normal for Lakeside and Tonicron to battle this issue out with the result being a winner, a loser, or a split-the-difference compromise. Suppose such a process took place—that Lakeside "won" outright, and that the parties agreed to restrict joint venture sales for, say, two years. Could both sides do better than this outcome? (Of course Lakeside is on both sides of this negotiation, but has a clear individual preference for the joint venture to observe sales restrictions.)

Let us push this analysis a bit. Suppose the two sides worked together to produce the data shown in Table Two, which illustrates the effect on the net sales both of Lakeside and the joint venture as a function of the length of time that the Lakeside-Tonicron venture would be restricted from selling to Lakeside's existing customers.

Agreement on a two-year restriction would result in net sales to Lakeside of $24 million and

Table One: Costs and Customers Relevant to Lakeside-Tonicron Joint Venture

	Lakeside Corp.	Tonicron Corp.
Cost of new debt	9%	7%
Cost of supplying semi-finished chips	$40/unit	$45/unit
Variable production costs (% of sales)	30%	22%
Existing customers	Yes	No

---

5 This assumes that the cost figures reflect true economic (opportunity) costs.
6 This aspect of the example is inspired by the El-Tek case series written by Bazerman and Neale.
7 See Bazerman and Neale (1992) for an elaboration.

$66 million to the Lakeside-Tonicron venture (however, the revenues from the latter were split between Lakeside and Tonicron). Could the two sides jointly do better than this? Suppose they reduced the restrictions to eighteen months; then Lakeside would get $22 million while the Lakeside-Tonicron project would net $74 million. Even though Lakeside would lose $2 million individually by this move relative to a two-year restriction, the gain to the joint venture—an $8 million increase from $66 to $74 million—would more than offset Lakeside's loss from relaxing the restriction. Indeed, by compensating Lakeside by an amount between $2 million and $8 million, both the joint venture and Lakeside would be better off with the eighteen-month restriction rather than a two-year ban. Similarly, by moving from eighteen months to a one-year restriction, both sides could again be made better off since the joint venture's gain ($9 million) could more than compensate Lakeside's loss ($4 million) from relaxing the restriction further. And moving to a six-month restriction could improve both sides yet more as the joint venture's incremental gain ($15 million) could more than compensate Lakeside's added loss ($4 million), leaving both better off. However, going all the way to remove the restriction entirely would cost Lakeside $14 million while benefiting the Lakeside-Tonicron project only by $2 million; there is no way that this extra move could result in a joint gain.

This reasoning makes clear that, with respect to the market restriction issue, a six-month restriction is, with appropriate allocation to Lakeside and Tonicron, better for *both* sides than any other outcome. Another way to see this is to look at the total benefit (to Lakeside individually plus the joint venture) for any option. From the data shown in Table Two, it is clear that a six-month restriction gives higher total projected net sales ($112 million) than unrestricted sales or any restrictions longer than six months. (The total benefits of moving from no restrictions to two years of them in six-month increments, in millions of dollars, are 100, 112, 101, 96, and 90.) As such, allocating the added benefit created by a six-month restriction can provide more benefits jointly and individually than other restrictions. In short, where value can be transferred in this manner, focusing on how to increase the *total net pie* is the right guide to creating value.[8]

Recall that the preferred negotiating positions of each side individually were completely incompatible: Lakeside wanted two years of restrictions while Tonicron, arguing on behalf of the joint venture, demanded total sales freedom. Viewed individually, and through the prism of the mythical fixed pie, these opposing positions were indeed the most valuable to each side: Lakeside wanted two years while Tonicron wanted no restrictions. But the six-month optimal outcome was *not* a compromise that each side could live with; it actually created value both jointly and individually relative to the other possible outcomes. (Note that a seemingly "fair" compromise—restrictions for a year—between the two individually preferred positions, of no restrictions versus two years of them, would leave $11 million on the table, as value uncreated.)

To find the most value-creating outcome requires a view toward maximizing the whole first, rather than taking the positions most preferred by individ-

Table TWO Timing and Restraints on Lakeside-Tonicron Sales

Length of restrictions on joint venture sales to Lakeside customers (years)	Net present value to Lakeside of sales to Lakeside customers ($million)	Net present value of total potential joint venture sales ($million)
None	$0	$100
Six months	$14	$98
One year	$18	$83
Eighteen months	$22	$74
Two years	$24	$66

8 We are using the term "total pie" in a loose sense. If value is transferable among the parties, there is no ambiguity. Otherwise, adding up value to each side involves illegitimate interpersonal comparisons of utility, per standard textbook treatments. More accurately, we are referring to pareto-optimal moves, that benefit each side at no cost to the other.

ual side. Then the added total value can be used to compensate any individual "losers," such that all parties are strictly better off. This is *not* an argument about sacrificing individual interest for the good of the whole. Individual positional bargaining generally suboptimizes relative to a focus on increasing the total, both on individual and collective bases.

Consider the potential value of such an approach in dealing with the siting of noxious facilities (such as waste treatment plants), which are often blocked by the so-called "NIMBY" problem—all agree that the facility is needed but "not in my backyard." The value to the region as a whole can be enormous. Particular groups who are able to block its siting near them clearly feel damaged by having such a facility nearby. Yet, the cost of the damage to them can easily be a small fraction of the aggregate value to the people of the region of having the facility available. Devising a mechanism that adequately compensates the abutters of the facility can unlock great value for the region as a whole (see Raiffa 1985).

In general, potential value-creating agreements between organizations are often blocked because individuals or groups within an organization believe that they will be hurt individually by the agreement. For example, pharmaceutical giants SmithKline Beecham and Glaxo announced plans for a merger in 1998, including the executive lineup of the new entity. Immediately, the combined market capitalization of the two companies rose by about $20 *billion*. Incredibly for the shareholders, this agreement was scuttled with renewed disputing between the two CEOs over who would hold which senior management roles. When the announced merger was called off, the combined market capitalization dropped back to previous levels.

One can imagine many approaches to better handling of such "social issues." Somewhat tongue-in-cheek, suppose the board were to offer whichever executive who agrees to leave a sum that could be ratcheted up until accepted by one side or the other in a kind of reverse Dutch auction. Even if the sum required were astronomical by ordinary compensation standards, such a deal still might have preserved the vast bulk of the shareholder value that would have been created by the 1998 merger proposal. (The value-creating merger was revived nearly two wasted years later, with one of the contending CEOs announcing his retirement.)

Principle: Focus away from directly seeking to maximize individual outcomes. Instead, as a means of optimizing individual results, seek to create an agreement with the highest total net value (e.g., manufacturing by the lower cost party, borrowing by the party with access to the least expensive credit, etc.). As necessary, devise legitimate compensation mechanisms to individuals to unlock higher total net value.

Basic Dealcrafting Orientation 2: A Relentless Focus on Differences as the Raw Material for Joint Gains

Given conventional wisdom that one negotiates to overcome differences and that differences divide us, typical negotiation advice exhorts negotiators to find "win-win" agreements by searching for common ground. While common ground—in the sense of accurate communication and trust along with the possibility that both sides want an identical outcome—is generally a good thing, we take the view that the most valuable sources of value in agreement are typically created because of *differences* among the parties. These include differences in relative cost or revenue structure; in priority or valuation; in forecasts or beliefs about the future; in attitudes toward risk; in attitudes towards time; in capabilities; in tax or accounting treatment; or in myriad other characteristics of the negotiators.

In many instances, the sources of value from negotiated agreement are obvious: appropriately motivating the parties, reaping economies of scale, cutting costs, or simply increasing the efficiency of production. Yet, based on our experience over the years, we consistently observe that important classes of difference exist, and that crafting a characteristic form of agreement can exploit each class of difference to mutual advantage. Our experience, backed up by considerable experimental study (see, e.g., Thompson 1998 or Bazerman and Neale 1992), is that negotiators frequently miss these sources of potential value. We believe that the principles made explicit and elaborated in the following sections can systematically guide negotiators' attention to unrealized value in many negotiations.

Differences in Cost/Revenue Structure

Return for a moment to the Lakeside-Tonicron joint venture and reexamine the source of joint gains. The simplest gains came from disaggregating the various joint venture tasks and allocating them to the low-cost party (with appropriate compensation in terms of ownership or profit sharing). At the most basic level, value was found here by focusing on cost/revenue *differences between the parties*. But push further to the potentially contentious sales restriction issue; when focused on its individual outcomes, Lakeside wanted two years of total sales restrictions while Tonicron wanted complete marketing freedom. As we showed, however, when sales restrictions were progressively relaxed from two years on down to six months, the gain to the joint Lakeside-Tonicron venture at each stage was larger than the loss to Lakeside. It is this difference that permitted the pie to expand and joint gains to be realized. If the cost of relaxing the restrictions to Lakeside were equal at each stage to the gain for the joint venture, no mutual benefit could be found; the negotiation over restrictions would be strictly zero-sum or a matter of pure value-claiming. But difference in this element, the cost/revenue structure, underlies the joint gain potential here (just as differences above in costs of borrowing, manufacturing, or furnishing semi-finished chips pointed the way to the optimal structure for the joint venture).

Principle: Craft deals so that differences in cost/revenue structure combine to create the largest net economic pie. This permits each party to get more than would be possible otherwise.

Differences in Capability

Closely related to net cost and revenue structure are complementary capabilities. Obviously, a company with strong production capabilities can combine forces with another firm that has great marketing and distribution channels to create value that neither could achieve otherwise. Similarly, a company with strong basic research and development activities may profitably combine forces with another firm that has strong applications engineering.

Principle: Craft deals so that complementary capabilities combine to create the largest net economic pie. With appropriate compensation, this permits each party to gain more than would be possible otherwise.

Differences in Interest and Priority

Parties with different interests and priorities can be the ingredients of trades that create value for both parties. This venerable principle underlying pure exchange-based gains from trade can be seen in very simple cases. Suppose Jerrold has three apples, which he intensely dislikes, while craving pears. Geraldine, by contrast, loathes pears, of which she has three, and dreams of eating apples. Precisely because of this difference of interest or priority, the apple-pear swap creates value for both, relative to no-trade.

In a more elaborate example, an American buyout group sought to purchase a money-losing luxury consumer brand company with a highly prestigious brand and a loyal following among elite consumers. The potential seller was a wealthy European family whose net worth would be enhanced by the sale but whose lives would likely not be materially affected. After considerable due diligence, which detailed the extent of the underlying business problems, the maximum price the buyout group was willing to pay was well below the minimum on which the family was firmly insisting. The gap was such that the buyout group had virtually concluded that no deal was likely and pursuing other opportunities was a better option.

Yet in reading carefully between the lines of the discussions, it became clear that the family wanted to be able to tell their equally wealthy friends that they had "gotten the best" of the American group: a high price and an option to buy a controlling stake back if the Americans could not improve the performance of the firm. Privately, the business-savvy family members also realized that the business itself was a mess and could not rationally fetch their asking price. Yet there was simply no way they would agree to a sale on the buyout group's terms; as word got out, it would be too humiliating.

Ultimately, however, the deal was done at the lower price and the family received options to buy back a major part of the firm—but only after an initial public offering of the stock, at which point the family would not actually be able to regain control. This satisfied the buyout group's priority interest in the economic and control aspects of the deal. What made the deal happen, however, was the fact that the terms were openly "leaked" by various credible third parties as having taken place at a higher price. Moreover, these third parties described the family's options as if they could regain control.[9] When the parties were just talking about price and control, there was an impasse between the conflicting positions of the two sides. Pushing behind these starkly incompatible positions to discover underlying priority differences, however, suggested that a deal could be possible. Then, unbundling appearance and substance—that is, widening the set of issues under negotiation to match the underlying different interests—permitted a trade to go through that was better for both parties than no deal.

Principle: Where the parties assign different priorities to different underlying interests, seek trades that give to each party what is relatively most important to it. Look behind apparently incompatible positions on a set of issues that bundle together differently valued interests; seek to unbundle these differently valued interests by way of

---

[9] The entire deal was entirely private and there were no public shareholders or regulatory authorities involved; otherwise such tactics would almost certainly have been both unethical and illegal.

a new set of issues that enables a mutually beneficial trade.

Implication: Agenda Management

When negotiating large contracts, it is common to have one party's attorney make a list of unresolved issues and have the group work down the list one issue at a time, attempting to get closure on each, before moving on to the next issue. While this method of agenda setting can help the parties to organize the remaining questions, it is almost guaranteed to leave value on the table for all parties. If the parties have opposing interests on each issue, they will typically reach mid-range settlements on each of the issues. Yet this fails to heed the principle laid out earlier, in which the party who places greatest weight on each issue should receive more favorable treatment on that issue in return for "compensation," such as giving the other(s) favorable treatment on the issues most important to them (providing the issues are of roughly similar importance). As such, the agreement reached by finalizing one issue at a time is likely to be substantially worse for all parties than that reached by a process that is geared to look for difference in interest and thereby to facilitate trades. Yet issue-by-issue agenda management is often the default procedure in many complex negotiations.

Examples: 3-D Moves—Adding Parties to Exploit Differences of Interest

The principle of seeking differences of interest or relative priority to craft mutually beneficial trades is well-known in its simple forms, but it is in its elaboration that it can provide dealmakers with surprising power. Consider the possibility of fashioning value-creating trades by adding parties with different interests. For example, in 1997, WorldCom (now MCI WorldCom) acquired CompuServe for $1.2 billion, largely to obtain CompuServe's Internet infrastructure, data transmission and key corporate customers.[10] However, CompuServe also had a large Internet content business and 2.6 million subscribers. WorldCom enhanced the value of the transaction by the addition of AOL, which wanted CompuServe's subscribers to augment its then 9 million subscribers. Obviously, AOL valued these subscribers differently (far more) than did WorldCom. AOL also received: (1) CompuServe's 850,000 European subscribers (three times AOL's then subscriber base in Europe), which AOL placed in a joint venture with Bertelsmann in return for $75 million; (2) $175 million from WorldCom; and (3) immediate use of 100,000 modems from WorldCom to relieve the congestion that, at that point, was sharply hurting AOL's performance and reputation. In return, WorldCom received AOL's Internet backbone network and data service to augment those it acquired in its purchases of UUnet and MFS along with a five-year major service contract to run much of AOL's network. By bringing in AOL as part of the CompuServe deal, WorldCom was able to bring in a player with complementary differences that facilitated several value-creating trades as part of this transaction.

In the diplomatic realm, potentially valuable bilateral deals can be impossible without a third party with complementary differences of interest. Janice Gross Stein (1985: 334) describes Henry Kissinger's role in Middle East negotiations:

> . . . *the circular structure of payment was essential to promoting agreement among the parties: Egypt improved the image of the United States in the Arab world, especially among the oil-producing states; the United States gave Israel large amounts of military and financial aid; and Israel supplied Egypt with territory. Indeed a bilateral exchange between Egypt and Israel would not have succeeded since each did not want what the other could supply.*

Overall, then, differences in relative priority, importance, or valuation can lead to mutually beneficial trades. Sometimes the differently valued interests are bundled; in which case creative unbundling can unlock value. And sometimes, moves away from the table to bring in a party that differentially values some of the elements of the deal can create value.

Differences in Forecast or Belief About the Future

Mark Twain once quipped that it is "differences of opinion that make horse races." Along these lines, differences in beliefs about how future events will unfold—e.g., what a key price will be, whether a technology will work, whether a permit will be granted or court suit won, etc.—can be the basis of mutually beneficial *contingent* agreements.

Example: Cogeneration Plant

In the early 1980s, an engineering firm was seeking to build plants that burned solid waste to generate electricity and be paid for disposing of the waste and selling the electricity. In its first deal, the firm found a city willing to supply waste and which would be able to use steam generated by such a plant in municipal facilities to augment electricity

---

10 For details, see various press reports, e.g., "Big Deals," *American Lawyer*, November 1997, p. 92; or Catherine Yang's report, "Answered Prayers at America Online," *Business Week*, 22 September 1997, p. 30.

it received from oil-fired plants. The firm and the city had reached agreement on a fixed (tipping) fee for disposing of the municipal waste but could not reach agreement on a fixed price for the steam that the city would purchase. Discussion revealed that the impasse resulted from different forecasts: the city planning department expected an oil glut and hence low electricity prices in the next few years while the firm expected oil prices to rise.

The parties were able to get beyond impasse by structuring an agreement in which the steam price varied but was tied to oil prices. Note that each party placed high value on this agreement precisely because of differing beliefs: the city expected to pay a low price for steam because it believed oil would be cheap while the engineering firm expected to receive a much higher price because it believed oil would be expensive. Although each side expected incompatible outcomes, each was willing to take the risk that it would be wrong and permit an agreement to go forward that, in an ex ante sense, created value for both sides relative to no deal.[11]

The contingent agreement should be structured, however, to be *sustainable* once the underlying uncertainty is resolved. It would be self-defeating, for example, (1) to permit the price of steam to drop below a level that provided for debt service and plant maintenance; (2) to rise to levels that would be politically unsustainable. Sustainability could easily be enhanced, for example, by setting floor and ceiling prices for the steam or partially indexing its price to the oil price. (A 3-D negotiation move might have been contemplated for the two parties to hedge future oil prices by using sufficiently long-dated futures or options written by third parties or markets with different effective future expectations and risk attitudes.)

Example: Earnouts

As the introductory example in this article described, when an entrepreneur seeks to sell her company to a much larger corporation, there is often a gap between the price the buyer will maximally pay and the seller will minimally accept. The entrepreneur often sees much brighter future prospects for the company but needs capital and organizational scale to reach the perceived potential, whereas the prospective buyer has a positive but typically more skeptical view.

The two sides may be able to bridge this characteristic value gap by structuring a contingent agreement called an earnout in which the seller pays a fixed amount today and then subsequent amounts that are contingent upon the future performance of the firm. Thus, the more optimistic entrepreneur believes the value of the payments she receives through the earnout will be higher than the buyer expects; both are happy to do the deal given their forecasts. Without the earnout, an otherwise mutually beneficial deal may well languish. Earnouts, sometimes of very large magnitude relative to the nominal deal value, are quite common.[12]

In addition to enabling parties to trade based on differences in belief, contingent deals can create incentives for particular behavior. For example, if the entrepreneur running the company after it has been purchased will receive large payments based on profits over the next three years, she has a strong incentive to maximize profits. It is important, therefore, to analyze carefully whether the contingent agreement creates perverse incentives. To return to the earnout example, the entrepreneur may well seek to optimize against whatever performance measure is used to compute the earnout while the corporation may have an incentive to depress this measure. For example, if the performance measure is profit-after-tax over the first three years after the sale, the entrepreneur may have an incentive to neglect investments that would only pay off after three years. Thus, one needs to think through the incentives created by agreements when the variable upon which the outcome is contingent can be influenced by the parties.

Contingent agreements can also act as a "truth serum" for parties who are prone to misstate their beliefs. To return to the example of an entrepreneur negotiating the sale of her company for a fixed price, what happens if she tells prospective buyers that she is highly confident that her few large customers will stay with the company over the next few years, even when she has some grounds for uncertainty? An astute buyer might structure an agreement whose value depends on whether the customers stay, in other words asking the seller to absorb the risk (which she asserts is negligible) that these customers leave. Had the seller contemplated a payment based on whether these customers stay, she would have had an incentive to be more truthful about her forecast. Indeed, to the extent that the discussion switches from a fixed purchase price to a contingent arrangement, the entrepreneur may be forced to backpedal from her overstated beliefs.

---

11 This example is based on a situation described by Prof. David E. Bell of the Harvard Business School.
12 Numerous current examples are discussed at the following Web site: http://www.thedailydeal.com/topstories/A21955-2000May3.html.

Principle: When forecasts of future events differ, contingent agreements may create expected value for the parties. Typically, such agreements give to each side the outcome it values most in the state of the world it forecasts as most likely. Such agreements need careful structuring both (1) to induce desirable behavior and avoid perverse incentives; and (2) to be sustainable once the uncertain quantity underlying the contingent agreement has been resolved.[13]

Contingent Agreements Based on Forecast Differences: A 3-D Extension

This principle—dovetailing expectational differences by way of contingent contracts—can sometimes be extended by bringing in third parties with different beliefs. In the mid-1990s, Ahmanson, a major California thrift institution, was negotiating to acquire a smaller competitor, Coast Financial Savings.[14] The acquisition would have made Ahmanson the second largest thrift in the United States, raising its share of the California market from 7.5 to 9.1 percent. The value of Coast's banking assets, given likely cost savings and synergies, suggested a purchase price of about $900 million.

Beyond this value, Coast had acquired weaker competitors consistent with agreements with the relevant regulatory bodies during the U.S. savings and loan crisis of the 1980s. These agreements also involved promises about the regulatory and accounting treatment that Coast would receive with regard to the acquired assets. Later, the regulators dramatically shortened the write-off period for these assets, precipitating disastrous financial results for Coast. In a legal action similar to that of a number of other institutions, Coast sued the federal government for $1.1 billion, alleging an arbitrary shortening of the write-off period. Coast had received favorable preliminary judgments in lower courts and some observers were confident that it would win a sizeable award, but were uncertain as to the amount and timing.

Given the size of the potential settlement relative to the value of the banking assets themselves, the negotiation dynamic involved Coast arguing for a higher price based on its argument that the payout would be large and soon; predictably, Ahmanson argued for a much lower price, based on its assertion that the likely payout would be smaller and farther into the future.

Instead of trying to negotiate whose projection was more accurate, or even trying to structure a contingent agreement based on the outcome of the litigation, the parties overcame the potential impasse by a more interesting device: structuring an acquisition in which Coast shareholders received $900 million in Ahmanson stock along with "litigation participation certificates." These certificates would pay in cash all proceeds ultimately received from the lawsuit, net of expenses. This contingent agreement enabled each side to value the uncertain outcome of the lawsuit using its own forecasts. However, these certificates were created to trade publicly, which allowed *additional* value creation. Coast shareholders who were skeptical of Coast's chance in its suit could sell the certificates at a price in excess of their valuation to other investors who valued them more highly, implicitly bringing in investors who had the most optimistic forecasts about the outcome of the suit. Relative to a straightforward Coast-Ahmanson deal on price, spinning out the litigation participation certificates and making them tradable created value.

Differences in Attitudes Toward Risk

The next important extensions of the differences principle involve differences in the parties' attitudes toward risk, specifically differences in the ability to bear, influence, or assess particular risks.

Example: A Restaurant in Arbitration

A restaurant owner was selling his highly successful restaurant to his head chef. The restaurant had a dispute with the contractor who had renovated the restaurant and had withheld $1,000,000 that the contractor felt she was owed. The dispute was in arbitration and likely to be completed soon. Both the owner and the chef agreed that there was a 50 percent chance that the contractor would win and be owed $1,000,000 and a 50 percent chance that nothing would be owed. Thus there was no difference in forecasts for the future.

However, because the chef was putting the bulk of his assets into the purchase, he was quite averse to the risk of paying additional money to the contractor. The chef and restaurant owner had agreed on a purchase price of $1 million under the assumption that the chef would have to pay the contractor if the

---

13 All sorts of tricky analytical issues are buried in this discussion, most obviously, the extent to which differences in probabilistic assessment are a function of differential information heritage. These issues are considered at length in the technical portions of Sebenius (1984).
14 For details, see various *Wall Street Journal* articles, including Steven Lipin's report, "Ahmanson agrees to acquire Coast Savings for $900 million," *Wall Street Journal Interactive Edition*, 6 October 1997; or Paul Sweeney's article, "How to win big in court and never see a lawyer," *New York Times*, 11 January 1998, p. C10.

restaurant lost its suit. The chef valued the restaurant at $2 million if he did not have to bear the arbitration risk, but only $1.3 million if he had to bear the risk. In short, the chef's risk aversion caused his valuation of the restaurant to drop by $700,000 if he bore the risk—even though the expected cost of the dispute with the chef was only $500,000.

By contrast, the restaurateur was already wealthy and would add a significant amount to his assets with a sale. He was much less averse to the arbitration risk and would not pay a premium to avoid it. Indeed, he valued the risk at its expected value and thus would pay up to $500,000 to avoid it. Given their different risk profiles, therefore, if the chef paid the owner $1.6 million for the restaurant with the current owner bearing the construction dispute risk, both sides would gain relative to the original offer. The chef would be paying $600,000 to avoid a risk that it was willing to pay up to $700,000 to avoid, for a net gain of $100,000. Similarly, the owner was receiving $600,000 to accept a risk that he valued at $500,000, for a gain of $100,000. Both sides would be better off if the risk were allocated to the less risk-averse party, who would see it as less costly than a more risk averse individual, and if he were compensated for bearing that risk in the price paid by the more risk-averse party. In other words, the total net cost of risk bearing to both parties would be reduced by this allocation.

Example: Specialty Steel Joint Venture

A marginally profitable, publicly traded, risk-averse steel company was discussing a joint venture with a highly profitable, privately held scrap metal company. The proposal on the table was to jointly build and operate a modern specialty steel facility that would use scrap metal as an input that would be operated by the steel company. There was no disagreement about the forecasts of future expenses and profits. However, the proposed deal that both parties were considering called for an even split of the investment costs, operating costs, future funding obligations, and returns. Even though this seemed fair to both sides, this proposed deal structure led to an impasse. The publicly traded steel company was highly averse to the risk of any losses that could hurt its earnings, reduce its share price, and increase its cost of capital. Yet the scrap company was far more aggressive in terms of its risk attitudes. The two firms were able to reconcile their interests by structuring an agreement in which the scrap company accepted more than a pro rata share of the losses in return for a larger share of the profit. Both parties strongly preferred limiting the steel company's downside in return for a higher share of the upside to the scrap company. In short, value was created by allocating more risk to the less risk-averse party and compensating it with a higher prospective return.

Example: Public-Private Real Estate Development

A city with a blighted downtown section was seeking a developer for a major mixed use project with office, retail, and residential components. The city was prepared to commit significant resources to assist in the development of the public-private project. Getting approval of the local Zoning Board, however, could be a significant hurdle. Although its members were appointed by the current and previous mayors, the board was intended to function as a quasi-independent body. Moreover, market risk loomed large: would the project generate the acceptable occupancy rates and rents in a reasonable time frame? Significant costs would be borne in developing a proposal for the Zoning Board (e.g., architects, consultants, environmental analyses, traffic planning, land acquisition, lobbying, public relations, etc.) Much larger costs would be incurred in construction of the project.

In early negotiations, the city's attorney proposed that the city and developer split all project development costs evenly, even if the proposal were turned down by the Zoning Board. The developer rejected this proposal. He believed that the mayor could have much greater de facto influence on the outcome of the Zoning Board review and thus that the city should bear the costs of failure there. Similarly, he believed that, as a developer, he would have much greater influence over the project's success in the market and was prepared to take the bulk of the risk at that stage. Relative to equally sharing costs and risks, the agreement between the city and the developer largely followed his suggestion, in which the party who had the greatest influence over a particular risk bore the largest share of that risk; this deal structure also created appropriate incentives.

Example: Selling a Waste Disposal Plant

Pushing this line of analysis further, differences in the ability to assess risk can drive its appropriate allocation. In one instance, a small developer of a waste disposal facility was deadlocked in his negotiation to sell the environmental permits he had obtained for a site to a large firm in the waste management industry. A quirk of state law seemed to create a crucial ambiguity: while the permits would legally transfer to a buyer if a facility were actually built, there was some question as to whether the permits would legally transfer if no facility had yet been built. When the large corporate buyer's attorney asked the seller for a representation of transferability, the seller was uncomfortable with this proposal.

While this anxiety could have been interpreted as an indication of his superior knowledge that the permits were, in fact, *not* transferable, the real explanation was simpler: The seller was an entrepreneur who had begun his career driving garbage trucks and was far less capable of assessing the transferability risk than the large waste management firm, which had specialized legal and regulatory compliance staffs. Indeed, the seller would have been willing to pay something to avoid the risk of nontransferability. A joint gain was created by (1) splitting the premium the seller was willing to pay to avoid the risk; and (2) transferring the risk to the buyer, who now had a very strong incentive to use its superior risk assessment and mitigation capabilities.

Risk-Profile Differences: 3-D Extensions

A predominantly value-claiming negotiation can develop when two parties to a negotiation with very similar risk attitudes seek to shift a large risk in the transaction to the other party. In such cases, changing the game by bringing in a third party or the market—with an effectively different risk profile—may be a value-creating move. Recall the cogeneration case in which the city believed oil prices would rise and the construction firm had opposite views. Suppose each party was also averse to the risks involved in fluctuating prices. Then laying off that risk to the market through various options, futures, or derivative instruments based on future oil prices could reduce the net cost of risk-bearing to the two parties; indeed this could be true even if both sides agreed on oil price forecasts.

Or consider a supplier of goods to retail stores who is highly averse to the risks of late payment or nonpayment. Such a supplier may insist on much tougher payment terms than the stores were willing to offer, leading to an impasse in the supplier-retailer negotiations. Yet bringing in a factoring firm that will purchase the supplier's retail accounts receivable at a discount may permit the transaction to go forward on less onerous payment terms. Adding a third party with different risk attitudes (as well as differential collection capabilities and reputation) may reduce risk-bearing costs. In fact, this move may actually lessen the magnitude of the risks themselves, leading to the potential for joint gains.

Principles: When one party is more risk averse than the other, seek to create value by shifting risk from the more risk-averse party to the less risk-averse one in return for a greater share of the rewards (or other form of compensation). When parties have influence over different risks, seek to create value by shifting risks to the parties that can best minimize them, again with appropriate compensation. When there is a difference in the parties' abilities to assess a particular risk, consider shifting that risk to the party best able to assess it in return for compensation in other dimensions. In some cases, changing the game by bringing in third parties or markets with different risk attitudes than the principals to a negotiation may create value.

Differences in Attitudes Toward Time

The next important extension of the differences principle involves the parties' attitudes toward time, which again can be understood to imply differences in expected value of the present value of a deal.

In the simplest case, one party is more impatient than another; equivalently, one party has a higher discount rate. For example, a venture capital group had provided an early round of financing to a promising biotechnology firm that was now seeking additional financing. The biotech firm had contacted a large European pharmaceutical company that was impressed with the biotech firm's technology and was interested in making a later-stage investment. The pharmaceutical company placed a high value on this investment as a window into a new area of biotechnology. Using its own hurdle rate, the European firm negotiated the terms of an investment that provided a 10 percent projected rate of return. However, the pharmaceutical firm wanted to see others invest at the same time and asked the existing venture capitalists to invest in this next round alongside it. The venture capitalists refused, which caused the pharmaceutical company to worry that they had lost confidence in the venture.

Discussion over how to break this impasse, however, revealed that, at this stage of development, the venture capitalists would require a projected 35 percent rate of return. To break the apparent deadlock, the biotech firm's managers negotiated terms that provided the venture capitalists with a higher share of the early profits and the pharmaceutical company with a higher share of the later profits. Although both value early distributions more than later distributions, the much stronger preference of the venture capitalists for early returns means that to get a disproportionate share of the early distributions, they could compensate the pharmaceutical company with a much larger share of later distributions. Since the venture capitalists would discount later returns so much more highly (when using a 35 percent discount rate) than the pharmaceutical firm (which used a 10 percent rate), it was a value-creating move to shift the pharmaceutical firm's return further out and increase its magnitude disproportionately.

In other settings, the parties' time preferences are not easily captured by a hurdle or discount rate. For example, government officials in grant-making agencies that have not allocated all their funds often have a strong interest in allocating all the funds before their fiscal year-end. The officials may be eager to do so because (1) the fund will have to be returned, unspent, to the Treasury; and (2) the agency's budget may well decline for the following year if some of this year's funds went unspent. At a more prosaic level, companies often have annual budgets for consultants or certain kinds of supplies. It is often much easier to negotiate a large agreement at the beginning of a new budget year when they have the funds than at the end of the last year when their ability to allocate new funds is low. Similarly, sales organizations often have quarterly goals. It may well be possible for a consumer to get better prices and terms at the end of the quarter, when the sales force is stretching to reach its goals, than at the beginning of the quarter. Someone who knows that she will be switching to a new overseas job at year-end may care much more about the effects of an agreement under negotiation on the next few months' results than about the effects after she is overseas. Each of these de facto differences in time attitudes offers the potential for joint gain among the involved parties—though one should be cautious about costs to others who are not party to the immediate deal.

Principle: Match payments and benefits received to relative time preferences. The relatively impatient should get more earlier but later compensate the other. In general, people should receive benefits at the times they value the benefits most highly in return for providing others with benefits at the times that the others value them most highly. Similarly, minimize the present value of costs to be borne by differentially allocating the timing of costs to parties to accord with their relative time preferences (and compensating accordingly).

Differences in Tax Status

Parties often differ in their tax status. For example, an individual in the United States cannot deduct interest from a loan used to purchase an automobile. However, if a corporation borrows money to purchase the same car and leases it to the individual, that party can deduct the interest from the loan. Assuming that the credit risk is not significant, it is often feasible and mutually beneficial to share the reduction in taxes experienced by the lessor rather than have the individual borrow and purchase the car directly. This is the simplest and most familiar form of tax arbitrage—with the joint gain effectively funded by the government. Tax-driven transaction structures, are, of course, legion; the following example is but one of myriad possibilities underpinned by differences in tax situation.

Example: Converting Ordinary Income to Capital Gains

For a number of years, U.S. investors in hedge funds that traded securities frequently were taxed each year at an ordinary rate on gains realized but not distributed to investors (rather than at the lower capital gains rate). Several investment banks developed "swap" instruments that transformed the ordinary income taxed each year into capital gains taxed only upon redemption from the fund. The investor would buy a bond whose face value was equal to the amount she wished to invest in the fund, and swap it for a promise from the investment bank to pay the total return of the fund (less a fee) to the investor when the investor chose to redeem. By virtue of its business status, the investment bank would not pay taxes on the income the fund generated because this asset was matched directly by its promise to pay out the income. When the investor redeemed the swap, she would receive the principal and the returns that had accumulated in the fund less any fees to the investment bank. As an added bonus, if she had held it long enough, the investor could treat it as a capital gain for tax purposes. The difference in the tax treatment accorded the investor and the tax treatment accorded the investment bank facilitated trades of substantial mutual value.

Principle: Look for differences in tax treatment. Where feasible, the party with the lower tax rate should receive taxable income and the party with the higher tax rate should receive deductions. The joint gain from these actions can then be shared for mutual benefit.

Differences in Accounting Treatment and Reporting Sensitivity

Parties may also differ in the accounting treatment they receive and the appearance of a transaction to key constituencies. For example, privately held financial firms and publicly traded companies can have very different perspectives on good will and on the debt-equity ratio changes created by a proposed acquisition. The private firm may be centrally concerned about cash flow and risk while the publicly traded firm may be more focused on how an acquisition will affect its reported earnings (since good will from an acquisition reduces reported earnings). At the same time, the good will increases tax deductions and thus increases cash flow, which often is of greater value to the owners of privately held financial firms. In addition, a publicly traded firm may be more concerned about its reported debt-equity ratio.

If these differences in attitudes toward good will and capital structure are present, the public firm can partner with the private firm to make acquisitions for the publicly traded firm. By giving majority control of the partnership to the private financial firm, the acquiring entity can be structured in such a way that the public firm does not need to consolidate the acquisition debt or write off the good will. Such agreements typically allow for the public firm to exercise an option to buy the remainder of the firm after good will and debt have been reduced and for the private firm to be able to force the public firm to buy it after a period of time. The differences in accounting treatment (and their implications in capital markets) enable the publicly traded firm to make a profitable acquisition it might otherwise shun while providing healthy profits for the private firm. These differences are the chief bases for so-called "industrial-financial partnerships."

Principle: Differences in accounting treatment and sensitivity to various constituencies can be used to create mutual benefit.

Additional Differences

There are myriad other ways in which people may value the same things differently. If one firm has liquidity and another firm is in tremendous need of capital to exploit a new technology, the liquid firm can provide capital in return for an attractive percentage of the profits generated by the new technology. One player may place great value on the deal at hand while another may focus primarily on the relationship. In some organizations, decision makers may be more concerned about the appearance of or precedents set by an agreement while others may only care about the substance of today's deal. In many, many such cases, the differences among the parties enable mutually beneficial dealcrafting.

Crafting Value from a Variety of Differences

Creative dealmakers frequently realize value from a variety of differences. For example, in settling personal injury litigation, insurers and plaintiffs can often dramatically improve the value to each side relative to a straight cash settlement. This value can derive from differences in attitudes towards time, tax status, capabilities, cost structure, forecasts, and risk aversion.

- *Attitude toward time.* Differences in attitudes toward time are common among parties in dispute; consider, for instance, injured plaintiffs in a battle with an insurance company who often have a lower discount rate than the insurers' cost of capital. Thus, insurers and plaintiffs can sometimes gain by settling with higher aggregate amounts spread over longer time periods. There may be a symbolic joint gain as well; injured plaintiffs sometimes care intensively about maximizing the undiscounted sum of a settlement amount—the total payout—while insurers evaluate the stream of payments by calculating the discounted cash flow.

- *Tax status.* Income to a plaintiff generated by investing a cash settlement is taxable to the plaintiff. In contrast, annuity payments are not taxable to the plaintiff as long as the plaintiff has not and does not control the principal amount. Exploiting this difference in tax status, the insurer and plaintiff can both gain by structuring the settlement as an annuity and implicitly splitting the (considerable) tax savings.

- *Investment expertise, opportunities, and cost.* In many situations, a difference in investment capability typically exists. Relative to an individual plaintiff, the insurance company generally has greater skill and resources as an investor. Thus, having the insurance company invest can often be better for both parties than having the individual plaintiff responsible for his or her investments. By virtue of its size, moreover, the insurer is likely to be able to obtain lower commissions and better investment opportunities. Thus, having the insurance company invest can often be better than having the individual plaintiff be responsible for his or her investments.

- *Forecasts.* Insurers and plaintiffs are likely to have different forecasts about the plaintiffs' life expectancies. Plaintiffs often believe that their life expectancy is equivalent to that of noninjured persons of their age. However, injuries often shorten life expectancy. Thus, plaintiffs may value the payment stream based on a longer forecasted life expectancy than that predicted by the insurer's actuarial tables.

- *Differences in attitudes toward risk.* Some plaintiffs are concerned their resources may not last over their lifetime; they may highly value the peace of mind from knowing that they have an assured income. Insurers provide this peace of mind at little cost.

In this example, the effects of these differences can be closely entwined: agreement on an annuity may bundle joint gains based on differential forecasts, time and risk profiles, tax status, as well as expertise investment options. The broader point remains, however: when a variety of differences exist among the parties, substantial value can be created from the perspective of each by devising agreements that reflect the whole array of these differences.

Conclusion

In sum, one-dimensional negotiators primarily see negotiation as an interpersonal *process* at the table. A two-dimensional approach complements this process view of negotiation with an understanding of the substantive principles behind value creation. Knowing what you are looking for can counteract powerful psychological biases toward seeing the world in "fixed-pie" terms that assume interests are incompatible. We have suggested three broad prescriptions for effective dealcrafting, the core work the a 2-D negotiator needs to do.

First, rather than seeking directly to increase individual shares via a value-claiming orientation, we argued that a joint focus on maximally expanding the total net economic pie, then allocating shares, can offer superior individual as well as joint results.

Second, rather than looking mainly for common ground and shared interests, as important as they are and as naturally as they are sought, 2-D negotiators understand the potential power of *differences* in creating value when accompanied by legitimate and appropriate forms of "compensation." Differences in cost and revenue structure point to arrangements of highest net value. Complementary differences in capability can be profitably combined. Differences in priority or relative importance lead to mutually beneficial trades or creative solutions that unbundle underlying interests. Differences in beliefs about the future can lead to joint gains from carefully crafted contingent agreements. Differences in attitudes toward risk—assessing, bearing, or influencing it—can lead to mutually preferable mechanisms. Differences in attitudes toward time, whether simple discount rate differences or more complex manifestations, can suggest collectively worthwhile intertemporal reallocations. And many other differences—in tax status, accounting or regulatory treatment, sensitivity to constituencies, etc.—can profitably be arbitraged by sophisticated dealcrafters to create value on a sustainable basis.

Finally, by looking outside the locus of the immediately involved parties and issues, a differences orientation can often suggest 3-D moves away from the table to change the game—by adding or subtracting parties and issues that manifest complementary differences—for mutual benefit.

About the Authors

David A. Lax is a principal in Lax Sebenius LLC and Summa Capital, a consulting firm and hedge fund, respectively, with offices in the Boston area. His e-mail address is: lax@negotiate.com. **James K. Sebenius** is the Gordon Donaldson Professor of Business Administration at the Harvard Business School, Soldiers Field, Boston, MA 02163. E-mail: jsebenius@hbs.edu. Lax and Sebenius have worked together on a variety of negotiation projects over the years; they are coauthors of one of the best-known books in the field, *The Manager as Negotiator* (New York: The Free Press, 1986).

References

The ideas presented in this essay have evolved from a number of sources over the years. Chapter Five of Lax and Sebenius (1986) lays out a more elaborate version of the sources of value creation in negotiation. A technical version of these ideas is developed in Sebenius (1984) while a general discussion of these concepts can be found in Raiffa (1982).

Arrow, K. J., R. H. Mnookin, L. Ross, A. Tversky, and R. Wilson eds. 1995. *Barriers to conflict resolution*. New York: W. W. Norton.

Bazerman, M. and M. Neale. 1992. *Negotiating rationally*. New York: The Free Press.

Hart, O. 1995. *Firms, contracts, and financial structure* (Clarendon Lectures in Economics). Oxford: Oxford University Press.

Kim, W. C. and R. Mauborgne. 1997. Fair process: Managing in the knowledge economy. *Harvard Business Review*, July–August 1997: 65–75.

Lax, D. A. and J. K. Sebenius. 1986. *The manager as negotiator*. New York: The Free Press.

Raiffa, H. 1982. *The art and science of negotiation*. Cambridge, Mass.: Harvard University Press.

———. 1985. Creative compensation: Maybe "in my backyard." *Negotiation Journal* 1(3): 197–203.

Sebenius, J. K. 1984. *Negotiating the law of the sea*. Cambridge, Mass.: Harvard University Press.

Stein, J. G. 1985. Structure, strategies, and tactics of mediation: Kissinger and Carter in the Middle East. *Negotiation Journal* 1(4): 331–347.

Susskind, L. and J. Cruikshank. 1987. *Breaking the impasse: Consensual approaches to resolving disputes.* New York: Basic Books.

Thompson, L. 1998. *The mind and heart of the negotiator.* New York: Prentice Hall.

Ury, W. L. 1991. *Getting past no: Negotiating your way from confrontation to cooperation.* New York: Bantam Books.

Breakthrough Bargaining

by Deborah M. Kolb and Judith Williams

Sometimes the hardest part of an informal negotiation is persuading the other side to deal with the issues. Understanding the dynamics of the "shadow negotiation" can help get things rolling.

Negotiation was once considered an art practiced by the naturally gifted. To some extent it still is, but increasingly we in the business world have come to regard negotiation as a science—built on creative approaches to deal making that allow everyone to walk away winners of sorts. Executives have become experts at "getting to yes," as the now-familiar terminology goes.

Nevertheless, some negotiations stall or, worse, never get off the ground. Why? Our recent research suggests that the answers lie in a dynamic we have come to call the "shadow negotiation"—the complex and subtle game people play before they get to the table and continue to play after they arrive. The shadow negotiation doesn't determine the "what" of the discussion, but the "how." Which interests will hold sway? Will the conversation's tone be adversarial or cooperative? Whose opinions will be heard? In short, how will bargainers deal with each other?

The shadow negotiation is most obvious when the participants hold unequal power—say, subordinates asking bosses for more resources or new employees engaging with veterans about well-established company policies. Similarly, managers who, because of their race, age, or gender, are in the minority in their companies may be at a disadvantage in the shadow negotiation. Excluded from important networks, they may not have the personal clout, experience, or organizational standing to influence other parties. Even when the bargainers are peers, a negotiation can be blocked or stalled—undermined by hidden assumptions, unrealistic expectations, or personal histories. An unexamined shadow negotiation can lead to silence, not satisfaction.

It doesn't have to be that way. Our research identified strategic levers—we call them power moves, process moves, and appreciative moves—that executives can use to guide the shadow negotiation. In situations in which the other person sees no compelling need to negotiate, *power moves* can help bring him or her to the table. When the dynamics of decision making threaten to overpower a negotiator's voice, *process moves* can reshape the negotiation's structure. And when talks stall because the other party feels pushed or misunderstandings cloud the real issues, *appreciative moves* can alter the tone or atmosphere so that a more collaborative exchange is possible. These strategic moves don't guarantee that bargainers will walk away winners, but they help to get stalled negotiations out of the dark of unspoken power plays and into the light of true dialogue.

Power Moves

In the informal negotiations common in the workplace, one of the parties can be operating from a one-down position. The other bargainer, seeing no apparent advantage in negotiating, stalls. Phone calls go unanswered. The meeting keeps being postponed or, if it does take place, a two-way conversation never gets going. Ideas are ignored or overruled, demands dismissed. Such resistance is a natural part of the informal negotiation process. A concern will generally be accorded a fair hearing only when someone believes two things: the other party has something desirable, and one's own objectives will not be met without giving something in return. Willingness to negotiate is, therefore, a confession of mutual need. As a result, a primary objective in the shadow negotiation is fostering the perception of mutual need.

Source: Reprinted by permission of *Harvard Business Review.* From "Breakthrough Bargaining" by Deborah M. Kolb and Judith Williams, Jan/Feb 2001. Copyright © 2001 by the Harvard Business School Publishing Corporation; all rights reserved.

Power moves can bring reluctant bargainers to the realization that they must negotiate: they will be better off if they do and worse off if they don't. Bargainers can use three kinds of power moves. Incentives emphasize the proposed value to the other person and the advantage to be gained from negotiating. Pressure levers underscore the consequences to the other side if stalling continues. And the third power move, enlisting allies, turns up the volume on the incentives or on the pressure. Here's how these strategies work.

Offer Incentives

In any negotiation, the other party controls something the bargainer needs: money, time, cooperation, communication, and so on. But the bargainer's needs alone aren't enough to bring anyone else to the table. The other side must recognize that benefits will accrue from the negotiation. These benefits must not only be visible—that is, right there on the table—but they must also resonate with the other side's needs. High-tech executive Fiona Sweeney quickly recognized this dynamic when she tried to initiate informal talks about a mission-critical organization change.

Shortly after being promoted to head operations at an international systems company, Sweeney realized that the organization's decision-making processes required fundamental revamping. The company operated through a collection of fiefdoms, with little coordination even on major accounts. Sales managers, whose bonuses were tied to gross sales, pursued any opportunity with minimal regard for the company's ability to deliver. Production scrambled to meet unrealistic schedules; budgets and quality suffered. Sweeney had neither the authority nor the inclination to order sales and production to cooperate. And as a newcomer to corporate headquarters, her visibility and credibility were low.

Sweeney needed a sweetener to bring sales and production together. First, she made adjustments to the billing process, reducing errors from 7.1% to 2.4% over a three-month period, thereby cutting back on customer complaints. Almost immediately, her stock shot up with both of the divisions. Second, realizing that sales would be more reluctant than production to negotiate any changes in the organization's decision-making processes, she worked with billing to speed up processing the expense-account checks so that salespeople were reimbursed more quickly, a move that immediately got the attention of everyone in sales. By demonstrating her value to sales and production, Sweeney encouraged the two division managers to work with her on improving their joint decision-making process. (For the complete story of Fiona Sweeney's campaign to revamp operations, see the sidebar "The Shadow Campaign.")

Creating value and making it visible are key power moves in the shadow negotiation. A bargainer can't leave it up to the other party to puzzle through the possibilities. The benefits must be made explicit if they are to have any impact on the shadow negotiation. When value disappears, so do influence and bargaining power.

Put a Price on the Status Quo

Abba Eban, Israel's former foreign minister, once observed that diplomats have "a passionate love affair with the status quo" that blocks any forward movement. The same love affair carries over into ordinary negotiations in the workplace. When people believe that a negotiation has the potential to produce bad results for them, they are naturally reluctant to engage on the issues. Until the costs of *not* negotiating are made explicit, ducking the problem will be the easier or safer course.

To unlock the situation, the status quo must be perceived as less attractive. By exerting pressure, the bargainer can raise the cost of business-as-usual until the other side begins to see that things will get worse unless both sides get down to talking.

That is exactly what Karen Hartig, one of the women in our study did when her boss dragged his heels about giving her a raise. Not only had she been promoted without additional pay, but she was now doing two jobs because the first position had never been filled. Although her boss continued to assure her of his support, nothing changed. Finally, Hartig was so exasperated that she returned a headhunter's call. The resulting job offer provided her with enough leverage to unfreeze the talks with her boss. No longer could he afford to maintain the status quo. By demonstrating that she had another alternative, she gave him the push—and the justification—he needed to argue forcefully on her behalf with his boss and with human resources.

Enlist Support

Solo power moves won't always do the job. Another party may not see sufficient benefits to negotiating, or the potential costs may not be high enough to compel a change of mind. When incentives and pressure levers fail to move the negotiation forward, a bargainer can enlist the help of allies.

Allies are important resources in shadow negotiations. They can be crucial in establishing credibility, and they lend tangible support to incentives already proposed. By providing guidance or running interference, they can favorably position a bargainer's proposals before talks even begin. At a minimum,

> **About the Research**
>
> We became aware of the shadow negotiation as we interviewed, over a five-year period, more than 300 executive women to probe their work experiences in formal and informal negotiations. We spoke with lawyers and bankers, accountants and entrepreneurs, consultants and marketers, project managers and account executives across a range of industries and organization types. In each interview, we asked about the executive's best and worst negotiation experience. After describing these scenarios, the women wanted to talk with us not only about what worked and why but also about how they might have better handled challenging situations.
>
> During this interviewing and the subsequent writing of *The Shadow Negotiation,* we came to believe that these dialogues and the study's findings have implications for both men and women. The shadow negotiation is where issues of parity, or the equivalence of power, get settled. And parity—its presence or absence—determine to a great extent whether a negotiation takes place at all and on what terms.

their confidence primes the other party to listen and raises the costs of not negotiating seriously.

When a member of Dan Riley's squadron faced a prolonged family emergency, the air force captain needed to renegotiate his squadron's flight-rotation orders. The matter was particularly sensitive, however, because it required the consent of the wing commander, two levels up the chain of command. If Riley approached the commander directly, he risked making his immediate superior look bad since his responsibilities covered readiness planning. To bridge that difficulty, Riley presented a draft proposal to his immediate superior. Once aware of the problem, Riley and his superior anticipated some of the objections the commander might raise and then alerted the wing commander to the general difficulties posed by such situations. When Riley finally presented his proposal to the commander, it carried his immediate superior's blessing, and so his credibility was never questioned; only the merits of his solution were discussed.

Process Moves

Rather than attempt to influence the shadow negotiation directly through power moves, a bargainer can exercise another kind of strategic move, the process move. Designed to influence the negotiation process itself, such moves can be particularly effective when bargainers are caught in a dynamic of silencing—when decisions are being made without their input or when colleagues interrupt them during meetings, dismiss their comments, or appropriate their ideas.

While process moves do not address the substantive issues in a negotiation, they directly affect the hearing those issues receive. The agenda, the prenegotiation groundwork, and the sequence in which ideas and people are heard—all these structural elements influence others' receptivity to opinions and demands. Working behind the scenes, a bargainer can plant the seeds of ideas or can marshal support before a position becomes fixed in anyone's mind. Consensus can even be engineered so that the bargainer's agenda frames the subsequent discussion.

Seed Ideas Early

Sometimes parties to a negotiation simply shut down and don't listen; for whatever reason, they screen out particular comments or people. Being ignored in a negotiation doesn't necessarily result from saying too little or saying it too hesitantly. When ideas catch people off guard, they can produce negative, defensive reactions, as can ideas presented too forcefully. Negotiators also screen out the familiar: if they've already heard the speech, or a close variant, they stop paying attention.

Joe Lopez faced this dilemma. Lopez, a fast-track engineer who tended to promote his ideas vigorously in planning meetings, began to notice that his peers were tuning him out—a serious problem since departmental resources were allocated in these sessions. To remedy the situation, Lopez scheduled one-on-one lunch meetings with his colleagues. On each occasion, he mentioned how a particular project would benefit the other manager's department and how they could work together to ensure its completion. As a result of this informal lobbying,

The Shadow Campaign

A single strategic move seldom carries the day. In combination, however, such moves can jump-start workplace negotiations and keep them moving toward resolution.

Consider the case of Fiona Sweeney, the new operations chief introduced earlier in this article. She had neither the authority nor the personal inclination to order the sales and production divisions of her company to cooperate. Instead, she fashioned a series of strategic moves designed to influence the negotiations.

Power Moves. Having established her credibility with sales by increasing the turnaround time on expense-account reimbursements, Sweeney knew she needed to up the ante for maintaining the status quo, which created hardships for production and was frustrating customers. It was particularly important to bring pressure to bear on the sales division, since the informal reward systems, and many of the formal ones, currently worked to its benefit. To disturb the equilibrium, Sweeney began to talk in management meetings about a bonus system that would penalize the sales division whenever it promised more than production could deliver. Rather than immediately acting on this threat, however, she suggested creating a cross-divisional task force to explore the issues. Not surprisingly, sales was eager to be included. Moreover, the CEO let key people know that he backed Sweeney's proposal to base bonuses on profits, not revenues.

Process Moves. Sweeney then moved to exert control over the agenda and build support for the changes she and the CEO envisioned. She started an operations subgroup with the heads of quality control and production, mobilizing allies in the two areas most directly affected by the sales division's behavior. Soon they developed a common agenda and began working in concert to stem the influence of sales in senior staff meetings. On one occasion, for example, Sweeney proposed assigning a low priority to orders that had not been cleared by the operations subgroup. Quality control and production roundly supported the suggestion, which was soon implemented. Through these process moves, Sweeney built a coalition that shaped the subsequent negotiations. But she did something more.

Power and process moves often provoke resistance from the other side. Sweeney prevented resistance from becoming entrenched within the sales division through a series of appreciative moves.

Appreciative Moves. To deepen her understanding of the issues sales confronted, Sweeney volunteered her operations expertise to the division's planning team. By helping sales develop a new pricing-and-profit model, she not only increased understanding and trust on both sides of the table, but she also paved the way for dialogue on other issues—specifically the need for change in the company's decision-making processes.

Most important, Sweeney never forced any of the players into positions where they would lose face. By using a combination of strategic moves, she helped the sales division realize that change was coming and that it would be better off helping to shape the change than blocking it. In the end, improved communication and cooperation among divisions resulted in increases in both the company's top-line revenues and its profit margins. With better product quality and delivery times, sales actually made more money, and production no longer had the burden of delivering on unrealistic promises generated by sales. Customers—and the CEO—were all happy.

Lopez found he no longer needed to oversell his case in the meetings. He could make his ideas heard with fewer words and at a lower decibel level.

Preliminary work like this allows a bargainer to build receptivity where a direct or aggressive approach might encounter resistance. Once the seeds of an idea have been planted, they will influence how others view a situation, regardless of how firmly attached they are to their own beliefs and ideas.

Reframe the Process

Negotiators are not equally adept in all settings. Highly competitive approaches to problem solving favor participants who can bluff and play the game, talk the loudest, hold out the longest, and think fastest on their feet. Bargainers who are uncomfortable with this kind of gamesmanship can reframe the process, shifting the dynamic away from personal competition. That's what Marcia Philbin decided to do about the way in which space was allocated in her company. Extra room and equipment typically went to those who pushed the hardest, and Philbin never fared well in the negotiations. She also believed that significant organizational costs always accompanied the process since group leaders routinely presented the building administrator with inflated figures, making it impossible to assess the company's actual requirements.

Positioning herself as an advocate not only for her department but also for the company, Philbin proposed changing the process. Rather than allocating space in a series of discrete negotiations with the space administrator, she suggested, why not collaborate as a group in developing objective criteria for assessing need? Management agreed, and Philbin soon found herself chairing the committee created to produce the new guidelines. Heated arguments took place over the criteria, but Philbin was now positioned to direct the discussions away from vested and parochial interests toward a greater focus on organizational needs.

Within organizations or groups, negotiations can fall into patterns. If a bargainer's voice is consistently shut out of discussions, something about the way negotiations are structured is working against his or her active participation. A process move may provide a remedy because it will influence how the discussion unfolds and how issues emerge.

Build Consensus

Regardless of how high a bargainer is on the organizational ladder, it is not always possible—or wise—to impose change on a group by fiat. By lobbying behind the scenes, a bargainer can start to build consensus before formal decision making begins. Unlike the first process move, which aims at gaining a hearing for ideas, building consensus creates momentum behind an agenda by bringing others on board. The growing support isolates the blockers, making continued opposition harder and harder. Moreover, once agreement has been secured privately, it becomes difficult (although never impossible) for a supporter to defect publicly.

As CEO of a rapidly growing biotechnology company, Mark Chapin gradually built consensus for his ideas on integrating a newly acquired research boutique into the existing company. Chapin had two goals: to retain the acquired firm's scientific talent and to rationalize the research funding process. The second goal was at odds with the first and threatened to alienate the new scientists. To mitigate this potential conflict, Chapin focused his attention on the shadow negotiation. First, he met one-on-one with key leaders of the board and the research staffs of both companies. These private talks provided him with a strategic map that showed where he would find support and where he was likely to meet challenges. Second, in another round of talks, Chapin paid particular attention to the order in which he approached people. Beginning with the most supportive person, he got the key players to commit, one by one, to his agenda before opposing factions could coalesce. These preliminary meetings positioned him as a collaborator—and, equally important, as a source of expanding research budgets. Having privately built commitment, Chapin found that he didn't need to use his position to dictate terms when the principal players finally sat down to negotiate the integration plan.

Appreciative Moves

Power moves exert influence on the other party so that talks get off the ground. Process moves seek to change the ground rules under which negotiations play out. But still, talks may stall. Two strong advocates may have backed themselves into respective corners. Or one side, put on the defensive, even inadvertently, may continue to resist or raise obstacles. Communication may deteriorate, turn acrimonious, or simply stop as participants focus solely on their own demands. Wariness stifles any candid exchange. And without candor, the two sides cannot address the issues together or uncover the real conflict.

Appreciative moves break these cycles. They explicitly build trust and encourage the other side to participate in a dialogue. Not only do appreciative moves shift the dynamics of the shadow negotiation away from the adversarial, but they also hold out a hidden promise. When bargainers demonstrate appreciation for another's concerns, situation, or "face," they open the negotiation to the different perspectives held by that person and to the opinions, ideas, and feelings shaping those perspectives. Appreciative moves foster open communication so that differences in needs and views can come to the surface without personal discord. Frequently the participants then discover that the problem they were worrying about is not the root conflict, but a symptom of it. And at times, before a negotiation can move toward a common solution, the participants must first experience mutuality, recognizing where their interests and needs intersect. A shared problem can then become the basis for creative problem solving.

Help Others Save Face

Image is a concern for everyone. How negotiators look to themselves and to others who matter to them often counts as much as the particulars of an agreement. In fact, these are seldom separate. "Face" captures what people value in themselves and the qualities they want others to see in them. Negotiators go to great lengths to preserve face. They stick to their guns against poor odds simply to avoid losing face with those who are counting on them. If a bargainer treads on another's self-image—in front of a boss or colleague, or even privately—his or her demands are likely to be rejected.

Sensitivity to the other side's face does more than head off resistance: it lays the groundwork for trust. It conveys that the bargainer respects what the other is trying to accomplish and will not do anything to embarrass or undermine that person. This appreciation concedes nothing, yet as Sam Newton discovered, it can turn out to be the only way to break a stalemate.

Newton's new boss, transferred from finance, lacked experience on the operations side of the business. During departmental meetings to negotiate project schedules and funding, he always rejected Newton's ideas. Soon it was routine: Newton would make a suggestion and before he got the last sentence out, his boss was issuing a categorical veto.

Frustrated, Newton pushed harder, only to meet increased resistance. Finally, he took a step back and looked at the situation from his boss's perspective. Rubberstamping Newton's proposals could have appeared as a sign of weakness at a time when his boss was still establishing his credentials. From then on, Newton took a different tack. Rather than present a single idea, he offered an array of options and acknowledged that the final decision rested with his boss. Gradually, his boss felt less need to assert his authority and could respond positively in their dealings.

Bosses aren't the only ones who need to save face; colleagues and subordinates do, too. Team members avoid peers who bump a problem upstairs at the first sign of trouble, making everyone appear incapable of producing a solution. Subordinates muzzle their real opinions once they have been belittled or treated dismissively by superiors. In the workplace, attention to face is a show of respect for another person, whatever one's corporate role. That respect carries over to the shadow negotiation.

Keep the Dialogue Going

Sometimes, talks don't get off the ground because the timing is not right for a participant to make a decision; information may be insufficient, or he or she is simply not ready. People have good reasons—at least, reasons that make sense to them—for thinking it's not yet time to negotiate. Appreciating this disposition doesn't mean abandoning or postponing negotiation. Instead, it requires that a bargainer keep the dialogue going without pushing for immediate agreement. This appreciative move allows an opportunity for additional information to come to the surface and affords the other side more time to rethink ideas and adjust initial predilections.

Francesca Rossi knew instinctively that unless she kept the communication lines open, discussions would derail about the best way for her software firm to grow. The company had recently decided to expand by acquiring promising applications rather than developing them in-house from scratch. As head of strategic development, Rossi targeted a small start-up that designed state-of-the-art software for office computers to control home appliances. The director of research, however, was less than enthusiastic about acquiring the firm. He questioned the product's commercial viability and argued that its market would never justify the acquisition cost.

Needing his cooperation, Rossi pulled back. Instead of actively promoting the acquisition, she began to work behind the scenes with the start-up's software designers and industry analysts. As Rossi gathered more data in support of the application's potential, she gradually drew the director of research back into the discussions. He dropped his opposition once the analysis convinced him that the acquisition, far from shrinking his department's authority, would actually enlarge it. Rossi's appreciative move had given him the additional information and time he needed to reevaluate his original position.

Not everyone makes decisions quickly. Sometimes people can't see beyond their initial ideas or biases. Given time to mull over the issues, they may eventually reverse course and be more amenable to negotiating. As long as the issue isn't forced or brought to a preemptive conclusion—as long as the participants keep talking—there's a chance that the resistance will fade. What seems unreasonable at one point in a negotiation can become more acceptable at another. Appreciative moves that keep the dialogue going allow the other side to progress at a comfortable speed.

Solicit New Perspectives

One of the biggest barriers to effective negotiation and a major cause of stalemate is the tendency for bargainers to get trapped in their own perspectives. It's simply too easy for people to become overly enamored of their opinions. Operating in a closed world of their making, they tell themselves they are right and the other person is wrong. They consider the merits of their own positions but neglect the other party's valid objections. They push their agendas, merely reiterating the same argument, and may not pick up on cues that their words aren't being heard.

It's safe to assume that the other party is just as convinced that his or her own demands are justified. Moreover, bargainers can only speculate what another's agenda might be—hidden or otherwise. Appreciative moves to draw out another's perspectives help negotiators understand why the other party feels a certain way. But these moves serve more than an instrumental purpose, doing more than add information to a bargainer's arsenal. They signal to the other side that differing opinions and perspective are important. By creating opportunities to discover something new and unexpected, appreciative moves can break a stalemate. As understanding deepens on both sides of the table, reaching a mutual resolution becomes increasingly possible.

Everyone agreed that a joint venture negotiated by HMO executive Donna Hitchcock between her organization and an insurance company dovetailed with corporate objectives on both sides. The HMO could expand its patient base and the insurance carrier its enrollment.

Although the deal looked good on paper, implementation stalled. Hitchcock couldn't understand where the resistance was coming from or why. In an attempt to unfreeze the situation, she arranged a meeting with her counterpart from the insurance company. After a brief update, Hitchcock asked about any unexpected effects the joint venture was exerting on the insurance carrier's organization and on her counterpart's work life. That appreciative move ultimately broke the logjam. From the carrier's perspective, she learned, the new arrangement stretched already overworked departments and had not yet produced additional revenues to hire more staff. Even more important, her counterpart was personally bearing the burden of the increased work.

Hitchcock was genuinely sympathetic to these concerns. The extra work was a legitimate obstacle to the joint venture's successful implementation. Once she understood the reason behind her counterpart's resistance, the two were able to strategize on ways to alleviate the overload until the additional revenues kicked in.

Through these appreciative moves—actively soliciting the other side's ideas and perspectives, acknowledging their importance, and demonstrating that they are taken seriously—negotiators can encourage the other person to work with them rather than against them.

There's more to negotiation than haggling over issues and working out solutions. The shadow negotiation, though often overlooked, is a critical component. Whether a bargainer uses power, process, or appreciative moves in the shadow negotiation depends on the demands of the situation. Power moves encourage another party to recognize the need to negotiate in the first place. They help bring a reluctant bargainer to the table. Process moves create a context in which a bargainer can shape the negotiation's agenda and dynamic so that he or she can be a more effective advocate. Appreciative moves engage the other party in a collaborative exchange by fostering trust and candor in the shadow negotiation. While power and process moves can ensure that a negotiation gets started on the right foot, appreciative moves can break a stalemate once a negotiation is under way. By broadening the discourse, appreciative moves can also lead to creative solutions. Used alone or in combination, strategic moves in the shadow negotiation can determine the outcome of the negotiation on the issues.

About the Authors

Deborah M. Kolb is professor of management at the Simmons College Graduate School of Man-

---

Note: Most of the negotiating stories used in this article have been adapted form *The Shadow Negotiation: How Women Can Master the Hidden Agendas That Determine Bargaining Success* (Simon & Schuster, 2000) and the authors' interviews with businesspeople. To respect interviewees' candor and to protect their privacy, their identities and situations have been disguised, sometimes radically.

agement in Boston and codirector of its Center for Gender in Organizations. She is a former executive director of the Program on Negotiation at Harvard Law School, where she continues as codirector of the Negotiations in the Workplace Project.

Judith Williams, a former investment banker, is the founder of Anagram, a nonprofit corporation in Boston dedicated to the study of social and organizational change.

Index

accounting treatment differences, 33–34
agenda management, 28
agents, 8
agreements, contingent, 23, 28–30
allies, 37–38
alternative, best, 13
AOL (American Online), 28
appreciative moves, 17, 39, 40–42
assisted negotiation, 17–19
avoidance, 8

bargaining. *See* negotiation and conflict resolution
bargaining power, 13–14
barriers to creativity, 16
BATNA (best alternative to a negotiated agreement), 13, 14
best alternative to a negotiated agreement (BATNA), 13, 14
bias, incompatibility, 24
bridging, 16

capabilities, complementary, 27
capital gains, 33
Chapin, Mark, 40
characteristics of negotiators, 9–10
cogeneration plant contingent agreement, 28–29
collaborative relationships, 17
collective bargaining, 10
communication
    in distributive vs. integrative negotiations, 15
    maintaining dialog, 41–42
    revealing and withholding information, 12
compensation, nonspecific, 15
complementary capabilities, 27
CompuServe, 28
concessions, 14–15
conciliator-style negotiators, 9
conflict management. *See* negotiation and conflict resolution
conflict management, forms of, 7–8
consensus-building, 40
context of interests, 12
contingent agreements, 23, 28–30
cost cutting, 15–16
cost of status quo, 37
cost/revenue structure differences, 26–27
creativity, barriers to, 16
culture, national, 9
culture, organizational, 10

deadlocked negotiations, 17, 22–23
dealcrafting, 22–35
    accounting treatment and sensitivity differences, 33–34
    agenda management, 28
    capability differences, 27
    cogeneration plant example, 28–29
    cost/revenue structure differences, 26–27
    defined, 22
    differences principle, 26
    earnouts, 29
    forecasting belief differences, and contingent agreements, 28–30, 34
    interest and priority differences, 27–28
    Lakeside-Tonicron joint venture example, 24–26, 26–27
    maximum total value vs. individual results, 24–26
    risk attitude differences, 30–32, 34
    tax status differences, 33, 34
    third parties, bringing in, 28, 32
    three-dimensional perspective, 22–24
    time preference differences, 32–33, 34
    variety and combination of differences, 34
"Dealcrafting: The Substance of Three-Dimensional Negotiations" (Lax and Sebenius), 22–35
dealmaking
    bargaining power, 13–14
    distributive vs. integrative negotiations, 14–16
    interests and, 11–12
    issues and, 10
    parties to negotiations, 8–10
    process of, 8, 14–16
debt-equity ratio differences, 33–34
differences, value in negotiations, 26–28
dilemma, negotiator's, 12, 16
dirty tricks, 17
distributive negotiations, 14–15
"dose of reality" process, 18

earnouts, 29
Eban, Abba, 37
egocentrism, 14
enlightened self-interest, 15
ethical issues in power mobilization, 14
exchange-based trade gains, 27

fear of revealing information, 12
fiscal year-end, and grant-making negotiations, 33
fixed pie, 10
forcing behavior, 7
forecasting belief differences, 28–30, 34

gains, mutual, 15–16
gender, 9
Glaxo, 26
good will, 33–34

Hartig, Karen, 37
Hitchcock, Donna, 42

identity, 9–10
image, and saving face, 41
impressions, managing, 14, 17
incentives, 10, 37
incompatibility bias, 24
individualism, 10
industrial-financial partnerships, 34
information, revealing and withholding, 12
integrative negotiations, 15–16
interests, 11–12, 15, 27–28
interpersonal process, 22
intuitive-style negotiators, 9
investment capability, 34
issues, 10

Kissinger, Henry, 13, 28

labor unions, 10
Lakeside-Tonicron joint venture example, 24–26, 26–27
Lax, David A., 22
Lehman Brothers, 17
liquidity, differences in, 34
logrolling, 15
Lopez, Joe, 38, 40

Mango Systems role play, 4
Max, Sandy, 6–7
mediation, in negotiations, 8, 17–19
mergers and acquisitions
    earnouts, 29
    SmithKline Beecham and Glaxo, 26
    WorldCom, Compuserve, and AOL, 28
methods of eliciting interests, 12
mixed motives, 14, 16
moves and countermoves, 17
mutual gains negotiations, 15–16
mutual need, 36

negotiation, definition of, 7
negotiation and conflict resolution, overview of, 4, 7
negotiator's dilemma, 12, 16
neutrality, in mediation, 18
new organization model, 4, 6, 8, 19
Newton, Sam, 41
NIMBY (not in my backyard), 26
nonspecific compensation, 15

organizational culture, 10

parties to negotiations, 8–10
personal injury litigation, 34
perspectives, new, 42
persuasion, 14
Philbin, Marcia, 40
positioning, 13–14, 16
positions, 11, 15
postsettlement settlements, 18
power, bargaining, 13–14
power moves, 36–38
priority differences, 27–28
process, preoccupation with, 22
process moves, 38, 39, 40

questions, and eliciting interests, 12

racial issues, 9
rational analysts, 9
relationships
    among negotiating parties, 8
    collaborative, 17
    interests relative to, 11
reputation, 11, 14
resources, acquiring, 15
revealing information, 12
Riley, Dan, 38
risk differences, 30–32, 34
Rossi, Francesca, 41

saving face, 41
"second table" problem, 8
self-interest, enlightened, 15
settlements, postsettlement, 18
shadow negotiations, 4, 16–17, 36–42
    appreciative moves, 17, 39, 40–42
    defined, 36
    dirty tricks, 17
    managing impressions, 17
    power moves, 36–38, 39
    process moves, 38, 39, 40
SmithKline Beecham, 26
smoothing, 7
social issues, 26
socially constructed identity, 9
status quo, cost of, 37
Stein, Janice Gross, 28
stereotyping, 9–10
strategic moves, 14
styles of negotiators, 9–10
substantive interests, 11
support, enlisting, 37–38

tax status, 33, 34
third-parties brought into negotiations, 28, 32
third-party assistance in negotiations, 8, 12 17–19

Thompson, Leigh, 24
three-dimensional perspective on negotiations, 22–24
thug-style negotiators, 9
time preference differences, 32–33, 34
trade-offs, 15

value claiming
    information withholding and, 12
    negotiator's dilemma and, 16
    risk profiles and, 32
    in zero-sum negotiation, 10, 14
value creation. *See also* dealcrafting
    differences as sources of value, 26
    information withholding and, 12
    maximum total value vs. individual results, 24–26
    multiple issues and, 10
    negotiator's dilemma and, 16
    as power move, 37
    two-dimensional negotiation and, 22, 23

willingness to negotiate, 36
win-lose negotiations, 14–15
withholding information, 12
WorldCom, 28

zero sum negotiations, 14
zone of possible agreements (ZOPA), 15

MANAGING FOR THE FUTURE

Organizational Behavior & Processes

Change From Within: Roads to Successful Issue Selling

Susan J. Ashford
University of Michigan

Jane E. Dutton
University of Michigan

Module 13

MANAGING FOR THE FUTURE
Organizational Behavior & Processes, Third Edition

Deborah Ancona
Sloan School of Management
Massachusetts Institute of Technology

John Van Maanen
Sloan School of Management
Massachusetts Institute of Technology

Thomas A. Kochan
Sloan School of Management
Massachusetts Institute of Technology

D. Eleanor Westney
Sloan School of Management
Massachusetts Institute of Technology

Maureen Scully
Graduate School of Management
Simmons College

Dedicated to those who have inspired us to try to be better students and teachers.
Special thanks to: Professor Jack Barbash • Professor Arthur H. Gladstein • Professor Marius B. Jansen • Professor Joanne Martin • Professor Edgar H. Schein

VP/Editorial Director
Jack W. Calhoun

VP/Editor-in-Chief
Michael P. Roche

Senior Publisher
Melissa S. Acuña

Executive Editor
John Szilagyi

Senior Developmental Editor
Judith O'Neill

Marketing Manager
Jacquelyn Carrillo

Production Editor
Emily Gross

Manufacturing Coordinator
Rhonda Utley

Compositor
Trejo Production

Printer
Von Hoffmann Press, Inc.
Frederick, MD

Internal Designer
Bethany Casey

Cover Designer
Bethany Casey

Photographs
©PhotoDisc

Design Project Manager
Bethany Casey

COPYRIGHT ©2005
by South-Western, a division of Thomson Learning.
Thomson Learning™ is a trademark used herein under license.

Printed in the United States of America
1 2 3 4 5 07 06 05 04 03

For more information contact
South-Western College Publishing,
5191 Natorp Boulevard,
Mason, Ohio, 45040
Or you can visit our Internet site at:
http://www.swlearning.com

ALL RIGHTS RESERVED
No part of this work covered by the copyright hereon may be reproduced or used in any form or by any means—graphic, electronic, or mechanical, including photocopying, recording, taping, Web distribution or information storage and retrieval systems—without the written permission of the publisher.

For permission to use material from this text or product, contact us by
Tel: (800) 730-2214
Fax: (800) 730-2215
http://www.thomsonrights.com

Library of Congress Control Number: 2003113908
ISBN 0-324-05575-7

Contents

Change From Within: Roads to Successful Issue Selling

Overview		4

Core

Class Note	**Issue Selling From Within**	6
	The Choice to Sell Issues in Organizations 7	
	The Challenge of Charged Issues 10	
	Conclusion 11	
Exercise	**Issue Selling**	12
	Instructions 12	
	Chris Peters and the "People" Issue 12	
Case	**Inex**	14
	Inex Company 16	
	Company Structure 16	
	The Management Committee 19	
	Jones's Dilemma 19	

Elective

The Press	**Dinosaurs or Dynamos? Recognizing Middle Management's Strategic Role**	22
	Executive Overview 22	
	The Misunderstood Middle Manager 23	
	Competitive Advantage and Middle Management Strategic Roles 23	
	Championing Strategic Alternatives 24	
	Synthesizing Information 24	
	Facilitating Adaptability 24	
	Implementing Deliberate Strategy 25	
	Linking Strategic Roles to Core Capability 25	
	Middle Management's Role in the Reengineered Organization 26	
	Realizing Middle Management's Strategic Value 27	
	Everyone a Middle Manager? 29	
	About the Authors 29	

Index

Overview

This module is designed to increase your skills in influencing change from the middle of an organization. We propose that long before business professionals reach the tops of their organizational hierarchies, they want to make change. They do so through a variety of processes. One of these is what we call issue selling. Issue selling involves the manager's active steps to get issues on the organization's agenda. Issue selling is important for both the employee/manager and the organization. Today's organizations operate within complex environments where hierarchy is being deemphasized and speedy responses are required. Consequently, drawing out ideas and surface issues from within the organization's own management ranks is critical. Employees also are becoming increasingly impatient with organizational settings that aren't responsive to new ideas. Given these two trends, it is in the organization's best interest to create a context in which issues can be surfaced and communicated.

For the individual employee, the ability to make a difference is becoming an important talent differentiator. Employees who are able to affect change are highly valued in today's organization. It is important, therefore, that new management professionals develop skills not only in managing change when they are the leader in charge, but also in suggesting and promoting changes from below.

This module gives you insights into both how organizations can be better managed to promote change from within and how employees can effectively use this skill. The goal is to give you the capability to make change in the contexts you enter and, perhaps later, to better create a context as an organizational leader that promotes change from within.

This module is divided into three parts consisting of some academic input on the topic followed by an exercise and a case to involve you more directly in using these new skills. The academic perspective provided in the Class Note serves as an introduction and overview of this critical managerial skill. The **Inex** case then asks you to assess the issue-selling efforts of a particular case character and to evaluate the context that exists at Inex. Is it one that facilitates change? The exercise asks you to put yourself into a situation and evaluate whether and how you would raise a particular issue. We provide citations at the end of the module to help you find additional materials if you are interested in following up on this topic. Finally, students found an article by Steve Floyd and Bill Wooldridge to be useful in the past, so we included it as an elective reading.

Assignment Summary

1. Read the Class Note, which, as noted above, provides an academic perspective on issue selling from within the organizational ranks. Read, also, the elective reading, "Dinosaurs or Dynamos" if your instructor requires it.
2. Complete the issue-selling exercise and come to class prepared to discuss your issue-selling plan.
3. Work through the Inex case. Be prepared to discuss what Jones should do.

Change From Within: Roads to Successful Issue Selling

CORE

Module 13

Issue Selling From Within

Issue selling is important to both organizations and managers in today's newer, flatter, more dynamic organizational settings. Recent research evidence suggests that organizations gain from finding ways to foster input and involvement from below; organizations that involved middle managers in the strategy process outperformed organizations that did not. A simple argument may explain why. First, the world is becoming increasingly more complex. Organizations must respond to environments that are themselves changing rapidly. New firms enter the industry, and industries themselves change and evolve (consider, for example, the telephone industry, which now competes with computer companies, which are in turn being bought up by entertainment companies). Relationships with suppliers and distributors become more complicated and diverse (especially when we consider global companies). The complexity of companies' customer bases increases as they court new customers and respond to more individualized tastes and demands.

In the face of all of this complexity, it is increasingly difficult for one small group at the top of any organization to cope! Top managers' cognitive capacity is limited, to say nothing of their time. In light of these realities, an organization needs to have *multiple* avenues for importing critical environmental information into the organization and simple pathways for getting it into the hands of the appropriate decision maker(s). Issue selling is one of those potential pathways. Organizations that open pathways for managers to raise issues of importance to those above them reap two benefits. First, they direct *many* minds to consider what is most important for the organization's future. Second, minds closer to the problem (customers, suppliers, and technological developments) provide input into important priorities. Such firms are more adaptable—they learn quickly about new market opportunities and problems and react faster than other firms without these pathways. Middle managers in this view are an important source of change and renewal from within the firm (see work by Nonaka, 1988, for a similar view).[1] Clearly in order to make this work, top management teams (TMTs) need the ability to sort and process issues quickly, but recent research suggests that fast decision makers use more rather than less information.[2] Access to more information may make the TMT susceptible to information overload. However, in the long run, information overload may be less damaging to the firm than isolation from the marketplace. Issue selling is a critical process that prevents this form of isolation.

Organizations exist to get things done. They make cars, develop software, and market shoes. Action is coordinated, in part, by a strategic agenda that specifies what goals are important to the organization and what issues are "on the table" for organizational consideration. In some organizations, the strategic agenda is transparent; everyone knows the dominant goals: the top issues are recognized and shared by all. In other organizations, the strategic agenda is operating, but it is hidden, tacit, and generally difficult to sense. Whether explicit or implicit, the strategic agenda directs action in organizations.[3] For example, the agenda may indicate that the firm is most interested in increasing market share and that issues of product positioning, distribution, and advertising are directing action. The prominence of these issues focuses action. In our example, marketing departments will be busy and powerful while financial and human resource issues may have a more difficult time being heard. In this way, the strategic agenda helps to direct which decisions get attention in organizations. Issues that make it onto the organizational agenda are the ones attended to by important decision makers, while other issues fall by the wayside. However, organizational decision makers cannot attend to everything.[4] When key organizational members choose to focus on some issues, they also choose not to focus on others.

Who sets the organization's agenda? Common wisdom is that the top management team (TMT) sets the organization's goals and identifies the issues relevant to those goals. The top management team is a small group at the top of the organization, which typically include the CEO, the COO, various subsidiary presidents, and/or func-

---

[1] Ikujiro Nonaka. "Toward Middle-Up-Down Management: Accelerating Information Creation," *Sloan Management Review* (Spring 1988), pp. 9–18.
[2] K. M. Eisenhardt. "Making Fast Strategic Decisions in High-Velocity Environments," *Academy of Management Journal*, 32, no, 3 (1989), pp. 543–576.
[3] J. E. Dutton and R. B. Duncan. "The Influence of Strategic Planning on Strategic Change," *Strategic Management Journal*, 8, no. 3 (1987), pp. 279–295.
[4] W. Ocasio. "Toward an Attention-Based View of the Firm," *Strategic Management Journal*, 18 (1997), pp. 187–206.

tional vice presidents. The team, or group, can be formally named or may operate informally. They are the group with the formal authority to allocate resources. Once the top group sets goals and priorities, it sends marching orders down the organization so that its goals can be realized. Top management groups clearly do play this role in some organizations.

Recently, however, researchers began to question the completeness of this portrayal. They argued that in addition to this "top down" picture of how strategy works, significant "bottom up" processes also come into play. A new picture emerged that portrays middle-level managers as important participants in the strategy process.[5] These managers take active steps to get issues on the organization's agenda. They do so either because they believe that the issue is important for the organization and/or because their own or their department's interest is served if the firm addresses the issue. The TMT is still centrally involved. Indeed they play two critical roles. First, they are the recipients of influence attempts (often-called **issue selling**) from the managers below them. The TMT's limited time and attention forces lower-level managers compete to get its ear. Thus, the first important role of the TMT lies in its judgment regarding which issues are worthy of attention. In addition to simply reacting to ideas brought to them by middle managers, TMTs play an important second role. They can take active steps to create an organizational context that stimulates middle managers to participate in the strategy-setting process. Essentially, TMTs can invite middle managers into the strategy process or signal to them that their input is not wanted.

For managers too, issue selling is an important activity and skill. Managers need to be able to sell their ideas within a firm if they are to be successful. Managers who can articulate why the firm ought to attend to issues that they think are critical to the firm's survival will be seen as having the leadership skills necessary to fill top roles within the company. All managers must manage down, but managers at middle levels also need to manage up, and issue selling is part of that upward management. Managerial careers can be "made" or "broken" by associations with certain issues. For example, a manager who brings a firm's attention to an important transformational technological development, would likely be seen in a positive light due to association with this issue. At the same time, bringing issues perceived as unimportant or inappropriate to the attention of top management can hurt rather than help a manager's career.

The Choice to Sell Issues in Organizations

If issue selling can have positive consequences for both the firm and for the managers who undertake it, then it is important to understand middle managers' choice processes. What motivates them to participate in the strategy process in this way? What makes them choose to stay silent? Our research suggests that situational assessments drive this choice, but in ways that rely on individual psychology. People appear to be more willing to speak up for issues in contexts where they perceive that management will listen and where the context is experienced as supportive.[6] That support may come from a supportive culture in general or from supportive relationships that middle managers have with those above them. Both of these conditions increase the sense of safety that managers feel in raising potential controversial issues to those above them.

The context may enhance issue selling. For example, managers are sensitive to the presence of change in the organization. In one organization, managers believed the time was ripe for them to raise issues because the organization itself was going through a lot of change. With so much in flux, these managers felt that they could easily raise another issue to consider. By implication, staid, tradition-bound organizations may shut off the precise input that they need to adapt and change, while organizations that are good at change (or at least that are changing) invite even more input and ideas! Managers also see the context as more favorable for issue selling when top management is seen as open.

At the same time, the context may inhibit issue selling. For example, sellers see a conflict-avoiding culture as a barrier to effective issue selling. They also note that complex politics make selling more difficult. In these types of cultures, managers do not raise issues either because it is not normative to do so or because they are unable to figure out how to go about it.

Woven throughout most of the stories that managers told about their choices to sell issues or stay silent were concerns about damaging their reputations or images in the eyes of others. Sellers worried about how it might look if they raised particular issues in their organization. They expressed concerns that they might look critical, naïve, or weak.

---

5 S. W. Floyd and B. J. Wooldridge, *The Strategic Middle Manager* (San Francisco: Jossey-Bass, 1996).
6 J. E. Dutton, et al. "Reading the Wind: How Middle Managers Assess the Context for Selling Issues to Top Managers," *Strategic Management Journal*, 18, no. 5 (1997), pp. 407–425.

Many of the context factors that discouraged issue selling seemed to do so by heightening concerns about possible image damage. Not surprisingly, much of the advice sellers gave regarding how to raise issues effectively addressed protecting their own images.

Top managers play an important role in prompting issue selling. They set the context for initiatives of those below them. Understanding sellers' choice processes gives top management some insight into how to intervene to make the choice to speak up and raise issues more likely. Early indications suggest that top managers can enhance the likelihood of issue selling by reducing the perceived image costs of the act. Image costs can be reduced, in turn, by creating a supportive context, signaling openness, and creating norms supporting issue selling.[7] Top managers can reinforce their openness and create such norms by celebrating early issue sellers and initiating conversations about potential issues. Top managers can also institute forums in which possibilities, half-baked ideas, and preliminary analyses could be presented. One conservative hospital entertained issue discussions only after a full-blown analysis was conducted and recommendations prepared. Such sessions are hardly the venue for raising ideas that are unattached to solutions (and yet are important for the firm) or for which a better solution might be reached if it was worked on collectively.

Tactical Choices in the Issue-Selling Process

The question for managers lower down in the organization is not how to promote issue selling, but how to engage in it successfully. First, managers must actually get the TMT to give some time and attention to the issues raised. Second, managers must proceed in such a way that they "live to sell another day," that is, their images can't be so badly damaged in this selling effort that they lose all credibility for subsequent efforts. Our research suggests that managers face a variety of choices regarding how to sell an issue. These choices concern how the issue is bundled, framed, and moved throughout the organization. Figure 13.1 identifies critical issue selling choices.

Bundling. The first basic selling choice is whether to tie a new issue to other issues currently circulating within the organization. A seller might, for example, propose that a new technology issue is really a part of a bigger issue considered previously or another issue currently on the agenda. The advantages of bundling a new issue with others are several. By doing so, a seller taps into resources and communication currency the other issue may have. If the new issue is linked to an issue considered important by others, then the new issue gains by association. Some established routines or mechanisms for talking about the other issue may also benefit the new issue. For example, if a new technology issue becomes linked to a larger product development issue, then a cross-functional team designated to address the company's problems in getting new products up and running may already exist. The seller's new technology issue can then be channeled through this structure as a means of getting a hearing.

Of course, bundling an issue with other issues presents potential costs as well. If the old issue comes to be seen in a negative way, for example, the new issue that the seller carefully linked to it may also be tainted and viewed negatively. Ties to an "old issue" that has political enemies may activate conditions or political resistance that dampen enthusiasm for the new issue. In addition, links to

---

Figure 13.1 Issue Selling Process Choices

Connect issue to other issue	**Bundling**	Sell issue as an isolated concern
Business frame No implied TMT responsibility	**Framing**	Moral frame Implied TMT responsibility
Universal	**Language**	Particularistic
Go solo	**Involvement**	Involve others as co-sellers
Formal Public	**Approach**	Informal Private
Early Connected to waves of change	**Timing**	Late

---

[7] S. J. Ashford, N. Rothbard, S. Piderit and J. Dutton, "Out on a Limb: The Role of Context and Impression Management in Selling Gender-Equity Issues," *Administrative Science Quarterly* (June 1998).

an old issue may limit the range of solutions and participants connected to the neighborhood of the old issues. Thus, bundling needs to be a measured tactic used with care in the selling process.

Framing. Sellers implicitly or explicitly choose a framing for their issue by the ways they describe and present it. For example, they can choose to frame an issue as an opportunity for the company or as a threat the company faces. Framing the issue as an opportunity may induce greater participation,[8] more commitment to taking action,[9] and changes of lesser magnitude,[10] than if the issue is framed as a threat. To frame an issue effectively as an opportunity, managers must work hard to help others to see the issue as controllable, involving gain, and as positive in impact.

Another basic choice that any seller must make is whether to frame the issue to imply that the top group has a responsibility or obligation to address it. For example, managers interested in more environmental responsiveness from the organization can push this issue as a moral obligation for the firm. In this approach, managers emphasize the communal obligation of all parties and the morality of an affirmative response. Such framing makes getting the ear of the top more likely (in that they exert more pressure on this group), however, it may have attendant image costs. TMTs may not like feeling pushed and may think poorly of managers who take this kind of stand. Most sellers prefer a business frame to such a "hard sell" approach. With a business frame, managers use facts and figures to suggest the financial costs of, for example, not attending to the environment. With this framing, managers appeal to their target's "head" and a concern for instrumental outcomes. With a moral appeal, managers appeal to their target's "heart" and their sense of what is right. Both frames are powerful, and each may be useful in certain situations.

Language. Closely tied to tactics surrounding issue framing are choices regarding the use of language to describe an issue. Managers make language choices in their issue-selling attempts. For example, choosing a business frame for an issue requires one kind of language and a moral frame implies another. In choosing language to use, issue sellers need to be mindful of what a particular target is interested in hearing. Issue sellers choose whether to speak similarly about their issues to everyone or whether to customize language use to a specific target. Issue sellers often credit their successes to an attempt to communicate flexibly about their issues. Effective sellers are able to speak "numbers to the numbers person and morality with the idealists." These managers effectively become multilingual. By tailoring their approaches to particular targets, sellers appeal to the targets' different zones of acceptance for an issue, making them more likely to be effective.

A second language choice involves attempts to link an issue to important organizational goals (e.g., this issue fits well with our plans to . . .). Managers can also cast the issue as a solution to current organizational issues and problems. For example, closely aligning a potential issue with an organization's strategic targets of increasing customer satisfaction, energy costs, or reducing waste may motivate targets to invest more attention in an issue. Both connecting strategies make the language used consistent with what decision makers are ready to hear and to what has already been collectively affirmed as important in the organization. Sellers can thus more easily reach an ear for their issues.

Involvement. Managers must decide whether to push their issues alone or to involve others in any selling effort. Though sometimes managers have little choice (e.g., when no one wants to get involved with the issue), sellers indicate that often they are faced with deciding whom to involve. Many managers gave the advice that sellers should involve others with a stake in the issue. Sellers might consider who might be affected by their issue and try to include them in the selling attempt. This strategy co-opts people who might object to the issue being raised or those with a stake in how it gets implemented. The advantage here is that it gets these voices working "for" the issue rather than, potentially, speaking out against it. The disadvantage is that including those with additional and perhaps unique concerns can dilute the selling effort as the seller adds subissues or deletes central messages to appease the new "co-sellers."

A second group to be targeted for involvement are those who stand to gain from the issue being raised. Here the seller invites additional issue champions on board his or her selling effort. The advantages of such an invitation are twofold. First, more sellers mean a greater potential of being heard from the strength in numbers. Second, if the issue is badly received, the seller who has involved others in his or her selling effort risks less image damage. Any negative reactions may be attributed to the

---

8 D. P. Ashmos, D. Duchon, and W. D. Bodensteiner, "Swords into Plowshares: Strategic Decision Making and Response to 'Crisis' Issues in the Defense Industry." Working paper at University of Texas at San Antonio, 1990.
9 A. Ginsberg and N. Venkatraman, "Investing in New Information Technology: The Role of Competitive Posture and Issue Diagnosis," *Strategic Management Journal*, 13 (Summer 1992), pp. 37–53.
10 J. E. Dutton, and S. Jackson, "Categorizing Strategic Issues: Links to Organizational Action," *Academy of Management Review*, 12 (1987), pp. 76–90.

group. A cost may come with a high involvement strategy too, however. If the issue is welcomed, no one particular seller stands out as the champion.

Approach. Sellers must make choices about their selling approach. Here two decisions stand out. First, sellers decide whether to make a formal or informal appeal and second whether to make a public or private pitch for their issues. Research indicates that rather than make these selling choices independently, sellers tend to follow the dominant organizational recipe for this activity. For example, if people tend to raise issues in private forums using informal means, then issue sellers would be better off if they sold the issue using a similar approach. In contrast, in a firm with a formal presentation norm, sellers would be better off customizing their efforts to this type of approach. By following the prescriptive routines, issue sellers are more likely to find a hearing for their issue. This "recipe-following" tendency suggests that organizations might want to take a look at the prescribed routines in their settings. For example, remember the conservative hospital? A factor that blocked issue selling was the lack of room in the organization to "think out loud." One of the changes contemplated by senior management as a result of the study was to institute a "not ready for prime time" issue-discussion forum. In this forum, managers could raise issues that were not yet thoroughly worked out. By this mechanism, senior management hoped to get an earlier read on emerging issues than they were able to previously.

Timing. Managers in several different organizational settings express advice for how issues can be raised effectively. For example, managers emphasize the importance of being opportunistic about timing. One seller, for example, talked about an issue that she, "kept in her desk drawer," ready to raise when the time was right. More effective managers may pay attention to "waves" of thought, opinion, and political momentum when deciding whether to sell a particular issue. Researchers who studied politicians who effectively get issues on the congressional docket liken them to surfers.[11] Good docket setters (or good issue sellers) are able to sense the waves of changing sentiment in an organization. They capitalize on the momentum created by the changing tides of openness and opportunity that exist in an organization. Getting in front of one of those waves with one's issue may help to propel that issue onto the organizational agenda. On the other hand, a poorly timed selling attempt may stand little chance of getting on the agenda given the existing currents in the organization no matter how meritorious it is. Savvy managers learn how to read the context effectively and to initiate their selling at the right time.

Other Tactics

In addition, many sellers emphasize the importance of doing one's homework as part of the work of effective issue selling. Homework involves two elements. First, sellers need to become experts in the issue they are promoting. It might involve gathering external evidence on a new technology, articles from industry publications about a proposed practice or anecdotes from senior colleagues about a new technique. The goal is to not only have one's facts straight about the issue one is promoting, but also to gather evidence that will be seen as credible by those to whom one is selling. In addition to homework about the topic, issue sellers also need to do their political homework. It involves assessing the organizational history around an issue. Has it been brought up before? What happened then? The seller should also assess other people's agendas related to the issue. Who is likely to be for or against it? This knowledge will be crucial in tailoring the selling approach.

Doing one's political homework can also include informally testing the waters by stimulating early conversations about the issue of interest. In this way the seller can obtain valuable information about the issue and how others might view it. From these early, informal discussions, the seller can draw better inferences about how others higher up in the organization might respond and can modify his or her approach to better ensure obtaining their support. These early informal conversations are also crucial for assessing whether and how much image cost may come with pushing this issue. This assessment can be crucial in making decisions about both whether and how to proceed.

The Challenge of Charged Issues

The discussion to this point ignored the *nature* of the issue that sellers might be considering. Sellers, however, appear to think carefully about the content of the issue they are selling. Certain issues seem to be more worrisome in the minds of potential issue sellers. These issues have a characteristic nature. Sellers are reluctant to raise them in all different contexts. We call these issues "charged." By charged, we mean that the issue is tough. Some authors label them "undiscussables" in organizations. Our research suggests that charged issues are evaluated negatively, emotion laden, politically

---

[11] J. W. Kingdon, "How Do Issues Get on Public Policy Agendas?" Paper presented at the annual meeting of the American Sociological Association.

hot in that they are seen as having a divisive quality, and complex. We studied gender-equity concerns (whether men and women are treated equitably in organizations) as one example of a charged issue. Other such issues might be the treatment of employees with AIDS, the treatment of racial minorities, the treatment of the natural environment, or other social issues. These issues are often scary ones for managers to raise. Managers wonder whether they will be seen as rocking the boat. They worry too about being shunned by the group for bringing up issues that cause controversy. They also worry about being labeled. For the gender-equity issue, for example, managers worried about being labeled a troublemaker.

How do organizations handle such issues? Typically, top management creates defensive routines that reduce the likelihood that such issues will be expressed. For example, aggressive statements from the top regarding how wonderfully the organization is addressing the issue in question can send strong signals to those below that messages to the contrary are not wanted. The top thereby protects itself from hearing that all is not well. Our research suggests that middle managers collude in this protection. Out of an interest in remaining accepted by the group and maintaining their team player image, managers restrain themselves from going out on a limb for an issue they think will be controversial or emotional. Over time and by behaviors such as these, certain issues become undiscussable within an organization. One manager described his setting as a conflict-avoiding culture. Other managers would agree with him in private that an issue needed to be addressed, but no support would be offered in public settings. Many managers suggested that risk taking is not rewarded in their settings. Given these beliefs, such managers are unlikely to raise issues that entail risk.

Should organizations care that certain issues take on the quality of undiscussables? If the issue that causes concern continues, it will fester within the organization. Women feeling inequitably treated, for example, will continue to experience the issue. If they have no place to talk about this issue within the organization, they are more likely to leave. A high cost is attached to such a talent drain. In addition, if looming concerns (say over the need to be more environmentally responsive) are undiscussables, then the organization loses valuable time in formulating a response. The organization may have to respond to the concern more in a crisis mode (say when a lawsuit is brought against the firm) than it would if avenues for discussion were made available earlier.

Firms interested in opening up the corporate conversation to include discussion of charged issues such as the treatment of employees (in all its various guises) need to work hard to make the context supportive and to establish communication avenues that put issue sellers less at personal risk. For example, GE holds a town meeting forum in which managers from all over the world can anonymously call in their information and concerns about a variety of topics. The call is heard simultaneously by their top managers worldwide. Often these calls raise issues along the lines of "our competitor in Brazil appears to be coming out with a new product." An alternative way to use this management practice (which is also used by Wal-Mart) is to have people surface these more troubling concerns too (e.g., "our competitors are taking significant steps to address the environmental impact of their production processes, should we?"). If managers can create a supportive atmosphere, charged issues can more easily enter the broad-based "discussion" created by this use of computer technology. What was undiscussable becomes discussable—and by a broad range of organizational members simultaneously.

Conclusion

Survival in an increasingly changing environment demands that organizations develop effective engines for change that work inside the organization. Our research indicates that a vital source for change from within is created and perfected through the effective identification and selling of critical organizational issues. Issue selling is a skilled activity. It takes a mindset and a competence that can be developed. Effective issue sellers demonstrate a good sense of the full range of issue-selling choices, and they customize issue-selling efforts to the contexts in which they find themselves. Over time, they learn to make these choices, thoughtfully and enact them with skill. The best issue sellers undertake this activity as a natural part of their middle managerial jobs. These managers are seen as influential and able to get things done in the organization. In this way issue selling is an important political skill in fostering managerial success.

Issue Selling

Instructions

Read the case situation about Chris Peters, which follows.[1] Assume that Chris Peters is a manager who works at "your firm." For "your firm," think of a firm with which you are most familiar. It may be the firm in which you have done most of your full-time work or the firm that you worked in most recently (e.g., your summer internship firm). Your task is to give Chris Peters advice on how to "sell" an issue.

Please give the case some thought, then answer the questions that follow on pages 19 and 20 and write up an issue-selling plan. In your plan, use bullet points, be brief, but be sure to describe the complete set of steps that you think Chris Peters should follow in raising the "people" issue. Draw upon your understanding of Chris Peters's issue, as well as your own experience of how things get done in organizations.

Remember: This is an individual assignment.

Chris Peters and the "People" Issue

After a wonderful dinner at a fancy seafood restaurant, your friend, Chris Peters, pushes a memo across the dinner table. "Take a look at this and tell me what I should do," Chris asks. "I really need your advice." You have known Chris since your early college days and have followed Chris's career proudly. Chris has worked at your firm for ten years in the marketing department.

Chris wrote the attached memo because she thought it was time that someone at the top really knew what was going on at the company. Chris believes that the message is important, but does not know how it will be received. She really wants your advice.

TO: Mr. Peter Jones, CEO
FROM: Chris R. Peters
       Director of Product Marketing
DATE: February 5, 1998

I've been working in the marketing department for ten years. I have been stretched and have grown in this department, but have also had challenges. I've enjoyed being part of this dynamic and interesting company. Despite my general enthusiasm about the company and my job, however, I was taken aback when I received your memo announcing the resignations of Jan Sims and Lee Chambers, two of our firm's high ranking people. Just nine months ago, Noel Fredrickson resigned, and a year before that, it was Pat Hayes. The reasons that they gave seem surprisingly similar, they wanted to "spend more time with their families" or "explore new career directions."

I wonder if there is a pattern here? Why do such able, conscientious people who seem to be committed to their careers suddenly want to change course or spend more time with families? It's a question I've been thinking about and one that I want to raise with you.

Despite our firm's policies to hire and promote good people and your own efforts to recognize and reward people's contributions, the overall atmosphere in this company is one that seems to slowly erode people's sense of worth. I believe that top-level people are leaving our firm not because they are drawn to other pursuits but because they are tired of struggling against a climate of failure. Little things that happen daily send subtle messages that people are less important, less talented, less likely to make a difference than they really could.

Let me try to describe what I mean. I'll start with meetings, which happen all the time at our firm and seem devaluing for people. People are often talked over and interrupted; their ideas never seem to be heard. Last week, I attended a meeting with eleven people. As soon as the two started their presentation, several side conversations began. Their presentation skills were excellent, but they couldn't seem to get people's attention. When it was time to take questions, one man said dismissively, "We did something like this a couple of years ago, and it didn't work." They explained how their ideas differed, but the explanation fell on deaf ears. When I tried to give them support by expressing interest, I was interrupted.

---

[1] Adapted & reprinted by permission of *Harvard Business Review*. From "The Memo Every Woman Keeps in Her Desk" by Kathleen Reardon, Mar/Apr 1993. Copyright © 1993 by the Harvard Business School Publishing Corporation; all rights reserved.

But it's not just meetings. There are many things that make people feel unwelcome or unimportant. One department holds its biannual retreats at a country club where some don't feel welcomed. At the end of the sessions, some typically hang around at the bar and talk, while others quietly disappear. Needless to say, important information is often shared during those casual conversations.

Almost every formal meeting is followed by a series of informal ones behind closed doors. Some are rarely invited. Nor are they privy to the discussions before the formal meetings. As a result, they are often less likely to know what the boss has on his or her mind and therefore less prepared to react.

Any of these incidents on its own is a small thing. But together and in repetition, they are quite powerful. The people here fight to get their ideas heard and to crack the informal channels of information. Their energy goes into keeping up, not getting ahead, until they just don't have any more to give.

I can assure you that my observations are shared by many in the company. I can only speculate that Jan Sims and Lee Chambers shared them.

Our firm needs people if it is to become preeminent. We need to send stronger, clearer signals that people matter. And this kind of change can work only if it starts with strong commitment at the top. That's why I'm writing to you. If I can be of help, please let me know.

Part One

Now that you've read the memo and thought about Chris's situation, we are interested in whether you would raise (or sell) this issue to the top management team. **Assume that Chris has not yet sent this memo to the CEO when you answer the following questions.**

Can Chris sell this issue successfully to the top management team (where success is indicated by the top management team giving the issue their time and attention to it)? To what extent do you agree or disagree with the following (please circle one number on the scales for the each question):

1. I am confident that Chris could get the top levels of my firm to pay attention to this issue.

1	2	3	4	5	6	7
Strongly Disagree			Neither Agree or Disagree			Strongly Agree

2. Based on the scenario, how willing should Chris be to try to sell this issue to the top management team (using whatever approach or style that you think best)?

1	2	3	4	5	6	7
Not at all Willing						Extremely Willing

3. Please explain the rationale for the rating that you provided in question 2.

    _____
    _____
    _____
    _____

4. How much effort should Chris be willing to put into selling this issue to the TMT?

1	2	3	4	5	6	7
None at all						A great deal of effort

5. How much *time* should Chris be willing to spend in selling this issue?

1	2	3	4	5	6	7
Not at all Willing						Extremely Willing

continued on the next page

Part Two

What are the different steps that Chris might consider taking in selling this issue to the top management team? (What is your issue-selling plan?)

Inex

Nestled in California's "Silicon Valley" is a middle-sized firm called Inex, a minor player in what has recently been a booming computer industry. While generally considered a "clean" industry, many computer companies had been coming under increasing attack during the past decade from environmentalists, public groups, and politicians for emitting sulfuric and hydrochloric acid into the atmosphere.

These groups have not yet targeted Inex, given its size. However, their presence caused Inex's president, Sara Lightwood, concern. Sara Lightwood worried that Inex's turn in the spotlight might soon be coming. Lightwood worried that her company's carefully created image as a new-age, enlightened workplace might be damaged if Inex was cited for harming the environment. In addition, it was also possible that the government might get involved. Congress recently passed new, special regulations that would control pollution from computer companies. Lightwood faced a tough choice. She could do nothing and face potential penalties for noncompliance, or she could spend enormous sums to tackle the problem. Her long-run strategy for the firm might change if the penalties were a certainty—but right now she couldn't be sure.

President Lightwood's concerns were not without reason. Recently she learned that LTX in Tucson's "Silicon Desert" had undertaken a $330 million dollar program to install somewhat low-tech scrubbers in their production facilities. LTX spent nearly six years in legal battles with the state of Arizona over their air emissions. While Inex was near LTX's size, Inex had been listed in the EPA's toxic release inventory system as a noted air pollutant contributor. There had also been increasing publicity in recent months about air quality in the valley, allegedly caused by computer manufacturers.

In January, Lightwood met with Brad Jones, a young engineer who has worked at Inex for three years. He was hired based on Sara Lightwood's recommendation. A faculty member at the University of Michigan's School of Information recommended Jones highly to Lightwood. Jones had combined training in computer science with training in environmental engineering through Michigan's Corporate Environmental Management Program. Lightwood herself was a Michigan graduate and when Jones was hired, the two had a long meeting. They discussed Lightwood's vision for Inex, her management style, and the plans she had for Jones and other young computer-savvy engineers. As Jones remembered the conversation, Lightwood's message centered on personal initiative and the interconnectedness of organizational life. She said:

Source: "The Issue with Inex" adapted by Susan Ashford of the University of Michigan from "Pegasus Chemical Company," a case study by David Kuechle, Professor Emeritus, Harvard Graduate School of Education, 1981.

Even if you have the best ideas, your insights in Inex, or indeed in any organization, will only have power and real impact if you are able to "work" the organization. Managing well involves reading the context and managing up. Power and influence are not dirty words! They are the essence of managerial success!

Jones and Lightwood met at 2 P.M. on January 11 for a regularly scheduled meeting. After initial pleasantries, Jones explained that he had begun the process of looking for another job. Jones noted that he asked for the meeting because he didn't want Lightwood to hear it from others. According to Jones, new ideas didn't appear to be welcome within Inex. "Even top level line and staff personnel resist change," Jones said. Jones then described a recent experience in which he tried to convince Janet Brown, the sector manager of the company's CPU Division, to support an idea that Jones had for reducing toxic air emissions. Jones felt he had a process that could essentially eliminate toxic sulfuric and hydrochloric acid from the smoke going up Inex's stacks.

Lightwood had many contacts in the field. She had already heard about Jones's recent activities. She knew that Jones, with Brown's approval, had just completed a $60,000 pilot project designed to reduce toxic emissions. The project was apparently successful. Jones now recommended that the company spend $3.4 million dollars to purchase and install special filtered smokestack "scrubbers" able to do the job for the entire company for at least the next 11 years. Lightwood probed a bit regarding Brown's reaction. Jones summarized Janet Brown's concerns.

1. Why this much? Brown thought that Jones's scrubbers were more than what was needed and, therefore, too costly! The EPA didn't require the reduction of toxins to such an extreme level. So why should they do it?
2. Why now? The company was experiencing little pressure from community groups. The media and public groups hadn't yet focused on pollution in Silicon Valley. When they did, Brown argued, they would focus on firms much larger than Inex first.
3. Can we afford it? $3.4 million was a lot of money, and other company priorities required resources in the immediate future.

Sara Lightwood was most interested in Jones's personal opinion of the process he had invented—was it really good? Jones said he was convinced that it was. Jones also argued that the money required to install the scrubbers was inexpensive when you looked at what the same equipment would likely cost in even just a few years.

Lightwood listened carefully to Jones. After sitting in silence for a moment, Lightwood reminded Jones of their conversation just after he was hired. Lightwood noted that if the equipment was as good as Jones said, then he should be able to convince others of his plan. She wanted Jones to understand, though, that a convincing idea wasn't enough. In Lightwood's mind, new ideas rarely make it on pure merit. Ideas sell because the seller knows the political landscape of the organization and works the idea with sensitivity to the organization's power sources. In Lightwood's mind, it was this knowledge that separated mere ideas from ultimate organizational changes.

Lightwood told Jones that as president, she wouldn't decide on her own to spend the $3.4 million even if she were certain it would benefit the company. She said, "Personally, I like your idea. Your task now is to make it happen. If you believe in this idea put the heat on me! Pressure me through the organization. Have the organization convince me, the president, now that you've convinced me, the individual."

Lightwood encouraged Jones to stay on, stay with it, and work the context to make his idea a reality. Lightwood then hit Jones with the big one. She said that if he decided to stay and push for what he believed in, that he shouldn't tell anyone of their conversation. She said that if she were to hear that he did, he wouldn't work for Inex any longer. Lightwood supported her strong stand by noting that she didn't believe in management by command and that orders from the top never created effective change.

Their conversation that day was brief, and Jones remembered leaving feeling angry. It didn't make sense to him that the company wouldn't adopt his process right now! In Jones's mind, Inex had a societal responsibility to cease polluting the atmosphere. It didn't matter what bigger companies were doing or whether regulatory agencies were focused on Silicon Valley or not! Sara Lightwood seemed unwilling to back her words with action!

Jones took the next several days off and traveled to the Alexander Valley north of Sonoma. In the beauty of the vineyards and hills he sought some perspective. What would he gain by quitting? He would certainly lose credit for all the work done thus far. He saw that Lightwood had boxed him in—he would have to work the project through the organization. So he decided to go for it—to try to get the organization to pressure Lightwood to accept the value of the scrubbers. Jones figured he had two things going for him. First, he was known as an excellent engineer. He was recognized as having great potential to advance within the company. Second, his pilot was acknowledged by technically competent people to be effective. The filtered scrubbers were a good idea. In fact, the company was seeking patents for them. Other companies had also expressed interest in purchasing the rights even at this early stage.

Inex Company

Inex was a medium-sized computer company. It competed successfully with both small start-ups and with the giants in the industry. Inex's competitive advantages were competitive prices and a somewhat faster and more reliable delivery to regional customers.

The company had three major operating units. They were the Central Processing Unit (CPU) sector, the Peripherals/Processors sector, and the Storage Devices sector. Each sector was run as a profit center. Each had its own manufacturing, developmental research, and marketing operations. The sector managers reported to Lightwood. They were rewarded with a salary plus a bonus based on sector profits. In good years, bonuses for sector managers would amount to 35 to 49 percent of their base salaries.

Top and mid-level operating managers at Inex tended to be moved around a lot. Young, ambitious managers who desired top operating positions were especially likely to move. In Jones's opinion, the rapid movement of management along with the method the firm used to evaluate and pay managers was responsible for a general resistance to try out new ideas. Such ideas often had long-term profit potential and required managers to spend money in the short run. Line managers at Inex became so concerned with short-term results that they sometimes ignored important longer-run concerns like preventative maintenance. On occasion, managers also concealed safety violations as well as environmental issues. The hope seemed to be that by the time the consequences of such violations became obvious the manager would have moved on to another job. Movement into and out of Inex, both from and to other companies in the industry was also frequent. As a result, good ideas from one company could easily be picked up in others. Consequently, managers tended to be less-than-open with others in the organization.

Company Structure

In addition to the three operating sectors, there were several small staff groups. President Lightwood had a particular view of staff groups. She didn't like them. She felt that they tended to begin masterminding things. She wanted the operating sectors left to the sector managers (with small staff groups within each sector). Corporate staff groups were there to assist. Inex had five staff groups: marketing, production, research, finance, and personnel. Marketing and personnel were quite small (two staff assistants reporting to a VP), but research was much larger. Lightwood picked staff VPs for their knowledge. She saw their major responsibilities as keeping her and her Management Committee (MC) up-to-date as to major market and technological issues facing the business. The MC used this information in setting long-range strategy for the sectors. A second staff VP responsibility was to review one- and five-year plans submitted by the sectors and to review annual sector performance. Lightwood counted on these staff groups for the expertise to evaluate the specifics of sector goals and performance. Finally, the staff groups were charged with being helpful to the sector managers and sector staff personnel. They were to give them needed information on changes in their fields of expertise.

To ensure that staff personnel were responsive to line managers, staff vice presidents at Inex were paid a set salary. They were not eligible for bonuses. The president evaluated the vice presidents based on how well the line functions they supported performed. In making her evaluation, Lightwood placed a great weight on how line managers viewed the performance of corporate staff employees. Their division managers also evaluated staff managers working in the divisions.

When President Lightwood discussed staff personnel, she often placed them into four categories. There were those who were approaching senility. They tried to compete with line personnel to try to support their own existence. The second group were those who had been "kicked upstairs" to a position where they couldn't hurt the firm too badly. A third group contained the activity creators. These folks felt the need to have others see that they are busy "doing" something. These employees tended to put out volumes of paper and sought to put responsibility for decisions on others. When they send memos, they often contained "fudge factors" that made responsibility for a decision ambiguous. For example, they might say, "I am in agreement with the proposal broadly, however, I have concerns about the chance that. . . ." Sometimes they would refer in public to a memo that they never had sent. If the idea were seen as meritorious, then they would take the photocopy out of their file! In Lightwood's mind these folks were the "hiders" in the organization.

There was a fourth group, however. These were the "well balanced." These folks recognized that line employees drive the decisions. Staff groups can advise, but it was the line manager's right to say "take a hike!" In Lightwood's view, staff people would do well to remember that line managers really want acknowledgment. Well-balanced staff personnel find ways to put the line managers center stage and to stay out of the spotlights themselves.

Brad Jones's first position at Inex was as a section staff engineer in the CPU sector. He worked in the sector's largest plant. [Figure 13.2 shows an Inex organization chart.] Brad had worked in the plant less than eight months when his performance drew the attention of the sector's manager, Janet Brown. Brown felt that Jones was one of the smartest and one of the most hard-working young engineers she had ever met. Brown noted that Brad got along well with everyone. He could not only talk to professionals, but could relate well to hourly production workers. Brown tapped Brad for a special assignment, a project that the sector had been trying to get going for over two years. Brown was impressed because in four months Brad had gotten it in shape! Brown kept an eye on him and soon tapped Jones to be her special assistant. He worked as a point person on the important problems facing the sector. Brown commented that, "Brad handled them like a pro!" Brown was impressed that despite Brad's lack of experience, he had the sensitivity and the good sense to know when he doesn't have all the answers and where to go to get them. With Brad's talent, Brown was not surprised when Jim Sands soon "stole" Brad from her.

Jim Sands was the staff VP heading up production. He was viewed by opinion leaders in the company as the most knowledgeable person in the production area. Sara Lightwood had appointed him to the vice presidency two years prior to Brad Jones's arrival in the firm. When one of his two subordinates was stolen away to another computer company, Sands asked Brown if he could approach Jones about working in the production staff group for a year or two. His rationale was that he needed his talents and that this move would broaden Jones by giving him experience in the work of Inex's other two divisions.

"I didn't want to lose Brad," said Brown, "but this seemed like an opportunity too good for me to stand in his way. I predict that Brad Jones will be running one of our divisions before too long if we are lucky enough to keep him."

When he was offered the job, Jones was working on his filtered scrubber pilot program. He wasn't sure he was ready to move. He asked Sands for time to consider the offer. He explained that he wanted to complete the pilot before moving. Sands understood and offered Jones a six-month extension on the offer. That conversation took place this past August.

During the six months Jones wrote a detailed proposal for the incorporation of the scrubbers. Chris Davis, plant manager of the CPU Sector's Fremont, California, facility, helped Brad in his efforts. The proposal went into great detail. It contained drawings and a $1/3$-inch scale mock-up of the facility showing the smokestacks with the filter scrubbers. Jones had obtained four different construction estimates and had looked into a couple of different plans for financing. Jones was enthusiastic when he went to Brown in January to show her the plan. Brown, to Jones's surprise, did not share the enthusiasm.

She did concede that Jones made several good points, but she feared that he put too much stock on the pollution question. She commented that what Inex sent into the atmosphere was a pittance compared to what other companies in the industry were doing. She continued:

Sure, in time we'll have to act, but there hasn't been any recent pressure since the Silicon Desert incident. I believe it will be four years, at minimum, before the pressure on big companies really will get hot. Only then will they take real action. Our efforts now will not make any difference! We alone can't affect air quality. The costs of action are significant. The filter scrubbers would add hundreds of thousands of dollars to our sector's operating costs over the next several years. In addition, I worry about the indirect costs. It will be disruptive to install these new scrubbers. It could upset our whole production flow for a week or more if there are problems. The total expense, when you take disruption into account might be much more than what Brad was estimating.

Beyond these concerns, Brown also thought that the system was too much—that Inex could get by with other measures, perhaps that did only less than a top job, for far less money.

It was after this discussion that Jones seriously thought about quitting Inex. However, he felt then that he ought to try one more time. That try involved seeking out Sara Lightwood, and the two met on January 11.

Jones continued to be unhappy after the Lightwood meeting. After spending time in the wine country thinking things over, he called Jim Sands and asked if he might still take the staff assistant's job that Sands had extended more than six months earlier. Sands asked about how the filter scrubber project was going. Jones said he had stopped working on it for the present.

Jones went to work for Sands on March 20th. Sands asked him to evaluate the CPU sector's plans for production. These reviews were undertaken annually. They gave Sands the information

Figure 13.2 Partial Organization Chart for Inex Company

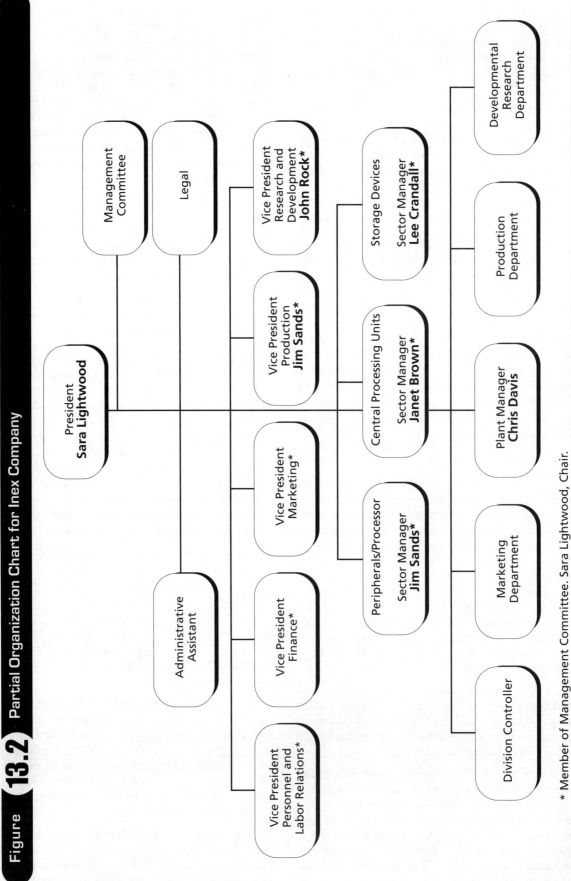

* Member of Management Committee. Sara Lightwood, Chair.

that he needed to be able to question the specific sector managers prior to bringing the total plan to President Lightwood and the Management Committee for evaluation. The staff review and the talks between staff and division personnel that they engendered often resulted in the issues being resolved without taking the time and attention of the president and other Management Committee members.

As Jones began his staff work with Sands, he remembered what Lightwood always said about the four types of staff personnel. He aspired to the "well balanced" group. In fact, Brad Jones aspired to a top-level position. Given that, Lightwood's views of staff managers challenged him. He would like to have recognition himself, but if he were going to be successful in **this** organization, he would have to set his own recognition aside as long as he worked in a staff area. If he didn't, he wouldn't have much chance of ever getting back to a line position. Jones did question whether Lightwood's ideas about staff actually worked. He worried that if staff managers gave away the limelight all the time, they might not be considered when promotions came up. It may be, too, that if they were really good at standing at the side and feeding the line managers' ego needs, the line manager might never want them to stop.

In his ruminations about staff roles at Inex, Jones's idea for the filtered scrubbers was never far from his mind. He knew that to get action on this issue, ultimately, the Management Committee would have to give it some attention. He needed to figure out how to work it through the organization to get it to the Management Committee. To get it there he would have to work both the line and the staff sides of the organization. The key, though, was the Management Committee.

The Management Committee

Sara Lightwood headed up the Management Committee. The committee consisted of the three sector managers, and the five staff vice presidents. It met once every two months to assess sector performance relative to the sector plans (one- and five-year plans) that the MC approved each year. Lightwood also used the committee for advice on cross-sector issues, issues that might influence the overall corporate direction, and on all requests for major capital investments (over $2 million). The tradition in Inex was that Lightwood approved proposals if she was satisfied that the proposal wouldn't "take the company under" or mean a significant new strategic direction and if the relevant sector manager and at least two staff vice presidents supported it. When the proposal involved two or more sectors, Lightwood also considered whether all who had a stake in the proposal had given their approval.

If all of these conditions were met, then Lightwood generally approved. When Lightwood approved, the MC tended to go along. Sometimes Lightwood asked for a straw vote at MC meetings, but formal paper ballot votes weren't done.

Often, there were "intense" discussions in MC meetings, but lingering conflicts were not the norm. Usually the pertinent staff and line people worked beforehand to build a consensus. In this process, many compromises and side deals were cut. Often managers traded off support for each other's proposals.

Jones's Dilemma

Jones didn't know how the MC members felt about his issue. He knew Lightwood liked it, but he wasn't allowed to mention this important fact. He had to build consensus among MC members. Of these, Janet Brown had already "trashed" the idea. Jones had to get Brown to change her mind! He also had to convince Sands, his current boss and Lee Crandall, the head of the Storage Devices sector.

Sands was taken by Jones's data. The pilot data were particularly impressive. The government fines that Jones cited as possible were also daunting. Sands knew that he could push the project through given what he knew about Lightwood's stand on pollution. Unfortunately, he could not take the issue up. He was currently involved in a dispute with another sector manager. He would have to take that one to the MC too. He did not feel he could also bring Jones's issue.

Sands did agree to get together with Brown to see if Brown would be willing to raise the issue herself in July. Sands reported back to Jones days later, however, that Brown was still reluctant. He said that he was sorry, but Brown wouldn't go along. Sands still felt the proposal had merit, but asked Jones to back off and to try again the following year.

Jones was let down. He didn't say much to Sands at the time but it bugged him. It was the principle that bothered him. It seemed like the managers all wanted someone else to take action. And meanwhile time was wasting. "They find all sorts of reasons not to 'make a big deal' out of something that *is* a big deal. I don't know what to do. I know compromise is needed, but where do I draw the line!? How do I proceed in my job of 'trying again next year.?"

Change From Within: Roads to Successful Issue Selling

ELECTIVE

Module 13

Dinosaurs or Dynamos? Recognizing Middle Management's Strategic Role

by Steven W. Floyd and Bill Wooldridge

Executive Overview

Reengineering has automated and obliterated middle management, and has diminished their number dramatically. What have also been lost in many delayering efforts, however, are the benefits of the strategic roles of middle managers.

This article describes how certain middle management behavior is crucial to developing organizational capability. This is a learning process which calls on organizations to interpret the world, uncover new market opportunities, focus existing resources, and accumulate new resources. In our research, we identified a middle management role with each of these elements and uncovered a strong relationship between the roles and organizational performance. Therefore, rethinking middle management's strategic role is a necessary part of the delayering process. The article closes by illustrating how to encourage strategic behavior in the reengineered organization.

Are middle managers becoming the dinosaurs of the business world? They once dominated the corporate landscape with salaries and perks that were the envy (and career goal) of every MBA. Now, like prehistoric reptiles, these behemoths of bureaucracy appear likely to succumb to a hostile environment.

In the past, when a company needed to grow, management simply added workers to the bottom and then filled in management layers above. This focused managers' attention on planning and control and provided the rationale for legions of middle managers. Growth slowed dramatically in the late 1980s, however, and today's priorities are higher quality, lower cost, flexibility, and, most important, speed.

People in the middle slow things down, increasing the distance between the customer and the corporate response. The current wave of reengineering is aimed at removing this obstacle by rethinking the division of work and reorganizing around "horizontal" processes. As part of this, "delayering" has entered the management jargon to represent the expected reduction in hierarchical levels.[1] Thus, for middle managers, the shift in emphasis from planning and control to speed and flexibility may mean the end of an epoch. Roughly twenty percent of the job losses since 1988 have come from middle management positions.[2]

There is growing evidence, however, that delayering often has unanticipated, adverse consequences. The consulting firm of Towers Perrin asked 350 senior managers in 275 major firms whether hoped-for cost reductions had been achieved, and half said "no."[3] Some firms lose valuable skills in the delayering process. Kodak, for example, slashed 12,000 positions between 1988 and 1992—many of them middle managers—but failed to achieve lasting performance improvement. Instead, innovation and creativity declined, and the company fell behind in the crucial race for new products.[4] Why doesn't delayering always work?

There are many things that can undermine successful organizational restructuring. But, at the heart of the problem in delayering seems to be the stereotypical "plan and control" view of middle management work. Seeing all middle managers from an operational viewpoint, top managers often fail to make distinctions about the variety of contributions made by middle managers, and, in particular, overlook the possibility that middle managers play strategic roles. Across-the-board or random influences (like attrition) become the *de facto* criteria for eliminating positions. As a result, delayering has the effect

---

Source: Steven W. Floyd and Bill Wooldridge, "Dinosaurs or Dynamos? Recognizing Middle Management's Strategic Role." *Academy of Management Executive: The Thinking Manager's Source.* Copyright 1994 by Academy of Management. Reproduced with permission of Academy of Management in the format Textbook via Copyright Clearance Center.

1. A host of terms related to organizational restructuring have entered the lexicon. For our purposes, restructuring is the most general, referring to all efforts aimed at radical reorganization. Consis-tent with Michael Hammer and James Champy's book, *Reengineering the Corporation* (Harper Business, 1993), we use *reengineering* to refer to the process-driven style of organizing. Delayering is one aspect of reengineering and refers to the reduction of managerial levels.
2. Touby, Laurel. 1993. "The Business of America Is Jobs," *Journal of Business Strategy*, pp. 21–31.
3. Fisher, Anne B. 1991. "Morale Crisis," *Fortune* (November 18).
4. Burrus, Daniel. 1994. Technotrends: *How You Can Go Beyond Your Competition by Applying Tomorrow's Technology Today.* New York: Harper-Collins.

of "throwing the baby out with the bath water"—curtailing vital strategic capability while eliminating middle management layers.

In this article, we take a fresh look at the contribution of middle managers and provide a framework for differentiating the baby from the bath water. We argue that sustaining an adaptive balance between industry forces and organizational resources depends on the *strategic* roles of middle management. The recognition of these roles fosters a discriminating approach to delayering that increases the organizational influence of surviving middle managers. More like the Phoenix bird than the dinosaur, a new breed of middle managers—whose roles are more strategic than operational—should be rising from the ashes of the delayered corporation.

The Misunderstood Middle Manager

Typically, middle managers have been seen as part of an organization's control system. Middle management does things which translate strategies defined at higher levels into actions at operating levels. This involves (1) defining tactics and developing budgets for achieving a strategy, (2) monitoring the performance of individuals and subunits, and (3) taking corrective action when behavior falls outside expectations. This description, or major elements of it, has applied for decades to the organization members we call middle managers, including functional department heads, project or product managers, brand managers, regional managers, and the like. In the language of strategic management, their role has been defined as "implementation."

In the reengineered organization, however, senior managers rely less and less on middle managers. Information and communications technologies make it easier for those at the top to monitor and control activities directly. In addition, empowerment and cross-functional teams allow operators to take responsibility for defining their own roles. The emphasis on business processes vastly reduces the relevance of functional departments and the accompanying managerial hierarchies. Such "stove pipes" gave rise to middle management in the first place, and as the layers disappear, so does the rationale for middle managers.

The withering of middle management's *operating* responsibilities undeniably justifies reductions in the number of middle managers. But our research shows that performance of middle managers' *strategic* roles remains as a crucial factor in organizational success. In a study of twenty companies, for example, we found that middle manager involvement in the *formulation* of strategic decisions was associated with higher financial performance.[5] This is not to say that implementation is unimportant. Strategies that lack middle management commitment suffer serious implementation problems.[6] What differentiated higher performing organizations in this study, however, was an arrangement in which middle managers actively participated in the "thinking" as well as the "doing" of strategy. Involvement is an important stimulus to strategic thinking, so that strategies formulated with middle management input are likely to be superior to those designed solely by top managers.

In short, middle managers are frequently misunderstood by corporate America. Typically, they are seen in strictly operational terms, and their potential for enhancing the quality of firm strategy is discounted or ignored. Yet, research shows that middle management's strategic contributions directly affect the bottom line. What are these strategic contributions, and how do they sustain competitive advantage? Further, which middle management positions are likely to be most important in strategy? To answer these questions, we initiated a second study of 259 middle managers within a diverse set of companies and industry circumstances. Before presenting the results, the following section details middle management's strategic roles and explains why they are related to an organization's economic performance.

Competitive Advantage and Middle Management Strategic Roles

In a number of widely read papers, Jay Barney, Gary Hamel, C. K. Prahalad, David Teece, and others have argued that competitive advantage results from unique organizational resources. According to this view, the most important strategic resources are the knowledge and skills accumulated collectively over time by organization members. The organizational capabilities associated with such human assets cannot be bought on an open market. They are acquired over an extended period and as part of complex interpersonal processes, and this makes capabilities difficult or impossible to imitate. When they effectively differentiate a firm from its competitors, they are

---

5 Wooldridge, Bill, and Steven W. Floyd. 1990. "The Strategy Process, Middle Management Involvement, and Organizational Performance," *Strategic Management Journal*, 11, pp. 213–241.
6 Guth, W. D., and Ian C. MacMillan. 1986. "Strategy Implementation Versus Middle Management Self-Interest," *Strategic Management Journal*, 7, pp. 313–327.

called "core capabilities." In comparison with specific products or technologies which can be copied, capabilities provide the potential for a more sustainable advantage. In principle, therefore, *dynamic capability*, or the ability to develop new capabilities, is the feature of organizations most likely to be associated with long-term economic performance.[7]

The striking correspondence between the nature of dynamic capability and our sense of how middle managers influence the quality of strategy provided impetus for our second study. Dynamic capability is a learning process which calls on organization members to interpret the world around them, to uncover new opportunities, to focus existing resources efficiently, and to accumulate new resources when existing ones become obsolete. Put simply, capabilities develop as the organization learns how to deliver what customers want and how to create new combinations of assets and skills. In other words, capabilities develop through the brains and nervous systems of middle managers.

After talking with dozens of middle managers and weaving our impressions from these interviews with the threads of prior research,[8] we developed a theoretical framework which captures the roles of middle managers in dynamic capability. Two principle dimensions underlie the roles. Each can be described as a dichotomy. Shown in Figure 1, the model combines upward and downward influence with integrative and divergent thinking to describe four roles: championing alternatives, synthesizing information, facilitating adaptability, and implementing deliberate strategy.[9]

Championing Strategic Alternatives

Sometimes, middle managers play an important part in bringing entrepreneurial and innovative proposals to top management's attention. Championing involves a complex sequence of activities. First, middle managers act as an initial screen, selecting from the broad array of business opportunities, new processes proposals, and administrative innovations suggested at operating levels. Living in the organizational space between strategy and operations, middle managers are uniquely qualified to make such judgments. Once committed, managers begin to nurture the idea, providing "seed" resources that allow experimentation. At this stage, the endeavor lacks formal sanction, and managers' effectiveness depends greatly on their ability to get informal cooperation and support. After gaining experience and building a credible proposal, middle managers take the initiative forward.

Synthesizing Information

Not all the ideas brought upward by middle managers are full-blown strategic proposals. Frequently, their role is to supply information to top management concerning internal and external events. Inevitably, middle managers are not objective channels of data, however. They saturate information with meaning through personal evaluation and explicit advice. Events are likely to be reported as "threats" or "opportunities," and these seemingly innocent labels are a powerful influence on how superiors come to see their situation.[10]

In conveying "facts," middle managers may be laying the foundation for a future agenda. An opportunity can be championed successfully only when all agree the "timing is right," and usually this requires a considerable amount of prior discussion. Accordingly, middle managers are often able to control, or at least influence, top management perceptions by framing information in certain ways. This role can be crucial in encouraging overly cautious top management teams to take needed risks.

Facilitating Adaptability

In her clinical analysis of a large computer manufacturer, Rosabeth Kanter describes the efforts of

---

7 Few managers would dispute the importance of core capabilities in competitive strategy, and numerous examples suggest a strong relationship to organizational performance. A widely circulated working paper by David Teece, Gary Pisano, and Amy Shuen summarizes the scholarly literature on the resource-based view of strategy and core capabilities: "Dynamic Capabilities and Strategic Management," University of California at Berkeley working paper, 1992.
8 The principal studies we relied on for an initial definition of middle managers' roles in strategy included: J. L. Bower. 1970. *Managing the Resource Allocation Process* (Boston, MA: Harvard Business School); R. A. Burgelman. 1983. "A Process Model of Internal Corporate Venturing in the Diversified Major Firm," *Administrative Science Quarterly*, 28, pp. 223–244; R. M. Kanter. 1983. *The Change Masters* (New York: Basic Books); T. Kidder. 1981. *The Soul of a New Machine* (Boston, MA: Little, Brown); I. Nonaka. 1988. "Toward Middle-Up-Down Management: Accelerating Information Creation," *Sloan Management Review*, Spring, pp. 9–18; and P. C. Nutt. 1987. "Identifying and Appraising How Managers Install Strategy," *Strategic Management Journal*, 8, pp. 1–14.
9 This model was first described in our article: S. W. Floyd and Bill Wooldridge. 1992. "Middle Management Involvement in Strategy and Its Association with Strategic Type," *Strategic Management Journal*, 13 (special issue), pp. 153–167.
10 See Jane E. Dutton and Susan E. Jackson. 1987. "Categorizing Strategic Issues: Links to Organization Action," *Academy of Management Review*, 12, pp. 76–90, for a more elaborate discussion. More recently, Jane E. Dutton and Susan J. Ashford published an article related directly to middle managers: "Selling Issues to Top Management," *Academy of Management Review*, 18, 1993, pp. 397–428.

Figure 1 — A Typology of Middle Management Roles in Strategy

	Behavioral Activity	
Cognitive Influences	Upward Influence	Downward Influence
Divergent	Championing Strategic Alternatives	Facilitating Adaptability
Integrative	Synthesizing Information	Implementing Deliberate Strategy

middle managers who sheltered and encouraged an employee involvement program in the midst of an emotional, top-down redesign of production processes.[11] Their efforts created an environment in which fears about the change could be brought into the discussion. Though participation helped the organization adopt the new work processes, the process diverged completely from top management's original intention. Without middle management's efforts to facilitate change, however, the reengineering would have met with considerably more resistance and could have failed.

Thus, while middle managers are often called change resisters, Kanter describes them as "change masters." We compare this role with the flexible, accordion-like structure between the two sections of a reticulated passenger bus. The shape and composition of the accordion overcomes the rigidities of the vehicle, while at the same time assuring that the front and back head in the same direction.

Implementing Deliberate Strategy

In championing, synthesizing, and facilitating, middle managers go beyond, or even ignore, the plans embedded in top management's deliberate strategy. The most commonly recognized strategic role, however, is the implementation of top management's intentions. Here, the strategic contribution rests on middle managers' efforts to deploy existing resources efficiently and effectively. Reports suggest a widening gap between intentions and implementations,[12] however, and the cause is often attributed to middle manager obstinacy. Our research suggests another reason.

Implementation is commonly perceived as a mechanical process where action plans are deduced and carried out from a master strategy conceived by top management. The reality is more complex. Even in fairly stable situations, priorities must be revised as conditions evolve and new information unfolds. Implementation, therefore, is best characterized as an ongoing series of interventions which are only partly anticipated in top management plans and which adjust strategic directions to suit emergent events.

In summary, the conception that top managers formulate strategy while middle managers carry it out is not only unrealistic, it is also self-defeating. Effective implementation requires that middle managers understand the strategic rationale behind the plan, in addition to the specific directives. Such understanding appears to result from broad participation in the strategic process,[13] and middle management's effectiveness in implementing strategy is thus directly related to their involvement in other roles. The "implementation gap" reflects a broader chasm between senior management's perception of implementation and what middle managers must know to get the job done. In an earlier *AME* article, we described the problem as lack of *strategic consensus* and outlined a process for narrowing the gap.[14]

Linking Strategic Roles to Core Capability

Seen through our own conceptual lens, anecdotal

---

11 Kanter, *op. cit.*
12 A study by Booz-Allen and Hamilton, Inc., "Making Strategy Work: The Challenge of the 1990s," was published in 1990. It is particularly articulate on this point and is available from their New York Office.
13 In this study cited under reference number 5, we found that middle managers who were involved in formulating as well as implementing strategy tended to understand the strategy better.
14 Floyd, Steven W., and Bill Wooldridge. 1992. "Managing Strategic Consensus: The Key to Effective Implementation," *Academy of Management Executive*, 6, pp. 27–39.

evidence suggested links between middle management and core capability. Because the argument countered prevailing wisdom, however, we wanted to go beyond logic and case study to examine the issue more systematically. Thus, we developed a questionnaire that would measure middle manager behavior in a large-scale, statistical survey. The research design called for observation of hundreds of middle managers across many organizations and drew from a combination of objective and subjective data. Because different strategies rely on different capabilities, we expected to tie the middle manager roles to the success of particular organizational strategies.

The results uncovered three convincing patterns.[15] First, in organizations whose strategy depended on product innovation and exploiting new market opportunities, we found significantly higher levels of middle management championing and facilitating. Since core capability in innovating firms is related to the discovery of new business opportunity and operational flexibility, these results suggested the centrality of middle management.

Second, certain middle managers within the innovating firms were greater champions than others, and in particular, the involvement of those in "boundary spanning" functions (i.e., marketing, sales, purchasing, and R&D) was highest overall. Ideas arose most often from interactions with customers, suppliers, and technologies, and we found championing highest where such exposure was most likely. Not only was innovative capability in the firm related to middle management championing and facilitating, then, but these behaviors were concentrated in certain positions. In other words, boundary-spanning middle managers appeared to use strategically important knowledge in ways that fostered the development of core capabilities.

These results supported our argument that middle management was important to strategy and that some middle management positions were more important than others. To establish a link to core capability, we needed to determine whether such behavior actually led to improved economic performance. We did not expect a simple linear relationship, however. In fact, this appeared to be a case where "more is not always better."

Rather than simply *more* of the strategic role behaviors, the successful development of core capability demands variety. A similar hypothesis was suggested by Stuart Hart and Catherine Banbury, who showed in a survey of top managers that firms who combined a diverse mix of strategy-making skills enjoyed enhanced capability and organizational performance. These skills included everything from formal planning procedures to informal experimentation, and even creating a "dream" about the company future.[16] Such skills and the behaviors associated with them are not likely to be distributed evenly throughout organizations. The successful formal planner, for example, is not likely to be the best dreamer. Similarly, middle managers are likely to differ widely in their ability and willingness to assume a strategic role at a particular point in time. As a result, one would expect considerable diversity in the levels of middle management strategic behavior within organizations that were successful in developing core capability.

Consistent with this, we asked top managers in each of the 25 companies we studied to assess the financial performance of their organization. Then we examined whether performance was associated with a statistical measure of diversity in middle management behavior. We found strong relationships between variation in the performance of the strategic roles and economic performance. This provided the first scientific evidence to support the proposition that middle managers are potential reservoirs of core capability.[17] But how does this change the way one thinks of middle managers in a world of flatter, reengineered organizations?

Middle Management's Role in the Reengineered Organization

At the beginning of this article we noted that middle managers in hierarchical organizations have been seen as the implementers of top management strategies. Thus, as organizations have been reengineered around horizontal processes, it is not surprising that the perceived need for middle managers has diminished. Unfortunately, the dominant, operational stereotype of middle managers has led to the diminution of their strategic contributions. Conversations with top and middle level managers reveal that the strategic roles we describe are misunderstood, considered secondary, almost always nonsanctioned, and often discouraged. Yet, reengineering's emphasis on responsiveness, flexibility, and speed puts a premium on the middle manager behavior associated with the development of new capabilities. In this section we first

---

15 These results were first described in the study cited in endnote number 9.
16 Hart, S., and C. Banbury. 1994. "How Strategy-Making Processes Can Make a Difference," *Strategic Management Journal*, 15, pp. 251–269.
17 The results on boundary-spanning middle managers and organized performance are reported in a working paper: S. W. Floyd and Bill Wooldridge. 1994. "Middle Management Behavior, Dynamic Capability, and Organizational Performance."

illustrate how organizations unwittingly discourage strategic behavior. The paper closes, then, with a set of guidelines for senior managers who want to encourage effective behavior in the reengineered organization.

The behavior associated with facilitating adaptability is often seen as risky and somewhat subversive. In his study of resource allocation, Joseph Bower describes how middle managers diverted resources and hid experimental programs from top management scrutiny in order to gain experience and acquire new capabilities. Not surprisingly, our interviews suggest that some top managers often view this role cynically. One CEO commented, "Oh, they've all got their own pet projects; I guess that's part of the price you pay." This view discourages the learning gained from experimentation and thereby lowers the level of dynamic capability.

Championing is generally recognized as a middle management activity, but its potential contribution is not always appreciated. One top manager described middle management championing as an "earned right," reserved only for a few in recognition of many years of "credible service." Similarly, many middle managers in our interviews observed that championing meant "spending currency" with top managers. It was pursued sparingly, as "an exception." Just as telling, some middle managers felt their real influence was minimal.

The role of middle managers as channels of communication and sources of information is well recognized. However, middle managers are often criticized for "putting their own spin on it." Senior managers use elaborate systems such as formal planning to objectify and rationalize middle management input. Unfortunately, formal, bureaucratic processes make the ongoing re-interpretation of events less likely and introduce undesirable rigidity into the decision-making process. Subjective interpretation is inevitable, and need not be considered pernicious.[18]

Realizing Middle Management's Strategic Value

In sum, our ongoing research on middle management's role in strategy suggests that as organizations move away from hierarchical toward more horizontal business structures, the importance of middle managers in achieving competitive advantage is likely to increase. While often unrecognized, their contributions in interpreting, nurturing, developing, and promoting new capabilities take on new importance as organizations strive to achieve increased levels of adaptability and responsiveness. Thus, the reengineered organization is likely to be delayered and certain to have fewer middle managers, but those remaining will be crucial to the firm's ongoing success. Senior managers interested in leveraging these human assets should reexamine middle management according to the following set of principles:

- **Recognize the link between middle management, core capability, and competitive advantage.** Most fundamentally, reengineering should occur with an awareness of the link between middle management and firm competitiveness. Effective delayering can be guided by an understanding of the contributions required of surviving middle managers. The goal is to cut cost and increase responsiveness, not cripple dynamic capability.

- **Identify middle managers with the appropriate skills, experiences, and potential to thrive within the new organization.** Not all middle managers are created equally, and certain middle managers are better equipped than others to thrive within the reengineered organization. Our research shows the importance of boundary spanning experience as one criterion for discriminating among middle managers. Another consideration is that middle management in the reengineered organization requires strategy and teaming skills. In the long run, developmental experiences that foster teamwork and a strategic mindset can be avoided only at the cost of eroding core capability.

- **Develop a better understanding of desired roles within the organization.** Few top- or middle-level managers fully understand the strategic roles described here. How many top managers have articulated their expectations along these lines to middle management? For reengineering to pay off, top managers need to analyze the changed role of middle management and begin to develop it within the organization. Interventions with middle managers can clarify expectations and encourage appropriate behavior.

- **Redesign the organization to leverage the knowledge and skills of a selected set of middle managers and encourage their influence on strategic priorities.** Delayering should be accompanied by reorganizing according to a process-oriented, horizontal logic. Though most top managers understand the idea of horizontal design, few appreciate the redistribution of power called for in the new arrangements.

Organizational boundaries are becoming

---

[18] The reader interested in pursuing this idea could begin by reading Richard Daft and Karl Weick's article, "Toward a Model of Organizations as Interpretation Systems," *Academy of Management Review*, 9, pp. 284–296.

Recognizing Middle Management's Strategic Value

The key to broadening middle management's participation beyond the implementation role is to bring them into the strategic communications loop. Unfortunately, most senior managers think of communicating strategy "to the troops" as an annual or quarterly effort handled in large auditoriums or in a video conference. The idea of discussing strategy eye to eye with middle managers, much less engaging in an ongoing strategic dialogue, seems like an unnatural act.

The restructuring effort of a large insurance firm provides an example. An early step involved assembling district managers at corporate headquarters for a week-long planning session. In prior years, the agenda had been limited to financial reporting and budgeting. Since the company hoped to decentralize as a part of the delayering, some of the week was set aside to "do strategic planning." When it was suggested that the regional managers were likely to generate ideas for new products and market opportunities, however, the reaction of top management went beyond skepticism. One of the executives commented "These people don't even understand the basics . . . and we're going to get new ideas about our strategy from *that* bunch?"

Much of the initial problem in this firm, as in most, was that upper and middle managers had lived wholly different realities in the organization and spoke a different language. Bridging this kind of communications chasm meant translating the strategy into a vision that could be interpreted across diverse perspectives.

This company was facing declining premium revenues as rivals chipped away at what had been a very comfortable niche. Senior management saw the problem as a need for new technical services that would differentiate them from rivals, retain customers, and build new business. It was far less clear, however, which particular services would appeal to customers or which ones the organization could deliver. These initiatives could have come from the field. But how do you solicit strategic initiatives when you really do not know what you want?

The answer came in creating a dialogue with regional managers about a strategic vision. The basis of the vision was captured by this admonition: to chart your own competitive future get to know the future of your customer's business. By communicating this simple idea, and more important, by talking about its implications one-on-one over a period of time, top management began getting substantive input from its middle management. These ideas provided the basis for reorganizing, redeploying managerial talent, and reinvigorating the competitive edge.

increasingly fuzzy as networks of suppliers, customers, and competitors are formed to cope with enormously complex and demanding circumstances. Organizations want to capture the influence of middle managers who relate to the market and technological environments. In order to open up the organization to environmental influence, boundary-spanning middle managers should become the owners of product development, order fulfillment, and other key business processes.

The need for power shifts—from functional to process leadership, for example—is often lost on those considering or undergoing a reengineering effort. Sometimes, senior managers expect middle managers to take charge of a process but give them very little real authority. Without the freedom to experiment, middle managers quickly become frustrated and cynical about top management's intent. "Slack" has become a dirty word, but the flexibility, experimentation, and learning which is the goal of horizontal organization does require resources.

- **Renegotiate the "psychological contract" by committing to the ongoing involvement of middle management in the strategy-making process.** Restructuring is often seen as destroying a time-honored employment contract and ". . . many companies have given no indication of what the new psychological contract is."[19] Most managers want to be loyal, but if the old vision is simply thrown out with nothing to replace it, management loyalty goes out the window, too. An unknown future does not inspire confidence. Instead, it encourages talented managers to leave, thereby draining the reservoirs of core capability and eroding competitive position. Disloyalty also contributes to foot dragging and even sabotage of a reengineering strategy.

In many of our conversations with middle- as well as senior-level managers, this set of consequences seems to be inevitable. One thing becoming clear where delayering has succeeded, however, is that surviving middle managers enjoy a renewed sense of power and contribution. This results from an acknowledgment by company executives that middle managers have strategic value. Delayering can enlist middle managers in new strategic roles, but this requires a vision, organizational redesign, and new power relationships. The insert on the facing page details one company's experience in realigning middle management's roles.

Everyone a Middle Manager?

The growth of the ranks of middle management during the postwar period allowed many Western companies to expand. Middle management provided the consistency and control so necessary to enterprise. While the resulting bureaucratic hierarchy may no longer fit today's demand for flexibility, wholesale elimination of the middle management role may be short-sighted. Some suggest middle management is a dying breed, but Tom Peters writes that everyone is becoming a middle manager.[20] This outlook is grounded in his customer- and change-dominated view of organization. There will be fewer layers and fewer managers overall, but the strategic roles of middle managers are likely to become more, rather than less, important in the organizations of tomorrow.

About the Authors

Steven W. Floyd and Bill Wooldridge are associate professors of strategic management at the University of Connecticut and University of Massachusetts at Amherst, respectively. Their recent research focuses on middle managers and the behaviors associated with developing and sustaining competitive advantage. In addition, the authors study the processes related to strategy formation and emergent adaptation within top management teams. Their work on strategic consensus and middle managers has been published previously in the *Academy of Management Executive*, and appeared frequently in the *Strategic Management Journal*. Jointly or independently, they have also published in the *Academy of Management Journal*, *Journal of Management Information Systems*, and the *Handbook of Business Strategy*. Currently, they are writing a book on the strategic roles of middle managers. As consultants, the authors apply a high-involvement approach to strategy making that helps organizations appreciate and elicit contributions from all managers.

---

19 The fading expectations of middle managers were expressed eloquently in an article titled "The Death of Corporate Loyalty," in *The Economist*, April 3, 1993, 63, which quoted David A. Nadler on this particular point.
20 See Tom Peters' book, *Thriving on Chaos* (New York: The Free Press, 1987).

Index

adaptability, facilitated by middle managers, 24–25, 27
agenda, strategic, 6
allies, 8, 9–10
approaches to issue selling, 8, 10

Banbury, Catherine, 26
Barney, Jay, 23
boundary-spanning, in middle managers, 26
Bower, Joseph, 27
Brown, Janet, 15, 17, 18, 19
bundling of issues, 8–9
business frame, 9

capability, core, 23, 27
capability, dynamic, 24
championing of strategic alternatives, 24, 27
change, and issue selling, 4
change, and middle managers, 25
charged issues, 10–11
choice processes, 7–8
communication, strategic, 28
competitive advantage, 23–24, 27
complexity, and issue selling, 6
context factors, 7–8
contracts, psychological, 29
core capability, 23, 25–26
Crandall, Lee, 18, 19

Davis, Chris, 17
delayering, 22–23, 27, 29
dynamic capability, 23–24

employee loyalty, 29
environmental issues, in Inex case, 14–19
EPA (Environmental Protection Agency), 14, 15

Floyd, Steven W., 22
forums for issue selling, 10
framing of issues, 8, 9

GE (General Electric), 11
goal-setting, by top management team, 6–7

Hamel, Gary, 23
hard sell approach, 9
Hart, Stuart, 26
hierarchical structure, and delayering, 22–23
horizontal processes, in reengineering, 22, 26
human resources, and dynamic capability, 23–24

implementation, by middle management, 23, 25
Inex case, 14–19
information synthesis, 24, 27
involvement in issue selling, 8, 9–10
issues, charged, 10–11

issue selling
  overview, 4
  exercise, 12–14
  importance of, 6

Jones, Brad, 14–15, 17, 19

Kanter, Rosabeth, 24–25

language, 8, 9
Lightwood, Sara, 14–19
loyalty, employee, 29
LTX, 14

management structure, 6–7
middle management
  boundary-spanning, 26
  championing of strategic alternatives, 24, 27
  delayering and, 22–23
  dynamic capabilities and competitive advantage, 23–24, 25–26, 27
  facilitation of adaptability, 24–25, 27
  implementation role, 23, 25
  issue selling and, 6, 7
  psychological contracts and, 29
  role in reengineered organization, 26, 27–29
  strategic value of, 27–29
  strategic vs. operational roles, 23
  synthesis of information, 24, 27

opportunity, framing issues as, 9
organizational restructuring, 22–23, 26, 27–29

Peters, Tom, 29
political homework, 10
power, redistributed in reengineering, 27, 29
Prahalad, C. K., 23
psychological contracts, 29

reengineering, 22–23, 26, 27–29
risk, in charged issues, 11
Rock, John, 18

Sands, Jim, 17, 18, 19
smokestack scrubbers, 14–19
status quo, cost of, 11
strategic agenda, 6
strategic behavior, discouragement of, 26–27
strategic roles of middle managers, 23–29
support factors, in issue selling, 7, 11
tactical choices, 8–10
Teece, David, 23
timing, 8, 10
top management teams (TMTs), 6–7

Wooldridge, Bill, 22

MANAGING FOR THE FUTURE

Organizational Behavior & Processes

Leadership

Deborah Ancona
Massachusetts Institute of Technology

Module 14

MANAGING FOR THE FUTURE
Organizational Behavior & Processes, Third Edition

Deborah Ancona
Sloan School of Management
Massachusetts Institute of Technology

Thomas A. Kochan
Sloan School of Management
Massachusetts Institute of Technology

Maureen Scully
Graduate School of Management
Simmons College

John Van Maanen
Sloan School of Management
Massachusetts Institute of Technology

D. Eleanor Westney
Sloan School of Management
Massachusetts Institute of Technology

Dedicated to those who have inspired us to try to be better students and teachers.
Special thanks to: Professor Jack Barbash • Professor Arthur H. Gladstein • Professor Marius B. Jansen • Professor Joanne Martin • Professor Edgar H. Schein

VP/Editorial Director
Jack W. Calhoun

VP/Editor-in-Chief
Michael P. Roche

Senior Publisher
Melissa S. Acuña

Executive Editor
John Szilagyi

Senior Developmental Editor
Judith O'Neill

Marketing Manager
Jacquelyn Carrillo

Production Editor
Emily Gross

Manufacturing Coordinator
Rhonda Utley

Compositor
Trejo Production

Printer
Von Hoffmann Press, Inc.
Frederick, MD

Internal Designer
Bethany Casey

Cover Designer
Bethany Casey

Photographs
©PhotoDisc

Design Project Manager
Bethany Casey

COPYRIGHT ©2005
by South-Western, a division of Thomson Learning. Thomson Learning™ is a trademark used herein under license.

Printed in the United States of America
1 2 3 4 5 07 06 05 04 03

For more information contact
South-Western College Publishing,
5191 Natorp Boulevard,
Mason, Ohio, 45040
Or you can visit our Internet site at:
http://www.swlearning.com

ALL RIGHTS RESERVED
No part of this work covered by the copyright hereon may be reproduced or used in any form or by any means—graphic, electronic, or mechanical, including photocopying, recording, taping, Web distribution or information storage and retrieval systems—without the written permission of the publisher.

For permission to use material from this text or product, contact us by
Tel: (800) 730-2214
Fax: (800) 730-2215
http://www.thomsonrights.com

Library of Congress Control Number: 2003113908
ISBN 0-324-05575-7

Contents

Leadership

Overview		4

Core

Class Note	**Leadership in an Age of Uncertainty** *The Framework 9* *The Four Capabilities 14* *The Change Signature 14* *References 16*	8
Exercise	**Your Change Signature** *Step 1: Past Self 19* *Step 2: Developed Self 19* *Step 3: Underdeveloped Self 20* *Step 4: Future Self 20* *Step 5: Integration 20*	19
Case	**Re-engineering MIT: How President Charles Vest Put MIT Back on Track**	21
Case	**Carly Fiorina: A Story of Leadership Development** *Early Fiorina 27* *The AT&T and Lucent Years 28* *HP 29* *Epilogue 32*	26

Elective

The Press	**What Should I Do With My Life?** *MONEY Doesn't Fund Dreams 37* *SMARTS Can't Answer The Question 38* *PLACE Defines You 39* *ATTITUDE Is the Biggest Obstacle 39*	36
The Press	**Excerpts from Geeks & Geezers: How Era, Values, and Defining Moments Shape Leaders** *The Power of the Crucible 42* *Creating Meaning Out of the Crucible Experience 43* *What Makes a Leader 44* *Crucibles of Leadership 44* *The Importance of Individual Factors 46* *Adaptive Capacity Is Key 46* *The Difference Between Fasting and Starving 48* *Adaptive Capacity as Applied Creativity 49* *Seeing the World in a New Light 51*	42

Index

Overview

This module is designed to help you learn about the theory and practice of leadership. It looks at what leadership is, examples of how leaders engage in the practice of leadership, and also how you can better develop as a leader. As defined in the module, leadership is distributed; that is, leadership is not solely the purview of the CEO but permeates all levels of the firm. Leadership in the complex, uncertain world that we inhabit today is the result of many people working together to make things happen.

The framework introduced in this module views leadership as consisting of four key *leadership capabilities* together with the leader's *change signature*. The four capabilities are sensemaking, relating, visioning, and inventing. These four capabilities represent a broad set in that they cover what is and what could be; people's trust in each other and the structures that coordinate their actions; their understanding of the environment and the ations they take to make things happen. The capabilities are complementary but they also create tensions that need to be managed. Whereas the capabilities represent what leaders do, the change signature affirms who the leader (individual or team) is. The change signature conveys the values that the leader embodies and the characteristic way that he or she makes things happen.

This leadership framework seems to be well suited to the organization of the future. As organizations become more networked, flat, and flexible, leaders are needed at all levels to manage across boundaries and to help adjust to a complex and rapidly changing environment. Cycles of sensemaking and inventing need to be carried out in this environment to maintain an understanding of what is going on at the moment and acting as necessary to adapt. Similarly, as organizations become more diverse and global, leaders need to become even better at understanding and working with others and at creating visions and structures that reach and connect a more varied set of individuals and groups.

The module contains a Class Note, two elective readings, one exercise, and two cases. The Class Note, "Leadership in an Age of Uncertainty," outlines a core leadership framework and provides numerous examples of how leaders mirror that framework. In addition to providing more explanation of sensemaking, relating, visioning, inventing, and the change signature, the Class Note also provides hints as to how to best improve these capabilities. Because the framework attempts to integrate a great deal of earlier work on leadership, a bibliography referencing work related to these capabilities is also provided.

The first elective reading, "What Should I Do With My Life?" (FastCompany, January 2003), doesn't seem to be about leadership at all at first glance. It summarizes some of the lessons learned from an in-depth study by Po Bronson of the life stories of 70 individuals who worked to identify who they really are and what kind of work is best suited to them. It is about people who showed the courage and commitment to create the kinds of lives they want to live, rather than trying to do what is right, or expected, or financially rewarding. This reading is included because leadership is about creating a picture of where you want to be and working to get there. This "visioning" needs to hold for the personal realm as well as the organizational one. Thus, the act of reflecting on who you are and what you want to do and who you want to be is a leadership act. This article examines the paths that some of these people chose to take as they attempted to answer *The Question:* What should I do with my life?

The second elective reading is a selection from the book, *Geeks and Geezers: How Era, Values, and Defining Moments Shape Leaders,* by Warren Bennis and Robert Thomas. This selection talks about "crucibles," or "intense, transformational experiences," that help leaders to discover who they are and what they are made of. This reading was selected to help students to know part of the process by which leaders come to know more about themselves and how change signatures are developed. From this reading students can learn not just about the crucibles that are thrust upon them but also about those that are chosen as a means of becoming a better leader and about the "adaptive capacity" necessary to successfully navigate through a crucible.

The two "cases," a *Boston Globe* article about Chuck Vest, the president of MIT, and a melding of newspaper and magazine articles about Carly Fiorina, the CEO of Hewlett-Packard, highlight two successful, but different, leaders. The cases provide the opportunity to examine how leaders actually engage in sensemaking, relating, visioning, and inventing, and what a change signature actually is. They also provide the opportunity to compare and contrast two leaders in terms of who they are, what they do, and the environments and situations that they face. Then the questions begin: do the leaders act the way they do because of who they are, or because of the circumstances that they face? How does each leader gain credibility in a new job, in a new organization, when many are betting against their success? What do these leaders do, and when do they do it, in order to buck the odds and make things happen?

Additional Activities

You can expand your learning about leadership in several ways. First, you can start observing the leaders around you. Pay attention to what these people do and whether you think they are effective. Observe whether they follow the leadership framework introduced here. What do they do, and how do they do it? Is there anything that you find intriguing about what they do that you might want to incorporate into your own leadership repertoire? What would you need to do to change in this way?

Another way to learn about leadership is to watch TV and videos. Many wonderful interviews and films portray great, good, and terrible leaders and provide lessons on how to lead and how not to lead. Such films and interviews can also provide a sense of how leaders develop over time. Recent interviews include Rudolf Guiliani, Lou Gerstner, and Kofi Annan. Videos include *Gandhi, Apollo 13, Norma Rae, Elizabeth, Twelve Angry Men,* and *Thirteen Days*. The *American Experience* series on PBS also highlights the lives of key American presidents.

Yet another tack is to engage in some self-assessment, reflection, feedback, and coaching to learn more about your own leadership style, strengths, and weaknesses. After reading this module you might want to sit down and think about how you go about sensemaking, relating, visioning, and inventing. Think about your own change signature. Then try to engage in some new leadership activity, to learn more about the kind of leader you are, and to try some new leader behaviors. If possible, get a friend, mentor, or coach to provide some feedback about how you are doing and to suggest some ways for you to improve.

Finally, think back over your leadership experiences of the past. Think about how you were able to engage in sensemaking, relating, visioning, and relating. Think about what differentiated your successful leadership experiences from your unsuccessful ones. How might you change as a result of this analysis?

References

Bass, B. M. 1985. *Leadership and Performance Beyond Expectations.* New York: Free Press.

Bennis, W. G., and R. J. Thomas. 2002. *Geeks and Geezers: How Era, Values, and Defining Moments Shape Leaders.* Boston: Harvard Business School Press.

Block, P. 1993. *Stewardship: Choosing Service Over Self-Interest.* San Francisco: Berrett Koehler

Bryman, A. 1996. Leadership in Organizations. In *Handbook of Organization Studies.* Thousand Oaks, CA: Sage Publications.

Conger, J. A. 1989. *The Charismatic Leader: Behind the Mystique of Exceptional Leadership.* San Francisco: Jossey-Bass.

Gabbaro, J. 1987. *Dynamics of Taking Charge.* Boston: Harvard Business School Press.

Hambrick, D. C., G. D. S. Fukutomi. 1991. The Seasons of a CEO's Tenure. *The Academy of Management Review* 16, 719–742.

House, R. J., W. D. Spangler, and J. Woycke. 1991. Personality and charisma in the U.S. presidency: A psychological theory of leader effectiveness. *Administrative Science Quarterly* 36, 364–396.

Kouzes, J., and B. Posner. 1993. *Credibility: How Leaders Gain and Lose It, Why People Demand It.* San-Francisco: Jossey-Bass.

Locke, E.A., et al. 1991. *The Essence of Leadership: The Four Keys to Leading Successfully.* New York: Lexington Books, Inc.

Pfeffer, J. 1992. *Managing with Power: Politics and Influence in Organizations.* Boston: Harvard Business School Press.

Schein, E. H. 1985. *Organizational Culture and Leadership.* San Francisco: Jossey-Bass.

Senge, P. 1996. Leading Learning Organizations: The Bold, the Powerful, and the Invisible. In F. Hesselbein et al., *The Leader of the Future.* San Francisco: Jossey-Bass.

Senge, P. 1990. The *Fifth Discipline: The Art & Practice of the Learning Organization.* New York: Doubleday.

Sutcliffe, K., and K. Weick. 2002. Managing the Unexpected: Assuring High Performance in an Age of Complexity. *European Management Journal* 20, 709–710.

Weick, K. 2001. *Making Sense of the Organization.* Malden, MA: Blackwell Publishing.

Yukl, G. A. 1998. *Leadership in Organizations,* 4th ed. Upper Saddle River, NJ: Prentice Hall.

Leadership

CORE

Module

Leadership in an Age of Uncertainty

by Deborah Ancona

The question "What is leadership?" has permeated society from our earliest times. The Romans wondered whether force or inspiration was more effective as a motivator. Our own culture glorifies the charismatic while preaching participation. We all struggle to identify a concept that is broad enough to capture Gandhi, Lou Gerstner, Nelson Mandela, and Eleanor Roosevelt. Interest in the what-is-leadership question has only intensified as we watch a new world order unfold in the aftermath of September 11th and as we are bombarded with images of corporate corruption—and attempts at reform. We all hunger to know what leadership is, yet the concept remains amorphous.

A search through the leadership research does not add clarity, because it yields almost as many definitions as there are scholars to propose them. The history of leadership theory started with an emphasis on traits—the notion that the makeup of the leader makes all the difference. Work on physical traits, abilities, and personality characteristics, such as introversion-extroversion (Bryman, 1996), dominated the research up to the late 1940s. Current work in this tradition suggests that our admired leaders are honest, forward looking, inspiring, competent (Kouzes and Posner, 1993), optimistic (Seligman, 1998), self-confident (Locke et al., 1991), and adaptive (Bennis and Thomas, 2002). But traits alone do not always accurately predict leadership effectiveness and thus the researchers shifted to the behavior or style of the leader. For example, some leaders are more task-oriented while others are more relationship-oriented; some are more autocratic while others are more democratic (Yukl, 1998). This research opened up the question of which behaviors are more effective.

The next wave of research, in the 1960s and 1970s, suggested a contingency approach suggesting that how one should act as a leader depends on the nature of the task and the environment. This approach led to elaborate "decision trees" for picking a leadership style. But something of the luster and dynamism of leadership seemed to get lost in this approach. So, in the 1980s and 1990s, the emphasis changed again to one of concentrating on change, and research on transformational, or charismatic leadership, took off (Bass, 1985; Conger, 1989; House et al., 1991). The charismatic leader provides a compelling vision that, clearly communicated, ignites the emotions and energy of followers. Another recent trend is the notion of the servant leader whose job is to sense and attend to the needs of followers (Block, 1993).

This Class Note communicates a framework that allows us to integrate a number of prior leadership theories while focusing on what leaders actually do. This framework seems particularly relevant in the uncertain and rapidly changing world in which we currently find ourselves. It allows us to view leadership not as a person, but as a capacity that individuals and groups possess. The framework carries several core assumptions:

1. **Leadership is distributed**. Leadership is not solely the purview of the CEO, but can permeate all levels of the firm (Senge, 1996). One can be a leader in a product development team as well as at the top of the corporation. Also, though one person may often get all the credit, leadership in today's complex, changing environment is the result of many people working together to make things happen (Malone, 1997).

2. **Leadership is personal and developmental.** There is no one way to lead. The best way to create change is to work with the particular capabilities that you have, while constantly striving to improve and expand those capabilities. Even though you might carefully study the key tactics of leaders who are "change masters," "power brokers," "charismatic," or "network builders," these monikers might or might not "fit" you as an individual. It is more important that you understand who you are and what works best for you, given your values, your skills, your likes, and your personality.

3. **Leadership is a process to create change.** Leadership is about making things happen, contingent on a context. Leaders may create change by playing a central role in the actual change process or by creating an environment in which others are empowered to act. Whichever route is taken, the nature of the change process depends on context. Change in a small company needs to be different from that in a large one, change with an experienced team will need to differ from that used with novices, and leadership under threat will have different requirements from other conditions. The key point is that leadership is about making things happen with a deep understanding of the environment in which change will occur.

4. **Leadership develops over time.** It is through practice, reflection, following role models, feedback, and theory that we learn leadership.

Some people undoubtedly come to leadership roles with more skills than others, but leadership can improve over time. Eric Schmidt shifted from a technical guru to a champion of change when he became the CEO of Novell. Tammy Savage and her group of "kiddie corps" moved from programmers to new product developers when they convinced the upper levels of Microsoft to support their "three degrees" software for the 13–24 set (*Newsweek*, February 24, 2003). By taking risks, trying new things, and learning from successes and failures, we move up the leadership learning curve.

The Framework

The framework presented here is one that evolved over the past several years from the collaborative work of Deborah Ancona, Tom Malone, Wanda Orlikowski, and Peter Senge. We combined our own research ideas with what we know of leadership practice, mixing in lots of feedback from the hundreds of students in our classes. The framework begins with four key leadership capabilities (see Figure 14.1): sensemaking, relating, visioning, and inventing. Added to these capabilities is the notion of a change signature—your own unique way of making change happen.

Leaders in business settings need all of these capabilities to be successful, and they need to cycle through them on an ongoing basis. *Sensemaking*, a term coined by Karl Weick (1995), is just what it sounds like, making sense of the world around us. Even though this concept sounds straightforward, in times of great change and uncertainty, sensemaking can be quite difficult. Managers wrestle with trying to figure out a new landscape; is it the old economy, the new economy, or something else? How will the new world order affect the role of business in society? Understanding and mapping the world in which we work is an ongoing and difficult task. *Relating* refers to the development of key relationships within and across organizations. Leadership is not a solo sport and, in our networked age, the ability to connect and build trusting relationships is a key competency. *Visioning* is the act of creating a compelling image of the future. While sensemaking creates a map of what is, visioning is a map of what could be. *Inventing* refers to creating new ways of working together. Once we have a vision, we need to invent structures and processes that enable us to realize that vision. We need constantly to invent new paths around roadblocks to change and to find new ways to create better organizations.

Although individual leaders need to exercise all four capabilities, they must also work with others who complement their skill portfolio. Thus, you can

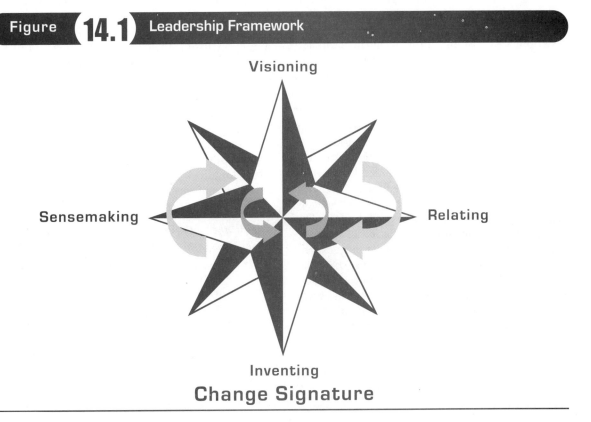

Figure 14.1 Leadership Framework

use this framework not only to talk about individual leadership but also to reference the leadership functions needed within a group or organization. New models of teams working in complex, dynamic situations suggest that a small core often collectively take on leadership responsibilities (see Module 6; and Ancona, Bresman, and Kaufer, 2002). In this way one person can be passionate about a new product, while another plans how to organize the team, another recruits and nurtures team members, and another makes sure that the product fits into the current organizational strategy. Thus, leadership is both an individual and a collective capacity.

Leaders appear to have one or two lead capabilities that distinguish their leadership. Andy Grove, chairman of Intel, is the quintessential sensemaker who continuously maps the competitive environment and recognizes "strategic inflection points" that can be exploited for competitive advantage. Lyndon Johnson, former president of the United States, was the quintessential power broker, leading primarily through his ability to use power and influence in his relationships with members of Congress. Eleanor Roosevelt, human rights activist and first lady to President Franklin Roosevelt, was a relationship builder, not only in her personal relationships but also in her work as chair of the United Nations Commission on Human Rights. Martin Luther King, Jr., a civil rights leader, was a true visionary who was able to paint a picture of the future, of a new and better world. His "I Have a Dream" speech provided a beacon for many others to follow in their quest for civil rights. Dave Kelly, the CEO of IDEO, a product development consulting firm, is an inventor. He formulated a whole new process for developing creative new products quickly. Later he founded a company that puts this process into practice and has won numerous design awards as a result.

Even as the four capabilities focus on what leaders actually need to do, the change signature focuses on who the leader actually is. It is the unique way that each individual leads change. Included here would the person's credo (Kouzes and Posner, 1993) or core set of values and beliefs. What does he actually stand for? What is she willing to fight for? The change signature also includes the leader's unique way of making change happen: What core experiences and skills does she bring to the situation? What tactics does he use to carry out the four capabilities? The remainder of this section will go through these core concepts in some detail before examining how they come together in the process of leading.

Sensemaking

Sensemaking is a process of coming to understand the context in which you are operating. Weick (2001) likens the process of sensemaking to cartography. As a mapmaker, you are trying to map the external terrain. What you map depends on where you look, what you focus on, what aspects of the terrain you choose to represent and what materials you use to represent them. Thus, there is no one best map and an "indefinite number of useful maps" (Weick, 2001). For example in this book we map the organization using strategic design, political, and cultural lenses that highlight the formal organization structure, centers of power and influence, and key norms, stories, and rituals, respectively. This mapping is further complicated by the fact that the terrain keeps changing so all we can do is create some temporary stability in a dynamic flow.

In other words the key here is to create a map that at least for the moment represents the current situation that the group or organization is facing. Certainly other maps may be applicable, but in order to function a group needs some shared map that members are all following. Better leaders are able to more quickly and effectively capture the complexity of their environments and yet explain them in simple terms. Better leaders are courageous enough to present a map as they see it, even if that map does not conform to the dominant one in use. For example, after Gandhi returned to India and spent a year learning about its culture, people, and issues, he told other Indian leaders that they did not understand the real India and courageously told them they were not so very different from the British. Finally, better leaders are able to meld observations, hard data, conversations, and gut feelings and let the map emerge, rather than trying to impose preexisting ideas. These leaders are constantly discussing their ideas with others, both to understand their own thinking and to incorporate the diverse views of others (Weick, 1995).

The need to make sense of the environment and map it is most apparent when that environment is changing rapidly and offers surprises for which we are not prepared. W. Brian Arthur (1996), an economist who studies the new economy, provides an analogy to a gambling casino to illustrate this new uncertain realm of business:

> *Imagine you are milling about in a large casino with the top figures in high-tech—the Gates, Gerstners, and Groves of their industries. Over at one table, a game is starting called Multimedia. Over at another is a game called Web Services. In the corner is Electronic Banking. There are many such tables. You sit at one.*

> *"How much to play?" you ask.*

> *"Three billion," the croupier replies.*

> *"Who'll be playing?" you ask.*

> *"We won't know until they show up," he replies.*

"What are the rules?"

"Those will emerge as the game unfolds," says the croupier.

"What are my odds of winning?" you wonder.

"We can't say," responds the house. *"Do you still want to play?" (Arthur, 1996)*

Arthur argues that, in this type of environment, sensemaking differentiates great leaders from average leaders. Great leaders are identified by "their ability to perceive the nature of the game and the rules by which it is played as they are playing it." In other words, the act of sensemaking is discovering the new terrain as you are inventing it. In the very process of mapping the new terrain, you are creating it.

Sensemaking may seem like an abstract concept, but it is practiced by leaders every day. When Jane Davis, a product development team leader in a large computer firm, saw how quickly the market was changing, she knew that her team would have to create a revolutionary design to succeed. Furthermore, she recognized that the changes in the industry went beyond technology to a whole new business model. She immediately went to talk to people in finance, marketing, and sales to jointly figure out what would be needed in this new environment. When John Reed, the former CEO of Citicorp, was in charge of back-office operations, he came to realize that the work done there was more in line with a factory than with a bank. The very use of the frame of factory served to shift the way that people structured and thought about the work to be done, their "sense" of it, and thus it became a factory. Similarly when he came to run the whole company, he said that one of the keys to his success was moving beyond the notion of Citicorp as a bank. "If we had been limited to that sense of who we were we would have missed many of the new opportunities that stretched us beyond common definitions of banking."

Tips for effective sensemaking include the following (building on the work of Sutcliffe and Weick, 2002):

1. Seek many types and sources of data. Get information from customers, suppliers, competitors, other departments, and investors. Combine financial data with visits to the shop floor.
2. Involve others in your sensemaking. Verbalizing what you think you are seeing will help you to hone your view. Input from others will help you test your view against other realities and develop a shared map of the situation.
3. Do not simply apply your existing frameworks and overlay them on the situation. Let the appropriate map emerge.
4. Move beyond stereotypes. Try not to describe the world as good guys and bad guys, victim and oppressor, or marketer and engineer—push for what's behind the labels.
5. Learn from small experiments. One of the best ways to figure out how any system works is to make a small change in the system and see what happens. Organizations are such systems.
6. Use images, metaphors, or stories to try to capture and communicate critical elements of your map.

Relating

Leadership texts are filled with the importance of interpersonal relationships. Leaders try to create trust, optimism, and harmony, but they often run into anger, cynicism, and conflict instead. The core capability of relating centers on the leader's ability to engage in inquiry, advocacy, and connecting. *Inquiry* and *advocacy* are terms coined in the pioneering work of Chris Argyris and Don Schon (1996), as well Peter Senge (1990). In order to enable effective interpersonal relationships, both practices are necessary. Inquiry means the ability to listen and understand what others are thinking and feeling. Inquiry involves trying to understand how the other person has moved from data to interpretation to assessment—rather than simply reacting to the assessment itself. Inquiry requires the leader to suspend judgment and to listen without imposing her own point of view. Instead the leader tries to understand the other's point of view, how he or she sees the world and what has happened.

Yet leadership also requires having opinions and taking a stand. Advocacy means being clear about what you think and how you moved from data to interpretation. It involves being clear about your own point of view and trying to influence others of its merits while also being open to alternative views (Pfeffer, 1992). Advocacy also means taking responsibility for your own biases and leaps to judgment. It means being able to say, "I was wrong. I jumped to conclusions based on insufficient data and overreacted." Yet often in business a great deal more advocacy takes place than inquiry. Often we are so busy trying to push our own ideas that we do not really listen to what others are saying. Worse there seems to be a great deal of emphasis on "winning" rather than on the effective interplay of inquiry and advocacy. If we are going to work together and come to trust one another, however, then some genuine interest in getting to know how and why others see the world as they do becomes a necessity.

The third area of relating is connecting. In a world in which boundaries are blurring, where people must work across units, functions, corporations, and countries, and where people are dependent on others to get the work done, we discover the real need to be able to connect with other people (Baker, 2000). Connecting involves cultivating a set of people who help each other to accomplish their goals. It is the ability to build collaborative relationships with others and to create coalitions for change. To test your ability at connecting you might ask yourself whether you have someone to call in case you needed to get career advice, technical expertise, information about new jobs, or help on a personal problem. On the other side, are you doing your part to help others by being on the receiving end of such requests? Do you support others in getting their jobs done? Going further, do you offer your services even before they are requested?

In his book, *The Dynamics of Taking Charge*, Jack Gabarro (1987) found that in executing change a leader needed to develop effective working relationships. Such development involved setting mutual expectations as well as building trust and mutual influence. A quote from the book shows how one person responded to a leader's attempts to develop an effective working relationship and also shows how inquiry, advocacy, and connecting are part of this process:

> *One thing that was very important to me was his just spending a hell of a lot of time being patient and listening to details.... He came down and became involved in understanding things his predecessor didn't have time for.... It's important to feel that you and your boss are talking on the same wavelength. You asked me why I didn't follow through on my resignation after he arrived. Well, this is a big part of it. You know that if you agree to something it's based on a real understanding. (Gabarro, p. 117)*

Tips for effective relating include the following:

1. Spend time trying to understand the perspective of others within the organization and try to withhold judgment while listening to others.
2. Encourage others to voice their opinions—What do they care about? How are they interpreting what is going on?
3. Be clear about what your stand is and how you got there.
4. When you have an idea, think about how others might react to it and how you might best explain it to them.
5. Think about your connections—Do you feel good about the nature of your relationships? How well do you relate to others in terms of giving and receiving career advice, help in getting work done, job hunting, thinking through difficult problems, and personal support. Think through how you can strengthen these relationships and build new ones.

Visioning

This capability centers on creating a compelling image of the future. Visions are important because they provide the motivation for people to give up their current views and ways of working to change. If a vision is compelling then this change occurs because people have actually changed their beliefs, not because they feel forced into a corner (Conger, 1989; House et al., 1991). When the vision is genuine (not just the ubiquitous vision statement), people excel and work hard because they want to (Senge, 1990). A vision also keeps people focused by helping to highlight what is important, and by implication, what is not important. One group's vision was illustrated by a hand, and each finger stood for a major activity that the organization would embody as it moved forward. When someone in a meeting started to move in a different direction, people didn't even have to say anything. They simply held up a hand and the meeting took a different direction.

Visions are clearly better to the extent that they are shared. It is the capacity to hold a shared picture of the future that enables people to act together. Shared values and mission enabled IBM to create an identity in "service" and Apple in "computing power for the masses." Through these shared visions, people become bound together around a common identity and sense of destiny (Senge, 1990).

Perhaps most importantly visions provide people with a sense of meaning about their work. Visions answer the questions "Why am I doing this?", "How are we trying to make the world a better place?", and "What makes us different?". Thus good leaders are able to frame visions in a way that emphasizes their importance along some important value dimensions. For example, Steve Jobs (a quintessential visionary) asked John Scully to leave Pepsi to come and work for a fledgling Apple. He asked, "Do you want to sell sugar water for the rest of your life or do you want to come and change the world?" To Jobs the importance of what Apple was doing went beyond "building a computer," it was about "changing the way that people work and learn," and this vision became part of the Macintosh team. In general people want to be doing something that will truly make a difference and effective leaders frame visions accordingly.

Much work has gone into describing how to craft a vision. Creating a compelling vision, letting people know that they have what it takes to realize the vision, and modeling appropriate behaviors have all been shown to be key (Conger, 1989; House et al., 1991; Schein, 1985). To create a compelling vision, you start with a sense of what the future could be and then use stories and metaphors to communicate the vision. Stories, metaphors, even sayings are remembered long after the PowerPoint slides with all of their accompanying statistics are forgotten. A vision is also more compelling to the extent that it actually lets people visualize what the future might be like and provides them with the words that capture the vision. Martin Luther King, Jr., painted a picture of "sons of former slaves and the sons of former slave owners will be able to sit down at a table of brotherhood" that allowed people to literally see a new world. He also provided the wording, "where people will not be judged by the color of their skin but by the content of their character."

This visioning capability should not be used simply as a framing exercise, however. Visions are most compelling and motivating when they come from a sincere belief in the cause—be it freedom from oppression, changing the way that people live and work, creating the most elegant computer design, getting the company out of the red ink, or saving the environment. Using such framing as a front for more selfish or political gains will usually be discovered. The result is often distrust and resentment, even rage. Thus, truly the best way to create a vision is to figure out what you feel most passionate about. It is easier to get others excited when you really care about the outcomes you are striving to achieve.

Tips for effective visioning include the following:

1. Develop a vision about something that excites you or that you think is important. Your own excitement will be catching. Listen to what others find exciting and important to them. Discover ways to blend visions and build a shared vision of the future.
2. Frame the vision with an ideological goal. Provide a rationale as to why people should care and what good can be achieved by the vision.
3. Use stories, metaphors, and analogies to paint a vivid picture of what the vision will accomplish.
4. Practice creating a vision in many arenas. For example, think about creating a vision for yourself as well as for your team, organization, or community group.
5. Enable those around you by pointing out that they have all the skills and capabilities needed to realize the vision.
6. Embody the key values and ideas contained in the vision. To prevent cynicism it is important that you "walk the talk."

Inventing

This capability involves changing the way people work together. It entails creating the processes and structures needed to make the vision a reality. Inventing might be on a very small or a very large scale. For example, a member of a manufacturing team demonstrated inventing when she suggested that her team take a trip to observe the practices at another firm as a way to overcome the inertia that was plaguing the team. On a grander scale, Dave Kelly, the CEO of IDEO created a whole company based on a new process of product development, and Henry Ford developed a new mode of manufacturing to realize his dream of a car for the average person.

Inventing can also be seen as an action aimed at overcoming a particular obstacle to change or a whole new way of approaching a task. What underlies these activities is a creative "can-do" attitude that is focused on doing whatever it takes to keep a group or organization moving toward its goals. Also inherent in this capability is a focus on continuous improvement in how work gets done. Inventing is related to creativity in that it often involves a new approach, new solutions, and new practices that have not been thought of before. So while inventing is very much an action-oriented activity—how do we change how we are working together to more effectively reach our goals—it is also a mindset that focuses people on creative problem solving and continuous improvement. Thus, inventing combines innovation and execution (Orlikowski and Hoffman, 1997).

Inventing often goes hand-in-hand with sensemaking. A leader who is constantly aware of what is going on with her work, her people, and the environment is also aware of problems that are arising and processes that are not working. This awareness begins a series of iterations between finding problems and then inventing solutions. Gail McGovern, the former president of Fidelity Personal Investments, showed just such a pattern. When she first came to Fidelity she discovered that the call centers were rewarded on how quickly operators answered the phone and when there were too many calls, they simply added more personnel. McGovern did some analysis to show that this kind of model would soon not be cost effective. She invented a new incentive scheme and a new proposal to move customers onto the Web site to ease the volume of calls. After a hugely successful campaign to get customers to use the Web site, McGovern and her team discovered that the Web format was not meeting their needs. This information inspired a new cycle of invention in which new improvements to Web services were created.

Tips for effective inventing include the following:

1. Maintain focus on improving the ways that people are working together in your team and organization.
2. When a new task or change effort emerges, think through how it will get done: who will

do what, by when, in what configuration. Consider what new things are needed to enable this action.
3. Play with new and different ways of organizing work—examine alternative ways of grouping people together, organizing their internal interaction, and linking across different groups.
4. Blend sensemaking and inventing. As new issues are discovered, use this knowledge as an opportunity to improve service to customers, suppliers, and employees.

The Four Capabilities

Taken together, sensemaking, relating, visioning, and inventing represent key leadership tools. You might want to picture them as a compass (see Figure 14.1), representing a full set of capabilities that covers all directions. They involve mapping the current situation even as it changes, creating a set of trusting relationships with people that together carry out the leadership activities and support one another, articulating a picture of a desired future that has meaning to its members, and the capacity to organize activity to meet work demands. Thus, the capabilities cover what is and what could be, people's hearts and minds and the structures that coordinate their actions. They entail understanding, acting, dreaming, and being together.

Leaders and teams must constantly iterate across sensemaking, relating, visioning, and inventing. The order of iteration may vary across contexts and individuals. In new jobs, research has shown that leaders often follow a sequence of sensemaking, then building relationships, inventing new solutions to existing problems, seeing what happens, then creating visions and inventing again on a larger scale (Gabarro, 1987; Hambrick, 1991). Then they repeat the cycle. In other situations it is impossible to understand without first acting, and sometimes the leader starts with a strong vision that molds all other activity. Other times external events intervene, reshaping any plans or priorities that may have existed before.

These capabilities are complementary. Without inventing, visions may just be dreams that never get realized. Inventing without a clear sense of the current situation and where you want to go can result in frenzied chaos. People want to know that they are operating with an accurate map of reality, not an outdated one and not one based on wishful thinking. They also want to know that they are working for something that is important. Finally while visions and new structures can result in lots of activity, in the absence of a base of people who are committed to working together to accomplish the work, any success may be short-lived.

These capabilities can also create tensions that need to be managed. It is difficult to hold an image of the future and the present simultaneously. Balancing people and processes, action and understanding, and individual and collective aspirations can be challenging. Yet it is inherent in the framework that managing these very tensions is the essence of leadership.

Leaders and teams can, in fact, derail when they get "stuck" in one or two quadrants of the compass. Whether due to comfort, prior success, or inertia, sometimes the balance and movement across capabilities gets lost. Then a preoccupation with the present can pull attention away from strategic thinking about where to go in the future. Too much analysis of what is going on can result in analysis paralysis and an inability to take any action. Too much action without analysis can result in a lot of wasted energy. A constant focus on interpersonal relationships may make it hard to think about what is important for the future, but a vision in the absence of broad commitment and understanding can result in low morale and even sabotage. Thus, it is important to monitor balance across capabilities and the tendency to favor one or two capabilities at the expense of others.

The Change Signature

The four capabilities, like the compass that they form, are only a tool. The change signature determines what the tool is used to do and how it is used. The change signature is the part of each of us that makes choices about where to aim the compass: What is it that we will spend time on? What are our priorities and goals? What is it that we will fight for? The capabilities focus on what leaders do, whereas the change signature is about who the leader is. A person's change signature shapes whether a person will use the leadership capabilities to cut costs or grow the business, to speed development of an electric car or try to slow legislation requiring cleaner air emissions, to go for the highest profits or maximize safety. A change signature develops slowly over time based on experience and skills, but it is a key part of the leadership model because it represents who we are as leaders.

Each person's change signature, like a fingerprint, is unique. Each person brings unique values, skills, experiences, tactics, and personality to the leader role. Each person finds a personal way of making change happen, although patterns certainly are evident across individuals. The change signature is made up of a credo and the characteristic way in which the leader creates change.

The term *credo* refers to your core values and beliefs for yourself and for the organization you are leading (this concept is built on that of Kouzes and Posner, 1993). Kouzes and Posner suggest that to understand your credo you might pretend that you are going away for a month and have only one paragraph to describe to people in your unit what they should be doing in your absence. For one leader working as a team might be key, while for another it might be customer service, and for both it might be to always treat others with honesty and respect. Another way to think about your credo is to think about how you want to be remembered. Jack Welch did an amazing job in terms of changing GE multiple times and bringing in great shareholder returns. He is also known for dumping lots of toxic waste and for adultery. When you think about your credo you need to think about what decisions you make and what those decisions say about your character as a leader and a human being.

The second aspect of the change signature is the way that you typically embody the four capabilities and the characteristic way in which you make change happen. What skills and abilities, tactics and modes of operating characterize how you carry out your leadership activities? For example, some people carry out sensemaking in an interpersonal manner, moving from office to office learning from everyone they meet. For others it is an analytic process that starts and ends on the computer. Some leaders favor inquiry while others are pure power brokers. Some leaders are great visionaries while others come to understand their visions only after the work is done. Finally, inventing can be done with a highly programmed approach or an innovative one. You might want to spend some time thinking about what distinguishes your mode of embodying the capabilities.

The change signature is not just about how you carry out the four capabilities, however. It is the overall pattern, the characteristic way in which you make things happen. For example, Chuck Vest, the president of MIT, is known for his problem-solving signature. He is an action-oriented leader who engages in deep sensemaking—talking to a wide range people, setting up committees, thinking through issues by himself and with others, and then inventing creative ways to deal with the issues that arise from sensemaking. Vest is also known as a moral leader, taking stands for what he believes is right even when those stands are not popular with alumni or shared by other schools. Carly Fiorina, the president and CEO of Hewlett-Packard is a much more dramatic, visionary leader who acts quickly. She is known for large-scale organizational change—moving fast and against internal and external opposition in a direction that she thinks is right. The cases that follow examine these leaders and their change signatures in greater depth.

Lyndon Baines Johnson, the former president of the United States, had his own distinct change signature. Speaking out against poverty and working to create a "Great Society" was the legacy he wanted to leave. But Johnson was a power broker. He used every form of power and influence that has been written about to cajole, beg, threaten, coerce, bribe, and debate others into supporting his legislation. Known as the "Johnson treatment" he would figure out what a member of Congress wanted, where he stood, and what skeletons were hidden in the closet, and then work on that person until a deal was reached. With this characteristic style he was able to pass civil rights legislation, to create Head Start, and wage a war on poverty. Unfortunately people had no idea whether he really cared about these causes or whether he was simply after more and more power. Furthermore, this same process did not work in Vietnam. The result was that Johnson was not able to leave the legacy he so desperately wanted to leave.

Change signatures are not only for the heads of organizations. One MBA graduate, Erik, went to work in the airline industry. He became known for his ability to change the culture, get along with others, and improve productivity through the use of teams. His "change signature" developed from several jobs. Erik went to work in a highly unionized production department. He was able to shift the culture to be much less antagonistic toward management by working with his people and giving them both responsibility and credit for their work. By creating cross-functional teams Erik was able to clear up existing bottlenecks in the production process and improve productivity. Having come from a consulting background, the use of teams was second nature to Erik and so he was able to make changes using an existing skill.

Change signatures develop over time. Leaders learn through experiences what is most important to them and how they can be most effective with others. This process is facilitated when leaders take the time to reflect on their experiences. Often people report that they learn more from failures than successes, but all experiences can help shed light on what kind of leader you are. Bennis and Thomas (2002) talk about "crucibles" or "intense, transformational experiences" (p. 14). They continue, "A crucible is a tipping point where new identities are weighed, where values are examined and strengthened or replaced, and where one's judgment and other abilities are honed. It is an incubator for new insights and a new conception of oneself" (p. 106). Sometimes crucibles are thrust upon us, but leaders can also choose to test themselves in new circumstances in order to learn more about themselves and see what they are capable of doing. Leaders can also learn more about their change signatures through active and structured reflection. A reflective exercise can be found on page 19.

Leadership, as presented here, is a combination of four capabilities plus a change signature. Leadership is distributed across individuals, and involves sensemaking, relating, visioning, and inventing. By engaging in these activities over time leaders begin to develop their own distinct way of making things happen. We call this characteristic way of leading the change signature. Through a variety of experiences leaders can further develop their capabilities, build leadership capacity in an organization, and create a better understanding of their own values and skills. We encourage you to take on these challenges.

References

Ancona, D., H. Bresman, and K. Kaeufer. 2002. The Comparative Advantage of X-Teams. *Sloan Management Review* 43, 33–39.

Argyris, C. and Schön, D. 1996. *Organizational Learning II: Theory, Method and Practice,* Reading, MA: Addison Wesley.

Arthur, W. B. 1996. Increasing Returns and the New World of Business. *Harvard Business Review,* July–August, 100–109.

Bailyn, L., J. Fletcher, and D. Kolb. 1997. Unexpected Connections: Considering Employees' Personal Lives Can Revitalize Your Business. *Sloan Management Review* 38, 11–19.

Baker, W. E. 2000. *Networking Smart: How to Build Relationships for Personal and Organizational Success.* Lincoln, NE: iUniverse.com, Inc. Originally published by McGraw-Hill.

Bass, B. M. 1985. *Leadership and Performance Beyond Expectations.* New York: Free Press.

Bass, B. M, and B. J. Avolio. 1993. Transformational Leadership: A Response to Critiques. In M. M Chemers and R. Ayman (Eds.), *Leadership Theory and Research: Perspectives and Directions.* New York: Academic Press.

Bennis, W. G., and R. J. Thomas. 2002. *Geeks and Geezers: How Era, Values, and Defining Moments Shape Leaders.* Boston: Harvard Business School Press.

Block, P. 1993. *Stewardship: Choosing Service Over Self-Interest.* San Francisco: Berrett Koehler.

Bryman, A. 1996. Leadership in Organizations. In *Handbook of Organization Studies.* Thousand Oaks, CA: Sage Publications.

Conger, J. A. 1989. *The Charismatic Leader: Behind the Mystique of Exceptional Leadership.* San Francisco: Jossey-Bass.

Gabbaro, J. 1987. *Dynamics of Taking Charge.* Boston: Harvard Business School Press.

Hambrick, D. C., G. D. S. Fukutomi. 1991. The Seasons of a CEO's Tenure. *The Academy of Management Review* 16, 719–742.

House, R. J., W. D. Spangler, and J. Woycke. 1991. Personality and Charisma in the U.S. Presidency: A Psychological Theory of Leader Effectiveness. *Administrative Science Quarterly* 36, 364–396.

Kouzes, J., and B. Posner. 1993. *Credibility: How Leaders Gain and Lose It, Why People Demand It.* San Francisco: Jossey-Bass.

Locke, E. A., et al. 1991. *The Essence of Leadership: The Four Keys to Leading Successfully.* New York: Lexington Books.

Malone, T. 1997. Is Empowerment Just a Fad? Control, Decision Making and IT. *Sloan Management Review* 38, 23–35.

Malone, T. Forthcoming. *Beyond Command and Control: Putting People at the Center of Business.* Boston: Harvard Business School Press.

Orlikowski, W., and J. Hofman. 1997. An Improvisational Model of Change Management: The Case of Groupware Technologies. *Sloan Management Review* 38, 11–21.

Pfeffer, J. 1992. *Managing with Power: Politics and Influence in Organizations.* Boston: Harvard Business School Press.

Schein, E. H. 1985. *Organizational Culture and Leadership.* San Francisco: Jossey-Bass.

Seligman, M. 1998. *Learned Optimism: How to Change Your Mind and Your Life.* New York: Pocket Books.

Senge, P. 1996. Leading Learning Organizations: The Bold, the Powerful, and the Invisible. In F. Hesselbein et al., *The Leader of the Future.* San Francisco: Jossey-Bass.

Senge, P. 1990. The *Fifth Discipline: The Art & Practice of the Learning Organization.* New York: Doubleday.

Sutcliffe, K., and K. Weick. 2002. Managing the Unexpected: Assuring High Performance in an Age of Complexity. *European Management Journal* 20, 709–710.

Weick, K. 1995. *Sensemaking in Organizations.* Thousand Oaks, CA: Sage Publications.

Weick, K. 2001. *Making Sense of the Organization.* Malden, MA: Blackwell Publishing.

Yukl, G. A. 1998. *Leadership in Organizations,* 4th ed. Upper Saddle River, NJ: Prentice Hall.

Your Change Signature

In order to learn more about your change signature, it is useful to think of yourself as having four parts: a past self, a developed self, an underdeveloped self, and a future self (see Figure 14.2). This exercise guides you through a set of questions in order to reflect on each of these parts.

Step 1: Past Self

Your past self represents you in your formative years. The past self often holds clues about your core values and skills. Take some time to think about your past by answering the following questions:

1. What values did your family stress? Did you adopt those values or fight against them?

2. Who were your heroes? What values did you take from them?

3. How did you gain recognition and self esteem? Were you a great athlete? An excellent student? A valued friend? The person who ran all the clubs?

4. What skills did you begin to develop in your formative years? What kinds of leadership experiences did you have in school? At home? With friends? How did you lead?

5. What values, skills, and patterns of leading are part of your past self?

Step 2: Developed Self

Of course over the years and through school and professional experiences you developed certain skills, abilities, and values and ignored others. Think about your developed self as it holds clues about the leader that you are right now.

1. What best describes the values and skills that you have honed?

2. What have conflicts—between work and family, between your team and the rest of the organization, between personal values and company demands—shown you about what is really important to you?

3. Are you best known as an analytic person, a problem solver, a visionary, or a people person?

4. What leadership challenges have you taken on?

5. What have you learned about yourself as a leader as a result of these challenges?

6. How would others describe your change signature?

Figure 14.2 Four Parts of the Self

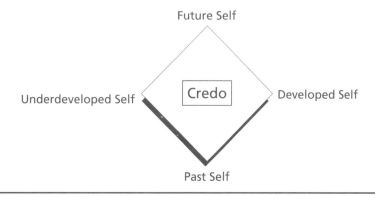

Step 3: Underdeveloped Self

Your underdeveloped self represents the part of you that has been somewhat ignored. Perhaps you have been working on your analytic skills and ignored your interpersonal ones. Or perhaps you have been so busy executing the plans of others that you have not given any thought to what is important to you and what you want to accomplish. Perhaps you have been totally occupied with your own career and have ignored the broader community.

1. Think about those parts of yourself that you have ignored. Are there any areas that you feel you want to begin to develop?

2. What kind of plan can you put together to move aspects of yourself from the underdeveloped to the developed side of the diamond?

Step 4: Future Self

Your future self represents the leader you want to be. Think about leaders in business, government, your community, or your family that you admire.

1. What aspects of their leadership would you like to incorporate into your own?

2. If you think about the end of your career, what would you want people to say about you?

3. If a head hunter called a colleague to ask about what kind of leader you are, what do you wish they would say? What skills, abilities, and values would you have to develop to get there?

4. If you think about the things you would like to do and the kind of person you would like to be, what would you need to do to be able to get there?

Step 5: Integration

Look back over your analysis of the four aspects of yourself.

1. Think through what is most important to you now. Do you want to work on honing those aspects of yourself that represent your past and current strengths? Do you want to add some new skills or rethink some values based on your experiences or aspirations for the future? Are your developed self and future self so different that you want to think about major changes in your change signature?

2. Create a plan that includes reading, skill development, reflection, looking at role models, and seeking jobs and experiences that will help you develop in the direction of your aspirations.

Re-engineering MIT

How president Charles Vest put MIT back on track

by David Mehegan

In the summer of 1994, three senior women professors in the School of Science at the Massachusetts Institute of Technology were unhappy—very unhappy. Full of energy and optimism when their MIT careers had started, they had come to believe as the years went by that they were being discriminated against in salary, office space, research support, and recognition.

They talked, compared notes, polled other women faculty, and discovered their feelings were widely shared. They decided to act. Sixteen of the 17 tenured women in the School of Science signed a statement alleging discrimination and asking the dean, Robert Birgeneau, to set up a committee to investigate.

Biology professor Nancy Hopkins, one of the three original activists, says the women doubted anything would change, and they were worried that they would be dismissed as whiners and troublemakers. "It's the easiest thing in the world for administrators to bury these sorts of initiatives," she says. "Most universities have done so. The women were scared of ruining their careers."

Birgeneau strongly supported the request, but most of the powerful department heads in the School of Science balked. The opposition view was: Why be so public? We can deal with this internally. The battle heated up, and the women were worried that Birgeneau might back down (though he says there was no chance of that). At last, Birgenau went to MIT president Charles M. Vest for advice. Vest listened, then said, "Just do it."

With Vest's support, Birgeneau appointed the committee, and it reported to him in 1996 that there was discrimination in the School of Science. Birgeneau quickly took steps to redress the glaring inequities. But some women faculty, convinced the problem was not limited to the School of Science, proposed to publicize the report by putting it in the faculty newsletter and on the MIT Web site. Because of the report's critical content, they needed Vest's approval.

Again, the women were pessimistic. Hopkins says, "I didn't believe it possible that the president of any major university would admit the unpopular truth about gender discrimination during my lifetime."

But Vest not only approved—the report was published in March of last year and is still on the MIT site—he wrote a supportive preface to the report: "I have always believed that gender discrimination within universities is part reality and part perception. I now understand that reality is by far the greater part of the balance. . . . I commend this study to all of my faculty colleagues. Please read it, contemplate its messages and information, and act upon it personally and collectively."

"Just do it" pretty well sums up the forceful, go-right-at-it style of Chuck Vest, 58, who will complete 10 years as president of MIT this fall. At a college known for its hands-on approach to everything, Vest appears to have the quintessential engineering attitude: There's a solution to every problem; find it and do it.

With that attitude, Vest has changed the university in major respects. From increasing diversity among the student body (now 42 percent female and 18 percent minority) to building up private research funding to revamping MIT's archaic housing policies, Vest has overseen changes that represent seismic shifts in the 139-year-old university's character. The differences may not seem dramatic to the outside world, but within MIT, the view is widespread that Vest has had a profound impact.

"Universities change slowly," says MIT provost Robert Brown, "and to change a university dramatically in a decade, as Chuck has done, is really an astounding thing."

It's not what anyone expected when Vest arrived 10 years ago. After all, he was an outsider. Most recent presidents have come from within, already immersed in MIT's quirky, inbred culture.

When president Paul Gray announced his retirement in 1989, the MIT search committee promptly nominated an insider to be president: molecular biologist Phillip A. Sharp. Sharp accepted the job, was publicly introduced, then flabbergasted the institute by changing his mind and deciding he'd rather stay in teaching and research. (In 1993, he was awarded the Nobel

Source: "Re-engineering MIT: How President Charles Vest Put MIT Back on Track" by David Mehegan, The *Boston Globe Magazine*, May 28, 2000. *Boston Globe Magazine* (as published in The *Boston Sunday Globe*) by David Mehegan. Copyright 2000 by Globe Newspaper Co. (MA). Reproduced with permission of Globe Newspaper Co. (MA) in the format Textbook via Copyright Clearance Center.

Prize for discoveries in genetics and this year was named head of the newly created McGovern Institute for Brain Research at MIT.)

A new committee went on a new president hunt and came back with the man who likes to be called Chuck: a genial, self-effacing, donnish mechanical engineer from the University of Michigan at Ann Arbor who tends to look away shyly when he talks or listens.

Some members of the MIT community were skeptical. Vest had spent his entire career at Michigan and had been provost there for only two months when he was tapped for the MIT presidency. "He wasn't a professor here," says Philip Khoury, dean of humanities and social science at MIT, "and no one had any idea whether he could have been. He was not a prize-winning scholar or perceived to be a major intellectual figure. Michigan is a very good school, but it's not in MIT's league. I didn't think he would be successful. I assumed the highfalutin attitude: 'Who is this guy from Ann Arbor, coming in here and thinking he can run things?'"

Vest himself had had no plans to leave Michigan. Though previous provosts had been lured away by other universities, he says, "I do not believe in job-hopping, and I intended to stay in that job for at least five years. I had not been willing even to talk to other colleges." But then—"to my utter amazement"—he got a call from the MIT search committee, which had heard good things about him as dean of engineering. He reconsidered his resolve to stay.

Recalling that time, in an interview in his wood-paneled office overlooking the Charles River, Vest shows a mix of down-home humility and self-confidence. "I remember receiving a note from an economist at Michigan that said, 'Dear Chuck, Boy from West Virginia becomes president of MIT. The American dream.' A lot of people would find that corny, but my entire life was devoted to engineering education, and MIT is the absolute pinnacle. So when the opportunity came, there really was no choice. I felt this position would offer a bully pulpit for science and technology; it was a call to national service."

After his appointment in June 1990, Vest asked Gray and provost John Deutch to stay until October. "This bought me a couple of months," he says. "I would come in here five days a week and just meet from morning to dinner, for an hour each, with faculty and administrators, asking them what they thought the big issues were."

That impressed the doubters. "I was a candidate for president," says Michael Dertouzos, director of the Laboratory for Computer Science. "John Deutch was another, and Phil Sharp. All of us were strong personalities with fixed agendas. But the faculty wanted someone who could listen. Chuck came and went around campus with a fat notebook and interviewed hundreds of people about what needed to be done. I've never seen anything like it."

Vest soon learned that the biggest issue was not in Cambridge but in Washington. "Public understanding and federal support for science and engineering were, at best, stable," Vest says, "and much more likely headed downhill, and I felt it was an important part of my role to try to articulate the importance of investment in research and advanced education."

Not that MIT was in danger. Its position in the top rank of scientific and technological institutions was unchallenged. Its endowment (now about $4 billion, a quarter of Harvard's) was healthy. Its 900 faculty and 10,000 students (half of them graduate students) were arguably the best in the world. Still, there were real worries about the future. For decades, MIT's vast research activities, the underpinning of its teaching culture, were funded primarily by the US government, largely through the Department of Defense, but also through NASA, the Department of Energy, and other agencies. In 1965, 92.3 percent of campus research was funded by the government, an all-time high.

The Cold War ended in 1989, and there were calls for big cutbacks in government spending in research, especially defense-related research. Then in 1991, Stanford University was found to be charging government research accounts for a yacht and for flowers and parties at the president's house. The hue and cry led to tighter control of the way research funds could be used for overhead. In that atmosphere, Vest decided a strong case needed to be made that federal funding for university research was a good public investment. Says Khoury: "It was important that we show that we were not taking this money, rolling it up, and lighting cigars with it."

Vest first set up an MIT office in Washington, with a full-time staff—essentially, a lobbying office. Then, he says, "Starting in June 1990, I would spend one day a month in Washington, talking to people in Congress and the executive branch about the importance of scientific and engineering research and advanced higher education to this nation, its economy and quality of life. The message has been simple, and I have tried to do a lot of it personally."

He was determined to speak not only for MIT but for research universities generally. "Over time," he says, "and I don't claim credit for this, we began to work with other institutions, and other presidents have become more active in this role."

The result, to be sure, has not been big increases in federal research funding in the last 10 years, but there has been no big collapse, either. In 1995, MIT got $245 million in federal funds for research; in 1999, the figure was $243 million. (This does not include $365 million for the Lincoln Laboratory in Lexington, a nonacademic electronics research center that MIT operates for the federal government.)

Vest's low-key but relentless lobbying, some observers say, gets part of the credit. "He is highly respected on the Hill," says Representative Vernon Ehlers (R-Mich.), vice chairman of the House science subcommittee. "He doesn't march in and say, 'This is the greatest project in the world, and any responsible legislator must support it,' which is what a lot of people do. He says, 'Let me explain this program. These are the funding needs; I hope you will support it.'"

While federal support has held up in dollar terms, it declined as a percentage of the university's total research budget—down from 1980's 83 percent to 69 percent of the campus total. Vest believed it would never be as high as it once was and that MIT had probably been overdependent on the federal trough, anyway. "What started as a problem also opened our sights to other views of the future and other ways of interacting with the world," he says. "We were nimble in finding new ways of serving society and at the same time creating new revenue streams from the private sector."

Individual faculty had always been free to seek private support for their research (the MIT Media Lab, which has for years aggressively courted corporate support for its research, may be the best example). But Vest sought to create higher-level connections. Since 1994, MIT has set up eight long-term research partnerships with U.S. companies, including Ford, Du Pont, Microsoft, Merck, and Merrill Lynch, that will generate $248 million over the next 12 years. Corporate sources provided 8.6 percent of the university's research funding in 1980; in 1998, it was 20 percent.

Vest strongly pushed these deals, and several come out of his personal contacts. The pact with Ford Motor Co., says chancellor Lawrence Bacow, is "a direct product of Chuck's personal relationship with [former Ford chairman] Alex Trotman. They served together on the IBM board. Alex one day said to Chuck, 'Is there something else that we could be doing together?' And Chuck said he had been thinking of how to develop close relationships with industrial companies."

Such relationships between universities and corporations have their critics. A government agency that gives money for research, according to Sheldon Krimsky, professor of public policy at Tufts University and a specialist in conflict-of-interest law, has no profit motive and therefore no financial interest in a particular finding. "You can't find out what they want," Krimsky says of government decision makers. "They want good research. But there have been cases where if private funders don't get what they want to hear, the funding stops."

If you get money to carry out research into a technological area because of its commercial potential, says Nicholas Ashford, professor of engineering and director of the Law and Technology Program at MIT, "you can't call that research balanced if it does not deal with the human side of it. The university is doing a great deal of research in biotechnology, as many universities are. Is anyone paying attention to the risk side of these assessments?"

Ashford doesn't believe any MIT faculty member would suppress or drop research under pressure from or fear of a sponsor, but, he says, "If the data is equivocal, concerned eyes might be cast in the direction of the funding source."

But Bacow, who oversees MIT's corporate partnerships, insists that the research agreements won't compromise academic or university integrity. For one thing, they center on basic research. The Merrill Lynch deal, worth $15 million, includes research in financial engineering and technology and a $5 million gift to establish a graduate minor in financial technology. The Ford agreement involves engineering and the environment, and the Microsoft agreement is in computer technology and education.

MIT retains the rights to all discoveries, Bacow says, though it may license their uses to the sponsor. Even then, all research is published. "We review each research agreement to ensure that publication rights are not limited," Bacow says. "Our conflict-of-interest rules prevent faculty from receiving research support from companies in which they have a financial interest. We require faculty to disclose such relationships."

President Vest insists that it's about more than money for MIT. The partnerships, he says, "have been driven as much if not more by educational objectives as by financial objectives. Manufacturing design, process, and production were not high on the academic agenda or prestige ladder. But a subset of our faculty has discovered there are some incredibly interesting challenges in the way industry works today: globalization, the speed with which scientific innovation moves into the marketplace."

In some ways, Chuck Vest resembles Dwight Eisenhower as a rising military officer: not a glamorous MacArthur or Patton, just a hard-working achiever with such manifest intelligence and ability to get things done that others seek him out.

He grew up in Morgantown, West Virginia, a small city with three main employers: coal mines, a glassware factory, and West Virginia University. He remembers his hometown with nostalgia: "It was a wonderful place to grow up. Pure Americana—good public education, and for the most part, kids mixed together with no one caring whether you were from a faculty, farm, or factory family. The schools were integrated when I was in junior high school, and race relations were rather good among the young people."

He describes his mother, Winifred, as a homemaker and gifted amateur genealogist. His father, Marvin, was a math professor at the university.

At an early age, Vest says, he was attracted to math and science. "I built radios, read about space as long as I can remember," he says. "I gave serious thought to studying history, but my strongest passion was science and technology." He went to West Virginia University, graduating in 1963 with a degree in mechanical engineering. While he was there, he took two advanced math courses with his father, who was, Vest recalls, "an absolutely superb teacher, delivering precise, well-organized lectures and expecting a lot from his students. I didn't ask a question once, and I earned an A in each. He was such a demanding teacher that my fellow students didn't even blink over the fact that I was in the class."

Vest and Rebecca McCue were married in June 1963, right after he graduated from college. He was 21; she was 20. They moved to Ann Arbor that same month, where he entered graduate school at the University of Michigan and she completed her last year of undergraduate study and went on to receive a master's degree in remedial reading. (They have two children, now grown, and one grandchild.)

He became immersed in the then-new field of holography and earned his PhD in 1967. (His field is holographic interferometry—the uses of holograms to visualize or measure thermal or mechanical phenomena—and some of his research was instrumental in the development of CT scanning.) He stayed at Michigan to teach and eventually became a full professor of engineering.

"I loved teaching," he says. "I always enjoyed explaining things and had some ability to do so. The thrill of guiding others to suddenly understand or discover something is wonderful. I had no aspirations to move into administration; I was never a department head and had a tendency to avoid committee assignments."

In 1981, he took a part-time job as associate dean of the College of Engineering as a favor to a colleague who had become dean. He intended to stay only for two years, but, he says, "One day I realized I was accomplishing more as an administrator than as a researcher and teacher. I enjoyed fostering the careers of younger faculty." He became dean of the College of Engineering in 1986, and three years later was named university provost and vice president for academic affairs.

If the MIT insiders raised eyebrows at the arrival of the West Virginia boy, Vest earned his chevrons early, as one dean put it, over the so-called overlap suit in 1991.

MIT and eight Ivy League colleges, plus several others, had a policy of admitting the best applicants without regard to affluence, then awarding financial aid to the neediest students. Often, the brightest needy students would apply to several of the top colleges and be accepted by all. To avoid bidding wars in the form of richer financial aid offers, the colleges shared information on admitted students and agreed to offer comparable financial aid packages.

But the U.S. Justice Department, under the Bush administration, called the sharing collusion and price-fixing and filed an antitrust suit against the colleges. The Ivies agreed to drop the practice, essentially saying, "We did nothing wrong, and we'll never do it again." But despite advice that he would never win in court, Vest refused to sign. He believed that if colleges did not cooperate, they would start using financial aid to bid for the most desirable students; there would be less aid for everyone else, which would hurt the neediest students.

MIT alone fought back in court. After losing an early decision, MIT won on appeal. Then, in 1993, President Clinton's Justice Department made a separate peace with MIT, dropping the suit and allowing MIT to do some information-sharing. The suit was filed "just as Chuck joined MIT," says Lawrence Bacow, "and the stakes were enormous. It was an antitrust suit with treble damages; there would have been huge fines levied. If we had lost that suit, it would have had profound consequences. MIT is traditionally not a place where the sons and daughters of privilege attend, and the concern was that if we did not protect our ability to allocate financial aid, needy students would not be able to come to MIT. And Chuck stood tall, did the principled thing, and earned tremendous respect."

Vest's interest in what is best for students came up most directly, perhaps, in 1997, when an 18-year-old freshman, Scott Krueger, died of alcohol poisoning during an initiation rite at Phi Gamma Delta, one of MIT's 30 fraternities. The chapter was disbanded. Two years later, another fraternity chapter, Sigma Alpha Epsilon, was disbanded for alcohol violations and two others were cited, one of them also for alcohol violations.

Vest was intensely disturbed by Krueger's death and appointed a task force to study the residential system. In the end, he ruled that all freshmen would live on campus, starting in 2001, after a new $40 million dormitory is finished.

It wasn't just the drinking that concerned Vest and others. It was the dearth of MIT student life, in general. Though there are dormitories, there never was much campus-based social or cultural life at MIT—nothing comparable to the Harvard residential houses, for example, which have concerts, art exhibitions, and lectures.

"Generations of students remember their MIT years in terms of where they lived and whom they lived with, and activities were based on that dispersed culture," says former president Gray.

About 30 percent of MIT's undergraduates, almost 1,200 students, live in the 28 fraternity houses or in "independent living groups"—off-campus group residences run by students and sanctioned officially by MIT. Instead of being assigned to housing before they come to school, incoming MIT freshmen attend Rush Week in August, where they are wooed by fraternities. If they decide to pledge rather than live in a dormitory or group house, the fraternity is where they live, usually for their whole MIT careers.

The system put a roof over students' heads, to be sure, but Vest and others believed that, combined with the intense workload of MIT students, it also separated them from their classmates and from the university.

"I have never been in an institution where people push harder, work longer hours, exhaust themselves," says Khoury, the dean of humanities. "Out there in the fraternities, they are isolated. We work them to death, and they hide out there—it's like a relief agency. Some fraternities are elegant, some are pretty bad. Vest has taken a courageous position on this and taken a lot of flak." There were student demonstrations against Vest's decision and angry complaints from certain alumni who fondly remembered their fraternity days. For the fraternities, there was a real money issue: Their financial viability depends on getting enough pledges to support the houses, and here was the university's president placing the freshmen class off-limits—in other words, eliminating one-quarter of the pool of potential pledges.

But Vest was firm. He maintains that MIT desperately needs a greater integration of residential and academic life and that faculty have to be more involved with students outside the classrooms and labs. The plan is eventually to have arts and intellectual programs in the dorms involving faculty members, as the Harvard houses do.

"If you look at the institute in the 1950s, '60s, '70s," Vest says, "students were virtually all white male engineers with fixed and similar career objectives. In 2000, it is nothing like this. It no longer serves a good purpose if students come here from these varied backgrounds and immediately move off into small, separated living groups. We are trying to build a broader sense of community and collegiality."

One thing almost everyone says about Charles Vest is that he works extremely hard—several who have worked closely with him say too hard. He answers all of his own e-mail, and administrators and faculty are accustomed to getting detailed messages from him posted at 2 or 3 A.M. He is said at times to show signs of sleep deprivation.

"He works amazingly hard," says provost Robert Brown. "It's very tough on people who have offices near him, because you know the volume and variety of things he's doing. You can't at the same time be talking to faculty about their individual problems and wondering about national issues without handling an enormous amount of work."

Meantime, Vest's interest in individual students is legendary. "The degree to which he gets involved in personal concerns that come to his attention is extraordinary," says Rosalind Williams, dean of students. "If someone is upset, he really wants to see if something can be done, and he will follow up with me: What happened with so and so? In most cases, it is someone who has run into bureaucracy, and he wants to be sure we act in a humane way."

Even so, he is not always working. He runs along the Charles River every morning ("to maintain my stability") and kayaks in the summer on New Hampshire's Lake Winnipesaukee. He no longer has time for the 100- and 200-mile bike rides he used to take, "but maybe someday I'll get back to it," Vest says. At home, he listens to music, mostly jazz and classical, and he says he and his wife "use movies as our primary diversion."

Vest's warm, low-key temperament and self-effacing humor are evident in conversation. When MIT offered him the top job, he recalls, "I thought one of the great benefits of going from public to private higher education would be that I wouldn't have to be going to Lansing to meet with the state Legislature." And although he is cutting-edge in terms of science, public policy, and society, Vest has a decidedly old-fashioned cast about him. He uses words like "service," "duty," and "community" with great seriousness, a kind of fiery mildness. Successful CEOs are often called hot-tempered, but Vest says, "Generally, I don't get very angry. I defuse angry situations with humor, when possible."

As for the challenges of running MIT, to say Chuck Vest has a positive attitude understates the case. "I honestly have never felt truly discouraged," he says, "but I certainly get frustrated when I do not believe I am rapidly accomplishing what I have a duty to do." As provost Robert Brown puts it, "It's hard to go to Chuck with an issue and paint it as an insurmountable problem. There just is no insurmountable problem."

Nevertheless, some problems have resisted even Vest's determination. When asked to name his greatest frustration, he says, "The toughest hill to climb is building diversity in the faculty. That's the area in which I feel least satisfied." Of MIT's 931 faculty, 144 are women; 15 of the women and 106 of the men are minorities. The positive attitude is also evident in Vest's handling of a personal crisis. On February 26, Rebecca Vest suffered cardiac arrest at home. Because of fast response by campus police and the Mount Auburn Hospital emergency room, she survived. She recently returned home after more than 40 days at Mount Auburn, Massachusetts General Hospital, and Spaulding Rehabilitation Hospital. Of her condition, Vest says, "Her recovery has been excellent, and we anticipate that she will continue to progress well."

Ten years is a long time to be president of MIT; only one president in this century has served significantly longer than that. Some have wondered whether his wife's health problems might break Vest's concentration. The answer is, evidently not. Though he spends a lot of time by her side, nobody reports any diminution of his energy or zest for his job.

And big things are brewing at MIT: a $300 million campus face lift, new ties with foreign universities, ambitious research initiatives in neuroscience and health, a $1.5 billion capital campaign (of which half is already pledged). Asked if he ever gets tired enough to consider stepping down, Vest replies in a characteristically emphatic way, "I am focused on doing my best during a period of change and excitement at MIT. I have not yet given a microsecond of thought to doing anything else."

Carly Fiorina

A story of leadership development

The key to success is not to wait for the perfect answer, but to seize the moment now, and make the best choices.
—Carly Fiorina, June 1999[1]

In February 1996, telecommunications giant AT&T readied itself for a bold move: spinning off its systems and technology unit. Two months later, the unit, renamed Lucent Technologies, issued an initial public offering (IPO) of stock. All signs pointed to Lucent's becoming a key player in mobility, optical, data, and voice-networking technologies.[2] During this exciting time, Carleton "Carly" Fiorina was president of AT&T's corporate relations. Overseeing strategy, business development, and corporate operations, she orchestrated the planning and implementation of Lucent's IPO and other launch activities.

Despite her natural confidence and rapid ascent up the corporate ladder, Fiorina faced a tough challenge in pitching the Lucent IPO.[3] In her recollections of these months, she acknowledged: "I think deep down I was scared I would screw it up. Fear of screwing up has been a very powerful motivator throughout my career."[4]

The spin-off was completed in September 1996, when AT&T distributed its shares of Lucent to AT&T shareholders. At $3 billion, the IPO ranked as the largest in the United States at the time.[5] Several years later, *Fortune* magazine named Fiorina the most powerful woman in American business. Indeed, many Wall Street observers lauded her marketing and customer-relations savvy. Some noted aspects of her personal charisma

---

Note: This case is based on information found in the business press and from recorded speeches.
1 Keynote: IEC Information Industry Luncheon SUPERCOMM'99, Atlanta, GA, http://www.lucent.com/news/speeches/docs/fiorina.html. Copyright @ 2002 Lucent Technologies.
2 http://www.lucent.com/corpinfo/history.html, "Globalization," Copyright © 2002 Lucent Technologies.
3 Copyright 1999 Newark Morning Ledger Co., February 14, 1999, *The Star-Ledger,* Newark, NJ, "A woman of substance," by Joseph R. Perone.
4 Copyright 1999 Newark Morning Ledger Co., February 14, 1999, *The Star-Ledger,* Newark, NJ, "A woman of substance," by Joseph R. Perone.
5 Copyright 1999 Globe Newspaper Company, *The Boston Globe,* July 20, 1999, City Edition, p. D1, "In landmark choice, HP taps Lucent's Fiorina for top post," by Diane E. Lewis.

as well, such as her ability to laugh easily, her direct gaze, and her willingness to speak her mind.[6] But above all, businesspeople pegged Fiorina as a leader who had a unique talent for making things happen quickly.

Early Fiorina

Carly's very name links her to a rich family history. During the American Civil War, her father's ancestors initiated a tradition of naming a son Carleton or a daughter Cara Carleton in every generation—to honor the memory of Carletons lost to the conflict. Carly Fiorina is the ninth daughter to receive the name since the Civil War.[7]

Yet the fact that Fiorina entered the corporate world is surprising in light of her early history. Her father, a law professor, changed employment so often that Carly attended five different high schools. Her mother was a homemaker and painter.[8] In Fiorina's words: "My own process of finding the soul to guide me brings me back once again to my parents. My mother was a stay-at-home wife and an artist, but [she], more than anyone else, taught me about the power of aspiration and courage."[9]

Fiorina graduated from Stanford University with a bachelor's degree in medieval history and philosophy. During one summer break, she worked as a secretary in Hewlett-Packard's shipping department.[10] There, she developed an admiration for the company's achievements and its decentralized culture.[11] At that time, she could not have foreseen the frustration she would experience many years later, as president of Lucent Technologies' largest division, in buying products from HP.[12]

After Stanford, Carly entered the University of California at Los Angeles' law school, intending to follow her father's professional path. But after just one semester, she knew she had little taste for the law. Informing her father that she was leaving UCLA counts among the hardest days of her life, she explained. However, the experience made her realize that she alone possesses the power and the responsibility to do what she wanted with her life.[13]

From such experiences, Fiorina learned about the importance of candor—of facing up to your own feelings and stating what's on your mind.[14]

"My parents were both very strong people," she pointed out. "I gained great strength from them. People sometimes interpret candor as toughness—and sometimes it's hard to tell the truth. But in the end, the truth sets you free. In Fiorina's view, the sooner and the more clearly you can tell the truth about what needs to be done, and clearly define what is and isn't acceptable performance, the more effective a leader you will be.[15]

After leaving law school, Fiorina went on to receive her MBA from the University of Maryland at College Park. She married and divorced, then spent some time working as a receptionist and teaching English to businessmen in Italy.[16] (She is also comfortable with French, Spanish, and some German.[17]) In 1989, she completed a master's of science degree at the MIT Sloan School of Management. Around that time, she married a man who worked for AT&T. She has raised two stepdaughters with him, at times trading off child-rearing and household duties for corporate work while her husband manages the home front and serves as a volunteer fireman in their community.[18]

---

6 Copyright 1999 Times Business Publications, *Business Times* (Singapore), October 29, 1999, p. 30, "Fiorina's fun formula for success," by Raju Chellam.
7 Copyright 1999 The McGraw-Hill Companies, Inc. *Business Week,* August 2, 1999, "The Boss—Resume: Cara Carleton S. Fiorina," by Peter Burrows with Peter Elstrom.
8 Copyright 1999 The McGraw-Hill Companies, Inc. *Business Week,* August 2, 1999, p. 76, "The Boss," by Peter Burrows with Peter Elstrom.
9 MIT Audio and Visual Services, Carly Fiorina, Massachusetts Institute of Technology Commencement, Cambridge, MA, June 2, 2000.
10 Copyright 1999 The Financial Times Limited, *Financial Times* (London), July 20, 1999, edition 1, p. 24, "HP secretary makes it to post of chief executive," by Louise Kehoe.
11 Copyright 2001 The McGraw-Hill Companies, Inc. *Business Week,* February 19, 2001, p. 70, "The Radical," by Peter Burrows.
12 Copyright 2001 The McGraw-Hill Companies, Inc. *Business Week,* February 19, 2001, p. 70, "The Radical," by Peter Burrows.
13 Copyright 1999 The McGraw-Hill Companies, Inc. *Business Week,* August 2, 1999, p. 76, "The Boss," by Peter Burrows with Peter Elstrom.
14 MIT Audio and Visual Services, Carly Fiorina, Massachusetts Institute of Technology Commencement, Cambridge, MA, June 2, 2000.
15 Copyright 1999 Times Business Publications, *Business Times* (Singapore), October 29, 1999, p. 30, "Fiorina's fun formula for success," by Raju Chellam.
16 Copyright 1999 *Newsweek,* August 2, 1999, Business, p. 56, "In a League of Her Own," by Michael Meyer.
17 Copyright 1999 Newark Morning Ledger Co., February 14, 1999, *The Star-Ledger,* Newark, NJ, "A woman of substance," by Joseph R. Perone.
18 Copyright 1999 *Newsweek,* August 2, 1999, Business; p. 56, "In a League of Her Own," by Michael Meyer.

The AT&T and Lucent Years

In 1980, Fiorina joined AT&T as a sales representative. She declined to participate in the company's savings plan because, as she remarked, "No way would I stay past two years."[19] Fiorina was just 25 and, like many young people, had not yet clarified her career goals.

But despite her misgivings about a long tenure at AT&T, she advanced quickly within the company. After setting up joint ventures for AT&T's equipment division, Network Systems (a Lucent precursor), in Asia, she became an officer at the division by age 35. She built a solid track record selling AT&T products to the U.S. government and by age 40 was running the company's North America sales. After the Lucent spin-off and IPO, she launched a $90-million brand-building campaign that helped transform AT&T from a mere phone-equipment maker into a key supplier of communications gear and Internet services. In 1998 she was promoted to the position of president of Lucent's global-service-provider business, stepping up product development to unprecedented levels.[20] Suddenly, she was managing revenues totaling $21 billion.[21]

Having started out in AT&T's core long-distance business, Fiorina next made a career move that many observers considered professional suicide: She jumped to the Network Systems group. "It wasn't the choice most people made," Daniel Stanzione, Lucent's co-chief operating officer later admitted. But "she's comfortable in uncomfortable situations."[22] Apparently, Fiorina had recognized the phone-equipment manufacturing unit's potential for growth in emerging markets such as Asia. Despite the risks, she thrived in the Network Systems group, burnishing her reputation further by brokering many important deals for the group.

In 1991, Fiorina joined a team of AT&T executives charged with negotiating with Telecom Italia to buy part of that company's equipment supplier, Italtel. The meetings did not go well. The Italians feared AT&T as a competitor and at times could not come to agreement on meeting agendas. The talks dragged on for three years. Finally, the Italians decided to sell a stake to Siemens instead of to AT&T. Yet some good still came of the effort. Fiorina managed to strike other deals with many of the same Telecom Italia executives who had participated in the Italtel negotiations, ultimately winning Lucent new contracts as well.[23]

A shrewd leader, Fiorina also developed a personal touch that inspired intense loyalty among her followers. For example, she publicly praised employees who landed big contracts by sending them balloons and flowers. And during the Lucent spin-off, she "burned the midnight oil" with AT&T's comptroller and other employees to ensure that every detail in the stock-offering prospectus was flawless. But Fiorina didn't limit her personal touch to just business: She also helped ill family members of Lucent employees to find medical advice, physicians, and support networks.[24]

Fiorina's time at Lucent also highlighted her savvy approach to customers. Her experience with AT&T customer Bell Atlantic Corp. is one example. In early 1998, Bell Atlantic set out to reduce the amount of time needed to order large-scale telephone equipment. The process typically took nine months. Fiorina defined—and achieved—a daring goal: whittling the time for critical orders from nine months to just three. "She stepped in and made sure it got done," said Paul A. Lacouture, Bell Atlantic's group president for network services.

Fiorina also knows that what customers need and what they ask for aren't necessarily the same things. To illustrate, when one large telecom company told Lucent it needed a new switch for its wireless business, Fiorina asked the company's executives to explain the thinking behind their request. They obliged—and their response made her realize that Lucent could supply them with a switch capable of handling both wireless and long-distance traffic. Even better, the switch she recommended would cost no more than the part the company had requested initially. A colleague pointed out, "She never just tries to sell a customer a box. We were talking with the chairman of a major Internet company and she asked, 'What keeps you up at night?' That's the attitude that she has."[25]

---

19 Copyright 1999 Globe Newspaper Company, *The Boston Globe,* July 20, 1999, City Edition, p. D1, "In landmark choice, HP taps Lucent's Fiorina for top post," by Diane E. Lewis.
20 Copyright 1999 The McGraw-Hill Companies, Inc. *Business Week,* August 2, 1999, p. 76, "The Boss," by Peter Burrows with Peter Elstrom.
21 Copyright 1999 Globe Newspaper Company, *The Boston Globe,* July 20, 1999, City Edition, p. D1, "In landmark choice, HP taps Lucent's Fiorina for top post," by Diane E. Lewis.
22 Copyright 1999 The McGraw-Hill Companies, Inc. *Business Week,* August 2, 1999, p. 76, "The Boss," by Peter Burrows with Peter Elstrom.
23 Copyright 1999 Newark Morning Ledger Co., February 14, 1999, *The Star-Ledger,* Newark, NJ, "A woman of substance," by Joseph R. Perone.
24 Copyright 1999 The McGraw-Hill Companies, Inc. *Business Week,* August 2, 1999, p. 76, "The Boss," by Peter Burrows with Peter Elstrom.
25 Copyright 1999 The McGraw-Hill Companies, Inc. *Business Week,* August 2, 1999, p. 76, "The Boss," by Peter Burrows with Peter Elstrom.

Fiorina worked at AT&T and Lucent for almost 20 years. In 1999, she contemplated a career move that would ultimately lead to the most pivotal professional experiences of her life.

HP

In 1999, even insiders knew that the "HP Way," a popular slogan representing Hewlett-Packard's decentralized, consensus-driven culture, was slowly killing the venerable firm. People were spending so much time trying to reach consensus on so many decisions that, ultimately, many tasks simply didn't get done. HP's emphasis on decentralization only further complicated matters. New product lines had splintered into autonomous units, and the company's four core businesses—ink-jet printers, laser printers, servers, and PCs—were riven by countless conflicting operations. Utter chaos resulted. For example, HP had manifold product logos and as many as one hundred different brand names—including OfficeJet, Pavilion, and Vectra. Its 34 customer databases remained unlinked. The different units used more than one hundred thousand vendors, engaging them through separate contracts. Advertising budgets were split among dozens of units—making it difficult to determine how much the company was spending on ads in total. "We never acknowledged publicly that we were in need of a change," recalled Antonio Perez, a top HP lieutenant. "It's hard, when you don't know what you're going to be."[26]

Why had HP become so bogged down in organizational inertia? The answer lies in part in the strength of its culture. Founded by two engineers in a garage, the company had set the standard by which other high-tech firms were judged. Over time, its management methods had been examined and praised in countless books and in case studies in numerous business schools.[27] In light of such a sterling reputation and legendary success, the current HP leadership wasn't likely to be interested in remaking the company's culture.

So HP set out to find a new CEO who could initiate the required transformation. The executive-search committee established a set of criteria, four of which played directly to Fiorina's strengths: ability to formulate and communicate broad strategies, a deep knowledge of operations, a talent for creating a sense of urgency around change, and ability to craft a compelling vision of HP's role in the Internet economy, then communicate that vision throughout the organization. The search committee evaluated three hundred potential candidates and identified four finalists. Ann Livermore, who headed HP's enterprise computing division, was among them. "But Carly was the best," recalled one committee member. "We see her being HP's CEO for a very long time."[28]

Fiorina had a strong ally in HP board member Richard Hackborn, 64, a retired forty-year HP veteran. Introduced during HP's 1999 CEO search, the two quickly established a connection. The reason for their rapid affinity? Both believed that HP had to be reinvented. As Hackborn put it, "We've got to do things differently." Aware of Fiorina's unique blend of strengths, Hackborn fought hard for her appointment. "He drove the search to bring Carly in. He was her strongest ally, and a good one to have," said Joe Schoendorf, a former eighteen-year HP veteran. Jeff Christian, the executive recruiter who placed Fiorina at HP, noted, "A vote of confidence from Dick goes a long way."[29]

On July 19, 1999, within hours of the announcement that she had been named HP's new CEO, Fiorina made a bold declaration: to expand the company in new directions at "Internet speed." "I think that in the Internet age, faster is always better than slower and first is always better than second," she maintained. In announcing her intent, Fiorina emphasized the need for a new leadership style and faster action over new policies: "We need to look at reinventing our speed, our sense of urgency, and our commitment to win."[30]

She used the crush of media attention following her appointment to build a star profile inside the company. Then she quickly turned her focus to the task at hand. Through interviewing managers, she arrived at some disturbing conclusions about the state of the business.[31] Within several weeks of taking HP's helm, she gathered the four members of her top team offsite for a meeting to discuss the major challenges facing the company. She urged

---

26 Copyright 1999 *Forbes* Inc., Forbes, December 13, 1999, "The Cult of Carly," by Quentin Hardy.
27 Copyright 2002 The Financial Times Limited, *Financial Times* (London), May 1, 2002, "Hewlett-Packard Verdict," p. 28, by Paul Abrahams, Louise Kehoe, Scott Morrison, and Elizabeth Wine.
28 Copyright 1999 The McGraw-Hill Companies, Inc. *Business Week*, August 2, 1999, p. 76, "The Boss," by Peter Burrows with Peter Elstrom.
29 Copyright 2001 Gannett Company, Inc., *USA Today*, December 4, 2001, p. 3B, "Many H-P employees oppose deal with Compaq," by Jon Swartz.
30 Copyright 1999 John Fairfax Publications Pty Ltd, *Australian Financial Review,* July 21, 1999, Computers; p. 28, "New HP Chief to Pep Up Growth," by David Crowe.
31 Copyright 1999 Forbes Inc., *Forbes,* December 13, 1999, "The Cult of Carly," by Quentin Hardy.

the team to focus again on key strategic growth areas—such as Internet services and imaging—and on customers rather than products. After considering her comments, team members told her that reviewing her change agenda would take about three months. The chief replied, "We don't have three months. Do it here, in three days." Someone later remembered that her demand required "a leap of faith, to unite us in a deep objective. She needed us, but we needed her."[32]

Fiorina's distinctive leadership style attracted notice among numerous top executives. For example, Robert Wayman, HP's CFO, said:

Shortly after Carly arrived here, we started discussions on a variety of matters, including the strategy of the company and the structure that would best support that strategy. We made some major announcements about changing from a series of mostly fully integrated, product-focused businesses to a more disintegrated approach, with pieces of the organization focused on what we term "product generation," and other pieces focused on the customer-facing activities—the sales and support activities....

At a three-day offsite about a month after she got here, I was struck by Carly's communication abilities. I still see her stepping up to the flip charts and choosing just the right numbers to help us immediately see where we were, compared with our competition. Obviously, she was new to our business, and didn't develop the strategy right then. But she drew out of us strategic options that we may not have imagined before, and got us focused on what was possible....

[She is] creating the tension and desire along with it, and translating it on the bottom line. She says to managers, "What can be done? There is no bag of money beyond what we have collectively here, and there is no free lunch."[33]

During her first year in the corner office, Fiorina made changes at breakneck speed.[34] Some examples:

- **Remaking HP's culture.**[35] Fiorina tackled the company's slow-moving, overly cautious culture first. Some units were disbanded; others, reorganized. HP's 86,000 employees had to adjust to new work processes and habits that, for some, seemed incompatible with "the HP way." But as Fiorina pointed out, too many people had begun using the HP way as an excuse for dragging their feet and avoiding taking risks. Some older cultural dicta had to be replaced. "Preserve the best," she advised, and "reinvent the rest."

  To that end, she drew up a series of "rules of the garage" that harked back to HP's earliest days. The rules included "No politics, no bureaucracy" and "Radical ideas are not bad ideas."[36] She backed up these changes by tying a higher portion of executives' pay to external performance benchmarks.[37]

  Likewise, Fiorina encouraged HP's long-neglected research arm, HP Labs, to explore "disruptive technologies" that had the potential to create entirely new markets and shake up the industry; for example, using molecules to build integrated circuits.[38] In her view, the division had decayed into a function that merely eked out incremental ideas for the product divisions.

- **Changing vision.** Fiorina shifted the firm's vision of itself as a provider of stand-alone products to a company that offered customers an integrated suite of information appliances, highly reliable IT infrastructure, and "e-services." She prodded the firm to pull all its products together into packages that provided e-services solutions. HP even began offering its own e-services, such as software for building internal company portals. It also developed "e-speak," a platform that enables it to quickly combine different types of online services into packages tailored specifically to customers' needs.[39]

- **Realigning organizational structure.** Fiorina knew that major shifts in vision and strategy need corresponding changes in organizational structure in order to succeed. With that principle in mind, she restructured HP into four organizations. Two of them focus on sales (consumer and corporate); the remaining two center on products (computers and printers/imaging). The company also slashed its number of product groups from 83 to 12—a far more manageable number.[40]

- **Marketing HP's new identity.** Fiorina also put HP's brand identity under her micro-

---

32 Copyright 1999 Forbes Inc., *Forbes*, December 13, 1999, "The Cult of Carly," by Quentin Hardy.
33 Copyright 2000 Gale Group, Inc. *Business and Management Practices*; Copyright 2000 CFO Publishing Corporation, *CFO The Magazine for Senior Financial Executives*, November 2000, vol. 16, pp. 70–71, 75, "Veteran's Day," by Roy Harris.
34 Copyright 2000 The Economist Newspaper Ltd., *The Economist*, July 15, 2000, U.S. Edition, "Rebuilding the garage."
35 Copyright 2000 Gale Group, Inc. *Business and Management Practices*; Copyright 2000 CFO Publishing Corporation, *CFO The Magazine for Senior Financial Executives*, November 2000, vol. 16, pp. 70–71, 75, "Veteran's Day," by Roy Harris.
36 Copyright 2000 The Economist Newspaper Ltd., *The Economist*, July 15, 2000, U.S. Edition, "Rebuilding the garage."
37 Copyright 2000 The Economist Newspaper Ltd., *The Economist*, July 15, 2000, U.S. Edition, "Rebuilding the garage."
38 Copyright 2000 The Economist Newspaper Ltd., *The Economist*, July 15, 2000, U.S. Edition, "Rebuilding the garage."
39 Copyright 2000 The Economist Newspaper Ltd., *The Economist*, July 15, 2000, U.S. Edition, "Rebuilding the garage."
40 Copyright 2000 The Economist Newspaper Ltd., *The Economist*, July 15, 2000, U.S. Edition, "Rebuilding the garage."

scope. As one of her first initiatives, she set aside $200 million for a branding campaign that would send a startling new message to customers, competitors, and industry partners: HP is a company of invention; we intend to democratize technology.[41]

To many observers, Fiorina came across as "a relentlessly executing, no-holds-barred, take-no-prisoners, be-in-front-with-the-shield-and-sword, go-to-war, stay-in-the-ditch-with-you executive." People inside and outside HP watched in awe as she eradicated fiefdoms, upended traditions, and put a fresh new face on the company's public image. With her "Challenge the mind and capture the heart" mantra,[42] she infused a new perspective into the company that emphasized speed and the "total customer experience."[43]

Her critics—and she did have them—painted Fiorina as a rude outsider who was violating HP's established practice of treating employees and shareholders as family. Some HP insiders warned of the dangers of speed for speed's sake and argued that Fiorina needed to communicate the reasoning behind her decisions more explicitly.[44]

But the new chief executive stayed the course she had defined. She centralized decision making and encouraged managers to fire their poorest-performing employees. But in her drive to shake up HP's overly comfortable culture, she also made some public relations blunders. For example, she allowed herself to be photographed standing before a mock-up of the garage where HP founders Bill Hewlett and David Packard had started the business in 1938. Employees considered the garage sacred turf and accused her of attaching herself to a legacy to which she had not contributed. Her tendency to eat lunch in places other than the company cafeteria, along with rumors that she had exclusive use of a corporate jet and chauffeur, earned her a reputation as an elitist—an insult in egalitarian Silicon Valley.[45]

Yet Fiorina explained the need for transformational change throughout HP in her own style:

As soon as you decide that people have to choose to change, then you have to engage them completely in "Why change?" Why do people want to change? They want to change because they are inspired by something that is in front of them, because they are excited by the power of aspiration, which is very strong in people, I believe, because they are afraid of failure.

To engage people in the choice to change means that people have to understand intellectually why it is necessary. One of the things I say inside HP is, we are not changing because you have a new CEO—that would be the worst reason to change. We are changing because the market is changing. We are changing because we have to continue to be successful.

People have to understand that intellectually. Then they have to be prepared and, yes, even inspired emotionally. That is why we go back to the legacy of our founders so often; that is why we talk about the rules of the garage—because in so many ways Bill and Dave had that spirit of constant change, constant invention, constant aspiration.[46]

The new CEO saw the market moving quickly and the pace of change accelerating. For that reason, she felt certain that no chief executive could hope to make every decision influencing his or her company. She initiated the phrase "Set the frame and set people free." By setting the frame, she meant making key choices about strategy, structure, profit, rewards, metrics, culture, and behavior—but then, within that frame, empowering people to invent creative solutions for customers.[47] In her view:

Effective leadership requires an understanding that you don't own people, that you can't control people. They must want to, they must choose to be in the company of others, oriented towards a particular mission. That means . . . a great deal of communication; it means using communication vehicles really creatively.[48]

Fiorina's emphasis on creative use of communication had one unfortunate consequence for her. As most female leaders might imagine, being a highly influential woman in a corporate world dominated by men isn't easy. Fiorina has endured epithets that go way beyond mere scrutiny of a

---

41 Copyright 2000 The Economist Newspaper Ltd., *The Economist,* July 15, 2000, U.S. Edition, "Rebuilding the garage."
42 Copyright 2000 Time Inc., *Fortune,* October 16, 2000, p. 130, "The 50 Most Powerful Women in Business," by Patricia Sellers.
43 Ann Livermore's quote on Carly Fiorina. (Ann was one of the candidates for HP CEO position.) Copyright 2000 Times Business Publications, *Business Times* (Singapore), February 14, 2000, Special Section, p. 1, SS2, "Going great guns under Carly," by Kenneth James.
44 Copyright 2002 The Daily Record Co., *The Daily Record,* Baltimore, MD, May 1, 2002, p. 7A.
45 Copyright 2002 The Financial Times Limited, *Financial Times* (London), May 1, 2002, "Hewlett-Packard Verdict," p. 28, by Paul Abrahams, Louise Kehoe, Scott Morrison, and Elizabeth Wine.
46 Copyright 2000 John Fairfax Publications Pty Ltd, *Australian Financial Review,* October 9, 2000, p.16, "Her Way."
47 Copyright 2000 John Fairfax Publications Pty Ltd, *Australian Financial Review,* October 9, 2000, p.16, "Her Way."
48 Copyright 2000 John Fairfax Publications Pty Ltd, *Australian Financial Review,* October 9, 2000, p.16, "Her Way."

new, untried leader. For example, on one Internet chat board frequented by HP employees, someone headlined a posting with "Back to the kitchen, Carly." And a *New York Observer* columnist snarled, "Pack it in, babe. You stink."[49]

Still, Fiorina has maintained her focus and determination. Among her favorite buzzwords is MBFA—management by flying around. At HP, she travels frequently to visit with customers and employees. With Hewlett-Packard now serving customers in 157 countries, she has ample reason to "manage by flying around."[50]

Yet owing to the company's sheer size, Fiorina has often employed internal Web and message boards to communicate with workers. This practice has prompted some to accuse her of being distant and out of touch. Such detractors contrast her approach to that of HP's founders, which was popularized as "management by walking around."[51]

Fiorina looks to her own management principles to guide her work. They include a list of short but potent commandments:

- Have fun.
- Love what you do.
- Stay focused.
- Believe in yourself.
- Strategy is zero, without execution.
- Do things more quickly.
- Take more risks.
- Seek out people who believe in your capabilities.
- Candor counts.
- Tell the truth quickly and clearly.
- Keep healthy—it makes a difference.[52]

Epilogue

Up to the end of 2000, Carly Fiorina was extolled as the belle of corporate America. The first woman to lead a blue-chip company in the Dow Jones industrial average, she generated an immense amount of press. Yet like many other corporate leaders, Fiorina could not shield her company completely against the larger forces tearing at the U.S. economy. As she continued her campaign to reorganize HP during 2001, the firm's stock plummeted by more than half.[53]

Things grew even shakier in September 2001, when Fiorina announced her intent to pursue a historical merger between computer giant Compaq and HP. Her rationale for the move was that the deal made sense in an economic climate that was tough for technology companies in particular. In her view, difficult times underscored the need for companies to become more cost effective and efficient.[54] She continued:

We're doing this deal because the technology landscape is changing fundamentally and has been for a couple of years now. Customers are demanding different things of their IT partners, and I mean consumers as well as businesses. If you look at the power of these two companies together—and we've looked at it very carefully—it's clear that we can deliver a much improved value proposition to customers. We're creating . . . a game-changing move here.[55]

Some analysts and press members noted that even before the Compaq merger, HP was in the grip of one of the farthest-reaching restructurings experienced by a modern technology company. They wondered: Was HP trying to do too much too soon?[56]

Perhaps their musings had merit. In November 2001, the HP-Compaq deal stumbled. Walter Hewlett, a board member and son of co-founder Bill Hewlett, had moved to halt the merger. Through family foundations, Hewlett controlled more than 5.5 percent of HP's stock. For some reason, Fiorina had failed to sell her vision of the merger to him. Though Hewlett had expressed reservations about the deal early on, controversy swirled around the question of how forcefully he communicated his objections to the rest of the board. He claimed he made his views crystal clear.

---

49 Copyright 2002 John Fairfax Publications Pty Ltd, *Australian Financial Review*, June 14, 2002, p. 56, "Yes, But Can She Cook?" by George Anders.
50 Copyright 2000 John Fairfax Publications Pty Ltd, *Australian Financial Review*, October 9, 2000, p.16, "Her Way".
51 Copyright 2001 Gannett Company, Inc., *USA Today*, December 4, 2001, p. 3B "Many H-P employees oppose deal with Compaq," by Jon Swartz.
52 Copyright 1999 Times Business Publications, *Business Times* (Singapore), October 29, 1999, p. 30, "Fiorina's fun formula for success," by Raju Chellam.
53 Copyright 2002 Los Angeles Times, *Los Angeles Times*, February 4, 2002, p. 4, "Technology Q&A; Fiorina's Fervor," by Joseph Menn.
54 Copyright 2001 Community Television Foundation of South Florida, Inc., September 4, 2001, Transcript # 090401cb.118, Business, Nightly Business Report, by Paul Kangas and Susie Gharib.
55 Copyright 2001 Community Television Foundation of South Florida, Inc., September 4, 2001, Transcript # 090401cb.118, Business, Nightly Business Report, by Paul Kangas and Susie Gharib.
56 Copyright 2002, Los Angeles Times, *Los Angeles Times*, February 4, 2002, p. 4, "Technology Q&A; Fiorina's Fervor," by Joseph Menn.

Moreover, he emphasized his right to vote his shares as he saw fit.[57] Upon news of the dispute, HP's share price rose 17 percent, perhaps because many investors felt unconvinced that a merger with Compaq would solve HP's problems.

Fiorina was left with a major battle: to win enough shareholder votes to gain approval for the deal. Hewlett, for his part, promised a proxy fight to persuade shareholders to vote against the merger.[58]

Hewlett made good on his word. The resulting five-month campaign proved the nastiest proxy battle in U.S. business history. To garner support for their camps, the two adversaries cranked out press releases, newspaper ads, faxes, and telephone calls extolling the virtues of their positions.[59]

The HP chief executive clearly had one aim in mind: to eradicate the widespread perception that the conflict centered on the fate of the soul of a Silicon Valley legend. The battle, she insisted, "is not about old versus new, not past versus future, not family versus company—it's not about any of that."[60]

Some would argue that Fiorina had only herself to blame for the battle. She and other HP directors never anticipated the opposition from Hewlett or his power to rally other opponents of the merger to his side. According to one institutional investor, the CEO's failure to convince Hewlett of the deal's merits from the start was a "sloppy" mistake. Indeed, Fiorina has contended that Hewlett's decision to oppose the merger came as a "complete surprise" to both her and HP's board.

But Fiorina also faced critics who challenged her personal record. Some, for instance, blamed her for Lucent's financial struggles during the late-1990s Internet downturn. "It's hard for me to see how I had anything to do with that," Fiorina has said. "We didn't miss numbers while I was there." She added that Lucent's problems cropped up after her departure.[61]

Other critics questioned Fiorina's ability to execute a massive, complex merger of two industry giants. Her response:

Well, I think we are confident we can do this and we are also sober about what it takes to do it. And . . . the fact that we're sober makes us confident.

There's no question there's a lot of work to do here. But . . . we have planned it out pretty carefully. In fact, we had done detailed business plans and detailed integration plans before we ever called the first banker. . . . We wanted to be sure: Are we aligned in terms of the value drivers of this combination?

We've thought about it, we've planned it, we have the key people in place, and we have the key decisions already made. . . . We are in a position when we get regulatory approval to execute with that discipline and speed and decisiveness. And we recognize we're going to have to prove that to people.[62]

In the spring of 2002, shareholders finally approved the merger with a slim majority of 51.4 percent.[63] Though HP's board claimed that it strongly supported the deal, analysts heard some midlevel managers echo earlier complaints that their chief executive wasn't doing things the "HP way." One analyst wrote:

When Carly Fiorina was brought in more than two years ago, the assumption was that she'd shake things up a little. The general feeling now is that she might've gone too far. A merger is expected to cut at least 15,000 jobs. It would also mean reorganization into four large units. Both moves would represent quite a break from HP's past. Until 2001, the maker of computers, software, and printers had avoided major layoffs. And its management had a strong sense of community, along with a decentralized style.[64]

Despite approval of the deal, Walter Hewlett wasn't finished with Fiorina. A week after the announcement of the voting results, he initiated a lawsuit claiming that HP had lied to shareholders about the status of its integration plans. He further stated that HP had coerced Deutsche Asset Management—the intermediary brokering the deal—into switching 17 million votes in favor of the deal

---

57 Copyright 2002 The Financial Times Limited, *Financial Times* (London), May 1, 2002, p. 28, by Paul Abrahams, Louise Kehoe, Scott Morrison, and Elizabeth Wine.
58 Copyright 2001 The Financial Times Limited, *Financial Times* (London), December 20, 2001, p. 18, "Interview with Carly Fiorina," by Scott Morrison and Richard Waters.
59 Copyright 2002 Sunday Business Group, *The Business,* March 24, 2002, p. 17, by Anna Stewart.
60 Copyright 2001 The Financial Times Limited, *Financial Times* (London), December 20, 2001, p. 18, "Interview with Carly Fiorina," by Scott Morrison and Richard Waters.
61 Copyright 2001 The Financial Times Limited, *Financial Times* (London), December 20, 2001, p. 18, "Interview with Carly Fiorina," by Scott Morrison and Richard Waters.
62 Copyright 2001 Community Television Foundation of South Florida, Inc., September 4, 2001, Transcript # 090401cb.118, Business, Nightly Business Report, by Paul Kangas and Susie Gharib.
63 Copyright 2002 The Financial Times Limited, *Financial Times* (London), May 1, 2002, "Hewlett-Packard Verdict," p. 28, by Paul Abrahams, Louise Kehoe, Scott Morrison, and Elizabeth Wine.
64 Copyright 2002 Investor's Business Daily, Inc. *Investor's Business Daily,* January 2, 2002, p. 8, "HP-Compaq Sparks Fireworks," by Murray Coleman.

just hours before the deadline. During a three-day trial in Delaware's Chancery Court, Fiorina took the witness stand. Over seven hours, she expertly fended off a hail of accusations and questions. Ultimately, Hewlett couldn't produce sufficient evidence to back up his claims.[65]

With all signs pointing to a merger that's now free to move ahead, Fiorina will need to shift her focus to how the deal will work in practice—no small feat indeed. As of this writing, the marriage of the two technology giants has gone better than expected. Once again, HP's chief has proven her mettle—though in the business world, one must continually do so. However, her track record so far has inspired numerous aspiring leaders, both male and female alike.

---

[65] Copyright 2002 The Financial Times Limited, *Financial Times* (London), May 1, 2002, "Hewlett-Packard Verdict," p. 28, by Paul Abrahams, Louise Kehoe, Scott Morrison, and Elizabeth Wine.

Leadership

ELECTIVE

Module 14

What Should I Do With My Life?

by Po Bronson

The real meaning of success—and how to find it.

It's time to define the new era. Our faith has been shaken. We've lost confidence in our leaders and in our institutions. Our beliefs have been tested. We've discredited the notion that the Internet would change everything (and the stock market would buy us an exit strategy from the grind). Our expectations have been dashed. We've abandoned the idea that work should be a 24-hour-a-day rush and that careers should be a wild adventure. **Yet we're still holding on.**

We're seduced by the idea that picking up the pieces and simply tweaking the formula will get the party started again. In spite of our best thinking and most searing experience, our ideas about growth and success are mired in a boom-bust mentality. Just as LBOs gave way to IPOs, the market is primed for the next engine of wealth creation. Just as we traded in the pinstripes and monster bonuses of the Wall Street era for T-shirts and a piece of the action during the startup revolution, we're waiting to latch on to the new trappings of success. (I understand the inclination. I've surfed from one boom to the next for most of my working life—from my early days as a bond trader to my most recent career as a writer tracking the migration of my generation from Wall Street to Silicon Valley.)

There's a way out. Instead of focusing on what's *next*, let's get back to what's *first*. The previous era of business was defined by the question, Where's the opportunity? I'm convinced that business success in the future starts with the question, What should I do with my life? Yes, that's right. The most obvious and universal question on our plates as human beings is the most urgent and pragmatic approach to sustainable success in our organizations. People don't succeed by migrating to a "hot" industry (one word: dotcom) or by adopting a particular career-guiding mantra (remember "horizontal careers"?). They thrive by focusing on the question of who they really are—and connecting that to work that they truly love (and, in so doing, unleashing a productive and creative power that they never imagined). Companies don't grow because they represent a particular sector or adopt the latest management approach. They win because they engage the hearts and minds of individuals who are dedicated to answering that life question.

This is not a new idea. But it may be the most powerfully pressing one ever to be disrespected by the corporate world. There are far too many smart, educated, talented people operating at quarter speed, unsure of their place in the world, contributing far too little to the productive engine of modern civilization. There are far too many people who look like they have their act together but have yet to make an impact. You know who you are. It comes down to a simple gut check: You either love what you do or you don't. Period.

Those who are lit by that passion are the object of envy among their peers and the subject of intense curiosity. They are the source of good ideas. They make the extra effort. They demonstrate the commitment. They are the ones who, day by day, will rescue this drifting ship. And they will be rewarded. With money, sure, and responsibility, undoubtedly. But with something even better too: the kind of satisfaction that comes with knowing your place in the world. We are sitting on a huge potential boom in productivity—if we could just get the square pegs out of the round holes.

Of course, addressing the question, What should I do with my life? isn't just a productivity issue: It's a moral imperative. It's how we hold ourselves accountable to the opportunity we're given. Most of us are blessed with the ultimate privilege: We get to be true to our individual nature. Our economy is so vast that we don't have to grind it out forever at jobs we hate. For the most part, we get to choose. That choice isn't about a career search so much as an identity quest. Asking The Question aspires to end the conflict between who you are and what you do. There is nothing more brave than filtering out the chatter that tells you to be someone you're not. There is nothing more genuine than breaking away from the chorus to learn the sound of your own voice. Asking The Question is nothing short of an act of courage: It requires a level of commitment and clarity that is almost foreign to our working lives.

Source: Po Bronson, "What Should I Do With My Life?" *FastCompany* 66 January, 2003, p. 69. Copyright © 2003 Gruner + Jahr USA Publishing. All rights reserved. FastCompany, 77 North Washington St., Boston, MA 02114. **Po Bronson** is the author of three best-selling books. This article is adapted from his new book, *What Should I Do with My Life? The True Story of People Who Answered the Ultimate Question* (Random House, January 2003). Contact him by e-mail (pobronson@pobronson.com).

During the past two years, I have listened to the life stories of more than 900 people who have dared to be honest with themselves. Of those, I chose 70 to spend considerable time with in order to learn how they did it. Complete strangers opened their lives and their homes to me. I slept on their couches. We went running together. They cried in my arms. We traded secrets. I met their families. I went to one's wedding. I witnessed many critical turning points.

These are ordinary people. People of all ages, classes, and professions—from a catfish farmer in Mississippi to a toxic-waste inspector in the oil fields of Texas, from a police officer in East Los Angeles to a long-haul trucker in Pennsylvania, from a financier in Hong Kong to a minister at a church on the Oregon coast. These people don't have any resources or character traits that give them an edge in pursuing their dream. Some have succeeded; many have not. Only two have what accountants call "financial independence." Only two are so smart that they would succeed at anything they chose (though having more choices makes answering The Question that much harder). Only one, to me, is saintly. They're just people who faced up to it, armed with only their weaknesses, equipped with only their fears.

What I learned from them was far more powerful than what I had expected or assumed. The first assumption to get busted was the notion that certain jobs are inherently cool and that others are uncool. That was a big shift for me. Throughout the 1990s, my basic philosophy was this: Work=Boring, *but* Work+Speed+Risk=Cool. Speed and risk transformed the experience into something so stimulating, so exciting, so intense, that we began to believe that those qualities defined "good work." Now, betrayed by the reality of economic uncertainty and global instability, we're casting about for what really matters when it comes to work.

On my journey, I met people in bureaucratic organizations and bland industries who were absolutely committed to their work. That commitment sustained them through slow stretches and setbacks. They never watched the clock, never dreaded Mondays, never worried about the years passing by. They didn't wonder where they belonged in life. They were phenomenally productive and confident in their value. In places unusual and unexpected, they had found their calling, and those callings were as idiosyncratic as each individual.

And this is where the second big insight came in: Your calling isn't something you inherently "know," some kind of destiny. Far from it. Almost all of the people I interviewed found their calling after great difficulty. They had made mistakes before getting it right. For instance, the catfish farmer used to be an investment banker, the truck driver had been an entertainment lawyer, a chef had been an academic, and the police officer was a Harvard MBA. Everyone discovered latent talents that weren't in their skill sets at age 25.

Most of us don't get epiphanies. We only get a whisper—a faint urge. That's it. That's the call. It's up to you to do the work of discovery, to connect it to an answer. Of course, there's never a single right answer. At some point, it feels right enough that you choose, and the energy formerly spent casting about is now devoted to making your choice fruitful.

This lesson in late, hard-fought discovery is good news. What it means is that today's confused can be tomorrow's dedicated. The current difficult climate serves as a form of reckoning. The tougher the times, the more clarity you gain about the difference between what really matters and what you only pretend to care about. The funny thing is that most people have good instincts about where they belong but make poor choices and waste productive years on the wrong work. Why we do this cuts to the heart of the question, What should I do with my life? These wrong turns hinge on a small number of basic assumptions that have ruled our working lives, career choices, and ambitions for the better part of two decades. I found hardly any consistencies in how the people I interviewed discovered what they love to do—the human soul resists taxonomy—*except* when it came to four misconceptions (about money, smarts, place, and attitude) that have calcified into hobbling fears. These are stumbling blocks that we need to uproot before we can find our way to where we really belong.

MONEY Doesn't Fund Dreams

Shouldn't I make money first—to fund my dream? The notion that there's an order to your working life is an almost classic assumption: Pay your dues, and then tend to your dream. I expected to find numerous examples of the truth of this path. But I didn't find any.

Sure, I found tons of rich guys who were now giving a lot away to charity or who had bought an island. I found plenty of people who had found something meaningful and original to do after making their money. But that's not what I'm talking about. I'm talking about the garden-variety fantasy: Put your calling in a lockbox, go out and make a ton of money, and then come back to the lockbox to pick up your calling where you left it.

It turns out that having the financial independence to walk away rarely triggers people to do just that. The reality is, making money is such hard work that it changes you. It takes twice as long as anyone plans for. It requires more sacrifices than anyone expects. You become so emotionally invested in that world—and psychologically adapted to it—that you don't really want to ditch it.

I met many people who had left the money behind. But having "enough" didn't trigger the change. It had to get personal: Something had to happen such as divorce, the death of a parent, or the recognition that the long hours were hurting one's children. (One man, Don Linn, left investment banking after he came home from a business trip and his two-year-old son *didn't recognize him*.)

The ruling assumption is that money is the *shortest* route to freedom. Absurdly, that strategy is cast as the "practical approach." But in truth, the opposite is true. The shortest route to the good life involves building the confidence that you can live happily within your means (whatever the means provided by the choices that are truly acceptable to you turn out to be). It's scary to imagine living on less. But embracing your dreams is surprisingly liberating. Instilled with a sense of purpose, your spending habits naturally reorganize, because you discover that you *need* less.

This is an extremely threatening conclusion. It suggests that the vast majority of us aren't just putting our dreams on ice—we're killing them. Joe Olchefske almost lost his forever. Joe started out in life with an interest in government. In the early 1980s, he made what seemed like a minor compromise: When he graduated from Harvard's Kennedy School of Government, he went into public finance. He wouldn't work *in* government, he'd work *with* government.

Joe went on to run Piper Jaffray in Seattle. By the mid-1990s, he realized that one little compromise had defined his life. "I didn't want to be a high-priced midwife," he said. "I wanted to be a mother. It was never *my* deal. It was my clients' deal. They were taking the risk. They were building hospitals and bridges and freeways, not me. I envied them for that."

One night, riding up the elevator of his apartment building, Joe met newly hired Seattle schools superintendent John Stanford. Soon after, Stanford offered Olchefske a job as his CFO—and partner in turning the troubled school system around. Olchefske accepted. Stanford rallied the city around school reform and earned the nickname Prophet of Hope. Meanwhile, Olchefske slashed millions from the budget and bloodlessly fired principals, never allowing his passions to interfere with his decisions. People called him Prophet of Doom.

Then Stanford died suddenly of leukemia. It was one of the great crises in the city's history. Who could fill this void? Certainly not the green-eyeshade CFO. But Stanford's death transformed Olchefske. It broke him open, and he discovered in himself a new ability to connect with people emotionally, not just rationally. As the new superintendent, he draws on that gift more than on his private-sector skills. He puts up with a lot of bureaucrap, but he says that avoiding crap shouldn't be the objective in finding the right work. The right question is, How can I find something that moves my heart, so that the inevitable crap storm is bearable?

SMARTS Can't Answer The Question

If the lockbox fantasy is a universal and eternal stumbling block when it comes to answering The Question, the idea that smarts and intensity are the essential building blocks of success and satisfaction is a product of the past decade. A set of twin misconceptions took root during the celebration of risk and speed that was the 90s startup revolution. The first is the idea that a smart, motivated individual with a great idea can accomplish *anything*. The corollary is that work should be fun, a thrill ride full of constant challenge and change.

Those assumptions are getting people into trouble. So what if your destiny doesn't stalk you like a lion? Can you *think* your way to the answer? That's what Lori Gottlieb thought. She considered her years as a rising television executive in Hollywood to be a big mistake. She became successful but felt like a fraud. So she quit and gave herself three years to analyze which profession would engage her brain the most. She literally attacked the question. She dug out her diaries from childhood. She took classes in photography and figure drawing. She interviewed others who had left Hollywood. She broke down every job by skill set and laid that over a grid of her innate talents. She filled out every exercise in *What Color Is Your Parachute?*

Eventually, she arrived at the following logic: Her big brain loved puzzles. Who solves puzzles? Doctors solve health puzzles. Therefore, become a doctor. She enrolled in premed classes at Pepperdine. Her med-school applications were so persuasive that every school wanted her. And then—can you see where this is headed?—Lori dropped out of Stanford Medical School after only two and a half months. Why? She realized that she didn't like hanging around sick people all day.

The point is, being smarter doesn't make answering The Question easier. Using the brain to solve this problem usually only leads to answers that make the brain happy and jobs that provide what I call "brain candy." Intense mental stimulation. But it's just that: *candy*. A synthetic substitute for other types of gratification that can be ultimately more rewarding and enduring. As the cop in East L.A. said of his years in management at Rockwell, "It was like cheap wood that burns too fast."

I struggled with this myself, but not until I had listened to hundreds of others did the pattern make itself shockingly clear. What am I good at? is the wrong starting point. People who attempt to *deduce* an answer usually end up mistaking intensity for passion. To the heart, they are vastly different. Intensity comes across as a pale *busyness,* while passion is meaningful and fulfilling. A simple test: Is your choice something that will stimulate you for a year or something that you can be passionate about for 10 years?

This test is tougher than it seems on paper. In the past decade, the work world has become a battleground for the struggle between the boring and the stimulating. The emphasis on intensity has seeped into our value system. We still cling to the idea that work should not only be challenging and meaningful—but also invigorating and entertaining. But really, work should be like life: sometimes fun, sometimes moving, often frustrating, and defined by meaningful events. Those who have found their place don't talk about how exciting and challenging and stimulating their work is. Their language invokes a different troika: meaningful, significant, fulfilling. And they rarely ever talk about work without weaving in their personal history.

PLACE Defines You

Every industry has a culture. And every culture is driven by a value system. In Hollywood, where praise is given too easily and thus has been devalued, the only honest metric is box-office receipts. So box-office receipts are all-important. In Washington, DC, some very powerful politicians are paid middling salaries, so power and money are not equal. Power is measured by the size of your staff and by how many people you can influence. In police work, you learn to be suspicious of ordinary people driving cars and walking down the street.

One of the most common mistakes is not recognizing how these value systems will shape you. People think that they can insulate themselves, that they're different. They're not. The relevant question in looking at a job is not *What will I do?* but *Who will I become?* What belief system will you adopt, and what will take on heightened importance in your life? Because once you're rooted in a particular system—whether it's medicine, New York City, Microsoft, or a startup—it's often agonizingly difficult to unravel yourself from its values, practices, and rewards. Your money is good anywhere, but respect and status are only a local currency. They get heavily discounted when taken elsewhere. If you're successful at the wrong thing, the mix of praise and opportunity can lock you in forever.

Don Linn, the investment banker who took over the catfish farm in Mississippi, learned this lesson the hard way. After years as a star at PaineWebber and First Boston, he dropped out when he could no longer bring himself to push deals on his clients that he knew wouldn't work. His life change smacked of foolish originality: 5.5 million catfish on 1,500 water acres. His first day, he had to clip the wings of a flock of geese. Covered in goose shit and blood, he wondered what he had gotten himself into. But he figured it out and grew his business into a $16 million operation with five side businesses. More important, the work reset his moral compass. In farming, success doesn't come at another farmer's expense. You learn to cooperate, sharing processing plants, feed mills, and pesticide-flying services.

Like Don, you'll be a lot happier if you aren't fighting the value system around you. Find one that enforces a set of beliefs that you can really get behind. There's a powerful transformative effect when you surround yourself with like-minded people. Peer pressure is a great thing when it helps you accomplish your goals instead of distracting you from them.

Carl Kurlander wrote the movie *St. Elmo's Fire* when he was 24. For years afterward, he lived in Beverly Hills. He wanted to move back to Pittsburgh, where he grew up, to write books, but he was always stopped by the doubt, Would it really make any difference to write from Pittsburgh instead of from Beverly Hills? His books went unwritten. Last year, when a looming Hollywood writers' strike coincided with a job opening in the creative-writing department at Pitt, he finally summoned the courage to move. He says that being in academia is like "bathing in altruism." Under its influence, he wrote his first book, a biography of the comic Louie Anderson.

ATTITUDE Is the Biggest Obstacle

Environment matters, but in the end, when it comes to tackling the question, What should I do with my life? it really is all in your head. The first psychological stumbling block that keeps people from finding themselves is that they feel guilty for simply taking the quest seriously. They think that it's a self-indulgent privilege of the educated upper class. Working-class people manage to be happy without trying to "find themselves," or so the myth goes.

But I found that just about anybody can find this question important. It's not just for free agents, knowledge workers, and serial entrepreneurs. I met many working-class people who found this question essential. They might have fewer choices, but they still care. Take Bart Handford. He went from working the graveyard shift at a Kimberley-Clark baby-wipes plant in Arkansas to running the Department of Agriculture's rural-development program. He didn't do this by just pulling up his bootstraps. His breakthrough came when his car was hit by a train, and he spent six months in bed exploring The Question.

Probably the most debilitating obstacle to taking on The Question is the fear that making a choice is a one-way ride, that starting down a path means closing a door forever.

"Keeping your doors open" is a trap. It's an excuse to stay uninvolved. I call the people who have the hardest time closing doors Phi Beta Slackers. They hop between esteemed grad schools, fat corporate gigs, and prestigious fellowships, looking as if they have their act together but still feeling like observers, feeling as if they haven't come close to living up to their potential.

Leela de Souza almost got lost in that trap. At age 15, Leela knew exactly what she wanted to be when she grew up: a dancer. She pursued that dream, supplementing her meager dancer's pay with work as a runway model. But she soon began to feel that she had left her intellect behind. So, in her early twenties, with several good years left on her legs, she took the SATs and applied to college. She paid for a $100,000 education at the University of Chicago with the money that she had earned from modeling and during the next seven years made a series of seemingly smart decisions: a year in Spain, Harvard Business School, McKinsey & Co., a White House Fellowship, high-tech PR. But she never got any closer to making a real choice.

Like most Phi Beta Slackers, she was cursed with tremendous ability and infinite choices. Figuring out what to do with her life was constantly on her mind. But then she figured something else out: Her need to look brilliant was what was keeping her from truly answering The Question. When she let go of that, she was able to shift gears from asking "What do I do next?" to making strides toward answering "To what can I devote my life?"

Asking "What Should I Do With My Life?" is the modern, secular version of the great timeless questions about our identity. Asking The Question aspires to end the conflict between who you are and what you do. Answering The Question is the way to protect yourself from being lathed into someone you're not. What is freedom for if not the chance to define for yourself who you are?

I have spent the better part of the past two years in the company of people who have dared to confront where they belong. They didn't always find an ultimate answer, but taking the question seriously helped get them closer. We are all writing the story of our own life. It's not a story of conquest. It's a story of discovery. Through trial and error, we learn what gifts we have to offer the world and are pushed to greater recognition about what we really need. The Big Bold Leap turns out to be only the first step.

One Size Does Not Fit All
Two different answers to one ultimate question

Organization Man

Of the 900 people who I talked to, only one has had the same employer for his entire adult life. His name is Russell Carpenter, he's 35, and he's an aerospace engineer at NASA Goddard. We can all learn from him. Russell began working at NASA during college. In exchange for his summers, they paid for his tuition and, later, financed his PhD. Russell is a GS-14, stuck to government pay scales. The money is okay, but it's never the reason to stay. He's building a guidance system for the newest type of satellite.

The halls and offices at NASA are quiet. These engineers are content with slowly pushing toward a solution. Which I took as Extractable Lesson number one: time frame. At NASA, Russell has found an intermediate time frame where he can accomplish the high-minded objectives that his division is charged with, but he's not under absurd pressure to do it all in 90 days.

Aerospace engineers are obsessed with redundancy and backup systems. Russell knows that metals give, that gears slip, and that motors overheat, and he plans for that in his designs. Not everything has to go right in order for it to work. And that way of thinking shows up in every aspect of his life, including how he achieves his ambitions. Which I took as Extractable Lesson number two: His backup plans do not lead to different destinations, such as "If I don't get into business school, I'll be a schoolteacher." His backup plans lead to the same destination, and if he has to arrive late by a back road, that's fine.

Later, Russell and I went to a baseball game, which clued me in to Extractable Lesson number three: Russell doesn't let himself get burned out. He doesn't think it's a big deal that he's only had one employer. His method is his secret, but it's no secret.

"So what do you do?" For five years, Marcela Widrig had a dream job that compensated her well, let her live in Barcelona, and paid for her frequent travel throughout Southern Europe. She sold modems for a big modem manufacturer. Modems were her means to her ends: money, travel, human connection.

When her company moved her to San Francisco, she suffered culture shock. The Internet was destroying everything that she loved about sales. The new ethos was speed. Get the deal done in a day! Don't even fly—email makes it so easy! The human contact was gone.

The worst part was constantly being asked The Inevitable Cocktail-Party Question: "What do you do?" Marcela had been away long enough to have forgotten about this disgusting American custom. She found it degrading and reductive and mercenary. I too used to think that The Inevitable Cocktail-Party Question was a scourge on our society. But I'm starting to see that it is really about freedom to choose. A status system has evolved that values being unique and true even more than it values being financially successful.

In other words, if you don't like The Inevitable Cocktail-Party Question, maybe it's partly because you don't like your answer.

Marcela no longer liked her answer. She endured migraines and insomnia. After flying all the way to Hong Kong for a meeting that didn't even last one hour, she vowed, "I cannot sell one more modem." But she didn't quit for two more years. On her vacations, she flew to Switzerland to train in a school for deep-tissue massage. It was her way to move toward genuine human contact. The day she returned from one of her Switzerland trips, the modem company went under, and she was forced into her new life.

It took her about a year to drop the business-suit persona and truly embrace her new profession. The Inevitable Cocktail-Party Question no longer bothers her. "I do body work," she says. "I love what I do, and I think that comes across."

Excerpts from Geeks & Geezers
How era, values, and defining moments shape leaders

by Warren G. Bennis and Robert J. Thomas

The Power of the Crucible

We found that every leader in our study, young or old, had undergone at least one intense, transformational experience. That transformational experience was at the very heart of becoming a leader. The descriptive term we found ourselves using is *crucible*. The *American Heritage Dictionary* defines crucible as "a place, time or situation characterized by the confluence of powerful intellectual, social, economic or political forces; a severe test of patience or belief; a vessel for melting material at high temperatures." A crucible was the vessel in which medieval alchemists attempted to turn base metals into gold. That the alchemists inevitably failed in their audacious attempts doesn't negate the power of the crucible as a metaphor for the circumstances that cause an individual to be utterly transformed.

As the event or relationship that forged a leader, the crucible is at the center of our model. The crucibles that produced our leaders were as varied as being mentored, mastering a martial art, climbing a mountain, and losing an election. Sometimes the crucible was an upbeat, even joyous experience. Video game expert Geoff Keighley, 21, remembers his whole life changing in second grade, when he made a magician's table out of a microwave box, put on a top hat, and performed a dazzling magic trick at a friend's birthday party. "It set me apart," said Keighley, remembering how the wonder and respect of his young audience filled him with a sense of power and uniqueness.

Sometimes the crucible is a tragedy. Pioneering television journalist Mike Wallace was uncertain whether he should give up his prestigious, well-paying job with a local station and try for a network slot when, in 1962, his oldest son, Peter, a student at Yale, fell off a mountain while on vacation in Greece. Two weeks after Peter disappeared, Wallace found the boy's body. "That was really the turning point when I said, 'To hell with it,'" Wallace recalled. "I'm going to quit everything and do what I want to do now."

One of the harshest crucibles in our study was that which shaped businessman Sidney Rittenberg, 79. In China in 1949 Rittenberg was jailed as a spy by former friends in Chairman Mao's government. He spent sixteen years in prison, the first year in solitary confinement and total darkness except when he was being interrogated and the remaining fifteen years in permanent lighting without the benefit of darkness. He emerged certain that absolutely nothing in professional life could break him.

The crucible need not be a horrendous ordeal. Motorola vice president Liz Altman, 34, didn't go to prison. But she was utterly transformed by the year she spent in a Sony factory in Japan, finding her way in an alien corporate world whose broad cultural differences—particularly its emphasis on groups over individuals—were both a shock and a challenge to a young American woman. Muriel Siebert, the first woman to own a seat on the New York Stock Exchange, was shaped by Wall Street of the 1950s and '60s, an arena so sexist that she couldn't get a job as a stockbroker until she took her first name off her resume and substituted a genderless initial. Thrust into the alpha-male world of Wall Street, Siebert wasn't broken or defeated. Instead, she emerged stronger, more focused, and determined to change the status quo that excluded her.

World War II was a crucible for almost all our older male leaders, many of whom were transformed by the terrible responsibility of leading other men into battle. The war was also a crucible for many in that it allowed them to recognize for the first time that they had the ability and desire to lead. Common Cause founder John Gardner, 89, identified his arduous training as a Marine as the crucible in which his leadership abilities emerged. "Some qualities were there waiting for life to pull those things out of me," he told us, with characteristic eloquence. The battlefield and basic training are recognized rites of passage after which people are different; their values and the way they see the world are forever changed. The quality of that change is captured in the observation by many Vietnam veterans that the war was in Technicolor, but everything before and after was in black and white.

Source: Reprinted by permission of Harvard Business School Press. From Geeks & Geezers by Warren G. Bennis and Robert J. Thomas, Boston, MA 2002, p. 14–21, 87–94, 98–108. Copyright © 2002 by the Harvard Business School Publishing Corporation; all rights reserved.

Mentor-protégé relationships constitute another, very powerful, kind of crucible. The importance of mentoring has become almost a cliché of management literature, but mentoring shares with other crucibles a powerful process of learning, adaptation, and transformation that is intensely individual, whether it occurs in a family or an organization. Consider, for example, Michael Klein, a young man who made millions in Southern California real estate while still in his teens. As Klein told us, his mentor was his grandfather, Max. S. Klein, who created the paint-by-numbers fad that swept the United States in the 1950s and '60s. Klein recalled that he was only 4 or 5 years old when his grandfather approached him and offered to share his expertise in business. The grandfather noted that Michael's father and aunt—Max's only children—had no interest in business and told young Michael, "You're never going to get any money from me . . . but I'll tell you anything you want to know and teach you anything that you want to learn from me." We learn from stories like Klein's that teaching is never solely the function of the mentor. The protégé can also be a teacher, a guide to the mindset and the skills of a younger generation that allows the mentor to continue learning and to cope more successfully with inexorable change.

Whether the crucible experience is an apprenticeship, an ordeal, or some combination of both, we came to think of it much like the hero's journey that lies at the heart of every myth, from *The Odyssey* to *Erin Brockovich*. It is both an opportunity and a test. It is a defining moment that unleashes abilities, forces crucial choices, and sharpens focus. It teaches a person who he or she is. People can be destroyed by such an experience. But those who are not emerge from it aware of their gifts and goals, ready to seize opportunities and make their future. Whether the crucible was harrowing or not, it is seen by the individual as the turning point that set him or her on the desired, even inevitable, course.

Creating Meaning Out of the Crucible Experience

Leaders create meaning out of events and relationships that devastate nonleaders. Even when battered by experience, leaders do not see themselves as helpless or find themselves paralyzed. They look at the same events that unstring those less capable and fortunate and see something useful, and often, a plan of action as well. A powerful example is that of Vernon E. Jordan, civil rights pioneer and presidential advisor. In his 2001 memoir *Vernon Can Read!*, Jordan describes the vicious baiting he received as a young man from his employer, Robert F. Maddox. Jordan served the racist former mayor of Atlanta at dinner, in a white jacket, with a napkin over his arm. He also functioned as Maddox's chauffeur. Whenever Maddox could, he would derisively announce, "Vernon can read!" as if the literacy of a young African American were a source of wonderment. So abused, a lesser man might have allowed Maddox to destroy him. But Jordan wrote his own interpretation of Maddox's sadistic heckling, a tale that empowered Jordan instead of embittering him. When he looked at Maddox through the rear-view mirror, Jordan did not see a powerful member of Georgia's ruling class. He saw a desperate anachronism who lashed out because he knew his time was up. As Jordan writes: "I do not mean just his physical time on earth—but I believe that the 'time' that helped shape him was on its way out. His half-mocking, half-serious comments about my education were the death rattle of his culture. When he saw that I was in the process of crafting a life for myself that would make me a man in some of the same ways he thought of being a man, he was deeply unnerved. The home in which Jordan was a servant was the crucible in which, consciously or not, Jordan imbued Maddox's cruelty with redemptive meaning. And thus are leaders made.

Nelson Mandela used his powerful character and imagination to thwart his jailers' attempts to dehumanize him. "If I had not been in prison," he told Oprah Winfrey in an interview in 2001, "I would not have been able to achieve the most difficult task in life, and that is changing yourself." Notice how Mandela made lemonade from the most bitter of lemons. He saw himself not as a passive victim—someone who was imprisoned by others—but as an individual who had been "in prison." Instead of allowing his jailers to define him, Mandela fashioned a heroic identity for himself—one that inspired millions in Africa and elsewhere and was instrumental in ending apartheid and creating a new, multicultural South Africa. For Mandela, the crucible was both an external reality and something he created in the process of imbuing it with meaning.

Much of the leadership literature focuses on the traits or habits of leaders. In fact, every individual has a unique set of obstacles as well as assets that he or she brings to the table. Whether the bar is poverty, insecurity based on some physical attribute (Mike Wallace's teenage acne), or ethnic or racial discrimination (architect Frank Gehry was so troubled by widespread anti-Semitism that he changed the family name from Goldberg shortly before his first child was born), everybody enters the lists with a burden, a perceived reason for not succeeding. Ford Motor Company executive (and geek) Elizabeth Kao expressed the concept well when she said: "Everybody has their own wall to climb." One of the key differences between leaders and nonleaders, we found, is the ability of leaders to transmogrify even the negatives in their lives into something that serves them. For leaders, the uses of adversity are genuinely sweet."

What Makes a Leader

An important part of our leadership model is what lies on the other side of the crucible—the qualities that define lifetime leaders and learners. The one key asset all our leaders share, whether young or old, is their adaptive capacity. The ability to process new experiences, to find their meaning and to integrate them into one's life, is the signature skill of leaders and, indeed, of anyone who finds ways to live fully and well. Of all our subjects, none showed a greater adaptive capacity than Sidney Rittenberg. Thrown into a Chinese jail, confined in a pitch-dark cell without any explanation, Rittenberg did not rail or panic. You wonder what you would do in such dreadful circumstances, if you would be able to come out whole. Within minutes, Rittenberg recalled matter-of-factly, a stanza of verse popped into his head, four lines read to him as a little boy:

> *They drew a circle that shut me out,*
> *Heretic, rebel, a thing to flout.*
> *But love and I had the wit to win.*
> *We drew a circle and took them in.*

That bit of verse (adapted from "Outwitted" by Edwin Markham) was the key to Rittenberg's survival. "My God," he thought to himself, "there's my strategy. There's my program." Evidence of the power of Rittenberg's ability to adapt and survive is Rittenberg Associates, the consulting firm that he founded and continues to run, which helps American companies do business with the Chinese. As his example so vividly reminds us, bitterness is maladaptive.

Optimism is an element of what health psychologists term *hardiness*, a rubric for the cluster of qualities that equip people for serial success. Tenacity and self-confidence are others. But leaders share less obvious assets as well. As Saul Bellow says of the character very like himself in his novel *Ravelstein,* they are all "first-class noticers." Being a first-class noticer allows you to recognize talent, identify opportunities, and avoid pitfalls. Leaders who succeed again and again are geniuses at grasping context. This is one of those characteristics, like taste, that is difficult to break down into its component parts. But the ability to weigh a welter of factors, some as subtle as how very different groups of people will interpret a gesture, is one of the hallmarks of a true leader.

One of the best ways to define good leadership is to study bad leaders. A single instance is instructive here: Shakespeare's tragic Roman general Coriolanus. A great warrior, a man with a strong moral compass, Coriolanus has only one flaw—his utter inability to reach out to the people of Rome and engage them in his vision. Rereading the play in the context of leadership, we couldn't help thinking of Coriolanus's mother, Volumnia, as the ancient Roman equivalent of an executive coach saddled with a particularly thick-headed client. Talk to the people, she encourages her son again and again. But Coriolanus doesn't get it. He fails to grasp the expectations of the people or how they respond to his aloofness. He is convinced that reaching out to the populace would be a form of pandering, that it would require him to sacrifice his integrity.

Finally, before we conclude this overview of our leadership model, we need to say something more about one of the most exciting ideas to emerge from our research. We discovered that every one of our geezers who continues to play a leadership role has one quality overriding importance: *neoteny*, a zoological term, as "the retention of youthful qualities by adults." Neoteny is more than retaining a youthful appearance, although that is often part of it. Neoteny is the retention of all those wonderful qualities that we associate with youth: curiosity, playfulness, eagerness, fearlessness, warmth, energy. Unlike those defeated by time and age, our geezers have remained much like our geeks—open, willing to take risks, hungry for knowledge and experience, courageous, eager to see what the new day brings. Time and loss steal the zest from the unlucky, and leave them looking longingly at the past. Neoteny is a metaphor for the quality—the gift—that keeps the fortunate of whatever age focused on all the marvelous undiscovered things to come. Frank Gehry designs buildings that make architects half his age gasp with envy. Neoteny is what makes him lace up his skates and whirl around the ice rink, while visionary buildings come to life and dance inside his head.

Walt Disney, of all people, did a good job describing his own neoteny. "People who worked with me say I am 'innocence in action,'" he wrote. "They say I have the innocence and unselfconsciousness of a child. Maybe I have. I still look at the world with uncontaminated wonder."

The capacity of "uncontaminated wonder," ultimately, is what distinguishes the successful from the ordinary, the happily engaged players of whatever era from the chronically disappointed and malcontent. Therein lies a lesson for geeks, geezers, and the sea of people who fall in between.

* * *

Crucibles of Leadership

Tara Church, one of our geeks and founder of Tree Musketeers, encountered her crucible on an outing with her Girl Scout troop. We were spellbound as she told us how she started the only nonprofit in the world run by children, an organization that has planted more than a million trees since 1987. As crucible stories so often are, hers is a tale of transformation that has the power and resonance of a fairy tale. Church recalled:

> *California was in the middle of a very severe drought at the time, and we were going someplace that had very little water. And [the adults] were encouraging us to conserve it whenever possible. My mother was our Girl Scout leader [and she told us we had to decide if we wanted to use paper plates]. As we did with all issues, we sat in a circle and discussed the pros and cons, and then my mother mentioned the fact that using paper plates meant that trees have to get cut down. . . . And then she mentioned that there is this problem with deforestation and rain forests being massacred at alarming rates, and that led to a discussion of how trees hold soil in place and how they filter pollutants from the air and there is this hole in the ozone layer. And she had this terrifying story, which we still haven't verified, that scientists were researching ways for the human race to live underground after the atmosphere is gone. And this all because there were not enough trees. . . . It was terrifying. It was the first time in my life that I remember being absolutely terrified. . . . All of a sudden I felt I was suspended in all of the horror of the world. This idea of living underground and not ever seeing the sunlight again, not able to play soccer, climb trees, all of these things. I thought I was with this mass of dying people, and, at the same time, I felt utterly alone. It was really horrible. And then we had an idea, and our idea was that we should plant a tree. So we did. We planted a tree. And that was the single most empowering experience of my life. Realizing that while terror, while challenges, while all of these roadblocks can obstruct our view of what lies ahead, something so simple as getting a shovel and digging a hole and putting a tree in it can change the world. And I could do that. I was eight years old.*

We will look at how our geeks and geezers and other leaders were transformed in their very personal crucibles. We will examine the nature of crucibles and what takes place in them. And we will focus on the key competency that all leaders, young and old, have in abundance—adaptive capacity. But before we tell more stories, it might be helpful to review our model of transformation again (see Figure 4.1).

Think of Tara Church's story, and you'll see each of these elements in play. A child of her time, with a vivid sense of how precious and fragile the Earth is, she is confronted with a terrifying vision of what thoughtless consumption of natural resources does to the planet. But unlike those less imaginative, less hardy souls who are reduced to morbidity by the prospect, Tara has qualities that allow her to find meaning in the crisis. Instead of an ecological apocalypse, she sees reason for hope and a course of action—the wholesale planting of trees. The qualities that allow her to become a leader, despite her youthfulness, are strengthened by her assuming a leadership role in creating the new organization, better preparing her for future successes.

Judge Nathaniel R. Jones of the U.S. Court of Appeals for the Sixth Circuit and one of our

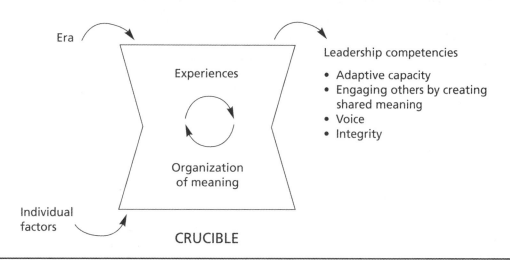

Figure 4.1 Our Leadership Development Model Elaborated

geezers, was transformed by the same process in a very different crucible: his interaction with a splendid mentor. As a teenager in Youngstown, Ohio, Jones "could have gone a very different way," he recalled, if it has not been for J. Maynard Dickerson, a successful attorney and editor of the local African-American newspaper.

Dickerson influenced Jones at many levels. The older man brought Jones behind the scenes to see how the great civil rights struggle of the 1950s was being waged, an experience that no doubt influenced the many important opinions Judge Jones has written in regard to civil rights. Dickerson was both a model and coach. His lessons covered every aspect of Jones's intellectual growth and presentation of self, including schooling in what we now call emotional intelligence. Dickerson set the highest standards for Jones, especially in the area of communication skills—a facility that we've found to be essential to leadership. Dickerson edited Jones's early attempts at writing a sports column with respectful ruthlessness, in red ink, as Jones remembers to this day.

Dickerson also expected the teenager to speak correctly at all times and would hiss discreetly in his direction if he stumbled. Great expectations are evidence of great respect, and as Jones learned all the complex, often subtle lessons of how to succeed, he was motivated in no small measure by his desire not to disappoint the man he still calls "Mr. Dickerson." Dickerson gave Jones the kind of intensive mentoring that was tantamount to grooming him for a kind of professional and moral succession—and Jones has indeed become an instrument for the profound societal change for which Dickerson fought so courageously as well. Jones found life-changing meaning in the attention paid to him by Dickerson, a conviction that he, too, though only a teenager, had a vital role to play in society and an important destiny.

The Importance of Individual Factors

We have said little so far about one element of our model, individual factors, shown in the bottom left of the diagram. We should explain why we are going to deal only briefly with the role individual factors play in creating leaders.

By individual factors, we mean "the hand you're dealt," the givens that any one of us brings to his or her encounters with the world. Traits and other individual factors have been among the most studied elements in the history of leadership. They are the essence of the argument in favor of the view—fallacious, we believe—that leaders are born, not made. If we were going to study the impact of class on the making of leaders, which we are not, we would include class under the rubric of "individual factors." It is undoubtedly true that, historically at least, being born male, white, and wealthy greatly increased the odds that an individual would achieve success, as both society and most individuals define it. That has certainly been the pattern in the United States, where leaders still tend to be male, white, and wealthy, despite affirmative action. But while those factors may be typical of the pool from which most current leaders come, they are largely irrelevant to the actual process of becoming a leader that we saw repeated over and over again. Wealth, for example, may smooth the way for high achievement, as it did for Franklin Roosevelt and John F. Kennedy. But it is no guarantee of it, as evidenced by the large number of wealthy nonentities in the world. Great intelligence helps individuals more often than it hinders them. But the only thing a high IQ is truly predictive of is an ability to solve the kinds of problems featured on IQ tests.

Much the same can be said for other factors often assumed to guarantee success. We found that most are significant only to the extent that they motivate or inhibit the individual who displays them. In theory, being gorgeous never hurts. In practice, it can paralyze a person as surely as it can benefit him or her. Our study confirmed our belief that traits and other individual factors are given far too much prominence in studies of leadership. Such factors rarely determine an individual's ultimate success. Leadership is much like other forms of creativity in this regard. The person who appears to hold the best genetic or socioeconomic hand doesn't necessarily win. The classic example is that of Poincaré and Einstein. Their mathematics professors would no doubt have predicted that the universally esteemed polymath Poincaré would have been the most important scientific thinker of his time, not Einstein, who looked, at least on paper, like a minor talent at best. There have indeed been great leaders whose emergence seemed inevitable as a result of their genius or some other fixed or genetic quality. But more often, success, including the kind of success we label leadership, emerges as a result of an individual's ability to adapt to a crisis or challenge (the event or situation we call a crucible).

Adaptive Capacity Is Key

To the extent that any single quality determines success, that quality is adaptive capacity. If you underline key points, that sentence is the one that should be swiped with yellow highlighter. When we look at who becomes a leader, we see enormous variance in IQ, birth order, family wealth, family stability, level of education, ethnicity, race, and gender. Certainly these factors cannot be dismissed entirely. But in studying both very young and older leaders, we found over and over again that much more important than a person's measured intelligence—to take just one factor—was his or her ability to transcend the limits that a particular IQ might impose. In the case of intelligence, this includes avoiding the trap of seeing oneself as highly intelligent, hopelessly average, or below average to the exclusion of other, more useful self-definitions. We emphatically agree with Ford's Elizabeth Kao that "everyone has their own wall to climb." And we believe that both the willingness to climb those walls and the ability to find ways to do so are the real measure of a leader.

Yes, adaptive capacity, which includes such critical skills as the ability to understand context and to recognize and seize opportunities, is the essential competence of leaders. But adaptive capacity, as we discovered in studying our geeks and geezers, is also the defining competence of everyone who retains his or her ability to live well despite life's inevitable changes and losses. It is no accident that psychiatrist George Vaillant called his analysis of the findings of the famed Grant study (in essence, a description of the stages of adult male development) *Adaptation to Life*. The Grant study examined the lives over many decades of 268 Harvard men, chosen as undergraduates between 1939 and 1942. (As in virtually all health studies of the period, women were regrettably excluded from the sample.) These men—in a very real sense, the brothers of our geezers—were chosen for their promise and relative mental and physical health because the psychiatrists and others conducting the study sensibly believed that science had tended to focus on illness so exclusively that we had failed to learn much about health. A crucial finding of the Grant study—one of the first to describe normal rather than abnormal psychology in adults—is that "soundness is a way of reacting to problems, not an absence of them." Like our geezers, the men of the Grant study encountered countless setbacks, heartbreaks, and difficulties, from the loss of loved ones to life-threatening illnesses. But the healthiest of Harvard men adapted to these crises; they didn't break. And those success adaptations, including one man's discovery and acceptance in mid-life of his homosexuality, allowed them to continue to grow.

To use the term of our model, people with ample adaptive capacity may struggle in the crucibles they encounter, but they don't become stuck or defined by them. They learn important lessons, including new skills that allow them to move on to new levels of achievement and new levels of learning. This ongoing process of challenge, adaptation, and learning prepares the individual for the next crucible, where the process is repeated. Whenever significant new problems are encountered and dealt with adaptively, new levels of competence are achieved, better preparing the individual for the next challenge. For those who become lifetime leaders, this extraordinary process of transformation, which provides the individual with new tools and new skills, leading to more successes and more growth, occurs over and over again. It is the process that has already distinguished our geeks from their less impressive contemporaries, and it is the process that will allow them, over time, to become distinguished geezers.

Early in 2002, Vaillant published a sequel to *Adaptation to Life*, entitled *Aging Well: Surprising Guideposts to a Happier Life from the Landmark Harvard Study of Adult Development*. This new book is based not just on the life experiences of the original Harvard study men but on those of gifted women and inner-city men as well. Some of Vaillant's most interesting new material describes the way the women, though hobbled by an era that limited their professional opportunities, adapted to their often mundane lives. One useful strategy a number of the women used was to rewrite their pasts in ways that downplayed the inequities they had experienced, allowing them to feel more useful emotions than the bitterness to which they were entitled. Like our study, the Harvard study found that the people who aged most successfully had great adaptive capacity, continued to learn new things, and looked forward, with eagerness and optimism, rather than dwelling on the past.

As we describe how the lives of our geeks and geezers were transformed in their personal crucibles, we will see the same thrilling process take place again and again, a process of change and growth that prepared each of them for future challenges and continued growth. Although none is a Pollyanna, all our geeks and geezers saw their crucibles, however punishing, as positive experiences, even as the high points of their lives, As we'll show, they not only survived their struggles, they were inspired and strengthened by them.

Aldous Huxley once observed: "Experience is not what happens to a man. It is what a man does with what happens to him." Even though Huxley's pronouns date him, he is right. The extraction of wisdom from the crucible experience is what distinguishes our successful leaders from those who are broken or burnt out by the comparable experiences. In every instance, our leaders carried the gold of meaning away from their crucibles. And they emerged with new tools as well. One invaluable take-home lesson to be learned from our geeks and geezers is that testing, however dire, is the hard but fertile soil that leads to continued growth, the process that liberates us from the past. As Vaillant so aptly describes in *Adaptation to Life*, "It is not stress that kills us. It is effective adaptation to stress that allows us to live." No matter how terrible their crucibles, our geeks and geezers wasted no time in ruing them. They all said, in essence: "I wouldn't have missed it for the world."

The Difference Between Fasting and Starving

Crucibles vary in duration (and in anticipated duration), in harshness, and in other ways. But there are two basic types: the ones you seek and the ones that find you. There is a world of difference between the two—the difference between jumping into an abyss and being pushed in, between fasting and starving, between emigration and exile. Some of our leaders had their crucibles forced upon them—Sidney Rittenberg's sixteen-year imprisonment may be the cruelest example. The majority of our leaders chose their crucibles, although rarely with a full understanding of what the experience would bring. Some, such as Arthur Levitt, Jr., became seekers of crucibles, constantly looking for the kinds of challenges that would stretch them. In a career of more than fifty years, Levitt served in the Air Force, was both a cattle broker and an editor at *Look* magazine, and served under President Clinton as chairman of the U.S. Securities and Exchange Commission. "What I believe is important in life is to keep as many doors open as possible," Levitt explained. "You close a door when you fall in love with a community and say you won't move. . . . I'll move any place. I couldn't care less where. . . . And I think that's important. You re-pot yourself."

Jack Coleman also consciously sought out tests and challenges. Now owner-editor of a weekly newspaper in Chester, Vermont, he has been a professor of economics, chairman of the Federal Reserve Bank of Philadelphia and president of Haverford College. But he is best known for taking time out of his privileged routine to experience the blue-collar lives of a garbage collector, a dishwasher, a prison guard, and an auxiliary police officer. He also lived for ten days on the streets of New York—a harsh crucible, reminiscent of George Orwell's experiences "down and out in Paris and London," but one that Coleman knew would end when his sabbatical was over and he returned to campus.

Whether imposed or sought out, crucibles are places where essential questions are asked: Who am I? Who could I be? Who *should* I be? How should I relate to the world outside myself? These are always places of reflection, but they are typically places where one transcends narrow self-regard and reflects on the self in relation to others. They are often places where one becomes increasingly aware of his or her connectedness. They are also places of choice, even when the choice is narrowed, as it was for Rittenberg and the long-imprisoned Nelson Mandela, to retaining or losing one's human dignity in the face of those who would strip it away. Crucibles are, above all, places or experiences from which one extracts meaning, meaning that leads to new definitions of self and new competencies that better prepare one for the next crucible.

The terrorist attacks on the United States on September 11, 2001, were an imposed crucible of the cruelest sort. We don't know how most of the thousands of people who experienced that event were changed. But we saw a vivid example of one man who seemed utterly transformed in Howard W. Lutnick. As head of the bond-trading firm of Cantor Fitzgerald, Lutnick would normally have been at his desk on the upper floors of the World Trade Center when it collapsed after being struck by two hijacked jets. Instead, he had taken his 5-year-old son to his first day of "big-boy school." The 40-year old executive arrived at the trade center that morning just as the attacks began. Inside were 1,000 employees of his firm. Six hundred died in the attacks and subsequent collapse, including Lutnick's 36-year-old brother, Gary.

We know what Lutnick was like before—a tough trader, with what the *New York Times* described as a "flinty edge." Known for his steel, not his compassion, Lutnick responded to the catastrophe by reaching out to the families of his employees. He wept openly in television interviews and gave his private home phone number to the families of every employee. Before the day was out, he had set up a family services center in a nearby hotel. "We have a new class of partners here—these families," he told the press, with tears in his eyes. By Thursday, the company was back doing business in makeshift quarters, and Lutnick had donated $1 million to a newly created Cantor Fitzgerald Foundation, to aid the families of anyone who died in the attacks, whomever they worked for. Later, angry members of the families of Cantor Fitzgerald dead would excoriate Lutnick for promptly sending out paychecks stamped "final" to their survivors. But whatever the ultimate truth, within hours, Lutnick seemed to have measured himself against a new reality and emerged different from the man he was before.

Crucibles are inevitably places where people play for mortal stakes. The test is often grueling, whether it is an institution-sanctioned rite of passage like Officers Candidate School or a novitiate. There is always a prize, whether it is the promise of freedom that kept Sidney Rittenberg alive or the promise of power that allows some of our geeks and geezers to endure the rankling orthodoxies of government service and corporate life. There is always a chance of failure—you don't know while you are in a crucible how the story is going to end or what your fate is going to be. But all our leaders saw their crucibles as propitious moments, dangerous perhaps, but also rich with opportunity. They believed, as FDR said in his second inaugural address: "This generation has a rendezvous with destiny." And even though our geeks and geezers knew they could fail, they had the optimist's expectation that they would win. They saw an arc to a desirable future that they believed they could travel. They were convinced that the goal was worth the struggle and that they would prevail.

Our study dealt with people who had passed through their crucibles and had emerged stronger and surer than before. If that were the universal experience, it would not be worth writing about. As we all know, while everyone is tested, some people fail. They learn nothing in a potential crucible, are broken in it, or emerge confused and demoralized. But to a person, our geeks and geezers came through in good psychological health, ready to tell their tales.

Adaptive Capacity as Applied Creativity

In essence, adaptive capacity is applied creativity. It is the ability to look at a problem or crisis and see an array of unconventional solutions. Adaptive capacity includes the quality Keats found essential to the genius of Shakespeare—negative capability. This gift, the poet explained in an 1817 letter to his younger brothers, is evident "when man is capable of being in uncertainties, mysteries, doubt without any irritable reaching after fact and reason." Those with negative capability may have considerable regard for fact and reason, but they also realize the wisdom of entertaining opposing views at the same time. John Gardner, for example, was able to see the past as "ballast and a teacher" and, at the same time, to realize that conventions and habits are limiting as well as comforting. "Beware," he said, of the prisons you build to protect yourself."

We spoke earlier of the gift our leaders have for thriving in chaos, for tolerating ambiguity and change. Studies of creativity by psychologist Theresa Amabile indicate that creative people are not only more tolerant of ambiguity than others, they also are able to consider multiple options for a longer period. They don't rule out possibilities prematurely and so they are able to make better, more artful choices. They can tolerate the nettle of uncertainty in situations where others long for closure. Most of our leaders have the requisite hungry patience to seek untested paths. But they also have the discipline necessary to achieve a desired goal. Even as they value unorthodoxy and change, they also finish dissertations and M.B.A.s because they know that such well-worn routes to success, even when they are tedious, are often worth the payoff.

Sidney Harman, octogenarian entrepreneur, former college president, and Carter cabinet undersecretary; showed a leader's attitude toward risk when he talked about the difference between recklessness and daring:

You proceed recklessly when you make no provision at all for an understanding of what the odds are or what the consequences are. You then must blindly move ahead, whether it's in a life decision or business decision. . . . Daring for me is an action you take understanding that the odds perhaps are against success, but having examined the whole network, understanding what the odds are, reckoning what the consequences can be, you make judgment that "I'm prepared to proceed against that knowledge."

Flexible, resilient people are not repelled by problems; they pounce on them, determined to find solutions to the puzzle, however painful they may be. Adaptive capacity allows individuals to confront unfamiliar situations with confidence and optimism. Those with well-developed adaptive capacity are not paralyzed by fear or undermined by anxiety in difficult situations. They believe that if they leap, a net will appear—or, if it doesn't, they will be able to find or fashion one in time. Where others see only chaos and confusion, they see opportunity. Bill Porter, who founded E*Trade in 1982, long before it was obvious that people would some day want to trade stocks at the speed of light, is a perfect example. "When you see a situation," he says, "you *go* for it."

Another example of someone who saw opportunity in chaos is a 30-year-old serial entrepreneur Sky Dayton. Asked if there was a particular point when the idea of Earthlink arrived, he thought for a moment and then laughed:

Wow, you know, there was. I was trying to get onto the Internet, and I had a book that I bought on how to do it, and I had an account that I'd gotten from an Internet service provider, and I had a Macintosh computer. And I spent eighty frustrating hours, banging on the computer, calling and trying to get help, not getting any. . . . I was tearing my hair out; it was horrible. I was sort of hacking my way through the jungle. And when I finally got connected, it was like I had arrived at this clearing in the jungle, and there was this golden pyramid, and I had a vine hanging around my neck and a leech stuck to my forehead. And so, some moment in late 1993, three A.M., when I finally made the thing work and I'm sitting at home, and I'm looking at this thing, and I'm like, "OK, this is it." A light bulb went off in my head: "I'm going to make it easy for anyone to get to this. And I'm going to bring the mass media to the masses." And that was it. I dropped everything else I was doing.

For Porter and Dayton, as for Thomas Edison and other giants of adaptive capacity, failure is a friend, not an enemy. When things don't turn out as they had hoped, they transmogrify failure into something palatable, even desirable. They see approaches that don't work not as something shameful, but as sources of valuable information that will eventually lead to a successful outcome.

Adaptive capacity allows people to embrace and explore new technologies, rather than demonize them. Former General Electric CEO Jack Welch is a good example. After initial resistance to using the Internet, Welch not only became enthusiastic, he assigned an electronically sophisticated geek to each of the company's 4,000 top managers. The compensation of the executives was linked to how readily they learned the skills taught by their young mentors. Indeed, seeking out expertise, wherever they find it, is one of the strengths of almost all our geeks and geezers. Our geeks tend to be stalkers of first-rate mentors. Our geezers don't hesitate to tap the wisdom of their children and grandchildren.

Old or young, our leaders have the ego strength to admit that there are things they don't know and to see learning as a reciprocal process. As Embark.com cofounder Young Shin put it: "We realized that we didn't have a lot of the operational experience we needed, so we brought in some senior managers. We had a lot to learn from them. But, at the same time, we knew some things they didn't, and we were proud of the things we knew."

Like other creative people, those with powerful adaptive capacity inevitably take pleasure in the problem-solving process. No matter how terrible the dilemma may be—a serious illness, a sick dot.com, an unjust and brutal imprisonment—grappling with it and finding a solution becomes a source of satisfaction, even pleasure. As the process of problem solving floods the person's brain with pleasure-giving endorphins, dealing creatively with the problem becomes both motivator and reward. The more a person uses his or her adaptive capacity, the stronger and more supple it becomes.

The crucible is the occasion for real magic, the creation of something more valuable than any alchemist could imagine. In it, the individual is transformed, changed, created anew. He or she grows in ways that change his or her definition of self. How do we know that people are changed? Often an observer can see the difference, but more important, the individual perceives it.

The crucible is a dividing line, a turning point, and those who have gone through it feel that they are different from the way they were before. In explaining how she had been changed by an early entrepreneurial failure, Ford's Elizabeth Kao recalled that she was at a "crossroads," a decision point at which she could either continue on the same less-than-satisfying road or jump the to next plateau." When pressed about what happened in the crucible, each of our geeks and geezers explains that he or she has acquired new insights, new skills, new qualities of mind or character that make it possible to function on a new, higher level—to "jump to the next plateau."

In the course of testing, the individual makes choices—to take a chance, to be selfless, to take responsibility, to start something new, to do the right thing. And when the testing is over, he or she emerges convinced that they were the right choices. This sense of having made personal choices that led to growth gives the individual a new, more generous self-perception. Believing that they have been transformed or have transformed themselves, those who survive the crucible are more confident, more willing to take future risks. That new self-confidence is grounded in the belief that he or she has done something hard and done it well.

Don Gevirtz (founder of Foothill Financial Group) spoke about this process in describing his initiation as ambassador to Fiji:

I'd been confirmed by the Senate and I got on the airplane with my wife and we flew out to what was a life-changing experience in Fiji. And also one that was very frightening in many ways. Frightening because the rookie ambassador walked into this place with instructions and approval from the State Department and the NSC to deal with human rights abuses that had occurred there, and in my first press conference, I was critical of the government and the human rights abuses. And I learned there what persona non grata meant. It meant that because the government was so angry at me, their government, that they were thinking of throwing me out of the country before I had a chance to get settled, unpack my bags in the wonderful ambassadorial residence. But eventually, in working closely with the prime minister and members of his cabinet, we were able to draw close together and work well as a team, the prime minister and his people, to build a really major record there. By the time I left, they had passed a new constitution, constitutional reform that I had sought and worked for behind the scenes and out front.

Many of our geeks and geezers had already prepared themselves for their crucibles by contemplating alternative selves. Success is, first of all, an act of imagination. Whatever their age, our leaders realized that they were not limited by the roles they had played in the past or the ways they had been defined by parents, teachers, or others. Our leaders have never been mired in the "now." Many have long been in the habit of dreaming about things they might do, a habit often acquired early in life. Jeff Wilke credits his stepfather with opening his eyes to worlds outside of blue-collar Pittsburgh. Because of his stepfather, Wilke considered schools other than nearby Penn State and careers other than his beloved baseball. Fantasizing about becoming a professional baseball player was Wilke's first step in transcending the givens of family and class (as dreaming of playing pro space football for Legacy Unlimited founder Brian Morris). Wilke's stepfather encouraged him to widen his repertoire of possible futures.

Seeing the World in a New Light

A crucible is a tipping point where new identities are weighed, where values are examined and strengthened or replaced, and where one's judgment and other abilities are honed. It is an incubator for new insights and a new conception of oneself. Often the transformational event in the crucible is a realization that one has the power that affects other people's lives. One of the life-changing lessons of any battlefield—or any medical school, for that matter—is that other people's lives are in your hands. Mike Wallace recalls how, during World War II, he was struck by the realization that American submariners depended for their very lives on his performance as a communications officer. Parenthood is another common crucible that makes one acutely aware of sobering power, responsibility, and interconnection.

While an undergraduate at the University of Michigan, with thoughts of becoming an English teacher, CBS News reported Mike Wallace happened upon the campus radio station and discovered that his distinctive gravelly voice worked well in news reporting. He literally "found his voice" in Ann Arbor, Michigan. But it was Navy duty in World War II that taught him the power of voice.

In the Navy you had a chance to think about yourself and what you wanted to do when you got back . . . and it turned out, the Navy turned out to be a remarkable chance to take a look inside yourself. What is it that you want to be? Mind you, I was still in my twenties. But what do you want to be? You're 26 years old, 27 years old. Only in retrospect do you realize that that's what you were doing. But the Navy game me a chance, gave me a pause to think about it. . . . All of a sudden you were in the position, forced into the position of being in charge, not just of yourself, but in charge of a job. And I was a communications officer. Started as an ensign. Wound up as a JG. But suddenly, I'm playing with strips or the ECM machine and talking to boats, the submarines out on patrol. And god damn it, I'm in charge! I was in a position of genuine responsibility.

The crucible makes the individual see the world in a new light. In the *Harvard Business Review*, civil and human rights activist Eleanor Josaitis recalls "to the exact moment, when my life changed." It was 1962, and she was an affluent housewife, 30 years old, raising five children in an all-white Detroit suburb. That evening, she was watching footage of the Nuremburg trails on TV when the show was interrupted with news of police using dogs, fire hoses, and cattle prods on peaceful civil rights marchers in Selma, Alabama. "I kept asking myself: 'what would I have done if I had lived in Germany during [the Third Reich]? Would I have pretended that I saw nothing?' . . . I also wondered: 'What am I doing about my own country?' I immediately became a strong supporter or Martin Luther King."

Josaitis found, or made, meaning where most others saw only tumult. So profoundly was she changed that she sold her house, moved to an integrated urban neighborhood, and devoted herself to racial justice. She never looked back, even when her mother tried to have her five children taken away from her and she was disowned.

The ability to find meaning and strength in adversity distinguishes leaders from nonleaders. When terrible things happen, less able people feel singled out and powerless. Leaders find purpose and resolve. In the crucible, to paraphrase former British prime minister Margaret Thatcher, iron enters the soul and turns to steel. Vernon Jordan was belittled and, instead of lashing out or being paralyzed with hatred, he saw the fall of the Old South. His ability to organize meaning around a potential crisis turned it into the crucible in which his leadership was forged.

Index

Adaptation to Life (Vaillant), 47, 48
adaptive capacity, 44, 46–48, 49–51
advocacy, 11, 12
African Americans, 46
Aging Well (Vaillant), 47
Altman, Liz, 42
Amabile, Theresa, 49
analysis paralysis, 14
applied creativity, 49–51
Arthur, W. Brian, 10–11
Ashford, Nicholas, 23
AT&T, 26, 28–29
attitude, 39–40

backup plans, 41
Bacow, Lawrence, 23, 24
beliefs and values, 14–15
Bell Atlantic Corp., 28
Birgeneau, Robert, 21
brain candy, 38–39
Brown, Robert, 25, 26

callings, 37
Cantor Fitzgerald, 48
capabilities, leadership, 4, 9–14
career development, 36–41
Carpenter, Russell, 40–41
change, creation of, 8
change signature, 4, 10, 14–16, 19–20
charismatic leader, 8
choice, and crucible experiences, 48–49, 50
Christian, Jeff, 29
Church, Tara, 44–45
Citicorp, 11
civil rights, 46
Coleman, Jack, 48
collective leadership, 10
Compaq, 32–34
complementary capabilities, 14
connecting, in leadership, 11–12
context, sensemaking and, 10
Coriolanus, 44
creativity, 13, 49–51
credo, 14–15, 20
crucible experiences
 adaptive capacity, 44, 46–48, 49–51
 applied creativity, 49–51
 change signatures and, 15
 development model, 44–45
 imposed or sought out, 48–49
 individual factors, 46
 intelligence and, 47
 meaning, creation of, 43–44, 51
 power of, 42–43
 qualities of leadership, 44

daring, 49
Davis, Jane, 11
Dayton, Sky, 49–50
Dertouzos, Michael, 22
de Souza, Leela, 40
Deutch, John, 22
developed self, 19
development, personal, 36–41
developmental nature of leadership, 8–9
development model of leadership, 44–45
Dickerson, J. Maynard, 46
discrimination, gender, 21
Disney, Walt, 44
distributed leadership, 8
diversity, 25
dreams, and money, 37–38
Dynamics of Taking Charge (Gabarro), 12

Ehlers, Vernon, 23
Einstein, Albert, 46
environment, external, 10–11
experiences, transformational, 15

failure, 50
Fiorina, Carleton "Carly," 15, 26–34
Ford Motor Company, 23
framework, leadership, 4, 9–16
framing, and vision, 13
future self, 20

Gabarro, Jack, 12
Gardner, John, 42, 49
"Geeks and Geezers" (Bennis and Thomas), 42–51
Gehry, Frank, 43, 44
gender discrimination, 21
Gevirtz, Don, 50
Gottlieb, Lori, 38
Grant study, 47
Gray, Paul, 21
Grove, Andrew S., 10

Hackborn, Richard, 29
Handford, Bart, 40
hardiness, 44
Harman, Sidney, 49
Hewlett, Walter, 32–33
Hewlett-Packard (HP), 29–34
history, theoretical, 8
Hopkins, Nancy, 21
Huxley, Aldous, 47

individual factors, 46
innovation, 13
inquiry, 11, 12

intelligence, 47
interpersonal relationships, 11
inventing, 9, 13–14

jobs, 36–41
Jobs, Steve, 12
Johnson, Lyndon B., 10, 15
Jones, Nathaniel R., 45–46
Jordan, Vernon E., 43, 51
Josaitis, Eleanor, 51

Kao, Elizabeth, 43, 47, 50
Keighley, Geoff, 42
Kelly, Dave, 10, 13
key leadership capabilities, 4, 9–14
Khoury, Philip, 22, 25
King, Martin Luther, Jr., 10, 13
Klein, Michael, 43
Krimsky, Sheldon, 23
Krueger, Scott, 24–25
Kurlander, Carl, 39

leadership
    overview, 4–5
    capabilities, key, 4, 9–14
    as change-creating process, 8
    change signature, 4, 10, 14–16, 19–20
    collective, 10
    crucible experiences and, 42–51
    development model, 44–45
    development of, 8–9
    as distributed, 8
    Fiorina case, 26–34
    framework for, 4, 9–16
    individual factors, 46
    inventing, 13–14
    meaning of, 8
    as personal, 8
    qualities of, 44
    relating, 9, 11–12
    sensemaking, 9, 10–11, 13
    theoretical history, 8
    traits of, 46
    transformational leader, 8
    Vest case, 21–26
    visioning, 4, 12–13, 30
Levitt, Arthur, Jr., 48
Linn, Don, 39
Lucent Technologies, 26, 28–29, 33
Lutnick, Howard W., 48

Maddox, Robert F., 43
Mandela, Nelson, 43
mapping, 10
McGovern, Gail, 13
meaning, 12, 43–44, 51
mentor-protégé relationships, 43, 50
merger, HP-Compaq, 32–34
metaphors, 12–13

MIT (Massachusetts Institute of Technology), 21–26
money, and dreams, 37–38

NASA, 40
neoteny, 44
Network Systems group, 28
new organization model, 4

Olchefske, Joe, 38
optimism, 44

past self, 19
personal development, 36–41
personal leadership, 8
place, and value systems, 39
plans, backup, 41
Poincaré, Jules-Henri, 46
Porter, Bill, 49, 50
power brokering, 15

qualities of leadership, 44
the Question, 36–41

recklessness, 49
Reed, John, 11
relating, 9, 11–12
relationships, interpersonal, 11
research funding, 22–23
Rittenberg, Sidney, 42, 44, 48

Schoendorf, Joe, 29
self, change signature and, 19–20
sensemaking, 9, 10–11, 13
September 11, 2001, terrorist attacks, 48
Shakespeare, William, 44, 49
shared visions, 12
Sharp, Phillip A., 21–22
Shin, Young, 50
Siebert, Muriel, 42
Stanford, John, 38
Stanzione, Daniel, 28
stories, vision and, 12–13

teams, 10
tensions, 14
terrorism, 48
Thatcher, Margaret, 51
theoretical history of leadership, 8
time frame, 40
traits of leadership, 46
transformation, model of, 45
transformational experiences, 15, 42. *See also* crucible experiences
transformational leader, 8

uncontaminated wonder, 44
underdeveloped self, 20

Vaillant, George, 47, 48
values, 14–15
value systems, 39
Vest, Charles "Chuck," 15, 21–26
visioning, 4, 9, 12–13, 30

Wallace, Mike, 42, 51
Wayman, Robert, 30
Welch, John F., Jr. (Jack), 15, 50
"What Should I Do With My Life?" (Bronson), 36–41

Widrig, Marcela, 41
Wilke, Jeff, 51
Williams, Rosalind, 25
women, at MIT, 21
wonder, uncontaminated, 44
work, meaningful, 36–41
World Trade Center, 48
World War II, 42, 51

youthful qualities, 44

Index

ABC Television, 10-8
abortion. *See* RU-486 case
Accenture, 5-16–5-17
access-and-legitimacy paradigm, 11-24, 11-35–11-36
Access Capital International case, 11-35–11-36
accountability, joint, 3-10
accounting treatment differences, in negotiations, 12-33–12-34
Acme Minerals Extraction Co. case, 8-22–8-25
"Action Company" paradigm, 2-71, 2-73
action steps, in organizational analysis, 2-84
adaptability, 13-24–13-25, 13-27
adaptation tasks, external, 2-72
Adaptation to Life (Vaillant), 14-47, 14-48
adaptive capacity, 14-44, 14-46–14-48, 14-49–14-51
"Addressing the Crisis in Confidence in Corporations" (Kochan), 7-58–7-61
advance factor endowments, 1-16
advertising, 10-38
advice networks, 2-40, 2-47–2-52
advocacy, in leadership, 14-11, 14-12
advocacy groups, 7-55, 9-25–9-26, 11-15–11-16
affective conflict, 5-13
affirmative action, 11-13, 11-14. *See also* diversity
African Americans. *See also* diversity
    caucus groups, 2-35, 11-12, 11-15, 11-16
    civil rights movement, 11-13, 14-46
    corporate advancement, 11-14
agenda, strategic, 13-6
agenda management, 12-28
agents, 12-8
Aging Well (Vaillant), 14-47
agreements, contingent, 12-23, 12-28–12-30
Aldrich, Howard, 8-6
alignment, 2-14, 2-15, 2-23–2-25, 2-26, 9-11
Allaire, Paul, 1-31, 1-37
alliances, inter-company, 1-13, 1-18–1-19
allies, 2-43–2-44, 12-37–12-38, 13-8, 13-9–13-10
Allina, 5-23–5-24
Altman, Liz, 14-42
Amabile, Theresa, 14-49
ambassadorial activities of teams, 6-8, 6-9, 6-10, 6-24
"The American Corporation as an Employer" (Kochan), 1-23
American Psychological Association (APA), 4-29
America Online (AOL), 8-7, 12-28
analysis, organizational, 2-8, 2-11. *See also* organizational analysis and action, lenses on
analysis paralysis, 14-14
analytical descriptive research, 2-68–2-69

analytic reasoning, 4-18
animation, 10-12, 10-52
antihormones, 9-23
anxiety, 2-25, 7-15, 7-19
AOL (America Online), 12-28
AOL-Time Warner, 8-7
APA (American Psychological Association), 4-29
appeals, inspirational, 5-12
appeals, personal, 5-12
appearance standards, at Disneyland, 10-14, 10-18, 10-37
Appelbaum, Eileen, 5-21
applied creativity, 14-49–14-51
Applied Materials, 7-37
appreciative moves, 12-17, 12-39, 12-40–12-42
apprentice system, 7-20
approaches to issue selling, 13-8, 13-10
approvals, in RAMMP matrix, 8-39
Ardai, Charles, 1-44–1-45
Arthur, W. Brian, 14-10–14-11
artifacts, 2-70
Ashford, Nicholas, 14-23
Asia, 1-10, 9-24–9-25, 9-30. *See also* China; Japan
Asian Americans, 11-14
Asian financial crisis, 10-46
assets, human. *See* human assets
assimilation, in diversity management, 11-34, 11-37
assisted negotiation, 12-17–12-19
Association for Conscientious Objectors to all Participation in Abortion, 9-25, 9-26
associations, and professionalism, 7-28
assumptions, 2-70–2-71, 2-73, 2-78
Aston, Wynn III, 6-11–6-12, 6-14
Aston-Blair case study, 6-11–6-17
atmosphere, in teams, 5-13–5-14
AT&T, 14-26, 14-28–14-29
attitude, 14-39–14-40
authority, 1-12, 1-37, 2-36, 2-38
automobile industry. *See* Nissan
avoidance, 12-8
awareness, situational, 11-21

backup plans, 14-41
Bacon, Michael, 6-11–6-17
Bacow, Lawrence, 14-23, 14-24
Bailyn, Lotte, 7-19
Banbury, Catherine, 13-26
banking, 1-42, 5-20–5-21
bargaining. *See* negotiation and conflict resolution
bargaining power, 12-13–12-14
Barnard, Chester, 7-26
Barney, Jay, 13-23

BATNA (best alternative to a negotiated agreement), 12-13, 12-14
Bauer, Victor, 9-30
Baugh, Robert, 5-23
Baulieu, Etienne-Emile, 9-23, 9-28, 9-29, 9-32
Bayamón, Puerto Rico, 1-32, 1-34
Beckhard, Richard, 8-12–8-13
Begun, Shelly, 7-39
behavioral science, 2-4, 8-12
beliefs and values. *See* values
Bell Atlantic Corp., 14-28
benefits, 2-35, 7-60, 11-12
Bernard, Jean, 9-24
best alternative to a negotiated agreement (BATNA), 12-13, 12-14
best practices, 8-40–8-41, 8-42
"Beyond the Hype" (Eccles and Nohria), 1-24
Bezos, Jeff, 1-44
bias, incompatibility, 12-24
Big Mac, as symbol, 2-58
Birgeneau, Robert, 14-21
black marketing, 9-27, 9-30
blame, culture of, 8-8
blockers and supporters, mapping, 2-42, 2-43
boards of directors, 7-60
Bodin, Emile, 6-12–6-17
body language, and bystanders, 11-23
Boeing, 5-20–5-21
bonding process, 7-35
Bossidy, Lawrence, 1-31, 1-32, 1-36, 1-37, 8-42
Boston Globe, 4-33–4-34
bottom-up change, 8-16, 8-17
boundaries
    in bureaucratic model, 1-12
    collective interests and, 2-34
    flat organizations and, 1-19
    permeability of, 1-13
    workforce management issues, 7-7
boundary management, by teams
    overview, 3-14, 6-4–6-5
    activities and processes of, 3-14, 6-8–6-10
    Aston-Blair case study, 6-11–6-17
    importance of, 6-4, 6-8, 6-9, 6-10
    rules of the game, 6-10
    styles of, 6-8–6-9
    task force management tips, 6-17–6-19
    X-teams, 6-22–6-29
boundary-spanners, 1-12, 1-13, 9-9, 13-26
bounded rationality, 2-65
Bourguignon, Philippe, 10-37
Bower, Joseph, 13-27
"bow ties," 2-54
boycotts, and RU-486 case, 9-25, 9-26
brain candy, 14-38–14-39
brain dominance, left and right, 4-22, 4-31–4-32
brands, American, 10-54–10-55
Brannen, Mary Yoki, 10-32
break schedules, 10-16

"Breakthrough Bargaining" (Kolb and Williams), 12-36–12-42
Bridgestone, 9-21
bridging, 12-16
Briggs, Katheryn, 4-4
British Petroleum (BP), 7-34–7-35
Brookhouse, Robert, 1-31, 1-35
Brower, Tim, 7-44–7-45, 7-46, 7-50
Brown, Janet, 13-15, 13-17, 13-18, 13-19
Brown, Robert, 14-25, 14-26
Browne, John, 7-34
Bryan, Lowell, 1-40, 1-42
Buck Breast Care Center, 5-16, 5-17
budgeting, of capital vs. talent, 7-32
Buehler, William, 1-31, 1-34
"Building Competitive Advantage Through People" (Bartell and Ghoshal), 7-29–7-36
bundling of issues, 13-8–13-9
bureaucracy. *See* old (bureaucratic) model
Burns, Jed, 6-12–6-17
Burt, Ron, 2-40
Bush, George, 9-31
business division structure, 2-17–2-18
business frame, 13-9
business/functional matrix, 2-19
business press, 1-6–1-7, 1-10, 1-30–1-31
business process reengineering (BPR), 1-30, 2-15. *See also* reengineering
business schools, 1-11
business units (BUs), 2-85–2-86
business unit solos, 2-18
"buy-in," getting, 2-42–2-43
buzzwords, 7-12
bystander awareness and skills
    overview, 11-16–11-17
    backlash, 11-21
    cultural variation and, 11-22–11-23
    definition of bystander, 11-6
    inaction, reasons for, 11-21
    nature of the bystander, 11-21, 11-22
    risks and benefits, 11-21–11-22
    scenarios, 11-25–11-29
    structural support for, 11-23–11-24
    tactics, 11-23
    value of, 11-20–11-21

Calico Commerce, 7-38–7-41
callings, 14-37
Camara, Wayne, 4-29
Cantor Fitzgerald, 14-48
capabilities
    complementary, 12-27, 14-14
    core, 1-24, 13-23, 13-25–13-26, 13-27
    dynamic, 13-23–13-24
    investment, 12-34
    leadership, 14-4, 14-9–14-14
    learning, 8-30–8-31
capital, 7-30, 7-32

capital, human. *See* human assets
capital, intellectual. *See* intellectual capital and talent
capital, social, 6-9
capital gains, 12-33
Cappelli, Peter, 7-14
career development. *See also* development of human capital
    flexibility and, 7-18
    generalized skills, 7-27, 7-28
    meaningful work, 14-36–14-41
    personality type and, 4-24–4-25
    success, conception of, 7-7
Carpenter, Russell, 14-40–14-41
Casey, Peter, 6-11–6-17
cast members, at Disneyland, 10-10, 10-28, 10-32
Catholic Church, 9-25, 9-28
caucus groups, 2-35, 11-12, 11-15, 11-16
Cemex, 1-43–1-44
Center for Effective Organization (USC), 5-21
centrality, and network position, 2-38–2-39
Centra Software, 5-16, 5-19
CEOs, 1-23–1-24, 7-59, 8-32–8-33. *See also* executives; leadership
chain of command, 1-12
chain stores, 1-25
Chambers, John T., 1-42, 1-44
championing of strategic alternatives, 13-24, 13-27
Champy, James, 1-31, 1-36, 1-37
change. *See also* innovation; new organization model
    overview, 8-4
    Acme Minerals Extraction Co. case, 8-22–8-25
    action steps, 8-18–8-19, 8-20
    advice on, 8-20–8-21
    communication about, 8-19–8-20
    compensation systems, 7-16
    compliance vs. commitment, 8-33
    consistency of, 8-18
    cultural evolution, 2-76–2-78
    cultural perspective, 8-7–8-8, 8-11, 8-19
    dimensions of, 8-15–8-18
    GE productivity case, 8-38–8-42
    inertia, organizational, 8-4, 8-6, 8-12, 8-13
    issue selling and, 13-4
    leadership and, 8-32–8-37, 14-8
    learning new roles, 8-10
    limiting processes, 8-29–8-31
    localization of, 8-18
    meaning of, 8-7, 8-34–8-35
    middle managers and, 13-25
    mistakes, avoiding, 8-19–8-20
    multidimensional jobs and, 7-16
    pacing of, 8-15
    policy changes, effecting, 7-7, 7-16, 7-51–7-52
    political perspective, 8-7, 8-10–8-11
    power and, 8-11
    pressures to, 8-6
    processes of, 8-16
    Proctor & Gamble case, 8-8–8-11, 8-16, 8-17
    profound, 8-34–8-35
    resistance to, 8-4, 8-6, 8-8, 8-12, 8-34
    Rosewell case, 8-18
    in schemas, 2-9
    scope of, 8-15
    sources of, 8-16
    stage models of, 8-11–8-15
    strategic design perspective, 8-7, 8-10–8-11, 8-18, 8-19
    success and failure of initiatives, 8-6, 8-28–8-29
    temporal sequencing of, 8-17–8-18, 8-20
    unanticipated consequences, 8-6–8-7, 8-10
Change Acceleration Process (CAP), 8-41–8-42
change signature, 14-4, 14-10, 14-14–14-16, 14-19–14-20
"The Changing Social Contract for White-Collar Workers" (Heckscher), 7-25–7-28
Chapin, Mark, 12-40
characteristics of negotiators, 12-9–12-10
charged issues, 13-10–13-11
charisma, 2-36–2-37
charismatic leader, 14-8
chief executive officers (CEOs), 1-23–1-24, 7-59, 8-32–8-33. *See also* executives; leadership
chief operating officer (COO), 3-11–3-12
childcare, 7-54, 7-57
children, 10-27, 10-46
China
    Hong Kong Disneyland, 10-45–10-49, 10-50–10-55
    political factors in, 10-46
    RU-486 and, 9-24–9-25, 9-30
    television in, 10-51, 10-53–10-54
China Central Television, 10-53–10-54
Chirac, Jacques, 10-35
choice, and crucible experiences, 14-48–14-49, 14-50
choice processes, in issue selling, 13-7–13-8
Christian, Jeff, 14-29
Church, Tara, 14-44–14-45
Cinderella's Castle, 10-30
Cisco Systems, 1-44, 7-37
Citicorp, 14-11
civil rights, 7-55, 11-13, 14-46. *See also* diversity
clarifying function, in teams, 5-10
class, and diversity, 11-39
classic model of formal organization, 1-11–1-12
Clearly, Michael J., 1-43
cleavage model of organizational culture, 2-62
climate, organizational, 2-68
clinical descriptive research, 2-69

Clinton, Bill, 9-31
coaching, 7-33
coalitions
    of allies, 2-43–2-44
    in change initiatives, 8-20
    dominant, 2-44
    network position and, 2-39–2-40
    in stakeholder model, 9-13
    as tactic for influence, 5-12
    in team dynamics, 5-11
    work-family integration, 7-57
"Coda to the New Organization" (Van Maanen), 1-24–1-25
codes of conduct, 10-19–10-21, 10-37
coercion as power, 2-36, 2-38
coercive isomorphism, 9-19
coercive theories, 2-60
cognitive processing, 2-8–2-9
cognitive style
    overview, 4-4
    brain dominance, left and right, 4-22, 4-31–4-32
    career development and, 4-24–4-25
    change, approaches to, 4-23–4-24
    composite types (Myers-Briggs), 4-20–4-21
    creativity and innovation and, 4-24
    decision-making style (thinking/feeling), 4-15, 4-18–4-19
    definition of, 4-4, 4-11
    hiring and promotion based on, 4-12, 4-30–4-31, 4-34
    homogeneity and cognitive diversity, 4-12–4-13
    honesty tests, 4-33–4-34
    information generation style (sensing/intuition), 4-15, 4-17–4-18
    Jungian approach, advantages of, 4-11–4-12
    learning styles and schools, 4-32–4-33
    management and, 4-13–4-15, 4-21–4-25
    Minnesota Multi-Phasic Inventory (MMPI), 4-29–4-30
    organizational issues, 4-11
    organizational structure and, 4-22–4-23
    popularity of, 4-28–4-29, 4-30
    Predictive Index, 4-29, 4-31
    priorities style (perceiving/judging), 4-15, 4-19–4-20
    problems with approach, 4-12, 4-29–4-31
    relationship style (extrovert/introvert), 4-15, 4-16–4-17
    self-assessment test, 4-6–4-9, 4-11
    shadow type, 4-24–4-25
    universities and, 4-34
Coleman, Jack, 14-48
collaboration, electronic, 3-12, 5-16–5-21
collaborative relationships, 7-7, 12-17. *See also* teams
collective bargaining, 12-10

collective interests, 2-34–2-35
collectivist vs. individualistic cultures, 3-12
college degree requirements, 11-38
Collier, Andrew, 10-54
collusion, and bystander awareness, 11-22
"The Coming of the New Organization (Drucker), 1-22
command-and-control system, 1-12
commitment. *See* loyalty and commitment
commitment, escalation of, 2-42
commitment chart, 2-42, 2-43
communication
    change initiatives and, 8-19–8-20
    cross-cultural, 1-20
    group patterns, 5-11–5-12
    manipulative and controlling, 5-14
    in negotiations, 12-12, 12-15, 12-41–12-42
    reduced costs of, 1-16
    strategic, and middle management, 13-28
    telecommunications technologies, 1-13–1-14
communication networks, 2-47, 2-48, 2-52–2-55
Communications Workers of America, 5-23
community builders, 8-36
community empowerment, 7-58
community groups, 7-55, 7-57
Compaq, 14-32–14-34
"The Comparative Advantage of X-Teams" (Ancona, Bresman, and Kaeufer), 6-22–6-29
compensation. *See also* incentives and rewards
    benefits, 7-60, 11-12
    bonding process and, 7-35
    boundary crossing and, 7-16
    executive, 7-59
    nonspecific, 12-15
    part-time partners and, 7-48, 7-52
    restructuring, and loss of living wage, 7-13
    Silicon Valley practices, 7-37
    teams and, 7-16
    wage inequities, 1-11, 7-13, 7-54
competencies, barriers to, 11-40–11-41
competency-based strategies, 7-29, 7-30
competition
    flat organization and, 1-14
    flexibility and, 1-15
    for human capital, 7-14, 7-29, 7-30, 7-35, 7-36, 7-51
    international, 1-13
    networking and, 1-14
    restructuring and, 7-14
competitive advantage, 2-14, 13-23–13-24, 13-27
competitive-strategy model, 7-29, 7-30, 7-36
competitors, in strategic design perspective, 9-9
complementary capabilities, 12-27, 14-14
complexity, and issue selling, 13-6
complexity of tasks, 2-14
compliance vs. commitment, 8-33, 8-38
comprehensive strategy, in boundary management, 6-9

compromising function, in teams, 5-10
CompuServe, 12-28
concessions, 12-14–12-15
conciliator-style negotiators, 12-9
condescension, 5-14
Condit, Philip, 5-20, 5-21, 5-23
conduct, codes of, 10-19–10-21, 10-37
Confederation of Associations of Catholic Families, 9-28-9-29
confidence, corporate, 7-6, 7-58–7-61, 10-40–10-41
conflict management. *See* negotiation and conflict resolution
congeneration plant contingent agreement, 12-28–12-29
congruence, 2-23
connecting, in leadership, 14-11–14-12
connotative meanings, 2-57
consensus-building, 5-9, 12-40
consensus testing, 5-10
consequences, observation of, 2-41
consistency of change, 8-18
consultation as influence tactic, 5-12
consulting firms, 1-25–1-26, 5-20
context. *See also* environment, external
    of interests, in negotiation, 12-12
    in issue selling, 13-7–13-8
    sensemaking and, 14-10
    of teams, 3-14, 5-8
contingent agreements, 12-23, 12-28–12-30
continuous change, 8-14, 8-15
contracts, psychological, 13-29. *See also* social contracts
contract workers, 7-14, 7-19, 7-35, 7-36–7-37
contribution plans, defined, 2-35
COO (chief operating officer), 3-11–3-12
cooperative family programs, 7-57
cooperative networks, 1-13
co-optation, 9-13
coordination mechanisms, in X-teams, 6-25–6-26
core capability, 1-24, 13-23, 13-25–13-26, 13-27
core-competency strategy, 7-29, 7-30
core members, of X-teams, 6-25
core process redesign, 1-35
core values and preferences, 4-14–4-15
Coriolanus, 14-44
Cornelius, Russell, 6-12–6-17
corporate confidence, 7-6, 7-58–7-61, 10-40–10-41
corporate domination, 7-26
Corporate Initiatives Group (GE), 8-42
cost cutting, 12-15–12-16
cost/revenue structure, 12-26–12-27
councils, work and family, 7-57, 7-58
Cox, Taylor, 11-10
Crandall, Lee, 13-18, 13-19
creation of culture, 2-75
creative individualism, 2-76

creativity. *See also* innovation
    adaptive capacity and, 14-49–14-51
    barriers to, in negotiations, 12-16
    inventing by leaders and, 14-13
    personality type and, 4-24
credo, 14-14–14-15, 14-20
critical incidents, 2-75
criticism, in teams, 5-14
cross-border cultural learning, 10-27, 10-38–10-39, 10-49
cross-border integration, 1-20
cross-cultural communication, 1-20
cross-functional teams, 2-31, 2-85–2-86, 3-11, 8-23–8-24
cross-marketing and synergies, by Disney, 10-8–10-9, 10-12, 10-52, 10-53–10-54
cross-training, 7-15
cross-unit groups, 2-22–2-23
Crozier, Michel, 2-37
crucible experiences
    adaptive capacity, 14-44, 14-46–14-48, 14-49–14-51
    applied creativity, 14-49–14-51
    development model, 14-44–14-45
    imposed or sought out, 14-48–14-49
    individual factors, 14-46
    intelligence and, 14-47
    meaning, creation of, 14-43–14-44, 14-51
    power of, 14-15, 14-42–14-43
    qualities of leadership, 14-44
Crum, R. Clayton, 1-34
culling of human resources, 7-33
cultural background, work perspectives and, 11-36–11-42
cultural differentiation, 2-77, 10-32
cultural diversity. *See* diversity
cultural dynamics, 2-75–2-78
cultural flow, 10-26–10-27, 10-28, 10-32–10-33
cultural imperialism, 10-27, 10-47, 10-50–10-51
cultural island, 2-68
cultural learning, cross-border, 10-27, 10-38–10-39, 10-49
cultural lens/perspective. *See also* organizational culture
    overview, 2-4, 2-11, 2-57
    on change, 2-76–2-78, 8-7–8-8, 8-11, 8-19
    definition of culture, 2-58–2-59
    diagnosis of organizations, 2-64–2-66
    on Disneyland, 10-4–10-5
    on diversity, 11-15
    external cultural context, 2-63–2-64
    on external environment, 9-4, 9-17–9-21, 9-22
    habits and history, 2-65
    identity and, 2-63, 2-64–2-65
    motivation and control, 2-60–2-61, 2-65
    "new" organization and, 2-66
    processes and products, cultural, 2-58–2-59

relativity, cultural, 2-65
structure and culture, 2-59
subcultures, 2-61–2-63, 2-65, 2-70, 2-77 (*See also* subcultures at Disneyland)
symbolism and meaning, 2-57–2-58, 2-64, 10-28, 10-32, 10-46
on team boundary management, 6-10
on workforce management, 7-6
culture, learning, 6-28–6-29
culture, organizational. *See* organizational culture
culture, popular, 10-47–10-48, 10-53. *See also* Disneyland
culture, youth, 10-17
cultures, individualistic vs. collectivist, 3-12
cultures, national, 2-63–2-64, 3-12, 9-19, 12-9. *See also* global and international business
cultures, worker. *See* subcultures and segmentation; subcultures at Disneyland
"currencies," and network construction, 2-44–2-45
custodial orientation, 2-76
customer division structure, 2-18–2-19, 2-32
customer loyalty, 7-38
customer needs
　at Disneyland, 10-20, 10-28–10-33
　flexibility and, 1-15, 1-19
　management by Web and, 1-41, 1-43
　in process management, 1-37
　worker self-management and, 1-32
customer productivity programs, 8-42
customization, mass, 1-41

The Dance of Change (Senge), 8-14
Daniels, Arnold, 4-29, 4-31
Daniels, Bill, 8-22–8-25
daring, 14-49
data gathering, and change, 8-12
dating among employees at Disney, 10-16–10-17
Davidson, Maury, 7-44–7-47
Davidson Interiors, 5-24
Davis, Chris, 13-17
Davis, Jane, 14-11
Dayton, Sky, 14-49–14-50
"Dealcrafting: The Substance of Three-Dimensional Negotiations" (Lax and Sebenius), 12-22–12-35
dealcrafting and dealmaking. *See also* negotiation and conflict resolution
　accounting treatment and sensitivity differences, 12-33–12-34
　agenda management, 12-28
　bargaining power, 12-13–12-14
　capability differences, 12-27
　cogeneration plant example, 12-28–12-29
　contingent agreements, 12-23, 12-29–12-30
　cost/revenue structure differences, 12-26–12-27
　defined, 12-22

　differences principle, 12-26
　distributive vs. integrative negotiations, 12-14–12-16
　earnouts, 12-29
　forecast differences, 12-28–12-30, 12-34
　interests and, 12-11–12-12, 12-27–12-28
　issues and, 12-10
　Lakeside-Tonicron joint venture example, 12-24–12-26, 12-26–12-27
　maximum total value vs. individual results, 12-24–12-26
　parties to negotiations, 12-8–12-10
　process of, 12-8, 12-14–12-16
　risk attitude differences, 12-30–12-32, 12-34
　tax status differences, 12-33, 12-34
　third parties, bringing in, 12-28, 12-32
　three-dimensional perspective, 12-22–12-24
　time preference differences, 12-32–12-33, 12-34
　variety and combination of differences, 12-34
　virtual sales, 5-17, 5-21
debt-equity ratio, 12-33–12-34
decision community software, 5-18
decision making
　flat structure and, 1-14
　personality and, 4-15, 4-18–4-19, 4-22, 4-34
　team process, 5-9–5-11
　transparent, in X-teams, 6-26
　values and, 4-19
decision rules, in teams, 6-26–6-27
defensive environments, in teams, 5-14
defined benefits vs. defined contribution plans, 2-35
Delage, Michel, 9-27
delayering, 13-22–13-23, 13-27, 13-29
delivery systems, 1-13, 1-43–1-44
Dell, Michael, 1-42
Dell Computer, 1-43
de Lorenzo, Francesco, 9-30
Delta Manufacturing case, 11-41
demeanor, standards of, 10-17, 10-48
Deming, W. Edward, 3-11
demographic diversity, 1-15, 7-17, 11-10, 11-19
demographic groups, and collective interests, 2-35
denotative meanings, 2-57
departments, and process reengineering, 1-34, 1-35–1-37
departments, boundaries between, 1-12, 1-13, 1-19. *See also* boundary management, by teams
dependency and counterdependence, 5-14
Dertouzos, Michael, 14-22
description, clear, 5-14
design, and team demographics, 11-12
design, strategic. *See* strategic design lens/perspective

"Designing Effective Organizations" (Goold and Campbell), 1-23
design of teams, 3-14
de Souza, Leela, 14-40
Deutch, John, 14-22
Devanna, Mary Anne, 8-13
developed self, 14-19
development, land. *See* property development, Disney
development, organizational (OD), 8-12
development, personal, 14-36–14-41
developmental nature of leadership, 14-8–14-19
development model of leadership, 14-44–14-45
development of human capital, 2-25, 7-32–7-33
Devine, Rob, 7-39
Dewey & Levin case, 11-37
Dickerson, J. Maynard, 14-46
differences, value in negotiations, 12-26–12-28
differentiation (strategic linking), 2-14
differentiation, cultural, 2-77, 10-32
differentiation, in diversity management, 11-37
difficult linkages, 2-23
Digital Equipment Corporation, 2-34
digitization, 1-42
dilemma, negotiator's, 12-12, 12-16
"Dinosaurs or Dynamos? Recognizing Middle Management's Strategic Role" (Floyd and Wooldridge), 13-22–13-29
dirty tricks in negotiations, 12-17
discovery, as bystander tactic, 11-23
discrimination. *See also* diversity
    affirmative action and equal opportunity, 11-13–11-14
    dominance and subordination, 11-40–11-41
    gender, 14-21
    personality tests and, 4-12, 4-30
    remaining challenges, 11-14
    work-family integration and, 7-55
discrimination-and-fairness paradigm, 11-24, 11-33–11-35
discussion, open, 11-40
Disney, as brand, 10-54–10-55
Disney, Roy, 10-12
Disney, Walt, 10-8, 10-9, 10-18, 10-51, 14-44
Disneyland
    overview, 10-4–10-5
    American theme, 10-4, 10-9, 10-26, 10-32, 10-33
    appearance standards, 10-14, 10-18, 10-37
    attendance, 10-25, 10-28, 10-36, 10-38, 10-42–10-43
    California park, 10-8–10-10
    conduct codes, formal and informal, 10-19–10-21, 10-37
    contrasts, 10-9–10-10, 10-29–10-30
    control of environment, 10-10
    corporate culture, 2-61, 10-4–10-5, 10-17, 10-21
    corporate operations, 10-51–10-52
    emotional management, 10-14, 10-22
    environmental issues, 10-48
    Euro Disney/Disneyland Paris, 10-35–10-39, 10-39–10-45
    financing, 10-35, 10-40–10-41, 10-45, 10-53
    firings, 10-19
    Florida development, 10-10–10-13
    guest misconduct, 10-20–10-21, 10-23
    "happiest place on earth," 10-9–10-10, 10-14, 10-36
    happiness and orderliness, 10-4, 10-9–10-10, 10-14, 10-29
    history and origins, 10-8–10-9
    Hong Kong, 10-45–10-49, 10-50–10-55
    hotel occupancy, 10-25, 10-37, 10-38, 10-43
    image problem, 10-40–10-41
    internationalization of, 10-4, 10-5
    language, control of, 10-17
    layout of park, 10-31
    lines, 10-10
    local opposition, 10-36–10-38, 10-45, 10-47, 10-48
    management of, 10-10, 10-12, 10-41
    overconfidence, 10-41
    personnel, categories of, 10-10
    pricing policies, 10-37, 10-38, 10-43
    as product, 10-9
    property development, 10-10–10-12, 10-25, 10-28, 10-35–10-36, 10-41–10-42, 10-45, 10-48
    public expectations, 10-20
    revenues, 10-12, 10-52
    screening of employees, 10-14
    security, 10-15, 10-21
    status ranking, employee, 10-15–10-16
    success of, 10-4, 10-27, 10-36–10-38
    supervisory practices, 10-19–10-20, 10-22
    synergies and cross-marketing, 10-8–10-9, 10-12, 10-52, 10-53–10-54
    Tokyo, 10-25–10-26, 10-27, 10-28–10-33, 10-52
    University of Disneyland and Disney University, 10-17–10-18, 10-36–10-37
    values emphasized at, 10-18
    worker subcultures, 10-13–10-23
Disney Sea (Japan), 10-52
Disney University, 10-36–10-37
Disney World (Florida), 10-10–10-13
"Displacing Disney: Some Notes on the Flow of Culture" (Van Maanen), 10-28–10-33
distancing mechanisms, 9-9
distinctive competitive advantage, 2-14
distributed leadership, 14-8
distributive negotiations, 12-14–12-15
diversity. *See also* bystander awareness and skills
    overview, 11-6–11-7

access-and-legitimacy paradigm, 11-24, 11-35–11-36
Access Capital International case, 11-35–11-36
backlash, 11-20
business case for, 11-11
celebrations of, 11-24, 11-35
cognitive, 4-12–4-13
in corporate ranks, 11-14
cultural differentiation, 10-32
cultural diversity, defined, 11-10
definition and meaning of, 11-10
Delta Manufacturing case, 11-41
demographic, 1-15, 7-17
Dewey & Levin case, 11-37
discrimination-and-fairness paradigm, 11-24, 11-33–11-35
Disneyland, minorities at, 10-14
elements of corporate programs, 11-14–11-15
First Interstate Bank case, 11-38–11-39
grassroots employee advocacy programs, 11-15–11-16
historical and policy context, 11-13–11-14
Iversen Dunham case, 11-34–11-35, 11-39
of labor force, 1-15
leadership commitment, 11-15
learning and, 11-12, 11-38
learning-and-effectiveness (work perspectives) paradigm, 11-24, 11-32–11-33, 11-36–11-37, 11-39–11-42
management implications, 1-19–1-20
Mastiff case, 11-39–11-40, 11-41
at MIT, 14-25
negotiations, value of differences in, 12-26–12-28
in new organization model, 1-15
organizational effectiveness and, 11-32, 11-33
organizational processes and, 11-17, 11-18
paradigm shift, 11-37–11-39
performance, effects on, 11-17
policy issues, 11-23–11-24
political perspective on, 11-14–11-15
societal, organizational, and managerial levels, 11-11, 11-13
strategic design, political, and cultural perspectives on, 11-14–11-15
structural solutions, 11-23–11-24
Torinno Food Company case, 11-40
training, 11-20
"valuing," 11-14, 11-20
work-family integration and, 7-17
workforce demographics, 1-15, 7-17, 11-10, 11-19
workforce management issues, 7-8
Diversity Council, 11-15
Diversity Research Network, 11-17

DMAIC (Define, Measure, Analyze, Improve, Control), 8-42
Dobier, Jack, 5-24
doctors, in virtual teams, 5-16, 5-17–5-18
dogmatism, in teams, 5-14
domestication, 10-29
domestic partner benefits, 11-12
dominance and subordination, 11-40–11-41
dominant coalition, 2-44
domination, corporate, 7-26
"dose of reality" process, 12-18
dot.com bubble, 7-13
dotted line hierarchical structure, 2-22
downsizing. *See* restructuring and downsizing
Draper Laboratory, 4-28
dreams, and money, 14-37–14-38
dress code, at Disneyland, 10-15, 10-18, 10-37
Driver, John, 7-40
Drucker, Peter, 1-31, 1-32, 4-13
dual agenda, 7-19
dual career ladder, 2-29
Duclos, Nancy, 4-32–4-33
Dynacorp case, 2-28–2-32, 2-85–2-90
dynamic capability, 13-23–13-24
dynamics, cultural, 2-75–2-78
Dynamics of Taking Charge (Gabarro), 14-12

earnouts, 12-29
Eban, Abba, 12-37
economic forecasting, 6-12, 6-15
"economic man," 2-34
economies of scope, 2-16
"ecosystem" of suppliers, partners, and contractors, 1-44–1-45
effectiveness. *See also* performance
diversity and, 11-32, 11-33
strategic design and, 2-14
of teams, 3-13–3-15, 5-8, 6-4, 6-9
efficiency, and strategic design perspective, 2-14
efficient networks, 2-39
ego, submersion of, 2-37
egocentrism, in negotiators, 12-14
Ehlers, Vernon, 14-23
Einstein, Albert, 14-46
Eisner, Michael, 10-12, 10-35, 10-38, 10-41, 10-42, 10-51
elaborating function, in teams, 5-10
electronic collaboration, 3-12, 5-16–5-21
Elkind, Manny, 4-31–4-32
emergent change, 8-16, 8-17
emotional issues in teams, 5-14
emotional management, at Disneyland, 10-14
empathy, 1-19–1-20, 5-14
employability, lifetime, 7-15
employees. *See also* human assets; subcultures at Disneyland; workforce management
as assets vs. costs, 7-16, 7-21
corporate scandals and, 7-59–7-60

exploitation, feelings of, 11-36
gay, lesbian, bisexual, and transgendered, 11-12
hours of work, 7-18, 7-36, 7-37, 7-57, 7-58
"ideal worker," 7-54, 7-55
labor reforms and, 7-60
loyalty, and psychological contracts, 13-29
making feel valued, 11-38
multi-skilled, 7-15–7-16
screening of, 10-14
as stakeholders, 9-13
as talent investors, 7-32
virtual, 7-19
employment, lifelong, 7-8, 7-14, 7-15
employment relationship. *See also* workforce management
alternatives, 7-20
changes in, 7-12–7-13
definition of, 7-6, 7-12
flexibility and, 7-12, 7-17–7-19
free agency, 7-26–7-27, 7-35, 7-36, 7-39
knowledge-based, 7-16, 7-20–7-21
long-term vs. short-term, 7-14, 7-20
market-mediated, 7-14
negotiation of, 7-28
old vs. new, 7-13–7-16
policy inconsistencies and, 7-21–7-22
social contracts, 7-8, 7-12, 7-14, 7-25–28, 7-39
employment security, 7-6, 7-15, 7-26
emWare Inc., 5-17
encouragement in teams, 5-10
energy, and power, 2-37
engineering, simultaneous, 9-12
English-only policies, 11-37
enlightened self-interest, 12-15
Enron Corporation, 1-42–1-43
enterprise groups, 2-63–2-64
environment, external
overview, 9-1–9-5
action tools, 9-9, 9-11, 9-13, 9-19, 9-22
and boundaries, in bureaucratic model, 1-12
competitors, 9-9
cultural perspective, and institutional field model, 9-4, 9-17–9-21, 9-22
diversity and, 1-15
"ecosystem" of suppliers, partners, and contractors, 1-44–1-45
flat organizations and, 1-19
flexibility and, 1-15, 1-19
global vs. international approach, 1-15–1-16
importance of interactions, 9-8
input set and output set, 9-8
integrated perspectives, 9-22
key external actors, 9-8
linking mechanisms and, 2-21, 9-9
national culture models, 9-19
national emphasis, 1-12, 1-15

networked organization's relations with, 1-13, 1-18–1-19
new organization model and, 9-9
organizational set model, 9-4, 9-8–9-12, 9-15, 9-22
outsourcing, 1-13, 9-4
political perspective, and the stakeholders model, 9-4, 9-13–9-16, 9-22
regulatory set, 9-8–9-9
RU-486 case, 9-4, 9-23–9-32
sensemaking and, 14-10–14-11
strategic design perspective, 2-26, 9-4, 9-8–9-12, 9-15, 9-22
environmental issues, 9-15, 10-48, 13-14–13-19
Environmental Protection Agency (EPA), 13-14, 13-15
EPCOT, 10-11
Epstein, Seymour, 4-29
equality in teams, 5-14
equalization, 1-16
equal opportunity, 11-13, 11-33–11-35. *See also* diversity
equilibrium, 8-12
equity partnerships, 7-48
escalation of commitment, 2-42
espoused values, 2-71
Esserman, Laura, 5-16, 5-17–5-18
ethic, professional, 7-27–7-28
ethical issues
downsizing, 7-25
negotiations and, 12-14
RU-486 case, 9-4, 9-25, 9-30–9-31
ethnography, 2-69, 10-14
Euro Disney/Disneyland Paris, 10-35–10-39, 10-39–10-45
Europe, 1-10, 9-29–9-30
Euvrard, Catherine, 9-27
evaluation. *See* performance measurement systems
"The Ever-Expanding, Profit-Maximizing, Cultural-Imperialist, Wonderful World of Disney" (Weber), 10-50–10-55
Evin, Claude, 9-28
evolution, cultural, 2-76–2-78
evolutionary model, 8-13–8-14
exchange, 2-44–2-45, 5-12
exchange-based trade gains, 12-27
exchange theories, 2-60
executives. *See also* leadership
compensation, and corporate scandals, 7-59
diversity among, 11-14
executive leaders, role of, 8-36–8-37
hero-CEO, myth of, 8-32–8-33
mind of the CEO, 1-23–1-24
Office of the President, 3-11–3-12
exhortation, change by, 8-19
experiences, cultural, 10-26–10-27, 10-32
experiences, transformational, 14-15
expertise, grouping by, 2-16–2-17

expertise and talent. *See* intellectual capital and talent
exploitation, employee feelings of, 11-36
extensive ties, in X-teams, 6-24
external activities of X-teams, 6-22, 6-24
external adaptation tasks, 2-72
external environment. *See* environment, external
external labor markets, 7-13–7-14
external stakeholders, 2-35, 9-13
extroversion. *See* Myers-Briggs Type Indicator (MBTI)

factionalism in networks, 2-54
failure, 14-50
family advocates, 7-55
family-friendly policies
    growth of, 7-17–7-18, 7-55
    holistic approach, 7-56
    parental leave, 7-49–7-51, 7-52–7-53, 7-58
Family Network, 10-55
family-work balance. *See* work-family integration
feedback, talent development and, 7-33
"feeling business" (Disney), 10-4, 10-14
fighting, in teams, 5-14
Fiorina, Carleton "Carly," 14-15, 14-26–14-34
First Interstate Bank case, 11-38–11-39
fiscal year-end, 12-33
Fisher, Pamela, 7-44–7-47, 7-48, 7-50, 7-51
Fitzpatrick, Robert, 10-43
fixed pie, 12-10
flat organizations. *See also* hierarchical structure
    communication networks and, 2-52
    diversity management and, 11-38
    horizontal structures, 1-33, 1-36, 1-37
    incentives in, 2-24
    management implications, 1-19
    in new organization model, 1-14
    social networks, and influence, 2-38
    unbiased information flow, and culture, 2-66
    workforce management issues, 7-7, 7-15
    X-teams and, 6-29
Fleet Securities, 5-20–5-21
Fletcher, Don, 1-31, 1-35
flexibility
    in benefits package, 11-12
    job rotation, 7-15
    management implications, 1-19
    in new organization model, 1-14–1-15, 1-19–1-20
    part-time partner case, 7-44–7-53
    as power source, 2-37
    of time, 7-18, 7-44–7-53, 10-16
    types of arrangements, 7-18–7-19
    work-family integration and, 7-58
    workforce diversity and, 7-17
    workforce management issues, 7-7–7-8, 7-12
    in X-team membership, 6-25
Flexible Bright, 5-24

flex time, 7-18
Flickinger, Burt, III, 8-9
flow, cultural, 10-26–10-27, 10-28, 10-32–10-33
Floyd, Steven W., 13-22
fluid membership, in X-teams, 6-25
focus, and power, 2-37
force field, 8-12
forcing behavior, 12-7
Ford, Henry, 1-39
Ford Motor Company, 11-12, 14-23
forecasting, economic, 6-12, 6-15
forecasting, sales, 6-11–6-17
forecasting differences, in negotiations, 12-28–12-30, 12-34
formal reporting structures, 2-21–2-22
formal vs. informal organization, 2-47
Forster, Scott, 5-23
fragmentation, 2-62
framing, and vision, 14-13
framing of issues, 13-8, 13-9
France. *See* Euro Disney/Disneyland Paris; RU-486 case
free agency, 7-26–7-27, 7-35, 7-36, 7-39
friendship networks, 2-40
front/back structure, 2-20, 2-21, 2-32, 2-85–2-86
functional grouping structure, 2-16–2-17, 2-28–2-30, 2-32
functional/product matrix, 2-19, 2-32
future self, 14-20
future state, 8-12, 8-16

Gabarro, Jack, 14-12
gaijin ("outside person"), 10-32
gains, mutual, 12-15–12-16
Gardner, John, 14-42, 14-49
gatekeeping, in teams, 5-10
gay, lesbian, bisexual, and transgendered (GLBT) employees, 11-12
"Geeks and Geezers" (Bennis and Thomas), 14-42–14-51
Gehry, Frank, 14-43, 14-44
gender. *See also* diversity
    discrimination at MIT, 14-21
    leadership and, 7-56, 7-58
    negotiation and, 12-9
    schema changes and, 2-9
    work-family integration and, 7-55, 7-56, 7-58
    workforce demographics, 7-17, 11-19
General Electric (GE), 1-32, 1-34, 8-38–8-42, 13-11
General Motors (GM), 2-64
Genzyme, 7-35
geographic grouping structure, 2-18–2-19, 2-29, 8-8–8-9
Germany, 7-20
Gerstner, Lou, 8-6, 8-8, 8-11

getting "buy-in," 2-42
Gevirtz, Don, 14-50
Ghasn, Carlos, 8-8
Gitell, J. H., 3-14–3-15
"Give Me an E. Give Me an S." (Golden), 4-28–4-35
Glaxo, 12-26
global and international business
    Access Capital International case, 11-35–11-36
    Euro Disney/Disneyland Paris, 10-35–10-39, 10-39–10-45
    geographic grouping, 2-18–2-19
    global vs. international approach, 1-15
    Hong Kong Disneyland, 10-45–10-49, 10-50–10-55
    job security anxiety, 7-15
    political factors in China, 10-46
    Tokyo Disneyland, 10-25–10-26, 10-27, 10-28–10-33
global business units (GBUs), 8-8–8-9
global dimension of new organizations
    cross-border learning, 10-27, 10-38–10-39, 10-49
    cross-cultural communication and, 1-20
    cultural flow, 10-26–10-27, 10-28, 10-32–10-33
    cultural variation, and bystanders, 11-22–11-23
    diversity and, 11-10–11-11
    electronic collaboration and virtual teams, 3-12, 5-16–5-21
    employee involvement, 1-16
    growing importance of, 1-16
    international trends, 1-10
    international vs. global approach, 1-15
    local responsiveness, 1-20
    management implications, 1-20
    of markets, 1-16
    networks across borders, 1-15–1-16
    organizational patterns and cultural context, 10-4
    talent and resources, global, 1-41, 1-45
    teams, transnational, 3-12
    workforce management issues, 7-8, 7-14
globalization
    cross-border integration, 1-20
    cross-cultural context and, 2-63
    cultural imperialism, 10-26, 10-47, 10-50–10-51
    cultural meanings and, 10-46
    cultural processes and, 2-66
    external environment and, 9-4
    global organizational fields, 9-19–9-20
    homogenization, 10-26–10-27, 10-33, 10-49
    individualistic vs. collectivist cultures, 3-12
    localization and, 10-49, 10-55
    stakeholders and, 9-15

goals
    assumptions, changes in, 7-21
    strategic design and, 9-9
    "stretch," 8-42
    as team issue, 5-14
    top management team and, 13-6–13-7
"Godfather" strategy, 2-38
gold, price of, 6-11
Goldstein, Marilyn, 7-50
Goodnight, Jim, 7-35, 7-37
good will, 12-33–12-34
Gottlieb, Lori, 14-38
government
    professionalism, role in, 7-28
    reinvention of, 1-10
    as stakeholder, 9-14
    work-family integration and, 7-57
Grant study, 14-47
grassroots employee advocacy programs, 11-15–11-16
Gray, Paul, 14-21
Gregorc, Anthony, 4-32
grouping, strategic, 2-14, 2-15, 2-16–2-20, 2-26
groupthink, 5-13
groupware systems, 11-12
Grove, Andrew S., 1-41, 14-10
growth patterns, 8-29

Hackborn, Richard, 14-29
Hall, D. Timothy, 7-51–7-52
Hallmark, 1-35
Hamel, Gary, 1-45, 13-23
Hammer, Mike, 1-31, 1-35
Handford, Bart, 14-40
"happiest place on earth," 10-9–10-10, 10-13, 10-36
happiness trade, at Disneyland, 10-4, 10-14
harassment policy, 11-24
hardiness, 14-44
hard sell approach, in issue selling, 13-9
Harman, Sidney, 14-49
harmonizing function, in teams, 5-10
Harris, Reuben T., 8-12–8-13
Hart, Stuart, 13-26
Hartig, Karen, 12-37
Hartwig, George, 7-44–7-47, 7-51, 7-52
headquarters, 1-41
Hermann Brain Dominance Instrument, 4-31–4-32
hero-CEO, myth of, 8-32–8-33
Herrmann, Ned, 4-31
Hewlett, Walter, 14-32–14-33
Hewlett-Packard (HP), 7-40, 14-29–14-34
hierarchical authority, 8-36
hierarchical structure. *See also* flat organizations; strategic design lens/perspective
    communication networks and, 2-52

delayering, and middle management, 13-22–13-23
flattening of, in new model, 1-14
in functional organizations, 2-17
information technology, effect of, 1-14
in law firms, 1-37
loyalism in, 7-25–7-28
in old model, 1-12
as strategic grouping, 2-21–2-22
team leadership in Office of the President, 3-11–3-12
teams, hierarchy of, 5-20–5-21
vertical power systems and, 2-38
workforce management issues, 7-7
high fliers, 2-37
high-involvement workplace, 1-32
high-performance work systems, 7-16
high-performing teams, 3-10, 5-21. *See also* X-teams
Hilger, Wolfgang, 9-26, 9-28
hiring. *See* recruitment
Hispanics, 11-14
historical method, 2-69
Hitchcock, Donna, 12-42
Hoechst. *See* RU-486 case
Hogan, Robert, 4-29
holidays, at Tokyo Disneyland, 10-25
holistic approach to work-family integration, 7-54–7-58
hollow corporations, 1-13
Holt, Robert, 6-12–6-17
home, balancing with work. *See* work-family integration
homo economicus ("economic man"), 2-34
homogeneity among personnel, 4-12–4-13. *See also* diversity
homogenization, global, 10-26–10-27, 10-33, 10-49
Honda, 9-11, 9-20
honesty, 7-27, 7-39
honesty tests, 4-33–4-34
Hong Kong Disneyland, 10-45–10-49, 10-50–10-55
Hopkins, Nancy, 14-21
horizontal organizations, 1-33, 1-36, 1-37. *See also* flat organizations
horizontal power systems, 2-38
horizontal processes, 13-22, 13-26
hot groups, 3-11
hours of work
impact of long hours, 7-36, 7-37
trends in, 7-18
work-family integration and, 7-57, 7-58
human assets. *See also* intellectual capital and talent
building of, 7-32–7-33
competition for, 7-29, 7-30, 7-36, 7-51
development of, and alignment, 2-25

knowledge-based work systems and, 7-16, 7-20–7-21
restructuring, and risk distribution, 7-59–7-60
as strategic resource, 7-29–7-36
human resource development, 9-11
human resources managers, 7-31–7-36
Huxley, Aldous, 14-47
hybrid grouping structures, 2-19–2-20

IBM, 8-8
ideal types, 1-16–1-17
"ideal worker," 7-54, 7-55
identification with leaders, 2-75
identity
cultural perspective, 2-63, 2-64–2-65
at Disneyland, 10-22
negotiation and, 12-9–12-10
"social," 11-10, 11-15
socially constructed, 12-9
as team issue, 5-14
identity-group affiliations, 11-32–11-33, 11-35, 11-38, 11-39. *See also* diversity
IDEO, 6-29
illusion of influence, 2-42–2-43
image, and saving face, 12-41
imagineers, 10-10, 10-12, 10-25
immigration, 11-10
impartiality, 1-12
imperialism, cultural, 10-27, 10-47, 10-50–10-51
implementation by middle management, 13-23, 13-25
imploded relationships in networks, 2-53
impressions, managing, 12-14, 12-17
incentives and rewards. *See also* compensation
as alignment mechanism, 2-24–2-25, 9-11
entrepreneurial incubation, 1-45
in flat organizations, 1-19
negotiation dynamics and, 12-10, 12-29, 12-37
principles for, 2-24
promotion, 1-19
in teams, 3-14
inclusion, as bystander tactic, 11-23
income partnerships, 7-48
incompatibility bias, 12-24
incremental change, 8-15, 8-17
independent contractors, 7-14, 7-19, 7-35, 7-36–7-37
individualism, 2-76, 12-10
individualistic vs. collectivist cultures, 3-12
individual retirement accounts, 2-35
industrial-financial partnerships, 12-34
inertia, organizational, 8-4, 8-6, 8-12, 8-13
Inex case, 13-14–13-19
influence. *See also* political lens/perspective; power
in boundary management, 6-8, 6-10

of grassroots advocacy groups, 11-16
negotiation skills and, 2-45
network-building and, 2-44–2-45
perception and illusion of, 2-42–2-43
as power, 2-36
in stakeholder model, 9-13, 9-14
tactics of, 5-12
in teams, 5-12–5-13
informal networks, 2-38–2-40, 2-47–2-55
informal systems and processes, 2-25
information
  accessibility, and teams, 6-28
  bits vs. atoms, 1-41
  culture and, 2-66
  gathering of, 4-15, 4-17–4-18, 8-12
  learning culture, 6-28–6-29
  liaison roles, 2-22
  in negotiations, 12-12
  network position and, 2-39, 2-40
  sharing of, 1-13, 5-10
  synthesis by middle managers, 13-24, 13-27
  workers, well-informed, 7-39
  X-teams and, 6-28, 6-29
information activity, in boundary management, 6-8, 6-9, 6-10, 6-24
information-based organizations, 1-22
information technology (IT)
  digitization, 1-42
  electronic collaboration and virtual teams, 3-12, 5-16–5-21
  flattening of hierarchy and, 1-14
  knowledge management and, 7-34
  as linking mechanism, 9-9
  "Management by Web" (Byrne), 1-39–1-45
  networking and, 1-13–1-14
  process reengineering and, 1-37
  strategic linking and, 2-23
ingratiation, 5-12
initiating function, in teams, 5-10
initiating-sustaining-redesigning model, 8-14–8-15
innovation. *See also* change; creativity
  in bureaucratic organization subunits, 1-12
  diversity and, 1-15
  evolutionary model of change and, 8-13
  flexibility and, 1-14–1-15
  ideational, 2-59
  internal networkers and, 8-36
  inventing by leaders, 14-13
  personality type and, 4-24
  professional ethic and, 7-28
  team boundary management and, 6-8
  workforce management and, 7-7
  in X-teams, 6-22
input/throughput/output system, 9-8–9-11
inquiry, 14-11, 14-12
INSERM (Institut National de la Sante et de la Recherche Medicale), 9-23

"In Silicon Valley, Loyalty Means Paying a High Price" (Berenson), 7-38–7-41
inspirational appeals, 5-12
institutional field model, 9-4, 9-17–9-21, 9-22
institutionalization, 9-17
integrated learning process, 8-42
"Integrating Work and Family Life: A Holistic Approach" (Bailyn, Drago, and Kochan), 7-54–7-58
integration (strategic linking), 2-14, 2-15, 2-20–2-23
integration, in diversity management, 11-37
integration tasks, internal, 2-72
integration teams, 5-23
integrative negotiations, 12-15–12-16
integrator roles, 2-22, 2-23
intellectual capital and talent. *See also* human assets
  competition for, 7-29, 7-30, 7-36, 7-51
  diversity and, 11-11
  expertise, management of, 1-12, 1-36
  globalization of, 1-41, 1-45
  recruitment and development of, 7-32–7-33
  scarce and valued expertise as power, 2-37
  scarcity as resource, 7-30
  strategy based on, 7-29–7-36
intelligence, and leadership, 14-47
interactions, organizational. *See* political lens/perspective
interdependence in teams, 3-10
interdependence of tasks, 2-14–2-15, 2-16, 2-20–2-21
interdependent networks, 1-13, 9-9
interests
  coalitions of allies, 2-43–2-44
  collective, 2-34–2-35
  definition of, 2-34
  dynamic nature of, 2-36
  mapping, 2-41–2-42
  multiple and competing, 2-35
  in negotiation, 12-11–12-12, 12-15, 12-27–12-28
  political perspective and, 2-34–2-36
  in stakeholder model, 9-13, 9-14–9-15, 9-16
  subunit, 8-11
  of workers, 7-6
internal boycott, 9-26
internal integration tasks, 2-72
internal labor markets, 7-13–7-14
internal networkers, 8-36
internal stakeholders, 2-35, 9-13
internal team process, 3-13–3-14
international business. *See* global and international business; global dimension of new organizations; globalization
International Federation of Gynecology and Obstetrics, 9-28

International Planned Parenthood Federation, 9-29
International Right to Life Federation, 9-25
Internet, 1-39–1-45, 10-55, 14-50. *See also* electronic collaboration
interviewing, 6-9
In the Age of the Machine (Zuboff), 1-34
intimacy, as team issue, 5-14
IntraLinks, 5-20–5-21
introversion. *See* Myers-Briggs Type Indicator (MBTI)
intuition. *See* Myers-Briggs Type Indicator (MBTI)
intuitive-style negotiators, 12-9
inventing, as leadership capability, 14-9, 14-13–14-14
investment capability, 12-34
investors, and corporate scandals, 7-59
involvement in issue selling, 13-8, 13-9–13-10
isolationist teams, 6-9
isomorphism, 9-17, 9-19, 9-20
issues, charged, 13-10–13-11
issues, in dealmaking, 12-10
issue selling
    overview, 13-4
    charged issues, 13-10–13-11
    choice processes and context factors, 13-7–13-8, 13-11
    exercise, 13-12–13-14
    importance of, 13-6
    Inex case, 13-14–13-19
    management structure and, 13-6–13-7
    middle managers as champions and facilitators, 13-24–13-25
    strategic behavior, discouragement of, 13-26–13-27
    tactical choices, 13-8–13-10
IT. *See* information technology (IT)
Italy, 9-29–9-30
Iversen Dunham case, 11-34–11-35, 11-39

Jacobson, Ralph, 4-28
Jager, Durk, 8-8, 8-9, 8-11, 8-16
Japan
    Disney Sea, 10-52
    language, and culture, 2-64
    lifetime employment, 7-15
    middle-up-down change pattern, 8-16
    quality circles in, 3-11
    Tokyo Disneyland, 10-25–10-26, 10-27, 10-28–10-33, 10-52
    workforce management, 7-20
    work methods and practices, 2-63
Jarrosiak, Philip, 1-31, 1-34
Jimenez, Karen, 8-22–8-25
job ladder, 7-18
jobs. *See also* work-family integration
    doing what you love, 14-36–14-41
    flexibility in, 7-18
    meaningful work, 14-36–14-41
    multitasked or multidimensional, 7-15–7-16
    notion of, called into question, 7-16
    posting, and diversity, 11-12
    rotation of, 7-15
    specialized and hierarchical, in old model, 1-12
Jobs, Steve, 14-12
job security, 7-6, 7-15, 7-26
job sharing, 7-18
Johnson, Lyndon B., 14-10, 14-15
Johnson, Michael, 10-52
jokes, offensive, 11-20
Joly, Pierre, 9-27, 9-28
Jones, Brad, 13-14–13-15, 13-17, 13-19
Jones, Ivan, 4-30
Jones, Nathaniel R., 14-45–14-46
Jordan, Vernon E., 14-43, 14-51
Josaitis, Eleanor, 14-51
journals, business. *See* press, business
journal-writing, 5-5
judgmentalism, in teams, 5-14
Julien, Jacques, 9-25, 9-28
Jung, Carl, 4-4, 4-11–4-12, 4-14
Juno Online Services, 1-44–1-45
just-in-time delivery systems, 1-13

Kanally, David, 10-37
Kanter, Rosabeth, 2-37–2-38, 13-24–13-25
Kao, Elizabeth, 14-43, 14-47, 14-50
Katzenbach, Jeff, 10-12
Keen, Peter G. W., 4-22
Keighley, Geoff, 14-42
Keller, David, 8-23–8-24
Kelly, Dave, 14-10, 14-13
key external actors, 9-8
Khoury, Philip, 14-22, 14-25
Kilmann, Ralph H., 4-22–4-23, 4-24
King, Martin Luther, Jr., 8-35, 14-10, 14-13
Kirton, Michael J., 4-24
Kissinger, Henry, 12-13, 12-28
Klein, Michael, 14-43
Kleinmuntz, Benjamin, 4-33
Knight-Ridder newspaper chain, 4-30, 4-34
knowledge-based work systems, 7-16, 7-20–7-21
knowledge management, 7-34–7-35
Kodak, 1-35
Kolodzieski, Aleida, 7-38, 7-40
Koogle, Tim, 2-4
Kotter, John, 8-28
Kraft, Kenneth, 4-29
Krimsky, Sheldon, 14-23
Kroeger, Otto, 4-28
Kronish, Miriam, 4-32
Krueger, Scott, 14-24–14-25
Kummerow, Jean, 4-34

Kundun (film), 10-47, 10-51
Kurlander, Carl, 14-39

labor laws, reform of, 7-60
labor/management divide, 2-62, 8-22–8-25
labor markets, internal vs. external, 7-13–7-14
labor unions. *See* unions
Lafley, Alan G., 8-9–8-10
Lakeside-Tonicron joint venture example, 12-24–12-26, 12-26–12-27
Landauer, Sally C., 7-48
land development. *See* property development, Disney
language
    cultural context and, 2-64
    at Disneyland Paris, 10-38
    English-only policies, 11-37
    in issue selling, 13-8, 13-9
    at Tokyo Disneyland, 10-31, 10-32
law firms, structure of, 1-37
Lawler, Edward, 5-21
layoffs. *See* restructuring and downsizing
leadership
    overview, 14-4–14-5
    Asian Americans and, 11-14
    assumptions, changes in, 7-21
    capabilities, key, 14-4, 14-9–14-14
    as change-creating process, 14-8
    change signature, 14-4, 14-10, 14-14–14-16, 14-19–14-20
    collective, 14-10
    crucible experiences and, 14-42–14-51
    cultural evolution and, 2-77
    definition of, 8-35
    development model, 14-44–14-45
    development of, 14-8–14-9
    as distributed, 14-8
    diversity programs, commitment to, 11-15, 11-41–11-42
    effective, 8-37
    executive leaders, role of, 8-36–8-37
    Fiorina case, 14-14–14-26–14-14–14-34
    framework for, 14-4, 14-9–14-16
    hero-CEO, myth of, 8-32–8-33
    identification with, 2-75
    individual factors, 14-46
    internal networkers, 8-36
    inventing, 14-13–14-14
    local line leaders, 8-35–8-36
    meaning of, 14-8
    as personal, 14-8
    qualities of, 14-44
    relating, 14-9, 14-11–14-12
    sensemaking, 14-9, 14-10–14-11, 14-13
    theoretical history, 14-8
    traits of, 14-46
    transformational leader, 8-13, 14-8
    Vest case, 14-21–14-26
    visioning, 14-4, 14-12–14-13, 14-30
    women in, 7-56, 7-58
leadership communities, 8-35–8-36
"The Leadership of Profound Change" (Senge), 8-32–8-37
learning
    cross-border, 10-27, 10-38–10-39, 10-49
    as culture, 2-69
    diversity and, 11-12, 11-38
    in flexible organizations, challenge of, 1-19
    integrated learning process, 8-42
    perpetual, at GE's Bayamón factory, 1-34
    styles of, 4-32–4-33
    in teams, 3-10
learning-and-effectiveness (work perspectives) paradigm, 11-24, 11-32–11-33, 11-36–11-37, 11-39–11-42
learning capabilities, 8-30–8-31
learning culture, 6-28–6-29
learning organization approach, 8-14, 8-30–8-31
leave policy, 7-49–7-51, 7-52–7-53, 7-58
Leavitt, Harold J., 4-22
Leers, David, 2-49–2-52
legitimating tactics, 5-12
Lehman Brothers, 12-17
Le Monde, 9-24
lenses. *See* organizational analysis and action, lenses on
Levitt, Arthur, Jr., 14-48
Lewin, Kurt, 8-11–8-12, 8-14
LG, 7-33
liaison positions, 9-9
liaison roles, 2-22
Liemandt, Joe, 1-45
"The Life Cycle of Typical Change Initiatives" (Senge), 8-28–8-31
lifelong employment, 7-8, 7-14, 7-15
lifetime employability, 7-15
Lightwood, Sara, 13-14–13-19
limiting processes, in change initiatives, 8-29–8-31
linking, and knowledge management, 7-34–7-35
linking, strategic, 2-14, 2-15, 2-20–2-23, 2-24, 9-9
Linn, Don, 14-39
The Lion King (film), 10-52
liquidity, differences in, 12-34
listening skills, 1-19–1-20
"Little Emperors and Empresses," 10-46
lobbying, 9-9
local government as stakeholder, 9-14
localization, 10-49, 10-55
local line leaders, 8-35–8-36
local responsiveness, 1-20
location, and institutional fields, 9-19
logical thinking, 4-18
logrolling, 12-15
long-distance collaboration, 3-12, 5-16–5-21

long-term employment relationships, 7-12, 7-14, 7-20
Lopez, Joe, 12-38, 12-40
Lord, Ellen, 5-24
loyalty and commitment
    bonding process, 7-35
    Calico Commerce case, 7-38–7-41
    compliance vs. commitment, 8-33, 8-38
    cultural meaning and, 2-65
    customer loyalty, 7-38
    downsizing and, 7-19
    fragmentation and, 2-62
    honesty with employees and, 7-27, 7-39
    middle management and, 13-29
    networking and, 7-7
    policy consistency and, 7-21–7-22
    professionalism vs. loyalism, 7-25–7-28
    Silicon Valley practices and, 7-38
    workforce management and, 7-6
LTX, 13-14
Lucent Technologies, 2-22, 14-26, 14-28–14-29, 14-33
Lutnick, Howard W., 14-48

Maag, William, 5-21
macroeconomic forecasting, 6-12
Maddox, Robert F., 14-43
Maestas, Lisa, 5-18
magazines, business. *See* press, business
maintenance functions, for teams, 5-9, 5-10
"Making Differences Matter" (Thomas and Ely), 11-32–11-42
Malloy, Richard, 1-35
management. *See also* leadership; middle management
    cognitive style and, 4-13–4-15, 4-21–4-25
    contradictory demands on, 1-18
    human resources development and, 7-31
    issue selling and, 13-6–13-7
    labor/management divide, 2-62
    listening skills and empathy, 1-19–1-20
    slow transformation of, 7-29–7-30
    talent-based strategy and, 7-29–7-36
    team issues, 5-4
    of teams, 3-15
"Management by Web" (Byrne), 1-39–1-45
management consultants, 1-25–1-26, 5-20
Mandela, Nelson, 14-43
Mango Systems role play, 12-4
Manpower, Inc., 7-19
mapping
    of interests and power, 2-41–2-42
    of managerial styles, 4-13–4-25
    "Mapping Your Organization" form, 1-27–1-28
    of networks, 2-47–2-55
    sensemaking as, 14-10
"Mapping Managerial Styles" (Margerison and Lewis), 4-13–4-25
Marinucci, Elena, 9-29–9-30
market, grouping by, 2-18–2-19
Marketing Development Organizations (MDOs), 8-9
marketing synergies, at Disney, 10-8–10-9, 10-12, 10-52, 10-53–10-54
market-mediated employment relationship, 7-14
markets, globalization of, 1-16
Marne-la-Vallée, France, 10-35, 10-38
Massachusetts Institute of Technology (MIT), 14-21–14-26
mass customization, 1-41
massification, 10-33
Mastiff case, 11-39–11-40, 11-41
matrix, payoff, 8-40
matrix, RAMMP, 8-38–8-40
matrix structure, 2-19–2-20
the Matthew effect, 2-38
Matthews, Dave, 8-24
Maturana, Humberto, 8-31
Max, Sandy, 12-6–12-7
Maxmin, H. James, 1-31, 1-32
Mayden, Barbara Mendel, 7-50–7-51
MBTI. *See* Myers-Briggs Type Indicator
McDermand, Nancy, 7-39–7-40
McDonald's, 1-25, 2-58, 10-27
McGovern, Gail, 14-13
McGregor, Douglas, 7-21
McKenney, James L., 4-22
McKinnon, D. W., 4-24
McKinsey & Co., 1-36, 7-33, 7-36
McLane, Jeff, 5-20–5-21
McMorrow, Joanne, 5-20
McNamee, Roger, 7-39
meaning
    crucible experiences, 14-43–14-44, 14-51
    cultural, 2-57–2-58, 2-64, 10-28, 10-32, 10-46
    denotative and connotative, 2-57
    sense of, 14-12
measures, in RAMMP matrix, 8-39
mechanism, organization as, 2-14
media, in institutional fields, 9-17, 9-19
mediation, diversity issues and, 11-24
mediation, in negotiations, 12-8, 12-17–12-19
medical industry, 5-16, 5-17–5-18
Meeker, Needham & Ames (MN&A), 7-44–7-52
meetings, 5-18–5-19, 8-39. *See also* electronic collaboration
Meir, Randy, 6-12–6-17
membership of X-teams, flexible, 6-25
memory system, transactive, 5-8
mentor-protégé relationships, 14-43, 14-50
Merck & Co., Inc., 7-50
mergers and acquisitions
    AOL-Time Warner, 8-7
    earnouts, 12-29

Glaxo-SmithKline Beecham, 12-26
HP-Compaq, 14-32–14-34
organizational culture and, 2-71, 2-77–2-78
WorldCom, CompuServe, and AOL, 12-28
metaphors, 14-12–14-13
Mickey Mouse
on Chinese television, 10-51, 10-53–10-54
cross-cultural variations, 10-33, 10-45
exportability of, 10-52
in Japan, 10-25, 10-33
Microsoft Corporation, 1-15, 7-32–7-33
middle management. *See also* management
boundary-spanning, 13-26
championing of strategic alternatives, 13-24, 13-27
delayering and, 13-22–13-23
design changes and, 8-10
dynamic capabilities and competitive advantage, 13-23–13-24, 13-25–13-26, 13-27
facilitation of adaptability, 13-24–13-25, 13-27
implementation role, 13-23, 13-25
issue selling and, 13-6, 13-7
psychological contracts and, 13-29
reengineered organization, role in, 13-26, 13-27–13-29
social contract and, 7-25
strategic value of, 13-27–13-29
strategic vs. operational roles, 13-23
synthesis of information, 13-24, 13-27
middle-up-down change pattern, 8-16
mifepristone, 9-24
Miller, Evan, 5-18
Miller, Jerry, 5-20
Mills, Quinn, 1-31, 1-37
mimetic isomorphism, 9-19
"The Mind of the CEO" (Garten), 1-23–1-24
Minnesota Multi-Phasic Inventory (MMPI), 4-29–4-30
minorities, at Disneyland, 10-14
minorities and diversity. *See* diversity
Mintzberg, Henry, 4-22
mission statements, 11-13, 11-38
MIT (Massachusetts Institute of Technology), 14-21–14-26
Mitroff, Ian I., 4-22–4-23, 4-24
MMPI (Minnesota Multi-Phasic Inventory), 4-29–4-30
mobilization of interests, 9-13
models, formal, 2-10. *See also* organizational analysis and action, lenses on
models, new and old organization. *See* new organization model; old (bureaucratic) model
money, and dreams, 14-37–14-38
moral issue in downsizing, 7-25
motivation, 2-60–2-61, 2-65, 7-6, 7-7
motives, mixed, 12-14, 12-16

Motorola, 8-42
"Mouse Trap" (Gumbel and Turner), 10-39–10-43
movies, Disney, 10-12, 10-47, 10-52
MTV, 10-55
MTW Corporation, 7-37
Mulan (film), 10-47, 10-51
"Multi Company" paradigm, 2-73–2-74
multiculturalism, 11-35
multidimensional grouping structures, 2-19–2-20
multidivisional structure, 2-17–2-18
multitasking, 1-19, 7-15–7-16
Murdoch, James, 10-55
mutual gains, 7-6, 12-15–12-16
mutual need, in negotiations, 12-36
Myers, Douglas, 1-38
Myers, Isabel, 4-4
Myers-Briggs Type Indicator (MBTI). *See also* cognitive style
career development and, 4-24–4-25
change, approaches to, 4-23–4-24
Cognitive Style Self-Assessment, 4-6–4-9, 4-11
composite types, 4-20–4-21
corporate use examples, 4-28, 4-34
creativity and innovation and, 4-24
extrovert/introvert (relationships), 4-16–4-17
hiring decisions and, 4-34
managerial style and decision making, 4-22
organizational structure and, 4-22–4-23
perceiving/judging (priority-setting), 4-15, 4-19–4-20
relationship management and, 4-15
sensing/intuition (information generation), 4-15, 4-17–4-18
shadow type, 4-24–4-25
thinking/feeling (decision making), 4-15, 4-18–4-19
in universities, 4-34
MyLearning.com, 5-20
Myrdal, Gunnar, 11-10

Nadler, David, 1-31, 2-24, 2-26
NASA, 14-40
national context, emphasis on, 1-12
national culture models, 9-19
Naumann, Alan, 7-38
Navickas, Leon, 5-16
negative feedback loop, in downsizing, 7-20
negotiation and conflict resolution. *See also* deal-crafting and dealmaking
overview, 12-4, 12-7
appreciative moves, 12-17, 12-39, 12-40–12-42
bargaining power, 12-13–12-14
BATNA (best alternative to a negotiated agreement), 12-13, 12-14

characteristics and styles of negotiators, 12-9–12-10
contingent agreements, 12-23, 12-28–12-30
deadlocked negotiations, 12-17, 12-22–12-23
dealmaking process, 12-8, 12-14–12-16
definition of negotiation, 12-7
distributive (win-lose) negotiations, 12-14–12-15
diverse organizations, conflict in, 1-20
flat organizations and, 1-19
forms of conflict management, 12-7–12-8
incentives, 12-10, 12-29, 12-37
influence, and negotiation skills, 2-45
integrative (mutual gains) negotiations, 12-15–12-16
interests, 12-11–12-12, 12-15, 12-27–12-28
issues and, 12-10
Mango Systems role play, 12-4
moves and countermoves, 12-17
negotiator's dilemma, 12-12, 12-16
organizational culture and, 12-10
parties in, 12-8–12-10
postsettlement settlements, 12-18
power moves, 12-36–12-38
process moves, 12-38, 12-39, 12-40
"pushing up" conflict to higher authority, 2-36
revealing and withholding information, 12-12
roots of conflict, 2-33
saving face, 12-41
shadow negotiations, 12-4, 12-16–12-17, 12-36–12-42
status quo, cost of, 12-37
substantive vs. affective conflict, 5-13
teams, conflict in, 5-10, 5-13, 5-23–5-24
third parties and, 12-8, 12-17–12-19, 12-28, 12-32
three-dimensional perspective, 12-22–12-24
toleration of conflict, 2-37
value in (*See* value claiming and creation, in negotiation)
willingness to negotiate, 12-36
neoteny, 14-44
network leaders, 8-36
networks
advice networks, 2-40, 2-47–2-52
analysis of social networks, 2-40
"bow ties," 2-54
caucuses, 11-15
communication networks, 2-47, 2-48, 2-52–2-55
connecting, in leadership, 14-11–14-12
construction of, 2-44–2-45
cooperative, 1-13
efficient vs. redundant, 2-39
factionalism in, 2-54
fragile structures, 2-54
friendship networks, 2-40
global approach, 1-15–1-16
holes in, 2-40, 2-54
imploded relationships, 2-53
informal, 2-38–2-40, 2-47–2-55
interdependence and, 9-9
internal networkers, 8-36
linking, and knowledge management, 7-34–7-35
"Management by Web" (Byrne), 1-39–1-45
management consultants and concept of, 1-25–1-26
management implications, 1-18–1-19
mapping and analysis, 2-47–2-55
in new organization model, 1-13–1-14, 1-23
outsourcing and, 1-13, 1-44–1-45, 9-4
power, and network position, 2-38–2-40
relationship networks, 2-47–2-52
size of, 2-38
solution testing, 2-54–2-55
of stakeholders, 9-15
structural hole theory, 2-40
task-related, 2-40
teams and, 3-6
trust networks, 2-47–2-52
virtual companies, 1-13
virtual teams and electronic collaboration, 3-12, 5-16–5-21
workforce management issues, 7-7
X-teams and, 6-22
Network Systems group, 14-28
neutrality, in mediation, 12-18
"The New Managerial Work" (Kanter), 1-22–1-23
new organization model. *See also* old (bureaucratic) model
overview, 1-6–1-7
appeal of, 1-17
assessments in business press, 1-22–1-26
assumptions, changes in, 7-21
challenges in shifting to, 1-10–1-11, 1-18, 1-20–1-21
characteristics of, 1-10
cognitive style variations and, 4-12
cultural processes and, 2-66
diverse aspect, 1-15
employment relationship and, 7-13–7-16
flat aspect, 1-14, 1-19
flexible aspect, 1-14–1-15, 1-19–1-20
global dimension, 1-15–1-16, 1-20
as ideal type, 1-16–1-17, 1-21
in international business, 1-10
leadership framework, 14-4
"Management by Web" (Byrne), 1-39–1-45
management implications, 1-18–1-21
"mapping your organization," 1-27–1-28
negotiation and conflict resolution in, 12-4, 12-6, 12-19

networked aspect, 1-13–1-14, 1-18–1-19, 1-23
old model, contrasts with, 1-17
organizational set model and, 9-9
relationships among negotiating parties, 12-8
"The Search for the Organization of Tomorrow (Stewart), 1-31–1-39
skepticism about, 1-24–1-26
society-business interactions, 1-23–1-24
teams and, 6-9
in U.S. government, 1-10
vertical vs. horizontal structure, 1-33
workforce management in, 1-19, 7-7–7-8
Newton, Sam, 12-41
NGOs (nongovernmental organizations), 1-16
Niermann, Jon, 10-53
NIMBY (not in my backyard), 12-26
Nissan, 8-8, 9-11–9-12, 9-15–9-16, 9-20–9-21
Nonaka, Ikujiro, 8-16
nonequity partnerships, 7-48
nonmarket strategies, 9-4
nonspecific compensation, 12-15
normative isomorphism, 9-19
norms, 2-60, 2-75, 11-20, 11-23
Nynex, 5-23

obligations, under professional ethic, 7-27
Obrand, Barry, 7-40
observation of consequences, 2-41
O'Connor, Joseph, 4-28
offensive jokes, 11-20
office, virtual, 7-18
Office of the President, 3-11–3-12
Olchefske, Joe, 14-38
old (bureaucratic) model
    career paths, linear, 7-18
    characteristics of, 1-11–1-13, 7-7
    diversity, lack of, 1-15
    employment relationship and, 7-13
    hierarchical structure, 1-12, 1-14, 1-37
    innovative subunits within, 1-12
    new model contrasted with, 1-17
    resiliency of, 1-11, 1-12
    Weber's model of bureaucracy, 1-11, 1-16–1-17
    workforce management in, 1-19, 7-7–7-8
operating procedures, flexible vs. rigid, 1-11, 1-12, 1-14–1-15
operational members, of X-teams, 6-25
operations, team, 3-13–3-14
opportunity, framing issues as, 13-9
optimism, 14-44
organization, concept of, 1-11
organization, team relations with. See boundary management, by teams
"Organization 2005" change initiative, 8-8–8-11
organizational analysis and action, lenses on, 2-4–2-5, 2-83–2-84. See also cultural lens/perspective; political lens/perspective; strategic design lens/perspective
organizational behavior, 2-68
organizational charts
    Dynacorp, 2-87, 2-88
    grouping structures, 2-16–2-20, 2-26
    as obsolete, 7-15
    and power systems, vertical and horizontal, 2-38
organizational congruence, 2-23
organizational culture
    overview, 2-59–2-60, 2-67
    "Action Company" paradigm, 2-71, 2-73
    artifacts, values, and assumptions, 2-70–2-71
    bonding process, 7-35
    changing, 8-7–8-8, 8-11
    content of, 2-71, 2-72
    definition of, 2-69–2-70
    Disney, 2-61, 10-4–10-5, 10-17, 10-21
    diversity paradigm shift and, 11-38
    dynamics, cultural, 2-75–2-78
    employee advocacy groups and, 11-16
    evolution, cultural, 2-76–2-78
    external cultural context, 2-63–2-64
    historical and theoretical background, 2-67–2-69
    levels of culture, 2-70–2-71
    "Multi Company" paradigm, 2-73–2-74
    negotiation and, 12-10
    research methods, 2-68–2-69, 2-78
    segmentalist model of, 2-62
    socialization, 2-75–2-76
    stories, circulation of, 2-61
    teams and, 3-14
    worker subcultures, 10-5, 10-13–10-23
    workforce management and, 7-6
"Organizational culture" (Schein), 2-67–2-82
organizational design. See strategic design lens/perspective
organizational development (OD), 8-12
organizational environment. See environment, external
organizational inertial, 8-4, 8-6, 8-12, 8-13
organizational patterns, and internationalization, 10-4
organizational processes, and diversity, 11-17, 11-18
organizational psychology, 2-68, 2-78
organizational restructuring. See restructuring and downsizing; strategic design lens/perspective
organizational set model, 9-4, 9-8–9-12, 9-15, 9-22
organizational status, 10-15–10-16
organizational structure. See strategic design lens/perspective
organization development, 2-69
"organization man," 7-18

organization model, new. *See* new organization model
organization model, old. *See* old (bureaucratic) model
Oriental Land Company, 10-25, 10-28, 10-52
Orlando, Florida, City of, 10-11
Osterman, Paul, 5-21
Ostroff, Frank, 1-31, 1-32, 1-34, 1-36
outer-net members, of X-teams, 6-25
output, grouping by, 2-17–2-18
output set, 9-8–9-11
outsiders, at Tokyo Disneyland, 10-32
outsourcing
    competition for talent, and bonding process, 7-35
    "ecosystem" of suppliers, partners, and contractors, 1-44–1-45
    external networking and, 9-4
    independent contractors, 7-14, 7-35, 7-36–7-37
    supplier relationships and, 1-13
    temporary workers, 1-15, 7-14, 7-19, 7-35
ownership, sharing, 2-42

pacing of change, 8-15
Pack, Richard, 6-11
Palermo, Richard, 1-31, 1-34
panel of experts, in virtual meetings, 5-19
parental leave, 7-49–7-51, 7-52–7-53, 7-58
parties to negotiations, 12-8–12-10
partnerships, 7-21, 7-44–7-53
"The Part-Time Partner" (Loveman), 7-44–7-52
part-time workers, 7-18, 7-44–7-53, 7-57
past performance, and power, 2-37–2-38
past self, 14-19
paternalism, 2-74, 7-25–7-26
payoff matrix, 8-40
peer assists, 7-34
Pells, Richard, 10-36
pension funds, 7-59, 7-60
Pepper, John, 8-8
perception of influence, 2-42–2-43
performance, 3-10, 11-17. *See also* effectiveness
performance measurement systems, 2-9, 2-24, 7-33, 9-11
performance record, and power, 2-37–2-38
performance standards, and diversity, 11-38
permanent cross-unit groups, 2-22
perpetual learning, 1-34
personal appeals, 5-12
personal characteristics, as source of power, 2-36–2-37
personal development, 14-36–14-41
personal injury litigation, 12-34
personality type. *See* cognitive style
personal leadership, 14-8
personal schemas, 2-8–2-10

perspectives. *See* organizational analysis and action, lenses on
persuasion, 5-12, 12-14
Peters, Tom, 13-29
Peterson, Jennifer, 8-24
Pettigrew, Andrew, 8-18
Pfeffer, Jeffrey, 2-34, 2-36, 2-40, 2-41–2-42
pharmaceuticals. *See* RU-486 case
Pharma Inc., 6-23, 6-26–6-29
Phase 2 Profile Integrity Status Inventory, 4-33
Philbin, Marcia, 12-40
pilot teams, 8-14
Pinotti, Jose, 9-29
place, and value systems, 14-39
PlaceWare, 5-19
planned change, 8-16, 8-17
Planned Parenthood, 9-29
plans, backup, 14-41
Platt, Lew, 11-11
Poincaré, Jules-Henri, 14-46
Polaroid Corp., 4-31-4-32
policies
    consistency in, 7-21–7-22
    diversity issues and, 11-24
    effecting change in, 7-7, 7-16, 7-51–7-52
    (*See also* change)
policies and procedures, in RAMMP matrix, 8-39
policy analysts, and work-family problems, 7-55
political lens/perspective. *See also* influence; power
    overview, 2-4, 2-10–2-11, 2-33
    on change, 8-7, 8-11
    on diversity, 11-14–11-15
    effective action and, 2-41–2-45
    on external environment, 9-4, 9-13–9-16, 9-22
    informal networks, analysis of, 2-47–2-55
    interests, 2-34–2-36
    political systems, 2-34
    power sources, 2-36–2-41
    on team boundary management, 6-10
    on workforce management, 7-6
politicians, and work-family problems, 7-55
pooled interdependence, 2-15, 2-20
popular culture, 10-47–10-48, 10-53. *See also* Disneyland
population ecology paradigm, 8-6, 8-13
Porter, Bill, 14-49, 14-50
Porter, Michael, 1-16
position, in networks, 2-38–2-40
positioning, 12-13–12-14, 12-16
positions, and negotiating interests, 12-11, 12-15
positions, work. *See* jobs
positive-sum game, 7-31
post-Fordism, 9-21
Post-It notes, 11-12
postsettlement settlements, 12-18
power. *See also* influence; negotiation and conflict

resolution; political lens/perspective
    assessment of, 2-41
    authority as, 2-36, 2-38
    bargaining power, 12-13–12-14
    "bow ties," 2-54
    brokering of, 14-15
    change and, 8-7, 8-11
    coercion as, 2-36, 2-38
    definitions of, 2-36
    ethical issues, 12-14
    flat organizations and, 7-7
    redistributed in reengineering, 13-27, 13-29
    sources of, 2-36–2-41
    in stakeholder model, 9-13
    and support or opposition, 2-34
    symbols of, 2-41
    as team issue, 5-12–5-13, 5-14
    vertical vs. horizontal, 2-38
power moves, 12-36–12-38
power struggles, 5-12–5-13
Prahalad, C. K., 13-23
predictability, 1-12
Predictive Index, 4-29, 4-31
preferences and personality. *See* cognitive style
present state, 8-12–8-13
press, business, 1-6–1-7, 1-10, 1-30–1-31
pressure, as influence tactic, 5-12
pricing at Disneyland Paris, 10-37, 10-38, 10-43
pricing of RU-486, 9-29
primary embedding mechanisms, 2-75
priority-setting, 4-15, 4-19–4-20, 12-27–12-28
problem orientation, in teams, 5-14
problem-solving, and flexibility, 1-14–1-15
problem-solving teams, 5-20
procedures, flexible vs. rigid, 1-11, 1-12, 1-14–1-15
processes, cultural, 2-58–2-59
processes, limiting, 8-29–8-31
processes, team. *See* team processes, internal
processes of change, 8-16
Process Improvement Teams (PMTs), 2-22
processing, cognitive, 2-8–2-9
process management, 1-35–1-36, 1-37
process maps, 8-41
process moves, 12-38, 12-39, 12-40
process reengineering. *See* reengineering
pro-choice movement. *See* RU-486 case
Proctor & Gamble, 1-34, 1-38, 8-8–8-11, 8-16, 8-17
procurement policy, 8-19
product division structure, 2-17–2-18, 2-32, 8-8–8-9
productivity, 7-37–7-38, 8-38–8-42
product manager position, 2-31
products, cultural, 2-58–2-59
professional associations, 7-56–7-57
professional ethic, 7-27–7-28
profound change, 8-34–8-35

pro-life movement. *See* RU-486 case
promotion
    college degree requirements, 11-38
    at Disneyland, 10-16
    diversity, and policies of, 11-24
    part-time partner case, 7-44–7-53
    personality tests and, 4-12
    scarcity of, in flat organizations, 1-19, 7-7, 7-15
property development, Disney
    Hong Kong, 10-45, 10-48
    Orlando, Florida, 10-10–10-11
    Paris, 10-35–10-36, 10-41–10-42
    Tokyo, 10-25, 10-28
prostaglandins, 9-24, 9-30
Proston, 9-25
provisionalism, 5-14
psychological contracts, 13-29. *See also* social contracts
psychological safety, 5-13
psychology, organizational, 2-68, 2-78
public opinion, in RU-486 case, 9-25–9-26, 9-28, 9-30–9-31
Puerto Rico, 1-32, 1-34
punctuated change, 8-15

quality, of part-time jobs, 7-57
quality circles, 3-11, 5-21
quality management, total (TQM), 2-15, 8-28, 9-21
"the Question," 14-36–14-41
"Question Manager" (PlaceWare), 5-19
questionnaires, for network analysis, 2-48–2-49
questions, in negotiation, 12-12
Quick Market Intelligence (QMI), 8-41

race. *See also* diversity
    discrimination-and-fairness paradigm and, 11-34–11-35
    influence on negotiation, 12-9
    source of conflict in U.S., 11-10
    workforce composition, 7-17, 11-19
radical change, 8-15, 8-16–8-17
RAMMP matrix, 8-38–8-40
rational analysts, 12-9
rationality, 2-26, 2-65
rational-legal bureaucracy, 1-11
rational persuasion, 5-12
reading critically, 1-30–1-31
Reagan, Ronald, 9-31
rebellion, 2-76
reciprocal interdependence, 2-15, 2-20
reciprocity, 1-24, 2-44
recklessness, 14-49
recruitment
    at Disneyland, 10-14
    personality tests and, 4-12

socialization and, 2-75
as strategic task, 7-32–7-33
redesign. *See* strategic design lens/perspective
redesigning, in change model, 8-14–8-15
redundant networks, 2-39
Reed, John, 14-11
Reedy Creek Improvement District, 10-11
reengineering
    definition of, 1-30, 1-35
    failure rate, 8-28
    linking of individual knowledge and, 7-34
    middle management and, 13-22–13-23, 13-26, 13-27–13-29
    "The Search for the Organization of Tomorrow (Stewart), 1-31–1-39
    task analysis and, 2-15
    teams and, 5-20, 5-23
    vertical vs. horizontal structure, 1-33
reference groups, 9-17
refreezing, 8-11–8-12
regulatory set, 9-8–9-12
Reich, Robert, 1-31, 1-38
Reichheld, Fred, 7-39
reinforcing growth processes, 8-29
Reiss, Vicki, 6-12–6-17
relating, as leadership capability, 14-9, 14-11–14-12
relationship networks, 2-47–2-52
relationships
    among negotiating parties, 12-8
    collaborative, 7-7, 12-17
    external environment and, 9-8, 9-9, 9-22
    interests relative to, 12-11
    leadership and, 14-11–14-12
    personality and, 4-15, 4-16–4-17
    shadow negotiations and, 12-4
relativity, cultural, 2-65
reliability, 1-12
remote-device technology, 5-17
reporting structures, formal, 2-21–2-22
reports, in RAMMP matrix, 8-38–8-39
representational indicators of power, 2-41
reputation, 2-41, 6-8, 12-11, 12-14
research funding, 14-22–14-23
resource-based strategy, 7-30
resource environment, 1-14, 9-4, 9-8
resources. *See also* human assets; intellectual capital and talent
    acquiring in negotiations, 12-15
    allocation of, 2-25, 9-11
    competition strategies, 7-29, 7-30
    human (*See* human assets)
    human capital, scarcity of, 7-30
restructuring and downsizing. *See also* strategic design lens/perspective
    costs of, 7-19–7-20, 7-20
    history of, 7-13
    human capital at risk, 7-59–7-60

    increase in layoffs, 1-10
    informal organization, effect on, 2-54
    long-term employment and, 7-14
    loyalty and, 7-25–7-28
    moral issue, 7-25
    teams and, 5-23
retention, in change model, 8-13
rethinking, in change model, 8-14–8-15
retirement plans, 2-35
rewards. *See* incentives and rewards
Richek, Herbert G., 4-23
rights, civil, 7-55, 11-13, 14-46. *See also* diversity
rights, labor, 7-60
Riley, Dan, 12-38
risk, 7-59–7-60, 12-30–12-32, 12-34, 13-11
Rittenberg, Sidney, 14-42, 14-44, 14-48
Ritzer, George, 1-25
Rock, John, 13-18
Rosewell case, 8-18
Ross, Julie, 7-45–7-52
Rossi, Francesca, 12-41
Roussel, Gaston, 9-23
Roussel, Jean-Claude, 9-23
Roussel-Uclaf. *See* RU-486 case
routinization of tasks, 2-14
Rowse, Mike, 10-53
Royal Dutch Shell, 9-15
RU-486 case
    overview, 9-4, 9-23
    in Asia, 9-24–9-25, 9-30
    chronology, 9-32
    debate on proceeding to market, 9-25–9-27
    decision not to distribute, 9-27–9-28
    distribution in France, 9-29
    in Europe, 9-29–9-30
    French government and, 9-24–9-25, 9-28–9-29
    history of Roussel-Uclaf, 9-23
    potential applications, 9-32
    pricing, 9-29
    the product, 9-23–9-24
    public reactions, 9-25–9-26, 9-28
    in United States, 9-30–9-32
rules
    in bureaucracies, 1-12
    decision, 6-26–6-27
    flexibility and, 1-14–1-15
    schemas and, 2-9

safety, and temporary workers, 7-19
safety, psychological, 5-13
Sakiz, Edouard, 9-23, 9-26, 9-28, 9-29, 9-30
sales, virtual, 5-17
sales forecasting, 6-11–6-17
San Diego Zoo, 1-38
Sands, Jim, 13-17, 13-18, 13-19
SAS Institute, 7-35, 7-37–7-38
satisfaction, among independent contractors, 7-19

saving face, in negotiations, 12-41
scandals, corporate, 7-6, 7-58–7-61
scarce expertise, 2-37
scheduling tools, in X-teams, 6-26
Schein, Ed, 2-34
schemas, 2-8–2-10
Schoendorf, Joe, 14-29
schools, 4-32–4-33
Schwartz, Joe, 7-38–7-39
"scientific management," 1-25, 2-15
scope, economies of, 2-16
scope of change, 8-15
Scott, Richard, 9-17
scouting activity, 6-8, 6-9, 6-10, 6-24
"The Search for the Organization of Tomorrow (Stewart), 1-31–1-39
secondary articulation and reinforcement mechanisms, 2-75
"second table" problem, 12-8
security, employment, 7-15, 7-16, 7-26
segmentalist model of organizational culture, 2-62
selection, in change model, 8-13
self, change signature and, 14-19–14-20
self-interest, amoral, 7-27
self-interest, enlightened, 12-15
self-managed teams, 3-11
self-management, worker, 1-32
self-other contrasts, at Tokyo Disneyland, 10-32
Semel, Terry, 2-4
Senge, Peter, 8-14, 8-16
sensemaking, as leadership capability, 14-9, 14-10–14-11, 14-13
sensitivity, and power, 2-37
September 11, 2001, terrorist attacks, 14-48
sequential interdependence, 2-14–2-15, 2-15, 2-16, 2-20
service industry, 10-4, 10-48. *See also* Disneyland
settlements, postsettlement, 12-18
sexual orientation, 11-12
shadow negotiations
    appreciative moves, 12-17, 12-39, 12-40–12-42
    defined, 12-36
    dirty tricks, 12-17
    managing impressions, 12-17
    power moves, 12-36–12-38, 12-39
    process moves, 12-38, 12-39, 12-40
    relationships and, 12-4
"shadow" personality type, 4-24–4-25
Shakespeare, William, 14-44, 14-49
Shalala, Donna, 9-31
Shanghai, China, 10-45, 10-53
Shapiro, Joe, 10-39
Share, Laura, 4-31
shared visions, 14-12
shareholder interests, and society, 7-20
sharing ownership, 2-42

Sharp, Phillip A., 14-21–14-22
Shaw, David E., 1-44
Shenzen, China, 10-46, 10-50
Shin, Young, 14-50
Shomber, Henry, 5-20
Siebert, Muriel, 14-42
sigmoidal growth patterns, 8-29
signaling, by bystanders, 11-23
Silicon Valley, 7-36–7-41
Simms, Marsha E., 7-48–7-49
Simon, Herman, 1-31, 1-34
Sims, Henry, 5-20
simultaneous engineering, 9-12
Singapore, 9-30
situational awareness, 11-21
Six Sigma Quality, 8-42
skills
    bystander (*See* bystander awareness and skills)
    generalized, 7-27, 7-28
    listening and empathy, 1-19–1-20
    multi-skilled employees, 7-15–7-16
    negotiation, 1-19
    teamwork, 1-18
Sloan, Alfred P., Jr., 1-39, 4-13–4-14
Sloan School of Management, MIT, 11-20
Slywotzky, Adrian J., 1-42, 1-44
"The Smile Factory: Work at Disneyland" (Van Maanen), 10-13–10-23
Smirov, Yuri, 7-40
Smith, Douglas, 1-31, 1-32, 1-35–1-36, 1-39
SmithKline Beecham, 12-26
smokestack scrubbers, 13-14–13-19
smoothing, 12-7
social actors, 9-4. *See also* environment, external
social capital, 6-9
social context, 1-23–1-24, 9-17
social contracts
    definition and history of, 7-12
    disappearance of, 7-39
    diversity and, 11-13
    employment relationship and, 7-8
    professionalism vs. loyalism, 7-25–7-28
    redefining, 7-14
social identities, 11-10, 11-15
social issues in negotiations, 12-26
socialization, 2-60–2-61, 2-75–2-76
socializing agents, 9-17
socially constructed identity, 12-9
social networks, 2-38–2-40, 7-34–7-35
social reference group, 9-17
societal interests, and shareholders, 7-20
sociograms, 5-11–5-12
software for electronic collaboration, 5-19
software for network mapping, 2-49
South Korea, 2-63–2-64
Southwest Airlines, 3-14–3-15
Souvaine, Emily, 4-34
space flexibility, 7-18

Spain, 10-35
specialization, 1-12, 1-36, 2-16
SPITS ("select a problem and implement a tailored solution"), 8-23–8-24
sponsorship, 6-8
spontaneity, in teams, 5-14
staffing. *See* workforce management
stage metaphor, 8-13
stage models of change, 8-11–8-15
stakeholders. *See also* strategic design lens/perspective
    Change Acceleration Process and, 8-41–8-42
    coalitions with, 1-13
    definition of, 2-35
    diversity of, 1-20
    employees as, 7-31
    in global organizations, 7-8
    interests, multiple, 2-35
    internal vs. external, 2-35
    mapping of interests, 2-42, 2-43
    team boundary management and, 6-9, 6-10
stakeholders model, 6-10, 9-4, 9-13–9-16, 9-22
Stanford, John, 14-38
Stanton, Steven, 1-35
Stanzione, Daniel, 14-28
Star Television, 10-55
status badges, 10-15
status quo, cost of, 12-37, 13-11
status rank ordering, at Disneyland, 10-15–10-16
Stein, Janice Gross, 12-28
stereotyping, 4-12, 12-9–12-10
Stewart, Rick, 7-44
stock options, 7-31, 7-36, 7-37, 7-38–7-41
stories, 2-61, 2-70, 14-12–14-13
stratagems in teams, 5-14
strategic agenda, 13-6
strategic behavior, discouragement of, 13-26–13-27
strategic design lens/perspective
    overview, 2-4, 2-10, 2-13–2-14
    alignment, 2-14, 2-15, 2-23–2-25, 2-26
    on change, 8-7, 8-11, 8-18, 8-19
    costs of redesign, 2-25–2-26
    definitions, 2-14
    design process, 2-25–2-26, 2-27
    on diversity, 11-14
    Dynacorp case, 2-28–2-32, 2-85–2-90
    environment, demands of, 2-26
    on external environment, 9-4, 9-8–9-12, 9-22
    grouping, 2-14, 2-15, 2-16–2-20, 2-26
    key elements, 2-14–2-15
    linking, 2-14, 2-15, 2-20–2-23
    network construction and, 2-44
    personality and, 4-22–4-23
    political lens compared to, 2-33
    rationality and, 2-26
    team analysis, 5-15
    team boundary management and, 6-10
    understanding an organization from, 2-26
    workforce management and, 7-6
strategic moves, 12-14
strategic planning groups, 2-23
strategic roles of middle managers, 13-23–13-29
strategy, evolving focus of, 7-29–7-31
strategy, talent-based, 7-29–7-36
"The Strategy That Wouldn't Travel" (Beer), 8-22–8-25
stresses, family, 7-54
stretch goals, 8-42
strong ties, 6-24
structural hole theory, 2-40
structural solutions to diversity issues, 11-23–11-24
structure and culture, 2-59
structures of organizations. *See* flat organizations; hierarchical structure; strategic design lens/perspective
structuring agencies, 9-17, 9-19
styles of boundary management, 6-8–6-9
styles of negotiators, 12-9–12-10
subcontractors. *See* independent contractors
subcultures and segmentation, 2-61–2-63, 2-65, 2-70, 2-77
subcultures at Disneyland
    appearance standards, 10-14, 10-18
    conduct codes, formal and informal, 10-19–10-21
    demeanor, standards of, 10-17–10-18
    emotional management, 10-14, 10-22
    guest misconduct and, 10-20–10-21, 10-23
    public interaction, 10-14–10-15, 10-18, 10-20–10-21
    socializing among workers, 10-16–10-17, 10-19–10-20
    status badges, personal, 10-15
    status rank ordering, 10-15–10-16
    supervisors and, 10-19–10-20, 10-22
    training and, 10-17–10-18
substantive conflict, 5-13
substantive interests, 12-11
subunit interests, 8-11
success, as source of power, 2-37–2-38
success, conception of, in flat organizations, 7-7
"Suits," Disney, 10-10, 10-35, 10-37
summarizing function, in teams, 5-10
supervision, at Disneyland, 10-19–10-20, 10-22
suppliers, 1-13, 9-12, 9-16, 9-21
supporters and blockers, mapping, 2-42, 2-43
support factors, in issue selling, 13-7, 13-11
supportive environments, in teams, 5-14
survey research, 2-48–2-49, 2-68
sustainable development, 9-22
sustaining, in change model, 8-14–8-15
Swallow team, 6-23–6-25

symbols, 2-57–2-58, 2-64
symbols of power, 2-41
synergies and cross-marketing, by Disney, 10-8–10-9, 10-12, 10-52, 10-53–10-54
systemic approach to work-family integration, 7-56, 7-57
systemic forces, and change initiatives, 8-13
systems perspective
    change models, 8-14
    organizational culture and, 2-68
    organizational design and, 2-14
    workforce management and, 7-7, 7-14

tactical choices, in issue selling, 13-8–13-10
Taiwan, 2-63–2-64
talent. *See* intellectual capital and talent
talent-based strategy, 7-29–7-36
talent investors, employees as, 7-32
Tandberg software, 5-19
Tang, Jun, 10-53, 10-54
Tapscott, Don, 1-41
task, as unit of activity, 2-14
task coordination, in boundary management, 6-8, 6-10, 6-24
task forces
    Aston-Blair case study, 6-11–6-17
    as cross-unit groups, 2-22–2-23
    definition of, 6-5
    Dynacorp case, 2-28, 2-30–2-32
    management tips, 6-17–6-19
    nature of, 6-4
task functions, for teams, 5-9, 5-10
task interdependence, 2-14–2-15, 2-16, 2-20–2-21
task-related networks, 2-40
tax status, in negotiations, 12-33, 12-34
Taylor, Frederick, 1-25, 2-15
TeamDisney, 10-12
team processes, internal
    overview, 5-4–5-5
    categories of, 5-4, 5-8
    communication patterns, 5-11–5-12
    conflict, 5-13
    decision making, 5-9, 5-11
    electronic collaboration, 3-12, 5-16–5-21
    emotional issues, 5-14
    individual members, 5-8
    influence and power, 5-12–5-13
    key processes, 3-13–3-14
    maintenance functions, 5-9, 5-10
    management issues, 5-4, 5-15
    observation and analysis, 5-8, 5-14–5-15
    organizational context, 5-8
    personalities, clashing, 5-23–5-24
    supportive vs. defensive atmosphere, 5-13–5-14
    task functions, 5-9, 5-10

"The Trouble with Teams (Dumaine), 5-21–5-24
    working with other teams, 5-20–5-21
teams. *See also* boundary management, by teams; networks
    overview, 3-6–3-7
    compensation and, 7-16
    conditions for implementing, 3-13
    context of, 3-14
    cross-functional, 2-31, 2-85–2-86, 3-11, 8-23–8-24
    cross-unit groups, 2-22–2-23
    definition of key terms, 3-10–3-11
    demographics, design, 11-12
    design of, 3-14
    effectiveness, and boundary management, 6-4, 6-9
    effectiveness model, 3-13–3-15, 6-4
    hierarchy of, 5-20–5-21
    high-performing, 3-10, 5-21
    individual work compared to, 3-12–3-13
    job loyalty and, 7-15
    leadership cores, 14-10
    management of, 3-15
    in networked organizations, 1-13, 3-6
    and new organization model, 6-9
    office of the president, 3-11–3-12
    operations of, 3-13–3-14
    pilot teams, 8-14
    problems with, 5-21–5-24
    project teams, 2-22–2-23
    reengineering and, 5-20, 5-23
    reputation of, 6-8
    satisfaction of, 6-9
    at Southwest Airlines, 3-14–3-15
    task forces (*See* task forces)
    team players, 3-11
    temporary structures, 1-15
    types of, 3-11–3-12, 5-20
    virtual, 3-12, 5-16–5-21
technology, changing assumptions of, 7-21
Teece, David, 13-23
telecommunications technologies, 1-13–1-14
telecommuting, 7-18
television
    in China, 10-51, 10-53–10-54
    Disney synergies with, 10-8, 10-12
    localization and, 10-55
temporal sequencing of change, 8-17–8-18, 8-20
temporary cross-unit groups, 2-22–2-23
temporary teams. *See* task forces
temporary workers
    competition for talent and, 7-35
    flexibility and, 1-15
    restructuring and, 7-14
    workforce management issues, 7-19
tensions, and leadership capabilities, 14-14
Termeer, Henri, 7-35

termination, at Disneyland, 10-19
terrorism, 10-50–10-51, 14-48
Texas Instruments (TI), 5-18–5-19
TFS (Tobias Fleishman Shapiro and Co.), 4-30–4-31
Thatcher, Margaret, 14-51
theater metaphor, 8-13
Theory X and Theory Y, 2-24
third-parties in negotiations, 12-8, 12-17–12-19, 12-28, 12-32
third-party mediation, diversity issues and, 11-24
Thompson, James, 2-14–2-15
Thompson, Leigh, 12-24
three-dimensional perspective on negotiations, 12-22–12-24
throughout-put systems, 2-26
thug-style negotiators, 12-9
Tichy, Noel M., 1-45, 8-13
Ticoll, David, 1-39, 1-43
tiers, in X-teams, 6-24–6-25, 6-26
ties, extensive, 6-24
time flexibility, 7-18, 7-44–7-53, 10-16
time frame, 14-40
time preference differences, in negotiations, 12-32–12-33, 12-34
time squeeze, in dual-earner families, 7-54
Time Warner, 8-7
timing, in issue selling, 13-8, 13-10
Tobias Fleishman Shapiro and Co. (TFS), 4-30–4-31
Tokyo Disneyland, 10-25–10-26, 10-27, 10-28–10-33, 10-52
top-down change, 8-16, 8-17
top management teams (TMTs), 13-6–13-7
Torinno Food Company case, 11-40
total quality management (TQM), 2-15, 8-28, 9-21
town meeting forum (GE), 8-38–8-40, 13-11
Toyota, 9-20
track record, and power, 2-37–2-38
trade-offs, and logrolling, 12-15
training. *See also* bystander awareness and skills
    alternative approaches, 7-20
    cross-training, 7-15
    cultural island concept and, 2-68
    Disney, 10-17–10-18, 10-29, 10-36–10-37
    diversity training, 11-20
    generalized skill development, 7-27, 7-28
    GE productivity programs, 8-38–8-42
    lifetime employability and, 7-15
    norm formation and, 2-75
    shorter-term employment and, 7-20
    standardization of, 1-12
traits of leadership, 14-46
transactive memory system, 5-8
"transformation," 8-34
transformation, model of, 14-45

transformational experiences, 14-15, 14-42. *See also* crucible experiences
transformational leader, 8-13, 14-8
transition state, 8-12–8-13
transnational teams, 3-12
transparent decision making, in X-teams, 6-26
transportation, international, 1-16
Trilogy Software, 1-45
Trosin, Walter R., 7-49–7-50
Trott, Chris, 6-11–6-17
"The Trouble with Teams" (Dumaine), 5-21–5-24
trust. *See also* loyalty and commitment
    diversity and, 11-41
    network construction and, 2-44
    networks of, 2-47–2-52
    workforce management and, 7-6, 7-22, 7-26
turnover, 7-36–7-37
Tushman, Michael, 2-24, 2-26
"The Twenty-first Century Firm" (DiMaggio), 1-25–1-26

UAW (United Automobile Workers), 9-16
unanticipated consequences of change, 8-6–8-7, 8-10
uncontaminated wonder, 14-44
underdeveloped self, 14-20
unfreezing-change-refreezing model, 8-11–8-12
uniforms, at Disneyland, 10-16, 10-17
unions
    changed employment relationships and, 7-28
    collective bargaining, 12-10
    decline of power, 7-14, 7-22, 7-59
    Disneyland Paris and, 10-37
    international variations in structure, 2-35
    Japanese auto firms and, 9-16, 9-21
    teams and, 5-23, 5-24
    work-family integration and, 7-55, 7-56–7-57
United Automobile Workers (UAW), 9-16
universal paid leave policy, 7-58
universal rules, 2-9
universities, 4-34
University of Disneyland, 10-17–10-18, 10-29
Upjohn, 9-25

Vaillant, George, 14-47, 14-48
value chains, 1-16
value claiming and creation, in negotiation. *See also* dealcrafting and dealmaking
    differences as sources of value, 12-26
    information withholding and, 12-12
    maximum total value vs. individual results, 12-24–12-26
    multiple issues and, 12-10
    negotiator's dilemma and, 12-16
    as power move, 12-37
    risk profiles and, 12-32

two-dimensional negotiation and, 12-22, 12-23
in zero-sum negotiation, 12-10, 12-14
value management, 7-31
values
credo and, 14-14–14-15
decision making and, 4-19
at Disneyland, 10-18
espoused, 2-71
as level of culture, 2-70, 2-71
managerial mapping and, 4-14–4-15
value systems, 14-39
variation-selection-retention model, 8-13
vertical organizations, 1-33
vertical power systems, 2-38
Vest, Charles (Chuck), 14-15, 14-21–14-26
videoconferencing. *See* electronic collaboration
virtual company, 1-13
virtual corporation, 7-19
virtual employees, 7-19
"Virtually There" (Overholt), 5-16–5-21
virtual meetings, 5-18–5-19
virtual office, 7-18
virtual sales, 5-17
virtual systems, 2-59
virtual teams, 3-12, 5-16–5-21
visioning, as leadership capability, 14-4, 14-9, 14-12–14-13, 14-30
vitality index, 7-33
voice, worker, 7-58
volatility, 1-14, 1-15

Wackenhut Corp., 4-33
wage gap, 1-11
wages, low, 7-13, 7-54
Wagner Act, 7-25, 7-28
Wallace, Mike, 14-42, 14-51
Wal-Mart, 1-38, 8-40–8-41
Walt Disney Company, 10-51–10-52, 10-55
Walt Disney Studios Park, 10-38
Walt Disney World (Florida), 10-10–10-13
Watts, Steven, 10-8, 10-9, 10-10
Wayman, Robert, 14-30
weak ties, 6-24
Weber, Max, 1-11, 1-16–1-17, 2-14, 2-36–2-37, 2-59
WebEx, 5-18–5-19, 5-19
Web technology. *See* electronic collaboration; Internet
"weenies," 10-10
Weick, Karl, 8-17
Weisbord, Marvin, 1-31, 1-32
Welch, Jim, 7-44–7-46, 7-50, 7-51
Welch, John F., Jr. (Jack), 1-42, 7-33, 8-16, 8-42, 14-15, 14-50
Wells, Frank, 10-12, 10-41
Western culture, opposition to, 10-54

"What Should I Do With My Life?" (Bronson), 14-36–14-41
"What's Wrong with Management Practices in Silicon Valley? A Lot" (Pfeffer), 7-36–7-38
WHO (World Health Organization), 9-24, 9-27, 9-30
Widrig, Marcela, 14-41
Wilke, Jeff, 14-51
Williams, Rosalind, 14-25
willingness to negotiate, 12-36
Willke, John, 9-25, 9-30–9-31
"Will the Organization of the Future Make the Mistakes of the Past?" (Pfeffer), 1-24
Wilson, Gary, 10-41
Window on the World theme park, 10-50
win-lose negotiations, 12-14–12-15
withdrawing, in teams, 5-14
women in the workforce
demographics, 7-17, 11-19
in leadership positions, 7-56, 7-58
at MIT, 14-21
schema changes and, 2-9
work-family integration and, 7-55, 7-56, 7-58
Women's Bar Association of Massachusetts, 7-53
wonder, uncontaminated, 14-44
"The Wonderful World of Disney" (TV), 10-12
Wooldridge, Bill, 13-22
work, meaningful, 14-36–14-41
work, nature of, 7-21
work design, 7-56, 7-58. *See also* jobs
worker self-management, 1-32
worker subcultures. *See* subcultures at Disneyland
work-family integration
costs of, 7-54
dual agenda, 7-19
holistic approach, 7-54–7-58
part-time partner case, 7-49–7-51
workforce diversity and, 7-17
workforce demographics, 1-15, 7-17
workforce management. *See also* employment relationship
alternative responses, 7-20
assumptions, 7-21
dimensions of, 7-6
employee representation models, 7-22
flexibility and, 7-7–7-8, 7-12, 7-17–7-19
human capital and knowledge, 7-16, 7-20–7-21
interests of workers, 7-6
in old and new models, 1-19, 7-7–7-8, 7-13–7-16
options, 7-20
policy inconsistencies, 7-21–7-22
systems perspective, 7-7, 7-14
work hours. *See* hours of work
Working Family Summit, 7-58
working groups, 3-10

working poor, 7-13
Working Today, 7-22, 7-28
work methods, and culture, 2-63
Work-Outs program, 8-38–8-40
work perspectives, connecting diversity to, 11-24, 11-36–11-42
work styles. *See* cognitive style
work systems, knowledge-based or high-performance, 7-16
"World Bazaar," 10-31
WorldCom, 12-28
World Congress of Gynecology and Obstetrics, 9-28, 9-29
World Health Organization (WHO), 9-24, 9-27, 9-30
World Trade Center, 14-48
World War II, 14-42, 14-51

Xerox, 1-37, 2-35, 11-12, 11-15
X-teams
    overview, 6-22
        components of, 6-22, 6-24–26, 6-27
        creating, 6-28
        research parameters, 6-23
        suitability of, 6-29
        supporting, 6-26–6-29

young adults, 10-27
youth culture, 10-17
youthful qualities, 14-44

Zambrano, Lorenzo H., 1-43–1-44
Zeigler, Reinhard, 5-17, 5-20
zero-sum game, 7-31
zero sum negotiations, 12-14
zone of possible agreements (ZOPA), 12-15
Zoological Society of San Diego, 1-38
Zuboff, Shoshanna, 1-31, 1-34